international marketing

international marketing

fourteenth edition

Philip R. Cateora
FELLOW, ACADEMY OF INTERNATIONAL BUSINESS
UNIVERSITY OF COLORADO

Mary C. Gilly
UNIVERSITY OF CALIFORNIA, IRVINE

John L. Graham
UNIVERSITY OF CALIFORNIA, IRVINE

McGraw-Hill
Irwin

Boston   Burr Ridge, IL   Dubuque, IA   New York   San Francisco   St. Louis
Bangkok   Bogotá   Caracas   Kuala Lumpur   Lisbon   London   Madrid   Mexico City
Milan   Montreal   New Delhi   Santiago   Seoul   Singapore   Sydney   Taipei   Toronto

McGraw-Hill
Irwin

INTERNATIONAL MARKETING

Published by McGraw-Hill/Irwin, a business unit of The McGraw-Hill Companies, Inc., 1221 Avenue of the Americas, New York, NY, 10020.

This book is printed on acid-free paper.

2 3 4 5 6 7 8 9 0 CCI/CCI 0 9

ISBN: 978-0-07-338098-8
MHID: 0-07-338098-9

Editorial director: *Brent Gordon*
Publisher: *Paul Ducham*
Executive Editor: *John Weimeister*
Editorial coordinator: *Sara Knox Hunter*
Marketing manager: *Katie Mergen*
Senior project manager: *Harvey Yep*
Lead production supervisor: *Carol Bielski*
Designer: *JoAnne Schopler*
Senior photo research coordinator: *Lori Kramer*
Photo researcher: *David Tietz, Editorial Image, LLC*
Media project manager: *Joyce Chappetto*
Cover design: *JoAnne Schopler*
Typeface: *10/12 Times New Roman*
Compositor: *Aptara Corporation*
Printer: *Courier–Kendalville*

Photo credits (chapter openers): page 2: AP Photo/Str; page 26: AP Photo/The Gazette, Cliff Jette; page 50: © Edro Lobo/Bloomberg News/Landov; page 92; AP Photo/Maxim Marmur; page 124: © David Coll Blanco; page 160: Reuters/Corbis; page 184: AP Photo/Christian Schwetz; page 214: © Cary Wolinsky; page 244: © Tomas Munita; page 274: © John Graham; page 304: © John Graham; page 334: Courtesy of The Disney/ABC Television Group: page 368: © John Graham; page 394: Courtesy of Marriott; page 428: © Macduff Everton/Corbis; page 462: © Tom Purslow/ Manchester United via Getty Images; page 500: © Roger Ressmeyer/Corbis; page 526: AP Photo; page 556: Copyrighted and used by permission of KARRASS, LTD. Beverly Hills, CA.; page 583: Goh Chai Hin/AFP Getty Images; page 593: © John Graham; page 611: AP Photo/Anat Givon; page 639: © John Graham; page 657: © Neil Thomas/africanpictures.net

Library of Congress Cataloging-in-Publication Data

Cateora, Philip R.
  International marketing / Philip R. Cateora, Mary C. Gilly, John L. Graham.—14th ed.
    p. cm.
  Includes index.
  ISBN-13: 978-0-07-338098-8 (alk. paper)
  ISBN-10: 0-07-338098-9 (alk. paper)
  1. Export marketing. 2. International business enterprises. I. Gilly, Mary C. II. Graham, John L. III. Title.
HF1416.C375 2009
658.8'4—dc22

                                    2008036578

www.mhhe.com

To William J. Stanton Friend, colleague and mentor

To the people who led me down this career path:
Richard Burr, Trinity University
Tom Barry, Southern Methodist University
Betsy Gelb, University of Houston

To Edward T. Hall

Philip R. Cateora

Professor Emeritus, The University of Colorado at Boulder. Received his Ph.D. from the University of Texas at Austin where he was elected to Beta Gamma Sigma. In his academic career at the University of Colorado he has served as Division Head of Marketing, Coordinator of International Business Programs, Associate Dean, and Interim Dean. His teaching has spanned a range of courses in marketing and international business from fundamentals through the doctoral level. He received the University of Colorado Teaching Excellence Award and the Western Marketing Educator's Association's Educator of the Year Award.

Professor Cateora has conducted faculty workshops on internationalizing principles of marketing courses for the AACSB and participated in designing and offering similar faculty workshops under a grant by the Department of Education. In conjunction with these efforts, he co-authored *Marketing: An International Perspective,* a supplement to accompany principles of marketing texts. Professor Cateora has served as consultant to small export companies as well as multinational companies, served on the Rocky Mountain Export Council, and taught in management development programs. He is a Fellow of the Academy of International Business.

Mary C. Gilly

Professor of Marketing at the Paul Merage School of Business, University of California, Irvine. She received her B.A. from Trinity University in San Antonio, Texas, her M.B.A. from Southern Methodist University in Dallas, Texas, and her Ph.D. from the University of Houston. Dr. Gilly has been at UCI since 1982 and has served as Vice Dean, Associate Dean, Director of the Ph.D. Program and Faculty Chair in the school of business as well as the Associate Dean of Graduate Studies for the campus. She has been on the faculties of Texas A&M University and Southern Methodist University, and has been a visiting professor at the Madrid Business School and Georgetown University. Professor Gilly has been a member of the American Marketing Association since 1975 and has served that organization in a number of capacities, including Marketing Education Council, President, Co-Chair, 1991 AMA Summer Educators' Conference, and member and chair of the AMA-Irwin Distinguished Marketing Educator Award Committee. She currently serves as Academic Director for the Association for Consumer Research. Professor Gilly has published her research on international, cross-cultural, and consumer behavior topics in the *Journal of Marketing, Journal of Consumer Research, Journal of Retailing, California Management Review* and other venues.

John L. Graham

Professor of International Business and Marketing at the Paul Merage School of Business, University of California, Irvine. He has been Associate Dean and Director, UCI Center for Citizen Peacebuilding, Visiting Scholar, Georgetown University School of Business, Visiting Professor at Madrid Business School in Spain, and Associate Professor, University of Southern California. Before beginning his doctoral studies at UC Berkeley, he worked for a division of Caterpillar Tractor Co. and served as an officer in the U.S. Navy Underwater Demolition Teams. Professor Graham is the author (with William Hernandez Requejo) of *Global Negotiation: The New Rules*, Palgrave-Macmillan, 2008; (with N. Mark Lam) of *China Now, Doing Business in the World's Most Dynamic Market,* McGraw-Hill, 2007; (with Yoshihiro Sano and James Hodgson, former U.S. Ambassador to Japan) of *Doing Business with the New Japan,* Rowman & Littlefield, 4th edition, 2008); and editor (with Taylor Meloan) of *Global and International Marketing,* Irwin, 2nd edition, 1997. He has published articles in publications such as the *Harvard Business Review, Journal of Marketing, Journal of International Business Studies, Strategic Management Review*, and *Marketing Science.* Excerpts of his work have been read into the *Congressional Record* and his research on business negotiation styles in 20 cultures was the subject of an article in the January 1988 issue of *Smithsonian.* His 1994 paper in *Management Science* received a citation of excellence from the Lauder Institute at the Wharton School of Business.

At the start of the last millennium the Chinese were the preeminent international traders. Although a truly global trading system would not evolve until some 500 years later, Chinese silk had been available in Europe since Roman times.

At the start of the last century the British military, merchants, and manufacturers dominated the seas and international commerce. Literally, the sun did not set on the British Empire.

At the start of the last decade, Japan's economic successes had rendered the military competition between the United States and the Soviet Union obsolete. Pundits circa 1990 predicted a Pacific Century, wherein trans-Pacific trade would surpass trans-Atlantic trade. Other Asian economies would follow the lead of Japan. No one then foresaw the ascendancy and impact of the American-created information technology revolution.

What surprises do the new decade, century, and millennium hold in store for all of us? Toward the end of the current decade natural disasters and wars have hampered commerce and human progress. The battle to balance economic growth and stewardship of the environment continues. The globalization of markets has certainly accelerated through almost universal acceptance of the democratic free enterprise model and new communication technologies, including cell phones and the Internet. Which will prove the better, Chinese gradualism or the Russian big-bang approach to economic and political reform? Will the information technology boom of the previous decade be followed by a demographics bust when American baby boomers begin to try to retire after 2010? Or will NAFTA and the young folks in Mexico provide a much needed demographic balance? Ten years out the debate about global warming should be settled—more data and better science will yield the answers. What unforeseen advances or disasters will the biological sciences bring us? Will we conquer AIDS/HIV in Africa? Will weapons and warfare become obsolete?

International marketing will play a key role in providing positive answers to all these questions. We know that trade causes peace and prosperity by promoting creativity, mutual understanding, and interdependence. Markets are burgeoning in emerging economies in eastern Europe, the Commonwealth of Independent States, China, Indonesia, Korea, India, Mexico, Chile, Brazil, and Argentina—in short, globally. These emerging economies hold the promise of huge markets in the future. In the more mature markets of the industrialized world, opportunity and challenge also abound as consumers' tastes become more sophisticated and complex and as increases in purchasing power provide consumers with new means of satisfying new demands.

Opportunities in today's global markets are on a par with the global economic expansion that existed after World War II. Today, however, the competitive environment within which these opportunities exist is vastly different from that earlier period when United States multinationals dominated world markets. From the late 1940s through the 1960s, multinational corporations (MNCs) from the United States had little competition; today, companies from almost all the world's nations vie for global markets. Fareed Zakaria reports: "During the last two years, 124 countries grew their economies at over 4 percent a year. That includes more than 30 countries in Africa. Over the last two decades, lands outside the industrialized West have been growing at rates that were once unthinkable. While there have been booms and busts, the overall trend has been unambiguously upward. Antoine van Agtmael, the fund manager who coined the term 'emerging markets,' has identified the 25 companies most likely to be the world's next great multinationals. His list includes four companies each from Brazil, Mexico, South Korea, and Taiwan; three from India, two from China, and one each from Argentina, Chile, Malaysia, and South Africa. This is something much broader than the much-ballyhooed rise of China or even Asia. It is the rise of the rest—the rest of the world."[1]

---

[1] Fareed Zakaria, "The Rise of the Rest," *Newsweek*, May 3, 2008.

The economic, political, and social changes that have occurred over the last decade have dramatically altered the landscape of global business. Consider the present and future impact of the following:

- The ever-present threat of global terrorism as represented by the September 11, 2001, attacks
- Major armed conflicts in sub-Saharan Africa and the Middle East
- The potential global recession emanating from the United States
- The emerging markets in eastern Europe, Asia, and Latin America, where more than 75 percent of the growth in world trade over the next 20 years is expected to occur
- The reunification of Hong Kong, Macau, and China, which finally puts all of Asia under the control of Asians for the first time in over a century
- The European Monetary Union and the successful switch from local-country currencies to one monetary unit for Europe, the euro
- The rapid move away from traditional distribution structures in Japan, Europe, and many emerging markets
- The growth of middle-income households the world over
- The continued strengthening and creation of regional market groups such as the European Union (EU), the North American Free Trade Area (NAFTA), the Central American Free Trade Area (CAFTA), ASEAN Free Trade Area (AFTA), the Southern Cone Free Trade Area (Mercosur), and the Asia-Pacific Economic Cooperation (APEC)
- The successful completion of the Uruguay Round of the General Agreement on Tariffs and Trade (GATT) and the creation of the World Trade Organization (WTO), the latter now including China and Taiwan
- The restructuring, reorganizing, and refocusing of companies in telecommunications, entertainment, and biotechnology, as well as in traditional smokestack industries around the world
- The continuing integration of the Internet and cell phones into all aspects of companies' operations and consumers' lives

These are not simply news reports. These changes affect the practice of business worldwide, and they mean that companies will have to constantly examine the way they do business and remain flexible enough to react rapidly to changing global trends to be competitive.

As global economic growth occurs, understanding marketing in all cultures is increasingly important. *International Marketing* addresses global issues and describes concepts relevant to all international marketers, regardless of the extent of their international involvement. Not all firms engaged in overseas marketing have a global perspective, nor do they need to. Some companies' foreign marketing is limited to one country; others market in a number of countries, treating each as a separate market; and still others, the global enterprises, look for market segments with common needs and wants across political and economic boundaries. All, however, are affected by competitive activity in the global marketplace. It is with this future that the fourteenth edition of *International Marketing* is concerned.

Emphasis is on the strategic implications of competition in different country markets. An environmental/cultural approach to international marketing permits a truly global orientation. The reader's horizons are not limited to any specific nation or to the particular ways of doing business in a single nation. Instead, the book provides an approach and framework for identifying and analyzing the important cultural and environmental uniqueness of any nation or global region. Thus, when surveying the tasks of marketing in a foreign milieu, the reader will not overlook the impact of crucial cultural issues.

The text is designed to stimulate curiosity about management practices of companies, large and small, seeking market opportunities outside the home country and to raise the reader's consciousness about the importance of viewing international marketing management strategies from a global perspective.

Although this revised edition is infused throughout with a global orientation, export marketing and the operations of smaller companies are also included. Issues specific to exporting are discussed where strategies applicable to exporting arise, and examples of marketing practices of smaller companies are examined.

New and Expanded Topics in This Edition

The new and expanded topics in this fourteenth edition reflect issues in competition, changing marketing structures, ethics and social responsibility, negotiations, and the development of the manager for the 21st century. Competition is raising the global standards for quality, increasing the demand for advanced technology and innovation, and increasing the value of customer satisfaction. The global market is swiftly changing from a seller's market to a buyer's market. This is a period of profound social, economic, and political change. To remain competitive globally, companies must be aware of all aspects of the emerging global economic order.

Additionally, the evolution of global communications and its known and unknown impact on how international business is conducted cannot be minimized. In the third millennium people in the "global village" will grow closer than ever, and will hear and see each other as a matter of course. An executive in Germany can routinely connect via VoIP (Voice over Internet Protocol) to hear and see his or her counterpart in an Australian company or anywhere else in the world. In many respects (time zone differences is a prominent exception), geographic distance is becoming irrelevant.

Telecommunications, fax machines, the Internet, and satellites are helping companies optimize their planning, production, and procurement processes. Information—and, in its wake, the flow of goods—is moving around the globe at lightning speed. Increasingly powerful networks spanning the globe enable the delivery of services that reach far beyond national and continental boundaries, fueling and fostering international trade. The connections of global communications bring people all around the world together in new and better forms of dialogue and understanding.

This dynamic nature of the international marketplace is reflected in the number of substantially improved and expanded topics in this fourteenth edition, including the following:

- A deeper look at the causes of cultural differences
- The Internet and cell phones and their expanding role in international marketing
- Negotiations with customers, partners, and regulators
- Big emerging markets (BEMs)
- Evolving global middle-income households
- Bottom of the pyramid markets
- World Trade Organization
- Free trade agreements
- Asia-Pacific Economic Cooperation
- Multicultural research
- Qualitative and quantitative research
- Country-of-origin effect and global brands
- Industrial trade shows
- A growing emphasis on both consumer and industrial services
- Trends in channel structures in Europe, Japan, and developing countries
- Ethics and socially responsible decisions
- Green marketing
- Changing profiles of global managers

Structure of the Text

The text is divided into six parts. The first two chapters, Part 1, introduce the reader to the environmental/cultural approach to international marketing and to three international marketing management concepts: domestic market expansion, multidomestic marketing, and global marketing. As companies restructure for the global competitive rigors of the 21st century, so too must tomorrow's managers. The successful manager must be globally aware and have a frame of reference that goes beyond a country, or even a region, and encompasses the world. What global awareness means and how it is acquired is discussed early in the text; it is at the foundation of global marketing.

Chapter 2 focuses on the dynamic environment of international trade and the competitive challenges and opportunities confronting today's international marketer. The importance of the creation of the World Trade Organization, the successor to GATT, is fully explored. The growing importance of cell phones and the Internet in conducting international business is considered, creating a foundation on which specific applications in subsequent chapters are presented.

The five chapters in Part 2 deal with the cultural environment of global marketing. A global orientation requires the recognition of cultural differences and the critical decision of whether it is necessary to accommodate them.

Geography and history (Chapter 3) are included as important dimensions in understanding cultural and market differences among countries. Not to be overlooked is concern for the deterioration of the global ecological environment and the multinational company's critical responsibility to protect it.

Chapter 4 presents a broad review of culture and its impact on human behavior as it relates to international marketing. Specific attention is paid to Geert Hofstede's study of cultural values and behavior. The elements of culture reviewed in Chapter 4 set the stage for the in-depth analyses in Chapters 5, 6, and 7 of business customs and the political and legal environments. Ethics and social responsibility are presented in the context of the dilemma that often confronts the international manager, that is, balancing corporate profits against the social and ethical consequences of his or her decisions.

The three chapters in Part 3 are concerned with assessing global market opportunities. As markets expand, segments grow within markets; as market segments across country markets evolve, marketers are forced to understand market behavior within and across different cultural contexts. Multicultural research, qualitative and quantitative research, and the Internet as a tool in the research task are explored in Chapter 8.

Chapters 9 and 10 in Part 3 explore the impact of the three important trends in global marketing: the growth and expansion of the world's big emerging markets; the rapid growth of middle-income market segments; and the steady creation of regional market groups that include NAFTA, the European Union, CAFTA, APEC, and the evolving Free Trade Area of the Americas (FTAA). Also discussed is the growing number of trade agreements that have been executed by the European Union and Japan with the FTAA and some Latin American countries.

The strategic implications of the dissolution of the Soviet Union and the emergence of new independent republics, the shift from socialist-based to market-based economies in Eastern Europe, and the return of South Africa and Vietnam to international commerce are examined. Attention is also given to the efforts of the governments of India and many Latin American countries to reduce or eliminate barriers to trade, open their countries to foreign investment, and privatize state-owned enterprises.

These political, social, and economic changes that are sweeping the world are creating new markets and opportunities, making some markets more accessible while creating the potential for greater protectionism in others.

In Part 4, Developing Global Marketing Strategies, planning and organizing for global marketing is the subject of Chapter 11. The discussion of collaborative relationships, including strategic alliances, recognizes the importance of relational collaborations among firms, suppliers, and customers in the success of the global marketer. Many multinational companies realize that to fully capitalize on opportunities offered by global markets, they must have strengths that often exceed their capabilities. Collaborative relationships can provide technology, innovations, productivity, capital, and market access that strengthen a company's competitive position.

Chapters 12 and 13 focus on product and services management, reflecting the differences in strategies between consumer and industrial offerings and the growing importance in world markets for both consumer and business services. Additionally, the discussion on the development of global offerings stresses the importance of approaching the adaptation issue from the viewpoint of building a standardized product/service platform that can be adapted to reflect cultural differences. The competitive importance in today's global market for quality, innovation, and technology as the keys to marketing success is explored.

Chapter 14 takes the reader through the distribution process, from home country to the consumer in the target country market. The structural impediments to market entry imposed by a country's distribution system are examined in the framework of a detailed presentation of the Japanese distribution system. Additionally, the rapid changes in channel structure that are occurring in Japan, as well as in other countries, and the emergence of the World Wide Web as a distribution channel are presented.

In Chapter 15, the special issues involved in moving a product from one country market to another, and the accompanying mechanics of exporting, are addressed. The importance of the Internet in assisting the exporter to wade through the details of exporting is discussed in the context of the revised export regulations.

Chapter 16 covers advertising and addresses the promotional element of the international marketing mix. Included in the discussion of global market segmentation are recognition of the rapid growth of market segments across country markets and the importance of market segmentation as a strategic competitive tool in creating an effective promotional message. Chapter 17 discusses personal selling and sales management and the critical nature of training, evaluating, and controlling sales representatives.

Price escalation and ways it can be lessened, countertrade practices, and price strategies to employ when the dollar is strong or weak relative to foreign currencies are concepts presented in Chapter 18.

In Part 5, Chapter 19 is a thorough presentation of negotiating with customers, partners, and regulators. The discussion stresses the varying negotiation styles found among cultures and the importance of recognizing these differences at the negotiation table.

Pedagogical Features of the Text

The text portion of the book provides a thorough coverage of its subject, with subject emphasis on the planning and strategic problems confronting companies that market across cultural boundaries.

The use of the Internet as a tool of international marketing is stressed throughout the text. On all occasions where data used in the text originated from an Internet source, the Web address is given. Problems that require the student to access the Internet are included with end-of-chapter questions. Internet-related problems are designed to familiarize the student with the power of the Internet in his or her research, to illustrate data available on the Internet, and to challenge the reader to solve problems using the Internet. Many of the examples, illustrations, and exhibits found in the text can be explored in more detail by accessing the Web addresses that are included.

Current, pithy, sometimes humorous, and always relevant examples are used to stimulate interest and increase understanding of the ideas, concepts, and strategies presented in emphasizing the importance of understanding cultural uniqueness and relevant business practices and strategies.

Each chapter is introduced with a Global Perspective, a real-life example of company experiences that illustrates salient issues discussed in the chapter. Companies featured in the Global Perspectives range from exporters to global enterprises.

The boxed Crossing Borders, an innovation of the first edition of *International Marketing,* have always been popular with students. They reflect contemporary issues in international marketing and can be used to illustrate real-life situations and as the basis for class discussion. They are selected to be unique, humorous, and of general interest to the reader.

The book is presented in full color, allowing maps to depict of geographical, cultural, and political boundaries and features more easily. Color also allows us to better communicate through that medium the intricacies of international symbols and meanings in marketing communications. New photographs of current and relevant international marketing events are found throughout the text—all in color.

The Country Notebook—A Guide for Developing a Marketing Plan, found in Part 6, Supplementary Material, is a detailed outline that provides both a format for a complete cultural and economic analysis of a country and guidelines for developing a marketing plan.

In addition to The Country Notebook, Part 6 comprises a selection of short and long cases. The short cases focus on a single problem, serving as the basis for discussion of a specific concept or issue. The longer, more integrated cases are broader in scope and focus on more than one marketing management problem; new cases focus on services, marketing, and marketing strategy. The cases can be analyzed by using the information provided. They also lend themselves to more in-depth analysis, requiring the student to engage in additional research and data collection.

Supplements

We have taken great care to offer new features and improvements to every part of the teaching aid package. Following is a list of specific features:

- **Instructor's Manual and Test Bank.** The Instructor's Manual, prepared by the authors, contains lecture notes or teaching suggestions for each chapter. A section called Changes to This Edition is included to help instructors adapt their teaching notes to the fourteenth edition. A case correlation grid at the beginning of the case note offers alternative uses for the cases.

The Test Bank is prepared by John Karonika, University of Houston, and is also available on the Online Learning Center for ease of use. The Test Bank contains more than 2,000 questions, including true/false, critical thinking, and essay formats. Computerized testing software with an online testing feature is also available.

- **Videos.** The video program has been revised for the fourteenth edition and contains new footage of companies, topics videos, and unique training materials for international negotiations. Teaching notes and questions relevant to each chapter in the text are available in the Instructor's Manual and at the Web site.

- **PowerPoint slides.** This edition has PowerPoint slides for both the instructor and students, the latter of which are narrated. The PowerPoint presentation that accompanies *International Marketing,* fourteenth edition, contains exhibits from the text and other sources. The PowerPoint slides are prepared by Monika Czehak.

- **Instructor's CD-ROM.** This presentation manager, available to adopters of the textbook, contains the Instructor's Manual, Test Bank, and PowerPoint. Instructors have the ability to customize their lectures with this powerful tool.

- **Web site:** www.mhhe.com/cateora14e. Included on the site are instructor resources such as downloadable files for the complete Instructor's Manual, PowerPoint slides, and links to current events and additional resources for the classroom. Instructors can also link to PageOut to create their own course Web site and access the complete Test Bank. For students, our site provides links to Web sites, an interactive version of the Country Notebook, online quizzing, and narrated chapter PowerPoint Slides.

Acknowledgments

The success of a text depends on the contributions of many people, especially those who take the time to share their thoughtful criticisms and suggestions to improve the text.

We would especially like to thank the following reviewers who gave us valuable insights into this revision:

Delores Barsellotti
California State Polytechnic University, Pomona

Andrew Bergstein
Penn State University

Janice Blankenburg
University of Wisconsin-Milwaukee

Trini Callava
Miami Dade College

Phillip Corse
Northwestern University

Richard Ettenson
Thunderbird School of Global Management

Rajani Ganesh Pillai
University of Central Florida

Daekwan Kim
Florida State University

Mike Mayo
Kent State University

Michael Mullen
Florida Atlantic University

Fred Pragasam
University of North Florida

Alexia Vanides
University of California Berkeley Extension

Y. Henry Xie
College of Charleston

We appreciate the help of all the many students and professors who have shared their opinions of past editions, and we welcome their comments and suggestions on this and future editions of *International Marketing*.

A very special thanks to Paul Ducham, John Weimeister, Sara Hunter, Katie Mergen, Harvey Yep, JoAnne Schopler, Joyce Chappetto, Lori Kramer, and Sri Potluri from McGraw-Hill/Irwin, whose enthusiasm, creativity, constructive criticisms, and commitment to excellence have made this edition possible.

Philip R. Cateora
Mary C. Gilly
John L. Graham

WALKTHROUGH
A quick look at the new edition

International Marketing by Cateora, Gilly, and Graham has always been a pioneer in the field of international marketing. The authors continue to set the standard in this edition with new and expanded topics that reflect the swift changes of an expanding competitive global market as well as an increased coverage of technology's impact on the international market arena.

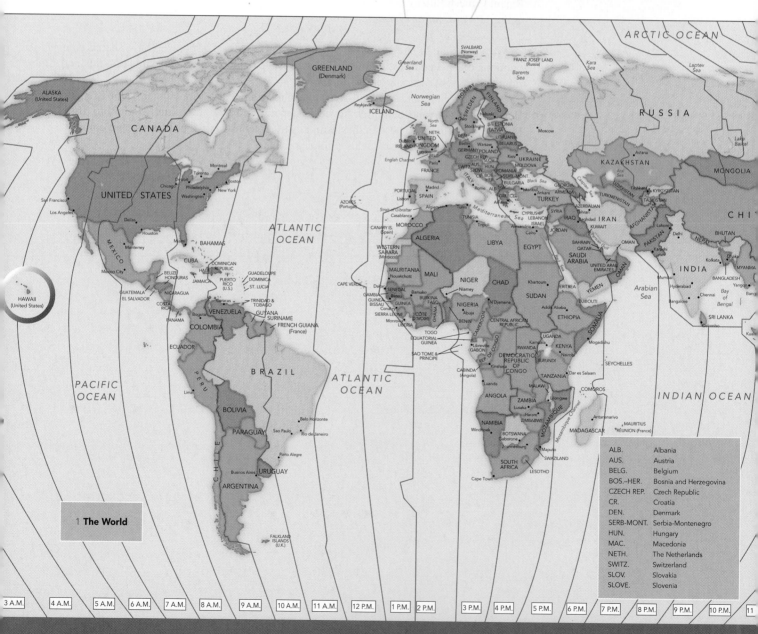

1 The World

ALB.	Albania
AUS.	Austria
BELG.	Belgium
BOS.–HER.	Bosnia and Herzegovina
CZECH REP.	Czech Republic
CR.	Croatia
DEN.	Denmark
SERB-MONT.	Serbia-Montenegro
HUN.	Hungary
MAC.	Macedonia
NETH.	The Netherlands
SWITZ.	Switzerland
SLOV.	Slovakia
SLOVE.	Slovenia

3 A.M. | 4 A.M. | 5 A.M. | 6 A.M. | 7 A.M. | 8 A.M. | 9 A.M. | 10 A.M. | 11 A.M. | 12 P.M. | 1 P.M. | 2 P.M. | 3 P.M. | 4 P.M. | 5 P.M. | 6 P.M. | 7 P.M. | 8 P.M. | 9 P.M. | 10 P.M.

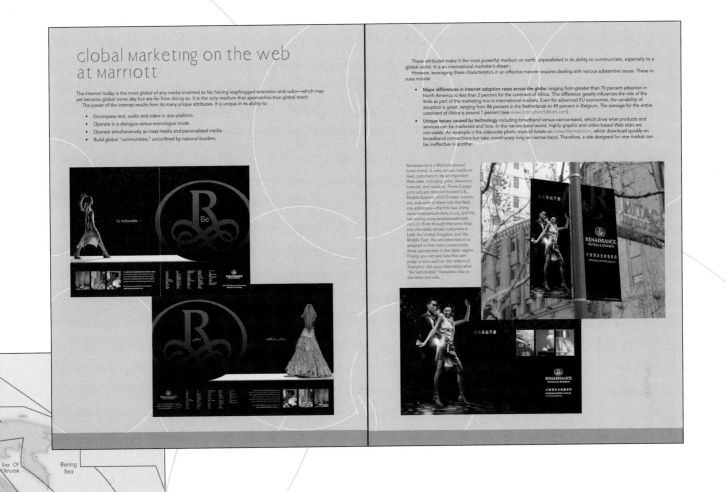

4-Color Design

New color maps and exhibits allow for improved pedagogy and a clearer presentation of international symbols and cultural meanings in marketing and advertising. In addition, photos that depend on full color for maximum impact easily bring many global examples to life. This visually stimulating combination works together to make the text material reader-friendly and accessible for both instructors and students.

Chapter Openers

A Chapter Outline provides students an at-a-glance overview of chapter topics, while Chapter Learning Objectives summarize the chapter's goals and focus. Each chapter is introduced with a Global Perspective, a real-life example of company experiences that illustrates significant issues discussed in the chapter. Companies featured in the Global Perspective vignettes range from exporters to global enterprises.

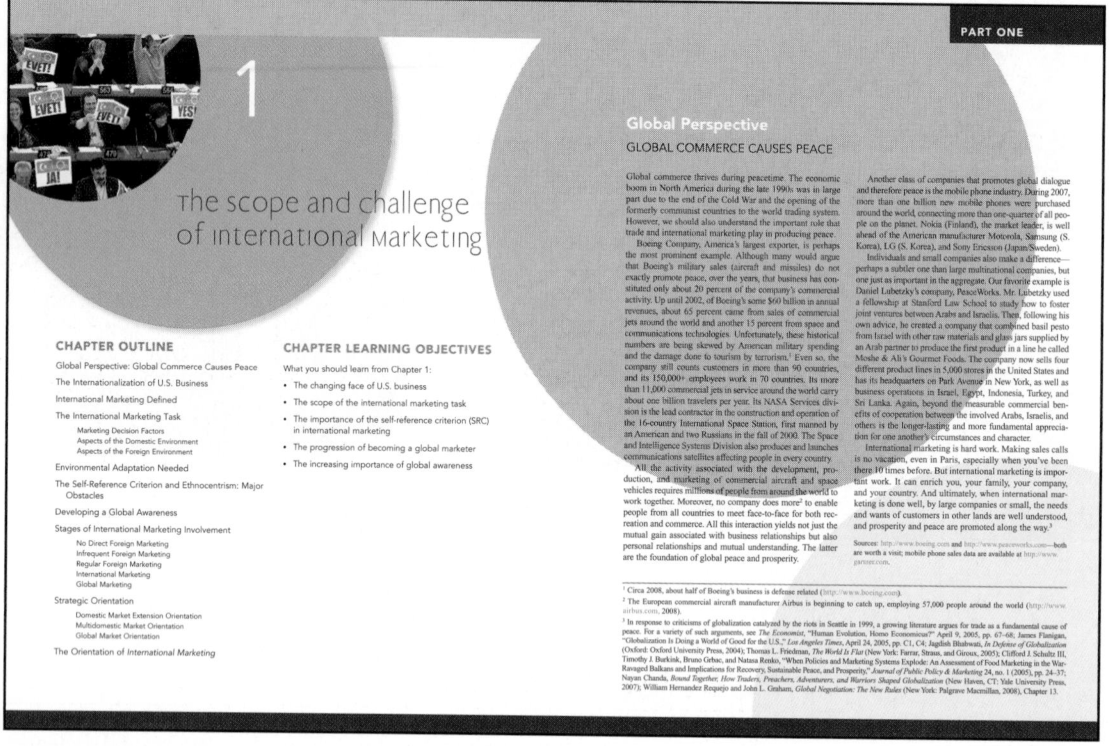

PART ONE

1

The scope and challenge of international Marketing

CHAPTER OUTLINE

Global Perspective: Global Commerce Causes Peace
The Internationalization of U.S. Business
International Marketing Defined
The International Marketing Task
- Marketing Decision Factors
- Aspects of the Domestic Environment
- Aspects of the Foreign Environment

Environmental Adaptation Needed
The Self-Reference Criterion and Ethnocentrism: Major Obstacles
Developing a Global Awareness
Stages of International Marketing Involvement
- No Direct Foreign Marketing
- Infrequent Foreign Marketing
- Regular Foreign Marketing
- International Marketing
- Global Marketing

Strategic Orientation
- Domestic Market Extension Orientation
- Multidomestic Market Orientation
- Global Market Orientation

The Orientation of *International Marketing*

CHAPTER LEARNING OBJECTIVES

What you should learn from Chapter 1:

- The changing face of U.S. business
- The scope of the international marketing task
- The importance of the self-reference criterion (SRC) in international marketing
- The progression of becoming a global marketer
- The increasing importance of global awareness

Global Perspective

GLOBAL COMMERCE CAUSES PEACE

Global commerce thrives during peacetime. The economic boom in North America during the late 1990s was in large part due to the end of the Cold War and the opening of the formerly communist countries to the world trading system. However, we should also understand the important role that trade and international marketing play in producing peace.

Boeing Company, America's largest exporter, is perhaps the most prominent example. Although many would argue that Boeing's military sales (aircraft and missiles) do not exactly promote peace, over the years, that business has constituted only about 20 percent of the company's commercial activity. Up until 2002, of Boeing's some $60 billion in annual revenues, about 65 percent came from sales of commercial jets around the world and another 15 percent from space and communications technologies. Unfortunately, these historical numbers are being skewed by American military spending and the damage done to tourism by terrorism.[1] Even so, the company still counts customers in more than 90 countries, and its 150,000+ employees work in 70 countries. Its more than 11,000 commercial jets in service around the world carry about one billion travelers per year. Its NASA Services division is the lead contractor in the construction and operation of the 16-country International Space Station, first manned by an American and two Russians in the fall of 2000. The Space and Intelligence Systems Division also produces and launches communications satellites affecting people in every country.

All the activity associated with the development, production, and marketing of commercial aircraft and space vehicles requires millions of people from around the world to work together. Moreover, no company does more[2] to enable people from all countries to meet face-to-face for both recreation and commerce. All this interaction yields not just the mutual gain associated with business relationships but also personal relationships and mutual understanding. The latter are the foundation of global peace and prosperity.

Another class of companies that promotes global dialogue and therefore peace is the mobile phone industry. During 2007, more than one billion new mobile phones were purchased around the world, connecting more than one-quarter of all people on the planet. Nokia (Finland), the market leader, is well ahead of the American manufacturer Motorola, Samsung (S. Korea), LG (S. Korea), and Sony Ericsson (Japan/Sweden).

Individuals and small companies also make a difference—perhaps a subtler one than large multinational companies, but one just as important in the aggregate. Our favorite example is Daniel Lubetzky's company, PeaceWorks. Mr. Lubetzky used a fellowship at Stanford Law School to study how to foster joint ventures between Arabs and Israelis. Then, following his own advice, he created a company that combined basil pesto from Israel with other raw materials and glass jars supplied by an Arab partner to produce the first product in a line he called Moshe & Ali's Gourmet Foods. The company now sells four different product lines in 5,000 stores in the United States and has its headquarters on Park Avenue in New York, as well as business operations in Israel, Egypt, Indonesia, Turkey, and Sri Lanka. Again, beyond the measurable commercial benefits of cooperation between the involved Arabs, Israelis, and others is the longer-lasting and more fundamental appreciation for one another's circumstances and character.

International marketing is hard work. Making sales calls is no vacation, even in Paris, especially when you've been there 10 times before. But international marketing is important work. It can enrich you, your family, your company, and your country. And ultimately, when international marketing is done well, by large companies or small, the needs and wants of customers in other lands are well understood, and prosperity and peace are promoted along the way.[3]

Sources: http://www.boeing.com and http://www.peaceworks.com—both are worth a visit; mobile phone sales data are available at http://www.gartner.com.

[1] Circa 2008, about half of Boeing's business is defense related (http://www.boeing.com).

[2] The European commercial aircraft manufacturer Airbus is beginning to catch up, employing 57,000 people around the world (http://www.airbus.com, 2008).

[3] In response to criticisms of globalization catalyzed by the riots in Seattle in 1999, a growing literature argues for trade as a fundamental cause of peace. For a variety of such arguments, see *The Economist*, "Human Evolution, Homo Economicus?" April 9, 2005, pp. 67–68; James Flanigan, "Globalization Is Doing a World of Good for the U.S.," *Los Angeles Times*, April 24, 2005, pp. C1, C4; Jagdish Bhabwati, *In Defense of Globalization* (Oxford: Oxford University Press, 2004); Thomas L. Friedman, *The World Is Flat* (New York: Farrar, Straus, and Giroux, 2005); Clifford J. Schultz III, Timothy J. Burkink, Bruno Grbac, and Natasa Renko, "When Policies and Marketing Systems Explode: An Assessment of Food Marketing in the War-Ravaged Balkans and Implications for Recovery, Sustainable Peace, and Prosperity," *Journal of Public Policy & Marketing* 24, no. 1 (2005), pp. 24–37; Nayan Chanda, *Bound Together, How Traders, Preachers, Adventurers, and Warriors Shaped Globalization* (New Haven, CT: Yale University Press, 2007); William Hernandez Requejo and John L. Graham, *Global Negotiation: The New Rules* (New York: Palgrave Macmillan, 2008), Chapter 13.

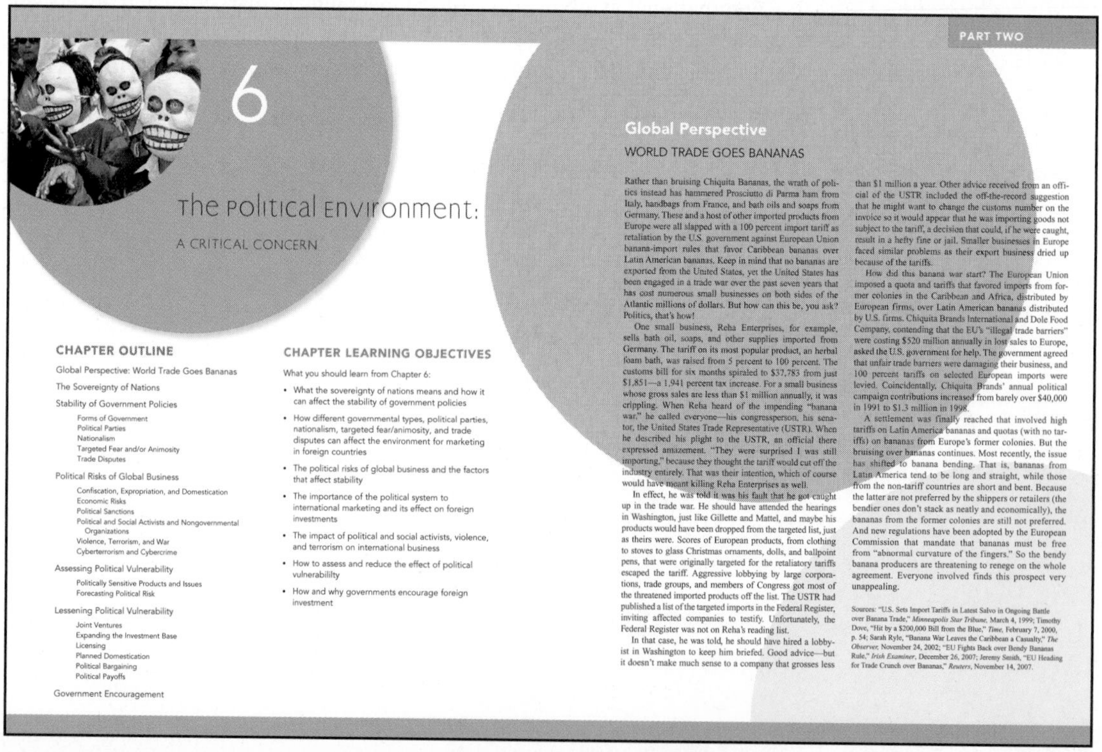

PART TWO

6

The political environment:

A CRITICAL CONCERN

CHAPTER OUTLINE

Global Perspective: World Trade Goes Bananas
The Sovereignty of Nations
Stability of Government Policies
- Forms of Government
- Political Parties
- Nationalism
- Targeted Fear and/or Animosity
- Trade Disputes

Political Risks of Global Business
- Confiscation, Expropriation, and Domestication
- Economic Risks
- Political Sanctions
- Political and Social Activists and Nongovernmental Organizations
- Violence, Terrorism, and War
- Cyberterrorism and Cybercrime

Assessing Political Vulnerability
- Politically Sensitive Products and Issues
- Forecasting Political Risk

Lessening Political Vulnerability
- Joint Ventures
- Expanding the Investment Base
- Licensing
- Planned Domestication
- Political Bargaining
- Political Payoffs

Government Encouragement

CHAPTER LEARNING OBJECTIVES

What you should learn from Chapter 6:

- What the sovereignty of nations means and how it can affect the stability of government policies
- How different governmental types, political parties, nationalism, targeted fear/animosity, and trade disputes can affect the environment for marketing in foreign countries
- The political risks of global business and the factors that affect stability
- The importance of the political system to international marketing and its effect on foreign investments
- The impact of political and social activists, violence, and terrorism on international business
- How to assess and reduce the effect of political vulnerabililty
- How and why governments encourage foreign investment

Global Perspective

WORLD TRADE GOES BANANAS

Rather than bruising Chiquita Bananas, the wrath of politics instead has hammered Prosciutto di Parma ham from Italy, handbags from France, and bath oils and soaps from Germany. These and a host of other imported products from Europe were all slapped with a 100 percent import tariff as retaliation by the U.S. government against European Union banana-import rules that favor Caribbean bananas over Latin American bananas. Keep in mind that no bananas are exported from the United States, yet the United States has been engaged in a trade war over the past seven years that has cost numerous small businesses on both sides of the Atlantic millions of dollars. But how can this be, you ask? Politics, that's how!

One small business, Reha Enterprises, for example, sells bath oil, soaps, and other supplies imported from Germany. The tariff on its most popular product, an herbal foam bath, was raised from 5 percent to 100 percent. The customs bill for six months spiraled to $37,783 from just $1,851—a 1,941 percent tax increase. For a small business whose gross sales are less than $1 million annually, it was crippling. When Reha heard of the impending "banana war," he called everyone—his congressperson, his senator, the United States Trade Representative (USTR). When he described his plight to the USTR, an official there expressed amazement. "They were surprised I was still importing," because they thought the tariff would cut off the industry entirely. That was their intention, which of course would have meant killing Reha Enterprises as well.

In effect, he was told it was his fault that he got caught up in the trade war. He should have attended the hearings in Washington, just like Gillette and Mattel, and maybe his products would have been dropped from the targeted list, just as theirs were. Scores of European products, from clothing to stoves to glass Christmas ornaments, dolls, and ballpoint pens, that were originally targeted for the retaliatory tariffs escaped the tariff. Aggressive lobbying by large corporations, trade groups, and members of Congress got most of the threatened imported products off the list. The USTR had published a list of the targeted imports in the Federal Register, inviting affected companies to testify. Unfortunately, the Federal Register was not on Reha's reading list.

In that case, he was told, he should have hired a lobbyist in Washington to keep him briefed. Good advice—but it doesn't make much sense to a company that grosses less than $1 million a year. Other advice received from an official of the USTR included the off-the-record suggestion that he might want to change the customs number on the invoice so it would appear that he was importing goods not subject to the tariff, a decision that could, if he were caught, result in a hefty fine or jail. Smaller businesses in Europe faced similar problems as their export business dried up because of the tariffs.

How did this banana war start? The European Union imposed a quota and tariffs that favored imports from former colonies in the Caribbean and Africa, distributed by European firms, over Latin American bananas distributed by U.S. firms. Chiquita Brands International and Dole Food Company, contending that the EU's "illegal trade barriers" were costing $520 million annually in lost sales to Europe, asked the U.S. government for help. The government agreed that unfair trade barriers were damaging their business, and 100 percent tariffs on selected European imports were levied. Coincidentally, Chiquita Brands' annual political campaign contributions increased from barely over $40,000 in 1991 to $1.3 million in 1998.

A settlement was finally reached that involved high tariffs on Latin America bananas and quotas (with no tariffs) on bananas from Europe's former colonies. But the bruising over bananas continues. Most recently, the issue has shifted to banana bending. That is, bananas from Latin America tend to be long and straight, while those from the non-tariff countries are short and bent. Because the latter are not preferred by the shippers or retailers (the bendier ones don't stack as neatly and economically), the bananas from the former colonies are still not preferred. And new regulations have been adopted by the European Commission that mandate that bananas must be free from "abnormal curvature of the fingers." So the bendy banana producers are threatening to renege on the whole agreement. Everyone involved finds this prospect very unappealing.

Sources: "U.S. Sets Import Tariffs in Latest Salvo in Ongoing Battle over Banana Trade," *Minneapolis Star Tribune*, March 4, 1999; Timothy Dove, "Hit by a $200,000 Bill from the Blue," *Time*, February 7, 2000, p. 54; Sarah Ryle, "Banana War Leaves the Caribbean a Casualty," *The Observer*, November 24, 2002; "EU Fights Back over Bendy Bananas Rule," *Irish Examiner*, December 26, 2007; Jeremy Smith, "EU Heading for Trade Crunch over Bananas," *Reuters*, November 14, 2007.

Crossing Borders Boxes

These invaluable boxes offer anecdotal company examples. These entertaining examples are designed to encourage critical thinking and guide students through topics ranging from ethical to cultural to global issues facing marketers today.

CROSSING BORDERS 2.2 Crossing Borders with Monkeys in His Pants

Robert Cusack smuggled a pair of endangered pygmy monkeys into the United States—in his pants! On June 13, 2002, a U.S. Fish and Wildlife Service special agent was called to Los Angeles International Airport after Cusack was detained by U.S. Customs on arrival from Thailand. Officials soon also discovered that Cusack had four endangered birds of paradise and 50 protected orchids with him. "When one of the inspectors opened up his luggage, one of the birds flew out," tells one official. "He had to go catch the bird." After finding the other purloined birds and exotic flowers, the inspectors asked, "Do you have anything else you should tell us about?" Cusack answered, "Yes, I have monkeys in my pants." The monkeys ended up in the Los Angeles Zoo, and the smuggler ended up in jail for 57 days. He also paid a five-figure fine.

Similarly, Wang Hong, a Chinese exporter, pleaded guilty to smuggling sea turtles into the United States. He didn't have them in his pants; instead, the sea turtle "parts" came in the form of shells and violin bows, among other things.

Smuggling isn't just a game played by sneaking individuals. Multinational companies can also get in the act. During the last year alone, convictions have come down for smuggling cell phones into Vietnam, cigarettes into Iraq and Canada, and platinum into China. In perhaps the biggest ever corporate case, after a nine-year lawsuit, Amway Corporation agreed to pay the Canadian government $38.1 million to settle charges it had avoided customs duties by undervaluing merchandise it exported from the United States to Canadian distributors over a six-year period. As long as there have been trade barriers, smuggling has been a common response. Indeed, Rudyard Kipling wrote some 100 years ago:

Five and twenty ponies trotting through the dark—
Brandy for the Parson, 'baccy for the clerk;
Laces for a lady, letters for a spy;
And watch the wall, my darling, while the Gentlemen go by!

Sources: "Amway Pays $38 Million to Canada," *Los Angeles Times*, September 22, 1989, p. 3; Patricia Ward Biederman, "Smuggler to Pay for Pocketing Monkeys," *Los Angeles Times*, December 19, 2002, p. B1; "Chinese National Pleads Guilty of Smuggling Protected Sea Turtles," Associated Press, January 3, 2008.

CROSSING BORDERS 10.3 Refusing to Pass along the Gas

Russia and Ukraine have escalated their dispute over natural gas supplies, raising the possibility that supplies of Russian fuel to Europe could be threatened if the tensions drag out. Seeking to force Kiev to sign new contracts and pay what it says are $600 million in debts, the Russian natural gas giant OAO Gazprom slashed gas supplies to Ukraine twice in two days and warned that further reductions could follow. Ukrainian state energy company NAK Naftogaz in turn threatened to dip into transit shipments of Russian natural gas to European customers to make up for the cuts. At least initially, those supplies weren't affected.

European Energy Commissioner Andris Piebalgs and Andrej Vajak, the economy minister of EU president Slovenia, insisted that supplies to the EU must remain uninterrupted. Despite Gazprom's supply cuts, Naftogaz said the combination of warm weather and ample natural gas in storage prevented the need for cutbacks to consumers in Ukraine or export flows—for now. Nonetheless, the latest ultimatum raised fears of a repeat of the January 2006 crisis in which European supplies were interrupted when Gazprom cut shipments to Ukraine in a price dispute. Gazprom quickly resumed pumping, but the episode sparked concerns across Europe about the company's reliability as a supplier. Europe gets about one-fourth of its gas from Russia, and the bulk of that is carried by pipeline across Ukraine.

Russian officials insist the current tensions are purely economic and blame Kiev for failing to fulfill a compromise deal on the debts. Critics denounced the Kremlin for using gas supplies as a political weapon, noting that Gazprom's threats came amid rising political tension in Kiev. Yet the presidents of two countries, Vladimir Putin and Viktor Yuschenko, claimed their differences had been resolved.

Sources: "Deadline Passes in Russian–Ukraine Gas Dispute," Agence France-Presse, March 2, 2008; Gregory L. White, "Gas-Supply Battle Escalates between Russia, Ukraine," *The Wall Street Journal* (online), March 4, 2008.

---

in kind. The war ended when the Europeans finally dropped pasta export subsidies. The EU and the United States also fought a similar trade war over bananas! Most recently, less developed countries are increasingly voicing complaints about American and European tariffs on agricultural products.[16]

Quotas. A quota is a specific unit or dollar limit applied to a particular type of good. Great Britain limits imported television sets, Germany has established quotas on Japanese ball bearings, Italy restricts Japanese motorcycles, and the United States has quotas on sugar, textiles, and, of all things, peanuts. Quotas put an absolute restriction on the quantity of a specific item that can be imported. When the Japanese first let foreign rice into their country, it was on a quota basis, but since 2000 the quotas have been replaced by tariffs.[17] Even more complicated, the banana war between the United States and the EU resulted in a mixed system wherein a quota of bananas is allowed into the EU with a tariff, then a second quota comes in tariff-free. Like tariffs, quotas tend to increase prices.[18] The U.S. quotas on textiles are estimated to add 50 percent to the wholesale price of clothing.

Voluntary Export Restraints. Similar to quotas are the *voluntary export restraints* (VERs) or *orderly market agreements* (OMAs). Common in textiles, clothing, steel, agriculture, and automobiles, the VER is an agreement between the importing country and the exporting country for a restriction on the volume of exports. Japan has a VER

---

[16] Allan Odhiambo, "EAC States in Row over Wheat Import Tariffs," *All Africa*, August 30, 2007.
[17] See the USA Rice Federation's Web site for details, http://www.usarice.com; also Hodgson et al., *Doing Business in the New Japan*.
[18] Peter T. Leach, "Is China Losing Its Edge?" *Journal of Commerce*, December 3, 2007.

The Americas[15]

Within the Americas, the United States, Canada, Central America, and South America have been natural if sometimes contentious trading partners. As in Europe, the Americas are engaged in all sorts of economic cooperative agreements, with NAFTA being the most significant and Mercosur and DR-CAFTA gaining in importance.

North American Free Trade Agreement (NAFTA)

Preceding the creation of the North American Free Trade Agreement (NAFTA), the United States and Canada had the world's largest bilateral trade agreement; each was the other's largest trading partner. Despite this unique commercial relationship, tariff and other trade barriers hindered even greater commercial activity. To further support trade activity, the two countries established the United States–Canada Free Trade Area (CFTA), designed to eliminate all trade barriers between the two countries. The CFTA created a single, continental commercial market for all goods and most services. The agreement between the United States and Canada was not a customs union like the European Community; no economic or political union of any kind was involved. It provided only for the elimination of tariffs and other trade barriers.

Shortly after both countries had ratified the CFTA, Mexico announced that it would seek free trade with the United States. Mexico's overtures were answered positively by the United States, and talks on a U.S.–Mexico free trade area began. Mexico and the United States had been strong trading partners for decades, but Mexico had never officially expressed an interest in a free trade agreement until the president of Mexico, Carlos Salinas de Gortari, announced that Mexico would seek such an agreement with the United States and Canada.

returned to more robust growth in large part due to the successful marketing of its vast energy resources.[14] All members of the CIS have had economic growth, and inflation has been held between a high of 5.9 percent for Tajikistan and a low of 0.2 percent for Kazakhstan.

[14] "Gazprom Eyes 10% of French Gas Market in 4–5 Years," *Dow Jones International News*, January 3, 2008.
[15] For a comprehensive list of all trade agreements in the Americas, with links to specific documents, visit http://www.oas-oas.org and select Trade Agreements.

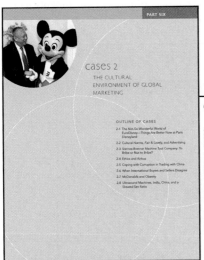

PART SIX

cases 2
THE CULTURAL ENVIRONMENT OF GLOBAL MARKETING

OUTLINE OF CASES

2-1 The Not-So-Wonderful World of EuroDisney—Things Are Better Now at Paris Disneyland
2-2 Cultural Norms, Fair & Lovely, and Advertising
2-3 Starnes-Brenner Machine Tool Company: To Bribe or Not to Bribe?
2-4 Ethics and Airbus
2-5 Coping with Corruption in Trading with China
2-6 When International Buyers and Sellers Disagree
2-7 McDonald's and Obesity
2-8 Ultrasound Machines, India, China, and a Skewed Sex Ratio

---

CASE 2–8 Ultrasound Machines, India, China, and a Skewed Sex Ratio

General Electric Co. and other companies have sold so many ultrasound machines in India that tests are now available in small towns like Indergarh, where there is no drinking water, electricity is infrequent, and roads turn to mud after a March rain shower. A scan typically costs $8, or a week's wages.

GE has waded into India's market as the country grapples with a difficult social issue: the abortion of female fetuses by families who want boys. Campaigners against the practice and some government officials are linking the country's widely reported skewed sex ratio with the spread of ultrasound machines. That's putting GE, the market leader in India, under the spotlight. It faces legal hurdles, government scrutiny, and thorny business problems in one of the world's fastest-growing economies.

"Ultrasound is the main reason the sex ratio is coming down," says Kalpana Bharmi, who is in charge of women and child welfare for the Datia district government, which includes Indergarh. Having a daughter is often viewed as incurring a lifetime of debt for parents because of the dowry payment at marriage. Compared with that, the cost of an ultrasound "is nothing," she says.

For more than a decade, the Indian government has tried to stop ultrasound technology from being used as a tool to determine gender. The devices are sound waves to produce images of fetuses or internal organs for a range of diagnostic purposes. India has passed laws forbidding doctors from disclosing the sex of fetuses, required official registrations of clinics, and stiffened punishments for offenders. Nevertheless, some estimate that hundreds of thousands of girl fetuses are aborted each year.

GE, by far the largest seller of ultrasound machines in India through a joint venture with the Indian outsourcing giant Wipro Ltd., introduced its own safeguards, even though that means forsaking sales. "We stress emphatically that the machines aren't to be used for sex determination," says V. Raja, chief executive of GE Healthcare South Asia. "This is not the root cause of female feticide in India."

But the efforts have failed to stop the problem, as a growing economy has made the scans affordable to more people. The skewed sex ratio is an example of how India's strong economy has, in unpredictable ways, exacerbated some nagging social problems, such as the traditional preference for boys. Some activists are accusing GE of not doing enough to prevent unlawful use of its machines to boost sales.

"There is a demand for a boy that's been completely exploited by multinationals," says Puneet Bedi, a New Delhi obstetrician. He says GE and others market the machines as an essential pregnancy tool, though the scans often aren't necessary for mothers in low-risk groups.

Prosecutors in the city of Hyderabad brought a criminal case against the GE venture with Wipro, as well as Erbis Engineering Co., the medical-equipment distributor in India for Japan's Toshiba Corp. In the suits, the district government alleged that the companies knowingly supplied ultrasound machines to clinics that were not registered with the government and were illegally performing sex-selection tests. The penalty is up to three months in prison and a fine of 1,000 rupees.

Both companies deny wrongdoing and say they comply with Indian laws. A GE spokesman said its legal team would be looking into the charges.

Vivek Paul, who helped build the early ultrasound business in India, first as a senior executive at GE and then at Wipro, says blame should be pinned on unethical doctors, not the machine's suppliers. "If someone drives a car through a crowded market and kills people, do you blame the car maker?" says Paul, who was Wipro's chief executive before he left the company in 2005. Paul is now a managing director at private equity specialists TPG Inc., formerly known as Texas Pacific Group.

India has been a critical market for GE. In outsourcing operations have helped the Fairfield, Connecticut, giant cut costs. The country also is a growing market for GE's heavy equipment and other products. The company won't disclose its ultrasound sales, but Wipro GE's overall sales in India, which includes ultrasounds and other diagnostic equipment, reached about $250 million in 2006, up from $30 million in 1995.

Annual ultrasound sales in India from all vendors also reached $77 million in 2006, up about 10 percent from the year before, according to an estimate from consulting firm Frost & Sullivan, which describes GE as the clear market leader. Other vendors include Siemens AG, Philips Electronics NV, and Mindray International Medical Ltd., a new Chinese entrant for India's price-sensitive customers.

India has long struggled with an inordinate number of male births, and female infanticide—the killing of newborn baby girls—remains a problem. The abortion of female fetuses is a more recent trend, but unless "urgent action is taken," it's poised to escalate as the use of ultrasound services expands, the United Nations Children's Fund said in a report. India's "alarming decline in the child sex ratio" is likely to exacerbate child marriage, trafficking of women for prostitution, and other problems, the report said.

The latest official Indian census, in 2001, showed a steep decline in the relative number of girls aged 0 to 6 years compared with the decade earlier: 927 girls for every 1,000 boys compared with 945 in 1991. In much of northwest India, the number of girls has fallen below 900 for every 1,000 boys. In the northern state of Punjab, the figure is below 800.

Only China today has a wider gender gap, with 832 girls born for every 1,000 boys among infants aged 0 to 4 years, according to UNICEF. GE sells about three times as many ultrasound machines in China as in India. In January, the Chinese government pledged to improve the gender balance, including tighter monitoring of ultrasounds. Some experts predict China will be more effective than India in enforcing its rules, given its success at other population-control measures.

Boys in India are viewed as wealth earners during life and lighters of one's funeral pyre at death. India's National Family Health Survey, released in February, showed that 90 percent of parents with two sons didn't want any more children. Of those with two daughters, 38 percent wanted to try again. Although there are restrictions on abortions in this Hindu-majority nation, the rules offer enough leeway for most women to get around them.

636

NEW Cases

New cases accompany the fourteenth edition, enlivening the material in the book and class discussions while broadening a student's critical thinking skills. These cases bring forth many of the topics discussed in the chapters and demonstrate how these concepts are dealt with in the real world.

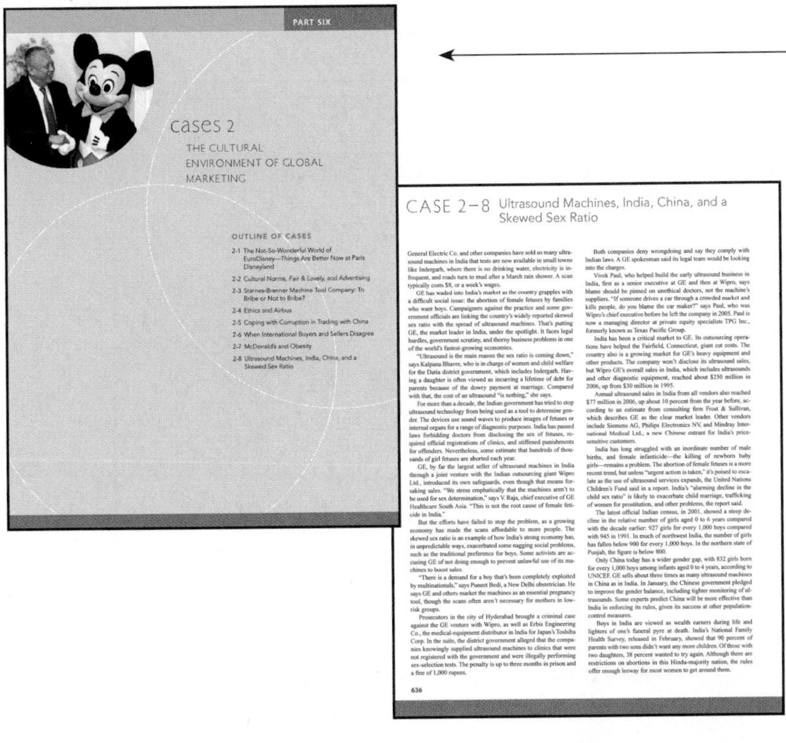

A Wealth of Supplements

Global Perspectives

At the beginning of each chapter, Global Perspectives give examples of current company experiences in global marketing. Illustrating chapter concepts, these profiles help students to combine the theory they read about with real-life application.

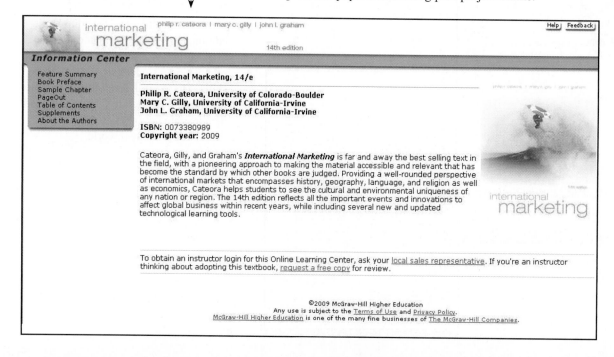

Online Learning Center

Numerous resources available for both instructors and students are online at www.mhhe.com/cateora14e. Instructor resources include downloadable versions of the Instructor's Manual, PowerPoint presentation, and Instructor Notes to accompany the videos. Student study tools include Chapter Quizzes, PowerPoint International Resource Links, and the Country Notebook Online with an interactive component so students can complete this popular marketing plan project online.

BRIEF CONTENTS

PART ONE

AN OVERVIEW

PART TWO

THE CULTURAL ENVIRONMENT OF GLOBAL MARKETS

PART THREE

ASSESSING GLOBAL MARKET OPPORTUNITIES

PART FOUR

DEVELOPING GLOBAL MARKETING STRATEGIES

PART FIVE

En los negocios no se cons
lo que se merece, se consi
lo que se negocia.

IMPLEMENTING GLOBAL MARKETING STRATEGIES

PART SIX

SUPPLEMENTARY MATERIAL

LIST OF CROSSING BORDERS BOXES

international marketing

1

the scope and challenge of international marketing

CHAPTER LEARNING OBJECTIVES

What you should learn from Chapter 1:

- The changing face of U.S. business

- The scope of the international marketing task

- The importance of the self-reference criterion (SRC)
  in international marketing

- The progression of becoming a global marketer

- The increasing importance of global awareness

Global Perspective

GLOBAL COMMERCE CAUSES PEACE

Global commerce thrives during peacetime. The economic boom in North America during the late 1990s was in large part due to the end of the Cold War and the opening of the formerly communist countries to the world trading system. However, we should also understand the important role that trade and international marketing play in producing peace.

Boeing Company, America's largest exporter, is perhaps the most prominent example. Although many would argue that Boeing's military sales (aircraft and missiles) do not exactly promote peace, over the years, that business has constituted only about 20 percent of the company's commercial activity. Up until 2002, of Boeing's some $60 billion in annual revenues, about 65 percent came from sales of commercial jets around the world and another 15 percent from space and communications technologies. Unfortunately, these historical numbers are being skewed by American military spending and the damage done to tourism by terrorism.[1] Even so, the company still counts customers in more than 90 countries, and its 150,000+ employees work in 70 countries. Its more than 11,000 commercial jets in service around the world carry about one billion travelers per year. Its NASA Services division is the lead contractor in the construction and operation of the 16-country International Space Station, first manned by an American and two Russians in the fall of 2000. The Space and Intelligence Systems Division also produces and launches communications satellites affecting people in every country.

All the activity associated with the development, production, and marketing of commercial aircraft and space vehicles requires millions of people from around the world to work together. Moreover, no company does more[2] to enable people from all countries to meet face-to-face for both recreation and commerce. All this interaction yields not just the mutual gain associated with business relationships but also personal relationships and mutual understanding. The latter are the foundation of global peace and prosperity.

Another class of companies that promotes global dialogue and therefore peace is the mobile phone industry. During 2007, more than one billion new mobile phones were purchased around the world, connecting more than one-quarter of all people on the planet. Nokia (Finland), the market leader, is well ahead of the American manufacturer Motorola, Samsung (S. Korea), LG (S. Korea), and Sony Ericsson (Japan/Sweden).

Individuals and small companies also make a difference—perhaps a subtler one than large multinational companies, but one just as important in the aggregate. Our favorite example is Daniel Lubetzky's company, PeaceWorks. Mr. Lubetzky used a fellowship at Stanford Law School to study how to foster joint ventures between Arabs and Israelis. Then, following his own advice, he created a company that combined basil pesto from Israel with other raw materials and glass jars supplied by an Arab partner to produce the first product in a line he called Moshe & Ali's Gourmet Foods. The company now sells four different product lines in 5,000 stores in the United States and has its headquarters on Park Avenue in New York, as well as business operations in Israel, Egypt, Indonesia, Turkey, and Sri Lanka. Again, beyond the measurable commercial benefits of cooperation between the involved Arabs, Israelis, and others is the longer-lasting and more fundamental appreciation for one another's circumstances and character.

International marketing is hard work. Making sales calls is no vacation, even in Paris, especially when you've been there 10 times before. But international marketing is important work. It can enrich you, your family, your company, and your country. And ultimately, when international marketing is done well, by large companies or small, the needs and wants of customers in other lands are well understood, and prosperity and peace are promoted along the way.[3]

Sources: http://www.boeing.com and http://www.peaceworks.com—both are worth a visit; mobile phone sales data are available at http://www.gartner.com.

---

[1] Circa 2008, about half of Boeing's business is defense related (http://www.boeing.com).

[2] The European commercial aircraft manufacturer Airbus is beginning to catch up, employing 57,000 people around the world (http://www.airbus.com, 2008).

[3] In response to criticisms of globalization catalyzed by the riots in Seattle in 1999, a growing literature argues for trade as a fundamental cause of peace. For a variety of such arguments, see *The Economist*, "Human Evolution, Homo Economicus?" April 9, 2005, pp. 67–68; James Flanigan, "Globalization Is Doing a World of Good for the U.S.," *Los Angeles Times*, April 24, 2005, pp. C1, C4; Jagdish Bhabwati, *In Defense of Globalization* (Oxford: Oxford University Press, 2004); Thomas L. Friedman, *The World Is Flat* (New York: Farrar, Straus, and Giroux, 2005); Clifford J. Schultz III, Timothy J. Burkink, Bruno Grbac, and Natasa Renko, "When Policies and Marketing Systems Explode: An Assessment of Food Marketing in the War-Ravaged Balkans and Implications for Recovery, Sustainable Peace, and Prosperity," *Journal of Public Policy & Marketing* 24, no. 1 (2005), pp. 24–37; Nayan Chanda, *Bound Together, How Traders, Preachers, Adventurers, and Warriors Shaped Globalization* (New Haven, CT: Yale University Press, 2007); William Hernandez Requejo and John L. Graham, *Global Negotiation: The New Rules* (New York: Palgrave Macmillan, 2008), Chapter 13.

Never before in American history have U.S. businesses, large and small, been so deeply involved in and affected by international business. A global economic boom, unprecedented in modern economic history, has been under way as the drive for efficiency, productivity, and open, unregulated markets sweeps the world. Powerful economic, technological, industrial, political, and demographic forces are converging to build the foundation of a new global economic order on which the structure of a one-world economic and market system will be built.

When we wrote those words eight years ago to open the eleventh edition of this book, the world was a very different place. The nation was still mesmerized by the information technology boom of the late 1990s. Most did not visualize the high-tech bust of 2001 or the associated Enron and WorldCom scandals. No one could have imagined the September 11, 2001, disasters, not even the perpetrators. The new wars in Afghanistan and Iraq were not on the horizon. The major international conflict grabbing headlines then was the series of diplomatic dustups among China, Taiwan, and the United States. Who could have predicted the disruptions associated with the 2003 SARS outbreak in Asia? The great Indian Ocean tsunami of 2004 was perhaps impossible to anticipate. Oil priced at more than $100 per barrel was also unthinkable then—the price seemed to have peaked at about $40 per barrel in late 2000.[4] We wrote about the promise of the space program and the international space station, whose future is now clouded by the Columbia shuttle tragedy and associated NASA budget cuts.

Through all these major events, American consumers continued to spend, keeping the world economy afloat. Layoffs at industrial icons such as United Airlines and Boeing and a generally tough job market didn't slow the booming American housing market until the fall of 2007. Lower government interest rates had yielded a refinancing stampede, distributing the cash that fueled the consumer spending, which finally flagging in early 2008. And seeing into the future is harder now than ever. Most experts expect global terrorism to increase, and the carnage in Bali, Madrid, and London seem to prove the point. Finally, as the global economy continues to wobble, international trade tensions take on new importance.[5] Competition from new Chinese companies has begun to raise concerns in the United States.[6] The steady growth of the U.S. trade and balance of payment deficits is particularly worrisome, particularly those with China.[7]

International marketing is affected by and affects all these things. For the first time in history, McDonald's has pulled out of international markets in both Latin America and the Middle East.[8] Slow economies, increasing competition, and anti-Americanism have impacted sales in both regions. Moreover, recall that the September 11 attacks targeted the *World Trade* Center in New York City. Indeed, the salient lesson for those involved in international commerce at the turn of the 21st century is to expect the unexpected. Any executive experienced in international business will verify that things never go as planned in global commerce. You still have to plan and forecast, but markets, particularly international ones, are ultimately unpredictable. The natural fluctuations in markets are best managed through building strong interpersonal and commercial relationships and broad portfolios of businesses. Flexibility means survival.

Perhaps now, more than ever, whether or not a U.S. company wants to participate directly in international business, it cannot escape the effects of the ever-increasing number of North American firms exporting, importing, and manufacturing abroad.

Aside from the tragic loss of life resulting from the terrorism of September 11, the event also represents a direct attack on the world trading system. The destruction of the New York City World Trade Center, it is hoped, will be the low point for global commerce and peace as the remainder of the second millennium unfolds. *(© Sean Adair/ Reuters/Corbis)*

[4] Niel King Jr., Chip Cummings, and Russell Gold, "Oil Hits $100, Jolting Markets," *The Wall Street Journal,* January 3, 2008, pp. A1, A6.

[5] Evelyn Iritani, "Trade Tension May Be Rising," *Los Angeles Times*, June 2, 2005, pp. C1, C6.

[6] Sara Bongiorni, *A Year Without "Made in China"* (New York: Wiley, 2007).

[7] Despite recent improvements, the trade deficit continues at dangerous levels. See Elizabeth Price and Brian Blackstone, "U.S. Trade Deficit Shrinks," *The Wall Street Journal*, November 12, 2007, p. 9.

[8] Richard Gibson, "McDonald's Swings to Loss on Sale of Restaurants," *The Wall Street Journal*, July 24, 2007.

[9] Bruce Wallace, "2 Trains Cross Korean Border," *Los Angeles Times*, May 17, 2007, p. A4; Moon Ihlwan, "A Capitalist Toehold in North Korea," *BusinessWeek*, June 11, 2007, p. 45; Associated Press, "North Korea Says It Gave Nuclear-Program List to U.S.," January 4, 2008.

Here the planet grows a little closer together. The European Parliament votes to start discussions with Turkey about joining the EU. Trade is beginning to bridge the religious divide between Christian Europe and Muslim Asia Minor. *(AP/Photo/Str)*

Nor can it ignore the number of foreign-based firms operating in U.S. markets, the growth of regional trade areas, the rapid growth of world markets, and the increasing number of competitors for global markets.

Of all the events and trends affecting global business today, four stand out as the most dynamic, the ones that will influence the shape of international business beyond today's "bumpy roads" and far into the future: (1) the rapid growth of the World Trade Organization and regional free trade areas such as the North American Free Trade Area and the European Union; (2) the trend toward the acceptance of the free market system among developing countries in Latin America, Asia, and eastern Europe; (3) the burgeoning impact of the Internet, mobile phones, and other global media on the dissolution of national borders; and (4) the mandate to manage the resources and global environment properly for the generations to come.

Today most business activities are global in scope. Technology, research, capital investment, and production, as well as marketing, distribution, and communications networks all have global dimensions. Every business must be prepared to compete in an increasingly interdependent global economic and physical environment, and all businesspeople must be aware of the effects of these trends when managing either a domestic company that exports or a multinational conglomerate. As one international expert noted, every American company is international, at least to the extent that its business performance is conditioned in part by events that occur abroad. Even companies that do not operate in the international arena are affected to some degree by the success of the European Union, the export-led growth in South Korea, the revitalized Mexican economy, the economic changes taking place in China, military conflicts in the Middle East, and global warming.

The challenge of international marketing is to develop strategic plans that are competitive in these intensifying

Trade also is easing tensions among North Korea, its close neighbors, and the United States. A rail link between North and South Korea has opened for the first time in nearly 60 years to provide transportation of raw materials and managers from the South, bound for a special economic development zone at Kaesong in the North.[9] *(AP/Photo/Lee Jin-man)*

CROSSING BORDERS 1.1

What Do French Farmers, Chinese Fishermen, and Russian Hackers Have in Common?

They can all disrupt American firms' international marketing efforts.

Thousands of supporters and activists gathered recently to show support for a French sheep farmer on trial for vandalizing a local McDonald's. Jose Bove has become an international legend of antiglobalization. Leader of the French Peasant Confederation, he has demonized the fast-food chain as the symbol of American trade "hegemony" and economic globalization. He and nine other farmers served six weeks in jail and paid fines for partially destroying the restaurant. Most recently, Bove has been thrown in jail again, this time for 10 months, for damaging fields of genetically modified rice and corn.

Local fishermen demanded suspension of the reclamation and dredging of a bay near Hong Kong, where Disney has built Hong Kong Disneyland. The fishermen claimed that the work has plunged water quality near the site to levels much worse than predicted, killing huge numbers of fish. The spokesman for the fishermen claims they have lost some $30 million because of depleted and diseased fish stocks.

St. Petersburg has, in a decade, become the capital of Russian computer hackers. These are the same folks that are reputed to have invaded Microsoft's internal network. Russia's science city has become the natural hub for high-tech computer crime. Dozens of students, teachers, and computer specialists hack into computers, seeing themselves as members of an exciting subculture that has flourished since the fall of communism. Before *glasnost* and *perestroika*, those who were dissatisfied with official Soviet culture turned to samizdat literature and bootleg tapes of Western pop music. But the Gorbachev era left little to rebel against. Today Russia's hackers, who even have their own magazine, entitled *Khacker*, have created a new underground culture that perhaps offers more excitement than passing around banned poetry. The city also benefits from being near the Baltic states. Programs are copied on the black market; the latest Windows pirate always arrives in Russia months before it appears in the West. Yes, fines and prison terms are consequences if caught. But computers are readily accessible at universities and increasingly in homes.

Sources: Agnes Lam, "Disney Dredging Killing Fish," *South China Morning Post*, November 5, 2000, p. 4; John Tagliabue, "Activist Jailed in Attack on Modified Crops," *The New York Times*, February 27, 2003, p. 6; Clifford J. Levy, "Russian Hackers: On the Right Side of Soft Laws," *International Herald Tribune*, October 22, 2007, p. 3.

global markets. For a growing number of companies, being international is no longer a luxury but a necessity for economic survival. These and other issues affecting the world economy, trade, markets, and competition are discussed throughout this text.

The Internationalization of U.S. Business

Current interest in international marketing can be explained by changing competitive structures, coupled with shifts in demand characteristics in markets throughout the world. With the increasing globalization of markets, companies find they are unavoidably enmeshed with foreign customers, competitors, and suppliers, even within their own borders. They face competition on all fronts—from domestic firms and from foreign firms. A huge portion of all consumer products—from CD players to dinnerware—sold in the United States is foreign made. Sony, Norelco, Samsung, Toyota, and Nescafé are familiar brands in the United States, and for U.S. industry, they are formidable opponents in a competitive struggle for U.S. and world markets.

Many familiar U.S. companies are now foreign controlled or headed in that direction.[10] When you drop in at a 7-Eleven convenience store or buy Firestone tires, you are buying directly from a Japanese company. Some well-known brands no longer owned by U.S. companies are Carnation (Swiss), *The Wall Street Journal* (Australian), and the all-American Smith & Wesson handgun that won the U.S. West, which is owned by a British firm. The last U.S.-owned company to manufacture TV sets was Zenith, but even

---

[10] Steven Stecklow and Martin Peers, "Murdoch's Role as Proprietor, Journalist Plan for Dow Jones," *The Wall Street Journal*, June 6, 2007.

Exhibit 1.1
Foreign Acquisitions of
U.S. Companies

Sources: Adapted from Kurt
Badenhausen, "Name Game,"
Forbes, July 24, 2000; "China Poised
to Take Over U.S. Huffy Bikes,"
Reuters, June 28, 2005; Michael
Barbaro and Andrew Ross Sorkin,
"Barneys New York Sold to Dubai
Government for $825 Million," *The
New York Times*, June 23, 2007.

U.S. Companies	Foreign Owner
Firestone (tires)	Japan
Ben & Jerry's (ice cream)	U.K.
Alpo (pet food)	Switzerland
Burger King (fast food)	U.K.
Random House (publishing)	Germany
TV Guide (magazine)	Australia
The Wall Street Journal (newspaper)	Australia
Oroweat (breads)	Mexico
Smith & Wesson (guns)	U.K.
RCA (televisions)	France/China
Chef America ("Hot Pockets" and other foods)	Switzerland
[IBM] ThinkPad (personal computers)	China
Huffy Corp. (bicycles)	China
Swift & Company (meatpacking)	Brazil
Barneys New York (retailer)	Dubai
Columbia Pictures (movies)	Japan

it was acquired by South Korea's LG Electronics, Inc., which manufactures Goldstar TVs and other products. Pearle Vision, Universal Studios, and many more are currently owned or controlled by foreign multinational businesses (see Exhibit 1.1). Foreign investment in the United States is more than $16.3 trillion, some $2.6 trillion more than American overseas investments. Companies from the United Kingdom lead the group of investors, with companies from the Netherlands, Japan, Germany, and Switzerland following, in that order.

Other foreign companies that entered the U.S. market through exporting their products into the United States realized sufficient market share to justify building and buying manufacturing plants in the United States. Honda, BMW, and Mercedes are all manufacturing in the United States. Investments go the other way as well. Ford bought Volvo; PacifiCorp acquired Energy Group, the United Kingdom's largest electricity supplier and second-largest gas distributor; and Wisconsin Central Transportation, a medium-sized U.S. railroad, controls all U.K. rail freight business and runs the queen's private train via its English, Welsh & Scottish Railway unit. It has also acquired the company that runs rail shuttles through the Channel Tunnel. Investments by U.S. multinationals abroad are nothing new.

Along with NAFTA have come two of Mexico's most prominent brand names. Gigante, one of Mexico's largest supermarket chains, now has several stores in southern California, including this one in Anaheim. On store shelves are a variety of Bimbo bakery products. Grupo Bimbo, a growing Mexican multinational, has recently purchased American brand-named firms such as Oroweat, Webers, and Mrs. Baird's Bread.

CROSSING BORDERS 1.2

Blanca Nieves, La Cenicienta y Bimbo (Snow White, Cinderella, and Bimbo)

Bimbo is a wonderful brand name. It so well demonstrates the difficulties of marketing across borders. Of course, to middle America, "bimbo" is slang for a dumb blonde. Even in *Webster's Dictionary* it's defined as ". . . a term of disparagement, a tramp."

Meanwhile, in Spain, Mexico, and other Spanish-speaking countries, the word "bimbo" has no pejorative meaning. Indeed, it is often simply associated with the little white bear logo of Bimbo brand bread. Bimbo is the most popular brand of bread in Mexico and, with the North American Free Trade Agreement (NAFTA), is stretching its corporate arms north and south. For example, the Mexican firm most recently acquired Mrs. Baird's Bread, the most popular local brand in Dallas, Texas, and Fargo, the most popular bread brand in Argentina. And you can now see 18-wheelers pulling truckloads of Bimbo products north on Interstate 5 toward Latino neighborhoods in Southern California and beyond.

Perhaps Bimbo is the reason the city leaders in Anaheim so feared Gigante's entrance into their city. Gigante, the Mexican-owned supermarket chain, features Bimbo buns, tomatillos, cactus pears, and other Latino favorites. Gigante already has three stores in Los Angeles County. But it was denied the city's permission to open a new market near the "Happiest Place on Earth." One has to wonder if Disneyland, Anaheim's biggest employer, may have been fretting over the juxtaposition of the Bimbo brand and its key characters, blonde, little, all-American Alice and her cinema sisters. Actually, a better case can be made that the Gigante–Anaheim imbroglio was more a matter of a mix of nationalism, xenophobia, and even racism. The city council eventually was forced to allow Gigante to open.

American firms have often run into similar problems as they have expanded around the world. Consider French nationalism. French farmers are famous for their protests—throwing lamb chops at their trade ministers and such. Or better yet, Culture Minister Jack Lang's comments about the U.S. Cartoon Network: "We must fight back against this American aggression. It is intolerable that certain North American audiovisual groups shamelessly colonize our countries."

Consider our own fear and loathing of "Japanese colonization" in both the 1920s and the 1980s. This apparent xenophobia turned to racism when Americans stoned Toyotas and Hondas but not Volkswagens and BMWs; when we decried Japanese takeovers of American firms and ignored Germany's recent gorging on the likes of Bankers Trust, Random House, and Chrysler.

PEMEX's current ban on American investments in the oil and gas industry in Mexico is a good example of nationalism. However, when British Petroleum buying ARCO is no problem, but Mexican cement giant CEMEX buying Houston's Southdown is, that's racism at work.

A cruel irony regarding Gigante's problems in Anaheim is well revealed by a quick drive around Tijuana. During the last decade, the change in Tijuana's retail facade has been remarkable. In this border town, after NAFTA, Blockbuster Video, Burger King, Costco, Smart & Final, and other American brands now dominate the signage.

Sources: John L. Graham, "Blanca Nieves, La Cenicienta, y Bimbo," *La Opinion*, February 22, 2002, p. C1 (translated from the Spanish); Denise M. Bonilla, "Latino Market Arrives with Giant Aspirations," *Los Angeles Times*, May 7, 2003, p. B6; Clifford Kraus, "New Accents in the U.S. Economy," *The New York Times*, May 2, 2007, pp. C1, C14.

Multinationals have been roaming the world en masse since the end of World War II, buying companies and investing in manufacturing plants. What is relatively new for U.S. companies is having their global competitors competing with them in "their" market, the United States. One of the more interesting new entrants is Chivas USA, a Mexican-owned soccer team that will play its matches in southern California.[11]

Once the private domain of domestic businesses, the vast U.S. market that provided an opportunity for continued growth must now be shared with a variety of foreign companies and products. Companies with only domestic markets have found increasing difficulty in sustaining their customary rates of growth, and many are seeking foreign markets in which to expand. Companies with foreign operations find that foreign earnings are making an important overall contribution to total corporate profits. A four-year Conference Board study of 1,250 U.S. manufacturing companies found that multinationals of all sizes and in

---

[11] Ivan Orozco, "Chivas USA: Guzan Keeper of the Year," *Los Angeles Daily News*, November 1, 2007, p. C5.

Exhibit 1.2
Selected U.S. Companies
and Their International
Sales

Source: Compiled from annual
reports of listed firms, 2007 and 2008.

Company	Global Revenues (billions)	Percent Revenues from Outside the U.S.
Wal-Mart	$345.0	22.3%
Ford Motor	160.3	46.1
General Electric	163.4	47.7
CitiGroup	89.6	42.6
Hewlett-Packard	91.7	65.0
Boeing	61.5	37.4
Intel	35.4	> 78.0
Coca-Cola	24.1	> 71.0
Apple	24.0	~ 40.0
Starbucks	7.8	17.0

all industries outperformed their strictly domestic U.S. counterparts. They grew twice as fast in sales and earned significantly higher returns on equity and assets. Furthermore, the U.S. multinationals reduced their manufacturing employment, both at home and abroad, more than domestic companies. Another study indicates that despite the various difficulties associated with internationalization, on average, firm value is increased by global diversification.[12] Indeed, at least periodically, profit levels from international ventures exceed those from domestic operations for many multinational firms.[13]

Exhibit 1.2 illustrates how important revenues generated on investments abroad are to U.S. companies. In many cases, foreign sales were greater than U.S. sales, demonstrating the global reach of these American brands. Apple's performance has been most impressive, with total revenues exploding from just $6 billion in 2003 to $24 billion in 2007. Meanwhile, the company maintained its traditional level of 40 percent revenues from outside the United States.

Companies that never ventured abroad until recently are now seeking foreign markets. Companies with existing foreign operations realize they must be more competitive to succeed against foreign multinationals. They have found it necessary to spend more money and time improving their marketing positions abroad because competition for these growing markets is intensifying. For firms venturing into international marketing for the first time and for those already experienced, the requirement is generally the same: a thorough and complete commitment to foreign markets and, for many, new ways of operating.

International Marketing Defined

International marketing is the performance of business activities designed to plan, price, promote, and direct the flow of a company's goods and services to consumers or users in more than one nation for a profit. The only difference between the definitions of domestic marketing and international marketing is that in the latter case, marketing activities take place in more than one country. This apparently minor difference, "in more than one country," accounts for the complexity and diversity found in international marketing operations. Marketing concepts, processes, and principles are universally applicable, and the marketer's task is the same, whether doing business in Dimebox, Texas, or Dar es Salaam, Tanzania. Business's goal is to make a profit by promoting, pricing, and distributing products for which there is a market. If this is the case, what is the difference between domestic and international marketing?

The answer lies not with different concepts of marketing but with the environment within which marketing plans must be implemented. The uniqueness of foreign marketing comes from the range of unfamiliar problems and the variety of strategies necessary to cope with different levels of uncertainty encountered in foreign markets.

Competition, legal restraints, government controls, weather, fickle consumers, and any number of other uncontrollable elements can, and frequently do, affect the profitable outcome

---

[12] John A. Doukas and Ozgur B. Kan, "Does Global Diversification Destroy Firm Value?" *Journal of International Business Studies* 37 (2006), pp. 352–71.

[13] Justin Lahart, "Behind Stocks' Run at Record," *The Wall Street Journal*, April 25, 2007, pp. C1–2.

of good, sound marketing plans. Generally speaking, the marketer cannot control or influence these uncontrollable elements but instead must adjust or adapt to them in a manner consistent with a successful outcome. What makes marketing interesting is the challenge of molding the controllable elements of marketing decisions (product, price, promotion, distribution, and research) within the framework of the uncontrollable elements of the marketplace (competition, politics, laws, consumer behavior, level of technology, and so forth) in such a way that marketing objectives are achieved. Even though marketing principles and concepts are universally applicable, the environment within which the marketer must implement marketing plans can change dramatically from country to country or region to region. The difficulties created by different environments are the international marketer's primary concern.

The International Marketing Task

The international marketer's task is more complicated than that of the domestic marketer because the international marketer must deal with at least two levels of uncontrollable uncertainty instead of one. Uncertainty is created by the uncontrollable elements of all business environments, but each foreign country in which a company operates adds its own unique set of uncontrollable factors.

Exhibit 1.3 illustrates the total environment of an international marketer. The inner circle depicts the controllable elements that constitute a marketer's decision area, the second circle encompasses those environmental elements at home that have some effect on foreign-operation decisions, and the outer circles represent the elements of the foreign environment for each foreign market within which the marketer operates. As the outer circles illustrate, each foreign market in which the company does business can (and usually does) present separate problems involving some or all of the uncontrollable elements. Thus, the more foreign markets in which a company operates, the greater is the possible variety of foreign environmental factors with which to contend. Frequently, a solution to a problem in country market A is not applicable to a problem in country market B.

Marketing Decision Factors

The successful manager constructs a marketing program designed for optimal adjustment to the uncertainty of the business climate. The inner circle in Exhibit 1.3 represents the area under the control of the marketing manager. Assuming the necessary overall corporate resources, structures, and competencies that can limit or promote strategic choice,[14] the marketing manager blends price, product, promotion, channels-of-distribution, and research activities to capitalize on anticipated demand. The controllable elements can be altered in the long run and, usually, in the short run to adjust to changing market conditions, consumer tastes, or corporate objectives.

The outer circles surrounding the marketing decision factors represent the levels of uncertainty created by the domestic and foreign environments. Although the marketer can blend a marketing mix from the controllable elements, the uncontrollable factors are precisely that; the marketer must actively evaluate and, if needed, adapt. That effort—the adaptation of the marketing mix to these environmental factors—determines the outcome of the marketing enterprise.

Aspects of the Domestic Environment

The second circle in Exhibit 1.3 represents the aspects of the domestic environment that are often beyond the control of companies. These include home-country elements that can have a direct effect on the success of a foreign venture: political and legal forces, economic climate, and competition.

A political decision involving domestic foreign policy can have a direct effect on a firm's international marketing success. For example, the U.S. government placed a total ban on trade with Libya to condemn Libyan support for terrorist attacks, imposed restrictions on trade with South Africa to protest apartheid, and placed a total ban on trade with Iraq, whose actions were believed to constitute a threat to the national security of the United States and its allies. In each case, the international marketing programs of the U.S. company, whether it was IBM, Exxon,

---

[14] A. Verbke, "The Evolutionary View of the MNE and the Future of Internationalization Theory," *Journal of International Business Studies* 34, no. 6 (2003), pp. 498–504.

Exhibit 1.3
The International Marketing Task

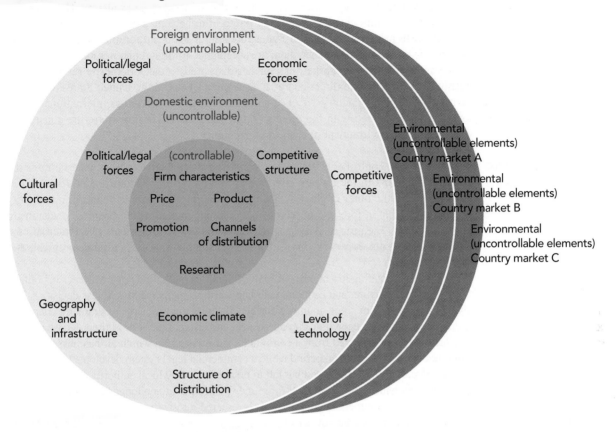

or Hawg Heaven Bait Company, were restricted by these political decisions. The U.S. government has the constitutional right to restrict foreign trade when such trade adversely affects the security or economy of the country or when such trade is in conflict with U.S. foreign policy.

Conversely, positive effects occur when changes in foreign policy offer countries favored treatment. Such were the cases when South Africa abolished apartheid and the embargo was lifted and when the U.S. government decided to uncouple human rights issues from foreign trade policy and grant permanently normalized trade relations (PNTR) status to China, paving the way for its entry into the World Trade Organization (WTO). In both cases, opportunities were created for U.S. companies. Finally, note that on occasion, companies can exercise a controversially high degree of influence over such legislation in the United States. Recall that it is Congress' responsibility to regulate business, not vice versa. Indeed, in the case of PNTR for China, companies with substantial interests there, such as Boeing and Motorola, lobbied hard for the easing of trade restrictions.

The domestic economic climate is another important home-based uncontrollable variable with far-reaching effects on a company's competitive position in foreign markets. The capacity to invest in plants and facilities, either in domestic or foreign markets, is to a large extent a function of domestic economic vitality. It is generally true that capital tends to flow toward optimum use; however, capital must be generated before it can have mobility. Furthermore, if internal economic conditions deteriorate, restrictions against foreign investment and purchasing may be imposed to strengthen the domestic economy.

Competition within the home country can also have a profound effect on the international marketer's task.[15] For more than a century, Eastman Kodak dominated the U.S. film

---

[15] G. R. G. Benito, B. Grogaard, and R. Narula, "Environmental Influences on MNE Subsidiary Roles: Economic Integration and the Nordic Countries," *Journal of International Business Studies* 34, no. 5 (2003), pp. 443–56.

market and could depend on achieving profit goals that provided capital to invest in foreign markets. Without having to worry about the company's lucrative base, management had the time and resources to devise aggressive international marketing programs. However, the competitive structure changed when Fuji Photo Film became a formidable competitor by lowering film prices in the United States, opening a $300 million plant, and gaining 12 percent of the U.S. market. Since then, the acceptance of digital photography, with Canon, from Japan, leading the market, has further disrupted Kodak's domestic business. As a result, Kodak has had to direct energy and resources back to the United States. Competition within its home country affects a company's domestic as well as international plans. Inextricably entwined with the effects of the domestic environment are the constraints imposed by the environment of each foreign country.

Aspects of the Foreign Environment

In addition to uncontrollable domestic elements, a significant source of uncertainty is the number of factors in the foreign environment that are often uncontrollable (depicted in Exhibit 1.3 by the outer circles). A business operating in its home country undoubtedly feels comfortable in forecasting the business climate and adjusting business decisions to these elements. The process of evaluating the uncontrollable elements in an international marketing program, however, often involves substantial doses of cultural, political, and economic shock.

A business operating in a number of foreign countries might find polar extremes in political stability, class structure, and economic climate—critical elements in business decisions. The dynamic upheavals in some countries further illustrate the problems of dramatic change in cultural, political, and economic climates over relatively short periods of time. A case in point is China, which has moved from a communist legal system in which all business was done with the state to a transitional period while a commercial legal system develops. In this transitional phase, new laws are passed but left to be interpreted by local authorities, and confusion prevails about which rules are still in force and which rules are no longer applicable.

For example, commercial contracts can be entered into with a Chinese company or individual only if that company or person is considered a "legal person." To be a legal person in China, the company or person must have registered as such with the Chinese government. To complicate matters further, binding negotiations may take place only with "legal representatives" of the "legal person." So if your company enters into negotiations with a Chinese company or person, you must ask for signed legal documents establishing the right to do business. The formalities of the signature must also be considered. Will a signature on a contract be binding, or is it necessary to place a traditional Chinese seal on the document? Even when all is done properly, the government still might change its mind. Coca-Cola had won approval for its plan to build a new facility to produce product for its increasing Chinese market share, but before construction began, the Chinese parliament objected that Coca-Cola appeared to be too successful in China, so negotiations continued delaying the project. Such are the uncertainties of the uncontrollable political and legal factors of international business.

The more significant elements in the uncontrollable international environment, shown in the outer circles of Exhibit 1.3, include political/legal forces, economic forces, competitive forces, level of technology,[16] structure of distribution, geography and infrastructure, and cultural forces.[17] These forces constitute the principal elements of uncertainty an international marketer must cope with in designing a marketing program. Although each will be discussed in depth in subsequent chapters, consider the level of technology and political/legal forces as illustrations of the uncontrollable nature of the foreign environment.

The level of technology is an uncontrollable element that can often be misread because of the vast differences that may exist between developed and undeveloped countries. A marketer cannot assume that understanding of the concept of preventive maintenance for machinery is the same in other countries as in the United States. Technical expertise may not be available

---

[16] Shih-Fen S. Chen, "Extending Internationalization Theory: A New Perspective on International Technology Transfer and Its Generalization," *Journal of International Business Studies* 36 (2005), pp. 231–45.

[17] Laszlo Tihany, David A. Griffith, and Craig J. Russell, "The Effect of Cultural Distance on Entry Mode Choice, International Diversification, and MNE Performance: A Meta-Analysis," *Journal of International Business Studies* 36, no. 3 (2005), pp. 270–83.

CROSSING BORDERS 1.3 | Mobile Phones, Economic Development, and Shrinking the Digital Divide

Wedged between stalls of dried fish and mounds of plastic goods, a red shipping container is loaded with Coca-Cola bottles. The local distributor for Soweto market, located in a tatty corner of Zambia's capital city, Lusaka, sells all its stock every few days. A full load costs 10m kwacha (about $2,000). In cash, this amount can be hard to get hold of, takes ages to count, and—being 10 times the average annual wage—is tempting to thieves. So Coca-Cola now tells its 300 Zambian distributors to pay for deliveries not in cash but by sending text messages from their mobile phones. The process takes about 30 seconds, and the driver issues a receipt. Faraway computers record the movement of money and stock. Coca-Cola is not alone. Around the corner from the market, a small dry-cleaning firm lets customers pay for laundry using their phones. So do Zambian petrol stations and dozens of bigger shops and restaurants.

This is just one example of the many innovative ways in which mobile phones are being used in the poorest parts of the world. Anecdotal evidence of mobile phones' ability to boost economic activity is abundant: They enable fishermen or farmers to check prices at different markets before selling produce, make it easier for people to look for jobs, and prevent wasted journeys. Mobile phones reduce transaction costs, broaden trade networks, and substitute for costly physical transport. They are of particular value when other means of communication (such as roads, post, or fixed-line phones) are poor or nonexistent.

This importance can be hard for people in affluent countries to understand, because the ways in which mobile phones are used in low-income countries are so different. In particular, phones are widely shared. One person in a village buys a mobile phone, perhaps using a microcredit loan. Others then rent it out by the minute; the small profit margin enables its owner to pay back the loan and make a living. When the phone rings, its owner carries it to the home of the person being called, who then takes the call. Other entrepreneurs set up as "text message interpreters," sending and receiving text messages (which are generally cheaper than voice calls) on behalf of their customers, who may be illiterate. So though the number of phones per 100 people is low by affluent-world standards, they still make a big difference.

Source: *The Economist*, "Economics Focus, Calling across the Divide," March 12, 2005, p. 74; Bruce Meyerson, "Skype Takes Its Show on the Road," *BusinessWeek*, October 29, 2007, p. 38.

at a level necessary for product support, and the general population may not have an adequate level of technical knowledge to maintain equipment properly. In such situations, a marketer will have to take extra steps to make sure that the importance of routine maintenance is understood and carried out. Furthermore, if technical support is not readily available, local people will have to be specially trained, or the company will have to provide support.

Political and legal issues face a business, whether it operates at home or in a foreign country. However, the issues abroad are often amplified by the "alien status" of the company, which increases the difficulty of properly assessing and forecasting the dynamic international business climate. The alien status of a foreign business has two dimensions: It is alien in that foreigners control the business and in that the culture of the host country is alien to management. The alien status of a business means that, when viewed as an outsider, it can be seen as an exploiter and receive prejudiced or unfair treatment at the hands of politicians, legal authorities, or both. Political activists can rally support by advocating the expulsion of the "foreign exploiters," often with the open or tacit approval of authorities. The Indian government, for example, gave Coca-Cola the choice of either revealing its secret formula or leaving the country. The company chose to leave. When it was welcomed back several years later, it faced harassment and constant interference in its operations from political activists, inspired by competing soft drink companies.

Furthermore, in a domestic situation, political details and the ramifications of political and legal events are often more transparent than they are in some foreign countries. For instance, whereas in the United States, each party in a dispute has access to established legal procedures and due process, legal systems in many other countries are still evolving. In many foreign countries, corruption may prevail, foreigners may receive unfair treatment, or the laws may be so different from those in the home country that they are misinterpreted. The point is that a foreign company is foreign and thus always subject to the political whims of the local government to a greater degree than a domestic firm.

Masai tribesmen in Tanzania with their cell phones. Competition is fierce among carriers in burgeoning markets like Tanzania. Both Celtel and Vodacom provide paint for local stores and houses. Here you see the bright Celtel yellow and red, which goes nicely with the colorful garb of local customers. Vodacom blue is at a disadvantage there. We imagine the ear lobe "carrying case" makes it easy to hear the ring but hard to dial! *(right: © Neil Thomas/africanpictures.net)*

Political/legal forces and the level of technology are only two of the uncontrollable aspects of the foreign environment that are discussed in subsequent chapters. The uncertainty of different foreign business environments creates the need for a close study of the uncontrollable elements within each new country. Thus a strategy successful in one country can be rendered ineffective in another by differences in political climate, stages of economic development, level of technology, or other cultural variations.

Environmental Adaptation Needed

To adjust and adapt a marketing program to foreign markets, marketers must be able to interpret effectively the influence and impact of each of the uncontrollable environmental elements on the marketing plan for each foreign market in which they hope to do business. In a broad sense, the uncontrollable elements constitute the culture; the difficulty facing the marketer in adjusting to the culture lies in recognizing their impact. In a domestic market, the reaction to much of the environment's (cultural) impact on the marketer's activities is automatic; the various cultural influences that fill our lives are simply a part of our socialization, and we react in a manner acceptable to our society without consciously thinking about it.

The task of cultural adjustment, however, is the most challenging and important one confronting international marketers; they must adjust their marketing efforts to cultures to which they are not attuned. In dealing with unfamiliar markets, marketers must be aware of the frames of reference they are using in making their decisions or evaluating the potential of a market, because judgments are derived from experience that is the result of acculturation in the home country. Once a frame of reference is established, it becomes an important factor in determining or modifying a marketer's reaction to situations—social and even nonsocial.

For example, time-conscious Americans are not culturally prepared to understand the culturally nuanced meaning of time to Latin Americans. Such a difference must be learned to avoid misunderstandings that can lead to marketing failures. Such a failure occurs every time sales are lost when a "long waiting period" in the outer office of a Latin American customer is misinterpreted by an American sales executive. Cross-cultural misunderstandings can also occur when a simple hand gesture has a number of different meanings in different parts of the world. When wanting to signify something is fine, many people in the United States raise a hand and make a circle with the thumb and forefinger. However, this same hand gesture means "zero" or "worthless" to the French, "money" to the Japanese, and a general sexual insult in Sardinia and Greece. A U.S. president sent an unintentional message to some Australian protesters when he held up his first two fingers with the back of his hand to the protesters. Meaning to give the "victory" sign, he was unaware that in Australia, the same hand gesture is equivalent to holding up the middle finger in the United States.

Cultural conditioning is like an iceberg—we are not aware of nine-tenths of it. In any study of the market systems of different peoples, their political and economic structures, religions, and other elements of culture, foreign marketers must constantly guard against measuring and assessing the markets against the fixed values and assumptions of their own cultures. They must take specific steps to make themselves aware of the home cultural reference in their analyses and decision making.

The Self-Reference Criterion and Ethnocentrism: Major Obstacles

The key to successful international marketing is adaptation to environmental differences from one market to another. Adaptation is a conscious effort on the part of the international marketer to anticipate the influences of both the foreign and domestic uncontrollable factors on a marketing mix and then to adjust the marketing mix to minimize the effects.

The primary obstacles to success in international marketing are a person's self-reference criterion (SRC) and an associated ethnocentrism. The SRC is an unconscious reference to one's own cultural values, experiences, and knowledge as a basis for decisions. Closely connected is ethnocentrism, that is, the notion that people in one's own company, culture, or country knows best how to do things. Ethnocentrism is particularly a problem for American managers at the beginning of the 21st century because of America's dominance in the world economy during the late 1990s. Ethnocentrism is generally a problem when managers from affluent countries work with managers and markets in less affluent countries. Both the SRC and ethnocentrism impede the ability to assess a foreign market in its true light.

When confronted with a set of facts, we react spontaneously on the basis of knowledge assimilated over a lifetime—knowledge that is a product of the history of our culture. We seldom stop to think about a reaction; we simply react. Thus when faced with a problem in another culture, our tendency is to react instinctively and refer to our SRC for a solution. Our reaction, however, is based on meanings, values, symbols, and behavior relevant to our own culture and usually different from those of the foreign culture. Such decisions are often not good ones.

To illustrate the impact of the SRC, consider misunderstandings that can occur about personal space between people of different cultures. In the United States, unrelated individuals keep a certain physical distance between themselves and others when talking or in groups. We do not consciously think about that distance; we just know what feels right without thinking. When someone is too close or too far away, we feel uncomfortable and either move farther away or get closer to correct the distance. In doing so, we are relying on our SRC. In some cultures, the acceptable distance between individuals is substantially less than that which is comfortable for Americans. When someone from another culture approaches an American too closely, the American, unaware of that culture's acceptable distance, unconsciously reacts by backing away to restore the proper distance (i.e., proper by American standards), and confusion results for both parties. Americans assume foreigners are pushy, while foreigners assume Americans are unfriendly and literally "standoffish." Both react according to the values of their own SRCs, making both victims of a cultural misunderstanding.

Your self-reference criterion can prevent you from being aware of cultural differences or from recognizing the importance of those differences. Thus you might fail to recognize the need to take action, you might discount the cultural differences that exist among countries, or you might react to a situation in a way offensive to your hosts. A common mistake made by Americans is to refuse food or drink when offered. In the United States, a polite refusal is certainly acceptable, but in Asia or the Middle East, a host is offended if you refuse hospitality. Although you do not have to eat or drink much, you do have to accept the offering of hospitality. Understanding and dealing with the SRC are two of the more important facets of international marketing.

Ethnocentrism and the SRC can influence an evaluation of the appropriateness of a domestically designed marketing mix for a foreign market. If U.S. marketers are not aware, they might evaluate a marketing mix based on U.S. experiences (i.e., their SRC) without fully appreciating the cultural differences that require adaptation. Esso, the brand name of a gasoline, was a successful name in the United States and would seem harmless enough for foreign countries; however, in Japan, the name phonetically means "stalled car," an undesirable image for gasoline. Another example is the "Pet" in Pet Milk. The name has been used for decades, yet in France, the word *pet* means, among other things, "flatulence"—again, not the desired image for canned milk. Both of these examples were real mistakes made by major companies stemming from their reliance on their SRC in making a decision.

When marketers take the time to look beyond their own self-reference criteria, the results are more positive. A British manufacturer of chocolate biscuits (cookies, in American English), ignoring its SRC, knows that it must package its biscuits differently to accommodate the Japanese market. Thus, in Japan, McVitie's chocolate biscuits are wrapped individually, packed in presentation cardboard boxes, and priced about three times higher than in the United Kingdom—the cookies are used as gifts in Japan and thus must look and be perceived as special. Unilever, appreciating the uniqueness of its markets, repackaged and reformulated its detergent for Brazil. One reason was that the lack of washing machines among poorer Brazilians made a simpler soap formula necessary. Also, because many people wash their clothes in rivers, the powder was packaged in plastic rather than paper so it would not get soggy. Finally, because the Brazilian poor are price conscious and buy in small quantities, the soap was packaged in small, low-priced packages. Even McDonald's modifies its traditional Big Mac in India, where it is known as the Maharaja Mac. This burger features two mutton patties, because most Indians consider cows sacred and don't eat beef. In each of these examples, had the marketers' own self-reference criteria been the basis for decisions, none of the necessary changes would have been readily apparent based on their home-market experience.

The most effective way to control the influence of ethnocentrism and the SRC is to recognize their effects on our behavior. Although learning every culture in depth and being aware of every important difference is almost humanly impossible, an awareness of the need to be sensitive to differences and to ask questions when doing business in another culture can help you avoid many of the mistakes possible in international marketing. Asking the appropriate question helped the Vicks Company avoid making a mistake in Germany. It discovered that in German, "Vicks" sounds like the crudest slang equivalent of "intercourse," so it changed the name to "Wicks" before introducing the product.

Be aware, also, that not every activity within a marketing program is different from one country to another; indeed, there probably are more similarities than differences. For example, the McVitie's chocolate biscuits mentioned earlier are sold in the United States in the same package as in the United Kingdom. Such similarities, however, may lull the marketer into a false sense of apparent sameness. This apparent sameness, coupled with the self-reference criterion, is often the cause of international marketing problems. Undetected similarities do not cause problems; however, the one difference that goes undetected can create a marketing failure.

To avoid errors in business decisions, the knowledgeable marketer will conduct a cross-cultural analysis that isolates the SRC influences and maintain a vigilance regarding ethnocentrism. The following steps are suggested as a framework for such an analysis.

1. Define the business problem or goal in home-country cultural traits, habits, or norms.

2. Define the business problem or goal in foreign-country cultural traits, habits, or norms through consultation with natives of the target country. Make no value judgments.

3. Isolate the SRC influence in the problem and examine it carefully to see how it complicates the problem.

4. Redefine the problem without the SRC influence and solve for the optimum business goal situation.

An American sales manager newly posted to Japan decided that his Japanese sales representatives did not need to come into the office every day for an early morning meeting before beginning calls to clients in Tokyo. After all, that was how things were done in the United States. However, the new policy, based on both the American's SRC and a modicum of ethnocentrism, produced a precipitous decline in sales performance. In his subsequent discussions with his Japanese staff, he determined that Japanese sales representatives are motivated mostly by peer pressure. Fortunately, he was able to recognize that his SRC and his American "business acumen" did not apply in this case in Tokyo. A return to the proven system of daily meetings brought sales performance back to previous levels.

The cross-cultural analysis approach requires an understanding of the culture of the foreign market as well as one's own culture. Surprisingly, understanding one's own culture may require additional study, because much of the cultural influence on market behavior remains at a subconscious level and is not clearly defined.

Developing a Global Awareness

Opportunities in global business abound for those who are prepared to confront myriad obstacles with optimism and a willingness to continue learning new ways. The successful businessperson in the 21st century will have global awareness and a frame of reference that goes beyond a region or even a country and encompasses the world. To be globally aware is to have (1) tolerance of cultural differences and (2) knowledge of cultures, history, world market potential, and global economic, social, and political trends.

Tolerance for cultural differences is crucial in international marketing. Tolerance is understanding cultural differences and accepting and working with others whose behaviors may be different from yours. You do not have to accept as your own the cultural ways of another, but you must allow others to be different and equal. For example, the fact that punctuality is less important in some cultures does not make them less productive, only different. The tolerant person understands the differences that may exist between cultures and uses that knowledge to relate effectively.

A globally aware person is knowledgeable about cultures and history. Knowledge of cultures is important in understanding behavior in the marketplace or in the boardroom. Knowledge of history is important because the way people think and act is influenced by their history. Some Latin Americans' reluctance toward foreign investment or Chinese reluctance to open completely to outsiders can be understood better if you have a historical perspective.

Global awareness also involves knowledge of world market potentials and global economic, social, and political trends. Over the next few decades, enormous changes will take place in the market potentials in almost every region of the world, all of which a globally aware person must continuously monitor. Finally, a globally aware person will keep abreast of the global economic, social, and political trends because a country's prospects can change as these trends shift direction or accelerate. The former republics of the Soviet Union, along with Russia, eastern Europe, China, India, Africa, and Latin America, are undergoing economic, social, and political changes that have already altered the course of trade and defined new economic powers. The knowledgeable marketer will identify opportunities long before they become evident to others. It is the authors' goal in this text to guide the reader toward acquiring global awareness.

Global awareness can and should be built into organizations using several approaches. The obvious strategy is to select individual managers specifically for their demonstrated global awareness. Global awareness can also be obtained through personal relationships in other countries. Indeed, market entry is very often facilitated through previously established social ties. Certainly, successful long-term business relationships with foreign customers often result in an organizational global awareness based on the series of interactions required by commerce. Foreign agents and partners can help directly in this regard. But perhaps the most effective approach is to have a culturally diverse senior executive staff or board of directors. Unfortunately, American managers seem to see relatively less value in this last approach than managers in most other countries.

Stages of International Marketing Involvement

Once a company has decided to go international, it has to decide the degree of marketing involvement and commitment it is prepared to make. These decisions should reflect considerable study and analysis of market potential and company capabilities—a process not always followed. Research has revealed a number of factors favoring faster internationalization: (1) Companies with either high-technology and/or marketing-based resources appear to be better equipped to internationalize than more traditional manufacturing kinds of companies;[18] (2) smaller home markets and larger production capacities appear to favor internationalization;[19] and (3) firms with key managers well networked internationally are able to accelerate the internationalization process.[20] Many companies begin tentatively in international marketing, growing as they gain experience and gradually changing strategy and tactics as they become more committed.[21] Others enter international marketing after much research and with fully developed long-range plans, prepared to make investments to acquire a market position and often evincing bursts of international activities.[22] One study suggests that striking a balance between the two approaches may actually work best,[23] with a variety of conditions and firm characteristics to be evaluated.

Regardless of the means employed to gain entry into a foreign market, a company may make little or no actual market investment—that is, its marketing involvement may be limited to selling a product with little or no thought given to the development of market control. Alternatively, a company may become totally involved and invest large sums of money and effort to capture and maintain a permanent, specific position in the market. In general, one of five (sometimes overlapping) stages can describe the international marketing involvement of a company.[24] Although the stages of international marketing involvement are presented here in a linear order, the reader should not infer that a firm progresses from one stage to another; quite to the contrary, a firm may begin its international involvement at any one stage or be in more than one stage simultaneously. For example, because of a short product life cycle and a thin but widespread market for many technology products, many high-tech companies, large and small, see the entire world, including their home market, as a single market and strive to reach all possible customers as rapidly as possible.

No Direct Foreign Marketing

A company in this stage does not actively cultivate customers outside national boundaries; however, this company's products may reach foreign markets. Sales may be made to trading companies as well as foreign customers who directly contact the firm. Or products may reach foreign markets via domestic wholesalers or distributors who sell abroad without the explicit encouragement or even knowledge of the producer. As companies develop Web sites on the Internet, many receive orders from international Web surfers. Often an unsolicited order from a foreign buyer is what piques the interest of a company to seek additional international sales.

Infrequent Foreign Marketing

Temporary surpluses caused by variations in production levels or demand may result in infrequent marketing overseas. The surpluses are characterized by their temporary nature; therefore, sales to foreign markets are made as goods become available, with little or no intention of maintaining continuous market representation. As domestic demand increases and absorbs surpluses, foreign sales activity is reduced or even withdrawn. In this stage, little or no change is seen in the company organization or product lines. However, few

---

[18] Chiung-Hui Tseng, Patriya Tansuhaj, William Hallagan, and James McCullough, "Effects of Firm Resources on Growth in Multinationality," *Journal of International Business Studies* 38 (2007), pp. 961–74.

[19] Terence Fan and Phillip Phan, "International New Ventures: Revisiting the Influences behind the 'Born-Global' Firm," *Journal of International Business Studies* 38 (2007), pp. 1113–31.

[20] Susan Freeman and S. Tamer Cavusgil, "Toward a Typology of Commitment States among Managers of Born-Global Firms: A Study of Accelerated Internationalization," *Journal of International Marketing* 15 (2007), pp. 1–40.

[21] Marian V. Jones and Nicole E. Coviello, "Internationalisation: Conceptualising an Entrepreneurial Process of Behaviour in Time," *Journal of International Business Studies* 36, no. 3 (2005), pp. 284–303.

[22] Elizabeth Maitland, Elizabeth L. Rose, and Stephen Nicholas, "How Firms Grow: Clustering as a Dynamic Model of Internationalization," *Journal of International Business Studies* 36 (2005), pp. 435–51.

[23] Harry G. Barkema and Rian Drogendijk, "Internationalizing in Small, Incremental or Larger Steps?" *Journal of International Business Studies* 38 (2007), pp. 1132–48.

[24] Alan M. Rugman and Alain Verbeke, "Extending the Theory of the Multinational Enterprise: Internationalization and Strategic Management Perspectives," *Journal of International Business Studies* 3 (2003), pp. 125–37.

companies fit this model today, because customers around the world increasingly seek long-term commercial relationships. Furthermore, evidence suggests that financial returns from initial international expansions are limited.[25]

Regular Foreign Marketing

At this level, the firm has permanent productive capacity devoted to the production of goods to be marketed in foreign markets. A firm may employ foreign or domestic overseas intermediaries, or it may have its own sales force or sales subsidiaries in important foreign markets. The primary focus of operations and production is to service domestic market needs. However, as overseas demand grows, production is allocated for foreign markets, and products may be adapted to meet the needs of individual foreign markets. Profit expectations from foreign markets move from being seen as a bonus in addition to regular domestic profits to a position in which the company becomes dependent on foreign sales and profits to meet its goals.

Meter-Man, a small company (25 employees) in southern Minnesota that manufactures agricultural measuring devices, is a good example of a company in this stage.[26] In 1989, the 35-year-old company began exploring the idea of exporting; by 1992 the company was shipping product to Europe. Today, one-third of Meter-Man's sales are in 35 countries, and soon the company expects international sales to account for about half of its business. "When you start exporting, you say to yourself, this will be icing on the cake," says the director of sales and marketing. "But now I say going international has become critical to our existence."

International Marketing

Companies in this stage are fully committed to and involved in international marketing activities. Such companies seek markets all over the world and sell products that are a result of planned production for markets in various countries. This planning generally entails not only the marketing but also the production of goods outside the home market. At this point, a company becomes an international or multinational marketing firm.

The experience of Fedders, a manufacturer of room air conditioners, typifies that of a company that begins its international business at this stage.[27] Even though it is the largest manufacturer of air conditioners in the United States, the firm faced constraints in its domestic market. Its sales were growing steadily, but sales of air conditioners (the company's only product) are seasonal, and thus, domestic sales at times do not even cover fixed costs. Furthermore, the U.S. market is mature, with most customers buying only replacement units. Any growth would have to come from a rival's market share, and the rivals, Whirlpool and Matsushita, are formidable. Fedders decided that the only way to grow was to venture abroad.

Fedders decided that Asia, with its steamy climate and expanding middle class, offered the best opportunity. China, India, and Indonesia were seen as the best prospects. China was selected because sales of room air conditioners had grown from 500,000 units to over 4 million in five years, which still accounted for only 12 percent of the homes in cities like Beijing, Shanghai, and Guangzhou. The company saw China as a market with terrific growth potential. After careful study, Fedders entered a joint venture with a small Chinese air conditioner company that was looking for a partner; a new company, Fedders Xinle, formed. The company immediately found that it needed to redesign its product for this market. In China, air conditioners are a major purchase, seen as a status symbol, not as a box to keep a room cool, as in the United States. The Chinese also prefer a split-type air conditioner, with the unit containing the fan inside the room and the heat exchanger mounted on a wall outside. Because Fedders did not manufacture split models, it designed a new product that is lightweight, energy efficient, and packed with features, such as a remote control and an automatic air-sweeping mechanism.

---

[25] Farok J. Contractor, Sumit K. Kundu, and Chin-Chun Hsu, "A Three-Stage Theory of International Expansion: The Link between Multinationality and Performance in the Service Sector," *Journal of International Business Studies* 34, no. 1 (2003), pp. 5–18.

[26] See http://www.meter-man.com for its product line and other details.

[27] See http://www.fedders.com for details about the company.

CROSSING BORDERS 1.4   Orange County, CA, Travels East and West

For $500,000 you can now buy a four-bedroom house in Orange County—in China!

The homes are designed by Southern California architects and built with American features but are located in a new development an hour's drive north of Beijing. The country road can be icy and is lined by fields and populated by trucks and sheep. The landscape is a far cry from palm-ringed golf courses and "Surfin' USA." A bit after Sun City, another half-built gated community, the tidy homes of Orange County come into view. Finally, you drive through a stone portal, past advertisements showing men fly-fishing in cowboy hats and such, and pull up before the impressive mansions of Watermark-Longbeach, the epicenter of *faux* L.A. in China. Says homeowner Nasha Wei, a former army doctor turned business-woman, "I liked it immediately—it is just like a house in California." By the way, in other neighborhoods around Beijing, you can also buy a large home in a development of French villas called "Palais de Fortune" or an eco-friendly Toronto-designed home in "Maple Town."

And apparently, in France, the waves can actually be better than in California. Check out the 60-footers at Belharra Reef off St. Jean de Luz. Or hang ten along the surfwear shops nearby in the hamlet of Hossegor in southwest France. They're all there: Roxy, Rip Curl Girl, Billabong, and Quicksilver Boardriders Club. And the kids in the neighborhoods and sidewalk cafés are decked out in Volcom sweatshirts, Vans sneakers, and jeans.

The $5-billion plus surfwear industry, rooted in Orange County, California, has established a beach-head in Europe. So many U.S. surfwear companies have international headquarters, subsidiaries, and stores in Pays Basque that it has a new nickname: *la petite Californie*. "This is the best place to observe the market," says Petra Holtschneider, who is organiz-ing the first Action Sports Retailer trade show in the area this summer. "So if you're not here, you're not getting it."

Finally, perhaps the scariest OC exports are the television programs about the place. First it was Fox's *The OC*, then MTV's *Laguna Beach: The Real Orange County*, which has now morphed into *Newport Harbor: The Real Orange County*. The latter is now showing an entirely new generation of Europeans the latest kinds of misbehavior going on in "paradise" while influenc-ing teen fashions globally. And there's a British spin-off in the works, *Alderley Edge, Cheshire*. Perhaps it will make its way back to the United States in the form of "educational TV"—those British accents make them sound so smart!

Sources: Elisabeth Rosenthal, "North of Beijing, California Dreams Come True," *The New York Times*, February 3, 2003, p. A3; Geoffrey A. Fowler, "Let 100 McMansions Bloom," *The Wall Street Journal*, October 19, 2007, pp. W1, W10; Leslie Earnest, "Riding a French New Wave," *Los Angeles Times*, May 11, 2003, p. C1; Cristina Kinon, "The Laguna Effect: MTV's Sexy Soaps Are Changing the Face of Fashion, Mags, and the Way Teens Speak," *New York Daily News*, August 13, 2007, p. 33; "Rich Kids to Get an Edge," *Daily Star* (UK), February 23, 2007, p. 36.

The joint venture appears to be successful, and the company is exploring the possibility of marketing to other Asian markets and maybe even back to the United States with the new product that it developed for the Chinese market. As Fedders expands into other mar-kets and makes other commitments internationally, it continues to evolve as an interna-tional or multinational company. The company may remain in this stage, as most companies do, or go through a change in orientation and become a global company.

Global Marketing   At the global marketing level, the most profound change is the orientation of the com-pany toward markets and associated planning activities. At this stage, companies treat the world, including their home market, as one market. Market segmentation decisions are no longer focused on national borders. Instead, market segments are defined by income levels, usage patterns, or other factors that frequently span countries and regions.[28] Often this transition from international marketing to global marketing is catalyzed by a company's crossing the threshold at which more than half its sales

---

[28] Frenkel Ter Hofstede, Jan-Benedict E. M. Steenkamp, and Michel Wedel, "International Market Segmentation Based on Consumer-Product Relations," *Journal of Marketing Research* 36 (February 1999), pp. 1–17.

North of Beijing, China, new development is being marketed as Orange County, China. The gardens and stucco and tile exteriors are all intended to replicate the Mediterranean look and feel of homes in Newport Beach, California. (© Robyn Beck/AFP/ Getty Image)

revenues comes from abroad. The best people in the company begin to seek international assignments, and the entire operation—organizational structure, sources of finance, production, marketing, and so forth—begins to take on a global perspective.[29]

The example of Coca-Cola's transition from international to global is instructive. Coca-Cola had actually been a global company for years; the mid-1990s organizational change was the last step in recognizing the changes that had already occurred. Initially, all international divisions reported to an executive vice president in charge of international operations, who, along with the vice president of U.S. operations, reported to the president. The new organization consists of six international divisions. The U.S. business unit accounts for about 20 percent of profits and has been downgraded to just part of one of the six international business units in the company's global geographic regions. The new structure does not reduce the importance of the company's North American business; it just puts other areas on an equal footing. It represents the recognition, however, that future growth is going to come from emerging markets outside the United States.

International operations of businesses in global marketing reflect the heightened competitiveness brought about by the globalization of markets, interdependence of the world's economies, and the growing number of competing firms from developed and developing countries vying for the world's markets. *Global companies* and *global marketing* are terms frequently used to describe the scope of operations and marketing management orientation of companies in this stage.

---

[29] One author argues for a middle ground on the issue of global markets: See Pankaj Ghemawat, "Semiglobalization and International Business Strategy," *Journal of International Business Studies* 34 (2003), pp. 139–52.

Orange County has also come to France in the form of the southern California surfing culture and clothiers. The OC's Quiksilver opened its European headquarters in southwest France in 1984. Last year, European sales amounted to over $1 billion. Part of the firm's success in Europe can be attributed to hiring local nationals in key marketing positions. Maritxu Darrigrand, former French women's surfing champion, is now Quiksilver's marketing director for Europe. The OC has also come to the U.K. as *Laguna Beach: The Real Orange County*. The MTV program brings California beach culture—clothes, music, and misbehavior—to Europe. (*right:* © The McGraw-Hill Companies, Inc.)

Strategic Orientation

The stages of international marketing involvement described previously do not necessarily coincide with managers' thinking and strategic orientations. Often companies are led into international and even global markets by burgeoning consumer or customer demands, and strategic thinking is secondary to "filling the next order." But putting strategic thinking on the back burner has resulted in marketing failures for even the largest companies.

The consensus of researchers and authors[30] in this area reveals three relatively distinctive approaches that seem to dominate strategic thinking in firms involved in international markets:

1. Domestic market extension concept

2. Multidomestic market concept

3. Global marketing concept

Differences in the complexity and sophistication of a company's marketing activity depend on which orientation guides its operations. The ideas expressed in each strategic orientation reflect the philosophical orientation that also should be associated with successive stages in the evolution of the international operations in a company.

Domestic Market Extension Orientation

The domestic company seeking sales extension of its domestic products into foreign markets illustrates this orientation to international marketing. It views its international operations as secondary to and an extension of its domestic operations; the primary motive is to market excess domestic production. Domestic business is its priority, and foreign sales are seen as a profitable extension of domestic operations. Even though foreign markets may be vigorously pursued, the firm's orientation remains basically domestic. Its attitude toward international sales is typified by the belief that if it sells in St. Louis, it will sell anywhere else in the world. Minimal, if any, efforts are made to adapt the marketing mix to foreign markets; the firm's orientation is to market to foreign customers in the same manner in which the company markets to domestic customers. It seeks markets in which demand is similar to the home market and its domestic product will be acceptable. This domestic market extension strategy can be very profitable; large and small exporting companies approach international marketing from this perspective. Firms with this marketing approach are classified as ethnocentric. Meter-Man, discussed previously, could be said to follow this orientation.

Multidomestic Market Orientation

Once a company recognizes the importance of differences in overseas markets and the importance of offshore business to the organization, its orientation toward international business may shift to a multidomestic market strategy. A company guided by this concept has a strong sense that country markets are vastly different (and they may be, depending on the product) and that market success requires an almost independent program for each country. Firms with this orientation market on a country-by-country basis, with separate marketing strategies for each country.

Subsidiaries operate independently of one another in establishing marketing objectives and plans, and the domestic market and each of the country markets have separate marketing mixes with little interaction among them. Products are adapted for each market with little coordination with other country markets; advertising campaigns are localized, as are the pricing and distribution decisions. A company with this concept does not look for similarity among elements of the marketing mix that might respond to standardization; rather, it aims for adaptation to local country markets. Control is typically decentralized to reflect the belief that the uniqueness of each market requires local marketing input and control. Firms with this orientation would be classified as polycentric. Fedders, as it progresses in its plans, fits this orientation.

Global Market Orientation

A company guided by a global marketing orientation or philosophy is generally referred to as a global company; its marketing activity is global, and its market coverage is the world.

---

[30] A seminal paper in this genre is Yorum Wind, Susan P. Douglas, and Howard V. Perlmutter, "Guidelines for Developing International Marketing Strategy," *Journal of Marketing*, April 1973, pp. 14–23; also important is Anne-Wil Harzing, "An Empirical Analysis and Extension of the Bartlett and Ghoshal Typology of Multinational Companies," *Journal of International Business Studies* 31, no. 1 (2000), pp. 101–20.

A company employing a global marketing strategy strives for efficiencies of scale by developing a standardized marketing mix applicable across national boundaries. Markets are still segmented, but the country or region is considered side by side with a variety of other segmentation variables, such as consumer characteristics (age, income, language group), usage patterns, and legal constraints. The world as a whole is viewed as the market, and the firm develops a global marketing strategy. The global marketing company would fit regiocentric or geocentric classifications. The Coca-Cola Company, Ford Motor Company, and Intel are among the companies that can be described as global companies.

The global marketing concept views an entire set of country markets (whether the home market plus just 1 other country or the home market and 100 other countries) as a unit, identifying groups of prospective buyers with similar needs as a global market segment and developing a marketing plan that strives for standardization wherever it is cost and culturally effective. This effort might mean a company's global marketing plan has a standardized product but country-specific advertising, or has a standardized theme in all countries with country- or cultural-specific appeals to a unique market characteristic, or has a standardized brand or image but adapts products to meet specific country needs, and so on. In other words, the marketing planning and marketing mix are approached from a global perspective, and where feasible in the marketing mix, efficiencies of standardization are sought. Wherever cultural uniqueness dictates the need for adaptation of the product, its image, and so on, it is accommodated. For example, McDonald's standardizes its processes, logos, most of its advertising, and store decor and layouts whenever and wherever possible. However, you will find wine on the menu in France and beer in Germany, a Filipino-style spicy burger in Manila, and pork burgers in Thailand—all to accommodate local tastes and customs. The point is, being global is a mind-set, a way of looking at the market for commonalties that can be standardized across regions or country-market groups. And such a global mind-set can work alike for the largest companies and small companies[31] that take aggressive strategies toward learning.[32]

As the competitive environment facing U.S. businesses becomes more internationalized—and it surely will—the most effective orientation for many firms engaged in marketing in another country will be a global orientation. This orientation means operating as if all the country markets in a company's scope of operations (including the domestic market) were approachable as a single global market and standardizing the marketing mix where culturally feasible and cost effective. It does not, however, mean a slavish adherence to one strategic orientation. Depending on the product and market, other orientations may make more marketing sense. For example, Procter & Gamble may pursue a global strategy for disposable diapers but a multidomestic strategy in Asian markets for detergents.

The Orientation of International Marketing

Most problems encountered by the foreign marketer result from the strangeness of the environment within which marketing programs must be implemented. Success hinges, in part, on the ability to assess and adjust properly to the impact of a strange environment. The successful international marketer possesses the best qualities of the anthropologist, sociologist, psychologist, diplomat, lawyer, prophet, and businessperson.

In light of all the variables involved, with what should a textbook in foreign marketing be concerned? It is the opinion of the authors that a study of foreign marketing environments, people, and cultures and their influences on the total marketing process is of primary concern and is the most effective approach to a meaningful presentation. Our views are supported by the most recent ranking of countries on their extent of globalization—see Exhibit 1.4.[33] Yes, the United States is near the top of the list, and most of the "Global Top

---

[31] Gary A. Knight and S. Tamer Cavusgil, "Innovation, Organizational Capabilities, and the Born-Global Firm," *Journal of International Business Studies* 35, no. 2 (2004), pp. 124–41.

[32] Sylvie Chetty and Colin Campbell-Hunt, "A Strategic Approach to Internationalization: A Traditional versus a 'Born-Global' Approach," *Journal of International Marketing* 12, no. 1 (2004), pp. 57–81.

[33] "Measuring Globalization," *Foreign Policy*, November/December 2007, pp. 68–77.

Exhibit 1.4
Foreign Policy's Global Top 20

The countries that top the charts in trade, travel, technology, and links to the rest of the world

Source: *Foreign Policy*, November/December 2007, pp. 68–77. Copyright 2007 by *Foreign Policy*. Reproduced with permission of *Foreign Policy* via Copyright Clearance Center.

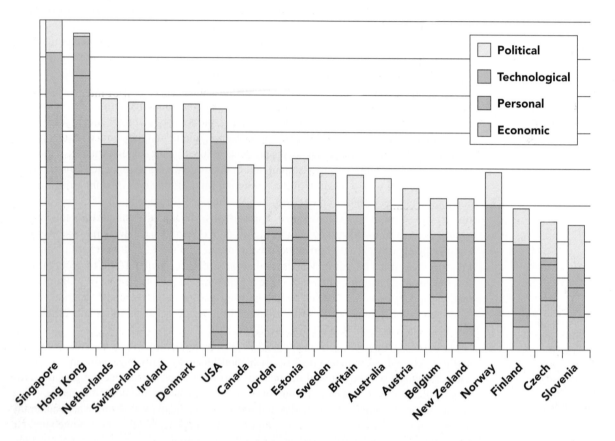

ECONOMIC INTEGRATION:

Trade and foreign direct investment

TECHNOLOGICAL CONNECTIVITY:

Internet users, Internet hosts, and secure servers

PERSONAL CONTACT:

International travel and tourism, international telephone traffic, and remittances and personal transfers (including worker remittances, compensation to employees, and other person-to-person and non-governmental transfers)

POLITICAL ENGAGEMENT:

Membership in international organizations, personnel and financial contributions to U.N. peacekeeping missions, international treaties ratified, and governmental transfers

20" are small countries. However, the key conclusion to be drawn from the graph is the dominance of "technological connectivity" for America. In particular, notice that as a country, the United States is weakest on the "personal contact" dimension. Compared with folks in other countries, Americans generally do not experience foreign environments. This lack is the gap our book focuses on.

Consequently, the orientation of this text can best be described as an environmental/cultural approach to international strategic marketing. By no means is it intended to present principles of marketing; rather, it is intended to demonstrate the unique problems of international marketing. It attempts to relate the foreign environment to the marketing process and to illustrate the many ways in which culture can influence the marketing task. Although marketing principles are universally applicable, the cultural environment within which the marketer must implement marketing plans can change dramatically from country to country. It is with the difficulties created by different environments that this text is primarily concerned.

The text is concerned with any company marketing in or into any other country or groups of countries, however slight the involvement or the method of involvement. Hence this discussion of international marketing ranges from the marketing and business practices of small exporters, such as a Colorado-based company that generates more than 50 percent of its $40,000 annual sales of fish-egg sorters in Canada, Germany, and Australia, to the practices of global companies such as Motorola, Avon, and Johnson & Johnson, all of which generate more than 50 percent of their annual profits from the sales of multiple products to multiple country-market segments all over the world.

The first section of *International Marketing* offers an overview of international marketing, including a brief discussion of the global business environment confronting the marketer. The next section deals exclusively with the uncontrollable elements of the environment and their assessment, followed by chapters on assessing global market opportunities. Then, management issues in developing global marketing strategies are discussed. In each chapter, the impact of the environment on the marketing process is illustrated.

Space prohibits an encyclopedic approach to all the issues of international marketing; nevertheless, the authors have tried to present sufficient detail so that readers will appreciate the real need to do a thorough analysis whenever the challenge arises. The text provides a framework for this task.

Summary

The internationalization of American business is proceeding with increasing pace. The globalization of markets and competition necessitates all managers pay attention to the global environment. International marketing is defined as the performance of business activities, including pricing, promotion, product, and distribution decisions, across national borders. The international marketing task is made more daunting because environmental factors such as laws, customs, and cultures vary from country to country. These environmental differences must be taken into account if firms are to market products and services at a profit in other countries.

Key obstacles facing international marketers are not limited to environmental issues. Just as important are difficulties associated with the marketer's own self-reference criteria and ethnocentrism. Both limit the international marketer's abilities to understand and adapt to differences prevalent in foreign markets. A global awareness and sensitivity are the best solutions to these problems, and they should be nurtured in international marketing organizations.

Three different strategic orientations are found among managers of international marketing operations. Some see international marketing as ancillary to the domestic operations. A second kind of company sees international marketing as a crucial aspect of sales revenue generation but treats each market as a separate entity. Finally, a global orientation views the globe as the marketplace, and market segments are no longer based solely on national borders—common consumer characteristics and behaviors come into play as key segmentation variables applied across countries.

Questions

1. Define the following terms:

international marketing	foreign uncontrollables
controllable elements	marketing relativism
uncontrollable elements	self-reference criterion (SRC)
domestic uncontrollables	global awareness

2. "The marketer's task is the same whether applied in Dimebox, Texas, or Dar es Salaam, Tanzania." Discuss.

3. How can the increased interest in international marketing on the part of U.S. firms be explained?

4. Discuss the four phases of international marketing involvement.

5. Discuss the conditions that have led to the development of global markets.

6. Differentiate between a global company and a multinational company.

7. Differentiate among the three international marketing concepts.

8. Prepare your lifelong plan to be globally aware.

9. Discuss the three factors necessary to achieve global awareness.

10. Define and discuss the idea of global orientation.

11. Visit the Bureau of Economic Analysis homepage (http://www.bea.doc.gov). Select the section "International articles" and find the most recent information on foreign direct investments in the United States. Which country has the highest dollar amount of investment in the United States? Second highest?

2

the Dynamic Environment of international Trade

CHAPTER OUTLINE

CHAPTER LEARNING OBJECTIVES

What you should learn from Chapter 2:

- The basis for the reestablishment of world trade following World War II

- The importance of balance-of-payment figures to a country's economy

- The effects of protectionism on world trade

- The seven types of trade barriers

- The provisions of the Omnibus Trade and Competitiveness Act

- The importance of GATT and the World Trade Organization

- The emergence of the International Monetary Fund and the World Bank Group

Global Perspective

TRADE BARRIERS—AN INTERNATIONAL MARKETER'S MINEFIELD

We all know the story about U.S. trade disputes with Japan. Japan has so many trade barriers and high tariffs that U.S. manufacturers are unable to sell in Japan as much as Japanese companies sell in the United States. The Japanese claim that "unique" Japanese snow requires skis made in Japan, and U.S. baseballs are not good enough for Japanese baseball. Even when Japan opened its rice market, popular California rice had to be mixed and sold with inferior grades of Japanese rice. And, at this writing, the Japanese government continues to exclude American beef from the Japanese diet based on disputes about mad cow disease.[1]

However, the Japanese are not alone; every country seems to take advantage of the open U.S. market while putting barriers in the way of U.S. exports. The French, for example, protect their film and broadcast industry from foreign competition by limiting the number of American shows that can appear on television, the percentage of American songs broadcast on radio, and the proportion of U.S. movies that can be shown in French theaters. Most recently, France launched its own "French" version of CNN with strong government financial support. Not only do these barriers and high tariffs limit how much U.S. companies can sell, they also raise prices for imported products much higher than they sell for in the United States.

Consider the fiscal hazards facing international marketing managers at a company like Neutrogena[2] as it contemplates exporting its products to Russia. Upon arrival there, the firm's products might be classified by Russian customs officers into any one of three separate categories for the purposes of assigning tariffs: pharmaceuticals at a 5 percent duty, soap at 15 percent, or cosmetics at 20 percent. Of course, Neutrogena managers would argue for the lowest tariff by pointing out that their "hypoallergenic soaps are recommended by dermatologists." And, as long as shipments remain relatively small, the customs officers might not disagree. However, as exports to Russia grow from cartons to container loads, product classifications receive more scrutiny. Simple statements on packaging, such as "Pure Neutrogena skin and hair care products are available at drug stores and cosmetic counters," would give the Russians reason to claim the highest duty of 20 percent.

Barriers to trade, both tariff and nontariff, are one of the major issues confronting international marketers. Nations continue to use trade barriers for a variety of reasons: some rational, some not so rational. Fortunately, tariffs generally have been reduced to record lows, and substantial progress has been made on eliminating nontariff barriers. And work continues around the world to further reduce these pesky hurdles to peace and prosperity.

Sources: Adapted from Todd G. Buchholz, "Free Trade Keeps Prices Down," *Consumers' Research Magazine*, October 1995, p. 22; Tomas Kellner, "What Gaul!" *Forbes*, April 28, 2003, p. 52; http://www.neutrogena.com; Jonathan Lynn, "WTO Negotiators to Tackle Obstacles to Farm Deal," *Reuters News*, January 3, 2008.

---

[1] See James Day Hodgson, Yoshihiro Sano, and John L. Graham, *Doing Business in the New Japan, Succeeding in America's Richest Foreign Market* (Boulder, CO: Rowman & Littlefield, 2008) for the complete story.

[2] Neutrogena has been a division of Johnson & Johnson since 1994. See Susan Warner, "From Band-Aids to Biotech," *The New York Times*, April 10, 2005, p. 1.

Exhibit 2.1
Top Ten 2007 U.S. Trading
Partners ($ billions,
merchandise trade)

Source: http://www.census.gov/
foreign-trade/top, 2008.

Country	Total Trade	Exports	Imports	Balance
Canada	$562.0	$248.9	$313.1	$−64.2
China	386.7	65.2	321.5	−256.3
Mexico	347.3	136.5	210.8	−74,3
Japan	208.1	62.7	145.5	−82.2
Germany	144.0	49.7	94.4	−44.7
United Kingdom	107.2	50.3	56.9	−6.3
South Korea	82.3	34.7	47.6	−12.9
France	69.0	27.4	41.6	−14.2
Taiwan	64,7	26.4	38.3	−11.9
Netherlands	51.4	18.4	33.0	−14.6

Yesterday's competitive market battles were fought in western Europe, Japan, and the United States; tomorrow's competitive battles will extend to Latin America, eastern Europe, Russia, China, India, Asia, and Africa as these emerging markets continue to open to trade. More of the world's people, from the richest to the poorest, will participate in the world's growing prosperity through global trade. The emerging global economy brings us into worldwide competition with significant advantages for both marketers and consumers. Marketers benefit from new markets opening and smaller markets growing large enough to become viable business opportunities. Consumers benefit by being able to select from the widest range of goods produced anywhere in the world at the lowest prices.

Bound together by satellite communications and global companies, consumers in every corner of the world are demanding an ever-expanding variety of goods. As Exhibit 2.1 illustrates, world trade is an important economic activity. Because of this importance, the inclination is for countries to attempt to control international trade to their own advantage. As competition intensifies, the tendency toward protectionism gains momentum. If the benefits of the social, political, and economic changes now taking place are to be fully realized, free trade must prevail throughout the global marketplace. The creation of the World Trade Organization (WTO) is one of the biggest victories for free trade in decades.

This chapter briefly surveys the United States' past and present role in global trade and some concepts important for understanding the relationship between international trade and national economic policy. A discussion of the logic and illogic of protectionism, the major impediment to trade, is followed by a review of the General Agreement on Tariffs and Trade (GATT) and its successor, the World Trade Organization (WTO), two multinational agreements designed to advance free trade.

The Twentieth to the Twenty-First Century
At no time in modern economic history have countries been more economically interdependent, have greater opportunities for international trade existed, or has the potential for increased demand existed than now, at the opening of the 21st century. In the preceding 100 years, world economic development was erratic.

The first half of the 20th century was marred by a major worldwide economic depression that occurred between two world wars that all but destroyed most of the industrialized world. The last half of the century, while free of a world war, was marred by struggles between countries espousing the socialist Marxist approach and those following a democratic capitalist approach to economic development. As a result of this ideological split, traditional trade patterns were disrupted.

After World War II, as a means to dampen the spread of communism, the United States set out to infuse the ideal of capitalism throughout as much of the world as possible. The Marshall Plan to assist in rebuilding Europe, financial and industrial development assistance to rebuild Japan, and funds channeled through the Agency for International Development and other groups designed to foster economic growth in the underdeveloped world were used to help create a strong world economy. The dissolution of colonial powers

Even though the John Deere tractors lined up for shipment from its Waterloo, Iowa, plant appear impressive, the Hyundai cars stacked up by the water in Ulsan, South Korea, headed for the United States dwarf their numbers. The juxtaposition of the two pictures aptly reflects the persistence of America's broader merchandise trade deficit. *(left: AP Photo/The Gazette, Cliff Jette; right: AP Photo/The Gazette, Cliff Jette)*

created scores of new countries in Asia and Africa. With the striving of these countries to gain economic independence and the financial assistance offered by the United States, most of the noncommunist world's economies grew, and new markets were created.

The benefits from the foreign economic assistance given by the United States flowed both ways. For every dollar the United States invested in the economic development and rebuilding of other countries after World War II, hundreds of dollars more returned in the form of purchases of U.S. agricultural products, manufactured goods, and services. This overseas demand created by the Marshall Plan and other programs[3] was important to the U.S. economy since the vast manufacturing base built to supply World War II and the swelling labor supply of returning military created a production capacity well beyond domestic needs. The major economic boom and increased standard of living the United States experienced after World War II were fueled by fulfilling pent-up demand in the United States and the demand created by the rebuilding of war-torn countries of Europe and Asia. In short, the United States helped make the world's economies stronger, which enabled them to buy more from us.

In addition to U.S. economic assistance, a move toward international cooperation among trading nations was manifest in the negotiation of the General Agreement on Tariffs and Trade (GATT). International trade had ground to a halt following World War I when nations followed the example set by the U.S. passage of the Smoot-Hawley Act (1930), which raised average U.S. tariffs on more than 20,000 imported goods to levels in excess of 60 percent. In retaliation, 60 countries erected high tariff walls, and international trade stalled, along with most economies. A major worldwide recession catapulted the world's economies into the Great Depression when trade all but dried up.[4]

Determined not to repeat the economic disaster that followed World War I, world leaders created GATT, a forum for member countries to negotiate a reduction of tariffs and

---

[3] The Organization for Economic Cooperation and Development (OECD) was a direct result of the Marshall Plan. See Pam Casellas, "America Does Earn Its Stripes," *West Australian*, January 6, 2005, p. 15.

[4] David M. Kennedy, Lizabeth Cohen, and Thomas A. Bailey, *The American Pageant*, 13th ed. (Boston: Houghton Mifflin, 2005).

other barriers to trade. The forum proved successful in reaching those objectives. With the ratification of the Uruguay Round agreements, the GATT became part of the World Trade Organization (WTO), and its 117 original members moved into a new era of free trade.

World Trade and U.S. Multinationals

The rapid growth of war-torn economies and previously underdeveloped countries, coupled with large-scale economic cooperation and assistance, led to new global marketing opportunities. Rising standards of living and broad-based consumer and industrial markets abroad created opportunities for American companies to expand exports and investment worldwide. During the 1950s, many U.S. companies that had never before marketed outside the United States began to export, and others made significant investments in marketing and production facilities overseas.

At the close of the 1960s, U.S. multinational corporations (MNCs) were facing major challenges on two fronts: resistance to direct investment and increasing competition in export markets. Large investments by U.S. businesses in Europe and Latin America heightened the concern of these countries about the growing domination of U.S. multinationals. The reaction in Latin American countries was to expropriate direct U.S. investments or to force companies to sell controlling interests to nationals. In Europe, apprehension manifested itself in strong public demand to limit foreign investment. Concern even in Britain that they might become a satellite with manufacturing but no determination of policy led to specific guidelines for joint ventures between British and U.S. companies. In the European Community, U.S. multinationals were rebuffed in ways ranging from tight control over proposed joint ventures and regulations covering U.S. acquisitions of European firms to strong protectionism laws.

The threat felt by Europeans was best expressed in the popular book *The American Challenge*, published in 1968, in which the French author J. J. Servan-Schreiber wrote:

> Fifteen years from now it is quite possible that the world's third greatest industrial power, just after the United States and Russia, will not be Europe but American Industry in Europe. Already, in the ninth year of the Common Market, this European market is basically American in organization.[5]

Servan-Schreiber's prediction did not come true for many reasons, but one of the more important was that American MNCs confronted a resurgence of competition from all over the world. The worldwide economic growth and rebuilding after World War II was beginning to surface in competition that challenged the supremacy of American industry. Competition arose on all fronts; Japan, Germany, most of the industrialized world, and many developing countries were competing for demand in their own countries and looking for world markets as well. Countries once classified as less developed were reclassified as newly industrialized countries (NICs). Various NICs such as Brazil, Mexico, South Korea, Taiwan, Singapore, and Hong Kong experienced rapid industrialization in selected industries and became aggressive world competitors in steel, shipbuilding, consumer electronics, automobiles, light aircraft, shoes, textiles, apparel, and so forth. In addition to the NICs, developing countries such as Venezuela, Chile, and Bangladesh established state-owned enterprises (SOEs) that operated in other countries. One state-owned Venezuelan company has a subsidiary in Puerto Rico that produces canvas, cosmetics, chairs, and zippers; there are also Chilean and Colombian companies in Puerto Rico; in the U.S. state of Georgia, a Venezuelan company engages in agribusiness; and Bangladesh, the sixth largest exporter of garments to the United States, also owns a mattress company in Georgia.

In short, economic power and potential became more evenly distributed among countries than was the case when Servan-Schreiber warned Europe about U.S. multinational domination. Instead, the U.S. position in world trade is now shared with other countries. For example, in 1950, the United States represented 39 percent of world gross national product (GNP), but by 2008, it represented 25 percent. In the meantime, however, the global GNP grew much larger, as did the world's manufacturing output—all countries

---

[5] J. J. Servan-Schreiber, *The American Challenge* (New York: Atheneum Publishers, 1968), p. 3.

Exhibit 2.2

The Nationality of the World's 100 Largest Industrial Corporations (size measured by annual revenues)

Source: "2007 Global 500," *Fortune*, http://www.fortune.com, 2008.

	1963	1979	1984	1990	1996	2000	2005	2007
United States	67	47	47	33	24	36	33	34
Germany	13	13	8	12	13	12	15	12
Britain	7	7	5	6	2	5	10	9
France	4	11	5	10	13	11	10	9
Japan	3	7	12	18	29	22	12	8
Italy	2	3	3	4	4	3	3	4
Netherlands–United Kingdom	2	2	2	2	2	2	1	
Netherlands	1	3	1	1	2	5	2	4
Switzerland	1	1	2	3	5	3	4	4
Argentina				1				
Belgium		1	1	1		1		1
Belgium–Netherlands							1	1
Brazil			1	1				1
Canada		2	3					
India			1					
Kuwait			1					
Mexico		1	1	1	1		1	1
Venezuela		1	1	1	1			
South Korea			4	2	4		1	4
Sweden			1	2				
South Africa			1	1				
Spain				2			1	3
Russia								1
China						2	1	3
Norway							1	1

shared in a much larger economic pie. This change was reflected in the fluctuations in the growth of MNCs from other countries as well. Exhibit 2.2 reflects the dramatic changes between 1963 and 2007. In 1963, the United States had 67 of the world's largest industrial corporations. By 1996, that number had dropped to a low of 24, while Japan moved from having 3 of the largest to 29 and South Korea from 0 to 4. And following the great economic boom in the late 1990s in the United States, 36 of the largest companies were American, only 22 Japanese, and none were Korean. Most recently, GAZPROM, the Russian natural gas giant, is the first eastern European entrant into the top 100 global firms, ranking number 52 in the most recent *Fortune* list.[6]

Another dimension of world economic power, the balance of merchandise trade, also reflected the changing role of the United States in world trade. Between 1888 and 1971, the United States sold more to other countries than it bought from them; that is, the United States had a favorable balance of trade. By 1971, however, the United States had a trade deficit of $2 billion that grew steadily until it peaked at $160 billion in 1987. After that, the deficit in merchandise trade declined to $74 billion in 1991 but began increasing again and by 2007 had surpassed $800 billion. However, with the continued weakness in the U.S. dollar, the trade deficit began to abate some in the fall of 2007.[7]

The heightened competition for U.S. businesses during the 1980s and early 1990s raised questions similar to those heard in Europe two decades earlier: how to maintain the competitive strength of American business, to avoid the domination of U.S. markets by foreign MNCs, and to forestall the buying of America. In the 1980s, the United States saw its competitive position in capital goods such as computers and machinery erode sharply. From

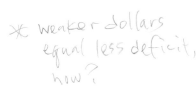

* weaker dollars equal less deficit, how?

---

[6] "GASPROM Eyes 10% of French Gas Market in 4–5 Years," *Dow Jones International News*, January 3, 2008.

[7] Elizabeth Price and Brian Blackstone, "U.S. Trade Deficit Shrinks—Rising Prices Dampen Demand for Imports, Could Fuel Inflation," *The Wall Street Journal Asia*, November 12, 2007, p. 9.

1983 to 1987, almost 70 percent of the growth of the merchandise trade deficit was in capital goods and automobiles. At the time, those were America's high-wage, high-skill industries. But U.S. industry got a wake-up call and responded by restructuring its industries, in essence, "getting lean and mean." By the late 1990s, the United States was once again holding its own in capital goods, particularly with trade surpluses in the high-tech category.

Among the more important questions raised were those concerning the ability of U.S. firms to compete in foreign markets and the fairness of international trade policies of some countries. Trade friction revolved around Japan's sales of autos and electronics in the United States and Japan's restrictive trade practices. The United States, a strong advocate of free trade, was confronted with the dilemma of how to encourage trading partners to reciprocate with open access to their markets without provoking increased protectionism. In addition to successfully pressuring Japan to open its markets for some types of trade and investment, the United States was a driving force behind the establishment of the WTO.

By the last decade of the 20th century, profound changes in the way the world would trade were already under way. The continuing integration of the countries of the European Union, the creation of NAFTA[8] and the American Free Trade Area (AFTA), and the rapid evolution of the Asia-Pacific Economic Cooperation Conference (APEC) are the beginnings of global trading blocks that many experts expect to dominate trade patterns in the future. With the return of Hong Kong in 1997 and Macao in 2000 to China, all of Asia is now controlled and managed by Asians for the first time in 400 years. During the decades since World War II, the West set the patterns for trade, but increasingly, Asia will be a major force, if not the leading force.

Beyond the First Decade of the Twenty-First Century

The unprecedented and precipitous growth of the U.S. economy in the late 1990s has slowed dramatically in the last few years. Growth in most of the rest of the world has followed suit, with the exception of China. The Organization for Economic Cooperation and Development (OECD) estimates that the economies of member countries will expand an average of 3 percent annually for the next 25 years, the same rate as in the past 25 years. Conversely, the economies of the developing world will grow at faster rates—from an annual rate of 4 percent in the past quarter century to a rate of 6 percent for the next 25 years. Their share of world output will rise from about one-sixth to nearly one-third over the same period. The World Bank estimates that five countries—Brazil, China, India, Indonesia, and Russia—whose share of world trade is barely one-third of that of the European Union will by 2020 have a 50 percent higher share than that of the European Union. As a consequence, economic power and influence will move away from industrialized countries—Japan, the United States, and the European Union—to countries in Latin America, eastern Europe, Asia, and Africa.

This shift does not mean that markets in Europe, Japan, and the United States will cease to be important; those economies will continue to produce large, lucrative markets, and the companies established in those markets will benefit. It does mean that if a company is to be a major player in the 21st century, now is the time to begin laying the groundwork. How will these changes that are taking place in the global marketplace impact international business? For one thing, the level and intensity of competition will change as companies focus on gaining entry into or maintaining their position in emerging markets, regional trade areas, and the established markets in Europe, Japan, and the United States.

Companies are looking for ways to become more efficient, improve productivity, and expand their global reach while maintaining an ability to respond quickly and deliver products that the markets demand. For example, large MNCs such as Matsushita of Japan continue to expand their global reach. Nestlé is consolidating its dominance in global consumer markets by acquiring and vigorously marketing local-country major brands. Samsung of South Korea has invested $500 million in Mexico to secure access to markets in the North American Free Trade Area. Whirlpool, the U.S. appliance manufacturer, which secured first place in the global appliance business by acquiring the European division of the appliance maker N. V. Philips, immediately began restructuring itself into its version of

---

[8] Jenalia Moreno, "Trade Tariffs End, Making NAFTA a Milestone," *Houston Chronicle*, January 2, 2008.

a global company. These are a few examples of changes that are sweeping multinational companies as they gear up for the rest of the 21st century.

Global companies are not the only ones aggressively seeking new market opportunities. Smaller companies are using novel approaches to marketing and seeking ways to apply their technological expertise to exporting goods and services not previously sold abroad. A small midwestern company that manufactures and freezes bagel dough for supermarkets to bake and sell as their own saw opportunities abroad and began to export to Japan. International sales, though small initially, showed such potential that the company sold its U.S. business to concentrate on international operations. Other examples of smaller companies include Nochar Inc., which makes a fire retardant it developed a decade ago for the Indianapolis 500. The company now gets 32 percent of its sales overseas, in 29 countries. The owner of Buztronics Inc., a maker of promotional lapel buttons, heard from a friend that his buttons, with their red blinking lights, would "do great" in Japan. He made his first entry in exporting to Japan, and after only a year, 10 percent of Buztronics sales came from overseas. While 50 of the largest exporters account for 30 percent of U.S. merchandise exports, the rest come from middle- and small-sized firms like those just mentioned. The business world is weathering a flurry of activity as companies large and small adjust to the internationalization of the marketplace at home and abroad.

As is always true in business, the best-laid plans can fail or be slowed by dramatic changes in the economy. When the U.S. economy was less involved in international trade, economic upheavals abroad often went unnoticed except by the very largest companies. But in 1997, when the stock market in Hong Kong dropped precipitously and South Korea and several Southeast Asia economies faltered shortly thereafter, the U.S. stock market reacted with its largest daily drop in several years. The fear was the potential negative impact on U.S. technology industries if the economies of Asian customers slowed. Four years later, most of the world's emerging markets were on a somewhat slower but nevertheless positive growth path than before the financial crisis of 1997.

Balance of Payments

When countries trade, financial transactions among businesses or consumers of different nations occur. Products and services are exported and imported, monetary gifts are exchanged, investments are made, cash payments are made and cash receipts received, and vacation and foreign travel occurs. In short, over a period of time, there is a constant flow of money into and out of a country. The system of accounts that records a nation's international financial transactions is called its *balance of payments*.

A nation's balance-of-payments statement records all financial transactions between its residents and those of the rest of the world during a given period of time—usually one year. Because the balance-of-payments record is maintained on a double-entry bookkeeping system, it must always be in balance. As on an individual company's financial statement, the assets and liabilities or the credits and debits must offset each other. And like a company's statement, the fact that they balance does not mean a nation is in particularly good or poor financial condition. A balance of payments is a record of condition, not a determinant of condition. Each of the nation's financial transactions with other countries is reflected in its balance of payments.

A nation's balance-of-payments statement presents an overall view of its international economic position and is an important economic measure used by treasuries, central banks, and other government agencies whose responsibility is to maintain external and internal economic stability. A balance of payments represents the difference between receipts from foreign countries on one side and payments to them on the other. On the plus side of the U.S. balance of payments are merchandise export sales; money spent by foreign tourists; payments to the United States for insurance, transportation, and similar services; payments of dividends and interest on investments abroad; return on capital invested abroad; new foreign investments in the United States; and foreign government payments to the United States.

On the minus side are the costs of goods imported, spending by American tourists overseas, new overseas investments, and the cost of foreign military and economic aid. A deficit results when international payments are greater than receipts. It can be reduced or eliminated by

Exhibit 2.3

U.S. Current Account by
Major Components, 2007
($ billions)

Exports	
Goods	$ 1149
Services	479
Income receipts	779
Imports	
Goods	−1965
Services	−372
Income payments	−698
Unilateral current transfers, net	−104
Current account balance	−739

increasing a country's international receipts (i.e., gain more exports to other countries or more tourists from other countries) and/or reducing expenditures in other countries. A balance-of-payments statement includes three accounts: the *current account*, a record of all merchandise exports, imports, and services plus unilateral transfers of funds; the *capital account*, a record of direct investment, portfolio investment, and short-term capital movements to and from countries; and the official *reserves account*, a record of exports and imports of gold, increases or decreases in foreign exchange, and increases or decreases in liabilities to foreign central banks. Of the three, the current account is of primary interest to international business.

The *current account* is important because it includes all international merchandise trade and service accounts, that is, accounts for the value of all merchandise and services imported and exported and all receipts and payments from investments.[9] Exhibit 2.3 gives the current account calculations for the United States in 2007.

Since 1971, the United States has had a favorable current account balance (as a percentage of GDP) in only a few years—see Exhibit 2.4. The imbalances resulted primarily from

---

[9] "Financial Globalization and U.S. Current Account Deficit," *US Fed News,* January 3, 2008.

Exhibit 2.4

U.S. Current Account Balance (% of GDP)

Percent

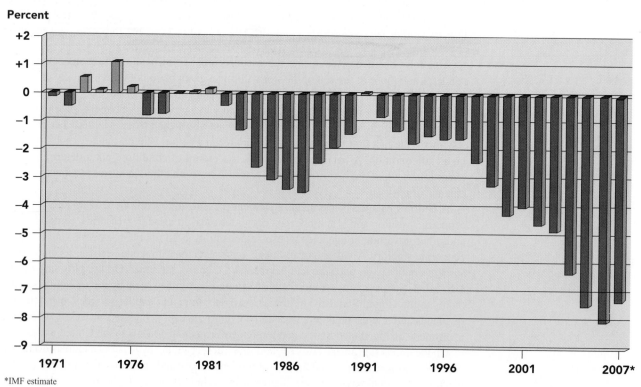

*IMF estimate

Exhibit 2.5

What Would One U.S. Dollar Buy?

Source: *The Wall Street Journal*, 2008.

	1985	1988	1992	1995	1999	2000	2005	2008
British pound	0.86	0.54	0.56	0.63	0.62	0.68	0.57	0.51
French franc	9.6	5.4	5.29	4.95	6.49	7.28		
Japanese yen	250.23	123.7	126.7	93.96	102.58	112.21	112.3	103.0
Swiss franc	2.25	1.29	1.41	1.18	1.58	1.68	1.31	0.96
Euro			1.01	0.90	0.92	1.08	0.79	0.65
Mexico peso	0.37	2.28	3.12	6.45	9.43	9.47	10.8	10.4

U.S. demand for oil,[10] petroleum products, cars, consumer durables, and other merchandise. Indeed, the merchandise trade deficit for 2007 was $816 billion, a substantial improvement over the two previous years.[11] Still, such imbalances have drastic effects on the balance of payments and, therefore, the value of U.S. currency in the world marketplace. Factors such as these eventually require an adjustment through a change in exchange rates, prices, and/or incomes.[12] In short, once the wealth of a country whose expenditures exceed its income has been exhausted, that country, like an individual, must reduce its standard of living. If its residents do not do so voluntarily, the rates of exchange of its money for foreign monies decline, and through the medium of the foreign exchange market, the purchasing power of foreign goods is transferred from that country to another. As can be seen in Exhibit 2.5, the U.S. dollar strengthened against most of the other major currencies during the 1990s but has weakened recently.

As the U.S. trade deficit has grown, pressures have begun to push the value of the dollar to lower levels. And when foreign currencies can be traded for more dollars, U.S. products (and companies) are less expensive for the foreign customer and exports increase, and foreign products are more expensive for the U.S. customer and the demand for imported goods is dampened. Likewise, investments in dollar-denominated equities and such investment goods become less attractive. Indeed, the dollar itself becomes less useful as a global currency.[13]

Protectionism

International business must face the reality that this is a world of tariffs, quotas, and nontariff barriers designed to protect a country's markets from intrusion by foreign companies. Although the World Trade Organization has been effective in reducing tariffs, countries still resort to measures of protectionism. Nations utilize legal barriers, exchange barriers, and psychological barriers to restrain the entry of unwanted goods.[14] Businesses work together to establish private market barriers, while the market structure itself may provide formidable barriers to imported goods. The complex distribution system in Japan, as will be detailed in Chapter 14, is a good example of a market structure creating a barrier to trade. However, as effective as it is in keeping some products out of the market, in a legal sense, it cannot be viewed as a trade barrier.

Protection Logic and Illogic

Countless reasons to maintain government restrictions on trade are espoused by protectionists, but essentially all arguments can be classified as follows: (1) protection of an infant industry, (2) protection of the home market, (3) need to keep money at home, (4) encouragement of capital accumulation, (5) maintenance of the standard of living and real wages, (6) conservation of natural resources, (7) industrialization of a low-wage nation, (8) maintenance of

---

[10] Terence Poon, "China to Steady Prices Amid Inflation Worries," *The Wall Street Journal*, January 10, 2008.

[11] "Financial Globalization and U.S. Current Account Deficit," *US Fed News,* January 3, 2008.

[12] Some disagree with this conventional wisdom. See Diana Farrell, "America's External Deficit," *Milken Institute Review* 2 (2005), pp. 10–17.

[13] Mark Whitehouse, "Foreign Investors View Dollar as 'Refuge Currency' Despite Recent Tumult," *The Wall Street Journal*, August 20, 2007, p. A2.

[14] "Europe's New Protectionism," *The Economist*, July 2, 2005, p. 49.

Ommibus Trade Act

CROSSING BORDERS 2.1   Trade Barriers, Hypocrisy, and the United States

The United States thinks of itself as the leader in free trade and frequently brings actions against nations as unfair trade partners. Section 301* of the Omnibus Trade and Competitiveness Act authorizes the U.S. government to investigate and retaliate against specific foreign trade barriers judged to be unfair and to impose up to 100 percent tariffs on exports to the United States from guilty nations unless they satisfy U.S. domestic demands. But critics say the United States is somewhat hypocritical in some of the stances taken, since it is just as guilty of protecting its markets with trade barriers. A Japanese government study alleges that the United States engages in unfair trade practices in 10 of 12 policy areas reviewed in the study. Notably, the United States imposes quotas on imports, has high tariffs, and abuses antidumping measures. Are the critics correct? Is the United States being hypocritical when it comes to free trade? You be the judge.

The United States launched a Section 301 investigation of Japanese citrus quotas. "The removal of Japan's unfair barriers could cut the price of oranges for Japanese consumers by one-third," said the U.S. trade representative. Coincidentally, the United States had a 40 percent tariff on Brazilian orange juice imports when the investigation was initiated.

The United States brought a 301 case against Korea for its beef import quotas even though the United States has beef import quotas that are estimated to

cost U.S. consumers $873 million annually in higher prices. Another 301 case was brought against Brazil, Korea, and Taiwan for trade barriers on footwear even though the United States maintains tariffs as high as 67 percent on footwear imports.

Can you believe that we have two phone book–sized volumes of the U.S. customs code that include restrictions on such innocuous items as scissors, sweaters, leather, costume jewelry, tampons, pizzas, cotton swabs, ice cream from Jamaica, and even products we do not produce, such as vitamin B_{12}? We also have restrictions on more sensitive products such as cars, supercomputers, lumber, and every type of clothing imaginable. Would-be Latin American exporters find hundreds of their most promising export products, such as grapes, tomatoes, onions, steel, cement, asparagus, and shoes, on the customs list. Visit www.usitc.gov/tata/index.htm and select the Interactive Tariff Database to see some other examples.

So, is the U.S. as guilty as the rest or not?

*Section 301, a provision of U.S. trade law, enables the U.S. government to take action against countries deemed to have engaged in "unreasonable, unjustifiable, or discriminatory" practices that restrict U.S. commerce.

Sources: Abstracted from James Bovard, "A U.S. History of Trade Hypocrisy," *The Wall Street Journal*, March 8, 1994, p. A10; Brian Hindley and Fredrik Erixon, "Dumping Protectionism," *The Wall Street Journal*, November 1, 2007, p. 12.

employment and reduction of unemployment, (9) national defense, (10) increase of business size, and (11) retaliation and bargaining. Economists in general recognize as valid only the arguments for infant industry, national defense, and industrialization of underdeveloped countries. The resource conservation argument becomes increasingly valid in an era of environmental consciousness[15] and worldwide shortages of raw materials and agricultural commodities. A case might be made for temporary protection of markets with excess productive capacity or excess labor when such protection could facilitate an orderly transition. Unfortunately such protection becomes long term and contributes to industrial inefficiency while detracting from a nation's realistic adjustment to its world situation.

To give you some idea of the cost to the consumer, consider the results of a recent study of 21 protected industries. The research showed that U.S. consumers pay about $70 billion per year in higher prices because of tariffs and other protective restrictions. On average, the cost to consumers for saving one job in these protected industries was $170,000 per year, or six times the average pay (wages and benefits) for manufacturing workers. Those figures represent the average of 21 protected industries, but the cost is much higher in selected industries. In the steel industry, for example, countervailing duties and antidumping penalties on foreign suppliers of steel since 1992 have saved the jobs of 1,239 steelworkers at a

---

[15] John Carey, "Global Warming, Suddenly the Climate in Washington Is Changing," *BusinessWeek*, June 27, 2005, p. 91.

cost of $835,351 each. Unfortunately, protectionism is politically popular, but it rarely leads to renewed growth in a declining industry. And the jobs that are saved are saved at a very high cost, which constitutes a hidden tax that consumers unknowingly pay.

Trade Barriers

To encourage development of domestic industry and protect existing industry, governments may establish such barriers to trade as tariffs, quotas, boycotts, monetary barriers, nontariff barriers, and market barriers. Barriers are imposed against imports and against foreign businesses. While the inspiration for such barriers may be economic or political, they are encouraged by local industry. Whether or not the barriers are economically logical, the fact is that they exist.

Tariffs.

A tariff, simply defined, is a tax imposed by a government on goods entering at its borders. Tariffs may be used as revenue-generating taxes or to discourage the importation of goods, or for both reasons. In general, tariffs:

Increase	Inflationary pressures.
	Special interests' privileges.
	Government control and political considerations in economic matters.
	The number of tariffs (they beget other tariffs via reciprocity).
Weaken	Balance-of-payments positions.
	Supply-and-demand patterns.
	International relations (they can start trade wars).
Restrict	Manufacturers' supply sources.
	Choices available to consumers.
	Competition.

In addition, tariffs are arbitrary, are discriminatory, and require constant administration and supervision. They often are used as reprisals against protectionist moves of trading partners. In a dispute with the European Union over pasta export subsidies, the United States ordered a 40 percent increase in tariffs on European spaghetti and fancy pasta. The EU retaliated against U.S. walnuts and lemons. The pasta war raged on as Europe increased tariffs on U.S. fertilizer, paper products, and beef tallow, and the United States responded

Exhibit 2.6
Types of Nontariff Barriers

Specific Limitations on Trade	**Governmental Participation in Trade**
Quotas	Government procurement policies
Import licensing requirements	Export subsidies
Proportional restrictions of foreign to domestic goods (local-content requirements)	Countervailing duties
	Domestic assistance programs
Minimum import price limits	
Embargoes	**Charges on Imports**
	Prior import deposit requirements
Customs and Administrative Entry Procedures	Administrative fees
Valuation systems	Special supplementary duties
Antidumping practices	Import credit discriminations
Tariff classifications	Variable levies
Documentation requirements	Border taxes
Fees	
	Others
Standards	Voluntary export restraints
Standards disparities	Orderly marketing agreements
Intergovernmental acceptances of testing methods and standards	
Packaging, labeling, marking standards	

Source: Reprinted from A. D. Cao, "Nontariff Barriers to U.S. Manufactured Exports," *Journal of World Business*, vol. 15, p. 94. Copyright © 1980, with permission from Elsevier.

CROSSING BORDERS 2.2   Crossing Borders with Monkeys in His Pants

Robert Cusack smuggled a pair of endangered pygmy monkeys into the United States—in his pants! On June 13, 2002, a U.S. Fish and Wildlife Service special agent was called to Los Angeles International Airport after Cusack was detained by U.S. Customs on arrival from Thailand. Officials soon also discovered that Cusack had four endangered birds of paradise and 50 protected orchids with him. "When one of the inspectors opened up his luggage, one of the birds flew out," tells one official. "He had to go catch the bird." After finding the other purloined birds and exotic flowers, the inspectors asked, "Do you have anything else you should tell us about?" Cusack answered, "Yes, I have monkeys in my pants." The monkeys ended up in the Los Angeles Zoo, and the smuggler ended up in jail for 57 days. He also paid a five-figure fine.

Similarly, Wang Hong, a Chinese exporter, pleaded guilty to smuggling sea turtles into the United States. He didn't have them in his pants; instead, the sea turtle "parts" came in the form of shells and violin bows, among other things.

Smuggling isn't just a game played by sneaking individuals. Multinational companies can also get into the act. During the last year alone, convictions have

come down for smuggling cell phones into Vietnam, cigarettes into Iraq and Canada, and platinum into China. In perhaps the biggest ever corporate case, after a nine-year lawsuit, Amway Corporation agreed to pay the Canadian government $38.1 million to settle charges it had avoided customs duties by undervaluing merchandise it exported from the United States to Canadian distributors over a six-year period. As long as there have been trade barriers, smuggling has been a common response. Indeed, Rudyard Kipling wrote some 100 years ago:

Five and twenty ponies trotting through the dark—

Brandy for the Parson, 'baccy for the clerk;

Laces for a lady, letters for a spy;

And watch the wall, my darling, while the Gentlemen go by!

Sources: "Amway Pays $38 Million to Canada," *Los Angeles Times*, September 22, 1989, p. 3; Patricia Ward Biederman, "Smuggler to Pay for Pocketing Monkeys," *Los Angeles Times*, December 19, 2002, p. B1; "Chinese National Pleads Guilty of Smuggling Protected Sea Turtles," *Associated Press*, January 3, 2008.

in kind. The war ended when the Europeans finally dropped pasta export subsidies. The EU and the United States also fought a similar trade war over bananas! Most recently, less developed countries are increasingly voicing complaints about American and European tariffs on agricultural products.[16]

Quotas.   A quota is a specific unit or dollar limit applied to a particular type of good. Great Britain limits imported television sets, Germany has established quotas on Japanese ball bearings, Italy restricts Japanese motorcycles, and the United States has quotas on sugar, textiles, and, of all things, peanuts. Quotas put an absolute restriction on the quantity of a specific item that can be imported. When the Japanese first let foreign rice into their country, it was on a quota basis, but since 2000 the quotas have been replaced by tariffs.[17] Even more complicated, the banana war between the United States and the EU resulted in a mixed system wherein a quota of bananas is allowed into the EU with a tariff, then a second quota comes in tariff-free. Like tariffs, quotas tend to increase prices.[18] The U.S. quotas on textiles are estimated to add 50 percent to the wholesale price of clothing.

Voluntary Export Restraints.   Similar to quotas are the *voluntary export restraints* (VERs) or *orderly market agreements* (OMAs). Common in textiles, clothing, steel, agriculture, and automobiles, the VER is an agreement between the importing country and the exporting country for a restriction on the volume of exports. Japan has a VER

---

[16] Allan Odhiambo, "EAC States in Row over Wheat Import Tariffs," *All Africa*, August 30, 2007.

[17] See the USA Rice Federation's Web site for details, http://www.usarice.com; also Hodgson et al., *Doing Business in the New Japan*.

[18] Peter T. Leach, "Is China Losing Its Edge?" *Journal of Commerce*, December 3, 2007.

on automobiles to the United States; that is, Japan has agreed to export a fixed number of automobiles annually. When televisions were still manufactured in the United States, Japan signed an OMA limiting Japanese color television exports to the United States to 1.56 million units per year. However, Japanese companies began to adjust their strategies by investing in television manufacturing in the United States and Mexico, and as a result, they regained the entire market share that had been lost through the OMA, eventually dominating the entire market. A VER is called voluntary because the exporting country sets the limits; however, it is generally imposed under the threat of stiffer quotas and tariffs being set by the importing country if a VER is not established.

Boycotts and Embargoes.
A government boycott is an absolute restriction against the purchase and importation of certain goods and/or services from other countries. This restriction can even include travel bans, like the one currently in place for Chinese tourists; the Beijing government refuses to designate Canada as an approved tourism destination. Officials in Beijing have not been forthcoming with explanations, even after three years of complaints by and negotiations with their Canadian counterparts, but most believe it has to do with Canada's unrelenting criticism of Chinese human rights policies.[19] An embargo is a refusal to sell to a specific country. A public boycott can be either formal or informal and may be government sponsored or sponsored by an industry. The United States uses boycotts and embargoes against countries with which it has a dispute. For example, Cuba[20] and Iran still have sanctions imposed by the United States. Among U.S. policymakers, there is rising concern, however, that government-sponsored sanctions cause unnecessary harm for both the United States and the country being boycotted without reaching the desired results. It is not unusual for the citizens of a country to boycott goods of other countries at the urging of their government or civic groups. Nestlé products were boycotted by a citizens group that considered the way Nestlé promoted baby milk formula in less developed countries misleading to mothers and harmful to their babies.

Monetary Barriers.
A government can effectively regulate its international trade position by various forms of exchange-control restrictions. A government may enact such restrictions to preserve its balance-of-payments position or specifically for the advantage or encouragement of particular industries. Three barriers should be considered: blocked currency, differential exchange rates, and government approval requirements for securing foreign exchange.

Blocked currency is used as a political weapon or as a response to difficult balance-of-payments situations. In effect, blockage cuts off all importing or all importing above a certain level. Blockage is accomplished by refusing to allow an importer to exchange its national currency for the sellers' currency.

The *differential exchange rate* is a particularly ingenious method of controlling imports. It encourages the importation of goods that the government deems desirable and discourages importation of goods that the government does not want. The essential mechanism requires the importer to pay varying amounts of domestic currency for foreign exchange with which to purchase products in different categories. For example, the exchange rate for a desirable category of goods might be one unit of domestic money for one unit of a specific foreign currency. For a less desirable product, the rate might be two domestic currency units for one foreign unit. For an undesirable product, the rate might be three domestic units for one foreign unit. An importer of an undesirable product has to pay three times as much for the foreign exchange as the importer of a desired product.

Government approval to secure foreign exchange is often used by countries experiencing severe shortages of foreign exchange. At one time or another, most Latin American and East European countries have required all foreign exchange transactions to be

---

[19] "Canada Threatens China with WTO Action over Tourism Ban," *Agence France-Presse*, January 8, 2008.

[20] Cornelia Dean, "Cuba After the Embargo," *The New York Times News Service, Edmonton Journal*, January 6, 2008, p. E8.

Cracker Jack invented the toy-with-candy promotion back in 1912. However, the Italian chocolatier Ferrero took things much further. Its milk chocolate Kinder eggs contain "sopresas" that kids enjoy in 37 countries around the world. The product is unavailable in the United States because of choking hazards. The product pictured is produced in Argentina for sale in Mexico, and it includes a warning label regarding kids under three years of age. Cracker Jack has had to eliminate many of the cool little toys it put in the packages for the same reason. Nestlé introduced a product similar to Kinder eggs in the U.S. market in the late 1990s but had to withdraw it for safety reasons. Wonderball is the latest version, but it has edible chocolate figures inside. See www.ferrero.com.ar and www.crackerjack.com for more details. Toys must be larger than the diameter of the plastic tube pictured on the right to meet the U.S. safety standard. *(left: © Sharon Hoogstraten; right: AP Photo/Conn. Attorney General)*

[handwritten: can't they buy with domestic or foreign money either is fine right? Why exchange?]

approved by a central minister. Thus, importers who want to buy a foreign good must apply for an exchange permit, that is, permission to exchange an amount of local currency for foreign currency.

The exchange permit may also stipulate the rate of exchange, which can be an unfavorable rate depending on the desires of the government. In addition, the exchange permit may stipulate that the amount to be exchanged must be deposited in a local bank for a set period prior to the transfer of goods. For example, Brazil has at times required funds to be deposited 360 days prior to the import date. This requirement is extremely restrictive because funds are out of circulation and subject to the ravages of inflation. Such policies cause major cash flow problems for the importer and greatly increase the price of imports. Clearly, these currency-exchange barriers constitute a major deterrent to trade.

Standards.   Nontariff barriers of this category include standards to protect health, safety, and product quality. The standards are sometimes used in an unduly stringent or discriminating way to restrict trade, but the sheer volume of regulations in this category is a problem in itself. A fruit content regulation for jam varies so much from country to country that one agricultural specialist says, "A jam exporter needs a computer to avoid one or another country's regulations." Different standards are one of the major disagreements between the United States and Japan. The size of knotholes in plywood shipped to Japan can determine whether or not the shipment is accepted; if a knothole is too large, the shipment is rejected because quality standards are not met.

The United States and other countries require some products (automobiles in particular) to contain a percentage of "local content" to gain admission to their markets. The North American Free Trade Agreement (NAFTA) stipulates that all automobiles coming from member countries must have at least 62.5 percent North American content to deter foreign car makers from using one member nation as the back door to another.

Antidumping Penalties.   Historically tariffs and nontariff trade barriers have impeded free trade, but over the years, they have been eliminated or lowered through the efforts of the GATT and WTO. Now there is a new nontariff barrier: antidumping laws that have emerged as a way of keeping foreign goods out of a market. Antidumping laws were designed to prevent foreign producers from "predatory pricing," a practice whereby a foreign producer intentionally sells its products in the United States for less than the cost of production to undermine the competition and take control of the market. This barrier was intended as a kind of antitrust law for international trade. Violators are assessed "antidumping" duties for selling below cost and/or assessed "countervailing duties" to prevent the use of foreign government subsidies to undermine American industry. Many countries have similar laws, and they are allowed under WTO rules.

Recent years have seen a staggering increase in antidumping cases in the United States. In one year, 12 U.S. steel manufacturers launched antidumping cases against 82 foreign steelmakers in 30 countries. Many economists felt that these antidumping charges were unnecessary because of the number of companies and countries involved; supply and demand could have been left to sort out the best producers and prices. And, of course, targeted countries have complained as well. Nevertheless, antidumping cases are becoming de facto trade barriers. The investigations are very costly, they take a long time to resolve, and until they are resolved, they effectively limit trade. Furthermore, the threat of being hit by an antidumping charge is enough to keep some companies out of the market.

Easing Trade Restrictions

Lowering the trade deficit has been a priority of the U.S. government for a number of years. Of the many proposals brought forward, most deal with fairness of trade with some of our trading partners instead of reducing imports or adjusting other trade policies. Many believe that too many countries are allowed to trade freely in the United States without granting equal access to U.S. products in their countries. Japan was for two decades the trading partner with which we had the largest deficit and which elicited the most concern about fairness. The Omnibus Trade and Competitiveness Act of 1988 addressed the trade fairness issue and focused on ways to improve U.S. competitiveness. At the turn of the century, China took over from Japan as America's number one "trade problem."

The Omnibus Trade and Competitiveness Act

The *Omnibus Trade and Competitiveness Act of 1988* is many faceted, focusing on assisting businesses to be more competitive in world markets as well as on correcting perceived injustice in trade practices.[21] The trade act was designed to deal with trade deficits, protectionism, and the overall fairness of our trading partners. Congressional concern centered on the issue that U.S. markets were open to most of the world but markets in Japan, western Europe, and many Asian countries were relatively closed. The act reflected the realization that we must deal with our trading partners based on how they actually operate, not on how we want them to behave. Some see the act as a protectionist measure, but the government sees it as a means of providing stronger tools to open foreign markets and to help U.S. exporters be more competitive. The bill covers three areas considered critical in improving U.S. trade: market access, export expansion, and import relief.

The issue of the openness of markets for U.S. goods is addressed as *market access*. Many barriers restrict or prohibit goods from entering a foreign market. Unnecessarily restrictive technical standards, compulsory distribution systems, customs barriers, tariffs, quotas, and restrictive licensing requirements are just a few. The act gives the U.S. president authority to restrict sales of a country's products in the U.S. market if that country imposes unfair restrictions on U.S. products. Furthermore, if a foreign government's procurement rules discriminate against U.S. firms, the U.S. president has the authority to impose a similar ban on U.S. government procurement of goods and services from the offending nation.

Besides emphasizing market access, the act recognizes that some problems with U.S. export competitiveness stem from impediments on trade imposed by U.S. regulations and export disincentives. Export controls, the Foreign Corrupt Practices Act (FCPA), and

---

[21] Caroline Baum, "China Isn't a Currency Manipulator," *Today* (Singapore), June 20, 2007, p. 35.

The billboard overlooking a busy shopping district in Beijing proclaims the importance of China's space technology to all passersby. Meanwhile, Boeing and Hughes have had to pay $32 million in a settlement with the U.S. government for allegedly giving the Chinese sensitive space technology in the middle 1990s. The restrictions on technology sales have rendered American high-tech firms less competitive in international markets even beyond China, such as Canada.

export promotion were specifically addressed in the *export expansion* section of the act. Export licenses could be obtained more easily and more quickly for products on the export control list. In addition, the act reaffirmed the government's role in being more responsive to the needs of the exporter. Two major contributions facilitating export trade were computer-based procedures to file for and track export license requests and the creation of the National Trade Data Bank (NTDB) to improve access to trade data.

Export trade is a two-way street: We must be prepared to compete with imports in the home market if we force foreign markets to open to U.S. trade. Recognizing that foreign penetration of U.S. markets can cause serious competitive pressure, loss of market share, and, occasionally, severe financial harm, the *import relief* section of the Omnibus Trade and Competitiveness Act provides a menu of remedies for U.S. businesses adversely affected by imports. Companies seriously injured by fairly traded imports can petition the government for temporary relief while they adjust to import competition and regain their competitive edge.

The act has resulted in a much more flexible process for obtaining export licenses, in fewer products on the export control list, and in greater access to information and has established a basis for negotiations with India, Japan, and other countries to remove or lower barriers to trade. However, since a 1999 congressional report (accusing China of espionage regarding defense technology), restrictions on exports of many high-tech products have again been tightened for national security reasons.[22]

As the global marketplace evolves, trading countries have focused attention on ways of eliminating tariffs, quotas, and other barriers to trade. Four ongoing activities to support the growth of international trade are GATT, the associated WTO, the International Monetary Fund (IMF), and the World Bank Group.

General Agreement on Tariffs and Trade

Historically, trade treaties were negotiated on a bilateral (between two nations) basis, with little attention given to relationships with other countries. Furthermore, they tended to raise barriers rather than extend markets and restore world trade. The United States and 22 other countries signed the *General Agreement on Tariffs and Trade (GATT)* shortly after World War II.[23] Although not all countries participated, this agreement paved the way for the first effective worldwide tariff agreement. The original agreement provided a process to reduce tariffs and created an agency to serve as watchdog over world trade. The GATT's agency director and staff offer nations a forum for negotiating trade and related issues. Member nations seek to resolve their trade disputes bilaterally; if that fails, special GATT panels are set up to recommend action. The panels are only advisory and have no enforcement powers.

The GATT treaty and subsequent meetings have produced agreements significantly reducing tariffs on a wide range of goods. Periodically, member nations meet to reevaluate trade barriers and establish international codes designed to foster trade among members. In general, the agreement covers these basic elements: (1) trade shall be conducted on a nondiscriminatory basis; (2) protection shall be afforded domestic industries through customs tariffs, not through such commercial measures as import quotas; and (3) consultation shall be the primary method used to solve global trade problems.

---

[22] Elaine Kurtenbach, "China Says Bids Due from Three Global Nuclear Power Companies," *Associated Press*, February 25, 2005.

[23] Florence Chong, "As GATT Turns 60, Crean Pledges to Revive the Great Struggle for World Trade Liberalization," *The Australian*, January 2, 2008, p. 17.

According to the U.S. government, you can't call it a "catfish" unless it's grown in America. Vietnamese are producing filets in flooded rice paddies at about $1.80 a pound at wholesale. American fish farmers are charging about $2.80. Neither consumers nor ichthyologists can tell the difference between the Asian and American fish, but Uncle Sam has stepped in anyway. The congressional claim on the "catfish" name has forced the United States to stifle its own protests about Europeans claiming exclusive rights to the name "herring." (© Tom McHugh/ Photo Researchers, Inc.)

Since GATT's inception, eight "rounds" of intergovernmental tariff negotiations have been held. The most recently completed was the Uruguay Round (1994), which built on the successes of the Tokyo Round (1974)—the most comprehensive and far-reaching undertaken by GATT up to that time. The Tokyo Round resulted in tariff cuts and set out new international rules for subsidies and countervailing measures, antidumping, government procurement, technical barriers to trade (standards), customs valuation, and import licensing. While the Tokyo Round addressed nontariff barriers, some areas that were not covered continued to impede free trade.

In addition to market access, there were issues of trade in services, agriculture, and textiles; intellectual property rights; and investment and capital flows. The United States was especially interested in addressing services trade and intellectual property rights, since neither had been well protected. On the basis of these concerns, the eighth set of negotiations (Uruguay Round) was begun in 1986 at a GATT Trade Minister's meeting in Punta del Este, Uruguay, and finally concluded in 1994. By 1995, 80 GATT members, including the United States, the European Union (and its member states), Japan, and Canada, had accepted the agreement.

The market access segment (tariff and nontariff measures) was initially considered to be of secondary importance in the negotiations, but the final outcome went well beyond the initial Uruguay Round goal of a one-third reduction in tariffs. Instead, virtually all tariffs in 10 vital industrial sectors with key trading partners were eliminated. This agreement resulted in deep cuts (ranging from 50 to 100 percent) in tariffs on electronic items and scientific equipment and the harmonization of tariffs in the chemical sector at very low rates (5.5 to 0 percent).

An important objective of the United States in the Uruguay Round was to reduce or eliminate barriers to international trade in services. The *General Agreement on Trade in Services (GATS)* was the first multilateral, legally enforceable agreement covering trade and investment in the services sector. It provides a legal basis for future negotiations aimed at eliminating barriers that discriminate against foreign services and deny them market access. For the first time, comprehensive multilateral disciplines and procedures covering trade and investment in services have been established. Specific market-opening concessions from a wide range of individual countries were achieved, and provision was made for continued negotiations to liberalize telecommunications and financial services further.

Equally significant were the results of negotiations in the investment sector. *Trade-Related Investment Measures (TRIMs)* established the basic principle that investment restrictions can be major trade barriers and therefore are included, for the first time, under GATT procedures. As a result of TRIMs, restrictions in Indonesia that prohibit foreign firms from opening their own wholesale or retail distribution channels can be challenged. And so can investment restrictions in Brazil that require foreign-owned manufacturers to buy most of their components from high-cost local suppliers and that require affiliates of foreign multinationals to maintain a trade surplus in Brazil's favor by exporting more than they sell within.

Another objective of the United States for the Uruguay Round was achieved by an agreement on *Trade-Related Aspects of Intellectual Property Rights (TRIPs)*. The TRIPs agreement establishes substantially higher standards of protection for a full range of intellectual property rights (patents, copyrights, trademarks, trade secrets, industrial designs, and semiconductor chip mask works) than are embodied in current international agreements, and it provides for the effective enforcement of those standards both internally and at the border.

The Uruguay Round also includes another set of improvements in rules covering anti-dumping, standards, safeguards, customs valuation, rules of origin, and import licensing. In each case, rules and procedures were made more open, equitable, and predictable, thus leading to a more level playing field for trade. Perhaps the most notable achievement of the Uruguay Round was the creation of a new institution as a successor to the GATT—the World Trade Organization.

World Trade Organization[24]

At the signing of the Uruguay Round trade agreement in Marrakech, Morocco, in April 1994, U.S. representatives pushed for an enormous expansion of the definition of trade issues. The result was the creation of the *World Trade Organization (WTO)*, which encompasses the current GATT structure and extends it to new areas not adequately covered in the past. The WTO is an institution, not an agreement as was GATT. It sets many rules governing trade among its 148 members, provides a panel of experts to hear and rule on trade disputes among members, and, unlike GATT, issues binding decisions. It will require, for the first time, the full participation of all members in all aspects of the current GATT and the Uruguay Round agreements, and, through its enhanced stature and scope, provide a permanent, comprehensive forum to address the trade issues of the 21st-century global market.

All member countries will have equal representation in the WTO's ministerial conference, which will meet at least every two years to vote for a director general, who will appoint other officials. Trade disputes, such as that swirling around genetically modified foods, are heard by a panel of experts selected by the WTO from a list of trade experts provided by member countries. The panel hears both sides and issues a decision; the winning side will be authorized to retaliate with trade sanctions if the losing country does not change its practices. Although the WTO has no means of enforcement, international pressure to comply with WTO decisions from other member countries is expected to force compliance. The WTO ensures that member countries agree to the obligations of all the agreements, not just those they like. For the first time, member countries, including developing countries (the fastest growing markets of the world), will undertake obligations to open their markets and to be bound by the rules of the multilateral trading system.

The World Trade Organization provision of the Uruguay Round encountered some resistance before it was finally ratified by the three superpowers: Japan, the European Union (EU), and the United States. A legal wrangle among European Union countries centered on whether the EU's founding treaty gives the European Commission the sole right to negotiate for its members in all areas covered by the WTO.

In the United States, ratification was challenged because of concern for the possible loss of sovereignty over its trade laws to WTO, the lack of veto power (the U.S. could have a decision imposed on it by a majority of the WTO's members), and the role the United States would assume when a conflict arises over an individual state's laws that might be challenged by a WTO member. The GATT agreement was ratified by the U.S. Congress, and soon after, the EU, Japan, and more than 60 other countries followed. All 117 members of the former GATT supported the Uruguay agreement. Since almost immediately after its inception on January 1, 1995, the WTO's agenda has been full with issues ranging from threats of boycotts and sanctions and the membership of Iran[25] and Russia.[26] Indeed, a major event in international trade during recent years is China's 2001 entry into the WTO. Instead of waiting for various "rounds" to iron out problems, the WTO offers a framework for a continuous discussion and resolution of issues that retard trade.

---

[24] See http://wto.org.

[25] Tom Wright, "WRTO to Open Talks on Iran's Membership," *International Herald Tribune*, May 27, 2005, p. 1.

[26] "Mexico Backs Russia's WTO Bid, Welcomes Russian Energy Investment," *Agence France-Presse*, June 21, 2005.

The WTO has its detractors, but from most indications it is gaining acceptance by the trading community. The number of countries that have joined and those that want to become members is a good measure of its importance. Another one is its accomplishments since its inception: It has been the forum for successful negotiations to opening markets in telecommunications and in information technology equipment, something the United States had sought for the last two rounds of GATT. It also has been active in settling trade disputes, and it continues to oversee the implementation of the agreements reached in the Uruguay Round. But with its successes come other problems, namely, how to counter those countries that want all the benefits of belonging to WTO but also want to protect their markets. Indeed, the latest multilateral initiative, dubbed the "Doha Round" for the city of Qatar where the talks began in 2001, has been stalled with little progress. However, the pluses associated with freer trade attracted experts from 151 countries to agree to continue the talks again in Geneva in 2008.[27]

Skirting the Spirit of GATT and WTO

Unfortunately, as is probably true of every law or agreement, since its inception there have been those who look for loopholes and ways to get around the provisions of the WTO. For example, China was asked to become a member of the WTO, but to be accepted it had to show good faith in reducing tariffs and other restrictions on trade. To fulfill the requirements to join the WTO, China reduced tariffs on 5,000 product lines and eliminated a range of traditional nontariff barriers to trade, including quotas, licenses, and foreign exchange controls. At the same time, U.S. companies began to notice an increase in the number and scope of technical standards and inspection requirements. As a case in point, China recently applied safety and quality inspection requirements on such seemingly benign imported goods as jigsaw puzzles. It also has been insisting that a long list of electrical and mechanical imports undergo an expensive certification process that requires foreign companies but not domestic companies to pay for on-site visits by Chinese inspection officials. Under WTO rules, China now must justify the decision to impose certain standards and provide a rationale for the inspection criteria. However, the foreign companies will have to request a review before the WTO will investigate. The WTO recognizes the need for standards (safety, health, and so on), and it advocates worldwide harmonization of product standards.

The previously mentioned antidumping duties are becoming a favorite way for nations to impose new duties. Indeed, following the example of the United States, the region's most prolific user of antidumping cases, Mexico and other Latin American countries have increased their use as well. The WTO continues to fight these new, creative barriers to trade.

Finally, frustrated with the slow progress of the most recent round of WTO trade negotiations, several countries are negotiating bilateral trade agreements. For example, the United States is currently negotiating free-trade agreements with Peru, Colombia, Panama, and South Korea.[28] The European Union is engaged in similar activities with South American countries. To the extent that the bilateral talks ultimately lead to multilateral concessions, such activities are not inconsistent with WTO goals and aspirations.

The International Monetary Fund and World Bank Group

The International Monetary Fund[29] and the World Bank[30] Group are two global institutions created to assist nations in becoming and remaining economically viable. Each plays an important role in the environment of international trade by helping maintain stability in the financial markets and by assisting countries that are seeking economic development and restructuring.

---

[27] "Doha Free Trade Talks Resume at WTO," *Voice of America Press Release*, January 3, 2008.

[28] http://www.ustr.gov, 2008.

[29] http://www.imf.org.

[30] http://www.worldbank.org.

Inadequate monetary reserves and unstable currencies are particularly vexing problems in global trade. So long as these conditions exist, world markets cannot develop and function as effectively as they should. To overcome these particular market barriers that plagued international trading before World War II, the *International Monetary Fund (IMF)* was formed. Originally 29 countries signed the agreement; now 184 countries are members. Among the objectives of the IMF are the stabilization of foreign exchange rates and the establishment of freely convertible currencies to facilitate the expansion and balanced growth of international trade. Member countries have voluntarily joined to consult with one another to maintain a stable system of buying and selling their currencies so that payments in foreign money can take place between countries smoothly and without delay. The IMF also lends money to members having trouble meeting financial obligations to other members. Argentina and Turkey have recently received such help from the IMF, but the results have been mixed.

To cope with universally floating exchange rates, the IMF developed *special drawing rights (SDRs)*, one of its more useful inventions. Because both gold and the U.S. dollar have lost their utility as the basic medium of financial exchange, most monetary statistics relate to SDRs rather than dollars. The SDR is in effect "paper gold" and represents an average base of value derived from the value of a group of major currencies. Rather than being denominated in the currency of any given country, trade contracts are frequently written in SDRs because they are much less susceptible to exchange-rate fluctuations. Even floating rates do not necessarily accurately reflect exchange relationships. Some countries permit their currencies to float cleanly without manipulation (clean float), whereas other nations systematically manipulate the value of their currency (dirty float), thus modifying the accuracy of the monetary marketplace. Although much has changed in the world's monetary system since the IMF was established, it still plays an important role in providing short-term financing to governments struggling to pay current account debts.

Although the International Monetary Fund has some severe critics,[31] most agree that it has performed a valuable service and at least partially achieved many of its objectives. To be sure, the IMF proved its value in the financial crisis among some Asian countries in 1997. The impact of the crisis was lessened substantially as a result of actions taken by the IMF. During the financial crisis, the IMF provided loans to several countries including Thailand, Indonesia, and South Korea. Had these countries not received aid ($60 billion to Korea alone), the economic reverberations might have led to a global recession. As it was, all the major equity markets reflected substantial reductions in market prices, and the rate of economic growth in some countries was slowed.

Sometimes confused with the IMF, the *World Bank Group* is a separate institution that has as its goal the reduction of poverty and the improvement of living standards by promoting sustainable growth and investment in people. The bank provides loans, technical assistance, and policy guidance to developing country members to achieve its objectives.[32] The World Bank Group has five institutions, each of which performs the following services: (1) lending money to the governments of developing countries to finance development projects in education, health, and infrastructure; (2) providing assistance to governments for developmental projects to the poorest developing countries (per capita incomes of $925 or less); (3) lending directly to the private sector to help strengthen the private sector in developing countries with long-term loans, equity investments, and other financial assistance; (4) providing investors with investment guarantees against "noncommercial risk," such as expropriation and war, to create an environment in developing countries that will attract foreign investment; and (5) promoting increased flows of international investment by providing facilities for the conciliation and arbitration of disputes between governments and foreign investors. It also provides advice, carries out research, and produces publications in the

---

[31] Krishna Guha, "Watchdog Calls on IMF to Curb Loan Conditions," *Financial Times*, January 4, 2008, p. 4.

[32] Thomas Pearmain, "Tanzanian Power Sector Faces Difficult Year," *Global Insight*, January 2, 2008.

area of foreign investment law. Since their inception, these institutions have played a pivotal role in the economic development of countries throughout the world and thus contributed to the expansion of international trade since World War II.

Protests against Global Institutions[33]

Beginning in 1999, what some are calling "anticapitalist protesters" began to influence the workings of the major global institutions described previously. The basic complaint against the WTO, IMF, and others is the amalgam of unintended consequences of globalization: environmental concerns, worker exploitation and domestic job losses, cultural extinction, higher oil prices, and diminished sovereignty of nations. The antiglobalization protests first caught the attention of the world press during a WTO meeting in Seattle in November 1999. Then came the World Bank and IMF meetings in April in Washington, DC, the World Economic Forum in Melbourne, Australia, in September, and IMF/World Bank meetings in Prague, also in September 2000. Some 10,000 protesters faced some 11,000 police in Prague. The protesters have established Web sites associated with each event, labeled according to the respective dates. The Web sites and the Internet have proved to be important media aiding organizational efforts. And the protests[34] and violence have continued at other meetings of world leaders regarding economic issues, such as the G8 meetings in Evian, France, in 2003, and in individual countries affected by the IMF. Tragically, the terrorism in London was most likely timed to coincide with the G8 meetings in Scotland in 2005.[35]

---

[33] "Anti-Capitalist Protests: Angry and Effective," *The Economist*, September 23, 2000, pp. 85–87.

[34] "Pakistani Farmers Stage Protests in Lahore against WTO Regime," *BBC Monitoring South Asia*, April 18, 2007.

[35] Mark Rice-Osley, "Overshadowed by Terrorism, G-8 Summit Still Secures Debt Relief," *Christian Science Monitor*, July 11, 2005, p. 7.

Three kinds of antiglobalization protests: the photo on this page and the two photos on the next. Gifford Myers showed this sculpture *Object (Globalization)–2001* in Faenza, Italy, as a peaceful protest. (*"Globalization" by Gifford Myers, Altadena, CA, 2001.*)

Starbucks may be replacing McDonald's as the American brand foreigners most love to hate. Here local police fail to stop anti–World Trade Organization rioters in Seattle from breaking windows close to home. (© Mike Nelson/AFP Getty Images)

And, finally, protest of the deadly sort. Terrorists maim and kill those aboard the classic red London double-deck bus (you can see the pieces in the street). (AP Photo/Jane Mingay)

The protest groups, some of them with responsible intent, have affected policy. For example, "antisweatshop" campaigns, mostly in America and mostly student-led, have had effects beyond college campuses. A coalition of nongovernmental organizations, student groups, and UNITE (the textile workers' union) recently sued clothing importers, including Calvin Klein and The Gap, over working conditions in the American commonwealth of Saipan in the Pacific. Faced with litigation and extended public campaigns against their brands, 17 companies settled, promising better working conditions. Similarly, a World Bank project in China, which involved moving poor ethnic Chinese into lands that were traditionally Tibetan, was abandoned after a political furor led by a relatively small group of pro-Tibetan activists.

Given the apparent previous successes associated with the generally peaceful grassroots efforts to influence policy at these global institutions, we can expect more of the same in the future. But to predict the consequences of the terrorism apparently being added to the mix of protestation is impossible.

Summary

Regardless of the theoretical approach used in defense of international trade, the benefits from an absolute or comparative advantage clearly can accrue to any nation. Heightened competitors from around the world have created increased pressure for protectionism from every region of the globe at a time when open markets are needed if world resources are to be developed and utilized in the most beneficial manner. And though market protection may be needed in light of certain circumstances and may be beneficial to national defense or the encouragement of infant industries in developing nations, the consumer seldom benefits from such protection.

Free international markets help underdeveloped countries become self-sufficient, and because open markets provide new customers, most industrialized nations have, since World War II, cooperated in working toward freer trade. Such trade will always be partially threatened by various governmental and market barriers that exist or are created for the protection of local businesses. However, the trend has been toward freer trade. The changing economic and political realities are producing unique business structures that continue to protect certain major industries. The future of open global markets lies with the controlled and equitable reduction of trade barriers.

Questions

1. Define the following terms:

   GATT

   balance of payments

   balance of trade

   current account

   tariff

   IMF

   nontariff barriers

   voluntary export restraint (VER)

   protectionism

   WTO

2. Discuss the globalization of the U.S. economy.

3. Differentiate among the current account, balance of trade, and balance of payments.

4. Explain the role of price as a free market regulator.

5. "Theoretically, the market is an automatic, competitive, self-regulating mechanism which provides for the maximum consumer welfare and which best regulates the use of the factors of production." Explain.

6. Interview several local businesspeople to determine their attitudes toward world trade. Furthermore, learn if they buy or sell goods produced in foreign countries. Correlate the attitudes with their commercial experience and report on your findings.

7. What is the role of profit in international trade? Does profit replace or complement the regulatory function of pricing? Discuss.

8. Why does the balance of payments always balance, even though the balance of trade does not?

9. Enumerate the ways in which a nation can overcome an unfavorable balance of trade.

10. Support or refute each of the various arguments commonly used in support of tariffs.

11. France exports about 18 percent of its gross domestic product, while neighboring Belgium exports 46 percent. What areas of economic policy are likely to be affected by such variations in exports?

12. Does widespread unemployment change the economic logic of protectionism?

13. Review the economic effects of major trade imbalances such as those caused by petroleum imports.

14. Discuss the main provisions of the Omnibus Trade and Competitiveness Act of 1988.

15. The Tokyo Round of GATT emphasized the reduction of nontariff barriers. How does the Uruguay Round differ?

16. Discuss the impact of GATS, TRIMs, and TRIPs on global trade.

17. Discuss the evolution of world trade that led to the formation of the WTO.

18. Visit www.usitc.gov/taffairs.htm (U.S. Customs tariff schedule) and look up the import duties on leather footwear. You will find a difference in the duties on shoes of different value, material composition, and quantity. Using what you have learned in this chapter, explain the reasoning behind these differences. Do the same for frozen and/or concentrated orange juice.

19. The GATT has had a long and eventful history. Visit www.wto.org/wto/about/about.htm and write a short report on the various rounds of GATT. What were the key issues addressed in each round?

3

HISTORY and Geography:

THE FOUNDATIONS OF CULTURE

CHAPTER LEARNING OBJECTIVES

What you should learn from Chapter 3:

- The importance of history and geography in understanding international markets

- The effects of history on a country's culture

- How culture interprets events through its own eyes

- How the United States moved west, and how this move affected attitudes

- The effect of geographic diversity on economic profiles of a country

- Why marketers need to be responsive to the geography of a country

- The economic effects of controlling population growth versus aging population

- Communications are an integral part of international commerce

Global Perspective

BIRTH OF A NATION—PANAMA IN 67 HOURS

The Stage Is Set

June 1902	The United States offers to buy the Panama Canal Zone from Colombia for $10 million.
August 1903	The Colombian Senate refuses the offer. Theodore Roosevelt, angered by the refusal, refers to the Colombian Senate as "those contemptible little creatures in Bogotá." Roosevelt then agrees to a plot, led by secessionist Dr. Manuel Amador, to assist a group planning to secede from Colombia.
October 17	Panamanian dissidents travel to Washington and agree to stage a U.S.-backed revolution. The revolution is set for November 3 at 6:00 p.m.
October 18	A flag, constitution, and declaration of independence are created over the weekend. Panama's first flag was designed and sewn by hand in Highland Falls, New York, using fabric bought at Macy's.

Philippe Jean Bunau-Varilla, a French engineer associated with the bankrupt French–Panamanian canal construction company and not a permanent resident in Panama, is named Panama's ambassador to the United States.

A Country Is Born

Tuesday, November 3	Precisely at 6:00 p.m., the Colombian garrison is bribed to lay down their arms. The revolution begins, the U.S.S. *Nashville* steams into Colón harbor, and the junta proclaims Panama's independence.
Friday, November 6	By 1:00 p.m., the United States recognizes the sovereign state of Panama.
Saturday, November 7	The new government sends an official delegation from Panama to the United States to instruct the Panamanian ambassador to the United States on provisions of the Panama Canal Treaty.

Wednesday, November 18	At 6:40 p.m., the Panamanian ambassador signs the Panama Canal Treaty. At 11:30 p.m., the official Panamanian delegation arrives at a Washington, DC, railroad station and is met by their ambassador, who informs them that the treaty was signed just hours earlier.

The Present

1977	The United States agrees to relinquish control of the Panama Canal Zone on December 31, 1999.
1997	Autoridad del Canal de Panama, the canal authority that will assume control from the U.S. Panama Canal Commission, is created.
1998	Panama gives a Chinese company the right to build new port facilities on both the Pacific and Atlantic sides, to control anchorages, to hire new pilots to guide ships through the canal, and to block all passage that interferes with the company's business.
January 1, 2000	"The canal is ours" is the jubilant cry in Panama.
January 17, 2000	The Pentagon sees a potential Chinese threat to the Panama Canal.
July 2002	China pressures Panama to extend diplomatic recognition to China and drop recognition of Taiwan.
2005	The Panama Canal is expected to reach maximum capacity by 2010. The administrative board proposes a $5 billion expansion to add a parallel set of locks in response to the threat of a competing project to build canals or "multimodal" systems across Mexico's Tehuantepec isthmus. Either expand or "run the risk of eventually becoming just a regional canal."
2020	????

This story is a good illustration of how history and geography can affect public and political attitudes in the present and far into the future. To the Panamanians and much of Latin America, the Panama Canal is but one example of the many U.S. intrusions during the early 20th century that have tainted U.S.–Latin American relations. For the United States, the geographical importance of the Panama Canal for trade (shipping between the two coasts via the canal is cut by 8,000 miles) makes control of the canal a sensitive issue, especially if that control could be potentially hostile. That a Chinese-owned company has operational control of both the Pacific and Atlantic ports and could pose an indirect threat to the Panama Canal Zone concerns the U.S. government. The recent history of U.S. conflict with China and the history of Western domination of parts of China create in the minds of many an adversarial relationship between the two countries. Furthermore, some wonder if Panama would be reluctant to ask the United States to intervene at some future date, perhaps fearing that the Americans might stay another 98 years. Although the probability of China sabotaging the canal is slim at best, historical baggage makes one wonder what would happen should U.S. relations with China deteriorate to the point that the canal were considered to be in jeopardy.

Sources: Bernard A. Weisberger, "Panama: Made in U.S.A.," *American Heritage*, November 1989, pp. 24–25; Juanita Darling, "'The Canal Is Ours' Is Jubilant Cry in Panama," *Los Angeles Times*, January 1, 2000, p. A1; Chris Kraul, "$5-Billion Expansion of Panama Canal Is Considered," *Los Angeles Times*, January 22, 2005, p. A15; Rainbow Nelson, "Panama Canal Hits Milestone," *Lloyd's List*, November 1, 2007, p. 4.

Here we begin the discussion of the Cultural Environment of Global Markets. *Culture* can be defined as a society's accepted basis for responding to external and internal events. To understand fully a society's actions and its points of view, you must have an appreciation for the influence of historical events and the geographical uniqueness to which a culture has had to adapt. To interpret a culture's behavior and attitudes, a marketer must have some idea of a country's history and geography.

The goal of this chapter is to introduce the reader to the impact of history and geography on the marketing process. The influence of history on behavior and attitudes and the influence of geography on markets, trade, and environmental issues are examined in particular.

Historical Perspective in Global Business

History helps define a nation's "mission," how it perceives its neighbors, how it sees its place in the world, and how it sees itself. Insights into the history of a country are important for understanding attitudes about the role of government and business, the relations between managers and the managed, the sources of management authority, and attitudes toward foreign corporations.

To understand, explain, and appreciate a people's image of itself and the attitudes and unconscious fears that are reflected in its view of foreign cultures, it is necessary to study

1000 First millennium ends; Y1K problem overblown—widespread fear of the end of the world proved unfounded
1000 Vikings settle Newfoundland
1004 Chinese unity crumbles with treaty between the Song and the Liao giving the Liao full autonomy; China will remain fractured until the Mongol invasion in the 13th century (see 1206)
1025 Navy of Cholas in southern India crushes the empire of Srivijaya in modern Myanmar to protect its trade with China
1054 Italy and Egypt formalize commercial relations

1066 William the Conqueror is victorious over Harold II in the Battle of Hastings, establishing Norman rule in England and forever linking the country with the continent
1081 Venice and Byzantium conclude a commercial treaty (renewed in 1126)
1095 First of the crusades begins; Pope Urban II calls on Europe's noblemen to help the Byzantines repel the Turks; the crusaders' travel, stories, and goods acquired along the way help increase trade across Europe and with the Mediterranean and Asia; eighth major crusade ends—Syria expels the Christians

1100 Japan begins to isolate itself from the rest of the world, not really opening up again until the mid-19th century (see 1858)
1100 China invents the mariner's compass and becomes a force in trade; widespread use of paper money also helps increase trade and prosperity
1100 Inca Empire in the Andes begins to develop, eventually encompassing about 12 million people until its destruction by the Spanish in 1553; cities specialize in certain farming and trade with others for what they don't make
1132 Corporate towns in France grant charters by Henry I to protect commerce

1189 German merchants conclude treaty with Novgorod in Russia
1200 Islam is introduced by spice traders to Southeast Asia
1200 More than 60,000 Italian merchants work and live in Constantinople
1206 Genghis Khan becomes the Great Khan, controlling most of northern China; after his death in 1227, the Khan clan conquers much of Asia by midcentury and promotes trade and commerce, reviving the ancient Silk Road that linked Chinese and Western traders

the culture as it is now as well as to understand the culture as it was—that is, a country's history.

History and Contemporary Behavior

Most Americans know the most about European history, even though our major trading partners are now to our west and south. Circa 2008, China has become a hot topic in the United States. It was back in 1776 as well. In a sense, American history really begins with China. Recall the Boston Tea Party: Our complaint then was the British tax, and more important, the British prohibition against Yankee traders dealing directly with merchants in Canton. So it is worthwhile to dwell for a few moments on a couple of prominent points in the history of the fast burgeoning market that is modern-day China. James Day Hodgson, former U.S. Labor Secretary and Ambassador to Japan, suggests that anyone doing business in another country should understand at least the encyclopedic version of the people's past as a matter of politeness, if not persuasion.[1] We first offer a few glimpses of the past that continues to influence U.S.–Chinese relations even today.

First Opium War and the Treaty of Nanjing (1839–1842).

During the early 1800s, the British taste for tea was creating a huge trade deficit with China. Silver bullion was flowing fast in an easterly direction. Of course, other goods were being traded too. Exports from China also included sugar, silk, mother-of-pearl, paper, camphor, cassia, copper and alum, lacquer ware, rhubarb, various oils, bamboo, and porcelain. The British "barbarians" returned cotton and woolen textiles, iron, tin, lead, carnelian, diamonds, pepper, betel nuts, pearls, watches and clocks, coral and amber beads, birds' nests and shark fins, and foodstuffs such as fish and rice. But the tea-for-silver swap dominated the equation.

Then came the English East India Company epiphany: Opium. Easy to ship, high value to volume and weight ratios, and addicting to customers—what a great product! At the time, the best opium came from British India, and once the full flow began, the tea-caused trade deficit disappeared fast. The Emperor complained and issued edicts, but the opium trade burgeoned. One of the taller skyscrapers in Hong Kong today is the Jardine-Matheson Trading House.[2] Its circular windows are reminiscent of the portholes of its clipper-ship beginnings in the opium trade.

---

[1] James Day Hodgson, Yoshihiro Sano, and John L. Graham, *Doing Business in the New Japan, Succeeding in America's Richest Foreign Market* (Latham, MD: Rowman & Littlefield, 2008).

[2] In a very interesting paper, it is argued that choices made by Jardine's and Swire's (trading houses) in Asia today, for example, are an outgrowth of strategic choices first in evidence more than a century ago! See Geoffrey Jones and Tarun Khanna, "Bringing History (Back) into International Business," *Journal of International Business Studies* 37 (2006), pp. 453–68.

1215 Magna Carta, a pact between the English king and his subjects, is signed by King John, who becomes subject to the rule of law

1229 German merchants sign trade treaty with the Prince of Smolensk in Russia

1252 First gold coins issued in the West since the fall of Rome, in Florence

1269 England institutes toll roads

1270 Venetian Marco Polo and his father travel through Asia and the Middle East, becoming the first European traders to establish extensive links with the region

1279 Kublai Khan unites China and creates the Yuan (Origin) dynasty; by the time he dies in 1294, he has created a unified Mongol Empire extending from China to eastern Europe

1300 The early stirrings of the Renaissance begin in Europe as people are exposed to other cultures, primarily through merchants and trade; trade fairs are held in numerous European cities

1315 A great famine hits Europe, lasting two years, more widespread and longer than any before

1348 The Plague (the Black Death) kills one-fourth to one-third of the population

in Europe (25 million people) in just three years, disrupting trade as cities try to prevent the spread of the disease by restricting visitors; it likely started in Asia in the 1320s; massive inflation took hold, because goods could only be obtained locally; serfs were in high demand and began moving to higher wage payers, forever altering Europe's labor landscape

1358 German Hanseatic League officially forms by the Hansa companies of merchants for trade and mutual protection, eventually encompassing more than 70 cities and lasting nearly 300 years

1375 Timur Lang the Turk conquers lands from Moscow to Delhi

1381 English rioters kill foreign Flemish traders as part of the 100,000-strong peasant rebellion against Richard II, which was led by Wat Tyler in a failed attempt to throw off the yoke of feudalism

1392 England prohibits foreigners from retailing goods in the country

1400 Koreans develop movable-type printing (see 1450)

1404 Chinese prohibit private trading in foreign countries, but foreign ships may trade in China with official permission

In 1836 some high-ranking Chinese officials advocated legalizing opium. The foreign suppliers boosted production and shipments in anticipation of exploding sales. Then the Emperor went the opposite direction and ordered the destruction of the inventories in Canton (now known as Guangzhou). By 1839 the trade was dead. The British responded by sinking junks in the Pearl River and blockading all Chinese ports.

The "magically accurate" British cannon pointed at Nanjing yielded negotiations there in 1842. The Chinese ceded Hong Kong and $21 million pounds to the British. Ports at Xiamen, Fuzhou, Ningbo, and Shanghai were opened to trade and settlement by foreigners. Hong Kong thus became the gateway to a xenophobic China, particularly for the past 50 years. Perhaps most important, China recognized for the first time its loss of great power status.

Ultimately the Opium War became about foreign access to Chinese trade, and the treaty of Nanjing really didn't settle the issue. A second Opium War was fought between 1857 and 1860. In that imbroglio, British and French forces combined to destroy the summer palace in Beijing. Such new humiliations yielded more freedoms for foreign traders; notably, the treaty specifically included provisions allowing Christian evangelism throughout the realm.

Taiping Rebellion (1851–1864).

One consequence of the humiliation at the hands of foreigners was a loss of confidence in the Chinese government. The resulting disorder came to a head in Guangxi, the southernmost province of the Empire. The leader of the uprising was a peasant who grew up near Guangzhou. Hong Xiuquan aspired to be a civil servant but failed the required Confucian teachings–based exam. When in Guangzhou for his second try at the exam, he came in contact with Protestant Western missionaries and later began to have visions of God.

After flunking the exam for a fourth time in 1843, he began to evangelize, presenting himself as Christ's brother. In the next seven years, he attracted 10,000 followers. In 1851 he was crowned by his followers as the "Heavenly King" of the "Heavenly Kingdom of Peace." Despite their adopted label, they revolted, cut off their pigtails in defiance of the ruling Manchus, and began to march north. With the fervor of the religious zealots they were, they fought their way through the capital at Nanjing and almost to Tianjing by 1855.

But then things started to unravel. Chinese opposition forces organized. Because foreigners appreciated neither Hong's interpretation of the scriptures, nor his 88 concubines, nor his attacks on Shanghai, they formed another army against him. Hong took his own life just before the final defeat and the recapture of Nanjing.

Estimates of the death toll from the Taiping Rebellion stand between 20 and 40 million people. We repeat: 20–40 million Chinese lives were lost. By contrast, "only" 2 million were killed in the 1949 Communist Revolution. The Taiping Rebellion is the single most horrific civil war in the history of the world. Surely Hong Xiuquan was insane. And other

1415 Chinese begin significant trading with Africa through government expeditions—some believe they sailed to North America as well in 1421	**1450** Renaissance takes hold in Florence, its traditional birthplace	**1479** Under the Treaty of Constantinople, in exchange for trading rights in the Black Sea, Venice agrees to pay tribute to the Ottoman Empire	**1500** Rise of mercantilism, the accumulation of wealth by the state to increase power, in western Europe; states without gold or silver mines try
1425 Hanseatic city of Brugge becomes the first Atlantic seaport to be a major trading center	**1450** Gutenberg Bible is first book printed with movable type; the ability to mass produce books creates an information revolution	**1482** English organize a postal system that features fresh relays of horses every 20 miles	to control trade to maintain a surplus and accumulate gold and silver; Englishman Thomas Mun was one of the great proponents in 1600, who realized that the overall balance of
1427 Aztec Empire is created by Itzcotl; it will encompass about 6 million people until its destruction in 1519	**1453** Byzantine Empire is destroyed as Muhammad II sacks Constantinople (renaming it Istanbul)	**1488** Bartolomeu Dias sails around the coast of Africa; this, along with the voyages of Christopher Columbus, ushers in the era of sea travel	trade was the important factor, not whether each individual trade resulted in a surplus
1430 Portuguese Prince Henry the Navigator explores west African coast to promote trade	**1464** French royal mail service established by Louis XI	**1492** Christopher Columbus "discovers" the New World	**1500** Slave trade becomes a major component of commerce
1441 Mayan Empire collapses as the city of Mayapán is destroyed in a revolt	**1470** Early trademark piracy committed by Persians who copy mass-produced Chinese porcelain to capitalize on its popularity in foreign countries	**1494** Portugal and Spain divide the unexplored world between them with the Treaty of Tordesillas	**1504** Regular postal service established among Vienna, Brussels, and Madrid

China did not want to be another India who had its resources strip away by the British and forced to be high on opium.

rebellions also occurred in China during this time; the Muslim one in the northwest is most notable (1862–78). However, based on these events in the mid-1800s, it is easy to see why the Chinese leadership has remained wary of foreign influences in general, and religious movements in particular, even today.[3]

History and Japan. Trade with Japan was a hot topic in the United States in both the 1850s and the 1980s. Likewise, unless you have a historical sense of the many changes that have buffeted Japan—seven centuries under the shogun feudal system, the isolation before the coming of Commodore Perry in 1853, the threat of domination by colonial powers, the rise of new social classes, Western influences, the humiliation of World War II, and involvement in the international community—you will have difficulty fully understanding its contemporary behavior. Why do the Japanese have such strong loyalty toward their companies? Why is the loyalty found among participants in the Japanese distribution systems so difficult for an outsider to develop? Why are decisions made by consensus? Answers to such questions can be explained in part by Japanese history (and geography).

Loyalty to family, to country, to company, and to social groups and the strong drive to cooperate, to work together for a common cause, permeate many facets of Japanese behavior and have historical roots that date back thousands of years. Historically, loyalty and service, a sense of responsibility, and respect for discipline, training, and artistry were stressed to maintain stability and order. Confucian philosophy, taught throughout Japan's history, emphasizes the basic virtue of loyalty "of friend to friend, of wife to husband, of child to parent, of brother to brother, but, above all, of subject to lord," that is, to country. A fundamental premise of Japanese ideology reflects the importance of cooperation for the collective good. Japanese achieve consensus by agreeing that all will unite against outside pressures that threaten the collective good. A historical perspective gives the foreigner in Japan a basis on which to begin developing cultural sensitivity and a better understanding of contemporary Japanese behavior.

History Is Subjective

History is important in understanding why a country behaves as it does, but history from whose viewpoint? Historical events always are viewed from one's own biases and self-reference criteria (SRC), and thus, what is recorded by one historian may not be what another records, especially if the historians are from different cultures. Historians traditionally try to be objective, but few can help filtering events through their own cultural biases.[4]

great point!

[3] N. Mark Lam and John L. Graham, *Doing Business in China Now, the World's Most Dynamic Marketplace* (New York: McGraw-Hill, 2007).

[4] An example of such biases is the differing perceptions of Turkey by European Union members in deciding on Turkey's membership in the EU. See "Which Turkey?" *The Economist*, March 17, 2005.

1520 First chocolate brought from Mexico to Spain
1521 Mexico is conquered by Hernán Cortés after Aztec ruler, Montezuma, is accidentally killed
1522 Magellan's expedition completes its three-year sail around the world; it is the first successful circumnavigation
1531 Antwerp stock exchange is the first exchange to move into its own building, signifying its importance in financing commercial enterprises throughout Europe and the rising importance of private trade and commerce; Antwerp emerges as a trading capital

1532 Brazil is colonized by the Portuguese
1534 English break from the Catholic Church, ending its dominance of politics and trade throughout Europe, as Henry VIII creates the Church of England
1553 South American Incan Empire ends with conquest by Spanish; the Incas had created an extensive area of trade, complete with an infrastructure of roads and canals
1555 Tobacco trade begins after its introduction to Europe by Spanish and Portuguese traders
1557 Spanish crown suffers first of numerous bankruptcies, discouraging cross-border lending

1561 Via Dutch traders, tulips come to Europe from Near East for first time
1564 William Shakespeare is born; many of his plays are stories of merchant traders
1567 Typhoid fever, imported from Europe, kills two million Indians in South America
1588 Spanish Armada defeated by British, heralding Britain's emergence as the world's greatest naval power; this power will enable Britain to colonize many regions of the globe and lead to its becoming the world's commercially dominant power for the next 300 years

1596 First flush toilet is developed for Britain's Queen Elizabeth I
1597 Holy Roman Empire expels English merchants in retaliation for English treatment of Hanseatic League
1600 Potatoes are brought from South America to Europe, where they quickly spread to the rest of world and become a staple of agricultural production
1600 Japan begins trading silver for foreign goods
1600 Britain's Queen Elizabeth I grants charter to the East India Company, which will dominate trade with the East until its demise in 1857

The Monumento de los Niños Heroes honors six young cadets who, during the Mexican–American War of 1847, chose death over surrender. The Mexican–American War is important in Mexican history and helps explain, in part, Mexico's love–hate relationship with the United States. (© Dave G. Houser/Corbis)

Our perspective not only influences our view of history but also subtly influences our view of many other matters. For example, maps of the world sold in the United States generally show the United States at the center, whereas maps in Britain show Britain at the center, and so on for other nations.

A crucial element in understanding any nation's business and political culture is the subjective perception of its history. Why do Mexicans have a love–hate relationship with the United States? Why were Mexicans required to have majority ownership in most foreign investments until recently? Why did dictator General Porfírio Díaz lament, "Poor Mexico, so far from God, so near the United States"? Why? Because Mexicans see the United States as a threat to their political, economic, and cultural sovereignty.

Most citizens of the United States are mystified by such feelings. After all, the United States has always been Mexico's good neighbor. Most would agree with President John F. Kennedy's proclamation during a visit to Mexico that "Geography has made us neighbors, tradition has made us friends." North Americans may be surprised to learn that most Mexicans "felt it more accurate to say 'Geography has made us closer, tradition has made us far apart.'"[5]

---

[5] For an insightful review of some of the issues that have affected relations between the United States and Mexico, see John Skirius, "Railroad, Oil and Other Foreign Interest in the Mexican Revolution, 1911–1914," *Journal of Latin American Studies*, February 2003, p. 25.

1601 France makes postal agreements with neighboring states
1602 Dutch charter their own East India Company, which will dominate the South Asian coffee and spice trade
1607 British colony of Jamestown built
1609 Dutch begin fur trade through Manhattan
1611 Japan gives Dutch limited permission to trade

1612 British East India Company builds its first factory in India
1620 *Mayflower* sails for the New World
1620 Father of the Scientific Revolution, Francis Bacon, publishes *Novum Organum*, promoting inductive reasoning through experimentation and observation
1625 Dutch jurist Hugo Grotius, sometimes called the father of

international law, publishes *On the Laws of War and Peace*
1636 Harvard University founded
1637 Dutch "tulip mania" results in history's first boom–bust market crash
1651 English pass first of so-called Navigation Acts to restrict Dutch trade by forcing colonies to trade only with English ships
1654 Spain and Germany develop hereditary land rights,

a concept that will help lead to the creation of great wealth in single families and thus to the development of private commercial empires
1687 Apple falling on Newton's head leads to his publication of the law of gravity
1694 The Bank of England is established; it offers loans to private individuals at 8 percent interest

Citizens of the United States feel they have been good neighbors. They see the Monroe Doctrine as protection for Latin America from European colonization and the intervention of Europe in the governments of the Western Hemisphere. Latin Americans, in contrast, tend to see the Monroe Doctrine as an offensive expression of U.S. influence in Latin America. To put it another way, "Europe keep your hands off—Latin America is only for the United States," an attitude perhaps typified by former U.S. President Ulysses S. Grant, who, in a speech in Mexico in 1880, described Mexico as a "magnificent mine" that lay waiting south of the border for North American interests.

United States Marines sing with pride of their exploits "from the halls of Montezuma to the shores of Tripoli." To the Mexican, the exploit to which the "halls of Montezuma" refers is remembered as U.S. troops marching all the way to the center of Mexico City and extracting as tribute 890,000 square miles that became Arizona, California, New Mexico, and Texas (see Exhibit 3.1). A prominent monument at the entrance of Chapultepec Park recognizes *Los Niños Heroes* (the boy heroes), who resisted U.S. troops, wrapped themselves in Mexican flags, and jumped to their deaths rather than surrender. Mexicans recount the heroism of *Los Niños Heroes*[6] and the loss of Mexican territory to the United States every September 13, when the president of Mexico, his cabinet, and the diplomatic corps assemble at the Mexico City fortress to recall the defeat that led to the *"despojo territorial"* (territorial plunder).

The Mexican Revolution, which overthrew the dictator Díaz and launched the modern Mexican state, is particularly remembered for the expulsion of foreigners—most notably North American businessmen who were the most visible of the wealthy and influential entrepreneurs in Mexico.

Manifest Destiny and the Monroe Doctrine

Manifest Destiny and the Monroe Doctrine were accepted as the basis for U.S. foreign policy during much of the 19th and 20th centuries.[7] Manifest Destiny, in its broadest interpretation, meant that Americans were a chosen people ordained by God to create a model society. More specifically, it referred to the territorial expansion of the United States from the Atlantic to the Pacific. The idea of Manifest Destiny was used to justify the U.S. annexation of Texas, Oregon, New Mexico, and California and, later, U.S. involvement in Cuba, Alaska, Hawaii, and the Philippines. Exhibit 3.1 illustrates when and by what means the present United States was acquired.

---

[6] When the United Nations recommended that all countries set aside a single day each year to honor children, Mexico designated April 30 as "Dia de Los Niños." Interestingly, this holiday is often included with Saint Patrick's Day celebrations, which include recognition of the San Patricios, the Irish-American battalion that fought with the Mexicans in the Mexican–American War. See Carol Sowers, "El Dia de Los Niños Adds International Touch to Celebration," *Arizona Republic*, April 29, 2005.

[7] Some say even into the 21st century. See "Manifest Destiny Warmed Up?" *The Economist*, August 14, 2003. Of course, others disagree. See Joseph Contreras, "Roll Over Monroe: The Influence the United States Once Claimed as a Divine Right in Latin America is Slipping away Fast," *Newsweek International*, December 10, 2007.

1698 First steam engine is invented

1719 French consolidate their trade in Asia into one company, the French East India Company; rival British East India Company maintains its grip on the region's trade, however, and French revert to individual company trading 60 years later

1725 Rise of Physiocrats, followers of the economic philosopher François Quesnay, who believed that production, not trade, created wealth and

that natural law should rule, which meant producers should be able to exchange goods freely; movement influenced Adam Smith's ideas promoting free trade

1740 Maria Theresa becomes empress of the Holy Roman Empire (until 1780); she ends serfdom and strengthens the power of the state

1748 First modern, scientifically drawn map, the Carte Géométrique de la France, comprising 182 sheets, was

authorized and subsequently drawn by the French Academy; Louis XV proclaimed that the new map, with more accurate data, lost more territory than his wars of conquest had gained

1750 Benjamin Franklin shows that lightning is a form of electricity by conducting it through the wet string of a kite

1750 Industrial Revolution begins and takes off with the manufacture, in 1780, of the steam engine to drive

machines—increased productivity and consumption follow (as do poor working conditions and increased hardships for workers)

1760 Chinese begin strict regulation of foreign trade to last nearly a century when they permit Europeans to do business only in a small area outside Canton and only with appointed Chinese traders

1764 British victories in India begin Britain's dominance of India, Eastern trade, and trade routes

Exhibit 3.1
Territorial Expansion of United States from 1783

The United States expanded westward to the Pacific through a series of financial deals, negotiated settlements, and forcible annexations. The acquisition of territory from Mexico began with the Battle of San Jacinto in 1836, when Texas staged a successful revolt against the rule of Mexico and became The Republic of Texas—later to join the Union in 1845. The Mexican War (1846–1848) resulted in Mexico ceding California and a large part of the West to the United States.

Source: From *Oxford Atlas of the World*, 10th ed., 2002. Copyright © 2002 Philip's Cartography.

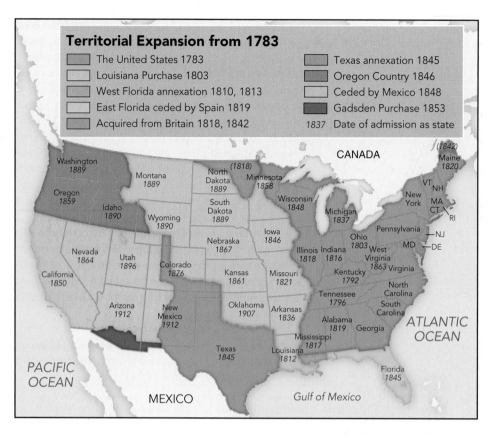

Territorial Expansion from 1783

- The United States 1783
- Louisiana Purchase 1803
- West Florida annexation 1810, 1813
- East Florida ceded by Spain 1819
- Acquired from Britain 1818, 1842
- Texas annexation 1845
- Oregon Country 1846
- Ceded by Mexico 1848
- Gadsden Purchase 1853
- *1837* Date of admission as state

The Monroe Doctrine, a cornerstone of early U.S. foreign policy, was enunciated by President James Monroe in a public statement proclaiming three basic dicta: no further European colonization in the New World, abstention of the United States from European political affairs, and nonintervention of European governments in the governments of the Western Hemisphere.

After 1870, interpretation of the Monroe Doctrine became increasingly broad. In 1881, its principles were evoked in discussing the development of a canal across the Isthmus of Panama. Theodore Roosevelt applied the Monroe Doctrine with an extension that became known as the Roosevelt Corollary. The corollary stated that not only would the United States prohibit non-American intervention in Latin American affairs, but it would also police the area and guarantee that Latin American nations met their international obligations. The corollary sanctioning American intervention was applied in 1905 when Roosevelt forced the Dominican Republic to accept the appointment of an American economic adviser, who quickly became the financial director of the small state. It was also used in the acquisition of the Panama Canal Zone from Colombia in 1903 and the formation of a provisional government in Cuba in 1906.

1764 British begin numbering houses, making mail delivery more efficient and providing the means for the development of direct mail merchants centuries later
1773 Boston Tea Party symbolizes start of American Revolution; impetus comes from American merchants trying to take control of distribution of goods that were being controlled exclusively by Britain

1776 American Declaration of Independence proclaims the colonies' rights to determine their own destiny, particularly their own economic destiny
1776 Theory of modern capitalism and free trade expressed by Adam Smith in *The Wealth of Nations*; he theorized that countries would only produce and export goods that they were able to produce more cheaply

than could trading partners; he demonstrates that mercantilists were wrong: It is not gold or silver that will enhance the state, but the *material* that can be purchased with it
1783 Treaty of Paris officially ends the American Revolution following British surrender to American troops at Yorktown in 1781
1787 U.S. Constitution approved; it becomes a model

document for constitutions for at least the next two centuries; written constitutions will help stabilize many countries and encourage foreign investment and trade with them
1789 French Revolution begins; it will alter the power structure in Europe and help lead to the introduction of laws protecting the individual and to limited democracy in the region

Exhibit 3.2
U.S. Intervention in Latin America Since 1945

Source: From *Oxford Atlas of the World*, 10th ed., 2002. Copyright © 2002 Philip's Cartography.

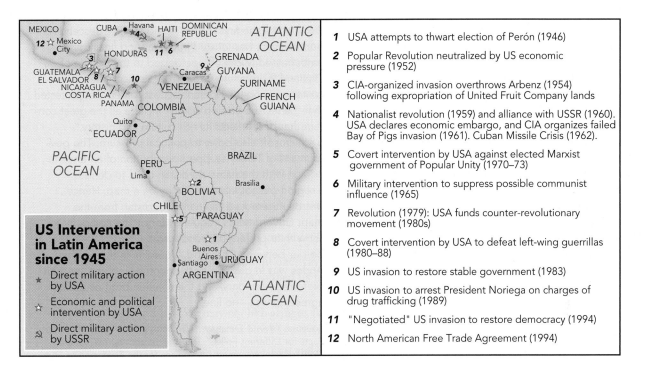

1   USA attempts to thwart election of Perón (1946)

2   Popular Revolution neutralized by US economic pressure (1952)

3   CIA-organized invasion overthrows Arbenz (1954) following expropriation of United Fruit Company lands

4   Nationalist revolution (1959) and alliance with USSR (1960). USA declares economic embargo, and CIA organizes failed Bay of Pigs invasion (1961). Cuban Missile Crisis (1962).

5   Covert intervention by USA against elected Marxist government of Popular Unity (1970–73)

6   Military intervention to suppress possible communist influence (1965)

7   Revolution (1979): USA funds counter-revolutionary movement (1980s)

8   Covert intervention by USA to defeat left-wing guerrillas (1980–88)

9   US invasion to restore stable government (1983)

10   US invasion to arrest President Noriega on charges of drug trafficking (1989)

11   "Negotiated" US invasion to restore democracy (1994)

12   North American Free Trade Agreement (1994)

The manner in which the United States acquired the land for the Panama Canal Zone typifies the Roosevelt Corollary—whatever is good for the United States is justifiable. As the Global Perspective at the beginning of this chapter illustrates, the creation of the country of Panama was a total fabrication of the United States.[8]

According to U.S. history, these Latin American adventures were a justifiable part of our foreign policy; to Latin Americans, they were unwelcome intrusions in Latin American affairs. This perspective has been constantly reinforced by U.S. intervention in Latin America since 1945 (see Exhibit 3.2). The way historical events are recorded and interpreted in

---

[8] For an interesting discussion of how past U.S. foreign interventions affect attitudes about U.S. involvement in Iraq, see "Anti-Americanism: The View from Abroad," *The Economist*, February 17, 2005.

1792 Gas lighting introduced; within three decades, most major European and U.S. cities will use gas lights
1804 Steam locomotive introduced; it will become the dominant form of transport of goods and people until the 20th century when trucks and airplanes become commercially viable
1804 Napoleon crowns himself emperor, overthrowing the French revolutionary government, and tries to conquer Europe (after already occupying

Egypt as a means of cutting off British trade with the East), the failure of which results in the redrawing of national boundaries in Europe and Latin America
1807 Robert Fulton's steamboat is the first to usher in a new age of transport when his *Clermont* sails from New York to Albany
1807 French Napoleonic Code issued and eventually becomes a model of civil law adopted by many nations around the world
1807 U.S. President Thomas Jefferson bans trade with

Europe in an effort to convince warring British and French ships to leave neutral U.S. trading ships alone
1810 Frenchman Nicolas Appert successfully cans food and prevents spoilage
1810 Following Napoleon's invasion of Spain and Portugal, Simón Bolivar begins wars of independence for Spanish colonies in Latin America, leading to new governments in Bolivia, Columbia, Ecuador, Peru, and Venezuela

1814 First practical steam locomotive is built by George Stephenson in England, leading to the birth of railroad transportation in 1825 with the first train carrying 450 passengers at 15 miles per hour
1815 Napoleon defeated at Battle of Waterloo and gives up throne days later
1815 British build roads of crushed stone, greatly improving the quality and speed of road travel

CROSSING BORDERS 3.2   Innovation and the Water Shortage, from Fog to Kid Power

When you live in Chungungo, Chile, one of the country's most arid regions with no nearby source of water, you drink fog. Of course! Thanks to a legend and resourceful Canadian and Chilean scientists, Chungungo now has its own supply of drinkable water after a 20-year drought. Before this new source of water, Chungungo depended on water trucks that came twice a week.

Chungungo has always been an arid area, and legend has it that the region's original inhabitants used to worship trees. They considered them sacred because a permanent flow of water sprang from the treetops, producing a constant interior rain. The legend was right—the trees produced rain! Thick fog forms along the coast. As it moves inland and is forced to rise against the hills, it changes into tiny raindrops, which are in turn retained by the tree leaves, producing the constant source of rain. Scientists set out to take advantage of this natural phenomenon.

The nearby ancient eucalyptus forest of El Tofo Hill provided the clue that scientists needed to create an ingenious water-supply system. To duplicate the water-bearing effect of the trees, they installed 86 "fog catchers" on the top of the hill—huge nets supported by 12-foot eucalyptus pillars, with water containers at their base. About 1,900 gallons of water are collected each day and then piped into town. This small-scale system is cheap (about one-fifth as expensive as having water trucked in), clean, and provides the local people with a steady supply of drinking water.

In sub-Saharan Africa, inventive folks have come up with a new way to bring water up from wells. A life-changing and life-saving invention—the PlayPump water system—provides easy access to clean drinking water, brings joy to children, and leads to improvements in health, education, gender equality, and economic development in more than 1,000 rural villages in South Africa, Swaziland, Mozambique, and Zambia. The PlayPump systems are innovative, sustainable, patented water pumps powered by children at play. Installed near schools, the PlayPump system doubles as a water pump and a merry-go-round. The PlayPump system also provides one of the only ways to reach rural and peri-urban communities with potentially life-saving public health messages. Please see the accompanying pictures of a new solution to one of humankind's oldest problems.

Sources: "Drinking Fog," *World Press Review*; "Silver Lining," *The Economist*, February 5, 2000, p. 75; "UNESCO Water Portal Weekly Update No. 89: Fog," April 15, 2005, http://www.unesco.org/water/news/newsletter/89.shtml; http://www.playpumps.org, 2008.

This section discusses the important geographic characteristics a marketer needs to consider when assessing the environmental aspects of marketing. Examining the world as a whole provides the reader with a broad view of world markets and an awareness of the effects of geographic diversity on the economic profiles of various nations. Climate and topography are examined as facets of the broader and more important elements of geography. A brief look at Earth's resources and population—the building blocks of world markets—completes the presentation on geography and global markets.

Climate and Topography

Altitude, humidity, and temperature extremes are climatic features that affect the uses and functions of products and equipment. Products that perform well in temperate zones may deteriorate rapidly or require special cooling or lubrication to function adequately in tropical zones. Manufacturers have found that construction equipment used in the United States requires extensive modifications to cope with the intense heat and dust of the Sahara

1848 The Communist Manifesto, by Germans Karl Marx and Friedrich Engels, is issued; it will become the basis for the communist movements of the 20th century
1851 First international world's fair held in London, showcasing new technology

1856 Declaration of Paris recognizes the principle of free movement for trade, even in wartime—blockades could only extend along the enemy's coast; it also establishes the practice of allowing the accession to treaties of nations other than the original signatories

1857 Russia and France sign trade treaty
1858 Ansei Commercial Treaties with Japan open the formerly closed country to trade with the West (treaties follow "opening" of Japan to the West by American Matthew Perry in 1854)

1860 The Cobden Treaty aims to create free trade by reducing or eliminating tariffs between Britain and France; also leads to most-favored-nation status in bilateral agreements and eventually to multilateral agreements

While children have fun spinning on the PlayPump merry-go-round, (1) clean water is pumped (2) from underground (3) into a 2,500-liter tank, (4) standing seven meters above the ground. A simple tap (5) makes it easy for adults and children to draw water. Excess water is diverted from the storage tank back down into the base hole (6). The water storage tank (7) provides rare opportunities to advertise to outlying communities. All four sides of the tank are leased as billboards, with two sides for consumer advertising and the other two sides for health and educational messages. The revenue generated from this unique model pays for pump maintenance. Capable of producing up to 1,400 liters of water per hour at 16 rpm from a depth of 40 meters, it is effective up to a depth of 100 meters. See http://www.play-pumps.org. *(right: © Frimmel Smith/PlayPumps)*

Desert. A Taiwanese company sent a shipment of drinking glasses to a buyer in the Middle East. The glasses were packed in wooden crates with hay used as dunnage to prevent breakage. The glasses arrived in shards. Why? When the crates moved to the warmer, less humid climate of the Middle East, the moisture content of the hay dropped significantly and shriveled to a point that it offered no protection.[14]

Within even a single national market, climate can be sufficiently diverse to require major adjustments. In Ghana, a product adaptable to the entire market must operate effectively in extreme desert heat and low humidity and in tropical rainforests with consistently high humidity. Bosch-Siemens washing machines designed for European countries require spin cycles to range from a minimum spin cycle of 500 rpm to a maximum of 1,600 rpm: Because the sun does not shine regularly in Germany or in Scandinavia, washing machines must have a 1,600 rpm spin cycle because users do not have the luxury of hanging them out to dry. In Italy and Spain, however, clothes can be damp, because the abundant sunshine is sufficient to justify a spin cycle speed of 500 rpm.

---

[14] Michael D. White, *International Marketing Blunders* (Novato, CA: World Trade Press, 2002), p. 79.

1860 Passports are introduced in the United States to regulate foreign travel
1866 The principle of the electric dynamo is found by German Werner Siemens, who will produce the first electric power transmission system
1866 The trans-Atlantic cable is completed, allowing nearly

instant (telegraphic) communication between the United States and Europe
1869 Suez Canal completed after 11 years of construction; the canal significantly cuts the time for travel between Europe and Asia, shortening, for example, the trip between Britain and India by 4,000 miles

1869 First U.S. transcontinental rail route is completed, heralding a boon for commerce; first commercially viable typewriter patented; until computer word processing becomes common more than a century later, the typewriter enables anyone to produce documents quickly and legibly

1873 United States adopts the gold standard to fix the international value of the dollar
1875 Universal Postal Union created in Switzerland to provide for an international mail service
1876 Alexander Graham Bell is granted a patent for the telephone, which will revolutionize communications

Different seasons between the northern and southern hemispheres also affect global strategies. JCPenney had planned to open five stores in Chile as part of its expansion into countries below the equator. It wanted to capitalize on its vast bulk buying might for its North American, Mexican, and Brazilian stores to provide low prices for its expansion into South America. After opening its first store in Chile, the company realized that the plan was not going to work—when it was buying winter merchandise in North America, it needed summer merchandise in South America. The company quickly sold its one store in Chile; its expansion into South America was limited to Brazil.[15]

South America represents an extreme but well-defined example of the importance of geography in marketing considerations. Economic and social systems are explained, in part, in terms of the geographical characteristics of the area. It is a continent 4,500 miles long and 3,000 miles wide at its broadest point. Two-thirds of it is comparable to Africa in its climate, 48 percent of its total area is made up of forest and jungle, and only 5 percent is arable. Mountain ranges cover South America's west coast for 4,500 miles, with an average height of 13,000 feet and a width of 300 to 400 miles. This natural, formidable barrier has precluded the establishment of commercial routes between the Pacific and Atlantic coasts. South America's natural barriers inhibit both national and regional growth, trade, and communication. It is a vast land area with population concentrations on the outer periphery and an isolated and almost uninhabited interior. In Colombia, mountain ranges are a major barrier to travel. The airtime from Bogotá to Medellín, the second-largest city in Colombia, is 30 minutes; by highway, the same trip takes 10 to 12 hours. Other regions of the world with extreme topographic and climatic variations are China, Russia, India, and Canada.

Mountains, oceans, seas, jungles, and other geographical features can pose serious impediments to economic growth and trade. Geographic hurdles have a direct effect on a country's economy, markets, and the related activities of communication and distribution. As countries seek economic opportunities and the challenges of the global marketplace, they invest in infrastructure to overcome such barriers. Once seen as natural protection from potentially hostile neighbors, physical barriers that exist within Europe are now seen as impediments to efficient trade in an integrated economic union.

For decades the British resisted a tunnel under the English Channel—they did not trust the French or any other European country and saw the channel as protection. But when they became members of the European Union, economic reality meant the channel tunnel had to be built to facilitate trade with other EU members. Now you can take a bullet train through the Chunnel, but even a decade after it opened, its finances are still a bit shaky,[16] and most recently, undocumented workers have tried to walk the underwater route to England.[17]

From the days of Hannibal, the Alps have served as an important physical barrier and provided European countries protection from one another. But with the EU expansion, the

---

[15] Miriam Jordan, "Penney Blends Two Business Cultures," *The Wall Street Journal*, April 5, 2001.

[16] Robert Lea, "Chunnel Rail Link Firm Heads for a Multi-Billion Break-Up," *Evening Standard*, November 1, 2007, p. 28.

[17] "Illegals in the Chunnel," *Daily Express*, January 4, 2008, p. 39.

1880 Thomas Edison creates first electric power station, after inventing the electric light in 1878, which lights New York City and starts a revolution in culture and business—making a truly 24-hour day and paving the way for electronic machines
1881 Zoopraxiscope, which shows pictures in motion, is developed
1884 The basis for establishing standard time and measuring the longitude of any spot in the world is created with the designation of Greenwich, England, as the prime meridian (0° longitude)
1886 American Federation of Labor founded, becoming a model for workers around the world to unite against management and gain higher pay and better working conditions
1901 Italian Guglielmo Marconi sends the first radio message; the radio could be said to spark the start of globalization because of the speed with which information is able to be transmitted
1903 First successful flight of an airplane, piloted by Orville Wright, takes place at Kitty Hawk, North Carolina
1904 First vacuum tube is developed by John Fleming, allowing alternating current to become direct current and helping create widespread use of the radio
1913 Assembly line introduced by Henry Ford; it will revolutionize manufacturing
1914 The first war to involve much of the world begins with the assassination of Archduke Francis Ferdinand and lasts four years; construction of Panama Canal is completed, making trade faster and easier
1917 Lenin and Trotsky lead Russian revolution, creating a living economic model that will affect trade (adversely) for the rest of the century

Alps became a major impediment to trade. Truck traffic between southern Germany and northern Italy, which choked highways through some of Switzerland's most treacherous mountain roads and pristine nature areas, was not only burdensome for all travelers but becoming economically unacceptable. The solution, the 21-mile Loetschberg Tunnel, which opened in 2007, burrows under the Alps and trims the time trains need to cross between Germany and Italy from a three-and-a-half-hour trip to less than two hours. By 2014, the 36-mile Gotthard Tunnel will provide additional rail coverage for the area and be the world's longest rail tunnel.

Other projects that help further integrate the European Union include the 10-mile-long Oresund Link, a bridge and tunnel across the Baltic Strait to continental Europe completed in 2000. It accommodates freight and high-speed passenger trains and reduces a five-hour trip between Copenhagen, Denmark, and Malmo, Sweden, to two-and-a-half hours. Ultimately, it will be possible to drive from Lapland in northernmost Scandinavia to Calabria in southern Italy and then on to Sicily when the bridge over the Messina Strait connecting Calabria to Sicily is completed—all tangible symbols that these nations are ending their political isolation from one another as they break down natural barriers in an increasingly borderless Europe.[18]

Geography, Nature, and Economic Growth

Always on the slim margin between subsistence and disaster, less-privileged countries suffer disproportionately from natural and human-assisted catastrophes.[19] Climate and topography coupled with civil wars, poor environmental policies, and natural disasters push these countries further into economic stagnation. Without irrigation and water management, droughts, floods, and soil erosion afflict them, often leading to creeping deserts that reduce the long-term fertility of the land.[20] Population increases, deforestation, and overgrazing intensify the impact of drought and lead to malnutrition and ill health, further undermining these countries' abilities to solve their problems. Cyclones cannot be prevented, nor can inadequate rainfall, but means to control their effects are available. Unfortunately, each disaster seems to push developing countries further away from effective solutions. Countries that suffer the most from major calamities are among the poorest in the world.[21] Many have neither the capital nor the technical ability to minimize the effects of natural phenomena; they are at the mercy of nature.

As countries prosper, natural barriers are overcome. Tunnels and canals are dug and bridges and dams are built in an effort to control or to adapt to climate, topography, and the recurring

---

[18] Bradley S. Klapper, "Swiss Complete Digging Alpine Tunnel," *Washington Post*, April 28, 2005.

[19] "Asia's Tsunami: Helping the Survivors," *The Economist*, January 5, 2005.

[20] See Map 2, "Global Climate," in the World Maps section for a view of the diversity of the world's climate. The climatic phenomenon of El Niño wreaks havoc with weather patterns and is linked to crop failures, famine, forest fires, dust and sand storms, and other disasters associated with either an overabundance or a lack of rain.

[21] "Water Shortage Fears in Darfur Camps," *All Africa*, December 10, 2007; "Northern Vietnam Likely to Face Water Shortages," *Xinhua News Agency*, January 4, 2008.

1919 First nonstop trans-Atlantic flight completed, paving the way for cargo to be transported quickly around the globe
1920 League of Nations created, establishing a model for international cooperation (though it failed to keep the peace)
1923 Vladimir Zworykin creates first electronic television, which will eventually help integrate cultures and consumers across the world

1929 Great Depression starts with crash of U.S. stock market
1930 Hawley-Smoot Tariff passed by U.S. Senate, plunging the world deeper into the Great Depression
1935 Radar developed in Britain; it will allow travel on ships and planes even when there is no visibility, enabling the goods to keep to a transport schedule (eventually allowing the development of just-in-time and other cost-savings processes)

1938 American Chester Carlson develops dry copying process for documents (xerography), which, among other things, will enable governments to require that multiple forms be filled out to move goods
1939 World War II begins with German invasion of Poland; over 50 million people will die
1943 The first programmable computer, Colossus I, is created in England at Bletchley Park; it helps to crack German codes

1944 Bretton Woods Conference creates basis for economic cooperation among 44 nations and the founding of the International Monetary Fund to help stabilize exchange rates
1945 Atomic weapons introduced; World War II ends; United Nations founded
1947 General Agreement on Tariffs and Trade signed by 23 countries to try to reduce barriers to trade around the world

Large trucks are dwarfed by the 185-meter-high sluice gates of the Three Gorges Dam. China began filling the reservoir in a major step toward completion of the world's largest hydroelectric project. The level is expected to reach 135 meters (446 feet), inundating thousands of acres, including cities and farms along the Yangtze. *(AP/Wide World Photos)*

A woman sits in the remains of demolished buildings below a water level marker on the bank of the Yangtze River. Many residents along the banks of the river moved their homes and farmland to higher ground but were, nevertheless, caught by rising water, which inundated their crops even though the high water level had been announced well in advance. *(AP Photo/Grey Baker)*

extremes of nature. Humankind has been reasonably successful in overcoming or minimizing the effects of geographical barriers and natural disasters, but as they do so, they must contend with problems of their own making. The construction of dams is a good example of how an attempt to harness nature for good has a bad side. Developing countries consider dams a cost-effective solution to a host of problems. Dams create electricity, help control floods, provide water for irrigation during dry periods, and can be a rich source of fish. However, there are side effects; dams displace people (the Three Gorges Dam in China will displace 1.3 million people[22] while attracting tourists[23]), and silt that ultimately clogs the reservoir is no longer carried downstream to replenish the soil and add nutrients. Similarly, the Narmada Valley Dam Project in India will provide electricity, flood control, and irrigation, but it has already displaced tens of thousands of people, and as the benefits are measured against social and environmental costs, questions of its efficacy are being raised. In short, the need for gigantic projects such as these must be measured against their social and environmental costs.[24]

As the global rush toward industrialization and economic growth accelerates, environmental issues become more apparent. Disruption of ecosystems, relocation of people, inadequate hazardous waste management, and industrial pollution are problems that must be addressed by the industrialized world and those seeking economic development.[25] The problems are mostly byproducts of processes that have contributed significantly to

---

[22] Anita Chang, "China: Three Gorges Dam Impact Not That Bad," *Associated Press*, November 22, 2007.

[23] "Tourist Arrivals to Three Gorges Dam Hit New High in 2007," *Asia Pulse*, January 8, 2008.

[24] "Dams Control Most of the World's Largest Rivers," *Environmental News Service*, April 15, 2005.

[25] Sandy Bauers, "Big Wake-Up to Global Warming," *Philadelphia Inquirer*, December 24, 2007, p. D1.

1948 Transistor is invented; it replaces the vacuum tube, starting a technology revolution
1949 People's Republic of China founded by Mao Zedong, which will restrict

access to the largest single consumer market on the globe
1957 European Economic Community (EEC) established by Belgium, France, West Germany, Italy, Luxembourg, and the

Netherlands, the precursor to today's European Union
1961 Berlin Wall is erected, creating Eastern and Western Europe with a physical and spiritual barrier

1964 Global satellite communications network established with INTELSAT (International Telecommunications Satellite Organization)

economic development and improved lifestyles. During the last part of the 20th century, governments and industry expended considerable effort to develop better ways to control nature and to allow industry to grow while protecting the environment.[26]

Social Responsibility and Environmental Management

Nations, companies, and people reached a consensus during the close of the last decade: Environmental protection is not an optional extra; it is an essential part of the complex process of doing business. Many view the problem as a global issue rather than a national issue and as one that poses common threats to humankind and thus cannot be addressed by nations in isolation. Of special concern to governments and businesses are ways to stem the tide of pollution and to clean up decades of neglect.

Companies looking to build manufacturing plants in countries with more liberal pollution regulations than they have at home are finding that regulations everywhere have gotten stricter. Many governments are drafting new regulations and enforcing existing ones. Electronic products contain numerous toxic substances that create a major disposal problem in landfills where inadequate disposal allows toxins to seep into groundwater. The EU, as well as other countries, has laws stipulating the amount and types of potentially toxic substances it will require a company to take back to recycle.[27] A strong motivator is the realization that pollution is on the verge of getting completely out of control.

An examination of rivers, lakes, and reservoirs in China revealed that toxic substances polluted 21 percent and that 16 percent of the rivers were seriously polluted with excrement. China has 16 of the world's 20 most polluted cities.[28] The very process of controlling industrial wastes leads to another and perhaps equally critical issue: the disposal of hazardous waste, a byproduct of pollution controls. Estimates of hazardous wastes collected annually exceed 300 million tons; the critical issue is disposal that does not simply move the problem elsewhere. Countries encountering increasing difficulty in the disposal of wastes at home are seeking countries willing to assume the burden of disposal. Waste disposal is legal in some developing countries as governments seek the revenues that are generated by offering sites for waste disposal. In other cases, illegal dumping is done clandestinely. A treaty among members of the Basel Convention that required prior approval before dumping could occur was later revised to a total ban on the export of hazardous wastes by developed nations. The influence and leadership provided by this treaty are reflected in a broad awareness of pollution problems by businesses and people in general.[29]

Governments, organizations, and businesses are becoming increasingly concerned with the social responsibility and ethical issues surrounding the problem of maintaining economic growth while protecting the environment for future generations. The Organization for Economic Cooperation and Development, the United Nations, the European Union, and international activist groups are undertaking programs to strengthen environmental policies.[30] The issue that concerns all is whether economic development and protection for

---

[26] Visit http://www.gemi.org for information on the Global Environmental Management Initiative, an organization of U.S. multinational companies dedicated to environmental protection. Also see Keith Bradsher, "Hong Kong Utilities Agree to Pollution-Linked Rates," *The New York Times*, January 10, 2008, p. C4.

[27] "Electronics, Unleaded," *The Economist*, March 10, 2005.

[28] Jim Yardley, "Consultant Questions Beijing's Claim of Cleaner Air," *The New York Times*, January 10, 2008, p. A3.

[29] For a comprehensive view of OECD programs, including environmental issues, visit http://www.oecd.org.

[30] William C. Clark, "Science and Policy for Sustainable Development," *Environment*, January–February 2005.

1965 *Unsafe at Any Speed* published by Ralph Nader, sparking a revolution in consumer information and rights
1967 European Community (EC) established by uniting

the EEC, the European Coal and Steel Community, and the European Atomic Energy Community
1971 First microprocessor produced by Intel, which leads to

the personal computer; communist China joins the United Nations, making it a truly global representative body
1971 United States abandons gold standard, allowing the

international monetary system to base exchange rates on perceived values instead of ones fixed in relation to gold
1972 One billion radios on the planet

CROSSING BORDERS 3.3   Garbage without a Country—The Final Solution?

Orange rinds, beer bottles, newspapers, and chicken bones—it was trash, like all trash, taken to an incinerator in Philadelphia for incineration. The ashes, like all ashes, were to be taken away to a landfill somewhere in Philadelphia. Joseph Paolino & Sons had a $6 million contract to remove the ash but kept having doors slammed in its face.

Paolino hired Amalgamated Shipping—operator of the *Khian Sea*, a 17-year-old, 466-foot rust bucket registered in Liberia—to dump the ash in the Bahamas, where Amalgamated was based. The Bahamian government rejected the ash, and the *Khian Sea* began its 16-year journey as the Flying Dutchman of debris.

Briefly returning to the United States, it took off for Puerto Rico, Bermuda, the Dominican Republic, Honduras, Guinea-Bissau, and the Netherlands Antilles, where it was turned away again and again. To make the cargo more appealing, the ash was described as "topsoil fertilizer," and the Haitian government agreed to accept the ship's cargo. About two-thirds of the ash (4,000 tons) had been unloaded when Greenpeace and local activists protested. The Haitian government then ordered the crew to reload the ash, but the ship departed, leaving the ash.

The ship returned to Philadelphia, hoping to find a place for the remaining ash, but to no avail. It left again, seeking a resting place. It sailed to Senegal and Cape Verde, Sri Lanka, Indonesia, and the Philippines, arriving in Singapore empty. Years later, the ship's captain admitted in court that the remaining ash, one-third of the original load, had been dumped in the Atlantic and Indian oceans.

Meanwhile, in Haiti, where the 4,000 tons of ash had been left on the beach, Greenpeace found that only 2,500 tons of the original 4,000 tons remained. Most had been carried off by wind and water, and Haitians said goats were dying.

Enter an unlikely hero: New York City. In 1996, to end mob involvement in the city's waste industry, Mayor Rudolph Giuliani established a Trade Waste Commission to oversee the awarding of trash removal. When Eastern Environmental Services applied to do business in New York, the Trade Waste Commission issued an ultimatum: If Eastern wanted to haul trash in New York, it had to deal with the *Khian Sea* ash.

Eastern agreed to find a place in its landfills, and what was left of the ash, 2,500 tons, was loaded on the *Khian Sea* and departed Haiti. Finally, after a 16-year odyssey, Philadelphia agreed to give the ash a final resting place.

The saga of the *Khian Sea* is not an isolated case of wandering toxic waste, albeit the longest journey. In 1999 the MV *Ulla* was loaded with 2,200 tons of ash from coal-fired power stations in Spain bound for Algeria. The cargo was refused by Algeria, and thus, it began a journey that ended in 2004 with the ship sinking off the Turkish coast, where it lay rusting until 2005, when Spain agreed to remove the toxic waste and the ship.

Unfortunately, one of the byproducts of economic and technological growth is toxic waste, and as countries such as China and India industrialize, toxic waste disposal will only become worse—there has to be a better solution than wandering ships, though we do not recommend the Naples solution: letting it collect in the streets.

Sources: "Wandering Waste's 14-Year Journey," *Toronto Star*, May 3, 2000; "Toxic Waste Returns," *Earth Island Journal*, Winter 2002–2003, p. 12; "Spain to Remove Sunken Ship with Toxic Cargo Off Turkish Coast," *Agence France-Presse*, February 2, 2005; "Italy Announces Emergency Steps for Naples' Garbage Crisis," *Dow Jones News*, January 8, 2008.

the environment can coexist. *Sustainable development,* a joint approach among those (governments, businesses, environmentalists, and others) who seek economic growth with "wise resource management, equitable distribution of benefits and reduction of negative efforts on people and the environment from the process of economic growth," is the concept that guides many governments and multinational companies today. Sustainable development is not about the environment or the economy or society. It is about striking a lasting balance between all of these. More and more companies are embracing the idea of sustain-

1973 Arab oil embargo jolts industrial world into understanding the totally global nature of supply and demand

1980 CNN founded, providing instant and common information the world over, taking another significant step in the process of globalization started by the radio in 1901
1987 ISO issues ISO 9000 to create a global quality standard

1988 One billion televisions on the planet
1989 Berlin Wall falls, symbolizing the opening of the East

A huge offshore discovery has the potential to make Brazil a new major petroleum exporter through its national oil company, Petrobras.[36] *Source:* The New York Times, *January 11, 2008, p. C1. (© Edro Lobo/Bloomberg News/Landov)*

able development as a "win–win" opportunity.[31] Responsibility for protecting the environment does not rest solely with governments, businesses, or activist groups, however; each citizen has a social and moral responsibility to include environmental protection among his or her highest goals.[32]

Resources

The availability of minerals[33] and the ability to generate energy are the foundations of modern technology. The locations of Earth's resources, as well as the available sources of energy, are geographic accidents. The world's nations are not equally endowed, and no nation's demand for a particular mineral or energy source necessarily coincides with domestic supply.

In much of the underdeveloped world, human labor provides the preponderance of energy. The principal supplements to human energy are animals, wood, fossil fuel, nuclear power, and, to a lesser and more experimental extent, the ocean's tides, geothermal power, and the sun. Of all the energy sources, oil and gas contribute over 60 percent of world energy consumption.[34] Because of petroleum's versatility and the ease with which it is stored and transported, petroleum-related products continue to dominate energy usage.[35] (See Exhibit 3.3.)

Many countries that were self-sufficient during much of their early economic growth have become net importers of petroleum during the past several decades and continue to become

---

[31] Visit http://www.oecd.org, the OECD Web site, for a directory and complete coverage of sustainable development.

[32] Visit http://www.webdirectory.com for the *Amazing Environmental Organization Web Directory*, a search engine with links to an extensive list of environmental subjects.

[33] "Global Copper Shortage Reaches 340,000t in H1," *China Industry Daily News*, September 21, 2007.

[34] Visit http://www.eia.doe.gov and search for "International Energy Outlook (most current year)" for details of production, use, and so forth.

[35] See Map 3, "Oil and Gas Production and Consumption," for a global view of the flow and uses of petroleum.

[36] Alexi Barrinuevo, "Hot Prospect for Oil's Big League," *The New York Times*, January 11, 2008, pp. C1, C4.

---

to the West for ideas and commerce
1991 Soviet Union formally abandons communism, as most formerly communist

states move toward capitalism and the trade it fosters; Commonwealth of Independent States (CIS) established among Russia, Ukraine, and Belarus

1993 NAFTA ratified by U.S. Congress; European Union created from the European Community, along with a framework for joint

security and foreign policy action, by the 1991 Maastricht Treaty on European Union; the EEC is renamed the EC

Exhibit 3.3
World Energy Consumption

Energy consumed by world regions, measured in quadrillion BTUs in 2001. Total world consumption was 381.8 quadrillion BTUs. The largest portion of the hydro/other category is hydroelectrical energy. Fuels such as wood, peat, animal waste, wind, solar, and geothermal account for less than 1.0 quadrillion BTUs in the other portion of the hydro/other category.

Sources: Data compiled from "Introduction to World Geography," *Oxford Atlas of the World* (New York: Oxford University Press, 2003) and Energy Information Administration (EIA), *International Energy Outlook 2004* (Washington, DC, 2005), http://www.eia.doe.gov/oiaf/ieo.

**Total World Energy Consumption
By Region and Fuel (Quadrillion BTU)**

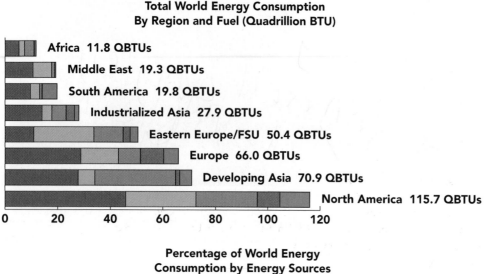

**Percentage of World Energy
Consumption by Energy Sources**

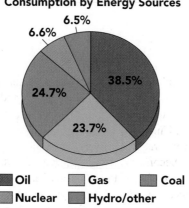

6.5%
6.6%
38.5%
24.7%
23.7%

■ Oil   ■ Gas   ■ Coal
■ Nuclear   ■ Hydro/other

increasingly dependent on foreign sources. A spectacular example is the United States, which was almost completely self-sufficient until 1942, became a major importer by 1950, and between 1973 and 2000 increased its dependency from 36 percent to over 66 percent of its annual requirements.[37] If present rates of consumption continue, predictions are that by the mid-2000s the United States will be importing more than 70 percent of its needs, that is, more than 17 million barrels of oil each day. Exhibit 3.3 compares North American domestic energy

---

[37] "U.S. Energy Bill Won't End Dependence on Foreign Oil," *Reuters News Service*, April 21, 2005.

1994 The Chunnel (Channel Tunnel) is opened between France and Britain, providing a ground link for commerce between the continent and Britain
1995 World Trade Organization (WTO) set up as successor of

GATT; by 2000 more than 130 members will account for over 90 percent of world trade
1997 Hong Kong, a world trading and financial capital and bastion of capitalism, is returned to communist Chinese control;

Pathfinder lands on Mars, and *Rover* goes for a drive but finds no one with whom to trade
1999 Euro introduced in 11 European Union nations, paving the way for the creation of a true trade union and trade bloc

1999 Seattle Round of WTO negotiations pits U.S. vs. EU, first great protest against globalization
1999 Control of the Panama Canal, a major trade lane, is returned to Panama

Cattle dung, which is used both as farmyard manure and, dried into cakes, as household fuel, is being carried to a local market in India. India's cattle produce enormous quantities of dung, which some studies suggest provide the equivalent of 10,000 megawatts of energy annually.

This Maasai woman of Tanzania put to good use both cow dung and urine in building her hut pictured, here in her family village (or boma). The semi-nomadic Maasai graze their cattle during the day but enclose them within the acacia bush boma at night to protect them from predators.

consumption with other world regions. It is interesting to note that though North America is currently a major consumer of energy, industrializing Asia and the three industrialized areas (as shown in Exhibit 3.3) do not lag far behind. In fact, China has become the world's second-largest oil importer after the United States, and demand continues to grow rapidly.[38]

Since World War II, concern for the limitless availability of seemingly inexhaustible supplies of petroleum has become a prominent factor. The dramatic increase in economic growth in the industrialized world and the push for industrialization in the remaining world has put tremendous pressure on Earth's energy resources. Unfortunately, as countries industrialize, energy sources are not always efficiently utilized. China, for example, spends three times the world average on energy (all sources) to produce one dollar of gross national product (GNP). In comparison with Japan, possibly the world's most efficient user of energy, where less than 5 ounces of oil is needed to generate $1 in GNP, in China, approximately 80 ounces of oil is needed.[39] The reasons for China's inefficient oil use are numerous, but the worst culprit is outdated technology.[40]

---

[38] Koh Chin Ling and Loretta Ng, "China's Crude Oil Imports Surge in March," *International Herald Tribune*, April 22, 2005.

[39] "Lessons from a Miser," *BusinessWeek*, April 11, 2005, p. 51.

[40] "Wasteful Ways," *BusinessWeek*, April 11, 2005, p. 50.

2000 Second millennium arrives, predicted computer problems are a non-event
2001 September 11 terrorist attack on the World Trade Center in New York

City and the Pentagon in Washington, DC; one billion mobile phones on the planet
2002 United States attacks Taliban in Afghanistan

2003 United States attacks regime of Saddam Hussein in Iraq
2004 Great Indian Ocean tsunami kills 500,000

2006 One billion personal computers on the planet
2008 Beijing Olympics
2040 The United Nations' earliest estimate for the world population to begin shrink due to the global decline of fertility

The growth of market-driven economies and an increasing reliance on petroleum supplies from areas of political instability—the Middle East, the former Soviet Union, and Latin America—create a global interdependence of energy resources. The net result is a profound impact on oil prices and on the economies of industrialized and industrializing countries.

The location, quality, and availability of resources will affect the pattern of world economic development and trade well into the 21st century. In addition to the raw materials of industrialization, an economically feasible energy supply must be available to transform resources into usable products. As the global demand for resources intensifies and prices rise, resources will continue to increase in importance among the uncontrollable elements of the international marketer's decisions.

Dynamics of Global Population Trends

Current population, rural/urban population shifts, rates of growth, age levels, and population control help determine today's demand for various categories of goods. Although not the only determinant, the existence of sheer numbers of people is significant in appraising potential consumer markets. Changes in the composition and distribution of population among the world's countries will profoundly affect future demand.

Recent estimates place world population at more than 6.7 billion people, and this number is expected to grow to about 9 billion by 2050. However, seemingly small differences in assumptions about fertility rates can make big differences in growth forecasts. One possible scenario put forth by United Nations experts suggests the planet's population may actually peak at about 8 billion and then begin to decline after 2040. All scenarios agree though that almost all of the projected growth for 2050 will occur in less-developed regions.[41] Exhibit 3.4 shows that 84 percent of the population will be concentrated in less-developed regions by 2025 and, if growth rates continue, 86 percent by 2050. The International Labor Organization estimates that 1.2 billion jobs must be created worldwide by 2025 to accommodate these new entrants. Furthermore, most of the new jobs will need to be created in urban areas where most of the population will reside.

Controlling Population Growth

Faced with the ominous consequences of the population explosion, it would seem logical for countries to take appropriate steps to reduce growth to manageable rates, but procreation is one of the most culturally sensitive uncontrollable factors. Economics, self-esteem,

---

[41] See *World Population Prospects, The 2004 and 2006 Revisions*, United Nations Economic and Social Affairs, http://www.unpopulation.org, 2008.

Exhibit 3.4
World Population by Region, 2005–2050, and Life Expectancy at Birth, 2005–2010 (millions)

Source: *World Population Prospects, The 2004 and 2006 Revisions*, United Nations Economic and Social Affairs, www.unpopulation.org, 2008.

Regions	Population (in millions)			Life Expectancy at Birth
	2005	**2025**	**2050**	**2005–2010**
World	6,465	7,905	9,076	67.2
More-developed regions*	1,211	1,249	1,236	76.5
Less-developed regions†	5,253	6,656	7,840	65.4
Least-developed regions‡	759	1,167	1,735	54.6
Africa	906	1,344	1,937	52.8
Asia	3,905	4,728	5,217	69.0
Europe	728	707	653	74.6
Latin America	561	697	783	73.3
Northern America	331	388	438	78.5
Oceania	33	41	48	75.2

*More-developed regions comprise all regions of Europe and Northern America, Australia, New Zealand, and Japan.
†Less-developed regions comprise all regions of Africa, Asia (excluding Japan), and Latin America and the regions of Melanesia, Micronesia, and Polynesia.
‡Least-developed regions, as defined by the United Nations General Assembly, include 48 countries, of which 33 are in Africa, 9 in Asia, 1 in Latin America, and 5 in Oceania. They are also included in less-developed regions.

religion, politics, and education all play a critical role in attitudes about family size. All this makes the impact of China's long-term enforcement of its one-child policies most remarkable.[42]

The prerequisites to population control are adequate incomes, higher literacy levels, education for women, universal access to healthcare, family planning, improved nutrition, and, perhaps most important, a change in basic cultural beliefs regarding the importance of large families. Unfortunately, minimum progress in providing improved living conditions and changing beliefs has occurred. India serves as a good example of what is happening in much of the world. India's population was once stable, but with improved health conditions leading to greater longevity and lower infant mortality, its population will exceed that of China by 2050, when the two will account for about 50 percent of the world's inhabitants.[43] The government's attempts to institute change are hampered by a variety of factors, including political ineptitude[44] and slow changes in cultural norms. Nevertheless, the government continues to pass laws with the intended purpose of limiting the number of births. The most recent attempt is a law that bars those with more than two children from election to the national Parliament and state assemblies. This rule would mean that many now in office could not seek reelection because of their family size.[45]

Perhaps the most important deterrent to population control is cultural attitudes about the importance of large families. In many cultures, the prestige of a man, whether alive or dead, depends on the number of his progeny, and a family's only wealth is its children. Such feelings are strong. Prime Minister Indira Gandhi found out how strong when she attempted mass sterilization of males, which reportedly was the main cause of her defeat in a subsequent election. Additionally, many religions discourage or ban family planning and thus serve as a deterrent to control.[46] Nigeria has a strong Muslim tradition in the north and a strong Roman Catholic tradition in the east, and both faiths favor large families. Most traditional religions in Africa encourage large families; in fact, the principal deity for many is the goddess of land and fertility.

Family planning and all that it entails is by far the most universal means governments use to control birthrates, but some economists believe that a decline in the fertility rate is a function of economic prosperity and will come only with economic development. Ample anecdotal evidence suggests that fertility rates decline as economies prosper. For example, before Spain's economy began its rapid growth in the 1980s, families had six or more children; now, Spain has one of the lowest birthrates in Europe, an average of 1.24 children per woman. Similar patterns have followed in other European countries as economies have prospered.

Rural/Urban Migration

Migration from rural to urban areas is largely a result of a desire for greater access to sources of education, healthcare, and improved job opportunities.[47] In the early 1800s, less than 3.5 percent of the world's people were living in cities of 20,000 or more and less than 2 percent in cities of 100,000 or more; today, more than 40 percent of the world's people are urbanites, and the trend is accelerating. Once in the city, perhaps three out of four migrants achieve some economic gains.[48] The family income of a manual worker in urban Brazil, for example, is almost five times that of a farm laborer in a rural area.

---

[42] Maureen Fan, "Officials Violating 'One-Child' Policy Forced Out in China," *Washington Post*, January 8, 2008, p. A16.

[43] "India to Surpass China in Population," *ExpressIndia*, May 18, 2005.

[44] Anand Giridharadas, "A Buoyant India Dares to Ask: Is a Billion So Bad?" *International Herald Tribune*, May 4, 2005.

[45] V. K. Paghunathan, "3 Tykes and You're Out," *Straits Times*, April 11, 2003.

[46] Huma Aamir Malik, "Aziz Seeks Scholars' Support to Control Population," *Arab News*, May 5, 2005.

[47] Tor Ching Li, "Urban Migration Drains Asian Coffee Farms' Work Force," *Dow Jones Commodities Service*, December 13, 2007.

[48] Diane Mosher, "Chinese Urban Migration Creates Opportunities for International Urban Planners," *Multi-Housing News*, April 2, 2007.

By 2030, estimates indicate that more than 61 percent of the world's population will live in urban areas (up from 49 percent in 2005, with similar changes across all regions), and at least 27 cities will have populations of 10 million or more, 23 of which will be in the less-developed regions. Tokyo has already overtaken Mexico City as the largest city on Earth, with a population of 26 million, a jump of almost 8 million since 1990.

Although migrants experience some relative improvement in their living standards, intense urban growth without investment in services eventually leads to serious problems. Slums populated with unskilled workers living hand to mouth put excessive pressure on sanitation systems, water supplies,[49] and other social services. At some point, the disadvantages of unregulated urban growth begin to outweigh the advantages for all concerned.

Consider the conditions that exist in Mexico City today. Besides smog, garbage, and pollution brought about by the increased population, Mexico City faces a severe water shortage. Local water supplies are nearly exhausted and in some cases are unhealthy.[50] Water consumption from all sources is about 16,000 gallons per second, but the underground aquifers are producing only 2,640 gallons per second. Water comes from hundreds of miles away and has to be pumped up to an elevation of 7,444 feet to reach Mexico City. This grim picture portrays one of the most beautiful and sophisticated cities in Latin America. Such problems are not unique to Mexico; throughout the developing world, poor sanitation and inadequate water supplies are consequences of runaway population growth. An estimated 1.1 billion people are currently without access to clean drinking water, and 2.8 billion lack access to sanitation services. Estimates are that 40 percent of the world's population, 2.5 billion people, will be without clean water if more is not invested in water resources.[51] Prospects for improvement are not encouraging, because most of the world's urban growth will take place in the already economically strained developing countries.

Population Decline and Aging

While the developing world faces a rapidly growing population,[52] the industrialized world's population is in decline and rapidly aging.[53] Birthrates in western Europe and Japan have been decreasing since the early or mid-1960s; more women are choosing careers instead of children, and many working couples are electing to remain childless. As a result of these and other contemporary factors, population growth in many countries has dropped below the rate necessary to maintain present levels. Just to keep the population from falling, a nation needs a fertility rate of about 2.1 children per woman. Not one major country has sufficient internal population growth to maintain itself, and this trend is expected to continue for the next 50 years. Europe's population could decline by as much as 88 million (from 375 million to 287 million) people if present trends continue to 2015.[54]

At the same time that population growth is declining in the industrialized world,[55] there are more aging people today than ever before.[56] Global life expectancy has grown more in the past 50 years than over the previous 5,000 years. Until the Industrial Revolution, no more than 2 or 3 percent of the total population was over the age of 65 years. Today in the developed world, the over-age-65 group amounts to 14 percent, and by 2030, this group will reach 25 percent in some 30 different countries. Furthermore, the number of "old old" will grow much faster than the "young old." The United Nations projects that by 2050, the number of people aged 65 to 84 years worldwide will grow from 400 million to 1.3 billion (a threefold increase), while the number of people aged 85 years and over will grow from 26 million to 175 million (a sixfold increase)—and the number aged 100 years and over will increase from

[49] "China Faces Worsening Water Woes," *Chicago Sun-Times*, March 24, 2005.

[50] "Nation Faces Water Shortage," *El Universal* (Mexico City), March 23, 2005.

[51] David Usorne, "The Water Crisis: One Billion People Lack Clean Supplies," *The (London) Independent*, March 23, 2005.

[52] Gerald Tenywa and Ben Okiror, "Population Growth Highest around Lake Victoria," *All Africa*, November 1, 2007.

[53] There are apparent exceptions; see "Finland Sees Record-High Population Growth in 2007," *Xinhua News Agency*, January 1, 2008.

[54] Mark Henderson, "Europe Shrinking as Birthrates Decline," *The Times Online* (UK), March 28, 2003.

[55] "Russia's Population Shrinks by 208,000 in 10 Months," *Russia & CIS Newswire*, December 21, 2007.

[56] "China Population Ageing Rapidly," *Associated Press Newswires*, December 17, 2007.

Exhibit 3.5
Age Density for World and Selected Countries

Source: From *Oxford Atlas of the World*, 10th ed., 2002. Copyright © 2002 Philip's Cartography.

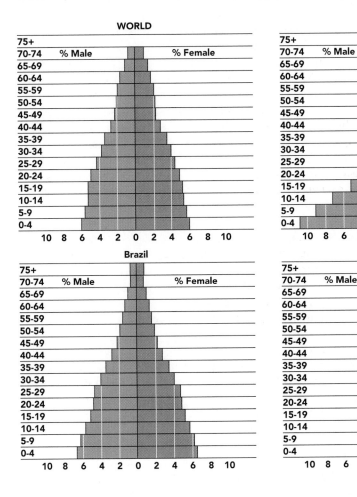

135,000 to 2.2 million (a sixteenfold increase). Exhibit 3.5 illustrates the disparity in aging that is typical among lesser-developed countries (Kenya), developing countries (Brazil), and an economically developed country (United Kingdom). Countries like Kenya, with a high proportion of young people, face high education and healthcare costs, whereas countries like the United Kingdom, with top-heavy population pyramids, face high pension and healthcare costs for the elderly with fewer wage earners to bear the burden.

Europe, Japan, and the United States epitomize the problems caused by an increasing percentage of elderly people who must be supported by a declining number of skilled workers. In 1998, Japan crossed a threshold anticipated with fear by the rest of the developed world: the point at which retirees withdrawing funds from the pension system exceeded those workers contributing to it.[57] The elderly require higher government outlays for healthcare and hospitals,[58] special housing and nursing homes, and pension and welfare assistance, but the workforce that supports these costs is dwindling. The part of the world with the largest portion of people over 65 years is also the part of the world with the fewest number of people under age 15 years. This disparity means that there will be fewer workers to support future retirees, resulting in an intolerable tax burden on future workers, more of the over-65 group remaining in the labor force, or pressure to change

---

[57] Sebastian Moffett, "Going Gray: For Ailing Japan, Longevity Begins to Take Its Toll," *The Wall Street Journal*, February 11, 2003, p. A1.

[58] Ben Shankland, "Government of Colombia Tries to Sell Beleaguered Hospital Again," *Global Insight Daily Analysis*, December 19, 2007.

CROSSING BORDERS 3.4   Where Have All the Women Gone?

Three converging issues in China have the potential of causing a serious gender imbalance:

- China, the world's most populous country, has a strict one-child policy to curb population growth.
- Traditional values dictate male superiority and a definite parental preference for boys.
- Prenatal scanning allows women to discover the sex of their fetuses and thereby abort unwanted female fetuses.

The first wave of children born under the one-child policy is reaching marriageable age, and there are far too few brides to go around. The ratio of males to females is unnaturally high, hovering between 117 to 119 boys for every 100 girls in 2000. Thus men in their 20s have to deal with the harsh reality of six bachelors for every five potential brides. So what is a desperate bachelor to do?

The shortage has prompted some parents to acquire babies as future brides for their sons. Infants are considered more appealing because they are less likely to run away, will look on their buyers as their own parents, and are cheaper than buying a teenage bride. Buying a baby girl can cost as little as $100 and won't result in the fines imposed on couples who violate birth control limits. Such fines can equal as much as six years' income.

Another alternative is to marry a relative. At age 20 years, with his friends already paired off, Liu found himself the odd man out. His parents, farmers in a small backwater village, could not raise the $2,000 required to attract a bride for their son. Desperate, Liu's mother asked her sister for a favor: Could she ask Hai, her daughter, to be Liu's bride? Young women like Hai are not likely to defy their parents. And so Liu and Hai were wed.

Chinese officials are starting to worry about the imbalance and have announced a raft of new programs to reverse the trend. These offers include cash payments for couples who have a daughter and let her live, along with privileges in housing, employment, and job training. Some families with girls will also be exempted from paying school fees. Even though the government staunchly defends its one-child policy, it is experimenting with allowing couples whose firstborn is a girl to have a second child. In the meantime and until the new policy results in more girls, today's 20-year-old men will just have to compete if they want a wife.

Sources: "Sex Determination before Birth," *Reuters News Service*, May 3, 1994; "China Breeding Frustrated Bachelors," *Vietnam Investment Review*, March 2004; "China to Make Sex-Selective Abortions a Crime," *ITV.com*, January 7, 2005; Nicholas Zamiska, "China's One-Child Policy Gets Wider Enforcement," *The Wall Street Journal Asia*, January 8, 2008, p. 10.

existing laws to allow mass migration to stabilize the worker-to-retiree ratio. No one solution is without its problems.[59]

Worker Shortage and Immigration

For most countries, mass immigration is not well received by the resident population. However, a recent report from the United Nations makes the strongest argument for change in immigration laws as a viable solution. The free flow of immigration will help ameliorate the dual problems of explosive population expansion in less-developed countries and worker shortage in industrialized regions.[60] Europe is the region of the world most affected by aging and thus by a steadily decreasing worker-to-retiree ratio. The proportion of older persons will increase from 20 percent in 1998 to 35 percent in 2050. The country with the largest share of old people will be Spain, closely followed by Italy. Recognizing the problem, Spain has changed immigration laws to open its borders to all South Americans of Spanish descent.[61] To keep the worker-to-retiree ratio from falling, Europe will need 1.4 billion immigrants over the next 50 years, while Japan and the United States[62] will need 600 million immigrants between now and 2050. Immigration will not help ameliorate the problem though if political and cultural opposition to immigration cannot be overcome.

---

[59] J. T. Young, "Failure of Social Security Reform Mustn't Derail Personal Accounts," *Investor's Business Daily*, January 3, 2008.

[60] "Russian Immigration Rules Could Cause Worker Shortage," *Associated Press, Charleston Gazette*, January 16, 2007, p. P2D.

[61] "Spain Grants Amnesty to 700,000 Migrants," *Guardian Unlimited*, May 9, 2005.

[62] "US Tech Sector Eyes Immigration Bill Revival, Cites Worker Shortage," *Agence France-Presse*, June 9, 2007.

CROSSING BORDERS 3.5

History, Geography, and Population Collide in America: Returning to Multigenerational Family Living

As pension systems, healthcare systems, and retirement plans continue to crumble under the weight of baby-boom numbers, we all will need to rely more on the strengths of family ties and remember the fundamental human characteristic of interdependence. The problem is that such remembrance is particularly hard for Americans, as opposed to all other peoples on the planet.

America started with The Declaration of Independence. On July 4, 1776, the founding fathers broke from the tyranny of England to form a new country. That document and the idea of independence represent the essence of being American and literally the most celebrated notion of the nation. Indeed, the goal of mainstream American parenting is to inculcate this notion into the noggins of children: We ensure they make their own beds, make their own lunches, wash their own clothes, do their own homework, drive their own cars, and so forth. How else can they become independent adults?

There are at least three problems with this American obsession with independence. First, it stigmatizes the burgeoning numbers of both boomerang kids and grandparents living with their grandchildren as families across America smartly reunite. According to the most recent U.S. Census figures, there are 22 million adult children living with their parents and 6 million grandparents living in three-generation households, and both numbers are growing fast. Second, teaching independence actually hasn't worked anyway, as we will see next. And third, there is really no such thing as independence anyway. There is only interdependence.

This American overemphasis on independence is now being recognized by the most independent-minded of all Americans, CEOs. In Bill George's wonderful book, *Authentic Leadership*, he argues that the job of chief executive depends on six constituencies. Without surprise, the former CEO of Medtronic lists shareholders, employees, customers, vendors, and the larger community. But what is unique, and perhaps even revolutionary, in his list is his own family. He recognizes that his own success as a CEO in part depended of the quality of his family life. Thus, he organized his executive team and responsibilities such that he had time to attend kids' soccer matches and such. Remarkable!

There's also another irony about American independence. We made a lot of tanks during World War II. Right after the war, the extra industrial capacity created during the war made cars cheap in this country. Thus, we have far more cars per family than any other nation. Cheap cars created freeways, suburbia, and shopping centers. With our cars, we can load up at the grocery store and become independent of the daily shopping routine that still faces households all around the world. Indeed, a car for every person in the family, and everyone is independent. "See the USA in a Chevrolet" made road trips attractive and promised a new freedom and independence from public transportation. The latest incarnation of the "car = independence" argument has been the billions of dollars spent selling Americans on unsafe, gas-guzzling SUVs, such as, "Go anywhere, any time in your Hummer. Your Hummer even gives you independence from roads (and traffic)."

So now, while we are independent of our local grocery store, as a nation, we Americans are completely dependent on our cars, big refrigerators, the continuous construction of new highways (for our sanity), and oil from foreign countries. The fuel burned in our cars pollutes the planet, changes global weather patterns, and, given the recent drowning of New Orleans and the polar ice melting, reduces the amount of land to live on. Perhaps the greatest irony of all is that the space taken up by all our cars limits our freedom to build sensible housing. Granny flats are often built above garages, yielding extra steps that will plague the coming elderly generation. And worst of all, providing the parking for our metal monsters subtracts from living space for American families as communities' codes mandate more and more parking spaces.

Source: Sharon G. Niederhaus and John L. Graham, *Together Again, A Creative Guide to Multigenerational Living* (Lanham, MD: Evans, 2007).

The trends of increasing population in the developing world, with substantial shifts from rural to urban areas, declining birthrates in the industrialized world, and global population aging, will have profound effects on the state of world business and world economic conditions. Without successful adjustments to these trends, many countries will experience slower economic growth, serious financial problems for senior retirement programs, and further deterioration of public and social services, leading to possible social unrest.[63]

[63] David J. Lynch, "Looming Pension Crisis in China Stirs Fears of Chaos," *USA Today*, April 19, 2005.

Exhibit 3.6
500 Years of Trade

U.S. negotiators seem miffed that Latin American countries didn't trip all over themselves to forge a free trade zone of the Americas pact. Indeed, the U.S. team blamed Brazil for the pact's failure to move further along.

But the United States often fails to recognize that many Latin American countries have strong relationships with Europe, Asia, and the rest of the world—and these relationships were in place long before the United States even existed.

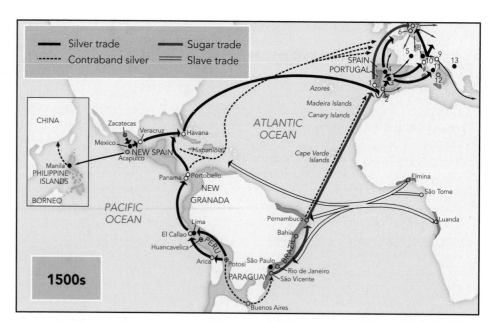

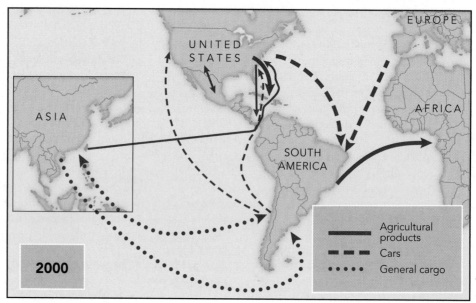

World Trade Routes

Trade routes bind the world together, minimizing distance, natural barriers, lack of resources, and the fundamental differences between peoples and economies. As long as one group of people in the world wants something that another group somewhere else has and there is a means of travel between the two, there is trade. Early trade routes were overland; later came sea routes, air routes, and, finally, some might say, the Internet to connect countries.

As Exhibit 3.6 illustrates, trade routes among Europe, Asia, and the Americas were well established by the 1500s. The Spanish empire founded the city of Manila in the Philippines to receive its silver-laden galleons bound for China. On the return trip, the ship's cargo of silk and other Chinese goods would be offloaded in Mexico, carried overland to the Atlantic, and put on Spanish ships to Spain. What we sometimes fail to recognize is that these same trades routes remain important today and that many Latin American countries have strong relationships with Europe, Asia, and the rest of the world that date back to the 1500s. The commodities traded have changed between the 1500s and today, but trade and the trade routes continue to be important. Today, instead of

CROSSING BORDERS 3.6

Is the Panama Canal Becoming Obsolete with Global Climate Change?

Although most worry about the potential environmental catastrophes associated with global warming and climate change, others see some advantages.

The Arctic is not just about oil and gas. A ship travelling at 21 knots between Rotterdam and Yokohama takes 29 days to make the voyage if it goes via the Cape of Good Hope, 22 days via the Suez Canal, and just 15 days if it goes across the Arctic Ocean. In coming years, the Arctic will dramatically alter the dynamics of global trade.

A combination of global warming melting the ice and new shipping technology means polar shipping routes will open up in the next few years, drastically reducing the time it takes for container traffic to travel from Asia's booming manufacturing centers to the West's consumer markets.

Although it may be possible for container ships to travel across the Arctic now, the amount of ice in winter makes travel extremely difficult, or too slow and expensive if the ships are accompanied by ice breakers. But these hindrances will all change as the ice disappears in coming years.

The emergence of a northern passage across the Arctic connecting the Atlantic and Pacific oceans could not be happening at a more propitious time as far as global trade routes are concerned. It is estimated that 90 percent of all the goods in the world, measured in tonnes, are transported by sea, and rapid global economic growth, fueled by China and India, means existing routes are becoming clogged. Container shipments on international routes have increased annually by between 5 and 7 percent in recent years, in line with world trade, meaning the volume of shipments approximately doubles every 10 to 15 years.

The Suez Canal can handle ships with a draught—the depth of water needed for a ship to float—of up to 19 meters, which is sufficient for the largest current container ships but not for the next generation. It is also operating at its maximum capacity, with between 16,000 and 18,000 ships passing through annually. Long queues are commonplace. The Panama Canal is suitable for ships with a draught of up to 11.3 meters, already too small for ships that are now common on longer shipping routes. The Panamanian government has plans to increase the capacity of the canal, build new locks, and deepen and widen the channels. But the planned extensions are not sufficient for a new generation of heavier vessels.

The Arctic thus is set to become an increasingly important route for world trade, highlighting the need for multilateral agreements over navigation rights and the application of international law in the region.

Sources: David Ibisonin, "Shippers Chart Polar Bypass for Clogged Global Trade," *Financial Times.com*, August 11, 2007; Mike Toner, "Accelerated Polar Melt Predicted Receding Ice Sheet Could Swamp Coast Areas," *Atlanta Journal-Constitution*, March 24, 2006, p. C1.

offloading goods in Mexico and carrying them on mule carts overland to the Atlantic, ships travel from the Pacific to the Atlantic via the Panama Canal. And ships too large for the canal offload their containers onto a railroad that crosses the Isthmus of Panama to be met by another container ship.[64]

Trade routes represent the attempts of countries to overcome economic and social imbalances created in part by the influence of geography. The majority of world trade is among the most industrialized and industrializing countries of Europe, North America, and Asia. It is no surprise that the trade flow, as seen in Map 8 at the end of this chapter links these major trading areas.

Communication Links

An underpinning of all commerce is effective communications—knowledge of where goods and services exist and where they are needed and the ability to communicate instantaneously across vast distances. Continuous improvements in electronic communications have facilitated the expansion of trade. First came the telegraph, then the telephone, television, satellites, the computer, and the Internet. Map 5 illustrates the importance of fiber optic cable and satellites in providing global communications. Each revolution in technology has had a profound effect on human conditions, economic growth, and the manner in which

---

[64] "Panama Canal Expansion Gets Environmental Approval," *Journal of Commerce Online*, November 13, 2007.

commerce functions. Each new communications technology has spawned new business models; some existing businesses have reinvented their practices to adapt to the new technology, while other businesses have failed to respond and thus ceased to exist.[65] The Internet revolution will be no different; it too affects human conditions, economic growth, and the manner in which commerce operates. As we discuss in subsequent chapters, the Internet has already begun to shape how international business is managed. However, as the Internet permeates the fabric of the world's cultures, the biggest changes are yet to come!

---

[65] For an interesting and insightful review of the impact information and communication technology will have on how business operates, see Jose de la Torre and Richard W. Moxon, "Introduction to the Symposium E-Commerce and Global Business: The Impact of the Information and Communication Technology Revolution on the Conduct of International Business," *Journal of International Business Studies* 32, no. 4 (2001), p. 617.

Summary

One British authority admonishes foreign marketers to study the world until "the mere mention of a town, country, or river enables it to be picked out immediately on the map." Although it may not be necessary for the student of foreign marketing to memorize the world map to that extent, a prospective international marketer should be reasonably familiar with the world, its climate, and topographic differences. Otherwise, the important marketing characteristics of geography could be completely overlooked when marketing in another country. The need for geographical and historical knowledge goes deeper than being able to locate continents and their countries. Geographic hurdles must be recognized as having a direct effect on marketing and the related activities of communications and distribution. For someone who has never been in a tropical rainforest with an annual rainfall of at least 60 inches (and sometimes more than 200 inches), anticipating the need for protection against high humidity is difficult. Likewise, someone who has never encountered the difficult problems caused by dehydration in constant 100-degrees-plus heat in the Sahara region will find them hard to comprehend. Indirect effects from the geographical ramifications of a society and culture ultimately may be reflected in marketing activities. Many of the peculiarities of a country (i.e., peculiar to the foreigner) would be better understood and anticipated if its history and geography were studied more closely. Without a historical understanding of a culture, the attitudes within the marketplace may not be fully understood.

Aside from the simpler and more obvious ramifications of climate and topography, history and geography exert complex influences on the development of the general economy and society of a country. In this case, the study of history and geography is needed to provide the marketer with an understanding of why a country has developed as it has rather than as a guide for adapting marketing plans. History and geography are two of the environments of foreign marketing that should be thoroughly understood and that must be included in foreign marketing plans to a degree commensurate with their influence on marketing effort.

Questions

1. Define the following terms:

   Manifest Destiny sustainable development

   Roosevelt Corollary Monroe Doctrine

2. Why study geography in international marketing? Discuss.

3. Why study a country's history? Discuss.

4. How does an understanding of history help an international marketer?

5. Why is there a love–hate relationship between Mexico and the United States? Discuss.

6. Some say the global environment is a global issue rather than a national one. What does this mean? Discuss.

7. Pick a country and show how employment and topography affect marketing within the country.

8. Pick a country, other than Mexico, and show how significant historical events have affected the country's culture.

9. Discuss the bases of world trade. Give examples illustrating the different bases.

10. The marketer "should also examine the more complex effect of geography on general market characteristics, distribution systems, and the state of the economy." Comment.

11. The world population pattern trend is shifting from rural to urban areas. Discuss the marketing ramifications.

12. Select a country with a stable population and one with a rapidly growing population. Contrast the marketing implications of these two situations.

13. "World trade routes bind the world together." Discuss.

14. Discuss how your interpretations of Manifest Destiny and the Monroe Doctrine might differ from those of a native of Latin America.

15. The telegraph, the telephone, television, satellites, the computer, and the Internet have all had an effect on how international business operates. Discuss how each of these communications innovations affects international business management.

maps

ARREAL
LANGLEY

ALANGLEY@
CCBCMD.EDU

1 **The World**

ALASKA
(United States)

GREENLAND
(Denmark)

Greenland
Sea

Norwegian
Sea

Reykjavik
ICELAND

North
Sea

CANADA

NETH.

Dublin
IRELAND

UNITED
KINGDOM

London

BELG.

GE

Montreal

English Channel

Paris

SW

Toronto

FRANCE

Detroit

Boston

Chicago

PORTUGAL

Madrid

Philadelphia

New York

Lisbon

SPAIN

UNITED   STATES

Washington

San Francisco

Los Angeles

AZORES
(Portugal)

Strait of Gibraltar

Algiers

Tu

ATLANTIC
OCEAN

CANARY IS.
(Spain)

Casablanca

MOROCCO

Dallas

Houston

Monterrey

MEXICO

Miami

BAHAMAS

CUBA

DOMINICAN
REPUBLIC

Mexico City

HAITI

BELIZE
HONDURAS

JAMAICA

GUATEMALA
EL SALVADOR

NICARAGUA

GUADELOUPE

DOMINICA

ST. LUCIA

PUERTO
RICO
(U.S.)

WESTERN
SAHARA
(Morocco)

ALGERIA

MAURITANIA

Nouakchott

MALI

Ni

CAPE VERDE

Dakar

SENEGAL

N

Bamako

GAMBIA

Bissau

BURKINA
FASO

HAWAII
(United States)

COSTA
RICA

Caracas

TRINIDAD &
TOBAGO

GUINEA-
BISSAU

GUINEA

Conakry

SIERRA LEONE

Monrovia

CÔTE
D'IVOIRE

GHANA

BE

Bogota

VENEZUELA

GUYANA

SURINAME

PANAMA

COLOMBIA

FRENCH GUIANA
(France)

LIBERIA

TOGO

EQUATORIAL
GUINEA

ECUADOR

SAO TOME &
PRINCIPE

P
E
R
U

BRAZIL

ATLANTIC
OCEAN

CA

Lima

PACIFIC
OCEAN

BOLIVIA

Belo Horizonte

PARAGUAY

Sao Paulo

Rio de Janeiro

C
H
I
L
E

Porto Alegre

Buenos Aires

URUGUAY

ARGENTINA

FALKLAND
ISLANDS
(U.K.)

| 3 A.M. | 4 A.M. | 5 A.M. | 6 A.M. | 7 A.M. | 8 A.M. | 9 A.M. | 10 A.M. | 11 A.M. | 12 P.M. | 1 P.M. | 2 P.M. |

ARCTIC OCEAN

FRANZ JOSEF LAND
(Russia)
Barents Sea
Kara Sea
Laptev Sea
East Siberian Sea

•Moscow

RUSSIA

•Kiev
UKRAINE
MOLDOVA
•ERB.-MONT.
BULGARIA
GEORGIA
•Istanbul
•Ankara
ARMENIA
AZERBAIJAN
TURKEY
CYPRUS
SYRIA
LEBANON
•Tehran
ISRAEL
JORDAN
•Alexandria
•Cairo
IRAQ
•Baghdad
KUWAIT
IRAN
BAHRAIN
QATAR
EGYPT
SAUDI ARABIA
UNITED ARAB EMIRATES
OMAN

Black Sea
KAZAKHSTAN
•Astana
Aral Sea
UZBEKISTAN
•Tashkent
KYRGYZSTAN
TURKMENISTAN
TAJIKISTAN
AFGHANISTAN
PAKISTAN
•Lahore
•Karachi

MONGOLIA

CHINA
•Shenyang
•Beijing
•Tianjin
Lake Baikal

Sea Of Okhotsk
Bering Sea

Sea of Japan (East Sea)
JAPAN
NORTH KOREA
•Seoul
SOUTH KOREA
•Tokyo
•Osaka

PACIFIC OCEAN

•Delhi
NEPAL
BHUTAN
•Shanghai
•Chongqing
East China Sea
•Taipei
TAIWAN

•Kolkata
•Dhaka
BANGLADESH
MYANMAR
•Guangzhou
•Hanoi
•Hong Kong
Macau

INDIA
•Mumbai
•Hyderabad
•Chennai
•Bangalore
Bay of Bengal
•Yangon
THAILAND
•Bangkok
LAOS
VIETNAM
CAMBODIA
South China Sea
Philippine Sea
•Manila
PHILIPPINES

Arabian Sea

SRI LANKA
•Colombo

•Ho Chi Minh City
BRUNEI
PALAU

FEDERATED STATES OF MICRONESIA

KHARTOUM•
SUDAN
ERITREA
YEMEN
DJIBOUTI
ETHIOPIA
•Addis Ababa
SOMALIA
AL AFRICAN REPUBLIC
UGANDA
•Kampala
RWANDA
KENYA
•Nairobi
BURUNDI
DEMOCRATIC REPUBLIC OF CONGO
•Mogadishu
SEYCHELLES
TANZANIA
•Dar es Salaam
MALAWI
•Lilongwe
COMOROS
ZAMBIA
•Lusaka
•Harare
ZIMBABWE
BOTSWANA
•Gaborone
•Joannesburg
SOUTH AFRICA
•Maputo
SWAZILAND
LESOTHO
MOZAMBIQUE
Mozambique Channel
•Antananarivo
MADAGASCAR
MAURITIUS
RÉUNION (France)

Kuala Lumpur
MALAYSIA
SINGAPORE
•Jakarta
•Surabaya
INDONESIA
TIMOR-LESTE

PAPUA NEW GUINEA
•Port Moresby
SOLOMON IS.

VANUATU
Coral Sea

INDIAN OCEAN

AUSTRALIA

•Sydney
•Melbourne
NEW ZEALAND
•Wellington
Tasman Sea

ALB.	Albania
AUS.	Austria
BELG.	Belgium
BOS.–HER.	Bosnia and Herzegovina
CZECH REP.	Czech Republic
CR.	Croatia
DEN.	Denmark
SERB-MONT.	Serbia and Montenegro
HUN.	Hungary
MAC.	Macedonia
NETH.	The Netherlands
SWITZ.	Switzerland
SLOV.	Slovakia
SLOVE.	Slovenia

| P.M. | 5 P.M. | 6 P.M. | 7 P.M. | 8 P.M. | 9 P.M. | 10 P.M. | 11 P.M. | 12 A.M. | 1 A.M. | 2 A.M. | 3 A.M. |

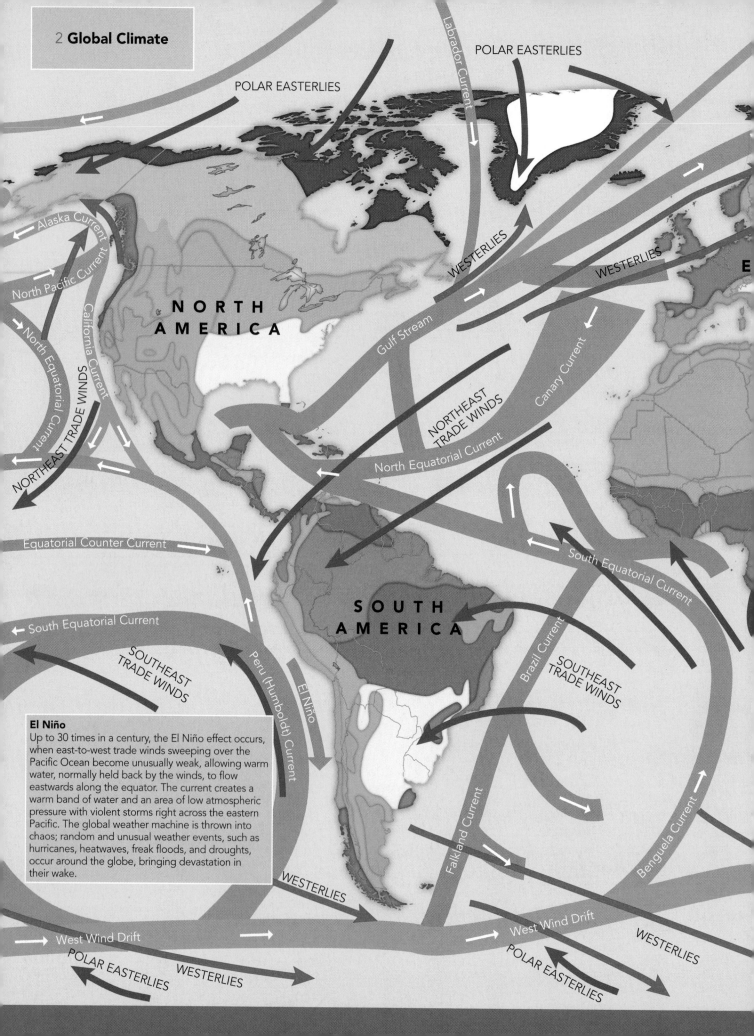

POLAR EASTERLIES

POLAR EASTERLIES

Labrador Current

WESTERLIES

WESTERLIES

E

Alaska Current

North Pacific Current

North Equatorial Current

California Current

NORTHEAST TRADE WINDS

**NORTH
AMERICA**

Gulf Stream

NORTHEAST
TRADE WINDS

Canary Current

North Equatorial Current

Equatorial Counter Current

South Equatorial Current

South Equatorial Current

SOUTHEAST
TRADE WINDS

Peru (Humboldt) Current

El Niño

**SOUTH
AMERICA**

Brazil Current

SOUTHEAST
TRADE WINDS

Falkland Current

Benguela Current

El Niño

Up to 30 times in a century, the El Niño effect occurs, when east-to-west trade winds sweeping over the Pacific Ocean become unusually weak, allowing warm water, normally held back by the winds, to flow eastwards along the equator. The current creates a warm band of water and an area of low atmospheric pressure with violent storms right across the eastern Pacific. The global weather machine is thrown into chaos; random and unusual weather events, such as hurricanes, heatwaves, freak floods, and droughts, occur around the globe, bringing devastation in their wake.

WESTERLIES

West Wind Drift

West Wind Drift

WESTERLIES

POLAR EASTERLIES   WESTERLIES

POLAR EASTERLIES

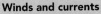

Winds and currents

The winds and currents that circulate across the surface of the planet act as a global heat exchange mechanism, transferring warmth from the tropics, which receive the most heat from the Sun, toward the cold polar regions. If air in one region of the globe is heated above the temperature of the surrounding air, it becomes less dense and rises. Cooler, denser air in another part of the atmosphere sinks—a constant cycle of heat exchange and air circulation, known as the prevailing winds. The surface currents of the ocean, which extend to depths of several hundred meters, are influenced by global wind patterns. The transfer of warm water polewards can have a strong influence on neighboring continents—the warm Gulf Stream in the Atlantic, for example, keeps northwestern Europe free of ice.

...TERLIES

...ic Drift

POLAR EASTERLIES

PE

ASIA

Kuro Siwo Current

North Equatorial Current

SOUTHWEST MONSOON (APR.–SEPT.)

NORTHEAST TRADE WINDS

ICA

Equatorial Counter Current

Equatorial Counter Current

NORTHEAST MONSOON (OCT.–MAR.)

South Equatorial Current

SOUTHEAST TRADE WINDS

South Equatorial Current

AUSTRALIA

West Australian Current

WESTERLIES

West Wind Drift

WESTERLIES

POLAR EASTERLIES

West Wind Drift

POLAR EASTERLIES

WESTERLIES

POLAR EASTERLIES

Climate Zones

- Ice cap
- Tundra
- Subarctic
- Highlands
- Marine west coast
- Humid continental
- Humid subtropical
- Mediterranean
- Arid
- Semiarid
- Tropical wet and dry
- Tropical wet

- Warm current
- Cool current

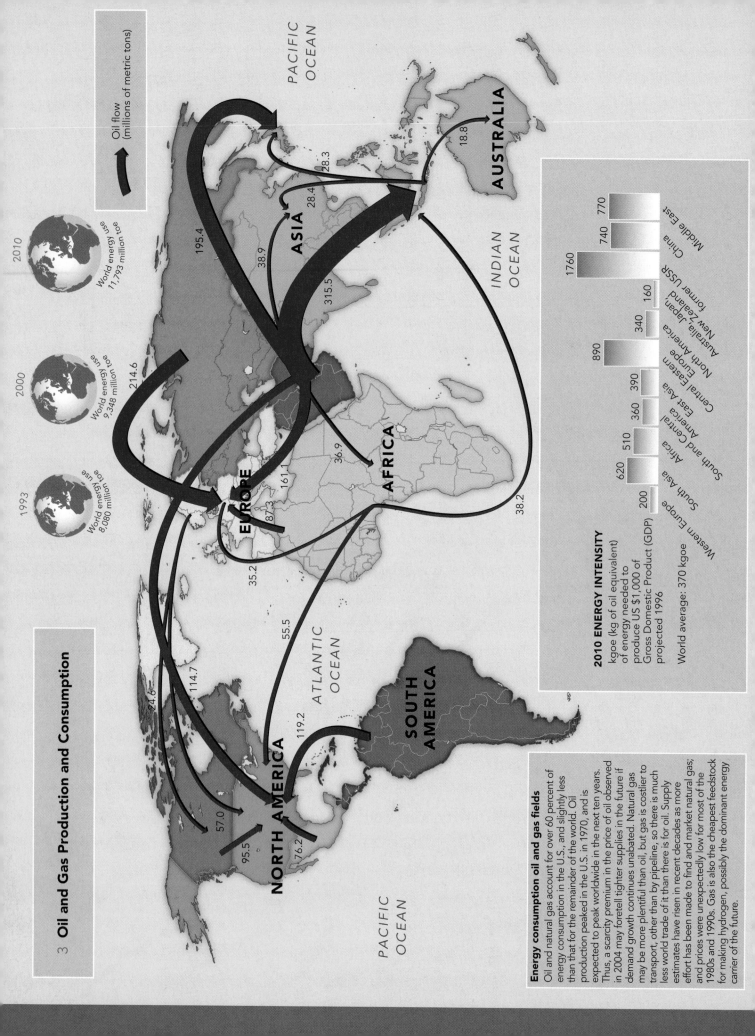

3 Oil and Gas Production and Consumption

Oil flow
(millions of metric tons)

2010

World energy use
11,793 million toe

2000

World energy use
9,348 million toe

1993

World energy use
8,080 million toe

PACIFIC
OCEAN

ATLANTIC
OCEAN

INDIAN
OCEAN

PACIFIC
OCEAN

NORTH AMERICA

SOUTH
AMERICA

EUROPE

AFRICA

ASIA

AUSTRALIA

195.4

214.6

38.9

28.4

28.3

315.5

36.9

161

87.3

35.2

55.5

119.2

76.2

95.5

57.0

114.7

24.6

18.8

38.2

2010 ENERGY INTENSITY

kgoe (kg of oil equivalent)
of energy needed to
produce US $1,000 of
Gross Domestic Product (GDP)
projected 1996

World average: 370 kgoe

South Asia	620
Africa	510
East Asia	360
Central/Eastern Europe	390
South and Central America	890
North America	340
Australia, Japan, New Zealand	160
Western Europe	200
China	740
former USSR	1760
Middle East	770

Energy consumption oil and gas fields

Oil and natural gas account for over 60 percent of
energy consumption in the U.S., and slightly less
than that for the remainder of the world. Oil
production peaked in the U.S. in 1970, and is
expected to peak worldwide in the next ten years.
Thus, a scarcity premium in the price of oil observed
in 2004 may foretell tighter supplies in the future if
demand growth continues unabated. Natural gas
may be more plentiful than oil, but gas is costlier to
transport, other than by pipeline, so there is much
less world trade of it than there is for oil. Supply
estimates have risen in recent decades as more
effort has been made to find and market natural gas;
and prices were unexpectedly low for most of the
1980s and 1990s. Gas is also the cheapest feedstock
for making hydrogen, possibly the dominant energy
carrier of the future.

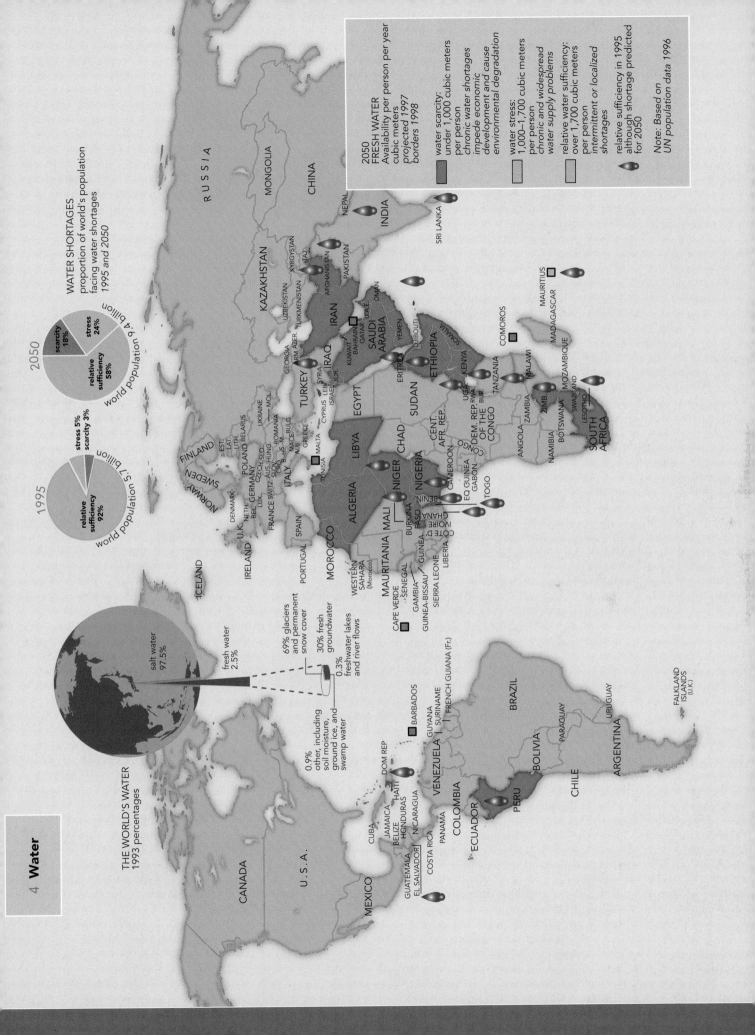

THE WORLD'S WATER
1993 percentages

salt water
97.5%

fresh water
2.5%

69% glaciers
and permanent
snow cover

30% fresh
groundwater

0.3%
freshwater lakes
and river flows

0.9%
other, including
soil moisture,
ground ice, and
swamp water

WATER SHORTAGES
proportion of world's population
facing water shortages
1995 and 2050

1995

world population 5.7 billion

relative
sufficiency
92%

stress 5%
scarcity 3%

2050

world population 9.4 billion

scarcity
18%

stress
24%

relative
sufficiency
58%

2050
FRESH WATER
Availability per person per year
cubic meters
projected 1997
borders 1998

water scarcity:
under 1,000 cubic meters
per person
chronic water shortages
impede economic
development and cause
environmental degradation

water stress:
1,000–1,700 cubic meters
per person
chronic and widespread
water supply problems

relative water sufficiency:
over 1,700 cubic meters
per person
intermittent or localized
shortages

relative sufficiency in 1995
although shortage predicted
for 2050

Note: Based on
UN population data 1996

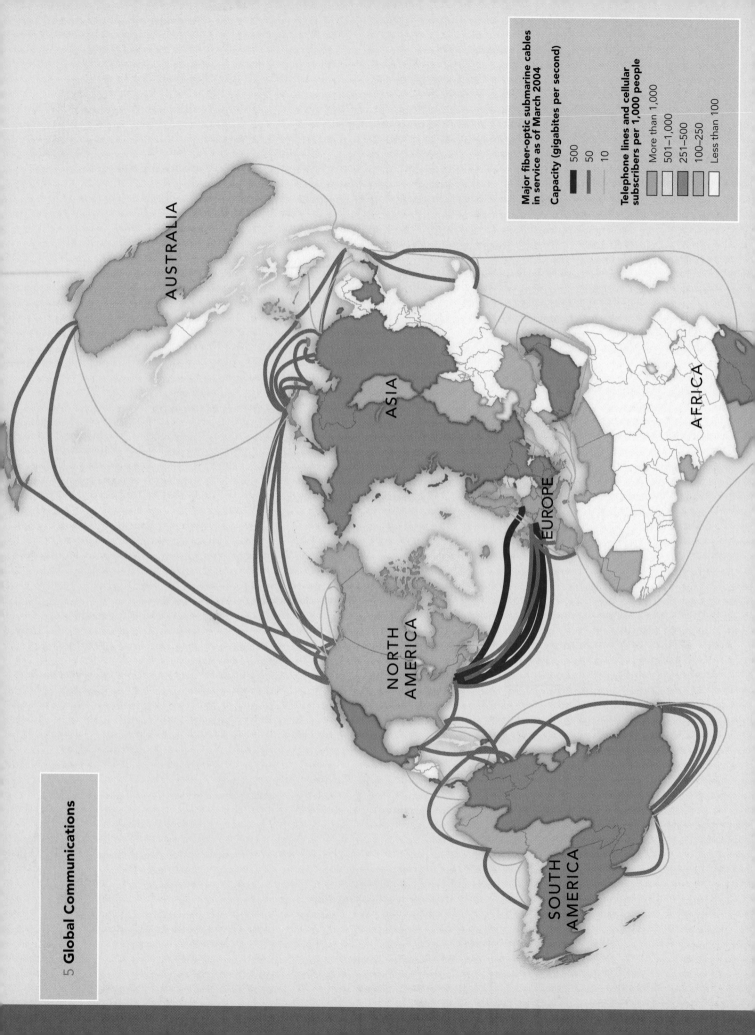

Major fiber-optic submarine cables in service as of March 2004

Capacity (gigabites per second)

500

50

10

Telephone lines and cellular subscribers per 1,000 people

More than 1,000

501–1,000

251–500

100–250

Less than 100

AUSTRALIA

ASIA

EUROPE

AFRICA

NORTH AMERICA

SOUTH AMERICA

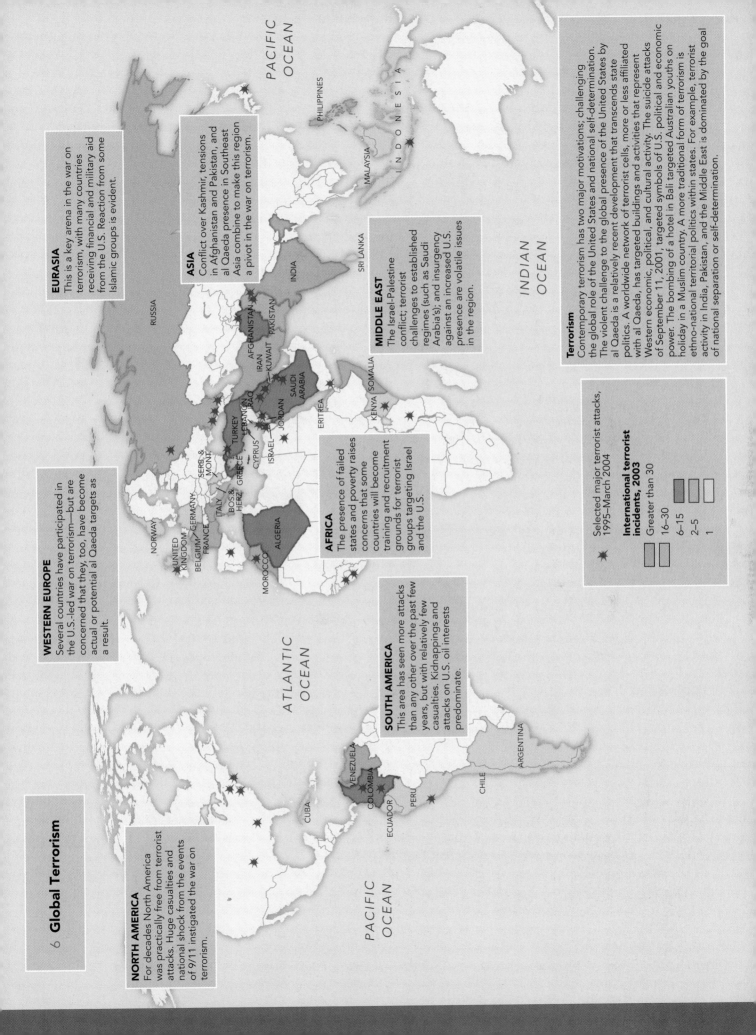

6 Global Terrorism

NORTH AMERICA
For decades North America was practically free from terrorist attacks. Huge casualties and national shock from the events of 9/11 instigated the war on terrorism.

WESTERN EUROPE
Several countries have participated in the U.S.-led war on terrorism—but are concerned that they, too, have become actual or potential al Qaeda targets as a result.

EURASIA
This is a key arena in the war on terrorism, with many countries receiving financial and military aid from the U.S. Reaction from some Islamic groups is evident.

ASIA
Conflict over Kashmir, tensions in Afghanistan and Pakistan; and al Qaeda presence in Southeast Asia combine to make this region a pivot in the war on terrorism.

MIDDLE EAST
The Israel-Palestine conflict; terrorist challenges to established regimes (such as Saudi Arabia's); and insurgency against an increased U.S. presence are volatile issues in the region.

AFRICA
The presence of failed states and poverty raises concerns that some countries will become training and recruitment grounds for terrorist groups targeting Israel and the U.S.

SOUTH AMERICA
This area has seen more attacks than any other over the past few years, but with relatively few casualties. Kidnappings and attacks on U.S. oil interests predominate.

Terrorism
Contemporary terrorism has two major motivations; challenging the global role of the United States and national self-determination. The violent challenge to the global presence of the United States by al Qaeda is a relatively recent development that transcends state politics. A worldwide network of terrorist cells, more or less affiliated with al Qaeda, has targeted buildings and activities that represent Western economic, political, and cultural activity. The suicide attacks of September 11, 2001, targeted symbols of U.S. political and economic power. The bombing of a hotel in Bali targeted Australian youths on holiday in a Muslim country. A more traditional form of terrorism is ethno-national territorial politics within states. For example, terrorist activity in India, Pakistan, and the Middle East is dominated by the goal of national separation or self-determination.

Selected major terrorist attacks, 1995–March 2004

International terrorist incidents, 2003
Greater than 30
16–30
6–15
2–5
1

PACIFIC OCEAN

ATLANTIC OCEAN

PACIFIC OCEAN

INDIAN OCEAN

RUSSIA

NORWAY
UNITED KINGDOM
BELGIUM
FRANCE
GERMANY
ITALY
BOS.& HERZ.
SERB. & MONT.
GREECE
CYPRUS
TURKEY
LEBANON
ISRAEL
JORDAN
SAUDI ARABIA
IRAQ
KUWAIT
IRAN
AFGHANISTAN
PAKISTAN
INDIA
SRI LANKA
MOROCCO
ALGERIA
ERITREA
SOMALIA
KENYA
MALAYSIA
INDONESIA
PHILIPPINES
CUBA
VENEZUELA
COLOMBIA
ECUADOR
PERU
CHILE
ARGENTINA

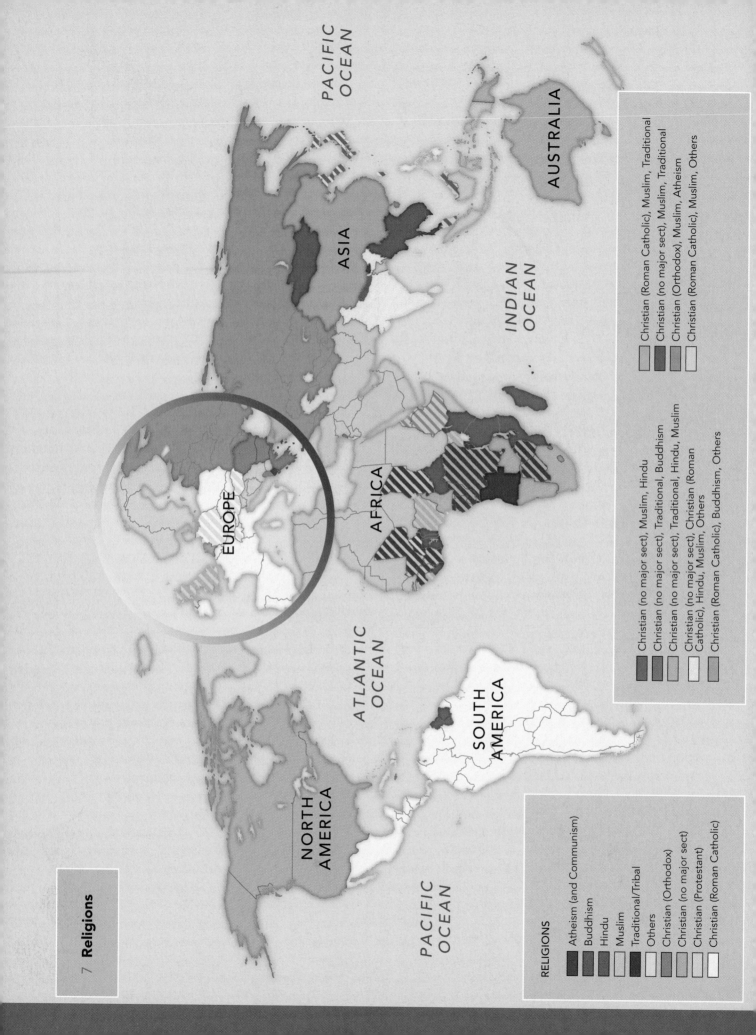

RELIGIONS

- Atheism (and Communism)
- Buddhism
- Hindu
- Muslim
- Traditional/Tribal
- Others
- Christian (Orthodox)
- Christian (no major sect)
- Christian (Protestant)
- Christian (Roman Catholic)

- Christian (no major sect), Muslim, Hindu
- Christian (no major sect), Traditional, Buddhism
- Christian (no major sect), Muslim, Traditional
- Christian (no major sect), Traditional, Hindu, Muslim
- Christian (no major sect), Christian (Roman Catholic), Hindu, Muslim, Others
- Christian (Roman Catholic), Buddhism, Others

- Christian (Roman Catholic), Muslim, Traditional
- Christian (no major sect), Muslim, Traditional
- Christian (Orthodox), Muslim, Atheism
- Christian (Roman Catholic), Muslim, Others

PACIFIC OCEAN

AUSTRALIA

ASIA

INDIAN OCEAN

AFRICA

EUROPE

ATLANTIC OCEAN

SOUTH AMERICA

NORTH AMERICA

PACIFIC OCEAN

Trade flow

The circling paths of trade between continents show just how interconnected the world's economies truly are. The richest countries, such as those in North America, western Europe, and the Far East, trade mostly with each other, exchanging different varieties of similar goods such as automobiles. However, trade also flows between higher- and lower-income regions. In those cases, the high-income countries typically provide more complex goods, such as electronic equipment, while low-income countries provide primary goods such as minerals. Smaller, poorer countries are more likely to be dependent on exporting a single commodity, such as coffee or petroleum. In general, poor, labor-abundant countries tend to export labor-intensive goods, such as textiles and shoes, and the countries rich in arable land will export foods such as grains.

AUSTRALIA

ASIA

EUROPE

AFRICA

NORTH
AMERICA

SOUTH
AMERICA

World economies

High income
Upper-middle income
Lower-middle income
Low income
No income data

World merchandise trade
(in billions of U.S. dollars)

Greater than 200
101–200
31–100
5–30
Less than 5

4

cultural Dynamics in assessing global markets

CHAPTER OUTLINE

CHAPTER LEARNING OBJECTIVES

What you should learn from Chapter 4:

- The importance of culture to an international marketer

- The origins and elements of culture

- The impact of cultural borrowing

- The strategy of planned change and its consequences

Global Perspective

EQUITIES AND EBAY—CULTURE GETS IN THE WAY

Two trillion dollars! That's about 200 trillion yen. Either way you count it, it's a lot of money. American brokerage houses such as Fidelity Investments, Goldman Sachs, and Merrill Lynch rushed new investment products and services to market in Japan to try to capture the huge capital outflow expected from 10-year time deposits, then held in the Japanese postal system. Liberalization of Japan's capital markets in recent years now gives Japanese consumers more freedom of choice in their investments. Post office time deposits still yield about a 2 percent return in Japan, and bank savings yields have been around 0. By American e-trading standards, that means an electronic flood of money moving out of the post offices and into the stock markets. Right?

However, Japan is not America. There is no American-style risk-taking culture among Japanese investors. The volume of stock trading in Japan is about one-sixth that of the United States. In Japan, only 12 percent of household financial assets are directly invested in stocks and a mere 2 percent in mutual funds. In contrast, about 55 percent of U.S. households own stock. Says one analyst, "Most of the population [in Japan] doesn't know what a mutual fund is." So will the flood be just a trickle? And what about online stock trading? Internet use in Japan has burgeoned—there are now some 85 million users in Japan. That's about the same percentage as in the United States. But the expected deluge into equities has been a dribble. Merrill Lynch and others are cutting back staff now as fast as they built it just a couple of years ago.

Making matters worse, for the Japanese, the transition into a more modern and trustworthy securities market has not been a smooth one. In 2005, an astounding transaction took place on the Tokyo Stock Exchange (TSE); instead of placing a small order of 1 share for 610,000 yen of J-Com, a trader with Mizuho Securities Co. mistakenly placed a sell order for 610,000 shares for 1 yen. Mizuho ended up losing 40 billion yen ($344 million) due to a simple computer glitch that ultimately led to the resignation of TSE president Takuo Tsurushima. Ouch!

A French firm is trying to break through a similar aversion to both e-trading and equities in France. That is, only about 26 million people use the Internet in France, and one-third of that number own stocks. The French have long shied away from stock market investments, seeing them as schemes to enrich insiders while fleecing novices. After the Enron and WorldCom scandals here, you could almost hear the chortling in the sidewalk cafés there. But even in France, investment preferences are beginning to change, especially now that the real estate market has turned. At the same time, the liberalization of Europe's financial services sector is bringing down transaction costs for institutional and retail investors alike.

eBay, the personal online auction site so successful in the United States, is running into comparable difficulties in both Japan and France. The lower rate of Internet use in France is just part of the problem. For Japanese it has been embarrassing to sell castoffs to anyone, much less buy them from strangers. Garage sales are unheard of. In France, eBay's founder Pierre Omidyar's country of birth, the firm runs into French laws restricting operations to a few government-certified auctioneers.

Based on a knowledge of differences in cultural values between the United States and both Japan and France, we should expect a slower diffusion of these high-tech Internet services in the latter two countries. E-trading and e-auctions have both exploded on the American scene. However, compared with those in many other countries, U.S. investors are averse to neither the risk and uncertainties of equity investments nor the impersonal interactions of online transactions.

Sources: William D. Echikson, "Rough Crossing for eBay," *BusinessWeek E.Biz*, February 7, 2000, p. EB48; Mark Scott, "Online Trading Blooms in Europe," *BusinessWeek Online*, November 27, 2007; Sang Lee, "Japan and the Future of Electronic Trading," *Securities Industry News*, November 5, 2007; *World Development Indicators*, World Bank, 2008.

Culture deals with a group's design for living. It is pertinent to the study of marketing, especially international marketing. If you consider the scope of the marketing concept—the satisfaction of consumer needs and wants at a profit—the successful marketer clearly must be a student of culture. For example, when a promotional message is written, symbols recognizable and meaningful to the market (the culture) must be used. When designing a product, the style, uses, and other related marketing activities must be made culturally acceptable (i.e., acceptable to the present society) if they are to be operative and meaningful. In fact, culture is pervasive in all marketing activities—in pricing, promotion, channels of distribution, product, packaging, and styling—and the marketer's efforts actually become a part of the fabric of culture. How such efforts interact with a culture determines the degree of success or failure of the marketing effort.

The manner in and amount[1] which people consume, the priority of needs and wants they attempt to satisfy, and the manner in which they satisfy them are functions of their culture that temper, mold, and dictate their style of living. Culture is the human-made part of human environment—the sum total of knowledge, beliefs, art, morals, laws, customs, and any other capabilities and habits acquired by humans as members of society.[2]

Markets constantly change; they are not static but evolve, expand, and contract in response to marketing effort, economic conditions, and other cultural influences. Markets and market behavior are part of a country's culture. One cannot truly understand how markets evolve or how they react to a marketer's effort without appreciating that markets are a result of culture. Markets are the result of the three-way interaction of a marketer's efforts, economic conditions, and all other elements of the culture. Marketers are constantly adjusting their efforts to cultural demands of the market, but they also are acting as *agents of change* whenever the product or idea being marketed is innovative. Whatever the degree of acceptance, the use of something new is the beginning of cultural change, and the marketer becomes a change agent.

This is the first of four chapters that focus on culture and international marketing. A discussion of the broad concept of culture as the foundation for international marketing is presented in this chapter. The next chapter, "Culture, Management Style, and Business Systems," discusses culture and how it influences business practices and the behaviors and thinking of managers. Chapters 6 and 7 examine elements of culture essential to the study of international marketing: the political environment and the legal environment.

This chapter's purpose is to heighten the reader's sensitivity to the dynamics of culture. It is neither a treatise on cultural information about a particular country nor a thorough marketing science or epidemiological study of the various topics. Rather, it is designed to emphasize the importance of cultural differences to marketers and the need to study each country's culture(s) and all its origins and elements, as well as point out some relevant aspects on which to focus.

Culture's Pervasive Impact

Culture affects every part of our lives, every day, from birth[3] to death,[4] and everything in between.[5] It affects how we spend money and how we consume in general. It even affects how we sleep. For example, we are told that Spaniards sleep less than

---

[1] It seems waistlines are expanding around the affluent world—in France, perhaps because people have more leisure. See "Obesity Rates Increase as French Become Idle," *The Wall Street Journal*, January 25, 2007, p. B6. Apparently obesity in the United States is causing Disney to have to deepen the stream on which its Small World boats float; they seem to be bottoming out more frequently. See Kimi Yoshino, "A Sinking Feeling on 'Small World' Ride," *Los Angeles Times*, November 9, 2007, p. C1. All these effects, despite our study of obesity, as in Adwiat Khare and J. Jeffrey Inman, "Habitual Behavior in American Eating Patterns: The Role of Meal Occasions," *Journal of Consumer Research* 32 (March 2006), pp. 567–82.

[2] An interesting Web site that has information on various cultural traits, gestures, holidays, language, religions, and so forth is www.culturegrams.com.

[3] "How to Deal with a Falling Population," *The Economist*, July 28, 2007, p. 11; "U.S. Defies Low-Birth Trend in Europe," *Associated Press*, January 15, 2008.

[4] Funerals vary in style and cost around the world. See Hiroko Tashiro and Brian Bremner, "Bereaved, but Not Broke in Japan," *BusinessWeek*, February 14, 2005, p. 10.

[5] A most important summary of research in the area of culture's impact on consumption behavior is Eric J. Arnould and Craig J. Thompson, "Consumer Culture Theory (CCT): Twenty Years of Research," *Journal of Consumer Research* 3, no. 2 (March 2005), pp. 868–82.

Exhibit 4.1
Birthrates (per 1,000 women)

Source: World Bank, *World Development Indicators*, 2008. Copyright © 2008 by World Bank. Reprinted with permission of World Bank via Copyright Clearance Center.

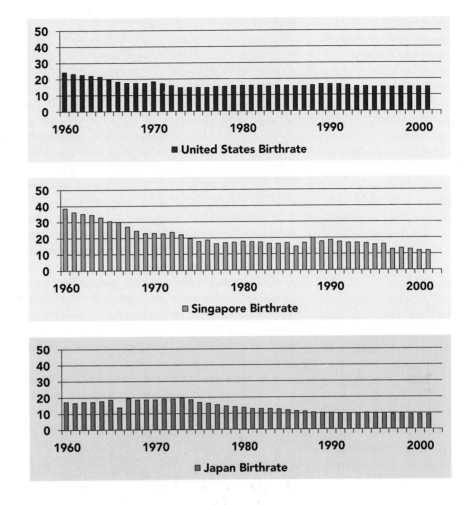

■ United States Birthrate

■ Singapore Birthrate

■ Japan Birthrate

other Europeans,[6] and Japanese children often sleep with their parents. You can clearly see culture operating in the birthrate tables in Exhibit 4.1. When you look across the data from the three countries, the gradual declines beginning in the 1960s are evident. As countries move from agricultural to industrial to services economies, birthrates decline. Immediate causes may be government policies and birth control technologies, but a global change in values is also occurring. Almost everywhere, smaller families are becoming favored. This cultural change now leads experts to predict that the planet's population will actually begin to decline after 2050 unless major breakthroughs in longevity intervene, as some predict.

But a closer look at the tables reveals even more interesting consequences of culture. Please notice the little peaks in 1976 and 1988 in the Singapore data. The same pattern can be seen in birthrate data from Taiwan. Those "extra" births are not a matter of random fluctuation. In Chinese cultures, being born in the Year of the Dragon (12 animals—dogs, rats, rabbits, pigs,[7] etc.—correspond to specific years in the calendar) is considered good luck. Such birthrate spikes have implications for sellers of diapers, toys, schools, colleges, and so forth in successive years in Singapore. However, superstitions have an even stronger influence on the birthrates in Japan, as shown in Exhibit 4.1. A one-year 20 percent drop in Japanese fertility rates in 1966 was caused by a belief that women born in the Year of the Fire Horse, which occurs every 60 years, will lead unhappy lives and perhaps murder their husbands. This sudden and substantial decline in fertility, which has occurred historically every 60 years since Japan started keeping birth records, reflects abstinence, abortions, and

---

[6] This seems a reasonable proposition to the authors, given that the best restaurants in Madrid are still serving the main course after midnight!

[7] "The Golden Pig Cohort: As China Enters an Auspicious Year, the Birth Rate is Expected to Soar," *The Economist*, February 10, 2007, p. 44.

Exhibit 4.2

Patterns of Consumption (annual per capita)

Source: EuroMonitor International, 2008.

Country	Cut Flowers (stems)	Chocolate (kg)	Fish (kg)	Pasta (kg)	Wine (lt)	Tobacco (sticks)
France	81	3.9	26.2	6.0	24.6	902 (–24)*
Germany	120	8.1	4.5	6.1	21.6	1,158 (–29)
Italy	87	2.5	22.0	18.9	26.5	1,593 (–6)
Netherlands	125	4.9	25.0	3.3	20.0	813 (–21)
Spain	33	2.0	35.9	4.0	11.7	1,932 (–15)
United Kingdom	48	10.5	16.0	2.0	17.9	783 (–16)
Japan	110	1.2	37.9	6.9	4.5	2,046 (–14)
United States	75	5.8	19.6	3.7	6.6	1,247 (–12)

*Five-year growth rate, percentage.

birth certificate fudging. This superstition has resulted in the stigmatization of women born in 1966 and had a large impact on market potential for a wide variety of consumer goods and services in Japan. It will be interesting to see how technological innovations and culture will interact in Japan in 2026, the next Year of the Fire Horse.[8]

Culture's influence is also illustrated in the consumption data[9] presented in Exhibit 4.2. The focus there is on the six European Union countries, but data from the two other major markets of affluence in the world—Japan and the United States—are also included. The products compared are those that might be included in a traditional (American) romantic dinner date.

First come the flowers and candy. The Dutch are the champion consumers of cut flowers,[10] and this particular preference for petals will be explored further in the pages to come. The British love their chocolate. Perhaps the higher consumption rate there is caused by Cadbury's[11] advertising, or perhaps the cooler temperatures have historically allowed for easier storage and better quality in the northern countries. At least among our six EU countries, per capita chocolate consumption appears to decline with latitude.

In Europe, the Spaniards are the most likely to feast on fish. They even come close to the Japanese preference for seafood. From the data in the table, one might conclude that being surrounded in Japan by water explains the preference for seafood. However, what about the British? The flat geography in England and Scotland allows for the efficient production of beef, and a bit later in this section, we consider the consequences of their strong preference for red meat. The Italians eat more pasta—not a surprise. History is important. The product was actually invented in China, but in 1270, Marco Polo is reputed to have brought the innovation back to Italy, where it has flourished. Proximity to China also explains the high rate of Japanese pasta (noodle) consumption.

How about alcohol and tobacco? Grapes grow best in France and Italy, so a combination of climate and soil conditions explains at least part of the pattern of wine consumption seen in Exhibit 4.2.[12] Culture also influences the laws, age limits, and such related to alcohol. The legal environment also has implications for the consumption of cigarettes. Indeed, the most striking patterns in the table are not the current consumption numbers; the

---

[8] Robert W. Hodge and Naohiro Ogawa, *Fertility Change in Contemporary Japan* (Chicago: University of Chicago Press, 1991).

[9] Thomas Fuller, "Fans Sour on Sweeter Version of Asia's Smelliest Fruit," *The New York Times International*, April 8, 2007, p. 3.

[10] See Amy Stewart, *Flower Confidential: The Good, the Bad, and the Beautiful in the Business of Flowers* (Chapel Hill, NC: Algonquin Books, 2007); Catherine Ziegler, *Favored Flowers: Culture and the Economy in a Global System* (Durham, NC: Duke University Press, 2007). Also see www.vba.nl if you wish to visit the Aalsmeer Flower Market near the Amsterdam airport.

[11] See Cadbury's Web site for the history of chocolate, www.cadbury.co.uk. Chocolate is also an important product in Switzerland, where the consumption per capita is more than 12 kg. The mountain climate is cooler, and of course, Nestlé has corporate headquarters there.

[12] Actually, Luxembourg, Hungary, and Ireland are the top three consuming countries (on a per capita basis) of alcohol.

Finding horse or donkey as your entree would not be romantic or even appetizing in most places around the world. Even though horse consumption is generally declining in France, here in Paris you can still buy a steed steak at the local *bouchers chevaleries*. Escargot *oui*, Eeyore *non!*

interesting data are the five-year growth rates. Demand is shrinking remarkably fast almost everywhere. These dramatic declines in consumption represent a huge cultural shift that the world seldom sees.

Any discussion of tobacco consumption leads immediately to consideration of the consequences of consumption. One might expect that a high consumption of the romance products—flowers, candy, and wine—might lead to a high birthrate. Reference to Exhibit 4.3 doesn't yield any clear conclusions. The Germans have some of the highest consumption levels of the romantic three but the lowest birthrate among the eight countries.

Perhaps the Japanese diet's[13] emphasis on fish yields them the longest life expectancy. But length of life among the eight affluent countries represented in the table shows little variation. How people die, however, does vary substantially across the countries.

---

[13] Notice we are not referring to the Japanese Diet, that country's legislature, though fishing rights are a hugely important international issue for that body.

Exhibit 4.3
Consequences of Consumption

Source: EuroMonitor 2008.

Country	Birthrate (per 100,000)	Life Expectancy	Death Rate per 100,000			
			Ischemic Heart Disease	Diabetes Mellitus	Lung Cancer	Stomach Cancer
France	12.8	81	25	22	45	8
Germany	8.2	79	179	29	49	14
Italy	9.2	81	134	31	59	19
Netherlands	11.3	80	80	23	60	9
Spain	10.7	80	89	23	47	13
United Kingdom	12.2	79	170	11	55	10
Japan	8.2	82	56	10	46	38
United States	13.9	79	174	25	54	4

The Floriad, the biggest exhibition of flowers on earth, happens once every decade. You can go to the next one in 2012.

Outside the Aalsmeer Flower Auction—notice the jet landing at nearby Schiphol Airport, which serves both Amsterdam and Aalsmeer.

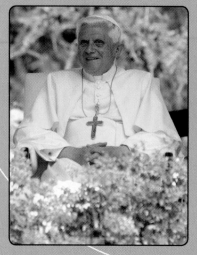

The Pope in St. Peter's Square on Easter Sunday surrounded by Dutch flowers. *(AP Photo/ Antonio Calanni)*

The Amsterdam flower market—a busy place for local consumers and tourists.

Four hundred years later, the one-dollar black tulip is available in the Amsterdam flower market.

A view of a Dutch harbor with trading ships circa 1600. *(© Archivo Iconografico, S.A./Corbis)*

we all love flowers. But for the Dutch, flowers are more important than that. For them, it's more like a national fascination, fixation, or even a fetish for flowers. why?

The answer is an instructive story about culture and international markets, the broader subjects of this chapter. The story starts with geography, goes through the origins and elements of culture, and ends with the Dutch being the masters of the exhibition, consumption, and production of flowers.

GEOGRAPHY. The rivers and the bays make the Netherlands a great trading country. But the miserable weather, rain, and snow more than 200 days per year make it a colorless place, gray nearly year-round. The Flying Dutchmen not only went to the Spice Islands for spice for the palate; they also went to the eastern Mediterranean for spice for the eyes. The vibrant colors of the tulip first came to Europe from the Ottoman Empire on a Dutch ship in 1561.

HISTORY. The Dutch enthusiasm for the new "visual drug" was great. Its most potent form was, ironically, the black tulip. Prices exploded, and speculators bought and sold promissory notes guaranteeing the future delivery of black tulip bulbs. This derivatives market yielded prices in today's dollars of $1 million or more for a single bulb, enough to buy a 5-story house in central Amsterdam today. Not only did the tulip mania create futures markets, it also caused the first great market bust in recorded history. Prices plummeted when the government took control in 1637. Now at the Amsterdam flower market, you can buy a black tulip bulb for about a dollar!

Inside Aalsmeer, 150 football fields of cut flowers, 20 million per day, are readied for auction.

The bidders in four huge auction rooms pay attention to the "clock" as high starting prices tick down. The wholesale buyer that stops the clock pays the associated price in this the archetypical "Dutch auction."

Technology and Economics.

The technology in the story comes in the name of Carolus Clusius, a botanist who developed methods for manipulating the colors of the tulips in the early 1600s. This manipulation added to their appeal and value, and the tulip trade became international for the Dutch.

Social Institutions.

Every Easter Sunday, the Pope addresses the world at St. Peter's Square in Rome reciting, "Bedankt voor bloemen." Thus, he thanks the Dutch nation for providing the flowers for this key Catholic ritual. The Dutch government, once every tenth year, sponsors the largest floriculture exhibition in the world, the Floriad. You can go next in 2012. Finally, at the Aalsmeer Flower Auction near Amsterdam, the prices are set for all flowers in all markets around the world. The Dutch remain the largest exporters of flowers (60 percent global market share), shipping them across Europe by trucks and worldwide by air freight.

Outside again at Aalsmeer, trucks are loaded for shipment by land across Europe and airfreight worldwide.

Cultural Values.

The high value the Dutch place on flowers is reflected in many ways, not the least of which is their high consumption rate, as seen in Exhibit 4.2.

Aesthetics as Symbols.

Rembrandt Van Rijn's paintings, including his most famous *Night Watch* (1642, Rijksmuseum, Amsterdam), reflect a dark palette. Artists generally paint in the colors of their surroundings. A quarter century later, his compatriot Vincent Van Gogh used a similar bleak palette when he worked in Holland. Later, when Van Gogh went to the sunny and colorful south of France, the colors begin to explode on his canvases. And, of course, there he painted flowers!

Rembrandt's *Night Watch*. (© Rijksmuseum, Amsterdam/SuperStock)

Van Gogh's *Vase with Fifteen Sunflowers*, painted in the south of France in 1889, and sold to a Japanese insurance executive for some $40 million in 1987, at the time the highest price ever paid for a single work of art. The Japanese are also big flower consumers—see Exhibit 4.2. (*AP Photo/Tsugufumi Matsumoto, file*)

Van Gogh's *Potato Eaters*, painted in The Netherlands in 1885. (© SuperStock, Inc./SuperStock)

CROSSING BORDERS 4.1   Human Universals: The Myth of Diversity?

Yes, culture's influence is pervasive. But as anthropologist Donald E. Brown correctly points out, we are all human. And since we are all of the same species, we actually share a great deal. Here's a few of the hundreds of traits we share:

Use metaphors

Have a system of status and roles

Are ethnocentric

Create art

Conceive of success and failure

Create groups antagonistic to outsiders

Imitate outside influences

Resist outside influences

Consider aspects of sexuality private

Express emotions with face

Reciprocate

Use mood-altering drugs

Overestimate objectivity of thought

Have a fear of snakes

Recognize economic obligations in exchanges of goods and services

Trade and transport goods

Indeed, the last two suggest that we might be characterized as the "exchanging animal."

Source: Donald E. Brown, *Human Universals* (New York: McGraw-Hill, 1991).

The influence of fish versus red meat consumption on the incidence of heart problems is easy to see. The most interesting datum in the table is the extremely high incidence of stomach cancer in Japan. The latest studies suggest two culprits: (1) salty foods such as soy sauce and (2) the bacterium *Helicobacter pylori*. The latter is associated with the unsanitary conditions prevalent in Japan immediately after World War II, and it is still hurting health in Japan today. Finally, because stomach cancer in Japan is so prevalent, the Japanese have developed the most advanced treatment of the disease, that is, both procedures and instruments. Even though the death rate is highest, the treatment success rate is likewise the highest in Japan. Whether you are in Tacoma, Toronto, or Tehran, the best medicine for stomach cancer may be a ticket to Tokyo. Indeed, this last example well demonstrates that culture not only affects consumption; it also affects production (of medical services in this case)!

The point is that culture matters.[14] It is imperative for foreign marketers to learn to appreciate the intricacies of cultures different from their own if they are to be effective in foreign markets.

Definitions and Origins of Culture

There are many ways to think about culture. Dutch management professor Geert Hofstede refers to culture as the "software of the mind" and argues that it provides a guide for humans on how to think and behave; it is a problem-solving tool.[15] Anthropologist and business consultant Edward Hall provides a definition even more relevant to international marketing managers: "The people we were advising kept bumping their heads against an invisible barrier. . . . We knew that what they were up against was a completely different way of organizing life, of thinking, and of conceiving the underlying assumptions about the family and the state, the economic system, and even Man himself."[16] The salient points in Hall's comments are that cultural differences are often invisible and that marketers who ignore them often hurt both their companies and careers. Finally, James

---

[14] Lawrence E. Harrison and Samuel P. Huntington (eds.), *Culture Matters* (New York: Basic Books, 2000).

[15] Geert Hofstede, *Culture's Consequences*, 2nd ed. (Thousand Oaks, CA: Sage, 2001); Susan P. Douglas, "Exploring New Worlds: The Challenge of Global Marketing," *Journal of Marketing*, January 2001, pp. 103–109.

[16] Edward T. Hall, *The Silent Language* (New York: Doubleday, 1959), p. 26.

Day Hodgson, former U.S. ambassador to Japan, describes culture as a "thicket."[17] This last metaphor holds hope for struggling international marketers. According to the ambassador, thickets are tough to get through, but effort and patience often lead to successes.

Most traditional definitions of culture center around the notion that culture is the sum of the *values, rituals, symbols, beliefs,* and *thought processes* that are *learned* and *shared* by a group of people,[18] then *transmitted* from generation to generation.[19] So culture resides in the individual's mind. But the expression "a culture" recognizes that large collectives of people can, to a great degree, be like-minded.

The best international marketers will not only appreciate the cultural differences pertinent to their businesses, but they will also understand the origins of these differences. Possession of the latter, deeper knowledge will help marketers notice cultural differences in new markets and foresee changes in current markets of operation. Exhibit 4.4 depicts the several causal factors and social processes that determine and form cultures and cultural

---

[17] James D. Hodgson, Yoshihiro Sano, and John L. Graham, *Doing Business in the New Japan, Succeeding in America's Richest Foreign Market* (Latham, MD: Rowman & Littlefield, 2008).

[18] Please note that the group may be smaller than that defined by nation. See Rosalie Tung, "The Cross-Cultural Research Imperative: The Need to Balance Cross-Cultural and Intra-National Diversity," *Journal of International Business Studies* 39 (2008), pp. 41–46; Jean-Francois Ouellet, "Consumer Racism and Its Effects on Domestic Cross-Ethnic Product Purchase: An Empirical Test in the United States, Canada, and France," *Journal of Marketing* 71 (2007), pp. 113–28.

[19] Melvin Herskovitz, *Man and His Works* (New York: Alfred A. Knopf, 1952), p. 634. See also Chapter 10, "Culture," in Raymond Scupin and Christopher R. Decorse, *Anthropology: A Global Perspective*, 6th ed. (Englewood Cliffs, NJ: Prentice Hall, 2005).

Exhibit 4.4
Origins, Elements, and Consequences of Culture

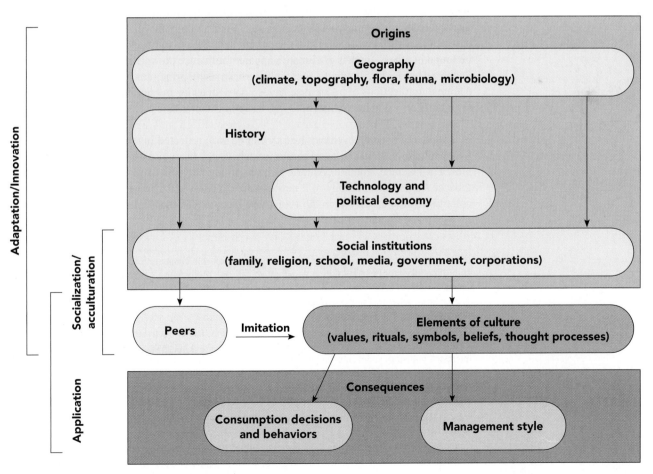

differences. Simply stated, humans make *adaptations* to changing environments through *innovation*. Individuals learn culture from social institutions through *socialization* (growing up) and *acculturation* (adjusting to a new culture). Individuals also absorb culture through role modeling, or imitation of their peers. Finally, people make decisions about consumption and production through *application* of their cultural-based knowledge. More details are provided below.

Geography

In the previous chapter, we described the immediate effects of geography on consumer choice. But geography exercises a more profound influence than just affecting the sort of jacket you buy. Indeed, geography (broadly defined here to include climate, topography, flora, fauna, and microbiology) has influenced history, technology,[20] economics, our social institutions, and, yes, our ways of thinking.[21] Geographical influences manifest themselves in our deepest cultural values developed through the millennia, and as geography changes, humans can adapt almost immediately. One sees the latter happening in the new interaction rituals evolving from the HIV/AIDS disaster or more recently the SARS outbreak in China. The ongoing cultural divides across the English Channel or the the Taiwan Strati are also representative of geography's historical salience in human affairs.

The ideas of two researchers are particularly pertinent to any discussion of geography's influence on everything from history to present-day cultural values. First, Jared Diamond,[22] a professor of physiology, tells us that historically, innovations spread faster east to west than north to south. Before the advent of transoceanic shipping, ideas flowed over the Silk Road but not across the Sahara or the Isthmus of Panama. He uses this geographical approach to explain the dominance of Euro-Asian cultures, with their superior technology and more virulent germs, over African and American cultures. Indeed, Diamond's most important contribution is his material on the influence of microbiology on world history.

Second, Philip Parker,[23] a marketing professor, argues for geography's deep influence on history, economics, and consumer behavior. For example, he reports strong correlations between the latitude (climate) and the per capita GDP of countries. Empirical support can be found in others' reports of climate's apparent influence on workers' wages.[24] Parker, like Diamond before him, explains social phenomena using principles of physiology. The management implications of his treatise have to do with using ambient temperature as a market segmentation variable. We return to this issue in Chapter 8.

History

The impact of specific events in history can be seen reflected in technology, social institutions, cultural values, and even consumer behavior.[25] Diamond's book is filled with examples. For instance, much of American trade policy has depended on the happenstance of tobacco (i.e., the technology of a new cash crop) being the original source of the Virginia colony's economic survival in the 1600s. In a like manner, the Declaration of Independence,

---

[20] Along with flowers, the Dutch are also champions at bicycle consumption. Their flat land makes their 20 million bikes for their 16 million people practical! See Molly More, "Bike Nation," *Washington Post*, June 24, 2007, p. 5A.

[21] Richard E. Nisbett, *The Geography of Thought: How Asians and Westerners Think Differently . . . and Why* (New York: The Free Press, 2003).

[22] Jared Diamond's *Guns, Germs and Steel: The Fates of the Human Societies* (New York: Norton, 1999) is a Pulitzer Prize winner, recipient of the Phi Beta Kappa Award in Science, and a wonderful read for anyone interested in history and/or innovation. PBS also has produced a video version of *Guns, Germs and Steel*. Also see Diamond's most recent book, *Collapse* (New York: Viking, 2005).

[23] Philip Parker's *Physioeconomics* (Cambridge, MA: MIT Press, 2000) is a data-rich discussion of global economics well worth reading.

[24] Evert Van de Vliert, "Thermoclimate, Culture, and Poverty as Country-Level Roots of Workers' Wages," *Journal of International Business* 34, no. 1 (2003), pp. 40–52.

[25] "France's 'Trust Deficit' Limits Its Growth Prospects," *The Wall Street Journal*, October 22, 2007, p. B12. The high state of distrust in French society is in part attributed to the German occupation in World War II.

and thereby Americans' values and institutions, was fundamentally influenced by the coincident 1776 publication of Adam Smith's *The Wealth of Nations*. Notice too that the military conflicts in the Middle East in 2003 bred new cola brands—Mecca Cola, Muslim Up, Arab Cola, and ColaTurka.[26]

The Political Economy

For most of the 20th century, four approaches to governance competed for world dominance: colonialism, fascism, communism, and democracy/free enterprise. Fascism fell in 1945. Colonialism was also a casualty of World War II, though its death throes lasted well into the second half of the century.[27] Communism crumbled in the 1990s.[28] One pundit even declared the "end of history."[29] Unfortunately, we have September 11 and the conflicts in the Middle East to keep the list of bad things growing. Much more detail is included in Chapters 6 and 7 on the influences of politics and the legal environment on the culture of commerce and consumption, so we will leave this important topic until then. The main point here is for you to appreciate the influence of the political economy on social institutions and cultural values and ways of thinking.

Technology

Sit back for a moment and consider what technological innovation has had the greatest impact on institutions and cultural values in the past 50 years in the United States. Seriously, stop reading, look out your window, and for a moment consider the question.

There are many good answers, but only one best one. Certainly jet aircraft, air conditioning, televisions, computers, and the Internet all make the list. But the best answer is most likely the pill.[30] That is, the birth control pill, or more broadly birth control techniques, have had a huge effect on everyday life for most Americans. Mainly, it has freed women to have careers and freed men to spend more time with kids. Before the advent of the pill, men's and women's roles were prescribed by reproductive responsibilities and roles. Now half the marketing majors in the United States are women. Now 10 percent of the crews on American navy ships are women. Before the pill, these numbers were unimaginable.

Obviously, not everyone is happy with these new "freedoms." For example, in 1968, the Roman Catholic Church forbade use of the birth control pill. But the technology of birth control undeniably has deeply affected social institutions and cultural values. Families are smaller, and government and schools are forced to address issues such as abstinence and condom distribution.

Social Institutions

Social institutions including *family, religion, school, the media, government*, and *corporations* all affect the ways in which people relate to one another, organize their activities to live in harmony with one another, teach acceptable behavior to succeeding generations, and govern themselves. The positions of men and women in society, the family, social classes, group behavior, age groups, and how societies define decency and civility are interpreted differently within every culture. In cultures in which the social organizations result in close-knit family units, for example, a promotion campaign aimed at the family unit is usually more effective than one aimed at individual family members. Travel advertising in culturally divided Canada has pictured a wife alone for the English-speaking market segment but a man and wife together for the French-speaking segments of the population, because the latter are traditionally more closely bound by family ties.

---

[26] See http://www.colaturka.com.tr.

[27] Indeed, some say it's still a problem. See Alex Salmond, "Scotland's Strong Independence Movement Is Hardly a 'Faint Blip,'" *The Wall Street Journal*, December 18, 2006, p. A17.

[28] Some might argue that communism has survived in North Korea, Cuba, or the Peoples' Republic of China, but at least in the last case, free enterprise is on the ascendancy. The former look more like dictatorships to most.

[29] Francis Fukuyama, *The End of History and the Last Man* (New York: The Free Press, 1992).

[30] Bernard Asbell, *The Pill: A Biography of the Drug that Changed the World* (New York: Random House, 1995).

The roles and status positions found within a society are influenced by the dictates of social institutions. The caste system in India is one such institution. The election of a low-caste person—once called an "untouchable"—as president made international news because it was such a departure from traditional Indian culture. Decades ago, brushing against an untouchable or even glancing at one was considered enough to defile a Hindu of high status. Even though the caste system has been outlawed, it remains a part of the culture.

Family.   Family forms and functions vary substantially around the world, even around the country. For example, whereas nepotism is seen as a problem in American organizations, it is more often seen as an organizing principle in Chinese[31] and Mexican[32] firms. Or consider the Dutch executive who lives with his mother, wife, and kids in a home in Maastricht that his family has owned for the last 300 years. Then there's the common practice of the high-income folks in Cairo buying an apartment house and filling it up with the extended family—grandparents, married siblings, cousins, and kids. Or how about the Japanese mother caring for her two children pretty much by herself, often sleeping with them at night, while her husband catches up on sleep during his four hours a day commuting via train. And there's the American family in California—both parents work to support their cars, closets, and kids in college, all the while worrying about aging grandparents halfway across the country in Texas.

Even the ratio of male to female children is affected by culture. In most European countries the ratio is about fifty-fifty. However, the gender percentage of boys aged one to six years is 52 in India and of those aged one to four years is 55 in China. Obviously these ratios have long-term implications for families and societies.[33] Moreover, the favoritism of boys is deep-seated in such cultures,[34] as demonstrated by the Chinese *Book of Songs*, circa 800 BC:

> When a son is born
> Let him sleep on the bed,
> Clothe him with fine clothes.
> And give him jade to play with. . . .
> When a daughter is born,
> Let her sleep on the ground,
> Wrap her in common wrappings,
> And give her broken tiles for playthings.

All these differences lead directly to differences in how children think and behave. For example, individualism is being taught the first night the American infant is tucked into her own separate bassinette. Values for egalitarianism are learned the first time Dad washes the dishes in front of the kids or Mom heads off to work or the toddler learns that both Grandpa and little brother are properly called "you." And there is some good news about gender equality to share: The education gap between men and women is narrowing in many places around the world.[35]

Religion.   In most cultures, the first social institution infants are exposed to outside the home takes the form of a church, mosque, shrine, or synagogue. The impact of religion on the value systems of a society and the effect of value systems on marketing must not be underestimated. For example, Protestants believe that one's relationship with God is a

---

[31] Kathy Chen, "China's Growth Places Strains on Family Ties," *The Wall Street Journal*, April 13, 2005, pp. A1, A15.

[32] Anabella Davila and Marta M. Elvira, "Culture and Human Resource Management in Latin America," in Marta M. Elvira and Anabella Davila (eds.), *Managing Human Resources in Latin America* (London: Routledge, 2005), pp. 3–24.

[33] Peter Wonacott, "India's Skewed Sex Ratio Puts GE Sales in Spotlight," *The Wall Street Journal*, April 18, 2007, pp. A1, A14.

[34] Margie Mason, "Bias for Boys Troubling, UN Says," *Chicago Tribune*, November 4, 2007, p. 24.

[35] "Learning and Equality," *The Economist*, November 3, 2007, p. 75.

personal one, and confessions are made directly through prayer. Alternatively, Roman Catholics confess to priests, setting up a hierarchy within the Church. Thus some scholars reason that Protestantism engenders egalitarian thinking. But no matter the details, religion clearly affects people's habits, their outlook on life, the products they buy, the way they buy them, and even the newspapers they read.

The influence of religion is often quite strong, so marketers with little or no understanding of a religion may readily offend deeply. One's own religion is often not a reliable guide to another's beliefs. Most people do not understand religions other than their own, and/or what is "known" about other religions is often incorrect. The Islamic religion is a good example of the need for a basic understanding of all major religions. Between 800 million and 1.2 billion people in the world embrace Islam, yet major multinational companies often offend Muslims. The French fashion house of Chanel unwittingly desecrated the Koran by embroidering verses from the sacred book of Islam on several dresses shown in its summer collections. The designer said he had taken the design, which was aesthetically pleasing to him, from a book on India's Taj Mahal and that he was unaware of its meaning.

In the United States, kids attend school 180 days per year; in China, they attend 251 days—that's six days a week. There's a great thirst for the written word in China—here children read books rented from a street vendor. (© Gary Wolinsky)

To placate a Muslim group that felt the use of the verses desecrated the Koran, Chanel had to destroy the dresses with the offending designs, along with negatives of the photos taken of the garments. Chanel certainly had no intention of offending Muslims, since some of its most important customers embrace Islam. This example shows how easy it is to offend if the marketer, in this case the designer, has not familiarized him- or herself with other religions.

School.   Education, one of the most important social institutions, affects all aspects of the culture, from economic development to consumer behavior. The literacy rate of a country is a potent force in economic development. Numerous studies indicate a direct link between the literacy rate of a country and its capability for rapid economic growth. According to the World Bank, no country has been successful economically with less than 50 percent literacy, but when countries have invested in education the economic rewards have been substantial. Literacy has a profound effect on marketing. Communicating with a literate market is much easier than communicating with one in which the marketer must depend on symbols and pictures. Increasingly, schools are seen as leading to positive cultural changes and progress across the planet.[36]

The Media.   The four social institutions that most strongly influence values and culture are schools, churches, families, and, most recently, the media. In the United States during the past 30 years, women have joined the workforce in growing numbers, substantially reducing the influence of family on American culture. Media time (TV and increasingly the Internet) has replaced family time—much to the detriment of American culture, some argue. At this time, it is hard to gauge the long-term effects of the hours spent with Bart Simpson or an EverQuest cleric-class character. Indeed, the British Prime Minister's cameo on *The Simpsons* reflects its prominence around the world.

American kids spend only 180 days per year in school. Contrast that with 251 days in China, 240 days in Japan, and 200 days in Germany. Indeed, Chinese officials are recognizing the national disadvantages of too much school—narrow minds. Likewise, Americans more and more complain about the detrimental effects of too much media.

---

[36] Emily Flynn Vencat, "The Race Is On," *Newsweek*, August 20, 2007, pp. 40–44.

Government.   Compared with the early (during childhood) and direct influences of family, religion, school, and the media, governments hold relatively little sway. Cultural values and thought patterns are pretty much set before and during adolescence. Most often governments try to influence the thinking and behaviors of adult citizens for the citizens' "own good." For example, the French government has been urging citizens to procreate since the time of Napoleon. Now the government is offering a new "birth bonus" of $800, given to women in their seventh month of pregnancy—despite France having the second highest fertility rate in the EU behind only Ireland (see Exhibit 4.1). Or notice the most recent French and British government-allowed bans of *hijabs* (head scarves worn by Muslim schoolgirls) or the Dutch government initiative to ban *burkas* in that country (full-body coverings warn by Muslim women).[37] Also, major changes in governments, such as the dissolution of the Soviet Union, can have noticeable impacts on personal beliefs and other aspects of culture.[38]

Of course, in some countries, the government owns the media and regularly uses propaganda to form "favorable" public opinions. Other countries prefer no separation of church and state—Iran is currently ruled by religious clerics, for example. Governments also affect ways of thinking indirectly, through their support of religious organizations and schools. For example, both the Japanese and Chinese governments are currently trying to promote more creative thinking among students through mandated changes in classroom activities and hours. Finally, governments influence thinking and behavior through the passage, promulgation, promotion, and enforcement of a variety of laws affecting consumption and marketing behaviors. The Irish government is newly concerned about its citizens' consumption of Guinness and other alcoholic products. Their studies suggest excessive drinking costs the country 2 percent of GDP, so to discourage underage drinking, the laws are being tightened again (see The end of Chapter 16 for more details).

Corporations.   Of course, corporations get a grip on us early through the media. But more important, most innovations are introduced to societies by companies, many times multinational companies. Indeed, merchants and traders have throughout history been the primary conduit for the diffusion of innovations, whether it be over the Silk Road or via today's air freight and/or the Internet.[39] Multinational firms have access to ideas from around the world. Through the efficient distribution of new products and services based on these new ideas, cultures are changed, and new ways of thinking are stimulated. The crucial role of companies as change agents is discussed in detail in the last section of this chapter.

Elements of Culture

Previously culture was defined by listing its five elements: values, rituals, symbols, beliefs, and thought processes. International marketers must design products, distribution systems, and promotional programs with due consideration of each of the five.

Cultural Values

Underlying the cultural diversity that exists among countries are fundamental differences in cultural values.[40] The most useful information on how cultural values influence various types of business and market behavior comes from seminal work by Geert

---

[37] "Dutch Governing Party Would Ban Burka," *International Herald Tribune*, November 16–18, 2006, pp. 1, 7.

[38] Shawn T. Thelen and Earl D. Honeycutt Jr., "Assessing National Identity in Russia between Generations Using the National Identity Scale," *Journal of International Marketing* 12, no. 2 (2004), pp. 58–81.

[39] Steve Hamm and Nandini Lakshman, "Widening Aisles for Indian Shoppers," *BusinessWeek*, April 30, 2007, p. 44.

[40] Ping Ping Fu, Jeff Kennedy, Jasmine Tata, Gary Yukl, Michael Harris Bond, Tai-Kuang Peng, Ekkirala S. Srinivas, Jon P. Howell, Leonel Prieto, Paul Koopman, Jaap J. Boonstra, Selda Pasa, Marie-Francoise Lacassagne, Hiro Higashide, and Adith Cheosakul, "The Impact of Societal Cultural Values and Individual Social Beliefs on the Perceived Effectiveness of Managerial Influence Strategies," *Journal of International Business Studies* 35, no. 4 (2004), pp. 284–305.

Exhibit 4.5
Hofstede's Indexes, Language, and Linguistic Distance

Source: Geert Hofstede, *Culture's Consequences* (Thousand Oaks, CA: Sage, 2001). Used by permission of Geert Hofstede.

Country	IDV Score	PDI Score	UAI Score	Primary Language	Distance from English
Arab countries	38	80	68	Arabic	5
Australia	90	36	51	English	0
Brazil	38	69	76	Portuguese	3
Canada	80	39	48	English (French)	0, 3
Colombia	13	67	80	Spanish	3
Finland	63	33	59	Finnish	4
France	71	68	86	French	3
Germany	67	35	65	German	1
Great Britain	89	35	35	English	0
Greece	35	60	112	Greek	3
Guatemala	6	95	101	Spanish	3
India	48	77	40	Dravidian	3
Indonesia	14	78	48	Bahasa	7
Iran	41	58	59	Farsi	3
Japan	46	54	92	Japanese	4
Mexico	30	81	82	Spanish	3
Netherlands	80	38	53	Dutch	1
New Zealand	79	22	49	English	0
Pakistan	14	55	70	Urdu	3
South Korea	18	60	85	Korean	4
Taiwan	17	58	69	Taiwanese	6
Turkey	37	66	85	Turkish	4
United States	91	40	46	English	0
Uruguay	36	61	100	Spanish	3
Venezuela	12	81	76	Spanish	3

Hofstede.[41] Studying more than 90,000 people in 66 countries, he found that the cultures of the nations studied differed along four primary dimensions. Subsequently, he and hundreds of other researchers have determined that a wide variety of business and consumer behavior patterns are associated with three of those four dimensions.[42] The four[43] dimensions are as follows: the Individualism/Collective Index (IDV), which focuses on self-orientation; the Power Distance Index (PDI), which focuses on authority orientation; the Uncertainty Avoidance Index (UAI), which focuses on risk orientation; and the Masculinity/Femininity Index (MAS), which focuses on assertiveness and achievement. The Individualism/Collectivism dimension has proven the most useful of the four dimensions, justifying entire books on the subject.[44] Because the MAS has proven least useful, we will not consider it further here. Please see Exhibit 4.5 for details.

During the 1990s, Robert House[45] and his colleagues developed a comparable set of data, more focused on values related to leadership and organizations. Their data are by themselves quite valuable, and aspects of their study nicely coincide with Hofstede's data,

[41] Geert Hofstede, *Culture's Consequences*, 2nd ed. (Thousand Oaks: CA: Sage, 2001).

[42] Debanjan Mitra and Peter N. Golder, "Whose Culture Matters? Near-Market Knowledge and Its Impact on Foreign Market Entry Timing," *Journal of Marketing Research* 39, no. 3 (August 2002), pp. 350–65; Boonghee Yoo and Naveen Donthu, "Culture's Consequences, a Book Review," *Journal of Marketing Research* 39, no. 3 (August 2002), pp. 388–89.

[43] In a subsequent study, a fifth dimension, Long-Term Orientation (LTO), was identified as focusing on cultures' temporal orientations. See Geert Hofstede and Michael Harris Bond, "The Confucius Connection," *Organizational Dynamics* 16, no. 4 (Spring 1988), pp. 4–21; Hofstede, 2001.

[44] Harry C. Triandis, *Individualism and Collectivism* (Boulder, CO: Westview Press, 1995).

[45] Robert J. House, Paul J. Hanges, Mansour Javidan, Peter W. Dorfman, and Vipin Gupta (eds.), *Culture, Leadership, and Organizations: The Globe Study of 62 Societies* (Thousand Oaks, CA: Sage, 2004).

collected some 25 years earlier. The importance of this work has yielded important criticisms and discussion.[46]

Individualism/Collectivism Index.

The Individualism/Collective Index refers to the preference for behavior that promotes one's self-interest. Cultures that score high in IDV reflect an "I" mentality and tend to reward and accept individual initiative, whereas those low in individualism reflect a "we" mentality and generally subjugate the individual to the group. This distinction does not mean that individuals fail to identify with groups when a culture scores high on IDV but rather that personal initiative and independence are accepted and endorsed. Individualism pertains to societies in which the ties between individuals are loose; everyone is expected to look after him- or herself and his or her immediate family. Collectivism, as its opposite, pertains to societies in which people from birth onward are integrated into strong, cohesive groups, which throughout people's lifetimes continue to protect them in exchange for unquestioning loyalty.

Power Distance Index.

The Power Distance Index measures the tolerance of social inequality, that is, power inequality between superiors and subordinates within a social system. Cultures with high PDI scores tend to be hierarchical, with members citing social roles, manipulation, and inheritance as sources of power and social status. Those with low scores, in contrast, tend to value equality and cite knowledge and respect as sources of power. Thus people from cultures with high PDI scores are more likely to have a general distrust of others (not those in their groups) because power is seen to rest with individuals and is coercive rather than legitimate. High PDI scores tend to indicate a perception of differences between superior and subordinate and a belief that those who hold power are entitled to privileges. A low score reflects more egalitarian views.

Uncertainty Avoidance Index.

The Uncertainty Avoidance Index measures the tolerance of uncertainty and ambiguity among members of a society. Cultures with high UAI scores are highly intolerant of ambiguity and as a result tend to be distrustful of new ideas or behaviors. They tend to have a high level of anxiety and stress and a concern with security and rule following. Accordingly, they dogmatically stick to historically tested patterns of behavior, which in the extreme become inviolable rules. Those with very high UAI scores thus accord a high level of authority to rules as a means of avoiding risk. Cultures scoring low in uncertainty avoidance are associated with a low level of anxiety and stress, a tolerance of deviance and dissent, and a willingness to take risks. Thus those cultures low in UAI take a more empirical approach to understanding and knowledge, whereas those high in UAI seek absolute truth.

Cultural Values and Consumer Behavior.

A variety of studies have shown cultural values can predict such consumer behaviors as the propensity to complain[47] and movie preferences.[48] Going back to the e-trading example that opened this chapter, we can see how Hofstede's notions of cultural values might help us predict the speed of diffusion

---

[46] Bradley L. Kirkman, Kevin B. Lowe, and Cristina Gibson, "A Quarter Century of Cultures' Consequences: A Review of Empirical Research Incorporating Hofstede's Cultural Values Framework," *Journal of International Business Studies* 37 (2006), pp. 285–320; Kwock Leung, "Editor's Introduction to the Exchange between Hofstede and GLOBE," *Journal of International Business Studies* 37 (2006), p. 881; Geert Hofstede, "What Did GLOBE Really Measure? Researchers' Minds versus Respondents' Minds," *Journal of International Business Studies* 37 (2006), pp. 882–96; Mansour Javidan, Robert J. House, Peter W. Dorfman, Paul J. Hanges, and Mary Sully de Luque, "Conceptualizing and Measuring Cultures and Their Consequences: A Comparative Review of GLOBE's and Hostede's Approaches," *Journal of International Business Studies* 37 (2006), pp. 897–914; Peter B. Smith, "When Elephants Fight, the Grass Gets Trampled: The GLOBE and Hofstede Projects," *Journal of International Business Studies* 37 (2006), pp. 915–21; P. Christopher Earley, "Leading Cultural Research in the Future: A Matter of Paradigms and Taste," *Journal of International Business Studies* 37 (2006), pp. 922–31.

[47] Piotr Chelminski and Robin A. Coulter, "The Effects of Cultural Individualism and Self-Confidence on Propensity to Voice: From Theory to Measurement to Practice," *Journal of International Marketing* 15 (2007), pp. 94–118.

[48] J. Samuel Craig, William H. Greene, and Susan P. Douglas, "Culture Matters: Consumer Acceptance of U.S. Films in Foreign Markets," *Journal of International Marketing* 13 (2006), pp. 80–103.

CROSSING BORDERS 4.2   It's Not the Gift That Counts, but How You Present It

Giving a gift in another country requires careful attention if it is to be done properly. Here are a few suggestions.

Japan

Do not open a gift in front of a Japanese counterpart unless asked, and do not expect the Japanese to open your gift.

Avoid ribbons and bows as part of the gift wrapping. Bows as we know them are considered unattractive, and ribbon colors can have different meanings.

Always offer the gift with both hands.

Europe

Avoid red roses and white flowers, even numbers, and the number 13. Do not wrap flowers in paper.

Do not risk the impression of bribery by spending too much on a gift.

Arab World

Do not give a gift when you first meet someone. It may be interpreted as a bribe.

Do not let it appear that you contrived to present the gift when the recipient is alone. It looks bad unless you know the person well. Give the gift in front of others in less personal relationships.

Latin America

Do not give a gift until after a somewhat personal relationship has developed, unless it is given to express appreciation for hospitality.

Gifts should be given during social encounters, not in the course of business.

Avoid the colors black and purple; both are associated with the Roman Catholic Lenten season.

China

Never make an issue of a gift presentation—publicly or privately. But always deliver gifts with two hands.

Gifts should be presented privately, with the exception of collective ceremonial gifts at banquets or after speeches.

Russia

Generally speaking, Russians take pleasure in giving and receiving gifts—so take plenty. Something for the kids is a good idea.

When invited to a Russian home, bring chocolates or wine, but not vodka.

Bringing a bouquet of flowers is a good idea, but make it an odd number. Even numbers are for funerals.

United States

Gifts that are too ostentatious can cause big problems.

Source: http://www.executiveplanet.com, 2008; James Day Hodgson, Yoshiro Sano, and John L. Graham, *Doing Business in the New Japan* (Latham, MD: Rowman and Littlefield, 2008); Michelle Archer, "From Nose Hair to Networking, a Word of Advice," *USA Today*, July 11, 2005, p. B5.

of such new consumer services as equity investments and electronic auctions in Japan and France. As shown in Exhibit 4.5, the United States scores the highest of all countries on individualism, at 91, with Japan at 46 and France at 71. Indeed, in America, where individualism reigns supreme, we might predict that the "virtually social" activity of sitting alone at one's computer might be most acceptable. In both Japan and France, where values favor group activities, face-to-face conversations with stockbrokers and neighbors might be preferred to impersonal electronic communications.

Similarly, both Japan (92) and France (86) score quite high on Hofstede's Uncertainty Avoidance Index, and America scores low (46). Based on these scores, both Japanese and French investors might be expected to be less willing to take the risks of stock market investments—and indeed, the security of post office deposits or bank savings accounts is preferred. So in both instances, Hofstede's data on cultural values suggest that the diffusion of these innovations will be slower in Japan and France than in the United States. Such predictions are consistent with research findings that cultures scoring higher on individualism and lower on uncertainty avoidance tend to be more innovative.[49]

---

[49] Jan-Benedict E. M. Steenkamp, Frenkel ter Hofstede, and Michel Wedel, "A Cross-National Investigation into the Individual and National Cultural Antecedents of Consumer Innovativeness," *Journal of Marketing* 63 (April 1999), pp. 55–69.

Every Muslim is enjoined to make the hajj, or pilgrimage to Mecca, once in his or her lifetime if physically able. Here, some 2 million faithful come from all over the world annually to participate in what is the largest ritual meeting on Earth.[50] Meanwhile, televised rituals such as the Academy Awards and World Cup soccer draw billions in the form of virtual crowds. (© Mahmoud Mahmoud/ AFP/Getty Images)

Perhaps the most interesting application of cultural values and consumer behavior regards a pair of experiments done with American and Chinese students.[51] Both groups were shown print ads using other-focused emotional appeals (that is, a couple pictured having fun on the beach) versus self-focused emotional appeals (an individual having fun on the beach). The researchers predicted that the individualistic Americans would respond more favorably to the self-focused appeals and the collectivistic Chinese to the other-focused appeals. They found the opposite. The Americans responded better to the other-focused ads and the Chinese vice versa. Their second experiment helped explain these unexpected results. That is, in both cases, what the participants liked about the ads was their *novelty* vis-à-vis their own cultures. So, even in this circumstance, cultural values appear to provide useful information for marketers. However, the complexity of human behavior, values, and culture is manifest.

Rituals   Life is filled with rituals, that is, patterns of behavior and interaction that are learned and repeated. The most obvious ones are associated with major events in life. Marriage ceremonies and funerals are good examples. Perhaps the one most important to most readers of this book is the hopefully proximate graduation ritual—*Pomp and Circumstance*, funny hats, long speeches, and all. Very often these rituals differ across cultures. Indeed, there is an entire *genre* of foreign films about weddings.[52] Perhaps the best is *Monsoon Wedding*. Grooms on white horses and edible flowers are apparently part of the ceremony for high-income folks in New Delhi.

Life is also filled with little rituals, such as dinner at a restaurant or a visit to a department store or even grooming before heading off to work or class in the morning. In a nice restaurant in Madrid, dessert may precede the entrée, but dinner often starts at about

---

[50] Hassan M. Fattar, "The Price of Progress: Transforming Islam's Holiest Sight," *The New York Times International*, March 8, 2007, p. A4.

[51] Jennifer L. Aaker and Patti Williams, "Empathy vs. Pride: The Influence of Emotional Appeals across Cultures," *Journal of Consumer Research* 25 (December 1998), pp. 241–61.

[52] Other excellent films in this genre include *Cousin, Cousine* (French), *Four Weddings and a Funeral* (U.K.), *Bend It Like Beckham* (U.K., Asian immigrants), *Wedding in Galilee* (Palestine/Israel), and *The Wedding Banquet* (Taiwan). Also see Cam Simpson, "For Jordanians, Shotgun Weddings Can Be a Problem," *The Wall Street Journal*, June 5, 2007, pp. A1, A11.

midnight, and the entire process can be a three-hour affair. Walking into a department store in the United States often yields a search for an employee to answer questions. Not so in Japan, where the help bows at the door as you walk in. Visit a doctor in the States and a 15-minute wait in a cold exam room with nothing on but a paper gown is typical. In Spain the exams are often done in the doctor's office. There's no waiting, because you find the doctor sitting at her desk.

Rituals are important. They coordinate everyday interactions and special occasions. They let people know what to expect. In the final chapter of the text, we discuss the ritual of business negotiations, and that ritual varies across cultures as well.

Symbols   Anthropologist Edward T. Hall tells us that culture is communication. In his seminal article about cultural differences in business settings, he talks about the "languages" of time, space, things, friendships, and agreements.[53] Indeed, learning to interpret correctly the symbols that surround us is a key part of socialization. And this learning begins immediately after birth, as we begin to hear the language spoken and see the facial expressions and feel the touch and taste the milk of our mothers.[54] We begin our discussion of symbolic systems with language, the most obvious part and the part that most often involves conscious communication.

Language.

We should mention that for some around the world, language is itself thought of as a social institution, often with political importance. Certainly the French go to extreme lengths and expense to preserve the purity of their *français*. In Canada the language has been the focus of political disputes including secession, though things seem to have calmed down there most recently. Unfortunately, as the number of spoken languages continues to decline worldwide, so does the interesting cultural diversity of the planet.

The importance of understanding the language of a country cannot be overestimated, particularly if you're selling your products in France! The successful international marketer must achieve expert communication, which requires a thorough understanding of the language as well as the ability to speak it. Advertising copywriters should be concerned less with obvious differences between languages and more with the idiomatic and symbolic[55] meanings expressed. It is not sufficient to say you want to translate into Spanish, for instance, because across Spanish-speaking Latin America, the language vocabulary varies widely. *Tambo*, for example, means a roadside inn in Bolivia, Colombia, Ecuador, and Peru; a dairy farm in Argentina and Uruguay; and a brothel in Chile. If that gives you a problem, consider communicating with the people of Papua New Guinea. Some 750 languages, each distinct and mutually unintelligible, are spoken there. This crucial issue of accurate translations in marketing communications is discussed further in Chapters 8 and 16.

The relationship between language and international marketing is important in another way. Recent studies indicate that a new concept, *linguistic distance*, is proving useful to marketing researchers in market segmentation and strategic entry decisions. Linguistic distance has been shown to be an important factor in determining the amount of trade between countries.[56] The idea is that crossing "wider" language differences increases transaction costs.

---

[53] Edward T. Hall, "The Silent in Overseas Business," *Harvard Business Review*, May–June 1960, pp. 87–96. A discussion of the salience of Hall's work appears in John L. Graham, "Culture and Human Resources Management," in Alan M. Rugman and Thomas L. Brewer (eds.), *The Oxford Handbook of International Business* (Oxford: Oxford University Press, 2008), pp. 503–36.

[54] The spices a nursing mother consumes actually affect the flavor of the milk she produces.

[55] Eric Yorkston and Gustavo E. De Mello, "Linguistic Gender Marking and Categorization," *Journal of Consumer Research* 32 (2005), pp. 224–34.

[56] Pankaj Ghemawat, "Distance Still Matters: The Hard Reality of Global Expansion," *Harvard Business Review*, September 2001, pp. 137–47; Jennifer D. Chandler and John L. Graham, "Using Formative Indicators to Discern the Meaning of Corruption and Its Implications for International Marketing," working paper, University of California, Irvine, 2008.

Over the years, linguistics researchers have determined that languages around the world conform to family trees[57] based on the similarity of their forms and development. For example, Spanish, Italian, French, and Portuguese are all classified as Romance languages because of their common roots in Latin. Distances can be measured on these linguistic trees. If we assume English[58] to be the starting point, German is one branch away, Danish two, Spanish three, Japanese four, Hebrew five, Chinese six, and Thai seven. These "distance from English" scores are listed for a sampling of cultures in Exhibit 4.5.

Other work in the area is demonstrating a direct influence of language on cultural values, expectations, and even conceptions of time.[59] For example, as linguistic distance from English increases, individualism decreases.[60] These studies are among the first in this genre, and much more work needs to be done. However, the notion of linguistic distance appears to hold promise for better understanding and predicting cultural differences in both consumer and management values, expectations, and behaviors.

Moreover, the relationship between language spoken and cultural values holds deeper implications. That is, as English spreads around the world via school systems and the Internet, cultural values of individualism and egalitarianism will spread with it. For example, both Chinese Mandarin speakers and Spanish speakers must learn two words for "you" (*ni* and *nin* and *tu* and *usted*, respectively). The proper use of the two depends completely on knowledge of the social context of the conversation. Respect for status is communicated by the use of *nin* and *usted*. In English there is only one form for "you."[61] Speakers can ignore social context and status and still speak correctly. It's easier, and social status becomes less important. *Français* beware!

Aesthetics as Symbols.
Art communicates. Indeed, Confucius is reputed to have opined, "A picture is worth a thousand words." But, of course, so can a dance or a song. As we acquire our culture, we learn the meaning of this wonderful symbolic system represented in its aesthetics, that is, its arts,[62] folklore, music, drama, dance, dress,[63] and cosmetics.[64] Customers everywhere respond to images, myths, and metaphors that help them define their personal and national identities and relationships within a context of culture and product benefits. The uniqueness of a culture can be spotted quickly in symbols having distinct meanings.[65] Think about the subtle earth tones of the typical Japanese restaurant compared with the bright reds and yellows in the decor of ethnic Chinese restaurants. Similarly, a long-standing rivalry between the Scottish Clan Lindsay and Clan Donald caused McDonald's Corporation some consternation when it chose the Lindsay tartan design for new uniforms for its restaurant hosts and hostesses. Godfrey Lord Macdonald, Chief of Clan Donald, was outraged and complained that McDonald's

---

[57] For the most comprehensive representation of global linguistic trees, see Jiangtian Chen, Robert R. Sokal, and Merrit Ruhlen, "Worldwide Analysis of Genetic and Linguistic Relationships of Human Populations," *Human Biology* 67, no. 4 (August 1995), pp. 595–612.

[58] We appreciate the ethnocentricity in using English as the starting point. However, linguistic trees can be used to measure distance from any language. For example, analyses using French or Japanese as the starting point have proven useful as well.

[59] Lera Boroditsky, "Does Language Shape Thought? Mandarin and English Speakers' Conceptions of Time," *Cognitive Psychology* 43 (2001), pp. 1–22.

[60] Joel West and John L. Graham, "A Linguistics-Based Measure of Cultural Distance and Its Relationship to Managerial Values," *Management International Review* 44, no. 3 (2004), pp. 239–60.

[61] In English, there was historically a second second-person form. That is, "thee" was the informal form up until the last century. Even in some Spanish-speaking countries, such as Costa Rica, the "tu" is being dropped in a similar manner.

[62] Japanese-style animation is making a strong entry to pop American culture. See Ian Rowley, Chester Dawson, and Hiroko Tashiro, "The Anime Biz: Still an Adolescent," *BusinessWeek*, June 27, 2005, pp. 50–52.

[63] "Muslims and the Veil, the Meaning of Freedom," *The Economist*, May 12, 2007, pp. 63–64.

[64] Heather Timmons, "Telling India's Modern Women They Have Power, Even over Their Skin Tone," *The New York Times*, May 30, 2007, p. C5.

[65] Robert Frank, "Why Jewels Are Tops in Middle East, but Art Takes Lead in Europe," *The Wall Street Journal*, June 29, 2007, p. W2.

Exhibit 4.6
Metaphorical Journeys
through 23 Nations

Source: From Martin J. Gannon,
*Understanding Global Cultures,
Metaphorical Journeys through 23
Nations*, 2nd ed. Copyright © 2001.
Reprinted by permission of Sage
Publications.

The Thai Kingdom	The Traditional British House
The Japanese Garden	The Malaysian *Balik Kampung*
India: The Dance of Shiva	The Nigerian Marketplace
Bedouin Jewelry and Saudi Arabia	The Israeli Kibbutzim and Moshavim
The Turkish Coffeehouse	The Italian Opera
The Brazilian Samba	Belgian Lace
The Polish Village Church	The Mexican Fiesta
Kimchi and Korea	The Russian Ballet
The German Symphony	The Spanish Bullfight
The Swedish *Stuga*	The Portuguese Bullfight
Irish Conversations	The Chinese Family Altar
American Football	

had a "complete lack of understanding of the name." Of course, the plaid in the uniforms is now the least of the firm's worries as British consumers are becoming more concerned about health-related matters.

Without a culturally correct interpretation of a country's aesthetic values, a host of marketing problems can arise. Product styling must be aesthetically pleasing to be successful, as must advertisements and package designs. Insensitivity to aesthetic values can offend, create a negative impression, and, in general, render marketing efforts ineffective or even damaging. Strong symbolic meanings may be overlooked if one is not familiar with a culture's aesthetic values. The Japanese, for example, revere the crane as being very lucky because it is said to live a thousand years; however, the use of the number four should be avoided completely because the word for four, *shi*, is also the Japanese word for death. Thus teacups are sold in sets of five, not four, in Japan.

Finally, one author has suggested that understanding different cultures' metaphors is a key doorway to success. In Exhibit 4.6, we list the metaphors Martin Gannon[66] identified to represent cultures around the world. In the fascinating text, he compares "American Football" (with its individualism, competitive specialization, huddling, and ceremonial celebration of perfection) to the "Spanish Bullfight" (with its pompous entrance parade, audience participation, and the ritual of the fight) to the "Indian Dance of the Shiva" (with its cycles of life, family, and social interaction). Empirical evidence is beginning to accumulate supporting the notion that metaphors matter.[67] Any good international marketer would see fine fodder for advertising campaigns in the insightful descriptions depicted.

Beliefs   Of course, much of what we learn to believe comes from religious training. But to consider matters of true faith and spirituality adequately here is certainly impossible. Moreover, the relationship between superstition and religion is not at all clear. For example, one explanation of the origin about the Western aversion to the number 13 has to do with Jesus sitting with his 12 disciples at the Last Supper.

However, many of our beliefs are secular in nature. What Westerners often call superstition may play quite a large role in a society's belief system in another part of the world. For example, in parts of Asia, ghosts, fortune telling, palmistry, blood types, head-bump reading, phases of the moon, faith healers, demons, and soothsayers can all be integral elements of society. Surveys of advertisements in Greater China show a preference for an "8" as the last digit in prices listed—the number connotes "prosperity" in Chinese culture.[68] The Beijing Olympics started on 8–8–08 for a reason! And recall the Japanese concern about Year of the Fire Horse discussed earlier.

---

[66] Martin J. Gannon, *Understanding Global Cultures, Metaphorical Journeys through 23 Nations*, 2nd ed. (Thousand Oaks, CA: Sage, 2001).

[67] Cristina B. Gibson and Mary E. Zeller-Bruhn, "Metaphors and Meaning: An Intercultural Analysis of the Concept of Work," *Administrative Science Quarterly* 46, no. 2 (2001), pp. 274–303.

[68] Lee C. Simmons and Robert M. Schindler, "Cultural Superstitions and the Price Endings in Chinese Advertising," *Journal of International Marketing* 11, no. 2 (2003), pp. 101–111.

Marketers have two options when introducing an innovation to a culture: They can wait for changes to occur, or they can cause change. The former requires hopeful waiting for eventual cultural changes that prove their innovations of value to the culture; the latter involves introducing an idea or product and deliberately setting about to overcome resistance and to cause change that accelerates the rate of acceptance.[82] The folks at Fidelity Investments in Japan, for example, pitched a tent in front of Tokyo's Shinjuku train station and showered commuters with investment brochures and demonstrations of its Japanese language WebXpress online stock trading services to cause faster changes in Japanese investor behavior. However, as mentioned previously, the changes have not happened fast enough for most foreign firms targeting this business and similar financial services.[83]

Obviously not all marketing efforts require change to be accepted. In fact, much successful and highly competitive marketing is accomplished by a strategy of *cultural congruence*. Essentially this strategy involves marketing products similar to ones already on the market in a manner as congruent as possible with existing cultural norms, thereby minimizing resistance. However, when marketing programs depend on cultural change to be successful, a company may decide to leave acceptance to a strategy of unplanned change—that is, introduce a product and hope for the best. Or a company may employ a strategy of planned change—that is, deliberately set out to change those aspects of the culture offering resistance to predetermined marketing goals.

As an example of unplanned cultural change, consider how the Japanese diet has changed since the introduction of milk and bread soon after World War II.[84] Most Japanese, who were predominantly fish eaters, have increased their intake of animal fat and protein to the

---

[82] "Broadway in Paris: Musicals Change Their Tune in France," *The Wall Street Journal*, October 3, 2007, p. B11.

[83] Edwina Gibbs, "Tough Sell in Senior Market [in Japan]," *Los Angeles Times*, October 29, 2007, p. C5; Andy C. W. Chui and Chuck C. Y. Kwok, "National Culture and Life Insurance Consumption," *Journal of International Business Studies*, 39 (2008), 88-101.

[84] The articles we found did not mention this change in diet as a potential factor in the prevalence of stomach cancer in Japan. However, given that medical science has yet to completely understand the disease, one has to wonder. And the other major environmental catastrophe of the time, the atomic bombs, is not mentioned either.

MTV meets Mom in Mumbai (formerly Bombay), India. Culture does change—dress and even names of major cities! Even so, a local resident tells us everyone still calls it Bombay despite the official alteration. (© Joe McNally)

point that fat and protein now exceed vegetable intake. As many McDonald's hamburgers are likely to be eaten in Japan as the traditional rice ball wrapped in edible seaweed, and American hamburgers are replacing many traditional Japanese foods. Burger King purchased Japan's homegrown Morinaga Love restaurant chain, home of the salmon burger—a patty of salmon meat, a slice of cheese, and a layer of dried seaweed, spread with mayonnaise and stuck between two cakes of sticky Japanese rice pressed into the shape of a bun—an eggplant burger, and other treats. The chain was converted and now sells Whoppers instead of the salmon-rice burger.

The Westernized diet has caused many Japanese to become overweight. To counter this trend, the Japanese are buying low-calorie, low-fat foods to help shed excess weight and are flocking to health clubs. All this began when U.S. occupation forces introduced bread, milk, and steak to Japanese culture. The effect on the Japanese was unintentional, but nevertheless, change occurred. Had the intent been to introduce a new diet—that is, a strategy of planned change—specific steps could have been taken to identify resistance to dietary change and then to overcome these resistances, thus accelerating the process of change.

Marketing strategy is judged culturally in terms of acceptance, resistance, or rejection. How marketing efforts interact with a culture determines the degree of success or failure. All too often marketers are not aware of the scope of their impact on a host culture. If a strategy of planned change is implemented, the marketer has some responsibility to determine the consequences of such action.

Consequences of Innovation

When product diffusion (acceptance) occurs, a process of social change may also occur. One issue frequently raised concerns the consequences of the changes that happen within a social system as a result of acceptance of an innovation. The marketer seeking product diffusion and adoption may inadvertently bring about change that affects the very fabric of a social system. Consequences of diffusion of an innovation may be functional or dysfunctional, depending on whether the effects on the social system are desirable or undesirable. In most instances, the marketer's concern is with perceived functional consequences—the positive benefits of product use. Indeed, in most situations, innovative products for which the marketer purposely sets out to gain cultural acceptance have minimal, if any, dysfunctional consequences, but that cannot be taken for granted.

On the surface, it would appear that the introduction of a processed feeding formula into the diet of babies in underdeveloped countries where protein deficiency is a health problem would have all the functional consequences of better nutrition and health, stronger and faster growth, and so forth. Much evidence, however, suggests that in many situations, the dysfunctional consequences far exceed the benefits. In Nicaragua (and numerous other developing countries), as a result of the introduction of the formula, a significant number of babies annually were changed from breast feeding to bottle feeding before the age of six months. In the United States, with appropriate refrigeration and sanitation standards, a similar pattern exists with no apparent negative consequences. In Nicaragua, however, where sanitation methods are inadequate, a substantial increase in dysentery and diarrhea and a much higher infant mortality rate resulted.

A change from breast feeding to bottle feeding at an early age without the users' complete understanding of purification had caused dysfunctional consequences. This dysfunction was the result of two factors: the impurity of the water used with the formula and the loss of the natural immunity to childhood disease that a mother's milk provides. This situation was a case of planned change that resulted in devastating consequences. The infant formula companies set out to purposely change traditional breast feeding to bottle feeding. Advertising, promotions of infant formula using testimonials from nurses and midwives, and abundant free samples were used to encourage a change in behavior. It was a very successful marketing program, but the consequences were unintentionally dysfunctional. An international boycott of infant formula companies' products by several groups resulted in the company agreeing to alter its marketing programs to encourage breast feeding. This problem first occurred some 30 years ago and is still causing trouble for the company. The consequences of the introduction of an innovation can be serious for society and the company responsible, whether the act was intentional or not.[85]

Some marketers may question their responsibility beyond product safety as far as the consequences of their role as change agents are concerned. The authors' position is that the marketer has responsibility for the dysfunctional results of marketing efforts, whether intentional or not. Foreign marketers may cause cultural changes that can create dysfunctional consequences. If proper analysis indicates that negative results can be anticipated from the acceptance of an innovation, it is the responsibility of the marketer to design programs not only to gain acceptance for a product but also to eliminate any negative cultural effects.

---

[85] See the Nestlé Infant Formula case toward the end of this book for complete details regarding the ongoing infant formula controversy.

Summary

A complete and thorough appreciation of the origins (geography, history, political economy, technology, and social institutions) and elements (cultural values, rituals, symbols, beliefs, and ways of thinking) of culture may well be the single most important gain for a foreign marketer in the preparation of marketing plans and strategies. Marketers can control the product offered to a market—its promotion, price, and eventual distribution methods—but they have only limited control over the cultural environment within which these plans must be implemented. Because they cannot control all the influences on their marketing plans, they must attempt to anticipate the eventual effect of the uncontrollable elements and plan in such a way that these elements do not preclude the achievement of marketing objectives. They can also set about to effect changes that lead to quicker acceptance of their products or marketing programs.

Planning marketing strategy in terms of the uncontrollable elements of a market is necessary in a domestic market as well, but when a company is operating internationally, each new environment that is influenced by elements unfamiliar and sometimes unrecognizable to the marketer complicates the task. For these reasons, special effort and study are needed to absorb enough understanding of the foreign culture to cope with the uncontrollable features. Perhaps it is safe to generalize that of all the tools the foreign marketer must have, those that help generate empathy for another culture are the most valuable. Each of the cultural elements is explored in depth in subsequent chapters. Specific attention is given to business customs, political culture, and legal culture in the following chapters.

Questions

1. Define the following terms:

culture	cultural values
cultural sensitivity	linguistic distance
social institutions	cultural borrowing
factual knowledge	strategy of unplanned change
ethnocentrism	aesthetics
interpretive knowledge	strategy of planned change
strategy of cultural congruence	

2. Which role does the marketer play as a change agent?

3. Discuss the three cultural change strategies a foreign marketer can pursue.

4. "Culture is pervasive in all marketing activities." Discuss.

5. What is the importance of cultural empathy to foreign marketers? How do they acquire cultural empathy?

6. Why should a foreign marketer be concerned with the study of culture?

7. What is the popular definition of culture? Where does culture come from?

8. "Members of a society borrow from other cultures to solve problems that they face in common." What does this mean? What is the significance to marketing?

9. "For the inexperienced marketer, the 'similar-but-different' aspect of culture creates an illusion of similarity that usually does not exist." Discuss and give examples.

10. Outline the elements of culture as seen by an anthropologist. How can a marketer use this cultural scheme?

11. Social institutions affect culture and marketing in a variety of ways. Discuss, giving examples.

12. "Markets are the result of the three-way interaction of a marketer's efforts, economic conditions, and all other elements of the culture." Comment.

13. What are some particularly troublesome problems caused by language in foreign marketing? Discuss.

14. Suppose you were asked to prepare a cultural analysis for a potential market. What would you do? Outline the steps and comment briefly on each.

15. Cultures are dynamic. How do they change? Are there cases in which changes are not resisted but actually preferred? Explain. What is the relevance to marketing?

16. How can resistance to cultural change influence product introduction? Are there any similarities in domestic marketing? Explain, giving examples.

17. Innovations are described as either functional or dysfunctional. Explain and give examples of each.

18. Defend the proposition that a multinational corporation has no responsibility for the consequences of an innovation beyond the direct effects of the innovation, such as the product's safety, performance, and so forth.

19. Find a product whose introduction into a foreign culture may cause dysfunctional consequences and describe how the consequences might be eliminated and the product still profitably introduced.

5

culture, management style, and business systems

CHAPTER LEARNING OBJECTIVES

What you should learn from Chapter 5:

- The necessity for adapting to cultural differences

- How and why management styles vary around the world

- The extent and implications of gender bias in other countries

- The importance of cultural differences in business ethics

- The differences between relationship-oriented and information-oriented cultures

Global Perspective

DO BLONDES HAVE MORE FUN IN JAPAN?

Recounts one American executive, "My first trip to Japan was pretty much a disaster for several reasons. The meetings didn't run smoothly because every day at least 20, if not more, people came walking in and out of the room just to look at me. It is one thing to see a woman at the negotiation table, but to see a woman who happens to be blonde, young, and very tall by Japanese standards (5'8" with no shoes) leading the discussions was more than most of the Japanese men could handle."

"Even though I was the lead negotiator for the Ford team, the Japanese would go out of their way to avoid speaking directly to me. At the negotiation table I purposely sat in the center of my team, in the spokesperson's strategic position. Their key person would not sit across from me, but rather two places down. Also, no one would address questions and/or remarks to me—to everyone (all male) on our team—but none to me. They would never say my name or acknowledge my presence. And most disconcerting of all, they appeared to be laughing at me. We would be talking about a serious topic such as product liability, I would make a point or ask a question, and after a barrage of Japanese they would all start laughing."

Another example regards toys and consumer behavior. For years, Barbie dolls sold in Japan looked different from their U.S. counterparts. They had Asian facial features, black hair, and Japanese-inspired fashions.

Then about five years ago, Mattel Inc. conducted consumer research around the world and learned something surprising: The original Barbie, with her yellow hair and blue eyes, played as well in Hong Kong as it did in Hollywood. Girls didn't care if Barbie didn't look like them, at least if you believed their marketing research.

"It's all about fantasies and hair," says Peter Broegger, general manager of Mattel's Asian operations. "Blonde Barbie sells just as well in Asia as in the United States."

So Mattel began rethinking one of the basic tenets of its $55 billion global industry—that children in different countries want different playthings. The implications were significant for kids, parents, and particularly the company. In the past, giants such as Mattel, Hasbro Inc., and Lego Co. produced toys and gear in a variety of styles. But Mattel went the other direction, designing and marketing one version worldwide. Sales plummeted, forcing a Barbie makeover that most recently includes Hello Kitty clothes and a new video game, iDesign.

Sources: James D. Hodgson, Yoshihiro Sano, and John L. Graham, *Doing Business with the New Japan, Succeeding in America's Richest International Market* (Latham, MD: Rowman & Littlefield, 2008); Lisa Banon and Carlta Vitzthum, "One-Toy-Fits-All: How Industry Learned to Love the Global Kid," *The Wall Street Journal*, April 29, 2003, p. A1; Melinda Fulmer, "Mattel Sees Results from Barbie Makeover," *Los Angeles Times*, February 1, 2005, pp. C1, C12; "Barbie Dressed by Kitty," *Sunday Mail*, June 3, 2007, p. 2; "Barbie Takes to the Runway at the 2008 Consumer Electronics Show," *Business Wire*, January 7, 2008.

Perhaps nothing causes more problems for Americans negotiating in other countries than their impatience. Everyone around the world knows that delaying tactics work well against time-conscious U.S. bargainers.

Culture, including all its elements, profoundly affects management style and overall business systems. This is not a new idea. German sociologist Max Weber made the first strong case back in 1930.[1] Culture not only establishes the criteria for day-to-day business behavior but also forms general patterns of values and motivations.[2] Executives are largely captives of their heritages and cannot totally escape the elements of culture they learned growing up.

In the United States, for example, the historical perspective of individualism and "winning the West" seems to be manifest in individual wealth or corporate profit being dominant measures of success. Japan's lack of frontiers and natural resources and its dependence on trade have focused individual and corporate success criteria on uniformity, subordination to the group, and society's ability to maintain high levels of employment. The feudal background of southern Europe tends to emphasize maintenance of both individual and corporate power and authority while blending those feudal traits with paternalistic concern for minimal welfare for workers and other members of society. Various studies identify North Americans as individualists, Japanese as consensus oriented and committed to the group, and central and southern Europeans as elitists and rank conscious. Although these descriptions are stereotypical, they illustrate cultural differences that are often manifest in business behavior and practices. Such differences also coincide quite well with Hofstede's scores listed in Exhibit 4.5 in the last chapter.[3]

A lack of empathy for and knowledge of foreign business practices can create insurmountable barriers to successful business relations. Some businesses plot their strategies with the idea that their counterparts from other business cultures are similar to themselves and are moved by similar interests, motivations, and goals—that they are "just like us." Even though that may be true in some respects, enough differences exist to cause frustration, miscommunication, and, ultimately, failed business opportunities if these differences are not understood and responded to properly.

Knowledge of the *management style*—that is, the business culture, management values, and business methods and behaviors—existing in a country and a willingness to accommodate the differences are important to success in an international market. Unless marketers remain flexible by accepting differences in basic patterns of thinking, local business tempo, religious practices, political structure, and family loyalty, they are hampered, if not prevented, from reaching satisfactory conclusions to business transactions. In such situations, obstacles take many forms, but it is not unusual to have one negotiator's business proposition accepted over another's simply because "that one understands us."

This chapter focuses on matters specifically related to management style. Besides an analysis of the need for adaptation, it reviews differences in management styles and ethics and concludes with a discussion of culture's influence on strategic thinking.

Required Adaptation

Adaptation is a key concept in international marketing, and willingness to adapt is a crucial attitude. Adaptation, or at least accommodation, is required on small matters as well as large ones.[4] In fact, small, seemingly insignificant situations are often the most

[1] Max Weber, *The Protestant Ethic and Spirit of Capitalism* (London: George Allen & Unwin, 1930, 1976).

[2] Rohit Deshpande and John U. Farley, "Organizational Culture, Market Orientation, Innovativeness, and Firm Performance: An International Odyssey," *International Journal of Research in Marketing* 21, no. 1 (2004), pp. 3–22.

[3] Geert Hofstede, *Culture's Consequences*, 2nd ed. (Thousand Oaks, CA: Sage, 2001).

[4] Including strategic approaches—see Leo Y. M. Sin, Alan C. B. Tse, Oliver H. M. Yau, Raymond P. M. Chow, and Jenny Lee, "Market Orientation, Relationship Marketing Orientation, and Business Performance: The Moderating Effects of Economic Ideology and Industry Type," *Journal of International Marketing* 13, no. 1 (2005), pp. 36–57.

crucial. More than tolerance of an alien culture is required. Affirmative acceptance, that is, open tolerance may be needed as well. Through such affirmative acceptance, adaptation becomes easier because empathy for another's point of view naturally leads to ideas for meeting cultural differences.[5]

As a guide to adaptation, all who wish to deal with individuals, firms, or authorities in foreign countries should be able to meet 10 basic criteria: (1) open tolerance, (2) flexibility, (3) humility, (4) justice/fairness, (5) ability to adjust to varying tempos, (6) curiosity/interest, (7) knowledge of the country, (8) liking for others, (9) ability to command respect, and (10) ability to integrate oneself into the environment. In short, add the quality of adaptability to the qualities of a good executive for a composite of the successful international marketer. It is difficult to argue with these 10 items. As one critic commented, "They border on the 12 Boy Scout laws." However, as you read this chapter, you will see that it is the obvious that we sometimes overlook.

Degree of Adaptation

Adaptation does not require business executives to forsake their ways and change to local customs; rather, executives must be aware of local customs and be willing to accommodate to those differences that can cause misunderstandings. Essential to effective adaptation is awareness of one's own culture and the recognition that differences in others can cause anxiety, frustration, and misunderstanding of the host's intentions. The self-reference criterion (SRC) is especially operative in business customs. If we do not understand our foreign counterpart's customs, we are more likely to evaluate that person's behavior in terms of what is familiar to us. For example, from an American perspective a Brazilian executive interrupting frequently during a business meeting may seem quite rude, even though such behavior simply reflects a cultural difference in conversational coordination.

The key to adaptation is to remain American but to develop an understanding of and willingness to accommodate the differences that exist. A successful marketer knows that in China it is important to make points without winning arguments; criticism, even if asked for, can cause a host to lose face. In Germany, it is considered discourteous to use first names unless specifically invited to do so. Instead, address a person as Herr, Frau, or Fraulein with the last name. In Brazil, do not be offended by the Brazilian inclination to touch during conversation. Such a custom is not a violation of your personal space but rather the Brazilian way of greeting, emphasizing a point, or making a gesture of goodwill and friendship. A Chinese, German, or Brazilian does not expect you to act like one of them. After all, you are American, not Chinese, German, or Brazilian, and it would be foolish for an American to give up the ways that have contributed so notably to American success. It would be equally foolish for others to give up their ways. When different cultures meet, open tolerance and a willingness to accommodate each other's differences are necessary. Once a marketer is aware of cultural differences and the probable consequences of failure to adapt or accommodate, the seemingly endless variety of customs must be assessed. Where does one begin? Which customs should be absolutely adhered to? Which others can be ignored? Fortunately, among the many obvious differences that exist between cultures, only a few are troubling.

Imperatives, Electives, and Exclusives

Business customs can be grouped into *imperatives,* customs that must be recognized and accommodated; *electives,* customs to which adaptation is helpful but not necessary; and *exclusives,* customs in which an outsider must not participate. An international marketer must appreciate the nuances of cultural imperatives, cultural electives, and cultural exclusives.

Cultural Imperatives.

Cultural imperatives are the business customs and expectations that must be met and conformed to or avoided if relationships are to be successful. Successful businesspeople know the Chinese word *guanxi*,[6] the Japanese *ningen kankei,* or

[5] P. Christopher Earley and Elaine Mosakowski, "Cultural Intelligence," *Harvard Business Review,* October 2004, pp. 139–46.

[6] Alaka N. Rao, Jone L. Pearce, and Katherine Xin, "Governments, Reciprocal Exchange, and Trust Among Business Associates," *Journal of International Business Studies* 36 (2005), pp. 104–18; Kam-hon Lee, Gong-ming Qian, Julie H. Yu, and Ying Ho, "Trading Favors for Marketing Advantage: Evidence from Hong Kong, China, and the United States" *Journal of International Marketing* 13 (2005), pp. 1–35.

the Latin American *compadre*. All refer to friendship, human relations, or attaining a level of trust.[7] They also know there is no substitute for establishing friendship in some cultures before effective business negotiations can begin.

Informal discussions, entertaining, mutual friends, contacts, and just spending time with others are ways *guanxi*, *ningen kankei*, *compadre*, and other trusting relationships are developed. In those cultures in which friendships are a key to success, the businessperson should not slight the time required for their development. Friendship motivates local agents to make more sales, and friendship helps establish the right relationship with end users, which leads to more sales over a longer period. Naturally, after-sales service, price, and the product must be competitive, but the marketer who has established *guanxi*, *ningen kankei*, or *compadre* has the edge. Establishing friendship is an imperative in many cultures. If friendship is not established, the marketer risks not earning trust and acceptance, the basic cultural prerequisites for developing and retaining effective business relationships.

The significance of establishing friendship cannot be overemphasized, especially in those countries where family relationships are close. In China, for example, the outsider is, at best, in fifth place in order of importance when deciding with whom to conduct business. The family is first, then the extended family, then neighbors from one's hometown, then former classmates, and only then, reluctantly, strangers—and the last only after a trusting relationship has been established.

BEIJING, CHINA: German Chancellor Angela Merkel and Chinese Prime Minister Wen Jiabao toast after the EU–China Business Summit at the Great Hall of the People in Beijing. The summit was boosted by the settlement of a trade row that had left 80 million Chinese-made garments piled up in European seaports, unable to be delivered to shops under a quota pact agreed to at the time. Drinking half a bottle is a cultural elective, but taking a sip is more of an imperative in this case. *(Reuters/Landov)*

In some cultures, a person's demeanor is more critical than in other cultures. For example, it is probably never acceptable to lose your patience, raise your voice, or correct someone in public, no matter how frustrating the situation. In some cultures such behavior would only cast you as boorish, but in others, it could end a business deal. In Asian cultures it is imperative to avoid causing your counterpart to lose face. In China, to raise your voice, to shout at a Chinese person in public, or to correct one in front of his or her peers will cause that person to lose face.

A complicating factor in cultural awareness is that what may be an imperative to avoid in one culture is an imperative to do in another. For example, in Japan, prolonged eye contact is considered offensive, and it is imperative that it be avoided. However, with Arab and Latin American executives, it is important to make strong eye contact, or you run the risk of being seen as evasive and untrustworthy.

Cultural Electives. Cultural electives relate to areas of behavior or to customs that cultural aliens may wish to conform to or participate in but that are not required. In other words, following the custom in question is not particularly important but is permissible. The majority of customs fit into this category. One need not greet another man with a kiss (a custom in some countries), eat foods that disagree with the digestive system (so long as the refusal is gracious), or drink alcoholic beverages (if for health, personal, or religious reasons). However, a symbolic attempt to participate in such options is not only acceptable but also may help establish rapport. It demonstrates that the marketer has studied the culture. Japanese do not expect a Westerner to bow and to understand the ritual of bowing among Japanese, yet a symbolic bow indicates interest and some sensitivity to Japanese culture that is acknowledged as a gesture of goodwill. It may help pave the way to a strong, trusting relationship.

A cultural elective in one county may be an imperative in another. For example, in some cultures, one can accept or tactfully and politely reject an offer of a beverage, whereas in other cases, the offer of a beverage is a special ritual and to refuse it is an insult. In the Czech Republic, an aperitif or other liqueur offered at the beginning of a business meeting, even in the morning, is a way to establish goodwill and trust. It is a sign that you are being

---

[7] Srilata Zaheer and Akbar Zaheer, "Trust across Borders," *Journal of International Business Studies* 37 (2006), pp. 21–29.

welcomed as a friend. It is imperative that you accept unless you make it clear to your Czech counterpart that the refusal is because of health or religion. Chinese business negotiations often include banquets at which large quantities of alcohol are consumed in an endless series of toasts. It is imperative that you participate in the toasts with a raised glass of the offered beverage, but to drink is optional. Your Arab business associates will offer coffee as part of the important ritual of establishing a level of friendship and trust; you should accept, even if you only take a ceremonial sip. Cultural electives are the most visibly different customs and thus more obvious. Often, it is compliance with the less obvious imperatives and exclusives that is more critical.

Cultural Exclusives.   Cultural exclusives are those customs or behavior patterns reserved exclusively for the locals and from which the foreigner is barred. For example, a Christian attempting to act like a Muslim would be repugnant to a follower of Mohammed. Equally offensive is a foreigner criticizing or joking about a country's politics, mores, and peculiarities (that is, peculiar to the foreigner), even though locals may, among themselves, criticize such issues. There is truth in the old adage, "I'll curse my brother, but if you curse him, you'll have a fight." Few cultural traits are reserved exclusively for locals, but a foreigner must carefully refrain from participating in those that are reserved.

Foreign managers need to be perceptive enough to know when they are dealing with an imperative, an elective, or an exclusive and have the adaptability to respond to each. There are not many imperatives or exclusives, but most offensive behaviors result from not recognizing them. It is not necessary to obsess over committing a faux pas. Most sensible businesspeople will make allowances for the occasional misstep. But the fewer you make, the smoother the relationship will be. By the way, you can ask for help. That is, if you have a good relationship with your foreign counterparts, you can always ask them to tell you when and how you have "misbehaved."

The Impact of American Culture on Management Style

There are at least three reasons to focus briefly on American culture and management style. First, for American readers, it is important to be aware of the elements of culture influencing decisions and behaviors. Such a self-awareness will help American readers adapt to working with associates in other cultures. Second, for readers new to American culture, it is useful to better understand your business associates from the States. The U.S. market is the biggest export market in the world. And hopefully, this knowledge will help everyone be more patient while conducting business across borders. Third, since the late 1990s, American business culture has been exported around the world, just as in the 1980s Japanese management practices were imitated almost everywhere. Management practices developed in the U.S. environment will not be appropriate and useful everywhere.[8] That is clear. So understanding their bases will help everyone make decisions about applying, adapting, or rejecting American practices. Indeed, most often Peter Drucker's advice will apply: "Different people have to be managed differently."[9]

There are many divergent views regarding the most important ideas on which normative U.S. cultural concepts are based. Those that occur most frequently in discussions of cross-cultural evaluations are represented by the following:

- "Master of destiny" viewpoint.
- Independent enterprise as the instrument of social action.
- Personnel selection and reward based on merit.
- Decisions based on objective analysis.
- Wide sharing in decision making.

---

[8] See Michael Song, Jinhong Xie, and Barbara Dyer, "Antecedents and Consequences of Marketing Managers' Conflict-Handling Behaviors," *Journal of Marketing* 64 (January 2000), pp. 50–66, for an excellent discussion of the differences among Chinese, Japanese, U.K., and U.S. managers.

[9] Peter F. Drucker, *Management Challenges for the 21st Century* (New York: HarperBusiness, 1999), p. 17.

- Never-ending quest for improvement.
- Competition producing efficiency.

The "master of destiny" philosophy is fundamental to U.S. management thought. Simply stated, people can substantially influence the future; they are in control of their own destinies. This viewpoint also reflects the attitude that though luck may influence an individual's future, on balance, persistence, hard work, a commitment to fulfill expectations, and effective use of time give people control of their destinies. In contrast, many cultures have a more fatalistic approach to life. They believe individual destiny is determined by a higher order and that what happens cannot be controlled.

In the United States, approaches to planning, control, supervision, commitment, motivation, scheduling, and deadlines are all influenced by the concept that individuals can control their futures. Recall from Chapter 4 that the United States scored highest on Hofstede's individualism scale.[10] In cultures with more collectivistic and fatalistic beliefs, these good business practices may be followed, but concern for the final outcome is different. After all, if one believes the future is determined by an uncontrollable higher order, then what difference does individual effort really make?

The acceptance of the idea that *independent enterprise* is an instrument for social action is the fundamental concept of U.S. corporations. A corporation is recognized as an entity that has rules and continuity of existence and is a separate and vital social institution. This recognition can result in strong feelings of obligation to serve the company. Indeed, the company may take precedence over family, friends, or activities that might detract from what is best for the company. This idea is in sharp contrast to the attitudes held by Mexicans, who feel strongly that personal relationships are more important in daily life than work and the company, and Chinese, who consider a broader set of stakeholders as crucial.[11]

Consistent with the view that individuals control their own destinies is the belief that personnel selection and reward must be made on *merit*. The selection, promotion, motivation, or dismissal of personnel by U.S. managers emphasizes the need to select the best-qualified persons for jobs, retaining them as long as their performance meets standards of expectations and continuing the opportunity for upward mobility as long as those standards are met. In other cultures where friendship or family ties may be more important than the vitality of the organization, the criteria for selection, organization, and motivation are substantially different from those in U.S. companies. In some cultures, organizations expand to accommodate the maximum number of friends and relatives. If one knows that promotions are made on the basis of personal ties and friendships rather than on merit, a fundamental motivating lever is lost. However, in many other cultures, social pressure from one's group often motivates strongly. Superstitions can even come into play in personnel selection; in Japan, a person's blood type can influence hiring decisions![12]

The very strong belief in the United States that business decisions are based on *objective analysis* and that managers strive to be scientific has a profound effect on the U.S. manager's attitudes toward objectivity in decision making and accuracy of data. Although judgment and intuition are important tools for making decisions, most U.S. managers believe decisions must be supported and based on accurate and relevant information. Thus, in U.S. business, great emphasis is placed on the collection and free flow of information to all levels within the organization and on frankness of expression in the evaluation of business opinions or decisions. In other cultures, such factual and rational support for decisions is not as important; the accuracy of data and even the proper reporting of data are not prime prerequisites. Furthermore, existing data frequently are for the eyes of a select few. The frankness of expression and openness in dealing with data, characteristic of U.S. businesses, do not fit easily into some cultures.

---

[10] Hofstede, *Culture's Consequences.*

[11] Chung-Leung Luk, Oliver H. M. Yau, Alan C. B. Tse, Leo Y. M. Sin, and Raymond P. M. Chow, "Stakeholder Orientation and Business Performance: The Case of Service Companies in China," *Journal of International Marketing* 13, no. 1 (2005), pp. 89–110.

[12] David Picker, "Blood, Sweat, and Type O," *The New York Times*, December 14, 2006, p. C15.

Compatible with the views that one controls one's own destiny and that advancement is based on merit is the prevailing idea of *wide sharing in decision making*. Although decision making is not a democratic process in U.S. businesses, there is a strong belief that individuals in an organization require and, indeed, need the responsibility of making decisions for their continued development. Thus decisions are frequently decentralized, and the ability as well as the responsibility for making decisions is pushed down to lower ranks of management. In many cultures, decisions are highly centralized, in part because of the belief that only a few in the company have the right or the ability to make decisions. In the Middle East, for example, only top executives make decisions.

A key value underlying the American business system is reflected in the notion of a *never-ending quest for improvement*. The United States has always been a relatively activist society; in many walks of life, the prevailing question is "Can it be done better?" Thus management concepts reflect the belief that change is not only normal but also necessary, that nothing is sacred or above improvement. In fact, the merit on which one achieves advancement is frequently tied to one's ability to make improvements. Results are what count; if practices must change to achieve results, then change is in order. In other cultures, the strength and power of those in command frequently rest not on change but on the premise that the status quo demands stable structure. To suggest improvement implies that those in power have failed; for someone in a lower position to suggest change would be viewed as a threat to another's private domain rather than the suggestion of an alert and dynamic individual.

Perhaps most fundamental to Western management practices is the notion that *competition is crucial for efficiency*, improvement, and regeneration. Gordon Gekko put it most banally in the movie *Wall Street:* "Greed is good." Adam Smith in his *The Wealth of Nations* wrote one of the most important sentences in the English language: "By pursuing his own interests he frequently promotes that of the society more effectually than when he really intended to promote it."[13] This "invisible hand" notion justifies competitive behavior because it improves society and its organizations. Competition among salespeople (for example, sales contests) is a good thing because it promotes better individual performance and, consequently, better corporate performance. When companies compete, society is

---

[13] Adam Smith, *The Wealth of Nations*, Book IV (1776; reprint, New York: Modern Library, 1994), p. 485.

What's different about Adam Smith's, "By pursuing his own interests he frequently promotes that of society more effectually than when he really intended to promote it," and Gordon Gekko's, "Greed is good" statements? It's the adverb. Smith didn't say "always," "most of the time," or even "often." He said "frequently." Today many on Wall Street ignore this crucial difference. *(left: © Bettmann/CORBIS; right: 20th Century Fox/The Kobal Collection)*

better off, according to this reasoning. However, managers and policymakers in other cultures often do not share this "greed is good" view. Cooperation is more salient, and efficiencies are attained through reduced transaction costs. These latter views are more prevalent in collectivistic cultures such as China and Japan.

Management Styles around the World[14]

Because of the diverse structures, management values,[15] and behaviors encountered in international business, there is considerable variation in the ways business is conducted.[16] No matter how thoroughly prepared a marketer may be when approaching a foreign market, a certain amount of cultural shock occurs when differences in the contact level, communications emphasis, tempo, and formality of foreign businesses are encountered. Ethical standards differ substantially across cultures, as do rituals such as sales interactions and negotiations. In most countries, the foreign trader is also likely to encounter a fairly high degree of government involvement. Among the four dimensions of Hofstede's cultural values discussed in Chapter 4, the Individualism/Collectivism Index (IDV)[17] and Power Distance Index (PDI) are especially relevant in examining methods of doing business cross-culturally.

Authority and Decision Making

Business size, ownership, public accountability, and cultural values that determine the prominence of status and position (PDI) combine to influence the authority structure of business.[18] In high-PDI countries such as Mexico and Malaysia, understanding the rank and status of clients and business partners is much more important than in more egalitarian (low-PDI) societies such as Denmark and Israel. In high-PDI countries, subordinates are not likely to contradict bosses, but in low-PDI countries, they often do. Although the international businessperson is confronted with a variety of authority patterns that can complicate decision making in the global environment,[19] most are a variation of three typical patterns: top-level management decisions, decentralized decisions, and committee or group decisions.

Top-level management decision making is generally found in situations in which family or close ownership[20] gives absolute control to owners and businesses are small enough to allow such centralized decision making. In many European businesses, such as those in France, decision-making authority is guarded jealously by a few at the top who exercise tight control. In other countries, such as Mexico and Venezuela, where a semifeudal, land-equals-power heritage exists, management styles are characterized as autocratic and paternalistic.

---

[14] A Web site that provides information about management styles around the world is www.globalnegotiationresources.com.

[15] T. Lenartowich and J. P. Johnson, "A Cross-National Assessment of the Values of Latin American Managers: Contrasting Hues or Shades of Gray?" *Journal of International Business Studies* 34, no. 3 (2003), pp. 266–81.

[16] This includes how the notion of teamwork varies—see Cristina B. Gibson and Mary E. Zellmer-Bruhn, "Applying the Concept of Teamwork Metaphors to the Management of Teams in Multicultural Contexts," *Organizational Dynamics* 31, no. 2 (2002), pp. 101–16.

[17] Ping Ping Fu et al., "The Impact of Societal Cultural Values and Individual Social Beliefs on the Perceived Effectiveness of Managerial Influence Strategies: A Meso Approach," *Journal of International Business Studies* 35, no. 4 (2004), pp. 284–305.

[18] Michael K. Hui, Kevin Au, and Henry Fock, "Empowerment Effects across Cultures," *Journal of International Business Studies* 35, no. 1 (2004), pp. 46–60; William Newburry and Nevena Yakova, "Standardization Preferences: A Function of National Culture, Work Interdependence, and Local Embeddedness," *Journal of International Business Studies* 37 (2006), pp. 44–60.

[19] Xiao-ping Chen and Shu Li, "Cross-National Differences in Cooperative Decision-Making in Mixed-Motive Business Contexts: The Mediating Effect of Vertical and Horizontal Individualism," *Journal of International Business Studies* 36 (2005), pp. 622–36.

[20] Several researchers have empirically demonstrated the influence and downside of such authority structures. See Kathy Fogel, "Oligarchic Family Control, Social Economic Outcomes, and the Quality of Government," *Journal of International Business Studies* 37 (2006), pp. 603–22; Naresh Kharti, Eric W. K. Tsang, and Thomas M. Begley, "Cronyism: A Cross-Cultural Analysis," *Journal of International Business Studies* 37 (2006), pp. 61–75; Ekin K. Pellegrini and Terri A. Scandura, "Leader-Member Exchange (LMX), Paternalism, and Delegation in the Turkish Business Culture: An Empirical Investigation," *Journal of International Business Studies* 37 (2006), pp. 264–79.

CROSSING BORDERS 5.1 · Don't Beat Your Mother-in-Law!

The crowding and collectivism of Chinese culture provide fertile ground for hierarchy. Add in a little Confucian advice, and status relationships become central for understanding Chinese business systems. Confucius's teachings were the foundation for Chinese education for 2,000 years, until 1911. He defined five cardinal relationships: between ruler and ruled, husband and wife, parents and children, older and younger brothers, and friends. Except for the last, all relationships were hierarchical. The ruled, wives, children, and younger brothers were all counseled to trade obedience and loyalty for the benevolence of their ruler, husband, parents, and older brothers, respectively. Strict adherence to these vertical relations yielded social harmony, that being the antidote for the violence and civil war of his time.

Obedience and deference to one's superiors remain a strong value in Chinese culture. The story of the Cheng family illustrates the historical salience of social hierarchy and high power distance:

In October 1865, Cheng Han-cheng's wife had the insolence to beat her mother-in-law. This was regarded as such a heinous crime that the following punishment was meted out: Cheng and his wife were both skinned alive, in front of the mother, their skin displayed at city gates in various towns and their bones burned to ashes. Cheng's granduncle, the eldest of his close relatives, was beheaded; his uncle and two brothers, and the head of the Cheng clan, were hanged. The wife's mother, her face tattooed with the words "neglected the daughter's education," was paraded through seven provinces. Her father was beaten 80 strokes and banished to a distance of 3,000 *li*. The heads of the family in the houses to the right and left of Cheng's were beaten 80 strokes and banished to Heilung-kiang. The educational officer in town was beaten 60 strokes and banished to a distance of 1,000 *li*. Cheng's nine-month-old boy was given a new name and put in the county magistrate's care. Cheng's land was to be left in waste "forever." All this was recorded on a stone stele, and rubbings of the inscriptions were distributed throughout the empire.

We recommend you have your children read this story! But seriously, notice the authorities held responsible the entire social network for the woman's breach of hierarchy. Status is no joke among Chinese. Age and rank of executives and other status markers must be taken into account during business negotiations with Chinese. American informality and egalitarianism will not play well on the western side of the Pacific.

Sources: Dau-lin Hsu, "The Myth of the 'Five Human Relations' of Confucius," *Monumenta Sinica* 1970, pp. 29, 31, quoted in Gary G. Hamilton, "Patriarchalism in Imperial China and Western Europe: A Revision of Weber's Sociology of Domination," *Theory and Society* 13, pp. 393–425; N. Mark Lam and John L. Graham, *China Now, Doing Business in the World's Most Dynamic Market* (New York: McGraw-Hill, 2006).

Decision-making participation by middle management tends to be deemphasized; dominant family members make decisions that tend to please the family members more than to increase productivity. This description is also true for government-owned companies in which professional managers have to follow decisions made by politicians, who generally lack any working knowledge about management. In Middle Eastern countries, the top man makes all decisions and prefers to deal only with other executives with decision-making powers. There, one always does business with an individual per se rather than an office or title.

As businesses grow and professional management develops, there is a shift toward decentralized management decision making. Decentralized decision making allows executives at different levels of management to exercise authority over their own functions. As mentioned previously, this approach is typical of large-scale businesses with highly developed management systems, such as those found in the United States. A trader in the United States is likely to be dealing with middle management, and title or position generally takes precedence over the individual holding the job.

Committee decision making is by group or consensus. Committees may operate on a centralized or decentralized basis, but the concept of committee management implies something quite different from the individualized functioning of the top management and decentralized decision-making arrangements just discussed. Because Asian cultures and religions tend to emphasize harmony and collectivism, it is not surprising that group decision making predominates there. Despite the emphasis on rank and hierarchy in Japanese social structure, business emphasizes group participation, group harmony, and group decision making—but at the top management level.

The demands of these three types of authority systems on a marketer's ingenuity and adaptability are evident. In the case of the authoritative and delegated societies, the chief problem is to identify the individual with authority. In the committee decision setup, every committee member must be convinced of the merits of the proposition or product in question. The marketing approach to each of these situations differs.

Management Objectives and Aspirations

The training and background (i.e., cultural environment) of managers significantly affect their personal and business outlooks.[21] Society as a whole establishes the social rank or status of management, and cultural background dictates patterns of aspirations and objectives among businesspeople. One study reports that higher CEO compensation is found in Scandinavian firms exposed to Anglo-American financial influence and in part reflects a pay premium for increased risk of dismissal.[22] These cultural influences affect the attitude of managers toward innovation, new products, and conducting business with foreigners. To fully understand another's management style, one must appreciate an individual's values, which are usually reflected in the goals of the business organization and in the practices that prevail within the company. In dealing with foreign business, a marketer must be particularly aware of the varying objectives and aspirations of management.

Security and Mobility.

Personal security and job mobility relate directly to basic human motivation and therefore have widespread economic and social implications. The word *security* is somewhat ambiguous, and this very ambiguity provides some clues to managerial variation. To some, security means a big paycheck and the training and ability required for moving from company to company within the business hierarchy; for others, it means the security of lifetime positions with their companies; to still others, it means adequate retirement plans and other welfare benefits. European companies, particularly in the more hierarchical (PDI) countries, such as France and Italy, have a strong paternalistic orientation, and it is assumed that individuals will work for one company for the majority of their lives. For example, in Britain, managers place great importance on individual achievement and autonomy, whereas French managers place great importance on competent supervision, sound company policies, fringe benefits, security, and comfortable working conditions. French managers have much less mobility than British.

Personal Life.

For many individuals, a good personal and/or family life takes priority over profit, security, or any other goal. In his worldwide study of individual aspirations, David McClelland[23] discovered that the culture of some countries stressed the virtue of a good personal life as far more important than profit or achievement. The hedonistic outlook of ancient Greece explicitly included work as an undesirable factor that got in the way of the search for pleasure or a good personal life. Alternatively, according to Max Weber,[24] at least part of the standard of living that we enjoy in the United States today can be attributed to the hard-working Protestant ethic from which we derive much of our business heritage. Flextime arrangements that allow businesspeople more time to work from home are a compromise that may or may not work. Many U.S. companies are reconsidering such arrangements,[25] and Korean and Japanese have not yet adopted the idea, despite their excellent information technology resources.[26]

To the Japanese, personal life is company life. Many Japanese workers regard their work as the most important part of their overall lives. The Japanese work ethic—maintenance of a sense of purpose—derives from company loyalty and frequently results in the Japanese

---

[21] Ted Baker, Eric Gedajlovic, and Michael Lubatkin, "A Framework for Comparing Entrepreneurship Processes across Nations," *Journal of International Business Studies* 36 (2005), pp. 492–504.

[22] Lars Oxelheim and Trond Randoy, "The Anglo-American Financial Influence on CEO Compensation in non–Anglo-American Firms," *Journal of International Business Studies* 36 (2005), pp. 470–83.

[23] David C. McClelland, *The Achieving Society* (New York: The Free Press, 1985).

[24] Weber, *The Protestant Ethic.*

[25] Jena McGregor, "Flextime: Honing the Balance," *BusinessWeek*, December 11, 2006, pp. 64–65.

[26] Moon Ihlwan and Kenji Hall, "New Tech, Old Habits," *BusinessWeek*, March 26, 2007, pp. 48–49.

CROSSING BORDERS 5.2 The American Tourist and the Mexican Fisherman

An American tourist was at the pier of a small coastal Mexican village when a small boat with just one fisherman docked. Inside the small boat were several large yellowfin tuna. The tourist complimented the Mexican on the quality of the fish and asked how long it took to catch them.

The Mexican replied, "Only a little while."

The tourist then asked, "Why didn't you stay out longer and catch more fish?"

The Mexican replied, "With this I have enough to support my family's needs."

The tourist then asked, "But what do you do with the rest of your time?"

The Mexican fisherman said, "I sleep late, fish a little, play with my children, take a siesta with my wife, Maria, stroll into the village each evening where I sip wine and play guitar with my amigos. I have a full and busy life."

The tourist scoffed, "I can help you. You should spend more time fishing and with the proceeds, buy a bigger boat. With the proceeds from the bigger boat you could buy several boats. Eventually you would have a fleet of fishing boats. Instead of selling your catch to a middleman you could sell directly to the processor, eventually opening your own cannery. You would control the product, processing, and distribution. You could leave this small village and move to Mexico City, then Los Angeles, and eventually to New York City where you could run your ever-expanding enterprise."

The Mexican fisherman asked, "But, how long will this take?"

The tourist replied, "15 to 20 years."

"But what then?" asked the Mexican.

The tourist laughed and said, "That's the best part. When the time is right you would sell your company stock to the public and become very rich, you would make millions."

"Millions?. . . Then what?"

The American said, "Then you would retire. Move to a small coastal fishing village where you would sleep late, fish a little, play with your grandkids, take a siesta with your wife, stroll to the village in the evenings where you could sip wine and play your guitar with your amigos."

Source: Author unknown.

employee maintaining identity with the corporation. Although this notion continues to be true for the majority, strong evidence indicates that the faltering Japanese economy has affected career advancement patterns[27] and has moved the position of the Japanese "salary man" from that of one of Japan's business elite to one of some derision. Japan's business culture is gradually shifting away from the lifelong employment that led to the intense company loyalty.[28] Now even Japanese formality at the office is bowing to higher oil prices; ties and buttoned collars are being shed to leave thermostats set at 82 degrees.[29]

We can get some measure of the work–personal life trade-off made in different cultures with reference to Exhibit 5.1. As a point of reference, 40 hours per week times 50 weeks equals 2,000 hours. The Americans appear to be in the middle of hours worked, far above the Europeans and below the Southeast Asians. Most Americans are getting about two weeks of paid vacation, while in Europe they are taking between four and six weeks! In Singapore and Hong Kong, Saturday is a workday. Although we do not list the numbers for China, the new pressures of free enterprise are adding hours and stress there as well.[30] However, the scariest datum isn't in the table. While hours worked are decreasing almost everywhere, in the States, the numbers are increasing, up 36 hours from 1990.[31] Thank you Max Weber! We wonder: How will things be in 2020?[32]

---

[27] George Graen, Ravi Dharwadkar, Rajdeep Grewal, and Mitsuru Wakabayashi, "Japanese Career Progress: An Empirical Examination," *Journal of International Business Studies* 37 (2006), pp. 148–61.

[28] "Sayonara, Salaryman," *The Economist*, January 5, 2008, pp. 68–69.

[29] Sebastian Moffett, "Japan Sweats It Out As It Wages War on Air Conditioning," *The Wall Street Journal*, September 11, 2007, pp. A1, A16.

[30] Michelle Conlin, "Go-Go-Going to Pieces in China," *BusinessWeek*, April 23, 2007, p. 88.

[31] Molly Selvin, "Group Hopes Workers Take Time to Seek More Time Off," *Los Angeles Times*, October 20, 2007, p. C1.

[32] We notice that most predictions about the future of the workplace miss the mark substantially. See Elizabeth Woyke, "Brave New Rat Race," *BusinessWeek*, August 20/27, 2007, p. 95.

Exhibit 5.1
Annual Hours Worked

Source: International Labor
Organization, 2004.

Britain	1,719
Canada	1,776
Germany	1,480
Hong Kong	2,287
Japan	1,842
Norway	1,399
Singapore	2,307
United States	1,979

By the way, the worst work–personal life trade-off seems to be among junior doctors. In the United States, they work 80 hours per week and, because of the associated fatigue, make many mistakes. In Ireland they work 75 hours per week. In both countries, pressure is being put on the medical community to cut down.

Affiliation and Social Acceptance.   In some countries, acceptance by neighbors and fellow workers appears to be a predominant goal within business. The Asian outlook is reflected in the group decision making so important in Japan, and the Japanese place high importance on fitting in with their group. Group identification is so strong in Japan that when a worker is asked what he does for a living, he generally answers by telling you he works for Sumitomo or Mitsubishi or Matsushita, rather than that he is a chauffeur, an engineer, or a chemist.

Power and Achievement.   Although there is some power seeking by business managers throughout the world, power seems to be a more important motivating force in South American countries. In these countries, many business leaders are not only profit oriented but also use their business positions to become social and political leaders. Related, but different, are the motivations for achievement also identified by management researchers in the United States. One way to measure achievement is by money in the bank; another is high rank—both aspirations particularly relevant to the United States.

Communication Styles   Edward T. Hall, professor of anthropology and for decades a consultant to business and government on intercultural relations, tells us that communication involves much more than just words. His article "The Silent Language of Overseas Business," which appeared in the *Harvard Business Review* in 1960,[33] remains a most worthwhile read. In it he

---

[33] *Harvard Business Review*, May–June 1960, pp. 87–96.

Speaking of office space: Notice the individualism reflected in the American cubicles and the collectivism demonstrated by the Japanese office organization. (*left: © Ed Kashi/Corbis; right: © ANDY RAIN/Bloomberg News/Landov*)

Exhibit 5.2

Context, Communication, and Cultures: Edward Hall's Scale

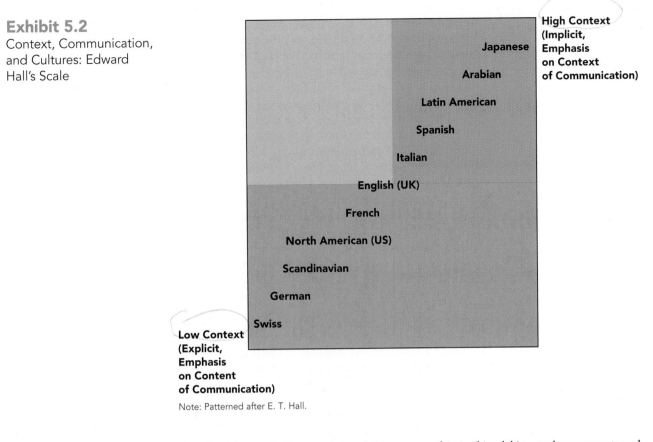

Note: Patterned after E. T. Hall.

describes the symbolic meanings of *time*, *space*, *things*, *friendships*, and *agreements* and how they vary across cultures. In 1960 Hall could not have anticipated the innovations brought on by the Internet. However, all of his ideas about cross-cultural communication apply to that medium as well. We begin here with a discussion of communication in the face-to-face setting and then move to the electronic media.

Face-to-Face Communication.   No language readily translates into another because the meanings of words differ widely among languages. For example, the word "marriage," even when accurately translated, can connote very different things in different languages—in one it may mean love, in another restrictions. Although language is the basic communication tool of marketers trading in foreign lands, managers, particularly from the United States, often fail to develop even a basic understanding of just one other language, much less master the linguistic nuances that reveal unspoken attitudes and information.

Verbal communication, no matter how imprecise, is at least explicit. But much business communication depends on implicit messages that are not verbalized. Edward Hall goes on to say, "In some cultures, messages are explicit; the words carry most of the information. In other cultures . . . less information is contained in the verbal part of the message since more is in the context."

On the basis of decades of anthropological fieldwork, Hall[34] places 11 cultures along a high-context/low-context continuum (see Exhibit 5.2). Communication in a high-context culture depends heavily on the contextual (*who* says it, *when* it is said, *how* it is said) or nonverbal aspects of communication, whereas the low-context culture depends more on explicit, verbally expressed communications.

A brief exemplar of the high-/low-context dimension of communication style regards an international marketing executive's description of a Los Angeles business entertainment

---

[34] Edward T. Hall, "Learning the Arabs' Silent Language," *Psychology Today*, August 1979, pp. 45–53. Hall has several books that should be read by everyone involved in international business, including *The Silent Language* (New York: Doubleday, 1959), *The Hidden Dimension* (New York: Doubleday, 1966), and *Beyond Culture* (New York: Anchor Press-Doubleday, 1976).

event: "I picked him [a German client] up at his hotel near LAX and asked what kind of food he wanted for dinner. He said, 'Something local.' Now in LA local food is Mexican food. I'd never met anyone that hadn't had a taco before! We went to a great Mexican place in Santa Monica and had it all, guacamole, salsa, enchiladas, burritos, a real Alka-Seltzer kind of night. When we were done I asked how he liked the food. He responded rather blandly, 'It wasn't very good.'"

The American might have been taken aback by his client's honest, and perhaps too direct, answer. However, the American knew well about German frankness[35] and just rolled with the "blow." Germans, being very low-context oriented, just deliver the information without any social padding. Most Americans would soften the blow some with an answer more like, "It was pretty good, but maybe a bit too spicy." And a high-context oriented Japanese would really pad the response with something like, "It was very good. Thanks." But then the Japanese would never order Mexican food again.

An American or German might view the Japanese response as less than truthful, but from the Japanese perspective, he was just preserving a harmonious relationship. Indeed, the Japanese have two words for truth, *honne* (true mind) and *tatemae* (official stance).[36] The former delivers the information, and the latter preserves the relationship. And in high-context Japan, the latter is often more important.

Internet Communications.

The message on a business-to-business Web site is an extension of the company and should be as sensitive to business customs as any other company representative would be. Once a message is posted, it can be read anywhere, at any time. As a consequence, the opportunity to convey an unintended message is infinite. Nothing about the Web will change the extent to which people identify with their own languages and cultures; thus language should be at the top of the list when examining the viability of a company's Web site.

Estimates are that 78 percent of today's Web site content is written in English, but an English e-mail message cannot be understood by 35 percent of all Internet users. A study of businesses on the European continent highlights the need for companies to respond in the languages of their Web sites. One-third of the European senior managers surveyed said they would not tolerate English online. They do not believe that middle managers can use English well enough to transact business on the Internet.

At the extreme are the French, who even ban the use of English terms. The French Ministry of Finance issued a directive that all official French civil service correspondence must avoid common English-language business words such as *start-up* and *e-mail;* instead, *jeune pousse* (literally, "a young plant") and *courrier électronique* are recommended.

The solution to the problem is to have country-specific Web sites, like those of IBM and Marriott. Dell Computer, for example, makes its Premier Pages Web sites, built for its business clients, available in 12 languages. A host of companies specialize in Web site translations; in addition, software programs are available to translate the company message into another language. However, cultural and linguistic correctness remains a problem with machine translation. If not properly done, English phrases are likely to be translated in a way that will embarrass or even damage a company. One way to avoid this issue is to prepare the original source material in easy-to-translate English, devoid of complicated phrases, idioms, or slang. Unfortunately, no machine translation is available that can manage all the nuances of language or syntax.

It would be ideal if every representative of your company spoke fluently the language of and understood the culture of your foreign customers or business associates; but that is an impossible goal for most companies. However, there is no reason why every person who

---

[35] Interestingly, the etymology of the term "frankness" has to do with the Franks, an ancient Germanic tribe that settled along the Rhine. This is not mere coincidence; it's history again influencing symbols (that is, language)!

[36] James D. Hodgson, Yoshihiro Sano, and John L. Graham, *Doing Business with the New Japan* (Boulder, CO: Rowman & Littlefield, 2000).

accesses a company's Web site should not be able to communicate in his or her own language if a company wants to be truly global.

In addition to being language friendly, a Web site should be examined for any symbols, icons, and other nonverbal impressions that could convey an unwanted message. Icons that are frequently used on Web sites can be misunderstood. For example, an icon such as a hand making a high-five sign will be offensive in Greece; an image of a thumb-to-index finger, the A-OK gesture, will infuriate visitors in Brazil; a two-fingered peace sign when turned around has a very crude meaning to the British; and AOL's "You've Got Mail" looks a lot like a loaf of bread to a European. Colors can also pose a problem; green is a sacred color in some Middle Eastern cultures and should not be used for something frivolous like a Web background.

Finally, e-mail use and usage rates by managers are also affected by culture. That is, businesspeople in high-context cultures do not use the medium to the same extent as those in low-context cultures. Indeed, the structure of the Japanese language has at least hindered the diffusion of Internet technologies in that country.[37] Moreover, businesspeople in Hong Kong behave less cooperatively in negotiations using e-mail than in face-to-face encounters.[38] Much of the contextual information so important in high-context cultures simply cannot be signaled via the computer.

Formality and Tempo

The breezy informality and haste that seem to characterize American business relationships appear to be American exclusives that businesspeople from other countries not only fail to share but also fail to appreciate. A German executive commented that he was taken aback when employees of his Indiana client called him by his first name. He noted, "In Germany you don't do that until you know someone for 10 years—and never if you are at a lower rank." This apparent informality, however, does not indicate a lack of commitment to the job. Comparing British and American business managers, an English executive commented about the American manager's compelling involvement in business: "At a cocktail party or a dinner, the American is still on duty."

Even though Northern Europeans seem to have picked up some American attitudes in recent years, do not count on them being "Americanized." As one writer says, "While using first names in business encounters is regarded as an American vice in many countries, nowhere is it found more offensive than in France," where formality still reigns. Those who work side by side for years still address one another with formal pronouns. France is higher on Hofstede's Power Distance Index (PDI) than the United States, and such differences can lead to cultural misunderstandings. For example, the formalities of French business practices as opposed to Americans' casual manners are symbols of the French need to show rank and Americans' tendency to downplay it. Thus the French are dubbed snobbish by Americans, while the French consider Americans crude and unsophisticated.

Haste and impatience are probably the most common mistakes of North Americans attempting to trade in the Middle East. Most Arabs do not like to embark on serious business discussions until after two or three opportunities to meet the individual they are dealing with; negotiations are likely to be prolonged. Arabs may make rapid decisions once they are prepared to do so, but they do not like to be rushed, and they do not like deadlines. The managing partner of the Kuwait office of KPMG Peat Marwick says of the "fly-in visit" approach of many American businesspeople, "What in the West might be regarded as dynamic activity—the 'I've only got a day here' approach—may well be regarded here as merely rude."

Marketers who expect maximum success have to deal with foreign executives in ways that are acceptable to the foreigner. Latin Americans depend greatly on friendships but establish these friendships only in the South American way: slowly, over a considerable

---

[37] Ibid.

[38] Guang Yang and John L. Graham, "The Impact of Computer-Mediated Communications on the Process and Outcomes of Buyer–Seller Negotiations," working paper, University of California, Irvine, 2006.

period of time. A typical Latin American is highly formal until a genuine relationship of respect and friendship is established. Even then the Latin American is slow to get down to business and will not be pushed. In keeping with the culture, *mañana* (tomorrow) is good enough. How people perceive time helps explain some of the differences between U.S. managers and those from other cultures.

P-Time versus M-Time

North Americans are a more time-bound culture than Middle Eastern and Latin cultures. Our stereotype of those cultures is "they are always late," and their view of us is "you are always prompt." Neither statement is completely true, though both contain some truth. What is true, however, is that we are a very time-oriented society—time is money to us—whereas in other cultures, time is to be savored, not spent.

Edward T. Hall defines two time systems in the world: monochronic and polychronic time. *M-time*, or *monochronic time*, typifies most North Americans, Swiss, Germans, and Scandinavians. These Western cultures tend to concentrate on one thing at a time. They divide time into small units and are concerned with promptness. M-time is used in a linear way, and it is experienced as almost tangible, in that one saves time, wastes time, bides time, spends time, and loses time. Most low-context cultures operate on M-time. *P-time*, or *polychronic time*, is more dominant in high-context cultures, where the completion of a human transaction is emphasized more than holding to schedules. P-time is characterized by the simultaneous occurrence of many things and by "a great involvement with people." P-time allows for relationships to build and context to be absorbed as parts of high-context cultures.

One study comparing perceptions of punctuality in the United States and Brazil found that Brazilian timepieces were less reliable and public clocks less available than in the United States. Researchers also found that Brazilians more often described themselves as late arrivers, allowed greater flexibility in defining *early* and *late*, were less concerned about being late, and were more likely to blame external factors for their lateness than were Americans.[39] Please see comparisons of 31 countries in Exhibit 5.3.

The American desire to get straight to the point and get down to business is a manifestation of an M-time culture, as are other indications of directness. The P-time system gives rise to looser time schedules, deeper involvement with individuals, and a wait-and-see-what-develops attitude. For example, two Latin colleagues conversing would likely opt to be late for their next appointments rather than abruptly terminate the conversation before it came to a natural conclusion. P-time is characterized by a much looser notion of being on time or late. Interruptions are routine, delays to be expected. It is not so much putting things off until *mañana* as it is the concept that human activity is not expected to proceed like clockwork.

Most cultures offer a mix of P-time and M-time behavior but have a tendency to adopt either more P-time or M-time with regard to the role time plays. Some are similar to Japan, where appointments are adhered to with the greatest M-time precision but P-time is followed once a meeting begins. The Japanese see U.S. businesspeople as too time bound and driven by schedules and deadlines that thwart the easy development of friendships.

When businesspeople from M-time and P-time meet, adjustments need to be made for a harmonious relationship. Often clarity can be gained by specifying tactfully, for example, whether a meeting is to be on "Mexican time" or "American time." An American who has been working successfully with the Saudis for many years says he has learned to take plenty of things to do when he travels. Others schedule appointments in their offices so they can work until their P-time friend arrives. The important thing for the U.S. manager to learn is adjustment to P-time in order to avoid the anxiety and frustration that comes from being out of synchronization with local time. As global markets expand, however, more businesspeople from P-time cultures are adapting to M-time.

---

[39] Robert Levine, *The Geography of Time* (New York: Basic Books, 1998).

Exhibit 5.3
Speed Is Relative

Rank of 31 countries for overall pace of life [combination of three measures: (1) minutes downtown pedestrians take to walk 60 feet, (2) minutes it takes a postal clerk to complete a stamp-purchase transaction, and (3) accuracy in minutes of public clocks].

Source: Robert Levine, "The Pace of Life in 31 Countries," *American Demographics,* November, 1997. Reprinted with permission from the November 1997 issue of *American Demographics.* Copyright, Crain Communications, Inc. 2004.

Overall Pace	Country	Walking 60 Feet	Postal Service	Public Clocks
1	Switzerland	3	2	1
2	Ireland	1	3	11
3	Germany	5	1	8
4	Japan	7	4	6
5	Italy	10	12	2
6	England	4	9	13
7	Sweden	13	5	7
8	Austria	23	8	9
9	Netherlands	2	14	25
10	Hong Kong	14	6	14
11	France	8	18	10
12	Poland	12	15	8
13	Costa Rica	16	10	15
14	Taiwan	18	7	21
15	Singapore	25	11	4
16	United States	6	23	20
17	Canada	11	21	22
18	South Korea	20	20	16
19	Hungary	19	19	18
20	Czech Republic	21	17	23
21	Greece	14	13	29
22	Kenya	9	30	24
23	China	24	25	12
24	Bulgaria	27	22	17
25	Romania	30	29	5
26	Jordan	28	27	19
27	Syria	29	28	27
28	El Salvador	22	16	31
29	Brazil	31	24	28
30	Indonesia	26	26	30
31	Mexico	17	31	26

Negotiations Emphasis

Business negotiations are perhaps the most fundamental commercial rituals. All the just-discussed differences in business customs and culture come into play more frequently and more obviously in the negotiating process than in any other aspect of business. The basic elements of business negotiations are the same in any country: They relate to the product, its price and terms, services associated with the product, and, finally, friendship between vendors and customers. But it is important to remember that the negotiating process is complicated, and the risk of misunderstanding increases when negotiating with someone from another culture.

Attitudes brought to the negotiating table by each individual are affected by many cultural factors and customs often unknown to the other participants and perhaps unrecognized by the individuals themselves. His or her cultural background conditions each negotiator's understanding and interpretation of what transpires in negotiating sessions. The possibility of offending one another or misinterpreting others' motives is especially high when one's self-reference criteria (SRC) is the basis for assessing a situation. One standard rule in negotiating is "know thyself" first and "know your counterpart" second. The SRC of both parties can come into play here if care is not taken. How business customs and culture influence negotiations is the focus of Chapter 19.

Marketing Orientation

The extent of a company's *marketing orientation* has been shown to relate positively to profits. Although American companies are increasingly embracing this notion (and marketing in general),[40] firms in other countries have not been so fast to change from the more

---

[40] John F. Gaski and Michael J. Etzel, "National Aggregate Consumer Sentiment toward Marketing: A Thirty-Year Retrospective and Analysis," *Journal of Consumer Research* 31 (2005), pp. 859–67.

traditional *production* (consumers prefer products that are widely available), *product* (consumers favor products that offer the best quality, performance, or innovative features), and *selling* (consumers and businesses alike will not buy enough without prodding) orientations.[41] For example, in many countries, engineers dominate corporate boards, and the focus is more toward a product orientation. However, more profitable American firms have adopted strong marketing orientations wherein everyone in the organization (from shop floor to finance) is encouraged to, and even receive rewards, if they generate, disseminate, and respond to marketing intelligence (that is, consumers' preferences, competitions' actions, and regulators' decisions). Recently researchers have empirically verified that, for a variety of complex reasons, including cultural explanations,[42] a marketing orientation is less prevalent in a number of other countries;[43] it can be difficult to encourage such an orientation across diverse business units in global companies.[44]

Gender Bias in International Business

The gender bias[45] against female managers that exists in some countries, coupled with myths harbored by male managers, creates hesitancy among U.S. multinational companies to offer women international assignments. Although women constitute nearly half of the U.S. workforce, they represent relatively small percentages of the

---

[41] Philip Kotler and Kevin Lane Keller, *Marketing Management* (Upper Saddle River, NJ: Prentice Hall, 2006).

[42] David Welch and Ian Rowley, "Toyota's All-Out Drive To Stay Toyota," *BusinessWeek*, December 3, 2007, pp. 54–55.

[43] Sin et al., "Marketing Orientation"; John Kuada and Seth N. Buatsi, "Market Orientation and Management Practices in Ghanaian Firms: Revisiting the Jaworski and Kohli Framework," *Journal of International Marketing* 13 (2005), pp. 58–88; Reto Felix and Wolfgang Hinck, "Market Orientation of Mexican Companies," *Journal of International Marketing* 13 (2005), pp. 111–27.

[44] Paul D. Ellis, "Distance, Dependence and Diversity of Markets: Effects on Market Orientation," *Journal of International Business Studies* 38 (2007), pp. 374–86.

[45] Gender bias is now taking on a new character that has long-term implications for the workplace. In a reversal of historical patterns, in most industrialized countries, women are now the majority on college campuses. Please see Michelle Colin, "The New Gender Gap," *BusinessWeek*, May 26, 2003, pp. 75–81; "The Conundrum of the Glass Ceiling," *The Economist*, July 23, 2005, pp. 63–65.

[46] "Eye on the World," *Marie Claire*, April 2007, p. 134.

Two ways to prevent the harassment of women. Mika Kondo Kunieda, a consultant at the World Bank in Tokyo explains, "I ride in a special women-only metro car that runs between 7:20 and 9:20 am. The cars were created in 2005 due to frequent complaints that women were being groped and sexually harassed. I was a victim a few times when I was younger, and it was—and still is—a humiliating experience. I had to learn how to position myself against moves even in the most overcrowded train. Now, I've seen a few men get visibly anxious when they realize they've accidentally boarded a car during women-only time!"[46] The Koran also specifies the cover-up pictured here in Riyadh, Saudi Arabia. *(left: © David Coll Blanco; right: AP PHOTO/Hasan Jamali)*

CROSSING BORDERS 5.3   Cultures Change, Albeit Slowly

Seoul

In a time-honored practice in South Korea's corporate culture, the 38-year-old manager at an online game company took his 10-person team on twice-weekly after-work drinking bouts. He exhorted his subordinates to drink, including a 29-year-old graphic designer who protested that her limit was two glasses of beer. "Either you drink or you get it from me tomorrow," the boss told her one evening.

She drank, fearing that refusing to do so would hurt her career. But eventually, unable to take the drinking any longer, she quit and sued. In May, in the first ruling of its kind, the Seoul High Court said that forcing a subordinate to drink alcohol was illegal, and it pronounced the manager guilty of a "violation of human dignity." The court awarded the woman $32,000 in damages for the incidents, which occurred in 2004.

The ruling was as much a testament to women's growing presence in corporate life there as a confirmation of changes already under way. As an increasing number of women have joined companies as professionals, corporate South Korea has struggled to change the country's corporate culture, starting with its attitude toward alcohol.

Tokyo

The experience of Kayoko Mura illustrates a big shift in attitudes of Japanese companies toward female workers. When Mura quit her accounting job 16 years ago, food giant Kagome Co. did little to stop her. She was getting married and felt she could not ask for a transfer to Tokyo, where she and her husband were to live.

But last summer, Kagome's Tokyo office sought out Mura, now 44 years old, and wooed her back to the same kind of job she had had before. It also assigned a system engineer to work with her until she got up to speed with the computer system. Kagome even accepted her request to work part-time, just three days a week, six hours a day. "There are many women who quit after we had spent time and money in training," says Tomoko Sone, a Kagome spokeswoman. "For the company, [not hiring them back] is such a waste."

Oslo

Beginning in 2008, all public companies in Norway were mandated to have at least 40 percent women among their board members. Before the law passed in 2003, 7 percent of corporate board members were women. But the number has risen quickly, as suggested in Exhibit 5.4, to 36 percent in 2008, though 75 companies have yet to meet the quota. Statoil's Chairman of the Board, Grace Reksten Skaugen, explains her gender's advantages: "Women feel more compelled than men to do their homework, and we can afford to ask the hard questions, because women are not always expected to know the answers." Reksten Skaugen was voted Norway's chairperson of the year for 2007.

Sources: Norimitsu Onishi, "Corporate Korea Corks the Bottle as Women Rise," *The New York Times*, June 10, 2007, pp. 1, 4; Miho Inada, "Japanese Companies Woo Women Back to Work," *The Wall Street Journal*, July 23, 2007, pp. B1, B3; "Girl Power," *The Economist*, January 5, 2008, pp. 54–55.

employees who are chosen for international assignments—only 18 percent. Why? The most frequently cited reason, the inability of women to succeed abroad. As one executive was quoted as saying, "Overall, female American executives tend not to be as successful in extended foreign work assignments as are male American executives." Unfortunately, such attitudes are shared by many and probably stem from the belief that the traditional roles of women in male-dominated societies preclude women from establishing successful relationships with host-country associates. An often-asked question is whether it is appropriate to send women to conduct business with foreign customers in cultures where women are typically not in managerial positions. To some, it appears logical that if women are not accepted in managerial roles within their own cultures, a foreign woman will not be any more acceptable.

In many cultures—Asian, Middle Eastern, and Latin American—women are not typically found in upper levels of management (see Exhibit 5.4), and men and women are treated very differently. Indeed, the scariest newspaper headline ever written may have been "Asia, Vanishing Point for as Many as 100 Million Women." The article, appearing in the *International Herald Tribune* in 1991,[47] points out that the birthrate in most countries around the world is about 105 boys for every 100 girls. However, in countries like the United States or

---
[47] January 7, 1991, p. 1.

6

the political environment:

A CRITICAL CONCERN

CHAPTER LEARNING OBJECTIVES

What you should learn from Chapter 6:

- What the sovereignty of nations means and how it can affect the stability of government policies

- How different governmental types, political parties, nationalism, targeted fear/animosity, and trade disputes can affect the environment for marketing in foreign countries

- The political risks of global business and the factors that affect stability

- The importance of the political system to international marketing and its effect on foreign investments

- The impact of political and social activists, violence, and terrorism on international business

- How to assess and reduce the effect of political vulnerabililty

- How and why governments encourage foreign investment

Global Perspective

WORLD TRADE GOES BANANAS

Rather than bruising Chiquita Bananas, the wrath of politics instead has hammered Prosciutto di Parma ham from Italy, handbags from France, and bath oils and soaps from Germany. These and a host of other imported products from Europe were all slapped with a 100 percent import tariff as retaliation by the U.S. government against European Union banana-import rules that favor Caribbean bananas over Latin American bananas. Keep in mind that no bananas are exported from the United States, yet the United States has been engaged in a trade war over the past seven years that has cost numerous small businesses on both sides of the Atlantic millions of dollars. But how can this be, you ask? Politics, that's how!

One small business, Reha Enterprises, for example, sells bath oil, soaps, and other supplies imported from Germany. The tariff on its most popular product, an herbal foam bath, was raised from 5 percent to 100 percent. The customs bill for six months spiraled to $37,783 from just $1,851—a 1,941 percent tax increase. For a small business whose gross sales are less than $1 million annually, it was crippling. When Reha heard of the impending "banana war," he called everyone—his congressperson, his senator, the United States Trade Representative (USTR). When he described his plight to the USTR, an official there expressed amazement. "They were surprised I was still importing," because they thought the tariff would cut off the industry entirely. That was their intention, which of course would have meant killing Reha Enterprises as well.

In effect, he was told it was his fault that he got caught up in the trade war. He should have attended the hearings in Washington, just like Gillette and Mattel, and maybe his products would have been dropped from the targeted list, just as theirs were. Scores of European products, from clothing to stoves to glass Christmas ornaments, dolls, and ballpoint pens, that were originally targeted for the retaliatory tariffs escaped the tariff. Aggressive lobbying by large corporations, trade groups, and members of Congress got most of the threatened imported products off the list. The USTR had published a list of the targeted imports in the Federal Register, inviting affected companies to testify. Unfortunately, the Federal Register was not on Reha's reading list.

In that case, he was told, he should have hired a lobbyist in Washington to keep him briefed. Good advice—but it doesn't make much sense to a company that grosses less than $1 million a year. Other advice received from an official of the USTR included the off-the-record suggestion that he might want to change the customs number on the invoice so it would appear that he was importing goods not subject to the tariff, a decision that could, if he were caught, result in a hefty fine or jail. Smaller businesses in Europe faced similar problems as their export business dried up because of the tariffs.

How did this banana war start? The European Union imposed a quota and tariffs that favored imports from former colonies in the Caribbean and Africa, distributed by European firms, over Latin American bananas distributed by U.S. firms. Chiquita Brands International and Dole Food Company, contending that the EU's "illegal trade barriers" were costing $520 million annually in lost sales to Europe, asked the U.S. government for help. The government agreed that unfair trade barriers were damaging their business, and 100 percent tariffs on selected European imports were levied. Coincidentally, Chiquita Brands' annual political campaign contributions increased from barely over $40,000 in 1991 to $1.3 million in 1998.

A settlement was finally reached that involved high tariffs on Latin America bananas and quotas (with no tariffs) on bananas from Europe's former colonies. But the bruising over bananas continues. Most recently, the issue has shifted to banana bending. That is, bananas from Latin America tend to be long and straight, while those from the non-tariff countries are short and bent. Because the latter are not preferred by the shippers or retailers (the bendier ones don't stack as neatly and economically), the bananas from the former colonies are still not preferred. And new regulations have been adopted by the European Commission that mandate that bananas must be free from "abnormal curvature of the fingers." So the bendy banana producers are threatening to renege on the whole agreement. Everyone involved finds this prospect very unappealing.

Sources: "U.S. Sets Import Tariffs in Latest Salvo in Ongoing Battle over Banana Trade," *Minneapolis Star Tribune,* March 4, 1999; Timothy Dove, "Hit by a $200,000 Bill from the Blue," *Time,* February 7, 2000, p. 54; Sarah Ryle, "Banana War Leaves the Caribbean a Casualty," *The Observer,* November 24, 2002; "EU Fights Back over Bendy Bananas Rule," *Irish Examiner,* December 26, 2007; Jeremy Smith, "EU Heading for Trade Crunch over Bananas," *Reuters,* November 14, 2007.

No company, domestic or international, large or small, can conduct business without considering the influence of the political environment within which it will operate. One of the most undeniable and crucial realities of international business is that both host and home governments are integral partners. A government reacts to its environment by initiating and pursuing policies deemed necessary to solve the problems created by its particular circumstances. Reflected in its policies and attitudes toward business are a government's ideas of how best to promote the national interest, considering its own resources and political philosophy. A government controls and restricts a company's activities by encouraging and offering support or by discouraging and banning or restricting its activities—depending on the pleasure of the government.

International law recognizes the sovereign right of a nation to grant or withhold permission to do business within its political boundaries and to control where its citizens conduct business. Thus the political environment of countries is a critical concern for the international marketer. This chapter examines some of the more salient political considerations in assessing global markets.

The Sovereignty of Nations

In the context of international law, a *sovereign state* is independent and free from all external control; enjoys full legal equality with other states; governs its own territory; selects its own political, economic, and social systems; and has the power to enter into agreements with other nations. *Sovereignty* refers to both the powers exercised by a state in relation to other countries and the supreme powers exercised over its own members.[1] A state sets requirements for citizenship, defines geographical boundaries, and controls trade and the movement of people and goods across its borders. Additionally, a citizen is subject to the state's laws even when beyond national borders. It is with the extension of national laws beyond a country's borders that much of the conflict in international business arises. This reasoning is especially true when another country considers its own sovereignty to be compromised.

Nations can and do abridge specific aspects of their sovereign rights to coexist with other nations. The European Union, North American Free Trade Agreement (NAFTA), North Atlantic Treaty Organization (NATO), and World Trade Organization (WTO)[2] represent examples of nations voluntarily agreeing to give up some of their sovereign rights to participate with member nations for a common, mutually beneficial goal. As indicated in Exhibit 1.4 (page 24), the United States' involvement in international political affiliations is surprisingly low (i.e., it is largely sovereign). Indeed, when it comes to participation in international treaty regimes, the United States is ranked near the bottom of the 72 countries included in *Foreign Policy* magazine rankings, tied with Iran and Israel (at 68th) and ahead of only Hong Kong and Taiwan. Most notably, the Kyoto Protocol[3] on global climate change and the International Criminal Court were rejected by the Bush administration, along with lesser known treaties such as the Basel Convention on the Control of Transboundary Movement of Hazardous Wastes.[4] This apparent lack of international political engagement is particularly hard to understand given the wide acceptance that such agreements lead to peace and mutual understanding.[5]

Countries that agree to relinquish some of their sovereignty often are subject to a nagging fear that too much has been given away. For example, the WTO is considered by some as the biggest threat so far to national sovereignty. Adherence to the WTO inevitably means the loss of some degree of national sovereignty, because the member nations have pledged to abide by

---

[1] For those interested in learning more about the concept of sovereignty, see Stephen D. Krasner (ed.), *Problematic Sovereignty* (New York: Columbia University Press, 2001).

[2] "Global Trade Talks Founder on Farm-Subsidy Issues," *The Wall Street Journal Online*, June 21, 2007.

[3] "More Than Hot Air," *The Economist*, July 16, 2005, p. 77.

[4] "Measuring Globalization," *Foreign Policy*, November/December 2007, pp. 68–77.

[5] John L. Graham, "The Big Secret of World Peace," *Journal of Commerce*, February 13, 1995, OPED page; John L. Graham, "Trade Brings Peace," in J. Runzo and N. Martin (eds.), *War and Reconciliation* (Cambridge: Cambridge University Press, 2008); Thomas L. Friedman, *The World Is Flat* (New York: Farrar, Straus, and Giroux, 2005).

international covenants and arbitration procedures that can override national laws and have far-reaching ramifications for citizens. Sovereignty was one of the issues at the heart of the spat between the United States and the European Union over Europe's refusal to lower tariffs and quotas on bananas (see the Global Perspective). And critics of the free trade agreements with both South Korea[6] and Peru[7] claim America's sacrifice of sovereignty is too great.

Foreign investment can also be perceived as a threat to sovereignty and thus become a rallying cry by opposing factions. The Chinese national oil company's proposed purchase of Unocal was opposed on such grounds. As American banks struggled to maintain liquidity during the 2008 home mortgage debacle, huge investments from overseas were solicited and received from one class of foreign investors that U.S. politicians particularly disfavored— the so-called "sovereign wealth funds" that entail vast pools of money controlled by foreign governments from China and the Middle East.[8] At the same time, members of the U.S. Congress have demanded that China raise the value of its currency, but that would make it even easier for Chinese firms and their government to buy American assets.[9] Of course, the Chinese resist the latter political pressure as a threat to their sovereignty. Ironically, Americans have criticized Mexico for hindering similar sorts of American investments. That is, Mexico badly needs privately financed electricity generating plants to meet electrical power demands and to upgrade the country's overloaded transmission network. The Mexican government entered into an agreement with a Belgian company to build a power plant that would bypass the state electricity monopoly and sell electricity directly to large Mexican manufacturers. But the Mexican constitution limits private ownership of utilities, and any exception requires a two-thirds vote of the legislature. The Institutional Revolutionary Party saw the attempt to open Mexico's protected energy industry as an assault on Mexican sovereignty and blocked the agreement. What all this conflict highlights is that national sovereignty is a critical issue in assessing the environment in which a firm operates.

Stability of Government Policies

The ideal political climate for a multinational firm is a stable, friendly government. Unfortunately, governments are not always stable and friendly, nor do stable, friendly governments remain so. Radical shifts in government philosophy when an opposing political party ascends to power,[10] pressure from nationalist and self-interest groups, weakened economic conditions, bias against foreign investment, or conflicts among governments are all issues that can affect the stability of a government. Because foreign businesses are judged by standards as variable as there are nations, the stability and friendliness of the government in each country must be assessed as an ongoing business practice.

At the top of the list of political issues concerning foreign businesses is the stability or instability of prevailing government policies. Governments might change[11] or new political parties might be elected, but the concern of the multinational corporation is the continuity of the set of rules[12] or codes of behavior and the continuation of the rule of law—regardless of which government is in power. A change in government, whether by election or coup, does not always mean a change in the level of political risk. In Italy, for example, more than 50 different governments have been formed since the end of World War II. While the

---

[6] Choe Sang-Hun, "U.S. and South Korea Agree to Sweeping Trade Deal," *The New York Times*, April 3, 2007, pp. C1, C8.

[7] Richard Simon, "Senate OKs Peru Free-Trade Pact," *Los Angeles Times*, December 5, 2007, p. C3.

[8] Peter S. Goodman and Louise Story, "Overseas Investors Buying U.S. Holdings at Record Pace," *The New York Times*, January 20, 2008, pp. 1, 14.

[9] "Lost in Translations," *The Economist*, January 19, 2008, pp. 73–75.

[10] Sabrina Tavernise, "Debate Intensifies in Turkey over Head Scarf Ban," *The New York Times*, January 19, 2008, p. A5.

[11] Sebastian Moffett, "Japanese Prime Minister Steps Down after Less than One Year in Office," *The Wall Street Journal Online*, September 12, 2007.

[12] "If You've Got It, Don't Flaunt It: The Sale of Luxury Goods in China Runs into Political Trouble," *The Economist*, June 2, 2007, p. 72.

political turmoil in Italy continues, business goes on as usual. In contrast, India has had as many different governments since 1945 as Italy, with several in the past few years favorable to foreign investment and open markets. However, much government policy remains hostile to foreign investment. Senior civil servants who are not directly accountable to the electorate but who remain in place despite the change of the elected government continue with former policies. Even after elections of parties favoring economic reform, the bureaucracy continues to be staffed by old-style central planners in India.

Conversely, radical changes in policies toward foreign business can occur in the most stable governments. The same political party, the Institutional Revolutionary Party (PRI), controlled Mexico from 1929 to 2000. During that period, the political risk for foreign investors ranged from expropriation of foreign investments to Mexico's membership in NAFTA and an open door for foreign investment and trade. In recent years, the PRI created a stable political environment for foreign investment in contrast to earlier expropriations and harassment. Beginning with the elections in 2000, however, a new era in Mexican politics emerged as a result of profound changes within the PRI brought about by then-president Ernesto Zedillo. Since 1929, the Mexican president had selected his successor, who, without effective challenge, was always elected. President Zedillo changed the process by refusing to nominate a candidate; instead he let the nomination be decided by an open primary—the first in seven decades. From a field of four candidates, the PRI selected Labastida Ochoa, and the opposing party PAN[13] selected Vicente Fox who, though considered a long shot, won the presidency. Although the PAN had gained strength for several years in the congress and among state governments, its presidential candidates never had a winning chance until the 2000 election.

Some African countries are unstable, with seemingly unending civil wars, boundary disputes, and oppressive military regimes. Even relatively stable and prosperous Kenya fell victim to political violence in 2008 that greatly disrupted growth in commerce in the entire region.[14] Sierra Leone has had three changes in government in five years; the most recent coup d'etat ended the country's brief experiment with democracy. Shortly after the coup, a civil war erupted, and UN peacekeeping forces have had to maintain peace. Central Africa, where ethnic wars have embroiled seven nations, is one of the most politically unstable

---

[13] PAN stands for Partido Accion National. PAN and PRI are the largest of eight political parties in Mexico.

[14] Michela Wrong, "Kenya's Turmoil Cuts off Its Neighbors," *Los Angeles Times*, January 14, 2008, p. C4.

Political disaster strikes Kenya. In the Nairobi slum of Kibera, supporters of opposition leader Raila Odinga tear up a key railway that ran from the coast to Uganda. They renamed the broken line "Odinga Highway." As many as 12 people were killed in the associated clashes. Of course, this destruction will do great damage to commerce and progress to all the countries in Eastern Africa. Let's hope the highway and international airport south of Nairobi stay intact, as they supply all of Europe with flowers from the burgeoning greenhouses in the area, and flower exports are a key source of revenue for the formerly thriving Kenyan economy. (© Carolyn Cole)

regions in the world. Africa is trapped in a vicious cycle. For its nations to prosper, they need foreign investment. But investment is leery of unstable nations, which is the status of most of Africa.[15] A recent World Bank study showed that the 47 nations of sub-Saharan Africa were attracting less than $2 billion annually in direct foreign investment—about one-tenth of what a developing nation such as Mexico attracts.

If there is potential for profit and if permitted to operate within a country, multinational companies can function under any type of government as long as there is some long-run predictability and stability. PepsiCo, for example, operated profitably in the Soviet Union when it had one of the world's most extreme political systems. Years before the disintegration of the USSR's Communist Party, PepsiCo established a very profitable countertrade business with the USSR. The company exchanged Pepsi syrup for Russian vodka thus avoiding the legally complicated financial transactions of the time.[16]

Socioeconomic and political environments invariably change, as they have in the Soviet Union and Mexico. There are five main political causes of instability in international markets: (1) some forms of government seem to be inherently unstable, (2) changes in political parties during elections can have major effects on trade conditions, (3) nationalism, (4) animosity targeted toward specific countries, and (5) trade disputes themselves.

Forms of Government

Circa 500 BC, the ancient Greeks conceived of and criticized three fundamental forms of government: rule by one, rule by the few, and rule by the many. The common terms for these forms in use today are monarchy (or dictatorship), aristocracy (or oligarchy), and democracy. About the same time in history Cyrus the Great, monarch of Persia, declared that the purpose of government was to serve the people, not vice versa. Cyrus's notion is embedded in the constitutions of most modern nations. Following the collapse of colonialism beginning with World War II and communism circa 1990, the world seemed to have agreed that free-enterprise democracy was the best solution to all the criticisms of government since the time of Aristotle, Cyrus, and the others.[17]

Thus of the more than 200 sovereign states on the planet, almost all have at least nominally representative governments with universal suffrage for those 18 years and over. In about 10 percent of the nations voting is required; in the rest it is voluntary. A few countries have some unusual rules for suffrage: In Bolivia, you can vote at 18 if you are married and at 21 if single; in Peru, police and military personnel cannot vote; in Croatia, you can vote at 16 if employed; in Lebanon, only women with at least an elementary education can vote (though all men can vote); and Saudi Arabia precludes women from voting. The last appears to be the only state still completely in the dark ages with regards to suffrage. Exhibit 6.1 lists a sampling of the countries that are currently taking a different approach to the conventional wisdom of representational democracy. More troubling though is the apparent backsliding of some countries toward autocracy and away from democracy, such as Nigeria, Kenya, Bangladesh, Venezuela, Georgia, and Kyrgyzstan.[18] Meanwhile we can all witness perhaps the world's greatest experiment in political and economic change: the race between Russian "big-bang" reform and Chinese gradualism as communism is left further behind in both countries.[19]

The Central Intelligence Agency[20] claims to have taken a look beyond the facade of constitutions in their descriptors. For example, Iran (modern Persia) is defined as a "theocratic

---

[15] Visit http://www.eiu.com for abstracts of the Economist Intelligence Unit's country reports of current political and economic data. Some information on this site is available for a fee only, but other sources are free.

[16] Visit the Pepsi Web site in Russia for a history of Pepsi in Russia, Pepsi advertising in Russia, and other information: http://www.pepsi.ru.

[17] Francis Fukuyama, *The End of History and the Last Man* (New York: The Free Press, 1992).

[18] "Freedom Marches Backwards," *The Economist*, January 19, 2008, pp. 63–64.

[19] Brian Bremmer, "The Dragon's Way or the Tiger's?" *BusinessWeek*, November 20, 2006, pp. 55–62; N. Mark Lam and John L. Graham, *Doing Business in China Now, The World's Most Dynamic Market* (New York: McGraw-Hill, 2007).

[20] http://www.cia.gov/cia/publications/factbook/, 2005.

Exhibit 6.1
A Sampling of
Government Types

Source: http://www.cia.gov/cia/
publications/factbook/, 2008.

Country	Government Type
Afghanistan	Islamic republic
Belarus	Republic in name, though in fact a dictatorship
Bosnia and Herzegovina	Emerging federal democratic republic
Burma (Myanmar)	Military junta
Canada	Confederation with parliamentary democracy
China	Communist state
Congo, Democratic Republic of the	Dictatorship, presumably undergoing a transition to representative government
Cuba	Communist state
Iran	Theocratic republic
Libya	Jamahiriya (a state of the masses) in theory, governed by the populace through local councils; in fact a military dictatorship
North Korea	Communist state, one-man dictatorship
Saudi Arabia	Monarchy
Somalia	No permanent national government; transitional, parliamentary federal government
Sudan	Authoritarian regime—ruling military junta
United Kingdom	Constitutional monarchy
United States	Constitutional federal republic
Uzbekistan	Republic; authoritarian presidential rule, with little power outside the executive branch
Vietnam	Communist state

republic," recognizing that the constitution codifies Islamic principles of government as interpreted from the Koran. Although political parties are allowed to function, they hold little political power. Instead, the Supreme Leader controls all-important decisions of the government, including who is allowed to run for president in Iran.

Political Parties

For most countries around the world, it is particularly important for the marketer to know the philosophies of all major political parties within a country, because any one of them

Eyes on the polls. Portraits of Ayatollah Ali Khamenei (the Supreme Leader) and the late Ayatollah Ruhollah Khomeini loom over Iranian women lined up to vote at a mosque south of Tehran. As mandated by law, women and men waited in separate lines at polling places with more than one ballot box. The current government also specifies the public dress of the women pictured. (© Behrouz Mehri/AFP/Getty Images)

might become dominant and alter prevailing attitudes and the overall business climate.[21] In countries where two strong political parties typically succeed one another in control of the government, it is important to know the direction each party is likely to take.[22] In Great Britain, for example, the Labour Party traditionally has been more restrictive regarding foreign trade than the Conservative Party. The Labour Party, when in control, has limited imports, whereas the Conservative Party has tended to liberalize foreign trade when it is in power. A foreign firm in Britain can expect to seesaw between the liberal trade policies of the Conservatives and the restrictive ones of Labour. Of course, in the United States in recent years, the Democratic Congress has been reluctant to ratify free trade pacts negotiated by the Republican administration in the White House.[23]

Even in Mexico, where a dominant party (PRI) maintained absolute control for seven decades, knowledge of the philosophies of all political parties is important. Over the years, the doctrines of opposing parties have had an influence on the direction of Mexican policy. With the election of the PAN party nominee for president, it was (and is) even more essential to know the philosophy and direction of both the PRI and PAN, the two major political parties in Mexico.

An astute international marketer must understand all aspects of the political landscape to be properly informed about the political environment. Unpredictable and drastic shifts in government policies deter investments, whatever the cause of the shift. In short, a current assessment of political philosophy and attitudes within a country is important in gauging the stability and attractiveness of a government in terms of market potential.

Nationalism

Economic and cultural nationalism, which exists to some degree within all countries, is another factor important in assessing business climate. *Nationalism* can best be described as an intense feeling of national pride and unity, an awakening of a nation's people to pride in their country. This pride can take an anti–foreign business bias, where minor harassment and controls of foreign investment are supported, if not applauded. Economic nationalism has as one of its central aims the preservation of national economic autonomy, in that residents identify their interests with the preservation of the sovereignty of the state in which they reside. In other words, national interest and security are more important than international relations.

Feelings of nationalism are manifested in a variety of ways, including a call to "buy our country's products only" (e.g., "Buy American"),[24] restrictions on imports, restrictive tariffs, and other barriers to trade. They may also lead to control over foreign investment, often regarded with suspicion, which then becomes the object of intensive scrutiny and control. Generally speaking, the more a country feels threatened by some outside force or the domestic economy declines, the more nationalistic it becomes in protecting itself against intrusions.

During the period after World War II, when many new countries were founded and many others were seeking economic independence, manifestations of militant nationalism were rampant. Expropriation of foreign companies, restrictive investment policies, and nationalization of industries were common practices in some parts of the world. During this period, India imposed such restrictive practices on foreign investments that companies such as Coca-Cola, IBM, and many others chose to leave rather than face the uncertainty of a hostile economic climate. In many Latin American countries, similar attitudes prevailed and led to expropriations and even confiscation of foreign investments.

---

[21] Paul M. Vaaler, Burkhard N. Schrage, and Steven A. Block, "Counting the Investor Vote: Political Business Cycle Effects on Sovereign Bond Spreads in Developing Countries," *Journal of International Business Studies* 36, no. 1 (2005), pp. 62–88.

[22] Joy C. Shaw, "Taiwan's KMT Wins Big in Legislative Elections," *The Wall Street Journal Online*, January 12, 2008.

[23] Steven R. Weisman, "Bush in Accord with Democrats on Trade Pacts," *The New York Times*, May 11, 2007, pp. 1, C7.

[24] Kent L. Granzin and John J. Painter, "Motivational Influences on 'Buy Domestic' Purchasing: Marketing Management Implications from a Study of Two Nations," *Journal of International Marketing* 9, no. 2 (2001), pp. 73–96.

CROSSING BORDERS 6.1   Coke's Back, and It Still Has the Secret

For almost 100 years, the formula for making Coca-Cola has been a closely guarded secret. Then the government of India ordered Coca-Cola to disclose it or cease operations in that country. A secret ingredient called 7-X supposedly gives Coke its distinctive flavor. The government's minister for industry told the Indian parliament that Coca-Cola's Indian branch would have to transfer 60 percent of its equity shares to Indians and hand over its know-how by April 1978 or shut down.

Indian sales accounted for less than 1 percent of Coca-Cola's worldwide sales, but the potential market in India, a country of 800 million, was tremendous. The government refused to let the branch import the necessary ingredients, and Coca-Cola—whose products were once as abundant as the bottled drinking water sold in almost every Indian town of more than 50,000—packed up its bags and left the country. The minister for industry said that Coca-Cola's activities in India "furnish a classic example of how multinational corporations operating in a low-priority, high-profit area in a developing country attain run-away growth and . . . trifle with the weaker indigenous industry."

Sixteen years later, India's attitudes toward foreign investment changed, and Coca-Cola reentered the market without having to divulge its formula. During

Coke's 16-year exile, however, Pepsi Cola came to India and captured a 26 percent market share. Not to worry; there is plenty of growth potential for both, considering that India's per capita consumption is just 3 eight-ounce bottles a year, versus about 12 for Pakistan and over 500 in Mexico. To forestall further political vulnerability, Coke sold 49 percent of its Indian bottler subsidiary to institutional investors and employees. The company hopes this move will put to rest an issue that concerned the Indian government, which wanted Indians to own part of Coke's local operation—in other words, Coke took steps to domesticate its operations.

But India is still a tough market. Most recently, a water quality dispute, domestic price competition, a pesticide scare, and cool weather have hurt Coke's sales in India, despite a general global rebound in revenues and profits.

Sources: "Indian Government Rejects Coke's Bid to Sell Soft Drinks," *The Wall Street Journal*, March 16, 1990, p. B5; "Coke Adds Fizz to India," *Fortune*, January 10, 1994, pp. 14–15; Manjeet Kripalani, "Finally, Coke Gets It Right," *BusinessWeek*, February 10, 2003, p. 47; Craig Simons, "India Coke Plant Still Closed as Water Woes Argued," *Atlanta Journal-Constitution*, December 16, 2007, p. F1; "Coke India Chief Bullish on India Becoming Top 5 Global Market," *Asia Pulse*, January 15, 2008.

By the late 1980s, militant nationalism had subsided; today, the foreign investor, once feared as a dominant tyrant that threatened economic development, is often sought as a source of needed capital investment.[25] Nationalism comes and goes as conditions and attitudes change, and foreign companies welcomed today may be harassed tomorrow and vice versa.

Although militant economic nationalism has subsided, nationalistic feelings can be found even in the most economically prosperous countries. When U.S. negotiators pushed Japan to import more rice to help balance the trade deficit between the two countries, nationalistic feelings rose to a new high. Deeply rooted Japanese notions of self-sufficiency, self-respect, and concern for the welfare of Japanese farmers caused Japan to resist any change for several years. It was only after a shortfall in the Japanese rice harvests that restrictions on rice imports were temporarily eased. Even then, all imported foreign rice had to be mixed with Japanese rice before it could be sold.

Targeted Fear and/or Animosity

It is important for marketers not to confuse nationalism, whose animosity is directed generally toward *all* foreign countries, with a widespread fear or animosity directed at a particular country. This confusion was a mistake made by Toyota in the United States in the late 1980s and early 1990s. Sales of Japanese cars were declining in the States, and an advertising campaign was designed and delivered that assumed the problem was American nationalism. However, nationalism was clearly not the problem, because sales of German cars were not experiencing the same kinds of declines. The properly defined problem was "Americans' *fear* of Japan." Indeed, at the time, Americans considered the economic threat

[handwritten: American attribute this same fear toward China now!]

---

[25] Muammar el Qaddafi, the leader of Libya, has changed his approach to international relations from supporting terrorism to supporting trade, for example. See "Rehabilitating Libya," *The New York Times* (editorial), January 8, 2007, p. 14.

Historically unfriendly neighbors begin to make friends. Manmohan Singh, India's Prime Minister, visits China and reviews the troops with Chinese Premier Wen Jiabao. Both countries have pledged to increase trade and military cooperation. (© *Andrew Wong/Getty Images*)

from Japan greater than the military threat from the Soviet Union. So when Toyota spent millions on an advertising campaign showing Toyotas being made by Americans in a plant in Kentucky, it may well have exacerbated the fear that the Japanese were "colonizing" the United States.

The World Is Not Merchandise, Who Is Killing France? The American Strategy, and *No Thanks Uncle Sam* have been best-selling titles in France that epitomize its animosity toward the United States. Although such attitudes may seem odd in a country that devours U.S. movies, eats U.S. fast foods, views U.S. soap operas, and shops at U.S. Wal-Mart stores, national animosity—whatever the cause—is a critical part of the political environment. The United States is not immune to the same kinds of directed negativism either. The rift between France and the United States over the Iraq–U.S. war led to hard feelings on both sides and an American backlash against French wine, French cheese, and even products Americans thought were French. French's mustard felt compelled to issue a press release stating that it is an "American company founded by an American named 'French.'"[26] Thus, it is quite clear that no nation-state, however secure, will tolerate penetration by a foreign company into its market and economy if it perceives a social, cultural, economic, or political threat to its well-being.

Trade Disputes   Finally, narrow trade disputes themselves can roil broader international markets. At the beginning of the chapter we discussed our favorite example—bananas. Among several hot issues circa 2008 were undervalued Chinese currency,[27] the ban on beef imports into Japan,[28] Chinese subsidies in apparent violation of WTO rules,[29] farm subsidies in developed countries, and the long-simmering AIRBUS–Boeing battle over subsidies. Any of these disputes might boil over and affect other aspects of international trade, but at least at this writing, cooler heads seem to be prevailing—along with the WTO dispute resolution processes.

Political Risks of Global Business

Issues of sovereignty, differing political philosophies, and nationalism are manifest in a host of governmental actions that enhance the risks of global business. Risks can range from confiscation, the harshest, to many lesser but still significant government rules and regulations, such as exchange controls, import restrictions, and price controls that directly affect the performance of business activities. Although not always officially blessed initially, social or political activist groups can provoke governments into actions that prove harmful to business. Of all the political risks, the most costly are those actions that result in a transfer of equity from the company to the government, with or without adequate compensation.

Confiscation, Expropriation, and Domestication   The most severe political risk is *confiscation*, that is, the seizing of a company's assets without payment. Two notable confiscations of U.S. property occurred when Fidel Castro became the leader in Cuba and later when the Shah of Iran was overthrown. Confiscation was most prevalent in the 1950s and 1960s when many underdeveloped countries saw confiscation, albeit ineffective, as a means of economic growth.

Less drastic, but still severe, is *expropriation*, where the government seizes an investment but makes some reimbursement for the assets. Often the expropriated investment is nationalized; that is, it becomes a government-run entity. A third type of risk is *domestication*,

---

[26] Floyd Norris, "French's Has an Unmentioned British Flavor," *The New York Times,* March 28, 2003. The news release failed to mention that French's is a subsidiary of Reckitt Benckiser P.L.C., a British firm—but the British did support the U.S. position.

[27] James T. Areddy, "Yuan's Surge Unlikely to Halt U.S. Criticism," *The Wall Street Journal Online,* December 31, 2007.

[28] "Japanese Food Chains Ask for Easing of U.S. Beef Rules," *Prism Insight,* December 26, 2006.

[29] "WTO Launches Formal Probe into Alleged Chinese Subsidies," *Associated Press,* August 31, 2007.

which occurs when host countries gradually cause the transfer of foreign investments to national control and ownership through a series of government decrees that mandate local ownership and greater national involvement in a company's management. The ultimate goal of domestication is to force foreign investors to share more of the ownership, management, and profits with nationals than was the case before domestication.

Rather than a quick answer to economic development, expropriation and nationalization have often led to nationalized businesses that were inefficient, technologically weak, and noncompetitive in world markets. Risks of confiscation and expropriation appear to have lessened over the last two decades (with exceptions in Latin America, particularly Venezuela),[30] because experience has shown that few of the desired benefits materialize after government takeover.[31] Today, countries often require prospective investors to agree to share ownership, use local content, enter into labor and management agreements, and share participation in export sales as a condition of entry; in effect, the company has to become domesticated as a condition for investment.

Countries now view foreign investment as a means of economic growth. As the world has become more economically interdependent, it has become obvious that much of the economic success of countries such as South Korea, Singapore, and Taiwan is tied to foreign investments. Nations throughout the world that only a few years ago restricted or forbade foreign investments are now courting foreign investors as a much needed source of capital and technology. Additionally, they have begun to privatize telecommunications, broadcasting, airlines, banks, railroads, and other nationally owned companies as a means of enhancing competition and attracting foreign capital.

The benefits of privatizing are many. In Mexico, for example, privatization of the national telephone company resulted in almost immediate benefits when the government received hundreds of millions of dollars of much needed capital from the sale and immediate investment in new telecommunications systems. A similar scenario has played out in Brazil, Argentina, India, and many eastern European countries. Ironically, many of the businesses that were expropriated and nationalized in earlier periods are now being privatized.

Economic Risks   Even though expropriation and confiscation are waning as risks of doing business abroad, international companies are still confronted with a variety of economic risks that can occur with little warning. Restraints on business activity may be imposed under the banner of national security to protect an infant industry, to conserve scarce foreign exchange, to raise revenue, or to retaliate against unfair trade practices, among a score of other real or imagined reasons. These economic risks are an important and recurring part of the political environment that few international companies can avoid.

Exchange Controls.

Exchange controls stem from shortages of foreign exchange held by a country. When a nation faces shortages of foreign exchange and/or a substantial amount of capital is leaving the country, controls may be levied over all movements of capital or selectively against the most politically vulnerable companies to conserve the supply of foreign exchange for the most essential uses. A recurrent problem for the foreign investor is getting profits in and out of the host country without loss of value, which can occur when a currency is devalued. Exhibit 6.2 illustrates how exchange controls can affect an international company's profits. Many countries maintain regulations for control of currency, and should an economy suffer a setback or foreign exchange reserves decline severely, the controls on convertibility are imposed quickly.

Local-Content Laws.

In addition to restricting imports of essential supplies to force local purchase, countries often require a portion of any product sold within the country to have local content, that is, to contain locally made parts. Thailand, for example, requires that all milk products contain at least 50 percent milk from local dairy farmers.

---

[30] Simon Romero, "Chavez Takes over Foreign-Controlled Oil Projects in Venezuela," *The New York Times*, May 2, 2007, p. A3.

[31] Marla Dickerson, "Woes Mount for Mexico's State Oil Titan," *Los Angeles Times*, January 2, 2008, pp. C1, C4.

Exhibit 6.2
How Complicated Things
Can Get!

Sources: "Myanmar's Crumbling
Kit," *Asiaweek*, March 2, 2001,
p. 8; Michael Vatikiotis, "Neighbors
Lean on Myanmar," *International
Herald Tribune*, February 2, 2005,
p. 7; "Myanmar Military Confirms No
Change in Fuel Rations," *Dow Jones
International*, December 31, 2007.

Exchange controls also are extended to products by applying a system of multiple exchange rates to regulate trade in specific commodities classified as necessities or luxuries. Necessary products are placed in the most favorable (low) exchange categories, while luxuries are heavily penalized with high foreign exchange rates. Myanmar (formerly known as Burma), for example, has three exchange rates for the kyat (Kt): the official rate (Kt6:U.S.$1), the market rate (Kt100–125:U.S.$1), and an import duty rate (Kt100:U.S.$1). Since the kyat is not convertible—that is, not officially exchangeable for currencies that can be spent outside the country—investors are severely affected by tax liability, and their ability to send profits outside the country is diminished. Under such exchange rates, tax liability can be very high. For instance, a profit of Kt135,000 is worth U.S.$22,500 at the official exchange rate of Kt6 to U.S.$1, but at the market rate, the investor has earned only U.S.$1,000. The exchange rate difference means that the investor has to pay tax on U.S.$21,500 of nonexistent, unearned income. It seems not much makes sense in Myanmar these days.

Contrary to popular belief, local-content requirements are not restricted to Third World countries. The European Union has had a local-content requirement as high as 45 percent for "screwdriver operations," a name often given to foreign-owned assemblers, and NAFTA requires 62 percent local content for all cars coming from member countries.

Import Restrictions.   Selective restrictions on the import of raw materials, machines, and spare parts are fairly common strategies to force foreign industry to purchase more supplies within the host country and thereby create markets for local industry. Although this restriction is done in an attempt to support the development of domestic industry, the result is often to hamstring and sometimes interrupt the operations of established industries. The problem then becomes critical when there are no adequately developed sources of supply within the country.

Tax Controls.   Taxes must be classified as a political risk when used as a means of controlling foreign investments. In such cases, they are raised without warning and in violation of formal agreements. India, for example, taxes PepsiCo and the Coca-Cola Company 40 percent on all soda bottled in India. And, using a different angle of attack, India is attempting to collect $40 million in taxes on travel tickets sold online from Sabre's (an airlines reservations service) data center in Tulsa, Oklahoma. The Indian government contends that Sabre has a permanent establishment in India in the form of data flows between Sabre's Tulsa processing center and the desktop computers of travel agents in India. To underdeveloped countries with economies constantly threatened with a shortage of funds, unreasonable taxation of successful foreign investments appeals to some government officials as the handiest and quickest means of finding operating funds. As the Internet grows in importance, countries will surely seize on Internet transactions as a lucrative source of revenue.

Price Controls.   Essential products that command considerable public interest, such as pharmaceuticals, food, gasoline, and cars, are often subjected to price controls. Such controls applied during inflationary periods can be used to control the cost of living. They also may be used to force foreign companies to sell equity to local interests. A side effect on the local economy can be to slow or even stop capital investment.

Labor Problems.   In many countries, labor unions have strong government support that they use effectively in obtaining special concessions from business. Layoffs may be forbidden, profits may have to be shared, and an extraordinary number of services may have to be provided. In fact, in many countries, foreign firms are considered fair game for the demands of the domestic labor supply. In France, the belief in full employment is almost religious in fervor; layoffs of any size, especially by foreign-owned companies, are regarded as national crises. We should also note that some multinational companies are more powerful than local labor unions. Wal-Mart closed a store in Quebec rather than let it be unionized.[32]

---

[32] "Union Loses Bid to Reopen Wal-Mart," *Montreal Gazette*, May 12, 2005, p. A11.

Political Sanctions

you said nation can't boycott another nation?

In addition to economic risks, one or a group of nations may boycott another nation, thereby stopping all trade between the countries, or may issue sanctions against the trade of specific products. The United States has long-term boycotts of trade with Cuba and Iran. The United States has come under some criticism for its demand for continued sanctions against Cuba and its threats of future sanctions against countries that violate human rights issues.

History indicates that sanctions are almost always unsuccessful in reaching desired goals, particularly when other major nations' traders ignore them. This lack of success is the case with Cuba, North Korea, and Iran, where the undesirable behavior that the sanctions were imposed to change continues, and the only ones who seem to be hurt are the people and companies that get caught in the middle. Moreover, the Chinese recently signed an agreement with Iran that will bring $70 billion of natural gas to China.[33] Please see Crossing Borders 6.2 for more on this issue.

Political and Social Activists and Nongovernmental Organizations

Although not usually officially sanctioned by the government, the impact of political and social activists (PSAs) can also interrupt the normal flow of trade. PSAs can range from those who seek to bring about peaceful change to those who resort to violence and terrorism to effect change. When well organized, the actions of PSAs can succeed.

One of the most effective and best-known PSA actions was against Nestlé due to the sale of baby formula in Third World markets. The worldwide boycott of Nestlé products resulted in substantial changes in the company's marketing. More recently, activists of the Free Burma Campaign (FBC) have applied enough pressure to cause several U.S. garment companies to stop importing textiles from Myanmar. Furthermore, activists on several U.S. college campuses boycotted Pepsi Cola drinks and PepsiCo.-owned Pizza Hut and Taco Bell stores, saying that the company's commercial activities contributed to the abysmal human rights in Myanmar. The results of the boycott were serious enough that PepsiCo. sold its stake in its joint venture in Myanmar and withdrew from that market. The concern was that potential losses in the United States outweighed potential profits in Myanmar. Holland's Heineken and Denmark's Carlsberg beer companies withdrew from Myanmar for similar reasons.

PSA groups such as Greenpeace and Consumers International have been successful in raising doubts about the safety of genetically modified (GM) food. Europeans' fears about "Frankenfood," as it is sometimes called, have spread throughout much of the world and persuaded some famine-ridden countries in Africa to reject GM grains. In some areas in Uganda, an airborne fungus is decimating 80 percent of the banana plants. Bananas are a food staple there. Ugandans eat banana pancakes, banana mash, and banana bread. They season their beans with banana salt, and they guzzle banana beer and sip banana gin.[34] Although a genetically modified plant has been developed that is immune to the leaf fungus, because of the fear of GM food, Uganda's legislature has not enacted laws that will permit bioengineered banana plants into the country.

The rather broad issue of globalization is the also the focus of many PSA groups. The demonstrations in Seattle during a 1999 WTO meeting and in Washington, DC, against the World Bank and the International Monetary Fund (IMF), along with similar demonstrations in other countries, reflect a growing concern about a global economy. Whether misguided, uninformed, or just "wackos," as they have been described, PSAs can be a potent force in rallying public opinion and are an important political force that should not be dismissed, as companies such as Nike, McDonald's, and Nestlé know.

They were "pirates" to some, "hostages" to others. But two anti-whaling activists (an Australian and a Briton from the Sea Shepherd Conservation Society) who drew global attention by forcibly boarding a Japanese harpoon ship in Antarctic waters have demonstrated how the emotional clash over Japan's annual whale hunt can disrupt even the best international friendships. *(Courtesy of Sea Shepherd Conservation Society)*

---

[33] Vivienne Walt, "Iran Looks East," *Fortune*, February 21, 2005, pp. 88–95.

[34] Roger Thurow, "As U.S., EU Clash on Biotech Crops, Africa Goes Hungry," *The Wall Street Journal*, February 26, 2002, p. A1.

CROSSING BORDERS 6.2   Trade Does Not Work as a Stick, Only as a Carrot

It was 1807 when Thomas Jefferson proposed trade sanctions as an innovation in diplomacy. The donkeys he endeavored to persuade were quite big and quite stubborn—England and France. The goal was to get these warring nations to leave American ships alone on the high seas. Lacking a competitive navy, our third president dreamed up the trade embargo; rather than using trade as a carrot, he planned to withhold trade and use it as a stick. However, instead of changing French or English policies and behaviors, Jefferson's policy actually endangered New England traders. They complained:

Our ships all in motion, once whiten'd the ocean;
They sail'd and return'd with a Cargo;
Now doom'd to decay, they are fallen a prey,
To Jefferson, worms, and EMBARGO.

Jefferson's embargo fell apart in just 15 months. Only the War of 1812 settled the problems with English aggression at sea.

Consider the track record of trade sanctions in the last century. In 1940 the United States told the Japanese to get out of China, and the ensuing embargo of gasoline and scrap metal led directly to the Pearl Harbor attack. Since 1948 Arab countries have boycotted Israel. Given that countries trade most with their close neighbors, you have to wonder how much this lack of trade has promoted the continuing conflicts in the area. Israel is still there. In 1959 Fidel Castro took over Cuba, and for the next 49 years, the United States has boycotted sugar and cigars, but Castro remained in charge for almost 50 years. OPEC's 1973 oil flow slowdown was intended to get America to stop supporting Israel. However, the dollars still flow fast to Israel and now Egypt as well.

In 1979 the United States told the Soviets to get out of Afghanistan. They refused. America boycotted the Moscow Olympics and stopped selling the Soviets grain and technology. The Soviet response: They continued to kill Afghans (and, by the way, Soviet soldiers) for another 10 years. Moreover, in 1984 they and their allies' athletes stayed away from the Olympics in Los Angeles. And the high-tech embargo didn't work anyway. A San Diego division of Caterpillar lost millions of dollars in service contracts for Soviet natural gas pipelines in the mid-1970s. These revenues were lost permanently, because the Soviets taught themselves how to do the maintenance and overhauls. In 1989 a Moscow weapons research facility had every brand of computer then available in the West: IBMs, Apples, and the best from Taiwan and Japan as well.

Perhaps the 1980s' multilateral trade sanctions imposed on South Africa hastened apartheid's demise. But look how well the world's 10-year embargo of Iraq changed policy there. Using trade as a weapon killed kids while Saddam Hussein celebrated at $12 million birthday parties. Indeed, the best prescription for Middle East peace (and American taxpayers' wallets, by the way) is all sides dropping all embargoes.

The end of the last century witnessed great strides in the elimination of ill-conceived trade sanctions. Perhaps most important was the U.S. Senate's and President's approvals of permanently normalized trade relations (PNTR) with China. However, other important steps were the relaxation of some of the trade restrictions on Vietnam, North Korea, Iran, and Cuba. Indeed, as a result of President Clinton's diplomacy, North and South Koreans marched together at the Sydney Olympics; Americans can now buy pistachio nuts and carpets from Tehran, and U.S. firms can sell medical supplies and services in Havana. Remarkable!

These same kinds of carrots need to be thrown in the direction of the other countries on America's blacklist—Myanmar, Angola, Libya, Sudan, and Syria. Be certain that the chorus of criticism regarding human rights, freedom of the press, and democracy should continue, loud and clear. But instead of dropping bombs (or threatening to), we should be selling them computers and Internet connections. The cost of a cruise missile is about the same as 2,000 Apple computers! And at the most fundamental level, coercion does not work. Exchange does.

Source: John L. Graham, "Trade Brings Peace," in Joseph Runzo and Nancy M. Martin (eds.), *War and Reconciliation* (Cambridge, MA: Cambridge University Press, 2008).

The Internet has become an effective tool of PSAs to spread the word about whatever cause they sponsor. During protest rallies against the U.S.–Iraq war, organizers were able to coordinate protest demonstrations in 600 cities worldwide and to disseminate information easily. A Google search for "peace protest" during that time (2003) resulted in 788,000 entries (about 660,000 in 2008), including news briefs, Web sites for peace organizations, online petitions for peace, where to show up with your placard, where to send your dollars, and how to write your member of Congress.[35]

Often associated with political activism, nongovernmental organizations (NGOs) are increasingly affecting policy decisions made by governments.[36] Many are involved in peaceful protests, lobbying, and even collaborations with governmental organizations. Many also are involved in mitigating much of the human misery plaguing parts of the planet. Some NGOs have received global recognition—the Red Cross and Red Crescent, Amnesty International, Oxfam, UNICEF, Care, and Habitat for Humanity are examples— for their good works, political influence, and even their brand power.[37]

Violence, Terrorism, and War

Although not usually government initiated, violence is another related risk for multinational companies to consider in assessing the political vulnerability of their activities. The State Department reported 3,200 terrorist incidents worldwide in 2004, up dramatically from previous years, given a new approach to counting.[38] Terrorism has many different goals. Multinationals are targeted to embarrass a government and its relationship with firms, to generate funds by kidnapping executives to finance terrorist goals, to use as pawns in political or social disputes not specifically directed at them, and to inflict terror within a country, as did September 11.

September 11 has raised the cost of doing business domestically and internationally. The dominance of the United States in world affairs exposes U.S. businesses to a multitude of uncertainties, from the growing danger of political violence to investment risks in emerging markets. In the past 30 years, 80 percent of terrorist attacks against the United States have been aimed at American businesses. Since September 11, McDonald's, KFC, and Pizza Hut combined have been bombed in more than 10 countries, including Turkey, Saudi Arabia, Russia, Lebanon, and China; most attacks have been linked with militant Islamic groups. There are reasons to expect that businesses will become increasingly attractive to terrorists, both because they are less well defended than government targets and because of what they symbolize. Based on the threats of terrorism and other violence, the U.S. State Department posts travel warnings on its Web site (see Exhibit 6.3 for a recent listing). However, many international travelers appear to regularly ignore those warnings.[39]

Finally, we note strong reasons to believe that international warfare is fast becoming obsolete. The number of wars has declined steadily since the end of the Cold War. Even though politicians in almost all countries use xenophobia to consolidate their own political power, the threat of one country attacking another is declining fast. Some predict a coming

---

[35] Mary Brown Malouf, "Web Unites Peace Rallies across Globe," *Salt Lake Tribune,* February 18, 2003.

[36] Hildy Teegen, Jonathan P. Doh, and Sushil Vachani, "The Importance of Non-Governmental Organizations (NGOs) in Global Governance and Value Creation: An International Business Research Agenda," *Journal of International Business Studies* 35, no. 6 (2004), pp. 463–83.

[37] See the excellent book by John A. Quelch and Nathalie Laidler-Kylander, *The New Global Brands: Managing Non-Governmental Organizations in the 21st Century* (Mason, OH: South-Western, 2006).

[38] Tim Reid, "The 28,000 Victims of Terrorism," *The Times of London,* July 7, 2005, p. 36.

[39] "Who Do We Trust?" *Condé Nast Traveler,* March 2005, pp. 53–62.

Exhibit 6.3
U.S. State Department Travel Warnings (in order of date of posting, most recent first)

Source: http://travel.state.gov/travel/, 2008.

Eritrea	Nigeria	Timor-Leste
Congo, Democratic Republic of	Uzbekistan	Sudan
Chad	Sri Lanka	Haiti
Iran	Kenya	Central African Republic
Algeria	Lebanon	Israel, the West Bank, and Gaza
Burundi	Indonesia	Colombia
Cote d'Ivoire	Yemen	Philippines
Somalia	Nepal	Afghanistan
Iraq	Syria	

Exhibit 6.4
Armed Conflicts Around the World

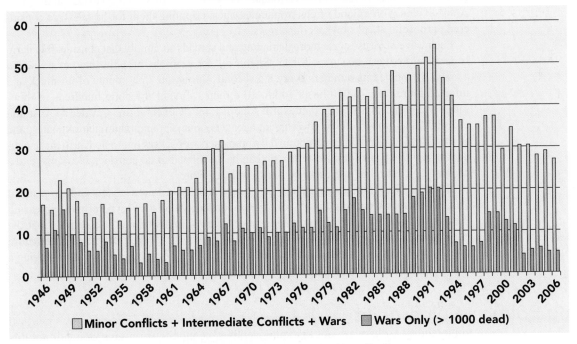

Armed Conflicts Around the World

☐ **Minor Conflicts + Intermediate Conflicts + Wars**   ■ **Wars Only (> 1000 dead)**

Source: The International Peace Research Institute, Oslo, http://www.prio.no/cwp/ArmedConflict.

war in space, with satellites used as weapons, but the multinational collaboration on the International Space Station makes such a possibility seem remote.[40] In 1996, political scientist Samuel Huntington[41] notoriously predicted a clash of civilizations. In his vision, the world was already divided up into nine civilizations (or cultural groupings): Western, Latin America, African, Islamic, Sinic, Hindu, Orthodox, Buddhist, and Japanese. This prediction reminds us of several others in the early 1990s who suggested the world would soon devolve into three spheres of influence based on trade, dominated by Japan, the European Union, and the United States. There may be some sense to the latter classification; time zones exercise an important influence on trade patterns that favor north–south exchanges. However, both theories oversimplify power and trade relations as they are unfolding. Both theories also ignore the successes of the World Trade Organization and the fast multiplying bilateral trade agreements, such as that between the United States and South Korea. And certainly the facts included in Exhibit 6.4 suggest that these warnings about a new clash of civilizations are off the mark. Although two of the five wars ongoing in 2006 were international ones (in Afghanistan and Iraq), the other three are better examples of civil wars (in Sri Lanka, Chad, and Sudan). Rather than state-to-state or civilization-to-civilization military action, the greater threats to peace and commerce for the 21st century remain civil strife and terrorism.

Cyberterrorism and Cybercrime

Always on the horizon is the growing potential for cyberterrorism and cybercrime.[42] Although still in its infancy, the Internet provides a vehicle for terrorist and criminal attacks by foreign and domestic antagonists wishing to inflict damage on a company with little chance of being caught. One problem in tracing cyberterrorists and criminals is that it is

---

[40] "Disharmony in the Spheres," *The Economist*, January 19, 2008, pp. 25–28.

[41] Samuel P. Huntington, *The Clash of Civilizations and the Remaking of the World Order* (New York: Simon and Schuster, 1996); Fouad Ajami, "The Clash," *The New York Times*, January 6, 2008.

[42] "Overseas Security Threats to U.S. Business Cited," *Los Angeles Times*, December 28, 2007, p. C2.

hard to determine if a cyberattack has been launched by a rogue state, a terrorist, or a hacker as a prank. The "I Love You" worm, which caused an estimated $25 billion in damage, was probably just an out-of-control prank. However, the Melissa virus and the denial of service (DoS) attacks that overloaded the Web sites of CNN, ZDNet, Yahoo!, and Amazon.com with a flood of electronic messages, crippling them for hours, were considered purposeful attacks on specific targets.

Each wave of viruses gets more damaging and spreads so rapidly that considerable harm is done before it can be stopped. The "Slammer," for example, brought Internet service to a crawl. It doubled its numbers every 8.5 seconds during the first minute of its attack and infected more than 75,000 hosts within 10 minutes.[43] After infecting hundreds of thousands of computers in Europe and North America, the "Goner worm" traveled to Australia overnight and brought down government agencies, financial and manufacturing sites, and at least 25 MNCs. Whether perpetrated by pranksters or hackers out to do harm, these incidents show that tools for cyberterrorism can be developed to do considerable damage to a company, an entire industry, or a country's infrastructure.

Because of mounting concern over the rash of attacks, business leaders and government officials addressed a Group of 8[44] conference convened to discuss cybercrime, expressing the urgent need for cooperation among governments, industry, and users to combat the growing menace of cybercrime. As the Internet grows, "it's only a matter of time before every terrorist, anarchist, thief, and prankster with a PC and a phone line will be waging a virtual war and inflicting real harm."

Assessing Political Vulnerability

There are at least as many reasons for a company's political vulnerability as there are political philosophies, economic variations, and cultural differences. Some companies appear to be more politically vulnerable than others, in that they receive special government attention. Depending on the desirability of a company, this special attention may result in positive actions toward the company or in negative attention.

Unfortunately, a marketer has no absolute guidelines to follow to determine whether a company and its products will be subject to political attention. Countries seeking investments in high-priority industries may well excuse companies from taxes, customs duties, quotas, exchange controls, and other impediments to investment. In a bid to attract foreign investment and increase exports, India announced a new trade policy that eases restraints and offers tax breaks for companies developing and maintaining infrastructure. Conversely, firms either marketing products not considered high priority or that fall from favor for some other reason often face unpredictable government restrictions.

As a case in point, Continental Can Company's joint venture to manufacture cans for the Chinese market faced a barrage of restrictions when the Chinese economy weakened. China decreed that canned beverages were wasteful and must be banned from all state functions and banquets. Tariffs on aluminum and other materials imported for producing cans were doubled, and a new tax was imposed on canned-drink consumption. For Continental Can, an investment that had the potential for profit after a few years was rendered profitless by a change in the attitude of the Chinese government.

Politically Sensitive Products and Issues

Although there are no specific guidelines to determine a product's vulnerability at any point, there are some generalizations that help identify the tendency for products to be politically sensitive. Products that have or are perceived to have an effect on the environment, exchange rates, national and economic security, and the welfare of people (and particularly children—recall the story of Barbie in Saudi Arabia from the previous chapter) or that are publicly visible, subject to public debate, or that are associated with their country of origin are more likely to be politically sensitive.

---

[43] For more information, see http://www.silicondefense.com.

[44] The Group of 8 consists of government representatives from Britain, Canada, France, Germany, Italy, Japan, Russia, and the United States who convene periodically to examine issues that affect the group.

Activists of the Bharatiya Janata Party wearing "evil" masks shout antigovernment slogans near the Union Carbide plant in the central Indian city of Bhopal on the eve of World Environment Day. The activists protested to draw the attention of the government to chemical waste and demanded the cleanup of hazardous waste in the area. The leak from the Union Carbide pesticide plant in 1984 was one of the world's worst industrial accidents, killing 3,000 people and leaving thousands of others with lifetime illnesses. (© Reuters/Corbis)

Fast-food restaurants, which are intended to be visible, have often been lightning rods for groups opposed to foreign companies. Authorities closed a KFC restaurant for health reasons (two flies were seen in the kitchen) after months of protesters arguing that foreign investment should be limited to high technology. "India does not need foreign investment in junk-food," said the leader of a protesting farmers' group. The store was later reopened by court order.

Health is often the subject of public debate, and products that affect or are affected by health issues can be sensitive to political concern. The European Union has banned hormone-treated beef for more than a decade. There is a question about whether the ban is a valid health issue or just protection for the European beef industry. The World Trade Organization concluded in 1989 that the ban had no scientific basis; nevertheless, Europe has yet to lift the ban. Reluctance to respond to the WTO directive may be the result of the recent outcry against genetically modified (GM) foods that has, for all practical purposes, caused GM foods to be banned in Europe. Public opinion against Frankenfood has been so strong that Unilever announced that it would stop using GM ingredients in all its products in Britain. Additionally, 11 leading restaurant chains, including McDonald's, Pizza Hut, Wimpy, and Burger King, have gone GM-free. The issue in the United States has not risen to the same level of concern as in Europe; to forestall such adverse public opinion, many U.S. companies are slowing the introduction of GM foods. Fearing a strong public reaction as in Europe, McDonald's has decided to stop using genetically modified potatoes for its french fries in its U.S. stores.

Forecasting Political Risk

In addition to qualitative measures of political vulnerability, a number of firms are employing systematic methods of measuring political risk.[45] Political risk assessment is an attempt to forecast political instability to help management identify and evaluate political events and their potential influence on current and future international business decisions. Perhaps the greatest risk to international marketers is the threat of the government actually failing, causing chaos in the streets and markets. *Foreign Policy* magazine uses 12 criteria to rank countries on its "Failed States Index."[46] The list of criteria includes demographic pressures, human flight, uneven development, and the like. (See Exhibit 6.5.)

Risk assessment is used to estimate the level of risk a company is assuming when making an investment and to help determine the amount of risk it is prepared to accept. In the former Soviet Union and in China, the risk may be too high for some companies, but stronger and better financed companies can make long-term investments in those countries that

[45] See http://www.prsgroup.com for a wealth of information on political risk assessments.
[46] "The Failed States Index," *Foreign Policy*, July/August 2007, pp. 54–65.

Exhibit 6.5

Top 20 States in Danger of Failing (ranked in order of closest to failure)

Source: From *Foreign Policy*, "Failed States Index," July/August 2007, pp. 54–65. Copyright 2007 by Foreign Policy. Reproduced with permission of *Foreign Policy* via Copyright Clearance Center.

Sudan	Afghanistan	Bangladesh
Iraq	Guinea	Nigeria
Somalia	Central African Republic	Nigeria
Zimbabwe	Haiti	Burundi
Chad	Pakistan	Timor-Leste
Ivory Coast	North Korea	
Democratic Republic of Congo	Burma (Myanmar)	
	Uganda	

CROSSING BORDERS 6.3

When States Fail: Dodging the Bullet in Former Yugoslavia

One pundit suggested that nations with McDonald's don't attack one another. Perhaps Yugoslavia was the exception that proves the rule?

During most of the 78-day air war against Yugoslavia in 1999, McDonald's kept the burgers flipping while NATO kept the bombs dropping. After only one night of air strikes, mobs of youths, whipped to patriotic fervor by the state-controlled media's attacks on the "NATO criminals and aggressors," targeted six McDonald's stores, smashing windows and scribbling insults on doors and walls. McDonald's Corporation was forced to temporarily close its 15 restaurants in Yugoslavia. Weeks later, when local managers flung the doors open again, they accomplished an extraordinary comeback using an unusual marketing strategy: They put McDonald's U.S. citizenship on the back burner.

Within a week after the attacks, they had launched a campaign to identify the plight of ordinary Serbs with the Mac. "McDonald's is sharing the destiny of all people here," read a sign at one branch. A key aspect of the campaign was to present McDonald's as a Yugoslav company. Restaurants promoted the McCountry, a domestic pork burger with paprika garnish, and lowered its price. Pork is considered the most Serbian of meats.

In a national flourish to evoke Serbian identity and pride, McDonald's produced posters and lapel buttons showing the golden arches topped with a traditional Serbian cap called the *sajkaca* (pronounced shy-KACH-a). The managing director said McDonald's needed to get

Serbs to view the company as their own. He masterminded the campaign to "Serbify" McDonald's. It was in this vein that he and his team decided to redesign the logo with the Serbian cap cocked at a haughty angle over one arch. Traditional national emblems, like the *sajkaca*, a strong, unique Serbian symbol, had undergone a revival in recent years with the rise of Serbian nationalism. "By adding this symbol of our cultural heritage, we hoped to denote our pride in being a local company."

Additionally, more than 3,000 free burgers were delivered to the participants of the Belgrade marathon, which was dominated by an anti-NATO theme. At the same time, the company announced that for every burger sold, it would donate one dinar (about a nickel) to the Yugoslav Red Cross to help victims of NATO's air strikes. It also handed out free cheeseburgers at anti-NATO rallies.

Once the war was over, the company basked in its success. Cash registers were ringing at prewar levels. McDonald's restaurants around the country were thronged with Serbs hungry for Big Macs and fries. And why not, asks 16-year-old Jovan Stojanovic, munching on a burger. "I don't associate McDonald's with America," he says. "Mac is ours." This claim is music to McDonald's ears. "We managed to save our brand."

Sources: Robert Block, "How Big Mac Kept from Becoming a Serb Archenemy," *The Wall Street Journal*, September 3, 1999; John Kozak, "McDonald's Can't Serve Up World Peace," *The Guardian*, April 26, 2005, p. 27.

will be profitable in the future. Additionally, one study found that compared with American and Japanese managers, French managers' market entry decisions appear to be more influenced by concerns about political risk in foreign markets.[47] Early risk is accepted in exchange for being in the country when the economy begins to grow and risk subsides.

During the chaos that arose after the political and economic changes in the Soviet Union, the newly formed republics were eager to make deals with foreign investors, yet the problems and uncertainty made many investors take a wait-and-see attitude. However, as one executive commented, "If U.S. companies wait until all the problems are solved, somebody else will get the business." Certainly the many companies that are investing in the former Soviet Union or China do not expect big returns immediately; they are betting on the future. For a marketer doing business in a foreign country, a necessary part of any market analysis is an assessment of the probable political consequences of a marketing plan, since some marketing activities are more susceptible to political considerations than others.

---

[47] Jennifer D. Chandler and John L. Graham, "Using Formative Indicators to Discern the Meaning of Corruption and Its Impact on International Marketing," working paper, University of California, Irvine, 2008.

Lessening Political Vulnerability

Although a company cannot directly control or alter the political environment of the country within which it operates, a specific business venture can take measures to lessen its degree of susceptibility to politically induced risks.

Foreign investors frequently are accused of exploiting a country's wealth at the expense of the national population and for the sole benefit of the foreign investor. This attitude is best summed up in a statement made by a recent president of Peru: "We have had massive foreign investment for decades but Peru has not achieved development. Foreign capital will now have to meet government and social goals." Such charges are not wholly unsupported by past experiences.

As long as these impressions persist, the political climate for foreign investors will continue to be hostile. Companies must manage external affairs in foreign markets to ensure that the host government and the public are aware of their contributions to the economic, social, and human development of the country. Relations between governments and MNCs are generally positive if the investment (1) improves the balance of payments by increasing exports or reducing imports through import substitution; (2) uses locally produced resources; (3) transfers capital, technology, and/or skills; (4) creates jobs; and/or (5) makes tax contributions.

In addition to the economic contributions a company makes, corporate philanthropy also helps create positive images among the general population. Many MNCs strive to benefit countries through their social programs, which polish their image as well. For example, Microsoft, recognizing that developing countries need sophisticated technical assistance, pledged more than $100 million in technology and training as part of a deal to put government services online in Mexico. Cisco Systems, the leading maker of Internet hardware, relies on nonprofit organizations to run its 10,000 networking academies, which train college and high school students to create computer networks in 150 countries. In China, Procter & Gamble is helping local schools and universities train and educate leaders. And in Malaysia, Motorola and Intel have instituted training programs to enhance the skills of local workers.

Merck, the pharmaceutical company, has developed a pill to fight river blindness in Africa and Latin America. River blindness is a parasitic disease transmitted to humans through the bite of the black fly commonly found along the riverbanks in some African countries. The parasite infiltrates, multiplies, and spreads throughout the body for as long as 15 years, causing acute skin rashes, terrible itching, and sometimes disfigurement or blindness. The pill is taken just once a year and has been proven to prevent the disease. Merck contributed millions of doses to fight the disease in developing countries.[48]

Although companies strive to become good corporate citizens in their host countries, political parties seeking publicity or scapegoats for their failures often serve their own interests by focusing public opinion on the negative aspects of MNCs, whether true or false. Companies that establish deep local roots and show by example, rather than meaningless talk, that their strategies are aligned with the long-term goals of the host country stand the best chance of overcoming a less than positive image. "In times like these," says one executive, "global citizenship is perhaps more important than ever."[49] An effective defense for the multinational company is to actively participate in improving the lives of local citizens.

In addition to corporate activities focused on the social and economic goals of the host country and good corporate citizenship, MNCs can use other strategies to minimize political vulnerability and risk.

Joint Ventures

Typically less susceptible to political harassment, joint ventures can be with locals or other third-country multinational companies; in both cases, a company's financial exposure is limited. A joint venture with locals helps minimize anti-MNC feelings, and a joint venture with another MNC adds the additional bargaining power of a third country.

---

[48] David Shook, "Merck Is Treating the Third World," *BusinessWeek Online,* October 10, 2002.

[49] Susan E. Reed, "Business; Technology Companies Take Hope in Charity," *The New York Times,* March 23, 2003, p. 17.

The most entertaining protest technique was pioneered by French farmers. Perhaps they were inspired by that American export, *Animal House*. In any case, French farmers like to throw their food. Here they tossed tomatoes and such at McDonald's; they've also lobbed lamb chops at their own trade ministers. Apparently they pay attention in Taiwan. Most recently, fishermen pitched perch in Taipei to protest the Japanese fishing fleet's presence in their waters. (*left: AP Photo/Claude Paris; right: AP Photo*)

Expanding the Investment Base

Including several investors and banks in financing an investment in the host country is another strategy. This approach has the advantage of engaging the power of the banks whenever any kind of government takeover or harassment is threatened. This strategy becomes especially powerful if the banks have made loans to the host country; if the government threatens expropriation or other types of takeover, the financing bank has substantial power with the government.

Licensing

A strategy that some firms find eliminates almost all risks is to license technology for a fee. Licensing can be effective in situations in which the technology is unique and the risk is high. Of course, there is some risk assumed, because the licensee can refuse to pay the required fees while continuing to use the technology.

Planned Domestication

In those cases in which a host country is demanding local participation, the most effective long-range solution is planned phasing out, that is, planned domestication. This method is not the preferred business practice, but the alternative of government-initiated domestication can be as disastrous as confiscation. As a reasonable response to the potential of domestication, planned domestication can be profitable and operationally expedient for the foreign investor. Planned domestication is, in essence, a gradual process of participating with nationals in all phases of company operations.

Political Bargaining

Multinational companies clearly engage in lobbying and other sorts of political bargaining to avoid potential political risks.[50] Mattel issued an extraordinary apology to China over the recall of Chinese-made toys, saying the items were defective because of Mattel's design flaws rather than faulty manufacturing.[51] In doing so, Mattel was (1) protecting the huge and all-important head of its value chain; (2) recognizing that it would be easier to fix its design and inspection routines than quickly affect manufacturing practices in China; and (3) uniquely for an American firm, publicly admitting its own very real culpability. On the other side of the

---

[50] Amy J. Hillman and William P. Wan, "The Determinants of MNE Subsidiaries' Political Strategies: Evidence of Institutional Duality," *Journal of International Business Studies* 36, no. 3 (2005), pp. 322–40.

[51] "Mattel Apologizes to China over Recall," *Associated Press*, September 21, 2007.

Political and economic aid in action, where everybody wins. The Japanese government has paid for the construction of a new highway that connects key safari tourism areas in Tanzania. Foreign tourism becomes more efficient, comfortable, and profitable for the Tanzanian company (and others) pictured—Kibo is one of the best in the country. The Japanese designers, consultants, and contractors involved make money on the work. And the road ultimately pays for itself in the form of lower warranty expenses on the armada of Toyota Land Cruisers that regularly ply the path between the Makuyuni and Ngorongoro animal preserves.

Pacific, Toyota has considered raising prices of its cars in the American market to "help" its ailing American competitors.[52] The Japanese government has set quotas on auto exports in the past as American car companies have struggled. And in the face of growing American and European criticism, China has agreed to put quotas on its exports of textiles[53] and to float its currency.[54] Finally, a cynical way to look at the motivation behind corporate social responsibility in general is its use as a bargaining chip with foreign publics and governments.[55]

Political Payoffs   One approach to dealing with political vulnerability is the political payoff—an attempt to lessen political risks by paying those in power to intervene on behalf of the multinational company. This choice is not an approach we recommend in any way. However, your competitors may use such a tactic, so beware. Political payoffs, or bribery, have been used to lessen the negative effects of a variety of problems. Paying heads of state to avoid confiscatory taxes or expulsion, paying fees to agents to ensure the acceptance of sales contracts, and providing monetary encouragement to an assortment of people whose actions can affect the effectiveness of a company's programs are decisions that frequently confront multinational managers and raise ethical questions.

Bribery poses problems for the marketer at home and abroad, because it is illegal for U.S. citizens to pay a bribe even if it is a common practice in the host country. Political payoffs may offer short-term benefits, but in the long run, the risks are high, and bribery is an untenable option. This issue is discussed in more detail in Chapter 7.

Government Encouragement

Governments, both foreign and U.S., encourage foreign investment as well as discourage it. In fact, within the same country, some foreign businesses may fall prey to politically induced harassment, while others may be placed under a government umbrella of protection and preferential treatment. The difference lies in the evaluation of a company's contribution to the nation's interest.

The most important reason to encourage foreign investment is to accelerate the development of an economy. An increasing number of countries are encouraging foreign investment

[52] "Toyota May Raise Prices to Avoid Backlash," *Associated Press*, April 26, 2005.

[53] "China to Put Quotas on Textile Exports," *Reuters*, June 22, 2005.

[54] Don Lee and Ching-Ching Ni, "China Revalues Currency in Action Sought by U.S.," *Los Angeles Times*, July 22, 2005, pp. A1, A4.

[55] Daniel Franklin, "Just Good Business," *The Economist*, January 18, 2008, pp. 1–24.

with specific guidelines aimed toward economic goals. Multinational corporations may be expected to create local employment, transfer technology, generate export sales, stimulate growth and development of local industry, conserve foreign exchange, or meet a combination of these expectations as a requirement for market concessions. Recent investments in China, India, and the former republics of the Soviet Union include provisions stipulating specific contributions to economic goals of the country that must be made by foreign investors.

The U.S. government is motivated for economic as well as political reasons to encourage American firms to seek business opportunities in countries worldwide, including those that are politically risky. It seeks to create a favorable climate for overseas business by providing the assistance that helps minimize some of the more troublesome politically motivated financial risks of doing business abroad. The Department of Commerce (DOC) at www.doc.gov is the principal agency that supports U.S. business abroad. The International Trade Administration (ITA) at www.ita.gov, a bureau of the DOC, is dedicated to helping U.S. business compete in the global marketplace. Other agencies that provide assistance to U.S. companies include:

- Export-Import Bank (Ex-Im Bank) underwrites trade and investments for U.S. firms. www.exim.gov

- Foreign Credit Insurance Association (FCIA), an agency of the Ex-Im Bank, provides credit insurance that minimizes nonpayment risk caused by financial, economic, or political uncertainties. It includes insurance against confiscation, civil disturbances, and the cancellation or restriction of export or import licenses. www.fcia.com

- The Agency for International Development (AID) provides aid to underdeveloped countries and has limited protection in support of "essential" projects in approved countries and for approved products. www.usaid.gov

- The Overseas Private Investment Corporation (OPIC) provides risk insurance for companies investing in less-developed countries. www.opic.gov

Summary

Vital to every marketer's assessment of a foreign market is an appreciation for the political environment of the country within which he or she plans to operate. Government involvement in business activities abroad, especially foreign-controlled business, is generally much greater than business is accustomed to in the United States. The foreign firm must strive to make its activities politically acceptable, or it may be subjected to a variety of politically condoned harassment. In addition to the harassment that can be imposed by a government, the foreign marketer frequently faces the problem of uncertainty of continuity in government policy.

As governments change political philosophies, a marketing firm accepted under one administration might find its activities undesirable under another. An unfamiliar or hostile political environment does not necessarily preclude success for a foreign marketer if the company becomes a local economic asset and responds creatively to the issues raised by political and social activists. The U.S. government may aid an American business in its foreign operations, and if a company is considered vital to achieving national economic goals, the host country often provides an umbrella of protection not extended to others.

Questions

1. Define the following terms:

   sovereignty   confiscation
   nationalism   domestication
   expropriation   PSAs
   NGOs

2. Why would a country rather domesticate than expropriate?

3. "A crucial fact when doing business in a foreign country is that permission to conduct business is controlled by the government of the host country." Comment.

4. What are the main factors to consider in assessing the dominant political climate within a country?

5. Why is a working knowledge of political party philosophy so important in a political assessment of a market? Discuss.

6. How can a change in the political party in power affect an investor? Discuss and give examples.

7. What are the most common causes of instability in governments? Discuss.

8. Discuss how governmental instability can affect marketing.

9. What are the most frequently encountered political risks in foreign business? Discuss.

10. Expropriation is considered a major risk of foreign business. Discuss ways in which this particular type of risk can be minimized somewhat as a result of company activities. Explain how these risks have been minimized by the activities of the U.S. government.

11. How do exchange controls impede foreign business? Discuss.

12. How do foreign governments encourage foreign investment? Discuss.

13. How does the U.S. government encourage foreign investment?

14. What are the motives behind U.S. government encouragement for foreign investment? Explain.

15. Discuss measures a company might take to lessen its political vulnerability.

16. Select a country and analyze it politically from a marketing viewpoint.

17. The text suggests that violence is a politically motivated risk of international business. Comment.

18. There is evidence that expropriation and confiscation are less frequently encountered today than just a few years ago. Why?

What other types of political risks have replaced expropriation and confiscation in importance?

19. You are an executive in a large domestic company with only minor interests in international markets; however, corporate plans call for major global expansion. Visit the home page of Control Risks Group (CRG) at www.crg.com. After thoroughly familiarizing yourself with the services offered by CRG, write a brief report to management describing how its services could possibly help with your global expansion.

20. Visit the Web site www.politicalresources.net/and select the Political Site of the Week. Write a brief political analysis highlighting potential problem areas for a company interested in investing in that country.

21. Search the Web for information about the activities of PSAs outside the United States and write a briefing paper for international management on potential problems.

22. Discuss ways the companies discussed in the Global Perspective could have minimized their losses in the banana wars.

23. Discuss any ethical and socially responsible issues that may be implied in the Global Perspective. Political disaster strikes Kenya. In the Nairobi slum of Kibera, supporters of opposition leader Raila Odinga tear up a key railway that ran from the coast to Uganda. They renamed the broken line "Odinga Highway."

7

The International Legal Environment:

PLAYING BY THE RULES

CHAPTER LEARNING OBJECTIVES

What you should learn from Chapter 7:

- The four heritages of today's legal systems

- The important factors in the jurisdiction of legal disputes

- Issues associated with the jurisdiction of legal disputes and the various methods of dispute resolution

- The unique problems of protecting intellectual property rights internationally

- How to protect against piracy and counterfeiting

- The legal differences between countries and how those differences can affect international marketing plans

- The different ways U.S. laws can be applied to U.S. companies operating outside the United States

- The many issues of evolving cyberlaw

Global Perspective

THE PAJAMA CAPER

Six headlines illustrate the entanglements possible when U.S. law, host-country law, and a multinational company collide:

- "Wal-Mart's Cuban-Made Pajamas Defy Embargo"
- "Wal-Mart Ignites Row by Pulling Cuban Pajamas off Shelves in Canada"
- "Canada, U.S. Wager Diplomatic Capital in a High-Stakes Pajama Game"
- "Cuban Quandary: Wal-Mart in Hot Water for Yanking Pajamas"
- "Canada Probes Wal-Mart Move against Cuban Pajamas"
- "Wal-Mart Puts Cuban Goods Back on Sale"

The controversy arose over a U.S. embargo forbidding U.S. businesses to trade with Cuba and concerned whether or not the embargo could be enforced in Canada. Wal-Mart was selling Cuban-made pajamas in Canada. When Wal-Mart officials in the United States became aware of the origin of manufacture, they issued an order to remove all the offending pajamas because it is against U.S. law (the Helms-Burton Act) for a U.S. company or any of its foreign subsidiaries to trade with Cuba. Canada was incensed at the intrusion of U.S. law on Canadian citizens. The Canadians felt they should have the choice of buying Cuban-made pajamas.

Wal-Mart was thus caught in the middle of conflicting laws in Canada and the United States and a Canada–U.S. foreign policy feud over the extraterritoriality of U.S. law. Wal-Mart Canada would be breaking U.S. law if it continued to sell the pajamas, and it would be subject to a million-dollar fine and possible imprisonment of its managers. However, if the company pulled the pajamas out of Canadian stores as the home office ordered, it would be subject to a $1.2 million fine under Canadian law. After discussion with Canadian authorities, Wal-Mart resumed selling the pajamas. Canada was upset with the United States for attempting to impose its laws on Canadian companies (Wal-Mart Canada is a subsidiary of Wal-Mart U.S.), while the United States says that Wal-Mart was violating its laws in not abiding by the boycott against Cuba. The situation illustrates the reality of the legal environment and international marketing—companies are subject to both home-country laws and host-country laws when doing business in another country. The federal government finally settled with Wal-Mart in 2003, and the pajama caper was finally closed.

Sources: *Boston Globe,* March 3, 1997; *St. Louis Post-Dispatch,* March 9, 1997; *Washington Post,* March 14, 1997, p. A6; *The Wall Street Journal,* March 14, 1997, p. B4; John W. Boscariol, "An Anatomy of a Cuban Pyjama Crisis," *Law and Policy in International Business,* Spring 1999, p. 439; Pablo Bachelet, "Hard-Liner Backs Easing Cuba Travel Ban," *Miami Herald,* March 22, 2007.

How would you like to play a game in which the stakes were high, there was no standard set of rules to play by, the rules changed whenever a new player entered the game, and, when a dispute arose, the referee used the other players' rules to interpret who was right? This game fairly well describes the international legal environment. Because no single, uniform international commercial law governing foreign business transactions exists, the international marketer must pay particular attention to the laws of each country within which it operates.[1] An American company doing business with a French customer has to contend with two jurisdictions (United States and France), two tax systems, two legal systems, and other supranational sets of European Union laws and WTO regulations that may override commercial laws of the countries. The situation is similar when doing business in Japan, Germany, or any other country. Laws governing business activities within and between countries are an integral part of the legal environment of international business.

The legal systems of different countries are so disparate and complex that it is beyond the scope of this text to explore the laws of each country individually. There are, however, issues common to most international marketing transactions that need special attention when operating abroad. Jurisdiction, dispute resolution, intellectual property, the extraterritoriality of U.S. laws, cyberlaw, and associated problems are discussed in this chapter to provide a broad view of the international legal environment. Although space and focus limit an in-depth presentation, the material presented should be sufficient for the reader to conclude that securing expert legal advice is a wise decision when doing business in another country. The foundation of a legal system profoundly affects how the law is written, interpreted, and adjudicated. The place to begin is with a discussion of the different legal systems.

Bases for Legal Systems

Four heritages form the bases for the majority of the legal systems of the world: (1) common law, derived from English law and found in England, the United States, Canada,[2] and other countries once under English influence; (2) civil or code law, derived from Roman law and found in Germany, Japan, France, and non-Islamic and non-Marxist countries; (3) Islamic law, derived from the interpretation of the Koran and found in Pakistan, Iran, Saudi Arabia, and other Islamic states; and (4) a commercial legal system in the Marxist–socialist economies of Russia and the republics of the former Soviet Union, Eastern Europe, China, and other Marxist–socialist states whose legal system centered on the economic, political, and social policies of the state. As each country moves toward its own version of a free market system and enters the global market, a commercial legal system is also evolving from those Marxist–socialist tenets. China has announced that it will adopt a constitution-based socialist legal system with Chinese characteristics.

The differences among these four systems are of more than theoretical importance because due process of law may vary considerably among and within these legal systems. Even though a country's laws may be based on the doctrine of one of the four legal systems, its individual interpretation may vary significantly—from a fundamentalist interpretation of Islamic law as found in Pakistan to a combination of several legal systems found in the United States, where both common and code law are reflected in the legal system.

One measure of the importance of the legal system in each country is the number of attorneys per capita. Please see Exhibit 7.1. Judging by that metric, the legal system is called upon to settle commercial disputes much more frequently in the United States than in China. As Japan continues to become more integrated in the global market, the need for attorneys is burgeoning. There are approximately 23,000 attorneys there now, and the Japanese government intends to grow that number to 50,000 by 2018.[3]

---

[1] Ilan Greenberg, "American Snared in Kazakh Legal Dispute," *The New York Times*, April 23, 2007, p. A11; Lorraine Woellert, "Made in China. Sued Here." *BusinessWeek*, July 9 and 16, 2007, p. 9.

[2] All the provinces of Canada have a common-law system with the exception of Quebec, which is a code-law province. All the states in the United States are common law except Louisiana, which is code law.

[3] Kana Inagaki, "Major Legal Reforms Expected to Bring Wave of New Lawyers in Japan," *Associated Press*, August 22, 2007.

Exhibit 7.1

Lawyers per 100,000 People in Selected Countries

Sources: Council of Bars and Law Societies of Europe (www.ccbe.org), 2005; "More than 2000 Counties Have No Lawyers," *People's Daily Online*, June 10, 2005; Kana Inagaki, "Major Legal Reforms Expected to Bring Wave of New Lawyers in Japan," *Associated Press*, August 22, 2007.

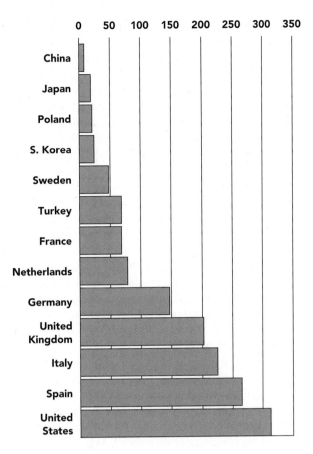

Common vs. Code Law

The basis for *common law*[4] is tradition, past practices, and legal precedents set by the courts through interpretations of statutes, legal legislation, and past rulings. Common law seeks "interpretation through the past decisions of higher courts which interpret the same statutes or apply established and customary principles of law to a similar set of facts." *Code law,*[5] in contrast, is based on an all-inclusive system of written rules (codes) of law. Under code law, the legal system is generally divided into three separate codes: commercial, civil, and criminal.

Common law is recognized as not being all-inclusive, whereas code law is considered complete as a result of catchall provisions found in most code-law systems. For example, under the commercial code in a code-law country, the law governing contracts is made inclusive with the statement that "a person performing a contract shall do so in conformity with good faith as determined by custom and good morals." Although code law is considered all-inclusive, it is apparent from the foregoing statement that some broad interpretations are possible in order to include everything under the existing code.

Steps are being taken in common-law countries to codify commercial law even though the primary basis of commercial law is common law, that is, precedents set by court decisions. An example of the new uniformity is the acceptance of the Uniform Commercial Code by most states in the United States. Even though U.S. commercial law has been codified to some extent under the Uniform Commercial Code, the philosophy of interpretation is anchored in common law.

As discussed later in the section on the protection of intellectual property, laws governing intellectual property offer the most striking differences between common-law and code-law systems. Under common law, ownership is established by use; under code law, ownership is determined by registration. In some code-law countries, certain agreements may not be enforceable unless properly notarized or registered; in a common-law country, the same

---

[4] Also known as English law.

[5] Also known as the Napoleonic Code.

agreement may be binding so long as proof of the agreement can be established. Although every country has elements of both common and code law, the differences in interpretation between common- and code-law systems regarding contracts, sales agreements, and other legal issues are significant enough that an international marketer familiar with only one system must enlist the aid of legal counsel for the most basic legal questions.

Another illustration of how fundamental differences in the two systems can cause difficulty is in the performance of a contract. Under common law in the United States, the impossibility of performance does not necessarily excuse compliance with the provisions of a contract unless compliance is impossible because of an act of God, such as some extraordinary occurrence of nature not reasonably anticipated by either party of a contract. Hence floods, lightning, earthquakes, and similar events are generally considered acts of God. Under code law, acts of God are not limited solely to acts of nature but are extended to include "unavoidable interference with performance, whether resulting from forces of nature or unforeseeable human acts," including such things as labor strikes and riots.

Consider the following situations: A contract was entered into to deliver a specific quantity of cloth. In one case, before the seller could make delivery, an earthquake caused the destruction of the cloth and compliance was then impossible. In the second case, pipes in the sprinkler system where the material was stored froze and broke, spilling water on the cloth and destroying it. In each case, loss of the merchandise was sustained and delivery could not be made. Were the parties in these cases absolved of their obligations under the contract because of the impossibility of delivery? The answer depends on the system of law invoked.

In the first situation, the earthquake would be considered an act of God under both common and code law, and impossibility of performance would excuse compliance under the contract. In the second situation, courts in common-law countries would probably rule that the bursting of the water pipes did not constitute an act of God if it happened in a climate where freezing could be expected. Therefore, impossibility of delivery would not necessarily excuse compliance with the provisions of the contract. In code-law countries, where the scope of impossibility of performance is extended considerably, the destruction might very well be ruled an act of God, and thus, release from compliance with the contract could be obtained.

Islamic Law

The basis for the *Shari'ah* (Islamic law) is interpretation of the Koran. It encompasses religious duties and obligations, as well as the secular aspect of law regulating human acts. Broadly speaking, Islamic law defines a complete system that prescribes specific patterns of social and economic behavior for all individuals. It includes issues such as property rights, economic decision making, and types of economic freedom. The overriding objective of the Islamic system is social justice.

Among the unique aspects of Islamic law is the prohibition against the payment of interest. The Islamic law of contracts states that any given transaction should be devoid of *riba,* which is defined as unlawful advantage by way of excess of deferment, that is, interest or usury. Prohibiting the receipt and payment of interest is the nucleus of the Islamic system. However, other principles of Islamic doctrine advocate risk sharing, individuals' rights and duties, property rights, and the sanctity of contracts. The Islamic system places emphasis on the ethical, moral, social, and religious dimensions to enhance equality and fairness for the good of society. Another principle of the Islamic legal system is the prohibition against investment in those activities that violate the *Shari'ah.* For example, any investment in a business dealing with alcohol, gambling, and casinos would be prohibited.

Prohibition against the payment of interest affects banking and business practices severely.[6] However, certain

Banking in Dubai, UAE, requires an understanding of Islamic law and customs. Prohibition against the payment of interest and prohibition against investments in businesses dealing with alcohol and gambling are two of the tenets of Islamic law that affect banking. *(© Derek Berwin/The Image Bank/Getty Images)*

---

[6] Sugata Ghosh, "Government Asks RBI to Draw up Roadmap for Islamic Banking," *Economic Times,* July 6, 2005.

acceptable practices adhere to Islamic law and permit the transaction of business. Mortgages for property are difficult because payment of interest is forbidden under Islamic law. Buyers of real property have to use a financier, who buys the property and then sells it to them in return for repayments of the capital. Instead of charging interest, a financier either sells the property at a higher price or sells it at the same price and takes additional payments to cover what would have been interest. Of the other ways to comply with Islamic law in financial transactions, trade with markup or cost-plus sale (*murabaha*) and leasing (*ijara*) are the most frequently used. In both *murabaha* and *ijara,* a mutually negotiated margin is included in the sale price or leasing payment. These practices meet the requirements of *Shari'ah* by enabling borrowers and lenders to share in the rewards as well as losses in an equitable fashion. They also ensure that the process of wealth accumulation and distribution in the economy is fair and representative of true productivity. Strict fundamentalists often frown on such an arrangement, but it is practiced and is an example of the way the strictness of Islamic law can be reconciled with the laws of non-Islamic legal systems.

Because the laws are based on interpretation of the Koran, the international marketer must have knowledge of the religion's tenets and understand the way the law may be interpreted in each region. Regional courts can interpret Islamic law from the viewpoint of fundamentalists (those that adhere to a literal interpretation of the Koran), or they may use a more liberal translation. A company can find local authorities in one region willing to allow payment of interest on deferred obligations as stipulated in a contract, while in another region, all interest charges may be deleted and replaced with comparable "consulting fees." In yet another, authorities may void a contract and declare any payment of interest illegal. Marketers conducting business in Islamic-law countries must be knowledgeable about this important legal system.

Marxist–Socialist Tenets

As socialist countries become more directly involved in trade with non-Marxist countries, it has been necessary to develop a commercial legal system that permits them to engage in active international commerce. The pattern for development varies among the countries because each has a different background, and each is at a different stage in its development of a market-driven economy. For example, central European countries such as the Czech Republic and Poland had comprehensive codified legal systems before communism took over, and their pre–World War II commercial legal codes have been revised and reinstituted. Consequently, they have moved toward a legal model with greater ease than some others have. Russia and most of the republics of the former Soviet Union and China have had to build from scratch an entire commercial legal system. Under the premise that law, according to Marxist–socialist tenets, is strictly subordinate to prevailing economic conditions, such fundamental propositions as private ownership, contracts, due process, and other legal mechanisms have had to be developed. China and Russia differ, however, in that each has taken a different direction in its political economic growth. Russia is moving toward a democratic system. China is attempting to activate a private sector within a multicomponent, or mixed, economy in a socialist legal framework; that is, it tries to "perform its functions according to law and contribute to the development of socialist democracy and political civilization in China."

Both countries have actively passed laws, though the process has been slow and often disjointed. China has implemented hundreds of new laws and regulations governing trade, yet the process is hampered by vaguely written laws, the lack of implementation mechanisms for the new laws, and an ineffective framework for dispute resolution and enforcement. A good example is China's attempt to control what goes on in Chinese cyberspace by applying the States Secrets Law to the Internet. The definition of a state secret is so broad that it can cover any information not cleared for publication with the relevant authorities.

Russia's experience has been similar to China's, in that vaguely worded laws have been passed without mechanisms for implementation. The situation in Russia is often described as chaotic because of the laws' lack of precision. For example, to illegally receive or disseminate commercial secrets has become a crime, but the law provides no exact definition of a commercial secret. Copyright law violations that cause "great damage" are listed but with no clear definition of how much damage constitutes "great." Both China and Russia are hampered by not having the heritage of a legal commercial code to build on, as many of the Eastern-bloc European countries had.

The international marketer must be concerned with the differences among common law, code law, Islamic law, and socialist legal systems when operating between countries; the rights of the principals of a contract or some other legal document under one law may be significantly different from their rights under the other. It should be kept in mind that there could also be differences between the laws of two countries whose laws are based on the same legal system. Thus the problem of the marketer is one of anticipating the different laws regulating business, regardless of the legal system of the country.

Jurisdiction in International Legal Disputes

Determining whose legal system has jurisdiction when a commercial dispute arises is another problem of international marketing. A frequent error is to assume that disputes between citizens of different nations are adjudicated under some supranational system of laws. Unfortunately, no judicial body exists to deal with legal commercial problems arising between citizens of different countries. Confusion probably stems from the existence of international courts such as the World Court at The Hague and the International Court of Justice, the principal judicial organ of the United Nations. These courts are operative in international disputes between sovereign nations of the world rather than between private citizens and/or companies.

Legal disputes can arise in three situations: between governments, between a company and a government, and between two companies. The World Court can adjudicate disputes between governments, whereas the other two situations must be handled in the courts of the country of one of the parties involved or through arbitration. Unless a commercial dispute involves a national issue between nation states, the International Court of Justice or any similar world court does not handle it. Because there is no "international commercial law," the foreign marketer must look to the legal system of each country involved—the laws of the home country, the laws of the countries within which business is conducted, or both.[7]

When international commercial disputes must be settled under the laws of one of the countries concerned, the paramount question in a dispute is: Which law governs? Jurisdiction is generally determined in one of three ways: (1) on the basis of jurisdictional clauses included in contracts, (2) on the basis of where a contract was entered into, or (3) on the basis of where the provisions of the contract were performed.

The most clear-cut decision can be made when the contracts or legal documents supporting a business transaction include a jurisdictional clause. A clause similar to the following establishes jurisdiction in the event of disagreements:

> That the parties hereby agree that the agreement is made in Oregon, USA, and that any question regarding this agreement shall be governed by the law of the state of Oregon, USA.

This clause establishes that the laws of the state of Oregon would be invoked should a dispute arise. If the complaint were brought in the court of another country, it is probable that the same Oregon laws would govern the decision. Cooperation and a definite desire to be judicious in foreign legal problems have led to the practice of foreign courts judging disputes on the basis of the law of another country or state whenever applicable. Thus, if an injured party from Oregon brings suit in the courts of Mexico against a Mexican over a contract that included the preceding clause, it would not be unusual for the Mexican courts to decide on the basis of Oregon law. This tendency assumes, of course, it has been recognized that Oregon law prevailed in this dispute, either as a result of the prior agreement by the parties or on some other basis.

---

[7] For a legal and thorough discussion of the globalization of jurisdiction, see Paul Schiff Berman, "The Globalization of Jurisdiction," *University of Pennsylvania Law Review*, December 2002, p. 311; Yadong Luo, "Transactional Characteristics, Institutional Environment, and Joint Venture Contracts," *Journal of International Business Studies* 36, no. 2 (2005), pp. 209–30.

International Dispute Resolution

When things go wrong in a commercial transaction—the buyer refuses to pay, the product is of inferior quality, the shipment arrives late, or any one of the myriad problems that can arise—what recourse does the international marketer have? The first step in any dispute is to try to resolve the issue informally, but if that fails, the foreign marketer must resort to more resolute action. Such action can take the form of conciliation, arbitration, or, as a last resort, litigation. Most international businesspeople prefer a settlement through arbitration rather than by suing a foreign company.

Conciliation

Most disputes that arise in commercial transactions are settled informally. When resolution is not forthcoming, however, conciliation can be an important first step in settling a dispute. *Conciliation* (also known as *mediation*) is a nonbinding agreement between parties to resolve disputes by asking a third party to mediate differences. The function of the mediator is to carefully listen to each party and to explore, clarify, and discuss the various practical options and possibilities for a solution with the intent that the parties will agree on a solution. Unlike arbitration and litigation, conciliation sessions are private, and all conferences between parties and the mediator are confidential; the statements made by the parties may not be disclosed or used as evidence in any subsequent litigation or arbitration. The track record for the conciliation process is excellent, with a majority of disputes reaching settlement and leading to the resumption of business between the disputants.

Conciliation is considered especially effective when resolving disputes with Chinese business partners, because they feel less threatened by conciliation than arbitration. The Chinese believe that when a dispute occurs, informal, friendly negotiation should be used first to solve the problem; if that fails, conciliation should be tried. In fact, some Chinese companies may avoid doing business with companies that resort first to arbitration. Conciliation can be either formal or informal. Both sides agreeing on a third party to mediate can establish informal conciliation. Formal conciliation is conducted under the auspices of some tribunal such as the Beijing Conciliation Center, which assigns one or two conciliators to mediate. If an agreement is reached, a conciliation statement based on the signed agreement is recorded. Although conciliation may be the friendly route to resolving disputes in China, it is not legally binding; thus an arbitration clause should be included in all conciliation agreements. Experience has shown that having an arbitration clause in the conciliation agreement makes it easier to move to arbitration if necessary.

Arbitration

If conciliation is not used or an agreement cannot be reached, the next step is *arbitration*. When all else fails, arbitration rather than litigation is the preferred method for resolving international commercial disputes. The usual arbitration procedure is for the parties involved to select a disinterested and informed party or parties as referees to determine the merits of the case and make a judgment that both parties agree to honor. Although informal arbitration is workable, most arbitration is conducted under the auspices of one of the more formal domestic and international arbitration groups organized specifically to facilitate the resolution of commercial disputes. These groups have formal rules for the process and experienced arbitrators to assist. In most countries, decisions reached in formal arbitration are enforceable under the law.

The popularity of arbitration has led to a proliferation of arbitral centers established by countries, organizations, and institutions. All have adopted standardized rules and procedures to administer cases, and each has its strengths and weaknesses. Some of the more active are the following:

- The Inter-American Commercial Arbitration Commission
- The Canadian-American Commercial Arbitration Commission (for disputes between Canadian and U.S. businesses)
- The London Court of Arbitration (decisions are enforceable under English law and English courts)
- The American Arbitration Association (www.adr.org/)
- The International Chamber of Commerce (www.iccwbo.org/; select Arbitration)

Litigation   Lawsuits in public courts are avoided for many reasons. Most observers of lawsuits between citizens of different countries believe that almost all victories are spurious because the cost, frustrating delays, and extended aggravation that these cases produce are more oppressive by far than any matter of comparable size. In India, for instance, there is a backlog of more than three million cases, and litigating a breach of contract between private parties can take a decade or more. The best advice is to seek a settlement, if possible, rather than sue. Other deterrents to litigation are the following:

- Fear of creating a poor image and damaging public relations.

- Fear of unfair treatment in a foreign court. (Fear that a lawsuit can result in unfair treatment, perhaps intentionally, is justifiable, because the decision could be made by either a jury or a judge not well versed in trade problems and the intricacies of international business transactions.)

- Difficulty in collecting a judgment that may otherwise have been collected in a mutually agreed settlement through arbitration.

- The relatively high cost and time required when bringing legal action. The Rheem Manufacturing Company, a billion-dollar manufacturer of heating and air conditioning systems, estimates that by using arbitration over litigation, it has reduced the time and cost of commercial-dispute resolution by half.

- Loss of confidentiality. Unlike arbitration and conciliation proceedings, which are confidential, litigation is public.

One authority suggests that the settlement of every dispute should follow four steps: first, try to placate the injured party; if this does not work, conciliate, arbitrate, and, finally, litigate. The final step is typically taken only when all other methods fail. Furthermore, in some cases, problem-solving approaches may be warranted within the context of even litigated disputes.[9] This approach is probably wise whether one is involved in an international dispute or a domestic one.

Protection of Intellectual Property Rights: A Special Problem   Companies

spend millions of dollars establishing brand names or trademarks to symbolize quality and design a host of other product features meant to entice customers to buy their brands to the exclusion of all others. Millions more are spent on research to develop products, processes, designs, and formulas that provide companies with advantages over their competitors. Such intellectual or industrial properties are among the more valuable assets a company may possess. Brand names such as Kodak, Coca-Cola, and Gucci, processes such as xerography, and computer software are invaluable. One financial group estimated that the Marlboro brand had a value of $33 billion, Kellogg's $9 billion, Microsoft $9.8 billion, and Levi's $5 billion; all have experienced infringement of their intellectual property rights. Normally, property rights can be legally protected to prevent other companies from infringing on such assets. Companies must, however, keep a constant vigil against piracy and counterfeiting. Moreover, with increasing frequency, companies are developing new technologies to prevent piracy, but counterfeiters are relentless in their criticism of and technological attacks on even the most sophisticated security measures.[10]

Counterfeiting and Piracy   Counterfeit and pirated goods come from a wide range of industries—apparel, automotive parts, agricultural chemicals, pharmaceuticals, books (yes, even management books such as the one you are reading right now),[11] records, films, computer software, baby formula, auto

---

[9] Chang Zhang, David A. Griffith, and S. Tamer Cavusgil, "The Litigated Dissolution of International Distribution Relationships: A Process Framework and Propositions," *Journal of International Marketing* 14, no. 2 (2006), pp. 85–115.

[10] Eric Schine, "Faking out the Fakers," *BusinessWeek*, June 4, 2007, pp. 75–79; Ethan Smith, "Napster Format Shift Would Enable More Players," *The Wall Street Journal*, January 7, 2008, p. B2.

[11] Don Lee, "Ripping Off Good Reads in China," *Los Angeles Times*, April 24, 2005, pp. C1, C10.

Exhibit 7.2

Piracy Rates for Computer Software, Top and Bottom 20

Source: From *2007 BSA and IDC Global Software Piracy Study*, Business Software Alliance, May 2005. Reprinted with permission. *Fourth Annual BSA and IDC Global Software Piracy Study* (Washington, DC: Business Software Alliance, 2007), www.bsa.org/globalstudy. One hundred two countries and regions are ranked.

Highest Piracy Rates		Lowest Piracy Rates	
Armenia	95%	Unites States	21%
Moldova	94	New Zealand	22
Azerbaijan	94	Japan	25
Zimbabwe	91	Denmark	25
Vietnam	88	Austria	26
Venezuela	86	Switzerland	26
Pakistan	86	Sweden	26
Indonesia	85	Finland	27
Ukraine	84	United Kingdom	27
Cameroon	84	Belgium	27
Algeria	84	Germany	28
Montenegro	82	Netherlands	29
El Salvador	82	Australia	29
Zambia	82	Norway	29
Bolivia	82	Israel	32
Ivory Coast	82	Canada	34
China	82	UAE	35
Nigeria	82	South Africa	35
Paraguay	82	Ireland	36
Guatemala	81	Singapore	39

parts, and even cars themselves.[12] Estimates are that more than 10 million fake Swiss time-pieces carrying famous brand names such as Cartier and Rolex are sold every year, netting illegal profits of at least $500 million. Although difficult to pinpoint, lost sales from the unauthorized use of U.S. patents, trademarks, and copyrights amount to more than $300 billion annually. That translates into more than two million lost jobs. Software, music, and movies are especially attractive targets for pirates because they are costly to develop but cheap to reproduce and distribute over the Internet. Pirated CD music sales are estimated to exceed $5 billion annually and are growing at 6 percent per year. And unauthorized U.S. software that sells for $500 in this country can be purchased for less than $10 in East Asia. The Business Software Alliance, a trade group, estimates that software companies lost over $11.6 billion in the Asia-Pacific region, $15.7 billion in Europe, and $8.1 billion in North America in 2006. One might conclude from perusing Exhibit 7.2 that China is the biggest piracy problem, given its high ranking and large size. However, the dollars lost in the Unites States because of software piracy are the most in the world at $7.3 billion, with China coming in a close second at $5.4 billion. The good news in the data is that piracy rates are dropping remarkably fast in China (down an impressive 10 percent from 2003), due primarily to education programs, enforcement, and Microsoft's historic agreement with Lenovo. We also note that other populous nations have made major progress in reducing software piracy (e.g., Russia down 7 percent, Japan and Vietnam both down 4 percent) between 2003 and 2006.[13]

Recent research implies that for companies like Microsoft, some level of piracy actually can serve the company. It can be seen as a kind of product trial that ultimately builds commitment. As updated versions of products become available, purchases may actually follow. Particularly as countries such as China begin to enforce WTO statutes on piracy, customers conditioned on pirated goods may indeed be willing and able to pay for the new versions.

Although counterfeit CDs, toys, and similar products cost companies billions of dollars in lost revenue and have the potential of damaging the product's brand image, the

---

[12] Mark Landler, "Germans See Imitation in Chinese Cars," *The New York Times*, September 12, 2007, p. B3.

[13] *Fourth Annual BSA and IDC Global Software Piracy Study* (Washington, DC: Business Software Alliance, 2007), http://www.bsa.org/globalstudy; Howard W. French, "China Media Battle Hints at Shift on Intellectual Property," *The New York Times*, January 6, 2007, p. A3; Bruce Einhorn and Steve Hamm, "A Big Windows Cleanup, China Is Discovering that It Pays to Sell PCs that Contain Legitimate Microsoft Software," *BusinessWeek*, June 4, 2007, p. 80.

counterfeiting of pharmaceuticals can do serious physical harm. In Colombia, investigators found an illegal operation making more than 20,000 counterfeit tablets a day of the flu drug Dristan, a generic aspirin known as Dolex, and Ponstan 500, a popular painkiller made by Pfizer. The counterfeited pills contained boric acid, cement, floor wax, talcum powder, and yellow paint with high lead levels, all used to replicate the genuine medications' appearance.

Counterfeit drugs range from copies that have the same efficacy as the original to those with few or no active ingredients to those made of harmful substances. A pharmaceutical manufacturers' association estimates that 2 percent of the $327 billion worth of drugs sold each year are counterfeit, or about $6 billion worth. In some African and Latin American nations, as much as 60 percent are counterfeit. The World Health Organization thinks 8 percent of the bulk drugs imported into the United States are counterfeit, unapproved, or substandard.

Another problem is collusion between the contract manufacturer and illegitimate sellers. In China, exact copies of New Balance shoes are fabricated by contract manufacturers who are or were New Balance suppliers. They flood the market with genuine shoes that are sold for as little as $20. Unilever discovered that one of its suppliers in Shanghai made excess cases of soap, which were sold directly to retailers. One of Procter & Gamble's Chinese suppliers sold empty P&G shampoo bottles to another company, which filled them with counterfeit shampoo. Counterfeiting and piracy of intellectual property constitute outright theft, but the possibility of legally losing the rights to intellectual property because of inadequate protection of property rights and/or a country's legal structure is another matter.

Finally, it should be mentioned that some critics argue that MNCs have pushed the current intellectual property regime too far in favor of the firms, particularly with the most recent WTO TRIPS Agreement, to be discussed in more detail subsequently.[14] The critics suggest that the so-called tight rein the firms hold on the production of intellectual property has actually served to limit creativity and the associated benefits to the people that the intellectual property (IP) laws are intended to serve. Such arguments pitch antitrust laws against IP laws. The argument goes on.

Inadequate Protection

The failure to protect intellectual property rights adequately in the world marketplace can lead to the legal loss of rights in potentially profitable markets. Because patents, processes, trademarks, and copyrights are valuable in all countries, some companies have found their assets appropriated and profitably exploited in foreign countries without license or reimbursement.[15] Furthermore, they often learn that not only are other firms producing and selling their products or using their trademarks but the foreign companies are the rightful owners in the countries where they operate.

There have been many cases in which companies have legally lost the rights to trademarks and have had to buy back these rights or pay royalties for their use. The problems of inadequate protective measures taken by the owners of valuable assets stem from a variety of causes. One of the more frequent errors is assuming that because the company has established rights in the United States, they will be protected around the world or that rightful ownership can be established should the need arise. This assumption was the case with McDonald's in Japan, where enterprising Japanese registered its golden arches trademark. Only after a lengthy and costly legal action with a trip to the Japanese Supreme Court was McDonald's able to regain the exclusive right to use the trademark in Japan. After having to "buy" its trademark for an undisclosed amount, McDonald's maintains a very active program to protect its trademarks.

---

[14] Susan Sell, *Power and Ideas, North–South Politics of Intellectual Property and Antitrust* (Albany: State University of New York Press, 1998); Susan Sell, *Intellectual Property Rights: A Critical History* (Boulder, CO: Lynne Rienners Publishers, 2006).

[15] John Hagedoorn, Danielle Cloodt, and Hans van Kranenburg, "Intellectual Property Rights and the Governance of International R&D Partnerships," *Journal of International Business Studies* 36, no. 2 (2005), pp. 156–74.

Similarly, a South Korean company legally used the Coach brand on handbags and leather goods. The company registered the Coach trademark first and has the legal right to use that mark in Korea. The result is that a Coach-branded briefcase that is virtually identical to the U.S. product can be purchased for $135 in South Korea versus $320 in the United States. A U.S. attorney who practices with a South Korean firm noted that he has seen several instances in which a foreign company will come to Korea and naively start negotiating with a Korean company for distribution or licensing agreements, only to have the Korean company register the trademark in its own name. Later, the Korean company will use that registration as leverage in negotiations or, if the negotiations fall apart, sell the trademark back to the company. Many businesses fail to take proper steps to legally protect their intellectual property. They fail to understand that some countries do not follow the common-law principle that ownership is established by prior use or to realize that registration and legal ownership in one country does not necessarily mean ownership in another.

Prior Use versus Registration

In the United States, a common-law country, ownership of IP rights is established by prior use—whoever can establish first use is typically considered the rightful owner. In many code-law countries, however, ownership is established by registration rather than by prior use—the first to register a trademark or other property right is considered the rightful owner. For example, a trademark in Jordan belongs to whoever registers it first in Jordan. Thus you can find "McDonald's" restaurants, "Microsoft" software, and "Safeway" groceries all legally belonging to Jordanians. After a lengthy court battle that went to the Spanish Supreme Court, Nike lost its right to use the "Nike" brand name for sports apparel in Spain. Cidesport of Spain had been using Nike for sports apparel since 1932 and sued to block Nike (U.S.) sportswear sales. Because Cidesport does not sell shoes under the Nike label, Nike (U.S.) will be able to continue selling its brand of sports shoes in Spain. A company that believes it can always establish ownership in another country by proving it used the trademark or brand name first is wrong and risks the loss of these assets.

Besides the first-to-register issue, companies may encounter other problems with registering. China has improved intellectual property rights protection substantially and generally recognizes "first to invent." However, a Chinese company can capture the patent for a product invented elsewhere; it needs only to reverse-engineer or reproduce the product from published specifications and register it in China before the original inventor. Latvia and Lithuania permit duplicate registration of trademarks and brand names. A cosmetics maker registered Nivea and Niveja cosmetics brands in the former Soviet Union in 1986 and again in Latvia in 1992, but a Latvian firm had registered and had been selling a skin cream called Niveja since 1964. Neither the Soviet nor the Latvian authorities notified either firm. Applicants are responsible for informing themselves about similar trademarks that are already registered. The case is being taken to the Supreme Court of Latvia. It is best to protect IP rights through registration. Several international conventions provide for simultaneous registration in member countries.

International Conventions

Many countries participate in international conventions designed for mutual recognition and protection of intellectual property rights. There are three major international conventions:

1. The Paris Convention for the Protection of Industrial Property, commonly referred to as the Paris Convention, includes the United States and 100 other countries.
2. The Inter-American Convention includes most of the Latin American nations and the United States.
3. The Madrid Arrangement, which established the Bureau for International Registration of Trademarks, includes 26 European countries.

In addition, the World Intellectual Property Organization (WIPO) of the United Nations is responsible for the promotion of the protection of intellectual property and for the administration of the various multilateral treaties through cooperation among its member states.[16] Furthermore, two multicountry patent arrangements have streamlined patent procedures in Europe. The first, the Patent Cooperation Treaty (PCT), facilitates the process for application for patents among its member countries. It provides comprehensive coverage, in that a single application filed in the United States supplies the interested party with an international search report on other patents to help evaluate whether or not to seek protection in each of the countries cooperating under the PCT. The second, the European Patent Convention (EPC), established a regional patent system allowing any nationality to file a single international application for a European patent. Companies have a choice between relying on national systems when they want to protect a trademark or patent in just a few member countries and applying for protection in all 15 member states. Trademark protection is valid for 10 years and is renewable; however, if the mark is not used within 5 years, protection is forfeited. Once the patent or trademark is approved, it has the same effect as a national patent or trademark in each individual country designated on the application.

The Trade-Related Aspects of Intellectual Property Rights (TRIPs) agreement, a major provision of the World Trade Organization, is the most comprehensive multilateral agreement on intellectual property to date. TRIPs sets standards of protection for a full range of intellectual property rights that are embodied in current international agreements. The three main provisions of the TRIPs agreement required that participating members be in compliance with minimum standards of protection by 2006, set procedures and remedies for the enforcement of IP rights, and made disputes between WTO members with respect to TRIPs obligations subject to the WTO's dispute settlement procedures.[17]

Once a trademark, patent, or other intellectual property right is registered, most countries require that these rights be used and properly policed. The United States is one of the few countries in which an individual can hold a patent without the patented entity being manufactured and sold throughout the duration of the patent period. Other countries feel that in exchange for the monopoly provided by a patent, the holder must share the product with the citizens of the country. Hence, if patents are not produced within a specified period, usually from one to five years (the average is three years), the patent reverts to public domain.

This rule is also true for trademarks; products bearing the registered mark must be sold within the country, or the company may forfeit its right to a particular trademark. McDonald's faced that problem in Venezuela. Even though the McDonald's trademark was properly registered in that code-law country, the company did not use it for more than two years. Under Venezuelan law, a trademark must be used within two years or it is lost. Thus a Venezuelan-owned "Mr. McDonalds," with accompanying golden arches, is operating in Venezuela. The U.S. McDonald's Corporation faces a potentially costly legal battle if it decides to challenge the Venezuelan company.

Individual countries expect companies to actively police their intellectual property by bringing violators to court. Policing can be a difficult task, with success depending in large measure on the cooperation of the country within which the infringement or piracy takes place. A lack of cooperation in some countries may stem from cultural differences regarding how intellectual property is viewed. In the United States, the goal of protection of IP is to encourage invention and to protect and reward innovative businesses. In Korea, the attitude is that the thoughts of one person should benefit all. In Japan, the intent is to share technology rather than protect it; an invention should serve a larger, national goal, with the rapid spread of technology among competitors in a manner that promotes cooperation. In light of such attitudes, the lack of enthusiasm toward protecting intellectual property can be better understood. The United States is a strong advocate of protection,

---

[16] Visit http://www.wipo.org, the home page of the WIPO, for detailed information on the various conventions and the activities of WIPO.

[17] For a discussion of TRIPs, visit http://www.wto.org and select Intellectual Property.

The three faces of piracy and/or reform, depending how you look at them. (1) American youths, particularly on college campuses, are protesting the current intellectual property laws and the associated enforcement tools. The fellow with the eyepatch was attending a seminar on the topic led by former Attorney General Alberto Gonzales.[18] *(Photography by Rick Loomis,* Los Angeles Times. *Copyright, 2005,* Los Angeles Times. *Reprinted with permission.)* (2) Aside from the United States, the biggest piracy problem is China. Here Jackie Chan helps the Chinese government crack down, forecasting the probable path of IP piracy in China. That is, pirates have turned into policemen historically in the United States, Japan, and Taiwan as the production of intellectual property took off in each country.[19] The same will happen in China during the next decade as artists, researchers, and entrepreneurs there produce new ideas worth protecting. *(© Mike Clarke/AFP/Getty Images)* (3) The HIV/AIDS epidemic is an economic and health catastrophe that many in sub-Saharan Africa and other developing countries[20] believe is exacerbated by drug companies' pricing policies and protection of intellectual property.[21] Here protestors march toward the U.S. embassy in Pretoria, South Africa. *(AP Photo/ Christian Schwetz)*

and at U.S. insistence, many countries are becoming more cooperative about policing cases of infringement and piracy. After decades of debate, European Union ministers agreed on a common continentwide system for patented inventions. Instead of being forced to submit an application in all EU countries' languages, inventors can submit only one, in English, French, or German.

---

[18] Lorenzo Munoz and Jon Healey, "Students Do Not Share Gonzales' View on Piracy," *Los Angeles Times,* April 29, 2005, pp. C1, C9.

[19] N. Mark Lam and John L. Graham, *China Now, Doing Business in the World's Most Dynamic Market* (New York: McGraw-Hill, 2007).

[20] Amelia Gentleman, "Battle Pits Patent Rights against Low-Cost Generic Drugs," *The New York Times,* January 30, 2007, p. C5; "Clinton, Drug Companies Strike Deal to Lower AIDS Drug Prices," *The Wall Street Journal,* May 8, 2007.

[21] John E. Cook and Roger Bate, "Pharmaceuticals and the Worldwide HIV Epidemic: Can a Stakeholder Model Work?" *Journal of Public Policy & Marketing* 23, no. 2 (2004), pp. 140–52.

Other Managerial Approaches to Protecting Intellectual Property

The traditional, but relatively feeble, remedies for American companies operating in countries such as China are several: (1) prevention, that is, engage local representation and diligently register IP with the appropriate agencies; (2) negotiation and alternative dispute resolution; (3) complaints to the Chinese authorities; and (4) complaints to the U.S. government and World Trade Organization (WTO). Beyond these traditional strategies, creative thinkers of enterprise have come up with several new ideas that we briefly describe next.[22]

Microsoft.   Bill Gates's negotiation strategy with Chinese software pirates demonstrates his guile, prescience, and patience. He accidentally revealed his strategy in 1998 in an interview at the University of Washington:

> Although about 3 million computers get sold every year in China, people don't pay for the software. Someday they will, though. And as long as they're going to steal it, we want them to steal ours. They'll get sort of addicted, and then we'll somehow figure out how to collect something in the next decade.

Well, it didn't take a decade for this marketing/product trial approach to work. On April 18, 2006, one day ahead of Chinese President Hu Jintao's arrival in Redmond, Washington, for dinner at Gates's home and on his way to a meeting with President George W. Bush, Gates inked a deal with Lenovo for $1.2 billion of software to be included in the Chinese firm's computers.

Philips.   One of the originators of "open innovation" is Philips Research in the Netherlands. Thirty years ago, it pioneered the concept of partnering to develop and market new ideas. Open innovation for Philips also means that it buys ideas from R&D partners and sells ideas to marketing partners, rather than developing and marketing only its own ideas. One current project exemplifies its innovative approach to developing and protecting intellectual property in China. The PHENIX Initiative is a commercial, industrial, and R&D project to develop mobile interactive digital services for the 2008 Olympics. Led by France Telecom, it involves financing and technology contributions form both European and Chinese corporations and governmental organizations.

Although many American firms have established design and R&D centers in China already, U.S. government restrictions on high-tech export and American executives' competitive angst prevent associations such as the PHENIX Initiative for U.S. firms in China. Thus our arm's-length relationships in China limit both the amount of technology we develop and the degree of protection afforded it compared with European and Asian competitors. Moreover, our pleas for the Chinese government to "protect *our* intellectual property" sound exploitative to both the authorities and the public there.

Warner Bros.   Finally, we suggest an excellent way for IP-rich firms to make money in China currently and in the near future, using the oldest pricing strategy of all: *Charge what the market will bear*. Even with the reluctant help of the Chinese authorities in enforcing the WTO/TRIPs agreement, Chinese consumers will continue the creative copying of foreign intellectual property until they are charged what they perceive as "reasonable" prices. Indeed, we applaud the recent heroic, albeit controversial, marketing strategies of Warner Bros. in China, which has nearly halved the prices of its DVDs to $1.88 and distributes the products within days of their release in theaters—earlier than anywhere else in the world.

This pricing approach is quite consistent with one we have long advocated, namely, adjusting prices on the basis of the comparative income levels in developing countries. That is, a fair price (from the Chinese point of view) would take into account the income and purchasing power differentials between consumers in the United States and China. For example, circa 2007, the ratio between U.S. and Chinese GDP per capita at purchase price parity is approximately $40,000 to $6,500. Adjusting the current U.S. price of about $10 for a DVD on Amazon.com, a "reasonable" price to charge in China would be about $1.50. And we particularly appreciate the tactical nuance of adding the $.38 to achieve the very lucky price the Warner Bros. marketers are both charging and getting in China—$1.88!

---

[22] Lam and Graham, *China Now*, for more details.

Commercial Law within Countries

When doing business in more than one country, a marketer must remain alert to the different legal systems. This problem is especially troublesome for the marketer who formulates a common marketing plan to be implemented in several countries. Although differences in languages and customs may be accommodated, legal differences between countries may still present problems for a marketing program.

Marketing Laws

All countries have laws regulating marketing activities in promotion, product development, labeling, pricing, and channels of distribution. Usually the discrepancies across markets cause problems for trade negotiators, particularly for managers and their firms. For example, the United States does not allow the buying or selling of human organs,[23] and it restricts the use of human stem cells in medical research to develop treatments for a variety of diseases.[24] Other nations have different laws.[25] The ethics of both issues are quite controversial, and adding an international dimension just complicates things even more. In the case of the current international trade in human organs, Europeans can legally travel to foreign countries for transplants. However, the European Union Parliament is considering making it a criminal offense to do so. Meanwhile, the U.S. government is considering relaxing laws regulating stem cell research as scientists in other nations, unfettered by similar restrictions, are making important advances in the field.

Some countries may have only a few marketing laws with lax enforcement; others may have detailed, complicated rules to follow that are stringently enforced. For example, Sweden banned all television advertising to children in 1991. Greece, Norway, Denmark, Austria, and the Netherlands all restrict advertising directed at children. Recently, the European Commission threatened to restrict all advertising of soft drinks and snack foods to children, and PepsiCo volunteered to curb its advertising to kids in response.[26] At the same time, the American food industry is arguing against such actions in the United States. It is interesting to note that the U.S. Federal Trade Commission and the sugared food and toy manufacturers went down a similar path toward restricting advertising to children in the late 1970s. The industry made a few minor concessions at the time but began ignoring previous commitments during the 1980s. All these developments will be interesting to follow as childhood obesity continues to be a major public health issue in all affluent countries.

There often are vast differences in enforcement and interpretation among countries with laws that cover the same activities. Laws governing sales promotions in the European Union offer good examples of such diversity. In Austria, premium offers, free gifts, or coupons are considered cash discounts and are prohibited. Premium offers in Finland are allowed with considerable scope as long as the word *free* is not used and consumers are not coerced into buying products. France also regulates premium offers, which are, for all practical purposes, illegal there because selling for less than cost price or offering a customer a gift or premium conditional on the purchase of another product is illegal. French law does permit sales twice a year, in January and August, which can legally last four to six weeks. This event is so popular that it is advertised on radio and TV, and special police are even required to control the crowds. One poll indicated that over 40 percent of the French set aside money during the year for sale time, and 56 percent will spend less money on essentials to buy things on sale. The good news here is that many of these restrictions on marketing activities are being softened. Most recently, holiday sales[27] and longer store hours[28] are being allowed in several European countries.

---

[23] Nancy Scheper-Hughes, "Organs without Borders," *Foreign Policy*, January/February 2005, pp. 26–27.

[24] Robert L. Paarlberg, "The Great Stem Cell Race," *Foreign Policy*, May/June 2005, pp. 44–51.

[25] Amelia Gentleman, "Transplant Scheme Preys on Poor Indians," *International Herald Tribune*, January 30, 2008, p. 2.

[26] Andrew Ward and Jeremy Grant, "PepsiCo Says It Has Curbed Advertising to Children," *Financial Times,* February 28, 2005, http://www.FT.com.

[27] Cecilie Rohwedder, "Achtung Christmas Shoppers!" *The Wall Street Journal*, December 24, 2007, pp. B1, B2.

[28] Marcus Walker, "Longer Store Hours in Germany," *The Wall Street Journal*, January 8, 2007, p. A5.

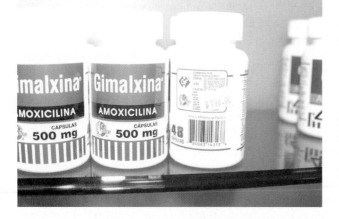

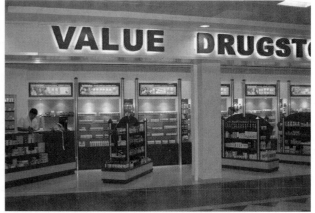

Laws regarding healthcare marketing differ substantially around the world. In Mexico prescriptions often are not required for powerful drugs. At this farmacia in the Cancun airport, tourists can buy the pictured antibiotic over the counter at bargain prices. Quality is an issue, but availability is not. In the Philippines and other developing countries, you can buy yourself a kidney on the black market—the global price is around $2,000. However, U.S. laws prohibit the buying and selling of human organs. In South Korea, the government supports stem cell research that is restricted in the United States by federal laws. (right: AP Photo/Pat Roque; bottom right: AP Photo/Jayanta Saha)

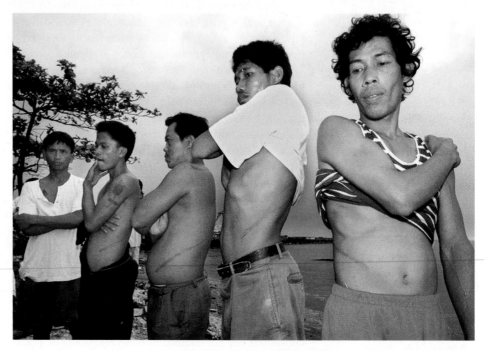

China has relaxed some of its restrictions on direct marketing that particularly affected companies such as Mary Kay.[29]

The various product comparison laws, a natural and effective means of expression, are another major stumbling block. In Germany, comparisons in advertisements are always subject to the competitor's right to go to the courts and ask for proof of any implied or stated superiority. In Canada, the rulings are even more stringent: All claims and statements must be examined to ensure that any representation to the public is not false or misleading. Such representation cannot be made verbally in selling or be contained in or on anything that comes to the attention of the public (such as product labels, inserts in products, or any other form of advertising, including what may be expressed in a sales letter). Courts have been directed by Canadian law to take into account, in determining whether a representation is false or misleading, the "general impression" conveyed by the representation as well as its literal meaning.[30] The courts are expected to apply the "credulous person standard," which means that if any reasonable person could possibly misunderstand the representation, the representation is misleading. In essence, puffery, an acceptable practice in the United States, could be interpreted in Canada as false and misleading advertising. Thus a statement such as "the strongest drive shaft in Canada" would be judged misleading unless the advertiser had absolute evidence that the drive shaft was stronger than any other drive shaft for sale in Canada.

China is experimenting with a variety of laws to control how foreign companies do business. Some regulations are being relaxed, such as those controlling foreign advertising companies. Censorship of advertising and program content[31] are constant concerns. Televised ads for "offensive" products such as feminine hygiene pads, hemorrhoid medications, and even athlete's food ointment are not allowed during the three daily mealtimes.[32] The Chinese authorities banned a LeBron James Nike TV ad because it "violates regulations that mandate all advertisements in China should uphold national dignity and interest and respect the motherland's culture."[33] Apparently LeBron battling a kung fu master isn't appropriate in the land of Confucius. Also, magazines have been ordered to use a direct translation of the often-obscure name that appears on their license or use no English name at all. Thus, *Cosmopolitan* would become "Trends Lady," *Woman's Day* would become "Friends of Health," and *Esquire* would become "Trends Man." Such diversity of laws among countries extends to advertising, pricing, sales agreements, and other commercial activities. Indeed, one study suggests that governmental policies actually forestall firms from taking a marketing orientation in their operations.[34]

There is some hope that the European Union will soon have a common commercial code. One step in that direction is the proposal to harmonize the pan-European regulation of promotions based on the conservative laws that cover promotions in Germany, Austria, and Belgium. However, this proposal is meeting with strong resistance from several groups

[29] Katherine Yung, "Mary Kay Sales Plans Get Beijing Blessing," *Dallas Morning News*, December 5, 2006, pp. D1, D7.

[30] Richard W. Pollay, "Considering the Evidence, No Wonder the Court Endorses Canada's Restrictions on Cigarette Advertising," *Journal of Public Policy & Marketing* 23, no. 1 (2004), pp. 80–88.

[31] "Bond in Beijing," *The Wall Street Journal*, January 31, 2007, p. A12; Don Lee and Jim Puzzanghera, "China Closing Curtains on U.S. Movies," *Los Angeles Times*, December 12, 2007, pp. C1, C4; Geoffrey A. Fowler, "Online-Video Firms Brace as China Tightens Rules," *The Wall Street Journal*, January 4, 2008.

[32] Geoffrey A. Fowler, "China Cracks Down on Commercials," *The Wall Street Journal*, February 19, 2004, p. B7.

[33] "China Bans Nike's LeBron Commercial," *Associated Press*, December 6, 2004.

[34] Rilian Qu and Christine T. Ennew, "Developing a Market Orientation in a Transitional Economy: The Role of Government Regulation and Ownership Structure," *Journal of Public Policy & Marketing* 24, no. 1 (2005), pp. 82–89.

A Greenpeace protester peers out from inside a plastic rubbish bin in Hong Kong, where activists were calling on the government to develop a comprehensive recycling industry that they claim will create 2,000 new jobs. A recent study by Greenpeace found that only 148 out of 18,200 rubbish bins in Hong Kong have waste separation compartments. It is calling on the government to revamp its current waste management procedures to facilitate a comprehensive system to reduce, recover, and recycle. (© AFP/Getty Images)

because of its complex restrictions.[35] Meanwhile, others push for even broader-based harmonization of marketing regulations involving the United States, United Nations, and the WTO.

Although the European Union may sometimes appear a beautiful picture of economic cooperation, there is still the reality of dealing with 27 different countries, cultures, and languages, as well as 27 different legal systems. Even though some of Germany's complicated trade laws were revoked in 2000, groups such as the Center for Combating Unfair Competition, an industry-financed organization, continue to work to maintain the status quo. Before the German law was revoked, the Center's lawyers filed 1,000 lawsuits a year, going after, for example, a grocery store that offered discount coupons or a deli that gave a free cup of coffee to a customer who had already bought 10; its efforts will surely continue.

Although the goal of full integration and a common commercial code has not been totally achieved in the European Union, decisions by the European Court continue to strike down individual-country laws that impede competition across borders. In a recent decision, the European Court ruled that a French cosmetics company could sell its wares by mail in Germany and advertise them at a markdown from their original prices, a direct contradiction of German law. As the Single European Market Act is implemented, many of the legal and trade differences that have existed for decades will vanish. Surprisingly enough, standards set by the European Union for food, software, cars, and other items affect U.S. product standards as well. In many cases, the reconciliation of so many different consumer protection standards that existed in European countries prior to the European Union resulted in rules more rigorous than those for many U.S. products. Consequently, many U.S. products have had to be redesigned to comply with European standards. For example, Carrier air conditioners have been redesigned to comply with European recycling rules; Microsoft has modified contracts with software makers; Internet service providers give consumers a wider choice of technologies; and McDonald's has ceased including soft plastic toys with its Happy Meals and has withdrawn all genetically engineered potatoes from its restaurants worldwide. All this change is because of the need to reconcile U.S. standards with those of the European Union.

Green Marketing Legislation

Multinational corporations also face a growing variety of legislation designed to address environmental issues. Global concern for the environment extends beyond industrial pollution, hazardous waste disposal, and rampant deforestation to include issues that focus directly on consumer products. Green marketing laws focus on environmentally friendly products and product packaging and its effect on solid waste management.

Germany has passed the most stringent green marketing laws that regulate the management and recycling of packaging waste. The new packaging laws were introduced in three phases. The first phase required all transport packaging, such as crates, drums, pallets, and Styrofoam containers, to be accepted back by the manufacturers and distributors for recycling. The second phase required manufacturers, distributors, and retailers to accept all returned secondary packaging, including corrugated boxes, blister packs, packaging designed to prevent theft, packaging for vending machine applications, and packaging for promotional purposes. The third phase requires all retailers, distributors, and manufacturers to accept returned sales packaging, including cans, plastic containers for dairy products, foil wrapping, Styrofoam packages, and folding cartons such as cereal boxes. The requirement for retailers to take back sales packaging has been suspended as long as the

---

[35] "EU Sets Cap on TV Ads and Product Placement," *International Herald Tribune*, November 14, 2006, p. 16.

voluntary green dot program remains a viable substitute. A green dot on a package identifies manufacturers that have agreed to ensure a regular collection of used packaging materials directly from the consumer's home or from designated local collection points.

Reclaiming recyclables extends beyond packaging to automobiles. Since 2006 manufacturers based in European Union nations must take back any cars they produced that no longer have resale value and pay for proper disposal. Similarly, 85 percent of a scrapped car's material must be recovered for future use.

Many European countries also have devised schemes to identify products that comply with certain criteria that make them more environmentally friendly than similar products. Products that meet these criteria are awarded an "ecolabel" that the manufacturer can display on packaging to signal to customers that it is an environmentally friendly product. The EU is becoming more aggressive in issuing new directives and in harmonizing ecolabeling and other environmental laws across all member states. Ecolabeling and EU packaging laws are discussed in more detail in the chapter on consumer products (Chapter 12).[36]

Foreign Countries' Antitrust Laws

With the exception of the United States, antitrust laws were either nonexistent or not enforced in most of the world's countries for the better part of the 20th century. However, the European Union,[37] Japan, and many other countries have begun to actively enforce their antitrust laws, patterned after those in the United States. Antimonopoly, price discrimination, supply restrictions, and full-line forcing are areas in which the European Court of Justice has dealt severe penalties. For example, before Procter & Gamble was allowed to buy VP-Schickedanz AG, a German hygiene products company, it had to agree to sell off one of the German company's divisions that produced Camelia, a brand of sanitary napkins. Because P&G already marketed a brand of sanitary napkins in Europe, the commission was concerned that allowing P&G to keep Camelia would give the company a controlling 60 percent of the German sanitary products market and 81 percent of Spain's.

The United States also intervenes when non-U.S. companies attempt to acquire American companies. Nestlé's proposed $2.8 billion acquisition of Dreyer's Grand Ice Cream hit a roadblock as U.S. antitrust officials opposed the deal on grounds that it would lead to less competition and higher prices for gourmet ice cream in the United States. At times, companies are subject to antitrust charges in more than one country. Microsoft had a partial victory against antitrust charges brought in the United States only to face similar anticompetitive charges against Microsoft's Windows operating system in the EU. The probe is based on possible competitive benefits to European software concerns if legal limits are placed on Microsoft. American companies have faced antitrust violations since the trust-busting days of President Theodore Roosevelt but much less so in other parts of the world. Enforcement of antitrust in Europe was almost nonexistent until the early stages of the European Union established antitrust legislation.

U.S. Laws Apply in Host Countries

All governments are concerned with protecting their political and economic interests domestically and internationally; any activity or action, wherever it occurs, that adversely threatens national interests is subject to government control. Leaving the political boundaries of a home country does not exempt a business from home-country laws. Regardless of the nation where business is done, a U.S. citizen is subject to certain laws of the United States. What is illegal for an American business at home can also be illegal by U.S. law in foreign jurisdictions for the firm, its subsidiaries, and licensees of U.S. technology.

---

[36] For information on the EU's environmental directives, as well as other information about the European Union, visit http://www.europa.eu.int. This address will take you to the home page, where you can search for topics and visit various information sources about the European Union.

[37] Charles Forelle, "Microsoft Yields in EU Antitrust Battle," *The Wall Street Journal*, October 23, 2007; Charles Forelle, "EU Probes Pharmaceutical Industry on Dwindling New Patents, Drugs," *The Wall Street Journal*, January 16, 2008.

CROSSING BORDERS 7.2   The Kind of Correspondence an International Marketer Doesn't Want to See

FOR IMMEDIATE RELEASE   CRM
  FRIDAY, MAY 20, 2005   (202) 514-2008
     WWW.USDOJ.GOV   TDD (202) 514-1888

DPC (TIANJIN) LTD. CHARGED WITH VIOLATING THE FOREIGN CORRUPT PRACTICES ACT

WASHINGTON, D.C.— Acting Assistant Attorney General John C. Richter of the Criminal Division today announced the filing of a one-count criminal information charging DPC (Tianjin) Co. Ltd.—the Chinese subsidiary of Los Angeles-based Diagnostic Products Corporation (DPC)—with violating the Foreign Corrupt Practices Act of 1977 (FCPA) in connection with the payment of approximately $1.6 million in bribes in the form of illegal "commissions" to physicians and laboratory personnel employed by government-owned hospitals in the People's Republic of China.

The company, a producer and seller of diagnostic medical equipment, has agreed to plead guilty to the charge, adopt internal compliance measures, and cooperate with ongoing criminal and SEC civil investigations. An independent compliance expert will be chosen to audit the company's compliance program and monitor its implementation of new internal policies and procedures. DPC Tianjin has also agreed to pay a criminal penalty of $2 million.

The bribes were allegedly paid from late 1991 through December 2002 for the purpose and effect of obtaining and retaining business with these hospitals. According to the criminal information and a statement of facts filed in court, DPC Tianjin made cash payments to laboratory personnel and physicians employed in certain hospitals in the People's Republic of China in exchange for agreements that the hospitals would obtain DPC Tianjin's products and services. This practice, authorized by DPC Tianjin's general manager, involved personnel who were employed by hospitals owned by the legal authorities in the People's Republic of China and, thus, "foreign officials" as defined by the FCPA.

In most cases, the bribes were paid in cash and hand-delivered by DPC Tianjin salespeople to the person who controlled purchasing decisions for the particular hospital department. DPC Tianjin recorded the payments on its books and records as "selling expenses." DPC Tianjin's general manager regularly prepared and submitted to Diagnostic Products Corporation its financial statements, which contained its sales expenses. The general manager also caused approval of the budgets for sales expenses of DPC Tianjin, including the amounts DPC Tianjin intended to pay to the officials of the hospitals in the following quarter or year.

The "commissions," typically between 3 percent and 10 percent of sales, totaled approximately $1,623,326 from late 1991 through December 2002, and allowed Depu to earn approximately $2 million in profits from the sales.

DPC Tianjin's parent company, Diagnostic Products Corporation, is the subject of an FCPA enforcement proceeding filed earlier today by the U.S. Securities and Exchange Commission. The SEC ordered the company to cease and desist from violating the FCPA and to disgorge approximately $2.8 million in ill-gotten gains, representing its net profit in the People's Republic of China for the period of its misconduct plus prejudgment interest . . .

Laws that prohibit taking a bribe, trading with the enemy, participating in a commercial venture that negatively affects the U.S. economy, participating in an unauthorized boycott such as the Arab boycott, or any other activity deemed to be against the best interests of the United States apply to U.S. businesses and their subsidiaries and licensees regardless of where they operate. Thus at any given time a U.S. citizen in a foreign country must look not only at the laws of the host country but at home law as well.

The question of jurisdiction of U.S. law over acts committed outside the territorial limits of the country has been settled by the courts through application of a long-established principle of international law, the "objective theory of jurisdiction." This concept holds that even if an act is committed outside the territorial jurisdiction of U.S. courts, those courts can nevertheless have jurisdiction if the act produces effects within the home country. The only possible exception may be when the violation is the result of enforced compliance with local law.

Foreign Corrupt Practices Act   Recall from Chapter 5 that the Foreign Corrupt Practices Act (FCPA) makes it illegal for companies to pay bribes to foreign officials, candidates, or political parties. Stiff penalties can be assessed against company officials, directors, employees, or agents found guilty of paying a bribe or of knowingly participating in or authorizing the payment of a bribe. However, also recall that bribery, which can range from lubrication to extortion, is a common business custom in many countries, even though illegal.[38]

The original FCPA lacked clarity, and early interpretations were extremely narrow and confusing. Subsequent amendments in the Omnibus Trade and Competitiveness Act clarified two of the most troubling issues. Corporate officers' liability was changed from having reason to know that illegal payments were made to knowing of or authorizing illegal payments. In addition, if it is customary in the culture, small (grease or lubrication) payments made to encourage officials to complete routine government actions such as processing papers, stamping visas, and scheduling inspections are not illegal per se.

The debate continues as to whether the FCPA puts U.S. businesses at a disadvantage. Some argue that U.S. businesses are at a disadvantage in international business transactions in those cases in which bribery payments are customary, whereas others contend that it has little effect and, indeed, that it helps companies to "just say no." The truth probably lies somewhere in between. The consensus is that most U.S. firms are operating within the law, and several studies indicate that the FCPA has not been as detrimental to MNCs' interests as originally feared, because exports to developed and developing countries continue to be favorable.

Although U.S. firms seem able to compete and survive without resorting to corruption in the most corrupt societies, it does not mean that violations do not occur or that companies are not penalized for violations. For example, a U.S. environmental engineering firm was found to have made corrupt payments to an Egyptian government official to assist the company in gaining a contract. The company agreed not to violate the FCPA in the future and agreed to pay a civil fine of $400,000 and to reimburse the Department of Justice for the costs of the investigation. Furthermore, the company agreed to establish FCPA compliance procedures and to provide certifications of compliance annually for five years. Other firms have paid even larger fines in recent years, and the Justice Department has agreed not to prosecute firms with "excellent" training programs in place.

National Security Laws

American firms, their foreign subsidiaries, or foreign firms that are licensees of U.S. technology cannot sell products to a country in which the sale is considered by the U.S. government to affect national security. Furthermore, responsibility extends to the final destination of the product, regardless of the number of intermediaries that may be involved in the transfer of goods.

An extensive export control system was created to slow the spread of sensitive technologies to the former Soviet Union, China, and other communist countries that were viewed as major threats to U.S. security. The control of the sale of goods considered to have a strategic and military value was extremely strict. But with the end of the Cold War, export controls were systematically dismantled until 1999, when a congressional committee reported Chinese espionage activities and American aerospace companies transferring sensitive technology irresponsibly. Following the report, legislation was passed again restricting the export of products or technologies that might be used by other countries for defense applications.

The events of September 11, 2001, added another set of restrictions related to weapons of mass destruction (WMD). Unfortunately, many of the products used in WMD are difficult to control because they have dual purposes; that is, they have legitimate uses as well as being important in manufacturing WMD. For example, Iraq, which was allowed to import medical equipment despite a U.N. embargo, purchased, under the pretext of medical benefits, six machines that destroy kidney stones. The manufacturer accepted the claim that Saddam Hussein was concerned about kidney stones in the Iraqi population and began shipping the machines. However, integral components of these machines are high-precision electronic switches that are also used to set off the chain reaction in thermonuclear weapons. When 120 additional switches as "spare parts" were ordered, a red flag went up, and the shipments were stopped.

---

[38] For discussions of the FCPA, updates, and other information, visit the FCPA home page at http://www.usdoj.gov/criminal/fraud/fcpa.html.

American doing !

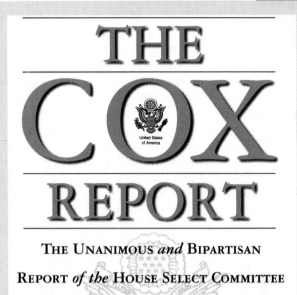

(© Editorial Image, LLC/PhotoEdit, Inc.)

In 1999 the Cox Report was published, making shocking claims about China's military aggressiveness toward the United States. The verbiage on the back cover delivered the gist of the argument:

China's Target: America

The unanimous, bipartisan Cox Report is one of the most stunning documents ever to come from the U.S. Congress—a shocking account of how the People's Republic of China has targeted America for subversion, high-tech theft, and nuclear challenge.

How Communist China has replaced the former Soviet Union as America's chief military rival—and acquired the means to target nuclear missiles on American cities. . . .

At the time, the report was widely criticized as politically motivated and shallow in substance. Moreover, the events of September 11 rendered the argument, at best, obsolete. But the combination of the political attack on China and the associated renewed restrictions on sales of high-technology goods and expertise has had a long-term chilling effect on U.S. sales in the world's fastest growing market. During 1999, the U.S. market share of merchandise exports to China fell from 10 percent to 8 percent, and the loss of competitiveness has remained permanent.

Sources: *The Cox Report* (Washington, DC: Regency, 1999); N. Mark Lam and John L. Graham, *China Now, Doing Business in the World's Most Dynamic Market* (New York: McGraw-Hill, 2007).

Countless numbers of dual-purpose technologies are exported from the United States. A sticking point with dual-purpose exports is the intent of the buyer. Silicon Graphics Inc. (SGI) sold computer equipment to a Russian nuclear laboratory that contended it was for nonmilitary use, which would have been legal. However, the Department of Justice ruled that since the sale was made to a government-operated facility involved in both civil and noncivil activities, SGI should have applied for the correct export license. Thus SGI paid a fine of $1 million plus a $500,000 fine for each of the export violations. National security laws prohibit a U.S. company, its subsidiaries, joint ventures, or licensees to sell controlled products without special permission from the U.S. government. The consequences of violation of the Trading with the Enemy Act can be severe: fines, prison sentences, and, in the case of foreign companies, economic sanctions.

Exports are controlled for the protection and promotion of human rights, as a means of enforcing foreign policy, because of national shortages, to control technology,[39] and for a host of other reasons the U.S. government deems necessary to protect its best interests. In years past, the government restricted trade with South Africa (human rights) and restricted the sale of wheat to the Soviet Union in retaliation for its invasion of Afghanistan (foreign policy). Currently, the government restricts trade with Iran (foreign policy) and the sale of leading-edge electronics (control of technology), and it prohibits the export of pesticides that have not been approved for use in the United States (to avoid the return of residue of unauthorized pesticides in imported food and protect U.S. consumers from the so-called circle of poison). In each of these cases, U.S. law binds U.S. businesses, regardless of where they operate.[40]

U.S. Antitrust Laws that Apply in Foreign Markets

Antitrust enforcement has two purposes in international commerce. The first is to protect American consumers by ensuring that they benefit from products and ideas produced by foreign competitors as well as by domestic competitors. Competition from foreign producers is important when imports are, or could be, a major source of a product or when a single firm dominates a domestic industry. This issue becomes relevant in many joint ventures, particularly if the joint venture creates a situation in which a U.S. firm entering a joint venture with a foreign competitor restricts competition for the U.S. parent in the U.S. market.

The second purpose of antitrust legislation is to protect American export and investment opportunities against any privately imposed restrictions. The concern is that all U.S.-based firms engaged in the export of goods, services, or capital should be allowed to compete on merit and not be shut out by restrictions imposed by bigger or less principled competitors.

The questions of jurisdiction and how U.S. antitrust laws apply are frequently asked but only vaguely answered. The basis for determination ultimately rests with the interpretation of Sections I and II of the Sherman Act. Section I states that "every contract, combination . . . or conspiracy in restraint of trade or commerce among the several states or with foreign nations is hereby declared to be illegal." Section II makes it a violation to "monopolize, or attempt to monopolize, or combine or conspire with any other person or persons, to monopolize any part of the trade or commerce among the several states, or with foreign nations."

The Justice Department recognizes that application of U.S. antitrust laws to overseas activities raises some difficult questions of jurisdiction. It also recognizes that U.S. antitrust-law enforcement should not interfere unnecessarily with the sovereign interest of a foreign nation. At the same time, however, the Antitrust Division is committed to controlling foreign transactions at home or abroad that have a substantial and foreseeable effect on U.S. commerce. When such business practices occur, there is no question in the Antitrust Division of the Department of Justice that U.S. laws apply.

Antiboycott Law

Under the antiboycott law,[41] U.S. companies are forbidden to participate in any unauthorized foreign boycott; furthermore, they are required to report any request to cooperate with a boycott. The antiboycott law was a response to the Arab League boycott of Israeli businesses. The Arab League boycott of Israel has three levels: A primary boycott bans direct trade between Arab states and Israel, a secondary boycott bars Arab governments from doing business with companies that do business with Israel, and a tertiary boycott bans Arab governments from doing business with companies that do business with companies doing business with Israel.[42]

---

[39] Deborah Zabarenko, "U.S. Policy Curbs Global Space Cooperation," *Reuters*, June 23, 2005; "U.S. in Talks with Boeing over Sensor Sales to China," *Reuters*, July 7, 2005; "Space Station, No Plan B for Outer Space," *The Economist*, March 12, 2005, pp. 75–76.

[40] Export controls will be discussed in more detail in Chapter 15.

[41] The antiboycott law applies only to those boycotts not sanctioned by the U.S. government. Sanctioned boycotts, such as the boycotts against trade with Cuba and Iran, are initiated by the United States and must be honored by U.S. firms.

[42] For those non-U.S. companies trading with the Arab League and complying with the boycott, each was required to include a statement on shipping invoices. On an invoice for 10 buses to be shipped from Brazil to Kuwait, the following statement appeared: "We certify that we are the producer and supplier of the shipped goods; we are neither blacklisted by the Arab Boycott of Israel nor are we the head office branch or subsidiary of a boycotted company. No Israeli capital is invested in this firm, no company capital or capital of its owners is invested in any Israeli company; our products are not of Israeli origin and do not contain Israeli raw material or labor."

When companies do not comply with the Arab League's boycott directives, their names are placed on a blacklist, and they are excluded from trade with members of the Arab League. Thus U.S. companies are caught in the middle: If they trade with Israel, the Arab League will not do business with them, and if they refuse to do business with Israel in order to trade with an Arab League member, they will be in violation of U.S. law.[43] One hospital supply company that had been trading with Israel was charged with closing a plant in Israel to get itself taken off the Arab League blacklist. After an investigation, the company pled guilty, was fined $6.6 million, and was prohibited from doing business in Syria and Saudi Arabia for two years. A less costly fine of $12,000 was paid by a freight forwarder who certified that the goods shipped for a third party were not of Israeli origin, were not shipped from Israel, and did not contain any material from Israel.

Extraterritoriality of U.S. Laws

The issue of the extraterritoriality of U.S. laws is especially important to U.S. multinational firms, because the long arm of U.S. legal jurisdiction causes anxiety for heads of state. Foreign governments fear the influence of American government policy on their economies through U.S. multinationals.[44]

Especially troublesome are those instances when U.S. law is in conflict with host countries' economic or political goals. Conflict arises when the host government requires joint ventures to do business within the country and the U.S. Justice Department restricts or forbids such ventures because of their U.S. anticompetitive effects. Host countries see this influence as evidence of U.S. interference. When U.S. MNCs' subsidiaries are prohibited from making a sale in violation of the U.S. Trading with the Enemy Act, host governments react with hostility toward the extraterritorial application of U.S. foreign policy. This chapter's Global Perspective is a good illustration of the extraterritoriality of U.S. law and how it has an impact on a friendly neighbor as well as a major multinational company.

In an interesting development, MNCs are being held liable for the human-rights abuses of foreign governments. Lawsuits are being brought in U.S. courts against U.S. MNCs, charging them with doing business with oppressive regimes. Unocal Corporation was sued for doing business with Burma's military regime, which forced peasants at gunpoint to help build a pipeline for Unocal. Unocal denied the charges. This case was brought under the Alien Claims Act, originally intended to reassure Europe that the fledgling United States would not harbor pirates or assassins. It permits foreigners to sue in U.S. courts for violations of the "the law of nations." Businesses like IBM, Citibank, and Coca-Cola worry that they may be socked with huge jury damages for the misdeeds of oppressive governments. Employment lawyers warn that multinational companies are likely to face more lawsuits from the Third World.

When the intent of any kind of overseas activity is to restrain trade, there is no question about the appropriateness of applying U.S. laws. There is a question, however, when the intent is to conclude a reasonable business transaction. If the U.S. government encourages U.S. firms to become multinational, then the government needs to make provisions for the resolution of differences when conflict arises between U.S. law and host-government laws.

Cyberlaw: Unresolved Issues

The Internet is by its nature a global enterprise for which no political or national boundaries exist. Although this global reach is its strength, it also creates problems when existing laws do not clearly address the uniqueness of the Internet and its related activities. Existing law is vague or does not completely cover such issues as gambling, the protection of domain names, taxes, jurisdiction in cross-border transactions, and contractual issues. The European Union, the United States, and many other countries are drafting legislation to address the myriad legal questions not clearly addressed by current law.

---

[43] For a list of current cases against firms violating antiboycott law, visit http://www.bxa.doc.gov and select Antiboycott Compliance, then Antiboycott Case Histories.

[44] Anthony Ferner, Phil Almond, and Trevor Colling, "Institutional Theory and the Cross-National Transfer of Employment Policy: The Case of 'Workforce Diversity' in U.S. Multinationals," *Journal of International Business Studies* 36, no. 3 (2005), pp. 304–21.

But until these laws apply worldwide, companies will have to rely on individual-country laws, which may or may not provide protection.[45]

Domain Names and Cybersquatters

Unfortunately, the ease with which Web names can be registered and the low cost of registering has led to thousands being registered. Cybersquatters (CSQs) buy and register descriptive nouns, geographic names, names of ethnic groups and pharmaceutical substances, and other similar descriptors and hold them until they can be sold at an inflated price. For example, a cybersquatter sold "www.themortgage.com" for $500,000; the record price paid so far is $7.5 million for the domain name "www.business.com." If a cybersquatter has registered a generic domain name that a company wants, the only recourse is to buy it.

Another ploy of CSQs is to register familiar names and known trademarks that divert traffic from intended destinations or to sell competing products. eBay, the world's largest online auction house, was embroiled in a dispute with an entrepreneur in Nova Scotia who registered "www.ebay.ca," thus forcing the U.S. company to use "www.ca.ebay.com" for its newly launched Canadian Web site until it was successful in regaining the use of "www.ebay.ca"; both Web addresses now go to the same site.

Cybersquatters register a well-known brand or trademark that misdirects a person to the CSQ's site or to a competing company's site. For example, an adult entertainment Web site registered "www.candyland.com." Hasbro, the toy company, markets a game for children called "Candy Land." Disturbed by the thought that customers might end up at an adult entertainment site, Hasbro wanted to have the site vacated. It had the option of suing to have it removed or buying the domain name. Hasbro elected to sue, and though the adult Web site was not directly infringing on its trademark, the courts deemed it to be damaging to the reputation of Hasbro and its children's game. The Web address now takes you directly to a Hasbro site.

Other cybersquatting abuses that can pose a serious threat to business include parody sites, protest sites, and hate sites. A good example is "www.walmartsucks.org," a site highly critical of Wal-Mart. This type of Web site may be difficult to prevent because the right to free speech is protected. The only defense Wal-Mart might have is to challenge the Web site's right to use a trade name to direct someone to the site.

It is easy to imagine many situations in which the actions of companies or information posted on a site can lead to a lawsuit when Internet content is unlawful in one country but not in the host country. For example, an American studio that makes a movie with nude scenes could be prosecuted in a country that bans nudity in movies. Not only would the movie studio be liable, but the Internet service provider could be liable for material posted on its Web site. Writers and publishers could face libel suits in countries with laws restrictive of free speech, where weak or nonexistent free speech protections are tools to intimidate and censor.[46] Internet publishers or individual Web site owners fear they can be sued for defamation from any or many jurisdictions, merely because their articles can be downloaded anywhere in the world. Lawsuits involving libel, defamation, and product liability cause companies to voluntarily restrict their Web sites to selected countries rather than leave themselves open to legal action. The Internet is not a libel-free zone.

Most country's courts are inclined to assert jurisdiction over online activity, wherever it originates, so long as harm is experienced locally and the sense is that the party responsible either knew or ought to have known that the harm was a likely consequence of its actions. Most agree, though, that laws that

Potential customers visit a Microsoft booth in Beijing. When Chinese bloggers use Microsoft's service to post messages and type in such terms as "democracy," "capitalism," "liberty," or "human rights," they get a yellow light and a computer warning: "This message includes forbidden language. Please delete the prohibited expression." Microsoft has agreed to this sort of censorship, explaining that it is just following local laws and that the company still provides a most useful service to its Chinese clients. The critics disagree. The argument goes on. *(AP Photo/ Ng Han Guan)*

---

[45] Jefferson Graham, "File-Sharing Beat Goes On," *USA Today*, June 29, 2005, p. 3B.

[46] Mark Magnier and Joseph Menn, "As China Censors the Internet, Money Talks," *Los Angeles Times*, June 17, 2005, pp. A1, A14.

are expressly designed to apply not just in a single country but worldwide are necessary to untangle the legal hassles that are occurring.

Of 100 business leaders polled by the International Chamber of Commerce, more than one-third said legal uncertainty covering Internet operations affected "significant business decisions." The most immediate impact, according to the ICC, is clear: Many online merchants refuse to sell outside their home countries.

Taxes

Another thorny issue in e-commerce concerns the collection of taxes. A typical tax system relies on knowing where a particular economic activity is located. But the Internet enables individual workers to operate in many different countries while sitting at the same desk. When taxes should be collected, where they should be collected, and by whom are all issues under consideration by countries around the world. In the past, a company was deemed to have a taxable presence in a country if it had a permanent establishment there. But whether the existence of a server or a Web site qualifies as such a presence is not clear. One proposal that has enthusiastic support from tax authorities is for servers to be designated as "virtual permanent establishments" and thus subject to local taxes.

To pinpoint when and where a sale takes place in cyberspace is difficult, and unless elusive taxpayers can be pinpointed, any tax may be difficult to collect. In "brick-and-mortar" sales, the retailer collects, but when the Internet site is in one country and the customer is in another, who collects? One proposal is to have shipping companies such as FedEx or credit card companies collect—obviously, neither party is receiving this suggestion enthusiastically.

The EU Commission has announced plans for a directive to force foreign companies to levy value-added tax (VAT) on services delivered via the Internet, television, or radio to customers in the European Union. Foreign companies with sales via the Internet of over €100,000 (~$155,000) inside the European Union would have to register in at least one EU country and levy VAT at that country's rate, somewhere between 15 percent and 25 percent. The tax is justified on the basis of leveling the playing field. That is, EU companies have to charge their EU customers VAT, whereas foreign companies supplying the same service to the same customers are duty free. However, U.S. companies are protesting, calling the proposal "e-protectionism." Although the EU plan is only a proposal now, as the value of Internet transactions increases, the taxman will sooner or later get his share.[47]

Jurisdiction of Disputes and Validity of Contracts

As countries realize that existing laws relating to commerce do not always clearly address the uniqueness of the Internet and its related activities, a body of cyberlaw is gradually being created. Two of the most troubling areas are determining whose laws will prevail in legal disputes between parties located in different countries and establishing the contractual validity of electronic communications. The European Union is having the most difficulty in reconciling the vast differences in the laws among its member states to create a uniform law. For example, a draft regulation debated in Brussels and other European capitals would have required vendors to comply with 27 different, and sometimes bizarre, sets of national rules on consumer protection—ranging from dozens of restrictions on advertising to France's requirement that all contracts must be concluded in French, regardless of whether businesses intend to sell goods for export to France.

The EU Commission has adopted an e-commerce directive that will permit online retailers to trade by the rules of their home country unless the seller had enticed or approached the consumer by way of advertising. Then, any legal action is to take place in the consumer's country of residence. The rationale is that if a company actively seeks customers in a given country, it ought to be willing to abide by that country's consumer protection laws. Whether the directive will be accepted by all 27 member states is still problematic.

The European Commission has begun to review the entire regulatory framework for the technological infrastructure of the information society. The commission is working on various pieces of legislation intended to place electronic commerce on an equal footing with

---

[47] For a report on a resolution on cross-border tax issues proposed by the OECD, see "OECD Launches Project on Improving the Resolution of Cross-Border Tax Disputes," http://www.oecd.org, and select Taxation. The OECD proposes a variety of issues related to the Internet, all of which can be found at this site.

conventional commerce. One of the first steps was to introduce an EU–wide computer network dubbed EEJ-net that provides an easy way to resolve small-scale disputes out of court. Problems over deliveries, defective products, or products that do not fit their description can be dealt with by a single one-stop national contact point, or clearinghouse, in each member state. The consumer will be able to find information and support in making a claim to the out-of-court dispute resolution system in the country where the product supplier is based.

Establishing the validity of contractual law for e-commerce is making substantial progress also. India, for example, recently passed a law that recognizes e-mail as a valid form of communication, electronic contracts as legal and enforceable, and digital signatures as binding. Several countries are preparing, or have passed, legislation similar to the United Kingdom's that allows digital signatures to be used in the creation of online contracts that are as legally binding as any paper-based original document.

Summary

Businesses face a multitude of problems in their efforts to develop successful marketing programs. Not the least of these problems is the varying legal systems of the world and their effect on business transactions. Just as political climate, cultural differences, local geography, different business customs, and the stage of economic development must be taken into account, so must such legal questions as jurisdictional and legal recourse in disputes, protection of intellectual property rights, extended U.S. law enforcement, and enforcement of antitrust legislation by U.S. and foreign governments. A primary marketing task is to develop a plan that will be enhanced, or at least not adversely affected, by these and other environmental elements. New to the international legal scene is the Internet, which, by its nature, creates a new set of legal entanglements, many of which have yet to be properly addressed. One thing is certain: The freedom that now exists on the World Wide Web will be only a faint memory before long. The myriad questions created by different laws and different legal systems indicate that the prudent path to follow at all stages of foreign marketing operations is one leading to competent counsel, well versed in the intricacies of the international legal environment.

Questions

1. Define the following terms:

   common law

   Islamic law

   prior use versus registration

   arbitration

   cybersquatters

   code law

   Marxist–socialist tenets

   conciliation

   litigation

2. How does the international marketer determine which legal system will have jurisdiction when legal disputes arise?

3. Discuss the state of international commercial law.

4. Discuss the limitations of jurisdictional clauses in contracts.

5. What is the "objective theory of jurisdiction"? How does it apply to a firm doing business within a foreign country?

6. Discuss some of the reasons seeking an out-of-court settlement in international commercial legal disputes is probably better than suing.

7. Illustrate the procedure generally followed in international commercial disputes when settled under the auspices of a formal arbitration tribunal.

8. What are intellectual property rights? Why should a company in international marketing take special steps to protect them?

9. In many code-law countries, registration rather than prior use establishes ownership of intellectual property rights. Comment.

10. Discuss the advantages to the international marketer arising from the existence of the various international conventions on trademarks, patents, and copyrights.

11. "The legal environment of the foreign marketer takes on an added dimension of importance since there is no single uniform international commercial law which governs foreign business transactions." Comment.

12. Why is conciliation a better way to resolve a commercial dispute than arbitration?

13. Differentiate between conciliation and arbitration.

14. Assume you are a vice president in charge of a new business-to-business e-commerce division of a well-known major international auto parts manufacturer. A cybersquatter has registered the company name as a domain Web name. What are your options to secure the domain name for your company? Discuss the steps you should take to ensure worldwide protection of your domain name.

15. Discuss the issues of a Web site owner being liable for information posted on the site.

16. Discuss the motives of a cybersquatter. What recourse does a company have to defend itself against a cybersquatter?

8

Developing a Global Vision through Marketing Research

CHAPTER OUTLINE

CHAPTER LEARNING OBJECTIVES

What you should learn from Chapter 8:

- The importance of problem definition in international research

- The problems of availability and use of secondary data

- Quantitative and qualitative research methods

- Multicultural sampling and its problems in less-developed countries

- Sources of secondary data

- How to analyze and use research information

Global Perspective

JAPAN—TEST MARKET FOR THE WORLD

It was 10:51 p.m. in Tokyo, and suddenly Google was hit with a two-minute spike in searches from Japanese mobile phones. "We were wondering: Was it spam? Was it a system error?" says Ken Tokusei, Google's mobile chief in Japan. A quick call to carrier KDDI revealed that it was neither. Instead, millions of cell phone users had pulled up Google's search box after a broadcaster offered free ringtone downloads of the theme song from *The Man Who Couldn't Marry*, a popular TV show, but had only briefly flashed the Web address where the tune was available.

The surge in traffic came as a big surprise to Tokusei and his team. They had assumed that a person's location was the key element of most mobile Internet searches, figuring that users were primarily interested in maps of the part of town they happened to be, timetables for the train home, or the address of the closest yakitori restaurant. The data from KDDI indicated that many Japanese were just as likely to use Google's mobile searches from the couch as from a Ginza street corner.

Japan's handset-toting masses, it seems, have a lot to teach the Internet giant. The country has become a vast lab for Google as it tries to refine mobile search technology. That's because Japan's 100 million cell phone users represent the most diverse—and discriminating—pool of mobile subscribers on the planet. Although Google also does plenty of testing elsewhere, the Japanese are often more critical because they are as likely to tap into the Internet with a high-tech phone as a PC and can do so at speeds rivaling fixed-line broadband. And because Japanese carriers have offered such services for years, plenty of Web sites are formatted for cell phones.

Tokyo's armies of fashion-obsessed shopaholics have long made the city figure prominently on the map of Western designers. Sure, the suit and tie remain the uniform of the salaryman, but for originality, nothing rivals Tokyo teenyboppers, who cycle in and out of fads faster than a schoolgirl can change out of her uniform and into Goth-Loli gear. (Think Little Bo Peep meets Sid Vicious.) For American and European brands, these young people are a wellspring of ideas that can be recycled for consumers back home.

But now, instead of just exporting Tokyo cool, some savvy foreign companies are starting to use Japan as a testing ground for new concepts. They're offering products in Japan before they roll them out globally, and more Western retailers are opening new outlets in Tokyo to keep an eye on trends. Ohio-based Abercrombie & Fitch and Sweden's H&M (Hennes & Mauritz) plan to set up shop in Tokyo in 2008, and Spain's Zara is expected to double its store count to 50 over the next three years. "Twenty-five or 30 years ago, major brands tested their new products in New York," says Mitsuru Sakuraba, who spent 20 years at French fashion house Charles Jourdan. "Now Japan has established a presence as a pilot market."

Some Western companies also have signed on with local partners who can better read the Japanese market. Gola, an English brand of athletic shoes and apparel, has teamed up with EuroPacific (Japan) Ltd., a Tokyo-based retailer of fashion footwear. EuroPacific tweaks Gola's designs for the Japanese market and, a few years ago, came up with the idea of pitching shin-high boxing boots to women. They were a hit with Japanese teens and twenty-somethings, prompting Gola to try offering them in other markets. "They've sold a hell of a lot in Europe," says EuroPacific Director Steve Sneddon.

Sources: Hiroko Tashiro, "Testing What's Hot in the Cradle of Cool," *BusinessWeek*, May 7, 2007, p. 46; Kenji Hall, "Japan: Google's Real-Life Lab," *BusinessWeek*, February 25, 2008, pp. 55–57.

It's crucial for top executives to get away from their desks and spend time in the marketplace. While detailed marketing research reports are important, decisions at the very top of the largest corporations must still be informed by a sense of the market and customers, obtainable only through direct contact by top executives. Here we see Bill Gates (left) and Steven Jobs (right) going east and west talking with and learning from their customers in the most direct way. Both have heavy international travel schedules, and both find face-to-face meetings with foreign vendors, partners, customers, and regulators to be an inescapable part of trying to understand their international markets. Most recently, to mark the 20th anniversary of Microsoft's entry into Mexico, Gates played and lost a game of Xbox 360 soccer to Mexican national player Rafael Marquez. We wonder: Did he throw the game?[1] *(left: AP Photo/Greg Baker; right: © Jim Watson/AFP/Getty Images)*

Information is the key component in developing successful marketing strategies and avoiding major marketing blunders. Information needs range from the general data required to assess market opportunities to specific market information for decisions about product, promotion, distribution, and price. Sometimes the information can be bought from trusted research vendors or supplied by internal marketing research staff. But sometimes even the highest-level executives have to "get their shoes dirty" by putting in the miles, talking to key customers, and directly observing the marketplace in action.[2] As an enterprise broadens its scope of operations to include international markets, the need for current, accurate information is magnified. Indeed, some researchers maintain that entry into a fast developing, new-to-the-firm foreign market is one of the most daunting and ambiguous strategic decisions an executive can face. A marketer must find the most accurate and reliable data possible within the limits imposed by time, cost, and the present state of the art.

Marketing research is traditionally defined as the systematic gathering, recording, and analyzing of data to provide information useful to marketing decision making. Although the research processes and methods are basically the same, whether applied in Columbus, Ohio, or Colombo, Sri Lanka, international marketing research involves two additional complications. First, information must be communicated across cultural boundaries. That is, executives in Chicago must be able to "translate" their research questions into terms that consumers in Guangzhou, China, can understand. Then the Chinese answers must be put into terms (i.e., reports and data summaries) that American managers can comprehend.

---

[1] "Microsoft's Bill Gates Loses Xbox Soccer Match," *CMP TechWeb*, March 21, 2007.

[2] Peter Drucker's wisdom improves with age. In his *The Wall Street Journal* article of May 11, 1990 (p. A15), he eloquently makes the case for direct observation of the marketplace by even the most senior executives. For the most substantive argument in that same vein, see Gerald Zaltman's description of emotional aspects of managerial decision making in "Rethinking Market Research: Putting People Back In," *Journal of Marketing Research* 34 (November 1997), pp. 424–37; Carol Hymowitz, "CEOs Are Spending More Quality Time with Their Customers," *The Wall Street Journal*, May 14, 2007, p. B1. Executives also learn about the "big picture" of the international business environment from mass media sources. Unfortunately, the effort to collect news around the world is shrinking fast as newspapers continue to cut reporting staffs, particularly at their international bureaus; see Trudy Rubin, "The Latest Casualty: Detailed Foreign News," *Dallas Morning News*, December 7, 2006, p. 23A.

Fortunately, there are often internal staff and research agencies that are quite experienced in these kinds of cross-cultural communication tasks.

Second, the environments within which the research tools are applied are often different in foreign markets. Rather than acquire new and exotic methods of research, the international marketing researcher must develop the capability for imaginative and deft applications of tried and tested techniques in sometimes totally strange milieus. The mechanical problems of implementing foreign marketing research often vary from country to country. Within a foreign environment, the frequently differing emphases on the kinds of information needed, the often limited variety of appropriate tools and techniques available, and the difficulty of implementing the research process constitute the challenges facing most international marketing researchers.

This chapter deals with the operational problems encountered in gathering information in foreign countries for use by international marketers. The emphasis is on those elements of data generation that usually prove especially troublesome in conducting research in an environment other than the United States.

Breadth and Scope of International Marketing Research

The basic difference between domestic and foreign market research is the broader scope needed for foreign research, necessitated by higher levels of uncertainty. Research can be divided into three types on the basis of information needs: (1) general information about the country, area, and/or market; (2) information necessary to forecast future marketing requirements by anticipating social, economic, consumer, and industry trends within specific markets or countries; and (3) specific market information used to make product, promotion, distribution, and price decisions and to develop marketing plans. In domestic operations, most emphasis is placed on the third type, gathering specific market information, because the other data are often available from secondary sources.

A country's political stability, cultural attributes, and geographical characteristics are some of the kinds of information not ordinarily gathered by domestic marketing research departments but required for a sound assessment of a foreign market. This broader scope of international marketing research is reflected in Unisys Corporation's planning steps, which call for collecting and assessing the following types of information:

1. **Economic and demographic.** General data on growth in the economy, inflation, business cycle trends, and the like; profitability analysis for the division's products; specific industry economic studies; analysis of overseas economies; and key economic indicators for the United States and major foreign countries, as well as population trends, such as migration, immigration, and aging.[3]

2. **Cultural, sociological, and political climate.** A general noneconomic review of conditions affecting the division's business. In addition to the more obvious subjects, it covers ecology, safety, and leisure time and their potential impacts on the division's business.[4]

3. **Overview of market conditions.** A detailed analysis of market conditions that the division faces, by market segment,[5] including international.

4. **Summary of the technological environment.** A summary of the state-of-the-art technology as it relates to the division's business, carefully broken down by product segments.

5. **Competitive situation.** A review of competitors' sales revenues, methods of market segmentation, products, and apparent strategies on an international scope.

---

[3] Hiroki Tashiro, "Here, Kid, Take the Wheel," *BusinessWeek*, July 23, 2007, p. 37.

[4] Debanjan Mitra and Peter N. Golder, "Whose Culture Matters? Near-Market Knowledge and Its Impacts on Foreign Market Entry Timing," *Journal of Marketing Research* 39, no. 3 (August 2002), pp. 350–65.

[5] Tammo H. A. Bijmolt, Leo J. Paas, and Jeroen K. Vermunt, "Country and Consumer Segmentation: Multi-Level Latent Class Analysis of Financial Product Ownership," *International Journal of Research in Marketing* 21, no. 4 (2004), pp. 323–40.

Exhibit 8.1

Top 20 Countries for Marketing Research Expenditures (millions of dollars)

Source: From *Marketing News*, July 15, 2007, pp. 26–27. Reprinted with permission of American Marketing Association.

United States	$7,722
United Kingdom	2,411
France	2,247
Germany	2,185
Japan	1,358
Italy	684
Canada	573
Australia	522
Spain	498
China	475
Brazil	350
Netherlands	346
Mexico	332
Sweden	323
S. Korea	282
Belgium	179
Switzerland	164
Poland	149
India	102
Taiwan	98

Such in-depth information is necessary for sound marketing decisions.[6] For the domestic marketer, most such information has been acquired after years of experience with a single market, but in foreign countries, this information must be gathered for each new market.

There is a basic difference between information ideally needed and that which is collectible and/or used. Many firms engaged in foreign marketing do not make decisions with the benefit of the information listed. Cost, time, and human elements are critical variables. Some firms have neither the appreciation for information nor adequate time or money for the implementation of research. As a firm becomes more committed to foreign marketing and the cost of possible failure increases, however, greater emphasis is placed on research. Indeed, marketing research expenditures reflect the size and growth of markets around the world. Please see Exhibit 8.1 for a listing of the top 20 markets for international marketing research.

The Research Process

A marketing research study is always a compromise dictated by the limits of time, cost, and the present state of the art. A key to successful research is a systematic and orderly approach to the collection and analysis of data. Whether a research program is conducted in New York or New Delhi, the research process should follow these steps:

1. Define the research problem and establish research objectives.✳
2. Determine the sources of information to fulfill the research objectives.
3. Consider the costs and benefits of the research effort.
4. Gather the relevant data from secondary or primary sources, or both.
5. Analyze, interpret, and summarize the results.
6. Effectively communicate the results to decision makers.

Although the steps in a research program are similar for all countries, variations and problems in implementation occur because of differences in cultural and economic development. Whereas the problems of research in England or Canada may be similar to those in the United States, research in Germany, South Africa, or Mexico may offer a multitude

---

[6] Apparently governments also get into the industrial competitive intelligence game. See Edward Iwata, "More U.S. Trade Secrets Walk out Door with Foreign Spies," *USA Today*, February 13, 2003, p. 5A; *The Economist*, "I Spy, You Spy," June 4, 2005, p. 61; Neil A. Lewis, "Justice Department Announces Arrests in 2 Chinese Espionage Cases," *The New York Times*, February 12, 2008, p. 14.

of difficult distinctions. These distinctions become apparent with the first step in the research process—formulation of the problem. The subsequent text sections illustrate some frequently encountered difficulties facing the international marketing researcher.

Defining the Problem and Establishing Research Objectives

After examining internal sources of data, the research process should begin with a definition of the research problem and the establishment of specific research objectives.[7] The major difficulty here is converting a series of often ambiguous business problems into tightly drawn and achievable research objectives. In this initial stage, researchers often embark on the research process with only a vague grasp of the total problem. A good example of such a loosely defined problem is that of Russian airline Aeroflot. The company undertook a branding study to inform its marketing decisions regarding improving its long-standing reputation for poor safety standards and unreliable service. This goal is a tough challenge for international marketing researchers.

This first, most crucial step in research is more critical in foreign markets because an unfamiliar environment tends to cloud problem definition. Researchers either fail to anticipate the influence of the local culture on the problem or fail to identify the self-reference

---

[7] Scholars in the field also struggle with defining the problem. See Mike W. Peng, "Identifying the Big Question in International Business Research," *Journal of International Business Studies* 35, no. 2 (2004), pp. 99–108; Susan B. Douglas and C. Samuel Craig, "On Improving the Conceptual Foundations of International Marketing Research," *Journal of International Marketing* 14, no. 1 (2006), pp. 1–22.

The first step in marketing research is defining the problem. The pilots in Gary Larson's cartoon eloquently reflect the major challenge in international marketing research. Defining the problem can be much more difficult in foreign markets, and more careful preliminary qualitative work is crucial in avoiding international marketing research "collisions with mountains"! By the way, this is not an Aeroflot joke. (*The Far Side*® by Gary Larson © 1983 FarWorks, Inc. All Rights Reserved. Used with permission.)

THE FAR SIDE®   **BY GARY LARSON**

"Say ... what's a mountain goat doing way up here in a cloud bank?"

criterion (SRC) and therefore treat the problem definition as if it were in the researcher's home environment. In assessing some foreign business failures, it becomes apparent that research was conducted, but the questions asked were more appropriate for the U.S. market than for the foreign one. For example, all of Disney's years of research and experience in keeping people happy standing in long lines could not help Disney anticipate the scope of the problems it would run into with Disneyland Paris. The firm's experience had been that the relatively homogeneous clientele at both the American parks and Tokyo Disneyland were cooperative and orderly when it came to queuing up. Actually, so are most British and Germans. But the rules about queuing in other countries such as Spain and Italy are apparently quite different, creating the potential for a new kind of intra-European "warfare" in the lines. Understanding and managing this multinational customer service problem has required new ways of thinking. Isolating the SRC and asking the right questions are crucial steps in the problem formulation stage.

Other difficulties in foreign research stem from failures to establish problem limits broad enough to include all relevant variables. Information on a far greater range of factors is necessary to offset the unfamiliar cultural background of the foreign market. Consider proposed research about consumption patterns and attitudes toward hot milk-based drinks. In the United Kingdom, hot milk-based drinks are considered to have sleep-inducing, restful, and relaxing properties and are traditionally consumed prior to bedtime. People in Thailand, however, drink the same hot milk-based drinks in the morning on the way to work and see them as invigorating, energy-giving, and stimulating. If one's only experience is the United States, the picture is further clouded, because hot milk-based drinks are frequently associated with cold weather, either in the morning or the evening, and for different reasons each time of day. The market researcher must be certain the problem definition is sufficiently broad to cover the whole range of response possibilities and not be clouded by his or her self-reference criterion.

Indeed, this clouding is a problem that Mattel Inc. ran into headlong. The company conducted a coordinated global research program using focus groups of children in several countries. Based on these findings, the firm cut back on customization and ignored local managers' advice by selling an unmodified Barbie globally. Not only was it dangerous to ignore the advice of local managers; it was also dangerous to ignore parents' opinions involving toys. Kids may like a blonde Barbie, but parents may not.[8] Unfortunately, our predictions about Barbie in a previous edition of this book proved correct: As we mentioned in previous chapters, sales of blonde Barbie dramatically declined in several foreign markets following the marketing research error. Now it seems that the doll's 2004 "makeover" only slowed the sagging sales of Mattel's most important product.[9]

Once the problem is adequately defined and research objectives established, the researcher must determine the availability of the information needed. If the data are available—that is, if they have been collected already by some other agency—the researcher should then consult these *secondary data* sources.

Problems of Availability and Use of Secondary Data

The U.S. government provides comprehensive statistics for the United States; periodic censuses of U.S. population, housing, business, and agriculture are conducted and, in some cases, have been taken for over 100 years. Commercial sources, trade associations, management groups, and state and local governments provide the researcher with additional sources of detailed U.S. market information. Often the problem for American marketing researchers is sorting through too much data!

---

[8] Lisa Bannon and Carlta Vitzhum, "One-Toy-Fits-All: How Industry Learned to Love the Global Kid," *The Wall Street Journal*, April 29, 2003, p. A1; Nicolas Casey, "Online Popularity Contest Next in Barbie–Bratz Brawl," *The Wall Street Journal*, July 23, 2007, pp. B1, B2.

[9] Melinda Fulmer, "Mattel Sees Results from Barbie Makeover," *Los Angeles Times*, February 1, 2005, pp. C1, C12.

CROSSING BORDERS 8.1   Headache? Take Two Aspirin and Lie Down

Such advice goes pretty far in countries such as Germany, where Bayer invented aspirin more than 100 years ago, and the United States. But people in many places around the world don't share such Western views about medicine and the causes of disease. Many Asians, including Chinese, Filipinos, Koreans, Japanese, and Southeast Asians, believe illnesses such as headaches are the result of the imbalance between *yin* and *yang*. *Yin* is the feminine, passive principle that is typified by darkness, cold, or wetness. Alternatively, *yang* is the masculine, active principle associated with light, heat, or dryness. All things result from their combination, and bad things like headaches result from too much of one or the other. Acupuncture and moxibustion (heating crushed wormwood or other herbs on the skin) are common cures. Many Laotians believe pain can be caused by one of the body's 32 souls being lost or by sorcerers' spells. The exact cause is often determined by examining the yolk of a freshly broken egg. In other parts of the world, such as Mexico and Puerto Rico, illness is believed to be caused by an imbalance of one of the four body humors: "blood— hot and wet; yellow bile—hot and dry; phlegm—cold and wet; and black bile—cold and dry." Even in the high-tech United States, many people believe that pain is often a "reminder from God" to behave properly.

Now Bayer is marketing aspirin as a preventive drug for other ailments, such as intestinal cancer and heart attack. But in many foreign markets for companies such as Bayer, a key question to be addressed in marketing research is how and to what extent aspirin can be marketed as a supplement to the traditional remedies. That is, will little white pills mix well with phlegm and black bile?

Sources: Larry A. Samovar, Richard E. Porter, and Lisa A. Stefani, *Communication between Cultures*, 3rd ed. (Belmont, CA: Wadsworth Publishing, 1998), pp. 224–25; the direct quote is from N. Dresser, *Multicultural Manners: New Rules for Etiquette for a Changing Society* (New York: John Wiley & Sons, 1996), p. 236; see also "Aspirin Truly Merits Consideration as One of the Wonders of World," *Star-Ledger*, September 18, 2007, p. 67.

Availability of Data

Unfortunately, the quantity and quality of marketing-related data available on the United States is unmatched in other countries. The data available on and in Japan is a close second, and several European countries do a good job of collecting and reporting data. Indeed, on some dimensions, the quality of data collected in these latter countries can actually exceed that in the United States. However, in many countries substantial data collection has been initiated only recently.[10] Through the continuing efforts of organizations such as the United Nations and the Organization for Economic Cooperation and Development (OECD), improvements are being made worldwide.

In addition, with the emergence of eastern European countries as potentially viable markets, a number of private and public groups are funding the collection of information to offset a lack of comprehensive market data. Several Japanese consumer goods manufacturers are coordinating market research on a corporate level and have funded dozens of research centers throughout eastern Europe. As market activity continues in eastern Europe and elsewhere, market information will improve in quantity and quality. To build a database on Russian consumers, one Denver, Colorado, firm used a novel approach to conduct a survey: It ran a questionnaire in Moscow's *Komsomolskaya Pravda* newspaper asking for replies to be sent to the company. The 350,000 replies received (3,000 by registered mail) attested to the willingness of Russian consumers to respond to marketing inquiries. The problems of availability, reliability, and comparability of data and of validating secondary data are described in the following sections.

Another problem relating to the availability of data is researchers' language skills. For example, though data are often copious regarding the Japanese market, being able to read Japanese is a requisite for accessing them, either online or in text. This problem may seem rather innocuous, but only those who have tried to maneuver through foreign data can appreciate the value of having a native speaker of the appropriate language on the research team.

---

[10] See GIS analyses based on the 2000 Census in China at http://www.geodemo.com, Demographic Consulting, Inc.

Reliability of Data

Available data may not have the level of reliability necessary for confident decision making for many reasons. Official statistics are sometimes too optimistic, reflecting national pride rather than practical reality, while tax structures and fear of the tax collector often adversely affect data.

Although not unique to them,[11] less-developed countries are particularly prone to being both overly optimistic and unreliable in reporting relevant economic data about their countries. China's National Statistics Enforcement Office recently acknowledged that it had uncovered about 60,000 instances of false statistical reports since beginning a crackdown on false data reporting several months earlier.[12] More recently the head of China's National Bureau of Statistics was fired for his involvement in an unfolding corruption scandal.[13] Seeking advantages or hiding failures, local officials, factory managers, rural enterprises, and others file fake numbers on everything from production levels to birthrates. For example, a petrochemical plant reported one year's output to be $20 million, 50 percent higher than its actual output of $13.4 million. Finally, if you believe the statistics, until 2000, the Chinese in Hong Kong were the world-champion consumers of fresh oranges—64 pounds per year per person, twice as much as Americans. However, apparently about half of all the oranges imported into Hong Kong, or some $30 million worth, were actually finding their way into the rest of China, where U.S. oranges were illegal.

Willful errors in the reporting of marketing data are not uncommon in the most industrialized countries either. Often print media circulation figures are purposely overestimated even in OECD countries. The European Union (EU) tax policies can affect the accuracy of reported data also. Production statistics are frequently inaccurate because these countries collect taxes on domestic sales. Thus some companies shave their production statistics a bit to match the sales reported to tax authorities. Conversely, foreign trade statistics may be blown up slightly because each country in the EU grants some form of export subsidy. Knowledge of such "adjusted reporting" is critical for a marketer who relies on secondary data for forecasting or estimating market demand.

Comparability of Data

Comparability of available data is the third shortcoming faced by foreign marketers. In the United States, current sources of reliable and valid estimates of socioeconomic factors and business indicators are readily available. In other countries, especially those less developed, data can be many years out of date as well as having been collected on an infrequent and unpredictable schedule. Naturally, the rapid change in socioeconomic features being experienced in many of these countries makes the problem of currency a vital one. Furthermore, even though many countries are now gathering reliable data, there are generally no historical series with which to compare the current information. Comparability of data can even be a problem when the best commercial research firms collect data across countries, and managers are well advised to query their vendors about this problem.

A related problem is the manner in which data are collected and reported. Too frequently, data are reported in different categories or in categories much too broad to be of specific value. The term *supermarket*, for example, has a variety of meanings around the world. In Japan a supermarket is quite different from its American counterpart. Japanese supermarkets usually occupy two- or three-story structures; they sell foodstuffs, daily necessities, and clothing on respective floors. Some even sell furniture, electric home appliances, stationery, and sporting goods; some have a restaurant. General merchandise stores, shopping centers, and department stores are different from stores of the same name in the United States.[14]

---

[11] *The Economist*, "Britain: The Numbers Game," March 26, 2005, pp. 35–36; *The Economist*, "Lies, Damned Lies," March 3, 2007, p. 18.

[12] Mark L. Clifford, "How Fast Is China Really Growing?" *BusinessWeek*, March 10, 2003, p. 65; Terence Poon, "World Bank Raises China Outlook," *The Wall Street Journal Online*, September 12, 2007.

[13] "Chinese Statistics Chief Fired in Scandal Inquiry," *International Herald Tribune*, October 20, 2006, p. 3.

[14] Matthew B. Myers, Roger J. Calantone, Thomas J. Page Jr., and Charles R. Taylor, "An Application of Multiple-Group Causal Models in Assessing Cross-Cultural Measurement Equivalence," *Journal of International Marketing* 8, no. 4 (2000), pp. 108–21.

Validating Secondary Data

The shortcomings discussed here should be considered when using any source of information. Many countries have similarly high standards for the collection and preparation of data as those generally found in the United States, but secondary data from any source, including the United States, must be checked and interpreted carefully. As a practical matter, the following questions should be asked to effectively judge the reliability of secondary data sources:

1. Who collected the data? Would there be any reason for purposely misrepresenting the facts?
2. For what purposes were the data collected?
3. How (by what methodology) were the data collected?
4. Are the data internally consistent and logical in light of known data sources or market factors?

Checking the consistency of one set of secondary data with other data of known validity is an effective and often-used way of judging validity. For example, a researcher might check the sale of baby products with the number of women of childbearing age and birthrates, or the number of patient beds in hospitals with the sale of related hospital equipment. Such correlations can also be useful in estimating demand and forecasting sales.

In general, the availability and accuracy of recorded secondary data increase as the level of economic development increases. There are exceptions; India is at a lower level of economic development than many countries but has accurate and relatively complete government-collected data.

Fortunately, interest in collecting high-quality statistical data rises as countries realize the value of extensive and accurate national statistics for orderly economic growth. This interest in improving the quality of national statistics has resulted in remarkable improvement in the availability of data over the last 25 years. However, when no data are available or the secondary data sources are inadequate, it is necessary to begin the collection of primary data.

The appendix to this chapter includes a comprehensive listing of secondary data sources, including Web sites on a variety of international marketing topics. Indeed, almost all secondary data available on international markets can now be discovered or acquired via the Internet. For example, the most comprehensive statistics regarding international finances, demographics, consumption, exports, and imports are accessible through a single source, the U.S. Department of Commerce at www.stat-usa.gov. Many other governmental, institutional, and commercial sources of data can be tapped into on the Internet as well. You can find supplementary information about this text at www.mhhe.com/cateora14e.

Gathering Primary Data: Quantitative and Qualitative Research

If, after seeking all reasonable secondary data sources, research questions are still not adequately answered, the market researcher must collect *primary data*—that is, data collected specifically for the particular research project at hand. The researcher may question the firm's sales representatives, distributors, middlemen, and/or customers to get appropriate market information. Marketing research methods can be grouped into two basic types: quantitative and qualitative research. In both methods, the marketer is interested in gaining knowledge about the market.

In *quantitative research*, usually a large number of respondents are asked to reply either verbally or in writing to structured questions using a specific response format (such as yes/ no) or to select a response from a set of choices. Questions are designed to obtain specific responses regarding aspects of the respondents' behavior, intentions, attitudes, motives, and demographic characteristics. Quantitative research provides the marketer with responses that can be presented with precise estimations. The structured responses received in a survey can be summarized in percentages, averages, or other statistics. For example, 76 percent of the respondents prefer product A over product B, and so on. Survey research is generally associated with quantitative research, and the typical instrument used is a questionnaire administered by personal interview, mail, telephone, and, most recently, over the Internet.

Scientific studies, including tightly designed experiments, often are conducted by engineers and chemists in product-testing laboratories around the world.[15] There, product designs and formulas are developed and tested in consumer usage situations. Often those results are integrated with consumer opinions gathered in concurrent survey studies. One of the best examples of this kind of marketing research comes from Tokyo. You may not know it, but the Japanese are the world champions of bathroom and toilet technology. Japan's biggest company in that industry, Toto, has spent millions of dollars developing and testing consumer products. Thousands of people have collected data (using survey techniques) about the best features of a toilet, and at the company's "human engineering laboratory," volunteers sit in a Toto bathtub with electrodes strapped to their skulls to measure brain waves and "the effects of bathing on the human body." Toto is now introducing one of its high-tech (actually low-tech compared with what it offers in Japan) toilets in the U.S. market. It's a $600 seat, lid, and control panel that attaches to the regular American bowl. It features a heated seat and deodorizing fan.

In *qualitative research*, if questions are asked, they are almost always open-ended or in-depth, and unstructured responses that reflect the person's thoughts and feelings on the subject are sought. Consumers' first impressions about products may be useful.[16] Direct observation of consumers in choice or product usage situations is another important qualitative approach to marketing research. One researcher spent two months observing birthing practices in American and Japanese hospitals to gain insights into the export of healthcare services. Nissan Motors sent a researcher to live with an American family (renting a room in their house for six weeks) to directly observe how Americans use their cars. Most recently the British retailer TESCO sent teams to live with American families to observe their shopping behaviors in advance of its new entry in the U.S. supermarket battleground with Wal-Mart and others.[17] Anderson Worldwide, Nynex, and Texas Commerce Bank have all employed anthropologists who specialize in observational and in-depth interviews in their marketing research. Qualitative research seeks to interpret what the people in the sample are like—their outlooks, their feelings, the dynamic interplay of their feelings and ideas, their attitudes and opinions, and their resulting actions.[18] The most often used form of qualitative questioning is the focus group interview. However, oftentimes, in-depth interviewing of individuals can be just as effective while consuming far fewer resources.

Qualitative research is used in international marketing research to formulate and define a problem more clearly and to determine relevant questions to be examined in subsequent research. It is also used to stimulate ad message ideas and where interest centers on gaining an understanding of a market rather than quantifying relevant aspects. For example, a small group of key executives at Solar Turbines International, a division of Caterpillar Tractor Company, called on key customers at their offices around the world. They discussed in great depth, with both financial managers and production engineers, potential applications and the demand for a new size of gas-turbine engine the company was considering developing. The data and insights gained during the interviews to a large degree confirmed the validity of the positive demand forecasts produced internally through macroeconomic modeling. The multimillion-dollar project was then implemented. During the discussions, new product features were suggested by the customer personnel that proved most useful in the development efforts.

Qualitative research is also helpful in revealing the impact of sociocultural factors on behavior patterns and in developing research hypotheses that can be tested in subsequent studies designed to quantify the concepts and relevant relationships uncovered in qualitative

[15] Patricia Sellers, "The World of Ideas: Where Do Good Ideas Come From? For Global 500 Companies, the Answer Could Be Anywhere," *Fortune*, July 25, 2005, special insert.

[16] Danielle Sacks, "The Accidental Guru," *Fast Company*, January 2005, pp. 64–68.

[17] Cecillie Rohwedder, "Tesco Studies Hard for U.S. Debut," *The Wall Street Journal*, June 28, 2007, pp. B1, B2.

[18] Paul E. Green, Yoram Wind, Abba M. Krieger, and Paul Saatsoglou, "Applying Qualitative Data," *Marketing Research* 12 (Spring 2000), pp. 17–25.

data collection.[19] Procter & Gamble has been one of the pioneers of this type of research—the company has systematically gathered consumer feedback for some 70 years. It was the first company to conduct in-depth consumer research in China. In the mid-1990s, P&G began working with the Chinese Ministry of Health to develop dental hygiene programs that have now reached millions there.

Oftentimes the combination of qualitative and quantitative research proves quite useful in consumer markets[20] and business-to-business marketing settings as well. In one study, the number of personal referrals used in buying financial services in Japan was found to be much greater than that in the United States.[21] The various comments made by the executives during interviews in both countries proved invaluable in interpreting the quantitative results, suggesting implications for managers and providing ideas for further research. Likewise, the comments of sales managers in Tokyo during in-depth interviews helped researchers understand why individual financial incentives did not work with Japanese sales representatives.[22]

As we shall see later in this chapter, using either research method in international marketing research is subject to a number of difficulties brought about by the diversity of cultures and languages encountered.

Problems of Gathering Primary Data

The problems of collecting primary data in foreign countries are different only in degree from those encountered in the United States. Assuming the research problem is well defined and the objectives are properly formulated, the success of primary research hinges on the ability of the researcher to get correct and truthful information that addresses the research objectives. Most problems in collecting primary data in international marketing research stem from cultural differences among countries and range from the inability or unwillingness[23] of respondents to communicate their opinions to inadequacies in questionnaire translation.

Ability to Communicate Opinions

The ability to express attitudes and opinions about a product or concept depends on the respondent's ability to recognize the usefulness and value of such a product or concept. It is difficult for a person to formulate needs, attitudes, and opinions about goods whose use may not be understood, that are not in common use within the community, or that have never been available. For example, someone who has never had the benefits of an office computer will be unable to express accurate feelings or provide any reasonable information about purchase intentions, likes, or dislikes concerning a new computer software package. The more complex the concept, the more difficult it is to design research that will help the respondent communicate meaningful opinions and reactions. Under these circumstances, the creative capabilities of the international marketing researcher are challenged.

No company has had more experience in trying to understand consumers with communication limitations than Gerber. Babies may be their business, but babies often can't talk, much less fill out a questionnaire. Over the years, Gerber has found that talking to and observing both infants and their mothers are important in marketing research. In one study, Gerber found that breast-fed babies adapted to solid food more quickly than bottle-fed

[19] Robert Levine, "MySpace Growth Faces Cultural Hurdles," *International Herald Tribune*, November 7, 2006, pp. 1, 17.

[20] Nguyen Thi Thyet, Kwon Jung, Garold Lantz, and Sandra G. Loeb, "An Exploratory Investigation of Impulse Buying in a Transitional Economy: A Study of Urban Consumers in Vietnam," *Journal of International Business Studies* 11, no. 2 (2003), pp. 13–35.

[21] R. Bruce Money, "Word-of-Mouth Referral Sources for Buyers of International Corporate Financial Services," *Journal of World Business* 35, no. 3 (Fall 2000), pp. 314–29.

[22] R. Bruce Money and John L. Graham, "Sales Person Performance, Pay, and Job Satisfaction: Tests of a Model Using Data Collected in the U.S. and Japan," *Journal of International Business Studies* 30, no. 1 (1999), pp. 149–72.

[23] Fang Wu, Rudolf R. Sinkovics, S. Tamer Cavusgil, and Anthony S. Roath, "Overcoming Export Manufacturers' Dilemma in International Expansion," *Journal of International Business Studies* 38 (2007), pp. 283–302.

babies because breast milk changes flavor depending on what the mother has eaten. For example, infants were found to suck longer and harder if their mother had recently eaten garlic. In another study, weaning practices were studied around the world. Indian babies were offered lentils served on a finger. Some Nigerian children got fermented sorghum, fed by the grandmother through the funnel of her hand. In some parts of tropical Asia, mothers "food-kissed" prechewed vegetables into their babies' mouths. Hispanic mothers in the United States tend to introduce baby food much earlier than non-Hispanic mothers and continue it well beyond the first year. All this research helps the company decide which products are appropriate for which markets. For example, the Vegetable and Rabbit Meat and the Freeze-Dried Sardines and Rice flavors popular in Poland and Japan, respectively, most likely won't make it to American store shelves.

Willingness to Respond

Cultural differences offer the best explanation for the unwillingness or the inability of many to respond to research surveys. The role of the male, the suitability of personal gender-based inquiries, and other gender-related issues can affect willingness to respond.

In some countries, the husband not only earns the money but also dictates exactly how it is to be spent. Because the husband controls the spending, it is he, not the wife, who should be questioned to determine preferences and demand for many consumer goods. In some countries, women would never consent to be interviewed by a man or a stranger. A French Canadian woman does not like to be questioned and is likely to be reticent in her responses. In some societies, a man would certainly consider it beneath his dignity to discuss shaving habits or brand preference in personal clothing with anyone—most emphatically not a female interviewer.

Anyone asking questions about any topic from which tax assessment could be inferred is immediately suspected of being a tax agent. Citizens of many countries do not feel the same legal and moral obligations to pay their taxes as do U.S. citizens. Tax evasion is thus an accepted practice for many and a source of pride for the more adept. Where such an attitude exists, taxes are often seemingly arbitrarily assessed by the government, which results in much incomplete or misleading information being reported. One of the problems revealed by the government of India in a recent population census was the underreporting of tenants by landlords trying to hide the actual number of people living in houses and flats. The landlords had been subletting accommodations illegally and were concealing their activities from the tax department.

In the United States, publicly held corporations are compelled by the Securities and Exchange Commission (SEC) to disclose certain operating figures on a periodic basis. In

Midnight in New Delhi—both customer service and telephone survey research are being outsourced to lower-wage English-speaking countries. Cost savings of such outsourcing must be balanced with consumer reluctance in cross-cultural communication settings, particularly those involving voluntary responses to marketing research. (© Brian Lee/Corbis)

many European countries, however, such information is seldom if ever released and then most reluctantly. For example, in Germany attempts to enlist the cooperation of merchants in setting up an in-store study of shelf inventory and sales information ran into strong resistance because of suspicions and a tradition of competitive secrecy. The resistance was overcome by the researcher's willingness to approach the problem step by step. As the retailer gained confidence in the researcher and realized the value of the data gathered, more and more requested information was provided. Besides the reluctance of businesses to respond to surveys, local politicians in underdeveloped countries may interfere with studies in the belief that they could be subversive and must be stopped or hindered. A few moments with local politicians can prevent days of delay.

Although such cultural differences may make survey research more difficult to conduct, it is possible. In some communities, locally prominent people could open otherwise closed doors; in other situations, professional people and local students have been used as interviewers because of their knowledge of the market. Less direct measurement techniques and nontraditional data analysis methods may also be more appropriate. In one study, Japanese supermarket buyers rated the nationality of brands (foreign or domestic) as relatively unimportant in making stocking decisions when asked directly; however, when an indirect, paired-comparison questioning technique was used, brand nationality proved to be the most important factor.[24]

Sampling in Field Surveys

The greatest problem in sampling stems from the lack of adequate demographic data and available lists from which to draw meaningful samples.[25] If current, reliable lists are not available, sampling becomes more complex and generally less reliable. In many countries, telephone directories, cross-index street directories, census tract and block data, and detailed social and economic characteristics of the population being studied are not available on a current basis, if at all. The researcher has to estimate characteristics and population parameters, sometimes with little basic data on which to build an accurate estimate.

To add to the confusion, in some South American, Mexican, and Asian cities, street maps are unavailable, and in some Asian metropolitan areas, streets are not identified and houses are not numbered. In contrast, one of the positive aspects of research in Japan and Taiwan is the availability and accuracy of census data on individuals. In these countries, when a household moves, it is required to submit up-to-date information to a centralized government agency before it can use communal services such as water, gas, electricity, and education.

The effectiveness of various methods of communication (mail, telephone, personal interview, and Internet) in surveys is limited. In many countries, telephone ownership is extremely low, making telephone surveys virtually worthless unless the survey is intended to cover only the wealthy. In Sri Lanka, fewer than 7 percent of the residents have landline telephones and less than 2 percent Internet access—that is, only the wealthy.[26] Even if the respondent has a telephone, the researcher may still be unable to complete a call.

The adequacy of sampling techniques is also affected by a lack of detailed social and economic information. Without an age breakdown of the total population, for example, the researcher can never be certain of a representative sample requiring an age criterion, because there is no basis of comparison for the age distribution in the sample. A lack of detailed information, however, does not prevent the use of sampling; it simply makes it more difficult. In place of probability techniques, many researchers in such situations rely on convenience samples taken in marketplaces and other public gathering places.

---

[24] Frank Alpert, Michael Kamins, Tomoaki Sakano, Naoto Onzo, and John L. Graham, "Retail Buyer Beliefs, Attitudes, and Behaviors toward Pioneer and Me-Too Follower Brands: A Comparative Study of Japan and the United States," *International Marketing Review* 18, no. 2 (2001), pp. 160–87.

[25] N. L. Reynolds, A. C. Simintiras, and A. Diamantopoulos, "Theoretical Justification of Sampling Choices in International Marketing Research: Key Issues and Guidelines for Researchers," *Journal of International Business Research* 34 (2003), pp. 80–89.

[26] World Bank, *World Development Indicators 2008* (Washington, DC: World Bank, 2008).

Internet is now China, with 111 million users at last count.[39] International Internet use is growing almost twice as fast as American use. Growth in countries such as Costa Rica was dramatically spurred by the local government's decision to reclassify computers as "educational tools," thus eliminating all import tariffs on the hardware. The demographics of users worldwide are as follows: 60 percent male and 40 percent female; average age about 32 years; about 60 percent college educated; median income of about $60,000; usage time about 2.5 hours per week; and main activities of e-mail and finding information. The percentage of home pages by language is as follows: English, 80 percent; Japanese, 4 percent; German, 3 percent; French, 2 percent; Spanish, 1 percent; and all others less than 1 percent each.

For many companies, the Internet provides a new and increasingly important medium for conducting a variety of international marketing research. Indeed, a survey of marketing research professionals suggests that the most important influences on the industry are the Internet and globalization. New product concepts and advertising copy can be tested over the Internet for immediate feedback. Worldwide consumer panels[40] have been created to help test marketing programs across international samples. Indeed, it has been suggested that there are at least eight different uses for the Internet in international research:

1. **Online surveys and buyer panels.** These can include incentives for participation, and they have better "branching" capabilities (asking different questions based on previous answers) than more expensive mail and phone surveys.

2. **Online focus groups.** Bulletin boards can be used for this purpose.

3. **Web visitor tracking.** Servers automatically track and time visitors' travel through Web sites.

4. **Advertising measurement.** Servers track links to other sites, and their usefulness can therefore be assessed.

5. **Customer identification systems.** Many companies are installing registration procedures that allow them to track visits and purchases over time, creating a "virtual panel."

6. **E-mail marketing lists.** Customers can be asked to sign up on e-mail lists to receive future direct marketing efforts via the Internet.

7. **Embedded research.** The Internet continues to automate traditional economic roles of customers, such as searching for information about products and services, comparison shopping among alternatives, interacting with service providers, and maintaining the customer–brand relationship. More and more of these Internet processes look and feel like research processes themselves. The methods are often embedded directly into the actual purchase and use situations and therefore are more closely tied to actual economic behavior than traditional research methods. Some firms even provide the option of custom designing products online—the ultimate in applying research for product development purposes.

8. **Observational research.** Chat rooms, blogs, and personal Web sites can all be systematically monitored to assess consumers' opinions about products and services.

Clearly, as the Internet continues to grow, even more types of research will become feasible, and the extent to which new translation software has an impact on marketing communications and research over the Internet will be quite interesting to watch. Some companies now provide translation services for questionnaires, including commonly used phrases such as "rate your satisfaction level."[41] Surveys in multiple languages can be produced

---

[39] "The Great Internet Race," *BusinessWeek*, June 13, 2005, pp. 54–55.

[40] Information regarding worldwide Internet panels is available at http://www.decisionanalyst.com.

[41] See, for example, http://www.markettools.com.

quickly, given the translation libraries now available from some application service providers. Finally, as is the case in so many international marketing contexts, privacy is and will continue to be a matter of personal and legal considerations. A vexing challenge facing international marketers will be the cross-cultural concerns about privacy and the enlistment of cooperative consumer and customer groups.

The ability to conduct primary research is one of the exciting aspects about the Internet. However, the potential bias of a sample universe composed solely of Internet respondents presents some severe limitations, and firms vary substantially in their abilities to turn data collected into competitive advantages.[42] Nevertheless, as more of the general population in countries gain access to the Internet, this tool will be all the more powerful and accurate for conducting primary research. Also, the Internet can be used as one of several methods of collecting data, offering more flexibility across countries.[43]

Today the real power of the Internet for international marketing research is the ability to easily access volumes of secondary data. These data have been available in print form for years, but now they are much easier to access and, in many cases, are more current. Instead of leafing through reference books to find two- or three-year-old data, as is the case with most printed sources, you can often find up-to-date data on the Internet. Such Internet sites as www.stat-usa.gov provide almost all data that are published by the U.S. government. If you want to know the quantity of a specific product being shipped to a country, the import duties on a product, and whether an export license is required, it's all there, via your computer. A variety of private firms also provide international marketing information online. See the Appendix of this chapter for more detail.

Estimating Market Demand

In assessing current product demand and forecasting future demand, reliable historical data are required.[44] As previously noted, the quality and availability of secondary data frequently are inadequate; nevertheless, estimates of market size must be attempted to plan effectively. Despite limitations, some approaches to demand estimation are usable with minimum information.[45] The success of these approaches relies on the ability of the researcher to find meaningful substitutes or approximations for the needed economic, geographic,[46] and demographic relationships.

When the desired statistics are not available, a close approximation can be made using local production figures plus imports, with adjustments for exports and current inventory levels. These data are more readily available because they are commonly reported by the United Nations and other international agencies. Once approximations for sales trends are established, historical series can be used as the basis for projections of growth. In any straight extrapolation however, the estimator assumes that the trends of the immediate past will continue into the future. In a rapidly developing economy, extrapolated figures may not reflect rapid growth and must be adjusted accordingly. Given the greater uncertainties and data limitations associated with foreign markets, two methods of forecasting demand are particularly suitable for international marketers: expert opinion and analogy.

---

[42] Tho D. Nguyen and Nigel J. Barrett, "The Knowledge-Creating Role of the Internet in International Business: Evidence from Vietnam," *Journal of International Marketing* 14, no. 2 (2006), pp. 116–47.

[43] Janet Ilieva, Steve Baron, and Nigel M. Healey, "Online Surveys in Marketing Research; Pros and Cons," *International Journal of Marketing Research* 44, no. 3 (2002), pp. 361–76.

[44] Although more than 20 years old, still the best summary of forecasting methods and their advantages, disadvantages, and appropriate applications is David M. Georgoff and Robert G. Murdick, "Manager's Guide to Forecasting," *Harvard Business Review*, January–February 1986, pp. 110–20.

[45] Manoj K. Argawal, "Developing Global Segments and Forecasting Market Shares: A Simultaneous Approach Using Survey Data," *Journal of International Marketing* 11, no. 4 (2003), pp. 56–80.

[46] For a fascinating description of the potential role of ambient temperature (and latitude) in forecasting demand, see Philip M. Parker and Nader T. Tavassoli, "Homeostasis and Consumer Behavior across Cultures," *International Journal of Research in Marketing* 17, no. 1 (March 2000), pp. 33–53.

Expert Opinion

For many market estimation problems, particularly in foreign countries that are new to the marketer, expert opinion is advisable. In this method, experts are polled for their opinions about market size and growth rates. Such experts may be the companies' own sales managers or outside consultants and government officials. The key in using expert opinion to help forecast demand is *triangulation*, that is, comparing estimates produced by different sources. One of the tricky parts is how best to combine the different opinions.

Developing scenarios is useful in the most ambiguous forecasting situations, such as predicting demand for accounting services in emerging markets such as China and Russia or trying to predict the impact of SARS on tourism to Hong Kong. Moreover, statistical analyses of past data are fundamentally weak, because they cannot capture the potential impacts of extreme events[47] such as SARS. Experts with broad perspectives and long experience in markets will be better able to anticipate such major threats to stability and/or growth of market demand.

Analogy

Another technique is to estimate by analogy. This method assumes that demand for a product develops in much the same way in all countries, as comparable economic development occurs in each country.[48] First, a relationship must be established between the item to be estimated and a measurable variable[49] in a country that is to serve as the basis for the analogy. Once a known relationship is established, the estimator then attempts to draw an analogy between the known situation and the country in question. For example, suppose a company wanted to estimate the market growth potential for a beverage in country X, for which it had inadequate sales figures, but the company had excellent beverage data for neighboring country Y. In country Y, per capita consumption is known to increase at a predictable ratio as per capita gross domestic product (GDP) increases. If per capita GDP is known for country X, per capita consumption for the beverage can be estimated using the relationships established in country Y.

Caution must be used with analogy though because the method assumes that factors other than the variable used (in the preceding example, GDP) are similar in both countries, such as the same tastes, taxes, prices, selling methods, availability of products, consumption patterns,[50] and so forth. For example, the 13 million WAP (Wireless Access Protocol) users in Japan led to a serious overestimation of WAP adoptions in Europe—the actual figure of 2 million was less than the 10 million forecasted. Or consider the relevance of the adoption rate of personal computers or cell phones in the Unites States as they help predict adoption rates in the other four countries listed in Exhibit 8.2. How might Apple Computer use the American data to help predict demand in Japan? Despite the apparent drawbacks to analogy, it can be useful when data are limited.

All the methods for market demand estimation described in this section are no substitute for original market research when it is economically feasible and time permits. Indeed, the best approach to forecasting is almost always a combination of macroeconomic database approaches and interviews with potential and current customers. As more adequate data sources become available, as would be the situation in most of the economically developed countries, more technically advanced techniques such as multiple regression analysis or input–output analysis can be used.

---

[47] Pierpaolo Andriani and Bill McKelvey, "Beyond Gaussian Averages: Redirecting International Business and Management Research toward Extreme Events and Power Laws," *Journal of International Business Studies* 38 (2007), pp. 1212–30.

[48] Such an approach is now being used to predict the depth of the housing market decline in the United States and other markets by making comparisons to the housing boom–bust cycle experienced by Japan in the 1980s and 1990s. See Robert J. Shiller, "Things that Go Boom," *The Wall Street Journal*, February 8, 2007, p. A15.

[49] These variables may include population and other demographics or usage rates or estimates, and so forth. Using combinations of such variables is also referred to as a *chain-ratio* approach to forecasting.

[50] Gerard J. Tellis, Stefan Stremerch, and Eden Yin, "The International Takeoff of New Products: The Role of Economics, Culture, and Country Innovativeness," *Marketing Science* 22, no. 2 (2003), pp. 188–208; Sean Dwyer, Hani Mesak, and Maxwell Hsu, "An Exploratory Examination of the Influence of National Culture on Cross-National Product Diffusion," *Journal of International Marketing* 13, no. 2 (2005), pp. 1–27; Roger J. Calantone, David A. Griffith, and Goksel Yalcinkaya, "An Empirical Examination of a Technology Adoption Model for the Context of China," *Journal of International Marketing* 14, no. 4 (2006), pp. 1–27.

Exhibit 8.2
(*a*) Personal Computer and (*b*) Mobile Phone Diffusion Rate (per 1,000 people)

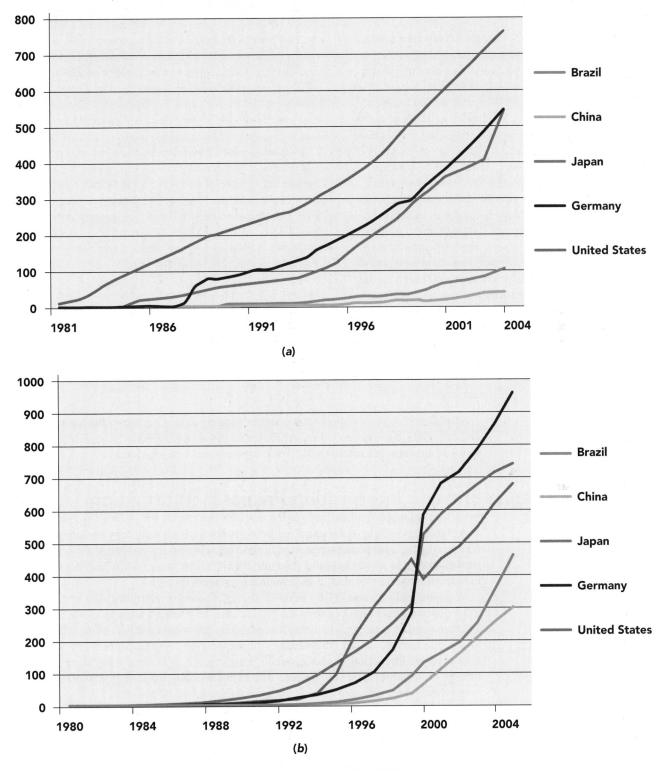

(*a*)

(*b*)

Source: World Bank, *World Development Indicators 2008* (Washington, DC: World Bank, 2008).

CROSSING BORDERS 8.2   Forecasting the Global Healthcare Market

In 2000, Johns Hopkins Hospital in Baltimore treated more than 7,500 patients from foreign countries. That's up from just 600 in 1994. And there were no hassles with insurance companies and HMOs. In fact, many of these patients paid cash—even for $30,000 surgical procedures! The Mayo Clinic in Rochester, Minnesota, has been serving foreigners for decades. The number there has jumped by about 15 percent in five years to more than 1,000 per year. Similar growth is happening in places such as Mount Sinai Hospital in Miami, the University of Texas Cancer Center, and the UCLA Medical Center. The Mayo Clinic has even set up a Muslim prayer room to make patients and their families feel more comfortable. Fast growth, yes (some say exponential), but will it continue? Forecasting this demand so that decisions can be made about staffing and numbers of beds is a daunting project indeed.

Demand in Mexico and Latin America seems to be coming primarily for treatment of infectious and digestive diseases and cancer. Demand from the Middle East stems more from genetic diseases, heart diseases, can-

cer, and asthma. From Asia, wealthy patients are coming mainly to California for treatment of cancer and coronary diseases. Europeans travel to the United States for mental illness services, cancer and heart disease, and AIDS treatments. Given that Japan has the world's best success rate for treating stomach cancer, one would forecast that to be a growth sector in the future.

But perhaps the strangest market to forecast is global war wounded. Recently Johns Hopkins contracted to replace limbs for soldiers involved in a border clash between Ecuador and Peru at $35,000 per patient. The description in *The Wall Street Journal* article might have been a bit overzealous: "There are wars all over the world, bombs all over the world. Casualty patients are a new and enriching market niche."

Sources: "U.S. Hospitals Attracting Patients from Abroad," *USA Today*, July 22, 1997, p. 1A; Ron Hammerle, "Healthcare Becoming a Lot Less Local," *Modern Healthcare*, March 20, 2000, p. 40; Pamela Fayerman, "Risk of Blood Clots Jumps with Travel for Surgery," *National Post* (CanWest News Service), June 30, 2005, p. A8.

Finally, it should go without saying that forecasting demand is one of the most difficult and important business activities. All business plans depend entirely on forecasts of a future that no one can see. Even the best companies make big mistakes.

Problems in Analyzing and Interpreting Research Information   Once data have been collected, the final steps in the research process are the analysis and interpretation of findings in light of the stated marketing problem. Both secondary and primary data collected by the market researcher are subject to the many limitations just discussed. In any final analysis, the researcher must take into consideration these factors and, despite their limitations, produce meaningful guides for management decisions.

Accepting information at face value in foreign markets is imprudent. The meanings of words, the consumer's attitude toward a product, the interviewer's attitude, or the interview situation can distort research findings. Just as culture and tradition influence the willingness to give information, so they influence the information given. Newspaper circulation figures, readership and listenership studies, retail outlet figures, and sales volume can all be distorted through local business practices. To cope with such disparities, the foreign market researcher must possess three talents to generate meaningful marketing information.

First, the researcher must possess a high degree of cultural understanding of the market in which research is being conducted. To analyze research findings, the social customs, semantics, current attitudes, and business customs of a society or a subsegment of a society must be clearly understood. At some level, it will be absolutely necessary to have a native of the target country involved in the interpretation of the results of any research conducted in a foreign market.

Second, a creative talent for adapting research methods is necessary. A researcher in foreign markets often is called on to produce results under the most difficult circumstances and short deadlines. Ingenuity and resourcefulness, willingness to use "catch as catch can" methods to get facts, patience (even a sense of humor about the work), and a willingness to be guided by original research findings even when they conflict with popular opinion or prior assumptions are all considered prime assets in foreign marketing research.

Third, a skeptical attitude in handling both primary and secondary data is helpful. For example, it might be necessary to check a newspaper pressrun over a period of time to get accurate circulation figures or to deflate or inflate reported consumer income in some areas by 25 to 50 percent on the basis of observable socioeconomic characteristics. Indeed, where data are suspect, such triangulation through the use of multiple research methods will be crucial.

These essential traits suggest that a foreign marketing researcher should be a foreign national or should be advised by a foreign national who can accurately appraise the data collected in light of the local environment, thus validating secondary as well as primary data. Moreover, regardless of the sophistication of a research technique or analysis, there is no substitute for decision makers themselves getting into the field for personal observation.

Responsibility for Conducting Marketing Research

Depending on the size and degree of involvement in foreign marketing, a company in need of foreign market research can rely on an outside, foreign-based agency or on a domestic company with a branch within the country in question. It can conduct research using its own facilities or employ a combination of its own research force with the assistance of an outside agency.

Many companies have an executive specifically assigned to the research function in foreign operations; he or she selects the research method and works closely with foreign management, staff specialists, and outside research agencies. Other companies maintain separate research departments for foreign operations or assign a full-time research analyst to this activity. For many companies, a separate department is too costly; the diversity of markets would require a large department to provide a skilled analyst for each area or region of international business operations.

A trend toward decentralization of the research function is apparent. In terms of efficiency, local analysts appear able to provide information more rapidly and accurately than a staff research department. The obvious advantage to decentralization of the research function is that control rests in hands closer to the market. Field personnel, resident managers, and customers generally have a more intimate knowledge of the subtleties of the market and an appreciation of the diversity that characterizes most foreign markets. One

Both Ford and Philips keep track of European technology and consumers and develop products for global markets at their research centers in Aachen, Germany. The best technical universities are close by in Belgium, the Netherlands, and Germany.

disadvantage of decentralized research management is possible ineffective communications with home-office executives. Another is the potential unwarranted dominance of large-market studies in decisions about global standardization. That is to say, larger markets, particularly the United States, justify more sophisticated research procedures and larger sample sizes, and results derived via simpler approaches that are appropriate in smaller countries are often erroneously discounted.

A comprehensive review of the different approaches to multicountry research suggests that the ideal approach is to have local researchers in each country, with close coordination between the client company and the local research companies. This cooperation is important at all stages of the research project, from research design to data collection to final analysis. Furthermore, two stages of analysis are necessary. At the individual-country level, all issues involved in each country must be identified, and at the multicountry level, the information must be distilled into a format that addresses the client's objectives. Such recommendations are supported on the grounds that two heads are better than one and that multicultural input is essential to any understanding of multicultural data. With just one interpreter of multicultural data, there is the danger of one's self-reference criterion resulting in data being interpreted in terms of one's own cultural biases. Self-reference bias can affect the research design, questionnaire design, and interpretation of the data.

If a company wants to use a professional marketing research firm, many are available. Most major advertising agencies and many research firms have established branch offices worldwide. Moreover, foreign-based research and consulting firms have seen healthy growth. Of the 10 largest marketing research firms in the world (based on revenues), 4 are based in the United States, including the largest; 3 are in the United Kingdom; 1 is in France; 1 is in Germany; and 1 is in the Netherlands. The latest count of marketing research firms in China is more than 400 and growing fast. In Japan, where understanding the unique culture is essential, the quality of professional marketing research firms is among the best. A recent study reports that research methods applied by Japanese firms and American firms are generally similar, but with notable differences in the greater emphasis of the Japanese on forecasting, distribution channels, and sales research. A listing of international marketing research firms is printed annually in April as an advertising supplement in *Marketing News.*

An increasingly important issue related to international marketing research is the growing potential for governmental controls on the activity. In many countries, consumer privacy issues are being given new scrutiny as the Internet expands companies' capabilities to gather data on consumers' behaviors.

Communicating with Decision Makers

Most of the discussion in this chapter has pertained to getting information from or about consumers, customers, and competitors. It should be clearly recognized, however, that getting the information is only half the job. Analyses and interpretation of that information must also be provided to decision makers in a timely manner.[51] High-quality international information systems design will be an increasingly important competitive tool as commerce continues to globalize, and resources must be invested accordingly.[52]

Decision makers, often top executives, should be directly involved not only in problem definition and question formulation but also in the fieldwork of seeing the market and hearing the voice of the customers in the most direct ways when the occasion warrants (as in new foreign markets). Top managers should have a "feel" for their markets that even the best marketing reports cannot provide.

[51] Anne L. Souchon, Adamantios Diamantopoulos, Hartmut H. Holzmuller, Catherine N. Axxin, James M. Sinkula, Heike Simmet, and Geoffrey R. Durden, "Export Information Use: A Five-Country Investigation of Key Determinants," *Journal of International Marketing* 11, no. 3 (2003), pp. 106–27.

[52] Nicoli Juul Foss and Torben Pedersen, "Organizing Knowledge Processes in the Multinational Corporation: An Introduction," *Journal of International Business Studies* 35, no. 5 (2004), pp. 340–49; Ram Mudambi and Pietro Navarra, "Is Knowledge Power? Knowledge Flows, Subsidiary Power and Rent-Seeking within MNCs," *Journal of International Business Studies* 35, no. 5 (2004), pp. 385–406.

Exhibit 8.3
Managing the Cultural Barrier in International Marketing Research

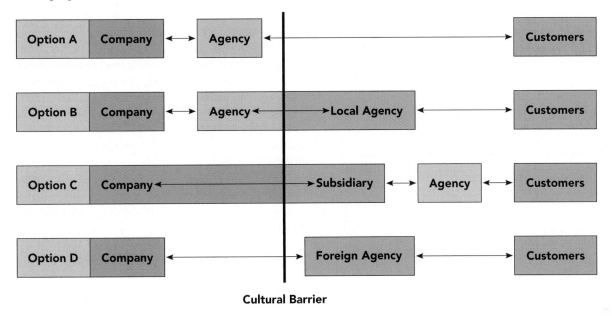

Cultural Barrier

Finally, international marketers face an additional obstacle to obtaining the best information about customers. At the most basic level, marketing research is mostly a matter of interaction with customers. Marketing decision makers have questions about how best to serve customers, and those questions are posed and answered often through the media of questionnaires and research agencies. Even when both managers and customers speak the same language and are from the same culture, communication can become garbled in either direction. That is, customers misunderstand the questions and/or managers misunderstand the answers. Throw in a language/cultural barrier, and the chances of misinformation expand dramatically.

The four kinds of company–agency–customer relationships possible are presented in Exhibit 8.3. Options B and C are better suited for managing the cultural barrier across the chain of communication. That is, in both cases, the cultural barrier is bridged *within* a company wherein people that have a common corporate culture and work together on an everyday basis. In B the translation (in the broadest sense of the term—that is, of both questionnaires and reports) is worked out between employees of the international marketing research agency. In C the translation is managed within the company itself. In cases A and D, both cultural and organizational barriers are being crossed simultaneously, thus maximizing the chances for miscommunication. Indeed, these same company–agency–customer considerations are pertinent to other kinds of communications between companies and customers, such as advertising and distribution channel control, and this uniquely international topic will be addressed again in subsequent chapters.

Summary

The basic objective of the market research function is providing management with information for more accurate decision making. This objective is the same for domestic and international marketing. In foreign marketing research, however, achieving that objective presents some problems not encountered on the domestic front.

Customer attitudes about providing information to a researcher are culturally conditioned. Foreign market information surveys must be carefully designed to elicit the desired data and at the same time not offend the respondent's sense of privacy. Besides the cultural and managerial constraints involved in gathering information for primary data, many foreign markets have inadequate or unreliable bases of secondary information. Such challenges suggest three keys to successful international marketing research: (1) the inclusion of natives of the foreign culture on research teams; (2) the use of multiple methods and triangulation; and (3) the inclusion of decision makers, even top executives, who must on occasion talk directly to or directly observe customers in foreign markets.

Questions

1. Define the following terms:

marketing research	international marketing research
research process	primary data
secondary data	multicultural research
back translation	parallel translation
expert opinion	decentering
analogy	

2. Discuss how the shift from making "market entry" decisions to "continuous operations" decisions creates a need for different types of information and data.

3. Discuss the breadth and scope of international marketing research. Why is international marketing research generally broader in scope than domestic marketing research?

4. The measure of a competent researcher is the ability to utilize the most sophisticated and adequate techniques and methods available within the limits of time, cost, and the present state of the art. Comment.

5. What is the task of the international marketing researcher? How is it complicated by the foreign environment?

6. Discuss the stages of the research process in relation to the problems encountered. Give examples.

7. Why is the formulation of the research problem difficult in foreign market research?

8. Discuss the problems of gathering secondary data in foreign markets.

9. "In many cultures, personal information is inviolably private and absolutely not to be discussed with strangers." Discuss.

10. What are some problems created by language and the ability to comprehend the questions in collecting primary data? How can a foreign market researcher overcome these difficulties?

11. Discuss how decentering is used to get an accurate translation of a questionnaire.

12. Discuss when qualitative research may be more effective than quantitative research.

13. Sampling presents some major problems in market research. Discuss.

14. Select a country. From secondary sources found on the Internet, compile the following information for at least a five-year period prior to the present:

principal imports	principal exports
gross national product	chief of state
major cities and population	principal agricultural crop

15. "The foreign market researcher must possess three essential capabilities to generate meaningful marketing information." What are they? Discuss.

Appendix: Sources of Secondary Data

For almost any marketing research project, an analysis of available secondary information is a useful and inexpensive first step. Although there are information gaps, particularly for detailed market information, the situation on data availability and reliability is improving. The principal agencies that collect and publish information useful in international business are presented here, with some notations regarding selected publications.

A. Web Sites for International Marketing

1. www.stat-usa.gov STAT-USA/Internet is clearly the single most important source of data on the Internet. STAT-USA, a part of the U.S. Department of Commerce's Economics and Statistics Administration, produces and distributes at a nominal subscription fee the most extensive government-sponsored business, economic, and trade information databases in the world today, including the National Trade Data Bank, Economic Bulletin Board, and Global Business Procurement Opportunities.

2. www.trade.gov/index.asp The Web site of the Commerce Department's International Trade Administration provides export assistance, including information about trade events, trade statistics, tariffs and taxes, marketing research, and so forth.

3. www.usatradeonline.gov Provides import and export information on more than 18,000 commodities, but the user must subscribe.

4. www.census.gov/foreign-trade/www/ The U.S. Census Bureau provides a variety of international trade statistics.

5. www.cia.gov/library/publications/the-world-factbook/ Find the CIA *World Factbook* here, as well as other pertinent trade information.

6. www.customs.ustreas.gov The U.S. Customs Service provides information regarding customs procedures and regulations.

7. www.opic.gov The Overseas Private Investment Corporation (OPIC) provides information regarding its services.

8. www.exim.gov The Export-Import Bank of the United States (Ex-Im Bank) provides information related to trade financing services provided by the U.S. government.

9. www.imf.org The International Monetary Fund (IMF) provides information about the IMF and international banking and finance.

10. www.wto.org The World Trade Organization (WTO) provides information regarding its operations.

11. www.oecd.org The Organization of Economic Cooperation and Development (OECD) provides information regarding OECD policies and associated data for 29 member countries.

12. www.jetro.go.jp The Japan External Trade Organization (JETRO) is the best source for data on the Japanese market.

13. www.euromonitor.com Euromonitor is a company providing a variety of data and reports on international trade and marketing.

14. publications.worldbank.org *World Development Indicators (WDI) Online* offers the World Bank's comprehensive database on development data, covering more than 600 indicators, 208 economies, and 18 regional income groups.

15. University-based Web sites. The best such site is the Michigan State University's Center for International Business Education and Research (http://globaledge.msu.edu/resourceDesk/).

16. www.worldchambers.com The World Network of Chambers of Commerce and Industry provides data and addresses regarding chambers of commerce around the world.

17. www.ipl.org/ref/RR/static/bus4700.html The Internet Public Library provides Internet addresses for dozens of sources of trade data worldwide.

18. http://world.wtca.org The World Trade Centers Association provides information about services provided by the World Trade Centers in the United States, including export assistance, trade leads, training programs, and trade missions.

19. www.worldtrademag.com *World Trade* magazine provides its annual Resource Guide to products, goods, and services for international trade.

20. www.mhhe.com/cateora14e The online learning center that accompanies this text provides supplementary support materials for both instructors and students.

B. U.S. Government Sources

The U.S. government actively promotes the expansion of U.S. business into international trade. In the process of keeping U.S. businesses informed of foreign opportunities, the U.S. government generates a considerable amount of general and specific market data for use by international market analysts. The principal source of information from the U.S. government is the Department of Commerce, which makes its services available to U.S. businesses in a variety of ways. First, information and assistance are available either through personal consultation in Washington, DC, or through any of the US&FCS (U.S. and Foreign Commercial Service) district offices of the International Trade Administration of the Department of Commerce located in key cities in the United States. Second, the Department of Commerce works closely with trade associations, chambers of commerce, and other interested associations in providing information, consultation, and assistance in developing international commerce. Third, the department publishes a wide range of information available to interested persons at nominal cost.

1. National Trade Data Bank (NTDB). The Commerce Department provides a number of the data sources mentioned previously, plus others in its computerized information system in the National Trade Data Bank. The NTDB is a one-step source for export promotion and international trade data collected by 17 U.S. government agencies. Updated each month and released on the Internet, the NTDB enables the reader to access more than 100,000 trade-related documents. The NTDB contains the latest census data on U.S. imports and exports by commodity and country; the complete CIA (Central Intelligence Agency) *World Factbook*; current market research reports compiled by the U.S. and Foreign Commercial Service; the complete *Foreign Traders Index*, which contains over 55,000 names and addresses of individuals and firms abroad that are interested in importing U.S. products; State Department country reports on economic policy and trade practices; the publications *Export Yellow Pages, A Basic Guide to Exporting* and the *National Trade Estimates Report on Foreign Trade Barriers*; the *Export Promotion Calendar*; and many other data series. The NTDB is also available at over 900 federal depository libraries nationwide.

In addition, the Department of Commerce provides a host of other information services. Beyond the material available through the Department of Commerce, consultation and information are available from a variety of other U.S. agencies. For example, the Department of State, Bureau of the Census, and Department of Agriculture can provide valuable assistance in the form of services and information for an American business interested in international operations.

2. www.export.gov/tradeleads/index.asp This Web site connects you to the Export.gov Trade Leads Database, which contains prescreened, time-sensitive leads and Government Tenders gathered through U.S. Commercial Service offices around the world. You can search leads and receive notification when new leads are posted.

3. buyusa.gov Provides details about the services offered by the U.S. Commercial Service.

C. Other Sources

1. Directories

a. Directory of American Firms Operating in Foreign Countries. New York: World Trade Academy Press. Alphabetically lists U.S. firms with foreign subsidiaries and affiliates operating in over 125 countries; also lists the foreign operations grouped by countries.

b. Directory of United States Importers and United States Exporters. New York: Journal of Commerce. Annual. (Also on CD-ROM.) Contain verified business profiles on a total of 60,000 active trading companies. These annual guides also include a product index with the Harmonized Commodity Code numbers, customs information, foreign consulates, embassies, and international banks.

c. Encyclopedia of Global Industries. Detroit: Gale. Alphabetically covers 125 vital international industries, providing in-depth information including statistics, graphs, tables, charts, and market share.

d. Export Yellow Pages. Washington, DC: Venture Publishing–North America; produced in cooperation with the Office of Export Trading Company Affairs and International Trade Administration. Annual. Provides detailed information on over 12,000 export service providers and trading companies, agents, distributors, and companies outside the United States; also includes a product/service index and an alphabetical index.

e. World Directory of Trade and Business Associations. London: Euromonitor, 1995. (Also on CD-ROM.) Contains entries from a broad range of sectors, giving details of publications produced, aims and objectives of the association, and whether they provide assistance in further research.

2. Marketing Guides

a. Exporters Encyclopaedia. Wilton, CT: Dun & Bradstreet. Annual. Comprehensive world marketing guide, in five sections; section two, "Export Markets," gives important market information on 220 countries (import and exchange regulations, shipping services, communications data, postal information, currency, banks, and embassies); other sections contain general export information. Also available are regional guides for Asia-Pacific, Europe, and Latin America and export guides for single countries.

b. U.S. Custom House Guide. Hightstown, NJ: K-III Directory Co. Annual. Provides a comprehensive guide to importing, including seven main sections: import how-to, ports sections, directory of services, tariff schedules (Harmonized Tariff Schedules of the United States), special and administrative provisions, custom regulations, and samples of import documents.

3. General sources of international business and economic data and customized reports. These exemplary Web sites are generally accessible for corporations with substantial research needs and budgets:

a. Economist Intelligence Unit www.eiu.com The Economist Intelligence Unit (EIU) describes itself as providing "a constant flow of analysis and forecasts on more than 200 countries and eight key industries." It helps "executives make informed business decisions through dependable intelligence delivered online, in print, in customized research as well as through conferences and peer interchange." The EIU represents a very high level of analysis. Its products are for sale (an annual subscription runs in the four figures), it facilitates the initial aggregation of information, and it undertakes preliminary analyses. At an intermediate level, within the industries it targets, we have found EIU to be very helpful.

b. Oxford Analytica www.oxan.org Oxford Analytica is self-described as "an international, independent consulting firm drawing on a network of over 1,000 senior faculty members at Oxford and other major universities and research institutions around the world." If the CIA Factbook is a Chevy sort of resource and the EIU is a Cadillac, then Oxan is a Lamborghini. Fees run to the five figures, depending on what you order. Among the publicly accessible sources, Oxford Analytica is one of the very best. Its reputation rests "on its ability to harness the expertise of pre-eminent scholar experts to provide business and government leaders with timely and authoritative analysis of world events. It is a unique bridge between the world of ideas and the world of enterprise." A review of its clients clearly indicates the level of professionalism the firm strives for and apparently attains.

9

emerging markets

CHAPTER OUTLINE

CHAPTER LEARNING OBJECTIVES

What you should learn from Chapter 9:

- The political and economic changes affecting global marketing

- The connection between the economic level of a country and the marketing task

- Marketing's contribution to the growth and development of a country's economy

- The growth of developing markets and their importance to regional trade

- The political and economic factors that affect stability of regional market groups

- The NIC growth factors and their role in economic development

Global Perspective

WAL-MART, TIDE, AND THREE-SNAKE WINE

Developing markets are experiencing rapid industrialization, growing industrial and consumer markets, and new opportunities for foreign investment. Consider the following illustration: In China, it is just a few shopping days before the advent of the Year of the Ox, and the aisles at the local Wal-Mart Supercenter are jammed with bargain hunters pushing carts loaded high with food, kitchen appliances, and clothing. It could be the preholiday shopping rush in any Wal-Mart in Middle America, but the shoppers here are China's nouveau riche. Superstores have proven popular with Chinese consumers, who devote a large part of their spending to food and daily necessities. Wal-Mart has been able to tap into the Chinese sense of social status by offering membership cards that confer not only eligibility for special discounts but social status as well.

Alongside Campbell's soup and Bounty paper towels are racks of dried fish and preserved plums. One shelf is stacked high with multiple brands of *congee*, a popular southern Chinese breakfast dish, and another has *nam yue* peanuts and packets of bamboo shoots. In the liquor section in the back of the store is three-snake rice wine, complete with the dead serpents' bodies coiled together in the potent liquid. About 95 percent of what Wal-Mart sells in China is sourced locally. Gone are the efforts to sell big extension ladders or a year's supply of soy sauce to customers living in tiny apartments.

At present Wal-Mart operates 2,980 units in thirteen foreign countries, including almost 200 in China. Revenues and profits are growing nicely for its international operations, and overseas expansion is set to continue particularly in China since its entry into the World Trade Organization. As one executive commented, "It boggles the mind to think if everybody washed their hair every day, how much shampoo you would sell [in China]."

The Chinese market can be difficult to tap and may not be profitable for many years for many companies. Most foreign retailers are in a learning mode about the ways and tastes of Asia, which are very different from those on Main Street U.S.A. For example, Pricesmart designed its Beijing store with two huge loading docks to accommodate full-sized diesel trucks in anticipation of the big deliveries needed to keep shelves well packed. What the company found was Chinese distributors arriving with goods in car trunks, on three-wheel pedicabs, or strapped to the backs of bicycles.

Procter & Gamble offered powdered Tide detergent in large quantities, but China's oppressive summer humidity turned it into unwieldy clumps. Stocking large quantities of paper towels and disposable diapers didn't work well either—most customers didn't know what a paper towel was, and disposable diapers were too expensive a luxury for most. Package sizes also posed a problem—small Chinese apartments could not handle the large American-sized packages.

How do you sell $75 jeans or $150 wireless phones in a country where the per capita gross domestic product is only a couple of thousand dollars a year? Marketing researchers have found that extended families are showering their money on the kids, a common form of conspicuous consumption in the developing world. Even in China, the spending power of youth is nothing to discount. Studies have shown that the average 7- to 12-year-old in a large city has $182 a year in spending money—admittedly less than the $377 in France or $493 in the United States, but still a significant amount considering the huge population.

Sources: Keith B. Richburg, "Attention Shenzen Shoppers! U.S. Retail Giants Are Moving into China, and Finding the Learning Curve Formidable," *Washington Post*, February 12, 1997; David Barboza, "The Bold Struggle for China's Belly," *The New York Times*, March 6, 2003, p. C1; http://www.walmartstores.com, 2008.

The distribution of Coca-Cola is often one of the first signs of a country transforming from a command economy to one of free enterprise. Here the cyclo driver transports a promotional refrigerator in Ho Chi Minh City (formerly Saigon), Vietnam. (© Hoang Dinh Nam/AFP/Getty Images)

Not many years ago, large parts of the developing world were hostile to foreign investment and imposed severe regulatory barriers to foreign trade.[1] But few nations are content with the economic status quo; now, more than ever, they seek economic growth, improved standards of living, and an opportunity for the good life most people want as part of the global consumer world.[2] China and other emerging markets throughout the world will account for 75 percent of the world's total growth in the next two decades and beyond, according to U.S. Department of Commerce estimates. The transition from socialist to market-driven economies, the liberalization of trade and investment policies in developing countries, the transfer of public-sector enterprises to the private sector, and the rapid development of regional market alliances are changing the way countries will trade and prosper in the 21st century.

China, South Korea, Poland, Argentina, Brazil, Mexico, Turkey, India, and Vietnam[3] are some of the countries undergoing impressive changes in their economies and emerging as vast markets. These and other countries have an ever-expanding and changing demand for goods and services. As countries prosper and their people are exposed to new ideas and behavior patterns via global communications networks, old stereotypes, traditions, and habits are cast aside or tempered, and new patterns of consumer behavior emerge. Luxury cars in China;[4] Avon cosmetics in South Korea; Wal-Mart discount stores in Argentina, Brazil, Mexico, China, and Thailand; McDonald's beefless Big Macs in India; Whirlpool washers and refrigerators in eastern Europe; Sara Lee food products in Indonesia; and Amway products in the Czech Republic represent opportunities in emerging markets.

A pattern of economic growth and global trade that will extend well into the 21st century appears to be emerging. It consists of three multinational market regions that comprise major trading blocs: Europe, Asia, and the Americas. Within each trading bloc are fully industrialized countries, as typified by Germany, Japan, and the United States; rapidly industrializing countries such as Mexico, Poland, and South Korea that are close on the heels of the fully industrialized; and other countries that are achieving economic development but at more modest rates. Outside the triad of Europe, Asia, and the Americas are others at different levels of development striving to emulate their more prosperous neighbors. Indonesia, Malaysia, Thailand, and the Philippines are beginning to chase the leaders' tails, though from much lower levels of income. All four groups are creating enormous global markets. This chapter and the next explore the emerging markets and the multinational market regions and market groups that comprise the global trading blocs of the future.

Marketing and Economic Development

The economic level of a country is the single most important environmental element to which the foreign marketer must adjust the marketing task. The stage of economic growth within a country affects the attitudes toward foreign business activity,[5] the demand for goods, the distribution systems found within a country, and the entire marketing process.[6] In static economies, consumption patterns

---

[1] James C. McKinley Jr., "For U.S. Exporters in Cuba, Business Trumps Politics," *The New York Times*, November 12, 2007, p. A3.

[2] Stephen Kotkin, "First World, Third World (Maybe Not in That Order)," *The New York Times*, May 6, 2007, p. 7.

[3] "WTO—Landmark of Vietnam's 20-Year Renewal Process," *Asia Pulse*, January 2, 2008.

[4] Jason Leow and Gordon Fairclough, "Rich Chinese Fancy Luxury Cars," *The Wall Street Journal*, April 12, 2007, pp. B1, B6.

[5] Terrance H. Witkowski, "Antiglobal Challenges to Marketing in Developing Countries: Exploring the Ideological Divide," *Journal of Public Policy & Marketing* 24, no. 1 (2005), pp. 7–23.

[6] Ramarao Desiraju, Harikesh Nair, and Pradeep Chintagunta, "Diffusion of New Pharmaceutical Drugs in Developing and Developed Nations," *International Journal of Research in Marketing* 21, no. 4 (2004), pp. 341–57.

become rigid, and marketing is typically nothing more than a supply effort. In a dynamic economy, consumption patterns change rapidly.[7] Marketing constantly faces the challenge of detecting and providing for new levels of consumption, and marketing efforts must be matched with ever-changing market needs and wants.

Economic development presents a two-sided challenge. First, a study of the general aspects of economic development is necessary to gain empathy regarding the economic climate within developing countries. Second, the state of economic development must be studied with respect to market potential, including the present economic level and the economy's growth potential. The current level of economic development dictates the kind and degree of market potential that exists, while knowledge of the dynamism of the economy allows the marketer to prepare for economic shifts and emerging markets.[8]

Economic development is generally understood to mean an increase in national production that results in an increase in the average per capita gross domestic product (GDP).[9] Besides an increase in average per capita GDP, most interpretations of the concept also imply a widespread distribution of the increased income. Economic development, as commonly defined today, tends to mean rapid economic growth and increases in consumer demand—improvements achieved "in decades rather than centuries."

Stages of Economic Development

The United Nations classifies a country's stage of economic development on the basis of its level of industrialization. It groups countries into three categories:

MDCs (more-developed countries). Industrialized countries with high per capita incomes, such as Canada, England, France, Germany, Japan, and the United States. Exhibit 9.1 summarizes data regarding the standards of living in a variety of countries across the spectrum of development. The reader will notice that those at the lowest levels of development often do not collect or report data suitable for international resources such as Euromonitor International or the World Bank.

LDCs (less-developed countries). Industrially developing countries just entering world trade, many of which are in Asia and Latin America, with relatively low per capita incomes.

LLDCs (least-developed countries). Industrially underdeveloped, agrarian, subsistence societies with rural populations, extremely low per capita income levels, and little world trade involvement. Such LLDCs are found in Central Africa and parts of Asia. Violence and the potential for violence are often associated with LLDCs.

The UN classification has been criticized because it no longer seems relevant in the rapidly industrializing world. In addition, many countries that are classified as LDCs are industrializing at a very rapid rate, whereas others are advancing at more traditional rates of economic development. It is interesting to note in Exhibit 9.1 the differences in consumer spending among the Latin American countries and the United States.

Countries that are experiencing rapid economic expansion and industrialization and do not exactly fit as LDCs or MDCs are more typically referred to as *newly industrialized countries (NICs)*. These countries have shown rapid industrialization of targeted industries and have per capita incomes that exceed other developing countries. They have moved away from restrictive trade practices and instituted significant free market reforms; as a result, they attract both trade and foreign direct investment. Chile, Brazil, Mexico, South Korea, Singapore, and Taiwan are some of the countries that fit this description. These

---

[7] Seung Ho Park, Shaomin Li, and David K. Tse, "Market Liberalization and Firm Performance During China's Economic Transition," *Journal of International Business Studies* 37 (2006), pp. 127–47.

[8] Kevin Zheng Zhou, David K. Tse, and Julie Juan Li, "Organizational Changes in Emerging Economies: Drivers and Consequences," *Journal of International Business Studies* 37 (2006), pp. 248–63.

[9] Gross domestic product (GDP) and gross national product (GNP) are two measures of a country's economic activity. GDP is a measure of the market value of all goods and services produced within the boundaries of a nation, regardless of asset ownership. Unlike gross national product, GDP excludes receipts from that nation's business operations in foreign countries, as well as the share of reinvested earnings in foreign affiliates of domestic corporations.

Exhibit 9.1
Standards of Living of Selected Countries

Country	Population (millions)	GDP/Capita* ($000s)	Medical Resources per 1000 Persons		Household Ownership %		
			Doctors	Hospital Beds	Color TV	Refrigerator	Shower
United States	303.0	$44.9	3.0	3.1	98.8%	100.0%	99.1%
Mexico	109.2	11.5	1.7	1.9	93.9	80.0	71.3
Cuba	11.3	—	6.3	6.0	—	—	—
Venezuela	27.6	8.2	1.4	1.9	88.9	96.8	93.1
Brazil	193.0	10.5	1.0	2.5	93.4	89.9	79.4
Netherlands	16.4	38.9	4.0	4.8	98.5	98.5	98.3
Germany	82.3	33.0	3.8	8.3	97.9	99.2	99.1
Poland	38.1	16.6	1.7	5.4	98.7	97.6	77.3
Russia	141.7	13.4	4.5	9.2	95.1	96.1	62.5
Turkey	73.9	9.8	1.5	2.7	92.4	98.2	78.7
Libya	6.2	14.0	—	3.9	—	—	—
Egypt	74.7	5.2	0.6	2.5	83.4	89.1	77.6
Nigeria	149.8	1.3	0.3	—	35.3	21.9	60.9
Kenya	38.0	1.3	0.1	1.8	—	—	—
S. Africa	50.6	13.2	0.8	—	64.5	52.5	61.0
India	1148.9	4.1	0.6	0.9	78.9	18.1	44.7
China	1319.0	8.8	1.5	2.5	98.6	92.2	44.1
Vietnam	86.0	3.7	0.8	2.3	76.5	26.9	38.8
S. Korea	47.9	26.2	1.5	8.0	99.3	99.6	95.3
Japan	127.7	34.0	2.2	13.9	99.6	99.4	99.7

*At purchase price parity.

Source: Euromonitor International 2008.

NICs have become formidable exporters of many products, including steel, automobiles, machine tools, clothing, and electronics, as well as vast markets for imported products.

Brazil provides an example of the growing importance of NICs in world trade, exporting everything from alcohol to carbon steel. Brazilian orange juice, poultry, soybeans, and weapons (Brazil is the world's sixth-largest weapons exporter) compete with U.S. products for foreign markets. Embraer, a Brazilian aircraft manufacturer, has sold planes to more than 60 countries and provides a substantial portion of the commuter aircraft used in the United States and elsewhere. Even in automobile production, Brazil is a world player; it ships more than 200,000 cars, trucks, and buses to Third World countries annually. Volkswagen has produced more than 3 million VW Beetles in Brazil and has invested more than $500 million in a project to produce the Golf and Passat automobiles. The firm also recently announced a deal to sell $500 million worth of auto parts to a Chinese partner. General Motors has invested $600 million to create what it calls "an industrial complex"— a collection of 17 plants occupied by suppliers such as Delphi, Lear, and Goodyear to deliver preassembled modules to GM's line workers. All in all, auto and auto parts makers are investing more than $2.8 billion aimed at the 200 million people in the Mercosur market, the free trade group formed by Argentina, Brazil, Paraguay, and Uruguay.

Among the NICs, South Korea, Taiwan, Hong Kong, and Singapore have had such rapid growth and export performance that they are known as the "Four Tigers" of Southeast Asia. The Four Tigers have almost joined the ranks of developed economies in terms of GDP per capita. These countries have managed to dramatically improve their living standards by deregulating their domestic economies and opening up to global markets. From typical Third World poverty, each has achieved a standard of living equivalent to that of industrialized nations, with per capita incomes in Hong Kong and Singapore rivaling those of the wealthiest Western nations.

Another sign of Vietnam's emergence in the world economy is the dramatic effect new production (on left) has had on world coffee prices in recent years. World prices crashed from a high of $1.85 per pound in 1997 to about $0.50 in 2001, adversely affecting growers in Brazil (on right) and all other countries. (© *Christopher Anderson/Magnum Photos*)

These four countries began their industrialization as assemblers of products for U.S. and Japanese companies. They are now major world competitors in their own right. Korea exports such high-tech goods as petrochemicals, electronics, machinery, and steel, all of which are in direct competition with Japanese and U.S.-made products. In consumer products, Hyundai, Kia, Samsung, and Lucky-Goldstar are among the familiar Korean-made brand names in automobiles, microwaves, and televisions sold in the United States. Korea is also making sizable investments outside its borders. A Korean company recently purchased 58 percent of Zenith, the last remaining TV manufacturer in the United States. At the same time, Korea is dependent on Japan and the United States for much of the capital equipment and components needed to run its factories.

NIC Growth Factors

The UN's designations of stages of economic development reflect a static model, in that they do not account for the dynamic changes in economic, political, and social conditions in many developing countries, especially among NICs. Why some countries have grown so rapidly and successfully while others with similar or more plentiful resources languish or have modest rates of growth is a question to which many have sought answers. Is it cultural values, better climate, more energetic population, or just an "Asian Miracle"? There is ample debate as to why the NICs have grown while other underdeveloped nations have not. Some attribute their growth to cultural values, others to cheap labor, and still others to an educated and literate population. Certainly all of these factors have contributed to growth, but other important factors are present in all the rapidly growing economies, many of which seem to be absent in those nations that have not enjoyed comparable economic growth.

One of the paradoxes of Africa is that its people are for the most part desperately poor, while its land is extraordinarily rich.[10] East Asia is the opposite: It is a region mostly poor in resources that over the last few decades has enjoyed an enormous economic boom. When several African countries in the 1950s (for example, Congo, the former Zaire) were at the same income level as many East Asian countries (for example, South Korea) and were blessed with far more natural resources, it might have seemed reasonable for the African countries to have prospered more than their Asian counterparts. Although there is no doubt that East Asia enjoyed some significant cultural and historical advantages, its economic boom relied on other factors that have been replicated elsewhere but are absent in Africa. The formula for success in East Asia was an outward-oriented, market-based economic policy coupled with an emphasis on education and health care. Most newly industrialized countries have followed this model in one form or another.

---

[10] "Kenya, Going Up or Down?" *The Economist*, June 9, 2007, pp. 49–50.

The factors that existed to some extent during the economic growth of NICs were as follows:

- Political stability in policies affecting their development.

- Economic and legal reforms. Poorly defined and/or weakly enforced contract and property rights are features the poorest countries have in common.

- Entrepreneurship. In all of these nations, free enterprise in the hands of the self-employed was the seed of the new economic growth.

- Planning. A central plan with observable and measurable development goals linked to specific policies was in place.

- Outward orientation. Production for the domestic market and export markets with increases in efficiencies and continual differentiation of exports from competition was the focus.

- Factors of production. If deficient in the factors of production—land (raw materials), labor, capital, management, and technology—an environment existed where these factors could easily come from outside the country and be directed to development objectives.

- Industries targeted for growth. Strategically directed industrial and international trade policies were created to identify those sectors where opportunity existed. Key industries were encouraged to achieve better positions in world markets by directing resources into promising target sectors.

- Incentives to force a high domestic rate of savings and to direct capital to update the infrastructure, transportation, housing, education, and training.

- Privatization of state-owned enterprises (SOEs) that had placed a drain on national budgets. Privatization released immediate capital to invest in strategic areas and gave relief from a continuing drain on future national resources. Often when industries are privatized, the new investors modernize, thus creating new economic growth.

Despite world-class scientists, the Indian pharmaceutical industry (with its ownership restrictions, price controls, and weak intellectual property restrictions) does not benefit from innovations and international investments compared to more open emerging economies such as China. *(AP Photo/Sherwin Crasto)*

The final factors that have been present are large, accessible markets with low tariffs. During the early growth of many of the NICs, the first large open market was the United States, later joined by Europe and now, as the fundamental principles of the World Trade Organization (WTO) are put into place, by much of the rest of the world.

Although it is customary to think of the NIC growth factors as applying only to industrial growth, the example of Chile shows that economic growth can occur with agricultural development as its economic engine. Chile's economy has expanded at an average rate of 7.2 percent since 1987 and is considered one of the least risky Latin American economies for foreign investment. However, since 1976, when Chile opened up trade, the relative size of its manufacturing sector declined from 27.3 percent of GDP in 1973 to 17.6 percent in 2005.[11] Agriculture, in contrast, has not declined. Exports of agricultural products have been the star performers. Chile went from being a small player in the global fruit market, exporting only apples in the 1960s, to one of the world's largest fruit exporters in 2000. Sophisticated production technology and management methods were applied to the production of table grapes, wine, salmon from fish farms, and a variety of other processed and semiprocessed agricultural products. Salmon farming, begun in the early 1980s, has made salmon a major export item. Salmon exports to the United States are 40,000 tons annually, whereas U.S. annual production of farm-raised salmon is only 31,000 tons. Chile is also a major exporter of the fishmeal that is fed to hatchery-raised salmon.

[11] World Bank, World Development Indicators, 2008.

Chile's production technology has resulted in productivity increases and higher incomes. Its experience indicates that manufacturing is not the only way for countries to grow economically. The process is to continually adapt to changing tastes, constantly improve technology, and find new ways to prosper from natural resources. Contrast Chile today with the traditional agriculturally based economies that are dependent on one crop (e.g., bananas) today and will still be dependent on that same crop 20 years from now. This type of economic narrowness was the case with Chile a few decades ago when it depended heavily on copper. To expand its economy beyond dependency on copper, Chile began with what it did best—exporting apples. As the economy grew, the country invested in better education and infrastructure and improved technology to provide the bases to develop other economic sectors, such as grapes, wine, salmon, and tomato paste.

Regional cooperation and open markets are also crucial for economic growth. As will be discussed in Chapter 10, being a member of a multinational market region is essential if a country is to have preferential access to regional trade groups. As steps in that direction, in 2003 Chile and in 2005 Central American countries (including banana producers) signed free trade agreements with the United States.[12]

Information Technology, the Internet, and Economic Development

In addition to the growth factors previously discussed, a country's investment in information technology (IT) is an important key to economic growth. The cellular phone,[13] the Internet, and other advances in IT open opportunities for emerging economies to catch up with richer ones.[14] New, innovative electronic technologies can be the key to a sustainable future for developed and developing nations alike.

Because the Internet cuts transaction costs and reduces economies of scale from vertical integration, some argue that it reduces the economically optimal size for firms. Lower transaction costs enable small firms in Asia or Latin America to work together to develop a global reach. Smaller firms in emerging economies can now sell into a global market. It is now easier, for instance, for a tailor in Shanghai to make a suit by hand for a lawyer in Boston, or a software designer in India to write a program for a firm in California. One of the big advantages that rich economies have is their closeness to wealthy consumers, which will erode as transaction costs fall.

The Internet accelerates the process of economic growth by speeding up the diffusion of new technologies to emerging economies. Unlike the decades required for many developing countries to benefit from railways, telephones, or electricity, the Internet is spreading rapidly throughout Asia, Latin America, and eastern Europe. Information technology can jump-start national economies and allow them to leapfrog from high levels of illiteracy to computer literacy.

The Internet also facilitates education, a fundamental underpinning for economic development. The African Virtual University, which links 24 underfunded and ill-equipped African campuses to classrooms and libraries worldwide, grants degrees in computer science, computer engineering, and electrical engineering. South Africa's School Net program links 1,035 schools to the Internet, and the government's Distance Education program brings multimedia teaching to rural schools.

Mobile phones and other wireless technologies greatly reduce the need to lay a costly telecom infrastructure to bring telephone service to areas not now served.[15] In Caracas, Venezuela, for example, where half of the city's 5 million people lives in nonwired slums, cell phones with pay-as-you-go cards have provided service to many residents for the first time. The Grameen Bank, a private commercial enterprise in Bangladesh, developed a program to supply phones to 300 villages. There are only eight land phones lines for every

---

[12] "Chile and U.S. Sign Accord on Free Trade," *The New York Times*, June 7, 2003, p. 3; David Armstrong, "CAFTA Signed into Law," *San Francisco Chronicle*, August 3, 2005, p. C1.

[13] Nandini Lakshman, "Nokia: Lessons Learned, Reward Reaped," *BusinessWeek*, July 30, 2007, p. 32.

[14] Simon Cox, "High-Tech Hopefuls, A Special Report on Technology in India and China," *The Economist*, November 10, 2007, pp. 1–25.

[15] Jack Ewing and Edel Rodriguez, "Upwardly Mobile in Africa," *BusinessWeek*, September 4, 2007, pp. 64–71.

1,000 people in Bangladesh, one of the lowest phone-penetration rates in the world. The new network is nationwide, endeavoring to put every villager within two kilometers of a cellular phone. Already cell phone penetration has exploded, growing from 4 per 1,000 to 63.5 per 1,000 during the last four years.[16]

The Internet allows for innovative services at a relatively inexpensive cost. For example, cyber post offices in Ghana offer e-mail service for the price of a letter. Telecenters in five African countries provide public telephone, fax, computer, and Internet services where students can read online books and local entrepreneurs can seek potential business partners. Medical specialists from Belgium help train local doctors and surgeons in Senegal via video linkups between classrooms and operating centers and provide them with Internet access to medical journals and databases. Traveling there to teach would be prohibitively expensive; via Internet technology, it costs practically nothing.

India not only stands firmly at the center of many success stories in California's Silicon Valley (Indian engineers provide some 30 percent of the workforce there) but is also seeing Internet enthusiasm build to a frenzy on its own shores. Indian entrepreneurs and capital are creating an Indian Silicon Valley, dubbed "Cyberabad," in Bangalore. Exports there are growing 50 percent annually, and each worker adds $27,000 of value per year, an extraordinary figure in a country where per capita GDP is about $500. After a little more than a decade of growth, the Indian industry has an estimated 280,000 software engineers in about 1,000 companies.

Similar investments are being made in Latin America and eastern Europe as countries see the technology revolution as a means to dramatically accelerate their economic and social development. As one economist commented, "Traditional economic reforms in the 1980s and 1990s managed to stop hyper-inflation and currency crises, but further change will not produce significant new growth needed to combat poverty. Governments must work to provide public access to the Internet and other information technologies."

The IT revolution is not limited to broad, long-range economic goals; as Crossing Borders 9.1 illustrates, it can have an almost immediate impact on the poorest inhabitants of an emerging country.

Objectives of Developing Countries

A thorough assessment of economic development and marketing should begin with a brief review of the basic facts and objectives of economic development.

Industrialization is the fundamental objective of most developing countries.[17] Most countries see in economic growth the achievement of social as well as economic goals. Better education,[18] better and more effective government, the elimination of many social inequities, and improvements in moral and ethical responsibilities are some of the expectations of developing countries. Thus economic growth is measured not solely in economic goals but also in social achievements. Regarding the last, consider for a moment the tremendous efforts China undertook in preparing for the 2008 Olympics.[19]

Because foreign businesses are outsiders, they often are feared as having goals in conflict with those of the host country. Considered exploiters of resources, many multinational firms were expropriated in the 1950s and 1960s. Others faced excessively high tariffs and quotas, and foreign investment was forbidden or discouraged. Today, foreign investors are seen as vital partners in economic development. Experience with state-owned businesses proved to be a disappointment to most governments. Instead of being engines for accelerated economic growth, state-owned enterprises were mismanaged, inefficient drains on state treasuries. Many countries have deregulated industry, opened their doors to foreign investment, lowered trade barriers, and begun privatizing SOEs. The trend toward privatization is currently a major economic phenomenon in industrialized as well as in developing countries.

---

[16] World Bank, World Development Indicators, 2008.

[17] "Chocolate, Thinking out of the Box," *The Economist*, April 7, 2007, p. 65.

[18] Somini Sengupta, "Push for Education Yields Little for India's Poor," *The New York Times*, January 17, 2008, pp. A1, A16.

[19] Mei Fong, "Spit's Out, Polish In as Beijing Primps for the Olympics," *The Wall Street Journal*, February 9, 2007, pp. B1, B6.

CROSSING BORDERS 9.1 — The Benefits of Information Technology in Village Life

Delora Begum's home office is a corrugated metal and straw hut in Bangladesh with a mud floor, no toilet, and no running water. Yet in this humble setting, she reigns as the "phone lady," a successful entrepreneur and a person of standing in her community. It's all due to a sleek Nokia cell phone. Begum acquired the handset in 1999. Her telephone "booth" is mobile: During the day, it's the stall on the village's main dirt road; at night, callers drop by her family hut to use the cell phone.

Once the phone hookup was made, incomes and quality of life improved almost immediately for many villagers. For as long as he can remember, a brick factory manager had to take a two-and-a half-hour bus ride to Dhaka to order furnace oil and coal for the brick factory. Now, he avoids the biweekly trip: "I can just call if I need anything, or if I have any problems." The local carpenter uses the cell phone to check the current market price of wood, so he ensures a higher profit for the furniture he makes.

The only public telecom link to the outside world, this unit allows villagers to learn the fair value of their rice and vegetables, cutting out middlemen notorious for exploiting them. They can arrange bank transfers or consult doctors in distant cities and, in a nation where only 45 percent of the population can read and write, the cell phone allows people to dispense with a scribe to compose a letter. It also earns some $600 a year for its owner—twice the annual per capita income in Bangladesh.

When members of the Grand Coast Fishing Operators cooperative salt and smoke the day's catch to prepare it for market, it may seem light years away from cyberspace, but for these women, the Internet is a boon. The cooperative has set up a Web site that enables its 7,350 members to promote their produce, monitor export markets, and negotiate prices with overseas buyers before they arrive at markets in Senegal. Information technology has thus improved their economic position.

Sources: Miriam Jordan, "It Takes a Cell Phone," *The Wall Street Journal*, June 25, 1999, p. B1; 7; World Bank, World Development Indicators, 2008.

Infrastructure and Development

One indicator of economic development is the extent of social overhead capital, or infrastructure, within the economy. *Infrastructure* represents those types of capital goods that serve the activities of many industries. Included in a country's infrastructure are paved roads,[20] railroads,[21] seaports, communication networks,[22] financial networks,[23] and energy supplies—all necessary to support production and marketing. The quality of an infrastructure directly affects a country's economic growth potential and the ability of an enterprise to engage effectively in business. See Exhibit 9.2 for some comparisons of infrastructure among countries at different levels of economic development.

Infrastructure is a crucial component of the uncontrollable elements facing marketers. Without adequate transportation facilities, for example, distribution costs can increase substantially, and the ability to reach certain segments of the market is impaired. The lack of readily available educational assets hampers not only the ability to communicate to residents (literacy) but also firms' ability to find qualified local marketing managers. To a marketer, the key issue is the impact of a country's infrastructure on a firm's ability to market effectively. Business efficiency is affected by the presence or absence of financial and commercial service infrastructure found within a country—such as advertising agencies, warehousing storage facilities, credit and banking facilities, marketing research agencies, and satisfactory specialized middlemen. Generally speaking, the less developed a country is, the less adequate the

---

[20] Cherin Thomas, "The Boom in India Now Heard Overseas," *Los Angeles Times*, January 14, 2008, p. C4.

[21] "Bullet Time, the Old China Meets the New on the Nation's New High-Speed Trains," *The Economist*, May 19, 2007, p. 70; David Lague, "China's Achilles' Heel, Storm Exposes Fragility of Rail Network," *International Herald Tribune*, February 1, 2008, p. 14.

[22] David Barboza, "Internet Boom in China is Built on Virtual Fun," *The New York Times*, February 5, 2007, pp. A1, A4.

[23] Keith Epstein and Geri Smith, "The Ugly Side of Micro-Lending," *BusinessWeek*, December 24, 2007, pp. 39–46.

Exhibit 9.2
Infrastructure of Selected Countries

Country	Roads (000s km)	Rail (000s km)	Passenger Cars/1000 People	Energy Consumption (tonnes oil equivalent per capita)	Computers in Use per 1000	Mobile Phones in Use per 1000	Literacy Rate %	College Students (000s)
United States	6611.2	157.5	459.1	7.7	717.3	766.4	99.9%	14569.8
Mexico	359.3	26.7	134.4	1.5	184.1	518.9	93.3	2540.9
Cuba	60.9	4.4	1.1	—	161.1	10.5	97.5	467.1
Venezuela	96.2	0.6	79.7	2.6	87.1	592.6	94.6	629.7
Brazil	1759.6	30.0	98.6	1.1	150.0	600.5	89.6	5198.7
Netherlands	130.7	2.8	461.9	5.7	556.5	1027.9	99.5	205.2
Germany	231.5	35.0	574.9	4.0	527.6	1030.5	99.9	2133.7
Poland	475.8	19.8	335.3	2.5	206.0	922.6	99.7	560.7
Russia	858.0	85.0	190.7	5.1	195.4	1062.3	99.7	7499.2
Turkey	426.9	8.7	83.4	1.4	72.7	747.8	88.6	2073.4
Libya	91.0	—	145.5	—	—	33.7	85.9	316.4
Egypt	106.1	9.6	3.0	0.8	36.4	302.2	60.9	2279.7
Nigeria	192.8	3.5	11.9	—	8.4	258.0	73.5	721.3
Kenya	62.9	2.7	10.1	—	16.5	188.0	88.6	85.6
S. Africa	366.0	18.8	86.2	2.4	106.4	728.5	87.9	699.2
India	2676.2	62.8	11.8	0.4	23.1	129.9	62.6	12697.3
China	2002.1	76.8	14.8	1.4	96.0	401.7	89.2	14285.4
Vietnam	225.1	2.8	1.8	—	28.6	186.6	93.6	1563.6
S. Korea	104.4	3.1	244.6	4.8	600.9	864.7	98.5	1888.4
Japan	1190.4	20.0	465.9	4.1	443.8	794.9	99.9	2891.9

Source: Euromonitor International 2008.

infrastructure is for conducting business. Companies do market in less-developed countries, but often they must modify their offerings and augment existing levels of infrastructure.

Countries begin to lose economic development ground when their infrastructure cannot support an expanding population and economy. A country that has the ability to produce commodities for export may be unable to export them because of an inadequate infrastructure. For example, Mexico's economy has been throttled by its archaic transport system. Roads and seaports are inadequate, and the railroad system has seen little modernization since the 1910 Revolution. Please see Exhibit 9.2 for some of the numbers associated with this problem. If it were not for Mexico's highway system (though it, too, is in poor condition), the economy would have come to a halt; Mexico's highways have consistently carried more freight than its railroads. Conditions in other Latin American countries are no better. Shallow harbors and inadequate port equipment make a container filled with computers about $1,000 more expensive to ship from Miami to San Antonio, Chile (about 3,900 miles), than the same container shipped from Yokohama, Japan, to Miami (8,900 miles).

Marketing's Contributions

How important is marketing to the achievement of a nation's goals? Unfortunately, marketing (or distribution) is not always considered meaningful to those responsible for planning. Economic planners frequently are more production oriented than marketing oriented and tend to ignore or regard distribution as an inferior economic activity. Given such attitudes, economic planners generally are more concerned with the problems of production, investment, and finance than the problems of efficiency of distribution.

Although it is difficult to compete with China's low manufacturing costs, imagine marketing in a country with production but little disposable income, no storage, limited transportation that goes to the wrong markets, and no middlemen or facilitating agents to activate the flow of goods from the manufacturer to the consumer. When such conditions exist in

Seeing the rough weave of traffic on the streets of old Delhi, India, you likely can understand the need for the elevated expressways. The introduction of Tata Motor's new $2,500 car, the Nano, will only make congestion worse. The country just raised the national speed limit from 80 kph to 100 kph, spurred by a roads revolution, the centerpiece of which is the 3,650-mile golden Quadrilateral highway linking Delhi, Mumbai (Bombay), Chennai (Madras), and Kolkata (Calcutta), the most expensive public works project in the nation's history. However, we wonder: How will the traffic police keep the ubiquitous sacred cows off expressway on-ramps? *(left: © Tomas Munita; right: © Amit Bhargava/ Bloomberg News/Landov)*

developing markets, marketing and economic progress are retarded. To some degree, this problem faces China and many of the republics of the former Soviet Union. In China, for example, most of the 1.3 billion potential consumers are not accessible because of a poor or nonexistent distribution network. Indeed, the true consumer market in China is probably limited to no more than 20 percent of those who live in the more affluent cities. No distribution and channel system exists to effectively distribute products, so companies must become resourceful to compensate for poor infrastructure.

For example, after nearly a decade of frustration in trying to effectively market and service its products in China, IBM took a bold step[24] and entered a venture with the Railways Ministry that allowed IBM to set up IBM service centers dubbed the "Blue Express." The agreement created a national network of service centers in railway stations that has enabled IBM to ship computer parts via the railroad around the country within 24 hours; competitors must book cargo space weeks in advance. In addition, the ministry's staff of more than 300 computer engineers helps out by providing customer services on IBM products.

Such innovative thinking by IBM and other marketers often accelerates the development of a more efficient market system.[25] IBM's service centers set an example of effective service before and after sales—important marketing activities. Management training for the thousands of employees of franchises such as Pizza Hut, McDonald's, and KFC has spread expertise throughout the marketing system as the trainees move on to more advanced positions and other companies.

Marketing is an economy's arbitrator between productive capacity and consumer demand. The marketing process is the critical element in effectively utilizing production resulting from economic growth; it can create a balance between higher production and higher consumption. An efficient distribution and channel system and all the attendant liaisons match production capacity and resources with consumer needs, wants, and purchasing power.

---

[24] MNCs are becoming more creative in their approaches to investment and operations in developing countries. See Ravi Ramamurti, "Developing Countries and MNEs: Extending and Enriching the Research Agenda," *Journal of International Business Studies* 35, no. 4 (2004), pp. 277–83.

[25] Klaus E. Meyer, "Perspectives on Multinational Enterprises in Emerging Economies," *Journal of International Business Studies* 35, no. 4 (2004), pp. 259–76.

CROSSING BORDERS 9.2   Infrastructure: India

Animals in India provide 30,000 megawatts (MW) of power, more than the 29,000 MW provided by electricity.

Because of the religious ban on the slaughter of cattle in almost all states in the country, India has the highest cattle population in the world—perhaps as many as 360 million head. Bullocks are used for plowing fields, turning waterwheels, working crushers and threshers, and above all for hauling carts. The number of bullock carts has doubled to 15 million since India's independence in 1947. Bullocks haul more tonnage than the entire railway system (though over a much shorter distance); in many parts of rural India, they are the only practical means of moving things about.

As a bonus, India's cattle produce enormous quantities of dung, which is used both as farmyard manure and, when dried in cakes, as household fuel. Each animal produces an estimated average of 3 kilograms of dung per day. Some studies suggest that these forms of energy are the equivalent of another 10,000 MW.

Although Indian farmers prefer machines for plowing and hauling carts, bullocks and other draft animals are still in demand. Because it will take a long time for farmers to replace these draft animals with machines and there is concern that the better breeds may degenerate or become extinct, the government has developed an artificial insemination program to preserve the best breeds.

Sources: "Bullock Manure," *The Economist*, October 17, 1981, p. 88; S. Rajendran, "India: Scheme to Preserve Local Cattle Breed on Anvil," *The Hindu*, August 9, 1997; "Not Enough Bulls to Till the Land," *Times of India*, May 9, 2000; Randeep Ramesh, "India's Drivers Feel the Need for Speed," *The Guardian*, December 6, 2007, p. 29.

Marketing in a Developing Country

A marketer cannot superimpose a sophisticated marketing strategy on an underdeveloped economy.[26] Marketing efforts must be keyed to each situation, custom tailored for each set of circumstances. A promotional program for a population that is 50 percent illiterate is vastly different from a program for a population that is 95 percent literate. Pricing in a subsistence market poses different problems from pricing in an affluent society. In evaluating the potential in a developing country, the marketer must make an assessment of the existing level of market development and receptiveness within the country, as well as the firm's own capabilities and circumstances.[27]

Level of Market Development

The level of market development roughly parallels the stages of economic development. Exhibit 9.3 illustrates various stages of the marketing process as it evolves in a growing economy. The table is a static model representing an idealized evolutionary process. As discussed previously, economic cooperation and assistance, technological change, and political, social, and cultural factors can and do cause significant deviations in this evolutionary process. However, the table focuses on the logic and interdependence of marketing and economic development. The more developed an economy, the greater the variety of marketing functions demanded, and the more sophisticated and specialized the institutions become to perform marketing functions.

As countries develop, the distribution and channel systems develop. In the retail sector,[28] specialty stores, supermarkets, and hypermarkets emerge, and mom-and-pop stores and local brands[29] often give way to larger establishments. In short, the number of retail stores declines, and the volume of sales per store increases. Additionally, a defined channel

---

[26] Y. Luo, "Market-Seeking MNEs in an Emerging Marke*t: H*ow Parent–Subsidiary Links Shape Overseas Success," *Journal of International Business Studies* 35, no. 4 (2003), pp. 290–309.

[27] Donna L. Paul and Rossitza B. Wooster, "Strategic Investments by US Firms in Transition Economies," *Journal of International Business Studies* 39 (March 2008), pp. 249–66; "Indian Retailing, Getting Cheaper and Better," *The Economist*, February 3, 2007, pp. 64–65.

[28] Giana M. Eckhardt, "Local Branding in a Foreign Product Category in an Emerging Market," *Journal of International Marketing* 13, no. 4 (2005), pp. 57–79.

[29] Anna Smolchenko, "They've [Russians] Driven a Ford Lately," *BusinessWeek*, February 26, 2007, p. 52.

Exhibit 9.3
Evolution of the Marketing Process

Stage	Substage	Example	Marketing Functions	Marketing Institutions	Channel Control	Primary Orientation	Resources Employed	Comments
Agricultural and raw materials	Self-sufficient	Nomadic or hunting tribes	None	None	Traditional authority	Subsistence	Labor Land	Labor intensive No organized markets
	Surplus commodity product	Agricultural economy, such as coffee, bananas	Exchange	Small-scale merchants, traders, fairs, export-import	Traditional authority	Entrepreneurial Commercial	Labor Land	Labor and land intensive Product specialization Local markets Import oriented
Manufacturing	Small scale	Cottage industry	Exchange Physical distribution	Merchants, wholesalers, export-import	Middlemen	Entrepreneurial Financial	Labor Land Technology Transportation	Labor intensive Product standardization and grading Regional and export markets Import oriented
	Mass production	U.S. economy, 1885–1914	Demand creation Physical distribution	Merchants, wholesalers, traders, and specialized institutions	Producer	Production and finance	Labor Land Technology Transportation Capital	Capital intensive Product differentiation National, regional, and export markets
Marketing	Commercial—transition	U.S. economy, 1915–1929	Demand creation Physical distribution Market information	Large-scale and chain retailers	Producer	Entrepreneurial Commercial	Labor Land Technology Transportation Capital Communication	Capital intensive Changes in structure of distribution National, regional, and export markets
	Mass distribution	U.S. economy, 1950 to present	Demand creation Physical distribution Market information Market and product planning, development	Integrated channels of distribution Increase in specialized middlemen	Producer Retailer	Marketing	Labor Land Technology Transportation Capital Communication	Capital and land intensive Rapid product innovation National, regional, and export markets

structure from manufacturer to wholesaler to retailer develops and replaces the import agent that traditionally assumed all the functions between importing and retailing.

Advertising agencies, facilities for marketing research, repair services,[30] specialized consumer-financing agencies,[31] and storage and warehousing facilities are facilitating agencies created to serve the particular needs of expanded markets and economies. These institutions do not come about automatically, and the necessary marketing structure does not simply appear. Part of the marketer's task when studying an economy is to determine what in the foreign environment will be useful and how much adjustment will be necessary to carry out stated objectives. In some developing countries, it may be up to the marketer to institute the foundations of a modern market system.

The limitation of Exhibit 9.3 in evaluating the market system of a particular country is that the system is in a constant state of flux. To expect a neat, precise progression through each successive growth stage, as in the geological sciences, is to oversimplify the dynamic nature of marketing development. So some ventures will not succeed no matter how well planned—eBay learned that lesson the hard way in China and closed its auction site. A significant factor in the acceleration of market development is that countries or areas of countries have been propelled from the 18th to the 21st century in the span of two decades via borrowed technology.

Marketing structures of many developing countries are simultaneously at many stages. It is not unusual to find traditional small retail outlets functioning side by side with advanced, modern markets. This situation is especially true in food retailing, where a large segment of the population buys food from small produce stalls, while the same economy supports modern supermarkets equal to any found in the United States. On the same street as the Wal-Mart store described in the Global Perspective are mom-and-pop food stands.

Demand in Developing Countries

The data in Exhibit 9.4 represent the diversity of consumption patterns across types of countries. Notice the higher percentages of expenditures for food in developing countries, whereas the costs of housing are more important in affluent countries. Also note the high costs of health goods and medical services associated with the mostly private-sector healthcare system of the United States. You may recall from Chapter 4 that the government-based, tax-dollar supported systems in many other affluent countries deliver equal or better longevity to their citizens, particularly in Japan. Affluence also allows higher proportions to be spent on leisure activities than is the case in developing countries.

Estimating market potential in less-developed countries involves additional challenges. Most of the difficulty arises from the coexistence of three distinct kinds markets in each country: (1) the traditional rural/agricultural sector, (2) the modern urban/high-income sector, and (3) the often very large transitional sector usually represented by low-income urban slums. The modern sector is centered in the capital city and has jet airports, international hotels, new factories, and an expanding Westernized middle class. The traditional rural sector tends to work in the countryside, as it has for centuries. Directly juxtaposed to the modern sector, the transitional sector contains those moving from the country to the large cities. Production and consumption patterns vary across the three sectors. India is a good example. The eleventh largest industrial economy in the world, India has a population of approximately 1 billion, of which 200 million to 250 million are considered middle class. The modern sector demands products and services similar to those available in any industrialized country; the remaining 750 million in the transitional and rural sectors, however, demand items more indigenous and basic to subsistence. As one authority on India's markets observed, "A rural Indian can live a sound life without many products. Toothpaste, sugar, coffee, washing soap, bathing soap, kerosene are all bare necessities of life to those who live in semi-urban and urban areas." One of the greatest challenges of the 21st century is to manage and market to the transitional sector in developing countries. The large-city slums perhaps present the greatest problems for smooth economic development.

---

[30] Ian Alum, "New Service Development Process: Emerging versus Developed Markets," *Journal of Global Marketing* 20, no. 2/3 (2007), pp. 43–56.

[31] Katrijn Gielens and Marnik G. Dekimpe, "The Entry Strategy of Retail Firms into Transition Economies," *Journal of Marketing* 71 (2007), pp. 196–212; Datie Hafner and Brad Stone, "EBay is Expected to Close Its Auction Site in China," *The New York Times*, December 19, 2006, pp. C1, C12.

Exhibit 9.4

Consumption Patterns in Selected Countries

Country	Occupants per household	Food	Alcohol, Tobacco	Clothing	Housing	Health Goods, Medical Services	Transportation	Communications	Leisure	Education
						Percentage of Household Expenditures				
United States	2.6	6.9%	2.1%	4.4%	17.3%	19.4%	11.4%	1.6%	9.0%	2.6%
Mexico	4.3	24.0	2.5	3.0	13.7	4.8	17.4	1.7	2.5	3.9
Cuba	3.7	—	—	—	—	—	—	—	—	—
Venezuela	4.5	29.7	3.1	4.2	12.0	4.8	9.3	4.2	9.8	6.4
Brazil	3.7	24.6	1.9	3.5	15.1	4.4	12.9	5.3	33.3	7.1
Netherlands	2.3	10.2	2.9	5.3	22.9	5.6	11.4	4.6	10.5	0.7
Germany	2.1	11.5	3.5	5.1	24.6	4.7	13.4	2.9	9.5	0.5
Poland	2.8	21.4	7.3	4.1	25.6	4.4	12.9	1.7	6.7	1.5
Russia	2.7	28.5	2.3	9.6	12.8	2.7	12.0	4.2	7.3	2.7
Turkey	4.6	24.8	4.2	6.1	27.0	2.2	13.5	4.2	2.2	2.2
Libya	4.7	—	—	—	—	—	—	—	—	—
Egypt	4.4	39.0	2.2	6.7	20.3	4.6	6.5	2.3	2.4	3.8
Nigeria	5.3	39.4	2.5	7.0	17.6	4.5	7.2	2.2	2.4	3.9
Kenya	4.7	—	—	—	—	—	—	—	—	—
S. Africa	3.9	20.8	4.7	5.4	12.8	9.3	14.1	3.9	3.9	3.3
India	5.3	32.9	2.3	5.1	10.8	7.1	19.1	2.0	2.0	2.4
China	3.5	34.8	2.7	8.6	12.1	7.8	2.7	10.1	2.9	6.2
Vietnam	3.2	39.0	2.8	4.1	4.1	7.1	13.4	1.3	1.3	6.3
S. Korea	2.7	15.4	2.6	4.1	17.3	5.1	11.1	5.5	7.1	6.1
Japan	2.6	14.6	3.2	3.1	25.2	4.4	10.4	3.8	11.4	2.2

Source: Euromonitor International 2008.

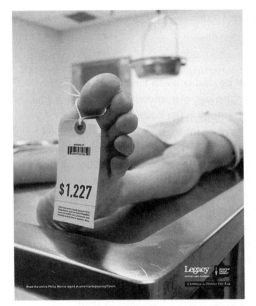

As demand for tobacco declines in more-developed countries, manufacturers direct more marketing efforts in the direction of emerging economies. Indeed, recently Philip Morris published a report estimating the cost savings for the Czech government at $1,227 every time a smoker dies. Apparently, the company did not think through the public relations implications of this grisly bit of research. *(Courtesy of American Legacy Foundation, American Cancer Society, and Campaign for Tobacco Free Kids)*

despite the recent backsliding of a few countries in the region, such as Venezuela. Privatization of state-owned enterprises and other economic, monetary, and trade policy reforms show a broad shift away from the inward-looking policies of import substitution (that is, manufacturing products at home rather than importing them) and protectionism so prevalent in the past. The trend toward privatization of SOEs in the Americas followed a period in which governments dominated economic life for most of the 20th century. State ownership was once considered the ideal engine for economic growth. Instead of economic growth, however, they ended up with inflated public-sector bureaucracies, complicated and unpredictable regulatory environments, the outright exclusion of foreign and domestic private ownership, and inefficient public companies. Fresh hope for trade and political reforms is now being directed even to communist Cuba.[40]

Today many Latin American countries are at roughly the same stage of liberalization that launched the dynamic growth in Asia during the 1980s and 1990s. In a positive response to these reforms, investors have invested billions of dollars in manufacturing plants, airlines, banks, public works, and telecommunications systems. Because of its size and resource base, the Latin American market has always been considered to have great economic and market possibilities. The population of nearly 460 million is one-half greater than that of the United States and 100 million more than the European Community.

The strength of these reforms was tested during the last decade, a turbulent period both economically and politically for some countries. Argentina, Brazil, and Mexico, the three BEMs in Latin America, were affected by the economic meltdown in Asia and the continuing financial crisis in Russia. The Russian devaluation and debt default caused a rapid deterioration in Brazil's financial situation; capital began to flee the country, and Brazil devalued its currency. Economic recession in Brazil—coupled with the sharp devaluation of the real—reduced Argentine exports, and Argentina's economic growth slowed. Mexico was able to weather the Russian debt default partly because of debt restructuring and other changes after the major devaluation and recession in the early 1990s. However, competition with Chinese manufacturing has yielded slower growth than predicted at the time of passage of the North American Free Trade Agreement (NAFTA). Other Latin American countries suffered economic downturns that led to devaluations and, in some cases, political instability. Nevertheless, Latin America is still working toward economic reform.

Eastern Europe and the Baltic States

Eastern Europe and the Baltic states, satellite nations of the former Soviet Union, have moved steadily toward establishing postcommunist market reforms. New business opportunities are emerging almost daily, and the region is described as anywhere from chaotic with big risks to an exciting place with untold opportunities. Both descriptions fit as countries continue to adjust to the political, social, and economic realities of changing from the restrictions of a Marxist–socialist system to some version of free markets and capitalism. However, these countries have neither all made the same progress nor had the same success in economic reform and growth.[41]

Eastern Europe.   It is dangerous to generalize beyond a few points about eastern Europe because each of the countries has its own economic problems and is at a different stage in its evolution from a socialist to a market-driven economy. Most eastern European countries are privatizing state-owned enterprises, establishing free market pricing systems, relaxing import controls, and wrestling with inflation. The very different paths taken toward market

[40] Katherine Yung, "When Cuba Opens Up . . . " *Dallas Morning News*, March 11, 2007, pp. D1, D6.

[41] Clifford J. Schultz II, Timothy J. Burkink, Bruno Grbac, and Natasa Renko, "When Policies and Marketing Systems Explode: An Assessment of Food Marketing in the War-Ravaged Balkans and Implications for Recovery, Sustainable Peace, and Prosperity," *Journal of Public Policy & Marketing* 24, no. 1 (2005), pp. 24–37.

Some in Warsaw suggest the picture includes two icons of imperialism. Soviet dictator Joseph Stalin "gave" the people of Poland his 1950s version of great architecture. The Poles have now turned his infamous Palace of Culture and Science into a movie theater (Kinoteka) and office tower. Others see Coca-Cola and its ever-present, powerful advertising as a new kind of control. The argument about globalization goes on.

economies have resulted in different levels of progress. Countries such as the Czech Republic, which moved quickly to introduce major changes, seem to have fared better than countries[42] such as Hungary, Poland, and Romania, which held off privatizing until the government restructured internally. Moving quickly allows the transformation to be guided mainly by the spontaneity of innovative market forces rather than by government planners or technocrats. Those countries that took the slow road permitted the bureaucrats from communist days to organize effectively to delay and even derail the transition to a market economy.

Yugoslavia has been plagued with internal strife over ethnic divisions, and four of its republics (Croatia, Slovenia, Macedonia, and Bosnia/Herzegovina) seceded from the federation, leaving Serbia and Montenegro in the reduced Federal Republic of Yugoslavia. Soon after seceding, a devastating ethnic war broke out in Croatia and Bosnia/Herzegovina that decimated their economies. A tentative peace, maintained by United Nations peacekeepers, now exists, but for all practical purposes the economies of Croatia and Bosnia are worse now than ever before. Most recently, the Kosovo region of Serbia also declared its independence, and political tension remains.[43]

Nevertheless, most countries in the region continue to make progress in building market-oriented institutions and adopting legislation that conforms to that of advanced market economies. The Czech Republic, Hungary, the Slovak Republic, and Poland have become members of the OECD.[44] Joining the OECD means they accept the obligations of the OECD to modernize their economies and to maintain sound macroeconomic policies and market-oriented structural reforms. The four also became members of the European Union in 2004, along with Bulgaria and Romania in 2007. And they are eager to stabilize their developing democracies and their westward tilt in foreign and security policies.

The Baltic States.   The Baltic states—Estonia, Latvia, and Lithuania—are a good example of the difference that the right policies can make. All three countries started off with roughly the same legacy of inefficient industry and Soviet-style command economies. Estonia quickly seized the lead by dropping the ruble, privatizing companies and land, letting struggling banks fail, and adopting the freest trading regime of the three countries. Its economic growth has handily outpaced Latvia's and Lithuania's. Since regaining independence in 1991, Estonia's economic reform policy has led to a liberalized, nearly tariff-free, open-market economy.

Although Latvia and Lithuania have made steady progress, government bureaucracy, corruption, and organized crime—common problems found in the countries of the former Soviet Union—continue. These issues represent the most significant hurdles to U.S. trade and investment. The governments and all major political parties support a free market system, yet traces of the Soviet methodology and regulatory traditions at the lower levels of bureaucracy remain visible. All three Baltic countries are WTO members and, as of 2004, EU members.

Asia   Asia has been the fastest-growing area in the world for the past three decades, and the prospects for continued economic growth over the long run are excellent. Beginning in 1996, the leading economies of Asia (Japan, Hong Kong, South Korea, Singapore, and Taiwan) experienced a serious financial crisis, which culminated in the meltdown of the Asian stock market. A tight monetary policy, an appreciating dollar, and a deceleration of

---

[42] Judy Dempsey, "In a Car, a Lesson in Russian-European Trade," *The New York Times*, January 1, 2008.

[43] Tracy Wilkinson, "Kosovo Takes a Big Leap of Faith," *Los Angeles Times*, February 18, 2008, pp. A1, A6.

[44] http://www.oecd.org.

exports all contributed to the downturn. Despite this economic adjustment, the 1993 estimates by the International Monetary Fund (IMF) that Asian economies would have 29 percent of the global output by the year 2000 were on target. Both as sources of new products and technology and as vast consumer markets, the countries of Asia—particularly those along the Pacific Rim—are just beginning to gain their stride.

Asian-Pacific Rim.   The most rapidly growing economies in this region are the group sometimes referred to as the Four Tigers (or Four Dragons): Hong Kong, South Korea, Singapore, and Taiwan. Often described as the "East Asian miracle," they were the first countries in Asia, besides Japan, to move from a status of developing countries to newly industrialized countries. In addition, each has become a major influence in trade and development in the economies of the other countries within their spheres of influence. The rapid economic growth and regional influence of the member countries of the Association of Southeast Nations (ASEAN) over the last decade has prompted the U.S. Trade Representative to discuss free-trade agreements—Singapore has already signed up. They are vast markets for industrial goods and, as will be discussed later, important emerging consumer markets.

The Four Tigers are rapidly industrializing and extending their trading activity to other parts of Asia. Japan was once the dominant investment leader in the area and was a key player in the economic development of China, Taiwan, Hong Kong, South Korea, and other countries of the region. But as the economies of other Asian countries have strengthened and industrialized, they are becoming more important as economic leaders. For example, South Korea is the center of trade links with north China and the Asian republics of the former Soviet Union. South Korea's sphere of influence and trade extends to Guangdong and Fujian, two of the most productive Chinese Special Economic Zones, and is becoming more important in interregional investment as well.

China.   Aside from the United States and Japan, there is no more important single market than China.[45] The economic and social changes occurring in China since it began actively seeking economic ties with the industrialized world have been dramatic. China's dual economic system, embracing socialism along with many tenets of capitalism, produced an economic boom with expanded opportunity for foreign investment that has resulted in annual GNP growth averaging nearly 10 percent since 1970. Most analysts predict that an 8 to 10 percent average for the next 10 to 15 years is possible. At that rate, China's GNP should equal that of the United States by 2015. All of this growth is dependent on China's ability to deregulate industry, import modern technology, privatize overstaffed and inefficient SOEs, and continue to attract foreign investment. The prospects look good.

Two major events that occurred in 2000 are having a profound effect on China's economy: admission to the World Trade Organization and the United States' granting normal trade relations (NTR) to China on a permanent basis (PNTR). The PNTR status and China's entry to the WTO cut import barriers previously imposed on American products and services. The United States is obligated to maintain the market access policies that it already applies to China, and has for over 20 years, and to make its normal trade relation status permanent. After years of procrastination, China has begun to comply with WTO provisions and has made a wholehearted and irrevocable commitment to creating a market economy that is tied to the world at large.

An issue that concerns many is whether China will follow WTO rules when it has to lower its formidable barriers to imported goods. Enforcement of the agreement will not just happen. Experience with many past agreements has shown that gaining compliance on some issues is often next to impossible. Some of China's concessions are repeats of unfulfilled agreements extending back to 1979. The United States has learned from its experience with Japan that the toughest work is yet to come. A promise to open markets to U.S. exports can be just the beginning of a long effort at ensuring compliance.

A vendor delivers a Christmas tree in Beijing. Since China's reforms and loosening of controls on religion at the end of the 1970s, the number of Christians has risen from 2 million to 50 million. Although restrictions on freedom of religion continue, as economic freedom grows, so do political freedoms. (© Goh Chai Hin/AFP/Getty Images)

45 "How China Runs the World Economy," *The Economist*, July 30, 2005, pp. 11, 61–63; Keith Bardsher, "China's Trade Surplus Near Record Last Month," *The New York Times*, March 13, 2007, p. C3.

Because of China's size, diversity,[46] and political organization, it can be more conveniently thought of as a group of six regions rather than a single country. There is no one-growth strategy for China. Each region is at a different stage economically and has its own link to other regions as well as links to other parts of the world. Each has its own investment patterns, is taxed differently, and has substantial autonomy in how it is governed. But while each region is separate enough to be considered individually, each is linked at the top to the central government in Beijing.

China has two important steps to take if the road to economic growth is to be smooth: improving human rights and reforming the legal system. The human rights issue has been a sticking point with the United States because of the lack of religious freedom, the Tiananmen Square massacre in 1989, the jailing of dissidents, and China's treatment of Tibet. The U.S. government's decision to award PNTR reflected, in part, the growing importance of China in the global marketplace and the perception that trade with China was too valuable to be jeopardized over a single issue. However, the issue remains delicate both within the United States and between the United States and China.

Despite these positive changes, the American embassy in China has seen a big jump in complaints from disgruntled U.S. companies fed up with their lack of protection under China's legal system. Outside the major urban areas of Beijing, Shanghai, and Guangzhou, companies are discovering that local protectionism and cronyism make business tough even when they have local partners. Many are finding that Chinese partners with local political clout can rip off their foreign partner and, when complaints are taken to court, influence courts to rule in their favor.

Actually there are two Chinas—one a maddening, bureaucratic, bottomless money pit, the other an enormous emerging market. There is the old China, where holdovers of the Communist Party's planning apparatus heap demands on multinational corporations, especially in politically important sectors such as autos, chemicals, and telecom equipment. Companies are shaken down by local officials, whipsawed by policy swings, railroaded into bad partnerships, and squeezed for technology. But there is also a new, market-driven China that is fast emerging. Consumer areas, from fast food to shampoo, are now wide open. Even in tightly guarded sectors, the barriers to entry are eroding as provincial authorities, rival ministries, and even the military challenge the power of Beijing's technocrats.

No industry better illustrates the changing rules than information technology. Chinese planners once limited imports of PCs and software to promote homegrown industries, but the Chinese preferred smuggled imports to the local manufacturers. Beijing eventually loosened the restraints, and Microsoft is now the dominant PC operating system. A market whose modernization plan calls for imports of equipment and technology of over $100 billion per year, with infrastructure expenditures amounting to $250 billion through the remainder of the decade, is worth the effort. Indeed, China is now the second biggest market for personal computers, following only the United States.

In the long run, the economic strength of China will not be as an exporting machine but as a vast market. The economic strength of the United States comes from its resources, productivity, and vast internal market that drives its economy. China's future potential might better be compared with America's economy, which is driven by domestic demand, than with Japan's, driven by exports. China is neither an economic paradise nor an economic wasteland, but a relatively poor nation going through a painfully awkward transformation from a socialist market system to a hybrid socialist–free market system, not yet complete and with the rules of the game still being written.

Hong Kong. After 155 years of British rule, Hong Kong reverted to China in 1997 when it became a special administrative region (SAR) of the People's Republic of China. The Basic Law of the Hong Kong SAR forms the legal basis for China's "one country, two

[46] Diversity across regions also provides other dimensions suitable for market segmentation. See Kineta H. Hung, Flora Fang Gu, and Chi Kin (Bennett) Yim, "A Social Institutional Approach to Identifying Generation Cohorts in China with a Comparison with American Consumers," *Journal of International Business Studies* 38 (2007), pp. 836–53.

systems" agreement that guarantees Hong Kong a high degree of autonomy. The social and economic systems, lifestyle, and rights and freedoms enjoyed by the people of Hong Kong prior to the turnover were to remain unchanged for at least 50 years. The Hong Kong government negotiates bilateral agreements (which are then "confirmed" by Beijing) and makes major economic decisions on its own. The central government in Beijing is responsible only for foreign affairs and defense of the SAR.

The Hong Kong dollar continues to be freely convertible, and foreign exchange, gold, and securities markets continue to operate as before. Hong Kong is a free society with legally protected rights. The Hong Kong SAR government continues to pursue a generally noninterventionist approach to economic policy that stresses the predominant role of the private sector. The first test came when the Hong Kong financial markets had a meltdown in 1997 that reverberated around the financial world and directly threatened the mainland's interests. Beijing's officials kept silent; when they said anything, they expressed confidence in the ability of Hong Kong authorities to solve their own problems.

The decision to let Hong Kong handle the crisis on its own is considered strong evidence that the relationship is working for the best for both sides, considering that China has so much riding on Hong Kong. Among other things, Hong Kong is the largest investor in the mainland, investing more than $100 billion over the last few years for factories and infrastructure. The Hong Kong stock market is the primary source of capital for some of China's largest state-owned enterprises. China Telcom, for example, recently raised $4 billion in an initial public offering.

Most business problems that have arisen stem from fundamental concepts such as clear rules and transparent dealings that are not understood the same way on the mainland as they are in Hong Kong. Many thought the territory's laissez-faire ways, exuberant capitalism, and gung-ho spirit would prove unbearable for Beijing's heavy-handed communist leaders. But, except for changes in tone and emphasis, even opponents of communist rule concede that Beijing is honoring the "one country, two systems" arrangement.

Taiwan. The presidential victory of longtime Taiwan opposition leader and independence advocate Chen Shui-bian fanned fears in Beijing that the island, which it regards as part of China, would finally declare independence from the mainland. However, Chen quickly assuaged those fears when he promised not to formally declare independence unless China attacked Taiwan. Mainland–Taiwan economic ties are approaching a crossroads as both countries enter the World Trade Organization. As both sides implement WTO provisions, they will have to end many restrictions and implement direct trade—not that they have not been trading. Taiwanese companies have invested about $40 billion in China, and about 250,000 Taiwanese-run factories are responsible for about 12 percent of China's exports. Estimates of real trade are even higher if activities conducted through Hong Kong front companies are taken into consideration.

It is best to wrap future talks on the One China debate inside a bundle of more concrete issues, such as establishing the "three direct links"—transportation, trade, and communications. The three direct links issue must be faced because each country has joined the WTO, and the rules insist that members communicate about trade disputes and other issues. Trade fits well with both countries' needs. Taiwanese companies face rising costs at home; China offers a nearly limitless pool of cheap labor and engineering talent. Taiwan's tech powerhouses also crave access to China's market.

For Beijing, the Taiwanese companies provide plentiful jobs at a time when bloated SOEs are laying off millions. They also bring the latest technology and management systems, which China needs as it joins the WTO. In any case, Taiwan continues to stand tall in the East Asian economy—indeed, as of 2004 the tallest building in the world is in Taipei, its capital.

India. The wave of change that has been washing away restricted trade, controlled economies, closed markets, and hostility to foreign investment in most developing countries has finally reached India. Since its independence in 1950, the world's largest democracy had set a poor example as a model for economic growth for other developing countries and was among the last of the economically important developing nations to throw off traditional insular policies. As a consequence, India's growth had been constrained and shaped by policies of

Here we see the start of economic development. As rough as conditions are in this rural school in Lahtora, India, they're even more difficult in Tanzania. But in both places, students are eager to learn. *(Left: © Ruth Fremson/The New York Times/Redux)*

import substitution and an aversion to free markets. While other Asian countries were wooing foreign capital, India was doing its best to keep it out. Multinationals, seen as vanguards of a new colonialism, were shunned. Aside from textiles, Indian industrial products found few markets abroad other than in the former Soviet Union and eastern Europe.

Now however, times have changed, and India has embarked on the most profound transformation since it won political independence from Britain. A five-point agenda that includes improving the investment climate; developing a comprehensive WTO strategy; reforming agriculture, food processing, and small-scale industry; eliminating red tape; and instituting better corporate governance has been announced. Steps already taken include the following:

- Privatizing state-owned companies as opposed to merely selling shares in them. The government is now willing to reduce its take below 51 percent and to give management control to so-called strategic investors.

- Recasting the telecom sector's regulatory authority and demolishing the monopolies enjoyed by SOEs.

- Signing a trade agreement with the United States to lift all quantitative restrictions on imports.

- Maintaining the momentum in reform of the petroleum sector.

- Planning the opening of domestic long-distance phone services, housing, and real estate and retail trading sectors to foreign direct investment.

Leaders have quietly distanced themselves from campaign rhetoric that advocated "computer chips and not potato chips" in foreign investment and a *swadeshi* (made-in-India) economy. The new direction promises to adjust the philosophy of self-sufficiency that had been taken to extremes and to open India to world markets. India now has the look and feel of the next China or Latin America.

Foreign investors and Indian reformers still face problems, however. Although India has overthrown the restrictions of earlier governments, reforms meet resistance from bureaucrats, union members, and farmers, as well as from some industrialists who have lived comfortably behind protective tariff walls that excluded competition. Socialism is not dead in the minds of many in India, and religious, ethnic, and other political passions flare easily.

For a number of reasons, India still presents a difficult business environment. Tariffs are well above those of developing world norms, though they have been slashed to a maximum of 65 percent from 400 percent. Inadequate protection of intellectual property rights remains a serious concern. The antibusiness attitudes of India's federal and state bureaucracies continue to hinder potential investors and plague their routine operations. Policymakers have dragged their feet on selling money-losing SOEs, making labor laws flexible, and deregulating banking.

In addition, widespread corruption and a deeply ingrained system of bribery make every transaction complicated and expensive. One noted authority on India declared that corrupt practices are not the quaint custom of *baksheesh* but pervasive, systematic, structured, and degraded corruption running from the bottom to the top of the political order. Nevertheless, a survey of U.S. manufacturers shows that 95 percent of respondents with Indian operations plan on expanding, and none say they are leaving. They are hooked on the country's cheap, qualified labor and the potential of a massive market.

Despite these uncertainties, being included among the BEMs reflects the potential of India's market. With a population now over 1 billion, India is second in size only to China, and both contain enormous low-cost labor pools. India has a middle class numbering some 250 million, about the population of the United States. Among its middle class are large numbers of college graduates, 40 percent of whom have degrees in science and engineering. India has a diverse industrial base and is developing as a center for computer software. India may be on the threshold of an information technology boom. After establishing a reputation among foreign corporations by debugging computer networks in time for Y2K, Indian companies now supply everything from animation work to browsers used on new-generation wireless phones to e-commerce Web sites. As discussed previously, India has been an exporter of technical talent to the U.S. Silicon Valley, and now many of these individuals are returning to establish IT companies of their own. Finally, there is a competitive advantage to being on the other side of the world–wide-awake English speakers are available there for 24/7 services for the United States while their American counterparts sleep.

India has the capacity to be one of the more prosperous nations in Asia if allowed to develop and live up to its potential. Some worry, however, that the opportunity could be lost if reforms don't soon reach a critical mass—that point when reforms take on a life of their own and thus become irreversible.

Newest Emerging Markets

The United States' decision to lift the embargo against Vietnam and the United Nations' lifting of the embargo against South Africa resulted in the rapid expansion of these economies. Because of their growth and potential, the U.S. Department of Commerce designated both as BEMs.

Vietnam's economy and infrastructure were in a shambles after 20 years of socialism and war, but this country of more than 84 million is poised for significant growth. A bilateral trade agreement between the United States and Vietnam led to NTR status for Vietnam and will lower tariffs on Vietnamese exports to the United States from an average of 40 percent to less than 3 percent. For example, Vietnamese coffee is now in almost every pantry in America, and the new competitiveness has caused prices to sharply decline on the world market. If Vietnam follows the same pattern of development as other Southeast Asian countries, it could become another Asian Tiger. Many of the ingredients are there: The population is educated and highly motivated, and the government is committed to economic growth. Some factors are a drag on development, however, including poor infrastructure, often onerous government restrictions, minimal industrial base, and a lack of capital and technology, which must come primarily from outside the country. Most of the capital and technology are being supplied by three of the Asian Tigers—Taiwan, Hong Kong, and South Korea. American companies such as Intel are also beginning to make huge investments now that the embargo has been lifted.

South Africa's economic growth has increased significantly now that apartheid is officially over and the United Nations has lifted the economic embargo that isolated that nation from much of the industrialized world. Unlike Vietnam, South Africa has an industrial base that will help propel it into rapid economic growth, with the possibility of doubling its GNP in as few as 10 years. The South African market also has a developed infrastructure—airports, railways, highways, telecommunications—that makes it important as a base for serving nearby African markets too small to be considered individually but viable when coupled with South Africa.

Upbeat economic predictions, a stable sociopolitical environment, and the reinforced vigor of the South African government in addressing the issues of privatization and deregulation while maintaining the long-term goal of making the country more investor friendly bode well for U.S. businesses seeking trading, investment, and joint venture opportunities in South Africa. The country has a fair-sized domestic market of nearly $500 billion with significant growth potential and is increasingly becoming free market oriented. It has yet to develop to its full potential, however, because of years of isolation, former inward-looking trade and investment policies, a low savings rate, and a largely unskilled labor force with attendant low productivity.

Vietnam and South Africa have the potential to become the newest emerging markets, but their future development will depend on government action and external investment by other governments and multinational firms. In varying degrees, foreign investors are leading the way by making sizable investments.

Strategic Implications for Marketing

Surfacing in the emerging markets is a vast population whose expanding incomes are propelling them beyond a subsistence level to being viable consumers. As a country develops, incomes change, population concentrations shift, expectations for a better life adjust to higher standards, new infrastructures evolve, and social capital investments are made. Market behavior changes and eventually groups of consumers with common tastes and needs (i.e., market segments) arise.[47]

When incomes rise, new demand is generated at all income levels for everything from soap to automobiles. By some measures, per capita income in China is only about $1,500 a year. But nearly every independent study by academics and multilateral agencies puts incomes, adjusted for black market activity and purchasing power parity, at four or five times that level.[48] Furthermore, large households can translate into higher disposable incomes. Young working people in Asia and Latin America usually live at home until they marry. With no rent to pay, they have more discretionary income and can contribute to household purchasing power. Countries with low per capita incomes are potential markets for a large variety of goods; consumers show remarkable resourcefulness in finding ways to buy what really matters to them. In the United States, the first satellite dishes sprang up in the poorest parts of Appalachia. Similarly, the poorest slums of Calcutta are home to 70,000 VCRs, and in Mexico, homes with color televisions outnumber those with running water.

As incomes rise to middle-class range, demand for more costly goods increases for everything from disposable diapers to automobiles. Incomes for the middle class in emerging markets are less than those in the United States, but spending patterns are different, so the middle class has more to spend than comparable income levels in the United States would indicate. For example, members of the middle class in emerging markets do not own two automobiles and suburban homes, and healthcare and housing in some cases are subsidized, freeing income to spend on refrigerators, TVs, radios, better clothing, and special treats. Exhibit 9.4 illustrates the percentage of household income spent on various classes of goods and services. More household money goes for food in emerging markets than in developed markets, but the next category of high expenditures for emerging and developed countries alike is appliances and other durable goods. Spending by the new rich, however, is a different story. The new rich want to display their wealth; they want to display status symbols such as Rolex watches, Louis Vuitton purses, and Mercedes-Benz automobiles.

A London securities firm says that a person earning $250 annually in a developing country can afford Gillette razors; at $1,000, he or she can become a Sony television owner. A Nissan or Volkswagen could be possible with a $10,000 income. Whirlpool estimates that in eastern Europe, a family with an annual income of $1,000 can afford a

---

[47] Peter G. P. Walters and Saeed Samiee, "Marketing Strategy in Emerging Markets: The Case of China," *Journal of International Marketing* 11, no. 1 (2003), pp. 97–106.

[48] The *CIA Factbook 2008* reports it to be $5,300 (not at purchase price parity), for example.

refrigerator, and with $2,000, they can buy an automatic washer as well. Estimates are that a sustainable growth in the car market will occur in China when average annual income of $5,000 is achieved. Although that will not likely happen until 2010, more than one million cars were sold in 2005—making the Chinese market as large as all of South Asia combined.

Recognizing the growth in Asia, Whirlpool has invested $265 million to buy controlling interest in four competitors in China and two in India. The attraction is expanding incomes and low appliance ownership rates. Fewer than 10 percent of Chinese households have air conditioners, microwave ovens, or washers. At the same time, incomes are reaching levels where demand for such appliances will grow.

One analyst suggests that as a country passes the $5,000 per capita GNP level, people become more brand conscious and forgo many local brands to seek out foreign brands they recognize. At $10,000, they join those with similar incomes who are exposed to the same global information sources. They join the "$10,000 Club" of consumers with homogeneous demands who share a common knowledge of products and brands. They become global consumers. If a company fails to appreciate the strategic implications of the $10,000 Club, it will miss the opportunity to participate in the world's fastest growing global consumer segment. More than 1 billion people in the world now have incomes of $10,000 or better. Companies that look for commonalties among these 1 billion consumers will find growing markets for global brands.

Markets are changing rapidly, and identifiable market segments with similar consumption patterns are found across many countries. Emerging markets will be the growth areas of the 21st century.

Emerging Competition

Finally, we cannot leave this topic of emerging markets without briefly considering the associated competitors emerging in these fast growing countries.[49] Perhaps the most visible sign of growing global competition comes from the automobile makers surging onto the world scene from China,[50] Russia,[51] and India.[52] But this new competition is actually rising across broad categories of products—computers, space technology, appliances, and commercial aircraft, to mention the most obvious. Moreover, firms in emerging countries are making substantial investments in many regions around the world, even the most affluent ones.[53] We consider this new competition as a growing opportunity associated with the growth of these emerging markets, but others do not share our views. Emerging competition deserves, and is now getting, close attention.[54] And there is little doubt that the global market will be revitalized and reorganized by these new corporate powerhouses.

---

[49] "The Challengers, A New Breed of Multinational Company Has Emerged," *The Economist*, January 12, 2008, pp. 62–64.

[50] Norihiko Shirouzu, "Obscure Chinese Car Maker Seeks U.S. Presence," *The Wall Street Journal*, January 3, 2007, pp. B1, B2; Ken Bensinger, "China Seeks Inroads into U.S. Car Market," *Los Angeles Times*, January 15, 2008, pp. A1, A12.

[51] Jason Bush, "From Soviet Clunker to Speed Demon," *BusinessWeek*, November 20, 2006, p. 52.

[52] David Kiley, "Baseball, Apple Pie . . . and Mahindra?" *BusinessWeek*, November 5, 2007, pp. 61–63; David Welch and Nandini Lakshman, "My Other Car Is a Tata," *BusinessWeek*, January 14, 2008, pp. 33–34.

[53] Bruce Stanley, "China's AVIC I Looks to Invest in Airbus Plants," *The Wall Street Journal* (online), June 20, 2007.

[54] Yadong Luo and Rosalie Tung, "International Expansion of Emerging Market Enterprises: A Springboard Perspective," *Journal of International Business Studies* 38 (2007), pp. 481–98; Peter J. Buckley, L. Jeremy Clegg, Adam R. Cross, Xiin Liu, Hinrich Voss, and Ping Zheng, "The Determinants of Chinese Outward Foreign Direct Investment," *Journal of International Business Studies* 38 (2007), pp. 499–518; Daphne W. Yiu, ChingMing Lau, and Garry D. Bruton, "International Venturing by Emerging Economy Firms: The Effects of Firm Capabilities, Home Country Networks, and Corporate Entrepreneurship," *Journal of International Business Studies* 38 (2007), pp. 519–40; Igor Filatotchev, Roger Strange, Jennifer Piesse, and Yung-Chih Lien, "FDI by Firms from Newly Industrialized Economies in Emerging Markets: Corporate Governance, Entry Mode, and Location," *Journal of International Business Studies* 38 (2007), pp. 556–72.

Summary

The ever-expanding involvement in world trade of more and more people with varying needs and wants will test old trading patterns and alliances. The global marketer of today and tomorrow must be able to react to market changes rapidly and to anticipate new trends within constantly evolving market segments that may not have existed as recently as last year. Many of today's market facts will likely be tomorrow's historical myths.

Along with dramatic shifts in global politics, the increasing scope and level of technical and economic growth have enabled many nations to advance their standards of living by as much as two centuries in a matter of decades. As nations develop their productive capacity, all segments of their economies will feel the pressure to improve. The impact of these political, social, and economic trends will continue to be felt throughout the world, resulting in significant changes in marketing practices. Furthermore, the impact of information technology will speed up the economic growth in every country. Marketers must focus on devising marketing plans designed to respond fully to each level of economic development. China and Russia continue to undergo rapid political and economic changes that have brought about the opening of most socialist-bloc countries to foreign direct investments and international trade. And though big emerging markets present special problems, they are promising markets for a broad range of products now and in the future. Emerging markets create new marketing opportunities for MNCs as new market segments evolve.

Questions

1. Define the following terms:

   underdeveloped   BEMs

   economic development   infrastructure

   NICs   BOPMs

2. Is it possible for an economy to experience economic growth as measured by total GNP without a commensurate rise in the standard of living? Discuss fully.

3. Why do technical assistance programs by more affluent nations typically ignore the distribution problem or relegate it to a minor role in development planning? Explain.

4. Discuss each of the stages of evolution in the marketing process. Illustrate each stage with a particular country.

5. As a country progresses from one economic stage to another, what in general are the marketing effects?

6. Select a country in the agricultural and raw materials stage of economic development and discuss what changes will occur in marketing when it passes to a manufacturing stage.

7. What are the consequences of each stage of marketing development on the potential for industrial goods within a country? For consumer goods?

8. Discuss the significance of economic development to international marketing. Why is the knowledge of economic development of importance in assessing the world marketing environment? Discuss.

9. The Internet accelerates the process of economic growth. Discuss.

10. Discuss the impact of the IT revolution on the poorest countries.

11. Select one country in each of the three stages of economic development. For each country, outline the basic existing marketing institutions and show how their stages of development differ. Explain why.

12. Why should a foreign marketer study economic development? Discuss.

13. The infrastructure is important to the economic growth of an economy. Comment.

14. What are the objectives of economically developing countries? How do these objectives relate to marketing? Comment.

15. Using the list of NIC growth factors, evaluate India and China as to their prospects for rapid growth. Which factors will be problems for India or for China?

16. What is marketing's role in economic development? Discuss marketing's contributions to economic development.

17. Discuss the economic and trade importance of the big emerging markets.

18. What are the traits of those countries considered big emerging markets? Discuss.

19. Discuss how the economic growth of BEMs is analogous to the situation after World War II.

20. Discuss the problems a marketer might encounter when considering the Marxist–socialist countries as a market.

21. One of the ramifications of emerging markets is the creation of a middle class. Discuss.

22. The needs and wants of a market and the ability to satisfy them are the result of the three-way interaction of the economy, culture, and the marketing efforts of businesses. Comment.

23. Discuss the strategic implications of marketing in India.

24. "Too much emphasis is usually laid—by Chinese policy makers as well as by foreign businessmen—on China's strength as an export machine. China is so big that its economic potential might more usefully be compared with continental America's." Discuss fully.

10

multinational market regions and market groups

CHAPTER LEARNING OBJECTIVES

What you should learn from Chapter 10:

- The reasons for economic union

- Patterns of international cooperation

- The evolution of the European Union

- Strategic implications for marketing in Europe

- Evolving patterns of trade as eastern Europe and the former Soviet states embrace the free-market system

- The trade linkage of NAFTA and South America and its regional effects

- The development of trade within the Asian-Pacific Rim

Global Perspective

MIGHT FREE TRADE BRING PEACE TO THE MIDDLE EAST?

The nearly complete destruction of the continental European economies by World War II seriously endangered the stability of Europe's social and political institutions. Europe's leaders knew that to rebuild from the ruins, it was essential to form new kinds of international institutions to ensure prosperity, stability, and peace in the region. The first of these institutions was the European Coal and Steel Community, established in 1952 to integrate the coal and steel industries of France, West Germany, Italy, Belgium, the Netherlands, and Luxembourg. Fifty years later, based on the success of this first small experiment in economic interdependence, we now see the European Union with 27 member nations and 3 candidate countries set to join during the next few years. The economies have burgeoned, but more important, peace has persisted.

Might such an approach work in the war-torn Middle East? Let's consider the possibilities and potential of a Middle Eastern Union. The crux of the problem is Jerusalem. The holy Old City is a matter of faith to so many. For Christians it is sacred because of its associations with Christ. For Jews it has served as the center for their people—not only in a national way but, more important, in a religious sense. For Muslims only Mecca and Medina are more important spiritual places. And the fighting over the real estate that represents its spiritual events appears perpetual.

Jerusalem can be a primary part of the solution. But we must look beyond the rockets and bombs of the day. We must imagine a safe, prosperous, and peaceful place. Imagine an international shrine. Perhaps the Old City would be administered by Buddhists or Norwegians or the United Nations. Israel would have its grand capital to the west, in the New City, and the Palestinians to the east a bit.

Religious tourism would feed the economies in both countries, as well as the surrounding area. Imagine the possibilities! In 2000, before the most recent insanity of violence, tourism brought in $3.2 billion in revenues for Israel. Compare that with Disneyland in Orange County, California. That park's yearly 10 million visitors spend about $100 each on tickets, food, and souvenirs. Add in the transportation, hotel, and restaurant revenues appreciated in the neighborhood, and that's more than a couple of billion dollars a year coming to the Anaheim environs.

The Church of the Holy Sepulcher (built over the tomb of Jesus) would draw Christians. The Wailing Wall is the most holy place for Jews. Muslims would flock to the Dome of the Rock (Mohammed was carried by the angel Gabriel for a visit to Heaven after praying at the Rock). The most enlightened tourists would visit all three. Disney might consult on the queuing problems. Staying open 24/7

would expand capacity by allowing jet-lagged pilgrims access to the more popular places. And outside the Old City are Bethlehem, Hebron, Nazareth, Jericho, the Sea of Galilee, the Dead Sea, and the Red Sea, to name only the more obvious attractions. We're talking $10 billion to $20 billion in annual revenues if things are done right—that's about 10 to 15 percent of the current GDP of Israel.

To the east, the new Hijaz Railway Corp. is already working on a line connecting Iran and Jordan via Syria and is talking about lines connecting Iraq, Turkey, and Europe as well—all for the sake of religious tourism. Indeed, the line's original purpose was taking pilgrims to Medina from Damascus; that was before Lawrence of Arabia severed it for carrying arms and troops during World War I. The current company executives reckon the two-day trip from Tehran to Amman will cost only about $30, and the Shiite Muslims of Iran will flock to their holy sights in the area. Why not run the line all the way to east Jerusalem?

How about Jerusalem as the site for the 2020 Olympic games? That's another $5 billion in revenues. And ignoring the dollars for a moment, please consider the sentiments associated with "the 2020 Jerusalem Games" juxtaposed with the disaster of Munich in 1972. And ignoring the dollars for another moment, imagine the spiritual splendor for so many millions visiting the sources of their faith, treading some of the original paths of David, Jesus, and Mohammed.

This little fantasy presumes a peaceful political division of Israel and Palestine along the lines reaffirmed in the Oslo Accords. It presumes a dropping of all commercial boycotts in the region. It presumes that Palestinians won't have to risk being shot while "hopping the fence" to work in Israel. It presumes that companies like Nestlé will be able to integrate the operations of their complementary plants in the area. It presumes that the United States and other countries will send to the region legions of tourists rather than boatloads of weapons. It presumes an open, international, and, most important, a whole Old City of Jerusalem. And it presumes free trade and travel among all nations in the region allowing all to prosper in new ways.

Finally, as Pulitzer Prize–winner Jared Diamond points out, the Middle East, historically referred to as the Fertile Crescent, was the cradle of civilization. It became so long ago because of innovation and trade in the region. One can only imagine what free trade in the area would produce now.

Sources: John L. Graham, "Trade Brings Peace," paper delivered at the Global Ethics and Religion Forum; Clare Hall, Cambridge University conference, *War and Reconciliation: Perspectives of the World Religions*, May 26, 2003, Cambridge, England; Jared Diamond, *Collapse: How Societies Choose to Fail or Succeed* (New York: Viking, 2005).

Within a short walk of one another in the Old City of Jerusalem are three of the most important holy sights for Muslims (the Dome of the Rock), Jews (the Wailing Wall), and Christians (the Church of the Holy Sepulchre). Peace in the region would yield a bonanza of religious tourism.

Following the success of aforementioned European Steel and Coal Community, a global economic revolution began in 1958 when the European Economic Community was ratified and Europe took the step that would ultimately lead to the present-day European Union (EU). Until then, skeptics predicted that the experiment would never work and that the alliance would fall apart quickly. It was not until the single market was established that the United States, Japan, and other countries gave serious thought to creating other alliances. The establishment of common markets, coupled with the trend away from planned economies to the free market system in Latin America, Asia, and eventually the former Soviet Union, created fertile ground that sparked the drive to form trade alliances and free markets the world over. Nation after nation embraced the free market system, implementing reforms in their economic and political systems with the desire to be part of a multinational market region in the evolving global marketplace. Traditions that are centuries old are being altered, issues that cannot be resolved by decree are being negotiated to acceptable solutions, governments and financial systems are restructuring, and companies are being reshaped to meet new competition and trade patterns.

The evolution and growth of *multinational market regions*—those groups of countries that seek mutual economic benefit from reducing interregional trade and tariff barriers—are the most important global trends today. Organizational form varies widely among market regions, but the universal goals of multinational cooperation are economic benefits for the participants and the associated peace between [1] and within countries.[2] The world is awash in economic cooperative agreements as countries look for economic alliances to expand access to free markets. Indeed, part of the efforts of the 192 member countries in the United Nations include mutual economic development; the World Trade Organization, with its 151 members and 31 observers, is wholly dedicated to making trade among nations more efficient.

---

[1] By far the strongest evidence for the "trade causes peace" notion is that provided by Solomon W. Polachek, "Why Democracies Cooperate More and Fight Less: The Relationship between International Trade and Cooperation," *Review of International Economics* 5, no. 3 (1997), pp. 295–309; additional evidence is supplied at http://www.cpbp.org, click on Peace Monitor, then Countries; Jonathan Schell, *The Unconquerable World* (New York: Metropolitan Books, 2003); Thomas Friedman, *The World Is Flat* (New York: Farrar, Straus, and Giroux, 2005).

[2] New studies of the causes of civil wars supports their belief; see Paul Collier, "The Market for Civil War," *Foreign Policy*, May/June 2003, pp. 38–45.

Regional economic cooperative agreements have been around since the end of World War II. The most successful one is the European Union (EU), the world's largest multinational market region and foremost example of economic cooperation. Multinational market groups form large markets that provide potentially significant opportunities for international business. As it became apparent in the late 1980s that the European Union was to achieve its long-term goal of a single European market, a renewed interest in economic cooperation followed, with the creation of several new alliances. The North American Free Trade Agreement (NAFTA) and the Latin American Integration Association (LAIA) in the Americas and the Association of Southeast Asian Nations (ASEAN) and Asia-Pacific Economic Cooperation (APEC) in the Asian-Pacific Rim are all relatively new or reenergized associations that are gaining strength and importance as multinational market regions.

Along with the growing trend of economic cooperation, concerns about the effect of such cooperation on global competition are emerging. Governments and businesses worry that the EU, NAFTA, and other cooperative trade groups will become regional trading blocs without trade restrictions internally but with borders protected from outsiders. But as each of these trade groups continues to create new agreements with other countries and groups, the networked global economy and free trade are clearly on the ascendance. The benefits are clear for consumers; however, global companies face richer and more intense competitive environments.

La Raison d'Etre

Successful economic union requires favorable economic, political, cultural, and geographic factors as a basis for success. Major flaws in any one factor can destroy a union unless the other factors provide sufficient strength to overcome the weaknesses. In general, the advantages of economic union must be clear-cut and significant, and the benefits must greatly outweigh the disadvantages before nations forgo any part of their sovereignty. Many of the associations formed in Africa and Latin America have had little impact because perceived benefits were not sufficient to offset the partial loss of sovereignty.

Economic Factors

Every type of economic union shares the development and enlargement of market opportunities as a basic orientation; usually, markets are enlarged through preferential tariff treatment for participating members, common tariff barriers against outsiders, or both. Enlarged, protected markets stimulate internal economic development by providing assured outlets and preferential treatment for goods produced within the customs union, and consumers benefit from lower internal tariff barriers among the participating countries. In many cases, external and internal barriers are reduced because of the greater economic security afforded domestic producers by the enlarged market.

Nations with complementary economic bases are least likely to encounter frictions in the development and operation of a common market unit. However, for an economic union to survive, it must have agreements and mechanisms in place to settle economic disputes. In addition, the total benefit of economic integration must outweigh individual differences that are sure to arise as member countries adjust to new trade relationships. The European Union includes countries with diverse economies, distinctive monetary systems, developed agricultural bases, and different natural resources. It is significant that most of the problems encountered by the EU have arisen over agriculture and monetary policy. In the early days of the European Community (now the European Union), agricultural disputes were common. The British attempted to keep French poultry out of the British market, France banned Italian wine, and the Irish banned eggs and poultry from other member countries. In all cases, the reason given was health and safety, but the stronger motives were the continuation of the age-old policies of market protection. Such skirmishes are not unusual, but they do test the strength of the economic union. In the case of the EU, the European Commission was the agency used to settle disputes and charge the countries that violated EU regulations.

The demise of the Latin American Free Trade Association (LAFTA) was the result of economically stronger members not allowing for the needs of the weaker ones. Many of the less

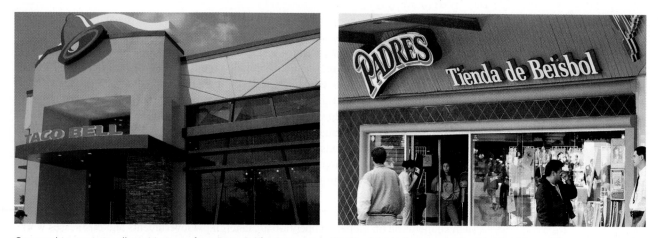

Geographic proximity allows Mexicans from Baja, California, to attend Padres baseball games in close-by San Diego. The team maintains this successful store just across the border in Plaza Rio shopping center in Tijuana. And of course, historically, Padre Junipero Serra had visited both places in the late 1700s while establishing the chain of missions in old Spanish California. NAFTA also has given Taco Bell a second shot at making it in Mexico; the company's 1992, pre-NAFTA incursion failed. *(left: AP Photo/Monica Rueda)*

well-known attempts at common markets have languished because of economic incompatibility that could not be resolved and the uncertainty of future economic advantage.

Political Factors

Political amenability among countries is another basic requisite for the development of a supranational market arrangement. Participating countries must have comparable aspirations and general compatibility before surrendering any part of their national sovereignty. State sovereignty is one of the most cherished possessions of any nation and is relinquished only for a promise of significant improvement of the national position through cooperation.

Economic considerations are the basic catalyst for the formation of a customs union group, but political elements are equally important. The uniting of the original European Union countries was partially a response to the outside threat of the Soviet Union's great political and economic power; the countries of western Europe were willing to settle their "family squabbles" to present a unified front to the Russian bear. The communist threat no longer exists, but the importance of political unity to fully achieve all the benefits of economic integration has driven European countries to form the Union (EU).

Geographic and Temporal Proximity

Although geographic and temporal proximity are not absolutely imperative for cooperating members of a customs union, such closeness does facilitate the functioning of a common market. Indeed, the most recent research demonstrates that more important than physical distance are differences across time zones.[3] That is, trade tends to travel more easily in north–south directions than it did in ancient times. However, transportation networks (basic to any marketing system) are likely to be interrelated and well developed when countries are close together. Issues of immigration, legal and illegal, also promote closer economic integration between close neighbors. One of the first major strengths of the European Union was its transportation network; the opening of the tunnel between England and France further bound this common market. Countries that are widely separated geographically have major barriers to overcome in attempting economic fusion. However, with increasing efficiencies in communication and transportation, the importance of such factors appears to be waning.

Cultural Factors

The United States has bilateral free trade agreements with, among others, Israel, Jordan, Morocco, Bahrain, Chile, Australia, and Singapore, and has several other agreements in various stages of completion with Colombia, Panama, South Korea, Peru, Oman, Malaysia,

---

[3] Contrast Jared Diamond's *Guns, Germs, and Steel* (New York: W. W. Norton, 1999) and Jennifer Chandler and John L. Graham, "Corruption and the Attractiveness of International Markets," working paper, Paul Merage School of Business, University of California, Irvine, 2009.

Thailand, and the United Arab Emirates.[4] These agreements are in addition to its multilateral agreements, such as NAFTA and DR-CAFTA (Dominican Republic, Central American Countries, and the U.S.). But generally, cultural similarity eases the shock of economic cooperation with other countries. The more similar the culture, the more likely an agreement is to succeed, because members understand the outlook and viewpoints of their colleagues. Although there is great cultural diversity in the European Union, key members share a long-established Christian heritage and are commonly aware of being European. However, even this aspect of diversity may be unimportant as negotiations proceed with Turkey about EU membership. Language, as a part of culture, has not created as much a barrier for EU countries as was expected. Nearly every educated European can do business in at least two or three languages, so the linguistic diversity of several major languages did not impede trade.

Patterns of Multinational Cooperation

Of course, at the most general level, the World Trade Organization represents the most important and comprehensive trade agreement in history. At this writing, it appears that Russia will be invited to join the WTO.[5] However, beyond the WTO, multinational market groups take several other forms, varying significantly in the degree of cooperation, dependence, and interrelationship among participating nations. There are five fundamental groupings for regional economic integration, ranging from regional cooperation for development, which requires the least amount of integration, to the ultimate integration of political union.

Regional Cooperation Groups.   The most basic economic integration and cooperation is the *regional cooperation for development (RCD)*. In the RCD arrangement, governments agree to participate jointly to develop basic industries beneficial to each economy. Each country makes an advance commitment to participate in the financing of a new joint venture and to purchase a specified share of the output of the venture. An example is the project between Colombia and Venezuela to build a hydroelectric generating plant on the Orinoco River. They shared jointly in construction costs, and they share the electricity produced.

Free Trade Area.   A *free trade area (FTA)* requires more cooperation and integration than the RCD. It is an agreement between two or more countries to reduce or eliminate customs duties and nontariff trade barriers among partner countries while members maintain individual tariff schedules for external countries. Essentially, an FTA provides its members with a mass market without barriers to impede the flow of goods and services.[6]

Customs Union.   A *customs union* represents the next stage in economic cooperation. It enjoys the free trade area's reduced or eliminated internal tariffs and adds a common external tariff on products imported from countries outside the union. The customs union is a logical stage of cooperation in the transition from an FTA to a common market. The European Union was a customs union before becoming a common market. Customs unions exist between France and Monaco, Italy and San Marino, and Switzerland and Liechtenstein, to name some examples.

Common Market.   A *common market* agreement eliminates all tariffs and other restrictions on internal trade, adopts a set of common external tariffs, and removes all restrictions on the free flow of capital and labor among member nations. Thus a common market is a common marketplace for goods as well as for services (including labor) and for capital. It is a unified economy and lacks only political unity to become a political union. The Treaty of Rome, which established the European Economic Community (EEC) in 1957, called for common external tariffs and the gradual elimination of intramarket tariffs, quotas, and other trade barriers. The treaty also called for the elimination of restrictions on the movement of services, labor, and capital; prohibition of cartels;

---

[4] http://www.ustr.gov/Trade_Agreements/, 2008.

[5] Stephen Castle, "EU to Fast-Track Russia on WTO," *International Herald Tribune*, January 26–27, 2008, p. 13.

[6] The European Free Trade Area is a good example. http://www.efta.int/, 2008.

coordinated monetary and fiscal policies; common agricultural policies; use of common investment funds for regional industrial development; and similar rules for wage and welfare payments. The EEC existed until the Maastricht Treaty created the European Union, an extension of the EEC into a political union.

Latin America boasts three common markets: the Central America Common Market (CACM), the Andean Common Market, and the Southern Cone Common Market (Mercosur). The three have roughly similar goals and seek eventual full economic integration.

Political Union.   *Political union* is the most fully integrated form of regional cooperation. It involves complete political and economic integration, either voluntary or enforced. The most notable enforced political union was the Council for Mutual Economic Assistance (COMECON), a centrally controlled group of countries organized by the Soviet Union. With the dissolution of the Soviet Union and the independence of the Eastern European bloc, COMECON was disbanded.

A *commonwealth* of nations is a voluntary organization providing for the loosest possible relationship that can be classified as economic integration. The British Commonwealth includes Britain and countries formerly part of the British Empire. Some of its members still recognize the British monarch as their symbolic head, though Britain has no political authority over any commonwealth country. Its member states had received preferential tariffs when trading with Great Britain, but when Britain joined the European Community, all preferential tariffs were abandoned. A commonwealth can best be described as the weakest of political unions and is mostly based on economic history and a sense of tradition. Heads of state meet every three years to discuss trade and political issues they jointly face, and compliance with any decisions or directives issued is voluntary.

Two new political unions came into existence in the 1990s: the Commonwealth of Independent States (CIS), made up of the republics of the former Soviet Union, and the European Union (EU). The European Union was created when the 12 nations of the European Community ratified the Maastricht Treaty. The members committed themselves to economic and political integration. The treaty allows for the free movement of goods, persons, services, and capital throughout the member states; a common currency; common foreign and security policies, including defense; a common justice system; and cooperation between police and other authorities on crime, terrorism, and immigration issues. Although not all the provisions of the treaty have been universally accepted, each year the EU members become more closely tied economically and politically. Now that the Economic and Monetary Union is put in place and all participating members share a common currency, the EU is headed toward political union as well.

Global Markets and Multinational Market Groups   The globalization of markets, the restructuring of the eastern European bloc into independent market-driven economies, the dissolution of the Soviet Union into independent states, the worldwide trend toward economic cooperation, and enhanced global competition make it important that market potential be viewed in the context of regions of the world rather than country by country.

This section presents basic information and data on markets and market groups in Europe, the Americas, Africa, Asia, and the Middle East. Existing economic cooperation agreements within each of these regions are reviewed. The reader must appreciate that the status of cooperative agreements and alliances among nations has been extremely fluid in some parts of the world. Many are fragile and may cease to exist or may restructure into a totally different form. Several decades will probably be needed for many of the new trading alliances that are now forming to stabilize into semipermanent groups.

Europe

Within Europe, every type of multinational market grouping exists. The European Union, European Economic Area, and the European Free Trade Area are the most established cooperative groups (see Exhibits 10.1 and 10.2). The careful reader will note the discrepancies

Exhibit 10.1
European Market Regions

Association	Member (year entered union) e = eurozone	Population (millions)	GDP* (billions)	GDP* per Capita at PPP	Imports of Goods and Services* (billions)	Exports of Goods and Services* (billions)
European Union (EU)						
	Belgium (founder)e	10.5	$ 257.3	$30,004	$215.6	$222.9
	Denmark (1973)	5.4	176.7	31,422	82.5	87.8
	Germany (founder)e	82.4	2026.7	27,438	742.0	837.2
	Greece (1981)e	11.1	148.2	21,675	43.5	30.4
	Spain (1986)e	43.5	704.5	24,681	250.7	193.0
	France (founder)e	61.0	1458.7	28,877	436.7	417.6
	Ireland (1973)e	4.2	132.2	36,238	94.7	116.3
	Italy (founder)e	58.6	1154.3	26,496	298.3	288.5
	Luxembourg (founder)e	0.5	25.3	59,853	35.6	40.6
	Netherlands (founder)e	16.4	414.7	31,306	292.6	323.3
	Austria (1995)e	8.2	215.2	30,736	105.7	116.1
	Portugal (1986)e	10.6	117.8	18,966	84.9	37.9
	Finland (1995)e	5.3	142.3	30,420	50.0	61.5
	Sweden (1995)	9.0	282.3	30,392	111.0	139.2
	United Kingdom (1973)	60.4	1664.9	30,237	543.4	466.3
	Czech Republic (2004)	10.2	71.9	19,700	68.1	67.0
	Estonia (2004)	1.3	9.3	15,885	9.3	8.4
	Cyprus (2004)e	0.8	10.3	20,203	–	–
	Latvia (2004)	2.3	13.0	13,724	8.1	5.4
	Lithuania (2004)	3.4	17.8	14,020	13.7	10.8
	Hungary (2004)	10.1	61.6	16,928	60.7	62.7
	Malta (2004)e	0.4	3.9	17,079	–	–
	Poland (2004)	38.1	210.4	13,349	84.9	81.2
	Slovenia (2004)e	2.0	24.1	20,890	17.6	17.2
	Slovak	5.4	27.6	15,409	28.3	27.5
	Republic (2004)	7.7	17.4	8,754	15.2	
	Bulgaria (2007)	21.5	52.6	8,722	28.4	12.1
	Romania (2007)					22.6
EU Candidate Countries						
	Croatia	4.4	24.2	12,164	15.3	12.4
	Macedonia, FYR	2.0	4.0	6,580	2.4	1.8
	Turkey	72.9	261.2	7,842	102.1	92.6
European Free Trade Area (EFTA)						
	Iceland	0.3	10.7	33,610	5.1	3.7
	Liechtenstein	0.03	–	–	–	–
	Norway	4.6	190.1	37,667	58.9	82.4
	Switzerland	7.4	265.6	32,775	107.5	121.3

*Constant 2000 dollars.

Source: World Bank, 2008. Copyright © 2008 by World Bank. Reproduced with permission of World Bank via the Copyright Clearance Center.

between Exhibit 9.1 from the previous chapter and Exhibit 10.1 here. For example, in the case of Germany in Exhibit 9.1, we reported GDP per capita at PPP to be "$33,000," whereas in Exhibit 10.1, it is $27,438. We point out this discrepancy to demonstrate that comparing such statistics across international databases is fraught with potential problems. For Exhibit 9.1, we used Euromonitor as a source; for Exhibit 10.1, we use the World Bank. Neither "estimate" of per capita income is necessarily inaccurate; they are just based on different assumptions and different data collection methods.

Of escalating economic importance are the fledgling capitalist economies of eastern Europe and the three Baltic states that gained independence from the Soviet Union just prior

Exhibit 10.2
The European Economic
Area: EU, EFTA, and
Associates

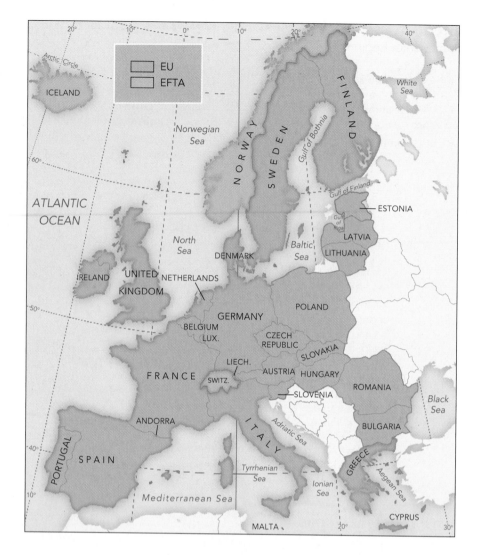

to its breakup. Key issues center on their economic development and economic alliance with the EU. Also within the European region is the Commonwealth of Independent States. New and untested, this coalition of 12 former USSR republics may or may not survive in its present form to take its place among the other multinational market groups.

European Integration

Of all the multinational market groups, none is more secure in its cooperation or more important economically than the European Union (Exhibit 10.3). From its beginning, it has made progress toward achieving the goal of complete economic integration and, ultimately, political union. However, many people, including Europeans, had little hope for the success of the European Economic Community, or the European Common Market as it is often called, because of the problems created by integration and the level of national sovereignty that would have to be conceded to the community. After all, 1,000 years of economic separatism had to be overcome, and the European Common Market is quite heterogeneous. There are language and cultural differences, individual national interests, political differences, and centuries-old restrictions designed to protect local national markets.

Historically, standards have been used to effectively limit market access. Germany protected its beer market from the rest of Europe with a purity law requiring beer sold in Germany to be brewed only from water, hops, malt, and yeast. Italy protected its pasta market by requiring that pasta be made only from durum wheat. Incidentally, the European Court of Justice has struck down both the beer and pasta regulations as trade violations. Such restrictive standards kept competing products, whether from other European countries or elsewhere, out of their respective markets. Skeptics, doubtful that such cultural, legal, and social differences could ever be overcome, held little hope for a unified Europe. Their skepticism has proved wrong. Today, many marvel at how far the European Union has come. Although complete integration has not been fully achieved, a review of the structure of the EU, its authority over member states, the Single European Act, the European Economic Area, the Maastricht Treaty, and the Amsterdam Treaty will show why the final outcome of full economic and political integration now seems more certain.

Exhibit 10.3

From the European Coal and Steel Community to Monetary Union

Source: "Chronology of the EU," http://www.europa.eu.int/ (select Abc). Reprinted with permission from the European Communities.

Year	Event	Description
1951	Treaty of Paris	European Coal and Steel Community (ECSC) (founding members are Belgium, France, Germany, Italy, Luxembourg, and the Netherlands).
1957	Treaty of Rome	Blueprint, European Economic Community (EEC).
1958	European Economic Community	Ratified by ECSC founding members. Common market is established.
1960	European Free Trade Association	Established by Austria, Denmark, Norway, Portugal, Sweden, Switzerland, and United Kingdom.
1973	Expansion	Denmark, Ireland, and United Kingdom join EEC.
1979	European monetary system	The European Currency Unit (ECU) is created. All members except the UK agree to maintain their exchange rates within specific margins.
1981	Expansion	Greece joins EEC.
1985	1992 Single Market Program	White paper for action introduced to European Parliament.
1986	Expansion	Spain and Portugal join EEC.
1987	Single European Act	Ratified, with full implementation by 1992.
1992	Treaty on European Union	Also known as Maastricht Treaty. Blueprint for Economic and Monetary Union (EMU).
1993	Europe 1992	Single European Act in force (January 1, 1992).
1993	European Union	Treaty on European Union (Maastricht Treaty) in force, with monetary union by 1999.
1994	European Economic Area	The EEA was formed with EU members and Norway and Iceland.
1995	Expansion	Austria, Finland, and Sweden join EU.
1997	Amsterdam Treaty	Established procedures for expansion to Central and Eastern Europe.
1999	Monetary union	Conversion rates are fixed, and euro used by banking and finance industry. Consumer prices are quoted in local currency and in euros.
2002	Banknotes and coins	Circulation of euro banknotes and coins begins January 1, and legal status of national banknotes and coins canceled July 1, 2002.
2004	Expansion	Ten new countries join EU.
2007	Expansion	Bulgaria and Romania join.

Each month the European Parliament meets for three weeks here in Brussels, Belgium, and then moves for one week to meet in Strasbourg, France. The inconvenience of the fourth week move was a concession to French pride—or perhaps the cheese is better there.

Even though several member states are not fully implementing all the measures, they are making progress. The proportion of directives not yet implemented in all 27 member states has fallen dramatically. Taxation has been one of the areas where implementation lags and reform continues to be necessary. Value-added and registration taxes for automobiles, for example, at one time ranged from 15 percent in Luxembourg to 218 percent in Denmark. Then a midsized Mercedes in Haderslev, Denmark, cost $90,000, nearly triple the amount you would have paid in Flensburg, Germany, just 30 miles south. A Honda Civic cost the British consumer 89 percent more than it cost continental customers. Scotch in Sweden had an $18 tax, nine times the amount levied in Italy. The EU finance ministers have addressed these issues and made some progress, even though tax-raising ability is a sacred power of the nation-state. The full implementation of the legislation is expected to take several years. Although all proposals have not been met, the program for unification has built up a pace that cannot be reversed.

European Union[7]

EU Institutions. The European Union's institutions form a federal pattern with executive, parliamentary, and judicial branches: the European Commission, the Council of Ministers, the European Parliament, and the Court of Justice. Their decision-making processes have legal status and extensive powers in fields covered by common policies. The European Union uses three legal instruments: (1) regulations binding the member states directly and having the same strength as national laws; (2) directives also binding the member states but allowing them to choose the means of execution; and (3) decisions addressed to a government, an enterprise, or an individual, binding the parties named. Over the years, the Union has gained an increasing amount of authority over its member states.

The European Commission initiates policy and supervises its observance by member states, and it proposes and supervises execution of laws and policies. Commission members act only in the interest of the EU, and their responsibilities are to ensure that the EU rules and the principles of the common market are respected.

The Council of Ministers is the decision-making body of the EU; it is the Council's responsibility to debate and decide which proposals of the Single European Act to accept as binding on EU members. The Council can enact into law all proposals by majority vote except for changes in tax rates on products and services, which require unanimous vote. The Council, for example, drafted the Maastricht Treaty, which was presented to member states for ratification.

[7] http://europa.eu.int, 2008.

CROSSING BORDERS 10.1 Lost in Translation

There are any number of things that Europeans don't like about the European Union—including its very declaration. Sharp-eyed professors have spotted what they say is evidence of the "political translation" of the EU's Berlin Declaration. Specifically, both the Danish and English versions downplay the emotional language of the original German, they claim. Instead of stating that the EU member states are united in "happiness," the translation notes they have united "for the better" or "for the common good."

An EU spokesman argues the texts had been agreed by the national governments. The German-language version of the declaration reads: "We, the citizens in the European Union, are united *zu unserem Gluck*." The controversy stems from that final phrase, which might be rendered in English as "united in our fortune/ happiness." Instead, the English-language version reads: "We, the citizens of the European Union, have united for the better."

In the Danish version, the word "*Gluck*" has been replaced with "*vor faelles bedste*," meaning "for the common good." Professor Henning Koch from Copenhagen University told the Danish paper *Politiken* that the low-key translation could be no coincidence. "It would come as a big surprise to me if the translators are bad at German. So then it's a political translation," he said. Gushing added that emotional terms were something Danes feared.

Professor Rudinger Gorner, head of the German department at University of London, echoed Koch's point, looking at the English version of the Declaration. He told the BBC that the German phrase used in the declaration implies that it is "really a fortunate thing we have united." Instead, he said, "The English rendering certainly downplays the meaning. There's no doubt that if one wanted to express the German sentiment, one could do so." He also noted a subtle difference, in that the English version "suggests something happening in the future."

Mats Persson of the Eurosceptic thinktank Open Europe, which focuses on EU reform, concedes the clear struggle over the translation of the declaration: "It is quite common that people use the maximum room available to accommodate shades of meaning." He also noted, "The Swedish version . . . reads quite awkwardly. The Berlin Declaration is a reflection of a political compromise, and this is reflected in the translations."

Finally, a spokesman for the EU Council said all the translations of the declaration were "official" and had been agreed to by the national delegations of the member states.

Sources: "EU Effusion 'Lost in Translation,'" *BBC News*, March 27, 2007; D. Cooper, "Berlin Declaration Bypasses EU's Citizens," *Financial Times*, June 23, 2007, p. 8.

The European Parliament originally had only a consultative role that passed on most Union legislation. It can now amend and adopt legislation, though it does not have the power to initiate legislation. It also has extensive budgetary powers that allow it to be involved in major EU expenditures.

The European Court of Justice (ECJ) is the European Union's Supreme Court. It is responsible for challenging any measures incompatible with the Treaty of Rome and for passing judgment, at the request of a national court, on the interpretation or validity of points of EU law. The court's decisions are final and cannot be appealed in national courts. For example, Estée Lauder Companies appealed to the ECJ to overrule a German court's decision to prohibit it from selling its Clinique product. The German court had ruled that the name could mislead German consumers by implying medical treatment. The ECJ pointed out that Clinique is sold in other member states without confusing the consumer and ruled in favor of Estée Lauder. This decision marked a landmark case, because many member countries had similar laws that were in essence nontariff trade barriers designed to protect their individual markets. If the German court ruling against Estée Lauder had been upheld, it would have made it difficult for companies to market their products across borders in an identical manner. This case is but one example of the ECJ's power in the EU and its role in eliminating nontariff trade barriers.

Economic and Monetary Union.

The EMU, a provision of the Maastricht Treaty, established the parameters of the creation of a common currency for the EU, the *euro,* and established a timetable for its implementation. In 2002, a central bank was established,

Exhibit 10.4
The Euro

Source: Euro, http://www.europa. eu.int/euro. Reprinted with permission from the European Communities.

Notes. There are seven euro notes in different colors and sizes, denominated in 500, 200, 100, 50, 20, 10 and 5 euros. The designs symbolize Europe's architectural heritage, with windows and gateways on the front side as symbols of the spirit of openness a nd cooperation in the EU. The reverse side features a bridge from a particular age, a metaphor for communication among the people of Europe and the rest of the world.

Coins. There are eight euro coins, denominated in 2 and 1 euros, then 50, 20, 10, 5, 2, and 1 cent. Every coin will carry a common European face—a map of the European Union against a background of transverse lines to which are attached the stars of the European flag. On the obverse, each member state will decorate the coins with their own motifs, for example, the King of Spain or some national hero. Regardless of the motif, every coin can be used and will have the same value in all the member states.

Sign. The graphic symbol for the euro was inspired by the Greek letter epsilon, in reference to the cradle of European civilization and to the first letter of the word *Europe*. It looks like an *E* with two clearly marked, horizontal parallel lines across it. The parallel lines are meant to symbolize the stability of the euro. The official abbreviation is "EUR."

conversion rates were fixed, circulation of euro banknotes and coins was completed (see Exhibit 10.4), and the legal tender status of participating members' banknotes and coins was canceled. To participate, members must meet strict limits on several financial and economic criteria, including national deficit, debt, and inflation. The 12 member states employing the euro beginning in January 1, 2001, were Austria, Belgium, Finland, France, Germany, Greece, Ireland, Italy, Luxembourg, the Netherlands, Portugal, and Spain. Denmark voted in 2000 not to join the monetary union, leaving Britain and Sweden still undecided. Denmark's rejection of the euro caused a broader debate about the EU's future. Anti-euro advocates exploited fears of a "European superstate" and local interference from Brussels rather than relying on economic arguments when pushing for rejection. However, in 2007 Slovenia and in 2008 both Malta and Cyprus switched their currencies to the euro. Others may choose to follow as the euro continues to strengthen against the U.S. dollar.[8]

The original 40-year-old operating rules of the EC were proving to be inadequate in dealing with the problems that confront the EU today. Expansion beyond its present 27 members (see Exhibit 10.1), managing the conversion to the euro and EMU, and speaking with one voice on foreign policy that directly affects the European continent are all issues that require greater agreement among members and thus more responsibility and authority for the institutions of the EU. The Amsterdam Treaty increases the authority of the institutions of the EU and is designed to accommodate the changes brought about by the monetary union and the admission of new members.

It took some selling for the Greeks to adopt the euro instead of the 2,500-year-old drachma. The truck seen here in Athens's Syntagma Square was equipped with video projectors and euro information stands and traveled to 40 Greek towns, informing folks about the new currency. (© AFP/Getty Images)

Expansion of the European Union. The process of enlargement has been the most important item on the EU's agenda. Ten new countries were added in 2004, some ahead of schedule. Bulgaria and Romania entered as planned in 2007, and talks with Turkey,[9] Macedonia, and Croatia are continuing. One of the main preoccupations is the prospect of illegal immigrants from former Soviet states surging across poorly guarded borders of the newer and/or candidate states and making their way farther west within the

[8] "Cyprus, Malta Change to the Euro," *The Wall Street Journal* (online), January 2, 2008.

[9] For a complete rundown on Turkey's entrance into the EU, see "Looking to Europe," *The Economist*, March 19, 2005, insert pp. 1–16.

CROSSING BORDERS 10.2   The Death of the Drachma

Having officially joined the European Union on January 1, 2001, Greece began phasing out the drachma, Europe's oldest currency and the survivor of some 2,500 years of war and economic turmoil. Below, highlights from its storied history.
—MEGAN JOHNSTON

Source: March 2001 *Money*. Used by permission of *Money* magazine.

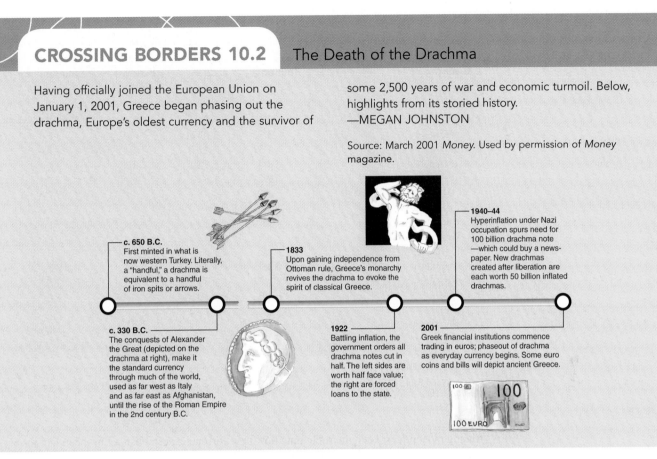

c. 650 B.C.
First minted in what is now western Turkey. Literally, a "handful," a drachma is equivalent to a handful of iron spits or arrows.

c. 330 B.C.
The conquests of Alexander the Great (depicted on the drachma at right), make it the standard currency through much of the world, used as far west as Italy and as far east as Afghanistan, until the rise of the Roman Empire in the 2nd century B.C.

1833
Upon gaining independence from Ottoman rule, Greece's monarchy revives the drachma to evoke the spirit of classical Greece.

1922
Battling inflation, the government orders all drachma notes cut in half. The left sides are worth half face value; the right are forced loans to the state.

1940–44
Hyperinflation under Nazi occupation spurs need for 100 billion drachma note —which could buy a newspaper. New drachmas created after liberation are each worth 50 billion inflated drachmas.

2001
Greek financial institutions commence trading in euros; phaseout of drachma as everyday currency begins. Some euro coins and bills will depict ancient Greece.

EU. The EU is demanding that borders be sealed, but the new and candidate states are reluctant to jeopardize relations with neighboring communities. Furthermore, the EU fears a flood of cheap labor even if the borders are closed; it wants a long transition period before freedom of movement of labor, whereas the applicants say their citizens should be allowed to work anywhere in the EU once they are members.

In 2007 the European Union celebrated its golden anniversary. Most would agree that it has been a tremendous success, delivering peace and prosperity to hundreds of millions of people that previously had lived with frequent wars and accompanying economic and social hardships. The challenges facing the Union in the next 50 years appear to fall into three categories: (1) improving the Union's economic performance, (2) deciding how to limit the political aspects of union, and (3) deciding about further enlargement. The last problem may well disappear as both multilateral and bilateral agreements continue to multiply around the world and as the WTO continues to gain influence and traction in trade barrier reduction.[10]

The Commonwealth of Independent States

Europe (and Asia) has one other trade group that has emerged and persisted since the dissolution of the Soviet Union: the Commonwealth of Independent States (CIS).[11] The series of events after the aborted coup against Mikhail Gorbachev led to the complete dissolution of the USSR. The first Soviet republics to declare independence were the Baltic states, which quickly gained recognition by several Western nations. The remaining 12 republics of the former USSR, collectively known as the Newly Independent States (NIS), regrouped into the Commonwealth of Independent States (see Exhibit 10.5).

The CIS is a loose economic and political alliance with open borders but no central government. The main provisions of the commonwealth agreement are to repeal all Soviet laws and assume the powers of the old regimes; launch radical economic reforms, including

---

[10] John Peet, "Fit at 50? A Special Report of the European Union," *The Economist*, March 17, 2007.
[11] http://www.cisstat.com, 2008.

Exhibit 10.5
Commonwealth of
Independent States (CIS)

Country	Population (millions)	GDP* (billions)	GDP* per Capita at PPP	Imports of Goods and Services* (billions)	Exports of Goods and Services* (billions)
Russia	142.4	$373.2	$10,350	$171.8	$183.3
Ukraine	46.6	48.4	6,605	26.9	24.1
Belarus	9.7	20.1	7,810	15.1	12.3
Armenia	3.0	3.9	5,011	1.9	1.2
Moldova	3.8	1.9	2,151	2.0	1.4
Azerbaijan	8.5	13.4	5,953	8.8	7.0
Uzbekistan	26.5	19.2	1,942	3.9	4.4
Turkmenistan (associate member, withdrew 2005)	4.9	2.9	3,416	2.5	5.3
Tajikistan	6.7	1.6	1,257	0.9	1.5
Kazakhstan	15.3	33.1	7,652	11.3	15.8
Kyrgyzstan	5.2	1.7	1,749	1.3	0.6
Georgia (outside defense pact, withdrew 2006)	4.4	4.8	3,304	1.8	1.0

*Constant 2000 dollars.

Source: World Bank, 2008. Copyright © 2008 by World Bank. Reproduced with permission of World Bank via Copyright Clearance Center.

freeing most prices; keep the ruble but allow new currencies; establish a European Union–style free trade association; create joint control of nuclear weapons; and fulfill all Soviet foreign treaties and debt obligations.

The 12 members of the CIS share a common history of central planning, and their close cooperation could make the change to a market economy less painful, but differences over economic policy, currency reform, and control of the military may break them apart. How the CIS will be organized and what its ultimate importance will be is anyone's guess.

The three Slavic republics of Russia, Ukraine, and Belarus have interests and history in common, as do the five Central Asian republics. But the ties between these two core groups of the CIS are tenuous and stem mainly from their former Soviet membership. At this writing, Russia and Ukraine are involved in a nasty dispute over the price and payments of gas shipped by the former to the latter.[12] The CIS is by no means coming apart, though it has not solidified to the point of having a stable membership and purpose.[13] Under Vladimir Putin, Russia has shown renewed interest in the CIS, and a free trade zone, which Russia had blocked since the CIS was created, may become a reality.

Of all the former republics, Azerbaijan, Georgia, and Armenia have been the most economically successful since leaving the former USSR. After the USSR collapsed, their economies had all imploded to less than half their peak size during Soviet days. Now, however, they are showing sustained signs of commercial renewal—and multinational icons like Intel have made investments in the area. Although initially Russia experienced serious economic problems, it now has

The hammer and sickle logo of the old USSR has been replaced by signs of free enterprise in Russia. Here in the main shopping district of St. Petersburg, Nike Sport is prominent, along with Coca-Cola red umbrellas.

[12] Gregory L. White, "Gas-Supply Battle Escalates Between Russia, Ukraine," *The Wall Street Journal* (online), March 4, 2008.

[13] The Economist Intelligence Unit, "Kazakhstan: Transport and Communications," *Views Wire*, September 1, 2005, p. 15.

CROSSING BORDERS 10.3   Refusing to Pass along the Gas

Russia and Ukraine have escalated their dispute over natural gas supplies, raising the possibility that supplies of Russian fuel to Europe could be threatened if the tensions drag out. Seeking to force Kiev to sign new contracts and pay what it says are $600 million in debts, the Russian natural gas giant OAO Gazprom slashed gas supplies to Ukraine twice in two days and warned that further reductions could follow. Ukrainian state energy company NAK Naftogaz in turn threatened to dip into transit shipments of Russian natural gas to European customers to make up for the cuts. At least initially, those supplies weren't affected.

European Energy Commissioner Andris Piebalgs and Andrej Vizjak, the economy minister of EU president Slovenia, insisted that supplies to the EU must remain uninterrupted. Despite Gazprom's supply cuts, Naftogaz said the combination of warm weather and ample natural gas in storage prevented the need for cutbacks to consumers in Ukraine or export flows—for now. Nonetheless, the latest ultimatum raised fears of

a repeat of the January 2006 crisis in which European supplies were interrupted when Gazprom cut shipments to Ukraine in a price dispute. Gazprom quickly resumed pumping, but the episode sparked concerns across Europe about the company's reliability as a supplier. Europe gets about one-fourth of its gas from Russia, and the bulk of that is carried by pipeline across Ukraine.

Russian officials insist the current tensions are purely economic and blame Kiev for failing to fulfill a compromise deal on the debts. Critics denounced the Kremlin for using gas supplies as a political weapon, noting that Gazprom's threats came amid rising political tension in Kiev. Yet the presidents of two countries, Vladimir Putin and Viktor Yuschenko, claimed their differences had been resolved.

Sources: "Deadline Passes in Russian–Ukraine Gas Dispute," *Agence France-Presse*, March 2, 2008; Gregory L. White, "Gas-Supply Battle Escalates between Russia, Ukraine," *The Wall Street Journal* (online), March 4, 2008.

returned to more robust growth in large part due to the successful marketing of its vast energy resources.[14] All members of the CIS have had economic growth, and inflation has been held between a high of 5.9 percent for Tajikistan and a low of 0.2 percent for Kazakhstan.

The Americas[15]

Within the Americas, the United States, Canada, Central America, and South America have been natural if sometimes contentious trading partners. As in Europe, the Americas are engaged in all sorts of economic cooperative agreements, with NAFTA being the most significant and Mercosur and DR-CAFTA gaining in importance.

North American Free Trade Agreement (NAFTA)

Preceding the creation of the North American Free Trade Agreement (NAFTA), the United States and Canada had the world's largest bilateral trade agreement; each was the other's largest trading partner. Despite this unique commercial relationship, tariff and other trade barriers hindered even greater commercial activity. To further support trade activity, the two countries established the United States–Canada Free Trade Area (CFTA), designed to eliminate all trade barriers between the two countries. The CFTA created a single, continental commercial market for all goods and most services. The agreement between the United States and Canada was not a customs union like the European Community; no economic or political union of any kind was involved. It provided only for the elimination of tariffs and other trade barriers.

Shortly after both countries had ratified the CFTA, Mexico announced that it would seek free trade with the United States. Mexico's overtures were answered positively by the United States, and talks on a U.S.–Mexico free trade area began. Mexico and the United States had been strong trading partners for decades, but Mexico had never officially expressed an interest in a free trade agreement until the president of Mexico, Carlos Salinas de Gortari, announced that Mexico would seek such an agreement with the United States and Canada.

---

[14] "Gazprom Eyes 10% of French Gas Market in 4–5 Years," *Dow Jones International News*, January 3, 2008.

[15] For a comprehensive list of all trade agreements in the Americas, with links to specific documents, visit http://www.sice.oas.org and select Trade Agreements.

CROSSING BORDERS 10.4 | Taco Bell Tries Again

It sounds like a fast-food grudge match: Taco Bell is taking on the homeland of its namesake by reopening for the first time in 15 years in Mexico. Defenders of Mexican culture see the chain's reentry as a crowning insult to a society already overrun by U.S. chains, from Starbucks and Subway to KFC. "It's like bringing ice to the Arctic," complained pop culture historian Carlos Monsivais.

In Mexico, the company is projecting a more "American" fast-food image by adding french fries—some topped with cheese, sour cream, ground meat, and tomatoes—to the menu of its first store, which opened in late September 2007 in the northern city of Monterrey. Other than the fries and sales of soft-serve ice cream, "our menu comes almost directly from the U.S. menu," said Managing Director Steven Pepper.

Some of the names have been changed to protect the sacred: the hard-shelled items sold as "tacos" in the United States have been renamed "tacostadas." This made-up word is a play on "tostada," which for Mexicans is a hard, fried disk of cornmeal that is always served flat, with toppings. But while Mexicans eagerly buy many American brands, the taco holds a place of honor in the national cuisine. Mexicans eat them every-where, any time of day, buying them from basket-toting street vendors in the morning or slathering them in salsa at brightly lit taquerias to wrap up a night on the town.

Taco Bell has taken pains to say that it's not trying to masquerade as a Mexican tradition. "One look alone is enough to tell that Taco Bell is not a 'taqueria,'" the company said in a half-page newspaper ad. "It is a new fast-food alternative that does not pretend to be Mexican food." It's still a mixed message for Mexicans like Marco Fragoso, a 39-year-old office worker sitting down for lunch at a traditional taqueria in Mexico City, because the U.S. chain uses traditional Mexican names for its burritos, gorditas, and chalupas. "They're not tacos," Fragoso said. "They're folded tostadas. They're very ugly."

Taco Bell failed with an earlier, highly publicized launch in Mexico City in 1992, when it opened a few outlets next to KFC restaurants. Now Taco Bell, KFC, and Pizza Hut are owned by Yum Brands. But Mexicans were less familiar with foreign chains back then, the economy was on the verge of a crisis, and NAFTA had yet to be signed. The restaurants didn't even last two years. Since then, free trade and growing migration have made U.S. brands ubiquitous in Mexico, influencing everything from how people dress to how they talk.

Graham Allan, president of Yum Brands, says two years of market research have convinced him that the firm will succeed this time. The company is building its second store in another Monterrey suburb and plans to open between 8 and 10 more locations in 2008, with plans to eventually reach 300 stores. The first stores will be company-owned, and franchise opportunities will open up in later years.

Sources: Michael Arndt, "Tacos without Borders," *BusinessWeek*, September 3, 2007, p. 12; Mark Stevenson, "Another Run for the Border," *Los Angeles Times*, October 15, 2007, p. C4.

Despite the disparity between Mexico's economy and the economies of the other two countries, there were sound reasons for such an alliance. Canada is a sophisticated industrial economy, resource rich, but with a small population and domestic market. Mexico desperately needs investment, technology, exports, and other economic reinforcement to spur its economy.[16] Even though Mexico has an abundance of oil and a rapidly growing population, the number of new workers is increasing faster than its economy can create new jobs. The United States needs resources (especially oil) and, of course, markets. The three need one another to compete more effectively in world markets, and they need mutual assurances that their already dominant trading positions in the others' markets are safe from protection pressures. When NAFTA was ratified and became effective in 1994, a single market of 360 million people with a $6 trillion GNP emerged.

NAFTA required the three countries to remove all tariffs and barriers to trade over 15 years, and beginning in 2008, all tariff barriers were officially dropped.[17] Some nagging disagreements still persist, such as allowing Mexican trucks and truckers free access to

---

[16] John O'Dell, "A Toyota Factory Revs Up in Tijuana," *Los Angeles Times*, February 23, 2005, pp. C1, C4.

[17] Jenalia Moreno, "Trade Tariffs End, Marking a NAFTA Milestone: U.S., Mexico Tout New Growth, but Some Farmers Feel Squeezed Out," *Houston Chronicle*, January 2, 2008.

U.S. roads. But for the most part, NAFTA is a comprehensive trade agreement that addresses, and in most cases improves, all aspects of doing business within North America. See Exhibit 10.6 for some of the key provisions of the trade agreement. The elimination of trade and investment barriers among Canada, Mexico, and the United States creates one of the largest and richest markets in the world. Cross-border cooperation seems to ameliorate other long-standing areas of conflict such as legal and illegal immigration. NAFTA also

Exhibit 10.6
Key Provisions of NAFTA

Market access
Within 10 years of implementation, all tariffs will be eliminated on North American industrial products traded among Canada, Mexico, and the United States. All trade between Canada and the United States not already duty free will be duty free as provided for in CFTA. Mexico will immediately eliminate tariffs on nearly 50 percent of all industrial goods imported from the United States, and remaining tariffs will be phased out entirely within 15 years.

Nontariff barriers
In addition to the elimination of tariffs, Mexico will eliminate nontariff barriers and other trade-distorting restrictions. The U.S. exporters will benefit immediately from the removal of most import licenses that have acted as quotas, essentially limiting the importation of products into the Mexican market. NAFTA also eliminates a host of other Mexican barriers, such as local-content, local-production, and export-performance requirements that have limited U.S. exports.

Rules of origin
NAFTA reduces tariffs only for goods made in North America. Tough rules of origin will determine whether goods qualify for preferential tariff treatment under NAFTA. Rules of origin are designed to prevent free riders from benefiting through minor processing or transshipment of non-NAFTA goods. For example, Japan could not assemble autos in Mexico and avoid U.S. or Canadian tariffs and quotas unless the auto had a specific percentage of Mexican (i.e., North American) content. For goods to be traded duty free, they must contain substantial (62.5 percent) North American content. Because NAFTA rules of origin have been strengthened, clarified, and simplified over those contained in the U.S.–Canada Free Trade Agreement, they supersede the CFTA rules.

Customs administration
Under NAFTA, Canada, Mexico, and the United States have agreed to implement uniform customs procedures and regulations. Uniform procedures ensure that exporters who market their products in more than one NAFTA country will not have to adapt to multiple customs procedures. Most procedures governing rules-of-origin documentation, record keeping, and verification will be the same for all three NAFTA countries. In addition, the three will issue advanced rulings, on request, about whether or not a product qualifies for tariff preference under the NAFTA rules of origin.

Investment
NAFTA will eliminate investment conditions that restrict the trade of goods and services to Mexico. Among the conditions eliminated are the requirements that foreign investors export a given level or percentage of goods or services, use domestic goods or services, transfer technology to competitors, or limit imports to a certain percentage of exports.

Services
NAFTA establishes the first comprehensive set of principles governing services trade. Both U.S. and Canadian financial institutions are permitted to open wholly owned subsidiaries in Mexico, and all restrictions on the services they offer will be lifted. NAFTA opens Mexico's market for international truck, bus, and rail transport and eliminates the requirement to hand off cargo to a Mexican vehicle upon entry into Mexico, saving U.S. industry both time and money. Also, U.S. truck and bus companies will have the right to use their own drivers and equipment for cross-border cargo shipment and passenger service with Mexico.

Intellectual property
NAFTA will provide the highest standards of protection of intellectual property available in any bilateral or international agreement. The agreement covers patents, trademarks, copyrights, trade secrets, semiconductor integrated circuits, and copyrights for North American movies, computer software, and records.

Government procurement
NAFTA guarantees businesses fair and open competition for procurement in North America through transparent and predictable procurement procedures. In Mexico, PEMEX (the national oil company), CFE (the national electric company), and other government-owned enterprises will be open to U.S. and Canadian suppliers.

Standards
NAFTA prohibits the use of standards and technical regulations used as obstacles to trade. However, NAFTA provisions do not require the United States or Canada to lower existing health, environmental, or safety regulations, nor does NAFTA require the importation of products that fail to meet each country's health and safety standards.

has paved the way for Wal-Mart to move into Mexico and the Mexican supermarket giant Gigante to move into the United States. Other cross-border services are also thriving, including entertainment and healthcare.

Furthermore, U.S. and foreign investors with apparel and footwear factories in Asia have been encouraged to relocate their production operations to Mexico. For example, Victoria's Secret lingerie chain opened a new manufacturing plant near Mexico City. The company previously had used contractors in Asia for its lingerie line. Even with wages in Mexico three times the monthly wages in Sri Lanka, the company will still come out ahead because moving goods from Mexico City to the United States is cheaper and faster than moving them from Colombo—the time needed to make a sample can be cut from weeks to days. Mexican goods have no tariffs, whereas Sri Lankan goods carry a 19 percent duty.

Total foreign direct investment in Mexico has averaged $11 billion a year since 1995 as companies from all over the world poured money into auto and electronics plants, telecommunications, petrochemicals, and a host of other areas. A large chunk of investment is earmarked for factories that will use Mexico as an export platform for the rest of North America, and increasingly the rest of Latin America.

Job losses have not been as drastic as once feared, in part because companies such as Lucent Technologies have established *maquiladora* plants in anticipation of the benefits from NAFTA. The plants have been buying more components from U.S. suppliers, while cutting back on Asian sources. Miles Press, a $2 million maker of directory cards, saw orders from Lucent grow 20 percent in just a few months. Berg Electronics, a $700 million component maker, expects to triple sales to Lucent's Guadalajara plant next year. This ripple effect has generated U.S. service-sector jobs as well. Fisher Price shifted toy production for the U.S. market from Hong Kong to a plant in Monterrey. Celadon Trucking Services, which moves goods produced for Fisher Price from Mexico to the United States, has added 800 new U.S. drivers to the payroll.

NAFTA is a work in progress. It is still too early to pass judgment; after all, the EU has been in existence for more than 50 years and has had its ups and downs. NAFTA is a mere babe in arms in comparison. What is happening is that economic relationships among the three countries are becoming more intense each day, for the most part quietly and profitably. In short, at least 20 years are needed for an objective evaluation of NAFTA to be possible.

Most recently, during the protracted economic slump following the dot-com bust in the United States, *maquiladora* plants have been closing at an uncomfortable rate. Manufacturing is migrating to other low-paying countries such as China, Guatemala, and Vietnam. However, the firms operating in Tijuana and other border cities are responding with investments in technology and increased marketing efforts.

United States–Central American Free Trade Agreement–Dominican Republic Free Trade Agreement (DR-CAFTA)

In August 2005, President George Bush signed into law a comprehensive free trade agreement among Costa Rica, the Dominican Republic, El Salvador, Guatemala, Honduras, Nicaragua, and the United States. The agreement includes a wide array of tariff reductions aimed at increasing trade and employment among the seven signatories. Thus, DR-CAFTA represents another important step toward the ultimate goal of a free trade agreement encompassing all the Americas. See Exhibit 10.7 for a listing of American countries involved in trade associations.

Southern Cone Free Trade Area (Mercosur)[18]

Mercosur (including Argentina, Bolivia, Brazil, Chile, Paraguay, and Uruguay) is the second-largest common-market agreement in the Americas after NAFTA. The Treaty of Asunción, which provided the legal basis for Mercosur, was signed in 1991 and formally inaugurated in 1995. The treaty calls for a common market that would eventually allow for the free movement of goods, capital, labor, and services among the member countries, with

---

[18] See http://www.mercosur.org.uy/.

Exhibit 10.7
Market Regions of the Americas

Association	Member	Population (millions)	GDP* (billions)	GDP* per Capita at PPP	Imports of Goods and Services* (billions)	Exports of Goods and Services* (billions)
North American Free Trade Agreement (NAFTA)						
	United States	299.0	$11,411.0	$38,165	$1719.2	$1117.9
	Mexico	104.2	665.6	9,967	261.6	240.0
	Canada	32.6	832.2	30,278	312.3	331.6
Dominican Republic–Central American Free Trade Agreement (DR-CAFTA)						
	Guatemala	12.9	22.9	4,150	8.3	4.1
	Costa Rica	4.4	21.0	9,646	9.7	9.9
	El Salvador	7.0	15.2	4,776	7.0	4.5
	Nicaragua	5.2	4.7	3,539	2.6	1.5
	Honduras	7.4	7.5	3,170	5.4	3.6
	Dominican Republic	9.6	25.9	7,618	11.0	9.0
	United States	as above	–			–
Caribbean Community and Common Market (CARICOM)						
	Antigua and Barbuda	0.1	0.9	12,318	0.5	0.4
	Barbados	0.3	2.5	9,256	1.3	1.2
	Belize	0.3	1.1	6,646	0.6	0.7
	Dominica	0.1	0.3	6,047	0.2	0.1
	Grenada	0.1	0.4	7,378	0.3	0.2
	Guyana	0.8	0.8	4,204	0.8	0.7
	Haiti	8.6	3.8	1,479	1.9	0.6
	Jamaica	2.7	9.0	3,907	4.9	3.4
	Montserrat St. Kitts-Nevis	0.05	0.4	12,521	0.2	0.1
	St. Lucia	0.2	0.8	6,482	–	–
	Surinam	0.5	1.2	7,231	0.5	0.2
	Trinidad-Tobago	1.3	13.4	14,708	6.1	6.5
Latin American Integration Association (LAIA, aka ALADI)						
	Argentina	39.1	340.1	13,652	36.6	47.6
	Bolivia	9.3	10.2	2,579	3.4	2.6
	Brazil	188.7	765.1	7,826	98.4	111.5
	Chile	16.5	96.2	10,939	39.3	33.2
	Colombia	45.6	105.6	6,886	27.6	22.4
	Ecuador	13.4	21.4	3,982	10.3	8.6
	Mexico	as above	–	–	–	–
	Paraguay	6.0	8.3	4,368	4.7	3.5
	Peru	28.4	70.6	5,725	14.2	14.5
	Uruguay	3.3	23.2	9,898	5.1	5.5
	Venezuela	27.0	146.6	6,485	41.4	37.1

*Constant 2000 dollars.

a uniform external tariff. Because Mercosur members were concerned about sacrificing sovereign control over taxes and other policy matters, the agreement envisioned no central institutions similar to those of the European Union institutions.

Since its inception, Mercosur has become the most influential and successful free trade area in South America. With the addition of Bolivia and Chile in 1996, Mercosur became a market of 220 million people with a combined GDP of nearly $1 trillion and is the third largest free trade area in the world. More recently Colombia and Ecuador have also become associate members, with Venezuela to follow shortly; Mexico has observer status as well. Mercosur has demonstrated greater success than many observers expected. The success can be attributed to the willingness of the region's governments to confront some very tough issues caused by dissimilar economic policies related to the automobile and textile trade and to modify antiquated border customs procedures that initially created a bottleneck to smooth border crossings. The lack of surface and transportation infrastructure to facilitate trade and communications is a lingering problem that is being addressed at the highest levels.

Mercosur has pursued agreements aggressively with other countries and trading groups. For example, there are concrete negotiations under way to create a free trade program with Mexico, talks with Canada regarding a free trade agreement, and talks between Chile and Mercosur aimed at gradual and reciprocal trade liberalization.

In addition, negotiations have been under way since 1999 for a free trade agreement between the EU and Mercosur, the first region-to-region free trade accord. A framework agreement was signed in 1995, and the long-term objective is to reach convergence in all areas—cooperation, trade, market access, intellectual property, and political dialogue. The two blocs propose the largest free trade area in the world. The advantages of the accord to Mercosur will mainly come from lifting trade barriers on agricultural and agro-industrial products, which account for the lion's share of Mercosur exports to Europe. However, that point will also be a major stumbling block if the EU is unwilling to open its highly protected agricultural sector to Brazilian and Argentine imports. Nevertheless, one official of the EU indicated that the EU was already in the process of reforming its Common Agricultural Policy. Although negotiations will not be easy, Mercosur and the EU should be able to reach an accord. As we shall see in the next section, Mercosur has assumed the leadership in setting the agenda for the creation of a free trade area of the Americas or, more likely, a South American Free Trade Area (SAFTA).

Latin American Economic Cooperation

Besides the better-known NAFTA and Mercosur, other Latin American market groups (Exhibit 10.8) have had varying degrees of success. Plagued with tremendous foreign debt, protectionist economic systems, triple-digit inflation, state ownership of basic industries, and overregulation of industry, most Latin American countries were in a perpetual state of economic chaos. In such conditions, trade or integration among member countries stagnated. But as discussed previously, sparked by the success of Mercosur and NAFTA, Latin America has seen a wave of genuine optimism about the economic miracle under way, spurred by political and economic reforms from the tip of Argentina to the Rio Grande. Coupled with these market-oriented reforms is a desire to improve trade among neighboring countries by reviving older agreements or forming new ones. Many of the trade groups are seeking ties to Mercosur, the European Union, or both.

Latin American Integration Association.

The long-term goal of the LAIA, better known by its Spanish acronym, ALADI,[19] is a gradual and progressive establishment of a Latin American common market. One of the more important aspects of LAIA that differs from LAFTA, its predecessor, is the differential treatment of member countries according to their level of economic development. Over the years, negotiations among member countries have lowered duties on selected products and eased trade tensions over quotas, local-content requirements, import licenses, and other trade barriers. An important feature of LAIA is the provision that permits members to establish bilateral trade

---

[19] http://www.aladi.org, 2008.

Exhibit 10.8
Far Eastern Market Group

Association	Member	Population (millions)	GDP* (billions)	GDP* per Capita at PPP	Imports of Goods and Services* (billions)	Exports of Goods and Services* (billions)
ASEAN Free Trade Area (AFTA)						
	Brunei	0.4	$ 4.8	$ –	$ —	$ —
	Cambodia	14.4	6.3	2,629	4.6	4.0
	Indonesia	223.0	219.3	3,570	78.9	95.6
	Laos	5.8	2.5	2,013	1.2	0.8
	Malaysia	25.8	119.1	10,091	130.9	153.1
	Myanmar	51.0	–	–	–	–
	Philippines	84.6	99.4	4,731	56.5	57.3
	Singapore	4.4	121.6	28,305	–	–
	Thailand	64.7	165.0	8,065	103.9	116.7
	Vietnam	84.1	48.4	2,925	41.4	40.6
ASEAN +3						
	China	1311.8	2092.2	6,621	602.9	802.3
	Japan	127.6	5102.7	27,992	510.4	638.8
	South Korea	48.4	671.3	23,416	318.6	388.0

*Constant 2000 dollars.

Source: World Bank, 2008. Copyright © 2008 by World Bank. Reproduced with permission of World Bank via Copyright Clearance Center.

agreements among member countries. It is under this proviso that trade agreements have been developed among LAIA members.

Caribbean Community and Common Market (CARICOM).[20]   The success of the Caribbean Free Trade Association led to the creation of the Caribbean Community and Common Market. CARICOM member countries continue in their efforts to achieve true regional integration. The group has worked toward a single-market economy and in 2000 established the CSME (CARICOM Single Market and Economy) with the goal of a common currency for all members. The introduction of a common external tariff structure was a major step toward that goal. CARICOM continues to seek stronger ties with other groups in Latin America and has signed a trade agreement with Cuba.

NAFTA to FTAA or SAFTA?

Initially NAFTA was envisioned as the blueprint for a free trade area extending from Alaska to Argentina. The first new country to enter the NAFTA fold was to be Chile, then membership was to extend south until there was a Free Trade Area of the Americas (FTAA) by 2005. The question now is whether there will be an FTAA or whether there will be a tricountry NAFTA in the north and a South American Free Trade Area (SAFTA) led by Brazil and the other member states of Mercosur in the south. The answer to this question rests in part with the issue of fast-track legislation and the policies of the new American president.

Asian-Pacific Rim

After decades of dependence on the United States and Europe for technology and markets, countries in the Asian-Pacific Rim are preparing for the next economic leap driven by trade, investment, and technology, aided by others in the region. Though few in number, trade agreements among some of the Asian newly industrialized countries (NICs) are seen as movement toward a regionwide, intra-Asian trade area, with Japan and China[21] at the center of this activity.

---

[20] http://www.caricom.org, 2008.

[21] Carlos H. Conde, "China and ASEAN in Services Pact," *The New York Times*, January 15, 2007, p. C2.

Although the United States is Japan's single largest trading partner, markets in China and Southeast Asia are increasingly more important in Japanese corporate strategy for trade and direct investment. Once a source of inexpensive labor for products shipped to Japan or to third markets, these countries are now seen as viable markets. Furthermore, Japanese investment across a number of manufacturing industries is geared toward serving local customers and building sophisticated local production and supplier networks.

Present trade agreements include one multinational trade group, the Association of Southeast Asian Nations (ASEAN), which is evolving into the ASEAN Free Trade Area (AFTA); ASEAN+3, a forum for ASEAN ministers plus ministers from China, Japan, and South Korea; and the Asia-Pacific Economic Cooperation (APEC), a forum that meets annually to discuss regional economic development and cooperation.

Association of Southeast Asian Nations

The primary multinational trade group in Asia is ASEAN.[22] Like all multinational market groups, ASEAN has experienced problems and false starts in attempting to unify the combined economies of its member nations. Most of the early economic growth came from trade outside the ASEAN group. Similarities in the kinds of products they had to export, in their natural resources, and other national assets hampered earlier attempts at intra-ASEAN trade. The steps countries took to expand and diversify their industrial base to foster intraregional trade when ASEAN was first created have resulted in the fastest growing economies in the region and an increase in trade among members (see Exhibit 10.8).

Four major events account for the vigorous economic growth of the ASEAN countries and their transformation from cheap-labor havens to industrialized nations: (1) the ASEAN governments' commitment to deregulation, liberalization, and privatization of their economies; (2) the decision to shift their economies from commodity based to manufacturing based; (3) the decision to specialize in manufacturing components in which they have a comparative advantage (which created more diversity in their industrial output and increased opportunities for trade); and (4) Japan's emergence as a major provider of technology and capital necessary to upgrade manufacturing capability and develop new industries.[23]

Although there has never been an attempt to duplicate the supranational government of the European Union, each year the group becomes more interrelated. ASEAN Vision 2020 is the most outward-looking commitment to regional goals ever accepted by the group. Among the targets that will lead to further integration is the commitment to implementing fully and as rapidly as possible the ASEAN Free Trade Area.

Just as was the case in the EU, businesses are drafting plans for operation within a free trade area. The ability to sell in an entire region without differing tariff and nontariff barriers is one of the important changes that will affect many parts of the marketing mix. Distribution can be centralized at the most cost-effective point rather than having distribution points dictated by tariff restrictions. Some standardization of branding will be necessary because large customers will buy at the regional level rather than bit by bit at the country level. Pricing can be more consistent, which will help reduce the smuggling and parallel importing that occur when different tariff schedules create major price differentials among countries. In essence, marketing can become more regionally and centrally managed.

One result of the Asian financial crisis of 1997 to 1998 was the creation of ASEAN+3 (ASEAN plus China, Japan, and South Korea) to deal with trade and monetary issues facing Asia. Most of East Asia felt that they were both let down and put upon by the West, whom they felt created much of the problem by pulling out in the midst of the crisis. The leading financial powers seemingly either declined to take part in the rescue operations, as the United States did in Thailand, or proposed unattainable solutions. The result was the creation of ASEAN+3, consisting of the foreign and finance ministers of each country, which meets annually after ASEAN meetings. The first meeting was devoted to devising a system whereby the member countries share foreign exchange reserves to defend their

---

[22] See http://www.aseansec.org.

[23] Shisei Kaku, "Japan Walks the Path of Peace," *The Age*, September 6, 2005, p. 13.

currencies against future attack. Although they were only tentative, the members of ASEAN+3 also discussed creating a common market and even a single currency or, perhaps, a new Asian entity encompassing both Northeast and Southeast Asia. Closer links between Southeast Asia and Northeast Asia are seen as a step toward strengthening Asia's role in the global economy and creating a global three-bloc configuration.

Asia-Pacific Economic Cooperation

The other important grouping that encompasses the Asian-Pacific Rim is the Asia-Pacific Economic Cooperation.[24] Formed in 1989, APEC provides a formal structure for the major governments of the region, including the United States and Canada, to discuss their mutual interests in open trade and economic collaboration. APEC is a unique forum that has evolved into the primary regional vehicle for promoting trade liberalization and economic cooperation. APEC includes all the major economies of the region and the most dynamic, fastest growing economies in the world. APEC has as its common goals a commitment to open trade, to increase economic collaboration, to sustain regional growth and development, to strengthen the multilateral trading system, and to reduce barriers to investment and trade without detriment to other economies.

Representatives from APEC member nations meet annually to discuss issues confronting the group, to propose solutions to problems arising from the growing interdependence among their economies, and to continue their quest for ways to lower barriers to trade. Although APEC is still far from being a free trade area, each meeting seems to advance it another step in that direction, notwithstanding the objections of some members.

Africa

Africa's multinational market development activities can be characterized as a great deal of activity but little progress. All the countries on the continent (save Morocco) have joined a loosely defined African Union, and they are listed in Exhibit 10.9. Including bilateral agreements,[25] an estimated 200 other economic arrangements exist among African countries. Despite the large number and assortment of paper organizations, there has been little actual economic integration because of the political instability that has characterized Africa in recent decades and the unstable economic base on which Africa has had to build. The United Nations Economic Commission for Africa (ECA) has held numerous conferences but has been hampered by governmental inexperience, undeveloped resources, labor problems, and chronic product shortages.

Cell phone service is available even in African countries with per capita incomes among the lowest in the world.

The Economic Community of West African States (ECOWAS) and the Southern African Development Community (SADC) are the two most active regional cooperative groups. A 15-nation group, ECOWAS has an aggregate gross domestic product of more than $60 billion and is striving to achieve full economic integration. The 20th ECOWAS summit in 1997 approved a plan to accelerate subregional economic integration and development, with emphasis on a full commitment to regional monetary integration and the eventual adoption of a single West African currency. Unfortunately, ECOWAS continues to be plagued with financial problems, conflict within the group, and inactivity on the part of some members. After 30 years, the ECOWAS treaty and its many defined objectives and the way they are to be achieved over a 15-year period in three stages languishes; nothing has been achieved, and free trade remains a deferred dream.

The Southern African Development Community is the most advanced and viable of Africa's regional organizations. Its 14 members encompass a landmass of 6.6 million

---

[24] See http://www.apec.org.

[25] Isaya Muriwo Sithole, "Zimbabwe, SA in Perspective," *All Africa*, September 2, 2005, p. 16.

Exhibit 10.9
African Union Countries and Other Market Groups

Country	Population (millions)	GDP* (billions)	GDP* per Capita at PPP	Imports of Goods and Services* (billions)	Exports of Goods and Services* (billions)
Algeria	0.1	$ –	$ –	$ –	$ –
Angola[3]	16.4	17.1	2,314	–	–
Benin[2]	8.7	2.8	1,016	0.7	0.7
Botswana[3]	1.8	8.4	11,313	2.3	4.0
Burkina Faso[2]	13.6	3.6	1,143	–	–
Burundi[4]	7.8	0.8	622	–	–
Cameroon	16.7	12.5	2,079	3.3	2.6
Cape Verde[2]	0.5	0.7	5,381	0.4	0.2
Central African Republic	4.1	0.9	1,111	–	–
Comoros	0.6	0.2	1,744	0.1	–
Congo, DR[3]	59.3	5.5	649	2.8	1.4
Congo, R	4.1	4.2	1,159	–	–
Cote d'Ivoire[2]	18.5	10.6	1,471	5.4	5.7
Djibouti	0.8	0.7	1,982	0.3	0.2
Egypt	75.4	127.9	4,031	31.1	26.9
Equatorial Guinea	0.5	3.6	14,306	3.1	3.5
Eritrea	4.5	0.7	947	0.4	0.1
Ethiopia	72.7	11.3	1,030	4.0	1.9
Gabon	1.4	5.6	5,835	1.6	2.9
Gambia[2]	1.6	0.5	1,745	0.3	0.3
Ghana[2]	22.5	6.8	2,299	4.9	3.3
Guinea Bissau[2]	1.6	0.2	745	0.1	0.1
Guinea[2]	9.2	3.7	2,108	0.8	0.8
Kenya[4]	35.1	16.0	1,137	5.2	4.1
Lesotho[3]	1.8	1.0	3,105	1.0	0.4
Liberia[2]	3.4	0.5	–	–	–
Libya	6.0	42.7	–	–	–
Madagascar[3]	19.1	4.6	840	2.1	1.2
Malawi[3]	13.2	2.2	631	0.8	0.6

*Constant 2000 $s.

square kilometers containing abundant natural resources and a population of over 200 million. South Africa, the region's dominant economy, has a GDP of over $160 billion and accounts for 76.8 percent of SADC market share. After years of negotiations, 11 members of SADC approved a free trade agreement aimed at phasing out a minimum of 85 percent of tariffs within eight years and all tariffs by the end of 2012.

Middle East

The Middle East has been less aggressive in the formation of successfully functioning multinational market groups. The Arab Common Market has set goals for free internal trade but has not succeeded. The aim is to integrate the economies of the 22 Arab countries, but before that will be feasible, a long history of border disputes and persisting ideological differences will have to be overcome. The idea is still alive, however, and is a topic of discussion whenever Arab foreign ministers meet. The Arab Gulf states, Egypt, and Morocco have worked out an agreement on an Arab Free Trade Area, sometimes called the Greater Arab Free Trade Area (GAFTA). This 2005 agreement is still in its early stages of implementation, and its success is thus uncertain.

Iran, Pakistan, and Turkey, formerly the Regional Cooperation for Development (RCD), have renamed their regional group the Economic Cooperation Organization (ECO). Since reorganizing, Afghanistan and six of the newly independent states were

Country	Population (millions)	GDP* (billions)	GDP* per Capita at PPP	Imports of Goods and Services* (billions)	Exports of Goods and Services* (billions)
Mali[2]	13.9	3.5	942	1.3	1.1
Mauritania	3.2	1.5	2,161	1.6	0.5
Mauritius[3]	1.3	5.7	11,622	3.4	3.5
Morocco[1]	30.5	43.9	4,346	15.7	14.5
Mozambique[3]	20.1	6.2	1,162	2.1	2.0
Namibia[3]	2.1	4.5	7,038	2.0	2.1
Niger[2]	14.4	2.3	700	–	–
Nigeria[2]	144.7	63.5	1,008	30.8	29.7
Rwanda[4]	9.2	2.5	1,105	0.7	0.4
Sao Tome and Principe	0.2	–	–	–	–
Senegal[2]	11.9	5.6	1,599	2.5	1.6
Seychelles[3]	0.1	0.6	15,105	0.7	0.8
Sierra Leone[2]	5.6	1.3	753	–	–
Somalia	8.5	–	–	–	–
South Africa[3]	47.4	168.8	10,338	56.4	43.8
Sudan	37.0	18.9	2,050	2.5	2.8
Swaziland[3]	1.1	1.6	4,440	1.6	1.4
Tanzania[3,4]	39.5	13.2	650	2.8	2.9
Chad	10.0	2.8	1,341	1.1	1.7
Togo[2]	6.3	1.5	1,306	0.8	0.6
Tunisia	10.1	25.5	7,758	10.8	10.8
Uganda[4]	29.9	8.2	1,313	2.5	1.1
Western Sahara	0.4	—	—	—	—
Zambia[3]	11.9	4.3	949	1.9	1.4
Zimbabwe[3]	13.1	5.3	1,739	1.9	1.9

[1] Morocco withdrew from the predecessor of the African Union in 1984.

[2] Member of Economic Community of West African States (ECOWAS).

[3] Member of Southern African Development Community (SADC).

[4] Member of East African Community.

Source: World Bank, 2008. Copyright © 2008 by World Bank. Reproduced with permission of World Bank via Copyright Clearance Center.

accepted into the ECO. Impressive strides in developing basic industrial production were being made when the RCD was first organized, but the revolution in Iran ended any economic activity. ECO has as its primary goal the development of its infrastructure to pave the way for regional cooperation. Unfortunately, trade volume among ECO members constitutes only 7 percent of their total trade. However, a recent announcement from ECO indicated that there has been an agreement to reduce tariff and nontariff barriers to boost trade.

The other activity in the region, led by Iran, is the creation of the Organization of the Islamic Conference (OIC), a common market composed of Islamic countries. A preferential tariff system among the member states of the OIC and the expansion of commercial services in insurance, transport, and transit shipping are among the issues to be debated at the next conference of Islamic countries. The OIC represents 60 countries and over 650 million Muslims worldwide. The member countries' vast natural resources, substantial capital, and cheap labor force are seen as the strengths of the OIC.

Implications of Market Integration

The degree of differences across regions in economic integration is manifest. The European Union continues to be the global pacesetter, and therefore serves as the best model for understanding and predicting the processes of change in the other regions described above. We can expect lessons learned there to be useful for international marketers contemplating entry and operations in the other regions in earlier stages of integration.

Strategic Implications

The complexion of the entire world marketplace has been changed significantly by the coalition of nations into multinational market groups. To international business firms, multinational groups spell opportunity in bold letters through access to greatly enlarged markets with reduced or abolished country-by-country tariff barriers and restrictions. Production, financing, labor, and marketing decisions are affected by the remapping of the world into market groups.

World competition will continue to intensify as businesses become stronger and more experienced in dealing with large market groups. For example, in an integrated Europe, U.S. multinationals had an initial advantage over expanded European firms because U.S. businesses were more experienced in marketing to large, diverse markets and are accustomed to looking at Europe as one market. These U.S. firms did not carry the cumbersome baggage of multiple national organizations dealing in many currencies, with differentiated pricing and administration, with which most EU firms had to contend. The advantage, however, was only temporary as mergers, acquisitions, and joint ventures consolidated operations of European firms in anticipation of the benefits of a single European market. Individual national markets still confront international managers with the same problems of language, customs, and instability, even though they are packaged under the umbrella of a common market. However, as barriers come down and multicountry markets are treated as one common market, a global market will be one notch closer to reality.

Regulation of business activities has been intensified throughout multinational market groups; each group now has management and administrative bodies specifically concerned with business. In the process of structuring markets, rules and regulations common to the group are often more sophisticated than those of the individual countries.[26] Despite the problems and complexities of dealing with the new markets, the overriding message to the astute international marketer continues to be opportunity and profit potential.

Opportunities.

Economic integration creates large mass markets. Many national markets, too small to bother with individually, take on new dimensions and significance when combined with markets from cooperating countries. Large markets are particularly important to businesses accustomed to mass production and mass distribution because of the economies of scale and marketing efficiencies that can be achieved. In highly competitive markets, the benefits derived from enhanced efficiencies are often passed along as lower prices that lead to increased purchasing power.

Most multinational groups have coordinated programs to foster economic growth as part of their cooperative efforts. Such programs work to the advantage of marketers by increasing purchasing power, improving regional infrastructure, and fostering economic development. Despite the problems that are sure to occur because of integration, the economic benefits from free trade can be enormous.

Major savings will result from the billions of dollars now spent in developing different versions of products to meet a hodgepodge of national standards.[27] Philips and other European companies invested a total of $20 billion to develop a common switching system for Europe's several different telephone networks. This figure compares with the $3 billion spent in the United States for a common system and $1.5 billion in Japan for a single system.

---

[26] Kevin J. O'Brien, "EU Considers a Telecommunications 'Superregulator,'" *International Herald Tribune*, August 13, 2007, p. 10.

[27] John W. Miller, "EU Food-Safety Agency Backs Products from Cloned Animals," *The Wall Street Journal* (online), January 12, 2008.

Market Barriers.   The initial aim of a multinational market is to protect businesses that operate within its borders. An expressed goal is to give an advantage to the companies within the market in their dealings with other countries of the market group. Analysis of the interregional and international trade patterns of the market groups indicates that such goals have been achieved.

Companies willing to invest in production facilities in multinational markets may benefit from protectionist measures because these companies become a part of the market. Exporters, however, are in a considerably weaker position. This prospect confronts many U.S. exporters who face the possible need to invest in Europe to protect their export markets in the European Union. The major problem for small companies may be adjusting to the EU standards. A company selling in one or two EU member countries and meeting standards there may find itself in a situation of having to change standards or be closed out when an EU-wide standard is adopted.

A manufacturer of the hoses used to hook up deep-fat fryers and other gas appliances to gas outlets faced such a problem when one of its largest customers informed the company that McDonald's was told it could no longer use that manufacturer's hoses in its British restaurants. The same thing happened at EuroDisney. Unfortunately, when the common standards were written, only large MNCs and European firms participated, so they had the advantage of setting standards to their benefit. The small company had only one choice: Change or leave. In this particular case, it appears that competitors were working to keep the company out of the market. There are, however, enough questions about threaded fittings and compatibility that the company worked with individual countries to gain entrance to their markets—just as it had before a single market existed.

Marketing Mix Implications   Companies are adjusting their marketing mix strategies to reflect anticipated market changes in the single European market. In the past, companies often charged different prices in different European markets. Nontariff barriers between member states supported price differentials and kept lower-priced products from entering those markets where higher prices were charged. For example, Colgate-Palmolive Company adapted its Colgate toothpaste into a single formula for sale across Europe at one price. Before changing its pricing practices, Colgate sold its toothpaste at different prices in different markets.

Beddedas Shower Gel is priced in the middle of the market in Germany and as a high-priced product in the United Kingdom. As long as products from lower-priced markets could not move to higher-priced markets, such differential price schemes worked. Now, however, under the EU rules, companies cannot prevent the free movement of goods, and parallel imports from lower-priced markets to higher-priced markets are more likely to occur. Price standardization among country markets will be one of the necessary changes to avoid the problem of parallel imports. With the adoption of the euro, price differentials are much easier to spot, and the consumer can search for the best bargains in brand-name products more easily. Furthermore, the euro is making marketing on the Internet a much simpler task for European firms. On balance, a single currency will make competition in Europe a lot fairer and also a lot tougher.

In addition to initiating uniform pricing policies, companies are reducing the number of brands they produce to focus advertising and promotion efforts. For example, Nestlé's several brands of yogurt in the EU were reduced to a single brand. Unilever winnowed its 1,600 brands down to focus on 400 core brands. It plans to develop master brands in certain markets such as the EU and to market others globally. A major benefit from an integrated Europe is competition at the retail level. Europe lacks an integrated and competitive distribution system that would support small and midsized outlets. The elimination of borders could result in increased competition among retailers and the creation of Europewide distribution channels.

Finally, all international marketers should see market integration around the world in a positive light. Trade among close neighbors will always be important—distance does make a difference. But, overall local integration ultimately serves globalization and harmonization of the world trading system, thus reducing the costs of business and delivering greater choice to consumers and greater opportunities to marketers.

Summary

The experiences of the multinational market groups developed since World War II point up both the successes and the hazards such groups encounter. The various attempts at economic cooperation represent varying degrees of success and failure, but almost without regard to their degree of success, the economic market groups have created great excitement among marketers. In the near future, these regional groupings will continue to form trade agreement ties with other nations and regions, thus paving the way for truly globalized markets where consumers dominate.

For companies the economic benefits possible through cooperation relate to more efficient marketing and production. Marketing efficiency is effected through the development of mass markets, encouragement of competition, improvement of personal income, and various psychological market factors. Production efficiency derives from specialization, mass production for mass markets, and the free movement of the factors of production. Economic integration also tends to foster political harmony among the countries involved; such harmony leads to stability and peace, which are beneficial to the marketer as well as the countries' citizens.

The marketing implications of multinational market groups may be studied from the viewpoint of firms located inside the market or of firms located outside, which wish to sell to the markets. For each viewpoint the problems and opportunities are somewhat different; regardless of the location of the marketer, however, multinational market groups provide great opportunity for the creative marketer who wishes to expand volume. Market groupings make it economically feasible to enter new markets and to employ new marketing strategies that could not be applied to the smaller markets represented by individual countries. At the same time, market groupings intensify competition by protectionism within a market group but may foster greater protectionism between regional markets. Mercosur and ASEAN+3, for example, suggest the growing importance of economic cooperation and integration. Such developments will continue to confront the international marketer by providing continually growing market opportunities and challenges.

Questions

1. Define the following terms:

multinational market region	customs union
EMU	common market
Single European Act	political union
NAFTA	Maastricht Treaty
Mercosur	Treaty of Amsterdam
APEC	ASEAN+3
free trade area	

2. Elaborate on the problems and benefits that multinational market groups represent for international marketers.

3. Explain the political role of multinational market groups.

4. Identify the factors on which one may judge the potential success or failure of a multinational market group.

5. Explain the marketing implications of the factors contributing to the successful development of a multinational market group.

6. Imagine that the United States was composed of many separate countries with individual trade barriers. What marketing effects might be visualized?

7. Discuss the possible types of arrangements for regional economic integration.

8. Differentiate between a free trade area and a common market. Explain the marketing implications of the differences.

9. It seems obvious that the founders of the European Union intended it to be a truly common market, so much so that economic integration must be supplemented by political integration to accomplish these objectives. Discuss.

10. The European Commission, the Council of Ministers, and the Court of Justice of the European Union have gained power in the last decade. Comment.

11. Select any three countries that might have some logical basis for establishing a multinational market organization and illustrate their compatibility as a regional trade group. Identify the various problems that would be encountered in forming multinational market groups of such countries.

12. U.S. exports to the European Union are expected to decline in future years. What marketing actions might a company take to counteract such changes?

13. "Because they are dynamic and because they have great growth possibilities, the multinational markets are likely to be especially rough-and-tumble for the external business." Discuss.

14. Differentiate between a customs union and a political union.

15. Why have African nations had such difficulty in forming effective economic unions?

16. Discuss the implications of the European Union's decision to admit eastern European nations to the group.

17. Discuss the consequences to the United States of not being a part of SAFTA.

18. Discuss the strategic marketing implications of NAFTA.

19. How is the concept of reciprocity linked to protectionism?

20. Visit the Web pages for NAFTA and Mercosur and locate each group's rules of origin. Which group has the most liberal rules of origin? Why is there a difference?

21. Using the factors that serve as the basis for success of an economic union (political, economic, social, and geographic), evaluate the potential success of the EU, NAFTA, and Mercosur.

22. For each regional trade group—EU, NAFTA, ASEAN+3, and Mercosur—cite which of the factors for success are the strongest and which are the weakest. Discuss each factor.

23. What is the motive behind ASEAN+3, and what are the probable implications for global trade?

24. NAFTA has been in existence for several years—how has it done? Review Exhibit 10.6, which discusses the initial provisions of the agreement, and, using the Internet, evaluate how well the provisions have been met.

11

global marketing management:

PLANNING AND ORGANIZATION

CHAPTER LEARNING OBJECTIVES

What you should learn from Chapter 11:

- How global marketing management differs from international marketing management

- The increasing importance of international strategic alliances

- The need for planning to achieve company goals

- The important factors for each alternative market-entry strategy

Global Perspective

GLOBAL GATEWAYS

With their domestic market crowded with competitors, Yahoo!, Lycos, America Online (AOL), and others are rushing to establish their brands in Europe, Asia, and Latin America before local competitors can create dominant franchises of their own.

Recently, Lycos Europe, a joint venture between Lycos Inc. and Germany's Bertelsmann AG, had its initial public offering on Germany's Neuer Markt. Many more such offerings are expected, because U.S. Web executives and investors believe that the Internet will continue to grow faster abroad than at home. The U.S. share of Internet users fell from 42 percent in 1997 to 15 percent in 2008.

The battle has been hottest in Europe among the portals that serve as starting points for Web surfers looking for news, shopping, and search services. Yahoo! and Lycos each operates about two dozen foreign portals, most with native-language news, shopping links, and other content custom tailored to the local population. Lycos's German site features tips on brewing beer at home and a program for calculating auto speeding fines. Yahoo!'s Singapore site offers real-time information on haze and smog in Southeast Asia. AOL has about a dozen international ventures, and Excite, the portal arm of At Home Corporation, has nine international partners.

The top U.S. players face tough homegrown competitors, who often have a better sense of local culture and Internet styles. In many countries, the dominant telephone companies offer portals, giving them a big leg up because customers are automatically sent to their home pages when they log on. Germany's leading portal, T-Online, is run by Deutsche Telekom. In France, No. 1 Wanadoo is operated by France Telecom.

The U.S. portals risk being viewed as digital colonists trying to flex their muscles around the world, according to industry analysts. Many advise that American companies hoping to set up shop abroad are better served by forming partnerships with local outfits that understand the culture.

Sources: Jon G. Auerbach, Bernard Wysocki Jr., and Neal E. Boudette, "For U.S. Internet Portals, the Next Big Battleground Is Overseas," *The Wall Street Journal,* March 23, 2000, p. B1; Daekwan Kim, "The Internationalization of U.S. Portals: Does It Fit the Model of Internationalization?" *Marketing Intelligence & Planning* 21, no. 1 (2003), pp. 23–36; Euromonitor 2008.

Confronted with increasing global competition for expanding markets, multinational companies are changing their marketing strategies and altering their organizational structures. Their goals are to enhance their competitiveness and to ensure proper positioning to capitalize on opportunities in the global marketplace. Comprehensive decisions must be made regarding key strategic choices, such as standardization versus adaptation, concentration versus dispersion, and integration versus independence.[1] Particularly as national borders become less meaningful, we see the rise of greater international corporate collaboration networks yielding new thinking about traditional concepts of competition and organization.[2]

A recent study of North American and European corporations indicated that nearly 75 percent of the companies are revamping their business processes, that most have formalized strategic planning programs, and that the need to stay cost competitive was considered the most important external issue affecting their marketing strategies. Change is not limited to the giant multinationals but includes midsized and small firms as well.

In fact, the flexibility of a smaller company may enable it to reflect the demands of global markets and redefine its programs more quickly than larger multinationals. Acquiring a global perspective is easy, but the execution requires planning, organization, and a willingness to try new approaches—from engaging in collaborative relationships to redefining the scope of company operations.

This chapter discusses global marketing management, competition in the global marketplace, strategic planning, and alternative market-entry strategies. It also identifies the elements that contribute to an effective international or global organization.

Global Marketing Management

In the 1970s, the market segmentation argument was framed as "standardization versus adaptation." In the 1980s, it was "globalization versus localization," and in the 1990s, it was "global integration versus local responsiveness." The fundamental question was whether the global homogenization of consumer tastes allowed global standardization of the marketing mix. The Internet revolution of the 1990s with its unprecedented global reach added a new twist to the old debate.

Even today, some companies are answering "global" as the way to go. For example, executives at Twix Cookie Bars tried out their first global campaign with a new global advertising agency, Grey Worldwide. With analysis, perhaps a global campaign does make sense for Twix. But look at the companies that are going in the other direction. Levi's jeans have faded globally in recent years. Ford has chosen to keep acquired nameplates such as Mazda, and Volvo. And perhaps the most global company of all, Coca-Cola, is peddling two brands in India—Coke and Thums Up. Coke's CEO explained at the time, "Coke has had to come to terms with a conflicting reality. In many parts of the world, consumers have become pickier, more penny-wise, or a little more nationalistic, and they are spending more of their money on local drinks whose flavors are not part of the Coca-Cola lineup."[3]

Part of this trend back toward localization is caused by the new efficiencies of customization made possible by the Internet and increasingly flexible manufacturing processes. Indeed, a good example of the new "mass customization" is Dell Computer Corporation, which maintains no inventory and builds each computer to order. Also crucial has been the apparent rejection of the logic of globalism by trade unionists, environmentalists, and consumers so well demonstrated in Seattle during the World

[1] Lewis K. S. Lim, Frank Acito, and Alexander Rusetski, "Development of Archetypes of International Marketing Strategy," *Journal of International Business Studies* 37 (2006), pp. 499–524.

[2] B. Elango and Chinmay Pattnaik, "Building Capabilities for International Operations through Networks: A Study of Indian Firms," *Journal of International Business Studies* 38 (2007), pp. 541–55; Victor K. Fung, William K. Fung, and Yoram (Jerry) Wind, *Competing in a Flat World* (Upper Saddle River, NJ: Wharton School Publishing, 2008).

[3] Rance Crain, "Agencies Press Get-Global Plans but Clients Face Local Realities," *Advertising Age*, February 14, 2000, p. 32.

The competition among soft drink bottlers in India is fierce. Here Coke and Pepsi combine to ruin the view of the Taj Mahal. Notice how the red of Coke stands out among its competitors in the picture. Of course, now Coca-Cola has purchased Thums Up, a prominent local brand—this is a strategy the company is applying around the world. But the red is a substantial competitive advantage both on store shelves and in outdoor advertising of the sort common in India and other developing countries. We're not sure who borrowed the "monsoon/thunder" slogans from whom.

Trade Organization meetings in 2000. Although there is a growing body of empirical research illustrating the risks and difficulties of global standardization,[4] contrary results also appear in the literature. Finally, prominent among firms' standardization strategies is Mattel's recently unsuccessful globalization of blonde Barbie. We correctly predicted in a previous edition of this book that a better approach was that of Disney, with its more culturally diverse line of "Disney Princesses" including Mulan (Chinese) and Jasmine (Arabic). Even though Bratz and Disney Princesses won this battle of the new "toy soldiers," the question is still not completely settled.[5]

Indeed, the debate about standardization versus adaptation is itself a wonderful example of the ethnocentrism of American managers and academics alike. That is, from the Euro-

---

[4] Carl Arthur Solberg, "The Perennial Issue of Adaptation or Standardization of International Marketing Communication: Organizational Contingencies and Performance," *Journal of International Marketing* 10, no. 3 (2002), pp. 1–21; Marios Theodosiou and Leonidas C. Leonidou, "Standardization versus Adaptation of International Marketing Strategy: An Integrative Assessment of the Empirical Research," *International Business Review* 12 (2003), pp. 141–71; Joan Enric Ricart, Michael J. Enright, Panjak Ghemawat, Stuart L. Hart, and Tarun Khanna, "New Frontiers in International Strategy," *Journal of International Business Studies* 35, no. 3 (2004), pp. 175–200.

[5] Erika Kinetz, "Putting Away Childish Things," *International Herald Tribune*, April 2–3, 2005, p. 16.

Items in the Disney Princess collection are on display at the Licensing International show at New York's Javits Convention Center. It will be interesting to see Barbie's (Mattel's) competitive response to the ethnic breadth of the Disney line. *(AP Photo/Richard Drew)*

pean or even the Japanese perspective, markets are by definition international, and the special requirements of the huge American market must be considered from the beginning. Only in America can international market requirements be an afterthought.

Moreover, as the information explosion allows marketers to segment markets ever more finely, it is only the manufacturing and/or finance managers in companies who argue for standardization for the sake of economies of scale. From the marketing perspective, customization is always best.[6] The ideal market segment size, if customer satisfaction is the goal, is *one.* According to one expert, "Forward-looking, proactive firms have the ability and willingness . . . to accomplish both tasks [standardization and localization] simultaneously."[7]

We believe things are actually simpler than that. As global markets continue to homogenize and diversify simultaneously, the best companies will avoid the trap of focusing on *country* as the primary segmentation variable. Other segmentation variables are often more important—for example, climate, language group, media habits, age,[8] or income. The makers of Twix apparently think that media habits (that is, MTV viewership) supersede country, according to their latest segmentation scheme. At least one industry CEO concurred regarding media-based segmentation: "With media splintering into smaller and smaller communities of interest, it will become more and more important to reach those audiences wherever [whichever country] they may be. Today, media companies are increasingly delivering their content over a variety of platforms: broadcast—both TV and radio—and cable, online and print, big screen video, and the newest portable digital media. And advertisers are using the same variety of platforms to reach their desired audience." Finally, perhaps a few famous Italian brands are the best examples: Salvatore Ferragamo shoes, Gucci leather goods, and Ferrari cars sell to

[6] Peggy A. Cloninger and Ziad Swaidan, "Standardization, Customization and Revenue from Foreign Markets," *Journal of Global Marketing* 20 (2007), pp. 57–70.

[7] Masaaki Kotabe, "Contemporary Research Trends in International Marketing: The 1960s," Chapter 17 in *Oxford Handbook of International Business*, 2nd edition, Alan Rugman and Thomas L. Brewer (eds.) (Oxford: Oxford University Press, 2008). Also consistent are the findings of Shouming Zou and S. Tamer Cavusgil, "The GMS: A Broad Conceptualization of Global Marketing Strategy and Its Effect on Firm Performance," *Journal of Marketing* 66, no. 4 (October 2002), pp. 40–57.

[8] Dannie Kjeldgaard and Soren Askegaard, "The Glocalization of Youth Culture: The Global Youth Segment as Structures of Common Difference," *Journal of Consumer Research* 33 (2006), pp. 21–27.

the highest-income segments globally. Indeed, for all three companies, their U.S. sales are greater than their Italian sales.

In the 21st century, standardization versus adaptation is simply not the right question to ask.[9] Rather, the crucial question facing international marketers is what are the most efficient ways to segment markets.[10] Country has been the most obvious segmentation variable, particularly for Americans. But as better communication systems continue to dissolve national borders, other dimensions of global markets are growing in salience.

The Nestlé Way: Evolution Not Revolution

Nestlé certainly hasn't been bothered by the debate on standardization versus adaptation. Nestlé has been international almost from its start in 1866 as a maker of infant formula. By 1920, the company was producing in Brazil, Australia, and the United States and exporting to Hong Kong. Today, it sells more than 8,500 products produced in 489 factories in 193 countries. Nestlé is the world's biggest marketer of infant formula, powdered milk, instant coffee, chocolate, soups, and mineral water. It ranks second in ice cream, and in cereals, it ties Ralston Purina and trails only Kellogg Company. Its products are sold in the most upscale supermarkets in Beverly Hills, California, and in huts in Nigeria, where women sell Nestlé bouillon cubes alongside homegrown tomatoes and onions. Although the company has no sales agents in North Korea, its products somehow find their way into stores there, too.

The "Nestlé way" is to dominate its markets. Its overall strategy can be summarized in four points: (1) Think and plan long term, (2) decentralize, (3) stick to what you know, and (4) adapt to local tastes. To see how Nestlé operates, take a look at its approach to Poland, one of the largest markets of the former Soviet bloc. Company executives decided at the outset that it would take too long to build plants and create brand awareness. Instead, the company pursued acquisitions and followed a strategy of "evolution not revolution." It purchased Goplana, Poland's second-best-selling chocolate maker (it bid for the No. 1 company but lost out) and carefully adjusted the end product via small changes every two months over a two-year period until it measured up to Nestlé's standards and was a recognizable Nestlé brand. These efforts, along with all-out marketing, put the company within striking distance of the market leader, Wedel. Nestlé also purchased a milk operation and, as it did in Mexico, India, and elsewhere, sent technicians into the field to help Polish farmers improve the quality and quantity of the milk it buys through better feeds and improved sanitation.

Nestlé's efforts in the Middle East are much longer term. The area currently represents only about 2 percent of the company's worldwide sales, and the markets, individually, are relatively small. Furthermore, regional conflicts preclude most trade among the countries. Nevertheless, Nestlé anticipates that hostility will someday subside, and when that happens, the company will be ready to sell throughout the entire region. Nestlé has set up a network of factories in five countries that can someday supply the entire region with different products. The company makes ice cream in Dubai and soups and cereals in Saudi Arabia. The Egyptian factory makes yogurt and bouillon, while Turkey produces chocolate. And a factory in Syria makes ketchup, a malted-chocolate energy food, instant noodles, and other products. If the obstacles between the countries come down, Nestlé will have a network of plants ready to provide a complete line to market in all the countries. In the meantime, factories produce and sell mostly in the countries in which they are located.

For many companies, such a long-term strategy would not be profitable, but it works for Nestlé because the company relies on local ingredients and markets products that consumers can afford. The tomatoes and wheat used in the Syrian factory, for example, are major local agricultural products. Even if Syrian restrictions on trade remain, there

---

[9] Panjak Ghemawat, "Semiglobalization and International Business Strategy," *Journal of International Business Studies* 34 (2003), pp. 138–52.

[10] Amanda J. Broderick, Gordon E. Greenley, and Rene Dentiste Mueller, "The Behavioral Homogeneity Evaluation Framework: Multi-Level Evaluations of Consumer Involvement in International Segmentation," *Journal of International Business Studies* 38 (2007), pp. 746–63.

are 14 million people to buy ketchup, noodles, and other products the company produces there. In all five countries, the Nestlé name and the bird-in-a-nest trademark appear on every product.

Nestlé bills itself as "the only company that is truly dedicated to providing a complete range of food products to meet the needs and tastes of people from around the world, each hour of their day, throughout their entire lives."

Benefits of Global Marketing

Few firms have truly global operations balanced across major regional markets.[11] However, when large market segments can be identified, economies of scale in production and marketing can be important competitive advantages for multinational companies. As a case in point, Black & Decker Manufacturing Company—makers of electrical hand tools, appliances, and other consumer products—realized significant production cost savings when it adopted a pan-European strategy. It was able to reduce not only the number of motor sizes for the European market from 260 to 8 but also 15 different models to 8. Similarly, Ford estimates that by unifying product development, purchasing, and supply activities across several countries, it saved up to $3 billion a year. Finally, while Japanese firms initially dominated the mobile phone business in their home market, international competitors now pose growing challenges via better technologies developed through greater global penetration.

Transfer of experience and know-how across countries through improved coordination and integration of marketing activities is also cited as a benefit of global operations. Global diversity in marketing talent leads to new approaches across markets.[12] Unilever successfully introduced two global brands originally developed by two subsidiaries. Its South African subsidiary developed Impulse body spray, and a European branch developed a detergent that cleaned effectively in European hard water. Aluminum Company of America's (Alcoa) joint-venture partner in Japan produced aluminum sheets so perfect that U.S. workers, when shown samples, accused the company of hand-selecting the samples. Line workers were sent to the Japanese plant to learn the techniques, which were then transferred to the U.S. operations. Because of the benefits of such transfers of knowledge, Alcoa has changed its practice of sending managers overseas to "keep an eye on things" to sending line workers and managers to foreign locations to seek out new techniques and processes.

Marketing globally also ensures that marketers have access to the toughest customers. For example, in many product and service categories, the Japanese consumer has been the hardest to please; the demanding customers are the reason that the highest-quality products and services often emanate from that country. Competing for Japanese customers provides firms with the best testing ground for high-quality products and services.

Diversity of markets served carries with it additional financial benefits.[13] Spreading the portfolio of markets served brings an important stability of revenues and operations to many global companies.[14] Companies with global marketing operations suffered less during the Asian market downturn of the late 1990s than did firms specializing in the area. Firms that market globally are able to take advantage of changing financial

---

[11] Alan M. Rugman and Alaine Verbeke, "A Perspective on Regional and Global Strategies of Multinational Enterprises," *Journal of International Business Studies* 35, no. 1 (2004), pp. 3–18.

[12] Janet Y. Murray and Mike C. H. Chao, "A Cross-Team Framework on International Knowledge Acquisition on New Product Development Capabilities and New Product Market Performance," *Journal of International Marketing* 13 (2005), pp. 54–78.

[13] N. Capar and M. Kotabe have noted that for services firms, the relationship between international diversification and firm performance can be curvilinear (that is, both not enough and too much are bad); see "The Relationship between International Diversification and Performance in Service Firms," *Journal of International Business Studies* 34, no. 4 (2003), pp. 345–55.

[14] Lee Li, Gongming Qian, and Zhengming Qian, "Product Diversification, Multinationality, and Country Involvement: What Is the Optimal Combination?" *Journal of Global Marketing* 20 (2007), pp. 5–25.

CROSSING BORDERS 11.1   Swedish Takeout

Fifty years ago in the woods of southern Sweden, a minor revolution took place that has since changed the concept of retailing and created a mass market in a category where none previously existed. The catalyst of the change was and is IKEA, the Swedish furniture retailer and distributor that virtually invented the idea of self-service, takeout furniture. IKEA sells high-quality, reasonably priced, and innovatively designed furniture and home furnishings for a global marketplace.

The name was registered in Agunnaryd, Sweden, in 1943 by Ingvar Kamprad—the IK in the company's name. He entered the furniture market in 1950, and the first catalog was published in 1951. The first store didn't open until 1958 in Almhult. It became so incredibly popular that a year later the store had to add a restaurant for people who were traveling long distances to get there.

IKEA entered the United States in 1985. Although IKEA is global, most of the action takes place in Europe, with about 85 percent of the firm's $7 billion in sales. Nearly one-fourth of that comes from stores in Germany. This compares to only about $1 billion in NAFTA countries.

One reason for the relatively slow growth in the United States is that its stores are franchised by Netherlands-based Inter IKEA Systems, which carefully scrutinizes potential franchisees—individuals or companies—for strong financial backing and a proven record in retailing. The IKEA Group, based in Denmark, is a group of private companies owned by a charitable foundation in the Netherlands; they operate more than 100 stores. The Group also develops, purchases, distributes, and sells IKEA products, which are available only in company stores. The items are purchased from more than 2,400 suppliers in 65 countries and shipped through 14 distribution centers.

Low price is built into the company's lines. Even catalog prices are guaranteed not to increase for one year. The drive to produce affordable products inadvertently put IKEA at the forefront of the environmental movement several decades ago. In addition to lowering costs, minimization of materials and packing addressed natural resource issues. Environmentalism remains an integral operational issue at IKEA. Even the company's catalog is completely recyclable and produced digitally rather than on film.

On the day that Russia's first IKEA store opened in 2000, the wait to get in was an hour. Highway traffic backed up for miles. More than 40,000 people crammed into the place, picking clean sections of the warehouse. The store still pulls in more than 100,000 customers per week. IKEA has big plans for Russia. Company officials dream of placing IKEA's simple shelves, kitchens, bathrooms, and bedrooms in millions of Russian apartments that haven't been remodeled since the Soviet days. And now IKEA has opened five new stores in China's biggest cities.

Sources: Colin McMahon, "Russians Flock to IKEA as Store Battles Moscow," *Chicago Tribune,* May 17, 2000; Katarina Kling and Ingela Goteman, "IKEA CEO Anders Dahlvig on International Growth and IKEA's Unique Corporate Culture and Brand Identity," *Academy of Management Executive,* February 2003, pp. 31–37; "IKEA to March into China's Second-tier Cities [Next]," *SinoCast China Business Daily News,* August 6, 2007, p. 1.

circumstances in other ways as well. For example, as tax and tariff rates ebb and flow around the world, the most global companies are able to leverage the associated complexity to their advantage.

Planning for Global Markets

Planning is a systematized way of relating to the future. It is an attempt to manage the effects of external, uncontrollable factors on the firm's strengths, weaknesses, objectives, and goals to attain a desired end. Furthermore, it is a commitment of resources to a country market to achieve specific goals. In other words, planning is the job of making things happen that might not otherwise occur.

Planning allows for rapid growth of the international function, changing markets, increasing competition, and the turbulent challenges of different national markets. The plan must blend the changing parameters of external country environments with corporate objectives and capabilities to develop a sound, workable marketing program. A strategic plan commits corporate resources to products and markets to increase competitiveness and profits.

CROSSING BORDERS 11.2   Apple Shops for Partners around the World

Apple has moved fast since its introduction of the iPhone, making distribution deals with U.S. and European operators. Now Steve Jobs is turning east, making plans to enter Japan, one of the biggest and most sophisticated mobile phone markets in the world.

People familiar with the situation say Jobs recently met with NTT DoCoMo Inc.'s president, Masao Nakamura, to discuss a deal to offer the iPhone in Japan through the nation's dominant mobile operator. These informants said Apple also has been talking to the No. 3 operator, Softbank Corp., and that executives from both companies have made multiple trips to Apple's Cupertino, California, headquarters. For Apple, finding a wireless partner soon in Japan is an important step in the company's oft-stated goal of gaining a 1 percent share of the global cell phone business by shipping about 10 million iPhones between the product's launch in late June 2007 and the end of 2008.

The world's second-largest economy, after the United States, is an attractive market because it not only has a strong base of iPod fans, but its nearly 100 million mobile phone users buy new phones every two years on average. Japanese consumers also are accustomed to shelling out hundreds of dollars for expensive phones with advanced capabilities, such as digital television, cameras, and music.

Yet Japan could be a difficult market to crack for Apple. More than 10 domestic mobile phone makers work closely with the three major operators to develop phones tailored to Japanese consumers' tastes. In the past, foreign mobile phone makers have not been willing to go to such lengths and generally have met with little success in selling their phones, especially when those phones do not contain essential Japanese features, such as the operators' proprietary mobile Internet technology or e-mail software that Japanese consumers are used to having.

The iPhone has been successful thus far in countries where it has been launched. Apple sold a total of 1.4 million iPhones by late September 2007. And though sales of the product did not quite meet some of the most bullish Wall Street forecasts, the iPhone has been one of the top-selling smart phones in the United States, where it is sold only through AT&T Inc., the nation's largest carrier by subscribers.

In Japan, Softbank has been widely believed to be interested in a partnership with Apple, but people familiar with the matter say DoCoMo is likely to be Apple's first choice because of the strong preference it has shown so far for signing agreements with top mobile operators.

Sources: John Markoff, "A Personal Computer to Carry in a Pocket," *The New York Times,* January 8, 2007, pp. C1, C3; Yukari Iwatani and Nick Wingfield, "Apple Meets with DoCoMo, Softbank on Launching iPhone in Japan," *The Wall Street Journal* (online), December 18, 2007.

Planning relates to the formulation of goals and methods of accomplishing them, so it is both a process and a philosophy. Structurally, planning may be viewed as corporate, strategic, or tactical. International *corporate planning* is essentially long term, incorporating generalized goals for the enterprise as a whole. *Strategic planning* is conducted at the highest levels of management and deals with products, capital, research, and the long- and short-term goals of the company. *Tactical planning,* or market planning, pertains to specific actions and to the allocation of resources used to implement strategic planning goals in specific markets. Tactical plans are made at the local level and address marketing and advertising questions.

A major advantage to a multinational corporation (MNC) involved in planning is the discipline imposed by the process. An international marketer who has gone through the planning process has a framework for analyzing marketing problems and opportunities and a basis for coordinating information from different country markets. The process of planning may be as important as the plan itself because it forces decision makers to examine all factors that affect the success of a marketing program and involves those who will be responsible for its implementation. Another key to successful planning is evaluating company objectives, including management's commitment and philosophical orientation to international business. Finally, the planning process is a primary medium of organizational learning.

Company Objectives and Resources

Defining objectives clarifies the orientation of the domestic and international divisions, permitting consistent policies. The lack of well-defined objectives has found companies rushing into promising foreign markets only to find activities that conflict with or detract from the companies' primary objectives.[15]

Foreign market opportunities do not always parallel corporate objectives; it may be necessary to change the objectives, alter the scale of international plans, or abandon them. One market may offer immediate profit but have a poor long-run outlook, while another may offer the reverse.[16] Only when corporate objectives are clear can such differences be reconciled effectively.

International Commitment

The planning approach taken by an international firm affects the degree of internationalization to which management is philosophically committed.[17] Such commitment affects the specific international strategies and decisions of the firm. After company objectives have been identified, management needs to determine whether it is prepared to make the level of commitment required for successful international operations—commitment in terms of dollars to be invested, personnel for managing the international organization, and determination to stay in the market long enough to realize a return on these investments.[18]

The degree of commitment to an international marketing cause reflects the extent of a company's involvement. A company uncertain of its prospects is likely to enter a market timidly, using inefficient marketing methods, channels, or organizational forms, thus setting the stage for the failure of a venture that might have succeeded with full commitment and support by the parent company. Any long-term marketing plan should be fully supported by senior management and have realistic time goals set for sales growth. Occasionally, casual market entry is successful, but more often than not, market success requires long-term commitment.[19]

Finally, a new series of studies is demonstrating a strong regional preference for multinational companies as they expand their operations.[20] Part of this preference is due to the challenges associated with cultural distance[21] and part with physical distance, particularly that related to the difficulties of doing business across time zones.[22] As we mentioned previously, most countries and companies trade most with their neighbors. Others report that firms also gain competitive advantages from clustering operations in specific

---

[15] Peter J. Buckley and Niron Hashai, "A Global System View of Firm Boundaries," *Journal of International Business Studies* 35, no. 1 (2004), pp. 33–45.

[16] Farok J. Contractor, Sumit K. Kundu, and Chin-Chun Hsu, "A Three-Stage Theory of International Expansion: The Link between Multinationality and Performance in the Service Sector," *Journal of International Business Studies* 34, no. 1 (2003), pp. 5–18.

[17] Orly Levy, Schon Beechler, Sully Taylor, and Nakiey A. Boyacigiller, "What We Talk about When We Talk about 'Global Mindset': Managerial Cognition in Multinational Corporations," *Journal of International Business Studies* 38 (2007), pp. 231–58.

[18] Thomas Hutzschenreuter, Torben Pedersen, and Henk W. Voldberda, "The Role of Path Dependency and Managerial Intentionality: A Perspective on International Business Research," *Journal of International Business Studies* 38 (2007), pp. 1055–68.

[19] Luis Felipe Lages, Sandy D. Jap, and David A. Griffith, "The Role of Past Performance in Export Ventures: A Short-Term Reactive Approach," *Journal of International Business Studies* 39 (2008), pp. 304–25.

[20] John H. Dunning, Masataka Fujita, and Nevena Yakova, "Some Macro-Data on the Regionalization/ Globalization Debate: A Comment on the Rugman/Verbeke Analysis," *Journal of International Business Studies* 38 (2007), pp. 177–99; Ricardo G. Flores and Ruth V. Aguilera, "Globalization and Location Choice: An Analysis of U.S. Multinational Firms in 1980 and 2000," *Journal of International Business Studies* 38 (2007), pp. 1187–210; Simon Collinson and Alan M. Rugman, "The Regional Nature of Japanese Multinational Business," *Journal of International Business Studies* 39 (2008), pp. 215–30.

[21] Lazlo Tihanyi, David A. Griffith, and Craig J. Russell, "The Effect of Cultural Distance on Entry Mode Choice, International Diversification, and MNE Performance: A Meta-Analysis," *Journal of International Business Studies* 36 (2005), pp. 270–83; Thomas Hutzschenreuter and Johannes C. Voll, "Performance Effects of 'Added Cultural Distance' in the Path of International Expansion: The Case of German Multinational Enterprises," *Journal of International Business Studies* 39 (2008), published online, http://www.jibs.net.

[22] Jennifer D. Chandler and John L. Graham, "Corruption and the Attractiveness of International Markets," working paper, University of California, Irvine, 2008.

regions.[23] Although some disagree,[24] researchers question the existence of global strategies, maintaining that only nine American Fortune 500 companies deserve the term "global" with respect to their operational coverage of the planet.[25] We can agree that strategic choices currently favor regional foci, but the trend is toward steadily increasing globalization of trade agreements, trade, and company strategies, as we mentioned in the previous chapter. Competition and the new ease of global communications is forcing managers around the world to make greater commitments to global marketing.

The Planning Process

Whether a company is marketing in several countries or is entering a foreign market for the first time, planning is essential to success. The first-time foreign marketer must decide what products to develop, in which markets, and with what level of resource commitment. For the company that is already committed, the key decisions involve allocating effort and resources among countries and product(s), deciding on new markets to develop or old ones to withdraw from, and determining which products to develop or drop. Guidelines and systematic procedures are necessary for evaluating international opportunities and risks and for developing strategic plans to take advantage of such opportunities.[26] The process illustrated in Exhibit 11.1 offers a systematic guide to planning for the multinational firm operating in several countries.

Phase 1: Preliminary Analysis and Screening—Matching Company and Country Needs.

Whether a company is new to international marketing or heavily involved, an evaluation of potential markets is the first step in the planning process. A critical first step in the international planning process is deciding in which existing country market to make a market investment.[27] A company's strengths and weaknesses,[28] products, philosophies,[29] and objectives must be matched with a country's constraining factors and market potential. In the first part of the planning process, countries are analyzed and screened to eliminate those that do not offer sufficient potential for further consideration. Emerging markets pose a special problem because many have inadequate marketing infrastructures, distribution channels are underdeveloped, and income level and distribution vary among countries.

The next step is to establish screening criteria against which prospective countries can be evaluated. These criteria are ascertained by an analysis of company objectives, resources, and other corporate capabilities and limitations. It is important to determine the reasons for

---

[23] Elizabeth Maitland, Elizabeth L. Rose, and Stephen Nicholas, "How Firms Grow: Clustering as a Dynamic Model of Internationalization," *Journal of International Business Studies* 36 (2005), pp. 435–51; Gongming Qian, Lee Li, Ji Li, and Zhengming Qian, "Regional Diversification and Firm Performance," *Journal of International Business Studies* 39 (2008), pp. 197–214; Stephanie A. Fernhaber, Brett Anitra Gilbert, and Patricia P. McDougall, "International Entrepreneurship and Geographic Location: An Empirical Examination of New Venture Internationalization," *Journal of International Business Studies* 39 (2008), pp. 267–90.

[24] Thomas Osegowitsch and Andre Sammartino, "Reassessing (Home-) Regionalization," *Journal of International Business Studies* 39 (2008), pp. 184–96.

[25] Alan M. Rugman and Alain Verbeke, "The Theory and Practice of Regional Strategy: A Response to Osegowitsch and Sammartino," *Journal of International Business Studies* 39 (2008), pp. 326–32.

[26] G. Thomas M. Hult, S. Tamer Cavusgil, Seyda Deligonul, Tunga Kiyak, and Katarine Lagerstrom, "What Drives Performance in Globally Focused Marketing Organizations? A Three Country Study," *Journal of International Marketing* 15 (2007), pp. 58–85.

[27] Peter J. Buckley, Timothy M. Devinney, and Jordan J. Louviere, "Do Managers Behave the Way Theory Suggests? A Choice-Theoretic Examination of Foreign Direct Investment Location Decision-Making," *Journal of International Business Studies* 38 (2007), pp. 1069–94.

[28] Yadong Luo and Oded Shankar, "The Multinational Corporation as a Multilingual Community: Language and Organization in a Global Context," *Journal of International Business Studies* 37 (2006), pp. 321–29; Carlos M. P. Sousa and Frank Bradley, "Cultural Distance and Psychic Distance: Two Peas in a Pod?" *Journal of International Marketing* 14 (2006), pp. 48–70; Paul A. Brewer, "Operationalizing Psychic Distance: A Revised Approach," *Journal of International Marketing* 15 (2007), pp. 44–66.

[29] Kevin Zheng Zhou, James R. Brown, Chekitan S. Dev, and Sanjeev Agarwal, "The Effects of Customer and Competitor Orientations on Performance in Global Markets: A Contingency Analysis," *Journal of International Business Studies* 38 (2007), pp. 303–19.

Exhibit 11.1
International Planning Process

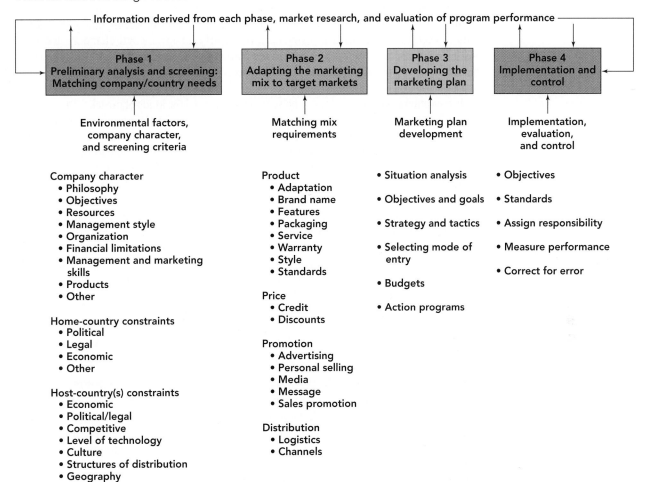

Information derived from each phase, market research, and evaluation of program performance

Phase 1
Preliminary analysis and screening:
Matching company/country needs

Phase 2
Adapting the marketing
mix to target markets

Phase 3
Developing the
marketing plan

Phase 4
Implementation and
control

Environmental factors,
company character,
and screening criteria

Matching mix
requirements

Marketing plan
development

Implementation,
evaluation,
and control

Company character
• Philosophy
• Objectives
• Resources
• Management style
• Organization
• Financial limitations
• Management and marketing
  skills
• Products
• Other

Home-country constraints
• Political
• Legal
• Economic
• Other

Host-country(s) constraints
• Economic
• Political/legal
• Competitive
• Level of technology
• Culture
• Structures of distribution
• Geography
• Competition

Product
• Adaptation
• Brand name
• Features
• Packaging
• Service
• Warranty
• Style
• Standards

Price
• Credit
• Discounts

Promotion
• Advertising
• Personal selling
• Media
• Message
• Sales promotion

Distribution
• Logistics
• Channels

• Situation analysis

• Objectives and goals

• Strategy and tactics

• Selecting mode of
  entry

• Budgets

• Action programs

• Objectives

• Standards

• Assign responsibility

• Measure performance

• Correct for error

entering a foreign market and the returns expected from such an investment. A company's commitment to international business and its objectives for going international are important in establishing evaluation criteria. Minimum market potential, minimum profit, return on investment, acceptable competitive levels, standards of political stability, acceptable legal requirements, and other measures appropriate for the company's products are examples of the evaluation criteria to be established.[30]

Once evaluation criteria are set, a complete analysis of the environment within which a company plans to operate is made. The environment consists of the uncontrollable elements discussed previously and includes both home-country and host-country constraints, marketing objectives, and any other company limitations or strengths that exist at the beginning of each planning period. Although an understanding of uncontrollable environments is important in domestic market planning, the task is more complex in foreign marketing because each country under consideration presents the foreign marketer with a

---

[30] Luis Filipe Lages, Carmen Lages, and Cristiana Raquel Lages, "Bringing Export Performance Metrics into Annual Reports: The APEV Scale and the PERFEX Scorecard," *Journal of International Marketing* 13 (2005), pp. 79–104; David Smith, "A Cross-Cultural Classification of Service Export Performance Using Artificial Neural Networks: Japan, Germany, United States," *Journal of Global Marketing* 20 (2006), pp. 5–20; Rosane K. Gertner, David Gertner, and Dennis Guthery, "The Implications of Export Performance Measurement for the Significance of the Determinants of Export Performance: An Empirical Investigation of Brazilian Firms," *Journal of Global Marketing* 20 (2006), pp. 21–38; Adamantios Diamantopoulos and Nikolaos Kakkos, "Managerial Assessments of Export Performance: Conceptual Framework and Empirical Illustration," *Journal of International Marketing* 15 (2007), pp. 1–31.

different set of unfamiliar environmental constraints. This stage in the planning process, more than anything else, distinguishes international from domestic marketing planning.

The results of Phase 1 provide the marketer with the basic information necessary to evaluate the potential of a proposed country market, identify problems that would eliminate the country from further consideration, identify environmental elements that need further analysis, determine which part of the marketing mix can be standardized and which part of and how the marketing mix must be adapted to meet local market needs, and develop and implement a marketing action plan.

Information generated in Phase 1 helps companies avoid the kinds of mistakes that plagued Radio Shack Corporation, a leading merchandiser of consumer electronic equipment in the United States, when it first went international. Radio Shack's early attempts at international marketing in western Europe resulted in a series of costly mistakes that could have been avoided had it properly analyzed the uncontrollable elements of the countries targeted for its first attempt at multinational marketing. The company staged its first Christmas promotion in anticipation of December 25 in Holland, unaware that the Dutch celebrate St. Nicholas Day and give gifts on December 6. Furthermore, legal problems in various countries interfered with some plans; the company was unaware that most European countries have laws prohibiting the sale of citizen-band radios, one of Radio Shack's most lucrative U.S. products and one it expected to sell in Europe. German courts promptly stopped a free flashlight promotion in German stores because giveaways violate German sales laws. In Belgium, the company overlooked a law requiring a government tax stamp on all window signs, and poorly selected store sites resulted in many of the new stores closing shortly after opening.

With the analysis in Phase 1 completed, the decision maker faces the more specific task of selecting country target markets and segments, identifying problems and opportunities in these markets, and beginning the process of creating marketing programs.

Phase 2: Adapting the Marketing Mix to Target Markets.   A more detailed examination of the components of the marketing mix is the purpose of Phase 2. Once target markets are selected, the marketing mix must be evaluated in light of the data generated in Phase 1. Incorrect decisions at this point lead to products inappropriate for the intended market or to costly mistakes in pricing, advertising, and promotion. The primary goal of Phase 2 is to decide on a marketing mix adjusted to the cultural constraints imposed by the uncontrollable elements of the environment that effectively achieves corporate objectives and goals.

The process used by the Nestlé Company is an example of the type of analysis done in Phase 2. Each product manager has a country fact book that includes much of the information suggested in Phase 1. The country fact book analyzes in detail a variety of culturally related questions. In Germany, the product manager for coffee must furnish answers to a number of questions. How does a German rank coffee in the hierarchy of consumer products? Is Germany a high or a low per capita consumption market? (These facts alone can be of enormous consequence. In Sweden the annual per capita consumption of coffee is 11.6 kilograms, in the United States 4.4, and in Japan it's only 3.6.)[31] How is coffee used—in bean form, ground, or powdered? If it is ground, how is it brewed? Which coffee is preferred—Brazilian Santos blended with Colombian coffee, or robusta from the Ivory Coast? Is it roasted? Do the people prefer dark roasted or blonde coffee? (The color of Nestlé's instant coffee must resemble as closely as possible the color of the coffee consumed in the country.)

As a result of the answers to these and other questions, Nestlé produces 200 types of instant coffee, from the dark robust espresso preferred in Latin countries to the lighter blends popular in the United States. Almost $50 million a year is spent in four research laboratories around the world experimenting with new shadings in color, aroma, and flavor. Do the Germans drink coffee after lunch or with their breakfast? Do they take it black or with cream or milk? Do they drink coffee in the evening? Do they sweeten it? (In France, the answers are clear: In the morning, coffee with milk; at noon, black coffee—that is, two totally different coffees.) At what age do people begin drinking coffee? Is it a traditional

---

[31] International Coffee Organization, http://www.ico.org, 2008.

As they say, as one door closes, another opens up—indeed, sometimes two! Given all the tea in China, it's particularly amazing that for almost eight years you could buy a mocha frappuccino in the Forbidden City in Beijing. The yellow roof symbolizes Imperial grounds, but we don't think the Emperor had grounds of the coffee sort in mind when he built the place in the 1400s. China joining the WTO some six centuries later opened up the market in new ways to franchisers from around the world. However, unlike the other 240 Starbucks stores in China, this one stirred strong protests by the local media, and was eventually closed in the summer of 2007. Meanwhile, about one month after the Forbidden City store was forbidden in China, the company's first Russian store opened in Moscow. On a cold afternoon in Moscow Russians and foreign tourists can now choose between grabbing a cappuccino at either Starbucks or McDonald's McCafe. The two are just a couple of blocks from one another on Moscow's most famous traditional shopping street, the Arbat. The American companies were smart enough this time around not to try Red Square.

beverage, as in France; is it a form of rebellion among the young, as in England, where coffee drinking has been taken up in defiance of tea-drinking parents; or is it a gift, as in Japan? There is a coffee boom in tea-drinking Japan, where Nescafé is considered a luxury gift item; instead of chocolates and flowers, Nescafé is toted in fancy containers to dinners and birthday parties. With such depth of information, the product manager can evaluate the marketing mix in terms of the information in the country fact book.

Phase 2 also permits the marketer to determine possibilities for applying marketing tactics across national markets. The search for similar segments across countries can often lead to opportunities for economies of scale in marketing programs. This opportunity was the case for Nestlé when research revealed that young coffee drinkers in England and Japan had identical motivations. As a result, Nestlé now uses principally the same message in both markets.

Frequently, the results of the analysis in Phase 2 indicate that the marketing mix would require such drastic adaptation that a decision not to enter a particular market is made. For example, a product may have to be reduced in physical size to fit the needs of the market, but the additional manufacturing cost of a smaller size may be too high to justify market entry. Also, the price required to be profitable might be too high for a majority of the market to afford. If there is no way to reduce the price, sales potential at the higher price may be too low to justify entry.

The answers to three major questions are generated in Phase 2:

1. Are there identifiable market segments that allow for common marketing mix tactics across countries?

2. Which cultural/environmental adaptations are necessary for successful acceptance of the marketing mix?

3. Will adaptation costs allow profitable market entry?

Based on the results in Phase 2, a second screening of countries may take place, with some countries dropped from further consideration. The next phase in the planning process is the development of a marketing plan.

Phase 3: Developing the Marketing Plan. At this stage of the planning process, a marketing plan is developed for the target market—whether it is a single country or a global market set. The marketing plan begins with a situation analysis and culminates in the selection of an entry mode and a specific action program for the market. The specific plan establishes what is to be done, by whom, how it is to be done, and when. Included are budgets and sales and profit expectations. Just as in Phase 2, a decision not to enter a specific market may be made if it is determined that company marketing objectives and goals cannot be met.

Phase 4: Implementation and Control.   Although the model is presented as a series of sequential phases, the planning process is a dynamic, continuous set of interacting variables with information continuously building among phases. The phases outline a crucial path to be followed for effective, systematic planning.

A "go" decision in Phase 3 triggers implementation of specific plans and anticipation of successful marketing. However, the planning process does not end at this point. All marketing plans require coordination and control during the period of implementation.[32] Many businesses do not control marketing plans as thoroughly as they could even though continuous monitoring and control could increase their success. An evaluation and control system requires performance-objective action, that is, bringing the plan back on track should standards of performance fall short. Such a system also assumes reasonable metrics of performance are accessible. A global orientation facilitates the difficult but extremely important management tasks of coordinating and controlling the complexities of international marketing.

Utilizing a planning process and system[33] encourages the decision maker to consider all variables that affect the success of a company's plan. Furthermore, it provides the basis for viewing all country markets and their interrelationships as an integrated global unit. By following the guidelines presented in Part Six of this text, "The Country Notebook—A Guide for Developing a Marketing Plan," the international marketer can put the strategic planning process into operation.

With the information developed in the planning process and a country market selected, the decision regarding the entry mode can be made. The choice of mode of entry is one of the more critical decisions for the firm because the choice will define the firm's operations and affect all future decisions in that market.

Alternative Market-Entry Strategies

When a company makes the commitment to go international, it must choose an entry strategy. This decision should reflect an analysis of market characteristics (such as potential sales, competition,[34] strategic importance, strengths of local resources,[35] cultural differences,[36] and country restrictions and deregulation[37]) and company capabilities and characteristics, including the degree of near-market knowledge, marketing involvement, and commitment that management is prepared to make.[38] Even so, many firms appear to simply imitate others in the industry or repeat their own successful

---

[32] Janell D. Townsend, Sengun Yeniyurt, Z. Seyda Deligonul, and S. Tamer Cavusgil, "Exploring Marketing Program Antecedents of Performance in a Global Company," *Journal of International Marketing* 12, no. 4 (2004), pp. 1–24.

[33] Anna Shaojie Cui, David A. Griffith, and S. Tamer Cavusgil, "The Influence of Competitive Intensity and Market Dynamism on Knowledge Management Capabilities of Multinational Corporation Subsidiaries" *Journal of International Marketing* 13 (2005), pp. 32–53.

[34] Geng Cui and Hon-Kwong Lui, "Order of Entry and Performance of Multinational Corporations in an Emerging Market: A Contingent Resource Perspective," *Journal of International Marketing* 13 (2005), pp. 28–56.

[35] Ted London and Stuart L. Hart, "Reinventing Strategies for Emerging Markets: Beyond the Transnational Model," *Journal of International Business Studies* 35, no. 5 (2004), pp. 350–70; Esther Sanchez-Peinado, "Strategic Variables that Influence Entry Mode Choice in Service Firms," *Journal of International Marketing* 15 (2007), pp. 66–91.

[36] Keith D. Brouthers, "Institutional, Cultural, and Transaction Cost Influences on Entry Mode Choice and Performance," *Journal of International Business Studies* 33, no. 2 (2002), pp. 203–31; Laszlo Tihanyi, David A. Griffith, and Craig Russell, "The Effect of Cultural Distance on Entry Mode Choice, International Diversification, and MNE Performance: A Meta-Analysis," *Journal of International Business Studies* 36, no. 3 (2005), pp. 270–83; Torben Pedersen and Bent Pedersen, "Learning about Foreign Markets: Are Entrant Firms Exposed to a 'Shock Effect?'" *Journal of International Marketing* 12, no. 1 (2004), pp. 103–23.

[37] Veronika Papyrina, "When, How, and with What Success? The Joint Effect of Entry Timing and Entry Mode on Survival of Japanese Subsidiaries in China," *Journal of International Marketing* 15 (2003), pp. 73–96.

[38] Naresh K. Malhotra, James Agarwal, and Francis M. Ulgado, "Internationalization and Entry Modes: A Multitheoretical Framework and Research Propositions," *Journal of International Marketing* 11, no. 4 (2003), pp. 1–31.

Exhibit 11.2
Alternative Market-Entry
Strategies

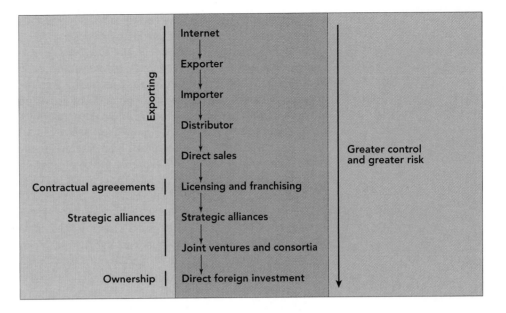

entry strategies—this is not what we recommend. The approach to foreign marketing can range from minimal investment with infrequent and indirect exporting and little thought given to market development to large investments of capital and management in an effort to capture and maintain a permanent, specific share of world markets.[39] Depending on the firm's objectives and market characteristics, either approach can be profitable.

Companies most often begin with modest export involvement.[40] As sales revenues grow, the firms often proceed down through the series of steps listed in Exhibit 11.2.[41] Successful smaller firms are often particularly adept at exploiting networks of personal and commercial relationships to mitigate the financial risks of initial entry.[42] Also, experience[43] in larger numbers of foreign markets can increase the number of entry strategies used. In fact, a company in several country markets may employ a variety of entry modes because each country market poses a different set of conditions.[44] For example, JLG Industries in Pennsylvania makes self-propelled aerial work platforms (cherry pickers) and sells them all over the world. The firm actually manufactured in Scotland and Australia beginning in the 1970s, but it was forced to close the plants in the 1990s. However, the company's international sales have burgeoned again. The growth in European business is allowing for a simplification of distribution channels through the elimination of middlemen; dealerships have been purchased in Germany, Norway, Sweden, and the United Kingdom. JLG set up dealership joint ventures in Thailand and Brazil, and sales have been brisk despite economic

[39] A. Delios and W. J. Henisz, "Policy Uncertainty and the Sequence of Entry by Japanese Firms, 1980–1998," *Journal of International Business Studies* 34, no. 3 (2003), pp. 227–41.

[40] Harry G. Barkema and Rian Drogendijk, "Internationalizing in Small, Incremental or Large Steps?" *Journal of International Business Studies* 39 (2008), pp. 1132–1148.

[41] Mauro F. Guillen, "Experience, Imitation, and the Sequence of Foreign Entry: Wholly Owned and Joint-Venture Manufacturing by South Korean Firms and Business Groups in China, 1987–1995," *Journal of International Business Studies* 34, no. 2 (2003), pp. 185–98.

[42] Susan Freeman, Ron Edwards, and Bill Schroder, "How Smaller Born-Global Firms Use Networks and Alliances to Overcome Constraints to Rapid Internationalization," *Journal of International Marketing* 14 (2006), pp. 33–63; Nicole E. Coveillo, "The Network Dynamics of International New Ventures," *Journal of International Business Studies* 37 (2006), pp. 713–31.

[43] Taewon Suh, Mueun Bae, and Sumit K. Kundu, "Smaller Firms' Perceived Cost and Attractiveness in International Markets," *Journal of Global Marketing* 21 (2007), pp. 5–18; Anna Nadolska and Harry G. Barkema, "Learning to Internationalise: The Pace and Success of Foreign Acquisitions," *Journal of International Business Studies* 38 (2007), pp. 1170–86.

[44] Nicholas C. Williamson, Nir Kshetri, Tim Heijwegen, and Andreea Fortuna Schiopu, "An Exploratory Study of the Functional Forms of Export Market Identification Variables," *Journal of International Marketing* 14 (2006), pp. 71–97.

problems in those countries. The company also has established sales and service businesses from scratch in Scotland, Italy, and South Africa.

A company has four different modes of foreign market entry from which to select: exporting, contractual agreements, strategic alliances, and direct foreign investment. The different modes of entry can be further classified on the basis of the equity or nonequity requirements of each mode. The amount of equity required by the company to use different modes affects the risk, return, and control that it will have in each mode. For example, indirect exporting requires no equity investment and thus has a low risk, low rate of return, and little control, whereas direct foreign investment requires the most equity of the four modes and creates the greatest risk while offering the most control and the potential highest return.

Exporting

Exporting accounts for some 10 percent of global economic activity.[45] Exporting can be either direct or indirect. With *direct exporting* the company sells to a customer in another country. This method is the most common approach employed by companies taking their first international step because the risks of financial loss can be minimized. In contrast, *indirect exporting* usually means that the company sells to a buyer (importer or distributor) in the home country, which in turn exports the product. Customers include large retailers such as Wal-Mart or Sears, wholesale supply houses, trading companies, and others that buy to supply customers abroad.

Early motives for exporting often are to skim the cream from the market or gain business to absorb overhead.[46] Early involvement may be opportunistic and come in the form of an inquiry from a foreign customer or initiatives from an importer in the foreign market. This motive is the case with Pilsner Urquell, the revered Czech beer, which for many years has sold in the United States through Guinness Bass Import Corporation (GBIC). However, the Czech firm severed its relationship with the importer because it wasn't getting the attention of the other imported beers in GBIC's portfolio. The firm established its own sales force of two dozen to handle five key metropolitan areas in the United States. Prices were reduced and a global media plan developed with a British ad agency. The firm may import other brands from the Czech parent as well.

Exporting is also a common approach for mature international companies with strong marketing capabilities.[47] Some of America's largest companies engage in exporting as their major market-entry method. Indeed, Boeing is the best example, as America's largest exporter. The mechanics of exporting and the different middlemen available to facilitate the exporting process are discussed in detail in Chapters 14 and 15.

The Internet. The Internet is becoming increasingly important as a foreign market entry method. Initially, Internet marketing focused on domestic sales.[48] However, a surprisingly large number of companies started receiving orders from customers in other countries, resulting in the concept of international Internet marketing (IIM). PicturePhone Direct, a mail-order reseller of desktop videoconferencing equipment, posted its catalog on the Internet expecting to concentrate on the northeastern United States. To the company's surprise, PicturePhone's sales staff received orders from Israel, Portugal, and Germany.

Other companies have had similar experiences and are actively designing Internet catalogs targeting specific countries with multilingual Web sites. Dell Computer Corporation

[45] Neil A. Morgan, Anna Kaleka, and Constantine S. Katsikeas, "Antecedents of Export Venture Performance: A Theoretical Model and Empirical Assessment," *Journal of Marketing* 68, no. 1 (2004), pp. 90–108.

[46] Luis Filipe Lages and Cristiana Raquel Lages, "The STEP Scale: A Measure of Short-Term Export Performance," *Journal of International Marketing* 12, no. 1 (2004), pp. 36–56.

[47] Shaoming Zou, Eric Fang, and Shuming Zhao, "The Effect of Export Marketing Capabilities on Export Performance: An Investigation of Chinese Exporters," *Journal of International Marketing* 11, no. 4 (2003), pp. 32–55.

[48] Ikechi Ekeledo and K. Sivakumar, "The Impact of E-Commerce on Entry-Mode Strategies of Services Firms: A Conceptual Framework and Research Propositions," *Journal of International Marketing* 12, no. 4 (2004), pp. 46–70.

has expanded its strategy of selling computers over the Internet to foreign sites as well. Dell began selling computers via the Internet to Malaysia, Australia, Hong Kong, New Zealand, Singapore, Taiwan, and other Asian countries through a "virtual store" on the Internet. The same selling mode has been launched in Europe.

Amazon.com jumped into the IIM game with both feet. It hired a top Apple Computer executive to manage its fast growing international business. Just 15 months after setting up book and CD e-tailing sites in Germany and the United Kingdom, the new overseas Amazon Web sites have surged to become the most heavily trafficked commercial venues in both markets. Among the companies with the most profitable e-tailing businesses are former catalog companies such as Lands' End and L.L. Bean. Interestingly, Lands' End's success in foreign markets was tainted by unexpected problems in Germany. German law bans "advertising gimmicks"—and that's what regulators there called Lands' End's "unconditional lifetime guarantee." Indeed, the firm took the dispute all the way to the German supreme court and lost. Moreover, the uncertainty swirling around the EU's approach to taxing Internet sales is continuing cause for great concern.

As discussed in Chapter 2, the full impact of the Internet on international marketing is yet to be determined. However, IIM should not be overlooked as an alternative market-entry strategy by the small or large company. Coupled with the international scope of credit card companies such as MasterCard and Visa and international delivery services such as UPS and Federal Express, deliveries to foreign countries can be relatively effortless.

Direct Sales.   Particularly for high-technology and big ticket industrial products, a direct sales force may be required in a foreign country. This requirement may mean establishing an office with local and/or expatriate managers and staff, depending of course on the size of the market and potential sales revenues. International sales management is one of the topics covered in detail in Chapter 17.

Contractual Agreements

Contractual agreements are long-term, nonequity associations between a company and another in a foreign market. Contractual agreements generally involve the transfer of technology, processes, trademarks, and/or human skills. In short, they serve as a means of transfer of knowledge rather than equity.

Licensing.   A means of establishing a foothold in foreign markets without large capital outlays is *licensing*. Patent rights, trademark rights, and the rights to use technological processes are granted in foreign licensing. It is a favorite strategy for small and medium-sized companies, though by no means limited to such companies. Common examples of industries that use licensing arrangements in foreign markets are television programming and pharmaceuticals. Not many confine their foreign operations to licensing alone; it is generally viewed as a supplement to exporting or manufacturing, rather than the only means of entry into foreign markets. The advantages of licensing are most apparent when capital is scarce, import restrictions forbid other means of entry, a country is sensitive to foreign ownership, or patents and trademarks must be protected against cancellation for nonuse. The risks of licensing are choosing the wrong partner, quality and other production problems, payment problems, contract enforcement, and loss of marketing control.

Although licensing may be the least profitable way of entering a market, the risks and headaches are less than those for direct investments. It is a legitimate means of capitalizing on intellectual property in a foreign market, and such agreements can also benefit the economies of target countries. Licensing takes several forms. Licenses may be granted for production processes, for the use of a trade name, or for the distribution of imported products. Licenses may be closely controlled or be autonomous, and they permit expansion without great capital or personnel commitment if licensees have the requisite capabilities. Not all experiences with licensing are successful because of the burden of finding, supervising, and inspiring licensees.

Franchising.   *Franchising* is a rapidly growing form of licensing in which the franchiser provides a standard package of products, systems, and management services, and

Maybe they can help you find a home with a view of the Black Sea here at the Century 21 office in Istanbul, Turkey. We know they'll be happy to sell you a piece of chicken from the Colonel's place in Eilat, Israel, just across the Red Sea from Aqaba, Jordan.

the franchisee provides market knowledge, capital, and personal involvement in management. The combination of skills permits flexibility in dealing with local market conditions and yet provides the parent firm with a reasonable degree of control. The franchiser can follow through on marketing of the products to the point of final sale. It is an important form of vertical market integration. Potentially, the franchise system provides an effective blending of skill centralization and operational decentralization; it has become an increasingly important form of international marketing. In some cases, franchising is having a profound effect on traditional businesses. In England, for example, annual franchised sales of fast foods are estimated at nearly $2 billion, which accounts for 30 percent of all foods eaten outside the home.

Prior to 1970, international franchising was not a major activity. A survey by the International Franchising Association revealed that only 14 percent of its member firms had franchises outside of the United States, and the majority of those were in Canada. Now more than 30,000 franchises of U.S. firms are located in countries throughout the world. Franchises include soft drinks, motels (including membership "organizations" like Best Western International), retailing, fast foods, car rentals, automotive services, recreational services, and a variety of business services from print shops to sign shops. Canada is the dominant market for U.S. franchisers, with Japan and the United Kingdom second and third in importance. The Asian-Pacific Rim has seen rapid growth as companies look to Asia for future expansion.

Despite temporary setbacks during the global economic downturn right after the turn of the millennium, franchising is still expected to be the fastest growing market-entry strategy. Franchises were often among the first types of foreign retail business to open in the emerging market economies of eastern Europe, the former republics of Russia, and China. McDonald's is in Moscow (its first store seated 700 inside and had 27 cash registers), and KFC is in China (the Beijing KFC store has the highest sales volume of any KFC store in the world). The same factors that spurred the growth of franchising in the U.S. domestic economy have led to its growth in foreign markets. Franchising is an attractive form of corporate organization for companies wishing to expand quickly with low capital investment. The franchising system combines the knowledge of the franchiser with the local knowledge and entrepreneurial spirit of the franchisee. Foreign laws and regulations are friendly toward franchising because it tends to foster local ownership, operations, and employment.

Lil'Orbits,[49] a Minneapolis-based company that sells donut-making equipment and ingredients to entrepreneurs, is an example of how a small company can use licensing and franchising to enter a foreign market. Lil'Orbits sells a donut maker that turns out

[49] http://www.lilorbits.com, 2005.

CROSSING BORDERS 11.3   The Men Who Would Be Pizza Kings

In more senses than one, pizza outlets are mushrooming all over India. The wait for pizza lovers in places like Surat, Kochi, and Bhubaneshwar is finally over. Domino's, the home delivery specialist, now has 180 stores across the nation, and Pizza Hut, a part of Yum! Brands, has increased its number of restaurants to 163. Chennai-based Pizza Corner, having established itself in the south, has now boldly ventured into the north—it has already opened three outlets in Delhi and is planning to increase the number to eight.

While Domino's is trying to dish out a pizza for every ethnic group, Pizza Hut is trying to expose Indians to the pizza's Chinese cousin. It has come up with the "Oriental," which has hot Chinese sauce, spring onions, and sesame seeds as its toppings. It was developed based on the Indian fondness for Chinese food. This

is not to say that Pizza Hut does not pay heed to the spice-soaked Indian version. Apart from the Oriental, it is also dishing out a spicy paneer tikka pizza. Milk shakes are on the menu, too. Most recently an Indian dairy company has been earning market share in both pizzas and ice cream. Things are getting interesting there fast. And, in spite of Kipling's prophesy that the two streams shall never meet, the Indianization of the pizza is truly here.

Sources: Smita Tripathi, "Butter Chicken Pizza in Ludhiana," *Business Standard*, June 17, 2000, p. 2; Rahul Chandawarkar, "Collegians Mix Money with Study Material," *Times of India*, June 22, 2000; Thomas L. Friedman, *The World Is Flat* (New York: Farrar, Straus, and Giroux, 2005); "Dominos Pizza India Plans 500 Stores in Country," *Indian Business Insight*, February 14, 2008, p. 20.

1.5-inch donuts while the customer waits. The typical buyer in the United States buys equipment and mix directly from the company without royalties or franchise fees. The buyer has a small shop or kiosk and sells donuts by the dozen for takeout or individually along with a beverage.

Successful in the United States, Lil'Orbits ran an advertisement in *Commercial News USA*, a magazine showcasing products and services in foreign countries, that attracted 400 inquiries. Pleased with the response, the company set up an international franchise operation based on royalties and franchise fees. Now a network of international franchised distributors markets the machines and ingredients to potential vendors. The distributors pay Lil'Orbits a franchise fee and buy machines and ingredients directly from Lil'Orbits or from one of the licensed vendors worldwide, from which Lil'Orbits receives a royalty. This entry strategy has enabled the company to enter foreign markets with minimum capital investment outside the home country. The company has over 20,000 franchised dealers in 85 countries. About 60 percent of the company's business is international.

Although franchising enables a company to expand quickly with minimum capital, there are costs associated with servicing franchisees. For example, to accommodate different tastes around the world, Lil'Orbits had to develop a more pastrylike, less sweet mix than that used in the United States. Other cultural differences have had to be met as well. For example, customers in France and Belgium could not pronounce the trade name, Lil'Orbits, so Orbie is used instead. Toppings also had to be adjusted to accommodate different tastes. Cinnamon sugar is the most widely accepted topping, but in China, cinnamon is considered a medicine, so only sugar is used. In the Mediterranean region, the Greeks like honey, and chocolate sauce is popular in Spain. Powdered sugar is more popular than granulated sugar in France, where the donuts are eaten in cornucopia cups instead of on plates.

Strategic International Alliances

A *strategic international alliance (SIA)* is a business relationship established by two or more companies to cooperate out of mutual need and to share risk in achieving a common objective. Strategic alliances have grown in importance over the last few decades as a competitive strategy in global marketing management. Strategic international alliances are sought as a way to shore up weaknesses and increase competitive strengths. Firms enter into SIAs for several reasons: opportunities for rapid expansion into new markets, access to new technology,[50] more efficient production and innovation, reduced marketing costs, strategic competitive moves, and access to additional sources of products[51] and capital. Finally, evidence suggests that SIAs often contribute nicely to profits.[52]

Perhaps the most visible SIAs are now in the airline industry. American Airlines, Cathay Pacific, British Airways, Japan Airlines, Finnair, Malev, Iberia, LAN, Royal Jordanian, and Quantas are partners in the Oneworld Alliance, which integrates schedules and mileage programs. Competing with Oneworld are the Star Alliance (led by United and Lufthansa) and SkyTeam (led by Air France, Northwestern, and KLM). These kinds of strategic international alliances imply that there is a common objective; that one partner's weakness is offset by the other's strength; that reaching the objective alone would be too costly, take too much time, or be too risky; and that together their respective strengths make possible what otherwise would be unattainable. For example, during the recent turmoil in the global airline industry, Star Alliance began moving in the direction of buying aircraft, a new strategic innovation. In short, an SIA is a synergistic relationship established to achieve a common goal in which both parties benefit.

An SIA with multiple objectives involves C-Itoh (Japan), Tyson Foods (United States), and Provemex (Mexico). It is an alliance that processes Japanese-style yakitori (bits of marinated and grilled chicken on a bamboo stick) for export to Japan and other Asian countries. Each company had a goal and made a contribution to the alliance. C-Itoh's goal was to find a lower-cost supply of yakitori; because it is so labor intensive, it was becoming increasingly costly and noncompetitive to produce in Japan. C-Itoh's contribution was access to its distribution system and markets throughout Japan and Asia. Tyson's goal was new markets for its dark chicken meat, a byproduct of demand for mostly white meat in the U.S. market. Tyson exported some of its excess dark meat to Asia and knew that C-Itoh wanted to expand its supplier base. But Tyson faced the same high labor costs as C-Itoh. Provemex, the link that made it all work, had as its goal expansion beyond raising and slaughtering chickens into higher value-added products for international markets. Provemex's contribution was to provide highly cost-competitive labor.

In the SkyTeam strategic alliance, U.S.-based Northwest Airlines and Dutch KLM share several aspects of their operations, including ticketing and reservations, catering, cargo, and airport slots. As the global airline industry continues to consolidate, more strategic partnerships are being formed.

Through the alliance, they all benefited. Provemex acquired the know-how to bone the dark meat used in yakitori and was able to vertically integrate its operations and secure a foothold in a lucrative export market. Tyson earned more from the sale of surplus chicken legs than was previously possible and gained an increased share of the Asian market. C-Itoh had a steady supply of competitively priced yakitori for its vast distribution and marketing network. Thus, three companies with individual strengths created a successful alliance in which each contributes and each benefits.

Many companies also are entering SIAs to be in a strategic position to be competitive and to benefit from the expected growth in the single European market. As a case in point, when

---

[50] Bernard L. Simonin, "An Empirical Investigation of the Process of Knowledge Transfer in International Strategic Alliances," *Journal of International Business Studies* 35, no. 5 (2004), pp. 407–27; John Hagedoorn, Danielle Cloodt, and Hans van Kraneburg, "Intellectual Property Rights and the Governance of International R&D Partnerships," *Journal of International Business Studies* 36 (2005), pp. 175–86; Marjorie A. Lyles and Jane E. Salk, "Knowledge Acquisition from Foreign Parents in International Joint Ventures: An Empirical Examination of the Hungarian Context," *Journal of International Business Studies* 38 (2007), pp. 3–18; Masaaki Kotabe, Denise Dunlap-Hinkler, Ronaldo Parente, and Harsh A. Mishra, "Determination of Cross-National Knowledge Transfer and Its Effect on Innovation," *Journal of International Business Studies* 38 (2007), pp. 259–82.

[51] Janet Y. Murray, Masaaki Kotabe, and Joe Nan Zhou, "Strategic Alliance–Based Sourcing and Market Performance: Evidence from Foreign Firms Operating in China," *Journal of International Business Studies* 36, no. 2 (2005), pp. 187–208.

[52] Africa Arino, "Measures of Strategic Alliance Performance: An Analysis of Construct Validity," *Journal of International Business Studies* 34, no. 1 (2003), pp. 66–79.

General Mills wanted a share of the rapidly growing breakfast-cereal market in Europe, it joined with Nestlé to create Cereal Partners Worldwide. The European cereal market was projected to be worth hundreds of millions of dollars as health-conscious Europeans changed their breakfast diet from eggs and bacon to dry cereal. General Mills's main U.S. competitor, Kellogg, had been in Europe since 1920 and controlled about half of the market.

For General Mills to enter the market from scratch would have been extremely costly. Although the cereal business uses cheap commodities as its raw materials, it is both capital and marketing intensive; sales volume must be high before profits begin to develop. Only recently has Kellogg earned significant profits in Europe. For General Mills to reach its goal alone would have required a manufacturing base and a massive sales force. Furthermore, Kellogg's stranglehold on supermarkets would have been difficult for an unknown to breach easily. The solution was a joint venture with Nestlé. Nestlé had everything General Mills lacked—a well-known brand name, a network of plants, and a powerful distribution system—except for the one thing that General Mills could provide: strong cereal brands.

The deal was mutually beneficial. General Mills provided the knowledge in cereal technology, including some of its proprietary manufacturing equipment, its stable of proven brands, and its knack for pitching these products to consumers. Nestlé provided its name on the box, access to retailers, and production capacity that could be converted to making General Mills's cereals. In time, Cereal Partners Worldwide intends to extend its marketing effort beyond Europe. In Asia, Africa, and Latin America, Cereal Partners Worldwide will have an important advantage over the competition because Nestlé is a dominant food producer.

As international strategic alliances have grown in importance, more emphasis has been placed on a systematic approach to forming them. Most experts in the field agree that the steps outlined in Exhibit 11.3 will lead to successful and high-performance strategic alliances.[53] In particular, we note the wide agreement regarding the importance of building trust in the interpersonal and institutional relationships as a prerequisite of success.[54] Of course, in international business there are no guarantees; the interface between differing ethical and legal systems often makes matters more difficult.[55] And a key activity in all the steps outlined in the exhibit is international negotiation, the subject of Chapter 19.[56]

International Joint Ventures.
International joint ventures (IJVs) as a means of foreign market entry have accelerated sharply during the last 30 years. Besides serving as a means of lessening political and economic risks by the amount of the partner's contribution to the venture, IJVs provide a way to enter markets that pose legal and cultural barriers that is less risky than acquisition of an existing company.

A *joint venture* is different from other types of strategic alliances or collaborative relationships in that a joint venture is a partnership of two or more participating companies that have joined forces to create a separate legal entity. Joint ventures are different from minority holdings by an MNC in a local firm.

Four characteristics define joint ventures: (1) JVs are established, separate, legal entities; (2) they acknowledge intent by the partners to share in the management of the JV; (3) they are partnerships between legally incorporated entities, such as companies,

[53] Robert E. Spekman, Lynn A. Isabella, with Thomas C. MacAvoy, *Alliance Competence* (New York: Wiley, 2000).

[54] Alaka N. Rao, Jone L. Pearce, and Katherine Xin, "Governments, Reciprocal Exchange and Trust among Business Associates," *Journal of International Business Studies* 36 (2005), pp. 104–18; David A. Griffith, Matthew B. Myers, and Michael G. Harvey, "An Investigation of National Culture's Influence on Relationship and Knowledge Resources in Interorganizational Relationships between Japan and the United States," *Journal of International Marketing* 14 (2006), pp. 1–36; Srilata Zaheer and Akbar Zaheer, "Trust across Borders," *Journal of International Business Studies* 37 (2006), pp. 21–29.

[55] Kam-hon Lee, Gong-ming Qian, Julie H. Yu, and Ying Ho, "Trading Favors for Marketing Advantage: Evidence from Hong Kong, China, and the United States," *Journal of International Marketing* 13 (2005), pp. 1–35.

[56] David G. Sirmon and Peter J. Lane, "A Model of Cultural Differences and International Alliance Performance," *Journal of International Business Studies* 35, no. 4 (2004), pp. 306–19.

Exhibit 11.3
Building Strategic Alliances

Primary Relationship Activity	Typical Actions, Interactions, Activities	Key Relationship Skill
Dating	Senior executives leveraging personal networks Wondering how to respond to inquiries Wondering how to seek out possibilities	Good radar; good relationship self-awareness
Imaging	Seeing the reality in possibilities Creating a shared vision from being together Involving trusted senior managers	Creating intimacy
Initiating	Bringing key executives into action Creating trust through face-to-face time	Trust building
Interfacing	Facilitating the creating of personal relationships at many levels Traveling to partner facilities and engaging in technical conversations Blending social and business time	Partnering
Committing	Demonstrating that managers are fully committed to the alliance and each other Managing the conflict inherent in making hard choices Accepting the reality of the alliance and its relationships	Commitment
Fine-tuning	Relying on mature and established relationships Facilitating interaction and relationships with future successors	Growing with another

Source: Adapted from Robert E. Spekman, Lynn A. Isabella, with Thomas C. MacAvoy, *Alliance Competence* (New York: Wiley, 2000), p. 81. Copyright © 2000, John Wiley & Sons, Inc. This material is used by permission of John Wiley & Sons, Inc.

chartered organizations, or governments, and not between individuals; and (4) equity positions are held by each of the partners.

However, IJVs can be hard to manage. The choice of partners and the qualities of the relationships[57] between the executives are important factors leading to success. Several other factors contribute to their success or failure as well: how control is shared,[58] relations with parents,[59] institutional (legal) environments,[60] and the extent to which

---

[57] Steven C. Currall and Andrew C. Inkpen, "A Multilevel Approach to Trust in Joint Ventures," *Journal of International Business Studies* 33, no. 3 (2003), pp. 479–95; Chris Styles and Lis Hersch, "Relationship Formation in International Joint Ventures: Insights from Australian-Malaysian International Joint Ventures," *Journal of International Marketing* 13 (2005), pp. 105–34.

[58] Nitin Pangarkar and Saul Klein, "The Impact of Control on IJV Performance: A Contingency Approach," *Journal of International Marketing* 12, no. 3 (2004), pp. 86–107; Chang-Bum Choi and Paul W. Beamish, "Split Management Control and IJV Performance," *Journal of International Business Studies* 35, no. 3 (2004), pp. 201–15; Yadong Luo and Seung H. Park, "Multiparty Cooperation and Performance in International Equity Joint Ventures," *Journal of International Business Studies* 35, no. 2 (2004), pp. 142–60; Jeffrey Q. Bardon, H. Kevin Steensma, and Marjorie A. Lyles, "The Influence of Parent Control Structure on Parent Conflict in Vietnamese IJVs: An Organizational Justice–Based Contingency Approach," *Journal of International Business Studies* 36, no. 2 (2005), pp. 156–74.

[59] Barden, Steensma, and Lyles, "The Influence of Parent Control Structure on Parent Conflict"; Yaping Gong, Oded Shenkar, Yadong Luo, and Mee-Kau Nyaw, "Human Resources and International Joint Venture Performance: A System Perspective," *Journal of International Business Studies* 36 (2005), pp. 505–18; Rene Belderbos and Jianglei Zou, "On the Growth of Foreign Affiliates: Multinational Plant Networks, Joint Ventures, and Flexibility," *Journal of International Business Studies* 38 (2007), pp. 1095–112.

[60] Yadong Luo, "Transactional Characteristics, Institutional Environment, and Joint Venture Contracts," *Journal of International Business Studies* 36, no. 2 (2005), pp. 209–30.

knowledge is shared across partners.[61] Despite this complexity, nearly all companies active in world trade participate in at least one international joint venture somewhere; many companies have dozens of joint ventures. A recent Conference Board study indicated that 40 percent of Fortune 500 companies were engaged in one or more IJVs. Particularly in telecommunications and Internet markets, joint ventures are increasingly favored.

In the Asian-Pacific Rim, where U.S. companies face unfamiliar legal and cultural barriers, joint ventures are preferred to buying existing businesses. Local partners can often lead the way through legal mazes and provide the outsider with help in understanding cultural nuances. A JV can be attractive to an international marketer when it enables a company to utilize the specialized skills of a local partner, when it allows the marketer to gain access to a partner's local distribution system, when a company seeks to enter a market where wholly owned activities are prohibited, when it provides access to markets protected by tariffs or quotas, and when the firm lacks the capital or personnel capabilities to expand its international activities.

In China, a country considered to be among the most challenging in Asia, more than 50,000 joint ventures have been established in the 30 years since the government began allowing IJVs there. Among the many reasons IJVs are so popular is that they offer a way of getting around high Chinese tariffs, allowing a company to gain a competitive price advantage over imports. Manufacturing locally with a Chinese partner rather than importing achieves additional savings as a result of low-cost Chinese labor. Many Western brands are manufactured and marketed in China at prices that would not be possible if the products were imported.

Consortia.   Consortia are similar to joint ventures and could be classified as such except for two unique characteristics: (1) They typically involve a large number of participants and (2) they frequently operate in a country or market in which none of the participants is currently active. Consortia are developed to pool financial and managerial resources and to lessen risks. Often, huge construction projects are built under a consortium arrangement in which major contractors with different specialties form a separate company specifically to negotiate for and produce one job. One firm usually acts as the lead firm, or the newly formed corporation may exist independently of its originators.

Without doubt, the most prominent international consortium has been Airbus, Boeing's European competitor in the global commercial aircraft market. Airbus Industrie was originally formed when four major European aerospace firms agreed to work together to build commercial airliners. In 2000, the four agreed to transform the consortium into a global company to achieve operations efficiencies that would allow it to compete better against Boeing. Meanwhile, Boeing is joining together with its own consortium to develop new 787 Dreamliner aircraft.[62]

Sematech, the other candidate for most prominent consortium, was originally an exclusively American operation. Sematech is an R&D consortium formed in Austin, Texas, during the 1980s to regain America's lead in semiconductor development and sales from Japan. Members included firms such as IBM, Intel, Texas Instruments, Motorola, and Hewlett-Packard. However, at the turn of the millennium even Sematech went international. Several of the founding American companies left and were replaced by firms from Taiwan, Korea, Germany, and the Netherlands (still none from Japan).

---

[61] Eric W. K. Tsang, Duc Tri Nguyen, and M. Krishna Erramilli, "Knowledge Acquisition and Performance in International Joint Ventures in the Transition Economy of Vietnam," *Journal of International Marketing* 12, no. 2 (2004), pp. 82–103; Charles Dhanaraj, Marjorie A. Lyles, H. Kevin Steensma, and Laszlo Tihanyi, "Managing Tacit and Explicit Knowledge Transfer in IJVs: The Role of Embeddedness and the Impact on Performance," *Journal of International Business Studies* 35, no. 5 (2004), pp. 428–42; Yan Zhang, Haiyang Li, Michael A. Hitt, and Geng Cui, "R&D Intensity and International Joint Venture Performance in an Emerging Market: Moderating Effects of Market Focus and Ownership Structure," *Journal of International Business Studies* 38 (2007), pp. 944–60.

[62] Peter Pae, "Japanese Helping 787 Take Wing," *Los Angeles Times*, May 9, 2005, pp. C1, C5.

CROSSING BORDERS 11.4

The Consortium Goes Corporate—Bad News for Boeing?

The partners in Airbus Industrie jacked up the competitive pressure on Boeing by turning their consortium into a corporation and officially starting to sell the A380 superjumbo jet. The announcement by the consortium companies came only hours before three of them launched the initial public offering of their merged company, the European Aeronautic Defence & Space Company (EADS), through which they planned to raise 3.5 billion euros.

Airbus was run by four companies—one French, one Spanish, one German, and one British. The four built planes as allied but independent companies and marketed them through their Airbus Industrie joint venture. Under the new agreement, they combined all their individual Airbus production assets and the joint venture (EADS) into a new French-registered company, the working name of which is Airbus Integrated Company (AIC).

The partners had said that creating the AIC was a prerequisite to launching the 550-seat A380. Developing the jet, which would be the world's largest

passenger plane, will cost $12 billion, and the partners had said that the complex consortium structure was too inefficient to support such a large project.

The A380 has already drawn interest and orders from at least eight airlines, among them Quantas, Singapore Airlines, and Air France. The superjumbo jet will compete with Boeing's 400+-seat 747 jumbo jets, a major source of profit for the Seattle company because it had a monopoly on building the biggest jets. The consolidation of Airbus should make it more nimble and profitable as well as help it compete against Boeing. The A380 project should break even within 10 years on sales of 250 planes. Airbus already has booked almost 200 orders. Are they sleepless in Seattle?

Sources: Daniel Michaels, "It's Official: Airbus Will Become a Company and Market A380 Jet," *The Wall Street Journal Europe*, June 26, 2000, p. 6; Stanley Holmes, "Boeing Is Choking on Airbus' Fumes," *BusinessWeek*, June 30, 2003, p. 50; "Airshow—Aibus has 196 Orders for A380 Superjumbo," *Reuters*, February 19, 2008.

The firm is also broadening its own investment portfolio to include a greater variety of international companies.

All strategic international alliances are susceptible to problems of coordination. For example, some analysts blamed the international breadth of Boeing's 787 Dreamliner consortium for the costly delays in manufacturing the new jet. Further, circumstances and/or partners can change in ways that render agreements untenable, and often such corporate relationships are short lived. Ford and Nissan launched a joint venture minivan in 1992 called the Mercury Villager/Nissan Quest. The car was mildly successful in the U.S. market, but in 2002 the joint venture stopped producing the cars—that's two years earlier than the original contract called for. Now that Nissan is controlled by French automaker Renault, it began producing its own minivan in 2003 for sale in the United States. When General Motors formed a joint venture with Daewoo, its purpose was to achieve a significant position in the Asian car market. Instead, Daewoo used the alliance to enhance its own automobile technology, and by the time the partnership was terminated, GM had created a new global competitor for itself.

Nestlé has been involved in a particularly ugly dissolution dispute with Dabur India. The Swiss firm owned 60 percent and the Indian firm 40 percent of a joint venture biscuit company, Excelcia Foods. Following months of acrimony, Dabur filed a petition with the Indian government accusing Nestlé of indulging in oppression of the minority shareholder and of mismanaging the JV company. In particular, Dabur alleged that Nestlé was purposefully running Excelcia into bankruptcy so that Nestlé could wriggle out of its "non-compete obligations and go after the India-biscuit market using another brand." Nestlé countered that the problem had more to do with the partners' inability to agree on a mutually acceptable business plan. The dispute was eventually settled out of court by Nestlé buying Dabur's 40 percent interest, shortly after which Excelcia was closed in lieu of restructuring.

Direct Foreign Investment

A fourth means of foreign market development and entry is *direct foreign investment*, that is, investment within a foreign country. Companies may invest locally to capitalize on low-cost labor, to avoid high import taxes, to reduce the high costs of transportation to market, to gain access to raw materials and technology,[63] or as a means of gaining market entry.[64] Firms may either invest in or buy local companies or establish new operations facilities. The local firms enjoy important benefits aside from the investments themselves, such as substantial technology transfers[65] and the capability to export to a more diversified customer base.[66] As with the other modes of market entry, several factors have been found to influence the structure and performance of direct investments: (1) timing—first movers have advantages but are more risky;[67] (2) the growing complexity[68] and contingencies of contracts;[69] (3) transaction cost structures;[70] (4) technology transfer;[71] (5) degree of product differentiation;[72] (6) the previous experiences and cultural diversity of acquired firms;[73] and (7) advertising and reputation barriers.[74] This mix of considerations and risks makes for increasingly difficult decisions about such foreign investments. But as legal restrictions continue to ease with WTO and other international agreements, more and more large firms are choosing to enter markets via direct investment.

The growth of free trade areas that are tariff free among members but have a common tariff for nonmembers creates an opportunity that can be capitalized on by direct investment. Similar to its Japanese competitors, Korea's Samsung has invested some $500 million to build television tube plants in Tijuana, Mexico, to feed the already huge NAFTA television industry centered there. Kyocera Corporation, a Japanese high-tech company, bought Qualcomm's wireless consumer phone business as a means of fast entry into the American market. Yahoo! paid $1 billion for a 40 percent stake in Chinese competitor Alibaba.[75] Finally, Nestlé is building a new milk factory in Thailand to serve the ASEAN Free Trade Area.

A hallmark of global companies today is the establishment of manufacturing operations throughout the world.[76] This trend will increase as barriers to free trade are eliminated and companies can locate manufacturing wherever it is most cost effective. The selection of an

---

[63] Sunil Venaik, David F. Midgley, and Timothy M. Devinney, "Dual Paths to Performance: The Impact of Global Pressures on MNC Subsidiary Conduct and Performance," *Journal of International Business Studies* 36 (2005), pp. 655–75; Tony S. Frost and Changhui Zhou, "R&D Co-Practice and 'Reverse' Knowledge Integration in Multinational Firms," *Journal of International Business Studies* 36 (2005), pp. 676–87.

[64] Donna L. Paul and Rossitza B. Wooster, "Strategic Investments by US Firms in Transition Economies," *Journal of International Business Studies* 39 (2008), pp. 249–66.

[65] Jasjit Singh, "Asymmetry of Knowledge Spillovers between MNCs and Host Country Firms," *Journal of International Business Studies* 38 (2007), pp. 764–86.

[66] Rashimi Banga, "The Export-Diversifying Impact of Japanese and US Foreign Direct Investments in the Indian Manufacturing Sector," *Journal of International Business Studies* 37 (2006), pp. 558–68.

[67] Andrew Delios and Shige Makino, "Timing of Entry and the Foreign Subsidiary Performance of Japanese Firms," *Journal of International Marketing* 11, no. 3 (2003), pp. 83–105.

[68] Peter J. Buckley and Pervez Ghauri, "Globalization, Economic Geography, and the Strategy of Multinational Enterprises," *Journal of International Business Studies* 35, no. 2 (2004), pp. 81–98.

[69] Jeffrey J. Reuer, Oded Shenkar, and Roberto Ragozzino, "Mitigating Risk in International Mergers and Acquisitions: The Role of Contingent Payouts," *Journal of International Business Studies* 35, no. 1 (2004), pp. 19–32.

[70] Hongxin Zhao, Yadong Luo, and Taewon Suh, "Transaction Cost Determinants and Ownership-Based Entry Mode Choice: A Meta-Analytic Review," *Journal of International Business Studies* 35, no. 6 (2004), pp. 524–44.

[71] Shih-Fen S. Chen, "Extending Internationalization Theory: A New Perspective on International Technology Transfer and Its Generalization," *Journal of International Business Studies* 36, no. 2 (2005), pp. 231–45.

[72] Lilach Nachum and Cliff Wymbs, "Product Differentiation, External Economies, and MNE Location Choices: M&A Global Cities," *Journal of International Business Studies* 36 (2005), pp. 415–34.

[73] Klaus Uhlenbruck, "Developing Acquired Foreign Subsidiaries: The Experience of MNEs in Transition Economies," *Journal of International Business Studies* 35, no. 2 (2004), pp. 109–23.

[74] Shin-Fen S. Chen and Ming Zeng, "Japanese Investors' Choice of Acquisition vs. Startups in the U.S.: The Role of Reputation Barriers and Advertising Outlays," *International Journal of Research in Marketing* 21, no. 2 (2004), pp. 123–36.

[75] Jason Dean and Jonathan Cheng, "Meet Jack Ma, Who Will Guide Yahoo in China," *The Wall Street Journal*, August 12, 2005, pp. B1, B3.

[76] John A. Doukas and L. H. P. Lang, "Foreign Direct Investment, Diversification, and Firm Performance," *Journal of International Business Studies* 34, no. 2 (2003), pp. 153–72.

entry mode and partners are critical decisions, because the nature of the firm's operations in the country market is affected by and depends on the choices made. The entry mode affects the future decisions because each mode entails an accompanying level of resource commitment, and changing from one entry mode to another without considerable loss of time and money is difficult.

Organizing for Global Competition

An international marketing plan should optimize the resources committed to company objectives. The organizational plan includes the type of organizational arrangements and management process to be used and the scope and location of responsibility.[77] Because organizations need to reflect a wide range of company-specific characteristics—such as size, level of policy decisions, length of chain of command, staff support, source of natural and personnel resources, degree of control, cultural differences in decision-making styles,[78] centralization, and type or level of marketing involvement—devising a standard organizational structure is difficult.[79] Many ambitious multinational plans meet with less than full success because of confused lines of authority, poor communications, and lack of cooperation between headquarters and subsidiary organizations.[80]

An organizational structure that effectively integrates domestic and international marketing activities has yet to be devised.[81] Companies face the need to maximize the international potential of their products and services without diluting their domestic marketing efforts. Companies are usually structured around one of three alternatives: (1) global product divisions responsible for product sales throughout the world; (2) geographical divisions responsible for all products and functions within a given geographical area; or (3) a matrix organization consisting of either of these arrangements with centralized sales and marketing run by a centralized functional staff, or a combination of area operations and global product management.

Companies that adopt the global product division structure are generally experiencing rapid growth and have broad, diverse product lines. General Electric is a good example, having reorganized its global operations into six product divisions—infrastructure, industrial, commercial financial services, NBC Universal, health care, and consumer finance.[82] Geographic structures work best when a close relationship with national and local governments is important.

The matrix form—the most extensive of the three organizational structures—is popular with companies as they reorganize for global competition. A matrix structure permits management to respond to the conflicts that arise among functional activity, product, and geography. It is designed to encourage sharing of experience, resources, expertise, technology, and information among global business units. At its core is better decision making, in

---

[77] Shichun Xu, S. Tamer Cavusgil, and J. Chris White, "The Impact of Strategic Fit among Strategy, Structure, and Processes on Multinational Corporation Performance: A Multi-Method Assessment," *Journal of International Marketing* 14 (2006), pp. 1–31.

[78] Gerald Albaum, Joel Herche, Julie Yu, Felicitas Evangelista, Brian Murphy, and Patrick Poon, "Differences in Marketing Managers' Decision Making Styles within the Asia-Pacific Region: Implications for Strategic Alliances," *Journal of Global Marketing* 21 (2007), pp. 63–72.

[79] Ingmar Bjorkman, Carl F. Fey, and Hyeon Jeong Park, "Institutional Theory and MNC Subsidiary HRM Practices: Evidence from a Three-Country Study," *Journal of International Business Studies* 38 (2007), pp. 430–46.

[80] Claude Obadia and Irena Vida, "Endogenous Opportunism in Small and Medium-Sized Enterprises' Foreign Subsidiaries: Classification and Research Propositions," *Journal of International Marketing* 14 (2006), pp. 57–86.

[81] Kelly Hewett and William O. Bearden, "Dependence, Trust, and Relational Behavior on the Part of Foreign Subsidiary Marketing Operations: Implications for Managing Global Marketing Operations," *Journal of Marketing* 65, no. 4 (October 2001), pp. 51–66.

[82] Kathryn Kranhold, "GE Reorganizes into Six Units, Names Three New Vice Chairmen," *The Wall Street Journal* (online), June 23, 2005.

Exhibit 11.4

Schematic Marketing Organization Plan Combining Product, Geographic, and Functional Approaches

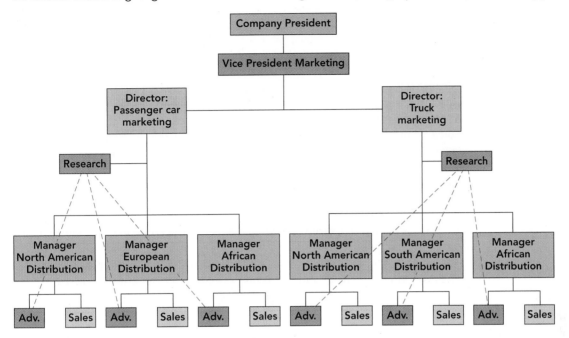

which multiple points of view affecting functional activity, product, and geography are examined and shared. A matrix organization can also better accommodate customers who themselves have global operations and global requirements.

A company may be organized by product lines but have geographical subdivisions under the product categories. Both may be supplemented by functional staff support. Exhibit 11.4 shows such a combination. Modifications of this basic arrangement are used by a majority of large companies doing business internationally.

The turbulence of global markets requires flexible organizational structures. Forty-three large U.S. companies studied indicated that they planned a total of 137 organizational changes for their international operations over a five-year period. Included were such changes as centralizing international decision making, creating global divisions, forming centers of excellence, and establishing international business units. Bausch & Lomb, one of the companies in the study, revamped its international organizational structure by collapsing its international division into a worldwide system of three regions and setting up business management committees to oversee global marketing and manufacturing strategies for four major product lines. Bausch & Lomb's goal was to better coordinate central activities without losing touch at the local level. "Global coordination is essential," according to the company's CEO, "but in a way that maintains the integrity of the foreign subsidiaries." More recently, General Motors dramatically revamped its global strategies through its network of strategic alliances.

To the extent that there is a trend, two factors seem to be sought, regardless of the organizational structure: a single locus for direction and control and the creation of a simple line organization that is based on a more decentralized network of local companies.

Locus of Decision   Considerations of where decisions will be made, by whom, and by which method constitute a major element of organizational strategy. Management policy must be explicit about which decisions are to be made at corporate headquarters, which at international headquarters, which at regional levels, and which at national or even local levels. Most companies also limit the amount of money to be spent at each level. Decision levels for determination of policy, strategy, and tactical decisions must be established. Tactical decisions normally should be made at the lowest possible level, without country-by-country duplication.[83] This guideline requires American headquarters managers to trust the expertise of their local managers.

Centralized versus Decentralized Organizations

An infinite number of organizational patterns for the headquarters activities of multinational firms exist, but most fit into one of three categories: centralized, regionalized, or decentralized organizations. The fact that all of the systems are used indicates that each has certain advantages and disadvantages. The chief advantages of centralization are the availability of experts at one location, the ability to exercise a high degree of control on both the planning and implementation phases, and the centralization of all records and information.[84]

Some companies effect extreme decentralization by selecting competent local managers and giving them full responsibility for national or regional operations. These executives are in direct day-to-day contact with the market but lack a broad company view, which can mean partial loss of control for the parent company.

In many cases, whether a company's formal organizational structure is centralized or decentralized, the informal organization reflects some aspect of all organizational systems. This reflection is especially true relative to the locus of decision making. Studies show that even though product decisions may be highly centralized, subsidiaries may have a substantial amount of local influence in pricing, advertising, and distribution decisions. If a product is culturally sensitive, the decisions are more likely to be decentralized.

---

[83] K. Hewett, M. S. Roth, and K. Roth, "Conditions Influencing Headquarters and Foreign Subsidiary Roles in Marketing Activities and Their Effects on Performance," *Journal of International Business Studies* 34, no. 6 (2003), pp. 567–85.

[84] Peter J. Buckley and Martin J. Carter, "A Formal Analysis of Knowledge Combinations in Multinational Enterprises," *Journal of International Business Studies* 35, no. 5 (2004), pp. 371–84.

Summary

Expanding markets around the world have increased competition for all levels of international marketing. To keep abreast of the competition and maintain a viable position for increasingly competitive markets, a global perspective is necessary. Global competition also requires quality products designed to meet ever-changing customer needs and rapidly advancing technology. Cost containment, customer satisfaction, and a greater number of players mean that every opportunity to refine international business practices must be examined in light of company goals. Collaborative relationships, strategic international alliances, strategic planning, and alternative market-entry strategies are important avenues to global marketing that must be implemented in the planning and organization of global marketing management.

Questions

1. Define the following terms:

   global marketing management   licensing
   corporate planning   franchising
   direct exporting   joint venture
   strategic planning   global market concept
   indirect exporting   SIA
   tactical planning

2. Define strategic planning. How does strategic planning for international marketing differ from domestic marketing?

3. Discuss the benefits to an MNC of accepting the global market concept. Explain the three points that define a global approach to international marketing.

4. Discuss the effect of shorter product life cycles on a company's planning process.

5. What is the importance of collaborative relationships to competition?

6. In Phases 1 and 2 of the international planning process, countries may be dropped from further consideration as potential markets. Discuss some of the conditions that may exist in a country that would lead a marketer to exclude a country in each phase.

7. Assume that you are the director of international marketing for a company producing refrigerators. Select one country in Latin America and one in Europe and develop screening criteria to use in evaluating the two countries. Make any additional assumptions that are necessary about your company.

8. "The dichotomy typically drawn between export marketing and overseas marketing is partly fictional; from a marketing standpoint, they are but alternative methods of capitalizing on foreign market opportunities." Discuss.

9. How will entry into a developed foreign market differ from entry into a relatively untapped market?

10. Why do companies change their organizations when they go from being an international to a global company?

11. Formulate a general rule for deciding where international business decisions should be made.

12. Explain the popularity of joint ventures.

13. Compare the organizational implications of joint ventures versus licensing.

14. Visit the Web sites of General Motors and Ford, both car manufacturers in the United States. Search their sites and compare their international involvement. How would you classify each—as exporter, international, or global?

15. Using the sources in Question 14, list the different entry modes each company uses.

16. Visit the Nestlé Corporation Web site (www.nestle.com/) and the Unilever Web site (www.unilever.com/). Compare their strategies toward international markets. In what ways (besides product categories) do they differ in their international marketing?

12

products and services
for consumers

CHAPTER OUTLINE

CHAPTER LEARNING OBJECTIVES

What you should learn from Chapter 12:

- The importance of offering a product suitable for the intended market

- The relationship between product acceptance and the market into which it is introduced

- The importance of quality and how quality is defined

- Country-of-origin effects on product image

- Physical, mandatory, and cultural requirements for product adaptation

- The need to view all attributes of a product in order to overcome resistance to acceptance

Global Perspective

HONG KONG—DISNEY ROLLS THE DICE AGAIN

With the opening of Disneyland in Anaheim in 1955, the notion of the modern theme park was born. The combination of the rides, various other attractions, and the Disney characters has remained irresistible. Tokyo Disneyland has also proved to be a big success, making modest money for Disney through licensing and major money for its Japanese partners. Three-fourths of the visitors at the Tokyo park are repeat visitors, the best kind.

Then came EuroDisney. Dissatisfied with the ownership arrangements at the Tokyo park, the EuroDisney deal was structured very differently. Disney negotiated a much greater ownership stake in the park and adjacent hotel and restaurant facilities. Along with the greater control and potential profits came a higher level of risk.

Even before the park's grand opening ceremony in 1992, protestors decried Disney's "assault" on the French culture. The location was also a mistake—the Mediterranean climate of the alternative Barcelona site seemed much more attractive on chilly winter days in France. Managing both a multicultural workforce and clientele proved daunting. For example, what language was most appropriate for the Pirates of the Caribbean attraction—French or English? Neither attendance nor consumer purchases targets were achieved during the early years: Both were off by about 10 percent. By the summer of 1994, EuroDisney had lost some $900 million. Real consideration was given to closing the park.

A Saudi prince provided a crucial cash injection that allowed for a temporary financial restructuring and a general reorganization, including a new French CEO and a new name, Paris Disneyland. The Paris park returned to profitability, and attendance increased. However, the temporary holiday on royalties, management fees, and leases is now expired, and profits are dipping again. Disney's response was to expand with a second "Disney Studios" theme park and an adjacent retail and office complex at the Paris location. Again in 2005, the Saudi prince injected another $33 million into the park.

In 2006 Hong Kong Disneyland opened for business. The Hong Kong government provided the bulk of the investment for the project (almost 80 percent of the $3 billion needed). As in Europe, the clientele is culturally diverse, though primarily Chinese. Performances are done in Cantonese (the local dialect), Mandarin (the national language), and English. The park drew 5.2 million visitors in 2006, but attendance fell sharply to about 4 million in 2007. Disney has had to renegotiate its financial structure and schedule as a consequence. On the positive side of the ledger, the firm and the Hong Kong government are still talking about expanding the park, and Disney inked a new joint venture agreement for the online delivery of entertainment services to customers in China. Indeed, it will be quite interesting to follow Mickey's international adventures, both the ups and downs.

Sources: http://www.disney.go.com; "Disney to Build Hong Kong Theme Park; Euro Disney's Profit Slumped," *Dow Jones News Service,* November 2, 1999; Richard Verrier, "Saudi Prince Helps Out EuroDisney," *Los Angeles Times,* January 12, 2005, p. C2; "Hong Kong Disney Crowds Disappoint for Second Year," *Reuters News*, December 12, 2007.

The opportunities and challenges for international marketers of consumer goods and services today have never been greater or more diverse. New consumers are springing up in emerging markets in eastern Europe, the Commonwealth of Independent States, China and other Asian countries, India, Latin America—in short, globally. Although some of these emerging markets have little purchasing power today, they promise to be huge markets in the future. In the more mature markets of the industrialized world, opportunity and challenge also abound as consumers' tastes become more sophisticated and complex, and as increases in purchasing power provide them with the means of satisfying new demands.

As described in the Global Perspective, Disney is the archetypal American exporter for global consumer markets. The distinction between products and services for such companies means little. Their DVDs are *products*, whereas cinema performances of the same movies are *services*. Consumers at the theme parks (including foreign tourists at domestic sites) pay around $60 to get in the gate, but they also spend about the same amount on hats, T-shirts, and meals while there. And the movies, of course, help sell the park tickets and the associated toys and clothing. Indeed, this lack of distinction between products and services has led to the invention of new terms encompassing both products and services, such as *market offerings*[1] and *business-to-consumer marketing*. However, the governmental agencies that keep track of international trade still maintain the questionable product–service distinction, and thus so do we in this chapter and the next.[2] The reader should also note that when it comes to U.S. exports targeting consumers, the totals are about evenly split among the three major categories of durable goods (such as cars and computers), nondurable goods (mainly food, drugs, toys), and services (for example, tourism and telecommunications).

The trend for larger firms is toward becoming global in orientation and strategy. However, product adaptation is as important a task in a smaller firm's marketing effort as it is for global companies. As competition for world markets intensifies and as market preferences become more global, selling what is produced for the domestic market in the same manner as it is sold at home proves to be increasingly less effective. Some products cannot be sold at all in foreign markets without modification; others may be sold as is, but their acceptance is greatly enhanced when tailored specifically to market needs. In a competitive struggle, quality products and services that meet the needs and wants of consumers at an affordable price should be the goal of any marketing firm.

Quality

Global competition is placing new emphasis on some basic tenets of business. It is shortening product life cycles and focusing on the importance of quality, competitive prices, and innovative products. The power in the marketplace is shifting from a sellers' to a customers' market, and the latter have more choices because more companies are competing for their attention. More competition and more choices put more power in the hands of the customer, and that of course drives the need for quality. Gone are the days when the customer's knowledge was limited to one or at best just a few different products. Today the customer knows what is best, cheapest, and highest quality, largely due to the Internet. It is the customer who defines quality in terms of his or her needs and resources. For example, cell phones that don't roam don't sell in Japan at any price, but in China, they do very well indeed. Just ask the folks at UTStarcom, a California firm that now sells in India and Vietnam, as well as China.[3]

American products have always been among the world's best, but competition is challenging us to make even better products. In most global markets, the cost and quality of a product

---

[1] For example, Philip Kotler and Kevin Lane Keller, *Marketing Management,* 13th ed. (Upper Saddle River, NJ: Prentice Hall, 2008).

[2] We hope that it is obvious that many of the points we make regarding the development of consumer products are pertinent to consumer services as well, and vice versa. Of course, some distinctions are still substantive. These are focused on in Chapter 12 the section entitled "Marketing Consumer Services Globally."

[3] Peter Burrows, "Ringing off the Hook in China," *BusinessWeek*, June 9, 2003, pp. 80–81; *The Economist*, "Calling an End to Poverty," July 9, 2005, p. 52.

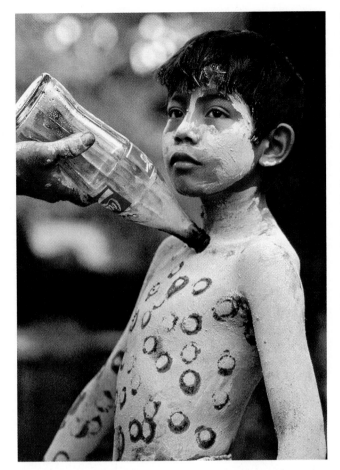

Products are not used in the same ways in all markets. Here a boy in an eastern Mexican village is prepared for a "Jaguar dance" to bring rain. Clay, ashes, and the globally ubiquitous Coke bottle make for the best cat costumes. (*© Kenneth Garrett/National Geographic Image Collection*)

are among the most important criteria by which purchases are made. For consumer and industrial products alike, the reason often given for preferring one brand over another is better quality at a competitive price. Quality, as a competitive tool, is not new to the business world, but many believe that it is the deciding factor in world markets. However, we must be clear about what we mean by quality.

Quality Defined   *Quality* can be defined on two dimensions: market-perceived quality and performance quality.[4] Both are important concepts, but consumer perceptions of a quality product often has more to do with market-perceived quality[5] than performance quality.[6] The relationship of quality conformance to customer satisfaction is analogous to an airline's delivery of quality. If viewed internally from the firm's perspective (performance quality), an airline has achieved quality conformance with a safe flight and landing. But because the consumer expects performance quality to be a given, quality to the consumer is more than compliance (a safe flight and landing). Rather, cost, timely service, frequency of flights, comfortable seating, and performance of airline personnel from check-in to baggage claim are all part of the customer's experience that is perceived as being of good or poor quality. Considering the number of air miles flown daily, the airline industry is approaching zero defects in quality conformance, yet who will say that customer satisfaction is anywhere near perfection? These market-perceived quality attributes are embedded in the total product, that is, the physical or core product and all the additional features the consumer expects.

In a competitive marketplace in which the market provides choices, most consumers expect performance quality to be a given. Naturally, if the product does not perform up to their standards, it will be rejected. Compare hybrid gas-electric systems for example—Toyota's is designed to save fuel in city driving, General Motors' performs best on the highway during long trips. Which drive system offers higher quality depends on the consumer's needs. Japanese consumers find themselves stuck in traffic more frequently, whereas Americans tend toward road trip types of activities.[7] When there are alternative products, all of which meet performance quality standards, the product chosen is the one that meets market-perceived quality attributes. Interestingly, China's leading refrigerator maker recognized the importance of these market-perceived quality attributes when it adopted a technology that enabled consumers to choose from 20 different colors and textures for door handles and moldings. For example, a consumer can design an off-white refrigerator with green marble handles and moldings. Why is this important? Because it lets consumers "update their living rooms," where most of Chinese refrigerators are parked. The company's motive was simple: It positioned its product for competition with multinational brands by giving the consumer another expression of quality.

[4] Xiaohua Lin and Richard Germain, "Product Quality Orientation and Its Performance Implications in Chinese State-Owned Enterprises," *Journal of International Marketing* 11, no. 2 (2003), pp. 59–78.

[5] There is much evidence that perceptions of quality vary across cultures. For example, see Terrence Witkowski and Mary Wolfinbarger, "Comparative Service Quality: German and American Ratings of Five Different Service Settings," *Journal of Business Research*, November 2002, pp. 875–81.

[6] Michael Laroche, Linda C. Ueltschy, Shuzo Abe, Mark Cleveland, and Peter P. Yannopoulos, "Service Quality Perceptions and Customer Satisfaction: Evaluating the Role of Culture," *Journal of International Marketing* 13, no. 3 (2004), pp. 58–85.

[7] Joseph B. White, "One System, Two Visions," *The Wall Street Journal* (online), May 7, 2007.

CROSSING BORDERS 12.1   The Quality of Food Is a Matter of Taste

Food preferences vary not only across countries but within them as well. For example, many Vietnamese still have to eat whatever they can lay their hands on. Pet birds and dogs are kept indoors to save them from the cooking pot. In 1998, the government tried to reduce the consumption of snakes and cats by banning their sale because the exploding rat population was damaging crops. Instead, peasants simply took to eating rats as well. The dwindling number of rats, in turn, has caused an explosion in the numbers of another tasty treat: snails.

Meanwhile, in nearby Ho Chi Minh City, the country's commercial capital, a recent survey found that 12.5 percent of children were obese—and the figure is rising. Local restaurants vie with one another in expense and luxury. Hoang Khai, a local businessman, recalls how his family always celebrated at home when he was young, because there was nowhere to go out.

He decided to change all that by plowing the returns from his textile business into a restaurant lavish enough to suit the city's business elite. The result is *Au Manoir de Khai*, a colonial villa smothered in gilt and silk where a meal with imported wine can set you back more than most Vietnamese earn in a year.

One has to wonder how ice cream from Fugetsudo, a small confectionary shop in northern Japan, would sell in either neighborhood in Vietnam. You can get fish, sea slug, whale meat, turtle, or cedar chip–flavored ice cream there. Fugetsudo's competition sells pickled-orchid, chicken-wing, shrimp, eel, and short-necked clam flavors. Yum!

Sources: "Eating Out in Vietnam," *The Economist*, December 21, 2002, pp. 49–50; Phred Dvorak, "Something Fishy Is Going On in Japan in the Ice-Cream Biz," *The Wall Street Journal*, September 4, 2002, p. 1; Eric Johnston, "Savour the Whale," *The Guardian*, July 4, 2005, p. 6.

Quality is also measured in many industries by objective third parties. In the United States, J.D. Power and Associates has expanded its auto quality ratings, which are based on consumer surveys, to other areas, such as computers. Customer satisfaction indexes developed first in Sweden are now being used to measure customer satisfaction across a wide variety of consumer products and services.[8] Finally, the U.S. Department of Commerce annually recognizes American firms for the quality of their international offerings—the Ritz Carlton Hotel chain has won the prestigious award twice.

Maintaining Quality

Maintaining performance quality is critical,[9] but frequently a product that leaves the factory with performance quality is damaged as it passes through the distribution chain. This damage is a special problem for many global brands for which production is distant from the market and/or control of the product is lost because of the distribution system within the market. When Mars Company's Snickers and other Western confectioneries were introduced to Russia, they were a big hit. Foreign brands such as Mars, Toblerone, Waldbaur, and Cadbury were the top brands—indeed, only one Russian brand placed in the top ten. But within five years, the Russian brands had retaken eight of the top spots, and only one U.S. brand, Mars's Dove bars, was in the top ten.

What happened? A combination of factors caused the decline. Russia's Red October Chocolate Factory got its act together; modernized its packaging, product mix, and equipment; and set out to capture the market. Performance quality was also an issue. When the Russian market opened to outside trade, foreign companies eager to get into the market dumped surplus out-of-date and poor-quality products. In other cases, chocolates were smuggled in and sold on street corners and were often mishandled in the process. By the

---

[8] Claes Fornell, Michael D. Johnson, Eugene W. Anderson, Jaesung Cha, and Barbara Everitt Bryant, "The American Consumer Satisfaction Index: Nature, Purpose, and Findings," *Journal of Marketing* 60, no. 4 (October 1996), pp. 35–46; http://www.cfigroup.com, 2008.

[9] Duncan I. Simester, John R. Hauser, Birger Wernerfelt, and Roland T. Rust, "Implementing Quality Improvement Programs Designed to Enhance Customer Satisfaction: Quasi-Experiments in the United States and Spain," *Journal of Marketing Research* 37 (February 2000), pp. 102–12; Mark Landler, "Missteps Haunt Smart Car," *International Herald Tribune*, April 2–3, 2005, pp. 1, 4.

time they made it to consumers, the chocolates were likely to be misshapen or discolored—poor quality compared with Russia's Red October chocolate.

Market-perceived quality was also an issue. Russian chocolate has a different taste because of its formulation—more cocoa and chocolate liqueur are used than in Western brands, which makes it grittier. Thus the Red October brand appeals more to Russian tastes, even though it is generally priced above Western brands. As evinced by this example, quality is not just desirable, it is essential for success in today's competitive global market, and the decision to standardize or adapt a product is crucial in delivering quality.

Physical or Mandatory Requirements and Adaptation

A product may have to change in a number of ways to meet the physical or mandatory requirements of a new market, ranging from simple package changes to total redesign of the physical core product. In many countries, the term *product homologation* is used to describe the changes mandated by local product and service standards. A recent study reaffirmed the often-reported finding that mandatory adaptations were more frequently the reason for product adaptation than adapting for cultural reasons.

Red October brand chocolate (on the left) still competes well against foreign rivals Nestlé and Mars on Moscow store shelves. One advertising executive in Moscow reports that Russians are experiencing a renewed nationalism in product preferences as their economy continues to surge along with world oil prices. We have no idea what the "for Men" appeal is all about, but it apparently works in Moscow?

Some changes are obvious with relatively little analysis; a cursory examination of a country will uncover the need to rewire electrical goods for a different voltage system, simplify a product when the local level of technology is not high, or print multilingual labels where required by law. Electrolux, for example, offers a cold-wash-only washing machine in Asian countries where electric power is expensive or scarce. Other necessary changes may surface only after careful study of an intended market.

Legal, economic, political, technological, and climatic requirements of the local marketplace often dictate product adaptation. During a period in India when the government strongly opposed foreign investment, PepsiCo. changed its product name to Lehar-Pepsi (in Hindi, *lehar* means "wave") to gain as much local support as possible. The name returned to Pepsi-Cola when the political climate turned favorable. Laws that vary among countries usually set specific package sizes and safety and quality standards. The World Health Organization is only beginning to regulate the marketing of high-carcinogen American cigarettes. But, most interesting, videogame content is regulated around the world according to violence levels and sexual content.

The less economically developed a market is, the greater degree of change a product may need for acceptance. One study found that only one in ten products could be marketed in developing countries without modification of some sort. To make a purchase more affordable in low-income countries, the number of units per package may have to be reduced from the typical quantities offered in high-income countries. Razor blades, cigarettes, chewing gum, and other multiple-pack items are often sold singly or two to a pack instead of the more customary 10 or 20. Cheetos, a product of PepsiCo.'s Frito-Lay, is packaged in 15-gram boxes in China so it can be priced at 1 yuan, or about 12 cents. At this price, even children with little spending money can afford Cheetos.

Changes may also have to be made to accommodate climatic differences.[10] General Motors of Canada, for example, experienced major problems with several thousand Chevrolet automobiles shipped to a Middle Eastern country; GM quickly discovered they were unfit for the hot, dusty climate. Supplementary air filters and different clutches had to be added to adjust for the problem. Similarly, crackers have to be packaged in tins rather than cardboard boxes for humid areas.

Because most products sold abroad by international companies originate in home markets and most require some form of modification, companies need a systematic process to identify products that need adaptation.

Green Marketing and Product Development

A quality issue of growing importance the world over, especially in Europe and the United States, is green marketing. Europe has been at the forefront of the "green movement," with strong public opinion and specific legislation favoring environmentally friendly marketing

[10] Philip M. Parker and Nader T. Tavossoli, "Homeostasis and Consumer Behavior across Cultures," *International Journal of Research in Marketing* 17, no. 1 (March 2000), pp. 33–53.

CROSSING BORDERS 12.2

In Germany, Video Games Showing Frontal Nudity Are OK, but Blood Is *Verboten*

Video game heroine Lara Croft is an adrenaline junkie unafraid of getting bloody. But in Germany, the buxom starlet of the "Tomb Raider" series doesn't bleed—even if she's being mauled by a tiger.

Although the $25 billion video game industry is global, the games themselves aren't. They reflect the distinct cultures and traditions of different markets, and game publishers carefully tweak their titles and other details to tone down offensive materials. And "offensive" varies from country to country.

Red blood in a game sold in the United States turns green in Australia. A topless character in a European title acquires a bikini in the United States. Human enemies in an American game morph into robots in Germany. Violent sex scenes in a Japanese game disappear in the American versions.

Of all countries, Germany is one of the trickiest to tackle, publishers say. The country has spent five decades developing one of the world's strictest decency standards for virtually all media, from books and comics to music and games.

If a game features blood splatterings, decapitations, or death cries, it runs the risk of being placed on a government list known as "the index." Being indexed means it can't be sold to anyone under 18, displayed in stores, or advertised on television, in newspapers, or in magazines. Games containing pornography or glorifications of war, Nazism, and racial hatred face the same fate. Most recently the government has announced plans to forbid the sales of such graphic video games to minors.

The scariest part of this story is not the games themselves but the newest use of them as political tools. A game indexed in Germany involves a prisoner of war camp for Turkish detainees. On the other side, Hezbollah, the terrorist organization known for killing 240 American marines in Lebanon in 1983, has published a new "click-and-kill" game. When are such games more than just entertainment?

Sources: A. Phan and S. Sandell, "In Germany, Video Games Showing Frontal Nudity Are OK, but Blood Is *Verboten*," *Los Angeles Times*, June 9, 2003, p. C1; "Germany Plans Crackdown on Violent Video Games, Films," *Deutsche Welle*, October 12, 2007.

and products. *Green marketing* is a term used to identify concern with the environmental consequences of a variety of marketing activities. In the United States, Japanese car manufacturers are taking advantage of their gas-guzzling American cousins as consumers become more concerned about the environmental effects of SUVs like General Motors' Hummer. The European Commission has passed legislation to control all kinds of packaging waste throughout the European Union. Two critical issues that affect product development are the control of the packaging component of solid waste and consumer demand for environmentally friendly products.

The European Commission issued guidelines for ecolabeling that became operational in 1992. Under the directive, a product is evaluated on all significant environmental effects throughout its life cycle, from manufacturing to disposal—a cradle-to-grave approach. A detergent formulated to be biodegradable and nonpolluting would be judged friendlier than a detergent whose formulation would be harmful when discharged into the environment. Aerosol propellants that do not deplete the ozone layer are another example of environmentally friendly products. No country's laws yet require products to carry an ecolabel to be sold, however. The designation that a product is "environmentally friendly" is voluntary, and environmental success depends on the consumer selecting the ecology-friendly product.

Since the introduction of the ecolabel idea, Hoover washing machines have been the only products that have gained approval for the ecolabel. Interestingly enough, the benefits of winning the symbol have resulted in Hoover tripling its market share in Germany and doubling its share of the premium sector of the U.K. washing-machine market. The approval process seems to be deterring many European manufacturers, many of whom are using their own, unofficial symbols. The National Consumer Council, a consumer watchdog group, reports that many consumers are so confused and cynical about the myriad symbols that they are giving up altogether on trying to compare the green credentials of similar products.

Laws that mandate systems to control solid waste, while voluntary in one sense, do carry penalties. The EU law requires that packaging material through all levels of distribution, from the manufacturer to the consumer, be recycled or reused. Currently, between 50 percent and 65 percent of the weight of the packaging must be recovered, and between 25 percent and 45 percent of the weight of the totality of packaging materials contained in packaging waste will be recycled.

Each level of the distribution chain is responsible for returning all packaging, packing, and other waste materials up the chain. The biggest problem is with the packaging the customer takes home; by law the retailer must take back all packaging from the customer if no central recycling locations are available. For the manufacturer's product to participate in direct collection and not have to be returned to the retailer for recycling, the manufacturer must guarantee financial support for curbside or central collection of all materials. The growing public and political pressure to control solid waste is a strong incentive for compliance.

Although the packaging and solid waste rules are burdensome, there have been successful cases of not only meeting local standards but also being able to transfer this approach to other markets. Procter & Gamble's international operations integrated global environmental concerns as a response to increasing demands in Germany. It introduced Lenor, a fabric softener in a superconcentrated form, and sold it in a plastic refill pouch that reduced packaging by 85 percent. This move increased brand sales by 12 percent and helped set a positive tone with government regulators and activists. The success of Lenor was transferred to the United States, where P&G faced similar environmental pressures. A superconcentrated Downy, the U.S. brand of fabric softener, was repackaged in refill pouches that reduced package sizes by 75 percent, thereby costing consumers less and actually increasing Downy market share. The global marketer should not view green marketing as a European problem; concern for the environment is worldwide and similar legislation is sure to surface elsewhere. This discussion is yet another example of the need to adapt products for global marketing.

Products and Culture

To appreciate the complexity of standardized versus adapted products, one needs to understand how cultural influences are interwoven with the perceived value and importance a market places on a product. A product is more than a physical item: It is a bundle of satisfactions (or *utilities*) that the buyer receives. These utilities include its form, taste, color, odor, and texture; how it functions in use; the package; the label; the warranty; the manufacturer's and retailer's servicing; the confidence or prestige enjoyed by the brand; the manufacturer's reputation; the country of origin; and any other symbolic utility received from the possession or use of the goods. In short, the market relates to more than a product's physical form and primary function.[11] The values and customs within a culture confer much of the importance of these other benefits. In other words, a product is the sum of the physical and psychological satisfactions it provides the user.

A product's physical attributes generally are required to create its primary function. The primary function of an automobile, for example, is to move passengers from point A to point B. This ability requires a motor, transmission, and other physical features to achieve its primary purpose. The physical features or primary function of an automobile generally are in demand in all cultures where there is a desire to move from one point to another by ways other than by foot or animal power. Few changes to the physical attributes of a product are required when moving from one culture to another. However, an automobile has a bundle of psychological features that are as important in providing consumer satisfaction as its physical features. Within a specific culture, other automobile

[11] C. K. Prahalad, *The Fortune at the Bottom of the Pyramid* (Philadelphia: Wharton School Publishing, 2005).

Cola Turka holds a surprisingly large percentage of shelf space vis-à-vis Coke and Pepsi in this supermarket in Istanbul. The 2-liter bottle is priced at 2.00 lira, just under Coke's 2.05 lira. Cola Turka's TV ads, initially featuring American actor Chevy Chase speaking Turkish, seem to have worked well.

features (color, size, design, brand name, price) have little to do with its primary function—the movement from point A to B—but do add value to the satisfaction received.

The meaning and value imputed to the psychological attributes of a product can vary among cultures and are perceived as negative or positive. To maximize the bundle of satisfactions received and to create positive product attributes rather than negative ones, adaptation of the nonphysical features of a product may be necessary. Coca-Cola, frequently touted as a global product, found it had to change Diet Coke to Coke Light when it was introduced in Japan. Japanese women do not like to admit to dieting, because the idea of a diet implies sickness or medicine. So instead of emphasizing weight loss, "figure maintenance" is stressed. Anti-American sentiment is also causing Coke problems with Muslim consumers. At least four new competitors have popped up recently—Mecca Cola, Muslim Up, Arab Cola, and Cola Turka. McDonald's is also responding to such problems with its new McArabia sandwich.

Adaptation may require changes of any one or all of the psychological aspects of a product. A close study of the meaning of a product shows the extent to which the culture determines an individual's perception of what a product is and what satisfaction that product provides.

The adoption of some products by consumers can be affected as much by how the product concept conforms with their norms, values, and behavior patterns as by its physical or mechanical attributes. For example, only recently have Japanese consumers taken an interest in dishwashers—they simply didn't have room in the kitchen. However, very compact designs by Mitsubishi, Toto (a Japanese toilet company), and others are making new inroads into Japanese kitchens. A novelty always comes up against a closely integrated cultural pattern, and this conflict is primarily what determines whether, when, how, and in what form it gets adopted. Some financial services have been difficult to introduce into Muslim countries because the pious have claimed they promoted usury and gambling, both explicitly forbidden in the Koran. The Japanese have always found all body jewelry repugnant. The Scots have a decided resistance to pork and all its associated products, apparently from days long ago when such taboos were founded on fundamentalist interpretations of the Bible. Filter cigarettes have failed in at least one Asian country because a very low life expectancy hardly places people in the age bracket most prone to fears of lung cancer—even supposing that they shared Western attitudes about death. All these sorts of problems require product offering adaptation by international marketers.

When analyzing a product for a second market, the extent of adaptation required depends on cultural differences in product use and perception between the market the product was originally developed for and the new market. The greater these cultural differences between the two markets, the greater the extent of adaptation that may be necessary.

When instant cake mixes were introduced in Japan, the consumers' response was less than enthusiastic. Not only do Japanese reserve cakes for special occasions, but they prefer the cakes to be beautifully wrapped and purchased in pastry shops. The acceptance of instant cakes was further complicated by another cultural difference: Many Japanese homes do not have ovens. An interesting sidebar to this example is the company's attempt to correct for that problem by developing a cake mix that could be cooked in a rice cooker, which all Japanese homes have. The problem with that idea was that in a Japanese kitchen, rice and the manner in which it is cooked have strong cultural overtones, and to use the rice cooker to cook something other than rice is a real taboo.

Examples are typically given about cultures other than American, but the need for cultural adaptation is often necessary when a foreign company markets a product in the United States too. A major Japanese cosmetics company, Shiseido, attempted to break into the U.S. cosmetic market with the same products sold in Japan. After introducing them in more than 800 U.S. stores, the company realized that American taste in cosmetics is very different from Japanese tastes. The problem was that Shiseido's makeup required a time-consuming series of steps, a point that does not bother Japanese women.

Success was attained after designing a new line of cosmetics as easy to use as American products.

The problems of adapting a product to sell abroad are similar to those associated with the introduction of a new product at home. Products are not measured solely by their physical specifications. The nature of the new product is what it does to and for the customer—habits, tastes, and patterns of life. The problems illustrated in the cake mix example have little to do with the physical product or the user's ability to make effective use of it and more with the fact that acceptance and use of the cake mixes would have required upsetting behavior patterns considered correct or ideal.

Finally, there are some interesting surprises in the area of adaptation. The most recent example is Harry Potter. About 20 percent of the sales of his last adventure book in Japan are in English. Japanese consumers are looking for ways to augment English lessons, and the books and associated audiotapes fill that particular need very well. For them Potter is not just entertainment; it's education.[12]

Innovative Products and Adaptation

An important first step in adapting a product to a foreign market is to determine the degree of newness as perceived by the intended market. How people react to newness and how new a product is to a market must be understood. In evaluating the newness of a product, the international marketer must be aware that many products successful in the United States, having reached the maturity or even decline stage in their life cycles, may be perceived as new in another country or culture and thus must be treated as innovations. From a sociological viewpoint, any idea perceived as new by a group of people is an innovation.

Whether or not a group accepts an innovation, and the time it takes to do so, depends on the product's characteristics. Products new to a social system are innovations, and knowledge about the *diffusion* (i.e., the process by which innovation spreads) of innovation is helpful in developing a successful product strategy. Sony's marketing strategies for the U.S. introduction of its PlayStation 2 were well informed by its wild successes achieved six months earlier during the product's introduction in Japan. Conversely, mid-1990s dips in Japanese sales of Apple computers were preceded by dips in Apple's home U.S. market.[13] Marketing strategies can guide and control, to a considerable degree, the rate and extent of new product diffusion because successful new product diffusion is dependent on the ability to communicate relevant product information and new product attributes.

A U.S. cake mix company entered the British market but carefully eliminated most of the newness of the product. Instead of introducing the most popular American cake mixes, the company asked 500 British housewives to bake their favorite cake. Since the majority baked a simple, very popular dry sponge cake, the company brought to the market a similar easy mix. The sponge cake mix represented familiar tastes and habits that could be translated into a convenience item and did not infringe on the emotional aspects of preparing a fancy product for special occasions. Consequently, after a short period of time, the second company's product gained 30 to 35 percent of the British cake mix market. Once the idea of a mix for sponge cake seemed acceptable, the introduction of other flavors became easier.

The goal of a foreign marketer is to gain product acceptance by the largest number of consumers in the market in the shortest span of time. However, as discussed in Chapter 4 and as many of the examples cited have illustrated, new products are not always readily accepted by a culture; indeed, they often meet resistance. Although they may ultimately be accepted, the time needed for a culture to learn new ways, to learn to accept a new product, is of critical importance to the marketer because planning reflects a time frame for investment and profitability. If a marketer invests with the expectation that a venture will break even in three years and seven are needed to gain profitable volume, the effort may have to

---

[12] "Potter's Japanese Adventure," *The Economist*, February 16, 2002, p. 39.

[13] Joel West, "Standards Competition and Apple Computers," unpublished doctoral dissertation, Graduate School of Management, University of California, Irvine, 2000.

be prematurely abandoned. The question comes to mind of whether the probable rate of acceptance can be predicted before committing resources and, more critically, if the probable rate of acceptance is too slow, whether it can be accelerated. In both cases, the answer is a qualified yes. Answers to these questions come from examining the work done in diffusion research—research on the process by which innovations spread to the members of a social system.

Diffusion of Innovations

Everett Rogers noted that "crucial elements in the diffusion of new ideas are (1) an innovation, (2) which is communicated through certain channels, (3) over time, (4) among the members of a social system."[14] Rogers continued with the statement that it is the element of time that differentiates diffusion from other types of communications research. The goals of the diffusion researcher and the marketer are to shorten the time lag between introduction of an idea or product and its widespread adoption.

Rogers and others[15] give ample evidence of the fact that product innovations have varying rates of acceptance. Some diffuse from introduction to widespread use in a few years; others take decades. Patterns of diffusion also vary substantially, and steady growth is the exception—high-tech products often demonstrate periods of slow growth interspersed with performance jumps[16] or early declines followed by broader takeoffs. Patterns of alcoholic beverage consumption converge across Europe only when a 50-year time frame is considered. Microwave ovens, introduced in the United States initially in the 1950s, took nearly 20 years to become widespread; the contraceptive pill was introduced during that same period and gained acceptance in a few years. In the field of education, modern math took only five years to diffuse through U.S. schools, whereas the idea of kindergartens took nearly 50 years to gain total acceptance. A growing body of evidence suggests that an understanding of diffusion theory may suggest ways to accelerate the process of diffusion. Knowledge of this process also may provide the foreign marketer with the ability to assess the time it takes for a product to diffuse—before a financial commitment is necessary.[17] It also focuses the marketer's attention on features of a product that provoke resistance, thereby providing an opportunity to minimize resistance and hasten product acceptance.

At least three extraneous variables affect the rate of diffusion of an object: the degree of perceived newness, the perceived attributes of the innovation, and the method used to communicate the idea.[18] Each variable has a bearing on consumer reaction to a new product and the time needed for acceptance. An understanding of these variables can produce better product strategies for the international marketer.

The more innovative a product is perceived to be, the more difficult it is to gain market acceptance. That is, at a fundamental level, innovations are often disruptive.[19] Consider alternative-fuel cars in the United States. Although they are popular with consumers, dealers did not appreciate their low maintenance requirements, which reduced after-sale

---

[14] Everett M. Rogers, *Diffusion of Innovations*, 4th ed. (New York: The Free Press, 1995). This book should be read by anyone responsible for product development and brand management, domestic or international.

[15] Marnik G. Dekimpe, Philip M. Parker, and Miklos Sarvary, "Global Diffusion and Technological Innovations: A Couple-Hazard Approach," *Journal of Marketing Research* 38 (February 2000), pp. 47–59; Gerard J. Tellis, Stefan Stremersch, and Eden Yin, "The International Takeoff of New Products: The Role of Economics, Culture, and Country Innovativeness," *Marketing Science* 22, no. 2 (2003), pp. 188–208; Sean Dwyer, Hani Mesak, and Maxwell Hsu, "An Exploratory Examination of the Influence of National Culture on Cross-National Product Diffusion," *Journal of International Marketing* 13, no. 2 (2005), pp. 1–27.

[16] Ashish Sood and Gerard J. Tellis, "Technological Evolution and Radical Innovation," *Journal of Marketing* 69 (2005), pp. 152–68.

[17] Stefan Stremersch and Gerard J. Tellis, "Understanding and Managing International Growth of New Products," *International Journal of Research in Marketing* 21, no. 4 (2004), pp. 421–38.

[18] Anita Elberse and Jehoshua Eliashberg, "Demand and Supply Dynamics for Sequentially Released Products in International Markets: The Case of Motion Pictures," *Marketing Science* 22, no. 3 (2003), pp. 329–54.

[19] Jared Diamond, *Collapse* (New York: Viking, 2005).

The Japanese and the Dutch are the world's champions in toilet innovations. Japan's long history of crowding has prompted the culture to focus on cleanliness, frequent bathing, and high-tech bathrooms. Thus, Matsushita's toilet reads your body weight, temperature, and blood pressure. Soon you will also be able to get a readout on glucose and protein levels in your urine! The Dutch are also worried about plumbing—much of their country is below sea level. Sphinx in Maastricht produces a urinal for women and a fly imbedded in the porcelain for their men's urinal. The latter reduces maintenance costs, as the company's research has shown that most men will aim for the fly, which is strategically placed to minimize splash. Either Dutch innovation can be seen in the Schiphol Airport outside of Amsterdam. *(top: © Michael Edrington/The Image Works)*

service revenues. Furthermore, the infrastructure to support hydrogen fuel cell cars has been expensive to build. Thus, some suggest that the technology is inappropriate for the United States, whereas China, without the established infrastructure, may be able to leapfrog the older, gasoline-fueled options.[20] Additionally, the perception of innovation can often be changed if the marketer understands the perceptual framework of the consumer, as has certainly proved to be the case with the fast global diffusion of Internet use, e-tailing, and health- and beauty-related products and services.

---

[20] Jane Lanhee Lee, "The Leapfrog Strategy: Fuel-Cell Advocates Say China Is Uniquely Positioned to Jump Past Petroleum," *The Wall Street Journal,* July 25, 2005, p. R6.

CROSSING BORDERS 12.3   Selling Coffee in Tea Drinking Japan

My first meeting with Nestlé executives and their Japanese advertising agency was very instructive. Their strategy, which today seems absurdly wrong, but wasn't as obviously so in the 1970s, was to try to convince Japanese consumers to switch from tea to coffee. Having spent some time in Japan, I knew that tea meant a great deal to this culture, but I had no sense of what emotions they attached to coffee. I decided to gather several groups of people together to discover how they imprinted the beverage. I believed there was a message there that could open a door for Nestlé.

I structured a three-hour session with each of the groups. In the first hour, I took on the persona of a visitor from another planet, someone who had never seen coffee before and had no idea how one "used" it. I asked for help understanding the product, believing their descriptions would give me insight into what they thought of it.

In the next hour, I had them sit on the floor like elementary school children and use scissors and a pile of magazines to make a collage of words about coffee. The goal here was to get them to tell me stories with these words that would offer further clues.

In the third hour, I had participants lie on the floor with pillows. There was some hesitation among members of every group, but I convinced them I wasn't entirely out of my mind. I put on soothing music and asked the participants to relax. What I was doing was calming their active brainwaves, getting them to that tranquil point just before sleep. When they reached this state, I took them on a journey back from their adulthood, past their teenage years, to a time when they were very young. Once they arrived, I asked them to think again about coffee and to recall their earliest

memory of it, the first time they consciously experienced it, and their most significant memory of it (if that memory was a different one).

I designed this process to bring participants back to their first imprint of coffee and the emotion attached to it. In most cases, though, the journey led nowhere. What this signified for Nestlé was very clear. While the Japanese had an extremely strong emotional connection to tea (something I learned without asking in the first hour of the sessions), they had, at most, a very superficial imprint of coffee. Most, in fact, had no imprint of coffee at all.

Under these circumstances, Nestlé's strategy of getting these consumers to switch from tea to coffee could only fail. Coffee could not compete with tea in the Japanese culture if it had such weak emotional resonance. Instead, if Nestlé was going to have any success in the market at all, they needed to start at the beginning. They needed to give the product meaning in this culture. They needed to create an imprint for coffee for the Japanese.

Armed with this information, Nestlé devised a new strategy. Rather than selling instant coffee to a country dedicated to tea, they created desserts for children infused with the flavor of coffee but without the caffeine. The younger generation embraced these desserts. Their first imprint of coffee was a very positive one, one they would carry throughout their lives. Through this, Nestlé gained a meaningful foothold in the Japanese market.

Coffee consumption has burgeoned since. And Starbucks can thank Nestlé for the help!

Source: Clotaire Rapaille, *The Culture Code* (New York: Broadway Books, 2006).

Analyzing the five characteristics of an innovation can assist in determining the rate of acceptance or resistance of the market to a product. A product's (1) *relative advantage* (the perceived marginal value of the new product relative to the old), (2) *compatibility* (its compatibility with acceptable behavior, norms, values, and so forth), (3) *complexity* (the degree of complexity associated with product use), (4) *trialability* (the degree of economic and/or social risk associated with product use), and (5) *observability* (the ease with which the product benefits can be communicated) affect the degree of its acceptance or resistance. In general, the rate of diffusion can be postulated as positively related to relative advantage, compatibility, trialability, and observability but negatively related to complexity.

By analyzing a product within these five dimensions, a marketer can often uncover perceptions held by the market that, if left unchanged, would slow product acceptance. Conversely, if these perceptions are identified and changed, the marketer may be able to accelerate product acceptance.

The evaluator must remember that it is the perception of product characteristics by the potential adopter, not the marketer, that is crucial to the evaluation. A market analyst's self-reference criterion (SRC) may cause a perceptual bias when interpreting the characteristics of a product. Thus, instead of evaluating product characteristics from the foreign user's frame of reference, the marketer might analyze them from his or her frame of reference, leading to a misinterpretation of the product's cultural importance.

Once the analysis has been made, some of the perceived newness or causes for resistance can be minimized through adroit marketing. The more congruent product perceptions are with current cultural values, the less resistance there will be and the more rapid product diffusion or acceptance will be. Finally, we should point out that the newness of the product or brand introduced can be an important competitive advantage; the pioneer brand advantage often delivers long-term competitive advantages in both domestic and foreign markets.[21]

⌐ Production of Innovations

Some consideration must be given to the inventiveness of companies[22] and countries.[23] For example, it is no surprise that most of the new ideas associated with the Internet are being produced in the United States.[24] The 187 million American users of the Internet far outnumber the 69 million Japanese users.[25] Similarly, America wins the overall R&D expenditure contest. Expenditures are about the same across member countries of the Organization for Economic Cooperation and Development, at about 2 to 3 percent of GDP, so America's large economy supports twice the R&D spending as does Japan, for example. This spending yields about three times the number of U.S. patents granted to American firms versus Japanese firms. Most interesting, the Japanese government had diagnosed the problem as a lack of business training. Japanese engineers are not versed in marketing and entrepreneurship, and American-style educational programs are being created at a record pace to fill the gap. Many Japanese firms also take advantage of American innovativeness by establishing design centers in the United States—most notable are the plethora of foreign auto design centers in southern California. At the same time, American automobile firms have established design centers in Europe. Recent studies have shown that innovativeness varies across cultures, and companies are placing design centers worldwide. Indeed, the Ford Taurus, the car that saved Ford in the 1980s, was a European design.

Research is also now focusing on the related issue of "conversion-ability" or the success firms have when they take inventions to market. Three main factors seem to favor conversion, at least in the global pharmaceutical industry: patience (nine years seems optimal for taking a newly patented drug to approval), focus on a few important innovations, and experience.[26] Another study demonstrates that strengthening patent protections tends to favor firms in developed countries differentially more than firms in developing countries.[27] If evidence continues to accumulate in this vein, policy makers will have to reconsider the current global application of a "one-size-fits-all" intellectual property system.

---

[21] Gerald Young Gao, Yigang Pan, David K. Tse, and Chi Kin (Bennett) Yim, "Market Share Performance of Foreign and Domestic Brands in China," *Journal of International Marketing* 14 (2006), pp. 32–51.

[22] Rhohit Deshpandé and John U. Farley, "Organizational Culture, Innovativeness, and Market Orientation in Hong Kong Five Years after Handover: What Has Changed?" *Journal of Global Marketing* 17, no. 4 (2004), pp. 53–75.

[23] Anyone interested in a wonderful book on this topic should read the Pulitzer Prize–winning *Guns, Germs, and Steel: The Fates of Human Societies* by Jared Diamond (New York: Norton, 1999); also see Subin Im, Cheryl Nakata, Heungsooa Park, and Young-Won Ha, "Determinants of Korean and Japanese New Product Performance: An Interrelational and Process View," *Journal of International Marketing* 11, no. 4 (2003), pp. 81–112. Also, one approach to innovation is copying—see Dexter Roberts, "Did Spark Spark a Copycat?" *BusinessWeek*, February 7, 2005, p. 64.

[24] Thomas L. Friedman, *The World Is Flat* (New York: Farrar, Straus, and Giroux, 2005).

[25] Euromonitor, 2008.

[26] Rajesh Chandy, Brigitee Hpostaken, Om Narasimhan, and Jaideep Prabhu, "From Invention to Innovation: Conversion Ability in Product Development," *Journal of Marketing Research* 43 (2006), pp. 494–508.

[27] Brent B. Allred and Walter G. Park, "Patent Rights and Innovative Activity: Evidence from National and Firm-Level Data," *Journal of International Business Studies* 38 (2007), pp. 878–900.

Although increasing numbers of Japanese employees at the largest and most diversified firms are going back to business school, their Korean conglomerate competitors are leveraging their vertical integration more successfully at the lower end of the consumer electronics business. Samsung has created a number of very successful innovations by tying together product development teams across semiconductors, telecom, digital appliance, and digital media units. Finally, it must be recognized that new ideas come from a growing variety of sources,[28] countries, acquisitions,[29] and even global collaborations (in both R&D and marketing),[30] the last now referred to as "open innovation."[31]

Analyzing Product Components for Adaptation

A product is multidimensional, and the sum of all its features determines the bundle of satisfactions (utilities) received by the consumer. To identify all the possible ways a product may be adapted to a new market, it helps to separate its many dimensions into three distinct components, as illustrated in Exhibit 12.1. By using this model, the impact of the cultural, physical, and mandatory

Exhibit 12.1
Product Component
Model

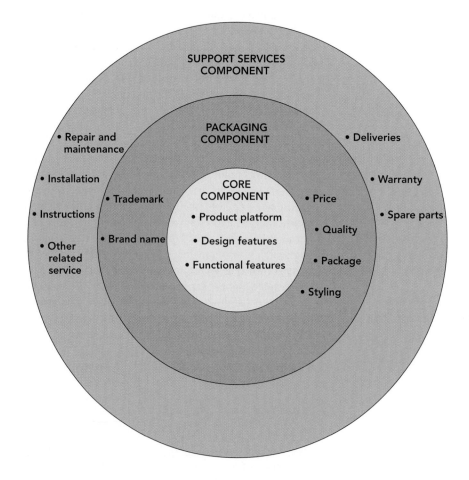

---

[28] Kwaku Atuahene-Gima and Janet Y. Murray, "Exploratory and Exploitative Learning in New Product Development: A Social Capital Perspective on New Technology Ventures in China," *Journal of International Marketing* 15 (2007), pp. 1–29; Francesca Sanna-Randaccio and Reinhilde Veugelers, "Multinational Knowledge Spillovers with Decentralized R&D: A Game Theoretic Approach," *Journal of International Business Studies* 38 (2007), pp. 47–63.

[29] Karen Ruckman, "Technology Sourcing through Acquisitions: Evidence from the U.S. Drug Industry," *Journal of International Business Studies* 36, no. 1 (2005), pp. 89–103.

[30] Several reporters, "The World of Ideas," *Fortune*, July 25, 2005, insert.

[31] Henry Chesbrough, *Open Innovation: The New Imperative from Creating and Profiting from Technology* (Boston, MA: Harvard Business School Press, 2006); Stephan J. Carson, "When to Give up Control of Outsourced New Product Development," *Journal of Marketing* 71 (2007), pp. 49–66.

factors (discussed previously) that affect a market's acceptance of a product can be focused on the core component, packaging component, and support services component. These components include all a product's tangible and intangible elements and provide the bundle of utilities the market receives from use of the product.

Core Component

The *core component* consists of the physical product—the platform that contains the essential technology—and all its design and functional features. It is on the product platform that product variations can be added or deleted to satisfy local differences. Major adjustments in the platform aspect of the core component may be costly because a change in the platform can affect product processes and thus require additional capital investment. However, alterations in design, functional features, flavors, color, and other aspects can be made to adapt the product to cultural variations. In Japan, Nestlé originally sold the same kind of corn flakes it sells in the United States, but Japanese children ate them mostly as snacks instead of for breakfast. To move the product into the larger breakfast market, Nestlé reformulated its cereals to more closely fit Japanese taste. The Japanese traditionally eat fish and rice for breakfast, so Nestlé developed cereals with familiar tastes—seaweed, carrots and zucchini, and coconut and papaya. The result was a 12 percent share of the growing breakfast cereal market.

For the Brazilian market, where fresh orange juice is plentiful, General Foods changed the flavor of its presweetened powdered juice substitute, Tang, from the traditional orange to passion fruit and other flavors. Changing flavor or fragrance is often necessary to bring a product in line with what is expected in a culture. Household cleansers with the traditional pine odor and hints of ammonia or chlorine popular in U.S. markets were not successful when introduced in Japan. Many Japanese sleep on the floor on futons with their heads close to the surface they have cleaned, so a citrus fragrance is more pleasing. Rubbermaid could have avoided missteps in introducing its line of baby furniture in Europe with modest changes in the core component. Its colors were not tailored to European tastes, but worst of all, its child's bed didn't fit European-made mattresses!

Functional features can be added or eliminated depending on the market. In markets where hot water is not commonly available, washing machines have heaters as a functional feature. In other markets, automatic soap and bleach dispensers may be eliminated to cut costs or to minimize repair problems. Additional changes may be necessary to meet safety and electrical standards or other mandatory (homologation) requirements. The physical product and all its functional features should be examined as potential candidates for adaptation.

Packaging Component

The *packaging component* includes style features, packaging, labeling, trademarks, brand name, quality, price, and all other aspects of a product's package. Apple Computer found out the hard way how important this component can be when it first entered the Japanese market. Some of its Macintosh computers were returned unused after customers found the wrapping on the instruction manual damaged! As with the core component, the importance of each of the elements in the eyes of the consumer depends on the need that the product is designed to serve.

Packaging components frequently require both discretionary and mandatory changes. For example, some countries require labels to be printed in more than one language, while others forbid the use of any foreign language. At Hong Kong Disneyland, the jungle cruise ride commentary is delivered in Cantonese, Mandarin, and English.[32] Several countries are now requiring country-of-origin labeling for food products. Elements in the packaging component may incorporate symbols that convey an unintended meaning and thus must be changed. One company's red-circle trademark was popular in some countries but was rejected in parts of Asia, where it conjured up images of the Japanese flag. Yellow flowers used in another company trademark were rejected in Mexico, where a yellow flower symbolizes death or disrespect.

---

[32] Don Lee and Kim Christensen, "Translating Anaheim for Asia," *Los Angeles Times*, September 6, 2005, pp. C1, C5.

CROSSING BORDERS 12.4   D'oh! Or Just Dough in Dubai?

When the Dubai-based Arab satellite TV network MBC decided to introduce Fox's *The Simpsons* to the Middle East, it knew the Simpson family would have to make some fundamental lifestyle changes.

"Omar Shamshoon," as he is called on the show, looks like the same Homer Simpson, but he has given up beer and bacon, which are both against Islam, and he no longer hangs out at "seedy bars with bums and lowlifes." In Arabia, Homer's beer is soda, and his hot dogs are barbequed Egyptian beef sausages. And the donut-shaped snacks he gobbles are the traditional Arab cookies called *kahk*.

An Arabized Simpsons—called *Al Shamshoon*—made its debut in the Arab world just in time for Ramadan, a time of high TV viewership. It uses the original Simpsons animation, but the voices are dubbed into Arabic, and the scripts have been adapted to make the show more accessible, and acceptable, to Arab audiences.

The family remains, as the producers describe them, "dysfunctional." They still live in Springfield, and "Omar" is still lazy and works at the local nuclear power plant. Bart (now called "Badr") is constantly cheeky to his parents and teachers and is always in trouble. Providing the characters' voices are several popular Egyptian actors, including Mohamed Heneidy, considered the Robert DeNiro of the Middle East.

Al Shamshoon is currently broadcast daily during an early-evening prime-time slot, starting with the show's first season. If it is a hit, MBC envisions Arabizing the other 16 seasons. But there's no guarantee of success. Many Arab blogs and Internet chat sessions have become consumed with how unfunny Al Shamshoon is: "They've ruined it! Oh yes they have, *sob*. . . . Why? Why, why oh why?!!!!" wrote a blogger, "Noors," from Oman.

Few shows have more obsessed fans than *The Simpsons*, and the vast online community is worried about whether classic Simpsons' dialogue can even be translated. One blogger wrote, "'Hi-diddly-ho, neighbors!' How the h— are they going to translate that? Or this great quote: Mr. Burns: 'Oooh, so Mother Nature needs a favor?! Well maybe she should have thought of that when she was besetting us with droughts and floods and poison monkeys! Nature started the fight for survival, and now she wants to quit because she's losing. Well I say, hard cheese'."

A blogger, who uses the name "Nibaq," wrote, "I am sure the effort [of] the people who made this show to translate it to Arabic could have made a good original show about an Egyptian family living in Egypt, dealing with religion, life and work and trying to keep a family together. That way they can proudly say Made in Egypt, instead of Made in USA Assembled in Egypt."

Most recently, *The Simpson's Movie* broke records worldwide. Indeed, it will be interesting to keep watching "D'oh!" being converted into dough in Dubai.

Sources: Yasmine El-Rashidi, "D'oh! Arabized Simpsons Aren't Getting Many Laughs," *The Wall Street Journal*, October 14, 2005, pp. B1, B2; "Microsoft Launches New Arabized Solutions and Localized Windows XP Theme Packs at Gitex 2005," *AME Info/Middle East Company News*, September 27, 2005; Frank Segers, "'Simpsons Movie' Reigns at Overseas Boxoffice," *Hollywood Reporter*, August 6, 2007.

A well-known baby-food producer that introduced small jars of baby food in Africa, complete with labels featuring a picture of a baby, experienced the classic example of misinterpreted symbols: The company was absolutely horrified to find that consumers thought the jars contained ground-up babies. In China, though not a problem of literacy per se, Brugel, a German children's cereal brand that features cartoon drawings of dogs, cats, birds, monkeys, and other animals on the package, was located in the pet foods section of a supermarket. The label had no Chinese, and store personnel were unfamiliar with the product. It is easy to forget that in low-literacy countries, pictures and symbols are taken literally as instructions and information.

Care must be taken to ensure that corporate trademarks and other parts of the packaging component do not have unacceptable symbolic meanings. Particular attention should be given to translations of brand names and colors used in packaging. When Ford tried to sell its Pinto automobile in Brazil, it quickly found out that the car model's name translated to "tiny male genitals." White, the color symbolizing purity in Western countries, is the color for mourning in others. In China, P&G packaged diapers in a pink wrapper. Consumers shunned the pink package—pink symbolized a girl, and in a country with a one-child-per-family rule where boys are preferred, you do not want anyone to think you have a girl, even if you do.

Reasons a company might have to adapt a product's package are countless. In some countries, laws stipulate specific bottle, can, and package sizes and measurement units. If a country uses the metric system, it will probably require that weights and measurements conform to the metric system. Such descriptive words as "giant" or "jumbo" on a package or label may be illegal. High humidity or the need for long shelf life because of extended distribution systems may dictate extra-heavy packaging for some products. As is frequently mentioned, Japanese attitudes about quality include the packaging of a product. A poorly packaged product conveys an impression of poor quality to the Japanese. It is also important to determine if the packaging has other uses in the market. Lever Brothers sells Lux soap in stylish boxes in Japan because more than half of all soap cakes there are purchased during the two gift-giving seasons. Size of the package is also a factor that may make a difference to success in Japan. Soft drinks are sold in smaller-size cans than in the United States to accommodate the smaller Japanese hand. In Japan, most food is sold fresh or in clear packaging, while cans are considered dirty. So when Campbell introduced soups to the Japanese market, it decided to go with a cleaner, more expensive pop-top opener.

Labeling laws vary from country to country and do not seem to follow any predictable pattern. In Saudi Arabia, for example, product names must be specific. "Hot Chili" will not do; it must be "Spiced Hot Chili." Prices are required to be printed on the labels in Venezuela, but in Chile putting prices on labels or in any way suggesting retail prices is illegal. Coca-Cola ran into a legal problem in Brazil with its Diet Coke. Brazilian law interprets *diet* to have medicinal qualities. Under the law, producers must give the daily recommended consumption on the labels of all medicines. Coca-Cola had to get special approval to get around this restriction. Until recently in China, Western products could be labeled in a foreign language with only a small temporary Chinese label affixed somewhere on the package. Under the new Chinese labeling law, however, food products must have their name, contents, and other specifics listed clearly in Chinese printed directly on the package—no temporary labels are allowed.

Labeling laws create a special problem for companies selling products in various markets with different labeling laws and small initial demand in each. In China, for example, there is demand for American- and European-style snack foods even though that demand is not well developed at this time. The expense of labeling specially to meet Chinese law often makes market entry costs prohibitive. Forward-thinking manufacturers with wide distribution in Asia are adopting packaging standards comparable to those required in the European Union by providing standard information in several different languages on the same package. A template is designed with space on the label reserved for locally required content, which can be inserted depending on the destination of a given production batch.

Marketers must examine each of the elements of the packaging component to be certain that this part of the product conveys the appropriate meaning and value to a new market. Otherwise they may be caught short, as was the U.S. soft-drink company that incorporated six-pointed stars as decoration on its package labels. Only when investigating weak sales did they find they had inadvertently offended some of their Arab customers, who interpreted the stars as symbolizing pro-Israeli sentiments.

The most controversial labeling and product content issue of all involves genetically modified (GM) foods, or what the critics are calling "Frankenfood." The disputes, primarily with the European Union, have huge implications for American firms, which lead the world in this technology. Japan, Australia, and New Zealand are adopting labeling requirements, and other countries are implementing bans and boycotts. And the problem has now spread to the United States itself, with government considering new labeling laws for domestic GM foods and products.

Support Services Component

The *support services* component includes repair and maintenance, instructions, installation, warranties, deliveries, and the availability of spare parts. Many otherwise successful marketing programs have ultimately failed because little attention was given to this product component. Repair and maintenance are especially difficult problems in developing countries. In the

CROSSING BORDERS 12.5   So, Your Computer Isn't Working?

Most people have two options when the desk beast starts acting up: Call the service center or read the manual. Both are becoming cross-cultural activities. With increasing frequency, service call centers are being staffed by folks in the Philippines, India, the Caribbean, and other developing countries where English is commonly spoken. The savings for the companies can be in the 90 percent range. But for consumers, it was tough enough bridging the technician–layperson gap. Now a cross-cultural layer is being added to the interaction.

At least many manufacturers are getting more adept at adapting user manuals. In some countries, the manuals are treasured for their entertainment value. Mike Adams of the translation and marketing firm Arial Global Reach explains, "Japanese people really enjoy reading documentation, but that's because Japanese documentation is actually fun to look at." Japanese manuals are often jazzed up with creative cartoons. Even program interfaces are animated. Microsoft's much-maligned Clippy the Paperclip is replaced in Japan with an animated dolphin, "And even highly technical Japanese engineers don't feel at all childish when they view or interact with these animations."

Put those cute characters in manuals in other countries and the customer will doubt the seriousness of the firm. Mark Katib, general manager of Middle East

Translation Services, says most customers in that part of the world, as do Americans, prefer uncluttered, nontechnical explanations. He spends most of his time making sure that information is presented in an acceptable manner, not impinging on people's beliefs.

Apparently you cannot give an Italian a command such as "never do this." The consequences for that kind of language are calls from Italians who have broken their machines by doing exactly "this." Instead, Italian manuals must use less demanding language, like "you might consider . . . ."

The Germans will reject manuals with embedded humor. Hungarians like to fix things themselves, so their manuals are more like machine shop guides. Finally, one software maker that developed a WAN (wide-area network) used a flowing stream of text, "WAN WAN WAN WAN" on the package. To a Japanese that's the sound a dog makes, and in Japan no one would buy a product advertising itself by a barking dog.

The main point here is that "technobabble" is hard to translate in any language.

Sources: Michelle Delio, "Read the F***ing Story, then RTFM," *Wired News,* http://www.wired.com, June 4, 2002; Pete Engardio, Aaron Bernstein, and Manjeet Kripalani, "Is Your Job Next?" *BusinessWeek,* February 3, 2003, pp. 50–60; Alli McConnon, "India's Competition in the Caribbean," *BusinessWeek,* December 24, 2007, p. 75.

United States, a consumer has the option of obtaining service from the company or from scores of competitive service retailers ready to repair and maintain anything from automobiles to lawn mowers. Equally available are repair parts from company-owned or licensed outlets or the local hardware store. Consumers in a developing country and in many developed countries may not have even one of the possibilities for repair and maintenance available in the United States, and independent service providers can be used to enhance brand and product quality.[33]

In some countries, the concept of routine maintenance or preventive maintenance is not a part of the culture. As a result, products may have to be adjusted to require less frequent maintenance, and special attention must be given to features that may be taken for granted in the United States.

The literacy rates and educational levels of a country may require a firm to change a product's instructions. A simple term in one country may be incomprehensible in another. In rural Africa, for example, consumers had trouble understanding that Vaseline Intensive Care lotion is absorbed into the skin. *Absorbed* was changed to *soaks into,* and the confusion was eliminated. The Brazilians have successfully overcome the low literacy and technical skills of users of the sophisticated military tanks it sells to Third World countries. The manufacturers include videocassette players and videotapes with detailed repair instructions as part of the standard instruction package. They also minimize spare parts

---

[33] Ikechi Ekeledo and Nadeem M. Firoz, "Independent Service Providers as a Competitive Advantage in Developing Economies," *Journal of Global Marketing* 20 (2007), pp. 39–54.

problems by using standardized, off-the-shelf parts available throughout the world. And, of course, other kinds of cultural preferences come into play even in service manuals. As noted, Japanese consumers actually read software manuals, and even find them entertaining, because the manuals often include cartoon characters and other diversions.

Complementary products must be considered increasingly in the marketing of a variety of high-tech products. Perhaps the best example is Microsoft's Xbox and its competitors. Sales of the Xbox have lagged those of Sony's and Nintendo's game consoles in Japan. Microsoft has diagnosed the problem as a lack of games that particularly attract Japanese gamers and therefore is developing a series of games to fill that gap. An early offering, a new role-playing game called *Lost Odyssey*, was developed by an all-Japanese team.[34]

The Product Component Model can be a useful guide for examining the adaptation requirements of products destined for foreign markets. A product should be carefully evaluated on each of the three components to determine any mandatory and discretionary changes that may be needed.

Marketing Consumer Services Globally

As mentioned at the beginning of the chapter, much of the advice regarding adapting products for international consumer markets also applies to adapting services. Moreover, some services are closely associated with products. Good examples are the support services just described or the customer services associated with the delivery of a Big Mac to a consumer in Moscow. However, services are distinguished by four unique characteristics—intangibility, inseparability, heterogeneity, and perishability—and thus require special consideration.[35]

Products are often classified as tangible, whereas services are *intangible*. Automobiles, computers, and furniture are examples of products that have a physical presence; they are things or objects that can be stored and possessed, and their intrinsic value is embedded within their physical presence. Insurance, dry cleaning, hotel accommodations, and airline passenger or freight service, in contrast, are intangible and have intrinsic value resulting from a process, a performance, or an occurrence that exists only while it is being created.

The intangibility of services results in characteristics unique to a service: It is *inseparable* in that its creation cannot be separated from its consumption;[36] it is *heterogeneous* in that it is individually produced and is thus unique; and it is *perishable* in that once created it cannot be stored but must be consumed simultaneously with its creation. Contrast these characteristics with a tangible product that can be produced in one location and consumed elsewhere, that can be standardized, whose quality assurance can be determined and maintained over time, and that can be produced and stored in anticipation of fluctuations in demand.

As is true for many tangible products, a service can be marketed as both an industrial (business-to-business) and a consumer service, depending on the motive of, and use by, the purchaser. For example, travel agents and airlines sell industrial or business services to a businessperson and a consumer service to a tourist. Financial services, hotels, insurance, legal services, and others may each be classified as either a business or a consumer service. As one might expect, the unique characteristics of services result in differences in the marketing of services and the marketing of consumer products.

Services Opportunities in Global Markets

International tourism is by far the largest services export of the United States, ranking behind only capital goods and industrial supplies when all exports are counted. Spending by foreign tourists visiting American destinations such as Orlando or Anaheim is roughly double that spent by foreign airlines on Boeing's commercial jets. Worldwide tourists spent some $3.5 trillion last year, and an agency of the United Nations projects that number will grow by four times by 2020. The industry employs some 200 million people all around the

---

[34] Yukari Iwatani Kane, "Microsoft Makes Big Push to Woo Japanese with New Xbox Games," *The Wall Street Journal* (online), September 12, 2007.

[35] Valarie A. Zeithaml and Mary Jo Bitner, *Services Marketing*, 3rd ed. (New York: McGraw-Hill, 2002).

[36] Bruce D. Keillor, G. Tomas M. Hult, and Destan Kandemir, "A Study of the Service Encounter in Eight Countries," *Journal of International Marketing* 12, no. 1 (2004), pp. 9–35.

Among the two best vistas in the world are Tahiti above the water (Bora Bora is silhouetted in the background) and the coral reefs off Belize under the water. Tourists flock to both from around the world. Services companies follow the tourists, including the Professional Association of Diving Instructors (PADI), which certifies scuba divers and instructors from its headquarters in Costa Mesa, California.

world. Furthermore, the same U.N. agency predicts that China will be followed by the United States, France, Spain, Hong Kong, Italy, Britain, Mexico, Russia, and the Czech Republic as the most popular destinations in the next century. Currently, France, Spain, the United States, Italy, and China are numbers one through five. Most tourists will be, as they are today, Germans, Japanese, and Americans; Chinese will be the fourth largest group. Currently, Japanese tourists contribute the most to U.S. tourism income, at some $20 billion. Overall, the tourism business is expected to grow at its traditionally brisk pace.[37]

The dramatic growth in tourism has prompted American firms and institutions to respond by developing new travel services attracting both domestic and foreign customers. For example, the Four Seasons Hotel in Philadelphia created a two-day package including local concerts and museum visits. In addition to its attractions for kids, Orlando, Florida, has offered its opera company with performances by world-class singers. The cities of Phoenix, Las Vegas, and San Diego formed a consortium and put together a $500,000 marketing budget specifically appealing to foreign visitors to stop at all three destinations in one trip. Even the smallest hotels are finding a global clientele on the Internet.

Other top consumer services exports include transportation, financial services, education, telecommunications, entertainment, information, and healthcare, in that order. Consider the following examples of each:

- American airlines are falling all over themselves to capture greater shares of the fast expanding Latin American travel market through investments in local carriers.

- Insurance sales are burgeoning in Latin America, with joint ventures between local and global firms making the most progress.

- Financial services in China are undergoing a revolution, with new services being offered at an incredible pace—new sources of investor information and National Cash Register ATMs popping up everywhere. Poles are just getting acquainted with ATMs as well.

- Merrill Lynch is going after the investment-trust business that took off after Japan allowed brokers and banks to enter that business for the first time in 1998.

- More than 600,000 foreign students (63,000 from China) spend some $11 billion a year in tuition to attend American universities and colleges in 2007. Executive training is also a viable export for U.S. companies.[38]

---

[37] Although tourists seem to be ignoring travel warnings more frequently; see "Who Do We Trust?" *Condé Nast Traveler*, March 2005, pp. 53–62.

[38] David M. Montgomery, "Asian Management Education: Some 21st Century Issues," *Journal of Public Policy & Marketing* 24, no. 1 (2005), pp. 150–54.

CROSSING BORDERS 12.6 | Even the Old Technology and a Telemarketer Can Save Your Life

Usually, outbound telemarketers are left out in the cold, saleswise. But Maria del Pilar Basto, a telemarketing agent for Bell South, recently reached a customer who was himself out in the cold—Colombian hiker Leonardo Diaz, trapped in an Andes mountain blizzard at an altitude above 12,500 feet. Stuck in the storm for 24 hours, Diaz had tried to call out on his cell phone but discovered that his prepaid minutes had run out. Basto's well-timed call initially was simply to offer to sell him more minutes. Once on the phone, though, she and her coworkers kept Diaz talking, to keep him awake and help stave off hypothermia, until rescuers arrived.

Imagine if Señor Diaz had packed some of the new stuff available now. How about Sanyo's picture phone with voice dialing (he wouldn't have had to take his hands out of his gloves), an electronic organizer (maybe he wouldn't have gotten lost in the first place), and

a built-in answering machine (Señorita del Pilar's call would have gone through even if he was frozen solid)? How about a wearable PC with a headband-mounted display? Even in a blizzard, that would be entertaining. Pokemon at 12,000 feet! An iPhone might have provided music and a current weather report and forecast. And then there's the Dick Tracey watch–phone combination, voice activated, with headphones. Perhaps Mr. Diaz might have kept better track of his minutes with that gadget.

Too bad Apple, Sanyo, Sony, or Samsung hadn't already come up with a combination compass–radar–hand warmer for Diaz. Maybe that's next?

Sources: Lisa M. Keefe, "Strange but True, Nice Save," *Marketing News*, December 9, 2002, p. 16; Janice Brand, "Beyond Pokemon, Hot Products," *CIO*, January 1, 2003, p. 62; Ben Charny, "Apple Targets Businesses with New iPhone Features," *The Wall Street Journal*, March 7, 2008, p. 6.

- Currently, phone rates in markets such as Germany, Italy, and Spain are so high that American companies cannot maintain toll-free information hotlines or solicit phone-order catalog sales. Other telecommunications markets are deregulating, creating opportunities for foreign firms. Wireless communications are taking Japan and Europe by storm.

- *Buffy the Vampire Slayer*, *Xena*, *Hercules*, and comparably "dumbed-down" (i.e., heavy on action, violence, and sex) video-game heroes are conquering electronic screens worldwide. Even movies on Pearl Harbor have successfully been exhibited in Japan.

- Cable TV is exploding in Latin America.

- The latest Gallup poll in China indicates that 43 percent of Beijing residents are aware of the Internet.

- Sporting events are being sold all over the world—Mexican football in Los Angeles, American football in Scotland and Turkey, American baseball in Mexico, and professional soccer in China.

- Finally, not only are foreigners coming to the United States for healthcare services in fast growing numbers, but North American firms are building hospitals abroad as well. Recently two infants, one from Sweden and one from Japan, received heart transplants at Loma Linda Hospital in California—laws in both their countries prohibit such life-saving operations. Beijing Toronto International Hospital will soon open its doors for some 250 Chinese patients; the services include a 24-hour satellite link for consultations with Toronto. Asian and Mexican competitors are also competing for this global market. Of course, the negative side of this trend is represented by the growing illegal global trade in organs for transplant.[39]

---

[39] Nancy Scheper-Hughes, "Organs without Borders," *Foreign Policy*, January/February 2005, pp. 26–27.

CROSSING BORDERS 12.7 Just to Go to School

Kofi Annan, the former secretary-general of the United Nations, did it; so did Vicente Fox of Mexico, Jacques Chirac of France, and King Abdullah of Jordan. All of them went to "college" in America (the French president enhanced his experience with a job scooping ice cream). Moreover, one-third of U.S. Nobel Prize winners were foreign born. But as the war for talent has given way to the war against terrorism, the welcome America extends to foreigners on its campuses is becoming much more guarded.

Last year, more than 600,000 foreign students enrolled at American universities and colleges. According to the Institute of International Education (IIE), about half came from Asia, mainly China and India. Fewer than 7 percent came from the Middle East. Students account for under 2 percent of all non-immigrant visas (though they have the right to stay for much longer than tourists). They spend $11 billion a year on tuition and living expenses, helping make higher education America's fifth-largest service export. And, as any visit to a Silicon Valley start-up reveals, they bring huge talent to the American economy.

Until September 11, 2001, the chief complaint was that America did not fully exploit this human capital.

Like other countries, it limits the amount of time foreign students can work in the country after they graduate. The IIE frets that America's share of the foreign-student market has dropped from 40 percent to under 30 percent in the past decade. It blames not only higher university fees in the United States and greater competition from Europe and Australia but also America's cumbersome visa process.

For college students from mostly Muslim Malaysia, it used to take about two weeks to get a student visa, but recently 20 Malay freshmen had to wait six months. They missed the fall semester. Undergraduate applications are declining nationwide. White House science adviser John H. Marburber III argues the delays do not reflect policies to exclude. However, Representative Dana Rohrabacher (R-Calif.) says that the appropriate objective is "to reduce the need to attract such a high percentage of foreign students."

Sources: "Student Visas: Chillier on Campus," *The Economist*, November 24, 2001, pp. 31–32; Catherine Arnst, "How the War on Terror Is Damaging the Brain Pool," *BusinessWeek*, May 19, 2003, pp. 72–73; James Boone, "Visa Crackdown Cost U.S. Cream of Foreign Students," *The Times* (London), November 29, 2004, p. 33; http://www.iie.org, 2008.

Barriers to Entering Global Markets for Consumer Services

Most other services—automobile rentals, airline services, entertainment, hotels, and tourism, to name a few—are inseparable and require production and consumption to occur almost simultaneously; thus exporting is not a viable entry method for them. The vast majority of services (some 85 percent) enter foreign markets by licensing, franchising, or direct investment. Four kinds of barriers face consumer services marketers in this growing sector of the global marketplace: protectionism, controls on transborder data flows, protection of intellectual property, and cultural requirements for adaptation.

Protectionism. The European Union is making modest progress toward establishing a single market for services. However, exactly how foreign service providers will be treated as unification proceeds is not clear. Reciprocity and harmonization, key concepts in the Single European Act, possibly will be used to curtail the entrance of some service industries into Europe. The U.S. film and entertainment industry seems to be a particularly difficult sector, although Vivendi's (a French company) purchase of Universal Studios made things a bit more interesting. A directive regarding transfrontier television broadcasting created a quota for European programs, requiring EU member states to ensure that at least 50 percent of entertainment air time is devoted to "European works." The European Union argues that this set-aside for domestic programming is necessary to preserve Europe's cultural identity. The consequences for the U.S. film industry are significant, because more than 40 percent of U.S. film industry profits come from foreign revenues.

Restrictions on Transborder Data Flows. There is intense concern about how to deal with the relatively new "problem" of transborder data transfers. The European Commission is concerned that data about individuals (e.g., income, spending preferences, debt repayment histories, medical conditions, employment) are being collected, manipulated, and transferred between companies with little regard to the privacy of the affected individuals. A proposed directive by the Commission would require the consent of the individual before data are collected or processed. A wide range of U.S. service companies would be affected by such a directive—insurance underwriters, banks, credit reporting firms, direct marketing companies, and tour operators are a few examples. The directive would have broad effects on data processing and data analysis firms because it would prevent a firm from electronically transferring information about individual European consumers to the United States for computer processing. Hidden in all the laws and directives are the unstated motives of most countries: a desire to inhibit the activities of multinationals and to protect local industry. As the global data transmission business continues to explode into the new century, regulators will focus increased attention in that direction.

Protection of Intellectual Property.

An important form of competition that is difficult to combat arises from pirated trademarks, processes, copyrights, and patents. You will recall that this topic was covered in detail in Chapter 7, so we just mention it here for completeness.

Cultural Barriers and Adaptation.

Because trade in services frequently involves people-to-people contact, culture plays a much bigger role in services than in merchandise trade.[40] Examples are many: Eastern Europeans are perplexed by Western expectations that unhappy workers put on a "happy face" when dealing with customers. But McDonald's requires Polish employees to smile whenever they interact with customers. Such a requirement strikes many employees as artificial and insincere. The company has learned to encourage managers in Poland to probe employee problems and to assign troubled workers to the kitchen rather than to the food counter. Japanese Internet purchasers often prefer to pay in cash and in person rather than trust the Internet transaction or pay high credit card fees.

As another example, notice if the Japanese student sitting next to you in class ever verbally disagrees with your instructor. Classroom interactions vary substantially around the world. Students in Japan listen to lectures, take notes, and ask questions only after class, if then. In Japan the idea of grading class participation is nonsense. Conversely, because Spaniards are used to large undergraduate classes (hundreds rather than dozens), they tend to talk to their friends even when the instructor is talking. Likewise, healthcare delivery systems and doctor–patient interactions reflect cultural differences. Americans ask questions and get second opinions. Innovative healthcare services are developed on the basis of extensive marketing research. However, in Japan the social hierarchy is reflected heavily in the patients' deference to their doctors. While Japanese patient compliance is excellent and longevity is the best in the world, the healthcare system there is relatively unresponsive to the expressed concerns of consumers.

Japanese also tend to take a few long vacations—7 to 10 days is the norm. Thus vacation packages designed for them are packed with activities. Phoenix, Las Vegas, and San Diego or Rome, Geneva, Paris, and London in 10 days makes sense to them. The Four Seasons Hotel chain provides special pillows, kimonos, slippers, and teas for Japanese guests. Virgin Atlantic Airways and other long-haul carriers now have interactive screens available for each passenger, allowing viewing of Japanese (or American, French, etc.) movies and TV.

Managing a global services workforce is certainly no simple task. Just ask the folks at UPS. Some of the surprises UPS ran into included indignation in France when drivers were told they couldn't have wine with lunch, protests in Britain when drivers' dogs were banned from delivery trucks, dismay in Spain when it was found that the brown UPS trucks resembled the local hearses, and shock in Germany when brown shirts were required for the first time since 1945 (brown shirts are associated with Nazi rule during World War II).

And while tips of 10 to 15 percent are an important part of services workers' incentives in the United States, this is not the case in Germany, where tips are rounded to the nearest euro. Thus closer management of service personnel is required in those countries to maintain high levels of customer satisfaction.

---

[40] Torsten Ringberg, Gaby Odekerken-Schroder, and Glenn L. Christensen, "A Cultural Models Approach to Service Recovery," *Journal of Marketing* 71 (2007), pp. 184–214.

Clearly, opportunities for the marketing of consumer services will continue to grow in the 21st century. International marketers will have to be quite creative in responding to the legal and cultural challenges of delivering high-quality services in foreign markets and to foreign customers at domestic locales.

Brands in International Markets

Hand in hand with global products and services are global brands. A *global brand* is defined as the worldwide use of a name, term, sign, symbol (visual and/or auditory),[41] design, or combination thereof intended to identify goods or services

---

[41] Nader T. Tavassoli and Jin K. Han, "Auditory and Visual Brand Identifiers in Chinese and English," *Journal of International Marketing* 10, no. 2 (November 2002), pp. 13–28.

Exhibit 12.2
Top Twenty Brands

Rank 2007/2006	2007 Brand Value (millions)	2006 Brand Value (millions)	Change (%)	Country of Ownership	Description
1/1 Coca-Cola	$65,324	$67,000	−3	U.S.	Still number 1, but consumers' shift away from soda in the West has hurt Coke. Success with Coke Zero hasn't made up for Coca-Cola Classic's continued loss of share
2/2 Microsoft	58,709	56, 926	3	U.S.	The launch of the Windows Vista operating system, coupled with its Xbox game console, keeps the software giant's latest technology in front of consumers.
3/3 IBM	57,091	56, 201	2	U.S.	Big Blue's ads promise to make customers feel "special." With powerful software, servers, and sophisticated services, it's delivering.
4/4 GE	51,569	48,907	5	U.S.	With big bets in China and an accelerating push to go green, GE aims to be the earth-friendly global brand.
5/6 Nokia	33,696	30,131	12	Finland	Nokia builds its brand at both ends of the market, with high-end multimedia handsets for upscale buyers and low-priced phones for emerging countries.
6/7 Toyota	32,070	27,941	15	Japan	Quality concerns have increased overall, but Toyota's reliability and its hybrid strategy are leaving auto rivals trailing.
7/5 Intel	30,954	32,319	−4	U.S.	Intel shored up its position as the world's leading chipmaker, but subbrands such as the Viiv entertainment PC and Core processors failed to resonate.
8/9 McDonald's	29,398	27,501	7	U.S.	McDonald's continues to move beyond its burgers-and-fries image with a growing selection of healthy foods and stylishly remodeled restaurants.
9/8 Disney	29,210	27,848	5	U.S.	Disney picks franchises it can sell throughout the Magic Kingdom, from movies to theme park rides. The strategy has paid off handsomely.
10/10 Mercedes-Benz	23,568	21,795	8	Germany	New models have helped repair a badly dented reputation for quality, but sales are up only 1.8 percent for the first half of the year, trailing gains by rivals BMW and Audi.

of one seller and to differentiate them from those of competitors. Much like the experience with global products, the question of whether or not to establish global brands has no single answer. However, the importance of a brand name, even in the nonprofit sector, is unquestionable.[42] Indeed, Exhibit 12.2 lists the estimated worth (equity) of the 20 top global brands. And as indicated in previous chapters, protecting brand names is also a big business.

A successful brand is the most valuable resource a company has. The brand name[43] encompasses the years of advertising, goodwill, quality evaluations, product experience, and other

---

[42] John A. Quelch and Nathalie Laidler-Kylander, *The New Global Brands* (Mason, OH: Southwestern, 2006).

[43] Yih Hwai Lee and Kim Soon Ang, "Brand Name Suggestiveness: A Chinese Language Perspective," *International Journal of Research in Marketing* 20, no. 4 (2003), pp. 323–35.

Rank 2007/2006	2007 Brand Value (millions)	2006 Brand Value (millions)	Change (%)	Country of Ownership	Description
11/11 Citi	$23,443	$21,458	9	U.S.	The folding of the Citi umbrella logo demonstrates that strong brands can transcend their visual identity and continue to add value during transitions.
12/13 Hewlett-Packard	22,197	20,458	9	U.S.	HP last fall edged out Dell as the world's largest PC maker by market share. Sleek new laptops are helping boost its consumer business.
13/15 BMW	21,612	19,617	10	Germany	It hit home runs with its revamp of the 3 series and the Z4 coupe. But with Mercedes on the mend and Audi and Lexus coming on, it can't afford any mistakes.
14/12 Marlboro	21,283	21,350	0	U.S.	Its latest brand extension, Marlboro Menthol, is a hit, but smoking bans and the threat of higher taxes have hurt.
15/14 American Express	20,827	19,641	6	U.S.	Although still the preeminent credit card brand, American Express's focus on points and cobranded cards could be risky to its long-term brand value.
16/16 Gillette	20,415	19,579	4	U.S.	Gillette owns the men's shaving category by innovating and spending heavily on advertising. Future growth depends on the women's shaving business.
17/17 Louis Vuitton	20,321	17,606	15	France	The world's most powerful luxury brand rolls on, expanding in China and other emerging markets as it introduces Vuitton-branded jewelry and eyewear.
18/18 Cisco	19,099	17,532	9	U.S.	Although its presence on the Internet is mostly behind the scenes, the networking giant continues to invest in pricey image ads in advance of a bigger push into consumer gear.
19/19 Honda	17,998	17,049	6	Japan	Small fuel-efficient cars and big investments in hybrids, "clean" diesels, and other green technologies make Honda the darling of the environmentalists.
20/24 Google	17,837	12,376	44	U.S.	Despite fears of Google's growing power as it moves into services beyond search, the brand still appeals to consumers and businesspeople.

Source: David Kiley, "Best Global Brands," *BusinessWeek,* August 6, 2007, pp. 56–64.

Copying is the highest form of flattery? Not so in the car business. The new QQ model from Chinese company Chery (left) resembles the *Matiz* or *Spark* from GM's Daewoo (right)—perhaps a bit too much. (© *Kevin Lee/Bloomberg News/Landov*)

beneficial attributes the market associates with the product. Brand image is at the very core of business identity and strategy. Research shows that the importance and impact of brands also vary with cultural values around the world.[44] Even so, customers everywhere respond to images,[45] myths, and metaphors that help them define their personal and national identities within a global context of world culture and product benefits.[46] Global brands play an important role in that process. The value of Sony, Coca-Cola, McDonald's, Toyota, and Marlboro is indisputable. One estimate of the value of Coca-Cola, the world's most valuable brand, places it at over $65 billion. In fact, one authority speculates that brands are so valuable that companies will soon include a "statement of value" addendum to their balance sheets to include intangibles such as the value of their brands.

Global Brands   Naturally, companies with strong brands strive to use those brands globally.[47] In fact, even perceived "globalness" can lead to increases in sales.[48] The Internet and other technologies accelerate the pace of the globalization of brands. Even for products that must be adapted to local market conditions, a global brand can be successfully used with careful consideration.[49] Heinz produces a multitude of products that are sold under the Heinz brand all over the world. Many are also adapted to local tastes. In the United Kingdom, for example, Heinz Baked Beans Pizza (available with cheese or sausage) was a runaway hit, selling over 2.5 million pizzas in the first six months after its introduction. In the

---

[44] Tulin Erdem, Joffre Swait, and Ana Valenzuela, "Brands as Signals: A Cross-Country Validation Study," *Marketing Science* 26 (2006), pp. 679–97.

[45] Pamela W. Henderson, Joseph A. Cote, Siew Meng Leong, and Berd Schmitt, "Building Strong Brands in Asia: Selecting the Visual Components of Image to Maximize Brand Strength," *International Journal of Research in Marketing* 20, no. 4 (2003), pp. 297–313.

[46] Douglas B. Holt, "What Becomes an Icon Most?" *Harvard Business Review*, March 2003, pp. 43–49.

[47] Isabelle Schuiling and Jean-Noel Kapferer, "Real Differences between Local and International Brands: Strategic Implications for International Marketers," *Journal of International Marketing* 12, no. 4 (2004), pp. 97–112.

[48] Jan-Benedict E. M. Steenkamp, Rajeev Batra, and Dana L. Alden, "How Perceived Brand Globalness Creates Brand Value," *Journal of International Business Studies* 34 (2003), pp. 53–65.

[49] Shi Zhang and Bernd H. Schmitt, "Creating Local Brands in Multilingual International Markets," *Journal of Marketing Research* 38 (August 2001), pp. 313–25; "Brand Name Translation: Language Constraints, Product Attributes, and Consumer Perceptions in East and Southeast Asia," *Journal of International Marketing* 10, no. 2 (November 2002), pp. 29–45; Giana M. Eckhardt and Michael J. Houston, "Cultural Paradoxes Reflected in Brand Meaning: McDonald's in Shanghai, China," *Journal of International Marketing* 10, no. 2 (November 2002), pp. 68–82.

British market, Heinz's brand of baked beans is one of the more popular products. The British consumer eats an average of 16 cans annually, for a sales total of $1.5 billion a year. The company realizes that consumers in other countries are unlikely to rush to stores for bean pizzas, but the idea could lead to the creation of products more suited to other cultures and markets.

Ideally a global brand gives a company a uniformly postive worldwide brand associations that enhances efficiency and cost savings when introducing other products with the brand name, but not all companies believe a single global approach is the best. Indeed, we know that the same brand does not necessarily hold the same meanings in different countries. In addition to companies such as Apple,[50] Kellogg, Coca-Cola, Caterpillar, and Levi's, which use the same brands worldwide, other multinationals such as Nestlé, Mars, Procter & Gamble,[51] and Gillette have some brands that are promoted worldwide and others that are country specific. Among companies that have faced the question of whether to make all their brands global, not all have followed the same path.[52] For example, despite BMW's worldwide successes, only recently did the company create its first global brand position.

Companies that already have successful country-specific brand names must balance the benefits of a global brand against the risk of losing the benefits of an established brand. And some brand names simply do not translate.[53] The cost of reestablishing the same level of brand preference and market share for the global brand that the local brand has must be offset against the long-term cost savings and benefits of having only one brand name worldwide. In those markets where the global brand is unknown, many companies are buying local brands of products that consumers want and then revamping, repackaging, and finally relaunching them with a new image. Unilever purchased a local brand of washing powder, Biopan, which had a 9 percent share of the market in Hungary; after relaunching, market share rose to about 25 percent.

When Mars, a U.S. company that includes candy and pet food among its product lines, adopted a global strategy, it brought all its products under a global brand, even those with strong local brand names. In Britain, the largest candy market in Europe, M&Ms previously were sold as Treets, and Snickers candy was sold under the name Marathon to avoid association with *knickers*, the British word for women's underpants. To bring the two candy products under the global umbrella, Mars returned the candies to their original names. The pet food division adopted Whiskas and Sheba for cat foods and Pedigree for dog food as the global brand name, replacing KalKan. To support this global division that accounts for over $4 billion annually, Mars also developed a Web site for its pet food brands. The site functions as a "global infrastructure" that can be customized locally by any Pedigree Petfoods branch worldwide. For instance, Pedigree offices can localize languages and information on subjects such as veterinarians and cat-owner gatherings.

Finally, researchers are beginning to address the sometimes difficult problem of brand extensions in global markets. Consumers in "Eastern" cultures may be more likely to understand and appreciate brand extensions because of their more holistic thinking than

---

[50] Deborah L. Vence, "Not Taking Care of Business," *Marketing News*, March 15, 2005, pp. 19–21.

[51] "The Rise of Superbrands," *The Economist*, February 5, 2005, pp. 63–65.

[52] Prominent among those arguing against global brands are David A. Aaker and Erich Joachimsthaler, "The Lure of Global Branding," *Harvard Business Review*, November–December 1999; Aysegul Ozsomer and Gregory E. Prussia, "Competing Perspectives in International Strategy: Contingency and Process Models," *Journal of International Marketing*, January 1, 2000, pp. 27–50. For an interesting view of the arguments for and against globalization of brands, see Anand P. Raman, "The Global Face Off," *Harvard Business Review*, June 2003, pp. 35–46.

[53] June Francis, Janet P. Y. Lam, and Jan Walls, "The Impact of Linguistic Differences on International Brand Name Standardization: A Comparison of English and Chinese Brand Names of Fortune 500 Companies," *Journal of International Marketing* 10, no. 1 (2002), pp. 98–116; Clement S. F. Chow, Esther P. Y. Tang, and Isabel S. F. Fu, "Global Marketers' Dilemma: Whether to Translated the Brand Name into Local Language," *Journal of Global Marketing* 20 (2007), pp. 25–38.

How do you sing "bop to the top" in Hindi? Rich Ross, President of Disney Channels Worldwide, says, "Localization really matters. We're pushing deeper into various countries. For the first [*High School Musical*] movie, we didn't do something special for the Netherlands. This time [*High School Musical 2*] we did. For India, 'bop to the top' became 'Pa Pa Pa Paye Yeh Dil,' which roughly translates back into English as 'the heart is full of happiness.'" Also in India, one of Disney's most important markets, the title song "All for One" becomes "Aaja Nachle," which translates into "come dance along."[54] *(Courtesy of The Disney/ABC Television Group)*

consumers in "Western" cultures, with their more analytical thinking patterns. Obviously more work needs to be done in this area, but important differences across cultures are readily discernable in the acceptance of brand extensions.[55]

National Brands

A different strategy is followed by the Nestlé Company, which has a stable of global and country-specific national brands in its product line. The Nestlé name itself is promoted globally, but its global brand expansion strategy is two-pronged. In some markets, it acquires well-established national brands when it can and builds on their strengths—there are 7,000 local brands in its family of brands. In other markets where there are no strong brands it can acquire, it uses global brand names. The company is described as preferring brands to be local, people to be regional, and technology to be global. It does, however, own some of the world's largest global brands; Nescafé is but one.

Unilever is another company that follows a strategy of a mix of national and global brands. In Poland, Unilever introduced its Omo brand detergent (sold in many other countries), but it also purchased a local brand, Pollena 2000. Despite a strong introduction of two competing brands, Omo by Unilever and Ariel by Procter & Gamble, a refurbished Pollena 2000 had the largest market share a year later. Unilever's explanation was that eastern European consumers are leery of new brands; they want brands that are affordable and in keeping with their own tastes and values. Pollena 2000 is successful not just because it is cheaper but because it is consistent with local values.

Multinationals must also consider increases in nationalistic pride that occur in some countries and their impact on brands. In India, for example, Unilever considers it critical that its brands, such as Surf detergent and Lux and Lifebuoy soaps, are viewed as Indian brands. Just as is the case with products, the answer to the question of when to go global

---

[54] Brooks Barnes, "Bopping in 17 Languages as Disney Milks Its Hits," *International Herald Tribune*, January 29, 2008, p. 13.

[55] Alokparna Basu Monga and Deborah Roedder John, "Cultural Differences in Brand Extension Evaluation: The Influence of Analytic versus Holistic Thinking," *Journal of Consumer Research* 33 (2007), pp. 529–36.

with a brand is, "It depends—the market dictates." Use global brands where possible and national brands where necessary. Finally, there is growing evidence that national brands' acceptance varies substantially across regions in countries, suggesting that even finer market segmentation of branding strategies may be efficient.[56]

Country-of-Origin Effect and Global Brands

As discussed previously, brands are used as external cues to taste, design, performance, quality, value, prestige, and so forth. In other words, the consumer associates the value of the product with the brand. The brand can convey either a positive or a negative message about the product to the consumer and is affected by past advertising and promotion, product reputation, and product evaluation and experience.[57] In short, many factors affect brand image. One factor that is of great concern to multinational companies that manufacture worldwide is the country-of-origin effect on the market's perception of the product.

Country-of-origin effect (COE) can be defined as any influence that the country of manufacture, assembly, or design has on a consumer's positive or negative perception of a product. A company competing in global markets today manufactures products worldwide; when the customer becomes aware of the country of origin, there is the possibility that the place of manufacture will affect product or brand images.[58]

The country, the type of product, and the image of the company and its brands all influence whether the country of origin will engender a positive or negative reaction. A variety of generalizations can be made about country-of-origin effects on products and brands.[59] Consumers tend to have stereotypes about products and countries that have been formed by experience, hearsay, myth, and limited information.[60] Following are some of the more frequently cited generalizations.

Consumers have broad but somewhat vague stereotypes about specific countries and specific product categories that they judge "best": English tea, French perfume, Chinese silk, Italian leather, Japanese electronics, Jamaican rum, and so on. Stereotyping of this nature is typically product specific and may not extend to other categories of products from these countries.

The importance of these types of stereotypes was emphasized recently as a result of a change in U.S. law that requires any cloth "substantially altered" (woven, for instance) in another country to identify that country on its label. Designer labels such as Ferragamo, Gucci, and Versace are affected in that they now must include on the label "Made in China," because the silk comes from China. The lure to pay $195 and up for scarves "Made in Italy" by Ferragamo loses some of its appeal when accompanied with a "Made in China" label. As one buyer commented, "I don't care if the scarves are made in China as long as it doesn't say so on the label." The irony is that 95 percent of all silk comes from China, which has the reputation for the finest silk but also a reputation of

---

[56] Bart J. Bronnenberg, Sanjay K. Dhar, and Jean-Pierre Dube, "Consumer Package Goods in the United States: National Brands, Local Branding," *Journal of Marketing Research* 44 (2007), pp. 4–13; M. Berk Ataman, Carl F. Mela, and Harald J. van Heerde, "Consumer Package Goods in France: National Brands, Regions Chains and Local Branding," *Journal of Marketing Research* 44 (2007), pp. 14–20.

[57] Jean-Claude Usunier and Ghislaine Cestre, "Product Ethnicity: Revisiting the Match between Products and Countries," *Journal of International Marketing* 15 (2007), pp. 32–72; Ravi Pappu, Pascale G. Quester, and Ray W. Cooksey, "Country Image and Consumer-Based Brand Equity: Relationships and Implications for International Marketing," *Journal of International Business Studies* 38 (2007), pp. 726–45.

[58] Svein Ottar Olsen and Ulf H. Olsson, "Multientity Scaling and the Consistency of Country-of-Origin Attitudes," *Journal of International Business Studies* 33, no. 1 (2002), pp. 149–67; Jill Gabrielle Klein, "Us Versus Them, or Us Versus Everyone? Delineating Consumer Aversion to Foreign Goods," *Journal of International Business Studies* 33, no. 2 (2002), pp. 345–63.

[59] Peeter W. J. Verleigh, Jan-Benedict E. M. Steenkamp, and Matthew T. G. Meulenberg, "Country-of-Origin Effects in Consumer Processing of Advertising Claims," *International Journal of Research in Marketing* 22, no. 2 (2005), pp. 127–39.

[60] Saeed Samiee, Terrance A. Shimp, and Subhash Sharma, "Brand Origin Recognition Accuracy: Its Antecedents and Consumers' Cognitive Limitations," *Journal of International Business Studies* 36 (2005), pp. 379–97.

producing cheap scarves. The "best" scarves are made in France or Italy by one of the haute couture designers.

Ethnocentrism can also have country-of-origin effects; feelings of national pride—the "buy local" effect, for example—can influence attitudes toward foreign products.[61] Honda, which manufactures one of its models almost entirely in the United States, recognizes this phenomenon and points out how many component parts are made in America in some of its advertisements. In contrast, others have a stereotype of Japan as producing the "best" automobiles. A recent study found that U.S. automobile producers may suffer comparatively tarnished images, regardless of whether they actually produce superior products.

Countries are also stereotyped on the basis of whether they are industrialized, in the process of industrializing, or developing. These stereotypes are less product specific; they are more a perception of the quality of goods and services in general produced within the country. Industrialized countries have the highest quality image, and products from developing countries generally encounter bias.

In Russia, for example, the world is divided into two kinds of products: "ours" and "imported." Russians prefer fresh, homegrown food products but imported clothing and manufactured items. Companies hoping to win loyalty by producing in Russia have been unhappily surprised. Consumers remain cool toward locally produced Polaroid cameras and Philips irons. Yet computers produced across the border in Finland are considered high quality. For Russians, country of origin is more important than brand name as an indicator of quality. South Korean electronics manufacturers have difficulty convincing Russians that their products are as good as Japanese ones. Goods produced in Malaysia, Hong Kong, or Thailand are more suspect still. Eastern Europe is considered adequate for clothing but poor for food or durables. Turkey and China are at the bottom of the heap.

One might generalize that the more technical the product, the less positive is the perception of something manufactured in a less developed or newly industrializing country. There is also the tendency to favor foreign-made products over domestic-made in less-developed countries. Foreign products fare not as well in developing countries because consumers have stereotypes about the quality of foreign-made products, even from industrialized countries. A survey of consumers in the Czech Republic found that 72 percent of Japanese products were considered to be of the highest quality, German goods followed with 51 percent, Swiss goods with 48 percent, Czech goods with 32 percent, and, last, the United States with 29 percent.

One final generalization about COE involves fads that often surround products from particular countries or regions in the world. These fads are most often product specific and generally involve goods that are themselves faddish in nature. European consumers' affection for American products is quite fickle. The affinity for Jeep Cherokees, Budweiser beer, and Bose sound systems of the 1990s has faded to outright animosity[62] toward American brands as a protest of American political policies. This reaction echoes the 1970s and 1980s backlash against anything American, but in the 1990s, American was in. In China, anything Western seems to be the fad. If it is Western, it is in demand, even at prices three and four times higher than those of domestic products. In most cases such fads wane after a few years as some new fad takes over.

---

[61] Aviv Shoham, Moshe Davidow, Jill G. Klein, and Ayalla Ruvio, "Animosity on the Home Front: The Intifada in Israel and Its Impact on Consumer Behavior," *Journal of International Marketing* 14 (2006), pp. 92–114; Peeter W. J. Verlegh, "Home Country Bias in Product Evaluation: The Complementary Roles of Economic and Socio-Psychological Motives," *Journal of International Business Studies* 38 (2007), pp. 361–73; Raymond A. Hopkins and Thomas L. Powers, " 'Buy National' and Altruistic Market Segments," *Journal of Global Marketing* 20 (2007), pp. 73–90.

[62] Edwin J. Nijssen and Susan P. Douglas, "Examining the Animosity Model in a Country with a High Level of Foreign Trade," *International Journal of Research in Marketing* 21, no. 1 (2004), pp. 23–38; Kevin Allison, "World Turning Its Back on Brand America," *Financial Times*, August 1, 2005, p. 3.

There are exceptions to the generalizations presented here, but it is important to recognize that country of origin can affect a product or brand's image significantly. Furthermore, not every consumer is sensitive to a product's country of origin.[63] A finding in a recent study suggests that more knowledgeable consumers are more sensitive to a product's COE than are those less knowledgeable. Another study reports that COE varies across consumer groups; Japanese were found to be more sensitive than American consumers.[64] The multinational company needs to take these factors into consideration in its product development and marketing strategy, because a negative country stereotype can be detrimental to a product's success unless overcome with effective marketing.

Once the market gains experience with a product, negative stereotypes can be overcome. Nothing would seem less plausible than selling chopsticks made in Chile to Japan, but it happened. It took years for a Chilean company to overcome doubts about the quality of its product, but persistence, invitations to Japanese to visit the Chilean poplar forests that provided the wood for the chopsticks, and a high-quality product finally overcame doubt; now the company cannot meet the demand for its chopsticks.

Country stereotyping—some call it "nation equity"[65]—can also be overcome with good marketing.[66] The image of Korean electronics and autos improved substantially in the United States once the market gained positive experience with Korean brands. Most recently in the United States the quality/safety of Chinese made products has been a source of problems for American branded toys, foods, and pharmaceuticals. It will be interesting to watch how the new Chinese brands themselves, such as Lenovo computers and Haier appliances, will work to avoid the current negative "nation equity" to which they are suffering association. All of this stresses the importance of building strong global brands like Sony, General Electric, and Levi's. Brands effectively advertised and products properly positioned can help ameliorate a less-than-positive country stereotype.

Private Brands

Private brands owned by retailers are growing as challengers to manufacturers' brands, whether global or country specific. Store brands are particularly important in Europe compared with the United States.[67] In the food retailing sector in Britain and many European countries, private labels owned by national retailers increasingly confront manufacturers' brands. From blackberry jam and vacuum cleaner bags to smoked salmon and sun-dried tomatoes, private-label products dominate grocery stores in Britain and many of the hypermarkets of Europe. Private brands have captured nearly 30 percent of the British and Swiss markets and more than 20 percent of the French and German markets. In some European markets, private-label market share has doubled in just the past five years.

Sainsbury, one of Britain's largest grocery retailers with 420 stores, reserves the best shelf space for its own brands. A typical Sainsbury store has about 16,000 products, of which 8,000 are Sainsbury labels. These labels account for two-thirds of store sales. The company avidly develops new products, launching 1,400 to 1,500 new private-label items each year, and weeds out hundreds of others no longer popular. It launched its own Novon brand laundry detergent; in the first year, its sales climbed past Procter & Gamble's

---

[63] This appears to be less the case when professional buyers make decisions. See John G. Knight, David K. Holdsworth, and Damien W. Mather, "Country-of-Origin and Choice of Food Imports: An In-Depth Study of European Distribution Chanel Gatekeepers," *Journal of International Business Studies* 38 (2007), pp. 107–25.

[64] Zeynep Gurhan-Canli and Durairaj Maheswaran, "Cultural Variations in Country of Origin Effects," *Journal of Marketing Research* 37 (August 2000), pp. 309–17.

[65] Durairaj Maheswaran, "Nation Equity: Incidental Emotions in Country-of-Origin Effects," *Journal of Consumer Research* 33 (2006), pp. 370–76.

[66] Lys S. Amine, Mike C. H. Chao, and Mark J. Arnold, "Exploring the Practical Effects of Origin, Animosity, and Price-Quality Issues: Two Case Studies of Taiwan and Acer in China," *Journal of International Marketing* 13, no. 2 (2005), pp. 114–50.

[67] Tulin Erdem, Ying Zhao, and An Valenzuela, "Performance of Store Brands: A Cross-Country Analysis of Consumer Store-Brand Preferences, Perceptions, and Risk," *Journal of Marketing Research* 41, no. 1 (2004), pp. 59–72.

and Unilever's top brands to make it the top-selling detergent in Sainsbury stores and the second-best seller nationally, with a 30 percent market share. The 15 percent margin on private labels claimed by chains such as Sainsbury helps explain why their operating profit margins are as high as 8 percent, or eight times the profit margins of their U.S. counterparts.

Private labels are formidable competitors, particularly during economic difficulties in the target markets. Buyers prefer to buy less expensive, "more local" private brands during recessions.[68] Private brands provide the retailer with high margins; they receive preferential shelf space and strong in-store promotions; and perhaps most important for consumer appeal, they are quality products at low prices. Contrast this characterization with manufacturers' brands, which traditionally are premium priced and offer the retailer lower margins than they get from private labels.

To maintain market share, global brands will have to be priced competitively and provide real consumer value. Global marketers must examine the adequacy of their brand strategies in light of such competition. This effort may make the cost and efficiency benefits of global brands even more appealing.

---

[68] Lien Lamey, Barbara Deleersnyder, Marnik G. Dekimpe, and Jan-Benedict E. M. Steenkamp, "How Business Cycles Contribute to Private-Label Success: Evidence from the United States and Europe," *Journal of Marketing* 76 (2007), pp. 1–15.

Summary

The growing globalization of markets that gives rise to standardization must be balanced with the continuing need to assess all markets for those differences that might require adaptation for successful acceptance. The premise that global communications and other worldwide socializing forces have fostered a homogenization of tastes, needs, and values in a significant sector of the population across all cultures is difficult to deny. However, more than one authority has noted that in spite of the forces of homogenization, consumers also see the world of global symbols, company images, and product choice through the lens of their own local culture and its stage of development and market sophistication. Each product must be viewed in light of how it is perceived by each culture with which it comes in contact. What is acceptable and comfortable within one group may be radically new and resisted within others, depending on the experiences and perceptions of each group. Understanding that an established product in one culture may be considered an innovation in another is critical in planning and developing consumer products for foreign markets. Analyzing a product as an innovation and using the Product Component Model may provide the marketer with important leads for adaptation.

Questions

1. Define the following terms:

   product diffusion   homologation
   Product Component Model innovation
   global brand   green marketing
   quality

2. Debate the issue of global versus adapted products for the international marketer.

3. Define the country-of-origin effect and give examples.

4. The text discusses stereotypes, ethnocentrism, degree of economic development, and fads as the basis for generalizations about country-of-origin effect on product perception. Explain each and give an example.

5. Discuss product alternatives and the three marketing strategies: domestic market extension, multidomestic markets, and global market strategies.

6. Discuss the different promotional/product strategies available to an international marketer.

7. Assume you are deciding to "go international." Outline the steps you would take to help you decide on a product line.

8. Products can be adapted physically and culturally for foreign markets. Discuss.

9. What are the three major components of a product? Discuss their importance to product adaptation.

10. How can knowledge of the diffusion of innovations help a product manager plan international investments?

11. Old products (that is, old in the U.S. market) may be innovations in a foreign market. Discuss fully.

12. "If the product sells in Dallas, it will sell in Tokyo or Berlin." Comment.

13. How can a country with a per capita GNP of $100 be a potential market for consumer goods? What kinds of goods would probably be in demand? Discuss.

14. Discuss the characteristics of an innovation that can account for differential diffusion rates.

15. Give an example of how a foreign marketer can use knowledge of the characteristics of innovations in product adaptation decisions.

16. Discuss "environmentally friendly" products and product development.

13

products and services for businesses

CHAPTER OUTLINE

CHAPTER LEARNING OBJECTIVES

What you should learn from Chapter 13:

- The importance of derived demand in industrial markets

- How demand is affected by technology

- Characteristics of an industrial product

- The importance of ISO 9000 certification

- The growth of business services and nuances of their marketing

- The importance of trade shows in promoting industrial goods

- The importance of relationship marketing for industrial products and services

Global Perspective

INTEL, THE BOOM, AND THE INESCAPABLE BUST

This is what we wrote here in the 1999 edition of this book:

Fortune's cover story, "Intel, Andy Grove's Amazing Profit Machine—and His Plan for Five More Years of Explosive Growth" is capped only by *Time*'s Man of the Year story, "Intel's Andy Grove, His Microchips Have Changed the World—and Its Economy." 1997 was the eighth consecutive year of record revenue ($25.1 billion) and earnings ($6.5 billion) for the company Grove helped found. Yet at the beginning of 1998 the real question was, Will the world change Intel? Judging from Intel's own forecasts for a flat first quarter in 1998, Chairman of the Board Grove and his associates were concerned that the financial meltdown in Asian markets would affect Intel's plans for "five more years of explosive growth." Some 30 percent of the firm's record 1997 revenues had come from Asian markets. Indeed, one pundit had earlier predicted, "I see no clear technology threats. The biggest long-term threat to Intel is that the market growth slows." Others warned there's something wrong out there: computer-industry overcapacity.

Actually Intel had an even longer list of threats all posted as a disclaimer to its published forecast: "Other factors that could cause actual results to differ materially are the following: business and economic conditions, and growth in the computing industry in various geographic regions; changes in customer order patterns, including changes in customer and channel inventory levels, and seasonal PC buying patterns; changes in the mixes of microprocessor types and speeds, motherboards, purchased components and other products; competitive factors, such as rival chip architectures and manufacturing technologies, competing software-compatible microprocessors and acceptance of new products in specific market segments; pricing pressures; changes in end users' preferences; risk of inventory obsolescence and variations in inventory valuation; timing of software industry product introductions; continued success in technological advances, including development, implementation and initial production of new strategic products and processes in a cost-effective manner; execution of manufacturing ramp; excess storage of manufacturing capacity; the ability to successfully integrate any acquired businesses, enter new market segments and manage growth of such businesses; unanticipated costs or other adverse effects associated with processors and other products containing errata; risks associated with foreign operations; litigation involving intellectual property and consumer issues; and other risk factors listed from time to time in the company's SEC reports.

Time's Man of the Year had a lot to worry about—most of all that industrial market booms are always followed by busts. Will the rise truly last five more years?

How is it that the brilliant Mr. Grove didn't see the inescapable bust coming? Hadn't he been in this cyclic business from the beginning? His boom did last another three and a half years beyond his 1997 prediction, not five. And the bust has been an ugly thing. Sales revenues declined by more than 20 percent during 2001, the stock price crashed from a high of $75 a share to below $20, shedding 80 percent of the company's value along the way, and 11,000 layoffs were announced. Ouch!

The lesson here is a simple one: In industrial markets, including the global ones, what goes up must come down!

Sources: David Kirkpatrick, "Intel Andy Grove's Amazing Profit Machine—And His Plan for Five More Years of Explosive Growth," *Fortune*, February 17, 1997, pp. 60–75; "Man of the Year," *Time*, January 5, 1998, pp. 46–99; Peter Burrow, Gary McWilliams, Paul C. Judge, and Roger O. Crockett, "There's Something Wrong Out There," *BusinessWeek*, December 29, 1997, pp. 38–49. And the bumps in the road continue for Intel; see Jordan Robertson, "Intel Stock Drops 12 Percent on Disappointing 4Q Results," *Associated Press Newswires*, January 16, 2008.

Exhibit 13.1
Major Categories of U.S. Exports

Category	Percentage
Services total	**29.6%**
Travel (hotels, etc.)	6.4
Transportation (fares, freight, and port services)	5.0
Commercial, professional, and technical services (advertising, accounting, legal, construction, engineering)	6.0
Financial services (banking and insurance)	2.1
Education and training services (mostly foreign student tuition)	1.1
Entertainment (movies, books, records)	1.0
Royalties and license fees	4.5
Insurance	0.5
Telecommunications	0.4
Other categories (telecommunications, information, healthcare)	7.6
Merchandise total	**70.4**
Foods, feeds, and beverages (wheat, fruit, meat)	4.8
Industrial supplies (crude oil, plastics, chemicals, metals)	17.5
Capital goods (construction equipment, aircraft, computers, telecommunications)	28.5
Automotive vehicles, engines, and parts	7.6
Consumer goods (pharmaceuticals, tobacco, toys, clothing)	8.8
Other categories	7.7

Note: The United States exports approximately $1.2 trillion worth of services and goods each year. Services exports are the more understated, so these percentages are only reasonable approximations of the importance of each category listed. Each U.S. Commerce Department category comprises many kinds of products or services, including (but certainly not limited to) those listed in parentheses.

Source: U.S. Department of Commerce, http://www.doc.gov, 2005.

Although everyone likely is familiar with most of the consumer brands described in Chapter 12, sales of such products and services do not constitute the majority of export sales for industrialized countries. Take the United States, for example. As can be seen in Exhibit 13.1, the main product the country sells for international consumption is *technology*. This dominance is reflected in categories such as capital goods and industrial supplies, which together account for some 46 percent of all U.S. exports of goods and services.[1] Technology exports are represented by both the smallest and the largest products—semiconductors and commercial aircraft, the latter prominently including America's export champions, Boeing's 747s. Two of the three most valuable companies in the world at this writing—Microsoft and General Electric—are sellers of high-technology industrial products.

The issues of standardization versus adaptation discussed in Chapter 12 have less relevance to marketing industrial goods than consumer goods because there are more similarities in marketing products and services to businesses across country markets than there are differences. The inherent nature of industrial goods and the sameness in motives and behavior among businesses as customers create a market where product and marketing mix standardization are commonplace. Photocopy machines are sold in Belarus for the same reasons as in Belgium: to make photocopies. Some minor modification may be necessary to accommodate different electrical power supplies or paper size, but basically, photocopy machines are standardized across markets, as are the vast majority of industrial goods. For industrial products that are basically custom made (specialized steel, customized machine tools, and so on), adaptation takes place for domestic as well as foreign markets.

---

[1] Internet jargon seems to be morphing the manager's lexicon toward B2B and B2C distinctions (that is, business-to-business and business-to-consumer) and away from the traditional industrial and consumer goods distinctions. International trade statistics, categories, and descriptors have not kept up with these changes. Consequently, we use the adjectives *industrial* and *business-to-business* interchangeably in this book.

CROSSING BORDERS 13.1   Trade Statistics Don't Tell the Whole Story

One reason U.S. manufacturers don't trumpet their export successes is that large companies no longer distinguish carefully between sales to Texas and those to Thailand. The totals could be worked up, but why bother? It's one world, after all. Besides, it's incredibly complicated in some cases to determine the net contribution a manufacturer makes to the U.S. balance of trade. Lucent Technologies' Microelectronics Group, which exports half of what it makes to customers in Europe and Asia, is an extreme example. A wafer of Lucent's integrated circuits is often designed at its laboratories in England or China; made in its plants in Pennsylvania, Florida, or Ireland; then shipped to Bangkok to be tested, diced, and packaged. After that the finished chips might move on to Germany to be used by Siemens in telecommunications equipment that, in turn, is shipped to BellSouth and installed in Charlotte, North Carolina.

Sources: Philip Siekman, "Industrial Management & Technology/Export Winners," *Fortune*, January 10, 2000, pp. 154–63; "Lucent CEO Sees China as Important Growth Area for Global Business," *Xinhua News Agency*, August 19, 2005; John Collins, "Buying in Ideas Gives Irish Firms License to Stay Ahead," *Irish Times*, September 9, 2005, p. 6.

Two basic factors account for greater market similarities among industrial goods customers than among consumer goods customers. First is the inherent nature of the product: Industrial products and services are used in the process of creating other goods and services; consumer goods are in their final form and are consumed by individuals. Second, the motive or intent of the users differ: Industrial consumers are seeking profit, whereas the ultimate consumer is seeking satisfaction. These factors are manifest in specific buying patterns and demand characteristics and in a special emphasis on relationship marketing as a competitive tool. Whether a company is marketing at home or abroad, the differences between business-to-business and consumer markets merit special consideration.

Along with industrial goods, business services are a highly competitive growth market seeking quality and value. Manufactured products generally come to mind when we think of international trade. Yet the most rapidly growing sector of U.S. international trade today consists of business services—accounting, advertising, banking, consulting, construction, hotels, insurance, law, transportation, and travel sold by U.S. firms in global markets. The intangibility of services creates a set of unique problems to which the service provider must respond. A further complication is a lack of uniform laws that regulate market entry. Protectionism, though prevalent for industrial goods, can be much more pronounced for the service provider.

This chapter discusses the special problems in marketing goods and services to businesses internationally, the increased competition and demand for quality in those goods and services, and the implications for the global marketer.

Demand in Global Business-to-Business Markets

Gauging demand in industrial markets can involve some huge bets. Shanghai's 30-kilometer, $1.2 billion bullet train line is one example. This product of a Sino–German joint venture is really a prototype for fast things to come in mass transit–dependent China. Indeed, plans are being drawn up for a 1,307-kilometer bullet train line from Shanghai to Beijing, and that's probably a $100 billion bet![2] And China does change its mind—in 2005 a multi-billion-dollar upgrade of its wireless networks was substantially scaled back.[3] Another big bet that went bad was Iridium LLC; its 72-satellite, $5 billion communications system was unable to sell the associated phones. Iridium badly miscalculated demand for its approach to global telecommunications and was sold in bankruptcy for $25 million. The system remains operational with the U.S. Department of Defence as its primary customer.

[2] Eric Ng, "French Energy Giant in Talks on China Ventures," *South China Morning Post*, June 20, 2005, p. 4.

[3] Rebecca Buckman, "China Shrinks Wireless Plan," *Washington Post*, June 30, 2005, p. D5.

Three factors seem to affect the demand in international industrial markets differently than in consumer markets. First, demand in industrial markets is by nature more volatile. Second, stages of industrial and economic development affect demand for industrial products. Third, the level of technology of products and services makes their sale more appropriate for some countries than others.

The Volatility of Industrial Demand

Consumer products firms have numerous reasons to market internationally—gaining exposure to more customers, keeping up with the competition, extending product life cycles, and growing sales and profits, to name a few. Firms producing products and services for industrial markets have an additional crucial reason for venturing abroad: dampening the natural

Servers are sold to companies; thus the demand for them is more volatile than the demand for personal computers being sold to individual consumers. Here Microsoft acknowledges the technology bust of 2000 in its ads for servers in both the United States and Japan. In both countries, the pressure was on CIOs to "do more with less." Both executives faced "larger projects" and "shrinking budgets." The American executive is working late; everyone else has gone home. The focus on the Japanese individual executive may look odd to older, more collectivistic Japanese managers. However, Microsoft acknowledged that things were changing in Japan—particularly, information technology decisions were more focused and less consensus-oriented. Younger Japanese will like the independence reflected in the image. Finally, do you think it's a coincidence that both executives are standing near windows? *(top: Courtesy of Microsoft Corporation. Photographer: Kiran Masters; bottom: Courtesy of Microsoft Corporation. Photographer: Tadayuki Minamoto; Talent: Takushi Yasumoto; CD/AD: Jun Asano; CW: Kenichi Okubo)*

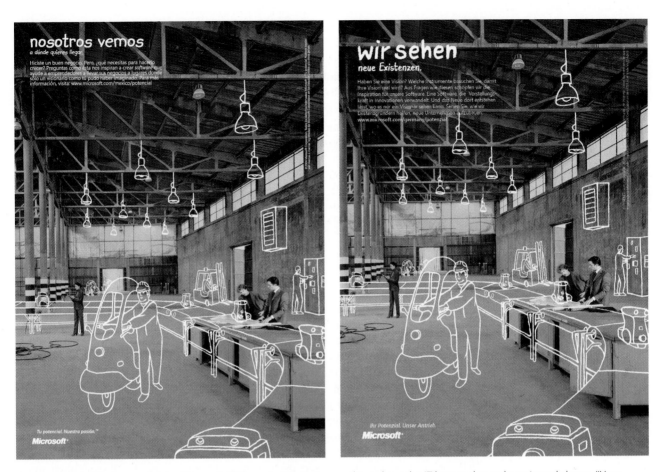

A more recent global campaign for Microsoft B2B products mentions nothing about the IT bust and uses the universal slogan "Your potential. Our passion" for both the Mexican and German markets, as in the United States. *(Courtesy of Microsoft Corporation.)*

volatility of industrial markets.[4] Indeed, perhaps the single most important difference between consumer and industrial marketing is the huge, cyclical swings in demand inherent in the latter.[5] It is true that demand for consumer durables such as cars, furniture, or home computers can be quite volatile. In industrial markets, however, two other factors come into play that exacerbate both the ups and downs in demand: Professional buyers tend to act in concert, and derived demand accelerates changes in markets.[6]

Purchasing agents at large personal computer manufacturers such as IBM, Apple, Acer, Samsung, and Toshiba are responsible for obtaining component parts for their firms as cheaply as possible and in a timely manner. They monitor demand for PCs and prices of components such as microprocessors or disk drives, and changes in either customer markets or supplier prices directly affect their ordering. Declines in PC demand or supplier prices can cause these professionals to slam on the brakes in their buying; in the latter case, they wait for further price cuts. And because the purchasing agents at all the PC companies, here and abroad, are monitoring the same data, they all brake (or accelerate) simultaneously. Consumers monitor markets as well, but not nearly to the same degree. Purchases of cola, clothing, and cars tend to be steadier.

---

[4] "The CEMEX Way," *The Economist*, June 16, 2001, pp. 75–76; Alan Clendenning, "Latin American Exporters Angling to Profit from Katrina Rebuilding, Get Tariffs Suspended," *Associated Press*, September 16, 2005.

[5] Russ Arensman, "When Slower Is Better," *Electronic Business*, March 2003, pp. 52–57.

[6] Ilan Brat, "Crane Migration Hinders Builders," *The Wall Street Journal*, June 18, 2007, pp. B1, B2.

Exhibit 13.2
Derived Demand Example

Time Period	Consumer Demand for Premolded Fiberglass Shower Stalls			Number of Machines in Use to Produce the Shower Stalls			Demand for the Machines		
Year	Previous Year	Current Year	Net Change	Previous Year	Current Year	Net Change	Replacement	New	Total
1	100,000	100,000	—	500	500	—	50	—	50
2	100,000	110,000	+10,000	500	550	+50	50	50	100
3	110,000	115,000	+5,000	550	575	+25	50	25	75
4	115,000	118,000	+3,000	575	590	+15	50	15	65
5	118,000	100,000	–18,000	590	500	–90	—	–40	–40
6	100,000	100,000	—	500	500	—	10	—	10

Source: Adapted from R. L. Vaile, E. T. Grether, and R. Cox, *Marketing in the American Economy* (New York: Ronald Press, 1952), p. 16. Appears in Robert W. Haas, *Business Marketing,* 6th ed. (Cincinnati, OH: Southwestern, 1995), p. 115.

For managers selling capital equipment and big-ticket industrial services, understanding the concept of derived demand is absolutely fundamental to their success. *Derived demand* can be defined as demand dependent on another source. Thus the demand for Boeing 747s is derived from the worldwide consumer demand for air travel services, and the demand for Fluor Corp's global construction and engineering services to design and build oil refineries in China is derived from Chinese consumers' demands for gasoline. Minor changes in consumer demand mean major changes in the related industrial demand. In the example in Exhibit 13.2, a 10 percent increase in consumer demand for shower stalls in year 2 translates into a 100 percent increase in demand for the machines to make shower stalls. The 15 percent decline in consumer demand in year 5 results in a complete shutdown of demand for shower-stall–making machines. For Boeing, the September 11 terrorist attacks, the continuing threat of more of the same, and the subsequent armed conflicts in the Middle East combined to dramatically reduce air travel (both vacation and commercial) worldwide, which in turn caused cancellations of orders for aircraft. Moreover, the airlines not only canceled orders, they also mothballed parts of their current fleets. During August 2003, there were 310 jetliners stored in a Mojave Desert facility awaiting demand to pick up again.[7] The commercial aircraft industry has always been and will continue to be one of the most volatile of all.

Industrial firms can take several measures to manage this inherent volatility, such as maintaining broad product lines[8] and broad market coverage,[9] raising prices faster and reducing advertising expenditures during booms, ignoring market share as a strategic goal, eschewing layoffs,[10] and focusing on stability. For most American firms, where corporate cultures emphasize beating competitors, such stabilizing measures are usually given only lip service. Conversely, German and Japanese firms value employees and stability more highly and are generally better at managing volatility in markets.[11]

[7] Edward Wong, "Airlines' Unwanted Fleet Grows in the Desert," *The New York Times*, June 7, 2003, p. C1; now demand has picked up, and the latest Mojave inventory number we could find is around 200 jets on the ground there.

[8] Nelson D. Schwartz, "Is G.E. Too Big for Its Own Good?" *The New York Times*, July 22, 2007, pp. 3-1,3-8.

[9] Ilan Brat and Bryan Gruley, "Global Trade Galvanizes Caterpillar," *The Wall Street Journal*, February 26, 2007, pp. B1, B7.

[10] Southwest Airlines management, different from almost all its competitors, has avoided layoffs during the recent bust in the industry. Refusing to make layoffs has been a founding principle of the organization. "Southwest Airlines December Traffic Rose 4%," *Dow Jones News Service*, January 4, 2008.

[11] Cathy Anterasian, John L. Graham, and R. Bruce Money, "Are American Managers Superstitious about Market Share?" *Sloan Management Review*, Summer 1996, pp. 667–77; John L. Graham, "Culture and Human Resources Management," Chapter 18 in Alan Rugman and Thomas L. Brewer (eds.), *The Oxford Handbook of International Business* (Oxford: Oxford University Press, 2nd edition, 2008); Rajiv Srinivasan, Arvind Rangaswamy, and Gary L. Lilien, "Turning Adversity into Advantage: Does Proactive Marketing During a Recession Pay Off?" *International Journal of Research in Marketing* 22, no. 2 (2005), pp. 109–25.

Some U.S. companies, such as Microsoft and especially General Electric,[12] have been quite good at spreading their portfolio of markets served. Late-1990s declines in Asian markets were somewhat offset by strong American markets, just as late-1980s increases in Japanese demand had offset declines in the United States. Indeed, one of the strange disadvantages of having the previously command economies go private is their integration into the global market. That is, prior to the breakup of the USSR, Soviets bought industrial products according to a national five-year plan that often had little to do with markets outside of the communist bloc. Their off-cycle ordering tended to dampen demand volatility for companies able to sell there. Now privately held Russian manufacturers watch and react to world markets just as their counterparts do all over the globe. The increasing globalization of markets will tend to increase the volatility in industrial markets as purchasing agents around the world act with even greater simultaneity. Managing this inherent volatility will necessarily affect all aspects of the marketing mix, including product/service development.

Stages of Economic Development

Perhaps the most significant environmental factor affecting the international market for industrial goods and services is the degree of industrialization. Although generalizing about countries is almost always imprudent, the degree of economic development can be used as a rough measure of a country's industrial market. Rostow's[13] five-stage model of economic development is useful here; demand for industrial products and services can be classified correspondingly.

Stage 1 (*the traditional society*). The most important industrial demand will be associated with natural resources extraction—think parts of Africa and the Middle East.

Stage 2 (*preconditions for takeoff*). Manufacturing is beginning. Primary needs will be related to infrastructure development[14]—for example, telecommunications, construction, and power generation equipment and expertise. Vietnam would fit this category.

Stage 3 (*takeoff*). Manufacturing of both semidurable and nondurable consumer goods has begun. Goods demanded relate to equipment and supplies to support manufacturing. Russian and Eastern European countries fit this category.

Stage 4 (*drive to maturity*). These are industrialized economies such as Korea and the Czech Republic. Their focus is more on low-cost manufacturing of a variety of consumer and some industrial goods. They buy from all categories of industrial products and services.

Stage 5 (*the age of mass consumption*). These are countries where design activities are going on and manufacturing techniques are being developed, and they are mostly service economies. Japan and Germany are obvious examples of countries that purchase the highest-technology products and services mostly from other Stage 5 suppliers and consumer products from Stage 3 and 4 countries.

Technology and Market Demand

Another important approach to grouping countries is on the basis of their ability to benefit from and use technology, particularly now that countries are using technology as economic leverage to leap several stages of economic development in a very short time.[15] Perhaps the best indicator of this dimension of development is the quality of the educational system. Despite relatively low levels of per capita GDP, many countries (e.g., China, the Czech Republic, Russia) place great emphasis on education, which affords them the potential to leverage the technology that is transferred.

---

[12] Claudia H. Deutsch, "[G.E.] At Home in the World," *The New York Times*, February 14, 2008, pp. C1, C4.

[13] Walt W. Rostow, *The Stages of Economic Growth*, 2nd ed. (London: Cambridge University Press, 1971).

[14] Anita Chang, "China: Three Gorges Dam Impact Not That Bad," *Associated Press Newswires*, November 22, 2007.

[15] Bruce Einhorn, "The Tech Dragon Stumbles," *BusinessWeek*, May 14, 2007, pp. 44–45.

Not only is technology the key to economic growth, but for many products, it is also the competitive edge in today's global markets. As precision robots and digital control systems take over the factory floor, manufacturing is becoming more science oriented, and access to inexpensive labor and raw materials is becoming less important. The ability to develop the latest information technology and to benefit from its application is a critical factor in the international competitiveness of managers, countries, and companies. Three interrelated trends spur demand for technologically advanced products: (1) expanding economic and industrial growth in Asia, particularly China and India; (2) the disintegration of the Soviet empire; and (3) the privatization of government-owned industries worldwide.

Beginning with Japan, many Asian countries have been in a state of rapid economic growth over the last 30 years. Although this growth has recently slowed, the long-term outlook for these countries remains excellent. Japan has become the most advanced industrialized country in the region, while South Korea, Hong Kong, Singapore, and Taiwan[16] (the "Four Tigers") have successfully moved from being cheap labor sources to becoming industrialized nations. The Southeast Asian countries of Malaysia, Thailand, Indonesia, and the Philippines are exporters of manufactured products to Japan and the United States now, and since overcoming most of their 1990s financial problems, they are continuing to gear up for greater industrialization. Countries at each of the first three levels of industrial development demand technologically advanced products for further industrialization, which will enable them to compete in global markets.

As a market economy develops in the Commonwealth of Independent States (CIS, former republics of the USSR) and other eastern European countries, new privately owned businesses will create a demand for the latest technology to revitalize and expand manufacturing facilities. The BEMs (big emerging markets) discussed in Chapter 9 are expected to account for more than $1.5 trillion of trade by 2010. These countries will demand the latest technology to expand their industrial bases and build modern infrastructures.

Concurrent with the fall of communism, which fueled the rush to privatization in eastern Europe, Latin Americans began to dismantle their state-run industries in hopes of reviving their economies. Mexico, Argentina, and Brazil are leading the rest of Latin America in privatizing state-owned businesses. The move to privatization will create enormous demand for industrial goods as new owners invest heavily in the latest technology. Telmex, a $4 billion joint venture between Southwestern Bell, France Telecom, and Teléfonos de Mexico, is investing hundreds of millions of dollars to bring the Mexican telephone system up to the most advanced standards. Telmex is only one of scores of new privatized companies from Poland to Paraguay that are creating a mass market for the most advanced technology.

The fast economic growth in Asia, the creation of market economies in eastern Europe and the republics of the former Soviet Union, and the privatization of state-owned enterprises in Latin America and elsewhere will create expanding demand, particularly for industrial goods and business services, well into the 21st century. The competition to meet this global demand will be stiff; the companies with the competitive edge will be those whose products are technologically advanced, of the highest quality, and accompanied by world-class service.

Quality and Global Standards

As discussed in Chapter 12, the concept of quality encompasses many factors, and the perception of quality rests solely with the customer. The level of technology reflected in the product, compliance with standards that reflect customer needs, support services and follow-through, and the price relative to competitive products are all part of a customer's evaluation and perception of quality. As noted, these requirements are different for consumers versus industrial customers because of differing end uses. The factors themselves also differ among industrial goods customers because their needs are varied. Finally, recent studies have demonstrated that perceptions of industrial product quality also can vary across cultural groups even in the most technologically developed countries.[17]

---

[16] Bruce Einhorn, "A Juggernaut in Electronics," *BusinessWeek*, June 18, 2007, p. 46.

[17] Christian Homburg, Sabine Kuester, Nikolas Beutin, and Ajay Menon, "Determinants of Customer Benefits in Business-to-Business Markets: A Cross-Cultural Comparison," *Journal of International Marketing* 13 (2005), pp. 1–31.

Business-to-business marketers frequently misinterpret the concept of quality. Good quality as interpreted by a highly industrialized market is not the same as that interpreted by standards of a less industrialized nation. For example, an African government had been buying hand-operated dusters for farmers to distribute pesticides in cotton fields. The duster supplied was a finely machined device requiring regular oiling and good care. But the fact that this duster turned more easily than any other on the market was relatively unimportant to the farmers. Furthermore, the requirement for careful oiling and care simply meant that in a relatively short time of inadequate care, the machines froze up and broke. The result? The local government went back to an older type of French duster that was heavy, turned with difficulty, and gave a poorer distribution of dust but that lasted longer because it required less care and lubrication. In this situation, the French machine possessed more relevant quality features and therefore, in marketing terms, possessed the higher quality.

Likewise, when commercial jet aircraft were first developed, European and American designs differed substantially. For example, American manufacturers built the engines slung below the wings, whereas the British competitor built the engines into the wings. The American design made for easier access and saved on repair and servicing costs, and the British design reduced aerodynamic drag and saved on fuel costs. Both designs were "high quality" for their respective markets. At the time, labor was relatively expensive in the United States, and fuel was relatively expensive in the United Kingdom.

Quality Is Defined by the Buyer

One important dimension of quality is how well a product meets the specific needs of the buyer. When a product falls short of performance expectations, its poor quality is readily apparent. However, it is less apparent but nonetheless true that a product that exceeds performance expectations can also be of poor quality. A product whose design exceeds the wants of the buyer's intended use generally has a higher price or is more complex, reflecting the extra capacity. Quality for many goods is assessed in terms of fulfilling specific expectations—no more and no less. Thus a product that produces 20,000 units per hour when the buyer needs one that produces only 5,000 units per hour is not a quality product, in that the extra capacity is unnecessary to meet the buyer's use expectations. Indeed, this point is one of the key issues facing personal computer makers. Many business buyers are asking the question, "Do we really need the latest $1,000 PC for everyone?" And more and more often the answer is no, the $500 machines will do just fine.

This price–quality relationship is an important factor in marketing in developing economies, especially those in the first three stages of economic development described earlier. Standard quality requirements of industrial products sold in the U.S. market that command commensurately higher prices may be completely out of line for the needs of the less developed markets of the world. Labor-saving features are of little importance when time has limited value and labor is plentiful. Also of lesser value is the ability of machinery to hold close tolerances where people are not quality-control conscious, where large production runs do not exist, and where the wages of skillful workers justify selective fits in assembly and repair work. Features that a buyer does not want or cannot effectively use do not enhance a product's quality rating.

This distinction does not mean quality is unimportant or that the latest technology is not sought in developing markets. Rather, it means that those markets require products designed to meet their specific needs, not products designed for different uses and expectations, especially if the additional features result in higher prices. This attitude was reflected in a study of purchasing behavior of Chinese import managers, who ranked product quality first, followed in importance by price. Timely delivery was third and product style/features ranked 11th out of 17 variables studied. Hence a product whose design reflects the needs and expectations of the buyer—no more, no less—is a quality product.

The design of a product must be viewed from all aspects of use. Extreme variations in climate create problems in designing equipment that is universally operable. Products that function effectively in western Europe may require major design changes to operate as well in the hot, dry Sahara region or the humid, tropical rain forests of Latin America. Trucks designed to travel the superhighways of the United States almost surely will experience operational difficulties in the mountainous regions of Latin America on roads that often barely resemble Jeep trails. Manufacturers must consider many variations in making products that will be functional in far-flung markets.

In light of today's competition, a company must consider the nature of its market and the adequacy of the design of its products. Effective competition in global markets means that overengineered and overpriced products must give way to products that meet the specifications of the customer at competitive prices. Success lies in offering products that fit a customer's needs—technologically advanced for some and less sophisticated for others, but all of high quality. To be competitive in today's global markets, the concept of total quality management (TQM)[18] must be a part of all MNCs' management strategy, and TQM starts with talking to customers.[19] Indeed, more and more frequently, industrial customers, including foreign ones, are directly involved in all aspects of the product development process, from generating new ideas to prototype testing.

A lack of universal standards is another problem in international sales of industrial products. The United States has two major areas of concern in this regard for the industrial goods exporter: a lack of common standards for manufacturing highly specialized equipment such as machine tools and computers, and the use of the inch-pound, or English, system of measurement. Conflicting standards are encountered in test methods for materials and equipment, quality control systems, and machine specifications. In the telecommunications industry, the vast differences in standards among countries create enormous problems for the expansion of that industry.

Efforts are being made through international organizations to create international standards. For example, the International Electrotechnical Commission is concerned with standard specifications for electrical equipment for machine tools. The search has also been engaged for ways in which an international roaming umbrella can be established for wireless communications. The U.S. Department of Commerce participates in programs to promote U.S. standards and is active in the development of the Global Harmonization Task Force, an international effort to harmonize standards for several industry sectors. The U.S. Trade Representative participates in negotiations to harmonize standards as well. Recently a key agreement was signed with the European Union to mutually recognize each other's standards in six sectors. The agreements will eliminate the need for double testing (once each on both sides of the Atlantic) and address inspection or certification in telecommunications, medical devices, electromagnetic compatibility, electrical safety, recreation craft, and pharmaceuticals. The agreements cover approximately $50 billion in two-way trade and are expected to equate to a 2 percent to 3 percent drop in tariffs.

In addition to industry and international organizations setting standards, countries often have standards for products entering their markets. Saudi Arabia has been working on setting standards for everything from light bulbs to lemon juice, and it has asked its trading partners for help. The standards, the first in Arabic, will most likely be adopted by the entire Arab world. Most countries sent representatives to participate in the standard setting. For example, New Zealand sent a representative to help write the standards for the shelf life of lamb. Unfortunately, the United States failed to send a representative until late in the discussions, and thus many of the hundreds of standards written favor Japanese and European products. Also, Saudi Arabia adopted the new European standard for utility equipment. The cost in lost sales to two Saudi cities by just one U.S. company, Westinghouse, was from $15 million to $20 million for U.S.-standard distribution transformers. Increasingly, American firms are waking up to the necessity of participating in such standards discussions early on.

In the United States, conversion to the metric system and acceptance of international standards have been slow. Congress and industry have dragged their feet for fear conversion would be too costly. But the cost will come from *not* adopting the metric system; the General Electric Company had a shipment of electrical goods turned back from a Saudi port because its connecting cords were six feet long instead of the required standard of two meters.

---

[18] Juan A. Magana-Campos and Elaine Aspinwall, "Comparative Study of Western and Japanese Improvement Systems," *TQM & Business Excellence* 14, no. 4 (June 2003), pp. 423–36.

[19] Ching-Chow Yang, "The Establishment of a TQM System for the Health Care Industry," *TQM* magazine 15, no. 2 (2003), pp. 93–98.

CROSSING BORDERS 13.2 Yes, Opinions Do Differ about the Metric System

In Canada, feelings about the metric system run high, as evinced by the following newspaper column:

A generation has not passed since Canada's traditional system of weights and measures was suppressed by bureaucratic edict, in a direct assault on the public will. Countless millions have since been spent—most of it imposed in costs to industry, but millions more taxed to feed Ottawa's metric police and propaganda machine. And after years of the most audacious brainwashing campaign ever attempted on our nation's children, this alien system has made some progress. I said "alien" not because metric is French, but because it is inhuman.

The metric system was originally imposed on France by the blood-soaked operatives of the Revolutionary Terror. It was then dragged across Europe by the armies of Napoleon. It met popular resistance wherever it appeared, and everywhere that resistance was quelled by force.

Yet to this day, in France, as in our old monarchist citadel of Quebec, there are workmen calculating in pieds (feet) and pouces (inches), in livres (pounds) and onces (ounces)—quietly, beyond the reach of the metric police and their informers. These are masons and carpenters and the like. Their eyes are wistful and they smile to themselves.

Ten is the magical number of tyranny. It can be halved only once, and can never go into thirds. It allows the deceptive ease of calculating in decimal places, such that when right we only approximately hit the boat, but when wrong we land in another ocean.

In America, metric boosters insist that the switch is happening, but in stealthy ways. More than 2,000 American businesses use the metric system in research, development, and marketing, according to the U.S. Metric Association, a California advocacy group. All of Eastman Kodak's product development is done in the metric system; Procter & Gamble's Scope mouthwash is sold in incremental liter bottles. The reason is financial. Making deals in pounds isn't easy when you're negotiating with someone who speaks in grams.

Britain duly converted to the metric system, selling its gasoline in liters and, more recently, its supermarket goods in grams. But small shopkeepers remained exempt until January 1, 2000. It was then that the new government regulations took effect, requiring every seller of loose goods—things like fruits, vegetables, carpets, window shades, loose candy, and meat—to begin selling in metric units.

The point, of course, was to harmonize with the rest of the European Union, a concept that was dear to the government of Prime Minister Tony Blair. But a healthy percentage of the country's 96,000 small shopkeepers do not feel much like harmonizing, especially not with the Germans and the French.

Sources: David Warren, "Ten: The Magical Number of Tyranny," *National Post* (Montreal), July 8, 2000, p. A14; Cassell Bryan-Low, "Pound for Pound, A Veggie Peddler Takes on the EU–East London's Ms. Devers Snubs the Metric System; Selling by the Bowl Is Alleged," *The Wall Street Journal*, January 22, 2008, p. A1.

As foreign customers on the metric system account for more and more American industrial sales, the cost of delaying standardization mounts. Measurement-sensitive products account for one-half to two-thirds of U.S. exports, and if the European Union bars nonmetric imports, as expected, many U.S. products will lose access to that market just as the European Union is on the threshold of major economic expansion. About half of U.S. exports are covered by the EU's new standards program.

To spur U.S. industry into action, the Department of Commerce indicated that accepting the metric system will not be mandatory unless you want to sell something to the U.S. government; all U.S. government purchases are to be conducted exclusively in metric. All federal buildings are now being designed with metric specifications, and highway construction funded by Washington uses metric units. Because the U.S. government is the nation's largest customer, this directive may be successful in converting U.S. business to the metric system. The Defense Department now requires metric specifications for all new weapons systems as well.

Despite the edicts from Washington, the National Aeronautics and Space Administration (NASA), which presides over some of the most advanced technology in the world, has resisted metrification. The $100 billion-plus[20] space station contains some metric parts, but most of the major components are made in the United States and are based on inches and pounds. NASA's excuse was that it was too far into the design and production to switch. Unfortunately, the space station is supposed to be an international effort with Russia as one of the partners, and this decision created large problems for systems integration. Worse yet, the cause of the 1999 failure of the $125 million Mars Climate Orbiter was a mix-up between metric and English measurement systems. NASA has agreed to make its next mission to the moon in 2020 metric.[21] Let's see if it keeps its promise. It is hard to believe that the only two countries not officially on the metric system are Myanmar and the United States. It is becoming increasingly evident that the United States must change or be left behind.

ISO 9000 Certification: An International Standard of Quality

With quality becoming the cornerstone of global competition, companies are requiring assurance of standard conformance from suppliers, just as their customers are requiring the same from them. ISO 9000[22] certification has also been found to positively affect the performance[23] and stock prices[24] of firms.

ISO 9000s, a series of five international industrial standards (ISO 9000–9004) originally designed by the International Organization for Standardization in Geneva to meet the need for product quality assurances in purchasing agreements, are becoming a quality assurance certification program that has competitive and legal ramifications when doing business in the European Union and elsewhere. The original ISO 9000 system was promulgated in 1994. In 2000 the system was streamlined, as it was again in 2006. ISO 9000 concerns the registration and certification of a manufacturer's quality system. It is a certification of the existence of a quality control system that a company has in place to ensure it can meet published quality standards. ISO 9000 standards do not apply to specific products. They relate to generic system standards that enable a company, through a mix of internal and external audits, to provide assurance that it has a quality control system. It is a certification of the production process only and does not guarantee that a manufacturer produces a "quality" product or service. The series describes three quality system models, defines quality concepts, and gives guidelines for using international standards in quality systems.

To receive ISO 9000 certification, a company requests a certifying body (a third party authorized to provide an ISO 9000 audit) to conduct a registration assessment—that is, an audit of the key business processes of a company. The assessor will ask questions about everything from blueprints to sales calls to filing. "Does the supplier meet promised delivery dates?" and "Is there evidence of customer satisfaction?" are two of the questions asked and the issues explored. The object is to develop a comprehensive plan to ensure that minute details are not overlooked. The assessor helps management create a quality manual, which will be made available to customers wishing to verify the organization's reliability. When accreditation is granted, the company receives certification. A complete assessment for recertification is done every four years, with intermediate evaluations during the four-year period.

Although ISO 9000 is generally voluntary, except for certain regulated products, the EU Product Liability Directive puts pressure on all companies to become certified. The directive holds that a manufacturer, including an exporter, will be liable, regardless of fault or negligence, if a person is harmed by a product that fails because of a faulty component. Thus customers in the EU need to be assured that the components of their products are

[20] The original cost estimate was $16 billion. "International Space Station Marks Its 10th Anniversary," *RIA Novosti*, January 29, 2008.

[21] David B. Williams, "Metric Mission," *Science World*, April 2, 2007, p. 6.

[22] ISO 14001, a parallel environmental management standard, has not experienced the same rate of diffusion as ISO 9000. See Magali Delmas and Ivan Montiel, "The Diffusion of Voluntary International Management Standards: Responsible Care, ISO 9000, and ISO 14001 in the Chemical Industry," *Policy Studies Journal* 36 (2008), pp. 65–82.

[23] Mile Terziovski, Damien Power, and Amrik S. Sohal, "The Longitudinal Effects of the ISO 9000 Certification Process on Business Performance," *European Journal of Operational Research*, May 1, 2003, pp. 580–95.

[24] Muli Rajan and Nabil Tamimi, "Payoff to ISO 9000 Registration," *Journal of Investing* 12, no. 1 (Spring 2003), pp. 71–77.

The Japanese manufacturer is quite proud of the ISO 9000 quality ratings for its plant in San Jose, Costa Rica.

free of defects or deficiencies. A manufacturer with a well-documented quality system will be better able to prove that products are defect free and thus minimize liability claims.

A strong level of interest in ISO 9000 is being driven more by marketplace requirements than by government regulations, and ISO 9000 is now an important competitive marketing tool in Europe and around the world.[25] As the market demands quality and more and more companies adopt some form of TQM, manufacturers are increasingly requiring ISO 9000 registration of their suppliers. Companies manufacturing parts and components in China are quickly discovering that ISO 9000 certification is a virtual necessity, and the Japanese construction industry now requires ISO 9000 as part of the government procurement process. More and more buyers, particularly those in Europe, are refusing to buy from manufacturers that do not have internationally recognized third-party proof of their quality capabilities. ISO 9000 may also be used to serve as a means of differentiating "classes" of suppliers, particularly in high-tech areas where high product reliability is crucial. In other words, if two suppliers are competing for the same contract, the one with ISO 9000 registration may have a competitive edge.

Although more and more countries (now more than 100) and companies continue to adopt ISO 9000 standards, many have complaints about the system and its spread. For example, 39 electronics companies battled against special Japanese software criteria for ISO 9000. Electronics companies also protested against the establishment of a new ISO Health and Safety Standard. Still others are calling for more comprehensive international standards along the lines of America's Malcolm Baldrige Award, which considers seven criteria—leadership, strategic planning, customer and market focus, information and analysis, human resource development, management, and business results. The telecommunications industry recently promulgated an industry-specific TL 9000 certification program, which combines aspects of ISO 9000 and several other international quality standards.

Perhaps the most pertinent kind of quality standard is now being developed by the University of Michigan Business School and the American Society for Quality Control.[26] Using survey methods, their American Customer Satisfaction Index (ACSI) measures customers' satisfaction and perceptions of quality of a representative sample of America's goods and services. The approach was actually developed in Sweden and is now being used in other European and Asian countries as well.[27] The appeal of the ACSI approach is its focus on results, that is, quality as perceived by product and service users. So far the ACSI approach has been applied only in consumer product and service contexts; however, the fundamental notion that customers are the best judges of quality is certainly applicable to international business-to-business marketing settings as well. Individual industrial marketing firms are seeking even better ways to implement quality improvement programs,[28] including using similar techniques as those employed by ACSI.

Business Services

For many industrial products, the revenues from associated services exceed the revenues from the products. Perhaps the most obvious case is cellular phones, in which the physical product is practically given away to gain the phone services contract. Or consider how inexpensive printers may seem until the costs of operation (i.e., ink cartridges) are included. Indeed,

[25] "China to Establish Industrial Garden in Nigeria," *Xinhua News Agency*, August 22, 2005.

[26] Claes Fornell, Michael D. Johnson, Eugene W. Anderson, Jaesung Cha, and Barbara Everitt Bryant, "The American Consumer Index: Nature, Purpose, and Findings," *Journal of Marketing* 60, no. 4 (October 1996), pp. 35–46; http://www.asq.org, 2008; http://www.cfigroup.com, 2008.

[27] Arti Mulchand, "Singapore's Own Quality Indicator," *Straits Times*, August 27, 2005.

[28] Duncan I. Simester, John R. Hauser, Birger Wernerfelt, and Roland T. Rust, "Implementing Quality Improvement Programs Designed to Enhance Customer Satisfaction: Quasi-Experiments in the United States and Spain," *Journal of Marketing Research* 37 (February 2000), pp. 102–12.

for many capital equipment manufacturers the margins on after-sale services (i.e., maintenance contracts, overhauls, repairs, and replacement parts) are much higher than the margins on the machinery itself. Furthermore, when companies lease capital equipment to customers, the distinction between products and services almost disappears completely. When a business customer leases a truck, is it purchasing a vehicle or transportation services?

Businesses also buy a variety of services that are not associated with products. Our favorite examples are the at-sea-satellite-launch services now provided by Boeing[29] and the Russian navy, the latter by submarine.[30] We also appreciate the Ukrainian cargo company that charges $24,000 an hour to rent space on its giant jets. Other professional services are purchased from advertising and legal agencies, transportation and insurance companies, oil field services, banks and investment brokers,[31] and healthcare providers, to name only a few. Both categories of business services are discussed in this section.

After-Sale Services

Effective competition abroad requires not only proper product design but effective service, prompt deliveries, and the ability to furnish spare and replacement parts without delay. For example, GE Medical Systems provides a wide range of after-sale services for hospitals that buy MRIs and other equipment—training, information technologies, associated healthcare services, and parts and accessories.[32] In the highly competitive European Union, it is imperative to give the same kind of service a domestic company or EU company can give.

For many technical products, the willingness of the seller to provide installation and training may be the deciding factor for the buyers in accepting one company's product over another's. South Korean and other Asian businesspeople are frank in admitting they prefer to buy from American firms but that Japanese firms often get the business because of outstanding after-sales service. Frequently heard tales of conflicts between U.S. and foreign firms over assistance expected from the seller are indicative of the problems of after-sales service and support. A South Korean executive's experiences with an American engineer and some Japanese engineers typify the situation: The Korean electronics firm purchased semiconductor-chip–making equipment for a plant expansion. The American engineer was slow in completing the installation; he stopped work at 5:00 p.m. and would not work on weekends. The Japanese, installing other equipment, understood the urgency of getting the factory up and running; without being asked, they worked day and night until the job was finished.

Unfortunately this example is not an isolated case. In another example, Hyundai Motor Company bought two multimillion-dollar presses to stamp body parts for cars. The presses arrived late, even more time was required to set up the machines, and Hyundai had to pay the Americans extra to get the machines to work correctly. Such problems translate into lost business for U.S. firms. Samsung Electronics Company, Korea's largest chipmaker, used U.S. equipment for 75 percent of its first memory-chip plant; when it outfitted its most recent chip plant, it bought 75 percent of the equipment from Japan. Of course, not all American companies have such problems. Indeed, in India Intel recently opened a data center comprising an Internet server farm of hundreds of servers. Already customers in many countries connect and store their servers and have them serviced by Intel at such centers.

Customer training is rapidly becoming a major after-sales service when selling technical products in countries that demand the latest technology but do not always have trained personnel. China demands the most advanced technical equipment but frequently has untrained people responsible for products they do not understand. Heavy emphasis on training programs and self-teaching materials to help overcome the common lack of skills to operate technical equipment is a necessary part of the after-sales service package in much of the developing world. While perhaps McDonald's Hamburger University is the most famous international customer training center, industrial sellers may soon catch up.

---

[29] "Spaceport Southbound," *Orange County Register*, June 9, 2005, pp. A1, B1.

[30] "Sail of the Century," *The Economist*, June 18, 2005, pp. 77–78.

[31] John U. Farley, Andrew F. Hayes, and Praveen K. Kopalle, "Choosing and Upgrading Financial Services Dealers in the U.S. and U.K.," *International Journal of Research in Marketing* 21, no. 4 (2004), pp. 359–75.

[32] See http://www.gehealthcare.com, 2008.

Cisco Systems, collaborating with the government and a university in Singapore,[33] established the first Cisco Academy Training Centre to serve that region of the world, and Intel established e-Business Solutions Centers in five European countries.

A recent study of international users of heavy construction equipment revealed that, next to the manufacturer's reputation, quick delivery of replacement parts was of major importance in purchasing construction equipment. Furthermore, 70 percent of those questioned indicated they bought parts not made by the original manufacturer of the equipment because of the difficulty of getting original parts. Smaller importers complain of U.S. exporting firms not responding to orders or responding only after extensive delay. It appears that the importance of timely availability of spare parts to sustain a market is forgotten by some American exporters that are used to quick deliveries in the domestic market. When companies are responsive, the rewards are significant. U.S. chemical production equipment manufacturers dominate sales in Mexico because, according to the International Trade Administration, they deliver quickly. The ready availability of parts and services provided by U.S. marketers can give them a competitive edge.

Some international marketers also may be forgoing the opportunity of participating in a lucrative aftermarket. Certain kinds of machine tools use up to five times their original value in replacement parts during an average life span and thus represent an even greater market. One international machine tool company has capitalized on the need for direct service and available parts by changing its distribution system from "normal" to one of stressing rapid service and readily available parts. Instead of selling through independent distributors, as do most machine tool manufacturers in foreign markets, this company established a series of company stores and service centers similar to those found in the United States. The company can render service through its system of local stores, whereas most competitors must dispatch service people from their home-based factories. The service people are kept on tap for rapid service calls in each of its network of local stores, and each store keeps a large stock of standard parts available for immediate delivery. The net result of meeting industrial needs quickly is keeping the company among the top suppliers in foreign sales of machine tools.

International small-package door-to-door express air services and international toll-free telephone service have helped speed up the delivery of parts and have made after-sales technical service almost instantly available. Amdahl, the giant mainframe computer maker, uses air shipments almost exclusively for cutting inventory costs and ensuring premium customer service, which is crucial to competing against larger rivals. With increasing frequency, electronics, auto parts, and machine parts sent by air have become a formidable weapon in cutting costs and boosting competitiveness. Technical advice is only a toll-free call away, and parts are air-expressed immediately to the customer. Not only does this approach improve service standards, but it also is often more cost effective than maintaining an office in a country, even though foreign-language speakers must be hired to answer calls.

After-sales services are not only crucial in building strong customer loyalty and the all-important reputation that leads to sales at other companies, but they are also almost always more profitable than the actual sale of the machinery or product.

Other Business Services

Trade creates demands for international services.[34] Most business services companies enter international markets to service their local clients abroad.[35] Accounting, advertising, and law[36] firms were among the early companies to establish branches or acquire local affiliations abroad to serve their U.S. multinational clients. Hotels and auto-rental agencies followed the business traveler abroad. Most recently, healthcare services providers have been

---

[33] "SMEs Set to Boost IT Services in Asia," *Business Times Singapore*, August 22, 2005.

[34] Perhaps one of the best examples of trade leading demand for services is the critical importance of Japanese trading companies to that country. See Anthony Goerzen and Shige Makino, "Multinational Corporation Internationalization in the Service Sector: A Study of Japanese Trading Companies," *Journal of International Business Studies* 38 (2007), pp. 1149–69.

[35] Lihong Qian and Andrew Delios, "Internationalization and Experience: Japanese Banks' International Expansion, 1980–1998," *Journal of International Business Studies* 39 (2008), pp. 231–48.

[36] John Tagliabue, "Law Firms from U.S. Invade Paris," *The New York Times*, July 25, 2007, pp. C1, C4.

Exhibit 13.3
Expansion of U.S. Law
Firms in Selected Cities
Worldwide

Sources: *National Law Journal,* "Top
250 Report," 2003; N. Mark Lam and
John L. Graham, *China Now, Doing
Business in the World's Most Dynamic
Market* (New York: McGraw-Hill, 2007).

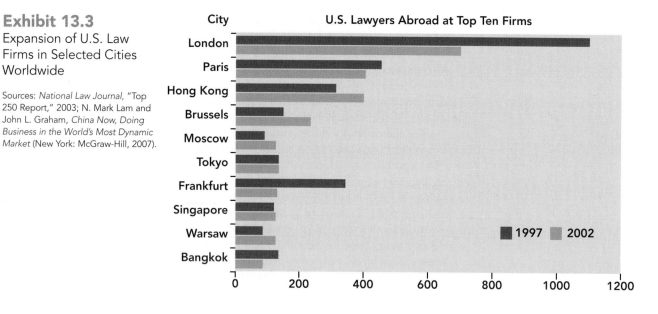

following firms abroad—Blue Cross is now selling HMO services to American companies operating in Mexico. Once established, many of these *client followers,* as one researcher refers to them, expand their client base to include local companies as well. As global markets grow, creating greater demand for business services, service companies become international market seekers. Indeed, notice in Exhibit 13.3 how American law firms have expanded (or contracted) overseas in recent years.

As mentioned in Chapter 12, the mode of entry for most consumer services firms is licensing, franchising, strategic alliances,[37] or direct. This tendency is so because of the inseparability of the creation and consumption of the services. However, because some business services have intrinsic value that can be embodied in some tangible form (such as a blueprint or architectural design), they can be produced in one country and exported to another. Data processing and data analysis services are good examples. The analysis or processing is completed on a computer located in the United States, and the output (the service) is transmitted via the Internet to a distant customer. Architecture and engineering consulting services are exportable when the consultant travels to the client's site and later returns home to write and submit a report or a design.

Business services firms face most of the same constraints and problems confronting merchandise traders. Protectionism is the most serious threat to the continued expansion of international services trade. The growth of international services has been so rapid during the last decade it has drawn the attention of local companies, governments, and researchers.[38] As a result, direct and indirect trade barriers have been imposed to restrict foreign companies from domestic markets. Every reason, from the protection of infant industries to national security, has been used to justify some of the restrictive practices. A list of more than 2,000 instances of barriers to the free flow of services among nations was recently compiled by the U.S. government. In response to the threat of increasing restriction, the United States has successfully negotiated to open business services markets through both NAFTA and GATT.

Until the GATT and NAFTA agreements, few international rules of fair play governed trade in services. Service companies faced a complex group of national regulations that impeded the movement of people and technology from country to country. At least one study

---

[37] One Chicago law firm has entered into a strategic alliance with a Chinese counterpart. See Nathan Koppel and Andrew Batson, "A U.S. Law Firm Takes a New Route into China," *The Wall Street Journal,* January 30, 2007, pp. B1, B2.

[38] Farok J. Contractor, Sumit K. Kundu, and Chin-Chun Hsu, "A Three-Stage Theory of International Expansion: The Link between Multinationality and Performance in the Service Sector," *Journal of International Business Studies* 34 (2003), pp. 5–19.

has demonstrated that personnel and intellectual property issues are key drivers of success and failure, particularly in knowledge-based services such as consulting, engineering, education, and information technology.[39] The United States and other industrialized nations want their banks, insurance companies, construction firms, and other business service providers to be allowed to move people, capital, and technology around the globe unimpeded. Restrictions designed to protect local markets range from not being allowed to do business in a country to requirements that all foreign professionals pass certification exams in the local language before being permitted to practice. In Argentina, for example, an accountant must have the equivalent of a high school education in Argentinean geography and history before being permitted to audit the books of a multinational company's branch in Buenos Aires.

Restrictions on cross-border data flows are potentially the most damaging to both the communications industry and other MNCs that rely on data transfers across borders to conduct business. Some countries impose tariffs on the transmission of data, and many others are passing laws forcing companies to open their computer files to inspection by government agencies or are tightly controlling transmission domestically. Most countries have a variety of laws to deal with the processing and electronic transmission of data across borders. In many cases, concern stems from not understanding how best to tax cross-border data flows.

As mentioned earlier, competition in all sectors of the services industry is increasing as host-country markets are being invaded by many foreign firms. The practice of following a client into foreign markets and then expanding into international markets is not restricted to U.S. firms. Service firms from Germany, Britain, Japan, and other countries follow their clients into foreign markets and then expand to include local business as well. Telecommunications, advertising, and construction are U.S. services that face major competition, not only from European and Japanese companies but also from representatives of Brazil, India, and other parts of the world.

Clearly opportunities for the marketing of business services will continue to grow well into the 21st century. International marketers will have to be quite creative in responding to the legal and cultural challenges of delivering high-quality business services in foreign markets and to foreign customers.

Trade Shows: A Crucial Part of Business-to-Business Marketing

The promotional problems encountered by foreign industrial marketers are little different from the problems faced by domestic marketers. Until recently there has been a paucity of specialized advertising media in many countries.[40] In the last decade, however, specialized industrial media have been developed to provide the industrial marketer with a means of communicating with potential customers, especially in western Europe and to some extent in eastern Europe, the Commonwealth of Independent States (CIS), and Asia.

In addition to advertising in print media and reaching industrial customers through catalogs, Web sites,[41] and direct mail, the trade show or trade fair has become the primary vehicle for doing business in many foreign countries. As part of its international promotion activities, the U.S. Department of Commerce sponsors trade fairs in many cities around the world. Additionally, local governments in most countries sponsor annual trade shows. African countries, for example, host more than 70 industry-specific trade shows.

Trade shows serve as the most important vehicles for selling products, reaching prospective customers, contacting and evaluating potential agents and distributors, and marketing in most countries. Firms that have successfully integrated trade show attendance and

---

[39] Chris Styles, Paul G. Patterson, and Vinh Q. La, "Exporting Services to Southeast Asia: Lessons from Australian Knowledge-Based Service Exporters," *Journal of International Marketing* 13 (2005), pp. 104–28.

[40] Of course, it should be noted that some industrial companies still use nonspecialized media, building brand awareness at all levels. Perhaps the best example is Intel's sponsorship of the official Web site of the Tour de France in 2002.

[41] For illustrative examples of the burgeoning information available to industrial customers on Web sites, see http://www.caterpillar.com, http://www.fluor.com, http://www.hewlett-packard.com, and http://www.qualcom.com.

So you want to buy a jet fighter? How about kicking the tires of one at the Paris Air Show, the world's biggest aerospace trade show? *(© PIERRE VERDY/AFP/Getty Images)*

follow-up personal selling efforts have been consistently shown to be more profitable.[42] Although important in the United States,[43] trade shows serve a much more important role in other countries. They have been at the center of commerce in Europe for centuries and are where most prospects are found. European trade shows attract high-level decision makers who are attending not just to see the latest products but to buy. Preshow promotional expenditures are often used in Europe to set formal appointments. The importance of trade shows to Europeans is reflected in the percentage of their media budget spent on participating in trade events and how they spend those dollars. On average, Europeans spend 22 percent of their total annual media budget on trade events, whereas comparable American firms typically spend less than 5 percent. Europeans tend not to spend money on circuslike promotions, gimmicks, and such; rather, they focus on providing an environment for in-depth dealings. More than 2,000 major trade shows are held worldwide every year. The Hanover Industry Fair (Germany), the largest trade fair in the world, has nearly 6,000 exhibitors, who show a wide range of industrial products to 600,000 visitors.

Trade shows provide the facilities for a manufacturer to exhibit and demonstrate products to potential users and to view competitors' products. They are an opportunity to create sales and establish relationships with agents, distributors, franchisees,[44] and suppliers that can lead to more nearly permanent distribution channels in foreign markets. In fact, a trade show may be the only way to reach some prospects. Trade show experts estimate that 80 to 85 percent of the people seen on a trade show floor never have a salesperson call on them. Several Web sites now specialize in virtual trade shows. They often include multimedia and elaborate product display booths that can be virtually toured. Some of these virtual trade shows last only a few days during an associated actual trade show.

The number and variety of trade shows are such that almost any target market in any given country can be found through this medium. Most remarkable was the Medical Expo in Havana in 2000—the first trade show to be sanctioned by both the U.S. and Cuban governments in more than four decades. Over 8,000 Cuban doctors, nurses, technicians, and hospital administrators attended. This initial event was followed in 2002 with a major

[42] Timothy Smith, Srinath Gopalakrishnan, and Paul M. Smith, "The Complementary Effect of Trade Shows on Personal Selling," *International Journal of Research in Marketing* 21, no. 1 (2004), pp. 61–76.

[43] David Pogue, "Fixated on TVs, and What's on Them," *The New York Times*, January 10, 2008, pp. C1, C7.

[44] Brad Fishman, "International Trade Shows: The Smartest Ticket for Overseas Research," *Franchising World*, April 2003, pp. 25–26.

CROSSING BORDERS 13.3   No More Aching Feet, but What about the 15-Ton Russian Tank?

During April 2000, the first stand-alone virtual trade show was staged by ISP Virtual Show. It was aimed at an appropriate audience—Internet service providers (ISPs). The address was ISPVirtualShow.com (the site is down now, but you can still reach take a look by Googling it). Technology for the show was provided by iTradeFair.com, a Web site worth the visit.

According to the promoters, "The advantages of a virtual trade show far outweigh those of the physical model. Exhibitors (booths start at $1,995) and attendees (tickets are $99) from all over the world will now be able to exhibit and attend direct from their desktops. There are endless benefits of a virtual show, including massive reductions in costs both in exhibiting and man-power terms, savings on booth space and buildings, accommodations, flights, expenses, the obligatory bar bills and costs of time spent out of the office."

The virtual trade show offers a fresh alternative to the traditional model. Using advanced technology, anyone anywhere in the world can visit the virtual show and access information in his or her own language—making language barriers a thing of the past. Also, if attendees and exhibitors would like to continue a discussion offline, clocks displaying times from all over the world make scheduling easy. Finally, weary executives attending the same trade shows year in, year out will no longer have to suffer aching feet, hot stuffy rooms without air-conditioning, and overpriced, plastic food.

Although this pitch sounds great, we believe that an aspect of real trade shows that the virtual ones miss is the face-to-face contact and the all-important interpersonal relationship building that goes on over drinks or during those plastic meals. And there is no virtual way to achieve the same effect as a Russian software developer who recently displayed a 15-ton Russian tank in his booth at Comtek Trade Show in Moscow. We shall see how this new promotional medium evolves.

Sources: "ISP Virtual Show: World's First Virtual Trade Show," *M2 Presswire*, October 26, 1999; Jeanette Borzo, "Moscow's Comtek Trade Show Confronts Internet Challenge," *Dow Jones News Service*, April 19, 2000; "ICUEE Is the Demo Expo," *Transmission & Distribution*, August 1, 2005, p. 74; www.iTradeFair.com, 2008.

food products trade show in Havana.[45] In eastern Europe, fairs and exhibitions offer companies the opportunity to meet new customers, including private traders, young entrepreneurs, and representatives of nonstate organizations. The exhibitions in countries such as Russia and Poland offer a cost-effective way of reaching a large number of customers who might otherwise be difficult to target through individual sales calls. Specialized fairs in individual sectors such as computers, the automotive industry, fashion, and home furnishings regularly take place.

In difficult economic and/or political circumstances, online trade shows become a useful, but obviously less than adequate, substitute.[46] A good example of the kinds of services being developed can be found in Crossing Borders 13.3. During the weakened global economy at the turn of the century, slimmer travel budgets and SARS scares dramatically reduced attendance, and even forced cancellations, of traditionally popular international trade fairs. Political conflicts between the EU and the United States over Middle East policies resulted in the U.S. Department of Defense discouraging American attendance at the 2003 Paris Air Show. Top American executives at Boeing, Lockheed, and the like dutifully stayed away. Exhibit space declined by 5 percent, and orders announced dropped from $45 billion in 2001 to $32 billion.[47] It is hard to estimate what the costs in terms of international orders are for firms such as Boeing when their top executives cannot mix with potential customers at such a crucial event. We do know that Airbus inked orders for dozens of commercial aircraft from

[45] Paul Richter, "Cuba Trade Show Kicks Off with a Hearty Welcome from Castro," *Los Angeles Times*, September 27, 2002, p. A3.

[46] Jennifer Saranow, "The Show Goes On: Online Trade Shows Offer Low-Cost, Flexible Alternatives for Organizers, Especially in These Days of Tight Travel Budgets," *The Wall Street Journal*, April 28, 2003, p. R4.

[47] "Plane Makers Land Fewer Deals at Paris Air Show," *Los Angeles Times*, June 23, 2003, p. C3.

If marketing goals are to be achieved, a product must be made accessible to the target market at an affordable price. Getting the product to the target market can be a costly process if inadequacies within the distribution structure cannot be overcome. Forging an aggressive and reliable channel of distribution may be the most critical and challenging task facing the international marketer. Moreover, some argue that meeting such challenges is a key catalyst to economic development.[1]

Each market contains a distribution network with many channel choices whose structures are unique and, in the short run, fixed. In some markets, the distribution structure is multilayered, complex, inefficient, even strange, and often difficult for new marketers to penetrate; in others, there are few specialized middlemen except in major urban areas; and in yet others, there is a dynamic mixture of traditional and new, evolving distribution systems available on a global scale. Regardless of the predominating distribution structure, competitive advantage will reside with the marketer best able to build the most efficient channels from among the alternatives available. And as global trade continues to burgeon and physical distribution infrastructures lag, the challenges will be even greater in the 21st century.[2]

This chapter discusses the basic points involved in making channel decisions: channel structures; distribution patterns; available alternative middlemen; factors affecting choice of channels; and locating, selecting, motivating, and terminating middlemen.

Channel-of-Distribution Structures

In every country and in every market, urban or rural, rich or poor, all consumer and industrial products eventually go through a distribution process. The *distribution process* includes the physical handling and distribution of goods, the passage of ownership (title), and—most important from the standpoint of marketing strategy—the buying and selling negotiations between producers and middlemen and between middlemen and customers.

A host of policy and strategic channel selection issues confronts the international marketing manager. These issues are not in themselves very different from those encountered in domestic distribution, but the resolution of the issues differs because of different channel alternatives and market patterns.

Each country market has a *distribution structure* through which goods pass from producer to user. Within this structure are a variety of middlemen whose customary functions, activities, and services reflect existing competition, market characteristics, tradition, and economic development.

In short, the behavior of channel members is the result of the interactions between the cultural environment and the marketing process. Channel structures range from those with little developed marketing infrastructure, such as those found in many emerging markets, to the highly complex, multilayered system found in Japan.

Import-Oriented Distribution Structure

Traditional channels in developing countries evolved from economies with a strong dependence on imported manufactured goods. In an *import-oriented* or *traditional distribution structure*, an importer controls a fixed supply of goods, and the marketing system develops around the philosophy of selling a limited supply of goods at high prices to a small number of affluent customers. In the resulting seller's market, market penetration and mass distribution are not necessary because demand exceeds supply, and in most cases, the customer seeks the supply from a limited number of middlemen.

This configuration affects the development of intermediaries and their functions. Distribution systems are local rather than national in scope, and the relationship between the importer and any middleman in the marketplace is considerably different from that found in a mass-marketing system. The idea of a channel as a chain of intermediaries performing specific activities and each selling to a smaller unit beneath it until the chain

---

[1] Paul Ellis, "Are International Trade Intermediaries Catalysts in Economic Development? A New Research Agenda," *Journal of International Marketing* 11, no. 1 (2003), pp. 73–96.

[2] Chip Cummins, "Istanbul Moment: Sir, There's a Ship in Your Bedroom," *The Wall Street Journal*, July 28, 2005, pp. A1, A7.

They're in China, but they aren't Peking ducks. The birds are for sale in Guangzhou's free market, the first farmers' market to be opened in China after the Cultural Revolution. This market was the place where free enterprise found its rebirth after the cultural revolution. Every kind of food is for sale here—from ducks to dogs, from scorpions to dried lizards on sticks.

reaches the ultimate consumer is not common in an import-oriented system.

Because the importer–wholesaler traditionally performs most marketing functions, independent agencies that provide advertising, marketing research, warehousing and storage, transportation, financing, and other facilitating functions found in a developed, mature marketing infrastructure are nonexistent or underdeveloped. Thus few independent agencies to support a fully integrated distribution system develop.

Contrast this situation with the distribution philosophy of mass consumption that prevails in the United States and other industrialized nations. In these markets, one supplier does not dominate supply, supply can be increased or decreased within a given range, and profit maximization occurs at or near production capacity. Generally a buyer's market exists, and the producer strives to penetrate the market and push goods out to the consumer, resulting in a highly developed channel structure that includes a variety of intermediaries, many of which are unknown in developing markets.

Obviously, few countries fit the import-oriented model today, though the channel structure for chewing gum illustrated in the Global Perspective comes closest to describing a traditional import-oriented structure. As China develops economically, its market system and distribution structure will evolve as well.[3] As already discussed, economic development is uneven, and various parts of an economy may be at different stages of development. Channel structures in countries that have historically evolved from an import-oriented base will usually have vestiges of their beginnings reflected in a less than fully integrated system. At the other extreme is the Japanese distribution system with multiple layers of specialized middlemen.

Japanese Distribution Structure

Distribution in Japan has long been considered the most effective nontariff barrier to the Japanese market.[4] Even though the market is becoming more open as many traditional modes of operation are eroding in the face of competition from foreign marketers, it still serves as an excellent case study for the pervasive impact culture plays on economic institutions such as national distribution systems. The Japanese distribution structure is different enough from its U.S. or European counterparts that it should be carefully studied by anyone contemplating entry. The Japanese system has four distinguishing features: (1) a structure dominated by many small middlemen dealing with many small retailers, (2) channel control by manufacturers, (3) a business philosophy shaped by a unique culture,[5] and (4) laws that protect the foundation of the system—the small retailer.

High Density of Middlemen.

The density of middlemen, retailers, and wholesalers in the Japanese market is unparalleled in any Western industrialized country.[6] The traditional Japanese structure serves consumers who make small, frequent purchases at small, conveniently located stores. An equal density of wholesalers supports the high density of small stores with small inventories. It is not unusual for consumer goods to go through three

[3] Lutz Kaufman and Andreas Jentzsch, "Internationalization Processes: The Case of Automotive Suppliers in China," *Journal of International Marketing* 14 (2006), pp. 52–84.

[4] For a detailed study on this subject, see Frank Alpert, Michael Kamins, Tokoaki Sakano, Naoto Onzo, and John L. Graham, "Retail Buyer Decision Making in Japan: What U.S. Sellers Need to Know," *International Business Review* 6, no. 2 (1997), pp. 91–104; Yoshinobu Sato, "Some Reasons Why Foreign Retailers Have Difficulties in Succeeding in the Japanese Market," *Journal of Global Marketing* 18, no. 1/2 (2004), pp. 21–44.

[5] Keysuk Kim and Changho Oh, "On Distributor Commitment in Marketing Channels for Industrial Products: Contrast between the United States and Japan," *Journal of International Marketing* 10, no. 1 (2002), pp. 72–97.

[6] Junji Nishimura, "The Linkage of Trades in Terms of Wholesale Business Formats in Japanese Distribution Systems," *Journal of Global Marketing* 18, no. 1 (2004), pp. 167–86.

Exhibit 14.1
Comparison of Distribution Channels between the United States and Japan

Automobile parts: Japan

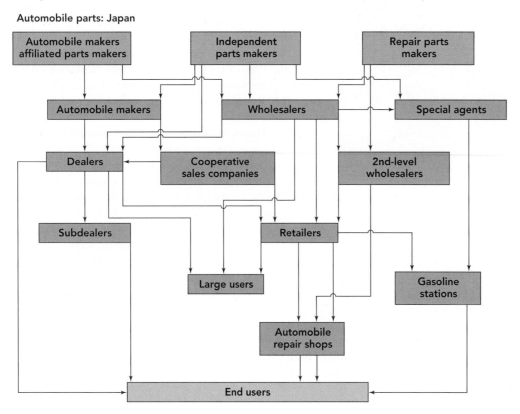

Automobile parts: United States

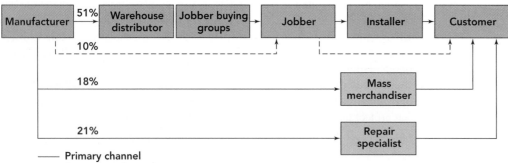

— Primary channel
--- Secondary channel

or four intermediaries before reaching the consumer—producer to primary, secondary, regional, and local wholesaler, and finally to retailer to consumer. Exhibits 14.1 and 14.2 illustrate the contrast between shorter U.S. channels and the long Japanese channels.

While other countries have large numbers of small retail stores, the major difference between small stores (nine or fewer employees) in Japan and the United States is the percentage of total retail sales accounted for by small retailers. In Japan, small stores (94.7 percent of all retail food stores) account for 59.1 percent of retail food sales; in the United States, small stores (90.0 percent of all retail food stores) generate 35.7 percent of food sales. A disproportionate percentage of nonfood sales are made in small stores in Japan as well. Such differences are also reflected in Exhibit 14.2. Notice the American emphasis on supermarkets, discount food stores, and department stores versus the Japanese prevalence of independent groceries and bakers.

Exhibit 14.2
Retail Structure in Three
Countries

Source: Euromonitor, 2008.

	Retail Outlets (000s)		
	Germany	**Japan**	**United States**
Food Stores			
Supermarkets and discounters	32.2	19.1	26.7
Hypermarkets	1.9	7.0	3.3
Small grocers	37.1	95.4	181.2
Food/drink/tobacco specialists	36.5	169.1	84.5
Other grocery retailers	4.1	79.6	7.9
Nonfood Stores			
Department stores	0.5	0.3	9.7
Variety stores	1.7	11.3	25.2
Mass merchandisers	0.1	1.7	4.3
Health and beauty retailers	42.7	81.0	87.2
Clothing and footwear retailers	40.0	163.0	117.5
Home furniture and household goods retailers	12.6	60.3	162.8
Durable goods retailers	11.8	55.8	37.0
Leisure and personal goods retailers	52.1	47.4	156.2
Other non-grocery retailers	9.1	145.5	42.8

As we shall see in a subsequent section, profound changes in retailing are occurring in Japan. Although it is still accurate to describe the Japanese market as having a high density of middlemen, the number of small stores is declining as they are being replaced by larger discount and specialty stores. The number of retail stores is down more 9 percent since 2002, and the number of retail stores with a staff of four or fewer dropped more than 15 percent. These small stores serve an important role for Japanese consumers. High population density; the tradition of frequent trips to the store; an emphasis on service, freshness, and quality; and wholesalers who provide financial assistance, frequent deliveries of small lots, and other benefits combine to support the high number of small stores.

Channel Control.   Manufacturers depend on wholesalers for a multitude of services to other members of the distribution network. Financing, physical distribution, warehousing, inventory, promotion, and payment collection are provided to other channel members by wholesalers. The system works because wholesalers and all other middlemen downstream are tied to manufacturers by a set of practices and incentives designed to ensure strong marketing support for their products and to exclude rival competitors from the channel. Wholesalers typically act as agent middlemen and extend the manufacturer's control through the channel to the retail level.

Control is maintained through the following elements:

1. **Inventory financing.** Sales are made on consignment with credits extending for several months.

2. **Cumulative rebates.** Rebates are given annually for any number of reasons, including quantity purchases, early payments, achieving sales targets, performing services, maintaining specific inventory levels, participating in sales promotions, remaining loyal to suppliers, maintaining manufacturer's price policies, cooperating, and contributing to overall success.

3. **Merchandise returns.** All unsold merchandise may be returned to the manufacturer.

4. **Promotional support.** Intermediaries receive a host of displays, advertising layouts, management education programs, in-store demonstrations, and other dealer aids that strengthen the relationship between the middleman and the manufacturer.

Business Philosophy.   Coupled with the close economic ties and dependency created by trade customs and the long structure of Japanese distribution channels is a relationship-oriented business philosophy that emphasizes loyalty, harmony, and friendship. The value system supports long-term dealer–supplier relationships that are difficult to change as long as each party perceives economic advantage. The traditional partner, the insider, generally has the advantage.

A general lack of price competition, the provision of costly services, and other inefficiencies render the cost of Japanese consumer goods among the highest in the world. Indeed, when you just compare paychecks at current exchange rates (that is, GDP per capita), Japanese at $40,000 outearn Americans at $38,165. However, if you take into consideration what those paychecks will buy [that is, GDP per capita at purchase price parity (PPP)], then Americans do better than Japanese at $27,992.[7] Such prices create a perfect climate for discounting, which is beginning to be a major factor. The Japanese consumer contributes to the continuation of the traditional nature of the distribution system through frequent buying trips, small purchases, favoring personal service over price, and a proclivity for loyalty to brands perceived to be of high quality. Additionally, Japanese law gives the small retailer enormous advantage over the development of larger stores and competition. All these factors have supported the continued viability of small stores and the established system, though changing attitudes among many Japanese consumers are beginning to weaken the hold traditional retailing has on the market.

Large-Scale Retail Store Law and Its Successor.   Competition from large retail stores had been almost totally controlled by *Daitenho*—the Large-Scale Retail Store Law (and its more recent incarnations). Designed to protect small retailers from large intruders into their markets, the law required that any store larger than 5,382 square feet (500 square meters) must have approval from the prefecture government to be "built, expanded, stay open later in the evening, or change the days of the month they must remain closed." All proposals for new "large" stores were first judged by the Ministry of International Trade and Industry (MITI). Then, if all local retailers *unanimously* agreed to the plan, it was swiftly approved. However, without approval at the prefecture level, the plan was returned for clarification and modification, a process that could take several years (10 years was not unheard of) for approval. Designed to protect small retailers against competition from large stores, the law had been imposed against both domestic and foreign companies. One of Japan's largest supermarket chains needed 10 years to get clearance for a new site. Toys "R" Us[8] fought rules and regulations for over three years before it gained approval for a store. In addition to the *Daitenho*, there were myriad licensing rules. One investigation of retail stores uncovered many different laws, each requiring a separate license that had to be met to open a full-service store.

Businesspeople in Japan and the United States see the Japanese distribution system as a major nontariff barrier, and Japanese see it as a major roadblock to improvement of the Japanese standard of living. However, pressure from the United States and the Structural Impediments Initiative (SII) negotiations to pry open new markets for American companies have resulted in relaxation of many of the more onerous restrictions on large retailers, both Japanese and foreign.

Changes in the Japanese Distribution System.   The Structural Impediments Initiative, deregulation, and most recently Wal-Mart[9] are causing changes in Japanese distribution practices. Ultimately, however, only local merchants challenging the traditional ways by giving the consumer quality products at competitive, fair prices can bring about the demise of the traditional distribution system. Specialty discounters are sprouting up everywhere, and entrepreneurs are slashing prices by buying direct and avoiding the distribution system altogether. For example, Kojima, a consumer electronics discounter, practices what it

---

[7] Constant 2000 international $, World Development Indicators, World Bank, 2008.

[8] Jungyim Baek, "How Does the Global Retailer Localize Its Format? The Case of Toys 'R' Us and Carrefour in Japan," *Journal of Global Marketing* 18, no. 1/2 (2004), pp. 151–66.

[9] Ann Zimmerman and Martin Fackler, "Wal-Mart's Foray into Japan Spurs a Retail Upheaval," *The Wall Street Journal* (online), September 19, 2003; Kay Itoi and George Wehrfritz, "A Dying Zombie," *NewsWeek*, August 30, 2004, pp. 34–35.

calls "global purchasing" and buys merchandise anywhere in the world as cheaply as possible. Kojima's tie with General Electric enables it to offer a 410-liter GE refrigerator for $640, down from the typical price of $1,925, and to reduce the 550-liter model from $3,462 to $1,585.

The "new" retailers are relatively few and account for no more than 5 percent of retail sales, compared with 14 percent for all specialty discounters in the United States. But the impact extends beyond their share of market because they are forcing the system to change.[10] Traditional retailers are modifying marketing and sales strategies in response to the new competition as well so as to take advantage of changing Japanese lifestyles. There are also indications that some wholesalers are modernizing and consolidating operations as more retailers demand to buy direct from the manufacturer or from the largest wholesalers. The process is slow because the characteristics of the distribution system are deeply rooted in the cultural history of Japan. However, the long supply chain consisting of many layers of middlemen in Japan is vulnerable to the efficiencies that business-to-business (B2B) commerce provides. Because the Internet allows suppliers and retailers to seek the cheapest price in the global market, it will be harder for the many Japanese middlemen to maintain the control they have had.

Similarly, traditional Japanese retailing is slowly giving ground to specialty stores, supermarkets, discounters, and convenience stores. Fast Retailing, a casual-clothing retailer, features good clothes at bargain prices. The store can sell cheaply without lowering quality because it shuns the traditional middlemen and designs its own clothes and sources them directly from factories in China. In 12 months, Fast Retailing's sales jumped by one-third to $927 million, just as Japanese retail sales showed their 36th consecutive monthly drop.

Konbini, as convenience stores are called in Japan, are among those retailers bringing about a revolution in Japanese retailing. Besides the traditional array of convenience goods, *konbini* are adding an Internet feature whereby customers can pay bills, bank, or purchase travel packages, music, and merchandise on in-store terminals or over the Internet at home. With its 8,000 outlets, 7-Eleven Japan has a joint venture with www.7dream.com. Instead of offering door-to-door delivery, 7dream wants to lure customers to the nearest 7-Eleven store to pay and pick up purchases. What seemed to be an impenetrable tradition-bound distribution system just a few years ago now appears to be on the verge of radical change. Japanese retailing seems to be following a direction similar to that of the United States decades earlier and may not be recognizable in a decade or two.

Trends: From Traditional to Modern Channel Structures

Today, few countries are sufficiently isolated to be unaffected by global economic and political changes. These currents of change are altering all levels of the economic fabric, including the distribution structure. Traditional channel structures are giving way to new forms, new alliances, and new processes—some more slowly than others, but all are changing.[11] Pressures for change in a country come from within and without. Multinational marketers are seeking ways to profitably tap market segments that are served by costly, traditional distribution systems. In India the familiar clutter[12] of traditional retailers is fast giving way to the wide aisles[13] of new local and foreign super markets. Direct marketing, door-to-door selling, hypermarkets, discount houses, shopping malls, catalog selling, the Internet, and other distribution methods are being introduced in an attempt to provide efficient distribution channels. Importers and retailers also are becoming more involved in new product development;[14] for example, the Mexican

---

[10] Adrian Slywotzky and Richard Wise, "An Unfinished Revolution," *Sloan Management Review*, Spring 2003, pp. 94–95.

[11] Suk-Ching Ho, "Evolution versus Tradition in Marketing Systems: The Hong Kong Food Retailing Experience," *Journal of Public Policy & Marketing* 24, no. 1 (2005), pp. 90–99; Ellyn Byron, "P&G's Global Target: Shelves of Tiny Stores," *The Wall Street Journal*, July 16, 2007, pp. A1, A10.

[12] Eric Bellman, "In India, a Retailer Finds Key to Success Is Clutter," *The Wall Street Journal*, August 8, 2007, pp. A1, A10.

[13] Steve Hamm and Nandini Lakshman, "Widening Aisles for Indian Shoppers," *BusinessWeek,* April 30, 2007, p. 44.

[14] Goksel Yalcinkaya, Roger J. Calantone, and David A. Griffith, "An Examination of Exploration Capabilities: Implications for Product Innovation and Market Performance," *Journal of International Marketing* 15 (2007), pp. 63–93.

CROSSING BORDERS 14.1 Big-Box Cookie-Cutter Stores Don't Always Work

Wal-Mart, JCPenney, Office Depot, and Starbucks are all going global with their successful U.S. operating strategies. However, adaptation is still important, and many have had to adapt their operating strategy to accommodate cultural and business differences. Growth strategies must be supported by three foundations: (1) The retailer must offer a competitively superior assortment of products as defined by local customers, (2) the retailer must be able to develop superior economies across the value chain that delivers the product to the local consumer, and (3) global retailers must be able to execute in the local environment.

Consider, for example, some of the problems U.S. retailers have had when building their global strategies on these three pillars.

- In fashion and clothing markets, personal taste is critical in the buying decision. Distinctions in culture, climate, and even physiology demand that products be tailored to each market. Tight skirts, blouses, and any other article that tightly hugs the female silhouette are sure sellers in southern Europe and are sure losers in the north. Dutch women bicycle to work, so tight skirts are out. French men insist that trousers be suitable for cuffs; German men cannot be bothered with cuffs. Rayon and other artificial fabrics are impossible to sell in Germany, but next door in Holland, artificial fabrics are popular because they are much cheaper.

- The best-selling children's lines in northern Europe don't have a significant following in France; the French dress their children as little adults, not as kids. One of the best sellers is a downsized version of a women's clothing line for girls.

- Operational costs vary too. Costs in the United States, where the minimum wage is $7.75 per hour, are dramatically different than in France, where the minimum wage is over $10.00, including employer social charges. As a consequence, Toys "R" Us has been forced to adapt its operating structure in France, where it uses one-third fewer employees per store than it does in the United States.

- The image of Sam Walton's English setter on packages of its private-label dog food, Ol' Roy, was replaced with a terrier after Wal-Mart's German executives explained that terriers are popular in Germany, while setters aren't familiar.

- Office Depot closed its U.S.-style cookie-cutter stores in Japan and reopened stores one-third the size of the larger ones. Customers were put off by the warehouselike atmosphere and confused by the English-language signs. The new stores have signs in Japanese and are stocked with office products more familiar to Japanese and purchased locally, such as two-ring loose-leaf binders rather than the typical three-ring binders sold in the United States.

Sources: Ernest Beck and Emily Nelson, "As Wal-Mart Invades Europe, Rivals Rush to Match Its Formula," *The Wall Street Journal,* October 6, 1999; Amy Chozick, "Foof Revives Starbucks Japan," *The Wall Street Journal Asia*, October 24, 2006, p. 19.

appliance and electronics giant Grupo Elektra has formed an alliance with Beijing Automobile Works Group to develop and build low-cost cars for Mexico and export markets.[15]

Some important trends in distribution will eventually lead to greater commonality than disparity among middlemen in different countries. Wal-Mart, for example, is expanding all over the world—from Mexico to Brazil and from Europe to Asia.[16] The only major disappointment for the American juggernaut has been it lack of scale and profits in South Korea; in 2006 the firm sold its five stores there.[17] Avon is expanding into eastern Europe; Mary Kay Cosmetics and Amway into China; and L.L. Bean and Lands' End have successfully entered the Japanese market. The effect of all these intrusions into the traditional distribution systems

[15] Marla Dickerson, "Mexican Retailer, Partner to Build Cars," *Los Angeles Times*, November 22, 2007, pp. C1, C4.

[16] Anand Giridharadas, "Megastores Gaze Longingly at India," *International Herald Tribune*, April 2–3, 2005, pp. 13, 15.

[17] "Wal-Mart Exits Korean Market," *Los Angeles Times*, May 23, 2006, p. C3.

is change that will make discounting, self-service, supermarkets, mass merchandising, and e-commerce concepts common all over the world, elevating the competitive climate to a level not known before.

As U.S. retailers have invaded Europe, staid, nationally based retailers have been merging with former competitors and companies from other countries to form Europewide enterprises.[18] Carrefour, a French global marketer, merged with Promodes, one of its fierce French competitors, to create, in the words of its CEO, "a worldwide retail leader." The U.K. supermarket giant Sainsbury has entered an alliance with Esselunga of Italy (supermarkets), Docks de France (hypermarkets, supermarkets, and discount stores), and Belgium's Delhaize (supermarkets). The alliance provides the four companies the opportunity to pool their experience and buying power to better face growing competition and opportunity afforded by the single European market and the euro.

While European retailers see a unified Europe as an opportunity for pan-European expansion, foreign retailers are attracted by the high margins and prices. Costco, the U.S.-based warehouse retailer, saw the high gross margins that British supermarkets command (7 to 8 percent compared with 2.5 to 3 percent in the United States) as an opportunity. Costco prices will initially be 10 to 20 percent cheaper than rival local retailers.

Expansion outside the home country, as well as new types of retailing, is occurring throughout Europe. El Corte Inglés, Spain's largest department store chain, not only is moving into Portugal and other European countries but also was one of the first retailers to offer a virtual supermarket on the Internet (www.elcorteingles.es) and to sponsor two 24-hour home shopping channels in Spain. Increasingly smaller retailers are also expanding overseas.[19] Another Spanish retailer, Mango, has opened a store in New York City and, along with other European competitors, is taking advantage of low costs of operation in the United States associated with the sinking dollar.[20]

One of Wal-Mart's strengths is its internal Internet-based system, which makes its transactions with suppliers highly efficient and lowers its cost of operations. Indeed, it is buying ailing retailers around the world with the intention of "saving them" with its distribution technologies. This same type of system is available on the Internet for both business-to-business and business-to-consumer transactions. For example, General Motors, Ford Motor Company, and DaimlerChrysler have created a single online site called Covisint (www.covisint.com) for purchasing automotive parts from suppliers, which is expected to save the companies millions of dollars. A typical purchase order costs Ford $150, whereas a real-time order via Covisint will cost about $15. Sears, Roebuck and Carrefour of France have created GlobalNetXchange (www.gnx.com), a retail exchange that allows retailers and their suppliers to conduct transactions online. Any company with a Web browser can access the exchange to buy, sell, trade, or auction goods and services. Described as "one of the most dramatic changes in consumer-products distribution of the decade," the exchange is expected to lower costs for both buyer and supplier. As more such exchanges evolve, one can only speculate about the impact on traditional channel middlemen.

We have already seen the impact on traditional retailing within the last few years caused by e-commerce retailers such as Amazon.com, Dell Computer, eBay, and others—all of which are expanding globally. Most brick-and-mortar retailers are experimenting with or have fully developed Web sites, some of which are merely extensions of their regular stores, allowing them to extend their reach globally. L.L. Bean, Eddie Bauer, and Lands' End are examples.

One of the most challenging aspects of Web sales is delivery of goods. As discussed previously, one of the innovative features of the 7dream program at 7-Eleven stores in Japan is the use of convenience stores for pick-up points for Web orders. It has worked

[18] John Dawson, "New Cultures, New Strategies, New Formats, and New Relationships in European Retailing: Some Implications for Asia," *Journal of Global Marketing* 18, no. 1/2 (2004), pp. 73–98.

[19] Karise Hutchinson, Nicholas Alexander, Barry Quinn, and Anne Marie Doherty, "Internationalization Motives and Facilitating Factors: Qualitative Evidence from Smaller Specialists Retailers," *Journal of International Marketing* 15 (2007), pp. 96–122.

[20] J. Alex Tarquinio, "Foreign Shops Invade New York," *International Herald Tribune*, January 30, 2008, pp. 9, 10.

Now that Russians can own their homes, they're spending fast in home improvement stores like this one in St. Petersburg. In English it would be called "Super Home."

so well in Japan that Ito-Yokado Corporation, owner of 7-Eleven Japan and 72 percent of the U.S. chain, is exporting the idea to U.S. stores. In the Dallas–Fort Worth area, 250 stores have installed ATM-like machines tied into a delivery and payment system that promises to make 7-Eleven stores a depot for e-commerce. FedEx, UPS, and other package delivery services that have been the backbone of e-commerce delivery in the United States are offering similar services for foreign customers of U.S. e-commerce companies, as well as for foreign-based e-commerce companies. When goods cross borders, UPS and others offer seamless shipments, including customs and brokerage. Most of these service companies are established in Europe and Japan and are building networks in Latin America and China.

The impact of these and other trends will change traditional distribution and marketing systems.[21] While this latest retailing revolution remains in flux, new retailing and middlemen systems will be invented, and established companies will experiment, seeking ways to maintain their competitive edge. Moreover, it is becoming more dangerous to think of competitors in terms of individual companies—in international business generally, and distribution systems particularly, a networks perspective is increasingly required. That is, firms must be understood in the context of the commercial networks of which they are a part.[22] These changes will resonate throughout the distribution chain before new concepts are established and the system stabilizes. Not since the upheaval that occurred in U.S. distribution after World War II that ultimately led to the Big-Box type of retailer has there been such potential for change in distribution systems. This time, however, such change will not be limited mostly to the United States—it will be worldwide.

Distribution Patterns

Even though patterns of distribution are in a state of change and new patterns are developing, international marketers need a general awareness of the traditional distribution base. The "traditional" system will not change overnight, and vestiges of it will remain for years to come. Nearly every international firm is forced by the structure of the market to use at least some middlemen in the distribution arrangement. It is all too easy to conclude that, because the structural arrangements of foreign and domestic distribution seem alike, foreign channels are the same as or similar to domestic channels of the same name. Only when the varied intricacies of actual distribution patterns are understood can the complexity of the

[21] Jung-Hee Lee and San-Chul Choi, "The Effects of Liberalization in Retail Markets on Economy and Retail Industry," *Journal of Global Marketing* 18, no. 1/2 (2004), pp. 121–32.

[22] Mats Forsgren, Ulf Holm, and Jan Johanson, *Managing the Embedded Multinational: A Business Network View* (Northampton, MA: Edward Elgar, 2005); see also the associated book review by Charles Dhanarah, *Journal of International Business Studies* 38 (2007), pp. 1231–33.

PEMEX (Petróleos Mexicanos), the Mexican national oil company, will not let foreign firms distribute there. However, in Malaysia, a Mobil station sits right across the boulevard from a government-owned PETRONAS (Petroliam Nasional) station.

distribution task be appreciated. The following description of differences in retailing should convey a sense of the variety of distribution patterns in general including wholesalers.

Retail Patterns

Retailing shows even greater diversity in its structure than does wholesaling.[23] In Italy and Morocco, retailing is composed largely of specialty houses that carry narrow lines, whereas in Finland, most retailers carry a more general line of merchandise. Retail size is represented at one end by Japan's giant department store Mitsukoshi, which reportedly enjoys the patronage of more than 100,000 customers every day, and at the other extreme by the market of Ibadan, Nigeria, where some 3,000 one- or two-person stalls serve not many more customers. Some manufacturers sell directly to consumers through company-owned stores such as Cartier and Disney,[24] and some sell through a half-dozen layers of middlemen.

Size Patterns.

The extremes in size in retailing are similar to those that predominate in wholesaling. Exhibit 14.3 dramatically illustrates some of the variations in size and number of retailers per person that exist in some countries. The retail structure and the problems it engenders cause real difficulties for the international marketing firm selling consumer goods. Large dominant retailers can be sold to directly, but there is no adequate way to reach small retailers who, in the aggregate, handle a great volume of sales. In Italy, official figures show there are 931,000 retail stores, or one store for every 63 Italians. Of the 269,000 food stores, fewer than 10,000 can be classified as large. Thus retailers are a critical factor in adequate distribution in Italy.

Underdeveloped countries present similar problems. Among the large supermarket chains in South Africa, there is considerable concentration. Of the country's 31,000 stores, 1,000 control 60 percent of all grocery sales, leaving the remaining 40 percent of sales to be spread among 30,000 stores. To reach the 40 percent of the market served by those 30,000 stores may be difficult. In black communities in particular, retailing is on a small scale—cigarettes are often sold singly, and the entire fruit inventory may consist of four apples in a bowl.

[23] Nobukazu J. Azuma, "The Paradox of Competition in the World of Volatility: An Analysis of the Drivers in the Middle Market of International Fashion Retailing," *Journal of Global Marketing* 18, no. 1/2 (2004), pp. 45–72.

[24] Richard Verrier, "Children's Place in Talks with Disney," *Los Angeles Times*, June 4, 2004, p. C2.

Exhibit 14.3
Retail Structure in Selected Countries

Source: Euromonitor, 2008.

Country	All Retailers (000)	People Served per Retailer	Internet Users (per 1,000)
United States	946	322	621
Canada	156	212	707
Argentina	422	91	206
Germany	281	294	513
Poland	333	115	368
Israel	49	145	647
South Africa	111	454	93
China	4,496	294	144
Japan	930	137	538
Australia	83	125	760

Retailing around the world has been in a state of active ferment for several years. The rate of change appears to be directly related to the stage and speed of economic development, and even the least developed countries are experiencing dramatic changes. Supermarkets of one variety or another are blossoming in developed and underdeveloped countries alike. Discount houses that sell everything from powdered milk and canned chili to Korean TVs and DVD players are thriving and expanding worldwide.[25]

Direct Marketing. Selling directly to the consumer through mail, by telephone, or door-to-door is often the approach of choice in markets with insufficient or underdeveloped distribution systems. The approach, of course, also works well in the most affluent markets. Amway, operating in 42 foreign countries, has successfully expanded into Latin America and Asia with its method of direct marketing. Companies that enlist individuals to sell their products are proving to be especially popular in eastern Europe and other countries where many people are looking for ways to become entrepreneurs. In the Czech Republic, for example, Amway Corporation signed up 25,000 Czechs as distributors and sold 40,000 starter kits at $83 each in its first two weeks of business. Avon is another American company that is expanding dramatically overseas.

Direct sales through catalogs have proved to be a successful way to enter foreign markets. In Japan, it has been an important way to break the trade barrier imposed by the Japanese distribution system. For example, a U.S. mail-order company, Shop America, teamed up with 7-Eleven Japan to distribute catalogs in its 4,000 stores. Shop America sells items such as compact discs, Canon cameras, and Rolex watches for 30 to 50 percent less than Tokyo stores; a Canon Autoboy camera sells for $260 in Tokyo and $180 in the Shop America catalog.

Many catalog companies are finding they need to open telephone service centers in a country to accommodate customers who have questions or problems. Hanna Andersson (the children's clothing manufacturer), for example, received complaints that it was too difficult to get questions answered and to place orders by telephone, so it opened a service center with 24 telephone operators to assist customers who generate over $5 million in sales annually. Many catalog companies also have active Web sites that augment their catalog sales.

Resistance to Change. Efforts to improve the efficiency of the distribution system, new types of middlemen, and other attempts to change traditional ways are typically viewed as threatening and are thus resisted.[26] A classic example is the restructuring of the film distribution business being caused by the fast changing technologies of digitization and piracy. Laws abound that protect the entrenched in their positions. In Italy, a new retail outlet must obtain a license from a municipal board composed of local tradespeople. In a two-year period, some 200 applications were made and only 10 new licenses granted. Opposition to retail innovation is everywhere, yet in the face of all the restrictions and hindrances,

[25] Manjeet Kripalani, "Here Come the Wal-Mart Wannabes," *BusinessWeek*, April 4, 2005, p. 56; Clay Chandler, "The Great Wal-Mart of China," *Fortune*, July 25, 2005, pp. 104–16.

[26] Seong Mu Suh, "Fairness and Relationship Quality Perceived by Local Suppliers: In Search of Critical Success Factors for International Retailers," *Journal of Global Marketing* 18, no. 1/2 (2004), pp. 5–20.

CROSSING BORDERS 14.2   It Depends on What "Not Satisfied" Means

Amway's policy is that dissatisfied customers can get a full refund at any time, no questions asked—even if the returned bottles are empty. This refund policy is a courtesy to customers and a testament that the company stands behind its products, and it is the same all over the world. But such capitalistic concepts are somewhat unfamiliar in China.

The best game in town for months among the rising ranks of Shanghai's entrepreneurs was an $84 investment for a box of soaps and cosmetics that they could sell as Amway distributors. Word of this no-lose proposition quickly spread, with some people repackaging the soap, selling it, and then turning in the containers for a refund. Others dispensed with selling altogether and scoured garbage bins instead, showing up at Amway's Shanghai offices with bags full of bottles to be redeemed.

One salesman got nearly $10,000 for eight sacks full of all kinds of empty Amway containers. And at least one barbershop started using Amway shampoos for free and returning each empty bottle for a full refund. In a few weeks, refunds were totaling more than $100,000 a day. "Perhaps we were too lenient," said Amway's Shanghai chief. Amway changed the policy, only to have hundreds of angry Amway distributors descend on the company's offices to complain that they were cheated out of their money. Amway had to call a press conference to explain that it wasn't changing its refund policy, simply raising the standard for what is deemed dissatisfaction. If someone returns half a bottle, fine, but for empties, Amway announced it would check records to see if the person had a pattern of return.

But the company did not anticipate the unusual sense of entitlement it had engendered in China. The satisfaction-guaranteed policy did not spell out specifically what dissatisfaction meant, something people in the Western world understood. "We thought that it would be understood here, too." The change in policy left some dissatisfied. One distributor protested, "Don't open a company if you can't afford losses." Despite these initial problems, Amway apparently is learning the market—the company doubled its sales last year in China to $2 billion.

Sources: Craig S. Smith, "Distribution Remains the Key Problem for Market Makers," *Business China*, May 13, 1996, p. 4; "In China, Some Distributors Have Really Cleaned Up with Amway," *The Wall Street Journal*, August 4, 1997, p. B1; "Avon Forays into Healthcare Sector via Direct Sales," *SinoCast China Business Daily News*, January 14, 2008, p. 1.

self-service, discount merchandising, liberal store hours, and large-scale merchandising continue to grow because they offer the consumer convenience and a broad range of quality product brands at advantageous prices. Ultimately the consumer does prevail.

Alternative Middleman Choices

A marketer's options range from assuming the entire distribution activity (by establishing its own subsidiaries and marketing directly to the end user) to depending on intermediaries for distribution of the product. Channel selection must be given considerable thought because once initiated, it is difficult to change, and if it proves inappropriate, future growth of market share may be affected.

The channel process includes all activities, beginning with the manufacturer and ending with the final consumer. This inclusion means the seller must exert influence over two sets of channels: one in the home country and one in the foreign-market country. Exhibit 14.4 shows some of the possible channel-of-distribution alternatives. The arrows show those to whom the producer and each of the middlemen might sell. In the home country, the seller must have an organization (generally the international marketing division of a company) to deal with channel members needed to move goods between countries. In the foreign market, the seller must supervise the channels that supply the product to the end user. Ideally, the company wants to control or be directly involved in the process through the various channel members to the final user. To do less may result in unsatisfactory distribution and the failure of marketing objectives. In practice, however, such involvement throughout the channel process is not always practical or cost effective. Consequently, selection of channel members and effective controls are high priorities in establishing the distribution process.

Exhibit 14.4
International Channel-of-Distribution Alternatives

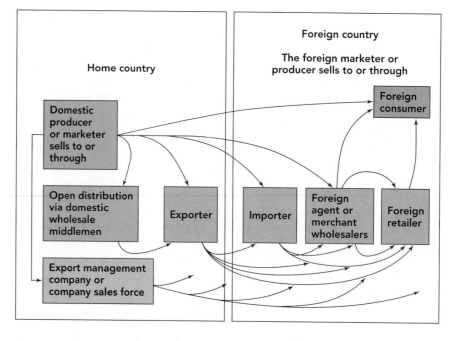

Once the marketer has clarified company objectives and policies, the next step is the selection of specific intermediaries needed to develop a channel. External middlemen are differentiated according to whether or not they take title to the goods: *Agent middlemen* work on commission and arrange for sales in the foreign country but do not take title to the merchandise. By using agents, the manufacturer assumes trading risk but maintains the right to establish policy guidelines and prices and to require its agents to provide sales records and customer information. *Merchant middlemen* actually take title to manufacturers' goods and assume the trading risks, so they tend to be less controllable than agent middlemen. Merchant middlemen provide a variety of import and export wholesaling functions involved in purchasing for their own account and selling in other countries. Because merchant middlemen primarily are concerned with sales and profit margins on their merchandise, they are frequently criticized for not representing the best interests of a manufacturer. Unless they have a franchise or a strong and profitable brand, merchant middlemen seek goods from any source and are likely to have low brand loyalty. Ease of contact, minimized credit risk, and elimination of all merchandise handling outside the United States are some of the advantages of using merchant middlemen.

Middlemen are not clear-cut, precise, easily defined entities. A firm that represents one of the pure types identified here is rare. Thus intimate knowledge of middlemen functions is especially important in international activity because misleading titles can fool a marketer unable to look beyond mere names. What are the functions of a British middleman called a stockist, or one called an exporter or importer? One exporter may, in fact, be an agent middleman, whereas another is a merchant. Many, if not most, international middlemen wear several hats and can be clearly identified only in the context of their relationship with a specific firm.

Only by analyzing middlemen functions in skeletal simplicity can the nature of the channels be determined. Three alternatives are presented: first, middlemen physically located in the manufacturer's home country; next, middlemen located in foreign countries; and finally, government-affiliated middlemen.

Home-Country Middlemen

Home-country middlemen, or *domestic middlemen*, located in the producing firm's country, provide marketing services from a domestic base. By selecting domestic middlemen as intermediaries in the distribution processes, companies relegate foreign-market distribution to others. Domestic middlemen offer many advantages for companies with small international sales volume, those inexperienced with foreign markets, those not wanting to become immediately involved with the complexities of international marketing, and those wanting to sell abroad with minimal financial and management commitment. A major

Remember for a moment the scene in the Pixar movie *Monsters Inc.*—millions of doors on conveyor belts. That scene is reminiscent of the inside of the Nike's European distribution center in Laakdal, Belgium. The shoes come from a variety of Asian low-cost manufacturers and arrive at the center via Rotterdam and Antwerp and the adjacent canal. Twelve hundred people work at the heavily automated facility where 8 million pairs of shoes are sorted and then shipped to customers all over the continent via truck. Even as sales grow, the company will not need to expand the center, because the trend is for the factories to ship directly to the major European retailers, including the Nike Sport in St. Petersburg pictured in Chapter 10.

trade-off when using home-country middlemen is limited control over the entire process. Domestic middlemen are most likely to be used when the marketer is uncertain or desires to minimize financial and management investment. A brief discussion of the more frequently used types of domestic middlemen follows.

Manufacturers' Retail Stores.
An important channel of distribution for a large number of manufacturers is the owned, or perhaps franchised, retail store. Disney, Benetton, and many of the classic Italian luxury goods makers take this approach.

Global Retailers.
As global retailers like IKEA, Costco, Sears Roebuck, Toys "R" Us, and Wal-Mart expand their global coverage, they are becoming major domestic middlemen for international markets.[27] Wal-Mart, with more than 3,000 stores in 13 foreign markets, is an attractive entry point to international markets for U.S. suppliers. Wal-Mart offers an effective way to enter international markets with a minimum of experience. For example, Pacific Connections, a California manufacturer of handbags with $70 million in sales, ventured into overseas markets in Argentina, Brazil, Canada, and Mexico through its ties to Wal-Mart. And as trade restrictions are eased through alliances such as NAFTA, new global retailers are being created—Gigante from Mexico is a good example of this trend.

Export Management Companies.
The *export management company (EMC)* is an important middleman for firms with relatively small international volume or those unwilling to involve their own personnel in the international function. These EMCs range in size from 1 person upward to 100 and handle about 10 percent of the manufactured goods exported. An example of an EMC is a Washington, D.C.–based company that has exclusive agreements with 10 U.S. manufacturers of orthopedic equipment and markets these products on a worldwide basis.

Typically, the EMC becomes an integral part of the marketing operations of its client companies. Working under the names of the manufacturers, the EMC functions as a low-cost, independent marketing department with direct responsibility to the parent firm. The working relationship is so close that customers are often unaware they are not dealing directly with the export department of the company (see Exhibit 14.5).

The export management company may take full or partial responsibility for promotion of the goods, credit arrangements, physical handling, market research, and information on financial, patent, and licensing matters. An EMC's specialization in a given field often enables it to offer a level of service that could not be attained by the manufacturer without years of groundwork. Traditionally, the EMC works on commission, though an increasing number are buying products on their own account.

Two of the chief advantages of EMCs are minimum investment on the part of the company to get into international markets, and no commitment of company personnel or major expenditure of managerial effort. The result, in effect, is an extension of the market for the firm with negligible financial or personnel commitments.

The major disadvantage is that EMCs seldom can afford to make the kind of market investment needed to establish deep distribution for products because they must have immediate sales payout to survive. Such a situation does not offer the market advantages gained by a company that can afford to use company personnel. Carefully selected EMCs can do an excellent job, but the manufacturer must remember that the EMC is dependent on sales volume for compensation and probably will not push the manufacturer's line if it is spread too thinly, generates too small a volume from a given principal, or cannot operate profitably in the short run. In such cases, the EMC becomes an order taker and not the desired substitute for an international marketing department.

---

[27] Peter Gwynne, "The Myth of Globalization?" *Sloan Management Review* 44, no. 2 (Winter 2003), p. 11.

Exhibit 14.5
How Does an EMC
Operate?

Source: "The Export Management
Company," U.S. Department of Commerce, Washington, DC.

Most export management companies offer a wide range of services and assistance, including the following:

Researching foreign markets for a client's products. Traveling overseas to determine the best method of distributing the product. Appointing distributors or commission representatives as needed in individual foreign countries, frequently within an already existing overseas network created for similiar goods. Exhibiting the client's products at international trade shows, such as U.S. Department of Commerce–sponsored commercial exhibitions at trade fairs and U.S. Export Development Offices around the world.

Handling the routine details in getting the product to the foreign customer—export declarations, shipping and customs documentation, insurance, banking, and instructions for special export packing and marking.

Granting the customary finance terms to the trade abroad and ensuring payment to the manufacturer of the product.

Preparing advertising and sales literature in cooperation with the manufacturer and adapting it to overseas requirements for use in personal contacts with foreign buyers.

Corresponding in the necessary foreign languages.

Making sure that goods being shipped are suitable for local conditions and meet overseas legal and trade norms, including labeling, packaging, purity, and electrical characteristics. Advising on overseas patent and trademark protection requirements.

Trading Companies.   Trading companies have a long and honorable history as important intermediaries in the development of trade between nations. *Trading companies* accumulate, transport, and distribute goods from many countries. In concept, the trading company has changed little in hundreds of years.

The British firm Gray MacKenzie and Company is typical of companies operating in the Middle East. It has some 70 salespeople and handles consumer products ranging from toiletries to outboard motors and Scotch whiskey. The key advantage to this type of trading company is that it covers the entire Middle East.

Large, established trading companies generally are located in developed countries; they sell manufactured goods to developing countries and buy raw materials and unprocessed goods. Japanese trading companies *(sogo shosha)* date back to the early 1700s and operate both as importers and exporters.[28] Some 300 are engaged in foreign and domestic trade through 2,000 branch offices outside Japan and handle over $1 trillion in trading volume annually. Japanese trading companies account for 61 percent of all Japanese imports and 39 percent of all exports, or about one-fifth of Japan's entire GDP.

For companies seeking entrance into the complicated Japanese distribution system, the Japanese trading company offers one of the easiest routes to success. The omnipresent trading companies virtually control distribution through all levels of channels in Japan. Because trading companies may control many of the distributors and maintain broad distribution channels, they provide the best means for intensive coverage of the market.[29]

U.S. Export Trading Companies.   The Export Trading Company (ETC) Act allows producers of similar products to form export trading companies. A major goal of the ETC Act was to increase U.S. exports by encouraging more efficient export trade services to producers and suppliers to improve the availability of trade finance and to remove antitrust disincentives to export activities. By providing U.S. businesses with an opportunity to obtain

[28] Roy Larke, "Expansion of Japanese Retailers Overseas," *Journal of Global Marketing* 18, no. 1/2 (2004), pp. 99–120.

[29] J. McGuire and S. Dow, "The Persistence and Implications of Japanese Keiretsu Organization," *Journal of International Business Studies* 34, no. 4 (2003), pp. 374–88; "The Mitsubishi Group, All in the Family," *The Economist*, May 29, 2004, p. 67.

antitrust preclearance for specified export activities, the ETC Act created a more favorable environment for the formation of joint export ventures. Through such joint ventures, U.S. firms can take advantage of economies of scale, spread risk, and pool their expertise. In addition, through joint selling arrangements, domestic competitors can avoid interfirm rivalry in foreign markets. Prior to the passage of the ETC Act, competing companies could not engage in joint exporting efforts without possible violation of antitrust provisions. The other important provision of the ETC Act permits bank holding companies to own ETCs.

Immediately after passage of the ETC Act, several major companies (General Electric, Sears Roebuck, Kmart, and others) announced the development of export trading companies. In most cases, these export firms did not require the protection of the ETC Act since they initially operated independently of other enterprises. They provided international sales for U.S. companies to a limited extent, but primarily they operated as trading companies for their own products. To date, many of the trading companies (particularly the bank-owned ones) established after passage of the ETC Act have closed their doors or are languishing.

Recall that the Japanese are the world-champion fish consumers at nearly 40 kg per person per year—see Exhibit 4.2. Consequently, just as world prices for cut flowers are set at the Aalsmeer Flower Auction in the Netherlands, world prices for fish are set at the Tsukigi fish market in Tokyo. A big fresh bluefin tuna caught in the Atlantic, iced and shipped by air to Tokyo, can bring $10,000 at auction, and then be shipped by air back to Boston for hungry sushi consumers. Perhaps the market is "too efficient," as the world now faces a shortage of such tuna.

Complementary Marketers.

Companies with marketing facilities or contacts in different countries with excess marketing capacity or a desire for a broader product line sometimes take on additional lines for international distribution; though the formal name for such activities is *complementary marketing*, it is commonly called *piggybacking*. General Electric Company has been distributing merchandise from other suppliers for many years. It accepts products that are noncompetitive but complementary and that add to the basic distribution strength of the company itself. The classic example was Gillette distributing batteries in less developed countries.

Most piggyback arrangements are undertaken when a firm wants to fill out its product line or keep its seasonal distribution channels functioning throughout the year. Companies may work either on an agency or merchant basis, but the greatest volume of piggyback business is handled on an ownership (merchant) purchase-and-resale arrangement. The selection process for new products for piggyback distribution determines whether (1) the product relates to the product line and contributes to it, (2) the product fits the sales and distribution channel presently employed, (3) the margin is adequate to make the undertaking worthwhile, and (4) the product will find market acceptance and profitable volume. If these requirements are met, piggybacking can be a logical way of increasing volume and profit for both the carrier and the piggybacker.

Manufacturer's Export Agent.

The *manufacturer's export agent (MEA)* is an individual agent middleman or an agent middleman firm providing a selling service for manufacturers. Unlike the EMC, the MEA does not serve as the producer's export department but has a short-term relationship, covers only one or two markets, and operates on a straight commission basis. Another principal difference is that MEAs do business in their own names rather than in the name of the client. Within a limited scope of operation, the MEAs provide services similar to those of the EMC.

Webb-Pomerene Export Associations.

Webb-Pomerene export associations (WPEAs) are another major form of group exporting. The Webb-Pomerene Act of 1918 allowed American business firms to join forces in export activities without being subject to the Sherman Antitrust Act. Thus WPEAs cannot participate in cartels or other international agreements that would reduce competition in the United States, but they can offer four major benefits: (1) reduction of export costs, (2) demand expansion through promotion, (3) trade barrier reductions, and (4) improvement of trade terms through bilateral bargaining. Additionally, WPEAs set prices, standardize products, and arrange for disposal of surplus products. Although they account for less than 5 percent of U.S. exports, WPEAs include some of America's blue-chip companies in agricultural products, chemicals and raw materials, forest products, pulp and paper, textiles, rubber products, motion pictures, and television.

Foreign Sales Corporation.   A *foreign sales corporation (FSC)* is a sales corporation set up in a foreign country or U.S. possession that can obtain a corporate tax exemption on a portion of the earnings generated by the sale or lease of export property. Manufacturers and export groups can form FSCs. An FSC can function as a principal, buying and selling for its own account, or a commissioned agent. It can be related to a manufacturing parent or can be an independent merchant or broker. The WTO in 2003 ruled FSCs to be in violation of international trade rules, thus starting a major trade dispute with the European Union that still simmers and occasionally sizzles.[30]

Foreign-Country Middlemen

The variety of agent and merchant middlemen in most countries is similar to that in the United States. International marketers seeking greater control over the distribution process may elect to deal directly with middlemen in the foreign market. They gain the advantage of shorter channels and deal with middlemen in constant contact with the market.

Using foreign-country middlemen moves the manufacturer closer to the market and involves the company more closely with problems of language, physical distribution, communications, and financing. Foreign middlemen may be agents or merchants, they may be associated with the parent company to varying degrees, or they may be hired temporarily for special purposes. Some of the more important foreign-country middlemen are manufacturer's representatives and foreign distributors.

Government-Affiliated Middlemen

Marketers must deal with governments in every country of the world. Products, services, and commodities for the government's own use are always procured through government purchasing offices at federal, regional, and local levels. In the Netherlands, the state's purchasing office deals with more than 10,000 suppliers in 20 countries. About one-third of the products purchased by that agency are produced outside the Netherlands. Finally, regarding the efficiency of the public sector versus the private sector, an important lesson was learned during the 2005 Hurricane Katrina disaster—Wal-Mart planned for and delivered aid better than FEMA (the U.S Federal Emergency Management Agency).[31]

Factors Affecting Choice of Channels

The international marketer needs a clear understanding of market characteristics and must have established operating policies before beginning the selection of channel middlemen. The following points should be addressed prior to the selection process:

1. Identify specific target markets within and across countries.
2. Specify marketing goals in terms of volume, market share, and profit margin requirements.
3. Specify financial and personnel commitments to the development of international distribution.
4. Identify control, length of channels, terms of sale, and channel ownership.

[30] "World Watch," *The Wall Street Journal*, July 25, 2005, p. A3.

[31] Ann Zimmerman and Valerie Bauerlein, "At Wal-Mart Emergency Plan Has a Big Payoff," *The Wall Street Journal*, September 12, 2005, pp. B1, B3.

Once these points are established, selecting among alternative middlemen choices to forge the best channel can begin. Marketers must get their goods into the hands of consumers and must choose between handling all distribution or turning part or all of it over to various middlemen.[32] Distribution channels vary depending on target market size, competition, and available distribution intermediaries.

Key elements in distribution decisions include the functions performed by middlemen (and the effectiveness with which each is performed), the cost of their services, their availability, and the extent of control that the manufacturer can exert over middlemen activities.

Although the overall marketing strategy of the firm must embody the company's profit goals in the short and long run, channel strategy itself is considered to have six specific strategic goals. These goals can be characterized as the six Cs of channel strategy: cost, capital, control, coverage, character, and continuity. In forging the overall channel-of-distribution strategy, each of the six Cs must be considered in building an economical, effective distribution organization within the long-range channel policies of the company. It should also be noted that many firms use multiple or hybrid[34] channels of distribution because of the trade-offs associated with any one option.[35] Indeed, both Dell selling computers at kiosks inside Japan's Jusco supermarkets and Toys "R" Us selling toys in food stores are good examples.

Cost

The two kinds of channel cost are (1) the capital or investment cost of developing the channel and (2) the continuing cost of maintaining it. The latter can be in the form of direct expenditure for the maintenance of the company's selling force or in the form of margins, markup, or commissions of various middlemen handling the goods. Marketing costs (a substantial part of which is channel cost) must be considered as the entire difference between the factory price of the goods and the price the customer ultimately pays for the merchandise. The costs of middlemen include transporting and storing the goods, breaking bulk, providing credit, local advertising, sales representation, and negotiations.

Despite the old truism that you can eliminate middlemen but you cannot eliminate their functions or cost, creative, efficient marketing does permit channel cost savings in many circumstances. Some marketers have found, in fact, that they can reduce cost by eliminating inefficient middlemen and thus shortening the channel. Mexico's largest producer of radio and television sets has built annual sales of $36 million on its ability to sell goods at a low price because it eliminated middlemen, established its own wholesalers, and kept margins low. Conversely, many firms accustomed to using their own sales forces in large-volume domestic markets have found they must lengthen channels of distribution to keep costs in line with foreign markets.

Capital Requirements

The financial ramifications of a distribution policy are often overlooked. Critical elements are capital requirement and cash-flow patterns associated with using a particular type of middleman. Maximum investment is usually required when a company establishes its own internal channels, that is, its own sales force. Use of distributors or dealers may lessen the capital investment, but manufacturers often have to provide initial inventories on consignment, loans, floor plans, or other arrangements. Coca-Cola initially invested in China with majority partners that met most of the capital requirements. However, Coca-Cola soon realized that it could not depend on its local majority partners to distribute its product aggressively in the highly competitive, market-share–driven business of carbonated beverages. To assume more control of distribution, it had to assume management control, and that meant greater capital investment from Coca-Cola. One of the highest costs of doing business in China is the capital required to maintain effective distribution.

---

[32] Alex Rialp, Catherine Axxin, and Sharon Tach, "Exploring Channel Internalization among Spanish Exporters," *International Marketing Review* 19, no. 2–3 (2002), pp. 133–55.

[34] Mika Gabrielsson, V. H. Manek Kirpalani, and Reijo Luostarinen, "Multiple Channel Strategies in the European Personal Computer Industry," *Journal of International Marketing* 10, no. 3 (2002), pp. 73–95.

[35] Rod B. McNaughton, "The Use of Multiple Export Channels by Small Knowledge-Intensive Firms," *International Marketing Review* 19, no. 2–3 (2002), pp. 190–203.

Control   The more involved a company is with the distribution, the more control it exerts. A company's own sales force affords the most control but often at a cost that is not practical. Each type of channel arrangement provides a different level of control;[33] as channels grow longer, the ability to control price,[34] volume, promotion, and type of outlets diminishes. If a company cannot sell directly to the end user or final retailer, an important selection criterion for middlemen should be the amount of control the marketer can maintain.[35] Of course, there are risks in international distribution relationships as well—opportunism and exploitation are two.[36] Finally, one of the most alarming examples of distribution channels out of control regards the current worldwide shortage of fish; retailers and distributors in affluent countries literally feed the demands of their voracious customers and kill the fisheries along the way.[37]

Coverage   Another major goal is full-market coverage to gain the optimum volume of sales obtainable in each market, secure a reasonable market share, and attain satisfactory market penetration. Coverage may be assessed by geographic segments, market segments, or both. Adequate market coverage may require changes in distribution systems from country to country or time to time. Coverage is difficult to extend both in highly developed areas and in sparse markets—the former because of heavy competition and the latter because of inadequate channels.

Many companies do not attempt full-market coverage but seek significant penetration in major population centers. In some countries, two or three cities constitute the majority of the national buying power. For instance, 60 percent of the Japanese population lives in the Tokyo-Nagoya-Osaka market area, which essentially functions as one massive city.

At the other extreme are many developing countries with a paucity of specialized middlemen except in major urban areas. Those that do exist are often small, with traditionally high margins. In China, for example, the often-cited billion-person market is, in reality, confined to fewer than 25 to 30 percent of the population of the most affluent cities. Even as personal income increases in China, distribution inadequacies limit marketers in reaching all those who have adequate incomes. In both extremes, the difficulty of developing an efficient channel from existing middlemen plus the high cost of distribution may nullify efficiencies achieved in other parts of the marketing mix.

To achieve coverage, a company may have to use many different channels—its own sales force in one country, manufacturers' agents in another, and merchant wholesalers in still another.

Character   The channel-of-distribution system selected must fit the character of the company and the markets in which it is doing business. Some obvious product requirements, often the first considered, relate to the perishability or bulk of the product, complexity of sale, sales service required, and value of the product.

Channel captains must be aware that channel patterns change; they cannot assume that once a channel has been developed to fit the character of both company and market, no more need be done. Great Britain, for example, has epitomized distribution through specialty-type middlemen, distributors, wholesalers, and retailers; in fact, all middlemen have traditionally worked within narrow product specialty areas. In recent years, however, there has been a trend toward broader lines, conglomerate merchandising, and mass marketing. The firm that neglects the growth of self-service, scrambled merchandising, or discounting may find it has lost large segments of its market because its channels no longer reflect the character of the market.

[33] C. Bello, Cristian Chelariu, and Li Zhang, "The Antecedents and Performance Consequences of Relationalism in Export Distribution Channels," *Journal of Business Research* 56, no. 1 (January 2003), pp. 1–16.

[34] Ting-Jui Chou and Fu-Tang Chen, "Retail Pricing Strategies in Recession Economies: The Case of Taiwan," *Journal of International Marketing* 12, no. 1 (2004), pp. 82–102.

[35] Michael Harvey and Milorad M. Novicevic, "Selecting Marketing Managers to Effectively Control Global Channels of Distribution," *International Marketing Review* 19, no. 4–5 (2002), pp. 525–44.

[36] Esra F. Gencturk and Preet S. Aulakh, "Norms- and Control-Based Governance of International Manufacturer-Distributor Relational Exchanges," *Journal of International Marketing* 15 (2007), pp. 92–125.

[37] "Japan's Tuna Crisis," *The New York Times*, June 27, 2007, p. A22; Elisabeth Rosenthal, "In Europe, the Catch of the Day is Often Illegal," *The New York Times*, January 15, 2008, pp. A1, A6.

You can buy just about anything at Stockmann's Department Store in Helsinki—men's and women's fashions, hardware (hammers, etc.) and software, bakery goods and garden supplies, fillet of reindeer and furniture, televisions—yes, everything from Audi A3s to zuccini. It even has cold storage services for your mink. But Stockmann's doesn't stock Samsung cell phones. The Korean company hasn't yet penetrated Nokia's home market. Of course, the product line is thin but rich at Cartier's in Paris. And you can find the Samsung at the Grand Bazaar (Kapali Carsi) in Istanbul, billed as the oldest and largest covered marketplace in the world. The 15th-century mall competes for customers with its 20th-century cousin, Akmerkez Etiler, in a high-income neighborhood about 10 miles away. Finally, Louis meets Lenin here on Red Square in Moscow. Russians now go for the luxury brands at the old government department store (still with the unattractive name, Gum), recently transformed into a 800,000 square foot in-door, high-end shopping mall. You can see St. Basil's Cathedral in the background, and just 200 meters across the square Comrade Vladimir Lenin's embalmed body is entombed in a chilly mausoleum. While the old communist isn't too happy about free enterprise disturbing his view, he certainly must be pleased about the 2008 resumption of the annual Red Square May Day military parade after its seventeen-year hiatus.

Continuity   Channels of distribution often pose longevity problems. Most agent middlemen firms tend to be small institutions. When one individual retires or moves out of a line of business, the company may find it has lost its distribution in that area. Wholesalers and especially retailers are not noted for their continuity in business either. Most middlemen have little loyalty to their vendors. They handle brands in good times when the line is making money but quickly reject such products within a season or a year if they fail to produce during that period. Distributors and dealers are probably the most loyal middlemen, but even with them, manufacturers must attempt to build brand loyalty downstream in a channel lest middlemen shift allegiance to other companies or other inducements.

Locating, Selecting, and Motivating Channel Members

The actual process of building channels for international distribution is seldom easy, and many companies have been stopped in their efforts to develop international markets by their inability to construct a satisfactory system of channels.

Construction of the middleman network includes seeking out potential middlemen, selecting those who fit the company's requirements, and establishing working relationships with them.[38] In international marketing, the channel-building process is hardly routine. The closer the company wants to get to the consumer in its channel contact, the larger the sales force required. If a company is content with finding an exclusive importer or selling agent for a given country, channel building may not be too difficult; however, if it goes down to the level of subwholesaler or retailer, it is taking on a tremendous task and must have an internal staff capable of supporting such an effort.

Locating Middlemen

The search for prospective middlemen should begin with study of the market and determination of criteria for evaluating middlemen servicing that market. The checklist of criteria differs according to the type of middlemen being used and the nature of their relationship with the company. Basically, such lists are built around four subject areas: productivity or volume, financial strength, managerial stability and capability, and the nature and reputation of the business. Emphasis is usually placed on either the actual or potential productivity of the middleman.

The major problems are locating information to aid in the selection and choice of specific middlemen and discovering middlemen available to handle one's merchandise. Firms seeking overseas representation should compile a list of middlemen from such sources as the following: the U.S. Department of Commerce; commercially published directories; foreign consulates; chamber-of-commerce groups located abroad; other manufacturers producing similar but noncompetitive goods; middlemen associations; business publications; management consultants; carriers—particularly airlines; and Internet-based services such as Unibex, a global technology services provider. Unibex provides a platform for small- to medium-sized companies and larger enterprises to collaborate in business-to-business commerce.

Selecting Middlemen

Finding prospective middlemen is less a problem than determining which of them can perform satisfactorily. Low volume or low potential volume hampers most prospects, many are underfinanced, and some simply cannot be trusted.[39] In many cases, when a manufacturer is not well known abroad, the reputation of the middleman becomes the reputation of the manufacturer, so a poor choice at this point can be devastating.

Screening.   The screening and selection process itself should include the following actions: an exploratory letter or email including product information and distributor requirements in the native language sent to each prospective middleman; a follow-up with the best respondents for specific information concerning lines handled, territory covered, size of firm, number of salespeople, and other background information; check of credit and references from other clients and customers of the prospective middleman; and, if possible, a personal check of the most promising firms. Obtaining financial information on prospective middlemen has become easier via such Internet companies as Unibex, which provides access to Dun & Bradstreet and other client information resources.

Experienced exporters suggest that the only way to select a middleman is to go personally to the country and talk to ultimate users of your product to find whom they consider to be the best distributors. Visit each possible middleman once before selecting the one to represent you; look for one with a key person who will take the new product to his or her heart and make it a personal objective to make the sale of that line a success. Furthermore, exporters stress that if you cannot sign one of the two or three customer-recommended distributors, you might be better off having no distributor in that country, because having a worthless one costs you time and money every year and may cut you out when you finally find a good one.

---

[38] Stephen Keysuk Kim, "A Cross-National Study of Interdependence Structure and Distributor Attitudes: The Moderating Effect of Group Orientation," *International Journal of Research in Marketing* 20, no. 2 (2003), pp. 193–214.

[39] C. Zhang, S. T. Cavusgil, and A. S. Roath, "Manufacturer Governance of Foreign Distributor Relationships: Do Relational Norms Enhance Competitiveness in the Export Market?" *Journal of International Business Studies* 34, no. 6 (2003), pp. 550–66.

The Agreement. Once a potential middleman has been found and evaluated, the task of detailing the arrangements with that middleman begins.[40] So far the company has been in a buying position; now it must shift into a selling and negotiating position to convince the middleman to handle the goods and accept a distribution agreement that is workable for the company. Agreements must spell out specific responsibilities of the manufacturer and the middleman, including an annual sales minimum. The sales minimum serves as a basis for evaluation of the distributor; failure to meet sales minimums may give the exporter the right of termination.

Some experienced exporters recommend that initial contracts be signed for one year only. If the first year's performance is satisfactory, they should be reviewed for renewal for a longer period. This time limit permits easier termination, and more important, after a year of working together in the market, a more suitable arrangement generally can be reached.

Motivating Middlemen

The level of distribution and the importance of the individual middleman to the company determine the activities undertaken to keep the middleman motivated. On all levels, the middleman's motivation is clearly correlated with sales volume. Motivational techniques that can be employed to maintain middleman interest and support for the product may be grouped into five categories: financial rewards, psychological rewards, communications, company support, and corporate rapport.

Obviously, financial rewards must be adequate for any middleman to carry and promote a company's products. Margins or commissions must be set to meet the needs of the middleman and may vary according to the volume of sales and the level of services offered. Without a combination of adequate margin and adequate volume, a middleman cannot afford to give much attention to a product.

Being human, middlemen and their salespeople respond to psychological rewards and recognition of their efforts. A trip to the United States or to the parent company's home or regional office is a great honor. Publicity in company media and local newspapers also builds esteem and involvement among foreign middlemen.

In all instances, the company should maintain a continuing flow of communication in the form of letters, newsletters, and periodicals to all its middlemen. The more personal these are, the better. One study of exporters indicated that the more intense the contact between the manufacturer and the distributor, the better the performance by the distributor. More and better contact naturally leads to less conflict and a smoother working relationship.

Finally, considerable attention must be paid to the establishment of close rapport between the company and its middlemen. In addition to methods noted, a company should be certain that the conflicts that arise are handled skillfully and diplomatically. Bear in mind that all over the world, business is a personal and vital thing to the people involved.

Terminating Middlemen

When middlemen do not perform up to standards or when market situations change, requiring a company to restructure its distribution, it may be necessary to terminate relationships. In the United States, this termination is usually a simple action regardless of the type of middlemen; they are simply dismissed. However, in other parts of the world, the middleman often has some legal protection that makes termination difficult. In Colombia, for example, if you terminate an agent, you are required to pay 10 percent of the agent's average annual compensation, multiplied by the number of years the agent served, as a final settlement.

Competent legal advice is vital when entering distribution contracts with middlemen. But as many experienced international marketers know, the best rule is to avoid the need to terminate distributors by screening all prospective middlemen carefully. A poorly chosen distributor may not only fail to live up to expectations but may also adversely affect future business and prospects in the country.

---

[40] S. Tamer Cavusgil, Seyda Deligonul, and Chun Zhang, "Curbing Foreign Distributor Opportunism: An Examination of Trust, Contracts, and the Legal Environment in International Channel Relationships," *Journal of International Marketing* 12, no. 2 (2004), pp. 7–27.

CROSSING BORDERS 14.3   No More Roses for My Miami Broker

Eight out of ten flowers you buy this year will have come from Colombia, our nation's leading supplier of cut flowers. Colombia's cut-flower industry now amounts to $580 million in exports annually. The majority of the flowers coming to the United States arrive in Miami aboard jets, bound for flower brokers who then hold them on consignment until U.S. wholesalers and retailers negotiate on price and place orders. In the past, growers often financed the supply chain and had no idea what a shipment would bring until sales were negotiated in Miami by brokers who charged an average of 15 percent for their services. That was the situation until the creation of the Flower Purchase Network (FPN) and its Floraplex Web site (www.floraplex.com), the first electronic marketplace in which flower growers, wholesalers, retailers, and consumers can meet online to conduct e-business.

The FPN system allows buyers to negotiate directly with the growers and provides growers with an opportunity to expand their markets and increase profits quickly and efficiently. Users can buy from Holland, Africa, and Israel with service through the Dutch auctions (refer to Chapter 4, pp. 100–101), as well as from South and North America with service through self-provided logistics providers. Floraplex members that utilize the marketplace receive all their invoices, orders, sales history, purchase history, and more by using the one-stop account summary page. This seamless link between buyer and seller means sellers can negotiate directly with buyers while simultaneously reducing the cost of middlemen. Floraplex applies a 3 to 8 percent service fee for system usage, depending on volume, whereas Miami brokers charge an average of 15 percent commission.

Owned by World Commerce Online, FPN handles roughly 1 million stems of flowers per week and actively trades flowers on six continents—after being on the Web for less than a year. The next Web launch will be Freshplex, designed to do for the entire produce industry what Floraplex is doing for the flower industry.

Sources: "Colombia's Hope: Less Coca, More Carnations," *Christian Science Monitor*, March 24, 2000; http://www.floraplex.com, 2008; Mike Candelaria, "Changing the Way the Fresh-Cut Flower Industry Does Business," *Latin Trade*, June 2000; T. Christian Miller, "Everything Is Coming Up Roses for Colombia's Flower Industry," *Los Angeles Times*, February 14, 2003, p. A3.

Controlling Middlemen

The extreme length of channels typically used in international distribution makes control of middlemen especially important. Marketing objectives must be spelled out both internally and to middlemen as explicitly as possible. Standards of performance should include sales volume objective, inventory turnover ratio, number of accounts per area, growth objective, price stability objective, and quality of publicity. Cultural differences enter into all these areas of management.[41]

Control over the system and control over middlemen are necessary in international business. The first relates to control over the distribution network, which implies overall controls for the entire system to be certain the product is flowing through desired middlemen. Some manufacturers have lost control through "secondary wholesaling" or parallel imports.[42] A company's goods intended for one country are sometimes diverted through distributors to another country, where they compete with existing retail or wholesale organizations.

The second type of control is at the middleman level. When possible, the parent company should know (and to a certain degree control) the activities of middlemen with respect

These greenhouses in the Jordan River Valley near Jericho are the beginning of a supply chain that delivers roses by air to the Aalsmeer Flower Market near Amsterdam, then to the United States and other countries. The mix of cultures in Israel is evident from the Bedouin shepherds in the foreground.

---

[41] Jody Evans and Felix T. Mavondo, "Psychic Distance and Organizational Performance: An Empirical Examination of International Retailing Operations," *Journal of International Business Studies* 33, no. 3 (2002), pp. 515–32; David A. Griffith and Matthew B. Myers, "The Performance Implications of Strategic Fit of Relational Norm Governance Strategies in Global Supply Chain Relationships," *Journal of International Business Studies* 36, no. 3 (2005), pp. 254–69.

[42] See the discussion of parallel imports in Chapter 18.

to their volume of sales, market coverage, services offered, prices, advertising, payment of bills, and even profit. Quotas, reports, and personal visits by company representatives can be effective in managing middleman activities at any level of the channel.

The Internet

The Internet is an important distribution method for multinational companies and a source of products for businesses and consumers. Indeed, a good argument can be made that the Internet has finally put the consumer in control of marketing and distribution globally.[43] Computer hardware and software companies and book and music retailers were the earliest e-marketers to use this method of distribution and marketing. More recently there has been an expansion of other types of retailing and business-to-business (B2B) services into e-commerce. Technically, e-commerce is a form of direct selling; however, because of its newness and the unique issues associated with this form of distribution, it is important to differentiate it from other types of direct marketing.

E-commerce is used to market B2B services, consumer services, and consumer and industrial products via the World Wide Web. It involves the direct marketing from a manufacturer, retailer, service provider, or some other intermediary to a final user. Some examples of e-marketers that have an international presence are Dell Computer Corporation[44] (www.dell.com), which generates nearly 50 percent of its total sales, an average of about $69 million a day, online; and Cisco Systems (www.cisco.com), which generates more than $1 billion in sales annually. Cisco's Web site appears in 14 languages and has country-specific content for 49 nations. Gateway has global sites in Japan, France, the Netherlands, Germany, Sweden, Australia, the United Kingdom, and the United States, to name a few (www.gateway.com). Sun Microsystems and its after-marketing company, SunExpress, have local-language information about more than 3,500 aftermarket products. SunPlaza enables visitors in North America, Europe, and Japan to get information online about products and services and to place orders directly in their native languages.

Besides consumer goods companies such as Lands' End, Levi, and Nike, many smaller[45] and less well-known companies have established a presence on the Internet beyond their traditional markets. An Internet customer from the Netherlands can purchase a pair of brake levers for his mountain bike from California-based Price Point. He pays $130 instead of the $190 that the same items would cost in a local bike store.

For a Spanish shopper in Pamplona, buying sheet music used to mean a 400-kilometer trip to Madrid. Now he crosses the Atlantic to shop—and the journey takes less time than a trip to the corner store. Via the Internet, he can buy directly from specialized stores and high-volume discounters in New York, London, and almost anywhere else.

E-commerce is more developed in the United States than the rest of the world partly because of the vast number of people who own personal computers and because of the much lower cost of access to the Internet than found elsewhere. (See Exhibit 14.3.) In addition language, legal, and cultural differences, the cost of local phone calls (which are charged by the minute in most European countries) initially discouraged extensive use and contributed to slower Internet adoption in Europe.

Services, the third engine for growth, are ideally suited for international sales via the Internet. All types of services—banking, education, consulting, retailing, hotels, gambling—can be marketed through a Web site that is globally accessible. As outsourcing of traditional in-house tasks such as inventory management, quality control, and accounting, secretarial, translation, and legal services has become more popular among companies, the Internet providers of these services have grown both in the United States and internationally.

---

[43] "Crowned at Last, A Survey of Consumer Power," *The Economist*, April 2, 2005, insert pp. 1–16.

[44] Evan Ramstad and Gary McWilliams, "For Dell, Success in China Tells a Tale of Maturing Market," *The Wall Street Journal*, July 5, 2005, pp. A1, A8.

[45] Oystein Moen, Iver Endresen, and Morten Gavlen, "Use of the Internet in International Marketing: A Case Study of Small Computer Software Firms," *Journal of International Marketing* 11, no. 4 (2003), pp. 129–49.

global marketing on the web at marriott

The Internet today is the most global of any media invented so far, having leapfrogged television and radio—which may yet become global some day but are far from doing so. It is the only medium that approaches true global reach.

The power of the Internet results from its many unique attributes. It is unique in its ability to:

- Encompass text, audio and video in one platform.
- Operate in a dialogue versus monologue mode.
- Operate simultaneously as mass media *and* personalized media.
- Build global "communities," unconfined by national borders.

These attributes make it the most powerful medium on earth, unparalleled in its ability to communicate, especially to a global world. It is an international marketer's dream.

However, leveraging these characteristics in an effective manner requires dealing with various substantive issues. These issues include:

- **Major differences in Internet adoption rates across the globe** ranging from greater than 70 percent adoption in North America to less than 2 percent for the continent of Africa. This difference greatly influences the role of the Web as part of the marketing mix in international markets. Even for advanced EU economies, the variability of adoption is great, ranging from 88 percent in the Netherlands to 49 percent in Belgium. The average for the entire continent of Africa is around 1 percent (see www.internetworldstats.com).

- **Unique issues caused by technology** including broadband versus narrow-band, which drive what products and services can be marketed and how. In the narrow-band world, highly graphic and video-based Web sites are not viable. An example is the elaborate photo tours of hotels on www.Marriott.com, which download quickly on broadband connections but take inordinately long on narrow band. Therefore, a site designed for one market can be ineffective in another.

Renaissance is a Marriott-owned hotel brand. It uses various media to lead customers to its all-important Web sites, including print, television, Internet, and outdoor. Three 2-page print ads are directed toward U.K., Middle Eastern, and Chinese customers, and each of them lists the Web site addresses—the first two citing www.renaissancehotels.co.uk, and the last noting www.renaissancehotels.com.cn. Even though the same Web site ultimately serves customers in both the United Kingdom and the Middle East, the ad presentation is adapted to the more conservative dress appropriate in the latter region. Finally, you can see how the campaign is also used on the streets of Shanghai. Ask your classmates what "Be fashionable" translates into on the latter two ads.

- **Costs to globalize** can be enormous if multiple language sites need to be built. For example, translating the 110,000-page Marriott.com Web site is a very costly undertaking, both on a one-time and ongoing basis. Add to that the costs of translating the back-end systems that feed the site, and the costs rise exponentially. For sites with a lot of constantly changing content and heavy dependence on back-end systems, maintaining foreign language sites can be prohibitively expensive.

- **Implications of differing labor costs** that affect return on investment (ROI). For example, in the United States, the cost of an online booking for Marriott is less than half that of a phone booking. That differential may not apply in many Third World countries, where labor costs are often very low, making it difficult to justify a Web site investment.

- **Different approaches to privacy, access, and infrastructure investment** also require changes to strategy by market.

  - On privacy. For example, EU laws are much more stringent than U.S. laws; as a result, the e-mail marketing strategy in the EU is much more cautious than in the United States.

  - On access. Some countries regulate access to the Internet. For example, China only allows access to approved sites, whereas the United States does not limit Internet access.

  - On infrastructure investment. Some countries have private investment fueling the development of the telecom technology systems required to enable Internet access (e.g., the United States), whereas in other countries, state-owned phone companies have this responsibility. In general, markets that have depended state investment have been laggards in the Internet space.

Apart from all of these issues, one of the most important challenges for companies contemplating a global Internet presence is determining whether they should build "foreign market sites" or "foreign language sites." In an ideal world, with infinite resources, the answer could be to build both. However, that option is rarely possible given resource constraints. This challenge has been a key issue for Marriott International, which has responded in different ways, depending on market situations. In some cases, the hotel company tried one approach before moving to the other. In fact, Marriott's experience in this area is an excellent illustration of the issue. To clarify the issue using France or French as an example, the question was:

Should we have a global site in French that caters to ALL French-speaking customers, no matter which country they live in

OR

Should we have a site in the French language, which addresses the needs of the LOCAL French market?

Having a French language site for a global French-speaking market had significant benefits, because there is a sizable French-speaking population in the world, which includes major parts of North and Central Africa and the Caribbean islands. However, in this case, Marriot decided in favor of a local site for France. In summary, the company found that

- The needs of French customers living in France were very different from the needs of customers in French-speaking Africa or Haiti. Customers living in France prefer different destinations than those living in other French-speaking areas, such as the Caribbean.

- Promotional approaches were also different for France than for other French-speaking countries. Using a U.S. example to illustrate, sweepstakes are far more popular and accepted in the United States than in Europe.

- Finally, the French market dwarfed all other French-speaking markets combined. Therefore, if Marriott could only afford to maintain one French site, it was more cost effective to address the largest French market, namely, France.

Paradoxically, when faced with the same question for Spanish—a Spanish-language site or a site for Spain/individual Spanish-speaking countries—Marriott decided to go for a Spanish-language site for several key reasons:

- None of the Spanish-speaking markets was very large for Marriott. Although Spain is the largest economy in the Spanish-speaking world, as of now, the company does not have enough hotels there or enough traffic from Spain to cost effectively build a site uniquely for Spain. That applies to all other Spanish-speaking countries.

The second series of banner ads might flash across a computer screen in China; the last panel asks visitors to click to go to the Marriott Web site there. Marriott maintains 11 Web sites to attract its global clientele to its 2,800 hotels around the world. The sites appeal to consumers in the following countries: the United States, the United Kingdom, Ireland, Australia and New Zealand, France, Germany, China, Japan, South Korea, Latin America (Spanish/Espanol), and Brazil.

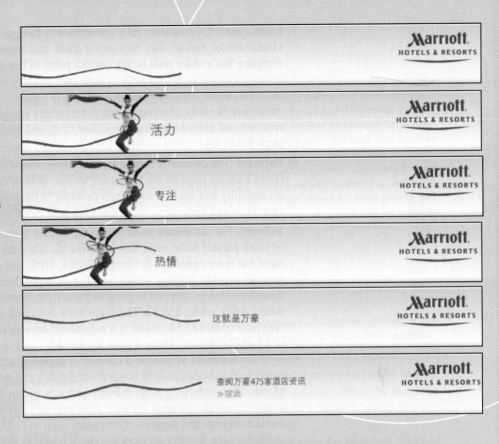

- There was greater commonality of destinations among many Spanish-speaking countries—especially the Latin American countries—than among French-speaking countries. For example, the United States is an equally popular destination for almost all Latin American countries.

Ironically, Marriott initially took the opposite approach to the same question, resulting in eight Spanish sites for various Latin American countries. However, it quickly found that it was impractical to build, manage, and maintain so many sites and get the returns on investment it desired. Although this scenario may and should change as the individual markets mature and gain critical mass, it appears that it will take some years. Until then, Marriott will maintain one Spanish-language site.

In summary, the international online marketplace is highly complex and continues to evolve. There is no single approach that fits every situation; even when that appears the case, it may not be for long, as is clear from the experience described. A key focus therefore should be on making good trade-off decisions and maintaining flexibility in strategy.

Source: Shafiq Khan, Senior Vice President eCommerce, Marriott International, 2008. (Photos Courtesy of Marriott.)

plant efficiency that will be gained should be worth the extra $20,000. Kang starts to call the bank to have the counter stacker added to the letter of credit but hesitates and thinks, "I'm sick of bank rhetoric, so we'll just wire them the additional funds before shipment. The amendment to the letter of credit will cost too much time and money."

Because a lot rides on this order, Kang decides he will schedule a trip to New Hampshire for the final acceptance test. He wants to be sure the machine will handle the paper stock the company uses. No one wants the machine to be delivered and then find out it won't work the way they expect. Too many complications arise if the equipment is paid for and delivered and it needs major adjustments.

Back in New Hampshire, Roberts is checking details to make sure the case maker will be shipped on time. "Things are getting hectic—so much to do, so little time. If they expect to ship this year, the customer must accept the machine by December 16. That gives us a week to break it down and skid it (bolt the machine to a wooden pallet) and a week to get it on a boat. We have very little room for error because of the holidays. Besides, the customer wants special packing in desiccant because of climatic conditions. So we'll need to send the shipment to a packing specialist before it goes to port."

November 1: Letter of Credit

Roberts sends the original letter of credit to his freight forwarder by second-day air and includes the bank invoice forms and marine insurance certificate.

December 2: Final Inspection and Shipping Schedules

In China, Kang thinks, "Roberts faxed me possible vessel dates. They're going for Friday, December 20, out of Montreal, and I'm booked to be in New Hampshire December 11–15. The vessel arrives in Shanghai January 25. That would be just right. I hope they'll be ready for the test run because our material will be a challenge for them to run."

Meanwhile, Roberts is thinking, "I'm glad our general manager decided to release the case maker as a stock machine during the DRUPA show. He OK'd it because the China Books deal looked firm. We'd never be able to ship it this year otherwise. Kang seems like a decent person—very bright. They got their material here two weeks ago for us to try, and since then manufacturing has been working hard trying to meet their specs. I hope we have a good week."

December 13: The Test Run

"The machine looks impressive," Kang observes after he watches the test run take place. "But I'm not convinced we can run a consistent 120 per minute. I insist we come in tomorrow for one more demo. They're close, so if they don't quite do it, I won't pay the installation bill until we're comfortable with production at our plant. Besides, Roberts told me the boat would probably leave late, so they have a little extra time to get the container to the pier."

A second test run takes place the next day. Kang asks for a few minor adjustments but is otherwise satisfied that China Books will get consistently good production from Austin's case maker.

In his office, Roberts wonders why all foreign shipments seem to occur at year-end. "Cheryl at Fast Forwarder (Austin's freight forwarder) said we should be ready first thing on Monday, December 16, if we want to get the container on board for a December 31 sailing. Since nothing happens during the last week of the year, it needs to be there this Friday morning to be processed by the line. The steamship companies will probably start the holidays at noon on the 24th. Red alert! Call Cheryl immediately and tell her the 40-footer (container) must have a wooden floor—with no room for surprises!"

January 2: It's on the Way

Kang is ecstatic. "Roberts just faxed me the ocean bill of lading. The case maker was on board the vessel *Tiger Shark* December 31, with an estimated arrival in Shanghai on January 30. They just made it!"

Analysis

Although this scenario may seem staggering, it is not intended to overwhelm you or make you wary of exporting. The point is that specific export mechanics occur when goods are shipped from one country to another, and though they may be tedious, you cannot escape them. The good news is that assistance is available for the exporter from government and private sources. This scenario occurred prior to widespread use of the Internet, and many of the steps can either be completed on the Internet or sped up by using the Internet, but they cannot be eliminated. According to one source, a bank's role in handling the risks in shipping and paying for goods has not changed much since the 17th century. What has changed is technology. Banks are adapting their trade finance to the electronic age. Instead of faxes, telegraph, and postal service as used in the Global Perspective, many banks take a direct feed from a client's purchase-order system, extract the data, use it to create a letter of credit, and provide real-time information on transaction status. For example, Bank One offers an Internet-based tool for creating, modifying, and sending letters of credit and collections. And in the future, banks will act as a hub to all parties involved in transactions—buyer, seller, bank, carrier, freight forwarder, insurance company, and customs authorities. The rules and regulations remain the same but the process is expedited, thanks to the benefits of the Internet. As you read this chapter, identify each of the places in this scenario where the Internet could be used to expedite the process.

Sources: Robert R. Costa, "Tales of Foreign Sales," *Financial Executive,* January–February 1997, pp. 43–46; Steve Marlin, "Banks Link Their Trade Platforms with the International Movement of Goods," *Information Week,* May 12, 2003, p. 48; "Short-Term Financing: Banker's Acceptances," *Economist Intelligence Unit—Country Finance,* February 19, 2008, p. 84.

Exhibit 15.1
The Exporting Process

Leaving the Exporting Country	Physical Distribution	Entering the Importing Country
Licenses	International shipping and logistics	Tariffs, taxes
General	Packing	**Nontariff barriers**
Validated	Insurance	Standards
Documentation		Inspection
Export declaration		Documentation
Commercial invoice		Quotas
Bill of lading		Fees
Consular invoice		Licenses
Special certificates		Special certificates
Other documents		Exchange permits
		Other barriers

Exporting is an integral part of all international business, whether the company is large or small, or whether it markets in one country or is a global marketer. Goods manufactured in one country and destined for another must be moved across borders to enter the distribution system of the target market. There are three kinds of barriers to exporting that face even the most enthusiastic international traders: managerial, organizational, and external.[1] All are pertinent to our discussion here about the nuts-and-bolts of exporting and logistics.

Most countries control the movement of goods crossing their borders, whether leaving (exports) or entering (imports). Export and import documents, tariffs, quotas, and other barriers to the free flow of goods between independent sovereignties are requirements that must be met by the exporter, the importer, or both.[2]

In addition to selecting a target market, designing an appropriate product, establishing a price, planning a promotional program, and selecting a distribution channel, the international marketer must meet the legal requirements involved in moving goods from one country to another. The exporting process (see Exhibit 15.1 above) includes the licenses and documentation necessary to leave the country, an international carrier to transport the goods, and fulfillment of the import requirements necessary to get the shipment legally into another country.[3]

Firms often have staff experienced in dealing with export mechanics, but agencies, government and private, are available to provide expert assistance to firms confronted with unfamiliar situations or a task that is too burdensome.[4] More and more, companies are finding it cost effective to outsource many exporting activities, especially since the terrorist attack on New York's World Trade Center (9/11) called for new security and compliance requirements.[5] In cases when exports are processed in-house, the necessary mechanics for

[1] Natalia Vila Lopez, "Export Barriers and Strategic Grouping," *Journal of Global Marketing* 20 (2007), pp. 17–30; Janet Y. Murray, Gerald Yong Gao, Masaaki Kotabe, and Nan Zhou, "Assessing Measurement Invariance of Export Orientation: A Study of Chinese and Non-Chinese Firms in China," *Journal of International Marketing* 15 (2007), pp. 41–62; John A. Mathews and Ivo Zander, "The International Entrepreneurial Dynamics of Accelerated Internationalization," *Journal of International Business Studies* 38 (2007), pp. 387–403.

[2] For a comprehensive review of trade barriers, see "2004 National Trade Estimate Report on Foreign Trade Barriers," http://www.ustr.gov, and select Search for Trade Barriers.

[3] Leonidas C. Leonidou, "An Analysis of the Barriers Hindering Small Business Export Development," *Journal of Small Business Management,* July 2004, discusses these issues in more detail.

[4] For a thorough discussion of the entire export-import process, see Evelyn Thomchick, Richard R. Young, and Kusumal Ruamsook, "Importing and Exporting: A Longitudinal Study of Process Component Importance and Expertise," *Transportation Journal,* Summer 2004, pp. 34–48.

[5] See, for example, Thomas A. Cook, Rennie Alston, and Kelly Raia, *Mastering Import and Export Management* (New York: American Management Association, 2004).

exporting can be largely completed using the Internet. These mechanics of exporting are sometimes considered the essence of foreign marketing; however, they should not be seen as the primary task of international marketing but as a necessary step in completing the process of marketing.

Countries impose some form of regulation and restriction on the exporting and importing of goods for many reasons. *Export regulations* may be designed to conserve scarce goods for home consumption or to control the flow of strategic goods to actual or potential enemies. *Import regulations* may be imposed to protect health, conserve foreign exchange, serve as economic reprisals, protect home industry, provide revenue in the form of tariffs, and ensure national security. To comply with various regulations, the exporter may have to acquire export licenses or permits from the home country and ascertain that the potential customer has the necessary permits for importing the goods. The rules and regulations that cover the exportation and importation of goods and their payment, and the physical movement of those goods between countries, are the special concerns of this chapter.

Export Restrictions

Although the United States requires no formal or special license to engage in exporting as a business, permission or a license to export may be required for certain commodities and certain destinations. Export licensing controls apply to exports of commodities and technical data from the United States; re-exports of U.S.-origin commodities and technical data from a foreign destination to another foreign destination; U.S.-origin parts and components used in foreign countries to manufacture foreign products for exports; and, in some cases, foreign products made from U.S.-origin technical data. Most items requiring special permission or a license for exportation are under the control of the Bureau of Industry and Security (BIS)[6] of the Department of Commerce.

The volume of exports and the number of companies exporting from the United States have grown spectacularly over the last decade. In an effort to alleviate many of the problems and confusions of exporting and to expedite the process, the Department of Commerce has published a revised set of export regulations known as the *Export Administration Regulations (EAR)*. They are intended to speed up the process of granting export licenses by removing a large number of items from specific export license control and by concentrating licensing on a specific list of items, most of which affect national security, nuclear nonproliferation, terrorism, or chemical and biological weapons. Along with these changes comes a substantial increase in responsibility on the part of the exporter since the exporter must now ensure that Export Administration Regulations are not violated.

The EAR is intended to serve the national security, foreign policy, and nonproliferation interests of the United States and, in some cases, to carry out its international obligations.[7] It also includes some export controls to protect the United States from the adverse impact of the unrestricted export of commodities in short supply, such as Western cedar. Items that do not require a license for a specific destination can be shipped with the notation NLR (no license required) on the Shipper's Export Declaration. Some export restrictions on high-technology products have been recently eased, which we hope marks the beginning of a new trend.[8]

Determining Export Requirements

The first step when complying with export licensing regulations is to determine the appropriate license for your product. Products exported from the United States require a general or a validated export license, depending on the product, where it is going, the

---

[6] Formerly known as the Bureau of Export Administration (BXA).

[7] For a primer on Commerce Department export controls, see "Introduction to Commerce Department Export Controls," http://www.bis.doc.gov, and select Export Control basics.

[8] James Auger, "United States to Ease Technology-Export Restrictions," *Global Insight Daily Analysis*, January 23, 2008. We note that other countries also restrict exports for a variety of reasons. For example see "Russian Government Mulls Additional Grain Export Restrictions," *Russia and CIS General Newswire, Interfax*, November 15, 2007.

end use, and the final user. The *general license* permits exportation of certain products that are not subject to EAR control with nothing more than a declaration of the type of product, its value, and its destination. The *validated license,* issued only on formal applications, is a specific document authorizing exportation within specific limitations designated under the EAR.

The responsibility of determining if a license is required rests with the exporter. This is a key point! The steps necessary to determine the type of license required and/or if an item can be shipped are as follows:

- The exporter is responsible for selecting the proper classification number, known as the *Export Control Classification Number (ECCN),* for the item to be exported. The ECCN leads to a description in the *Commerce Control List (CCL),* which indicates the exportability status of the item.

- The exporter must decide from the CCL if the items have end-use restrictions, for example, use in nuclear, chemical, and biological weapons. The exporter must also determine if the product has a dual use, that is, if it can be used in both commercial and restricted applications.

- The exporter is responsible for determining the ultimate end customer and end uses of the product, regardless of the initial buyer. This step includes carefully screening end users and uses of the product to determine if the final destination of the product is to an unapproved user or for an unapproved use. U.S. law requires firms to avoid shipments if the firm has knowledge that customers will use its products for illegal purposes or resell the product to unauthorized end users.

To illustrate, suppose you are an exporter of shotguns and you are beginning the process of fulfilling orders from Argentina (20-inch barrel shotguns), Australia (23-inch and 26-inch barrels), and Sudan (26-inch barrels).[9] The first step is to determine the proper Export Control Classification Number (ECCN) for the commodity to be exported. Each ECCN consists of five characters that identify its category, product group, type of control, and country group level. There are three general ways to determine a product's ECCN:

- If you are the exporter of the product but not its manufacturer, you can contact the manufacturer or developer to see if that firm already has an ECCN.

- Compare the general characteristics of the product to the Commerce Control List and find the most appropriate product category. Once the category is identified, you go through the entire category and identify the appropriate ECCN by determining the product's particular functions.

- Request a classification from the BIS. The request must include the end use, end user, and/or destination. The BIS will advise you whether a license is required or likely to be granted for a particular transaction. This type of request is known as an *advisory opinion.* An advisory opinion does not bind the BIS to issuing a license in the future, because government policies may change before a license is actually granted.

Once the proper ECCN has been obtained (in this illustration 0A984; see Exhibit 15.2), the second step is to locate the number in the Commerce Control List. Consulting the (CCL) for shotguns (see Exhibit 15.2), the description shows that the reasons for control are Crime Control (CC), Firearms Convention (FC), and U.N. sanctions (U.N.) and that there are different restrictions depending on the length of the shotgun barrel.

---

[9] This abbreviated example illustrates the general idea of the steps necessary to determine licensing requirements.

Exhibit 15.2
Illustration of Commerce Control List Requirements for ECCN 0A984

Source: Abstracted from Export Administration Regulations Database, Bureau of Industry and Security, http://www.bis.doc.gov.

0A984 Shotguns, barrel length 18 inches (45.72 cm) or over; buckshot shotgun shells; except equipment used exclusively to treat or tranquilize animals, and except arms designed solely for signal, flare, or saluting use; and parts, n.e.s.

License Requirements
Reason for Control: CC, FC, UN

Control(s)		Country Chart
FC applies to firearms		FC Column 1
CC 1	applies to shotguns with a barrel length greater than or equal to 18 in. (45.72 cm), but less than 24 in. (60.96 cm) or buckshot shotgun shells controlled by this entry, regardless of end-user.	CC Column 1
CC 2	applies to shotguns with a barrel length greater than or equal to 24 in. (60.96 cm), regardless of end user.	CC Column 2
CC 3	applies to shotguns with a barrel length greater than or equal to 24 in. (60.96 cm) if for sale or resale to police or law enforcement.	CC Column 3
UN	applies to UN sanctions that ban shipments of all firearms, regardless of type, to countries listed.	Rwanda; Serbia and Montenegro (formerly Yugoslavia)

List of Items Controlled
Unit: $ value
Related Controls: this entry does not control shotguns with a barrel length of less than 18 inches (45.72 cm). These items are subject to the export licensing authority of the Department of State.

The third step is to consult the *Commerce Country Chart (CCC)* (Exhibit 15.3), which helps you determine, based on the reason(s) for control associated with your item, if you need a license to export or re-export your item to a particular destination. In combination with the Commodity Control List, the CCC allows you to determine whether a license is required for items on the CCL exported to any country in the world.

In checking the CCC (Exhibit 15.3), you find Argentina, Australia, and Sudan all listed. Looking at the Crime Control and Firearms Convention columns and referencing the product description in the Commodity Control List, you see that the Argentinian order for

Exhibit 15.3
Commerce Country Chart: Reasons for Control (Selected Countries)

Country	Chemical & Biological Weapons			Nuclear Nonproliferation		National Security		Missile Tech	Regional Stability		Firearms Convention	Crime Control			Antiterrorism	
	CB 1	CB 2	CB 3	NP 1	NP 2	NS 1	NS 2	MT 1	RS 1	RS 2	FC 1	CC 1	CC 2	CC 3	AT 1	AT 2
Albania	x*	x		x		x	x	x	x	x		x	x			
Argentina	x					x	x	x	x	x	x	x		x		
Australia	x					x		x	x							
Canada	x										x					
China	x	x	x	x		x	x	x	x	x		x		x		
France	x					x		x	x							
India	x	x	x	x	x	x	x	x	x	x		x		x		
Mexico	x	x		x		x	x	x	x	x	x	x		x		
Sudan	x	x		x		x	x	x	x	x		x		x	x	x
Syria	x	x	x	x		x	x	x	x	x		x		x	x	

*special license required.

Source: Abstracted from Commerce Country Chart, http://www.bxa.doc.gov. Under *Rules, Regulations and Lists,* select *Go Direct to the Regs* and then select *part name, 738spir,* June 20, 2000.

shotguns with 20-inch barrels falls into CC Column 1 and FC Column 1, where the *x* indicates that the order cannot be shipped without a special license. The Australian orders for 23-inch and 26-inch shotguns (CC Columns 1 and 2) do not require special licenses.

Finally, an examination of the Sudanese order for 26-inch shotguns reveals in CC Column 2 that the product can be exported without a special license; however, CC Column 3 indicates that if the guns are for sale or resale to police or law enforcement, a special license is required. Because you are not sure if the shotguns are to be resold, more information will be needed before the order can be processed. If you determine that the guns will not be resold to police or law enforcement, they can be shipped without special license; otherwise, a license will have to be obtained before the shipment can take place.

But the challenge is not yet over. An exporter also must establish that the end user is not listed in the List of Denied Persons,[10] which lists those denied export privileges; no shipments may be made to any person or company on the denied persons list. In addition to checking the denial list, the exporter needs to make a general check to be sure there are no indications that the end-user's intentions will lead to an unauthorized use of the product.

Unfortunately, you cannot always rely on the buyer's word. Sun Microsystems sold one of its supercomputers to a Hong Kong firm that claimed the computer was destined for a scientific institute near Beijing, an authorized sale. A trace of the final destination revealed that the computer's final destination was a military research facility in China, an unauthorized end use and user. Because Sun Microsystems monitored the sale and reported the diversion, there were no legal consequences. Negotiations between China and the U.S. government resulted in the return of the computer to Sun Microsystems. To be alert to

Exhibit 15.4
Red Flags

Source: http://www.bxa.doc.gov;
select *Red Flags*.

The exporter has an important role to play in preventing exports and re-exports that might be contrary to the national security and foreign policy interests of the United States and to ensure that the shipment is not in violation of Bureau of Export Administration regulations. To assist in determining the motives of a buyer, the BXA proposes these indicators as possible signs that a customer is planning an unlawful diversion:

1. The customer or purchasing agent is reluctant to offer information about the end use of a product.
2. The product's capabilities do not fit the buyer's line of business; for example, a small bakery places an order for several sophisticated lasers.
3. The product ordered is incompatible with the technical level of the country to which the product is being shipped. For example, semiconductor-manufacturing equipment would be of little use in a country without an electronics industry.
4. The customer has little or no business background.
5. The customer is willing to pay cash for a very expensive item when the terms of the sale call for financing.
6. The customer is unfamiliar with the product's performance characteristics but still wants the product.
7. The customer declines routine installation, training, or maintenance services.
8. Delivery dates are vague, or deliveries are planned for out-of-the-way destinations.
9. A freight-forwarding firm is listed as the product's final destination.
10. The shipping route is abnormal for the product and destination.
11. Packaging is inconsistent with the stated method of shipment or destination.
12. When questioned, the buyer is evasive or unclear about whether the purchased product is for domestic use, export, or re-export.

---

[10] A database of all prohibited parties can be found on the "Prohibited Parties Database," which, in addition to the Denied Persons List, includes Debarred Parties, Entity List, and Specially Designated Nationals, Terrorists, Narcotics Traffickers, Blocked Persons and Vessels—all of whom must be screened before completing an export order. The list of denied persons can be found at http://www.bsi.doc.gov; select Denied Persons List under Rules, Regulations and Lists.

Chinese air force officers undergo a training session on the latest command center instruments at a training school in Beijing. China successfully test-fired a new type of long-range ground-to-ground missile within its territory as tensions between China and Taiwan intensified after Taiwan's president declared that relations between Taipei and Beijing should be regarded as "special state-to-state relations." Most recently China and the United States have both shot down their own "errant" satellites with missiles.[11] Much of the electronic technology used in long-range missiles is dual-use; that is, the technology can be used for both nonmilitary and military applications. It is the exporter's responsibility to ensure that the final user of restricted dual-use products complies with export restrictions. (© *Roger Ressmeyer/CORBIS*)

possible problems like the one Sun faced, the Export Administration Regulations suggest looking for red flags (Exhibit 15.4), which may give a clue that your customer is planning an unlawful diversion.

As is true of all the export mechanics that an exporter encounters, the details of exporting must be followed to the letter. Good record keeping, as well as verifying the steps undertaken in establishing the proper ECCN and evaluating the intentions of end users and end uses, is important should a disagreement arise between the exporter and the Bureau of Industry and Security. Penalties can entail denial of export privileges, fines, or both. For example, a five-year denial of export privileges was imposed on a resident of Pittsfield, Massachusetts, based on his conviction of illegally exporting 150 riot shields to Romania without the required export license. At the time of the shipment, the riot shields were controlled for export worldwide for foreign policy reasons. See Exhibit 15.5 for examples of violations and penalties.

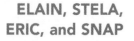

ELAIN, STELA, ERIC, and SNAP

Although the procedure for acquiring an export license may seem tedious on first reading, four electronic services facilitate the paperwork and reduce the time necessary to acquire export licenses.

- **ELAIN** (Export License Application and Information Network) enables exporters that have authorization to submit license applications via the Internet for all commodities except supercomputers to all free-world destinations. When approved, licensing decisions are conveyed back to the exporters via the Internet.

- **STELA** (System for Tracking Export License Applications), an automated voice-response system for tracking applications, can be accessed using a touch-tone phone. It provides applicants with the status of their license and classification applications and is available 24 hours a day, seven days a week. STELA can give exporters authority to ship their goods for those licenses approved without conditions.

- **ERIC** (Electronic Request for Item Classification), a supplementary service to ELAIN, allows an exporter to submit commodity classification requests via the Internet to the Bureau of Export administration.

---

[11] "China Confirms Anti-Satellite Test to US, Says Not a Threat," *AFX UK Focus*, January 22, 2007; Yochi J. Dreazen, "U.S. Missile Hits Satellite–Military Strike Raised Hackles in China; Test Charges Denied," *The Wall Street Journal*, February 22, 2008, p. A9.

Exhibit 15.5

Example of Violations and Penalties of BIS Export Controls

Source: "Don't Let This Happen to You—An Introduction to U.S. Export Control Law," Bureau of Industry and Security, U.S. Department of Commerce, April 2005, http://www.bis.doc.gov.

End Use/End-User Violation

A $12 million civil penalty was imposed against an American airframe manufacturer as part of a settlement of charges that the company violated federal export control laws by submitting false and misleading statements about the end use and end user of machine tools. In a related case, the BIS imposed a $1.32 million civil penalty and a denial of export privileges on a group of Chinese government–owned companies and their U.S. affiliates that had received the machine tools from the American firm.

Facilitating Export to Denied Persons

The Commerce Department imposed a $15,000 penalty on FedEx for allegedly facilitating the export of U.S.-origin semiconductor test equipment from the United States to Taiwan to a Denied Person and failure to maintain records of the subject transaction.

Duel-Use Products

Bushnell Corporation, which does business as Worldwide Sports & Recreation, pleaded guilty to conspiracy and violation of export regulations. For a period of two years, more than 500 Night Ranger night vision devices were shipped to Japan and 14 other countries without the required export license. The U.S. attorney warned that "distributors of equipment with potential military use must be vigilant about compliance with export restrictions. . . . Willful blindness and deliberate ignorance of the law is not an excuse when national security is at issue." Under a plea agreement, Bushnell agreed to pay a criminal fine of $650,000 and receive five years of corporate probation.

Violation of Antiboycott Provisions

St. Jude Medical Export GmbH agreed to pay a $30,000 penalty for violating the EAR when it failed to report in a timely manner its receipt of three requests from an Iraqi government agency to adhere to the rules of the Arab League boycott of Israel during a reporting period. On four occasions, St. Jude also violated the antiboycott provisions of the EAR by agreeing to refuse to do business with persons blacklisted by the Arab League.

Illegal Transshipping

All export privileges were denied for eight years to David Portnoy, convicted of violating the International Emergency Economic Powers Act by transshipping electronic components and telecommunications equipment through Switzerland to Libya (a U.S. boycott of Libya was in force) without the required export licenses.

- **SNAP** (Simplified Network Application Process), an alternative to paper license submissions, enables an exporter to submit export and re-export applications, high-performance computer notices, and commodity classification requests via the Internet. Acknowledgments of submissions will be received the same day, and electronic facsimiles of export licenses and other validations can be obtained online. SNAP is one of the changes made by the Department of Commerce to move it from being a paper-based bureaucracy to an all-digital department.

Import Restrictions

An exporter planning a sale to a foreign buyer must examine the export restrictions of the home country as well as the import restrictions and regulations of the importing country. Although the responsibility of import restrictions may rest with the importer, the exporter does not want to ship goods until it is certain that all import regulations of the destination country have been met. Goods arriving without proper documentation can be denied entry and returned to the shipper.

Besides import tariffs, many other trade restrictions are imposed by foreign countries. A few examples from the 30 basic barriers to exporting considered important by *Business International* include import licenses, quotas, and other quantitative restrictions; currency restrictions and allocation of exchange at unfavorable rates on payments for imports; devaluation; prohibitive prior import deposits, prohibition of collection-basis sales, and insistence on cash letters of credit; arbitrarily short periods in which to apply for import licenses; and delays resulting from pressure on overworked officials or from competitors' influence on susceptible officials.[12]

Trading with the European Union from outside the European Union or within member states, an exporter continues to be confronted with market barriers that have yet to be eliminated. One study of 20,000 EU exporting firms indicated that the most troublesome barriers were administrative roadblocks, border-crossing delays, and capital controls. Generally such barriers are challenged and ultimately dropped. As the European Union becomes more fully integrated, many of the barriers that exist among member countries will be eliminated, though not as rapidly as some expect.

The most frequently encountered trade restrictions, besides tariffs, are such nontariff barriers (NTBs) as exchange permits, quotas, import licenses, standards, boycotts, and voluntary agreements.

Tariffs

Recall that tariffs are the taxes or customs duties levied against goods imported from another country. All countries have tariffs for the purpose of raising revenue and protecting home industries from competition with foreign-produced goods.[13] Tariff rates are based on value or quantity or a combination of both. In the United States, for example, the types of customs duties used are classified as follows: (1) *ad valorem duties*, which are based on a percentage of the determined value of the imported goods; (2) *specific duties*, a stipulated amount per unit weight or some other measure of quantity; and (3) a *compound duty*, which combines both specific and ad valorem taxes on a particular item, that is, a tax per pound plus a percentage of value. Because tariffs frequently change, published tariff schedules for every country are available to the exporter on a current basis.[14]

Exchange Permits

Especially troublesome to exporters are exchange restrictions placed on the flow of currency by some foreign countries. To conserve scarce foreign exchange and alleviate balance-of-payment difficulties, many countries impose restrictions on the amount of their currency they will exchange for the currency of another country—in effect, they ration the amount of currency available to pay for imports. Exchange controls may be applied in general to all commodities, or a country may employ a system of multiple exchange rates based on the type of import. Essential products might have a very favorable exchange rate, while nonessentials or luxuries would have a less favorable rate of exchange. South Africa, for example, until recently had a two-tier system for foreign exchange: Commercial Rand and Financial Rand. At times, countries may not issue any exchange permits for certain classes of commodities.

In countries that use exchange controls, the usual procedure is for the importer to apply to the control agency of the importing country for an import permit; if the control agency approves the request, an import license is issued. On presentation to the proper government agency, the import license can be used to have local currency exchanged for the currency of the seller.

Receiving an import license, or even an exchange permit, however, is not a guarantee that a seller can exchange local currency for the currency of the seller. If local currency is in short supply—a chronic problem in some countries—other means of acquiring home-country currency are necessary. For example, in a transaction between the government of Colombia and a U.S. truck manufacturer, there was a scarcity of U.S. currency to exchange for the 1,000 vehicles Colombia wanted to purchase. The problem was solved through a series of exchanges. Colombia had a surplus of coffee that the truck manufacturer accepted and traded in Europe for sugar; the sugar was traded for pig iron; and finally the pig iron was traded for U.S. dollars.

---

[12] For a complete discussion of foreign trade barriers, see "2005 National Trade Estimate Report on Foreign Barriers, USTR (2005), http://www.ustr.gov, and select Foreign Trade Barriers.

[13] "China's Auto Tariff Policy Does Not Violate WTO Principles," *Xinhua China Facts and Figures*, March 3, 2008.

[14] The entire Harmonized Tariff Schedule of the United States can be downloaded, or accessed via an interactive tariff database, at USITC: http://www.usitc.gov; select Harmonized Tariff Schedule.

CROSSING BORDERS 15.1   Major Smuggling Ring Busted—A Sweet Deal

The United States maintains an artificial price for sugar to protect the cane and beet sugar industry. This feat is accomplished by placing a quota on sugar imports. The amount of sugar imported annually is determined by estimating the annual consumption less estimated U.S. production. In 2004, consumption was 10.2 tons, production was 8.4 tons; thus the quota for that year was 1.8 tons. This limit held U.S. domestic raw sugar prices to 23 cents per pound compared to 9 cents on the world market. Therefore, U.S. consumers spend about $2 billion yearly in higher prices for sugar and food items that contain sugar than if we had a free market in sugar. But while sugar costs more for the average citizen, it also means that if you could figure a way to buy sugar at 9 cents on the world market and sell it at 23 cents in the United States, you could make a pot full of money—but then there is that nasty quota standing in the way. Well, there may be a way around those quotas if we read the law carefully.

Eureka! After a careful reading of the categories of sugar and derivatives covered by the sugar quota, an enterprising importer spotted a category not included in the quota, a gooey brown sugar–based molasses that is good for little more than animal feed. The Customs Department was contacted about the molasses product, agreed that it was not covered by the sugar restrictions, and gave its explicit approval to import the mixture without paying high tariffs. The company built a processing plant in Canada to turn Brazilian sugar into the molasses and a refinery across the border in Michigan to reverse the process and produce precisely the sort of sugar syrup covered by the tariffs. It then sold the product to its usual customers: big makers of ice cream, confectionery, and breakfast cereals.

All went well until the ever-vigilant sugar lobby, one of the strongest lobbies in the United States, put pressure on prominent politicians from sugar-producing states to stop those "smugglers"—causing Customs to reverse itself. Alarmed that it might see its tariffs rise by some 7,000 percent, the company challenged the decision in the Court of International Trade (CIT). The court sided with the firm, dismissing the government's action as "arbitrary, capricious, and abuse of discretion," citing the precedent that products are classified according to the way they are imported, not their ultimate use. More pointedly, the court maintained that an importer had the right to design products specifically to get a lower duty. An internal memo from the agency said that under long-standing policy, what happened to a product after it was across the border didn't matter. The fact that, after importation, the product may be processed to allow it to compete directly with sugar subject to the quota is not relevant to classification. The agency has always tolerated a certain amount of tariff engineering. The judge said that car makers routinely import parts they later assemble in the United States to avoid high tariffs. The judge noted that even when pearls are imported ready for stringing, with holes already drilled in them, Customs classifies them as pearls, not jewelry, which carries a higher tax rate.

A month after the ruling, the litigators began an appeal to Congress to change the definition of the sugar syrup to one of ultimate use, rather than what it is when imported. This definition would make the Customs ruling and the court case irrelevant. It would also put the company out of business. However, until the law is rewritten, truckloads of molasses goop cross the border into the United States to become clear sugar syrup that is used, among other things, as a coating for your breakfast cereal.

Sources: Bill Walsh, "Smart or Smuggling?" *New Orleans Times-Picayune*, April 30, 2000, p. F9; David Whelan, "Even the Biggest Companies Screw Up on Export Rules," *Forbes*, May 2004; "CAFTA Cornucopia," *Washington Times*, May 5, 2005, p. A18; Alan Beattie, "Sugar Lobby Still Packs a Punch Despite Reform to Subsidies, *Financial Times*, March 30, 2006, p. 8.

This somewhat complicated but effective countertrade transaction is not uncommon. As will be discussed in Chapter 18, countertrade deals are often a result of the inability to convert local currency into home-country currency or of the refusal of a government to issue foreign exchange.

Quotas   Countries may also impose limitations on the quantity of certain goods imported during a specific period. These quotas may be applied to imports from specific countries or from all foreign sources in general. The United States, for example, has specific quotas for importing sugar,[15]

---

[15] Alan Beattie, "Sugar Lobby Still Packs a Punch Despite Reform to Subsidies, *Financial Times*, March 30, 2006, p. 8.

wheat, cotton, tobacco, textiles, and peanuts; in the case of some of these items, the amount imported from specific countries is also limited.[16] The most important reasons to set quotas are to protect domestic industry and to conserve foreign exchange. Some importing countries also set quotas to ensure an equitable distribution of a major market among friendly countries.

Import Licenses

As a means of regulating the flow of exchange and the quantity of a particular imported commodity, countries often require import licenses. The fundamental difference between quotas and import licenses as a means of controlling imports is the greater flexibility of import licenses over quotas. Quotas permit importing until the quota is filled; licensing limits quantities on a case-by-case basis.

Standards

Like many nontariff barriers, standards have legitimacy. Health standards,[17] safety standards, and product quality standards are necessary to protect the consuming public, and imported goods are required to comply with local laws. Unfortunately, standards can also be used to slow down or restrict the procedures for importing to the point that the additional time and cost required to comply become, in effect, trade restrictions.

Safety standards are a good example. Most countries have safety standards for electrical appliances and require that imported electrical products meet local standards. However, safety standards can be escalated to the level of an absolute trade barrier by manipulating the procedures used to determine if products meet the standards. The simplest process is for the importing nation to accept the safety standard verification used by the exporting country, such as Underwriters Laboratories (UL) in the United States. If the product is certified for sale in the United States, and if U.S. standards are the same as the importing country's, then U.S. standards and certification are accepted and no further testing is necessary. Most countries not interested in using standards as a trade barrier follow such a practice.

The extreme situation occurs when the importing nation does not accept the same certification procedure required by the exporting nation and demands all testing be done in the importing country. Even more restrictive is the requirement that each item be tested instead of accepting batch testing. In this case, the effect is the same as a boycott. Until recently, Japan required all electrical consumer products to be tested in Japan or tested in the United States by Japanese officials. Japan now accepts the UL's safety tests except for medical supplies and agricultural products, which still must be tested in Japan.

Boycotts

A boycott[18] is an absolute restriction against trade with a country or trade of specific goods. American firms must honor boycotts sanctioned by the U.S. government; however, a U.S. company participating in an unauthorized boycott could be fined for violating the U.S. antiboycott law. For example, U.S. companies are prohibited from participating in the Arab League boycott on trade with Israel. U.S. law forbids U.S. firms to comply with such unauthorized boycotts.[19] If an American firm refuses to trade with Israel in order to do business with an Arab nation, or in any other way participates in the Arab League boycott, it faces stiff fines. Boycotts are the most restrictive non-tariff barriers to trade (NTB) because they ban all trade, whereas other types of restrictions permit some trade.[20]

---

[16] "U.S. Begins Probe to Limit Imports of Chinese Textiles, Apparel," *Kyodo News International, Inc.*, April 11, 2005.

[17] Gordon Fairclough, "How Heparin Maker in China Tackles Risks," *The Wall Street Journal*, March 10, 2008, p. B1.

[18] Also referred to as an embargo.

[19] Hadas Manor, "Nestle's Israel Activity Brings Arab Boycott Threat," *Israel Business Arena*, July 9, 2006; "State Department Report on Steps Taken by U.S. Government to Bring about an End to Arab League Boycott of Israel Sent to House," *US Fed News*, April 5, 2007.

[20] "The Case against Embargoes," *BusinessWeek*, April 25, 2005.

NYK Line (Nippon Yusen Kaisha) brings automobiles from Japan to Aqaba, Jordan, on the Red Sea for delivery to other countries in the area, but not for neighboring Israel.

Voluntary Agreements   Foreign restrictions of all kinds abound, and the United States can be counted among those governments using restrictions. For over a decade, U.S. government officials have been arranging "voluntary" agreements with the Japanese steel and automobile industries to limit sales to the United States. Japan entered these voluntary agreements under the implied threat that if it did not voluntarily restrict the export of automobiles or steel to an agreed limit, the United States might impose even harsher restrictions, including additional import duties. Similar negotiations with the governments of major textile producers have limited textile imports as well. The cost of tariffs, quotas, and voluntary agreements on all fibers is estimated to be as much as $40 billion at the retail level. This number works out to be a hidden tax of almost $500 a year for every American family.

Other Restrictions   Restrictions may be imposed on imports of harmful products, drugs, medicines, and immoral products and literature. Products must also comply with government standards set for health, sanitation, packaging, and labeling. For example, in the Netherlands, all imported hen and duck eggs must be marked in indelible ink with the country of origin; in Spain, imported condensed milk must be labeled to show fat content if it is less than 8 percent fat; and in the European Union, strict import controls have been placed on beef and beef products imported from the United Kingdom because of mad cow disease. Add to this list all genetically modified foods, which are meeting stiff opposition from the European Union as well as activists around the world.

Failure to comply with regulations can result in severe fines, penalties, and delays in clearing customs. A shipment of pork sausages was delayed clearing customs for four months because the proper permit was not issued, even though prior shipments had cleared with a similar permit. Because requirements vary for each country and change frequently, regulations for all countries must be consulted individually and on a current basis. *Overseas Business Reports*, issued periodically by the Department of Commerce, provides the foreign marketer with the most recent foreign trade regulations of each country as well as U.S. regulations regarding each country.

Although sanitation certificates, content labeling, and similar regulations serve a legitimate purpose, countries can effectively limit imports by using such restrictions as additional trade barriers. Most of the economically developed world encourages foreign trade and works through the World Trade Organization (WTO) to reduce tariffs and nontariff barriers to a reasonable rate.[21] Yet in times of economic recession, countries revert to a protectionist philosophy and seek ways to restrict the importing of goods. Nontariff barriers have become one of the most potent ways for a country to restrict trade. The elimination of nontariff barriers has been a major concern of GATT negotiations in both the Tokyo and Uruguay Rounds and continues with the WTO.

Terms of Sale

Terms of sale, or *trade terms*, differ somewhat in international marketing from those used in the United States. In U.S. domestic trade, it is customary to ship FOB (free on board, meaning that the price is established at the door of the factory), freight collect, prepaid, or COD (cash, or collect, on delivery). International trade terms often sound similar to those used in domestic business but generally have different meanings. International terms indicate how buyer and seller divide risks and obligations and, therefore, the costs of specific kinds of international trade transactions. When quoting prices, it is important

---

[21] "The WTO: Free Trade's Best Friend," *The Economist*, January 20, 2005.

to make them meaningful. The most frequently used international trade terms include the following:

- **CIF** (cost, insurance, freight) to a named (that is, specified in writing) overseas port of import. A CIF quote is more meaningful to the overseas buyer because it includes the costs of goods, insurance, and all transportation and miscellaneous charges to the named place of debarkation.

- **C&F** (cost and freight) to a named overseas port. The price includes the cost of the goods and transportation costs to the named place of debarkation. The cost of insurance is borne by the buyer.

- **FAS** (free alongside) at a named U.S. port of export. The price includes cost of goods and charges for delivery of the goods alongside the shipping vessel. The buyer is responsible for the cost of loading onto the vessel, transportation, and insurance.

- **FOB** (free on board) at a named inland point, at a named port of exportation, or at a named vessel and port of export. The price includes the cost of the goods and delivery to the place named.

- **EX** (named port of origin). The price quoted covers costs only at the point of origin (for example, EX Factory). All other charges are the buyer's concern.

A complete list of terms and their definitions can be found in *Incoterms 2000,* a booklet published by the International Chamber of Commerce.[22] It is important for the exporter to understand exactly the meanings of terms used in quotations. A simple misunderstanding regarding delivery terms may prevent the exporter from meeting contractual obligations or make that person responsible for shipping costs he or she did not intend to incur. Exhibit 15.6 indicates who is responsible for a variety of costs under various terms.

---

[22] A list of Incoterms can be found at http://www.iccbooks.com.

Exhibit 15.6
Who's Responsible for Costs under Various Terms?

Cost Items/Terms	FOB, Inland Carrier at Factory	FOB, Inland Carrier at Point of Shipment	FAS, Vessel or Plane at Port of Shipment	CIF, at Port of Destination
Export packing*	Buyer	Seller	Seller	Seller
Inland freight	Buyer	Seller	Seller	Seller
Port charges	Buyer	Buyer	Seller	Seller
Forwarder's fee	Buyer	Buyer	Buyer	Seller
Consular fee	Buyer	Buyer	Buyer	Buyer†
Loading on vessel or plane	Buyer	Buyer	Buyer	Seller
Ocean freight	Buyer	Buyer	Buyer	Seller
Cargo insurance	Buyer	Buyer	Buyer	Seller
Customs duties	Buyer	Buyer	Buyer	Buyer
Ownership of goods passes	When goods on board an inland ocean carrier (truck, rail, etc.) or in hands of inland carrier	When goods unloaded by inland carrier	When goods alongside carrier, in hands of air or ocean carrier	When goods on board air or carrier at port of shipment

*Who absorbs export packing? This charge should be clearly agreed on. Charges are sometimes controversial.

†The seller has responsibility to arrange for consular invoices (and other documents requested by the buyer's government). According to official definitions, the buyer pays fees, but sometimes as a matter of practice, the seller includes fees in quotations.

Getting Paid: Foreign Commercial Payments

The sale of goods in other countries is further complicated by additional risks encountered when dealing with foreign customers.[23] Risks from inadequate credit reports on customers, problems of currency exchange controls, distance, and different legal systems, as well as the cost and difficulty of collecting delinquent accounts, require a different emphasis on payment systems.[24] In U.S. domestic trade, the typical payment procedure for established customers is an *open account*—that is, the goods are delivered, and the customer is billed on an end-of-the-month basis. However, the most frequently used term of payment in foreign commercial transactions for both export and import sales is a letter of credit, followed closely in importance by commercial dollar drafts or bills of exchange drawn by the seller on the buyer. Internationally, open accounts are reserved for well-established customers, and cash in advance is required of only the poorest credit risks or when the character of the merchandise is such that not fulfilling the terms of the contract may result in heavy loss. Because of the time required for shipment of goods from one country to another, advance payment of cash is an unusually costly burden for a potential customer and places the seller at a definite competitive disadvantage.

Terms of sales are typically arranged between the buyer and seller at the time of the sale. The type of merchandise, amount of money involved, business custom, credit rating of the buyer, country of the buyer, and whether the buyer is a new or old customer must be considered in establishing the terms of sale. The five basic payment arrangements—letters of credit, bills of exchange, cash in advance, open accounts, and forfaiting—are discussed in this section.

Letters of Credit

Export *letters of credit* opened in favor of the seller by the buyer handle most American exports. Letters of credit shift the buyer's credit risk to the bank issuing the letter of credit. When a letter of credit is employed, the seller ordinarily can draw a draft against the bank issuing the credit and receive dollars by presenting proper shipping documents.[25] Except for cash in advance, letters of credit afford the greatest degree of protection for the seller.

The procedure for a letter of credit begins with completion of the contract. (See Exhibit 15.7 for the steps in a letter-of-credit transaction.) Letters of credit can be revocable or irrevocable. An *irrevocable letter of credit* means that once the seller has accepted the credit, the buyer cannot alter it in any way without permission of the seller. Added protection is gained if the buyer is required to confirm the letter of credit through a U.S. bank. This irrevocable, confirmed letter of credit means that a U.S. bank accepts responsibility to pay regardless of the financial situation of the buyer or foreign bank. From the seller's viewpoint, this step eliminates the foreign political risk and replaces the commercial risk of the buyer's bank with that of the confirming bank. The confirming bank ensures payment against a confirmed letter of credit. As soon as the documents are presented to the bank, the seller receives payment.

The international department of a major U.S. bank cautions that a letter of credit is not a guarantee of payment to the seller. Rather, payment is tendered only if the seller complies exactly with the terms of the letter of credit. Because all letters of credit must be exact in their terms and considerations, it is important for the exporter to check the terms of the letter carefully to be certain that all necessary documents have been acquired and properly completed.

As illustrated in the Global Perspective at the beginning of this chapter, the process of getting a letter of credit can take days, if not weeks. Fortunately, this process is being shortened considerably as financial institutions provide letters of credit on the Internet. As one example, AVG Letter of Credit Management LLC uses eTrade Finance Platform (ETFP), an e-commerce trade transaction system that enables exporters, importers, freight forwarders, carriers, and trade banks to initiate and complete trade transactions over the Internet. The company advertises that the efficiencies afforded by the Internet make it possible to lower the cost of an export letter of credit from $500-plus to $25.[26]

---

[23] "International Payment Risk," *Financial Management,* March 2005.

[24] William Atkinson, "The International Obstacle Course," *Collections and Credit Risk,* January 2005.

[25] Unless, of course, the letter of credit is revoked: "Neuocrine Biosciences: $5M Letter of Credit Cancelled," *Dow Jones Corporate Filings Alert,* January 14, 2008.

[26] "QuestaWeb Offers Totally Automated Letter of Credit Feature," *Business Wire,* March 3, 2008.

Exhibit 15.7
A Letter-of-Credit Transaction

Here is what typically happens when payment is made by an irrevocable letter of credit confirmed by a U.S. bank. Follow the steps in the illustration below.

1. Exporter and customer agree on terms of sale.
2. Buyer requests its foreign bank to open a letter of credit.
3. The buyer's bank prepares an irrevocable letter of credit (LC), including all instructions, and sends the irrevocable letter of credit to a U.S. bank.
4. The U.S. bank prepares a letter of confirmation and letter of credit and sends to seller.
5. Seller reviews LC. If acceptable, arranges with freight forwarder to deliver goods to designated port of entry.
6. The goods are loaded and shipped.
7. At the same time, the forwarder completes the necessary documents and sends documents to the seller.
8. Seller presents documents, indicating full compliance, to the U.S. bank.
9. The U.S. bank reviews the documents. If they are in order, issues seller a check for amount of sale.
10. The documents are airmailed to the buyer's bank for review.
11. If documents are in compliance, the bank sends documents to buyer.
12. To claim goods, buyer presents documents to customs broker.
13. Goods are released to buyer.

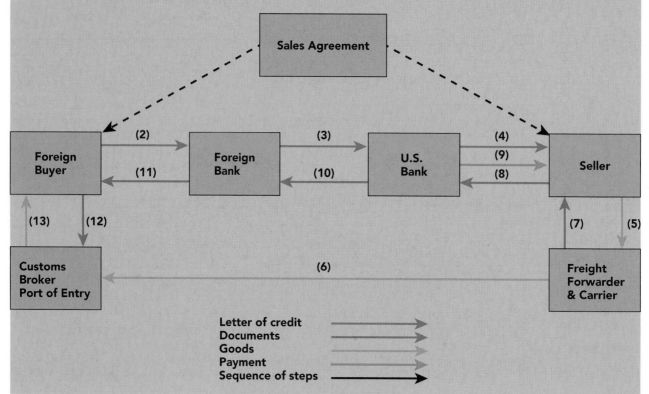

Source: Based on "A Basic Guide to Exporting," U.S. Department of Commerce, International Trade Administration, Washington, DC.

Bills of Exchange

Another important form of international commercial payment is *bills of exchange* drawn by sellers on foreign buyers. In letters of credit, the credit of one or more banks is involved, but with bills of exchange (also known as *dollar drafts*), the seller assumes all risk until the actual dollars are received. The typical procedure is for the seller to draw a draft on the buyer and present it with the necessary documents to the seller's bank for collection. The documents required are principally the same as for letters of credit. On receipt of the draft, the U.S. bank forwards it with the necessary documents to a correspondent bank in the buyer's country; the buyer is then presented with the draft for acceptance and immediate or later payment. With acceptance of the draft, the buyer receives the properly endorsed bill of lading that is used to acquire the goods from the carrier.

Dollar drafts have advantages for the seller because an accepted draft frequently can be discounted at a bank for immediate payment. Banks, however, usually discount drafts only with recourse; that is, if the buyer does not honor the draft, the bank returns it to the seller for payment. An accepted draft is firmer evidence in the case of default and subsequent litigation than an open account would be.

Cash in Advance

The volume of international business handled on a cash-in-advance basis is not large. Cash places unpopular burdens on the customer and typically is used when credit is doubtful, when exchange restrictions within the country of destination are such that the return of funds from abroad may be delayed for an unreasonable period, or when the American exporter for any reason is unwilling to sell on credit terms. Although full payment in advance is employed infrequently, partial payment (from 25 to 50 percent) in advance is not unusual when the character of the merchandise is such that an incomplete contract can result in heavy loss. For example, complicated machinery or equipment manufactured to specification or special design would necessitate advance payment, which would be, in fact, a nonrefundable deposit.

Open Accounts

Sales on open accounts are not generally made in foreign trade except to customers of long standing with excellent credit reputations or to a subsidiary or branch of the exporter. Open accounts obviously leave sellers in a position where most of the problems of international commercial finance work to their disadvantage. Sales on open accounts are generally not recommended when the practice of the trade is to use some other method, when special merchandise is ordered, when shipping is hazardous, when the country of the importer imposes difficult exchange restrictions, or when political unrest requires additional caution.

Forfaiting

Inconvertible currencies and cash-short customers can kill an international sale if the seller cannot offer long-term financing. Unless the company has large cash reserves to finance its customers, a deal may be lost. *Forfaiting* is a financing technique for such a situation.

The basic idea of a forfaiting transaction is fairly simple: The seller makes a one-time arrangement with a bank or other financial institution to take over responsibility for collecting the account receivable. The exporter offers a long financing term to its buyer but intends to sell its account receivable, at a discount, for immediate cash. The forfaiter buys the debt, typically a promissory note or bill of exchange, on a nonrecourse basis. Once the exporter sells the paper, the forfaiter assumes the risk of collecting the importer's payments. The forfaiting institution also assumes any political risk present in the importer's country.[27]

Forfaiting is similar to factoring, but it is not the same. In *factoring* a company has an ongoing relationship with a bank that routinely buys its short-term accounts receivable at a discount—in other words, the bank acts as a collections department for its client. In forfaiting, however, the seller makes a one-time arrangement with a bank to buy a specific account receivable.

Export Documents

Each export shipment involves many documents to satisfy government regulations that control exporting, as well as to meet requirements for international commercial payment transactions. The most frequently required documents are export declarations, consular invoices or certificates of origin, bills of lading, commercial invoices, and insurance

---

[27] For more information about forfaiting, visit http://www.afia-forfaiting.org.

certificates. Additional documents such as import licenses, export licenses, packing lists, and inspection certificates for agricultural products are often necessary.

The paperwork involved in successfully completing a transaction is considered by many to be the greatest of all nontariff trade barriers. There are 125 different documents in regular or special use in more than 1,000 different forms. A single shipment may require over 50 documents and involve as many as 28 different parties and government agencies or require as few as 5. Luckily, software is available that takes some of the burden out of this task. In one such program, the export information is entered once, and the program automatically completes more than two dozen standard export forms, which can then be either printed or e-mailed to freight forwarders, customs brokers, or customers.

Although documents can be prepared routinely, their importance should not be minimized; incomplete or improperly prepared documents lead to delays in shipment. For example, a Mexican Customs official noticed that a certain piece of documentation out of all the paperwork required for a complete trainload of containers lacked a required signature—just one signature. The officer held the train up for almost two days until every container was unloaded and opened to verify that the contents matched the contents listed on the manifest. In some countries, penalties, fines, or even confiscation of the goods could have resulted from errors in documentation.

Export documents are the result of requirements imposed by the exporting government, of requirements set by commercial procedures established in foreign trade, and, in some cases, of the supporting import documents required by the importing government. See Exhibit 15.8 for descriptions of the principal export documents.

Exhibit 15.8
Principal Export Documents

Source: Department of Commerce.

Export Documents Presented at the port of exit; includes the names and addresses of the principals involved, the destination of the goods, a full description of the goods, and their declared value.

Consular Invoice or Certificate of Origin Some countries require consular invoices obtained from the country's consulate and returned with two to eight copies in the language of the country, along with copies of other required documents (e.g., import license, commercial invoice, bill of lading), before certification is granted. Preparation of the document should be handled with extreme care because fines are levied for any errors uncovered. In most countries, the fine is shared with whoever finds the errors, so few go undetected.

Bill of Lading The bill of lading is the most important document required for establishing legal ownership and facilitating financial transactions. It serves the following purposes: (1) as a contract for shipment between the carrier and shipper, (2) as a receipt from the carrier for shipment, and (3) as a certificate of ownership or title to the goods.

Commercial Invoice Every international transaction requires a commercial invoice, that is, a bill or statement for the goods sold. This document often serves several purposes; some countries require a copy for customs clearance, and it is one of the financial documents required in international commercial payments.

Insurance Policy or Certificate The insurance policy or certificate of insurance is considered a key document in export trade.

Licenses Export or import licenses are additional documents frequently required in export trade. In those cases when import licenses are required by the country of entry, a copy of the license or license number is usually required to obtain a consular invoice. Whenever a commodity requires an export license, it must be obtained before an export declaration can be properly certified.

Other Documents Sanitary and health inspection certificates attesting to the absence of disease and pests may be required for certain agricultural products before a country allows goods to enter its borders. Packing lists with correct weights are also required in some cases.

Packing and Marking

In addition to completing all documentation, special packing and marking requirements must be considered for shipments destined to be transported over water, subject to excessive handling, or destined for parts of the world with extreme climates or unprotected outdoor storage. Packing that is adequate for domestic shipments often falls short for goods subject to the conditions mentioned. Protection against rough handling, moisture, temperature extremes, and pilferage may require heavy crating, which increases total packing costs as well as freight rates because of increased weight and size. Because some countries determine import duties on gross weight, packing can add a significant amount to import fees. To avoid the extremes of too much or too little packing, the marketer should consult export brokers, export freight forwarders, or other specialists.

All countries regulate the marking of imported goods and containers, and noncompliance can result in severe penalties. Recently announced Peruvian regulations require all imported foreign products to bear a brand name, country of origin, and an expiration date clearly inscribed on the product. In the case of imported wearing apparel, shoes, electric appliances, automotive parts, liquors, and soft drinks, the name and tax identity card number of the importer must also be added. Peruvian Customs refuse clearance to foreign products not fulfilling these requirements, and the importer has to reship the goods within 60 days of the customs appraisal date, or they are seized and auctioned as abandoned goods. Furthermore, goods already in Peru must meet the provisions of the decree or be subject to public auction.

The exporter must be careful that all markings on the container conform exactly to the data on the export documents, because Customs officials often interpret discrepancies as an attempt to defraud. A basic source of information for American exporters is the Department of Commerce pamphlet series entitled *Preparing Shipment to [Country]*, which details the necessary export documents and pertinent U.S. and foreign government regulations for labeling, marking, packing, and customs procedures.

Customs-Privileged Facilities

To facilitate export trade, countries designate areas within their borders as *customs-privileged facilities*, that is, areas where goods can be imported for storage and/or processing with tariffs and quota limits postponed until the products leave the designated areas. Foreign trade zones (also known as free trade zones), free ports, and in-bond arrangements are all types of customs-privileged facilities that countries use to promote foreign trade.[28]

Foreign Trade Zones

The number of countries with foreign trade zones (FTZs)[29] has increased as trade liberalization has spread through Africa, Latin America, eastern Europe, and other parts of Europe and Asia. Most FTZs function in a similar manner regardless of the host country.

In the United States, FTZs extend their services to thousands of firms engaged in a spectrum of international trade-related activities ranging from distribution to assembly and manufacturing.[30] More than 300 foreign trade zones are located throughout the United States,[31] including those in New York, New Orleans, San Francisco, Seattle, Toledo, Honolulu, Mayagües (Puerto Rico), Kansas City, Little Rock, and Sault St. Marie. Goods subject to U.S. customs duties and quota restrictions can be landed in these zones for storage or such processing as repackaging, cleaning, and grading before being brought into the United States or reexported to another country.[32] Merchandise

---

[28] Japan's version of the FTZ is called a foreign access zone (FAZ). It operates much like an FTZ. A complete description can be found on the JETRO Web site, http://www.jetro.go.jp; search for FAZ.

[29] For a review of FTZs, see http://www.ia.ita.doc.gov/ftzpage.

[30] "Santa Teresa Foreign Trade Zone Expands," *Associated Press Newswires*, February 4, 2008.

[31] Matt Myerhoff, "Duty-Free Designation Seen as Lure to Business, Development," *Los Angeles Business Journal*, March 14, 2005.

[32] Andrew P. Doornaert, "New Way to Reduce Costs with Foreign Trade Zones," *Kansas City Daily News*, March 10, 2005.

CROSSING BORDERS 15.2 — Underwear, Outerwear, Sony Playstations, and Pointed Ears—What Do They Have in Common?

What do underwear, outerwear, pointed ears, and Sony Playstation have in common? Quotas, that's what!

Call the first one the Madonna Effect. Madonna, the voluptuous pop star, affected the interpretation of outerwear/underwear when the ever-vigilant U.S. Customs Service stopped a shipment of 880 bustiers at the U.S. border. The problem was quota and tariff violations. The shipper classified them as underwear, which comes into the United States without quota and tariff. Outerwear imports, however, have a quota, and the Customs official classified the fashion item inspired by Madonna as "outerwear" and demanded the appropriate quota certificates.

"It was definitely outerwear. I've seen it; and I've seen the girls wearing it, and they're wearing it as outerwear." It took the importer three weeks to obtain sufficient outerwear quota allowances to cover the shipment; by that time, several retailers had canceled their orders.

Call the second the Video/Computer Effect. EU officials originally classified Sony's Playstation a video game and thus subject to a higher tariff than it would be if it were classified as a computer, which was Sony's desired classification. The Court of First Instance ruled that "it is intended mainly to be used to run video games," thus subject to millions of euros in customs duties as a video game. The appeals court sided with Sony on a technical error and reversed the decision. It really did not make much difference, because EU customs classifications were set to change six months later to allow computers and games consoles into the European Union with zero tariff.

Call the third the Vulcan Effect. EU officials applied the Vulcan death grip to *Star Trek* hero Spock. Likenesses of the pointy-eared Spock and other "nonhuman creatures" have fallen victim to an EU quota on dolls made in China. The EU Council of Ministers slapped a quota equivalent to $81.7 million on nonhuman dolls from China—but it left human dolls alone.

British Customs officials are in the unusual position of debating each doll's humanity. They have blacklisted teddy bears but cleared Batman and Robin. And though they turned away Spock because of his Vulcan origins, they have admitted *Star Trek*'s Captain Kirk. The Official Fan Club for *Star Trek* said the Customs officials "ought to cut Spock some slack" because his mother, Amanda, was human. But Britain's Customs office said, "We see no reason to change our interpretation. You don't find a human with ears that size."

Sources: Rosalind Resnick, "Busting Out of Tariff Quotas," *North American International Business* (now published as *International Business*), February 1991, p. 10; Dana Milbank, "British Customs Officials Consider Mr. Spock Dolls to Be Illegal Aliens," *The Wall Street Journal*, August 2, 1994, p. B1; "EU Rejects Sony Customs Claim," *(Salt Lake City) Deseret News*, October 6, 2003.

---

can be held in an FTZ even if it is subject to U.S. quota restrictions. When a particular quota opens up, the merchandise may then be immediately shipped into the United States. Merchandise subject to quotas may also be substantially transformed within a zone into articles that are not covered by quotas, and then shipped into the United States free of quota restrictions.

In situations in which goods are imported into the United States to be combined with American-made goods and re-exported, the importer or exporter can avoid payment of U.S. import duties on the foreign portion and eliminate the complications of applying for a *drawback*, that is, a request for a refund from the government of 99 percent of the duties paid on imports later re-exported. Other benefits for companies utilizing foreign trade zones include lower insurance costs, because greater security is required in FTZs; more working capital, since duties are deferred until goods leave the zone; the opportunity to stockpile products when quotas are filled or while waiting for ideal market conditions; significant savings on goods or materials rejected, damaged, or scrapped, for which no duties are assessed; and exemption from paying duties on labor and overhead costs incurred in an FTZ, which are excluded in determining the value of the goods.[33]

---

[33] See Chapter 18 for a discussion on using FTZs to help reduce price escalation.

Offshore Assembly (Maquiladoras)

Maquiladoras, in-bond companies, or *twin plants* are names given to a special type of customs-privileged facility that originated in Mexico in the early 1970s.[34] This type of facility has since expanded to other countries that have abundant, low-cost labor. Although in-bond operations vary from country to country, the original arrangement between Mexico and the United States remains the most typical. In 1971, the Mexican and U.S. governments established an in-bond program that created a favorable opportunity for U.S. companies to use low-cost Mexican labor.

The Mexican government allows U.S. processing, packaging, assembling, and/or repair plants located in the in-bond area to import parts and processed materials without import taxes, provided the finished products are re-exported to the United States or to another foreign country. In turn, the U.S. government permits the re-importation of the packaged, processed, assembled, or repaired goods with a reasonably low import tariff applied only to the value added while in Mexico.

The passage of NAFTA resulted in some changes in the rules governing maquiladoras. Preferential tariff treatment and all export performance requirements (for example, trade and foreign exchange balancing) have been eliminated for NAFTA countries. Also, 100 percent of all maquiladora-manufactured goods can be sold in Mexico versus the 50 percent permitted prior to NAFTA.

More than 2,600 companies participate in the maquiladoras program, with finished products valued at more than $30 billion annually. Although still dominated by U.S. companies, the maquiladoras are no longer only American. Heavy investments are pouring in from Asia and Europe, spurring expansion at close to 7 percent annually. Products made in maquiladoras include electronics, healthcare items, automotive parts, furniture, clothing, and toys. In most in-bond arrangements, special trade privileges are also part of the process. The maquiladora arrangement is becoming more cost efficient for many companies that previously operated in Asia as Asian wage rates increase. Higher costs in Mexico are offset by the wage increases in Asia and increased shipping costs from Asia to the United States rather than from Mexico. However, some companies are still finding manufacturing in Asia more attractive.[35]

Logistics

When a company is primarily an exporter from a single country to a single market, the typical approach to the physical movement of goods is the selection of a dependable mode of transportation that ensures safe arrival of the goods within a reasonable time for a reasonable carrier cost. As a company becomes global, such a solution to the movement of products could prove costly and highly inefficient for seller and buyer. As some global marketers say, the hardest part is not making the sale but getting the correct quantity of the product to customers in the required time frame at a cost that leaves enough margins for a profit.[36]

At some point in the growth and expansion of an international firm, costs other than transportation are such that an optimal cost solution to the physical movement of goods cannot be achieved without thinking of the physical distribution process as an integrated system. When an international marketer begins producing and selling in more than one country and becomes a global marketer, it is time to consider the concept of *logistics management,* a total systems approach to the management of the distribution process that includes all activities involved in physically moving raw material, in-process inventory, and finished goods inventory from the point of origin to the point of use or consumption.[37]

---

[34] For a detailed explanation of maquiladoras, visit the U.S Treasury Department's site at http://www.itds.treas.gov/maquiladora.html.

[35] Aaron Nelsen, "Matamoros Loses Maquiladora to China: Move Leaves 950 Jobless, Saves Littelfuse $7.4 Million," *The Brownsville Herald*, March 13, 2008.

[36] Clyde E. Witt, "International Hires Global Trade Management Specialists," *Material Handling Management,* May 2005.

[37] An excellent source on this subject is Donald F. Wood et al., *International Logistics,* 2nd ed. (New York: Amacom, 2002).

Getting the product to market can mean multiple transportation modes, from motorcycle delivery of moon cakes in Hanoi, to cargo containers in a U.S. port waiting to be loaded on to trucks, to air express service in Malaysia. More than 15 million containers are in use globally and, by value, account for about 90 percent of the world's internationally traded cargo. For products using high value and time-sensitive component parts manufactured worldwide, such air express services as provided by this DHL Worldwide Express Boeing 737 in Kuala Lumpur are vital. *(top: © Hoang Dinh Nam/AFP/Getty Images; left: © Macduff Everton/CORBIS; right: © JIMIN LAI/AFP/Getty Images)*

Interdependence of Physical Distribution Activities

A *physical distribution system* involves more than the physical movement of goods. It includes location of plants and warehousing (storage), transportation mode, inventory quantities, and packing. The concept of physical distribution takes into account the interdependence of the costs of each activity; a decision involving one activity affects the cost and efficiency of one or all others. In fact, because of their interdependence, the sum of each of the different activity costs entails an infinite number of "total costs." (*Total cost* of the system is defined as the sum of the costs of all these activities.)

The idea of interdependence can be illustrated by the classic example of airfreight. Exhibit 15.9 is an illustration of an actual company's costs of shipping 44,000 peripheral boards worth $7.7 million from a Singapore plant to the U.S. West Coast using two modes of transportation—ocean freight and the seemingly more expensive airfreight. When

Exhibit 15.9

Real Physical Distribution
Costs between Air and
Ocean Freight—Singapore
to the United States

Source: Adapted from "Air and
Adaptec's Competitive Strategy,"
International Business, September
1993, p. 44.

In this example, 44,000 peripheral boards worth $7.7 million are shipped from a Singapore plant to the U.S. West Coast. Cost of capital to finance inventories is 10 percent annually, or $2,109 per day, to finance $7.7 million.

	Ocean	Air
Transport costs	$ 31,790 (in transit 21 days)	$127,160 (in transit 3 days)
In-transit inventory financing costs	$ 44,289	$ 6,328
Total transportation costs	$ 76,179	$133,488
Warehousing inventory costs, Singapore and U.S.	(60 days @ $2,109 per day) $126,540	
Warehouse rent	$ 6,500	
Real physical distribution costs	$209,219	$133,488

considering only rates for transportation and carrying costs for inventory in transit, air transportation costs were approximately $57,000 higher than ocean freight. But notice that when total costs are calculated, airfreight was actually less costly than ocean freight because of other costs involved in the total physical distribution system.

To offset the slower ocean freight and the possibility of unforeseen delays and to ensure prompt customer delivery schedules, the company had to continuously maintain 30 days of inventory in Singapore and another 30 days' inventory at the company's distribution centers. The costs of financing 60 days of inventory and of additional warehousing at both points—that is, real physical distribution costs—would result in the cost of ocean freight exceeding air by more than $75,000. And ocean freight may even entail additional costs such as a higher damage rate, higher insurance, and higher packing rates.

Substantial savings can result from the systematic examination of logistics costs and the calculation of total physical distribution costs. A large multinational firm with facilities and customers around the world shipped parts from its U.S. Midwest plant to the nearest East Coast port, then by water route around the Cape of Good Hope (Africa), and finally to its plants in Asia, taking 14 weeks. Substantial inventory was maintained in Asia as a safeguard against uncertain water-borne deliveries. The transportation carrier costs were the least expensive available; however, delivery delays and unreliable service caused the firm to make emergency air shipments to keep production lines going. As a result, air shipment costs rose to 70 percent of the total transport bill. An analysis of the problem in the physical distribution system showed that trucking the parts to West Coast ports using higher-cost motor carriers and then shipping them to Asia by sea could lower costs. Transit time was reduced, delivery reliability improved, inventory quantities in Asia lowered, and emergency air shipments eliminated. The new distribution system produced annual savings of $60,000.

Although a cost difference will not always be the case, the examples illustrate the interdependence of the various activities in the physical distribution mix and the total cost. A change of transportation mode can affect a change in packaging and handling, inventory costs, warehousing time and cost, and delivery charges.

The concept behind physical distribution is the achievement of the optimum (lowest) system cost consistent with customer service objectives of the firm. If the activities in the physical distribution system are viewed separately, without consideration of their interdependence, the final cost of distribution may be higher than the lowest possible cost (optimum cost), and the quality of service may be adversely affected. Additional variables and costs that are interdependent and must be included in the total physical distribution decision heighten the distribution problems confronting the international marketer. As the international firm broadens the scope of its operations, the additional

Two giant pandas, four-year-old male Le Le and two-year-old female Ya Ye, are being loaded onto the Panda Express, a FedEx plane, that is airlifting them from China to the Memphis, Tennessee, zoo for a ten-year visit. Whether it is pandas, time-sensitive deliveries, or cost-saving solutions, FedEx delivers high-value shipments door-to-door to as many as 210 countries. Also, notice the white arrow embedded in the FedEx logo (between the E and the x) that connotes motion. *(AP Photo/Ng Han Guan)*

a factory in the United States to a final customer in Europe. Such services are now becoming available in Asia and Latin America as improvements in transportation services are being made in both areas.

Another innovation in transportation and logistics is the service provided by UPS, FedEx, and similar companies. In addition to providing air-express service for packages, these companies are offering complete logistics management services including support services for their clients—truly door-to-door delivery around the world. For example, FedEx will take a manufacturer's product, warehouse it, keep inventory, provide all the labor and technology, and move it throughout the world. FedEx can warehouse a computer system made in Malaysia, move it to Japan to be coupled with components from Taiwan, and then deliver a completed product to the final destination in yet another country. One client's experience illustrates how such a service can improve a company's distribution costs and service. The computer parts repair center of this company moved into a FedEx Express Distribution Center in Japan and was able to cut average total turn-around time from 45 days to 5 days while lowering cost. FedEx took over storage, control, and shipment of the parts using its own networks and aircraft. UPS offers similar services, including local parts stocking and defective return services in Europe, the Pacific Rim, and the Americas.

Distribution and its costs are an important part of every international transaction. Cheap labor may make Chinese clothing competitive in the United States, but if delays in shipment tie up working capital and cause winter coats to arrive in April, the advantage may be lost. Similarly, production machinery disabled for lack of a part can affect costs throughout the system, all of which might be avoided with a viable logistics system.

The globalization of marketing and manufacturing, in which component parts are made in several countries, assembled in some others, and serviced the world over, puts tremendous pressure on a company's ability to physically move goods. A narrow solution to physical movement of goods is the selection of transportation; a broader application is the concept of logistics management or physical distribution. When customers value broad product assortment, holding a great number of products or component parts in inventory increases the costs of the supplier. Although the need for warehousing can be reduced with direct deliveries from manufacturers, the value of direct deliveries is diminished when orders are received in several shipments and at different times. One solution to this problem is merge-in-transit, a distribution method in which goods shipped from several supply locations are consolidated into one final customer delivery point while they are in transit and then shipped as a unit to the customer. As distribution systems become more complex and costly, merge-in-transit is one system designed to increase customer value and decrease distribution costs.

Foreign Freight Forwarder

The *foreign freight forwarder*, licensed by the Federal Maritime Commission, arranges for the shipment of goods as the agent for an exporter. The forwarder is an indispensable agent for an exporting firm that cannot afford an in-house specialist to handle paperwork and other export trade mechanics.[39]

Even in large companies with active export departments capable of handling documentation, a forwarder is useful as a shipment coordinator at the port of export or at the destination port.[40] Besides arranging for complete shipping documentation, the full-service foreign freight forwarder provides information and advice on routing and scheduling, rates and related charges, consular and licensing requirements, labeling requirements, and export restrictions. Furthermore, the agent offers shipping insurance, warehouse storage, packing and containerization, and ocean cargo or airfreight space.

An astute freight forwarder will also double-check all assumptions made on the export declaration, such as commodity classifications, and will check the list of denied parties and end uses. Both large and small shippers find freight forwarders' wide range of services useful and well worth the fees normally charged. In fact, for many shipments, forwarders can save on freight charges because they can consolidate shipments into larger, more economical quantities. Although many forwarders are available, more and more companies are using those that have joined alliances with shippers and become part of the larger multifaceted integrators discussed previously. Experienced exporters regard the foreign freight forwarder as an important addition to in-house specialists.[41]

International Logistics and Supply Chain Management

As discussed previously, the essence of international logistics is to integrate all the steps necessary to move goods from supplier to manufacturer to customer. This goal means that a logistics system has to deal with an often disparate set of agents and activities—carriers, warehouses, export regulations, import regulations, customs agents, freight forwarders, and so on—each of which must be accessed individually by the logistics manager.[42] The goals are multidimensional and include cost minimization, increased levels of service, improved communication among customers or suppliers, and increased flexibility in terms of delivery and response time. The ability of firms to achieve these goals has been limited until recently because existing communication and knowledge links did not bring together all of the players in the process. The advent of information technology (IT) has allowed communication with the participants in real time via a single connection point.[43]

When a computer manufacturer has to coordinate supply chains that reach into China and Malaysia and Mexico and Portugal, software such as that provided by NextLinx,[44] Descartes,[45] and others is used to fully automate its supply chain systems. Trucks, ships,

---

[39] Marisa Mohd Isa, "International Freight Forwarding Made Easy," *New Straits Times,* January 17, 2005.

[40] "UPS Announces 8 New Products for Asian Companies," *Bernama Daily Malaysian News*, February 13, 2008; Hisane Masaki, "Kintetsu Targeting China, U.S. to Boost Revenue," *Journal of Commerce* (online), February 8, 2008.

[41] For insight on all that a fully integrated freight forwarder can provide for a shipper, visit http://www.ups-scs.com.

[42] Annie Gregory, "Avoiding Supply Chain Strangulation," *Works Management*, Spring 2005.

[43] Clyde E. Witt, "Online Interface Eases Global Distribution," *Material Handling Management,* May 2005.

[44] See "NextLinx-Trade Collaborator: Software for Import and Export," at http://www.nextlinx.com/trd_col.html.

[45] For more information about these two software applications, visit http://www.nextlinx.com and http://www.descartes.com.

trains, and planes cannot be made to travel much faster than they presently do; thus any additional speed has to come from better logistics management. An automated supply chain system can cut the time needed for deliveries from the Far East to warehouses in the United Kingdom from months to just 25 days.

For companies not wishing to maintain a fully automated supply chain system in-house, third-party logistics (3PL) providers[46] or integrators such as UPS Logistics Group[47] can process and store all inventory and then ship it within two hours to the precise plant location where it is needed.[48] They can also handle such tasks as customs clearance and return and repair of certain merchandise. Manufacturers can shift their supply chain structures much more rapidly and with less pain than is the case with vertically integrated operations.[49]

By providing inventory management, order fulfillment, and collections, integrators can assist e-commerce customers to enter new markets more quickly without having to invest in warehousing and distribution centers. The scramble is on to be able to fulfill orders that come from anywhere in the world without having to set up significant operations in such markets. The less onerous the process of moving products across a particular border, the easier it becomes for manufacturers to set up where it makes sense for business. Speed is perhaps the most essential goal for any manufacturer looking to develop a 21st-century supply chain.[50]

Terrorism and Logistics

Before the terrorist attack on New York's World Trade Center (9/11), international marketers had to contend with myriad details of exporting. Most companies had internal systems to manage documentation, customs, shipping, and other activities necessary to comply with cross-border marketing. "Security" referred to prevention of theft or pilferage. After 9/11, homeland security added a crucial step in logistics management—vigilance at each point in the export/import process. With more than 23 million sea, truck, and rail containers entering the United States each year,[51] guarding against the possibility that shipping will be used as a conduit into the United States for terrorists' weapons is critical. The Cargo and Container Security Initiative (CSI) is one of the U.S. government's first efforts to enhance post-9/11 security.[52]

Cargo and Container Security Initiative

The CSI (24-hour rule) requires sea carriers and NVOCC (Non-Vessel Operating Common Carriers)[53] to provide U.S. Customs with detailed descriptions (manifests) of the contents of containers bound for the United States 24 hours before a container is loaded on board a vessel. Trucking companies are also bound by the 24-hour rule and are expected to provide a manifest 4 hours before trucks are loaded with products entering the United States and 24 hours in advance when leaving the United States.

---

[46] A. Michael Knemeyer and Paul R. Murphy, "Exploring the Potential Impact or Relationship Characteristics and Customer Attributes on the Outcomes of Third-Party Logistics Arrangements," *Transportation Journal*, Winter 2005, pp. 5–19.

[47] For a survey of the various services provided by UPS, visit http://www.ups-scs.com/logistics.

[48] John D. Schultz, "Four Questions to Ask Before Hiring a 3PL," *Transport Topics,* March 21, 2005.

[49] See, for example, Edmund Prater and Soumen Ghosh, "Current Operational Practices of U.S. Small and Medium-Sized Enterprises in Europe," *Journal of Small Business Management,* April 2005, pp. 155–69; Gregory, "Avoiding Supply Chain Strangulation."

[50] James A. Cooke, "Customs to Ratchet Up C-TPAT Requirements for Importers," *Logistics Management,* February 2005, p. 16; "U.S. Senator Calls for Enhanced Security at U.S. Seaports," *Xinhua News Agency*, February 24, 2005.

[51] Trucks, railroads, and other nonocean carriers.

[52] Cooke, "Customs to Ratchet Up C-TPAT Requirements."

[53] Also, more effort is being put into security for foreign ports that ship to the United States. See R. G. Edmonson, "U.S. Puts Syria on Port Security Watch List," *Journal of Commerce* (online), March 7, 2008.

A U.S. Customs officer helps direct the use of a mobile gamma ray scanner to reveal the contents of a steel-shipping container, one of the 20 million closed containers that carry cargo into the United States each year. The device, used to help reveal nuclear, biological, or chemical threats inside, is one of more than 100 gamma and x-ray inspection devices deployed at major ports and border crossings into the United States. (*AP/Wide World Photos*)

The rule allows U.S. Customs officers time to analyze the contents of the container or truck and identify potential terrorist threats before the U.S.-bound shipment is loaded at a foreign port rather than after it arrives at a U.S. port. Cargo manifests must use precise terms as parts of the 24-hour rule; "Freight-All-Kinds" and "Said-to-Contain" or "General Merchandise," descriptions often used in the past, are no longer acceptable. If any discrepancy appears on the manifest and if it is not presented 24 hours before loading, the shipment can be denied loading and entry into a U.S. port. Whenever an invalid cargo description is used, a "Do Not Load" message is posted and loading is denied. Cargo bound for a foreign port loaded on a vessel with cargo bound for the United States must also have a valid manifest presented within 24 hours or it will not be allowed to be shipped. A violation of the 24-hour rule may prevent the vessel from loading or unloading any cargo, even if the violation applies to only one container.

In an effort to safeguard food against bioterrorism, U.S. Customs and Border Protection (CBP) requires the Food and Drug Administration (FDA) to receive prior notice of all food for humans and animals imported or offered for import into the United States. Carriers must file notice two hours before reaching a port of entry. Without prior notification, CBP will hold the goods at the port of entry or at an FDA-registered secure facility. Food offered for import with no prior notice or inadequate prior notice will be refused admission. Similar rules apply to drugs and medical devices.

Ports became the gatekeepers for the entire supply chain in preventing illegal entry of terrorists and weapons of mass destruction. They were expected to accomplish this task without interruption of service and without additional cost to shippers. Early on, government regulators saw that if the burden of compliance was not going to slow the movement of goods across borders to a snail's pace,[54] cooperation and compliance throughout the supply chain was necessary.[55]

Customs–Trade Partnership against Terrorism

The Customs–Trade Partnership against Terrorism (C-TPAT) is a joint initiative between government and business designed to augment the 24-hour rule by extending security procedures throughout the supply chain.[56] The C-TPAT requires importers to establish a documented program for security-risk assessment of overseas suppliers throughout the supply chain; therefore, companies ensure a more secure supply chain for their employees, suppliers, and customers, thus improving the flow of trade. Participation in C-TPAT means faster cargo processing at the border, fewer inspections, dedicated commercial lanes for more rapid border crossings, and an emphasis on self-policing rather than customs verification. Without C-TPAT accreditation, an importer will encounter countless inspections and delays.

C-TPAT certification requires members to:

- Conduct a comprehensive self-assessment of supply-chain security using C-TPAT guidelines jointly developed by U.S. Customs and the trade community.
- Submit a supply-chain security questionnaire to U.S. Customs.
- Identify and complete security checks of vendors and suppliers.[57]

---

[54] "Customs-Trade Partnership against Terrorism: A Year in Review," *Department of Homeland Security Documents,* January 31, 2008.

[55] "6 Areas Define Purchasing Role in Import Compliance" *Managing Exports,* June 2005, pp. 4–6.

[56] Raphael Madarang, "Tax Wise or Otherwise Stricter U.S. Customs Rules," *BusinessWorld,* May 12, 2005.

[57] A fact sheet with additional specific data about C-TPAT can be found at "C-TPAT Fact Sheet and Frequently Asked Questions," May 2005, http://www.customs.gov; search for C-TPAT facts.

- Record customs clearance documents and purchase orders.

- Ensure minimum-security standards and procedures for employee screening and facilities security by suppliers.

- Implement a program to communicate C-TPAT guidelines to companies in the supply chain and work toward building the guidelines into relationships with these companies.

- Maintain strict container security procedures, including security seals that are subject to periodic rigorous integrity examination and physical access controls in storage areas to eliminate unauthorized entry, pilferage, and sabotage.[58]

Even though C-TPAT applies only to U.S. importers, it is important for exporters outside the United States to know that they must also comply in order to be certified to remain in the supply chain[59] and thus benefit from faster processing at U.S. borders.

The C-TPAT is an evolving process, and Customs is continually seeking ways to ensure that suppliers and intermediaries, such as freight forwarders and carriers, have systems and processes in place to promote trustworthiness and to document shipments fully and precisely.[60] Innovative software,[61] advances in information technology (IT), and electronic tracking are integral components in the successful implementation of C-TPAT.

Electronic Tracking

To further strengthen C-TPAT, U.S. Customs and Border Protection (CBP) announced plans for electronic container tracking as an integral part of the process. Thus C-TPAT-Plus, as it is called, offers shippers immediate turnaround with no inspection upon arrival in exchange for including technologies that can electronically track incoming containers, monitor them for tampering from the point of origin, and provide a record of events[62] while in transit. Such tracking can include RFID[63] (radio frequency identification), GPS (global positioning systems), cellular, satellite, ultra-wide-band, "Bluetooth," bar codes, and optical character recognition. Although numerous technological devices are available, none has been more widely implemented than bar codes and RFID.

For nearly 10 years, the U.S. Department of Defense has been using RFID tags on freight containers (see Exhibit 15.10). The Defense Department asks its suppliers to affix RFID tags on cases and pallets they ship to key receiving sites.[64] The RFID tags provide different monitoring capabilities, but all track a container or pallet while in transit and, in some cases, communicate with a receiver at the border or elsewhere. Substantial disruptions in transit are avoided if security questions relating to a cargo shipment have been addressed prior to a vessel being loaded and sailing and then monitored while in transit.[65] In addition, RFID promises to deliver cost savings of up to $1.8 trillion globally. Domestically, Wal-Mart,[66] Gillette, Procter & Gamble, and Unilever are all adopting RFID.[67]

---

[58] "C-TPAT Must Succeed—Or World Trade Faces the Consequences," *Material Handling Management,* http://www.mhmonline.com.

[59] "New UPS Software Simplifies Trade by Tackling Compliance Obstacles," *Business Wire,* May 23, 2005.

[60] "Government Mandates Key to Electronic Container Tracking Success," *Microwave Journal,* March 2005.

[61] For a discussion of how RFID works and some of the problems and benefits associated with this system, see Perry A. Trunick and Dan Williams, "Stay Loose for the RFID Stretch Run," *Logistics Today,* March 2005.

[62] For a detailed discussion of how RFID was used successfully in Afghanistan and Iraq, see Peter Galuszka, "Lessons from Baghdad," *Chief Executive,* May 2005.

[63] "World Shipping Council President Chris Koch Testifies before Senate Committee; Urges Enhance Cargo Container Screening Overseas," *PR Newswire,* May 18, 2005.

[64] John S. McClenahen, "Wal-Mart's Big Gamble," *Industry Week,* April 2005, pp. 42–49.

[65] "Business Must Tune In to the Radio Frequency," *Sunday Herald (Glasgow, U.K.),* October 10, 2004.

[66] "Avante to License and Deploy Its RFID Cargo Seal to Secure Container Shipping," *Business Wire,* April 6, 2005.

[67] Diane Brady, "Secure Containers for $10 a Pop," *BusinessWeek,* January 12, 2005.

Exhibit 15.10
Radio Frequency Identification

As a potential for a security breach, each of the 42 million containers imported annually is a Trojan horse. Companies and customs are seeking ways to ensure the security of cargo without causing undue delays in the movement of goods. RFID is a flexible system that is adaptable to different needs and has the potential to provide both the shipper and customs with information in real time as goods move through the supply chain.

By attaching an RFID tag, any item—shipping container, pallet, packing crate, or package—can be located and/or tracked from point of origin to final destination, gathering information along the way.

The transponder (tag) is the backbone of the RFID system. It stores an identification code and other pertinent data and then transmits the data when the transceiver sends activation signals to it and receives identification data from the tag.

A read-only tag has an ID code plus other information such as the manifest, destination, shipping port, receiving port, and any other pertinent information the shipper desires. Each tag carries a mini-databank that identifies a particular item and contains accounting and inventory system information. Up to 70 pages of text can be coded on a tag. When a container with a tag passes an entry–exit point equipped with readers, its location is precisely recorded so managers can respond to any unanticipated changes. Furthermore, any data desired can be accessed and sent to the shipper, customs, or anyone else needing the information.

RFID is ideal for a shipping company. Multi-ton cargo containers in an Asian port, for example, can be tracked daily using RFID to assist in loading and unloading at numerous ship berths and countless truck loading areas. Transponders are embedded in the ground throughout the port. When cranes hoist cargo on and off ships and trucks, the lifting arm–mounted readers interrogate each transponder and match the code with the yard location. Managers have real-time information on the location and destination of each container, and these data can be relayed to customs authorities before the arrival, thereby expediting border crossings.

Besides the basic read-only tag, transponders also have read and write capabilities, which allow for data to be changed dynamically at any time. Read–write tags have the ability to receive information from a variety of sensors that can also be installed in a container. Sensors to detect changes in humidity within a container and others that detect changes in pressure and light to detect if the door has been opened can feed information to the RFID tag, which can then alert operators to the possibility of tampering or theft. An integrated environmental sensor module monitors temperature, humidity, and shock throughout the container's journey, allowing shippers, carriers, and logistics providers to detect spoilage or damage to goods. One system under development includes sensors that detect specific chemical, biological, and nuclear threats. The sensor data are sent in real time to a powerful transmitter on the ship, which can transmit the data via a satellite to authorities on shore. The system can also include sensors that monitor light, heat, motion, and shock, allowing it to detect conditions that might damage cargo. In addition, each container is monitored by GPS, so its location can be tracked worldwide.

Tags can verify that a container was loaded at a secure loading point, significantly reducing the likelihood that tampering will occur in transit; gather enough data to conduct a "virtual inspection" in advance of arrival; and guarantee that shipping containers meet governmental security regulations. Shipments that satisfy government regulations will avoid extensive delays in shipment and receipt and minimize cost of handling.

Sources: Mary Davis, "Smart Tags Bring Security to Containers Entering U.S.," *Modern Bulk Transporter*, July 2004; Tom Kevan, "High-Tech Container Security: Pressed to Protect Cargo from Damage, Theft, and Terrorists Threats, Business and Government Turn to Wireless Sensors and RFID Tags," *Frontline Solutions*, July 2004; Diane Brady, "Secure Containers for $10 a Pop," *BusinessWeek*, January 12, 2005; Brad Kenney, "10 Reasons to Adopt RFID," *Industry Week*, March 1, 2008, p. 69.

Satellite-based positioning systems that register when a container is taken off its predetermined route, weight sensors that register when a container weighs more than originally logged onto shipping documents, and radio tags that automatically report any in-transit intrusion to the destination customs and port authorities[68] are examples of some of the more advanced systems being developed and implemented.

Another promising tracking system, the Tamper Evident Secure Container (TESC), a palm-size device that is embedded in a container's wall, detects unauthorized access to any part of the door (including hinges) through a wireless network.[69] The technology can also be adapted to detect holes around the perimeter as well as humans inside the containers.

---

[68] Ann Keeton, "Sensors on Containers May Offer Safer Shipping," *The Wall Street Journal*, March 31, 2005, p. B4.

[69] Henry E. Teitelbaum, "Focus: Continued Risk Seen in Global Cargo Shipping," *The Wall Street Journal*, May 16, 2005.

Upon the delivery of a container, an inspector can use a wireless reader to check and disarm the device.

Even with all the checking and vetting, people in the supply chain are the weakest link, and without vigilance among warehouse managers, shippers, and port operators, technology can provide only part of the security needed to protect our borders. We are entering a security economy where everybody has to take responsibility for the safety of the supply chain.

Summary

An awareness of the mechanics of export trade is indispensable to the foreign marketer who engages in exporting goods from one country to another. Although most marketing techniques are open to interpretation and creative application, the mechanics of exporting are exact; they offer little room for interpretation or improvisation because of the requirements of export licenses, quotas, tariffs, export documents, packing, marking, and the various uses of commercial payments. The very nature of the regulations and restrictions surrounding importing and exporting can lead to frequent and rapid change. In handling the mechanics of export trade successfully, the manufacturer must keep abreast of all foreign and domestic changes in requirements and regulations pertaining to the product involved. For firms unable to maintain their own export staffs, foreign freight forwarders can handle many details for a nominal fee.

With paperwork completed, the physical movement of goods must be considered. Transportation mode affects total product cost because of the varying requirements of packing, inventory levels, time requirements, perishability, unit cost, damage and pilfering losses, and customer service. Transportation for each product must be assessed in view of the interdependent nature of all these factors. To ensure optimum distribution at minimal cost, a physical distribution system determines everything from plant location to final customer delivery in terms of the most efficient use of capital investment, resources, production, inventory, packing, and transportation. The seemingly endless rules, regulations of exporting, demands of efficient global logistics, and the absolute necessity to comply with national security regulations can be daunting. Fortunately, the continuous innovations in information technology, the Internet, and software programs can minimize much of the burden associated with global marketing.

Questions

1. Define and show the significance to international marketing of the following terms:

   Commerce Control List (CCL)

   Export Control Classification Number (ECCN)

   Commerce Country Chart (CCC)

   export regulations

   import regulations

   Export Administrative Regulations (EAR)

   logistics management

   consular invoice

   letter of credit

   bill of exchange

   24-hour rule

   C-TPAT

   CSI

   RFID

   bill of lading

   commercial invoice

   customs-privileged facilities

   foreign-trade zone

   maquiladora

   export control

   forfaiting

   physical distribution system

   merge-in-transit

   SNAP

   ELAIN

   STELA

   ERIC

2. Explain the reasoning behind the various regulations and restrictions imposed on the exportation and importation of goods.

3. What determines the type of license needed for exportation? Discuss.

4. Discuss the most frequently encountered trade restrictions.

5. What is the purpose of an import license? Discuss.

6. Explain foreign-trade zones and illustrate how an exporter may use them. How do foreign-trade zones differ from bonded warehouses?

7. How do in-bond areas differ from foreign-trade zones? How would an international marketer use an in-bond area?

8. Explain each of the following export documents:

   a. Bill of lading

   b. Consular invoice

   c. Commercial invoice

   d. Insurance certificate

9. Why would an exporter use the services of a foreign freight forwarder? Discuss.

10. Besides cost advantages, what are the other benefits of an effective physical distribution system?

11. Explain how merge-in-transit can be beneficial to all parties in the distribution process.

12. Discuss customs-privileged facilities. How are they used?

13. Why would a company engage the services of an intermodal transportation service instead of performing activities in-house?

14. You are the manager of a small company that manufactures and sells various types of personal restraints (e.g., handcuffs, leg irons). Your customers are law enforcement agencies, private security companies, and novelty stores. You receive a large order from an importer in Madrid that you have never done business with, though you have previously sold your product in Spain. Do you need a special export license? Outline the steps you would take to ensure that your transaction is legal. (Note: The solution to this problem cannot be completely answered from information in the text. Additional information will have to be obtained from sources on the Internet.)

15. You are the sales manager of a small company with sales in the United States. About 30 percent of your business is mail order, and the remainder is from your two retail stores. You recently created an e-store on the Web and a few days later received an order from a potential customer from a city near Paris, France. The shipping charges listed on the Web are all for locations in the United States. You don't want to lose this $350 order. You know you can use the postal service, but the customer indicated she wanted the item in about a week. Air express seems logical, but how much will it cost? Consult both the FedEx home page (www.fedex.com) and the UPS home page (www.ups.com) to get some estimates on shipping costs. Here are some details you will need: value $350; total weight of the package, 2.5 pounds; package dimensions, 4 inches high by 6 inches wide; U.S. zip code, 97035; and French zip code, 91400. (Note: It's not fair to call UPS or FedEx—use the Internet.)

16. Based on the information collected in Question 15, how practical would it be to encourage foreign sales? Your average order ranges from about $250 to $800. All prices are quoted plus shipping and handling. You handle a fairly exclusive line of Southwestern Indian jewelry that sells for about 15 to 20 percent higher in Europe than in the United States. The products are lightweight and high in value.

17. Discuss the principal requirements for gaining C-TPAT certification.

18. The Global Perspective illustrates a shipment from the United States to a Chinese customer. If the shipment had been from a Chinese manufacturer to a U.S. company, what would the U.S. company have to do to ensure compliance with all U.S. antiterrorism requirements?

16

integrated marketing communications and international Advertising

CHAPTER LEARNING OBJECTIVES

What you should learn from Chapter 16:

- Local market characteristics that affect the advertising and promotion of products

- The strengths and weaknesses of sales promotion and public relations in global marketing

- When global advertising is most effective; when modified advertising is necessary

- The effects of a single European market on advertising

- The effect of limited media, excessive media, and government regulations on advertising and promotion budgets

- The communication process and advertising misfires

Global Perspective

BARBIE VERSUS MULAN

For years, Barbie dolls sold in Japan looked different from their U.S. counterparts. They had Asian facial features, black hair, and Japanese-inspired fashions. Then Mattel Inc. conducted consumer research around the world and learned something surprising: The original Barbie, with her yellow hair and blue eyes, played as well in Hong Kong as it did in Hollywood. Girls didn't care if Barbie didn't look like them. "It's all about fantasies and hair," says Peter Broegger, general manager of Mattel's Asian operations. "Blond Barbie sells just as well in Asia as in the U.S."

Major toy makers are rethinking one of the basic tenets of their $55 billion global industry—that children in different countries want different playthings. The implications are significant for both kids and companies. In the past, giants such as Mattel, Hasbro Inc., and LEGO Co. produced toys and gear in a variety of styles. Increasingly, they are designing and marketing one version worldwide. This shift has led to a series of massive merchandise blitzkriegs, with companies deluging boys and girls around the globe simultaneously with identical dolls, cars, and gadgets.

For example, Mattel's Rapunzel Barbie, whose ankle-length blonde locks cascade down her pink ball gown, was released on the same day last fall in 59 countries including the United States—the company's biggest product launch ever. Since then, Rapunzel Barbie and related merchandise has generated $200 million in global sales, nearly half of that outside the United States. Mattel no longer makes Asian-featured Barbies.

Two recent developments are changing kids' tastes. One is the rapid worldwide expansion of cable and satellite TV channels, which along with movies and the Internet expose millions of kids to the same popular icons. For example, Walt Disney Co. now operates 24 Disney-branded cable and satellite channels in 67 countries outside the United States—up from 0 eight years ago. The other development is the widening international reach of retailing giants such as Wal-Mart Stores Inc., Toys "R" Us Inc., and Carrefour SA, which have opened some 2,300 stores outside their home markets. Increasingly, the mass retailers enter into exclusive deals with toy and consumer-products companies, allowing them to stage huge, coordinated promotional campaigns.

For example, when Rapunzel Barbie had its debut, Wal-Mart stores in South Korea and China hired local women to dress up like the doll and greet children as they entered. At the same time, the Mattel TV ad campaign was broadcast around the world in 15-, 20-, and 30-second spots—in 35 different languages. Mattel's Barbie Web site, which has eight language options, featured Rapunzel stories and games. A computer-animated movie, called *Barbie as Rapunzel*, was broadcast on TV and released on video and DVD around the world, and it was even shown in some theaters overseas.

In Madrid, the launch was accompanied by a "premiere" of the movie and special promotions of comb sets and other accessories at Carrefour stores across Spain. After attending the premiere, the kids could and did buy the dolls. For some parents, this means Christmas shopping later in the year at the often frenetic Toys "R" Us in Madrid for stuffed dragons from the movie or a Barbie laptop computer, a Barbie kitchen set, a Barbie travel van, and a host of other Barbie gadgets and accessories.

Some toys, games, and animated characters do not cross national boundaries. German children, for example, rarely play with action figures. According to the NPD Group, which tracks toy sales, action figures make up just 1 percent of the German toy market, compared with 5 percent of the U.S. and 6 percent of the U.K. toy markets. American kids want NASCAR toy cars, while European kids want Formula One models. Cheerleader-themed anything is irrelevant outside the United States. And few American companies sell toys in the Islamic world. Mattel, the world's largest toy company, has no plans to do so.

Perhaps Disney's Jasmine will well sell there, though she's actually inappropriately dressed for many of Islamic faith. Jasmine is just one of the new series of "Princess" dolls aimed directly at Barbie's dominance of the doll category. Snow White, Pocahontas, and Mulan are others in the band. Their diversity may have broader appeal. Disney uses pink in the packaging and Mattel objects. Disney is also mindful of the fashion-conscious Barbie critics. Disney Princess is more about tiaras and wands rather than handbags and high heels. Where Barbie is more a role model, and therefore more objectionable to parents, Disney is putting its emphasis on the fantasy. Too bad someone isn't emphasizing education.

Indeed, too bad for Mattel—despite the comprehensiveness of its integrated marketing communications plan, sales of Barbie have declined sharply. Competitors' more ethnically diverse product lines sold better, including Mulan, Bratz, and Fulla, as described in Chapter 5.

Sources: Lisa Bannon and Carlta Vitshum, "One-Toy-Fits-All: How Industry Learned to Love the Global Kid," *The Wall Street Journal*, April 29, 2003, p. A1; "A Challenge to Barbie, Toy Franchises," *The Economist*, April 19, 2003, p. 66; Christopher Palmeri, "Hair-Pulling in the Dollhouse," *BusinessWeek*, May 2, 2005, pp. 76–77.

integrated marketing communications (IMC) at quiksilver

In marketing high-quality branded lifestyle products, image is everything. Quiksilver has been one of the most innovative companies in creating new ways to deliver the "the mountain and the wave" images around the world.

With global revenues exceeding $2 billion in recent years, Quiksilver has grown quite fast since its 1969 beginnings in Torquay, Australia. There Alan Green had started working on prototypes for a new kind of board short, using aspects of wetsuit technology such as snaps and Velcro flies. The new design proved more suitable for the demands of big-wave wipeouts. The "mountain and wave" logo followed in 1970.

Now Quiksilver is headquartered in Huntington Beach, CA (aka Surf City), and is one of the leading firms in "Velcro Valley"—the actionwear capital of the world in Orange County. The Quiksilver brand family includes 15 brands, led by Quiksilver, Roxy, DC, and Rossignol. It counts among its markets six continents, over 90 countries, and 236 million youths. The majority of its sales are overseas with 45% in the Americas, 44% in Europe, and 11% in Asia Pacific. Quiksilver distributes its products worldwide through 406 company-owned stores, 245 licensed stores, and 56 stores in licensed and joint venture territories. The Quiksilver sales mix is composed of 58% apparel, 15% footwear, 14% winter sports equipment, and 13% accessories.

Exhibited on the front cover of this book (100% Sponsorship of Kelly Slater, the world's best surfer) and here is just a representative part of the breadth of Quiksilver's integrated marketing communications:

Greg Macias, Vice President of Marketing explains how IMC decisions are made:

A billboard and store front in Moscow, Russia.

Globally, Quiksilver has three major centers of management: U.S. (Huntington Beach, CA), Europe (Biarritz, France), and Asia Pacific (Torquay, Australia). There are other management offices in China, Indonesia, Korea, Brazil, Argentina, South Africa, Canada, and Japan.

The head marketers in each of the three major regions meet three times a year formally to discuss goals, strategy, and best practices. This also happens in the general management and retail disciplines.

Media decisions are made on a regional level. There are no "global buys."

Roxy's sponsorship of Sofia Mulanovich, South America's first champion surfer. (*Covered Images*)

At home in the OC the company supports the Ocean Institute financially and with a visit from its Indies Trade boat, which travels the world promoting clean water environments and, of course, the company image. (© Tom Cozad/Newport surfshots.com)

Quiksilver sponsored the 2005 Great Wall of China first-ever leap by Danny Way, a southern California skateboarder. (AP Photo/Greg Baker)

We do have a global brand manager and he oversees a budget that supports global initiatives, that is, initiatives that can have a significant global effect and can be utilized by each region. The best examples of this are athletes and Web casts of key events.

We agree to share a common brand promise, global goals, a singular logo and an annual art palette. Each region builds their own specific communication executions but many assets are shared so advertising looks fairly consistent.

The firm uses perhaps the broadest array of advertising media as well—from walls in Istanbul to an entertainment loaded Web site.

Like most businesses, we are constantly changing and trying to improve our message, products, relationships, and business practices. In my humble opinion, our biggest asset is our ability to evolve and not get entrenched in tradition.

Greg Macias
Huntington Beach, CA

CROSSING BORDERS 16.1   PR in the PRC

In 1999 an industry was born in China when the Ministry of Labor and Social Security recognized public relations as a profession. These excerpts from the *China Daily* illustrate how institutions evolve in emerging economies:

More laws are needed to regulate China's fledgling public relations profession, an industry leader said yesterday in Beijing. "To seize the enormous business opportunities promised by China's upcoming entry in the World Trade Organization, we need specific laws to regulate the market, curb malpractice and promote competency of local PR firms," said Li Yue, vice-director of the China International Public Relations Association. Her comments were made during a national symposium on public relations, also know as PR.

Symposium delegates said they were concerned about the disorder in the PR industry and the frequent personnel changes in PR firms. They urged the passage of more laws to put an end to what many consider to be the chaos in the profession. Industry insiders cited a limited talent pool, cut-throat price wars and low professional standards as the industry's major problems.

In the 1980s, most Chinese people would think of reception girls, lavish banquets, and the use of connections when public relations were mentioned. Now, public relations firms are seen as helping their clients gain better name recognition of their companies. They also manage corporate images.

To help the industry develop, the Labor and Social Security Ministry this year instituted a nationwide qualifying exam for PR professionals. In 1999, the industry reported a total business volume of $120 million, while employing 3,000 people. There are now more than 2,000 PR *firms* and business volume is over $500 million.

Sources: "China: More Regulation of PR Sought," *China Daily*, January 20, 2000, p. 3; "PRW: The Top European PR Consultancies 2000," *PR Week*, June 23, 2000, p. 7; "PR Firms Gaining Experience by Working with Multinational Firms," *Industry Updates*, June 20, 2005; "Ogilvy Public Relations Worldwide/China and JL McGregor Announce Strategic Alliance," *PR Newswire*, June 13, 2007.

standards and product safety recalls has become big business for companies serving corporate clients such as Mattel Toys,[4] McDonald's, and, of course, Nike. Fast growth is also being fueled by the expanding international communications industry. New companies need public relations consultation for "building an international profile," as the marketing manager of VDSL Systems explained when hiring MCC, a prominent British firm. Surprising growth is occurring in emerging markets like Russia as well. The industry itself is experiencing a wave of mergers and takeovers, including the blending of the largest international advertising agencies and the most well-established PR firms.

Corporate sponsorships might be classified as an aspect of public relations, though their connections to advertising are also manifest. Tobacco companies have been particularly creative at using sports event sponsorships to avoid countries' advertising regulations associated with more traditional media. Other prominent examples are Coca-Cola's sponsorship of European football (soccer) matches or Ford's sponsorship of the Australian Open tennis tournament. McDonald's executed a huge international IMC campaign surrounding its sponsorship of the 2000 Sydney Olympics. Included were Olympic-themed food promotions, packaging and in-store signs, TV and print ads, and Web chats with superstar athletes such as American basketball player Grant Hill. In addition to the various promotions targeting the 43 million daily customers in their 27,000 restaurants around the world, the firm targeted the athletes themselves. As the official restaurant partner, McDonald's got to operate seven restaurants in Sydney, including the two serving the Olympic Village. During the three weeks of the Games, nearly 1.5 million burgers were served to the athletes, officials, coaches, media staffers, and spectators. McDonald's has continued as official corporate sponsors of the Athens (2004) and Beijing (2008) games as well. Finally, one of the more innovative sponsorship arrangements was Intel's agreement with the Tour de France to support the official Tour Web site,

---

[4] "Mattel Apologizes to China over Recall," *Associated Press*, September 21, 2007.

www.letour.com. Of course, all these aspects of IMC work best when coordinated and reinforced with a consistent advertising campaign, the topic covered in the rest of the chapter.

International Advertising

Since the turn of the century, growth in global advertising expenditures has slowed with the global economy. Most estimates of total expenditures for 2007 are in the neighborhood of $600 billion, and one forecast has them growing to over $700 billion by 2012, despite the global financial difficulties starting in 2008.[5] A 4 percent annual growth rate was predicted through 2006, but that of course depended on a resurgence of growth in the general global economy. In this slow-growth global economic environment, the advertising industry continues to undergo substantial restructuring. Global mass media advertising is a powerful tool for cultural change, and as such, it receives continuing scrutiny by a wide variety of institutions. Even so, most scholars agree that we are just beginning to understand some of the key issues involved in international advertising.

Exhibits 16.1 and 16.2 illustrate the biggest companies and product categories for international advertising. Although automotive companies dominate the lists, Procter & Gamble was the global champion of spending. Also, notice the lack of growth across many of the categories and companies. We also broke out the spending patterns for two emerging markets in Exhibit 16.3. Demonstrated is a key difference in stages of development between China and Russia. Whereas the latter is dominated by foreign food firms, China is creating its own homegrown brands of pharmaceuticals. Judging by the relative progress of the two countries on this single criterion, China looks like it is further up the ladder of economic development.

Of all the elements of the marketing mix, decisions involving advertising are those most often affected by cultural differences among country markets. Consumers respond in terms of their culture, its style, feelings, value systems, attitudes, beliefs, and perceptions.

[5] Heidi Dawley, "Forecast–Web Will Halt Global Ad Slide," *MediaLife Magazine*, March 4, 2008, http://www.medialifemagazine.com.

Exhibit 16.1
Top 20 Global Advertisers ($ millions)*

2006	2005	Advertiser	Headquarters	2006	Percent Change
1	1	Procter & Gamble Co.	Cincinnati	$8,522	4.1
2	2	Unilever	London/Rotterdam	4,537	8.1
3	3	General Motors	Detroit	3,353	−17.4
4	5	L'Oreal	Paris	3,119	12.7
5	4	Toyota Motor Corp.	Toyota City, Japan	3,098	9.1
6	6	Ford Motor Co.	Dearborn, MI	2,869	8.5
7	7	Time Warner	New York	2,230	−13.8
8	10	Nestle	Vevey, Switzerland	2,114	0.2
9	8	Johnson & Johnson	New Brunswick, NJ	2,025	−13.2
10	9	DaimlerChrysler	Stuttgart, Germany	2,003	−5.4
11	11	Honda Motor Co.	Tokyo	1,910	4.2
12	14	Coca-Cola	Atlanta	1,893	7.9
13	12	Walt Disney Co.	Burbank, CA	1,755	−3.7
14	17	GlaxoSmithKline	Brentford, U.K.	1,754	9.3
15	13	Nissan Motor Co.	Tokyo	1,670	−6.2
16	19	Sony Corp.	Tokyo	1,620	5.4
17	18	McDonald's Corp.	Oak Brook, IL	1,611	3.7
18	16	Volkswagen	Wolfsburg, Germany	1,609	−0.1
19	21	Reckitt Benckiser	Slough, U.K.	1,550	7.2
20	15	PepsiCo	Purchase, NY	1,530	−8.4

*Figures are U.S. dollars in millions and are *AdvertisingAge* estimates.

Source: "21st Annual Global Marketers," reprinted with permission from the November 19, 2007, issue of *Advertising Age*. Copyright © 2007 Crain Communications, Inc.

Exhibit 16.2
Top 100 Advertisers'
Global Spending by
Category ($ millions)

Source: "Special Report Global
Marketing," reprinted with permission
from the November 19, 2007, issue
of *Advertising Age*. Copyright © 2007
Crain Communications, Inc.

Category	2006	Percent Change from 2005	Percent Total
Automotive	$22,195	−0.4	22.7
Personal care	19,526	6.2	20.0
Entertainment and media	9,538	−5.0	9.8
Food	7,793	2.0	8.0
Drugs	7,707	4.5	7.9
Electronics	4,023	5.9	4.1
Soft drinks	3,916	−0.6	4.0
Retail	3,576	6.6	3.7
Cleaners	3,571	7.5	3.7
Restaurants	3,553	5.3	3.6
Computers	3,247	0.7	3.3
Telephone	2,488	−15.8	2.5
Financial	2,433	−7.2	2.5
Beer, wine & liquor	2,050	−9.4	2.1
Candy	1,137	3.0	1.2

Because advertising's function is to interpret or translate the qualities of products and services in terms of consumer needs, wants, desires, and aspirations, the emotional appeals, symbols, persuasive approaches, and other characteristics of an advertisement must coincide with cultural norms if the ad is to be effective.

Reconciling an international advertising campaign with the cultural uniqueness of markets is the challenge confronting the international or global marketer. The basic framework and concepts of international advertising are essentially the same wherever employed. Seven steps are involved:

1. Perform marketing research.
2. Specify the goals of the communication.

Exhibit 16.3a
Russia's Top Ten
Advertisers ($ millions)

Source: "Special Report Global
Marketing," reprinted with permission
from the November 19, 2007, issue
of *Advertising Age*. Copyright © 2007
Crain Communications, Inc.

Advertiser	2006	Percent Change from 2005
Procter & Gamble Co.	$163.9	−20.5
L'Oreal	73.3	−9.8
Unilever	71.5	−12.8
Henkel	55.3	−0.8
Mars Inc.	55.1	−8.2
Wimm-Bill-Dann	50.9	−2.7
Vimpel-Communications	50.3	6.7
Nestlé	47.4	−21.5
Danone Group	45.5	−12.6
Mobile TeleSystems	42.8	−10.1

Exhibit 16.3b
China's Top Ten
Advertisers ($ millions)

Source: "Special Report Global
Marketing," reprinted with permission
from the November 19, 2007, issue
of *Advertising Age*. Copyright © 2007
Crain Communications, Inc.

Advertiser	2006	Percent Change from 2005
Procter & Gamble Co.	$977.8	3.1
Unilever	377.0	63.4
Harbin Pharma Group	353.5	22.5
Shanghai Goldenpartner Biology	179.3	10.6
China Mobile Telecom	178.3	48.2
Yum Brands	1333.3	67.1
Hayao Group Sanchine Pharmacy	126.0	41.2
L'Oreal	121.0	45.8
Colgate-Palmolive	108.0	−10.7
Nice Group	92.3	44.1

These vehicular ads make an effective advertising medium even in a dense London fog. Because most London cabs are black, the Snickers ad catches the eye immediately.

3. Develop the most effective message(s) for the market segments selected.

4. Select effective media.

5. Compose and secure a budget based on what is required to meet goals.

6. Execute the campaign.

7. Evaluate the campaign relative to the goals specified.

Of these seven steps, developing messages almost always represents the most daunting task for international marketing managers. So, that topic is emphasized here. Nuances of international media are then discussed. Advertising agencies are ordinarily involved in all seven steps and are the subject of a separate section. Finally, the chapter closes with a discussion of broader issues of governmental controls on advertising.

Advertising Strategy and Goals

The goals of advertising around the world vary substantially. For example, Chinese manufacturers are establishing new brands as their economy expands; Unilever is introducing a new product-line extension, Dove Shampoo, in East Asian markets; and Russia's airline Aeroflot is seeking to upgrade its quality image. All these marketing problems require careful marketing research and thoughtful and creative advertising campaigns in country, regional, and global markets.

Intense competition for world markets and the increasing sophistication of foreign consumers have led to the need for more sophisticated advertising strategies. Increased costs, problems of coordinating advertising programs in multiple countries, and a desire for a broader company or product image have caused multinational companies (MNCs) to seek greater control and efficiency without sacrificing local responsiveness. In the quest for more effective and responsive promotion programs, the policies covering centralized or decentralized authority,[6] use of single or multiple foreign or domestic agencies, appropriation and allocation procedures, copy, media, and research are being examined. More and more multinational companies can be seen to be managing the balance between standardization of advertising themes and customization.[7] And recently, as described in Chapter 12, more companies are favoring the latter.

---

[6] Carl Solberg, "The Perennial Issue of Adaptation or Standardization of International Marketing Communications: Organizational Contingencies and Performance," *Journal of International Marketing* 10, no. 3 (2002), pp. 1–21.

[7] Ali Kanso and Richard Alan Nelson, "Advertising Localization Overshadows Stardardization," *Journal of Advertising Research* 42, no. 1 (January–February 2002), pp. 79–89; Charles R. Taylor, "Who Standardizes Advertising More Frequently, and Why Do They Do So? A Comparison of U.S. and Japanese Subsidiaries' Advertising Practices in the European Union," *Journal of International Marketing* 14 (2006), pp. 98–120; Kineta H. Hung, Stella Yiyan Li, and Russell W. Belk, "Global Understandings: Female Readers' Perceptions of the New Woman in Chinese Advertising," *Journal of International Business Studies* 38 (2007), pp. 1034–51.

A case in point is the Gillette Company, which sells 800 products in more than 200 countries. Gillette has a consistent worldwide image as a masculine, sports-oriented company, but its products have no such consistent image. Its razors, blades, toiletries, and cosmetics are known by many names. Trac II blades in the United States are more widely known worldwide as G-II, and Atra blades are called Contour in Europe and Asia. Silkience hair conditioner is known as Soyance in France, Sientel in Italy, and Silkience in Germany. Whether or not global brand names could have been chosen for Gillette's many existing products is speculative. However, Gillette's current corporate philosophy of globalization provides for an umbrella statement, "Gillette, the Best a Man Can Get," in all advertisements for men's toiletries products in the hope of providing some common image.

A similar situation exists for Unilever, which sells a cleaning liquid called Vif in Switzerland, Viss in Germany, Jif in Britain and Greece, and Cif in France. This situation is a result of Unilever marketing separately to each of these countries. At this point, it would be difficult for Gillette or Unilever to standardize their brand names, because each brand is established in its market and therefore has equity. Nortel Networks has used a "local heroes" approach in its international advertising. The company picks local celebrities to pitch standardized messages across national markets for their telecommunications services.

In many cases, standardized products may be marketed globally. But because of differences in cultures, they still require a different advertising appeal in different markets.[8] For instance, Ford's model advertising varies by nation because of language and societal nuances. Ford advertises the affordability of its Escort in the United States, where the car is seen as entry level. But in India, Ford launched the Escort as a premium car. "It's not unusual to see an Escort with a chauffeur there," said a Ford executive.

Finally, many companies are using market segmentation strategies that ignore national boundaries—business buyers or high-income consumers across the globe are often targeted in advertising, for example.[9] Others are proposing newer global market segments defined by "consumer cultures" related to shared sets of consumption-related symbols—convenience, youth, America, internationalism, and humanitarianism are examples.[10] Other, more traditional segments are product and region related; those are discussed next.

Product Attribute and Benefit Segmentation

As discussed in the chapters on product and services development (Chapters 12 and 13), a market offering really is a bundle of satisfactions the buyer receives. This package of satisfactions, or utilities, includes the primary function of the product or service along with many other benefits imputed by the values and customs of the culture. Different cultures often seek the same value or benefits from the primary function of a product—for example, the ability of an automobile to get from point A to point B, a camera to take a picture, or a wristwatch to tell time. But while usually agreeing on the benefit of the primary function of a product, consumers may perceive other features and psychological attributes of the item differently.

Consider the different market-perceived needs for a camera. In the United States, excellent pictures with easy, foolproof operation are expected by most of the market; in Germany and Japan, a camera must take excellent pictures, but the camera must also be state of the art in design. In Africa, where penetration of cameras is less than 20 percent of the households, the concept of picture taking must be sold. In all three markets, excellent pictures are expected (i.e., the primary function of a camera is demanded), but the additional utility or satisfaction derived from a camera differs among cultures. Many products produce expectations beyond the common benefit sought by all.

Dannon's brand of yogurt promotes itself as the brand that understands the relationship between health and food, but it communicates the message differently, depending on the

---

[8] Henry F. L. Chung, "International Standardization Strategies: The Experiences of Australian and New Zealand Firms Operating in the Greater China Markets," *Journal of International Marketing* 11, no. 3 (2003), pp. 48–82.

[9] Greg Harris and Suleiman Attour, "The International Advertising Practices of Multinational Companies: A Content Analysis Study," *European Journal of Marketing* 37, no. 1–2 (2003), pp. 154–68.

[10] David A. Griffin, Aruna Chandra, and John K. Ryans Jr., "Examining the Intricacies of Promotion Standardization: Factors Influencing Advertising Message and Packaging," *Journal of International Marketing* 11, no. 3 (2003), pp. 30–47.

market.[11] In the United States, where Dannon yogurt is seen as a healthy, vibrant food, the brand celebrates its indulgent side. In France, however, Dannon was seen as too pleasure oriented. Therefore, Dannon created the Institute of Health, a real research center dedicated to food and education. The end result is the same message but communicated differently— a careful balance of health and pleasure.

The Blue Diamond Growers Association's advertising of almonds is an excellent example of the fact that some products are best advertised only on a local basis. Blue Diamond had a very successful ad campaign in the United States showing almond growers knee-deep in almonds while pleading with the audience, "A can a week, that's all we ask." The objective of the campaign was to change the perception of almonds as a special-occasion treat to an everyday snack food. The campaign was a success; in addition to helping change the perception of almonds as a snack food, it received millions of dollars worth of free publicity for Blue Diamond from regional and national news media. The successful U.S. ad was tested in Canada for possible use outside the United States. The Canadian reaction was vastly different; to them, the whole idea was just too silly. And further, Canadians prefer to buy products from Canadian farmers, not American farmers. This response led to the decision to study each market closely and design an advertisement for each country market. The only similarity among commercials airing in markets in New York, Tokyo, Moscow, Toronto, or Stockholm is the Blue Diamond logo.

In Japan, the Blue Diamond brand of almonds was an unknown commodity until Blue Diamond launched its campaign of exotic new almond-based products that catered to local tastes. Such things as almond tofu, almond miso soup, and Clamond—a nutritional snack concocted from a mixture of dried small sardines and slivered almonds—were featured in magazine ads and in promotional cooking demonstrations. Television ads featured educational messages on how to use almonds in cooking, their nutritional value, the versatility of almonds as a snack, and the California mystique and health benefits of almonds. As a result, Japan is now the association's largest importer of almonds.

In Korea, the emphasis was on almonds and the West. Commercials featured swaying palms, beach scenes, and a guitar-playing crooner singing "Blue Diamond" to the tune of "Blue Hawaii." And so it goes in the 94 countries where Blue Diamond sells its almonds. Blue Diamond assumes that no two markets will react the same, that each has its own set of differences—be they "cultural, religious, ethnic, dietary, or otherwise"—and that each will require a different marketing approach, a different strategy. The wisdom of adapting its product advertising for each market is difficult to question; two-thirds of all Blue Diamond's sales are outside the United States.

Regional Segmentation

The emergence of pan-European communications media is enticing many companies to push the balance toward more standardized promotional efforts. As media coverage across Europe expands, it will become more common for markets to be exposed to multiple messages and brands of the same product. To avoid the confusion that results when a market is exposed to multiple brand names and advertising messages, as well as for reasons of efficiency, companies strive for harmony in brand names, advertising, and promotions across Europe.

Mars, the candy company, traditionally used several brand names for the same product but has found it necessary to select a single name to achieve uniformity in its standardized advertising campaigns. As a result, a candy bar sold in some parts of Europe under the brand name Raider was changed to Twix, the name used in the United States and the United Kingdom.

Along with changes in behavior patterns, legal restrictions are slowly being eliminated, and viable market segments across country markets are emerging. Although Europe will never be a single homogeneous market for every product, that does not mean that companies should shun the idea of developing Europe-wide promotional programs. A pan-European promotional strategy would mean identifying a market segment across all European countries and designing a promotional concept appealing to market segment similarities. Mars candy is a good example of this strategy.

---

[11] Jae H. Pae, Saeed Samiee, and Susan Tai, "Global Advertising Strategy: The Moderating Role of Brand Familiarity and Execution Style," *International Marketing Review* 19, no. 2–3 (2002), pp. 176–89.

microsoft

microsoft annually spends more than a billion dollars on its global advertising. The company has nearly 100 subsidiaries around the world. The management processes traditionally used to develop the Corporate Brand and Office campaigns are instructive.

Things began with marketing research in selected countries regarding key market segments, most attractive product features, and potential themes. The data is analyzed, strategies established and then sent to advertising agencies' for the development of a set of universal value propositions and concepts.

In partnership with Microsoft corporate in Redmond, the agencies then produce the selected core concepts, video footage, photographic layouts, and copy themes that comprise the set of universal materials. Then, in cooperation with their local agencies, managers at each subsidiary chose the most appropriate materials for their particular consumers and markets. The most customization was and is required in Brazil, China, India, and Russia—all are plagued by major piracy problems and are in various stages of maturity. Also, since Japan has the firm's second-largest market behind only the United States, executives there have been given more freedom to adapt to local requirements and tastes.

corporate/brand image campaign

The purpose behind this corporate campaign is to complement the firm's heavy product-oriented marketing with a program that explains Microsoft's broader corporate mission. That is, "to help people and businesses throughout the world reach their full potential." The campaign serves to clarify the image of the firm and emphasizes the contribution its products and services have made to technology and the practical applications of personal computing in business, science, education, and so on. The program runs in more than 30 countries (here you see the versions used in Australia, Taiwan, and France) including TV ads with local copy, voice-overs, and other adaptations to the global theme. The majority of the ads are pre- and post-tested in multiple countries to check for cultural nuance. The print and TV ads are complemented by an associated PR, government, and community affairs campaign.

product-specific advertising

Here Microsoft Office is pitted against its toughest competitor—earlier versions of itself. So the goal of the campaign is to break up the inertia and facilitate an upgrade cycle. The key message is the way the world (of information workers) works is much different today than it was three to five years ago, or one or two versions ago of Office. The ads focus on the product's "new" facilitation of collaboration and teamwork as the key attribute.

Since there is so much satisfaction (85 percent with Office), the firm needs to do something different or risk just reinforcing with customers previous versions of Office. You can see the extent of local adaptation in the English, German, and Japanese versions of the ads. This theme was supplemented by a heavy public relations campaign about the changing information worker environment. In addition, in keeping with the evolution of media, this campaign had a heavy digital component with over half the media being in the on-line space. This allowed for greater trial/sampling of the new version of Office as well as more direct customer interaction and feedback.

Such programs are ordinarily run in more than 30 countries. The translations are done locally, so, for example, the copy is different between Mexico and Spain. A variety of themes and media (print and outdoor) are used across countries. And, in any one country, several themes and media may be used, particularly in the larger, more diverse markets.

Finally, the executions are then tested in each market and adjustments are made. This global approach makes sense for Microsoft because the product, its uses, and its market share are virtually the same across markets.

online behavioral advertising – the worldwide revolution

Finally, the last panel—an example of Microsoft's online advertising—reflects a key change in advertising practice for corporations around the world. That is, during the last few years companies' expenditures on online advertising have exploded to more than $20 billion in the United States alone. Expenditures

on traditional media (print, TV, etc.) are fast being replaced by online options. In 2007 a tipping point was reached with regard to targeting such expenditures via online tracking of consumer search, purchase, and usage behaviors. That year Microsoft itself made its largest corporate acquisition ever spending $6 billion for aQuantive, one of the leading firms in digital-ads located in nearby Seattle. The new technologies allow for more efficiently reaching potential customers with the most appropriate messages based on observations of specific online behavior patterns.

Most recently advertising regulators worldwide are trying to keep up with the fast-evolving technologies—in particular, international consumers and critics are concerned about protecting personal and corporate privacy and data security. In the United States the Federal Trade Commission has begun holding hearings on corporate practices. Microsoft touts its own online advertising best practices including "commitments to user notice, user control, anonymization, and security."

(Images Courtesy Microsoft Corporation)

With a common language (Brazil being the one exception), Latin America also lends itself to regionwide promotion programs. Eveready Battery has successfully developed a 16-country campaign with one message instead of the patchwork of messages that previously existed. Cable and satellite TV channels also provide regionwide media. For example, HBO promoted the American cable-TV hit *Six Feet Under* using a pan-Asian campaign.

The Message: Creative Challenges

Global Advertising and the Communications Process

International communications may fail for a variety of reasons: A message may not get through because of media inadequacy, the message may be received by the intended audience but not be understood because of different cultural interpretations, or the message may reach the intended audience and be understood but have no effect because the marketer did not correctly assess the needs and wants or even the thinking processes[12] of the target market.

In the international communications process, each of the seven identifiable steps ultimately can affect the accuracy of the process. As illustrated in Exhibit 16.4, the process consists of the following:

1. **An information source.** An international marketing executive with a product message to communicate.

2. **Encoding.** The message from the source converted into effective symbolism for transmission to a receiver.

3. **A message channel.** The sales force and/or advertising media that convey the encoded message to the intended receiver.

4. **Decoding.** The interpretation by the receiver of the symbolism transmitted from the information source.

5. **Receiver.** Consumer action by those who receive the message and are the target for the thought transmitted.

6. **Feedback.** Information about the effectiveness of the message that flows from the receiver (the intended target) back to the information source for evaluation of the effectiveness of the process.

---

[12] Jennifer Aaker, "Accessibility or Diagnosticity? Disentangling the Influence of Culture on Persuasion Processes and Attitudes," *Journal of Consumer Research* 26, no. 4 (March 2000), pp. 340–57.

Exhibit 16.4
The International Communications Process

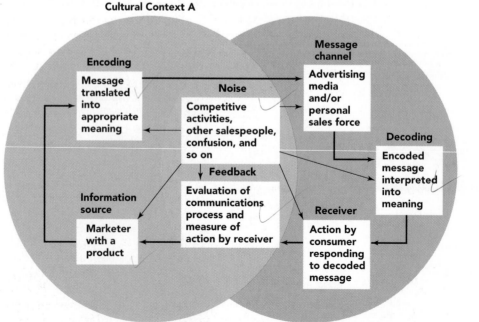

7. **Noise.** Uncontrollable and unpredictable influences such as competitive activities and confusion that detract from the process and affect any or all of the other six steps.

Unfortunately, the process is not as simple as just sending a message via a medium to a receiver and being certain that the intended message sent is the same one perceived by the receiver. In Exhibit 16.4, the communications process steps are encased in Cultural Context A and Cultural Context B to illustrate the influences complicating the process when the message is encoded in one culture and decoded in another. If not properly considered, the different cultural contexts can increase the probability of misunderstandings. Research in the area suggests that effective communication demands the existence of a "psychological overlap" between the sender and the receiver; otherwise, a message falling outside the receiver's perceptual field may transmit an unintended meaning. It is in this area that even the most experienced companies make blunders.

Most promotional misfires or mistakes in international marketing are attributable to one or several of these steps not properly reflecting cultural influences or a general lack of knowledge about the target market. Referring to Exhibit 16.4, the information source is a marketer with a product to sell to a specific target market. The product message to be conveyed should reflect the needs and wants of the target market; however, often the actual market needs and the marketer's perception of them do not coincide. This disconnect is especially true when the marketer relies more on the self-reference criterion (SRC) than on effective research. It can never be assumed that "if it sells well in one country, it will sell in another." For instance, bicycles designed and sold in the United States to consumers fulfilling recreational exercise needs are not sold as effectively for the same reason in a market where the primary use of the bicycle is transportation. Cavity-reducing fluoride toothpaste sells well in the United States, where healthy teeth are perceived as important, but has limited appeal in markets such as Great Britain and the French areas of Canada, where the reason for buying toothpaste is breath control. From the onset of the communications process, if basic needs are incorrectly defined, communications fail because an incorrect or meaningless message is received, even though the remaining steps in the process are executed properly.

The encoding step causes problems even with a "proper" message. At this step, such factors as color,[13] timing, values,[14] beliefs, humor,[15] tastes, and appropriateness of spokespersons[16] can cause the international marketer to symbolize the message incorrectly. For example, the marketer wants the product to convey coolness so the color green is used; however, people in the tropics might decode green as dangerous or associate it with disease. Another example of the encoding process misfiring was a perfume presented against a backdrop of rain that, for Europeans, symbolized a clean, cool, refreshing image but to Africans was a symbol of fertility. The ad prompted many viewers to ask if the perfume was effective against infertility. David Beckham may be a wonderful spokesperson in most of the world, but in the United States, even the greatest soccer players get little recognition.[17]

Problems of literacy,[18] media availability, and types of media create challenges in the communications process at the encoding step. Message channels must be carefully selected if an encoded message is to reach the consumer. Errors such as using the Internet as a medium when

---

[13] Thomas J. Madden, Kelly Hewett, and Martin S. Roth, "Managing Images in Different Cultures: A Cross-National Study of Color Meanings and Preferences," *Journal of International Marketing* 8, no. 4 (2000), pp. 108–21; Elizabeth G. Miller, "Shades of Meaning: The Effect of Color and Flavor Names on Consumer Choice," *Journal of Consumer Research* 32 (2005), pp. 86–92.

[14] Cheng Lu Wang and Allan K. K. Chan, "A Content Analysis of Connectedness vs. Separateness Themes Used in U.S. and PRC Print Advertisements," *International Marketing Review* 18, no. 2 (2001), pp. 145–60.

[15] Robert Guy Matthews, "KFC 'Soul' Ad Poses Global Issue," *The Wall Street Journal*, January 27, 2005, p. B6.

[16] Drew Martin and Arch G. Woodside, "Dochakuka: Melding Global Inside Local: Foreign-Domestic Advertising Assimilation in Japan," *Journal of Global Marketing* 21 (2007), pp. 19–32.

[17] Erin White and Maureen Tkacik, "Spend It Like Beckham," *The Wall Street Journal*, June 19, 2003, p. B1.

[18] Ivonne Torres, Betsy Gelb, and Jaime L. Noriega, "Warning and Informing the Domestic International Market," *Journal of Public Policy & Marketing* 22, no. 2 (2003), pp. 216–22.

Red Works! Since we first wrote about the color's power some 10 years ago, a lot has been happening. Notice the Coke advantage at work—the red contrasts with the outdoor environment, while the Cristal aqua blends more with the blue sky. Cristal is a popular brand of bottled water actually owned by Coca-Cola and sold in the Yucatan Peninsula in Mexico. The Coke ads are emblazoned on a café in the central plaza of Canas, Costa Rica. Or you can spend it like Beckham—in addition to Vodafone and Nike on his jersey, David Beckham, here in his Manchester United red (*© Tom Purslow/Manchester United via Getty Images*), also represents Pepsi, Adidas, Castrol, Upper Deck, Marks & Spencer, Police, Meiji, Tokyo Beauty Center, etc., etc., etc. The Spanish soccer power Real Madrid spent $40 million buying Beckham's contract from his British home team, and then the Los Angeles Galaxy moved him there. One disadvantage of the moves south—the white jerseys of the Spanish and American teams don't catch the eye as did the Manchester United red. Most recently Beckham has teamed up with the Red campaign (along with Oprah and Bono) to promote products of firms that donate revenues to the Global Fund to Fight AIDS. Other firms involved in the project include are Dell, Microsoft, American Express, Armani, Converse, Hallmark, Apple, and The Gap.[19] We also note that the world's most famous athlete is not Beckham, or even last-day-red-shirt-wearing Tiger Woods. Instead, it's Formula 1 racecar driver Michael Schumacher (*AP Photo/Mark Barker*). The 35-year-old German makes more money than any other sports figure as he dominates the sport most watched on television globally. And the flamboyant red jumpsuit and red Ferraris help. The other red brands—Marlboro and Vodafone—love him too. Finally, even PepsiCo is blushing over Coke's dominance: It's introducing an all-red can in China.[20] If it succeeds there, perhaps Pepsi will just match other countries' flags as well—red, white, and blue works not only in the United States but in Russia and France as well.

[19] Ron Nixon, "Little Green for (Red)," *The New York Times*, February 6, 2008, pp. C1, C5.

[20] Loretta Chao and Betsy McKay, "Pepsi Steps into Coke Realm: Red China," *The Wall Street Journal* (online), September 12, 2007.

City streets in Singapore are alive with advertising. California Fitness Centers in Southeast Asia are owned by America's 24-hour Fitness Centers. Obviously the image of "bodyland" southern California sells well around the world. However, there's an interesting irony in that brand name for Muslim customers. The word *California* first appears in the eleventh-century epic poem *The Song of Roland*; there it literally means the "caliph's domain"—the Caliph of Baghdad ruled the Islamic Empire then. The Spaniards who named California in the early 1500s thought they were in Asia! Moreover, the deeper meaning of the brand name is lost even on the modern Muslims who comprise 15 percent of Singapore's current population!

only a small percentage of an intended market has access to the Internet, or using print media for a channel of communications when the majority of the intended users cannot read or do not read the language in the medium, are examples of ineffective media channel selection in the communications process.

Decoding problems are generally created by improper encoding, which caused such errors as Pepsi's "Come Alive" slogan being decoded as "Come out of the grave." Chevrolet's brand name for the Nova model (which means new star) was decoded into Spanish as No Va!, meaning "it doesn't go." In another misstep, a translation that was supposed to be decoded as "hydraulic ram" was instead decoded as "wet sheep." In a Nigerian ad, a platinum blonde sitting next to the driver of a Renault was intended to enhance the image of the automobile. However, the model was perceived as not respectable and so created a feeling of shame. An ad used for Eveready Energizer batteries with the Energizer bunny was seen by Hungarian consumers as touting a bunny toy, not a battery.

Decoding errors may also occur accidentally, as was the case with Colgate-Palmolive's selection of the brand name Cue for toothpaste. The brand name was not intended to have any symbolism; nevertheless, it was decoded by the French into a pornographic word. In some cases, the intended symbolism has no meaning to the decoder. In an ad transferred from the United States, the irony of tough-guy actor Tom Selleck standing atop a mountain with a steaming mug of Lipton tea was lost on eastern Europeans.

Errors at the receiver end of the process generally result from a combination of factors: an improper message resulting from incorrect knowledge of use patterns, poor encoding producing a meaningless message, poor media selection that does not get the message to the receiver, or inaccurate decoding by the receiver so that the message is garbled or incorrect. Even bad luck comes into play. Recall that French's mustard was boycotted (along with French wines, fries, etc.) by Americans when the Paris government did not go along with the attack in Iraq in 2003—even though the brand name has nothing to do with the country.[21]

Finally, the feedback step of the communications process is important as a check on the effectiveness of the other steps. Companies that do not measure their communications efforts are likely to allow errors of source, encoding, media selection, decoding, or receiver to continue longer than necessary. In fact, a proper feedback system (ad testing) allows a company to correct errors before substantial damage occurs.

In addition to the problems inherent in the steps outlined, the effectiveness of the international communications process can be impaired by noise. *Noise* comprises all other external influences, such as competitive advertising, other sales personnel, and confusion at the receiving end, that can detract from the ultimate effectiveness of the communication. Noise is a disruptive force interfering with the process at any step and is frequently beyond the control of the sender or the receiver. As Exhibit 16.4 illustrates with the overlapping cultural contexts, noise can emanate from activity in either culture or be caused by the influences of the overlapping of the cultural contexts.

The model's significance is that one or all steps in the process, cultural factors,[22] or the marketer's SRC can affect the ultimate success of the communication. For example, the

---

[21] Floyd Norris, "It's French's Mustard. What's in a Name these Days?" *International Herald Tribune,* March 29, 2003, p. 13.

[22] Donnel A. Briley and Robert S. Wyer Jr., "The Effect of Group Membership Salience on the Avoidance of Negative Outcomes: Implications for Social and Consumer Research," *Journal of Consumer Research* 29, no. 3 (December 2002), pp. 400–15.

Cultural Diversity

The problems associated with communicating to people in diverse cultures present one of the great creative challenges in advertising.[35] One advertising executive puts it bluntly: "International advertising is almost uniformly dreadful mostly because people don't understand language and culture." Communication is more difficult because cultural factors largely determine the way various phenomena are perceived.[36] If the perceptual framework is different, perception of the message itself differs.[37]

Existing perceptions based on tradition and heritages often render advertising campaigns ineffective or worse. For example, marketing researchers in Hong Kong found that cheese is associated with *Yeung-Yen* (foreigners) and thus rejected by some Chinese. Toyota introduced the Prado SUV in China only to learn that the name sounded like the Chinese word for "rule by force." This name reminded some Chinese of the 1937 invasion by Japan—not a nice memory at all.[38]

Procter & Gamble's initial advertisement for Pampers brand diapers failed because of cultural differences between the United States and Japan. A U.S. commercial that showed an animated stork delivering Pampers diapers to homes was dubbed into Japanese with the U.S. package replaced by the Japanese package and put on the air. To P&G's dismay, the advertisement failed to build the market. Some belated consumer research revealed that consumers were confused about why this bird was delivering disposable diapers. According to Japanese folklore, giant peaches that float on the river bring babies to deserving parents, not storks.

In addition to concerns with differences among nations, advertisers find that subcultures within a country require attention as well. People in Hong Kong have 10 different patterns of breakfast eating. The youth of a country almost always constitute a different consuming culture from the older people, and urban dwellers differ significantly from rural dwellers. Besides these differences, there is the problem of changing traditions. In all countries, people of all ages, urban or rural, cling to their heritage to a certain degree but are willing to change some areas of behavior. Indeed, due to the early efforts of Nestlé's and the most recent expansion by Starbucks, in tea-drinking Japan, coffee has become the fashionable beverage for younger people and urban dwellers who like to think of themselves as cosmopolitan and sophisticated.

Media Limitations

Media are discussed at length later, so here we note only that limitations on creative strategy imposed by media may diminish the role of advertising in the promotional program and may force marketers to emphasize other elements of the promotional mix. A marketer's creativity is certainly challenged when a television commercial is limited to 10 showings a year with no two exposures closer than 10 days, as is the case in Italy. Creative advertisers in some countries have even developed their own media for overcoming media limitations. In some African countries, advertisers run boats up and down the rivers playing popular music and broadcasting commercials into rural areas as they travel.

Production and Cost Limitations

Creativity is especially important when a budget is small or where there are severe production limitations, such as poor-quality printing and a lack of high-grade paper. For example, the poor quality of high-circulation glossy magazines and other quality publications in eastern Europe has caused Colgate-Palmolive to depart from its customary heavy use of print media in the West for other media. Newsprint is of such low quality in China that a

---

[35] Elzbieta Lepkowska-White, "Polish and American Print Ads: Functional, Individualistic, Collectivistic, and Experiential Appeals," *Journal of Global Marketing* 17, no. 4 (2004), pp. 75–92.

[36] Nader T. Tavassoli and Yih Hwai Lee, "The Differential Interaction of Auditory and Visual Advertising Elements with Chinese and English," *Journal of Marketing Research* 40, no. 4 (2003), pp. 468–80.

[37] Some of the most important work being done in the area of culture and advertising is represented by Jennifer Aaker and Patti Williams's "Empathy and Pride: The Influence of Emotional Appeals across Cultures," *Journal of Consumer Research* 25 (December 1998), pp. 241–61; Ulrich R. Orth and Denisa Holancova, "Men's and Women's Responses to Sex Role Portrayals in Advertisements," *International Journal of Research in Marketing* 21, no. 1 (2004), pp. 77–88.

[38] Geoffrey A. Fowler, "China's Cultural Fabric Is a Challenge to Marketers," *The Wall Street Journal*, January 21, 2004, p. B7.

CROSSING BORDERS 16.3   Objections to Indian Ad Not Taken Lightly

A financially strapped father laments his fate, saying, "Kaash agar mera beta hota" ("If I only had a son"), while his dark-skinned, plain-Jane daughter looks on, helpless and demoralized because she cannot bear the financial responsibility of her family. Fast-forward and plain Jane has been transformed into a gorgeous, light-skinned woman through the use of a "fairness cream." Now clad in a miniskirt, the woman is a successful flight attendant and can take her father to dine at a five-star hotel. She's happy and so is her father.

All's well that end's well—except not so for Hindustan Lever Ltd. (HLL). The company, a subsidiary of Unilever, launched this television campaign to promote its Fair & Lovely fairness cream in India. It withdrew the campaign two months later amid severe criticism for its portrayal of women. The incident underscores the changing social mores in India and highlights tensions among the government, consumer groups, and industry regulatory agencies.

While tanning is the rage in Western countries, skin lightening treatments have been historically popular in Asia. The Japanese market for such products is estimated to be around $6 billion and in India about $150 million.

It may be safe for the skin, but not for society, says the All India Women's Democratic Association. Three things were objectionable about the campaign to the group. It was racist, it promoted preferences for sons, and it was insulting to working women. A government ministry found the ads to be in violation of the Cable and Television Act of 1995, which in part forbids ads that "deride any race, caste, color, creed, and nationality." Industry regulators agreed and pressured the company to stop airing the ad. The company admitted no wrong doing, but complied.

Sources: Arundhati Parmar, "Objections to Indian Ad Not Taken Lightly," *Marketing News*, June 9, 2003, pp. 4–5; Heather Timmons, "Telling India's Modern Women They Have Power, Even over Their Skin Tone," *The New York Times*, May 30, 2007, p. C5.

---

color ad used by Kodak in the West is not an option. Kodak's solution has been to print a single-sheet color insert as a newspaper supplement.

The necessity for low-cost reproduction in small markets poses another problem in many countries. For example, hand-painted billboards must be used instead of printed sheets because the limited number of billboards does not warrant the production of printed sheets. In Egypt, static-filled television and poor-quality billboards have led companies such as Coca-Cola and Nestlé to place their advertisements on the sails of feluccas, boats that sail along the Nile. Feluccas, with their triangle sails, have been used to transport goods since the time of the pharaohs and serve as an effective alternative to attract attention to company names and logos.

Media Planning and Analysis

Tactical Considerations   Although nearly every sizable nation essentially has the same kinds of media, a number of specific considerations, problems, and differences are encountered from one nation to another. In international advertising, an advertiser must consider the availability, cost, coverage, and appropriateness of the media. And the constant competitive churn among these media makes for a tricky and dynamic landscape for making decisions.[39] For example, billboard ads next to highways cannot include paragraphs of text. Moreover, recent research has demonstrated that media effectiveness varies across cultures and product types. Local variations and lack of market data require added attention. Major multinationals are beginning to recognize the importance of planning communications channels as media companies continue to rationalize and evolve. Indeed, media giants such as Disney and Time Warner cover an increasingly broad spectrum of the electronic media, necessitating that MNCs rethink their relationships with media service providers.

---

[39] Manjeet Kripalani, "Read All about It: India's Media Wars," *BusinessWeek*, May 16, 2005, p. 47.

Imagine the ingenuity required of advertisers confronted with these situations:

- In Brazil, TV commercials are sandwiched together in a string of 10 to 50 commercials within one station break.
- National coverage in many countries means using as many as 40 to 50 different media.
- Specialized media reach small segments of the market only. In the Netherlands, there are Catholic, Protestant, socialist, neutral, and other specialized broadcasting systems.
- In Germany, TV scheduling for an entire year must be arranged by August 30 of the preceding year, with no guarantee that commercials intended for summer viewing will not be run in the middle of winter.
- In Vietnam, advertising in newspapers and magazines is limited to 10 percent of space and to 5 percent of time, or three minutes an hour, on radio and TV.

Availability.   One of the contrasts of international advertising is that some countries have too few advertising media and others have too many. In some countries, certain advertising media are forbidden by government edict to accept some advertising materials. Such restrictions are most prevalent in radio and television broadcasting. In many countries, there are too few magazines and newspapers to run all the advertising offered to them. Conversely, some nations segment the market with so many newspapers that the advertiser cannot gain effective coverage at a reasonable cost. One head of an Italian advertising agency commented about his country: "One fundamental rule. You cannot buy what you want."

In China the only national TV station, CCTV, has one channel that must be aired by the country's 27 provincial/municipal stations. Recently CCTV auctioned off the most popular break between the early evening news and weather; a secured year-long, daily five-second billboard ad in this break went for $38.5 million. For this price, advertisers are assured of good coverage—more than 70 percent of households have TV sets. One of the other options for advertisers is with the 2,828 TV stations that provide only local coverage.

Cost.   Media prices are susceptible to negotiation in most countries. Agency space discounts are often split with the client to bring down the cost of media. The advertiser may find that the cost of reaching a prospect through advertising depends on the agent's bargaining ability. The per contract cost varies widely from country to country. One study showed that the cost of reaching 1,000 readers in 11 different European countries ranged from $1.58 in Belgium to $5.91 in Italy; in women's service magazines, the page cost per 1,000 circulation ranged from $2.51 in Denmark to $10.87 in Germany. Shortages of advertising time on commercial television in some markets have caused substantial price increases. In Britain, prices escalate on a bidding system. They do not have fixed rate cards; instead, there is a preempt system in which advertisers willing to pay a higher rate can bump already-scheduled spots.

Coverage.   Closely akin to the cost dilemma is the problem of coverage. Two points are particularly important: One relates to the difficulty of reaching certain sectors of the population with advertising and the other to the lack of information about coverage. In many world marketplaces, a wide variety of media must be used to reach the majority of the markets. In some countries, large numbers of separate media have divided markets into uneconomical advertising segments. With some exceptions, a majority of the population of less developed countries cannot be reached readily through the traditional mass medium of advertising. In India, video vans are used to reach India's rural population with 30-minute infomercials extolling the virtues of a product. Consumer goods companies deploy vans year-round except in the monsoon season. Colgate hires 85 vans at a time and sends them to villages that research has shown to be promising.

Because of the lack of adequate coverage by any single medium in eastern European countries, companies must resort to a multimedia approach. In the Czech Republic, for example, TV advertising rates are high, and the lack of available prime-time spots has forced companies to use billboard advertising. In Slovenia the availability of adequate media is such a problem that companies resort to some unique approaches to get their messages out. For example, in the summer, lasers are used to project images onto clouds above major cities. Vehicle advertising includes cement-mixers, where Kodak ads have appeared. On the positive side, crime is so low that products can be displayed in freestanding glass cabinets on sidewalks; Bosch Siemens (Germany) and Kodak have both used this method.

Lack of Market Data.   Verification of circulation or coverage figures is a difficult task. Even though many countries have organizations similar to the Audit Bureau of Circulation in the United States, accurate circulation and audience data are not assured. For example, the president of the Mexican National Advertisers Association charged that newspaper circulation figures are grossly exaggerated. He suggested that as a rule, agencies should divide these figures in two and take the result with a grain of salt. The situation in China is no better; surveys of habits and market penetration are available only for the cities of Beijing, Shanghai, and Guangzhou. Radio and television audiences are always difficult to measure, but at least in most countries, geographic coverage is known. Research data are becoming more reliable as advertisers and agencies demand better quality data.

Even where advertising coverage can be measured with some accuracy, there are questions about the composition of the market reached. Lack of available market data seems to characterize most international markets; advertisers need information on income, age, and geographic distribution, but such basic data seem chronically elusive except in the largest markets. Even the attractiveness of global television (satellite broadcasts) is diminished somewhat because of the lack of media research available.

An attempt to evaluate specific characteristics of each medium is beyond the scope of this discussion. Furthermore, such information would quickly become outdated because of the rapid changes in the international advertising media field. It may be interesting, however, to examine some of the unique international characteristics of various advertising media. In most instances, the major implications of each variation may be discerned from the data presented.

Newspapers.   The newspaper industry is suffering from lack of competition in some countries and choking because of it in others. Most U.S. cities have just one or two major daily newspapers, but in many countries, there are so many newspapers that an advertiser has trouble achieving even partial market coverage. Uruguay, population 3 million, has 21 daily newspapers with a combined circulation of 553,000. Turkey has 380 newspapers, and an advertiser must consider the political position of each newspaper so that the product's reputation is not harmed through affiliation with unpopular positions. Japan has only five national daily newspapers, and the complications of producing a Japanese-language newspaper are such that they each contain just 16 to 20 pages. Connections are necessary to buy advertising space; *Asahi,* Japan's largest newspaper, has been known to turn down over a million dollars a month in advertising revenue.

In many countries, there is a long time lag before an advertisement can be run in a newspaper. In India and Indonesia, paper shortages delay publication of ads for up to six months. Furthermore, because of equipment limitations, most newspapers cannot be made larger to accommodate the increase in advertising demand.

Separation between editorial and advertising content in newspapers provides another basis for contrast on the international scene. In some countries, it is possible to buy editorial space for advertising and promotional purposes; the news columns are for sale to anyone who has the price. Because there is no indication that the space is paid for, it is impossible to tell exactly how much advertising appears in a given newspaper.

Magazines.   The use of foreign national consumer magazines by international advertisers has been notably low for many reasons. Few magazines have a large circulation or provide dependable circulation figures. Technical magazines are used rather extensively to promote export goods, but as with newspapers, paper shortages cause placement problems. Media planners are often faced with the largest magazines accepting up to twice as many advertisements as they have space to run them in—then the magazines decide what advertisements will go in just before going to press by means of a raffle.

CROSSING BORDERS 16.4   Advertising Themes that Work in Japan, Including a Polite Duck

Respect for tradition: Mercedes ads stress that it was the first to manufacture passenger cars.

Mutual dependence: Shiseido ads emphasize the partnership (with beauty consultants) involved in achieving beauty.

Harmony with nature: Toyotas are shown in front of Mt. Fuji.

Use of seasons: Commercials are often set in and products are often used in specific seasons only.

Newness and evolution: Products are shown to evolve from the current environment slowly.

Distinctive use of celebrities, including gaijin (foreigners): A recent study showed that 63 percent of all Japanese commercials featured hired celebrities.

Aging of society: Seniors are featured often.

Changing families: The changing role of fathers—more time spent at home—is a common theme.

Generation gaps and individualism: Younger characters are shown as more individualistic.

Self-effacing humor: A dented Pepsi can was used in an ad to demonstrate its deference to more popular Coke.

Polite ducks: The AFLAC duck is going to Japan but with a softer quack. Instead of the American version's abrasive quack, the Japanese actor portrays the duck with a more soothing tone. "The Japanese culture does not like being yelled at," says an AFLAC spokesperson. About 70 percent of the firm's international revenues come from Japan, or some $8 billion. Although this campaign is the first to be shot specifically for Japan, the Japanese have met the duck before. The company, now Japan's largest insurer in terms of individual policies, has also used dubbed voices of American ads, including the loud "quacker."

Sources: George Fields, Hotaka Katahira, and Jerry Wind, *Leveraging Japan, Marketing to the New Asia* (San Francisco: Jossey-Bass, 2000); "ALFAC Tames Its Duck for Japanese Market," *Los Angeles Times,* May 13, 2003, p. C7; Lavonne Kuykendall, "AFLAC Japan Looks to Fly Again," *The Wall Street Journal,* April 18, 2007, p. B3F.

Such local practices may be key factors favoring the growth of so-called international media that attempt to serve many nations. Increasingly, U.S. publications are publishing overseas editions. *Reader's Digest International* has added a new Russian-language edition to its more than 20 other language editions. Other American print media available in international editions range from *Playboy* to *Scientific American* and even include the *National Enquirer*, recently introduced to the United Kingdom. Advertisers have three new magazines through which to reach women in China: Hachette Filipachi Presse, the French publisher, is expanding Chinese-language editions of *Elle*, a fashion magazine; *Woman's Day* is aimed at China's "busy modern" woman; and *L'Evénement Sportif* is a sports magazine. These media offer alternatives for multinationals as well as for local advertisers.

Radio and Television.   Possibly because of their inherent entertainment value, radio and television have become major communications media in almost all nations. Now high-definition television (HDTV) appears to be starting to take off worldwide as well. In China, virtually all homes in major cities have a television, and most adults view television and listen to radio daily. Radio has been relegated to a subordinate position in the media race in countries where television facilities are well developed. In many countries, however, radio is a particularly important and vital advertising medium when it is the only one reaching large segments of the population.

Television and radio advertising availability varies between countries. Three patterns are discernible: competitive commercial broadcasting, commercial monopolies, and noncommercial broadcasting. Countries with free competitive commercial radio and television normally encourage competition and have minimal broadcast regulations. Elsewhere, local or national monopolies are granted by the government, and individual stations or networks may then accept radio or TV commercials according to rules established by the government. In some countries, commercial monopolies may accept all the advertising they wish; in others, only spot advertising is permissible, and programs may not be sponsored. Live commercials are not permitted in some countries; in still others, commercial stations must compete for audiences against the government's noncommercial broadcasting network.

Some countries do not permit any commercial radio or television, but several of the traditional noncommercial countries have changed their policies in recent years because television production is so expensive. Until recently, France limited commercials to a daily total of 18 minutes but now has extended the time limit to 12 minutes per hour per TV channel. South Korea has two television companies, both government owned, which broadcast only a few hours a day. They do not broadcast from midnight to 6:00 a.m, and they usually cannot broadcast between 10:00 a.m. and 5:30 p.m. on weekdays. Commercials are limited to 8 percent of airtime and shown in clusters at the beginning and end •f programs. One advertiser remarked, "We are forced to buy what we don't want to buy just to get on."

Lack of reliable audience data is another major problem in international marketing via radio and television. Measurement of radio and television audiences is always a precarious business, even with highly developed techniques. In most countries, either audience size is not audited or the existing auditing associations are ineffective. Despite the paucity of audience data, many advertisers use radio and television extensively. Advertisers justify their inclusion in the media schedule with the inherent logic favoring the use of these media or defend their use on the basis of sales results.

Satellite and Cable TV.

Of increasing importance in TV advertising is the growth and development of satellite TV broadcasting. Sky Channel, a United Kingdom–based commercial satellite television station, beams its programs and advertising into most of Europe to cable TV subscribers. The technology that permits households to receive broadcasts directly from the satellite via a dish the size of a dinner plate costing about $350 is adding greater coverage and the ability to reach all of Europe with a single message. The expansion of TV coverage will challenge the creativity of advertisers and put greater emphasis on global standardized messages. For a comparison of penetration rates by cable TV, computers, and the Internet in the several countries, see Exhibit 16.5.

Advertisers and governments are both concerned about the impact of satellite TV. Governments are concerned because they fear further loss of control over their airwaves and the spread of "American cultural imperialism." European television programming includes such U.S. shows as *The OC. Wheel of Fortune* is the most popular foreign show in the United Kingdom and France, where both the U.S. and French versions are shown. American imports are so popular in France and Germany that officials fear lowbrow U.S. game shows, sitcoms, and soap operas will crush domestic producers. This battle has even reached political levels associated with differences in worldviews represented in the news. The government of France invested in developing, not surprisingly, a French-language "CNN" called France 24, but has stopped subsidizing an English-language version.[40]

---

[40] "Sarkozy to Scrap English-Language France 24 Television–AFP," *Dow Jones International News,* January 8, 2008.

Exhibit 16.5
Media Penetration in Selected Countries (per 1,000 persons)

Country	TV	Cable TV	Satellite TV	Telephone Lines	Internet Users	Daily Newspapers
United States	871	255	284	645	621	196
Canada	707	253	280	548	707	168
Argentina	326	163	169	237	206	40
Germany	675	251	283	668	513	291
Poland	229	94	117	332	368	102
Israel	342	190	258	420	647	250
South Africa	177	58	96	97	93	25
China	350	75	57	318	144	59
Japan	785	193	182	455	538	566
Australia	722	76	102	574	770	161

Source: Euromonitor, World Bank (World Development Indicators), 2008.

Al-Jazeera, initially subsidized by Qatar government loans, is currently struggling to break even. Nevertheless, it is the now widely recognized Arabic "CNN" and is commensurately influential in the Middle East.

Parts of Asia and Latin America receive TV broadcasts from satellite television networks. Univision and Televisa are two Latin American satellite television networks broadcasting via a series of affiliate stations in each country to most of the Spanish-speaking world, as well as the United States. *Sabado Gigante,* a popular Spanish-language program broadcast by Univision, is seen by tens of millions of viewers in 16 countries. Star TV, a new pan-Asian satellite television network, has a potential audience of 2.7 billion people living in 38 countries from Egypt through India to Japan, and from Russia to Indonesia. Star TV was the first to broadcast across Asia but was quickly joined by ESPN and CNN. The first Asian 24-hour all-sports channel was followed by MTV Asia and a Mandarin Chinese–language channel that delivers dramas, comedies, movies, and financial news aimed at the millions of overseas Chinese living throughout Asia. Programs are delivered through cable networks but can be received through private satellite dishes.

One of the drawbacks of satellites is also their strength, that is, their ability to span a wide geographical region covering many different country markets. That means a single message is broadcast throughout a wide area. This span may not be desirable for some products; with cultural differences in language, preferences, and so on, a single message may not be as effective. PVI (Princeton Video Imaging) is an innovation that will make regional advertising in diverse cultures easier than it presently is when using cable or satellite television. PVI allows ESPN, which offers this service, to fill visual real estate—blank walls, streets, stadium sidings—with computer-generated visuals that look like they belong in the scene. For instance, if you are watching the "street luge" during ESPN's X-Games, you will see the racers appear to pass a billboard advertising Adidas shoes that really is not there. That billboard can say one thing in Holland and quite another in Cameroon. And if

Given the ubiquitous Guinness advertising in Dublin, it's not surprising that Irish livers need assurance. Ireland is behind only the Czech Republic when it comes to per capita consumption of beer. Actually, Royal Liver Assurance is a British pension/insurance company with offices in Dublin (it was established in the 1850s as the Liverpool Liver Burial Society). "Hurling" is a rather brutal form of field hockey popular in Ireland. The Irish government recognizes the causal effects of advertising on consumption—beer ads are not allowed on radio or TV before sports programs and may not be shown more than once per night on any one channel. See http://www.eurocare.org for more on the consumption of alcohol in Ireland and other European countries.

you are watching in Portland, Oregon, where Adidas might not advertise, you will see the scene as it really appears—without the billboard. These commercials can play in different languages, in different countries, and even under different brand names.

Most satellite technology involves some government regulation. Singapore, Taiwan, and Malaysia prohibit selling satellite dishes, and the Japanese government prevents domestic cable companies from rebroadcasting from foreign satellites. Such restrictions seldom work for long, however. In Taiwan, an estimated 1.5 million dishes are in use, and numerous illicit cable operators are in business. Through one technology or another, Asian households will be open to the same kind of viewing choice Americans have grown accustomed to and the advertising that it brings with it.

Direct Mail.   Direct mail is a viable medium in an increasing number of countries. It is especially important when other media are not available. As is often the case in international marketing, even such a fundamental medium is subject to some odd and novel quirks. For example, in Chile, direct mail is virtually eliminated as an effective medium because the sender pays only part of the mailing fee; the letter carrier must collect additional postage for every item delivered. Obviously, advertisers cannot afford to alienate customers by forcing them to pay for unsolicited advertisements. Despite some limitations with direct mail, many companies have found it a meaningful way to reach their markets. The Reader's Digest Association has used direct mail advertising in Mexico to successfully market its magazines.

In Southeast Asian markets, where print media are scarce, direct mail is considered one of the most effective ways to reach those responsible for making industrial goods purchases, even though accurate mailing lists are a problem in Asia as well as in other parts of the world. In fact, some companies build their own databases for direct mail. Industrial advertisers are heavy mail users and rely on catalogs and sales sheets to generate large volumes of international business. Even in Japan, where media availability is not a problem, direct mail is successfully used by marketers such as Nestlé Japan and Dell Computer. To promote its Buitoni fresh-chilled pasta, Nestlé is using a 12-page color direct mail booklet of recipes, including Japanese-style versions of Italian favorites.

In Russia, the volume of direct mail has gone from just over 150,000 letters per month to over 500,000 per month in one year. Although small by U.S. standards, the response rate to direct mailings is as high as 10 to 20 percent, compared with only 3 to 4 percent or less in the United States. One suggestion as to why it works so well is that Russians are flattered by the attention—needless to say, that will probably change as use of the medium grows.

The Internet.   Although still evolving, the Internet has emerged as a viable medium for advertising and should be included as one of the media in a company's possible media mix. Its use in business-to-business communications and promotion via catalogs and product descriptions is rapidly gaining in popularity.[41] Because a large number of businesses have access to the Internet, the Internet can reach a large portion of the business-to-business market.

Although limited in its penetration of households globally, the Internet is being used by a growing number of companies as an advertising medium for consumer goods. Many consumer goods companies have e-stores, and others use the Internet as an advertising medium to stimulate sales in retail outlets. Waterford Crystal of Ireland set up its Web site specifically to drive store traffic. The aim is to promote its products and attract people into stores that sell Waterford crystal. Sites list and display almost the entire catalog of the Waterford collection, while stores like Bloomingdale's that stock Waterford support the promotional effort by also advertising on their Web sites.

For consumer products, the major limitation of the Internet is coverage (see Exhibit 16.5). In the United States, growing numbers of households have access to a computer, but there are fewer in other countries. However, the growing number of Internet households

---

[41] Oystein Moen, Iver Endresen, and Morten Gavlen, "Use of the Internet in International Marketing: A Case Study of Small Computer Software Firms," *Journal of International Marketing* 11, no. 4 (2003), pp. 129–149.

Exhibit 16.6
Top Ten Web Sites in Three Countries (visitors per month)

	France 24.0 million visitors		Germany 32.1 visitors		Japan 54.1 visitors	
1.	Google.fr	15.4	Google.de	21.5	Yahoo.jp	42.2
2.	MSN.com	12.4	eBay.de	16.9	Rakuten.co.jp	24.9
3.	Orange.fr	12.2	Wikipedia.org	11.5	fc2.com	24.8
4.	Free.fr	12.2	Google.com	10.5	Nifty.com	23.5
5.	PagesJaunes.fr	9.8	MSN.de	10.3	Inforseek.co.jp	22.3
6.	Live.com	9.7	Microsoft.com	9.9	goo.ne.jp	21.5
7.	Hotmail.com	15.3	Web.de	9.8	Microsoft.com	20.2
8.	MSN.co.uk	14.3	Amazon.de	9.7	Google.co.jp	19.9
9.	MSN.fr	8.9	T-Online.de	9.6	BIGLOBE.ne.jp	19.8
10.	eBay.fr	8.6	MSN.com	9.4	Amazon.co.jp	18.7

Source: comScore Media Metrix, *International Herald Tribune*, October 30, 2006, p. 11.

accessible outside the United States generally constitutes a younger, better-educated market segment with higher-than-average incomes. For many companies, this group is an important market niche. Furthermore, this limitation is only temporary as new technology allows access to the Internet via television and as lower prices for personal computers expand the household base. Exhibit 16.6 gives you some idea of the distribution of Web site visitors in three major markets. Notice the American brand names included in the lists: 7 for France, 8 for Germany, and 4 for Japan. You also might notice that most of these examples are local language–dedicated Web sites, such as Google.fr, MSN.de, and Yahoo.co.jp. Interestingly, Germans are looking at both MSN.de and MSN.com. The most visited Web sites in the United States during the same month were Yahoo, Google, MSN, AOL, eBay, Microsoft, Live, MySpace, MapQuest, and Hotmail, in that order.

As the Internet continues to grow and countries begin to assert control over what is now a medium with few restrictions, increasing limitations will be set. Beyond the control of undesirable information, issues such as pay-per-view,[42] taxes, unfair competition, import duties, and privacy are being addressed all over the world. In Australia, local retailers are calling for changes in laws because of the loss of trade to the Internet; under current law, Internet purchases do not carry regular import duties. The Internet industry is lobbying for a global understanding on regulation to avoid a crazy quilt of confusing and contradictory rules.

Another limitation that needs to be addressed soon is the competition for Web surfers. The sheer proliferation of the number of Web sites makes it increasingly difficult for a customer to stumble across a particular page. Search engines have now become crucial directors of Web surfers' attention. Also, serious Internet advertisers or e-marketers will have to be more effective in communicating the existence of their Internet sites via other advertising media. Some companies are coupling their traditional television spots with a Web site; IBM, Swatch watches, AT&T, and Samsung electronics are among those going for a one–two punch of on-air and online presences. Television spots raise brand awareness of a product regionally and promote the company's Web site. In addition, a company can buy ad banners on the Web that will lead enthusiastic consumers to the company's site, which also promotes the product. Some TV networks offer a package deal: a TV spot and ad banners on the network's Web site. For example, the EBN (European Business News) channel offers a cross-media program that includes TV spots and the advertiser's ad banner on the EB Interactive page for $15,000 a quarter.

The online advertising business itself—for example, a banner ad for Amazon.com placed on *The Wall Street Journal* Web site—has come into its own. The industry is now conducting international festivals annually in Cannes, France. In 2005 more than $8 billion

---

[42] Ashutosh Prasad, Vijay Mahajan, and Bart Bronnenberg, "Advertising versus Pay-Per-View in Electronic Media," *International Journal of Research in Marketing* 20, no. 1 (March 2003), pp. 13–30.

was spent worldwide on online ads; continued dramatic growth is forecasted.[43] Of course, the creative possibilities (with global reach, hyperlinks, and such) are endless.

The New Social Media.

Word-of-mouth (WOM) advertising and peer recommendations have always been key influencers of brand choice, but the power of the Internet has changed the pace and reach of WOM. Social media (such as social networking, blogs, virtual worlds, and video sharing) can be powerful marketing tools, but marketers are just beginning to loosen control and let consumers interact with brands on their own terms. Consumer-generated content is having an impact on brands (both positive and negative), and new media are on the agendas of marketers of all products, not just those targeted at young people. Consumers will create content about brands whether the marketers of those brands like it or not. Thus, it is vital that marketers follow, and participate in, the conversations consumers are having online.

The Internet is not delineated by national boundaries. Rather, consumers from many different countries can and do interact online. We are just beginning to understand the potential uses and pitfalls of this medium and the characteristics of its users. One recent study[44] distinguishes between social network uses in the United States and a sample from abroad (that is, an aggregate of 11 countries: Brazil, Canada, China, France, Germany, India, Japan, Mexico, Russia, South Korea, and the United Kingdom). For the purposes of the study, the users consisted of consumers who had visited at least one social networking Web site, such as MySpace, Facebook, Cyworld, and/or Mixi.

More than half the Americans in the sample had watched TV shows or video streams online. In addition, the Americans were significantly more likely to download TV programs, burn or copy a movie or TV show, and download a feature-length film. The Americans also owned significantly more technology than their international counterparts, and both samples owned more technology than those who had never visited a social networking site. More than half of the Americans had used their mobile devices to send or receive SMS (short message service) text and e-mails, browse the Internet for news and information, and receive digital images (See Exhibit 16.7). Although the international users exhibited similar behaviors, their mobile devices were richer with features. For example, international users are significantly more likely to have MP3s on their mobile devices than those in the United States.

Other Media.

Restrictions on traditional media or their availability cause advertisers to call on lesser media to solve particular local-country problems. The cinema is an important medium in many countries, as are billboards and other forms of outside advertising. Billboards are especially useful in countries with high illiteracy rates. Hong Kong is clearly the neon capital of the world, with Tokyo's Ginza and New York's Times Square running close seconds. Indeed, perhaps the most interesting "billboard" was the Pizza Hut logo that appeared on the side of a Russian Proton rocket launched to carry parts of the international space station into orbit. Can extraterrestrials read? Do they like pizza?

In Haiti, sound trucks equipped with powerful loudspeakers provide an effective and widespread advertising medium. Private contractors own the equipment and sell advertising space, much as a radio station would. This medium overcomes the problems of illiteracy, lack of radio and television set ownership, and limited print media circulation. In Ukraine,

---

[43] *Advertising Age Factbook,* February 28, 2005, insert; http://www.medialifemagazine.com, 2005.

[44] "Social Networkers Are Also Heavy Technology Users," *Research Brief from the Center for Media Research,* November 14, 2007, http://www.centerformediaresearch.com.

Exhibit 16.7
Social Networking Goes
Mobile (% of respondents)

Source: Ipsos Insight, November 2007.

	American Users	International Users
Sent/received SMS text	60%	25%
Sent/received e-mail	59	42
Browsed Web for news/information	59	39
Sent/received digital pictures	54	29
Played video games	42	17

procter & gamble experiments with social media

P&G was one of the first companies to have their virtual world headquarters on an island in Second Life, the Web-based virtual world where users interact via avatars. Sergio dos Santos, Global Hair Care—Digital Marketing Manager and Gerry Tseng, Digital Marketing Innovation were involved in P&G's Second Life marketing effort. They explain:

This image was posted within the Second Life world to enroll participants in the Water Fight contest. It was not posted on other Web sites or used to advertise the contest to anyone outside of Second Life.

The corporate team sponsored a contest to find the right brand interested in co-creating a Second Life experiment. An open-invite P&G event was hosted in the form of a 2-hour "Second Life University" event to learn about the medium's capabilities, followed by a call-to-action for interested brands to participate in a contest to win co-sponsorship funding. It received seventy-one event attendees, ten contest entries, four close-scoring finalists, and the selection of one winner: Wella Shockwaves brand in Europe.

Shockwaves, with their tag line of "Style—Attract—Play" targets both young men and women with hair styling products such as gel, spray, mousse, and wax. They tested their hypothesis that branded functionality, which brought their "play" equity to life, would be receptive to and used by avatars. As an extension to their TV campaign, the brand created a virtual waterfight utility that allowed avatars to throw water balloons at each other. As incentive, a 3-wave contest was held to give fans the opportunity to team up and compete to win L$1 million (Linden dollars, the basic currency of Second Life) in each round. Each wave involved points for thrown water balloons and accumulated medallions from scavenger hunts, and allowed some time for Shockwaves to learn and adjust accordingly for the next wave.

While Shockwaves products were only sold in Western and Eastern Europe at the time, P&G found that people from the United States and elsewhere wanted to participate in the "Shockwaves Water Fight" with their avatars. Initially, P&G thought about excluding non-Europeans, but ultimately decided to allow all avatars to participate. While these consumers would be unable to purchase Shockwaves products, the brand elected to study the global nature and behaviors of Second Life.

P&G learned the following from the Second Life execution:

- Second Life is not a reach mechanism: Second Life is a small pond versus today's traditional Internet channels, best suited for experimentation, research, and press release in the areas of community and socialization. If a brand is simply interested in reaching as many eyeballs as possible; perhaps a well-designed flash site with provocative content on an Internet site would better suffice as reach in SL is more difficult to do. Due to today's Second Life learning curve for average users, one can expect avatars there to be generally more creative and competitive, perhaps ideal for a brand looking for co-contributors and creative partners. SL proves to be a thriving world for a specific consumer segment, the "critics" and "creators," who are producers themselves. In the end, match your needs to each platform's focus/strength. Perhaps the use of a more globally recognized brand with increased consumer awareness may have also further driven adoption/trial in this experiment.

- Fun, simple & socialization is more important: While a contest was employed as an incentive to trial, we now hypothesize that fun, simple & socialization are more important to SL avatars than prizes & complexity. Celebrity status of their avatars may also be more important than monetary gain as well. This is also supported by other learning from the development agency's SL experiments to date. We learned that in making the game more complex, we risk lower adoption/trial of the execution as avatars may have been intimidated by the process (i.e., game rules and prize money distribution across countries and winning team avatars, interpretation of traditional contest-required legal guidelines into virtual worlds).

- Community managers and media support are key: The experiment did not receive media support; however, we utilized a community manager from the development agency who brought the contest to life via ongoing communications and in-world activities throughout all 3 waves. Word of Mouth was the primary driver to promote the contest, which would have been enhanced with media support if taken beyond experimental expectations. Word of Mouth works in SL but not as well as traditional Internet mechanisms. Should Second Life be used in a future brand execution for its unique strengths, the use of appropriate media support should compensate and increase its trial.

- Keep experiment budgets low: Keeping the experiment costs low through simple design executions allows ongoing tests in new digital channels with less ROI risk and more learning opportunities. We learned that most of our experiment's cost went to making the game's complex elements but perhaps may have been better saved in creating a fun and simple build for avatars to play with each other. This particular experiment realized more accountability to ROI than learning as it approached spending levels close to other digital tools such as online advertising and sampling.

- Maintain appropriate guidelines and principles: Expect that consumers will find loopholes and plan to embrace/adjust for them. Our experiment's game rule complexity within each wave's contest resulted in unexpected cheating allegations within waves 2 & 3. It was interesting to see how competitively

The Shockwaves products shown are available in 15 European countries: Austria, Belgium, Denmark, Finland, Germany, Greece, Hungary, Netherlands, Norway, Poland, Portugal, Romania, Spain, Sweden, and the United Kingdom. See www.shockwaves.com for more details.

close wave 3 became as we apologized for a discovered loophole in wave 2, held to the principle that we'd stay within our predefined game rules, and encouraged players to be more competitive for wave 3. This loophole could have been better prevented through the use of agency experts proficient in traditional contest rules and regulations. However, for this purpose, the Shockwaves brand authorized its bypass due to our need to learn/experiment the application of traditional rules into virtual worlds. Eliminating the contest component would have also avoided this scenario.

- Passionate consumers may not be vocal outside SL: While we received many messages in-world, not everyone wanted to be heard publicly via our external non-SL blogs as we encouraged them to do. This may have been due to the barrier of having them leave SL to perform an action elsewhere despite our promise to act on it in future potential executions if they did.

- Online conversations assisted in trial: The experiment generated over 400 blog posts around the world, most of them linked or driving traffic to Shockwaves Second Life's Web site, which represented over 104,000 unique visitors in our Web site during the period of the experiment (September through November '07) without having any additional on-line advertising. This "popularity" positioned our Web site into 1st place on Google's results page when searching for "shockwaves water fight."

Source: Gerry Tseng, Digital Marketing Innovation for P&G and Sergio dos Santos, Global Hair Care —Digital Marketing Manager.

Two novel media are shown here: (1) Not only do the Russians sell space for space tourists on their rockets; they also sell advertising space! (2) The Japanese beverage company Suntory promotes its products with "Monitor Man" during a football match at National Stadium. "Monitor Man" puts on an LCD display, showing ads for Pepsi and other products, and walks around the stadium. The job requires some muscle, as the equipment weighs about 15 pounds. All this effort is perhaps purposely reminiscent of the Simpson's "Duff Man." Ohhh yaaaa! *(left: AP/Wide World Photos; right: © Tatsuyuki Tayama/Fujifotos/The Image Works)*

where the postal service is unreliable, businesses have found that the most effective form of direct business-to-business advertising is direct faxing.

In Spain, a new medium includes private cars that are painted with advertisements for products and serve as moving billboards as they travel around. This system, called *Publi-coche* (derived from the words *publicidad*, meaning advertising, and *coche*, meaning car), has 75 cars in Madrid. Car owners are paid $230 a month and must submit their profession and "normal" weekly driving patterns. Advertisers pay a basic cost of $29,000 per car per month and can select the type and color of car they are interested in and which owners are most suited to the campaign, based on their driving patterns.

Campaign Execution and Advertising Agencies
The development of advertising campaigns and their execution are managed by advertising agencies. Just as manufacturing firms have become international, so too have U.S., Japanese, and European advertising agencies expanded internationally to provide sophisticated agency assistance worldwide.[45] Local agencies also have expanded as the demand for advertising services by MNCs has developed. Thus the international marketer has a variety of alternatives available. In most commercially significant countries, an advertiser has the opportunity to employ a local domestic agency, its company-owned agency, or one of the multinational advertising agencies with local branches. There are strengths and weaknesses associated with each. The discussion regarding firm and agency relations in Chapter 8 on pages 238–239 and Exhibit 8.3 are quite pertinent here. Moreover, the agency–company relationships can be complicated and fragile in the international context—Ford and Disneyland Paris recently changed agencies, for example.

A local domestic agency may provide a company with the best cultural interpretation in situations in which local modification is sought, but the level of sophistication can be weak. Moreover, the cross-cultural communication between the foreign client and the local agency can be problematic. However, the local agency may have the best feel for the market, especially if the multinational agency has little experience in the market. Eastern Europe has been a problem for multinational agencies that are not completely attuned to

---

[45] "Advertising, Consumer Republic," *The Economist,* March 19, 2005, pp. 69–70.

Exhibit 16.8
World's Top Ten Advertising Agency Organizations

2006	Agency	Headquarters	Global Revenues 2006	Percent Change from 2005	U.S. Revenues 2006
1	Omnicom Group	New York	$11,377	8.5	$6,194
2	WPP Group	London	10,820	11.1	4,196
3	Interpublic Group	New York	6,274	−1.3	3,441
4	Publicis Groupe	Paris	5,871	7.3	2,677
5	Dentsu	Tokyo	2,951	2.2	47
6	Havas	Suresnes, France	1,841	1.8	687
7	Aegis Group	London	1,826	15.7	489
8	Hakuhodo DY Holdings	Tokyo	1,337	−2.0	0
9	aQuantive	Seattle	442	43.4	352
10	Asatsu-DK	Tokyo	430	−3.3	3

Source: http://www.adage.com, 2008. These rankings have remained relatively stable over the years. However, aQuantive (a specialist in Internet advertising) moved to the top 10 from #44 in 2005, boosted by its 2007 acquisition by Microsoft for $6 billion. Microsoft's motivation is to compete better with rivals Google and Yahoo! in the fast evolving Internet advertising business.[46]

the market. In Hungary, a U.S. baby care company's advertisement of bath soap, showing a woman holding her baby, hardly seemed risqué. But where Westerners saw a young mother, scandalized Hungarians saw an unwed mother. The model was wearing a ring on her left hand; Hungarians wear wedding bands on the right hand. It was obvious to viewers that this woman wearing a ring on her left hand was telling everybody in Hungary she wasn't married. A local agency would not have made such a mistake. Finally, in some emerging markets like Vietnam, local laws require a local advertising partner.

The best compromise is a multinational agency with local branches, because it has the sophistication of a major agency with local representation. Furthermore, a multinational agency with local branches is better able to provide a coordinated worldwide advertising campaign. This ability has become especially important for firms doing business in Europe. With the interest in global or standardized advertising, many agencies have expanded to provide worldwide representation. Many companies with a global orientation employ one, or perhaps two, agencies to represent them worldwide.

Compensation arrangements for advertising agencies throughout the world are based on the U.S. system of 15 percent commissions. However, agency commission patterns throughout the world are not as consistent as they are in the United States; in some countries, agency commissions vary from medium to medium. Companies are moving from the commission system to a reward-by-results system, which details remuneration terms at the outset. If sales rise, the agency should be rewarded accordingly. This method of sharing in the gains or losses of profits generated by the advertising is gaining in popularity and may become the standard. Services provided by advertising agencies also vary greatly, but few foreign agencies offer the full services found in U.S. agencies.

International Control of Advertising: Broader Issues

In a previous section, specific legal restrictions on advertising were presented. Here broader issues related to the past, present, and future of the international regulation of advertising are considered.

Consumer criticisms of advertising are not a phenomenon of the U.S. market only. Consumer concern with the standards and believability of advertising may have spread around the world more swiftly than have many marketing techniques. A study of a representative sample of European consumers indicated that only half of them believed advertisements gave consumers any useful information. Six of ten believed that advertising meant higher prices (if a product is heavily advertised, it often sells for more than brands that are seldom

---

[46] Jessica Mintz, "Microsoft's $6 aQuantive Buyout Gets Green Light from FTC," *Associated Press*, July 6, 2007.

The salesperson is a company's most direct tie to the customer; in the eyes of most customers, the salesperson is the company. As presenter of company offerings and gatherer of customer information, the sales representative is the final link in the culmination of a company's marketing and sales efforts.

Growing global competition, coupled with the dynamic and complex nature of international business, increases both the need and the means for closer ties with both customers and suppliers. Particularly in relationship-based cultures such as China, relationship marketing, built on effective communications between the seller and buyer, focuses on building long-term alliances rather than treating each sale as a one-time event.[1] Advances in information technology are allowing for increasingly higher levels of coordination across advertising, marketing research, and personal selling efforts, yielding new roles and functions in customer relationship management (CRM).[2] Similarly, such advances are changing the nature of personal selling and sales management, leading some to forecast substantial reductions in field sales efforts.

In this ever-changing environment of international business, the tasks of designing, building, training, motivating, and compensating an international sales group generate unique problems at every stage of management and development. This chapter discusses the alternatives and problems of managing sales and marketing personnel in foreign countries. Indeed, these problems are among the most difficult facing international marketers. In one survey of CEOs and other top executives, the respondents identified "establishing sales and distribution networks" and "cultural differences" as major difficulties in international operations.

Designing the Sales Force

The first step in managing a sales force is its design. Based on analyses of current and potential customers, the selling environment, competition, and the firm's resources and capabilities, decisions must be made regarding the numbers, characteristics, and assignments of sales personnel. All these design decisions are made more challenging by the wide variety of pertinent conditions and circumstances in international markets. Moreover, the globalization of markets and customers, as illustrated by the IBM–Ford story in Crossing Borders 17.1, makes the job of international sales manager quite interesting.

As described in previous chapters, distribution strategies will often vary from country to country. Some markets may require a direct sales force, whereas others may not. How customers are approached can differ as well. For example, banks are placing sales representatives in Russian appliance stores to sell credit, a new concept there. The hard sell that may work in some countries can be inappropriate in others. Automobiles have been sold door to door in Japan for years, and only recently have stocks been sold over the Internet in Europe. More than 100,000 of Singapore's 6 million inhabitants are involved in home product sales and other forms of multilevel marketing. The size of accounts certainly makes a difference as well—notice in Crossing Borders 17.1 that an IBM sales representative works inside Ford. Selling high-technology products may allow for the greater use of American expatriates, whereas selling consulting services will tend to require more participation by native sales representatives. Selling in information-oriented cultures such as Germany may also allow for greater use of expatriates. However, relationship-oriented countries such as Japan will require the most complete local knowledge possessed only by natives. Writing about Japan, two international marketing experts agree: "Personal selling as a rule has to be localized for even the most global of corporations and industries."[3]

---

[1] Xueming Luo, David A. Griffith, Sandra S. Liu, and Yi-Zheng Shi, "The Effects of Customer Relationships and Social Capital on Firm Performance: A Chinese Business Approach," *Journal of International Marketing* 12, no. 4 (2004), pp. 25–47.

[2] Linda H. Shi, Shaoming Zou, J. Chris White, Regina C. McNally, and S. Tamer Cavusgil, "Global Account Management Capability: Insights from Leading Suppliers," *Journal of International Marketing* 13, no. 2 (2005), pp. 93–113.

[3] Johny K. Johansson and Ikujiro Nonaka, *Relentless: The Japanese Way of Marketing* (New York: Harper Business, 1997), p. 97.

CROSSING BORDERS 17.1 Sales Force Management and Global Customers

Did IBM really need a major overhaul to its sales compensation plan? For proof, just ask Kevin Tucker. Tucker, an IBM global account manager dedicated to Ford Motor Company, closed a $7 million sale with the automotive giant's European operations. Ford wanted Tucker and his team of IBM representatives to install networking systems in its engineering facilities. The systems would run the applications that design the company's automobiles.

Ford's installation required help from an IBM sales executive in Germany, the project's headquarters. So Tucker, whose office sits in Ford's Dearborn, Michigan, headquarters, sent an e-mail requesting the executive's assistance. And that's when things turned ugly. Although the rep in Germany did not turn his back on the project, his initial reaction was less than enthusiastic. Ford wanted the systems installed throughout Europe, yet the compensation plan for IBM's Germany-based reps rewarded only the systems that were installed in that country. With 80 percent of the work scheduled outside of Germany, the executive was left wondering: Where's the payoff? Tucker and other IBM sales incentive managers wasted three weeks discussing ways to maximize the rep's incentive. Energy that could have been focused on the customer was wasted on a pay plan. "Ford was world-centric, we were country-centric," Tucker says. "The team in Germany was asking, 'Kevin, how can you make us whole?'"

They were not the only salespeople asking that question at IBM. Tucker's predicament represents just one of many problems that were rooted in IBM's "$72 billion" sales incentive plan—a plan that had been obviously put on the back burner as the company giant tinkered with its vision.

Bob Wylie, manager of incentive strategies for IBM Canada, says, "There was the attitude that if it's outside my territory and outside my measurements, I don't get paid for it, and I don't get involved. What's in my pay plan defines what I do." Not the best setup for a company that operates in 165 countries.

Apparently, IBM has solved many of these problems. Ford signed contracts for more than $300 million with IBM to create almost all of the car company's software, including Internet and e-commerce applications in Europe and North America. Details about IBM's global sales compensation program are provided later in this chapter. And IBM continues its impressive sales force coverage in burgeoning new markets like India, where it now employs more than 50,000 professionals who are generating almost $1 billion in revenues.

Sources: Michele Marchetti, "Gamble: IBM Replaced Its Outdated Compensation Plan with a Worldwide Framework. Is It Paying Off?" *Sales & Marketing Management*, July 1996, pp. 65–69; "Ford Motor and IBM," *The Wall Street Journal Europe*, January 13, 1999, p. UK5A; "IBM Aims at $1-b India Revenue by Year-End," *Business Line (The Hindu)*, December 9, 2007.

Once decisions have been made about how many expatriates, local nationals, or third-country nationals a particular market requires, the more intricate aspects of design can be undertaken, such as territory allocation and customer call plans. Many of the most advanced operations research tools developed in the United States can be applied in foreign markets, with appropriate adaptation of inputs, of course. For example, one company has provided tools to help international firms create balanced territories and find optimal locations for sales offices in Canada, Mexico, and Australia.[4] However, the use of such high-tech resource allocation tools requires intricate knowledge of not only geographical details but also appropriate call routines. Many things can differ across cultures—the length of sales cycles, the kinds of customer relationships, and the types of interactions with customers. Indeed, more than one study has identified substantial differences in the importance of referrals in the sales of industrial services in Japan vis-à-vis the United States.[5] The implications are that in Japan, sales calls must be made not only on customers but also on the key people, such as bankers, in the all-important referral networks.

---

[4] See the Web site for The TerrAlign Group, http://www.terralign.com, for more detailed information.

[5] R. Bruce Money, Mary C. Gilly, and John L. Graham, "National Culture and Referral Behavior in the Purchase of Industrial Services in the United States and Japan," *Journal of Marketing* 62, no. 4 (October 1998), pp. 76–87; Chanthika Pornpitakpan, "Trade in Thailand: A Three-Way Cultural Comparison," *Business Horizons*, March–April 2000, pp. 61–70.

Recruiting Marketing and Sales Personnel

The number of marketing management personnel from the home country assigned to foreign countries varies according to the size of the operation, the availability of qualified locals, and other firm characteristics.[6] Increasingly, the number of U.S. home-country nationals (expatriates) assigned to foreign posts is smaller as the pool of trained, experienced locals grows.

The largest personnel requirement abroad for most companies is the sales force, recruited from three sources: expatriates, local nationals, and third-country nationals. A company's staffing pattern may include all three types in any single foreign operation, depending on qualifications, availability, and company needs. Sales and marketing executives can be recruited via the traditional media of advertising (including newspapers, magazines, job fairs, and the Internet), employment agencies or executive search firms,[7] and the all-important personal referrals. The last source will be crucial in many foreign countries, particularly the relationship-oriented ones.

Expatriates

The number of companies relying on expatriate personnel is declining as the volume of world trade increases and as more companies use locals to fill marketing positions. However, when products are highly technical, or when selling requires an extensive background of information and applications, an expatriate sales force remains the best choice. The expatriate salesperson may have the advantages of greater technical training, better knowledge of the company and its product line, and proven dependability. Because they are not locals, expatriates sometimes add to the prestige of the product line in the eyes of foreign customers. And perhaps most important, expatriates usually are able to effectively communicate with and influence headquarters personnel.

The chief disadvantages of an expatriate sales force are the high cost, cultural and legal barriers, and the limited number of high-caliber personnel willing to live abroad for extended periods. Employees are reluctant to go abroad for many reasons: Some find it difficult to uproot families for a two- or three-year assignment, increasing numbers of dual-career couples often require finding suitable jobs for spouses, and many executives believe such assignments impede their subsequent promotions at home. Recall the comments of the executives in the Global Perspective. The loss of visibility at corporate headquarters plus the belief that "out of sight is out of mind" are major reasons for the reluctance to accept a foreign assignment. Companies with well-planned career development programs have the least difficulty. Indeed, the best international companies make it crystal clear that a ticket to top management is an overseas stint. Korn/Ferry International reports in a survey of 75 senior executives from around the world that "international experience" is the attribute identified as second most important for CEOs—experience in marketing and finance positions were first and third, respectively.[8]

Expatriates commit to foreign assignments for varying lengths of time, from a few weeks or months to a lifetime. Some expatriates have one-time assignments (which may last for years), after which they return to the parent company; others are essentially professional expatriates, working abroad in country after country. Still another expatriate assignment is a career-long assignment to a given country or region; this assignment is likely to lead to assimilation of the expatriate into the foreign culture to such an extent that the person may more closely resemble a local than an expatriate. Because expatriate marketing personnel are likely to cost substantially more than locals, a company must be certain of their effectiveness.

More and more American companies are taking advantage of American employees who are fluent in languages other than English. For example, many U.S. citizens speak Spanish as their first language. The large number of Puerto Ricans working for American

---

[6] Rene A. Belderbos and Marielle G. Heijltjes, "The Determinants of Expatriate Staffing by Japanese Multinationals in Asia: Control, Learning, and Vertical Business Groups," *Journal of International Business Studies* 36, no. 3 (2005), pp. 341–54.

[7] The largest international executive search firm is Korn/Ferry International (http://www.kornferry.com).

[8] See "Marketing Is Fastest Route to the Executive Suite," Korn/Ferry International (http://www.kornferry.com).

multinationals in places like Mexico City is well documented. Recent immigrants and their sons and daughters who learn their parents' languages and about their native cultures will continue to be invaluable assets for firms wishing to enter such markets. Certainly ethnic Chinese- and Vietnamese-Americans are serving as cultural bridges for commerce with those two nations. Indeed, throughout history patterns of commerce have always followed paths of immigration.

Virtual Expatriates

The Internet and other advances in communications technologies, along with the growing reluctance of executives to move abroad, are creating a new breed of expatriate, the virtual one. According to a PricewaterhouseCoopers survey of 270 organizations, there has been a substantial increase in shorter-term, commute, and virtual assignments in recent years. Virtual expatriates manage operations in other countries but do not move there.[9] They stay in hotels, make long visits, and maintain their families at home. Some spend up to 75 percent of their working time traveling. None leave home without the ubiquitous laptop and cell phone.

Close contact with subordinates and customers is, of course, tougher for virtual expatriates. Moreover, the travel can be a killer—that is, foreign bugs are often more virulent and easier to catch on long international flights (indeed, one doctor calls airplanes "germ tubes"), crime against expatriates and travelers in foreign cities is a real hazard, traffic and short-hop flights in less developed countries are dangerous,[10] and living in hotels is lonely. However, virtual expatriates' families do not have to be uprooted, and executives can stay in closer touch with the home office. Finally, from the firm's perspective, a virtual assignment may be the only option and often a good way to avoid the extra expenses of an actual executive move.

Local Nationals

The historical preference for expatriate managers and salespeople from the home country is giving way to a preference for local nationals. At the sales level, the picture is clearly biased in favor of the locals because they transcend both cultural[11] and legal barriers. More

---

[9] Nanette Byrnes, "Home Is Where the Airport Is," *BusinessWeek*, August 20–27, 2007, pp. 89–92.

[10] Daniel Michaels, "In Africa, Aviation Woes Defeat a Zealous Watchdog," *The Wall Street Journal*, December 24, 2007, pp. A1, A8.

[11] Dominique Rouzies and Anne Macquin, "An Exploratory Investigation of the Impact of Culture on Sales Force Management Control Systems in Europe," *Journal of Personal Selling & Sales Management* 23, no. 3 (2002), pp. 61–72.

A worker cleans an American Airlines plane detained at San Jose International Airport in California after a nonstop flight from Tokyo in which several passengers complained of symptoms similar to SARS, or severe acute respiratory syndrome. Officials found no threat after isolating passengers and crew for two hours. International travel can be a lot of work! (© David Paul Morris/Getty Images)

knowledgeable about a country's business structure and systems[12] than an expatriate would be, local salespeople are better able to lead a company through the maze of unfamiliar distribution systems and referral networks. Furthermore, pools of qualified foreign personnel available in some places cost less to maintain than a staff of expatriates.

In Europe and Asia, many locals have earned MBA degrees in the United States; thus a firm gets the cultural knowledge of the local meshed with an understanding of U.S. business management systems. Although expatriates' salaries may be no more than those of their national counterparts, the total cost of keeping comparable groups of expatriates in a country can be considerably higher (often three times the expense) because of special cost-of-living benefits, moving expenses, taxes, and other costs associated with keeping an expatriate abroad. As can be seen in Exhibit 17.1, only one of the most expensive cities in the world is in the United States.

The main disadvantage of hiring local nationals is the tendency of headquarters personnel to ignore their advice. Even though most foreign nationals are careful to keep relationships at the home office warm, their influence is often reduced by their limited English communication skills and lack of understanding of how home-office politics influence decision making. Another key disadvantage can be their lack of availability; one CEO of a consulting firm that specializes in recruiting managers in China reports that ten openings exist for every one qualified applicant. Moreover, whereas in the United States hiring experienced salespeople from competitors, suppliers, or vendors is common practice, the same approach in other countries may not work. In places like Japan, employees are much more loyal to their companies and therefore are difficult to lure away even for big money. College recruits can also be hard to hire in Japan because the smartest students are heavily recruited by the largest Japanese firms. Smaller firms and foreign firms are seen in Japan as much more risky employment opportunities.

One other consideration makes recruiting of local nationals as sales representatives more difficult in many foreign countries. We all know about Americans' aversion to being a salesperson. Personal selling is often derided as a career and represented in a negative light in American media—Arthur Miller's *Death of a Salesman* is of course the best example. Despite the bad press, however, personal selling is the most common job in the United States. Indeed, the United States has been described as "a nation of salesmen."[13] But as

---

[12] Anne Macquin, Dominique Rouzies, and Nathalie Prime, "The Influence of Culture on Personal Selling Interactions," *Journal of Euromarketing* 9 (2000), pp. 71–88; Syeda Nazli Wasti and Syeda Arzu Wasti, "Trust in Buyer-Supplier Relations: The Case of the Turkish Automotive Industry," *Journal of International Business Studies*, 39 (2008), pp. 118–31.

[13] See Earl Shorris's excellent and still pertinent book, *A Nation of Salesmen* (New York: Norton, 1994).

Locals hit the road. Japanese salesmen save on expenses in this "capsule hotel" in Osaka. Meanwhile, the Avon Lady calls on a customer in rural Brazil. *(left: © Roger Ressmeyer/Corbis; right: © John Maier, Jr./The Image Works)*

CROSSING BORDERS 17.2   Avon Calling—or Not?

In a gold-mining town near an Amazon tributary, Maria de Fatima Nascimento ambles among mud shacks hawking Honesty and Care Deeply, two beauty products by Avon. She is part of a several-thousand-member Avon army that travels via foot, kayak, riverboat, and small plane through the Amazon Basin. Latin America accounts for 35 percent of Avon's total sales, with Brazil being the firm's number two market after the United States; its success can be attributed to the company's willingness to adapt to local conditions. Cash payments are not required; many Brazilian customers barter for products with fruit, eggs, flour, or wood. Two dozen eggs buys a Bart Simpson roll-on deodorant, and miners pay from 1 to 4 grams of gold powder or nuggets for fragrances like Sweet Crystal Splash. "Ladies of the evening," who regard the cosmetics as a cost of doing business, are some of Nascimento's better customers. But then, so are miners. As one commented, "It's worth 1½ grams of gold to smell nice."

Despite the success of the Bart Simpson roll-on in some parts of the world, Avon is not rolling along in the old-fashioned way in others. In 1998 at least ten people were killed in China during antigovernment rioting in several cities. Many of the rioters were among the country's 200,000 Avon ladies. The Chinese government had banned direct selling, complaining in a directive that such practices spawn "weird cults, triads, superstitious groups, and hooliganism." Worse yet, the authorities criticized meetings of direct marketers that involved singing, chanting, and inspirational sermons. The *People's Daily* once even complained that direct sales encouraged "excessive hugging"!

The latest and perhaps most serious threat to the 2.6 million Avon ladies working worldwide in 135 countries is the Internet. Many fret that Avon.com may replace "Ding dong, it's Avon calling." But, no matter what, Avon's international sales keep rolling along.

Sources: "Avon Calling Near the Amazon," *U.S. News & World Report,* October 25, 1994, pp. 16–17; Andrew Higgins, "Avon Calling? Not in China," *The Guardian*, May 1, 1998, p. 18; Kate Quill, "Ding Dong, Gone . . . Farewell Avon Lady?" *Times* (London), February 7, 2000, p. 7; "Avon Invests in Perfumes and Cosmetics to Grow in Brazil," *Gazeta Mercantil*, March 12, 2008.

negatively as the selling profession is viewed in the United States, in many other countries, it is viewed in even worse ways. Particularly in the more relationship-oriented cultures such as France, Mexico, and Japan, sales representatives tend to be on the bottom rung of the social ladder. Thus recruiting the brightest people to fill sales positions in foreign operations can be very difficult indeed.

Third-Country Nationals

The internationalization of business has created a pool of third-country nationals (TCNs), expatriates from their own countries working for a foreign company in a third country. The TCNs are a group whose nationality has little to do with where they work or for whom. An example would be a German working in Argentina for a U.S. company. Historically, few expatriates or TCNs spent the majority of their careers abroad, but now a truly "global executive" has begun to emerge. The recently appointed chairman of a division of a major

Exhibit 17.1
The World's 20 Most Expensive Cities (in order)

Source: "The World's Most Expensive Cities," *CNNMoney.com* (Mercer), June 19, 2007.

Moscow	Milan
London	St. Petersburg (Russia)
Seoul	Paris
Tokyo	Singapore
Hong Kong	New York City
Copenhagen	Dublin
Geneva	Tel Aviv
Osaka	Rome
Zurich	Vienna
Oslo	Beijing

The cities are listed in order; Moscow is the most expensive and Beijing the least.

Netherlands company is a Norwegian who gained that post after stints in the United States, where he was the U.S. subsidiary's chairman, and in Brazil, where he held the position of general manager. At one time, Burroughs Corporation's Italian subsidiary was run by a French national, the Swiss subsidiary by a Dane, the German subsidiary by an Englishperson, the French subsidiary by a Swiss, the Venezuelan subsidiary by an Argentinean, and the Danish subsidiary by a Dutch person.

American companies often seek TCNs from other English-speaking countries to avoid the double taxation costs of their American managers. Americans working in Spain, for example, must pay both Spanish and U.S. income taxes, and most American firms' compensation packages for expatriates are adjusted accordingly. So, given the same pay and benefits, it is cheaper for an American firm to post a British executive in Spain than an American.

Overall, the development of TCN executives reflects not only a growing internationalization of business but also an acknowledgment that personal skills and motivations are not the exclusive property of one nation. These TCNs often are sought because they speak several languages and know an industry or foreign country well. More and more companies feel that talent should flow to opportunity, regardless of one's home country.

Host-Country Restrictions

The host government's attitudes toward foreign workers often complicate selecting expatriate U.S. nationals over locals. Concerns about foreign corporate domination, local unemployment, and other issues cause some countries to restrict the number of non-nationals allowed to work within the country. Most countries have specific rules limiting work permits for foreigners to positions that cannot be filled by a national. Furthermore, the law often limits such permits to periods just long enough to train a local for a specific position. Such restrictions mean that MNCs have fewer opportunities for sending home-country personnel to management positions abroad.

In earlier years, personnel gained foreign-country experience by being sent to lower management positions to gain the necessary training before eventually assuming top-level foreign assignments. Most countries, including the United States, control the number of foreigners allowed to work or train within their borders. Since September 11, 2001, U.S. immigration authorities have clamped down even harder on the issuance of all kinds of work visas.

Selecting Sales and Marketing Personnel

To select personnel for international marketing positions effectively, management must define precisely what is expected of its people. A formal job description can aid management in expressing long-range as well as current needs. In addition to descriptions for each marketing position, the criteria should include special requirements indigenous to various countries.

People operating in the home country need only the attributes of effective salespersons, whereas a transnational management position can require skills and attitudes that would challenge a diplomat. International personnel requirements and preferences vary considerably.[14] However, some basic requisites leading to effective performance should be considered because effective executives and salespeople, regardless of what foreign country they are operating in, share certain personal characteristics, skills, and orientations.

Maturity is a prime requisite for expatriate and third-country personnel. Managers and sales personnel working abroad typically must work more independently than their domestic counterparts. The company must have confidence in their ability to make

---

[14] Dominique Rouzies, Michael Segalla, and Barton A. Weitz, "Cultural Impact on European Staffing Decisions in Sales Management," *International Journal of Research in Marketing* 20, no. 1 (2003), pp. 67–85.

ethical[15] decisions and commitments without constant recourse to the home office, or they cannot be individually effective.

International personnel require a kind of *emotional stability* not demanded in domestic sales positions.[16] Regardless of location, these people are living in cultures dissimilar to their own; to some extent they are always under scrutiny and always aware that they are official representatives of the company abroad. They need sensitivity to behavioral variations in different countries, but they cannot be so hypersensitive that their behavior is adversely affected.

Managers or salespeople operating in foreign countries need considerable *breadth of knowledge* of many subjects both on and off the job. The ability to speak one or more other languages is always preferable.

The marketer who expects to be effective in the international marketplace needs to have a *positive outlook* on an international assignment. People who do not like what they are doing and where they are doing it stand little chance of success, particularly in a foreign country. Failures usually are the result of overselling the assignment, showing the bright side of the picture, and not warning about the bleak side.

An international salesperson must have a high level of *flexibility*, whether working in a foreign country or at home. Expatriates working in a foreign country must be particularly sensitive to the habits of the market; those working at home for a foreign company must adapt to the requirements and ways of the parent company.

Successful adaptation in international affairs is based on a combination of attitude and effort. A careful study of the customs of the market country should be initiated before the marketer arrives and should be continued as long as facets of the culture are not clear. One useful approach is to listen to the advice of national and foreign businesspeople operating in that country. *Cultural empathy* is clearly a part of the basic orientation, because anyone who is antagonistic or confused about the environment is unlikely to be effective.[17]

Finally, international sales and marketing personnel must be *energetic* and *enjoy travel*. Many international sales representatives spend about two-thirds of their nights in hotel rooms around the world. Going through the long lines of customs and immigration after a 15-hour flight requires a certain kind of stamina not commonly encountered. Some argue that frequent long flights can damage your health. Even the seductive lights of Paris nights fade after the fifth business trip there.

Most of these traits can be assessed during interviews and perhaps during role-playing exercises. Paper-and-pencil ability tests, biographical information, and reference checks are of secondary importance. Indeed, as previously mentioned, in many countries, referrals will be the best way to recruit managers and sales representatives, making reference checks during evaluation and selection processes irrelevant.

There is also evidence that some traits that make for successful sales representatives in the United States may not be important in other countries. One study compared sales representatives in the electronics industries in Japan and the United States. For the American representatives, pay and education were both found to be positively related to performance and job satisfaction. In Japan, they were not. That is, the Americans who cared more about money and were more educated tended to perform better and be more satisfied with their sales jobs. Conversely, the Japanese sales representatives tended to be more satisfied with

[15] Kam-hon Lee, Gong-ming Qian, Julie H. Yu, and Ying Ho, "Trading Favors for Marketing Advantage: Evidence from Hong Kong, China, and the United States," *Journal of International Marketing* 13, no. 1 (2005), pp. 1–35; Sergio Roman and Salvador Ruiz, "Relationship Outcomes of Perceived Ethical Sales Behavior: The Customer's Perspective," *Journal of Business Research* 58, no. 4 (2005), pp. 439–52.

[16] Willem Verbeke and Richard P. Bagozzi, "Exploring the Role of Self- and Customer-Provoked Embarrassment in Personal Selling," *International Journal of Research in Marketing* 20, no. 3 (2003), pp. 233–58.

[17] Don Y. Lee and Philip L. Dawes, "Gaunxi, Trust, and Long-Term Orientation in Chinese Business Markets," *Journal of International Marketing* 13, no. 2 (2005), pp. 28–56.

International sales is hard work. A typical week for this Canadian executive looks like this: Leave Singapore with the flu. Arrive home in Toronto to discover that a frozen pipe has burst. Immediately board a plane for a two-day trip to Chicago. Back to Toronto. On to Detroit, battling jet lag and the flu. Back to Toronto, running through the Detroit airport "like O.J. in the Hertz commercial" and throwing his briefcase into a closing door. Take a brief break in flooded house before boarding another plane to China. Reports waking up in a plane and asking his seatmate where they were landing. Seventeen flights in two weeks left him a bit confused. (© David McIntyre/Stock Photo)

their jobs when their values were consistent with those of their company.[18] The few systematic studies in this genre suggest that selection criteria must be localized, and American management practices must be adapted to foreign markets.

Selection mistakes are costly. When an expatriate assignment does not work out, hundreds of thousands of dollars are wasted in expenses and lost time. Getting the right person to handle the job is also important in the selection of locals to work for foreign companies within their home country. Most developing countries and many European countries have stringent laws protecting workers' rights. These laws are specific as to penalties for the dismissal of employees. Perhaps Venezuela has the most stringent dismissal legislation: With more than three months of service in the same firm, a worker gets severance pay amounting to one month's pay at severance notice plus 15 days' pay for every month of service exceeding eight months plus an additional 15 days' pay for each year employed. Furthermore, after an employee is dismissed, the law requires that person be replaced within 30 days at the same salary. Colombia and Brazil have similar laws that make employee dismissal a high-cost proposition.

Finally, new evidence indicates that a manager's culture affects personnel decisions. In a new line of international sales management research, one study reports "that managers given an identical [personnel selection] problem do not make the same decisions nor do they value the criteria often used in recruitment and promotion decisions equally. For example, they found that Austrian and German managers are more likely to hire compatriots than Italian managers."[19] Thus we are just scratching the surface of a variety of issues in the area of international sales management research.

---

[18] R. Bruce Money and John L. Graham, "Salesperson Performance, Pay, and Job Satisfaction: Tests of a Model Using Data Collected in the U.S. and Japan," *Journal of International Business Studies* 30, no. 1 (1999), pp. 149–72.

[19] Rouzies, Segalla, and Weitz, "Cultural Impact on European Staffing Decisions in Sales Management."

Training for International Marketing

The nature of a training program depends largely on both the home culture of the salesperson[20] and the culture of the business system in the foreign market.[21] Also important is whether expatriate or local personnel will be representing the firm. Training for expatriates focuses on the customs and the special foreign sales problems that will be encountered, whereas local personnel require greater emphasis on the company, its products, technical information, and selling methods. In training either type of personnel, the sales training activity is burdened with problems stemming from long-established behavior and attitudes. Local personnel, for instance, cling to habits continually reinforced by local culture. Nowhere is the problem greater than in China or Russia, where the legacy of the communist tradition lingers. The attitude that whether you work hard or not, you get the same rewards, has to be changed if training is going to stick. Expatriates are also captives of their own habits and patterns. Before any training can be effective, open-minded attitudes must be established.

Continual training may be more important in foreign markets than in domestic ones because of the lack of routine contact with the parent company and its marketing personnel. In addition, training of foreign employees must be tailored to the recipients' ways of

---

[20] Richard P. Bagozzi, Willem Verbeke, and Jacinto C. Gavino Jr., "Culture Moderates the Self-Regulation of Shame and Its Effects on Performance: The Case of Salespersons in the Netherlands and the Philippines," *Journal of Applied Psychology* 88, no. 2 (2003), pp. 219–33.

[21] Sergio Roman and Salvador Ruiz, "A Comparative Analysis of Sales Training in Europe: Implications for International Sales Negotiations," *International Marketing Review* 20, no. 3 (2003), pp. 304–26.

Exhibit 17.2
Personal Selling Tips, from Brussels to Bangkok

The best training programs are much more than just a list of tips. But a quick read of such tips provides a glimpse of the cultural variation facing sales representatives around the globe.

Belgium—Be able to identify the decision makers. In Flanders (Dutch-speaking region) group decisions are common, but in Wallonia (French-speaking region) the highest-level execs have the final say.

China—Expect to continue negotiations after a deal is inked. To Chinese, signing a contract is just the beginning of the business relationship; therefore, they expect both sides to continue working together to fix problems that arise.

Colombia—Business counterparts want to get to know you personally and form a strong friendship with you. Be sure not to change reps in midstream, because often a switch puts an end to negotiations.

Germany—Be prepared with data and empirical evidence that supports your sales proposition. German business-people are unimpressed by flashy advertising and brochures, so keep them serious and detailed, with unexaggerated information.

India—Make sure your schedule remains flexible. Indians are more casual about time and punctuality. Because of India's rigid hierarchy, decisions are made only by the highest-level boss.

Mexico—When planning a meeting, breakfast and lunch are preferable. Take your time and cultivate relationships with business contacts. Those relationships are generally considered more important than professional experience.

Peru—Peruvians relate to individuals and not corporate entities. Establish personal rapport and don't switch your representative in the middle of negotiations.

Russia—Your first meeting will be just a formality. Your Russian counterparts will take this time to judge your credibility, so it's best to be warm and approachable.

Scotland—Scottish people tend to be soft-spoken and private. It takes time to build relationships, but business counterparts seem friendlier after bonds are established. (By the way, Scotch is a drink, not a nationality—it's Scottish.)

South Korea—Status is important. Make sure your business card clearly indicates your title. Don't send a rep to meet with a Korean executive of higher status—it could be viewed as disrespectful.

Thailand—The Thai culture emphasizes nonconflict, so don't make assertive demands when making sales pitches.

Source: *Sales & Marketing Management* publishes these tips regularly in its magazine and on its Web site (www.salesandmarketing.com).

learning and communicating. For example, the Dilbert cartoon characters theme that worked so well in ethics training courses with a company's American employees did not translate well in many of its foreign offices.

One aspect of training is frequently overlooked: Home-office personnel dealing with international marketing operations need training designed to make them responsive to the needs of the foreign operations. The best companies provide home-office personnel with cross-cultural training and send them abroad periodically to increase their awareness of the problems of the foreign operations.

The Internet now makes some kinds of sales training much more efficient. Users can study text onscreen and participate in interactive assessment tests. Sun Microsystems estimates that its use of the Internet can shorten training cycles by as much as 75 percent. And in some parts of the world where telecommunications facilities are more limited, CD-ROM approaches have proven quite successful. Lockheed Martin uses an interactive CD-ROM–based system to train its employees worldwide on the nuances of the Foreign Corrupt Practices Act and associated corporate policies and ethics.

Motivating Sales Personnel

Motivation is especially complicated because the firm is dealing with different cultures, different sources, and different philosophies.[22] Marketing is a business function requiring high motivation regardless of the location of the practitioner. Marketing managers and sales managers typically work hard, travel extensively, and have day-to-day challenges. Selling is hard, competitive work wherever undertaken, and a constant flow of inspiration is needed to keep personnel functioning at an optimal level. National differences must always be considered in motivating the marketing force.[23] In one study, sales representatives in comparable Japanese and American sales organizations were asked to allocate 100 points across an array of potential rewards from work.[24] As shown in Exhibit 17.3, the results were surprisingly similar. The only real difference between the two groups was in social recognition, which, predictably, the Japanese rated as more important. However, the authors of the study concluded that though individual values for rewards may be similar, the social and competitive contexts still require different motivational systems.

---

[22] James P Neelankavil, Anil Mathur, and Yong Zang, "Determinants of Managerial Performance: A Cross-Cultural Comparison of the Perceptions of Middle-Level Managers in Four Countries," *Journal of International Business Studies* 31, no. 1 (2000), pp. 121–40; Evert Van de Vliert, "Thermoclimate, Culture, and Poverty as Country-Level Roots of Workers' Wages," *Journal of International Business Studies* 34, no. 1 (2003), pp. 40–52.

[23] Thomas E. DeCarlo, Raymond C. Rody, and James E. DeCarlo, "A Cross National Example of Supervisory Management Practices in the Sales Force," *Journal of Personal Selling & Sales Management* 19 (1999), pp. 1–14; Ping Ping Fu, Jeff Kennedy, Jasmine Tata, Gary Yukl, Michael Harris Bond, Tai-Kuang Peng, Ekkirala S. Srinivas, John P. Howell, Leonel Prieto, Paul Koopman, Jaap J. Boonstra, Selda Pasa, Marie-Francoise Lacassagne, Hiro Higashide, and Adith Cheosakul, "The Impact of Societal Cultural Values and Individual Social Beliefs on the Perceived Effectiveness of Managerial Influence Strategies: A Meso Approach," *Journal of International Business Studies* 35 (2004), pp. 284–305.

[24] Money and Graham, "Salesperson Performance, Pay, and Job Satisfaction."

Exhibit 17.3
Salespeople's Distribution of 100 Points among Rewards in Terms of Their Importance

Rewards	Relative Importance (mean)	
	Japanese	Americans
Job security	18.5	17.6
Promotion	13.7	14.9
Merit increase in pay	24.7	26.2
Feeling of worthwhile accomplishment	18.5	18.2
Social recognition (sales club awards)	8.1	5.2
Personal growth and development	16.6	17.8

Source: R. Bruce Money and John L. Graham, "Salesperson Performance, Pay, and Job Satisfaction: Tests of a Model Using Data Collected in the U.S. and Japan," *Journal of International Business Studies* 30, no. 1 (1999).

CROSSING BORDERS 17.3   How Important Are Those Meetings?

In Japan, they're really important. A former American sales manager tells this story:

> I worked as general manager of the Japanese subsidiary of an American medical equipment company. Our office was in downtown Tokyo, which made for a two-hour commute for most of our salesmen. Rather than have them come into the office before beginning sales calls every day, I instructed them to go to their appointments directly from home and to come to the office only for a weekly sales meeting. Although this was a common way for a U.S. sales force to operate, it was a disaster in Japan. Sales fell, as did morale. I quickly changed the policy and had everyone come to the office every day. Sales immediately climbed as the salesmen reinforced their group identity.

Now contrast that with how sales representatives are managed at Hewlett-Packard in the United States, as described by one of its sales executives: "We're really looking at this issue of work/family balance. If someone wants to work at home, they can, and we'll outfit their home offices at our expense, provided they have a good reason to want to work at home. If you want to drive productivity, getting people's work lives and home lives in balance is key."

Sam Palmisano, IBM's new CEO, puts it even more strongly: "To win, our players have to be on the field. We can't win the game in the locker room.... We want our people on the field in front of the customers, not in conference rooms talking to their managers or other staff organizations." At IBM, a new corporate policy limits sales meeting to one per week.

Sources: Clyde V. Prestowitz, *Trading Places—How We Are Giving Away Our Future to Japan and How to Reclaim It* (New York: Basic Books, 1989); Geoffrey Brewer et al., "The Top (25 Best Sales Forces in the U.S.)," *Sales & Marketing Management*, November 1, 1996, p. 38; Erin Strout, "Blue Skies Ahead?" *Sales & Marketing Management*, March 1, 2003, pp. 24–26; http://www.ibm.com, 2008.

Because the cultural differences reviewed in this and previous chapters affect the motivational patterns of a sales force, a manager must be extremely sensitive to the personal behavior patterns of employees.[25] Individual incentives that work effectively in the United States can fail completely in other cultures. For example, with Japan's emphasis on paternalism and collectivism and its system of lifetime employment and seniority, motivation through individual incentives does not work well because Japanese employees seem to derive the greatest satisfaction from being comfortable members of a group. Thus an offer of an individual financial reward for outstanding individual effort could be turned down because an employee would prefer not to appear different from peers and possibly attract their resentment. Japanese bonus systems are therefore based on group effort, and individual commission systems are rare. Japanese sales representatives are motivated more by the social pressure of their peers than by the prospect of making more money based on individual effort. Likewise, compensation packages in eastern European countries typically involve a substantially greater emphasis on base pay than in the United States, and performance-based incentives have been found to be less effective. Although some point out that motivational practices are changing even in Japan, such patterns do not change very quickly or without substantial efforts.

Part of the corporate culture (some say peer pressure) that motivates Japanese sales representatives is the morning calisthenics. (© Tom Wagner/Corbis)

Communications are also important in maintaining high levels of motivation; foreign managers need to know that the home office is interested in their operations, and in turn,

---

[25] Eric Fang, Robert W. Palmatier, and Kenneth R. Evans, "Goal-Setting Paradoxes? Trade-Offs between Working Hard and Working Smart: The United States versus China," *Journal of the Academy of Marketing Science* 32 (2004), pp. 188–202.

they want to know what is happening in the parent country. Everyone performs better when well informed. However, differences in languages, culture, and communication styles[26] can make mutual understanding between managers and sales representatives more difficult.

Because promotion and the opportunity to improve status are important motivators, a company needs to make clear the opportunities for growth within the firm. In truly global firms, foreign nationals can aspire to the highest positions in the firm. Likewise, one of the greatest fears of expatriate managers, which can be easily allayed, is that they will be forgotten by the home office. Blending company sales objectives and the personal objectives of the salespeople and other employees is a task worthy of the most skilled manager. The U.S. manager must be constantly aware that many of the techniques used to motivate U.S. personnel and their responses to these techniques are based on the seven basic cultural premises discussed in Chapter 5. Therefore, each method used to motivate a foreigner should be examined for cultural compatibility.

Designing Compensation Systems

For Expatriates   Developing an equitable and functional compensation plan that combines balance, consistent motivation, and flexibility is extremely challenging in international operations. This challenge is especially acute when a company operates in a number of countries, when it has individuals who work in a number of countries, or when the sales force is composed of expatriate and local personnel.[27] Fringe benefits play a major role in many countries. Those working in high-tax countries prefer liberal expense accounts and fringe benefits that are nontaxable instead of direct income subject to high taxes. Fringe-benefit costs are high in Europe, ranging from 35 to 60 percent of salary.

Pay can be a significant factor in making it difficult for a person to be repatriated. Often those returning home realize they have been making considerably more money with a lower cost of living in the overseas market; returning to the home country means a cut in pay and a cut in standard of living. In many countries expats can afford full-time domestic help due to the low wages abroad that they cannot afford back at home.

Conglomerate operations that include domestic and foreign personnel cause the greatest problems in compensation planning.[28] Expatriates tend to compare their compensation with what they would have received at the home office during the same time, and local personnel and expatriate personnel are likely to compare notes on salary. Although any differences in the compensation level may be easily and logically explained, the group receiving the lower amount almost always feels aggrieved and mistreated.

Short-term assignments for expatriates further complicate the compensation issue, particularly when the short-term assignments extend into a longer time. In general, short-term assignments involve payments of overseas premiums (sometimes called separation allowances if the family does not go along), all excess expenses, and allowances for tax differentials. Longer assignments can include home-leave benefits or travel allowances for the spouse. International compensation programs also provide additional payments for hardship locations and special inducements to reluctant personnel to accept overseas employment and to remain in the position.

---

[26] Alma Mintu-Wimsatt and Julie B. Gassenheimer, "The Moderating Effects of Cultural Context in Buyer-Seller Negotiation," *Journal of Personal Selling and Sales Management* 20, no. 1 (Winter 2000), pp. 1–9.

[27] Bronwyn Fryer, "In a World of Pay," *Harvard Business Review*, November 2003, pp. 31–40.

[28] For a still excellent discussion of the problems of constructing a compensation plan for expatriates, nationals, and third-country nationals, see Michael Harvey, "Empirical Evidence of Recurring International Compensation Problems," *Journal of International Business Studies*, 4th Quarter, 1993, pp. 785–99; Chao C. Chen, Jaepil Choi, and Shu-Chen Chi, "Making Sense of Local–Expatriate Compensation Disparity," *Academy of Management Journal* 45, no. 4 (August 2002), pp. 807–17.

Exhibit 17.4
Global Similarity to U.S. Compensation Plans

Countries/Regions		Degree of Plan Similarity with the United States					
		Eligibility	Performance Measures	Weighting	Plan Mechanics	Mix/ Leverage	Payout Frequency
Europe	United Kingdom						
	Scandinavia						
	France						
	Germany						
	Spain/Italy						
Southeast Asia	Hong Kong						
	Korea						
	Taiwan						
	Malaysia						
	Indonesia						
	(Singapore)						
	Australia						
Japan							
Canada							
South America							

▢ Similar   ▢ Varies   ▣ Dissimilar

Data represent multiple client projects conducted by the Alexander Group Inc. for primarily high-technology industry sales organizations.

Source: David G. Schick and David J. Cichelli, "Developing Incentive Compensation Strategies in a Global Sales Environment," *ACA Journal*, Autumn 1996; updated based on interview with David J. Cichelli, Vice President of the Alexander Group, April 2008.

For a Global Sales Force

Compensation plans of American companies vary substantially around the globe, reflecting the economic and cultural differences[29] in the diverse markets served. As reflected in Exhibit 17.4, some experts feel compensation plans in Japan and southern Europe are most different from the standard U.S. approach. Those same experts believe that generally compensation schemes around the world are becoming more similar to the U.S. system with its emphasis on commissions based on individual performance.[30] However, the data in Exhibit 17.4 still reflect the locations of the larger differences.[31]

One company has gone to great lengths to homogenize its worldwide compensation scheme. Beginning in the late 1990s, IBM rolled out what is perhaps the most global approach to compensating a worldwide sales force.[32] The main features of that plan,

---

[29] Nigel F. Piercy, George S. Low, and David W. Cravens, "Consequences of Sales Management's Behavior- and Compensation-Based Control Strategies in Developing Countries," *Journal of International Marketing* 12, no. 3 (2004), pp. 36–57; Marta M. Elvira and Anabella Davila, *Managing Human Resources in Latin America* (London: Routledge, 2005).

[30] David J. Cichelli, *Global Sales Compensation Practices Survey* (Irvine, CA: The Alexander Group, Inc., 2006)

[31] Personal interview with David J. Cichelli, Vice President, Alexander Group, August 2005.

[32] Michele Marchetti, "Gamble: IBM Replaces Its Outdated Compensation Plan with a World Wide Framework. Will It Pay Off?" *Sales & Marketing Management*, July 1996, pp. 65–69. IBM continues to globalize its sales management practices—see Erin Strout, "Blue Skies Ahead? IBM Is Transforming the Way Its Sales Force Does Business," *Sales & Marketing Management*, March 1, 2003, pp. 24–27.

Exhibit 17.5

A Compensation
Blueprint: How IBM Pays
140,000 Sales Executives
Worldwide

Source: Adapted from Michele
Marchetti, "Gamble: IBM Replaces
Its Outdated Compensation Plan
with a World Wide Framework.
Will It Pay Off?" *Sales & Marketing
Management,* July 1996, pp. 65–69.

Total Compensation

Benefits	Plan Components	Payout Frequency	Pay Measurements	Number of Measurements Used to Calculate
Variable Pay →	Corporate Objectives	Annually	**Bonus payment (based on)** • Profit • Customer satisfaction	2
Incentive Compensation →	Teamwork	Monthly	**20% of incentive compensation** • Work team performance • Industry performance	2
	Personal Contribution	Quarterly	**60% of incentive compensation** • Growth • Solutions • Channels/partners • Profit contribution	1–2
	Challenges/ Contests	As earned	**20% of incentive compensation** • National • Local	1–4
Recognition				
Base Salary				

which applies to 140,000 sales executives in 165 countries, are presented in Exhibit 17.5. The plan was developed in response to "global" complaints from sales representatives that the old plan was confusing and did not provide for work done outside one's territory (such as in the scenario presented in Crossing Borders 17.1) and that it therefore did not promote cross-border teamwork. IBM sales incentive managers from North America, Latin America, Asia Pacific, and Europe worked together with consultants on the design for some nine months. At first glance it may appear that IBM is making the cardinal error of trying to force a plan developed centrally onto sales offices literally spread around the world and across diverse cultures; however, the compensation plan still allows substantial latitude for local managers. Compensation managers in each country determine the frequency of incentive payouts and the split between base and incentive pay, while following a global scheme of performance measures. Thus the system allows for a high incentive component in countries like the United States and high base-salary components in countries like Japan.

Perhaps the most valuable information gained during IBM's process of revamping its sales compensation scheme was the following list of the "do's and don'ts" of global compensation:[33]

1. Do involve representatives from key countries.
2. Do allow local managers to decide the mix between base and incentive pay.
3. Do use consistent performance measures (results paid for) and emphasis on each measure.
4. Do allow local countries flexibility in implementations.
5. Do use consistent communication and training themes worldwide.
6. Don't design the plan centrally and dictate to local offices.
7. Don't create a similar framework for jobs with different responsibilities.
8. Don't require consistency on every performance measure within the incentive plan.
9. Don't assume cultural differences can be managed through the incentive plan.
10. Don't proceed without the support of senior sales executives worldwide.

---

[33] Ibid.

Evaluating and Controlling Sales Representatives

Evaluation and control of sales representatives in the United States is a relatively simple task. In many sales jobs, emphasis is placed on individual performance, which can easily be measured by sales revenues generated (often compared with past performance, forecasts, or quotas). In short, a good sales representative produces big numbers. However, in many countries the evaluation problem is more complex, particularly in relationship-oriented cultures, where teamwork is favored over individual effort and closer supervision is expected, and may even be appreciated.[34] Performance measures require closer observation and may include the opinions of customers, peers, and supervisors. Of course, managers of sales forces operating in relationship-oriented cultures may see measures of individual performance as relatively unimportant.

One study comparing American and Japanese sales representatives' performance illustrates such differences.[35] Supervisors' ratings of the representatives on identical performance scales were used in both countries. The distribution of performance of the Japanese was statistically normal—a few high performers, a few low, but most in the middle. The American distribution was different—a few high, most in the middle, but almost no low performers. In the United States, poor performers either quit (because they are not making any money), or they are fired. In Japan the poor performers stay with the company and are seldom fired. Thus sales managers in Japan have a problem their American counterparts do not: how to motivate poor performers. Indeed, sales management textbooks in the United States usually include material on how to deal with "plateaued" salespeople but say little about poor performers because the latter are not a problem.

The primary control tool used by American sales managers is the incentive system. Because of the Internet and fax machines, more and more American sales representatives operate out of offices in their homes and see supervisors infrequently. Organizations have become quite flat and spans of control increasingly broad in recent years. However, in many other countries spans of control can be quite narrow by American standards—even in Australia and particularly in Japan. In the latter country, supervisors spend much more time with fewer subordinates. Corporate culture and frequent interactions with peers and supervisors are the means of motivation and control of sales representatives in relationship-oriented cultures like Japan.

Preparing U.S. Personnel for Foreign Assignments

Estimates of the annual cost of sending and supporting a manager and his or her family in a foreign assignment range from 150 to 400 percent of base salary. The costs in money (some estimates are in the $300,000 to $600,000 range) and morale increase substantially if the expatriate requests a return home before completing the normal tour of duty (a normal stay is two to four years). In addition, if repatriation into domestic operations is not successful and the employee leaves the company, an indeterminately high cost in low morale and loss of experienced personnel results. To reduce these problems, international personnel management has increased planning for expatriate personnel to move abroad, remain abroad, and then return to the home country.[36] The planning process must begin prior to the selection of those who go abroad and extend to their specific assignments after returning home. Selection, training,

---

[34] William A. Weeks, Terry W. Loe, Lawrence B. Chonko, Carlos Ruy Martinez, and Kirk Wakefield, "Cognitive Moral Development and the Impact of Perceived Organizational Ethical Climate on the Search for Sales Force Excellence: A Cross-Cultural Study," *Journal of Personal Selling & Sales Management* 26 (2006), pp. 205–17.

[35] Money and Graham, "Salesperson Performance, Pay, and Job Satisfaction."

[36] Jeffrey P. Shay and Sally A. Baack, "Expatriate Assignment, Adjustment and Effectiveness: An Empirical Examination of the Big Picture," *Journal of International Business Studies* 35, no. 3 (2004), pp. 216–32.

compensation, and career development policies (including repatriation) should reflect the unique problems of managing the expatriate.

Besides the job-related criteria for a specific position,[37] the typical candidate for an international assignment is married, has two school-aged children, is expected to stay overseas three years, and has the potential for promotion into higher management levels. These characteristics of the typical expatriate are the basis of most of the difficulties associated with getting the best qualified personnel to go overseas, keeping them there, and assimilating them on their return.

Overcoming Reluctance to Accept a Foreign Assignment

Concerns for career and family are the most frequently mentioned reasons for a manager to refuse a foreign assignment. The most important career-related reservation is the fear that a two- or three-year absence will adversely affect opportunities for advancement.[38] This "out of sight, out of mind" fear (as exemplified in the opening Global Perspective) is closely linked to the problems of repatriation. Without evidence of advance planning to protect career development, better qualified and ambitious personnel may decline offers to go abroad. However, if candidates for expatriate assignments are picked thoughtfully, returned to the home office at the right moment, and rewarded for good performance with subsequent promotions at home, companies find recruiting of executives for international assignments eased.

Even though the career development question may be adequately answered with proper planning, concern for family may interfere with many accepting an assignment abroad. Initially, most potential candidates are worried about uprooting a family and settling into a strange environment. Questions about the education of the children (especially those with specific needs), isolation from family and friends, proper healthcare, and, in some countries, the potential for violence reflect the misgivings a family faces when relocating to a foreign country. Special compensation packages have been the typical way to deal with this problem. A hardship allowance, allowances to cover special educational requirements that frequently include private schools, housing allowances, and extended all-expense-paid vacations are part of compensation packages designed to overcome family-related problems with an overseas assignment. Ironically, the solution to one problem creates a later problem when that family returns to the United States and must give up those extra compensation benefits used to induce them to accept the position.

Reducing the Rate of Early Returns

Once the employee and family accept the assignment abroad, the next problem is keeping them there for the assigned time. The attrition rate of those selected for overseas positions can be very high, though some studies have suggested it is declining overall. One firm with a hospital management contract experienced an annualized failure rate of 20 percent—not high when compared with the construction contractor who started out in Saudi Arabia with 155 Americans and was down to 65 after only two months.

The most important reasons a growing number of companies are including an evaluation of an employee's family among selection criteria are the high cost of sending an expatriate abroad and increasing evidence that unsuccessful family adjustment[39] is the single most important reason for expatriate dissatisfaction and the resultant request for return home.[40] In fact, a study of personnel directors of over 300 international firms found that the inability of the manager's spouse to adjust to a different physical or

---

[37] Shung J. Shin, Frederick P. Morgeson, and Michael A. Campion, "What You Do Depends on Where You Are: Understanding How Domestic and Expatriate Work Requirements Depend upon the Cultural Context", *Journal of International Business Studies* 38 (2007), pp. 64–83.

[38] Mark C. Bolino, "Expatriate Assignments and Intra-Organizational Career Success: Implications for Individuals and Organizations," *Journal of International Business Studies* 38 (2007), pp. 819–35.

[39] Riki Takeuchi, David P. Lepak, Sophia V. Marinova, and Seokhwa Yun, "Nonlinear Influences of Stressors on General Adjustment: The Case of Japanese Expatriates and Their Spouses," *Journal of International Business Studies* 38 (2007), pp. 928–43.

[40] Greg Hardesty, "Crash Course on Life in Japan," *Orange County Register*, July 20, 2005, pp. 1, 10.

American expatriates flock to stores like this one in Amsterdam. Inside you'll find not only books in English, but also Kraft macaroni and cheese, Bisquick, and other hard-to-find-in-Europe staples of the American diet.

cultural environment was the primary reason for an expatriate's failure to function effectively in a foreign assignment. One researcher estimated that 75 percent of families sent to a foreign post experience adjustment problems with children or have marital discord. One executive suggests that there is so much pressure on the family that if there are any cracks in the marriage and you want to save it, think long and hard about taking a foreign assignment.

Dissatisfaction is caused by the stress and trauma of adjusting to new and often strange cultures. The employee has less trouble adjusting than family members; a company's expatriate moves in a familiar environment even abroad and is often isolated from the cultural differences that create problems for the rest of the family. And about half of American expatriate employees receive cross-cultural training before the trip—much more often than their families do.[41] Family members have far greater daily exposure to the new culture but are often not given assistance in adjusting. New consumption patterns must be learned, from grocery shopping to seeking healthcare services.[42] Family members frequently cannot be employed, and in many cultures, female members of the family face severe social restrictions. In Saudi Arabia, for example, the woman's role is strictly dictated. In one situation, a woman's hemline offended a religious official who, in protest, sprayed black paint on her legs. In short, the greater problems of culture shock befall the family. Certainly any recruiting and selection procedure should include an evaluation of the family's ability to adjust.[43]

Families that have the potential and the personality traits that would enable them to adjust to a different environment may still become dissatisfied with living abroad if they are not properly prepared for the new assignment. More and more companies realize the need for cross-cultural training to prepare families for their new homes. One- or two-day briefings to two- or three-week intensive programs that include all members of the family are provided to assist assimilation into new cultures. Language training, films, discussions, and lectures on cultural differences, potential problems, and stress areas in adjusting to a new way of life are provided to minimize the frustration of the initial cultural shock. This cultural training helps a family anticipate problems and eases adjustment. Once the family is abroad, some companies even provide a local ombudsman (someone experienced in the country) to whom members can take their problems and get immediate assistance. Although the cost of preparing a family for an overseas assignment may appear high, it must be weighed against estimates that the measurable cost of prematurely returned families could cover cross-cultural training for 300 to 500 families. Companies that do not prepare employees and their families for culture shock have the highest incidence of premature return to the United States.

Successful Expatriate Repatriation

A Conference Board study reported that many firms have sophisticated plans for executives going overseas but few have comprehensive programs to deal with the return home. Many have noted that too often repatriated workers are a valuable resource neglected or wasted by inexperienced U.S. management.

---

[41] Visit http://www.natwestoffshore.com for a quick overview of the kinds of services provided by expatriate preparation companies.

[42] Mary C. Gilly, Lisa Peñaloza, and Kenneth M. Kambara, "The Role of Consumption in Expatriate Adjustment and Satisfaction," working paper, Paul Merage School of Business, University of California, Irvine, 2008.

[43] James T. Areddy, "Deep Inside China American Family Struggles to Cope," *The Wall Street Journal*, August 2, 2005, pp. A1, A6.

Low morale and a growing amount of attrition among returning expatriates have many causes. Some complaints and problems are family related, whereas others are career related. The family-related problems generally pertain to financial and lifestyle readjustments. Some expatriates find that in spite of higher compensation programs, their net worths have not increased, and the inflation of intervening years makes it impossible to buy a home comparable to the one they sold on leaving. The hardship compensation programs used to induce the executive to go abroad also create readjustment problems on the return home. Such compensation benefits frequently permitted the family to live at a much higher level abroad than at home (employing yard boys, chauffeurs, domestic help, and so forth). Because most compensation benefits are withdrawn when employees return to the home country, their standard of living decreases, and they must readjust. Unfortunately, little can be done to ameliorate these kinds of problems, short of transferring the managers to other foreign locations. Current thinking suggests that the problem of dissatisfaction with compensation and benefits upon return can be lessened by reducing benefits when overseas. Rather than provide the family abroad with hardship payments, some companies are reducing payments and other benefits[44] on the premise that the assignment abroad is an integral requirement for growth, development, and advancement within the firm.

Family dissatisfaction, which causes stress within the family on returning home, is not as severe a problem as career-related complaints. A returning expatriate's dissatisfaction with the perceived future is usually the reason many resign their positions after returning to the United States. The problem is not unique to U.S. citizens; Japanese companies have similar difficulties with their personnel. The most frequently heard complaint involves the lack of a detailed plan for the expatriate's career when returning home. New home-country assignments are frequently mundane and do not reflect the experience gained or the challenges met during foreign assignment. Some feel their time out of the mainstream of corporate affairs has made them technically obsolete and thus ineffective in competing immediately on return. Finally, there is some loss of status, requiring an ego adjustment when an executive returns home.

Companies with the least amount of returnee attrition differ from those with the highest attrition in one significant way: personal career planning for the expatriate.[45] This planning begins with the decision to send the person abroad. The initial transfer abroad should be made in the context of a long-term company career plan. Under these circumstances, the individual knows not only the importance of the foreign assignment but also when to expect to return and at what level. Near the end of the foreign assignment, the process for repatriation begins. The critical aspect of the return home is to keep the executive completely informed regarding such matters as the proposed return time, new assignment and an indication of whether it is interim or permanent, new responsibilities, and future prospects. In short, returnees should know where they are going and what they will be doing next month and several years ahead.

A report on what MNCs are doing to improve the reentry process suggests five steps:

1. Commit to reassigning expatriates to meaningful positions.

2. Create a mentor program.[46] Mentors are typically senior executives who monitor company activities, keep the expatriate informed on company activities, and act as liaison between the expatriate and various headquarters departments.

3. Offer a written job guarantee stating what the company is obligated to do for the expatriate on return.

---

[44] Katherine Rosman, "Expat Life Gets Less Cushy," *The Wall Street Journal*, October 26, 2007, pp. W1, W10.

[45] Aimin Yan, Guorong Zhu, and Douglas T. Hall, "International Assignments for Career Building," *Academy of Management Review* 27, no. 3 (July 2002), pp. 373–91.

[46] John M. Mezias and Terri A. Scandura, "A Needs-Driven Approach to Expatriate Adjustment and Career Development: A Multiple Mentoring Perspective," *Journal of International Business Studies* 36 (2005), pp. 519–38.

4. Keep the expatriate in touch with headquarters through periodic briefings and headquarters visits.

5. Prepare the expatriate and family for repatriation once a return date is set.[47]

Some believe the importance of preparing the employee and family for culture shock upon return is on a par with preparation for going abroad.

Developing Cultural Awareness

Many businesses focus on the functional skills needed in international marketing, overlooking the importance of cultural intelligence.[48] Just as the idea that "if a product sells well in Dallas, it will sell well in Hong Kong" is risky, so is the idea that "a manager who excels in Dallas will excel in Hong Kong." Most expatriate failures are not caused by lack of management or technical skills but rather by lack of an understanding of cultural differences and their effect on management skills. As the world becomes more interdependent and as companies depend more on foreign earnings, there is a growing need for companies to develop cultural awareness among those posted abroad.

Just as we might remark that someone has learned good social skills (i.e., an ability to remain poised and be in control under all social situations), so too good cultural skills can be developed.[49] These skills serve a similar function in varying cultural situations; they provide the individual with the ability to relate to a different culture even when the individual is unfamiliar with the details of that particular culture. Cultural skills can be learned just as social skills can be learned. People with cultural skills can:

- Communicate respect and convey verbally and nonverbally a positive regard and sincere interest in people and their culture.

- Tolerate ambiguity and cope with cultural differences and the frustration that frequently develops when things are different and circumstances change.

- Display empathy by understanding other people's needs and differences from their point of view.

- Remain nonjudgmental about the behavior of others, particularly with reference to their own value standards.

- Recognize and control the SRC, that is, recognize their own culture and values as an influence on their perceptions, evaluations, and judgment in a situation.

- Laugh things off—a good sense of humor helps when frustration levels rise and things do not work as planned.

The Changing Profile of the Global Manager

Until recently the road to the top was well marked. Surveys of chief executives consistently reported that more than three-quarters had finance, manufacturing, or marketing backgrounds. As the post–World War II

---

[47] Mila B. Lazarova and Jean-Luc Cerdin, "Revisiting Repatriation Concerns: Organizational Support versus Career and Contextual Influences," *Journal of International Business Studies* 38 (2007), pp. 404–29.

[48] This is a topic of much current discussion; see P. Christopher Earley and Elaine Mosakowski, "Cultural Intelligence," *Harvard Business Review*, October 2004, pp. 139–46; James P. Johnson, Tomasz Lenartowicz, and Salvador Apud, "Cross-Cultural Competence in International Business: Toward a Definition and Model," *Journal of International Business Studies* 37 (2006), pp. 231–58; Orly Levy, Schon Beechler, Sully Taylor, and Nakiye A. Boyacigiller, "What We Talk about When We Talk about 'Global Mindset': Managerial Cognition in Multinational Corporations," *Journal of International Business Studies* 38 (2007), pp. 231–58; William Neburry, Liuba Y. Belkin, and Paradis Ansari, "Perceived Career Opportunities from Globalization: Globalization Capabilities and Attitudes toward Women in Iran and the U.S.," *Journal of International Business Studies* 39 (2008), http://www.jibs.net.

[49] Jon M. Shapiro, Julie L. Ozanne, and Bige Saatcioglu, "An Interpretive Examination of the Development of Cultural Sensitivity in International Business," *Journal of International Business Studies* 39 (2008), pp. 71–87.

period of growing markets and domestic-only competition fades, however, so too does the narrow one-company, one-industry chief executive. In the new millennium, increasing international competition, the globalization of companies, technology, demographic shifts, and the speed of overall change will govern the choice of company leaders. It will be difficult for a single-discipline individual to reach the top in the future.[50]

The executive recently picked to head Procter & Gamble's U.S. operations is a good example of the effect globalization is having on businesses and the importance of experience, whether in Japan, Europe, or elsewhere. The head of all P&G's U.S. business was born in the Netherlands, received an MBA[51] from Rotterdam's Eramus University, then rose through P&G's marketing ranks in Holland, the United States, and Austria. After proving his mettle in Japan, he moved to P&G's Cincinnati, Ohio, headquarters to direct its push into East Asia, and then to his new position. Speculation suggests that if he succeeds in the United States, as he did in Japan, he will be a major contender for the top position at P&G.

Fewer companies today limit their search for senior-level executive talent to their home countries. Coca-Cola's former CEO, who began his ascent to the top in his native Cuba, and the former IBM vice chairman, a Swiss national who rose through the ranks in Europe, are two prominent examples of individuals who rose to the top of firms outside their home countries.

Some companies, such as Colgate-Palmolive, believe that it is important to have international assignments early in a person's career, and international training is an integral part of its entry-level development programs. Colgate recruits its future managers from the world's best colleges and business schools. Acceptance is highly competitive, and successful applicants have a BA or MBA with proven leadership skills, fluency in at least one language besides English, and some experience living abroad. A typical recruit might be a U.S. citizen who has spent a year studying in another country or a national of another country who was educated in the United States.[52]

Trainees begin their careers in a two-year, entry-level, total-immersion program that consists of stints in various Colgate departments. A typical rotation includes time in the finance, manufacturing, and marketing departments and an in-depth exposure to the company's marketing system. During that phase, trainees are rotated through the firm's ad agency, marketing research, and product management departments and then work seven months as field salespeople. At least once during the two years, trainees accompany their mentors on business trips to a foreign subsidiary. The company's goal is to develop in their trainees the skills they need to become effective marketing managers, domestically or globally.

On the completion of the program, trainees can expect a foreign posting, either immediately after graduation or soon after an assignment in the United States. The first positions are not in London or Paris, as many might hope, but in developing countries such as Brazil, the Philippines, or maybe Zambia. Because international sales are so important to Colgate (60 percent of its total revenues are generated abroad), a manager might not return to the United States after the first foreign assignment but rather move from one overseas post to another, developing into a career internationalist, which could open to a CEO position.

Companies whose foreign receipts make up a substantial portion of their earnings and that see themselves as global companies rather than as domestic companies doing business in foreign markets are the most active in making the foreign experience an integrated part of a successful corporate career. Indeed for many companies, a key threshold seems to be

[50] Erin White, "Future CEOs May Need to Have Broad Liberal-Arts Foundation," *The Wall Street Journal*, April 12, 2005, p. B4.

[51] Laurie Goering, "Foreign Business Schools Fill a Huge Gap," *Los Angeles Times*, January 14, 2008, p. C4.

[52] Mary Beth Marklein, "Report: USA Sees First Increase in Foreign Students Since 9/11," *USA Today*, November 12, 2007, p. 6D.

CROSSING BORDERS 17.4 — A Look into the Future: Tomorrow's International Leaders? An Education for the 21st Century

A school supported by the European Union teaches Britons, French, Germans, Dutch, and others to be future Europeans. The European School in a suburb of Brussels has students from 12 nations who come to be educated for life and work, not as products of motherland or fatherland but as Europeans. The European Union runs 10 European Schools in western Europe, enrolling 17,000 students from kindergarten to twelfth grade. Graduates emerge superbly educated, usually trilingual, and very, very European.

The schools are a linguistic and cultural melange. Native speakers of 36 different languages are represented in one school alone. Each year students take fewer and fewer classes in their native tongue. Early on, usually in first grade, they begin a second language, known as the "working language," which must be English, French, or German. A third language is introduced in the seventh year, and a fourth may be started in the ninth.

By the time students reach their eleventh year, they are taking history, geography, economics, advanced math, music, art, and gym in the working language. When the students are in groups talking, they are constantly switching languages to "whatever works."

Besides language, students learn history, politics, literature, and music from the perspective of all the European countries—in short, European cultures. The curriculum is designed to teach the French, German, Briton, and those of other nationalities to be future Europeans.

This same approach is being taken at the MBA level as well. The well-respected European School of Management has campuses in several cities—Berlin, Paris, Oxford, and Madrid. Students spend part of their time at each of the campuses. American MBA programs are beginning to imitate such programs. The University of Chicago School of Business now has campuses in Barcelona, and Singapore. The Fuqua School at Duke offers a unique executive MBA program involving travel to several foreign countries and a substantial percentage of teaching delivered interactively over the Internet. This last program attracts students from all over the world who are willing to pay a six-figure tuition.

Sources: Glynn Mapes, "Polyglot Students Are Weaned Early Off Mother Tongue," *The Wall Street Journal*, March 6, 1990, p. A1. Reprinted by permission of *The Wall Street Journal*, © 1990 Dow Jones & Company, Inc. All Rights Reserved Worldwide. See also Kevin Cape, "Tips on Choosing the Right One, International Schools," *International Herald Tribune*, January 25, 2003, p. 7; http://www.fuqua.duke.edu/mba/executive/global/, 2008.

that when overseas revenues surpass domestic revenues, then the best people in the company want to work on international accounts. Such a global orientation then begins to permeate the entire organization—from personnel policies to marketing and business strategies. This shift was the case with Gillette, which in the 1990s made a significant recruitment and management-development decision when it decided to develop managers internally. Gillette's international human resources department implemented its international-trainee program, designed to supply a steady stream of managerial talent from within its own ranks. Trainees are recruited from all over the world, and when their training is complete, they return to their home countries to become part of Gillette's global management team.

Foreign-Language Skills

Opinions are mixed on the importance of a second language for a career in international business. There are those whose attitude about another language is summed up in the statement that "the language of international business is English." Indeed, one journalist quipped, "Modern English is the Wal-Mart of languages: convenient, huge, hard to avoid, superficially friendly, and devouring all rivals in its eagerness to expand."[53] Others feel that even if you speak one or two languages, you may not be needed in a country whose language you speak. So, is language important or not?

---

[53] Mark Abley, journalist.

Proponents of language skills argue that learning a language improves cultural understanding and business relationships.[54] Others point out that to be taken seriously in the business community, the expatriate must be at least conversational in the host language. Particularly when it comes to selling in foreign countries, languages are important. Says a Dutch sales training expert, "People expect to buy from sales reps they can relate to, and who understand their language and culture. They're often cold towards Americans trying to sell them products."

Some recruiters want candidates who speak at least one foreign language, even if the language will not be needed in a particular job. Having learned a second language is a strong signal to the recruiter that the candidate is willing to get involved in someone else's culture.

Although most companies offer short, intensive language-training courses for managers being sent abroad, many are making stronger efforts to recruit people who are bilingual or multilingual. According to the director of personnel at Coca-Cola, when his department searches its database for people to fill overseas posts, the first choice is often someone who speaks more than one language.

We the authors feel strongly that language skills are of great importance; if you want to be a major player in international business in the future, learn to speak other languages, or you might not make it—your competition will be those European students described in Crossing Borders 17.4. A joke that foreigners tell about language skills goes something like this: What do you call a person who speaks three or more languages? Multilingual. What do you call a person who speaks two languages? Bilingual. What do you call a person who speaks only one language? An American! Maybe the rest of the world knows something we don't.

---

[54] Kathyrn Kranhold, Dan Bilefsky, Matthew Karnitschnig, and Ginny Parker, "Lost in Translation?" *The Wall Street Journal*, May 18, 2004, pp. B1, B6; "Know Thine Enemy," *The Economist*, May 7, 2005, p. 28; Ellen Gamerman, "Just One Word: (That's Chinese for 'Plastics')," *The Wall Street Journal*, March 17–18, 2007, pp. P1, P5.

Summary

An effective international sales force constitutes one of the international marketer's greatest concerns. The company's sales force represents the major alternative method of organizing a company for foreign distribution and, as such, is on the front line of a marketing organization.

The role of marketers in both domestic and foreign markets is rapidly changing, along with the composition of international managerial and sales forces. Such forces have many unique requirements that are being filled by expatriates, locals, third-country nationals, or a combination of the three. In recent years, the pattern of develop-

ment has been to place more emphasis on local personnel operating in their own lands. This emphasis, in turn, has highlighted the importance of adapting U.S. managerial techniques to local needs.

The development of an effective marketing organization calls for careful recruiting, selecting, training, motivating, and compensating of expatriate personnel and their families to ensure the maximization of a company's return on its personnel expenditures. The most practical method of maintaining an efficient international sales and marketing force is careful, concerted planning at all stages of career development.

Questions

1. Define the following terms:

   relationship marketing   TCN
   expatriate   repatriation
   local nationals   separation allowance

2. Why may it be difficult to adhere to set job criteria in selecting foreign personnel? What compensating actions might be necessary?

3. Why does a global sales force cause special compensation problems? Suggest some alternative solutions.

4. Under which circumstances should expatriate salespeople be utilized?

5. Discuss the problems that might be encountered in having an expatriate sales manager supervising foreign salespeople.

6. "To some extent, the exigencies of the personnel situation will dictate the approach to the overseas sales organization." Discuss.

7. How do legal factors affect international sales management?

8. How does the sales force relate to company organization? To channels of distribution?

9. "It is costly to maintain an international sales force." Comment.

10. Adaptability and maturity are traits needed by all salespeople. Why should they be singled out as especially important for international salespeople?

11. Can a person develop good cultural skills? Discuss.

12. Describe the attributes of a person with good cultural skills.

13. Interview a local company that has a foreign sales operation. Draw an organizational chart for the sales function and explain why that particular structure was used by that company.

14. Evaluate the three major sources of multinational personnel.

15. Which factors complicate the task of motivating the foreign sales force?

16. Why do companies include an evaluation of an employee's family among selection criteria for an expatriate assignment?

17. "Concerns for career and family are the most frequently mentioned reasons for a manager to refuse a foreign assignment." Why?

18. Discuss and give examples of why returning U.S. expatriates are often dissatisfied. How can these problems be overcome?

19. If "the language of international business is English," why is it important to develop a skill in a foreign language? Discuss.

20. The global manager of 2020 will have to meet many new challenges. Draw up a sample résumé for someone who could be considered for a top-level executive position in a global firm.

18

pricing for international markets

CHAPTER OUTLINE

CHAPTER LEARNING OBJECTIVES

What you should learn from Chapter 18:

- Components of pricing as competitive tools in international marketing

- The pricing pitfalls directly related to international marketing

- How to control pricing in parallel import or gray markets

- Price escalation and how to minimize its effect

- Countertrading and its place in international marketing practices

- The mechanics of price quotations

Global Perspective

THE PRICE WAR

The battle between Procter & Gamble and Kimberly-Clark is bringing Pampers and Huggies, respectively, to places they have never been, forcing down diaper prices worldwide, and expanding the global market for disposable diapers. A battle in Brazil between the two giants gives an interesting glimpse of the global markets of tomorrow. Disposable diapers are still considered a luxury by the vast majority of Brazil's 160 million people, whose average annual income is under $4,000. Before P&G and Kimberly arrived, rich and poor alike generally made do with cloth or nothing at all. The disposables that were available were expensive, bulky, and leaky.

When less than 5 percent of the Brazilian mass market used disposable diapers, P&G launched Pampers Uni, a no-frills, unisex diaper. Before Uni, it cost more to pay for disposable diapers than to pay for a maid to wash the cloth ones. The introduction of the relatively cheap, high-quality Uni fundamentally changed the economics of the diaper market for most middle-class Brazilians.

The plan was to put such nonessentials as disposable diapers within the reach of millions of Brazilians for the first time. At the same time, the Brazilian economy was on the upswing—inflation had subsided, and overnight, the purchasing power of the poor increased by 20 percent. Low-priced products flew off the shelves. P&G had to truck in diapers from Argentina as it struggled to open new production lines.

But the good days did not last. Kimberly-Clark entered the market and began importing Huggies from Argentina. With the help of a Unilever unit as its Brazilian distributor, Kimberly-Clark gained immediate distribution across the country and quickly made deep inroads into the market. Unilever agreed to work with Kimberly-Clark because its archrival in soap was P&G, and Kimberly-Clark's archrival in diapers was P&G. The two companies previously had entered into a global alliance to look for win–win situations when it was in both their best interests to partner and help each other, from a competitive standpoint, against the dominant P&G. The Brazilian market was the perfect case for cooperation.

With Unilever's help, Kimberly-Clark "push girls" invaded markets to demonstrate the diaper's absorption. Sales rose rapidly and began to exceed production. To gain more product, Kimberly-Clark formed an alliance with Kenko do Brazil, P&G's largest home-grown rival, and created the "Monica" brand. "Monica's Gang," a comic strip similar to "Peanuts" in the United States, sells four million copies monthly. São Paulo malls were crowded with thousands of kids waiting to get an Easter photo taken with actors in Monica suits, an

honor that required the purchase of three packs of diapers. Monica diapers were a big hit, and Kimberly-Clark became number one in the Brazilian market.

It was a tough blow to P&G. The company had devoted an entire page of its annual report to how Pampers Uni had tripled its market share in Brazil, helping P&G "retain the number one position in a market that has grown fivefold." Now it suddenly found itself on the defensive. First it cut prices, a step P&G loathes. "Price cutting is like violence: No one wins," says the head of its Brazilian operation. Then it broadened its product range, rolling out an up-market diaper called Super-Seca, priced 25 percent higher than Pampers Uni. Later, in a flanking move, it also unveiled Confort-Seca, a bikini-style diaper originally developed for Thailand and priced 10 to 15 percent lower than the already-inexpensive Uni.

Kimberly-Clark fired back, matching the price cut and then introducing a cheaper version of Monica called Tippy Basic. Four weeks later, P&G cut prices another 10 percent on Super-Seca and Confort-Seca. Despite the price cuts, the two brands were still relatively expensive; then a wave of really cheap diapers arrived. Carrefour, a French retailer that is now Brazil's biggest supermarket chain, sells crudely made Bye-Bye Pipi diapers from Mexico. Despite their inferior quality, the cheap imports pulled down diaper prices across the board.

The real war started when lower prices became so attractive that consumers who otherwise could not afford diapers came into the market. As prices continued to drop, the market grew; that attracted more producers, which were mostly small, local Brazilian companies that offered even lower priced competitive diapers. One such company, Mili, saw its market share increase from 4.8 percent to 16.2 percent over a three-year period. What accounts for growth of these smaller companies? One analyst suggests that the multinationals are too sophisticated and, thus, too expensive for the Brazilian market: "Smaller companies are just supplying what consumers need at a price they can afford." But it also can be said that as prices drop, products become more attractive to a larger segment of the total market.

Sources: Raju Narisetti and Jonathan Friedland, "Disposable Income: Diaper Wars of P&G and Kimberly-Clark Now Heat Up in Brazil," *The Wall Street Journal,* June 4, 1997, p. A1; "Brazil: Procter & Gamble Increased Market Share," *SABI* (South American Business Information), May 31, 2000; Jonathan Birchall, "New Tactics in the Battle for Babies' Bottoms," *Financial Times* (http://www.FT.com), August 24, 2006. For more information, see Kimberly-Clark's Web site at http://www.kimberly-clark.com and Procter & Gamble's at http://www.pg.com.

Prices both evaluate and communicate in international markets.[1] For example, initially Hong Kong Disneyland's early attendance was lower than expected, in part driven by what some called an unaffordable opening-day price of $32 a ticket.[2] Setting the right price for a product or service can be the key to success or failure. Even when the international marketer produces the right product, promotes it correctly, and initiates the proper channel of distribution, the effort fails if the product is not properly priced. Although the quality of U.S. products is widely recognized in global markets, foreign buyers, like domestic buyers, balance quality and price in their purchase decisions. An offering's price must reflect the quality and value the consumer perceives in the product. Of all the tasks facing the international marketer, determining what price to charge is one of the most difficult. It is further complicated when the company sells its product to customers in multiple country's markets.

As globalization continues, competition intensifies among multinational and home-based companies. All are seeking a solid competitive position so they can prosper as markets reach full potential. The competition for the diaper market among Kimberly-Clark, P&G, and the smaller companies illustrates how price becomes increasingly important as a competitive tool and how price competition changes the structure of a market. Whether exporting or managing overseas operations, the manager's responsibility is to set and control the actual price of goods in multiple markets in which different sets of variables are to be found: different tariffs, costs, attitudes, competition, currency fluctuations, and methods of price quotation.

This chapter focuses on the basic pricing policy questions that arise from the special cost, market, and competitive factors found in foreign markets. A discussion of price escalation and its control and factors associated with price setting and leasing is followed by a discussion of the use of countertrade as a pricing tool and a review of the mechanics of international price quotation.

Pricing Policy

Active marketing in several countries compounds the number of pricing problems and variables relating to price policy. Unless a firm has a clearly thought-out, explicitly defined price policy, expediency rather than design establishes prices. The country in which business is being conducted, the type of product, variations in competitive conditions, and other strategic factors affect pricing activity. Price and terms of sale cannot be based on domestic criteria alone.

Pricing Objectives

In general, price decisions are viewed two ways: pricing as an active instrument of accomplishing marketing objectives, or pricing as a static element in a business decision. If prices are viewed as an active instrument, the company *sets* prices (rather than *following* market prices)[3] to achieve a specific objectives, whether targeted returns on profit, targeted market shares, or some other specific goals.[4] The company that follows the second approach, pricing as a static element, probably exports only excess inventory, places a low priority on foreign business, and views its export sales as passive contributions to sales volume. When U.S. and Canadian international businesses were asked to rate, on a scale of 1 to 5, several factors important in price setting, total profits received an average rating of 4.7, followed by return on investment (4.41), market share (4.13), and total sales volume (4.06). Liquidity ranked the lowest (2.19).

The more control a company has over the final selling price of a product, the better it is able to achieve its marketing goals. However, controlling end prices is not always possible. The broader the product line and the larger the number of countries involved, the more complex the process of controlling prices to the end user.[5]

[1] Lorraine Eden and Peter Rodriguez, "How Weak Are the Signals? International Price Indices and Multinational Enterprises," *Journal of International Business Studies* 36, no. 1 (2004), pp. 61–74.

[2] Don Lee, "Disneyland's Cost a Hurdle for Chinese," *Los Angeles Times*, September 10, 2005, pp. C1, C3.

[3] Carl Arthur Solberg, Barbara Stottinger, and Attila Yaprak, "A Taxonomy of the Pricing Practices of Exporting Firms: Evidence from Austria, Norway, and the United States," *Journal of International Marketing* 14 (2006), pp. 23–48.

[4] S. Tamer Cavusgil, Kwog Chan, and Chun Zhang, "Strategic Orientations in Export Pricing: A Clustering Approach to Create Firm Taxonomies," *Journal of International Marketing* 11, no. 1 (2003), p. 47.

[5] Matthew B. Meyers and Michael Harvey, "The Value of Pricing Control in Export Channels: A Governance Perspective," *Journal of International Marketing* 9, no. 4 (2001), p. 1.

CROSSING BORDERS 18.1   Inside the iPhone Gray Market

You could buy one (indeed, more than one) in Beijing even though they had not yet been shipped there by Apple or AT&T. The gray market for iPhones in China was bustling. Apparently 800,000 to 1 million iPhones, or about one-fourth of the total sold, were "unlocked"—that is, altered to be able to run on networks other than those of Apple's exclusive partners.

This iPhone aftermarket did not take long to develop. By the time the device went on sale on June 29, 2007, software hackers and companies that specialize in unlocking cell phones had already begun searching for ways to make the iPhone work on unsanctioned networks. Within weeks, online forums were buzzing with an answer that emanated from a tiny company based in Prague, Czech Republic.

Pavel Zaboj is a 36-year-old former math student who, together with friends, developed an electronic device called Turbo SIM that was designed to turn cell phones into mobile payment systems. Turns out, Turbo SIM also could be used to trick the iPhone into thinking it was operating on AT&T's network. By mid-August, Zaboj's 10-person firm, Bladox, was flooded with orders, particularly from Canada and Mexico, where Apple addicts did not have to venture far to get an iPhone. Bladox was totally unprepared and could not fill all the orders that rolled in. "We just sat there, open-mouthed," Zaboj says.

Bladox has sold devices used to unlock phones in roughly 100 countries, including French Polynesia and Afghanistan, Brazil, Canada, the Dominican Republic, Indonesia, Israel, Nigeria, Peru, Poland, Russia, and the United Arab Emirates.

The boom was fueled not just by the short supply of a hot product but also by scant evidence of interference from Apple or its partners. Apple-authorized partners—AT&T, O2, Orange, and Deutsche Telekom's T-Mobile—lost hundreds of dollars in monthly fees when subscribers avoided a two-year contract in favor of unlocking. But the bulk of the unlocking seems to have been occurring in places where customers had no authorized carrier to choose from anyway.

Apple took in hundreds of dollars per iPhone sale when customers activated service with one of its partners, but most analysts say the unlocking craze also helps spread Apple's brand awareness.

The gray market got another push forward from exchange rates. With the dollar falling, consumers from Europe and elsewhere could get a better deal on an iPhone during a trip to the United States than from buying it at home. Gray marketers saw the same opportunity and began recruiting a range of people to secure iPhones.

Sometimes, it is as simple as asking friends and family members to reach their iPhone limit: five phones at Apple and three at AT&T. One reseller admits he got a friend to print business cards and pose as a small business owner to dupe an Apple Store manager into letting him buy 100 iPhones for his "employees." Chinese retailers also admitted to "getting people like airline stewardesses to bring the iPhones over for us."

Some iPhones on the gray market may have leaked from points closer to the source: the big Chinese factories where they are assembled. One distributor says he believes his China-based source gets iPhones from factory workers.

Sources: Peter Burrows, "Inside the iPhone Gray Market," *BusinessWeek*, February 12, 2008; John Markoff, "Friends and Smugglers Meet Demand for iPhones," *The New York Times*, February 18, 2008, pp. A1, A8.

Parallel Imports   In addition to having to meet price competition country by country and product by product, companies have to guard against competition with their own subsidiaries or branches. Because of the different prices possible in different country markets, a product sold in one country may be exported to another and undercut the prices charged in that country. For example, to meet economic conditions and local competition, an American pharmaceutical company might sell its drugs in a developing country at a low price and then discover that these discounted drugs are being exported to a third country, where, as parallel imports, they are in direct competition with the same product sold for higher prices by the same firm. This practice is lucrative when wide margins exist between prices for the same products in different countries. A variety of conditions can create a profitable opportunity for a parallel market.

Restrictions brought about by import quotas and high tariffs also can lead to parallel imports and make illegal imports attractive. India has a three-tier duty structure on computer parts ranging from 50 to 80 percent on imports. As a result, estimates indicate that as much as 35 percent of India's domestic computer hardware sales are accounted for by the gray market.

The possibility of a parallel market occurs whenever price differences are greater than the cost of transportation between two markets. In Europe, because of different taxes and competitive price structures, prices for the same product vary between countries. When this situation occurs, it is not unusual for companies to find themselves competing in one country with their own products imported from another European country at lower prices. Pharmaceutical companies face this problem in Italy, Greece, and Spain because of price caps imposed on prescription drugs in those countries. For example, the ulcer drug Losec sells for only $18 in Spain but goes for $39 in Germany. The heart drug Plavix costs $55 in France and sells for $79 in London. Presumably such price differentials would cease once all restrictions to trade were eliminated in the European Union, and in most cases, this is true. However, the European Union does not prevent countries from controlling drug prices as part of their national health plans.

The drug industry has tried to stop parallel trade in Europe but has been overruled by European authorities. This time the industry is trying a different approach, restricting supplies to meet only local demand according to formulas based on prior demand and anticipated growth. The idea is that a country should receive just enough of a drug for its citizens. Wholesalers that order more with the intention of shipping the drugs to higher-priced markets will not have enough to do so. A number of major pharmaceutical companies have imposed similar restrictions. The companies say these measures are intended to streamline distribution, help prevent medicine shortages, and curtail excess inventory, whereas distributors claim the strategy is aimed at thwarting cross-border drug trading. The fact is, "half of all demand in Britain of several products is being met by imports from low-priced countries" and companies are attempting to curtail parallel imports.

Gray market pharmaceuticals moved from Canada to the United States are estimated to represent about $427 million annually—not a large amount when compared to the $135 billion U.S. drug market, but it can be substantial for specific drugs like Paxil, Zyban, and Viagra. Although importing prescription drugs from a foreign country, including Canada, is against U.S. law, a person can travel to Canada or Mexico to make purchases or buy over the Internet. Technically, buying over the Internet and having the drugs mailed to the United States is illegal. However, the government has taken a relatively lax view toward such purchases, provided the supply does not exceed 90 days.

Naturally, drug companies that have been hit the hardest want to put a stop to the traffic. Glaxo SmithKline, the prescription drug maker, has asked all Canadian pharmacies and wholesalers to "self-certify" that they are not exporting its drugs outside Canada. The company also is warning U.S. customers about imported drugs in a new advertising campaign.[6] Those that fail to comply will have their Glaxo supplies cut off—"Glaxo products are approved by Health Canada for sale in Canada only." Some feel that this move will not solve the problem even if Glaxo is able to stop Canadian sales because Americans will be able to find less expensive drugs in other markets, like Australia and Ireland. The Internet trade will be hard to shut down as long as large price differentials persist among markets. Furthermore, U.S. legislators are passing laws that allow such drug imports.[7]

Exclusive distribution, a practice often used by companies to maintain high retail margins to encourage retailers to provide extra service to customers, to stock large assortments, or to maintain the exclusive-quality image of a product, can create a favorable condition for parallel importing. Perfume and designer brands such as Gucci and Cartier are especially prone to gray markets. To maintain the image of quality and exclusivity, prices for such products traditionally include high profit margins at each level of distribution; characteristically, there are differential prices among markets and limited quantities of product, and distribution is restricted to upscale retailers. Wholesale prices for exclusive brands of fragrances are often 25 percent more in the United States than wholesale prices in other countries. These are ideal conditions for a lucrative gray market for unauthorized dealers in other countries who buy more than they need at wholesale prices lower than U.S.

---

[6] Barrie McKenna, "New Shot Fired in Net Drug Battle," *Toronto Globe and Mail*, June 2, 2005, p. B3.

[7] "Senate Passes Bill to Keep Drug Import Bans Out of Trade Deals," *FDA Week* 11, no. 37 (September 16, 2005).

Exhibit 18.1
How Gray Market Goods End Up in U.S. Stores

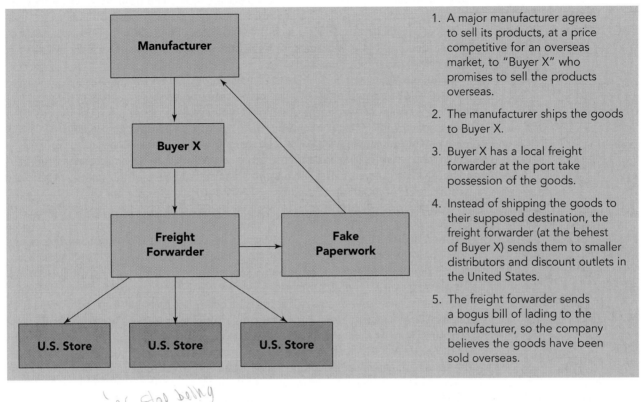

1. A major manufacturer agrees to sell its products, at a price competitive for an overseas market, to "Buyer X" who promises to sell the products overseas.

2. The manufacturer ships the goods to Buyer X.

3. Buyer X has a local freight forwarder at the port take possession of the goods.

4. Instead of shipping the goods to their supposed destination, the freight forwarder (at the behest of Buyer X) sends them to smaller distributors and discount outlets in the United States.

5. The freight forwarder sends a bogus bill of lading to the manufacturer, so the company believes the goods have been sold overseas.

wholesalers pay. They then sell the excess at a profit to unauthorized U.S. retailers but at a price lower than the retailer would have to pay to an authorized U.S. distributor.

The high-priced designer sportswear industry is also vulnerable to such practices. Nike, Adidas, and Calvin Klein were incensed to find their products being sold in one of Britain's leading supermarket chains, Tesco. Nike's Air Max Metallic trainers, which are priced at £120 ($196) in sports shops, could be purchased at Tesco for £50 ($80). Tesco had bought £8 million in Nike sportswear from overstocked wholesalers in the United States (Exhibit 18.1). To prevent parallel markets from developing when such marketing and pricing strategies are used, companies must maintain strong control over distribution and prices.

Companies that are serious about restricting the gray market must establish and monitor controls that effectively police distribution channels. In some countries they may get help from the courts. A Taiwan court ruled that two companies that were buying Coca-Cola in the United States and shipping it to Taiwan were violating the trademark rights of both the Coca-Cola Company and its sole Taiwan licensee. The violators were prohibited from importing, displaying, or selling products bearing the Coca-Cola trademark. In other countries, the courts have not always come down on the side of the trademark owner. The reasoning is that once the trademarked item is sold, the owner's rights to control the trademarked item are lost. In a similar situation in Canada, the courts did not side with the Canadian exporter who was buying 50,000 cases of Coke a week and shipping them to Hong Kong and Japan. The exporter paid $4.25 a case, plus shipping of $1.00 a case, and sold them at $6.00, a nifty profit of 75 cents a case. Coca-Cola sued, but the court ruled that the product was bought and sold legally.

When differences in prices between markets occur, the Internet makes it easy for individuals to participate in the gray market. Music CDs are especially vulnerable because of price differentials. Six foreign-owned record companies that maintain high prices through limited distribution dominate the Australian market and create a situation ripe for the gray market. There, CDs retail for an average of $24 but can be purchased for about 25 to

30 percent less from the many e-stores on the Internet. It is estimated that CDs purchased directly from the United States over the Internet have led to a 5 percent fall in Australian retail sales. In the United Kingdom, gray market CDs come from Italy, where they are about 50 percent cheaper and account for between 15 and 20 percent of sales in some releases. Sony believes that more than 100,000 copies of one of Celine Dion's best-selling albums sold in the United Kingdom were from parallel imports. The Internet has truly become a global price equalizer.

Parallel imports can do long-term damage in the market for trademarked products.[8] Customers who unknowingly buy unauthorized imports have no assurance of the quality of the item they buy, of warranty support, or of authorized service or replacement parts. Purchasers of computers, for example, may not be able to get parts because authorized dealers have no obligation to service these computers. In the case of software, the buyer may be purchasing a counterfeit product and will not be authorized for technical support. Furthermore, when a product fails, the consumer blames the owner of the trademark, and the quality image of the product is sullied.

Approaches to International Pricing

Whether the orientation is toward control over end prices or net prices, company policy relates to the net price received. Cost and market considerations are important; a company cannot sell goods below cost of production and remain in business, and it cannot sell goods at a price unacceptable in the marketplace. Firms unfamiliar with overseas marketing and firms producing industrial goods orient their pricing solely on a cost basis. Firms that employ pricing as part of the strategic mix, however, are aware of such alternatives as market segmentation from country to country or market to market, competitive pricing in the marketplace, and other market-oriented pricing factors,[9] including cultural differences in perceptions of pricing.[10]

Full-Cost versus Variable-Cost Pricing

Firms that orient their price thinking around cost must determine whether to use variable cost or full cost in pricing their goods. In *variable-cost pricing*, the firm is concerned only with the marginal or incremental cost of producing goods to be sold in overseas markets. Such firms regard foreign sales as bonus sales and assume that any return over their variable cost makes a contribution to net profit. These firms may be able to price most competitively in foreign markets, but because they are selling products abroad at lower net prices than they are selling them in the domestic market, they may be subject to charges of dumping. In that case, they open themselves to antidumping tariffs or penalties that take away from their competitive advantage. Nevertheless, variable-cost (or *marginal-cost*) pricing is a practical approach to pricing when a company has high fixed costs and unused production capacity. Any contribution to fixed cost after variable costs are covered is profit to the company.

In contrast, companies following the *full-cost pricing* philosophy insist that no unit of a similar product is different from any other unit in terms of cost and that each unit must bear its full share of the total fixed and variable cost.[11] This approach is suitable when a company has high variable costs relative to its fixed costs. In such cases, prices are often set on a cost-plus basis, that is, total costs plus a profit margin. Both variable-cost and full-cost policies are followed by international marketers.

---

[8] For an interesting look at how enforcement efforts work, see Kersi D. Anita, Mark E. Bergen, Shantanu Dutta, and Robert J. Fisher, "How Does Enforcement Deter Gray Market Incidence?" *Journal of Marketing* 70 (2006), pp. 92–106.

[9] Pradeep K. Chintagunta and Ramaroa Desiraju, "Strategic Pricing and Detailing Behavior in International Markets," *Marketing Science* 24, no. 1 (2005), pp. 67–80.

[10] Lee C. Simmons and Robert M. Schindler, "Cultural Superstitions and the Price Endings Used in Chinese Advertising," *Journal of International Marketing* 11, no. 2 (2003), pp. 101–111; Manoj Thomas and Vick Morwitz, "Penny Wise and Pound Foolish: The Left-Digit Effect in Price Cognition," *Journal of Consumer Research* 32, no. 2 (2005), pp. 54–64.

[11] For a research report on cost variables that influence price strategy, see Mary Anne Raymond, John F. Tanner Jr., and Joghoon Kim, "Cost Complexity of Pricing Decisions for Exporters in Developing and Emerging Markets," *Journal of International Marketing* 9, no. 3 (2001), p. 19.

CROSSING BORDERS 18.2   Don't Squeeze the Charmin, Mr. Whipple—Or Change the Color

The British pay twice as much as the Germans and the French, and nearly two-and-a-half times as much as Americans, for a standard four-roll pack of toilet paper. Why? Is it price gouging, the impact of the euro, the relative value of the English pound, or just culture?

The answer is rather simple: British consumers insist on a softer, more luxurious texture than their less discriminating continental and American cousins. British toilet paper is four grams heavier per square meter because it contains more fiber than European tissues. Extensive consumer testing has established that British consumers are not willing to be fobbed off with anything less.

Another factor distinguishes the British preference for a special toilet paper roll. Go to any supermarket, and you will be confronted by an extraordinary choice of more than 50 colors, sizes, and brands. Honeysuckle, warm pink, summer peach, pearl white, meadow green, breeze blue, and magnolia are just some of the shades on offer. The reason for this variety apparently is that the British shopper insists that toilet paper match the color scheme of the bathroom. On the continent, consumers settle happily for white, with pink thrown in as a wild alternative.

Procter & Gamble captured 10 percent of the market in less than five months after offering a stronger Charmin, but it may have gone too far. There were complaints that the "wet strength" of Charmin was unsuitable for U.K. toilets. The U.K. sewage system could handle Charmin alone, but the issue was whether the system would get clogged if several rival tissues adopted the stronger tissue. Procter & Gamble agreed to halve the strength of its Charmin toilet tissue, but will the price come down? And most recently, the P&G product has also been rated worst on a forest-friendly scale by Greenpeace. Complying with this latest criticism will surely raise costs.

Sources: "Going Soft," *The Economist,* March 4, 2000; "P&G Unblocks Sewage Row with Toilet Paper Revamp," *Reuters,* May 10, 2000; Timothy Kenny, "Eurasia: Of Toilet Paper, Escalators and Hope," *The Wall Street Journal Europe,* September 16, 2005, p. A9; "Skip it, Eco-Worrier," *The Times (London),* December 1, 2007, p. 11.

Skimming versus Penetration Pricing

Firms must also decide when to follow a skimming or a penetration pricing policy. Traditionally, the decision of which policy to follow depends on the level of competition, the innovativeness of the product, market characteristics, and company characteristics.[12]

A company uses *skimming* when the objective is to reach a segment of the market that is relatively price insensitive and thus willing to pay a premium price for the value received. If limited supply exists, a company may follow a skimming approach to maximize revenue and to match demand to supply. When a company is the only seller of a new or innovative product, a skimming price may be used to maximize profits until competition forces a lower price. Skimming often is used in markets with only two income levels: the wealthy and the poor. Costs prohibit setting a price that will be attractive to the lower-income market, so the marketer charges a premium price and directs the product to the high-income, relatively price-insensitive segment. Apparently this was the policy of Johnson & Johnson's pricing of diapers in Brazil before the arrival of P&G. Today such opportunities are fading away as the disparity in income levels is giving way to growing middle-income market segments. The existence of larger markets attracts competition and, as is often the case, the emergence of multiple product lines, thus leading to price competition.

A *penetration pricing policy* is used to stimulate market and sales growth by deliberately offering products at low prices.[13] Penetration pricing most often is used to acquire and hold share of market as a competitive maneuver. However, in country markets experiencing rapid and sustained economic growth, and where large shares of the population are moving into middle-income classes, penetration pricing may be used to stimulate market growth even with minimum competition. Penetration pricing may be a more profitable strategy than skimming if it maximizes revenues as a base for fighting the competition that is sure to come.

---

[12] Cavusgil, Chan, and Zhang, "Strategic Orientations in Export Pricing."

[13] Eric Bellman and Deborah Ball, "Unilever, P&G Wage Price War for Edge in India," *The Wall Street Journal,* August 11, 2004, pp. B1, B3.

Chinese wait to enter Beijing's first Wal-Mart outlet. Thousands crowded the Sam's Club store on the far western edge of Beijing as the world's biggest retailer made its first foray into a major Chinese city. Wal-Mart has more than 20 stores elsewhere in China; the first opened in 1996. The low-price-for-good-quality strategy of Wal-Mart and other mass retailers such as Costco and Carrefour, the French supermarket chain, have resulted in lower retail prices in China, Japan, and other Asian countries they have entered. (*AP Photo/Greg Baker*)

Regardless of the formal pricing policies and strategies a company uses, the market sets the effective price for a product. Said another way, the price has to be set at a point at which the consumer will perceive value received, and the price must be within reach of the target market. As a consequence, many products are sold in very small units in some markets to bring the unit price within reach of the target market. Warner-Lambert's launch of its five-unit pack of Bubbaloo bubble gum in Brazil failed—even though bubble gum represents over 72 percent of the overall gum sector—because it was priced above the target market. A relaunch of a single-unit "pillow" pack brought the price within range and enabled the brand to quickly gain a respectable level of sales.

As a country's economy grows and the distribution of wealth becomes more equitable, multiple income levels develop, distinct market segments emerge, and multiple price levels and price/quality perceptions increase in importance. As an example, the market for electronic consumer goods in China changed in just a few years. Instead of a market for imported high-priced and high-quality electronic goods aimed at the new rich versus cheaper, poorer quality, Chinese-made goods for the rest of the market, a multitiered market reflecting the growth of personal income has emerged.

Sony of Japan, the leading foreign seller of high-priced consumer electronic goods, was upstaged in the Chinese market when Aiwa, a competitor, recognized the emergence of a new middle-tier market for good-quality, modestly priced electronic goods. As part of a global strategy focused on slim margins and high turnover, Aiwa of Korea began selling hi-fi systems at prices closer to Chinese brands than to Sony's. Aiwa's product quality was not far behind that of Sony and was better than top Chinese brands, and the product resembled Sony's high-end systems. Aiwa's recognition of a new market segment and its ability to tap into it resulted in a huge increase in overall demand for Aiwa products.

Pricing decisions that were appropriate when companies directed their marketing efforts toward single market segments will give way to more sophisticated practices. As incomes rise in many foreign markets, the pricing environment a company encounters will be similar to that in the United States. As countries prosper and incomes become more equitably distributed, multiple market segments develop. As these segments emerge, Wal-Mart, Carrefour, and other mass retailers enter the market to offer price-conscious customers good value at affordable prices. This scenario seems to repeat itself in country after country. Within these markets, an effective pricing strategy becomes crucial.

Price Escalation

People traveling abroad often are surprised to find goods that are relatively inexpensive in their home country priced outrageously high in other countries. Because of the natural tendency to assume that such prices are a result of profiteering, manufacturers often resolve to begin exporting to crack these new, profitable foreign markets only to find that, in most cases, the higher prices reflect the higher costs of exporting. A case in point is a pacemaker for heart patients that sells for $2,100 in the United States. Tariffs and the Japanese distribution system add substantially to the final price in Japan. Beginning with the import tariff, each time the pacemaker changes hands, an additional cost is incurred. The product passes first through the hands of an importer, then to the company with primary responsibility for sales and service, then to a secondary or even a tertiary local distributor, and finally to the hospital. Markups at each level result in the $2,100 pacemaker selling for over $4,000 in Japan. Inflation results in price escalation, one of the major pricing obstacles facing the MNC marketer. This escalation is true not only for technical products like the pacemaker but for such products as crude oil, soft drinks, and beer. Estimates indicate that if tariffs and trade barriers on these products were abolished, the consumer would enjoy savings of 6.57 trillion yen.

Costs of Exporting

Excess profits exist in some international markets, but generally the cause of the disproportionate difference in price between the exporting country and the importing country, here termed *price escalation*, is the added costs incurred as a result of exporting products from one country to another. Specifically, the term relates to situations in which ultimate prices are raised by shipping costs, insurance, packing, tariffs, longer channels of distribution, larger middlemen margins, special taxes, administrative costs, and exchange rate fluctuations. The majority of these costs arise as a direct result of moving goods across borders from one country to another and often combine to escalate the final price to a level considerably higher than in the domestic market.

Taxes, Tariffs, and Administrative Costs

A Japanese wholesale store manager of a meat market in Tokyo arranges packs of beef imported from Australia. Earlier in the day, the government had announced Japan plans to raise its tariff on refrigerated beef imports to 50 percent from 38.5 percent, following a spike in imports. The price tag reads: "Premium beef, sirloin steak from Australia @ 258 yen [US$2.20] per 100 grams." Tariffs are one of the main causes of price escalation for imported products. (*AP Photo/Katsumi Kasahara*)

"Nothing is surer than death and taxes" has a particularly familiar ring to the ears of the international trader, because taxes include tariffs, and tariffs are one of the most pervasive features of international trading. Taxes and tariffs affect the ultimate consumer price for a product; in most instances, the consumer bears the burden of both. Sometimes, however, consumers benefit when manufacturers selling goods in foreign countries reduce their net return to gain access to a foreign market. Absorbed or passed on, taxes and tariffs must be considered by the international businessperson.

A tariff, or duty, is a special form of taxation. Like other forms of taxes, a tariff may be levied for the purpose of protecting a market or for increasing government revenue. A tariff is a fee charged when goods are brought into a country from another country. Recall from Chapter 15 that the level of tariff is typically expressed as the rate of duty and may be levied as specific, ad valorem, or compound. A specific duty is a flat charge per physical unit imported, such as 15 cents per bushel of rye. Ad valorem duties are levied as a percentage of the value of the goods imported, such as 20 percent of the value of imported watches. Compound duties include both a specific and an ad valorem charge, such as $1 per camera plus 10 percent of its value. Tariffs and other forms of import taxes serve to discriminate against all foreign goods.

Fees for import certificates or for other administrative processing can assume such levels that they are, in fact, import taxes. Many countries have purchase or excise taxes that apply to various categories of goods; value-added or turnover taxes, which apply as the product goes through a channel of distribution; and retail sales taxes. Such taxes increase the end price of goods but in general do not discriminate against foreign goods. Tariffs are the primary discriminatory tax that must be taken into account in reckoning with foreign competition.

In addition to taxes and tariffs, a variety of administrative costs are directly associated with exporting and importing a product. Export and import licenses, other documents, and the physical arrangements for getting the product from port of entry to the buyer's location mean additional costs. Although such costs are relatively small, they add to the overall cost of exporting.

Inflation

In countries with rapid inflation or exchange variation, the selling price must be related to the cost of goods sold and the cost of replacing the items. Goods often are sold below

Shoppers look at stacks of discount clothing jutting out on a sidewalk to attract potential buyers at Tokyo's Sugamo shopping district. With the stock market plunging to 16-year lows, talk of deflationary dangers, and a morass of confusion in its political leadership, Japan appeared to be headed toward a serious economic crisis. The central bank played down the possibility of deflation, saying that falling prices show the market is finally opening up to competition. *(AP Photo/Katsumi Kasahara)*

their cost of replacement plus overhead, and sometimes are sold below replacement cost. In these instances, the company would be better off not to sell the products at all. When payment is likely to be delayed for several months or is worked out on a long-term contract, inflationary factors must be figured into the price. Inflation and lack of control over price were instrumental in an unsuccessful new-product launch in Brazil by the H. J. Heinz Company; after only two years, Heinz withdrew from the market. Misunderstandings with the local partner resulted in a new fruit-based drink being sold to retailers on consignment; that is, they did not pay until the product was sold. Faced with a rate of inflation of over 300 percent at the time, just a week's delay in payment eroded profit margins substantially. Soaring inflation in many developing countries (Latin America in particular) makes widespread price controls a constant threat.

Because inflation and price controls imposed by a country are beyond the control of companies, they use a variety of techniques to inflate the selling price to compensate for inflation pressure and price controls. They may charge for extra services, inflate costs in transfer pricing, or break up products into components and price each component separately.

Inflation causes consumer prices to escalate, and consumers face ever-rising prices that eventually exclude many of them from the market. In contrast, deflation results in ever-decreasing prices, creating a positive result for consumers, but both put pressure to lower costs on everyone in the supply chain.

Deflation   The Japanese economy was in a deflationary spiral for a number of years. In a country better known for $10 melons and $100 steaks, McDonald's now sells hamburgers for 52 cents, down from $1.09; a flat screen 32-inch color television is down from $4,000 to $2,400; and clothing stores compete to sell fleece jackets for $8, down from $25 two years earlier.[14] Consumer prices have dropped to a point that they are similar to those Japanese once found only on overseas shopping trips. The high prices prevalent in Japan before deflation allowed substantial margins for everyone in the distribution chain. As prices continued to drop over several years, those less able to adjust costs to allow some margin with deflated prices fell by the wayside. Entirely new retail categories—100-yen discount shops, clothing chains selling low-cost imported products from China, and warehouse-style department stores—have become the norm. Sales at discount stores grew by 78 percent in the late 1990s. Discounting is the way to prosper in Japan, which again helps fuel deflation. While those in the distribution chain adjusted to a different competitive environment or gave up, Japanese consumers were reveling in their newfound spending power. Japanese tourists used to travel to the United States to buy things at much cheaper prices, but as one consumer commented, "Nowadays, I feel prices in Japan are going down and America is no longer cheaper." Although she was accustomed to returning from trips to the United States carrying suitcases of bargains, she returned from her last two-week vacation with purchases that fit in one fanny pack.

In a deflationary market, it is essential for a company to keep prices low and raise brand value to win the trust of consumers. Whether experiencing deflation or inflation, an exporter has to place emphasis on controlling price escalation.

Exchange Rate Fluctuations   At one time, world trade contracts could be easily written because payment was specified in a relatively stable currency. The American dollar was the standard, and all transactions could be related to the dollar. Now that all major currencies are floating freely relative to

---

[14] At least one exception in Japan is the Louis Vuitton brand of handbags, leather, and other luxury goods, which managed to raise prices twice in one year despite Japan's severe deflation. See Philippe Ries, "French Luxury Goods Hold Their Own in Japan Despite Euro's Rise," *Agence France-Presse*, March 2, 2003.

During the mid-1990s, Mexico knocked three zeroes off the peso in response to a major devaluation. Venezuela did the same in 2008.[19] In 2005 Turkey knocked six zeroes off its lira toward its potential alignment with the European Union. Both actions affected perceptions of key constituencies. Both bills are worth about 75¢.

one another, no one is quite sure of the future value of any currency.[15] Increasingly, companies are insisting that transactions be written in terms of the vendor company's national currency, and forward hedging is becoming more common. If exchange rates are not carefully considered in long-term contracts, companies find themselves unwittingly giving 15 to 20 percent discounts. The added cost incurred by exchange rate fluctuations on a day-to-day basis must be taken into account, especially where there is a significant time lapse between signing the order and delivery of the goods. Exchange rate differentials mount. Whereas Hewlett-Packard gained nearly half a million dollars additional profit through exchange rate fluctuations in one year, Nestlé lost a million dollars in six months. Other companies have lost or gained even larger amounts.[16]

Varying Currency Values

In addition to risks from exchange rate variations, other risks result from the changing values of a country's currency relative to other currencies,[17] such as consumers' perceptions of value.[18] Consider the situation in Germany for a purchaser of U.S. manufactured goods from mid-2001 to mid-2003. During this period, the value of the U.S. dollar relative to the euro went from a strong position (U.S.$1 to €1.8315) in mid-2001 to a weaker position in mid-2003 (U.S.$1 to €0.8499). A strong dollar produces price resistance because a larger quantity of local currency is needed to buy a U.S. dollar. Conversely, when the U.S. dollar is weak, demand for U.S. goods increases because fewer units of local currency are needed to buy a U.S. dollar. The weaker U.S. dollar, compared with most of the world's stronger currencies, that existed in mid-2003 stimulated exports from the United States. Consequently, when the dollar strengthens, U.S. exports will soften.

---

[15] Even China has begun to let its currency float within a defined range; Michael M. Phillips, "China Drops Yuan's Dollar Peg, Will Let Currency Float in Band," *The Wall Street Journal*, July 21, 2005, p. A1.

[16] Mark A. Stein, "Dollar's Fall Helps Some," *International Herald Tribune*, March 25, 2005, p. 17.

[17] Annually *The Economist* publishes its Big Mac index, which predicts currency fluctuations. See "Fast Food and Strong Currencies," June 11, 2005, p. 70.

[18] Klaus Wertenbrouch, Dilip Soman, and Amitava Chattopadhyay, "On the Perceived Value of Money: The Reference Dependence of Currency Numerosity Effects," *Journal of Consumer Research* 34 (2007), pp. 1–10.

[19] "Venezuela: Chavez's New Currency Targets Inflation," *Tulsa World*, January 1, 2008, p. A6.

A woman looks at a poster offering a half-priced bacon and lettuce hamburger, reduced from U.S.$3.20 to $1.60 during a monthly discount at a McDonald's restaurant in downtown Tokyo. McDonald's Japan announced that it would reduce the price of hamburgers by 30 percent for a month to return to customers the profit the company made by the strong yen against U.S. dollars in importing the raw materials from abroad. McDonald's move created goodwill among its customers at a time when it is forced to lower prices to "hike" sales in an economy that is suffering a major downturn. This move is a good example of how differences in the value of currencies can be positive for a company, as in this case, or negative when the value of the dollar is much stronger than the local currency. *(AP Photo)*

When the value of the dollar is weak relative to the buyer's currency (i.e., it takes fewer units of the foreign currency to buy a dollar), companies generally employ cost-plus pricing. To remain price competitive when the dollar is strong (i.e., when it takes more units of the foreign currency to buy a dollar), companies must find ways to offset the higher price caused by currency values. When the rupee in India depreciated significantly against the U.S. dollar, PC manufacturers faced a serious pricing problem. Because the manufacturers were dependent on imported components, their options were to absorb the increased cost or raise the price of PCs.

Currency exchange rate swings are considered by many global companies to be a major pricing problem. Because the benefits of a weaker dollar are generally transitory, firms need to take a proactive stance one way or the other. For a company with long-range plans calling for continued operation in foreign markets that wants to remain price competitive, price strategies need to reflect variations in currency values.

Innumerable cost variables can be identified depending on the market, the product, and the situation. The cost, for example, of reaching a market with relatively small potential may be high. High operating costs of small specialty stores like those in Mexico and Thailand lead to high retail prices. Intense competition in certain world markets raises the cost or lowers the margins available to world business. Even small things like payoffs to local officials can introduce unexpected costs to the unwary entrepreneur. Only experience in a given marketplace provides the basis for compensating for cost differences in different markets. With experience, a firm that prices on a cost basis operates in a realm of reasonably measurable factors.

Middleman and Transportation Costs

Channel length and marketing patterns vary widely, but in most countries, channels are longer and middleman margins higher than is customary in the United States. The diversity of channels used to reach markets and the lack of standardized middleman markups leave many producers unaware of the ultimate price of a product.

Besides channel diversity, the fully integrated marketer operating abroad faces various unanticipated costs because marketing and distribution channel infrastructures are underdeveloped in many countries. The marketer can also incur added expenses for warehousing and handling of small shipments and may have to bear increased financing costs when dealing with underfinanced middlemen.

Because no convenient source of data on middleman costs is available, the international marketer must rely on experience and marketing research to ascertain middleman costs. The Campbell Soup Company found its middleman and physical distribution costs in the United Kingdom to be 30 percent higher than in the United States. Extra costs were incurred because soup was purchased in small quantities—small English grocers typically purchase 24-can cases of assorted soups (each case being hand-packed for shipment). In the United States, typical purchase units are 48-can cases of one soup purchased by the dozens, hundreds, or carloads. The purchase habits in Europe forced the company into an extra wholesale level in its channel to facilitate handling small orders.

Exporting also incurs increased transportation costs when moving goods from one country to another. If the goods go over water, insurance, packing, and handling are additional costs not generally added to locally produced goods. Such costs add yet another burden because import tariffs in many countries are based on the landed cost, which includes transportation, insurance, and shipping charges. These costs add to the inflation of the final price. The next section details how a price in the home market may more than double in the foreign market.

Sample Effects of Price Escalation

Exhibit 18.2 illustrates some of the effects the factors discussed previously may have on the end price of a consumer item. Because costs and tariffs vary so widely from country to country, a hypothetical but realistic example is used. It assumes that a constant net price is received by the manufacturer, that all domestic transportation costs are absorbed by the various middleman and reflected in their margins, and that the foreign middlemen have the same margins as the domestic middlemen. In some instances, foreign middleman margins are lower, but it is equally probable that these margins could be greater. In fact, in many instances, middlemen use higher wholesale and retail margins for foreign goods than for similar domestic goods.

Notice that the retail prices in Exhibit 18.2 range widely, illustrating the difficulty of price control by manufacturers in overseas retail markets. No matter how much the manufacturer may wish to market a product in a foreign country for a price equivalent to US$10, there is little opportunity for such control. Even assuming the most optimistic conditions for Foreign Example 1, the producer would need to cut its net by more than one-third to absorb freight and tariff costs if the goods are to be priced the same in both foreign and domestic markets. Price escalation is everywhere: A man's dress shirt that sells for $40 in the United States retails for $80 in Caracas. A $20 U.S. electric can opener is priced in Milan at $70; a $35 U.S.-made automatic toaster is priced at $80 in France.

Unless some of the costs that create price escalation can be reduced, the marketer is faced with a price that may confine sales to a limited segment of wealthy, price-insensitive customers. In many markets, buyers have less purchasing power than in the United States and can be easily priced out of the market. Furthermore, once price escalation is set in motion, it can spiral upward quickly. When the price to middlemen is high and turnover is low, they may insist on higher margins to defray their costs, which, of course, raises the price even higher. Unless price escalation can be reduced, marketers find that the only buyers left are the wealthier ones. If marketers are to compete successfully in the growth of markets around the world, cost containment must be among their highest priorities. If costs can be reduced anywhere along the chain, from manufacturer's cost to retailer markups, price escalation will be reduced. A discussion of some of the approaches to reducing price escalation follows.

Exhibit 18.2
Sample Causes and Effects of Price Escalation

	Domestic Example	Foreign Example 1: Assuming the Same Channels with Wholesaler Importing Directly	Foreign Example 2: Importer and Same Margins and Channels	Foreign Example 3: Same as 2 but with 10 Percent Cumulative Turnover Tax	
Manufacturing net	$ 5.00	$ 5.00	$ 5.00	$ 5.00	
Transport, CIF	n.a.	6.10	6.10	6.10	
Tariff (20 percent CIF value)	n.a.	1.22	1.22	1.22	
Importer pays	n.a.	n.a.	7.32	7.32	
Importer margin when sold	n.a.	n.a.	1.83	1.83	
to wholesaler (25 percent				+0.73	Turnover
on cost)					Tax
Wholesaler pays landed cost	5.00	7.32	9.15	9.88	
Wholesaler margin	1.67	2.44	3.05	3.29	
(33⅓ percent on cost)				+0.99	
Retailer pays	6.67	9.76	12.20	14.16	Turnover
					Tax
Retail margin	3.34	4.88	6.10	7.08	
(50 percent on cost)				+1.42	Turnover
Retail price	$10.01	$14.64	$18.30	$22.66	Tax

Notes: All figures in U.S. dollars; CIF = cost, insurance, and freight; n.a. = not applicable. The exhibit assumes that all domestic transportation costs are absorbed by the middleman. Transportation, tariffs, and middleman margins vary from country to country, but for the purposes of comparison, only a few of the possible variations are shown.

Approaches to Reducing Price Escalation

Three methods used to reduce costs and lower price escalation are lowering the cost of goods, lowering tariffs, and lowering distribution costs.

Lowering Cost of Goods

If the manufacturer's price can be lowered, the effect is felt throughout the chain. One of the important reasons for manufacturing in a third country is an attempt to reduce manufacturing costs and thus price escalation. The impact can be profound if you consider that the hourly cost of skilled labor in a Mexican maquiladora is less than $3 an hour including benefits, compared with more than $10 in the United States.

In comparing the costs of manufacturing microwave ovens in the United States and in Korea, the General Electric Company found substantial differences. A typical microwave oven cost GE $218 to manufacture compared with $155 for Samsung, a Korean manufacturer. A breakdown of costs revealed that assembly labor cost GE $8 per oven and Samsung only 63 cents. Perhaps the most disturbing finding for GE was that Korean laborers delivered more for less cost: GE produced four units per person, whereas the Korean company produced nine.

Although Korea remains an important offshore manufacturing location, China is emerging as a global manufacturing powerhouse backed by an inexpensive labor force, rapidly improving production quality, new sources of capital, a more dynamic private sector, and a deliberately undervalued currency. China supplies a growing range of products to the global marketplace. Japan, the land of zero-defect quality control, is increasingly happy with the competence of Chinese workers. Star Manufacturing, a Japanese precision machine tool manufacturing company, moved 30 percent of its production to China because China's cheap labor and cheap resources reduced its production costs by 20 percent.

Eliminating costly functional features or even lowering overall product quality is another method of minimizing price escalation. For U.S.-manufactured products, the quality and additional features required for the more developed home market may not be necessary in countries that have not attained the same level of development or consumer demand. In the price war between P&G and Kimberly-Clark in Brazil, the quality of the product was decreased to lower the price. Remember that the grandmother in the grocery store chose the poorest quality and lowest priced brand of diaper. Similarly, functional features on washing machines made for the United States, such as automatic bleach and soap dispensers, thermostats to provide four different levels of water temperature, controls to vary water volume, and bells to ring at appropriate times, may be unnecessary for many foreign markets. Eliminating them means lower manufacturing costs and thus a corresponding reduction in price escalation. Lowering manufacturing costs can often have a double benefit: The lower price to the buyer may also mean lower tariffs, because most tariffs are levied on an ad valorem basis.

Lowering Tariffs

When tariffs account for a large part of price escalation, as they often do, companies seek ways to lower the rate. Some products can be reclassified into a different, and lower, customs classification. An American company selling data communications equipment in Australia faced a 25 percent tariff, which affected the price competitiveness of its products. It persuaded the Australian government to change the classification for the type of products the company sells from "computer equipment" (25 percent tariff) to "telecommunication equipment" (3 percent tariff). Like many products, this company's products could be legally classified under either category. One complaint against customs agents in Russia is the arbitrary way in which they often classify products. Russian customs, for instance, insists on classifying Johnson & Johnson's 2-in-1 Shower Gel as a cosmetic with a 20 percent tariff rather than as a soap substitute, which the company considers it, at a 15 percent tariff.

How a product is classified is often a judgment call. The difference between an item being classified as jewelry or art means paying no tariff for art or a 26 percent tariff for jewelry. For example, a U.S. customs inspector could not decide whether to classify a

CROSSING BORDERS 18.3

What Does It Mean To Be Human? 5.2 Percent, That's What

"What does it mean to be human?" asked Judge Barzilay in her chambers at the U.S. Court of International Trade. At the heart of the problem were some 60 little plastic figures of Marvel Enterprises' X-Men and other comic figures.

Marvel subsidiary Toy Biz Inc. sought to have its heroes from a range of comic characters declared nonhuman. At the time, tariffs were higher on dolls (12 percent) than toys (6.8 percent). According to the U.S. tariff code, human figures are dolls, whereas figures representing animals or "creatures," such as monsters and robots, are deemed toys.

Thus began the great debate over the figures' true being. Barbie is a doll. Pooh Bear's a toy. That much is easy. But what about Wolverine, the muscular X-Man with the metal claws that jut out from his fists? Wolverine has known many forms in his more than 40 years as a Marvel character. But is he human? Or consider Kraven, a famed hunter, who once vanquished Spiderman, thanks in part to the strength he gained from drinking secret jungle elixirs.

Toy Biz argued that the figures "stand as potent witnesses for their status as nonhuman creatures." How could they be humans if they possessed "tentacles, claws, wings or robotic limbs"? The U.S. Customs Service argued that each figure had a "distinctive individual personality." Some were Russians, Japanese, black, white, women, even handicapped. Wolverine, the government insisted, was simply "a man with prosthetic hands."

To weigh the question, Judge Barzilay sat down with a sheaf of opposing legal briefs and more than 60 action figures, including Wolverine, Storm, Rogue, Kraven, and Bonebreaker. Judge Barzilay described in her ruling how she subjected many of the figures to "comprehensive examinations." At times, that included "the need to remove the clothes of the figure." The X-Men, oddly, gave her the least trouble. They are

mutants, she declared, who "use their extraordinary and unnatural powers on the side of good or evil." Thus the X-Men are "something other than human." Tougher for the judge were figures from the Fantastic Four and Spiderman series. After careful examination and thought, the judge found Kraven exhibited "highly exaggerated muscle tone in arms and legs." He wore a "lion's mane-like vest." Both features helped relegate him to the netherworld of robots, monsters, and devils. Case closed.

Toy Biz Inc. was elated, but fans were incensed—no way are X-Men mere creatures. "Marvel's superheroes are supposed to be as human as you or I. They live in New York. They have families and go to work. And now they're no longer human?" The current author of Marvel's *Uncanny X-Men* comic book series is also incredulous. He worked hard for a year, he says, to emphasize the X-Men's humanity, to show "that they're just another strand in the evolutionary chain." But "Don't fret, Marvel fans, a decision that the X-Men figures indeed do have 'nonhuman' characteristics further proves our characters have special, out-of-this world powers."

Although this scenario may seem trivial, it highlights just how arbitrary tariff classification can be. It pays to argue your case if you believe a product can be classified at a lower rate. For every $100,000 of plastic figures Toy Biz imports, the reclassification saves it $5,200. Not a bad day's work, considering the hundreds of thousands of dollars worth of figures the company imports annually—not to mention the undisclosed sum Toy Biz can recoup from years of overpaid tariffs.

Sources: Niel King Jr., "Is Wolverine Human? A Judge Answers No; Fans Howl in Protest," *The Wall Street Journal*, January 20, 2003; Marie Beerens, "Marvel's Two Movies Should Fuel Demand," *Investor's Business Daily*, February 19, 2008.

$2.7 million Fabergé egg as art or jewelry. The difference was $0 tariff versus $700,000. An experienced freight forwarder/customs broker saved the day by persuading the customs agent that the Fabergé egg was a piece of art. Because the classification of products varies among countries, a thorough investigation of tariff schedules and classification criteria can result in a lower tariff.

Besides having a product reclassified into a lower tariff category, it may be possible to modify a product to qualify for a lower tariff rate within a tariff classification. In the footwear industry, the difference between "foxing" and "foxlike" on athletic shoes makes a substantial difference in the tariff levied. To protect the domestic footwear

Hugh Jackman portraying Wolverine, an X-Men fictional character from Marvel Enterprises. A tariff classification issue arose when the company declared the imported toy characters as nonhuman toys and U.S. Customs said that they were human figure dolls—tariffs on dolls at that time were 12 percent versus 6.8 percent for toys. U.S. Customs alleged that the X-Men figures were human figures and thus should be classified as dolls, not figures featuring animals or creatures, which would mean that they could be classified as toys. Product classifications are critical when tariffs are determined. See Crossing Borders 18.3 for more details on this case. (© 20th Century Fox/Marvel Entertainment Group/The Kobal Collection)

industry from an onslaught of cheap sneakers from the Far East, the tariff schedules state that any canvas or vinyl shoe with a foxing band (a tape band attached at the sole and overlapping the shoe's upper by more than one-quarter inch) be assessed at a higher duty rate. As a result, manufacturers design shoes so that the sole does not overlap the upper by more than one-quarter inch. If the overlap exceeds one-quarter inch, the shoe is classified as having a foxing band; less than one-quarter inch, a foxlike band. A shoe with a foxing band is taxed 48 percent and one with a foxlike band (one-quarter inch or less overlap) is taxed a mere 6 percent.

There are often differential rates between fully assembled, ready-to-use products and those requiring some assembly, further processing, the addition of locally manufactured component parts, or other processing that adds value to the product and can be performed within the foreign country. For example, a ready-to-operate piece of machinery with a 20 percent tariff may be subject to only a 12 percent tariff when imported unassembled. An even lower tariff may apply when the product is assembled in the country and some local content is added.

Repackaging also may help to lower tariffs. Tequila entering the United States in containers of one gallon or less carries a duty of $2.27 per proof gallon; larger containers are assessed at only $1.25. If the cost of rebottling is less than $1.02 per proof gallon, and it probably would be, considerable savings could result. As will be discussed shortly, one of the more important activities in foreign trade zones is the assembly of imported goods, using local and frequently lower cost labor.

Lowering Distribution Costs

Shorter channels can help keep prices under control. Designing a channel that has fewer middlemen may lower distribution costs by reducing or eliminating middleman markups. Besides eliminating markups, fewer middlemen may mean lower overall taxes. Some countries levy a value-added tax on goods as they pass through channels. Goods are taxed each time they change hands. The tax may be cumulative or noncumulative. A cumulative value-added tax is based on total selling price and is assessed every time the goods change hands. Obviously, in countries where value-added tax is cumulative, tax alone provides a special incentive for developing short distribution channels. Where that is achieved, tax is paid only on the difference between the middleman's cost and the selling price. While many manufacturers had to cut prices in wake of Japan's deflation, Louis Vuitton, a maker of branded boutique goods, was able to increase prices instead. A solid brand name and direct distribution have permitted Vuitton's price strategy. Vuitton's leather monogrammed bags have become a Japanese buyer's "daily necessity," and Vuitton distributes directly and sets its own prices.

Using Foreign Trade Zones to Lessen Price Escalation

Some countries have established foreign or free trade zones (FTZs) or free ports to facilitate international trade.[20] More than 300 of these facilities operate throughout the world, storing or processing imported goods. As free trade policies in Africa, Latin America, eastern Europe, and other developing regions expand, an equally rapid expansion has taken place in the creation and use of foreign trade zones. Recall from Chapter 15 that in a free port or FTZ, payment of import duties is postponed until the product leaves the FTZ area and enters the country. An FTZ is, in essence, a tax-free enclave

---

[20] Liu Li, "Free Trade Zone in Pipeline in Xinjiang," *China Daily*, September 20, 2005.

Exhibit 18.3
How Are Foreign Trade Zones Used?

There are more than 100 foreign trade zones (FTZs) in the United States, and FTZs exist in many other countries as well. Companies use them to postpone the payment of tariffs on products while they are in the FTZ. Here are some examples of how FTZs in the United States are used.

- A Japanese firm assembles motorcycles, jet skis, and three-wheel all-terrain vehicles for import as well as for export to Canada, Latin America, and Europe.

- A U.S. manufacturer of window shades and miniblinds imports and stores fabric from Holland in an FTZ, thereby postponing a 17 percent tariff until the fabric leaves the FTZ.

- A manufacturer of hair dryers stores its product in an FTZ, which it uses as its main distribution center for products manufactured in Asia.

- A European-based medical supply company manufactures kidney dialysis machines and sterile tubing using raw materials from Germany and U.S. labor. It then exports 30 percent of its products to Scandinavian countries.

- A Canadian company assembles electronic teaching machines using cabinets from Italy; electronics from Taiwan, Korea, and Japan; and labor from the United States, for export to Colombia and Peru.

In all these examples, tariffs are postponed until the products leave the FTZ and enter the United States. Furthermore, in most situations the tariff is at the lower rate for component parts and raw materials versus the higher rate that would be charged if products were imported directly as finished goods. If the finished products are not imported into the United States from the FTZ but are shipped to another country, no U.S. tariffs apply.

Sources: Lewis E. Leibowitz, "An Overview of Foreign Trade Zones," *Europe*, Winter–Spring 1987, p. 12; "Cheap Imports," *International Business*, March 1993, pp. 98–100; "Free-Trade Zones: Global Overview and Future Prospects," http://www.stat-usa.gov.

and not considered part of the country as far as import regulations are concerned. When an item leaves an FTZ and is imported officially into the host country of the FTZ, all duties and regulations are imposed.

Utilizing FTZs can to some extent control price escalation resulting from the layers of taxes, duties, surcharges, freight charges, and so forth. Foreign trade zones permit many of these added charges to be avoided, reduced, or deferred so that the final price is more competitive. One of the more important benefits of the FTZ in controlling prices is the exemption from duties on labor and overhead costs incurred in the FTZ in assessing the value of goods.

By shipping unassembled goods to an FTZ in an importing country, a marketer can lower costs in a variety of ways:

- Tariffs may be lower because duties are typically assessed at a lower rate for unassembled versus assembled goods.

- If labor costs are lower in the importing country, substantial savings may be realized in the final product cost.

- Ocean transportation rates are affected by weight and volume; thus unassembled goods may qualify for lower freight rates.

- If local content, such as packaging or component parts, can be used in the final assembly, tariffs may be further reduced.

All in all, a foreign or free trade zone is an important method for controlling price escalation. Incidentally, all the advantages offered by an FTZ for an exporter are also advantages for an importer. U.S. importers use over 100 FTZs in the United States to help lower their costs of imported goods. See Exhibit 18.3 for illustrations of how FTZs are used.

Dumping   A logical outgrowth of a market policy in international business is goods priced competitively at widely differing prices in various markets. Marginal (variable) cost pricing, as discussed previously, is a way prices can be reduced to stay within a competitive price range. The market and economic logic of such pricing policies can hardly be disputed, but the practices often are classified as dumping and are subject to severe penalties and fines. Various economists define *dumping* differently. One approach classifies international shipments as dumped if the products are sold below their cost of production. Another approach characterizes dumping as selling goods in a foreign market below the price of the same goods in the home market.[21]

World Trade Organization (WTO) rules allow for the imposition of a dumping duty when goods are sold at a price lower than the normal export price or less than the cost in the country of origin, increased by a reasonable amount for the cost of sales and profits, when this price is likely to be prejudicial to the economic activity of the importing country. A *countervailing duty* or *minimum access volume (MAV)*, which restricts the amount a country will import, may be imposed on foreign goods benefiting from subsidies, whether in production, export, or transportation.

For countervailing duties to be invoked, it must be shown that prices are lower in the importing country than in the exporting country and that producers in the importing country are being directly harmed by the dumping. A report by the U.S. Department of Agriculture indicated that levels of dumping by the United States hover around 40 percent for wheat and between 25 and 30 percent for corn, and levels for soybeans have risen steadily over the past four years to nearly 30 percent. These percentages, for example, mean that wheat is selling up to 40 percent below the cost of production. For cotton, the level of dumping for 2001 rose to a remarkable 57 percent, and for rice, it has stabilized at around 20 percent. The study indicated that these commodities are being dumped onto international markets by the United States in violation of WTO rules. The report found that after many years of accepting agricultural dumping, a few countries have begun to respond by investigating whether some U.S. agricultural exports are dumped. Brazil is considering a case against U.S. cotton before the WTO. In 2001, Canada briefly imposed both countervailing and antidumping duties on U.S. corn imports; the United States did the same for Chinese apple juice concentrate.[22]

Dumping is rarely an issue when world markets are strong. In the 1980s and 1990s, dumping became a major issue for a large number of industries when excess production capacity relative to home-country demand caused many companies to price their goods on a marginal-cost basis. In a classic case of dumping, prices are maintained in the home-country market and reduced in foreign markets.

Today, tighter government enforcement of dumping legislation is causing international marketers to seek new routes around such legislation. Assembly in the importing country is a way companies attempt to lower prices and avoid dumping charges. However, these *screwdriver plants,* as they are often called, are subject to dumping charges if the price differentials reflect more than the cost savings that result from assembly in the importing country. Another subterfuge is to alter the product so that the technical description will fit a lower duty category. To circumvent a 16.9 percent countervailing duty imposed on Chinese gas-filled, nonrefillable pocket flint lighters, the manufacturer attached a useless valve to the lighters so that they fell under the "nondisposable" category, thus avoiding the duty. Countries see through many such subterfuges and impose taxes. For example, the European Union imposed a $27 to $58 dumping duty per unit on a Japanese firm that assembled and sold office machines in the European Union. The firm was charged with valuing imported parts for assembly below cost.

The U.S. market is currently more sensitive to dumping than in the recent past. In fact, the Uruguay Round of the GATT included a section on antidumping that grew out of U.S. insistence on stricter controls on dumping of foreign goods in the United States at prices below those charged at home. Changes in U.S. law have enhanced the authority of the Commerce Department to prevent circumvention of antidumping duties and countervailing

[21] "U.S. Places Duties on TVs from China," *Bloomberg News*, May 15, 2005.

[22] Shannon Dininny, "Commerce Department Supports Continued Duties on Chinese Apple Juice Concentrate," *Associated Press*, September 9, 2005.

duties that have been imposed on a country for dumping. The United States and European Union have been the most ardent users of antidumping duties. A question asked by many though: Are dumping charges just a cover for protectionism? Previously, when an order was issued to apply antidumping and countervailing duties on products, companies charged with the violation would get around the order by slightly altering the product or by doing minor assembly in the United States or a third country. This effort created the illusion of a different product not subject to the antidumping order. The new authority of the Department of Commerce closes many such loopholes.

Leasing in International Markets

An important selling technique to alleviate high prices and capital shortages for capital equipment is the leasing system. The concept of equipment leasing has become increasingly important as a means of selling capital equipment in overseas markets. In fact, an estimated $50 billion worth (original cost) of U.S.-made and foreign-made equipment is on lease in western Europe.

The system of leasing used by industrial exporters is similar to the typical lease contracts used in the United States. Terms of the leases usually run one to five years, with payments made monthly or annually; included in the rental fee are servicing, repairs, and spare parts. Just as contracts for domestic and overseas leasing arrangements are similar, so are the basic motivations and the shortcomings. For example:

- Leasing opens the door to a large segment of nominally financed foreign firms that can be sold on a lease option but might be unable to buy for cash.
- Leasing can ease the problems of selling new, experimental equipment, because less risk is involved for the users.
- Leasing helps guarantee better maintenance and service on overseas equipment.
- Equipment leased and in use helps sell other companies in that country.
- Lease revenue tends to be more stable over a period of time than direct sales would be.

The disadvantages or shortcomings take on an international flavor. Besides the inherent disadvantages of leasing, some problems are compounded by international relationships. In a country beset with inflation, lease contracts that include maintenance and supply parts (as most do) can lead to heavy losses toward the end of the contract period. Furthermore, countries where leasing is most attractive are those where spiraling inflation is most likely to occur. The added problems of currency devaluation, expropriation, or other political risks are operative longer than if the sale of the same equipment were made outright. In light of these perils, leasing incurs greater risk than does outright sale; however, there is a definite trend toward increased use of this method of selling internationally.

Countertrade as a Pricing Tool

Countertrade is a pricing tool that every international marketer must be ready to employ, and the willingness to accept a countertrade will often give the company a competitive advantage. The challenges of countertrade must be viewed from the same perspective as all other variations in international trade. Marketers must be aware of which markets will likely require countertrades, just as they must be aware of social customs and legal requirements. Assessing this factor along with all other market factors will enhance a marketer's competitive position.

One of the earliest barter arrangements occurred between Russia and PepsiCo before the ruble was convertible and before most companies were trading with Russia. PepsiCo wanted to beat Coca-Cola into the Russian market. The only way possible was for PepsiCo to be willing to accept vodka (sold under the brand name Stolichnaya) from Russia and bottled wines (sold under the brand name of Premiat) from Romania to finance Pepsi bottling plants in those countries. From all indications, this arrangement was very profitable for Russia, Romania, and PepsiCo. Pepsi continues to use countertrade to expand its bottling plants. In a recent agreement between PepsiCo and Ukraine, Pepsi agreed to market $1 billion worth of Ukrainian-made commercial ships over an eight-year period. Some of the proceeds from the ship sales will be reinvested in the shipbuilding venture, and some will be used to buy soft-drink equipment and build five Pepsi bottling plants in Ukraine. PepsiCo dominates the cola market in Russia and all the former Soviet republics in part because of its exclusive countertrade agreement with Russia, which locked Coca-Cola out of the Russian cola market for more than 12 years. After the Soviet Union was dismembered, the Russian economy crashed, and most of the Russian payment system broke down into barter operations. Truckloads of aspirin were swapped by one company, then traded for poultry, which in turn was bartered for lumber, in turn to be exchanged for X-ray equipment from Kazakhstan—all to settle debts. Many of these transactions involved regional electricity companies that were owed money by virtually everyone.

Although cash may be the preferred method of payment, countertrades are an important part of trade with eastern Europe, the newly independent states, China,[23] and, to a varying degree, some Latin American and African nations. Barter or countertrades still constitute between 20 and 40 percent of all transactions in the economies of the former Soviet bloc. Corporate debts to suppliers, payment and services, even taxes—all have a noncash component or are entirely bartered. Many of these countries constantly face a shortage of hard currencies with which to trade and thus resort to countertrades when possible. A recent purchase of 48 F-16 Falcons from Lockheed Martin was pegged at $3.5 billion. The financial package included soft loans and a massive offset program—purchases from Polish manufacturers that more than erased the costs of the deal in foreign exchange. With an economy once short of hard currency, Russia has offered a wide range of products in barter for commodities it needed. For example, Russian expertise in space technology was offered for Malaysian palm oil and rubber, and military equipment was exchanged for crude palm oil or rice from Indonesia.[24] Today, an international company must include in its market-pricing toolkit some understanding of countertrading.

Types of Countertrade

Countertrade includes four distinct transactions: barter, compensation deals, counterpurchase, and buyback. *Barter* is the direct exchange of goods between two parties in a transaction. For example, the Malaysian government bought 20 diesel-electric locomotives from General Electric. Officials of the government said that GE would be paid with palm oil, to be supplied by a plantation company. The company will supply about 200,000 metric tons of palm oil over a period of 30 months. This agreement was GE's first barter deal for palm oil and palm products, though its division GE Trading has several other countertrade agreements worldwide. No money changed hands, and no third parties were involved. Obviously, in a barter transaction, the seller must be able to dispose of the goods at a net price equal to the expected selling price in a regular, for-cash transaction. Furthermore, during the negotiation stage of a barter deal, the seller must know the market and the price for the items offered in trade. In the General Electric example, palm oil has an established price and a global market for palm oil and palm products. But not all bartered goods have an organized market, and products can range from hams to iron pellets, mineral water to furniture to olive oil—all somewhat more difficult to price and to find customers.

Barter may also be used to reduce a country's foreign debt. To save foreign exchange reserves, the Philippine government offered some creditors canned tuna to repay part of a state $4-billion debt. If tuna is not enough, coconut oil and a seaweed extract, carrageenan, used as an additive in foods, toothpaste, cosmetics and ice cream, were offered. The seaweed and tuna exporters will be paid with pesos so no currency leaves the country.

---

[23] "Trade Financing and Insurance: Countertrade," *Economist Intelligence Unit–Country Finance*, January 22, 2008, p. 101.

[24] Zakki P. Hakim, "Ministry Eyes Rice-for-Planes Trade Deal," *Jakarta Post*, September 20, 2005, p. 13.

Compensation deals involve payment in goods and in cash. A seller delivers lathes to a buyer in Venezuela and receives 70 percent of the payment in convertible currency and 30 percent in tanned hides and wool. In an actual deal, General Motors Corporation sold $12 million worth of locomotives and diesel engines to Yugoslavia and took cash and $4 million in Yugoslavian cutting tools as payment. McDonnell Douglas agreed to a compensation deal with Thailand for eight top-of-the-range F/A-18 strike aircraft. Thailand agreed to pay $578 million of the total cost in cash, and McDonnell Douglas agreed to accept $93 million in a mixed bag of goods including Thai rubber, ceramics, furniture, frozen chicken, and canned fruit. In a move to reduce its current account deficit, the Thai government requires that 20 to 50 percent of the value of large contracts be paid for in raw and processed agricultural goods.

An advantage of a compensation deal over barter is the immediate cash settlement of a portion of the bill; the remainder of the cash is generated after successful sale of the goods received. If the company has a use for the goods received, the process is relatively simple and uncomplicated. However, if the seller has to rely on a third party to find a buyer, the cost involved must be anticipated in the original compensation negotiation if the net proceeds to the seller are to equal the market price.

Counterpurchase, or *offset trade*, is probably the most frequently used type of countertrade. For this trade, the seller agrees to sell a product at a set price to a buyer and receives payment in cash. However, two contracts are negotiated. The first contract is contingent on a second contract that includes an agreement by the original seller to buy goods from the buyer for the total monetary amount involved in the first contract or for a set percentage of that amount. This arrangement provides the seller with more flexibility than the compensation deal because there is generally a time period—6 to 12 months or longer—for completion of the second contract. During the time that markets are sought for the goods in the second contract, the seller has received full payment for the original sale. Furthermore, the goods to be purchased in the second contract are generally of greater variety than those offered in a compensation deal. Even greater flexibility is offered when the second contract is nonspecific; that is, the books on sales and purchases need to be cleared only at certain intervals. The seller is obligated to generate enough purchases to keep the books balanced or clear between purchases and sales.

Offset trades are becoming more prevalent among economically weak countries. Several variations of a counterpurchase or offset have developed to make it more economical for the selling company. For example, the Lockheed Martin Corporation entered into an offset trade with the United Arab Emirates (UAE) in a $6.4 billion deal for 80 F-16 fighter planes called Desert Falcons. Lockheed agreed to make a $160 million cash investment in a gas pipeline running from Qatar to UAE industrial projects and then on to Pakistan. The UAE requires that some of the proceeds from weapon sales be reinvested in the UAE. Such offsets are a common feature of arms deals, in which sellers build facilities ranging from hotels to sugar mills at the request of the buyer.

A *product buyback agreement* is the fourth type of countertrade transaction. This type of agreement is made when the sale involves goods or services that produce other goods and services, such as a production plant, production equipment, or technology. The buyback agreement usually involves one of two situations: The seller agrees to accept as partial payment a certain portion of the output, or the seller receives full price initially but agrees to buy back a certain portion of the output. One U.S. farm equipment manufacturer sold a tractor plant to Poland and was paid part in hard currency and the balance in Polish-built tractors. In another situation, General Motors built an auto manufacturing plant in Brazil and was paid under normal terms but agreed to the purchase of resulting output when the new facilities came online. Levi Strauss took Hungarian blue jeans, which it sells abroad, in exchange for setting up a jeans factory near Budapest.

An interesting buyback arrangement has been agreed on between the Rice Growers Association of California (RGAC) and the Philippine government. The RGAC will invest in Philippine farmlands and bring new technologies to enhance local rice production. In return, the RGAC will import rice and other food products in payment. A major drawback to product buyback agreements comes when the seller finds that the products bought back are in competition with its own similarly produced goods. Yet some have found that a product buyback agreement provides them with a supplemental source in areas of the world where there is demand but no available supply.

Problems of Countertrading

The crucial problem confronting a seller in a countertrade negotiation is determining the value of and potential demand for the goods offered. Frequently there is inadequate time to conduct a market analysis; in fact, it is not unusual to have sales negotiations almost completed before countertrade is introduced as a requirement in the transaction.

Although such problems are difficult to deal with, they can be minimized with proper preparation. In most cases where losses have occurred in countertrades, the seller has been unprepared to negotiate in anything other than cash. Some preliminary research should be done in anticipation of being confronted with a countertrade proposal. Countries with a history of countertrading are identified easily, and the products most likely to be offered in a countertrade often can be ascertained. For a company trading with developing countries, these facts and some background on handling countertrades should be a part of every pricing toolkit. Once goods are acquired, they can be passed along to institutions that assist companies in selling bartered goods.

Barter houses specialize in trading goods acquired through barter arrangements and are the primary outside source of aid for companies beset by the uncertainty of a countertrade. Although barter houses, most of which are found in Europe, can find a market for bartered goods, this effort requires time, which puts a financial strain on a company because capital is tied up longer than in normal transactions.

In the United States, there are companies that assist with bartered goods and their financing. Citibank has created a countertrade department to allow the bank to act as a consultant as well as to provide financing for countertrades. It is estimated that there are now about 500 barter exchange houses in the United States, many of which are accessible on the Internet. Some companies with a high volume of barter have their own in-house trading groups to manage countertrades. The 3M Company (Minnesota Mining and Manufacturing), for example, has a wholly owned division, 3M Global Trading (www.3m.com/globaltrading), which offers its services to smaller companies.

The Internet and Countertrading

The Internet may become the most important venue for countertrade activities. Finding markets for bartered merchandise and determining market price are two of the major problems with countertrades. Several barter houses have Internet auction sites, and a number of Internet exchanges are expanding to include global barter.

Some speculate that the Internet may become the vehicle for an immense online electronic barter economy, to complement and expand the offline barter exchanges that take place now. In short, some type of electronic trade dollar would replace national currencies in international trade transactions. This e-dollar would make international business considerably easier for many countries, because it would lessen the need to acquire sufficient U.S. or other hard currency to complete a sale or purchase.

TradeBanc, a market-making service, has introduced a computerized technology that will enable members of trade exchanges to trade directly, online, with members of other trade exchanges anywhere in the world, as long as their barter company is a TradeBanc affiliate (www.tradebanc.com). The medium of exchange could be the Universal Currency proposed by the International Reciprocal Trade Association (IRTA; www.irta.com), an association of trade exchanges with members including Russia, Iceland, Germany, Chile, Turkey, Australia, and the United States. The IRTA has proposed to establish and operate a Universal Currency Clearinghouse, which would enable trade exchange members to easily trade with one another using this special currency. When the system is in full swing, all goods and services from all the participating affiliates would be housed in a single database. The transactions would be cleared by the local exchanges, and settlement would be made using IRTA's Universal Currency, which could be used to purchase anything from airline tickets to potatoes.[25]

---

[25] You may want to visit the American Countertrade Association, http://www.countertrade.org, for a detailed discussion of the services offered by a countertrader.

Proactive Countertrade Strategy

Currently most companies have a reactive strategy; that is, they use countertrade when they believe it is the only way to make a sale. Even when these companies include countertrade as a permanent feature of their operations, they use it to react to a sales demand rather than using countertrade as an aggressive marketing tool for expansion. Some authorities suggest, however, that companies should have a defined countertrade strategy as part of their marketing strategy rather than be caught unprepared when confronted with a countertrade proposition

A proactive countertrade strategy is the most effective strategy for global companies that market to exchange-poor countries. Economic development plans in eastern European countries, the Commonwealth of Independent States (CIS), and much of Latin America will put unusual stress on their ability to generate sufficient capital to finance their growth. Furthermore, as countries encounter financial crises such as that in Latin America in 1996 and Asia in 1998, countertrade becomes especially important as a means of exchange. To be competitive, companies must be willing to include some countertraded goods in their market planning. Companies with a proactive strategy make a commitment to use countertrade aggressively as a marketing and pricing tool. They see countertrades as an opportunity to expand markets rather than as an inconvenient reaction to market demands.

In short, unsuccessful countertrades are generally the result of inadequate planning and preparation. One experienced countertrader suggests answering the following questions before entering into a countertrade agreement: (1) Is there a ready market for the goods bartered? (2) Is the quality of the goods offered consistent and acceptable? (3) Is an expert needed to handle the negotiations? (4) Is the contract price sufficient to cover the cost of barter and net the desired revenue?

Transfer Pricing Strategy

As companies increase the number of worldwide subsidiaries, joint ventures, company-owned distributing systems, and other marketing arrangements, the price charged to different affiliates becomes a preeminent question. Prices of goods transferred from a company's operations or sales units in one country to its units elsewhere, known as *intracompany pricing* or *transfer pricing*, may be adjusted to enhance the ultimate profit of the company as a whole. The benefits are as follows:

- Lowering duty costs by shipping goods into high-tariff countries at minimal transfer prices so that the duty base and duty are low.

- Reducing income taxes in high-tax countries by overpricing goods transferred to units in such countries; profits are eliminated and shifted to low-tax countries. Such profit shifting may also be used for "dressing up" financial statements by increasing reported profits in countries where borrowing and other financing are undertaken.

- Facilitating dividend repatriation when dividend repatriation is curtailed by government policy. Invisible income may be taken out in the form of high prices for products or components shipped to units in that country.

Government authorities have not overlooked the tax and financial manipulation possibilities of transfer pricing.[26] Transfer pricing can be used to hide subsidiary profits and to escape foreign-market taxes. Intracompany pricing is managed in such a way that profit is taken in the country with the lowest tax rate. For example, a foreign manufacturer makes a DVD player for $50 and sells it to its U.S. subsidiary for $150. The U.S. subsidiary sells it to a retailer for $200 but spends $50 on advertising and shipping so that it shows no profit and pays no U.S. taxes. Meanwhile, the parent company makes a $100 gross margin on

---

[26] Susan C. Borkowski, "Transfer Pricing Documentation and Penalties: How Much Is Enough?" *International Tax Journal,* Spring 2003, p. 31; Lorraine Eden, Luis F. Juarez, and Dan Li, "Talk Softly but Carry a Big Stick: Transfer Pricing Penalties and the Market Valuation of Japanese Multinationals in the United States," *Journal of International Business Studies* 36 (2005), pp. 398–414.

each unit and pays at a lower tax rate in the home country. If the tax rate were lower in the country where the subsidiary resides, the profit would be taken in the foreign country and no profit taken in the home country.[27]

When customs and tax regimes are high, companies have a strong incentive to trim fiscal liabilities by adjusting the transaction value of goods and services between subsidiaries. Pricing low cuts exposure to import duties; declaring a higher value raises deductible costs and thereby lightens the corporate tax burden. The key is to strike the right balance that maximizes savings overall.

The overall objectives of the intracompany pricing system include maximizing profits for the corporation as a whole; facilitating parent-company control; and offering management at all levels, both in the product divisions and in the international divisions, as an adequate basis for maintaining, developing, and receiving credit for their own profitability. Transfer prices that are too low are unsatisfactory to the product divisions because their overall results look poor; prices that are too high make the international operations look bad and limit the effectiveness of foreign managers.

An intracompany pricing system should employ sound accounting techniques and be defensible to the tax authorities of the countries involved. All of these factors argue against a single uniform price or even a uniform pricing system for all international operations. Four arrangements for pricing goods for intracompany transfer are as follows:

1. Sales at the local manufacturing cost plus a standard markup.
2. Sales at the cost of the most efficient producer in the company plus a standard markup.
3. Sales at negotiated prices.
4. Arm's-length sales using the same prices as quoted to independent customers.

Of the four, the arm's-length transfer is most acceptable to tax authorities and most likely to be acceptable to foreign divisions, but the appropriate basis for intracompany transfers depends on the nature of the subsidiaries and market conditions.

Although the practices described in this section are not necessarily improper, they are being scrutinized more closely by both home and host countries concerned about the loss of potential tax revenues from foreign firms doing business in their countries as well as domestic firms underreporting foreign earnings. The U.S. government is paying particular attention to transfer pricing in tax audits, as are other countries. This development has led to what some have described as a "tax war" between the United States and Japan over transfer pricing by MNCs, with each country bringing charges against foreign MNCs for underpayment of taxes because of transfer pricing practices. For example, the United States claimed that Nissan U.S. had inflated the prices it paid to its parent for finished cars it was importing to lower U.S. taxes. As a result, the United States levied a hefty multimillion-dollar tax penalty against Nissan. Japan retaliated by hitting Coca-Cola with a $145 million tax deficiency charge.

Governments are seeking tax revenues from their domestic MNCs as well. Prior to PepsiCo's decision to spin off its restaurant division into a separate company, the IRS charged PepsiCo $800 million after an audit of its foreign operations of Taco Bell, Pizza Hut, and KFC indicated an underreporting of profits of their foreign operations. Penalties can be as high as 40 percent of the amount underreported. The only certain way to avoid such penalties is to enter an *advanced pricing agreement (APA)* with the IRS. An APA is an agreement between the IRS and a taxpayer on transfer pricing methods that will be applied to some or all of a taxpayer's transactions with affiliates. Such agreements generally apply for up to five years and offer better protection against penalties than other methods. Otherwise, once the IRS charges underreporting, the burden of proof that a transfer price was fair rests with the company.

---

[27] For a detailed report on transfer pricing methods and their importance to an MNC with divisions located in different countries, see Thomas H. Stevenson and David W. E. Cabell, "Integrating Transfer Pricing Policy and Activity-Based Costing," *Journal of International Marketing* 10, no. 4 (2002), p. 77.

Price Quotations

In quoting the price of goods for international sale, a contract may include specific elements affecting the price, such as credit, sales terms, and transportation. Parties to the transaction must be certain that the quotation settled on appropriately locates responsibility for the goods during transportation and spells out who pays transportation charges and from what point. Price quotations must also specify the currency to be used, credit terms, and the type of documentation required. Finally, the price quotation and contract should define quantity and quality. A quantity definition might be necessary because different countries use different units of measurement. In specifying a ton, for example, the contract should identify it as a metric or an English ton and as a long or short ton. Quality specifications can also be misunderstood if not completely spelled out. Furthermore, there should be complete agreement on quality standards to be used in evaluating the product. For example, "customary merchantable quality" may be clearly understood among U.S. customers but have a completely different interpretation in another country. The international trader must review all terms of the contract; failure to do so may have the effect of modifying prices even though such a change was not intended.

Administered Pricing

Administered pricing is an attempt to establish prices for an entire market. Such prices may be arranged through the cooperation of competitors; through national, state, or local governments; or by international agreement. The legality of administered pricing arrangements of various kinds differs from country to country and from time to time. A country may condone price fixing for foreign markets but condemn it for the domestic market, for instance.

In general, the end goal of all administered pricing activities is to reduce the impact of price competition or eliminate it. Price fixing by business is not viewed as an acceptable practice (at least in the domestic market), but when governments enter the field of price administration, they presume to do it for the general welfare to lessen the effects of "destructive" competition.

The point at which comp_____ _____ _____ _pends largely on the country in question. To the Japan___ _____ ____ompetition in the home market that disturbs the existi__ ___ _____ _____ _ ___rket disruptions. Few countries apply more rigorous s___ ____ _____ ___ __ excessive than Japan, but no country favors or perm__ ___ _____ ____ists, the traditional champions of pure competition, acl__ ___ _____ ___s unlikely and agree that some form of workable comp_____ _____.

The pervasiveness o_ ___ _____ _____ ___ is reflected by the diversity of the language of admi_____ _____ts are known as agreements, arrangements, combine_ _____ _____ _____ties of profit, profit pools, licensing, trade associati__ _____ ____ _____icing, or informal interfirm agreements.[28] The arran_____ ___ __ _____completely informal, with no spoken or acknowled_____ _____ _____ed and structured arrangements. Any type of price-_____ _____ __ __l to international business, but of all the forms ment_____ ___ ____ _y associated with international marketing.

Cartels

A *cartel* exists when vari___ _____ _____ similar products or services work together to control markets for the types of goods and services they produce. The cartel association may use formal agreements to set prices, establish levels of production and sales for the participating companies, allocate market territories, and even redistribute profits. In some instances, the cartel organization itself takes over the entire selling function, sells the goods of all the producers, and distributes the profits.

---

[28] Dana Nunn and Miklos Sarvary, "Pricing Practices and Firms' Market Power in International Cellular Markets: An Empirical Study," *International Journal of Research in Marketing* 21, no. 4 (2004), pp. 377–95.

The economic role of cartels is highly debatable, but their proponents argue that they eliminate cutthroat competition and rationalize business, permitting greater technical progress and lower prices to consumers. However, most experts doubt that the consumer benefits very often from cartels.

The Organization of Petroleum Exporting Countries (OPEC) is probably the best known international cartel. Its power in controlling the price of oil has resulted from the percentage of oil production it controls. In the early 1970s, when OPEC members provided the industrial world with 67 percent of its oil, OPEC was able to quadruple the price of oil. The sudden rise in price from $3 a barrel to $11 or more a barrel was a primary factor in throwing the world into a major recession. In 2000, OPEC members lowered production, and the oil price rose from $10 to over $30, creating a dramatic increase in U.S. gasoline prices. Non-OPEC oil-exporting countries benefit from the price increases, while net importers of foreign oil face economic repercussions.

One important aspect of cartels is their inability to maintain control for indefinite periods. Greed by cartel members and other problems generally weaken the control of the cartel. OPEC members tend to maintain a solid front until one decides to increase supply, and then others rapidly follow suit. In the short run, however, OPEC can affect global prices. Indeed, at this writing, world oil prices are above $100 a barrel, but most analysts attribute this increase more to burgeoning demand[29] than OPEC's ability to control supply.[30]

A lesser-known cartel, but one that has a direct impact on international trade, is the cartel that exists among the world's shipping companies. Every two weeks about 20 shipping-line managers gather for their usual meeting to set rates on tens of billions of dollars of cargo. They do not refer to themselves as a cartel but rather operate under such innocuous names as "The Trans-Atlantic Conference Agreement" (www.tacaconf.com). Regardless of the name, they set the rates on about 70 percent of the cargo shipped between the United States and northern Europe. Shipping between the United States and Latin American ports and between the United States and Asian ports also is affected by shipping cartels. Not all shipping lines are members of cartels, but a large number are; thus they have a definite impact on shipping. Although legal, shipping cartels are coming under scrutiny by the U.S. Congress, and new regulations may soon be passed.

Another cartel is the diamond cartel controlled by De Beers. For more than a century, De Beers has smoothly manipulated the diamond market by keeping a tight control over world supply.[31] The company mines about half the world's diamonds and takes in another 25 percent through contracts with other mining companies. In an attempt to control the other 25 percent, De Beers runs an "outside buying office" where it spends millions buying up diamonds to protect prices. The company controls most of the world's trade in rough gems and uses its market power to keep prices high.

The legality of cartels at present is not clearly defined. Domestic cartelization is illegal in the United States, and the European Union also has provisions for controlling cartels. The United States does permit firms to take cartel-like actions in foreign markets, though it does not allow foreign-market cartels if the results have an adverse impact on the U.S. economy. Archer Daniels Midland Company, the U.S. agribusiness giant, was fined $205 million for its role in fixing prices for two food additives, lysine

Oil prices quadrupled in the mid-1970s because of OPEC's control of supplies. The $100 per barrel oil you see in this picture has been caused by burgeoning demand in China and around the world in 2008. Pertamina is the Indonesian national oil company. (© DADANG TRI/Reuters/Landov)

[29] "CPC to Continue Freeze on Oil Prices," *China Post*, March 2, 2008; Neil King Jr., Chip Cummins, and Russell Gold, "Oil Hits $100, Jolting Markets," *The Wall Street Journal* online, January 3, 2008, p. A1.

[30] Robert J. Samuelson, "The Triumph of OPEC," *Newsweek*, March 17, 2008, p. 45.

[31] Eric Onstad, "De Beers May Spurn Low-Margin Russian Supply," *Reuters News*, July 20, 2007.

The De Beers company is one of the world's largest cartels, and for all practical purposes, it controls most of the world's diamonds and thus is able to maintain artificially high prices for diamonds. One of the ways in which it maintains control is illustrated by a recent agreement with Russia's diamond monopoly, in which De Beers will buy at least $550 million in rough gem diamonds from Russia, or about half of the country's annual output. By controlling supply from Russia, the second largest producer of diamonds, the South African cartel can keep prices high. (© Susan Van Etten/Photo Edit, Inc.)

and citric acid. German, Japanese, Swiss, and Korean firms were also involved in the cartel. The group agreed on prices to charge and then allocated the share of the world market each company would get—down to the tenth of a decimal point. At the end of the year, any company that sold more than its allotted share was required to purchase in the following year the excess from a co-conspirator that had not reached its volume allocation target.

Although EU member countries have had a long history of tolerating price fixing, the European Union is beginning to crack down on cartels in the shipping, automobile, and cement industries, among others. The unified market and single currency have prompted this move. As countries open to free trade, powerful cartels that artificially raise prices and limit consumer choice are coming under closer scrutiny. However, the EU trustbusters are fighting tradition—since the trade guilds of the Middle Ages, cozy cooperation has been the norm. In each European country, companies banded together to control prices within the country and to keep competition out.

Government-Influenced Pricing

Companies doing business in foreign countries encounter a number of different types of government price setting. To control prices, governments may establish margins, set prices and floors or ceilings, restrict price changes, compete in the market, grant subsidies, and act as a purchasing monopsony or selling monopoly.[32] The government may also influence prices by permitting, or even encouraging, businesses to collude in setting manipulative prices. As an aside, of course, some companies need no help in price fixing—which often is illegal.[33]

The Japanese government traditionally has encouraged a variety of government-influenced price-setting schemes, However, in a spirit of deregulation that is gradually moving through Japan, Japan's Ministry of Health and Welfare will soon abolish regulation

---

[32] "Apple, EU Reach iTunes Pricing Deal," *The Wall Street Journal* (online), January 9, 2008.

[33] "Canada Probes Allegations of Chocolate Price-Fixing," *The Wall Street Journal* (online), November 28, 2007; John R. Wilke, "Two U.K. Airlines Settle Price-Fixing Claims," *Wall Street Journal* online, February 15, 2008, p. A4.

of business hours and price setting for such businesses as barbershops, beauty parlors, and laundries. Under the current practice, 17 sanitation-related businesses can establish such price-setting schemes, which are exempt from the Japanese Anti-Trust Law.

Governments of producing and consuming countries seem to play an ever-increasing role in the establishment of international prices for certain basic commodities. There is, for example, an international coffee agreement, an international cocoa agreement, and an international sugar agreement. And the world price of wheat has long been at least partially determined by negotiations between national governments.

Despite the pressures of business, government, and international price agreements, most marketers still have wide latitude in their pricing decisions for most products and markets.

Summary

Pricing is one of the most complicated decision areas encountered by international marketers. Rather than deal with one set of market conditions, one group of competitors, one set of cost factors, and one set of government regulations, international marketers must take all these factors into account, not only for each country in which they are operating but often for each market within a country. Market prices at the consumer level are much more difficult to control in international than in domestic marketing, but the international marketer must still approach the pricing task on a basis of established objectives and policy, leaving enough flexibility for tactical price movements. Controlling costs that lead to price escalation when exporting products from one country to another is one of the most challenging pricing tasks facing the exporter. Some of

the flexibility in pricing is reduced by the growth of the Internet, which has a tendency to equalize price differentials between country markets.

The continuing growth of Third World markets coupled with their lack of investment capital has increased the importance of countertrades for most marketers, making countertrading an important tool to include in pricing policy. The Internet is evolving to include countertrades, which will help eliminate some of the problems associated with this practice.

Pricing in the international marketplace requires a combination of intimate knowledge of market costs and regulations, an awareness of possible countertrade deals, infinite patience for detail, and a shrewd sense of market strategy.

Questions

1. Define the following terms:

dumping	barter
parallel imports	countervailing duty
exclusive distribution	compensation deal
buyback agreement	subsidy
administered pricing	cartel
variable-cost pricing	counterpurchase
full-cost pricing	transfer pricing
skimming	advanced pricing agreement
price escalation	countertrade

2. Discuss the causes of and solutions for parallel imports and their effect on price.

3. Why is it so difficult to control consumer prices when selling overseas?

4. Explain the concept of price escalation and why it can mislead an international marketer.

5. What are the causes of price escalation? Do they differ for exports and goods produced and sold in a foreign country?

6. Why is it seldom feasible for a company to absorb the high cost of international transportation and reduce the net price received?

7. Price escalation is a major pricing problem for the international marketer. How can this problem be counteracted? Discuss.

8. Changing currency values have an impact on export strategies. Discuss.

9. "Regardless of the strategic factors involved and the company's orientation to market pricing, every price must be set with cost considerations in mind." Discuss.

10. "Price fixing by business is not generally viewed as an acceptable practice (at least in the domestic market), but when governments enter the field of price administration, they presume to do it for the general welfare to lessen the effects of 'destructive' competition." Discuss.

11. Do value-added taxes discriminate against imported goods?

12. Explain specific tariffs, ad valorem tariffs, and compound tariffs.

13. Suggest an approach a marketer may follow in adjusting prices to accommodate exchange rate fluctuations.

14. Explain the effects of indirect competition and how they may be overcome.

15. Why has dumping become such an issue in recent years?

16. Cartels seem to rise, phoenixlike, after they have been destroyed. Why are they so appealing to business?

17. Discuss the different pricing problems that result from inflation versus deflation in a country.

18. Discuss the various ways in which governments set prices. Why do they engage in such activities?

19. Discuss the alternative objectives possible in setting prices for intracompany sales.

20. Why do governments so carefully scrutinize intracompany pricing arrangements?

21. Why are costs so difficult to assess in marketing internationally?

22. Discuss why countertrading is on the increase.

23. Discuss the major problems facing a company that is countertrading.

24. If a country you are trading with has a shortage of hard currency, how should you prepare to negotiate price?

25. Of the four types of countertrades discussed in the text, which is the most beneficial to the seller? Explain.

26. Why should a "knowledge of countertrades be part of an international marketer's pricing toolkit"? Discuss.

27. Discuss the various reasons purchasers impose countertrade obligations on buyers.

28. Discuss how FTZs can be used to help reduce price escalation.

29. Why is a proactive countertrade policy good business in some countries?

30. Differentiate between proactive and reactive countertrade policies.

31. One free trade zone is in Turkey. Visit www.esbas.com.tr and discuss how it might be used to help solve the price escalation problem of a product being exported from the United States to Turkey.

32. Visit Global Trading (a division of 3M) at www.mmm.com/globaltrading/edge.html and select "The Competitive Edge" and "Who We Are." Then write a short report on how Global Trading could assist a small company that anticipates having merchandise from a countertrade.

En los negocios no se consigue
lo que se merece, se consigue
lo que se negocia.

19

Negotiating with international customers, partners, and Regulators

CHAPTER OUTLINE

Global Perspective: A Japanese *Aisatsu*

The Dangers of Stereotypes

The Pervasive Impact of Culture on Negotiation
   Behavior

     Differences in Language and Nonverbal Behaviors
     Differences in Values
     Differences in Thinking and Decision-Making Processes

Implications for Managers and Negotiators

     Negotiation Teams
     Negotiation Preliminaries
     At the Negotiation Table
     After Negotiations

Conclusions

CHAPTER LEARNING OBJECTIVES

What you should learn from Chapter 19:

- The problems associated with cultural stereotypes

- How culture influences behaviors at the negotiation
  table

- Common kinds of problems that crop up during
  international business negotiations

- The similarities and differences in communication
  behaviors in several countries

- How differences in values and thinking processes
  affect international negotiations

- The important factors in selecting a negotiation team

- How to prepare for international negotiations

- Managing all aspects of the negotiation process

- The importance of follow-up communications and
  procedures

PART FIVE

Global Perspective

A JAPANESE *AISATSU*

It is not so much that speaking only English is a disadvantage in international business. Instead, it's more that being bilingual is a huge advantage. Observations from sitting in on an *aisatsu* (a meeting or formal greeting for high-level executives typical in Japan) involving the president of a large Japanese industrial distributor and the marketing vice president of an American machinery manufacturer are instructive. The two companies were trying to reach an agreement on a long-term partnership in Japan.

Business cards were exchanged and formal introductions made. Even though the president spoke and understood English, one of his three subordinates acted as an interpreter for the Japanese president. The president asked everyone to be seated. The interpreter sat on a stool between the two senior executives. The general attitude between the parties was friendly but polite. Tea and a Japanese orange drink were served.

The Japanese president controlled the interaction completely, asking questions of all Americans through the interpreter. Attention of all the participants was given to each speaker in turn. After this initial round of questions for all the Americans, the Japanese president focused on developing a conversation with the American vice president. During this interaction, an interesting pattern of nonverbal behaviors developed. The Japanese president would ask a question in Japanese. The interpreter then translated the question for the American vice president. While the interpreter spoke, the American's attention (gaze direction) was given to the interpreter. However, the Japanese president's gaze direction was at the American. Thus the Japanese president could carefully and unobtrusively observe the American's facial expressions and nonverbal responses. Conversely, when the American spoke, the Japanese president had twice the response time. Because the latter understood English, he could formulate his responses during the translation process.

What is this extra response time worth in a strategic conversation? What is it worth to be able to carefully observe the nonverbal responses of your top-level counterpart in a high-stakes business negotiation?

Source: James Day Hodgson, Yoshihiro Sano, and John L. Graham, *Doing Business with the New Japan* (Boulder, CO: Rowman & Littlefield, 2008).

I (John Graham) had been in China a couple of weeks. I was tired. The fog had delayed my flight from Xian to Shanghai by four hours. I was standing in a long line at the counter to check in *again*. I started chatting with the older chap in line ahead of me. Juhani Kari introduced himself as a Finnish sales manager at ABB. He asked me what I did for a living. I responded, "I teach international business." He replied, "There is no such thing as international business. There's only interpersonal business." A wise man, indeed!

Face-to-face negotiations are an omnipresent activity in international commerce.[1] Once global marketing strategies have been formulated, once marketing research has been conducted to support those strategies, and once product/service, pricing, promotion, and place decisions have been made, then the focus of managers turns to implementation of the plans. In international business, such plans are almost always implemented through face-to-face negotiations with business partners and customers from foreign countries. The sales of goods and services, the management of distribution channels, contracting for marketing research and advertising services, licensing and franchise agreements, and strategic alliances all require managers from different cultures to sit and talk with one another to exchange ideas and express needs and preferences.[2]

Executives must also negotiate with representatives of foreign governments who might approve a variety of their marketing actions or be the actual ultimate customer for goods and services. In many countries, governmental officials may also be joint venture partners and, in some cases, vendors. For example, negotiations for the television broadcast rights for the 2008 Summer Olympics in Beijing, China, included NBC, the International Olympic Committee, and Chinese governmental officials. Some of these negotiations can become quite complex, involving several governments, companies, and cultures.[3] Good examples are the European and North American talks regarding taxing the Internet, the continuing interactions regarding global environmental issues, or the ongoing WTO negotiations begun in Doha, Qatar, in 2001. All these activities demand a new kind of "business diplomacy."

One authority on international joint ventures suggests that a crucial aspect of all international commercial relationships is the negotiation of the original agreement. The seeds of success or failure often are sown at the negotiation table, vis-à-vis (face-to-face), where not only are financial and legal details agreed to but, perhaps more important, the ambiance of cooperation is established. Indeed, the legal details and the structure of international

---

[1] Several excellent books have been published on the topic of international business negotiations. Among them are Lothar Katz, *Negotiating International Business* (Charleston, SC: Booksurge, 2006); Camille Schuster and Michael Copeland, *Global Business, Planning for Sales and Negotiations* (Fort Worth, TX: Dryden, 1996); Robert T. Moran and William G. Stripp, *Dynamics of Successful International Business Negotiations* (Houston: Gulf, 1991); Pervez Ghauri and Jean-Claude Usunier (eds.), *International Business Negotiations* (Oxford: Pergamon, 1996); Donald W. Hendon, Rebecca Angeles Henden, and Paul Herbig, *Cross-Cultural Business Negotiations* (Westport, CT: Quorum, 1996); Sheida Hodge, *Global Smarts* (New York: Wiley, 2000); and Jeanne M. Brett, *Negotiating Globally* (San Francisco: Jossey-Bass, 2001). In addition, Roy J. Lewicki, David M. Saunders, and John W. Minton's *Negotiation: Readings, Exercises, and Cases*, 3rd ed. (New York: Irwin/McGraw-Hill, 1999) is an important book on the broader topic of business negotiations. The material from this chapter draws extensively on William Hernandez Requejo and John L. Graham, *Global Negotiation: The New Rules* (New York: Palgrave Macmillan, 2008); James Day Hodgson, Yoshihiro Sano, and John L. Graham, *Doing Business with the New Japan* (Boulder, CO: Rowman & Littlefield, 2008); and N. Mark Lam and John L. Graham, *China Now: Doing Business in the World's Most Dynamic Market* (New York: McGraw-Hill, 2007). See also http://www. GlobalNegotiationResources.com, 2008.

[2] David G. Sirmon and Peter J. Lane, "A Model of Cultural Differences and International Alliance Performance," *Journal of International Business Studies* 35, no. 4 (2004), pp. 306–19.

[3] R. Bruce Money provides an interesting theoretical perspective on the topic in "International Multilateral Negotiations and Social Networks," *Journal of International Business Studies* 29, no. 4 (1998), pp. 695–710. Lively anecdotes are included in Jiang Feng, "Courting the Olympics: Beijing's Other Face," *Asian Wall Street Journal*, February 26, 2001, p. 6; Ashling O'Connor, "After 54 Years, the Olympic Clock Is Ticking," *Times of London*, February 10, 2003, p. 35; Manjeet Kripalani, "Tata: Master of the Gentle Approach," *BusinessWeek*, February 25, 2008, pp. 64–66.

business ventures are almost always modified over time, usually through negotiations. But the atmosphere of cooperation initially established face-to-face at the negotiation table persists—or the venture fails.

Business negotiations between business partners from the same country can be difficult. The added complication of cross-cultural communication can turn an already daunting task into an impossible one.[4] However, if cultural differences are taken into account, oftentimes wonderful business agreements can be made that lead to long-term, profitable relationships across borders. The purpose of this final chapter is to help prepare managers for the challenges and opportunities of international business negotiations. To do this, we will discuss the dangers of stereotypes, the impact of culture on negotiation behavior, and the implications of cultural differences for managers and negotiators.

The Dangers of Stereotypes

The images of John Wayne, the cowboy, and the samurai, the fierce warrior, often are used as cultural stereotypes in discussions of international business negotiations.[5] Such representations almost always convey a grain of truth—an American cowboy kind of competitiveness versus a samurai kind of organizational (company) loyalty. One Dutch expert on international business negotiations argues, "The best negotiators are the Japanese because they will spend days trying to get to know their opponents. The worst are Americans because they think everything works in foreign countries as it does in the USA."[6] There are, of course, many Americans who are excellent international negotiators and some Japanese who are ineffective. The point is that negotiations are not conducted between national stereotypes; negotiations are conducted between people, and cultural factors often make huge differences.

Recall our discussion about the cultural diversity *within* countries from Chapter 4 and consider its relevance to negotiation. For example, we might expect substantial differences in negotiation styles between English-speaking and French-speaking Canadians. The genteel style of talk prevalent in the American Deep South is quite different from the faster speech patterns and pushiness more common in places like New York City. Experts tell us that negotiation styles differ across genders in America as well. Still others tell us that the urbane negotiation behaviors of Japanese bankers are very different from the relative aggressiveness of those in the retail industry in that country. Finally, age and experience can also make important differences. The older Chinese executive with no experience dealing with foreigners is likely to behave quite differently from her young assistant with undergraduate and MBA degrees from American universities.

The focus of this chapter is culture's influence on international negotiation behavior. However, it should be clearly understood that individual personalities and backgrounds and a variety of situational factors also heavily influence behavior at the negotiation table—and it is the manager's responsibility to consider these factors.[7] Remember: Companies and countries do not negotiate—people do. Consider the culture of your customers and business partners, but treat them as individuals.

---

[4] James K. Sebenius, "The Hidden Challenge of Cross-Border Negotiations," *Harvard Business Review*, March–April, 2002, pp. 76–82.

[5] Nurit Zaidman discusses how stereotypes are formed in "Stereotypes of International Managers: Content and Impact on Business Interactions," *Group & Organizational Management*, March 1, 2000, pp. 45–54.

[6] Samfrits Le Poole comments on the American stereotype in "John Wayne Goes to Brussels," in Roy J. Lewicki, Joseph A. Litterer, David M. Saunders, and John W. Minton (eds.), *Negotiation: Readings, Exercises, and Cases*, 2nd ed. (Burr Ridge, IL: Irwin, 1993). The quote is from the Spanish newspaper *Expansion*, November 29, 1991, p. 41.

[7] Stephen E. Weiss provides the most complete recent review of the international negotiations literature—"International Business Negotiations Research," in B. J. Punnett and O. Shenkar (eds.), *Handbook for International Management Research* (Ann Arbor: University of Michigan Press, 2004), pp. 415–74.

The Europeans stereotype themselves. This postcard was purchased at the European Parliament gift store in Brussels. Of course, not all Dutch are cheap; there are sober Irish, and so on. Now that the European Union has expanded to 27 countries, a larger card will be required. But we're fairly certain they'll have a humorous perspective on all the new entrants. (© J N Hughes-Wilson)

The Pervasive Impact of Culture on Negotiation Behavior

The primary purpose of this section is to demonstrate the extent of cultural differences in negotiation styles and how these differences can cause problems in international business negotiations. The material in this section is based on a systematic study of the topic over the last three decades in which the negotiation styles of more than 1,000 businesspeople in 17 countries (20 cultures) were considered.[8] The countries studied were Japan, Korea, Taiwan, China (Tianjin, Guangzhou, and Hong Kong), the Philippines, the Czech Republic, Russia, Israel, Norway, Germany, France, the United Kingdom, Spain, Brazil, Mexico, Canada (English-speaking and French-speaking), and the United States. The countries were chosen because they constitute America's most important present and future trading partners.

---

[8] The following institutions and people provided crucial support for the research upon which this material is based: U.S. Department of Education; Toyota Motor Sales USA, Inc.; Solar Turbines Inc. (a division of Caterpillar Tractors Co.); the Faculty Research and Innovation Fund and the International Business Educational Research (IBEAR) Program at the University of Southern California; Ford Motor Company; Marketing Science Institute; Madrid Business School; and Professors Nancy J. Adler (McGill University), Nigel Campbell (Manchester Business School), A. Gabriel Esteban (University of Houston, Victoria), Leonid I. Evenko (Russian Academy of the National Economy), Richard H. Holton (University of California, Berkeley), Alain Jolibert (Université des Sciences Sociales de Grenoble), Dong Ki Kim (Korea University), C. Y. Lin (National Sun-Yat Sen University), Hans-Gunther Meissner (Dortmund University), Alena Ockova (Czech Management Center), Sara Tang (Mass Transit Railway Corporation, Hong Kong), Kam-hon Lee (Chinese University of Hong Kong), and Theodore Schwarz (Monterrey Institute of Technology, Monterrey, CA).

Looking broadly across the several cultures, two important lessons stand out. The first is that regional generalizations very often are not correct.[9] For example, Japanese and Korean negotiation styles are quite similar in some ways, but in other ways, they could not be more different. The second lesson learned from this study is that Japan is an exceptional place: On almost every dimension of negotiation style considered, the Japanese are on or near the end of the scale. Sometimes Americans are on the other end. But actually, most of the time Americans are somewhere in the middle. The reader will see this evinced in the data presented in this section. The Japanese approach, however, is most distinct, even *sui generis*.

Cultural differences cause four kinds of problems in international business negotiations, at the levels of:[10]

1. Language

2. Nonverbal behaviors

3. Values

4. Thinking and decision-making processes

The order is important; the problems lower on the list are more serious because they are more subtle. For example, two negotiators would notice immediately if one were speaking Japanese and the other German. The solution to the problem may be as simple as hiring an interpreter or talking in a common third language, or it may be as difficult as learning a language. Regardless of the solution, the problem is obvious. Cultural differences in nonverbal behaviors, in contrast, are almost always hidden below our awareness. That is to say, in a face-to-face negotiation, participants nonverbally—and more subtly—give off and take in a great deal of information. Some experts argue that this information is more important than verbal information. Almost all this signaling goes on below our levels of consciousness.[11] When the nonverbal signals from foreign partners are different, negotiators are most likely to misinterpret them without even being conscious of the mistake. For example, when a French client consistently interrupts, Americans tend to feel uncomfortable without noticing exactly why. In this manner, interpersonal friction often colors business relationships, goes undetected, and, consequently, goes uncorrected. Differences in values and thinking and decision-making processes are hidden even deeper and therefore are even harder to cure. We discuss these differences here, starting with language and nonverbal behaviors.

Differences in Language and Nonverbal Behaviors

Americans are clearly near the bottom of the languages skills list, though Australians assert that Australians are even worse. It should be added, however, that American undergrads recently have begun to see the light and are flocking to language classes and study-abroad programs. Unfortunately, foreign language teaching resources in the United States are inadequate to satisfy the increasing demand. In contrast, the Czechs are now throwing away a hard-earned competitive advantage: Young Czechs will not take Russian anymore. It is easy to understand why, but the result will be a generation of Czechs who cannot leverage their geographic advantage because they will not be able to speak to their neighbors to the east.

The language advantages of the Japanese executive in the description of the *aisatsu* that opened the chapter were quite clear. However, the most common complaint heard from American managers regards foreign clients and partners breaking into side conversations in their native languages. At best, this is seen as impolite, and quite often American negotiators are likely to attribute something sinister to the content of the foreign talk—"They're plotting or telling secrets."

This perception is a frequent American mistake. The usual purpose of such side conversations is to straighten out a translation problem. For instance, one Korean may lean over to

---

[9] Rohit Deshpandé and John Farley, "High Performance Firms in a Complex New China: A Tale of Six Cities," *Journal of Global Marketing* 16, no. 1–2 (2002), pp. 207–209.

[10] For additional details, see William Hernandez Requejo and John L. Graham, *Global Negotiation: The New Rules* (New York: Palgrave Macmillan, 2008); http://www.GlobalNegotiationResources.com, 2008.

[11] Jan Ulijn, Anne Francoise Rutowski, Rajesh Kumar, and Yunxia Zhu, "Patterns of Feelings in Face-to-Face Negotiation: A Sino-Dutch Pilot Study," *Cross Cultural Management* 12, no. 3 (2005), pp. 103–118.

Japanese negotiators exchange business cards at the front end of a meeting. Even more important than the nonverbal demonstration of respect in the "little ritual" is the all-important information about the relative status of the negotiators, clearly communicated by job title and company. Japanese executives literally do not know how to talk to one another until the status relationship is determined, because proper use of the language depends on knowledge of the relative status of the negotiators.

(© Photodisc Green/Getty Images)

another and ask, "What'd he say?" Or the side conversation can regard a disagreement among the foreign team members. Both circumstances should be seen as positive signs by Americans—that is, getting translations straight enhances the efficiency of the interactions, and concessions often follow internal disagreements. But because most Americans speak only one language, neither circumstance is appreciated. By the way, people from other countries are advised to give Americans a brief explanation of the content of their first few side conversations to assuage the sinister attributions.

Data from simulated negotiations are also informative. In our study, the verbal behaviors of negotiators in 15 of the 21 cultures (six negotiators in each of the 15 groups) were videotaped. The numbers in the body of Exhibit 19.1 represent the percentages of statements that were classified into each category listed. That is, 7 percent of the statements made by Japanese negotiators were classified as promises, 4 percent as threats, 7 percent as recommendations, and so on. The verbal bargaining behaviors used by the negotiators during the simulations proved to be surprisingly similar across cultures. Negotiations in all 15 cultures studied were composed primarily of information-exchange tactics—questions and self-disclosures. Note that the Japanese appear on the low end of the continuum of self-disclosures. Their 34 percent (along with Spaniards and English-speaking Canadians) was the second lowest across all 15 groups, suggesting that they are the most reticent about giving information, except for the Israelis. Overall, however, the verbal tactics used were surprisingly similar across the diverse cultures.

Exhibit 19.2 provides analyses of some linguistic aspects and nonverbal behaviors for the 15 videotaped groups. Although these efforts merely scratch the surface of these kinds of behavioral analyses, they still provide indications of substantial cultural differences.[12] Note that, once again, the Japanese are at or next to the end of the continuum on almost every dimension of the behaviors listed. Their facial gazing and touching are the least among the 15 groups. Only the northern Chinese used the word *no* less frequently, and only the English-speaking Canadians and Russians used more silent periods than did the Japanese.

A broader examination of the data in Exhibits 19.1 and 19.2 reveals a more meaningful conclusion: The variation across cultures is greater when comparing linguistic aspects of language and nonverbal behaviors than when the verbal content of negotiations is considered. For example, notice the great differences between Japanese and Brazilians in Exhibit 19.1 vis-à-vis Exhibit 19.2.

Following are further descriptions of the distinctive aspects of each of the 15 cultural groups videotaped. Certainly, conclusions about the individual cultures cannot be drawn from an analysis of only six businesspeople in each culture, but the suggested cultural differences are worthwhile to consider briefly.

Japan.   Consistent with most descriptions of Japanese negotiation behavior, the results of this analysis suggest their style of interaction is among the least aggressive (or most polite). Threats, commands, and warnings appear to be deemphasized in favor of the more positive promises, recommendations, and commitments. Particularly indicative of their polite conversational style was their infrequent use of *no* and *you* and facial gazing, as well as more frequent silent periods.

Korea.   Perhaps one of the more interesting aspects of the analysis is the contrast of the Asian styles of negotiations. Non-Asians often generalize about Asians; the findings demonstrate, however, that this generalization is a mistake. Korean negotiators used considerably more punishments and commands than did the Japanese. Koreans used the word *no* and interrupted more than three times as frequently as the Japanese. Moreover, no silent periods occurred between Korean negotiators.

12 Thomas W. Leigh and John O. Summers, "An Initial Evaluation of Industrial Buyers' Impressions of Salespersons' Nonverbal Cues," *Journal of Personal Selling & Sales Management*, Winter 2002, pp. 41–53.

Exhibit 19.1
Verbal Negotiation Tactics (The "What" of Communications)

Bargaining Behaviors and Definitions	Cultures*														
	JPN	KOR	TWN	CHN**	RUSS	ISRL	GRM	UK	FRN	SPN	BRZ	MEX	FCAN	ECAN	USA
Promise. A statement in which the source indicates its intention to provide the target with a reinforcing consequence, which the source anticipates the target will evaluate as pleasant, positive, or rewarding.	7†	4	9	6	5	12	7	11	5	11	3	7	8	6	8
Threat. Same as promise, except that the reinforcing consequences are thought to be noxious, unpleasant, or punishing.	4	2	2	1	3	4	3	3	5	2	2	1	3	0	4
Recommendation. A statement in which the source predicts that a pleasant environmental consequence will occur to the target. Its occurrence is not under source's control.	7	1	5	2	4	8	5	6	3	4	5	8	5	4	4
Warning. Same as recommendation, except that the consequences are thought to be unpleasant.	2	0	3	1	0	1	1	1	3	1	1	2	3	0	1
Reward. A statement by the source that is thought to create pleasant consequences for the target.	1	3	2	1	3	2	4	5	3	3	2	1	1	3	2
Punishment. Same as reward, except that the consequences are thought to be unpleasant.	1	5	1	0	1	3	2	0	3	2	3	0	2	1	3
Normative appeals. A statement in which the source indicates that the target's past, present, or future behavior will conform with social norms or is in violation of social norms.	4	3	1	1	1	5	1	1	0	1	1	1	3	1	2
Commitment. A statement by the source to the effect that its future bids will not go below or above a certain level.	15	13	9	10	1	10	9	13	10	9	8	9	8	14	13
Self-disclosure. A statement in which the source reveals information about itself.	34	36	42	36	40	30	47	39	42	34	39	38	42	34	36
Question. A statement in which the source asks the target to reveal information about itself.	20	21	14	34	27	20	11	15	18	17	22	27	19	26	20
Command. A statement in which the source suggests that the target perform a certain behavior.	8	13	11	7	7	9	12	9	9	17	14	7	5	10	6

*For each, group n = 6.

**Northern China (Tianjin and environs).

†Read "7 percent of the statements made by Japanese negotiators were promises."

Source: From William Hernandez Requejo and John L. Graham, *Global Negotiation: The New Rules* (New York: Palgrave Macmillan, 2008).

CROSSING BORDERS 19.3   Fishing for Business in Brazil

How important is nontask sounding? Consider this description about an American banker's meeting in Brazil, as recounted by an observer:

Introductions were made. The talk began with the usual "How do you like Rio?" questions—Have you been to Ipanema, Copacabana, Corcovado, etc.? There was also talk about the flight down from New York. After about five minutes of this chatting, the senior American quite conspicuously glanced at his watch, and then asked his client what he knew about the bank's new services.

"A little," responded the Brazilian. The senior American whipped a brochure out of his briefcase, opened it on the desk in front of the client, and began his sales pitch.

After about three minutes of "fewer forms, electronic transfers, and reducing accounts receivables," the Brazilian jumped back in, "Yes, that should make us more competitive . . . and competition is important here in Brazil. In fact, have you been following the World Cup *fútbol* (soccer) matches recently? Great games." And so the reel began to whir, paying out that monofilament line, right there in that hot high-rise office.

After a few minutes' dissertation on the local *fútbol* teams, Pélé, and why *fútbol* isn't popular

in the United States, the American started to try to crank the Brazilian back in. The first signal was the long look at his watch, then the interruption, "Perhaps we can get back to the new services we have to offer."

The Brazilian did get reeled back into the subject of the sale for a couple of minutes, but then the reel started to sing again. This time he went from efficient banking transactions to the nuances of the Brazilian financial system to the Brazilian economy. Pretty soon we were all talking about the world economy and making predictions about the U.S. presidential elections.

Another look at his Rolex, and the American started this little "sport fishing" ritual all over again. From my perspective (I wasn't investing time and money toward the success of this activity), this all seemed pretty funny. Every time the American VP looked at his watch during the next 45 minutes, I had to bite my cheeks to keep from laughing out loud. He never did get to page two of his brochure. The Brazilian just wasn't interested in talking business with someone he didn't know pretty well.

Source: William Hernandez Requejo and John L. Graham, *Global Negotiation: The New Rules* (New York: Palgrave Macmillan, 2008).

first offers are more aggressive to reflect these expectations. "If the goal is 1 million, we better start at 2," makes sense there. Americans react to such aggressive first offers in one of two ways: They either laugh or get angry. And when foreign counterparts' second offers reflect deep discounts, Americans' ire increases.

A good example of this problem regards an American CEO shopping for a European plant site. When he selected a $20 million plot in Ireland, the Spanish real estate developer he had visited earlier called wondering why the American had not asked for a lower price for the Madrid site before choosing Dublin. He told the Spaniard that his first offer "wasn't even in the ballpark." He wasn't laughing when the Spaniard then offered to beat the Irish price. In fact, the American executive was quite angry. A potentially good deal was forgone because of different expectations about first offers. Yes, numbers were exchanged, but information was not. Aggressive first offers made by foreigners should be met with questions, not anger.

Persuasion.   In Japan, a clear separation does not exist between task-related information exchange and persuasion. The two stages tend to blend together as each side defines and refines its needs and preferences. Much time is spent in the task-related exchange of information, leaving little to "argue" about during the persuasion stage. Conversely, Americans tend to lay their cards on the table and hurry through the information exchange to persuasion. After all, the persuasion is the heart of the matter. Why hold a meeting unless someone's mind is to be changed? A key aspect of sales training in the United States is "handling objections." So the goal in information exchange among Americans is to quickly get those objections out in the open so they can be handled.

This handling can mean providing clients with more information. It can also mean getting mean. As suggested by Exhibit 19.2, Americans make threats and issue warnings in negotiations.[36] They do not use such tactics often, but negotiators in many other cultures use such tactics even less frequently and in different circumstances. For example, notice how infrequently the Mexicans and English-speaking Canadians used threats and warnings in the simulated negotiations. Others have found Filipino and Chinese negotiators to use a less aggressive approach than Americans.[37] Indeed, in Thailand or China, the use of such aggressive negotiation tactics can result in the loss of face and the destruction of important personal relationships. Such tough tactics may be used in Japan but by buyers only and usually only in informal circumstances—not at the formal negotiation table. Americans also get angry during negotiations and express emotions that may be completely inappropriate in foreign countries. Such emotional outbursts may be seen as infantile or even barbaric behavior in places like Hong Kong and Bangkok.

The most powerful persuasive tactic is actually asking more questions. Foreign counterparts can be politely asked to explain why they must have delivery in two months or why they must have a 10 percent discount. Chester Karrass, in his still useful book *The Negotiation Game*,[38] suggests that it is "smart to be a little dumb" in business negotiations. Repeat questions; for example, "I didn't completely understand what you meant—can you please explain that again?" If clients or potential business partners have good answers, then perhaps a compromise on the issue is best. Often, however, under close and repeated scrutiny, their answers are not very good. When their weak position is exposed, they are obliged to concede. Questions can elicit key information, the most powerful yet passive persuasive device. Indeed, the use of questions is a favored Japanese tactic, one they use with great effect on Americans.

You want him on your side! Banana salespeople such as this fellow in Agra, India, are known worldwide for their negotiation skills—they're hawking a perishable product that shows the wear. In Japan they even have a negotiation strategy named for them: Outrageously high first offers are derogated as *"banana no tataki uri,"* the banana sale approach.

Third parties and informal channels of communication are the indispensable media of persuasion in many countries, particularly the more relationship-oriented ones. Meetings in restaurants or meetings with references and mutual friends who originally provided introductions may be used to handle difficult problems with partners in other countries. The value of such informal settings and trusted intermediaries is greatest when problems are emotion laden. They provide a means for simultaneously delivering difficult messages and saving face. Although American managers may eschew such "behind the scenes" approaches, they are standard practice in many countries.

Concessions and Agreement.   Comments made previously about the importance of writing down concession-making strategies and understanding differences in decision-making styles—sequential versus holistic—are pertinent here. Americans often make concessions early, expecting foreign counterparts to reciprocate. However, in many cultures no concessions are made until the end of the negotiations. Americans often get frustrated and express anger when foreign clients and partners are simply following a different approach to concession making, one that can also work quite well when both sides understand what is going on.

[36] For more details, see Deborah A. Cai and Edward L. Fink, "Conflict Style Differences between Individualists and Collectivists," *Communication Monographs*, March 1, 2002, pp. 67–75.

[37] X. Michael Song, Jinhong Xie, and Barbara Dyer, "Antecedents and Consequences of Marketing Managers' Conflict Handling Procedures," *Journal of Marketing* 64 (January 2000), pp. 50–66; Alma Mintu-Wimsatt and Julie B. Gassenheimer, "The Moderating Effects of Cultural Context in Buyer–Seller Negotiation," *Journal of Personal Selling & Sales Management* 20, no. 1 (Winter 2000), pp. 1–9.

[38] Chester Karrass, *The Negotiation Game* (New York: Crowell, 1970).

After Negotiations

Contracts between American firms are often longer than 100 pages and include carefully worded clauses regarding every aspect of the agreement. American lawyers go to great lengths to protect their companies against all circumstances, contingencies, and actions of the other party. The best contracts are written so tightly that the other party would not think of going to court to challenge any provision. The American adversarial system requires such contracts.

In most other countries, particularly the relationship-oriented ones, legal systems are not depended upon to settle disputes. Indeed, the term *disputes* does not reflect how a business relationship should work. Each side should be concerned about mutual benefits of the relationship and therefore should consider the interests of the other. Consequently, in places like Japan written contracts are very short—two to three pages—are purposely loosely written, and primarily contain comments on principles of the relationship. From the Japanese point of view, the American emphasis on tight contracts is tantamount to planning the divorce before the wedding.

Tung Chee Hwa, Chief Executive of the Hong Kong Special Administrative Region, consummated the deal with the Mouse for Asia's new Walt Disney World, which opened in 2005. (AP Photo/Anat Givon)

In other relationship-oriented countries, such as China, contracts are more a description of what business partners view their respective responsibilities to be. For complicated business relationships, they may be quite long and detailed. However, their purpose is different from the American understanding. When circumstances change, then responsibilities must also be adjusted, despite the provisions of the signed contract. The notion of enforcing a contract in China makes little sense.

Informality being a way of life in the United States, even the largest contracts between companies are often sent through the mail for signature. In America, ceremony is considered a waste of time and money. But when a major agreement is reached with foreign companies, their executives may expect a formal signing ceremony involving CEOs of the respective companies. American companies are wise to accommodate such expectations.

Finally, follow-up communications are an important part of business negotiations with partners and clients from most foreign countries. Particularly in high-context cultures, where personal relationships are crucial, high-level executives must stay in touch with their counterparts. Letters, pictures, and mutual visits remain important long after contracts are signed. Indeed, warm relationships at the top often prove to be the best medicine for any problems that may arise in the future.

Conclusions

Despite the litany of potential pitfalls facing international negotiators, things are getting better. The stereotypes of American managers as "innocents abroad" or cowboys are becoming less accurate. Likewise, we hope it is obvious that the stereotypes of the reticent Japanese or the pushy Brazilian evinced in the chapter may no longer hold so true. Experience levels are going up worldwide, and individual personalities are important. So you can find talkative Japanese, quiet Brazilians, and effective American negotiators. But culture still does, and always will, count. We hope that it is fast becoming the natural behavior of American managers to take culture into account.

English author Rudyard Kipling said some one hundred years ago: "Oh, East is East, and West is West, and never the twain shall meet." Since then most have imbued his words with an undeserved pessimism. Some even wrongly say he was wrong.[39] The problem is that not many have bothered to read his entire poem, *The Ballad of East and West:*

> Oh, East is East, and West is West, and never the twain shall meet,
> Till Earth and Sky stand presently at God's great Judgment Seat;
> But there is neither East nor West, border, nor breed, nor birth,
> When two strong men stand face to face, though they come from the ends of the earth!

The poem can stand some editing for these more modern times. It should include the

[39] Michael Elliot, "Killing off Kipling," *Newsweek*, December 29, 1977, pp. 52–55.

other directions—North is North and South is South. And the last line properly should read, "When two strong *people* stand face to face." But Kipling's positive sentiment remains. Differences between countries and cultures, no matter how difficult, can be worked out when people talk to each other in face-to-face settings. Kipling rightly places the responsibility for international cooperation not on companies or governments but instead directly on the shoulders of individual managers, present and future, like you. Work hard!

Summary

Because styles of business negotiations vary substantially around the world, it is important to take cultural differences into account when meeting clients, customers, and business partners across the international negotiation table. In addition to cultural factors, negotiators' personalities and backgrounds also influence their behavior. Great care should be taken to get to know the individuals who represent client and customer companies. Cultural stereotypes can be quite misleading.

Four kinds of problems frequently arise during international business negotiations—problems at the level of language, nonverbal behaviors, values, and thinking and decision-making processes. Foreign-language skills are an essential tool of the international negotiator. Nonverbal behaviors vary dramatically across cultures, and because their influence is often below our level of awareness, problems at this level can be serious. Whereas most Americans value objectivity, competitiveness, equality, and punctuality, many foreign executives may not. As for thinking and decision making, Western business executives tend to address complex negotiations by breaking deals down into smaller issues and settling them sequentially; in many Eastern cultures, a more holistic approach is used in discussions.

Much care must be taken in selecting negotiation teams to represent companies in meetings with foreigners. Listening skills, influence at headquarters, and a willingness to use team assistance are important negotiator traits. Americans should be careful to try to match foreign negotiation teams in both numbers and seniority. The importance of cross-cultural training and investments in careful preparations cannot be overstated. Situational factors such as the location for meetings and the time allowed must also be carefully considered and managed.

All around the world, business negotiations involve four steps: nontask sounding, task-related information exchange, persuasion, and concessions and agreement. The time spent on each step can vary considerably from country to country. Americans spend little time on nontask sounding or getting to know foreign counterparts. Particularly in relationship-oriented cultures, it is important to let the customers bring up business when they feel comfortable with the personal relationship. Task-related information goes quickly in the United States as well. In other countries, such as Japan, the most time is spent on the second stage, and careful understandings of partners are the focus. Persuasion is the most important part of negotiations from the American perspective. Aggressive persuasive tactics (threats and warnings) are used frequently. Such persuasive tactics, though they may work well in some cultures, will cause serious problems in others. Finally, because Americans tend to be deal oriented, more care will have to be taken in follow-up communications with foreign clients and partners who put more emphasis on long-term business relationships.

Questions

1. Define the following terms:

   BATNA

   nontask sounding

   task-related information exchange

2. Why can cultural stereotypes be dangerous? Give some examples.

3. List three ways that culture influences negotiation behavior.

4. Describe the kinds of problems that usually come up during international business negotiations.

5. Why are foreign-language skills important for international negotiators?

6. Describe three cultural differences in nonverbal behaviors and explain how they might cause problems in international business negotiations.

7. Why is time an important consideration in international business negotiations?

8. What can be different about how a Japanese manager might address a complex negotiation compared with an American negotiator?

9. What are the most important considerations in selecting a negotiation team? Give examples.

10. What kinds of training are most useful for international business negotiators?

11. Name three aspects of negotiation situations that might be manipulated before talks begin. Suggest how this manipulation might be done.

12. Explain why Americans spend so little time on nontask sounding and Brazilians so much.

13. Why is it difficult to get negative feedback from counterparts in many foreign countries? Give examples.

14. Why won't getting mad work in Mexico or Japan?

15. Why are questions the most useful persuasive tactic?

The first stage in the planning process is a preliminary country analysis. The marketer needs basic information to evaluate a country market's potential, identify problems that would eliminate a country from further consideration, identify aspects of the country's environment that need further study, evaluate the components of the marketing mix for possible adaptation, and develop a strategic marketing plan. One further use of the information collected in the preliminary analysis is as a basis for a country notebook.

Many companies, large and small, have a *country notebook* for each country in which they do business. The country notebook contains information a marketer should be aware of when making decisions involving a specific country market. As new information is collected, the country notebook is continually updated by the country or product manager. Whenever a marketing decision is made involving a country, the country notebook is the first database consulted. New-product introductions, changes in advertising programs, and other marketing program decisions begin with the country notebook. It also serves as a quick introduction for new personnel assuming responsibility for a country market.

This section presents four separate guidelines for collection and analysis of market data and preparation of a country notebook: (1) guideline for cultural analysis, (2) guideline for economic analysis, (3) guideline for market audit and competitive analysis, and (4) guideline for preliminary marketing plan. These guidelines suggest the kinds of information a marketer can gather to enhance planning.

The points in each of the guidelines are general. They are designed to provide direction to areas to explore for relevant data. In each guideline, specific points must be adapted to reflect a company's products. The decision as to the appropriateness of specific data and the depth of coverage depends on company objectives, product characteristics, and the country market. Some points in the guidelines are unimportant for some countries or some products and should be ignored. Preceding chapters of this book provide specific content suggestions for the topics in each guideline.

I. CULTURAL ANALYSIS

The data suggested in the cultural analysis include information that helps the marketer make market planning decisions. However, its application extends beyond product and market analysis to being an important source of information for someone interested in understanding business customs and other important cultural features of the country.

The information in this analysis must be more than a collection of facts. Whoever is responsible for the preparation of this material should attempt to interpret the meaning of cultural information. That is, how does the information help in understanding the effect on the market? For example, the fact that almost all the populations of Italy and Mexico are Catholic is an interesting statistic but not nearly as useful as understanding the effect of Catholicism on values, beliefs, and other aspects of market behavior. Furthermore, even though both countries are predominantly Catholic, the influence of their individual and unique interpretation and practice of Catholicism can result in important differences in market behavior.

Guideline
I. Introduction
   Include short profiles of the company, the product to be exported, and the country with which you wish to trade.
II. Brief discussion of the country's relevant history
III. Geographical setting
   A. Location
   B. Climate
   C. Topography
IV. Social institutions
   A. Family
      1. The nuclear family
      2. The extended family
      3. Dynamics of the family
         a. Parental roles
         b. Marriage and courtship
      4. Female/male roles (changing or static?)
   B. Education
      1. The role of education in society
         a. Primary education (quality, levels of development, etc.)
         b. Secondary education (quality, levels of development, etc.)
         c. Higher education (quality, levels of development, etc.)
      2. Literacy rates
   C. Political system
      1. Political structure
      2. Political parties
      3. Stability of government
      4. Special taxes
      5. Role of local government

    D. Legal system
       1. Organization of the judiciary system
       2. Code, common, socialist, or Islamic-law country?
       3. Participation in patents, trademarks, and other conventions
    E. Social organizations
       1. Group behavior
       2. Social classes
       3. Clubs, other organizations
       4. Race, ethnicity, and subcultures
    F. Business customs and practices

V. Religion and aesthetics
    A. Religion and other belief systems
       1. Orthodox doctrines and structures
       2. Relationship with the people
       3. Which religions are prominent?
       4. Membership of each religion
       5. Any powerful or influential cults?
    B. Aesthetics
       1. Visual arts (fine arts, plastics, graphics, public art, colors, etc.)
       2. Music
       3. Drama, ballet, and other performing arts
       4. Folklore and relevant symbols

VI. Living conditions
    A. Diet and nutrition
       1. Meat and vegetable consumption rates
       2. Typical meals
       3. Malnutrition rates
       4. Foods available
    B. Housing
       1. Types of housing available
       2. Do most people own or rent?
       3. Do most people live in one-family dwellings or with other families?
    C. Clothing
       1. National dress
       2. Types of clothing worn at work
    D. Recreation, sports, and other leisure activities
       1. Types available and in demand
       2. Percentage of income spent on such activities
    E. Social security
    F. Healthcare

VII. Language
    A. Official language(s)
    B. Spoken versus written language(s)
    C. Dialects

VIII. Executive summary

After completing all of the other sections, prepare a *two-page* (maximum length) summary of the major points and place it at the front of the report. The purpose of an executive summary is to give the reader a brief glance at the critical points of your report. Those aspects of the culture a reader should know to do business in the country but would not be expected to know or would find different based on his or her SRC should be included in this summary.

IX. Sources of information

X. Appendixes

II. ECONOMIC ANALYSIS

The reader may find the data collected for the economic analysis guideline are more straightforward than for the cultural analysis guideline. There are two broad categories of information in this guideline: general economic data that serve as a basis for an evaluation of the economic soundness of a country, and information on channels of distribution and media availability. As mentioned previously, the guideline focuses only on broad categories of data and must be adapted to particular company and product needs.

Guideline

   I. Introduction
  II. Population
     A. Total
       1. Growth rates
       2. Number of live births
       3. Birthrates
     B. Distribution of population
       1. Age
       2. Sex
       3. Geographic areas (urban, suburban, and rural density and concentration)
       4. Migration rates and patterns
       5. Ethnic groups
 III. Economic statistics and activity
     A. Gross national product (GNP or GDP)
       1. Total
       2. Rate of growth (real GNP or GDP)
     B. Personal income per capita
     C. Average family income
     D. Distribution of wealth
       1. Income classes
       2. Proportion of the population in each class
       3. Is the distribution distorted?
     E. Minerals and resources
     F. Surface transportation
       1. Modes
       2. Availability
       3. Usage rates
       4. Ports
     G. Communication systems
       1. Types
       2. Availability
       3. Usage rates
     H. Working conditions
       1. Employer–employee relations
       2. Employee participation
       3. Salaries and benefits
     I. Principal industries
       1. What proportion of the GNP does each industry contribute?
       2. Ratio of private to publicly owned industries
     J. Foreign investment
       1. Opportunities?
       2. Which industries?
     K. International trade statistics
       1. Major exports
         a. Dollar value
         b. Trends
       2. Major imports
         a. Dollar value
         b. Trends
       3. Balance-of-payments situation

        a. Surplus or deficit?

        b. Recent trends

    4. Exchange rates

        a. Single or multiple exchange rates?

        b. Current rate of exchange

        c. Trends

L. Trade restrictions

    1. Embargoes

    2. Quotas

    3. Import taxes

    4. Tariffs

    5. Licensing

    6. Customs duties

M. Extent of economic activity not included in cash income activities

    1. Countertrades

        a. Products generally offered for countertrading

        b. Types of countertrades requested (barter, counterpurchase, etc.)

    2. Foreign aid received

N. Labor force

    1. Size

    2. Unemployment rates

O. Inflation rates

IV. Developments in science and technology

    A. Current technology available (computers, machinery, tools, etc.)

    B. Percentage of GNP invested in research and development

    C. Technological skills of the labor force and general population

V. Channels of distribution (macro analysis)

This section reports data on all channel middlemen available within the
market. Later, you will select a specific channel as part of your distribution
strategy.

    A. Retailers

        1. Number of retailers

        2. Typical size of retail outlets

        3. Customary markup for various classes of goods

        4. Methods of operation (cash/credit)

        5. Scale of operation (large/small)

        6. Role of chain stores, department stores, and specialty shops

    B. Wholesale middlemen

        1. Number and size

        2. Customary markup for various classes of goods

        3. Method of operation (cash/credit)

    C. Import/export agents

    D. Warehousing

    E. Penetration of urban and rural markets

VI. Media

This section reports data on all media available within the country or market.
Later, you will select specific media as part of the promotional mix and strategy.

    A. Availability of media

    B. Costs

        1. Television

        2. Radio

        3. Print

        4. Other media (cinema, outdoor, etc.)

    C. Agency assistance

    D. Coverage of various media

    E. Percentage of population reached by each medium

VII. Executive summary
After completing the research for this report, prepare a two-page (maximum) summary of the major economic points and place it at the front
VIII. Sources of information
IX. Appendixes

III. MARKET AUDIT AND COMPETITIVE MARKET ANALYSIS

Of the guidelines presented, this is the most product or brand specific. Information in the other guidelines is general in nature, focusing on product categories, whereas data in this guideline are brand specific and are used to determine competitive market conditions and market potential.

Two different components of the planning process are reflected in this guideline. Information in Parts I and II, Cultural Analysis and Economic Analysis, serve as the basis for an evaluation of the product or brand in a specific country market. Information in this guideline provides an estimate of market potential and an evaluation of the strengths and weaknesses of competitive marketing efforts. The data generated in this step are used to determine the extent of adaptation of the company's marketing mix necessary for successful market entry and to develop the final step, the action plan.

The detailed information needed to complete this guideline is not necessarily available without conducting a thorough marketing research investigation. Thus another purpose of this part of the country notebook is to identify the correct questions to ask in a formal market study.

Guideline

I. Introduction
II. The product
   A. Evaluate the product as an innovation as it is perceived by the intended market
      1. Relative advantage
      2. Compatibility
      3. Complexity
      4. Trialability
      5. Observability
   B. Major problems and resistances to product acceptance based on the preceding evaluation
III. The market
   A. Describe the market(s) in which the product is to be sold
      1. Geographical region(s)
      2. Forms of transportation and communication available in that (those) region(s)
      3. Consumer buying habits
         a. Product-use patterns
         b. Product feature preferences
         c. Shopping habits
      4. Distribution of the product
         a. Typical retail outlets
         b. Product sales by other middlemen
      5. Advertising and promotion
         a. Advertising media usually used to reach your target market(s)
         b. Sales promotions customarily used (sampling, coupons, etc.)
      6. Pricing strategy
         a. Customary markups
         b. Types of discounts available
   B. Compare and contrast your product and the competition's product(s)
      1. Competitor's product(s)
         a. Brand name
         b. Features
         c. Package
      2. Competitor's prices
      3. Competitor's promotion and advertising methods
      4. Competitor's distribution channels
   C. Market size

        1. Estimated industry sales for the planning year
        2. Estimated sales for your company for the planning year
    D. Government participation in the marketplace
        1. Agencies that can help you
        2. Regulations you must follow
IV. Executive summary
    Based on your analysis of the market, briefly summarize (two-page maximum) the major problems and opportunities requiring attention in your marketing mix, and place the summary at the front of the report.
  V. Sources of information
 VI. Appendixes

IV. PRELIMINARY MARKETING PLAN

Information gathered in Guidelines I through III serves as the basis for developing a marketing plan for your product or brand in a target market. How the problems and opportunities that surfaced in the preceding steps are overcome or exploited to produce maximum sales and profits are presented here. The action plan reflects, in your judgment, the most effective means of marketing your product in a country market. Budgets, expected profits and losses, and additional resources necessary to implement the proposed plan are also presented.

Guideline

I. The marketing plan
    A. Marketing objectives
        1. Target market(s) (specific description of the market)
        2. Expected sales year 20—
        3. Profit expectations year 20—
        4. Market penetration and coverage
    B. Product adaptation or modification—Using the product component model as your guide, indicate how your product can be adapted for the market.
        1. Core component
        2. Packaging component
        3. Support services component
    C. Promotion mix
        1. Advertising
            a. Objectives
            b. Media mix
            c. Message
            d. Costs
        2. Sales promotions
            a. Objectives
            b. Coupons
            c. Premiums
            d. Costs
        3. Personal selling
        4. Other promotional methods
    D. Distribution: From origin to destination
        1. Port selection
            a. Origin port
            b. Destination port
        2. Mode selection: Advantages/disadvantages of each mode
            a. Railroads
            b. Air carriers
            c. Ocean carriers
            d. Motor carriers
        3. Packing
            a. Marking and labeling regulations
            b. Containerization
            c. Costs

    4. Documentation required
      a. Bill of lading
      b. Dock receipt
      c. Air bill
      d. Commercial invoice
      e. Pro forma invoice
      f. Shipper's export declaration
      g. Statement of origin
      h. Special documentation
    5. Insurance claims
    6. Freight forwarder. If your company does not have a transportation or traffic management department, then consider using a freight forwarder. There are distinct advantages and disadvantages to hiring one.

E. Channels of distribution (micro analysis). This section presents details about the specific types of distribution in your marketing plan.
    1. Retailers
      a. Type and number of retail stores
      b. Retail markups for products in each type of retail store
      c. Methods of operation for each type (cash/credit)
      d. Scale of operation for each type (small/large)
    2. Wholesale middlemen
      a. Type and number of wholesale middlemen
      b. Markup for class of products by each type
      c. Methods of operation for each type (cash/credit)
      d. Scale of operation (small/large)
    3. Import/export agents
    4. Warehousing
      a. Type
      b. Location

F. Price determination
    1. Cost of the shipment of goods
    2. Transportation costs
    3. Handling expenses
      a. Pier charges
      b. Wharfage fees
      c. Loading and unloading charges
    4. Insurance costs
    5. Customs duties
    6. Import taxes and value-added tax
    7. Wholesale and retail markups and discounts
    8. Company's gross margins
    9. Retail price

G. Terms of sale
    1. EX works, FOB, FAS, C&F, CIF
    2. Advantages/disadvantages of each

H. Methods of payment
    1. Cash in advance
    2. Open accounts
    3. Consignment sales
    4. Sight, time, or date drafts
    5. Letters of credit

II. Pro forma financial statements and budgets
  A. Marketing budget
    1. Selling expense
    2. Advertising/promotion expense

      3. Distribution expense
      4. Product cost
      5. Other costs
   B. Pro forma annual profit and loss statement (first year and fifth year)
III. Resource requirements
   A. Finances
   B. Personnel
   C. Production capacity
IV. Executive summary
   After completing the research for this report, prepare a two-page (maximum) summary of the major points of your successful marketing plan, and place it at the front of the report.
 V. Sources of information
VI. Appendixes
   The intricacies of international operations and the complexity of the environment within which the international marketer must operate create an extraordinary demand for information. When operating in foreign markets, the need for thorough information as a substitute for uninformed opinion is equally important as it is in domestic marketing. Sources of information needed to develop the country notebook and answer other marketing questions are discussed in Chapter 8 and its appendix.

Summary

Market-oriented firms build strategic market plans around company objectives, markets, and the competitive environment. Planning for marketing can be complicated even for one country, but when a company is doing business internationally, the problems are multiplied. Company objectives may vary from market to market and from time to time; the structure of international markets also changes periodically and from country to country; and the competitive, governmental, and economic parameters affecting market planning are in a constant state of flux. These variations require international marketing executives to be especially flexible and creative in their approach to strategic marketing planning.

cases 1

AN OVERVIEW

CASE 1-1 Starbucks—Going Global Fast

The Starbucks coffee shop on Sixth Avenue and Pine Street in downtown Seattle sits serene and orderly, as unremarkable as any other in the chain bought years ago by entrepreneur Howard Schultz. A little less than three years ago however, the quiet storefront made front pages around the world. During the World Trade Organization talks in November 1999, protesters flooded Seattle's streets, and among their targets was Starbucks, a symbol, to them, of free-market capitalism run amok, another multinational out to blanket the earth. Amid the crowds of protesters and riot police were black-masked anarchists who trashed the store, leaving its windows smashed and its tasteful green-and-white decor smelling of tear gas instead of espresso. Says an angry Schultz: "It's hurtful. I think people are ill-informed. It's very difficult to protest against a can of Coke, a bottle of Pepsi, or a can of Folgers. Starbucks is both this ubiquitous brand and a place where you can go and break a window. You can't break a can of Coke."

The store was quickly repaired, and the protesters have scattered to other cities. Yet cup by cup, Starbucks really is caffeinating the world, its green-and-white emblem beckoning to consumers on three continents. In 1999, Starbucks Corp. had 281 stores abroad. Today, it has about 5,000—and it's still in the early stages of a plan to colonize the globe. If the protesters were wrong in their tactics, they weren't wrong about Starbucks' ambitions. They were just early.

The story of how Schultz & Co. transformed a pedestrian commodity into an upscale consumer accessory has a fairy-tale quality. Starbucks has grown from 17 coffee shops in Seattle 15 years ago to over 16,000 outlets in 44 countries. Sales have climbed an average of 20 percent annually since the company went public, to $9.4 billion in 2007, while profits bounded ahead an average of 30 percent per year, hitting $673 million last year.

Moreover, the Starbucks name and image connect with millions of consumers around the globe. Up until recently it was one of the fastest-growing brands in annual *BusinessWeek* surveys of the top 100 global brands. On Wall Street, Starbucks was one of the last great growth stories. Its stock, including four splits, soared more than 2,200 percent over a decade, surpassing Wal-Mart, General Electric, PepsiCo, Coca-Cola, Microsoft, and IBM in total return. In 2006 the stock price peaked at over $40, but now has declined to $18.

Schultz's team is hard-pressed to grind out new profits in a home market that is quickly becoming saturated. Amazingly, with over 11,000 stores scattered across the United States and Canada, there are still eight states in the United States with no Starbucks stores. Frappuccino-free cities include Butte, Montana, and Fargo, North Dakota. But big cities, affluent suburbs, and shopping malls are full to the brim. In coffee-crazed Seattle, there is a Starbucks outlet for every 9,400 people, and the company considers that the upper limit of coffee-shop saturation. In Manhattan's 24 square miles, Starbucks has 124 cafés, with more on the way. That's one for every 12,000 people—meaning that there could be room for even more stores. Given such concentration, it is likely to take annual same-store sales increases of 10 percent or more if the company is going to match its historic overall sales growth. That, as they might say at Starbucks, is a tall order to fill.

Indeed, the crowding of so many stores so close together has become a national joke, eliciting quips such as this headline in *The Onion*, a satirical publication: "A New Starbucks Opens in Restroom of Existing Starbucks." And even the company admits that while its practice of blanketing an area with stores helps achieve market dominance, it can cut sales at existing outlets. "We probably self-cannibalize our stores at a rate of 30 percent a year," Schultz says. Adds Lehman Brothers Inc. analyst Mitchell Speiser: "Starbucks is at a defining point in its growth. It's reaching a level that makes it harder and harder to grow, just due to the law of large numbers."

To duplicate the staggering returns of its first decade, Starbucks has no choice but to export its concept aggressively. Indeed, some analysts give Starbucks only two years at most before it saturates the U.S. market. The chain now operates 1,700 international outlets, from Beijing to Bristol. That leaves plenty of room to grow. Indeed, most of its planned new stores will be built overseas, representing a 35 percent increase in its foreign base. Starbucks expects to double the number of its stores worldwide in three years. During the past 12 months, the chain has opened stores in Vienna, Zurich, Madrid, Berlin, and even in far-off Jakarta. Athens comes next. And within the next year, Starbucks plans to move into Mexico and Puerto Rico. But global expansion poses huge risks for Starbucks. For one thing, it makes less money on each overseas store because most of them are operated with local partners. While that makes it easier to start up on foreign turf, it reduces the company's share of the profits to only 20 percent to 50 percent.

Moreover, Starbucks must cope with some predictable challenges of becoming a mature company in the United States. After riding the wave of successful baby boomers through the 1990s, the company faces an ominously hostile reception from its future consumers, the twenty- or thirtysomethings of Generation X. Not only are the activists among them turned off by the power and image of the well-known brand, but many others say that Starbucks' latte-sipping sophisticates and piped-in Kenny G music are a real turnoff. They don't feel wanted in a place that sells designer coffee at $3 a cup.

Even the thirst of loyalists for high-price coffee cannot be taken for granted. Starbucks' growth over the past decade coincided with a remarkable surge in the economy. Consumer spending has continued strong in the downturn, but if that changes, those $3 lattes might be an easy place for people on a budget to cut back. Starbucks executives insist that won't happen, pointing out that even in the weeks following the terrorist attacks, same-store comparisons stayed positive while those of other retailers skidded.

Starbucks also faces slumping morale and employee burnout among its store managers and its once-cheery army of baristas. Stock options for part-timers in the restaurant business was a Starbucks innovation that once commanded awe and respect from its employees. But now, though employees are still paid better than comparable workers elsewhere—about $7 per hour—many regard the job as just another fast-food gig. Dissatisfaction over odd hours and low pay is affecting the quality of the normally sterling service and even the coffee itself, say some customers and employees. Frustrated store managers among the company's roughly 470 California stores sued Starbucks in 2001 for allegedly refusing to pay legally mandated overtime. Starbucks settled the suit for $18 million, shaving $0.03 per share off an otherwise strong second quarter. However, the heart of the complaint—feeling overworked and underappreciated—doesn't seem to be going away.

To be sure, Starbucks has a lot going for it as it confronts the challenge of maintaining its growth. Nearly free of debt, it fuels expansion with internal cash flow. And Starbucks can maintain a tight grip on its image because stores are company-owned: There are no franchisees to get sloppy about running things. By relying on mystique and word of mouth, whether here or overseas, the company saves a bundle on marketing costs. Starbucks spends just $30 million annually on advertising, or roughly 1 percent of revenues, usually just for new flavors of coffee drinks in the summer and product launches, such as its new in-store Web service. Most consumer companies its size shell out upwards of $300 million per year. Moreover, unlike a McDonald's or a The Gap Inc., two other retailers that rapidly grew in the United States, Starbucks has no nationwide competitor.

Schultz remains the heart and soul of the operation. Raised in a Brooklyn public-housing project, he found his way to Starbucks, a tiny chain of Seattle coffee shops, as a marketing executive in the early 1980s. The name came about when the original owners looked to Seattle history for inspiration and chose the moniker of an old mining camp: Starbo. Further refinement led to Starbucks, after the first mate in *Moby-Dick*, which they felt evoked the seafaring romance of the early coffee traders (hence the mermaid logo). Schultz got the idea for the modern Starbucks format while visiting a Milan coffee bar. He bought out his bosses in 1987 and began expanding.

The company is still capable of designing and opening a store in 16 weeks or less and recouping the initial investment in three years. The stores may be oases of tranquility, but management's expansion tactics are something else. Take what critics call its "predatory real estate" strategy—paying more than market-rate rents to keep competitors out of a location. David C. Schomer, owner of Espresso Vivace in Seattle's hip Capitol Hill neighborhood, says Starbucks approached his landlord and offered to pay nearly double the rate to put a coffee shop in the same building. The landlord stuck with Schomer, who says: "It's a little disconcerting to know that someone is willing to pay twice the going rate." Another time, Starbucks and Tully's Coffee Corp., a Seattle-based coffee chain, were competing for a space in the city. Starbucks got the lease but vacated the premises before the term was up. Still, rather than let Tully's get the space, Starbucks decided to pay the rent on the empty store so its competitor could not move in. Schultz makes no apologies for the hardball tactics. "The real estate business in America is a very, very tough game," he says. "It's not for the faint of heart."

Still, the company's strategy could backfire. Not only will neighborhood activists and local businesses increasingly resent the tactics, but customers could also grow annoyed over having fewer choices. Moreover, analysts contend that Starbucks can maintain about 15 percent square-footage growth in the United States— equivalent to 550 new stores—for only about two more years. After that, it will have to depend on overseas growth to maintain an annual 20 percent revenue growth.

Starbucks was hoping to make up much of that growth with more sales of food and other noncoffee items, but has stumbled somewhat. In the late 1990s, Schultz thought that offering $8 sandwiches, desserts, and CDs in his stores and selling packaged coffee in supermarkets would significantly boost sales. The specialty business now accounts for about 16 percent of sales, but growth has been less than expected.

What's more important for the bottom line, though, is that Starbucks has proven to be highly innovative in the way it sells its main course: coffee. In 800 locations it has installed automatic espresso machines to speed up service. And several years ago, it began offering prepaid Starbucks cards, priced from $5 to $500, which clerks swipe through a reader to deduct a sale. That, says the company, cuts transaction times in half. Starbucks has sold $70 million of the cards.

When Starbucks launched Starbucks Express, its boldest experiment yet, it blended java, Web technology, and faster service. At about 60 stores in the Denver area, customers can pre-order and prepay for beverages and pastries via phone or on the Starbucks Express Web site. They just make the call or click the mouse before arriving at the store, and their beverage will be waiting—with their name printed on the cup. The company decided in 2003 that the innovation had not succeeded and eliminated the service.

And Starbucks continues to try other fundamental store changes. It announced expansion of a high-speed wireless Internet service to about 1,200 Starbucks locations in North America and Europe. Partners in the project—which Starbucks calls the world's largest Wi-Fi network—include Mobile International, a wireless subsidiary of Deutsche Telekom, and Hewlett-Packard. Customers sit in a store and check e-mail, surf the Web, or download multimedia presentations without looking for connections or tripping over cords. They start with 24 hours of free wireless broadband before choosing from a variety of monthly subscription plans.

Starbucks executives hope such innovations will help surmount their toughest challenge in the home market: attracting the next generation of customers. Younger coffee drinkers already feel uncomfortable in the stores. The company knows that because it once had a group of twentysomethings hypnotized for a market study. When their defenses were down, out came the bad news. "They either can't afford to buy coffee at Starbucks, or the only peers they see are those working behind the counter," says Mark Barden, who conducted the research for the Hal Riney & Partners ad agency (now part of Publicis Worldwide) in San Francisco. One of the recurring themes the hypnosis brought out was a sense that "people like me aren't welcome here except to serve the yuppies," he says. Then there are those who just find the whole Starbucks scene a bit pretentious. Katie Kelleher, 22, a Chicago paralegal, is put off by Starbucks' Italian terminology of grande and venti for coffee sizes. She goes to Dunkin' Donuts, saying: "Small, medium, and large is fine for me."

As it expands, Starbucks faces another big risk: that of becoming a far less special place for its employees. For a company modeled around enthusiastic service, that could have dire consequences for both image and sales. During its growth spurt of the mid- to late-1990s, Starbucks had the lowest employee turnover rate of any restaurant or fast-food company, largely thanks to its then unheard-of policy of giving health insurance and modest stock options to part-timers making barely more than minimum wage.

Such perks are no longer enough to keep all the workers happy. Starbucks' pay doesn't come close to matching the workload it requires, complain some staff. Says Carrie Shay, a former store manager in West Hollywood, California: "If I were making a decent living, I'd still be there." Shay, one of the plaintiffs in the suit against the company, says she earned $32,000 a year to run a store with 10 to 15 part-time employees. She hired employees, managed their schedules, and monitored the store's weekly profit-and-loss statement. But she was also expected to put in significant time behind the counter and had to sign an affidavit pledging to work up to 20 hours of overtime a week without extra pay—a requirement the company has dropped since the settlement. Smith says that Starbucks offers better pay, benefits, and training than comparable companies, while it encourages promotions from within.

For sure, employee discontent is far from the image Starbucks wants to project of relaxed workers cheerfully making cappuccinos. But perhaps it is inevitable. The business model calls for lots of low-wage workers. And the more people who are hired as Starbucks expands, the less they are apt to feel connected to the original mission of high service—bantering with customers and treating them like family. Robert J. Thompson, a professor of popular culture at Syracuse University, says of Starbucks: "It's turning out to be one of the great 21st century American success stories—complete with all the ambiguities."

Overseas, though, the whole Starbucks package seems new and, to many young people, still very cool. In Vienna, where Starbucks had a gala opening for its first Austrian store, Helmut Spudich, a business editor for the paper *Der Standard*, predicted that Starbucks would attract a younger crowd than the established cafés. "The coffeehouses in Vienna are nice, but they are old. Starbucks is considered hip," he says.

But if Starbucks can count on its youth appeal to win a welcome in new markets, such enthusiasm cannot be counted on indefinitely. In Japan, the company beat even its own bullish expectations, growing to 722 stores after opening its first in Tokyo in 1996. Affluent young Japanese women like Anna Kato, a 22-year-old Toyota Motor Corp. worker, loved the place. "I don't care if it costs more, as long as it tastes sweet," she says, sitting in the world's busiest Starbucks, in Tokyo's Shibuya district. Yet same-store sales growth has fallen in Japan, Starbucks' top foreign market, as rivals offer similar fare. Meanwhile in England, Starbucks' second-biggest overseas market, with over 400 stores, imitators are popping up left and right to steal market share.

Entering other big markets may be tougher yet. The French seem to be ready for Starbucks' sweeter taste, says Philippe Bloch, cofounder of Columbus Cafe, a Starbucks-like chain. But he wonders if the company can profitably cope with France's arcane regulations and generous labor benefits. And in Italy, the epicenter of European coffee culture, the notion that the locals will abandon their own 200,000 coffee bars en masse for Starbucks strikes many as ludicrous. For one, Italian coffee bars prosper by serving food as well as coffee, an area where Starbucks still struggles. Also, Italian coffee is cheaper than U.S. java and, say Italian purists, much better. Americans pay about $1.50 for an espresso. In northern Italy, the price is 67 cents; in the south, just 55 cents. Schultz insists that Starbucks will eventually come to Italy. It'll have a lot to prove when it does. Carlo Petrini, founder of the antiglobalization movement Slow Food, sniffs that Starbucks' "substances served in styrofoam" won't cut it. The cups are paper, of course. But the skepticism is real.

As Starbucks spreads out, Schultz will have to be increasingly sensitive to those cultural challenges. For instance, he flew to Israel several years ago to meet with then-Foreign Secretary Shimon Peres and other Israeli officials to discuss the Middle East crisis. He won't divulge the nature of his discussions. But subsequently,

at a Seattle synagogue, Schultz let the Palestinians have it. With Starbucks outlets already in Kuwait, Lebanon, Oman, Qatar, and Saudi Arabia, he created a mild uproar among Palestinian supporters. Schultz quickly backpedaled, saying that his words were taken out of context and asserting that he is "pro-peace" for both sides.

There are plenty more minefields ahead. So far, the Seattle coffee company has compiled an envious record of growth. But the giddy buzz of that initial expansion is wearing off. Now, Starbucks is waking up to the grande challenges faced by any corporation bent on becoming a global powerhouse.

In a 2005 bid to boost sales in its largest international market, Starbucks Corp. expanded its business in Japan, beyond cafés and into convenience stores, with a line of chilled coffee in plastic cups. The move gives the Seattle-based company a chance to grab a chunk of Japan's $10 billion market for coffee sold in cans, bottles, or vending machines rather than made-to-order at cafés. It is a lucrative but fiercely competitive sector, but Starbucks, which has become a household name since opening its first Japanese store, is betting on the power of its brand to propel sales of the new drinks.

Starbucks is working with Japanese beverage maker and distributor Suntory Ltd. The "Discoveries" line is the company's first foray into the ready-to-drink market outside North America, where it sells a line of bottled and canned coffee. It also underscores Starbucks' determination to expand its presence in Asia by catering to local tastes. For instance, the new product comes in two variations—espresso and latte—that are less sweet than their U.S. counterparts, as the coffee maker developed them to suit Asian palates. Starbucks officials said they hope to establish their product as the premium chilled cup brand, which, at 210 yen ($1.87), will be priced at the upper end of the category.

Starbucks faces steep competition. Japan's "chilled cup" market is teeming with rival products, including Starbucks lookalikes. One of the most popular brands, called Mt. Rainier, is emblazoned with a green circle logo that closely resembles that of Starbucks. Convenience stores also are packed with canned coffee drinks, including Coca-Cola Co.'s Georgia brand and brews with extra caffeine or made with gourmet coffee beans.

Schultz declined to speculate on exactly how much coffee Starbucks might sell through Japan's convenience stores. "We wouldn't be doing this if it wasn't important both strategically and economically," he said.

The company has no immediate plans to introduce the beverage in the United States, though it has in the past brought home products launched in Asia. A green tea frappuccino, first launched in Asia, was later introduced in the United States and Canada, where company officials say it was well received.

Starbucks has done well in Japan, although the road hasn't always been smooth. After cutting the ribbon on its first Japan store in 1996, the company began opening stores at a furious pace, and it now has more than 700. New shops attracted large crowds, but the effect wore off as the market became saturated. The company has since returned to profitability, and net profits jumped more than sixfold to 1.17 billion yen. It cleared another hurdle when sales at stores open at least 13 months rose from a year earlier for the first time in four years. It is focusing on continuing this trend by renovating stores and improving service.

Most recently in Japan, the firm has successfully developed a broader menu for its stores, including customized products—smaller sandwiches and less-sweet desserts. The strategy increased same store sales and overall profits. The firm also added 70 new stores in 2007, including some drive-through service. But

McDonald's also is attacking the Japan market with the introduction of its McCafé coffee shops.

QUESTIONS

As a guide use Exhibit 1.3 and its description in Chapter 1, and do the following:

1. Identify the controllable and uncontrollable elements that Starbucks has encountered in entering global markets.

2. What are the major sources of risk facing the company and discuss potential solutions.

3. Critique Starbucks' overall corporate strategy.

4. How might Starbucks improve profitability in Japan?

Visit www.starbucks.com for more information.

Sources: Stanley Holmes, Drake Bennett, Kate Carlisle, and Chester Dawson, "Planet Starbucks: To Keep Up the Growth It Must Go Global Quickly," *BusinessWeek,* December 9, 2002, pp. 100–110; Ken Belson, "Japan: Starbucks Profit Falls," *The New York Times,* February 20, 2003, p. 1; Ginny Parker Woods, "Starbucks Bets Drinks Will Jolt Japan Sales," *Asian Wall Street Journal,* September 27, 2005, p. A7; Amy Chozick, "Starbucks in Japan Needs A Jolt," *The Wall Street Journal,* October 24, 2006, p. 23; "McCafé Debuts in Japan, Challenging Starbucks, Other Coffee Shops," *Kyoto News,* August 28, 2007; "Starbucks Japan Sees 55% Pretax Profit Jump for April-December," *Nikkei Report,* February 6, 2008.

CASE I-2 Nestlé: The Infant Formula Controversy

Nestlé Alimentana of Vevey, Switzerland, one of the world's largest food-processing companies with worldwide sales of over $121 billion, has been the subject of an international boycott. For over 20 years, beginning with a Pan American Health Organization allegation, Nestlé has been directly or indirectly charged with involvement in the death of Third World infants. The charges revolve around the sale of infant feeding formula, which allegedly is the cause for mass deaths of babies in the Third World.

In 1974 a British journalist published a report that suggested that powdered-formula manufacturers contributed to the death of Third World infants by hard-selling their products to people incapable of using them properly. The 28-page report accused the industry of encouraging mothers to give up breast feeding and use powdered milk formulas. The report was later published by the Third World Working Group, a lobby in support of less developed countries. The pamphlet was entitled "Nestlé Kills Babies," and accused Nestlé of unethical and immoral behavior.

Although there are several companies that market infant baby formula internationally, Nestlé received most of the attention. This incident raises several issues important to all multinational companies. Before addressing these issues, let's look more closely at the charges by the Infant Formula Action Coalition and others and the defense by Nestlé.

THE CHARGES

Most of the charges against infant formulas focus on the issue of whether advertising and marketing of such products have discouraged breast feeding among Third World mothers and have led to misuse of the products, thus contributing to infant malnutrition and death. Following are some of the charges made:

- A Peruvian nurse reported that formula had found its way to Amazon tribes deep in the jungles of northern Peru. There, where the only water comes from a highly contaminated river—which also serves as the local laundry and toilet—formula-fed babies came down with recurring attacks of diarrhea and vomiting.

- Throughout the Third World, many parents dilute the formula to stretch their supply. Some even believe the bottle itself has nutrient qualities and merely fill it with water. The result is extreme malnutrition.

- One doctor reported that in a rural area, one newborn male weighed 7 pounds. At four months of age, he weighed 5 pounds. His sister, aged 18 months, weighed 12 pounds, what one would expect a four-month-old baby to weigh. She later weighed only 8 pounds. The children had never been breast fed, and since birth their diets were basically bottle feeding. For a four-month-old baby, one can of formula should have lasted just under three days. The mother said that one can lasted two weeks to feed both children.

- In rural Mexico, the Philippines, Central America, and the whole of Africa, there has been a dramatic decrease in the incidence of breast feeding. Critics blame the decline largely on the intensive advertising and promotion of infant formula. Clever radio jingles extol the wonders of the "white man's powder that will make baby grow and glow." "Milk nurses" visit nursing mothers in hospitals and their homes and provide samples of formula. These activities encourage mothers to give up breast feeding and resort to bottle feeding because it is "the fashionable thing to do or because people are putting it to them that this is the thing to do."

THE DEFENSE

The following points are made in defense of the marketing of baby formula in Third World countries:

- First, Nestlé argues that the company has never advocated bottle feeding instead of breast feeding. All its products carry a statement that breast feeding is best. The company states that it "believes that breast milk is the best food for infants and encourages breast feeding around the world as it has done for decades." The company offers as support of this statement one of Nestlé's oldest educational booklets on "Infant Feeding and Hygiene," which dates from 1913 and encourages breast feeding.

- However, the company does believe that infant formula has a vital role in proper infant nutrition as a supplement, when the infant needs nutritionally adequate and appropriate foods in addition to breast milk, and as a substitute for breast milk when a mother cannot or chooses not to breast feed. One doctor reports, "Economically deprived and thus dietarily deprived mothers who give their children only breast milk are raising infants whose growth rates begin to slow noticeably at about the age of three months. These mothers then turn to supplemental feedings that are often harmful to children. These include herbal teas and concoctions of rice water or corn water and sweetened, condensed milk. These feedings can also be prepared with contaminated water and are served in unsanitary conditions."

- Mothers in developing nations often have dietary deficiencies. In the Philippines, a mother in a poor family who is nursing a child produces about a pint of milk daily. Mothers in the United States usually produce about a quart of milk each day. For both the Filipino and U.S. mothers, the milk produced is equally nutritious. The problem is that there is less of it for the Filipino baby. If the Filipino mother doesn't augment the child's diet, malnutrition develops.

- Many poor women in the Third World bottle feed because their work schedules in fields or factories will not permit breast feeding. The infant feeding controversy has largely to do with the gradual introduction of weaning foods during the period between three months and two years. The average well-nourished Western woman, weighing 20 to 30 pounds more than most women in less developed countries, cannot feed only breast milk beyond five or six months. The claim that Third World women can breast feed exclusively for one or two years and have healthy, well-developed children is outrageous. Thus, all children beyond the ages of five to six months require supplemental feeding.

- Weaning foods can be classified as either native cereal gruels of millet or rice, or commercial manufactured milk formula. Traditional native weaning foods are usually made by mixing maize, rice, or millet flour with water and then cooking the mixture. Other weaning foods found in use are crushed crackers, sugar and water, and mashed bananas.

- There are two basic dangers to the use of native weaning foods. First, the nutritional quality of the native gruels is low. Second, microbiological contamination of the traditional weaning foods is a certainty in many Third World settings. The millet or the flour is likely to be contaminated, the water used in cooking will most certainly be contaminated, and the cooking containers will be contaminated; therefore, the native gruel, even after it is cooked, is frequently contaminated with colon bacilli, staph, and other dangerous bacteria. Moreover, large batches of gruel are often made and allowed to sit, inviting further contamination.

- Scientists recently compared the microbiological contamination of a local native gruel with ordinary reconstituted milk formula prepared under primitive conditions. They found both were contaminated to similar dangerous levels.

- The real nutritional problem in the Third World is not whether to give infants breast milk or formula but how to supplement mothers' milk with nutritionally adequate foods when they are needed. Finding adequate locally produced, nutritionally sound supplements to mothers' milk and teaching people how to prepare and use them safely are the issues. Only effective nutrition education along with improved sanitation and good food that people can afford will win the fight against dietary deficiencies in the Third World.

THE RESOLUTION

In 1974, Nestlé, aware of changing social patterns in the developing world and the increased access to radio and television there, reviewed its marketing practices on a region-by-region basis. As a result, mass media advertising of infant formula began to be phased out immediately in certain markets and, by 1978, was banned worldwide by the company. Nestlé then undertook to carry out more comprehensive health education programs to ensure that an understanding of the proper use of their products reached mothers, particularly in rural areas.

"Nestlé fully supports the WHO [World Health Organization] Code. Nestlé will continue to promote breast feeding and ensure that its marketing practices do not discourage breast feeding anywhere. Our company intends to maintain a constructive dialogue with governments and health professionals in all the countries it serves with the sole purpose of servicing mothers and the health of babies." This quote is from "Nestlé Discusses the Recommended WHO Infant Formula Code."

In 1977, the Interfaith Center on Corporate Responsibility in New York compiled a case against formula feeding in developing nations, and the Third World Institute launched a boycott against many Nestlé products. Its aim was to halt promotion of infant formulas in the Third World. The Infant Formula Action Coali-

tion (INFACT, successor to the Third World Institute), along with several other world organizations, successfully lobbied the World Health Organization to draft a code to regulate the advertising and marketing of infant formula in the Third World. In 1981, by a vote of 114 to 1 (three countries abstained, and the United States was the only dissenting vote), 118 member nations of WHO endorsed a voluntary code. The eight-page code urged a worldwide ban on promotion and advertising of baby formula and called for a halt to distribution of free product samples or gifts to physicians who promoted the use of the formula as a substitute for breast milk.

In May 1981 Nestlé announced it would support the code and waited for individual countries to pass national codes that would then be put into effect. Unfortunately, very few such codes were forthcoming. By the end of 1983, only 25 of the 157 member nations of the WHO had established national codes. Accordingly, Nestlé management determined it would have to apply the code in the absence of national legislation, and in February 1982, it issued instructions to marketing personnel that delineated the company's best understanding of the code and what would have to be done to follow it.

In addition, in May 1982 Nestlé formed the Nestlé Infant Formula Audit Commission (NIFAC), chaired by former Senator Edmund J. Muskie, and asked the commission to review the company's instructions to field personnel to determine if they could be improved to better implement the code. At the same time, Nestlé continued its meetings with WHO and UNICEF (United Nations Children's Fund) to try to obtain the most accurate interpretation of the code. NIFAC recommended several clarifications for the instructions that it believed would better interpret ambiguous areas of the code; in October 1982, Nestlé accepted those recommendations and issued revised instructions to field personnel.

Other issues within the code, such as the question of a warning statement, were still open to debate. Nestlé consulted extensively with WHO before issuing its label warning statement in October 1983, but there was still not universal agreement with it. Acting on WHO recommendations, Nestlé consulted with firms experienced and expert in developing and field testing educational materials, so that it could ensure that those materials met the code.

When the International Nestlé Boycott Committee (INBC) listed its four points of difference with Nestlé, it again became a matter of interpretation of the requirements of the code. Here, meetings held by UNICEF proved invaluable, in that UNICEF agreed to define areas of differing interpretation—in some cases providing definitions contrary to both Nestlé's and INBC's interpretations.

It was the meetings with UNICEF in early 1984 that finally led to a joint statement by Nestlé and INBC on January 25. At that time, INBC announced its suspension of boycott activities, and Nestlé pledged its continued support of the WHO code.

NESTLÉ SUPPORTS WHO CODE

The company has a strong record of progress and support in implementing the WHO code, including the following:

- Immediate support for the WHO code, May 1981, and testimony to this effect before the U.S. Congress, June 1981.

- Issuance of instructions to all employees, agents, and distributors in February 1982 to implement the code in all Third World countries where Nestlé markets infant formula.

- Establishment of an audit commission, in accordance with Article 11.3 of the WHO code, to ensure the company's compliance with the code. The commission, headed by Edmund S. Muskie, was composed of eminent clergy and scientists.

- Willingness to meet with concerned church leaders, international bodies, and organization leaders seriously concerned with Nestlé's application of the code.

- Issuance of revised instructions to Nestlé personnel, October 1982, as recommended by the Muskie committee to clarify and give further effect to the code.

- Consultation with WHO, UNICEF, and NIFAC on how to interpret the code and how best to implement specific provisions, including clarification by WHO/UNICEF of the definition of children who need to be fed breast milk substitutes, to aid in determining the need for supplies in hospitals.

NESTLÉ POLICIES

In the early 1970s, Nestlé began to review its infant formula marketing practices on a region-by-region basis. By 1978 the company had stopped all consumer advertising and direct sampling to mothers. Instructions to the field issued in February 1982 and clarified in the revised instructions of October 1982 to adopt articles of the WHO code as Nestlé policy include the following:

- No advertising to the general public
- No sampling to mothers
- No mothercraft workers
- No use of commission/bonus for sales
- No use of infant pictures on labels
- No point-of-sale advertising
- No financial or material inducements to promote products
- No samples to physicians except in three specific situations: a new product, a new product formulation, or a new graduate physician; limited to one or two cans of product
- Limitation of supplies to those requested in writing and fulfilling genuine needs for breast milk substitutes
- A statement of the superiority of breast feeding on all labels/materials
- Labels and educational materials clearly stating the hazards involved in incorrect usage of infant formula, developed in consultation with WHO/UNICEF

Even though Nestlé stopped consumer advertising, it was able to maintain its share of the Third World infant formula market. In 1988 a call to resume the seven-year boycott was made by a group of consumer activist members of the Action for Corporate Accountability. The group claimed that Nestlé was distributing free formula through maternity wards as a promotional tactic that undermined the practice of breast feeding. The group claimed that Nestlé and others, including American Home Products, have continued to dump formula in hospitals and maternity wards and that, as a result, "babies are dying as the companies are violating the WHO resolution." As late as 1997 the Interagency Group on Breastfeeding Monitoring (IGBM) claimed Nestlé continues to systematically violate the WHO code. Nestlé's response to these accusations is included on its Web site (see www.nestlé.com for details).

The boycott focus is Taster's Choice Instant Coffee, Coffee-mate Nondairy Coffee Creamer, Anacin aspirin, and Advil.

Representatives of Nestlé and American Home Products rejected the accusations and said they were complying with World Health Organization and individual national codes on the subject.

THE NEW TWISTS

A new environmental factor has made the entire case more complex: As of 2001 it was believed that some 3.8 million children around the world had contracted the human immunodeficiency virus (HIV) at their mothers' breasts. In affluent countries mothers can be told to bottle feed their children. However, 90 percent of the child infections occur in developing countries. There the problems of bottle feeding remain. Further, in even the most infected areas, 70 percent of the mothers do not carry the virus, and breast feeding is by far the best option. The vast majority of pregnant women in developing countries have no idea whether they are infected or not. One concern is that large numbers of healthy women will switch to the bottle just to be safe. Alternatively, if bottle feeding becomes a badge of HIV infection, mothers may continue breast feeding just to avoid being stigmatized. In Thailand, pregnant women are offered testing, and if found HIV positive, are given free milk powder. But in some African countries, where women get pregnant at three times the Thai rate and HIV infection rates are 25 percent compared with the 2 percent in Thailand, that solution is much less feasible. Moreover, the latest medical evidence indicates that extending breast feeding reduces the risk of breast cancer. Most recently the demand for infant formula in South Africa has outstripped supply as HIV-infected mothers make the switch to formula. Demand grew 20 percent in 2004 and the government is investigating the shortages as Nestlé scrambles to catch up with demand. The firm reopened a shuttered factory and began importing formula from Brazil.

THE ISSUES

Many issues are raised by this incident and the ongoing swirl of cultural change. How can a company deal with a worldwide boycott of its products? Why did the United States decide not to support the WHO code? Who is correct, WHO or Nestlé? A more important issue concerns the responsibility of an MNC marketing in developing nations. Setting aside the issues for a moment, consider the notion that, whether intentional or not, Nestlé's marketing activities have had an impact on the behavior of many people. In other words, Nestlé is a cultural change agent. When it or any other company successfully introduces new ideas into a culture, the culture changes and those changes can be functional or dysfunctional to established patterns of behavior. The key issue is, What responsibility does the MNC have to the culture when, as a result of its marketing activities, it causes change in that culture? Finally, how might Nestlé now participate in the battle against the spread of HIV and AIDS in developing countries?

QUESTIONS

1. What are the responsibilities of companies in this or similar situations?

2. What could Nestlé have done to have avoided the accusations of "killing Third World babies" and still market its product?

3. After Nestlé's experience, how do you suggest it, or any other company, can protect itself in the future?

4. Assume you are the one who had to make the final decision on whether or not to promote and market Nestlé's baby formula in Third World countries. Read the section titled "Ethical and Socially Responsible Decisions" in Chapter 5 as a guide to examine the social responsibility and ethical issues regarding the marketing approach and the promotion used. Were the decisions socially responsible? Were they ethical?

5. What advice would you give to Nestlé now in light of the new problem of HIV infection being spread via mothers' milk?

This case is an update of "Nestlé in LDCs," a case written by J. Alex Murray, University of Windsor, Ontario, Canada, and Gregory M. Gazda and Mary J. Molenaar, University of San Diego. The case originally appeared in the fifth edition of this text.

The case draws from the following: "International Code of Marketing of Breastmilk Substitutes" (Geneva: World Health Organization, 1981); INFACT Newsletter, Minneapolis, February 1979; John A. Sparks, "The Nestlé Controversy—Anatomy of a Boycott" (Grove City, PA: Public Policy Education Funds); "WHO Drafts a Marketing Code," *World Business Weekly*, January 19, 1981, p. 8; "A Boycott over Infant Formula," *BusinessWeek,* April 23, 1979, p. 137; "The Battle over Bottle-Feeding," *World Press Review*, January 1980, p. 54; "Nestlé and the Role of Infant Formula in Developing Countries: The Resolution of a Conflict" (Nestlé Company, 1985); "The Dilemma of Third World Nutrition" (Nestlé SA, 1985), 20 pp.; Thomas V. Greer, "The Future of the International Code of Marketing of Breastmilk Substitutes: The Socio-Legal Context," *International Marketing Review*, Spring 1984, pp. 33–41; James C. Baker, "The International Infant Formula Controversy: A Dilemma in Corporate Social Responsibility," *Journal of Business Ethic* 4 (1985), pp. 181–90; Shawn Tully, "Nestlé Shows How to Gobble Markets," *Fortune*, January 16, 1989, p. 75. For a comprehensive and well-balanced review of the infant formula issue, see Thomas V. Greer, "International Infant Formula Marketing: The Debate Continues," *Advances in International Marketing* 4 (1990), pp. 207–25. For a discussion of the HIV complication, see "Back to the Bottle?" *The Economist*, February 7, 1998, p. 50; Alix M. Freedman and Steve Stecklow, "Bottled Up: As UNICEF Battles Baby-Formula Makers, African Infants Sicken," *The Wall Street Journal*, December 5, 2000; Rone Tempest, "Mass Breast-Feeding by 1,128 Is Called a Record," *Los Angeles Times*, August 4, 2002, p. B1; "South Africa: Erratic Infant Formula Supply Puts PMTCT at Risk," All Africa/COMTEX, August 22, 2005; Hillary Parsons, "Response. We're Not Trying to Undermine the Baby-Milk Code," *The Guardian*, May 22, 2007, p. 35.

CASE I-3 Coke and Pepsi Learn to Compete in India

THE BEVERAGE BATTLEFIELD

In 2007, the President and CEO of Coca-Cola asserted that Coke has had a rather rough run in India; but now it seems to be getting its positioning right. Similarly, PepsiCo's Asia chief asserted that India is the beverage battlefield for this decade and beyond.

Even though the government had opened its doors wide to foreign companies, the experience of the world's two giant soft drinks companies in India during the 1990s and the beginning of the new millennium was not a happy one. Both companies experienced a range of unexpected problems and difficult situations that led them to recognize that competing in India requires special knowledge, skills, and local expertise. In many ways, Coke and Pepsi managers had to learn the hard way that "what works here" does not always "work there." "The environment in India is challenging, but we're learning how to crack it," says an industry leader.

THE INDIAN SOFT DRINKS INDUSTRY

In India, over 45 percent of the soft drinks industry in 1993 consisted of small manufacturers. Their combined business was worth $3.2 million dollars. Leading producers included Parle Agro (hereafter "Parle"), Pure Drinks, Modern Foods, and McDowells. They offered carbonated orange and lemon-lime beverage drinks. Coca-Cola Corporation (hereafter "Coca-Cola") was only a distant memory to most Indians at that time. The company had been present in the Indian market from 1958 until its withdrawal in 1977 following a dispute with the government over its trade secrets. After decades in the market, Coca-Cola chose to leave India rather than cut its equity stake to 40 percent and hand over its secret formula for the syrup.

Following Coca-Cola's departure, Parle became the market leader and established thriving export franchise businesses in Dubai, Kuwait, Saudi Arabia, and Oman in the Gulf, along with Sri Lanka. It set up production in Nepal and Bangladesh and served distant markets in Tanzania, Britain, the Netherlands, and the United States. Parle invested heavily in image advertising at home, establishing the dominance of its flagship brand, Thums Up.

Thums Up is a brand associated with a "job well done" and personal success. These are persuasive messages for its target market of young people aged 15 to 24 years. Parle has been careful in the past not to call Thums Up a cola drink so it has avoided direct comparison with Coke and Pepsi, the world's brand leaders.

The soft drinks market in India is composed of six product segments: cola, "cloudy lemon," orange, "soda" (carbonated water), mango, and "clear lemon," in order of importance. Cloudy lemon and clear lemon together make up the lemon-lime segment. Prior to the arrival of foreign producers in India, the fight for local dominance was between Parle's Thums Up and Pure Drinks' Campa Cola.

In 1988, the industry had experienced a dramatic shakeout following a government warning that BVO, an essential ingredient in locally produced soft drinks, was carcinogenic. Producers either had to resort to using a costly imported substitute, estergum, or they had to finance their own R&D in order to find a substitute ingredient. Many failed and quickly withdrew from the industry.

Competing with the segment of carbonated soft drinks is another beverage segment composed of noncarbonated fruit drinks. These are a growth industry because Indian consumers perceive fruit drinks to be natural, healthy, and tasty. The leading brand has traditionally been Parle's Frooti, a mango-flavored drink, which was also exported to franchisees in the United States, Britain, Portugal, Spain, and Mauritius.

OPENING INDIAN MARKET

In 1991, India experienced an economic crisis of exceptional severity, triggered by the rise in imported oil prices following the first Gulf War (after Iraq's invasion of Kuwait). Foreign exchange reserves fell as nonresident Indians (NRIs) cut back on repatriation of their savings, imports were tightly controlled across all sectors, and industrial production fell while inflation was rising. A new government took office in June 1991 and introduced measures to stabilize the economy in the short term, then launched a fundamental restructuring program to ensure medium-term growth. Results were dramatic. By 1994, inflation was halved, exchange reserves were greatly increased, exports were growing, and foreign investors were looking at India, a leading Big Emerging Market, with new eyes.

The turnaround could not be overstated; as one commentator said, "India has been in economic depression for so long that everything except the snake-charmers, cows and the Taj Mahal has faded from the memory of the world." The Indian government was viewed as unfriendly to foreign investors. Outside investment had been allowed only in high-tech sectors and was almost entirely prohibited in consumer goods sectors. The "principle of indigenous availability" had specified that if an item could be obtained anywhere else within the country, imports of similar items were forbidden. As a result, Indian consumers had little choice of products or brands and no guarantees of quality or reliability.

Following liberalization of the Indian economy and the dismantling of complicated trade rules and regulations, foreign investment increased dramatically. Processed foods, software, engineering plastics, electronic equipment, power generation, and petroleum industries all benefited from the policy changes.

PEPSICO AND COCA-COLA ENTER THE INDIAN MARKET

Despite its huge population, India had not been considered by foreign beverage producers to be an important market. In addition to the deterrents imposed by the government through its austere trade policies, rules, and regulations, local demand for carbonated drinks in India was very low compared with countries at a similar stage of economic development. In 1989, the average Indian was buying only three bottles a year, compared with per-capita consumption rates of 11 bottles a year in Bangladesh and 13 in Pakistan, India's two neighbors.

PepsiCo PepsiCo entered the Indian market in 1986 under the name "Pepsi Foods Ltd. in a joint venture with two local partners, Voltas and Punjab Agro." As expected, very stringent conditions were imposed on the venture. Sales of soft drink concentrate to local bottlers could not exceed 25 percent of total sales for the new venture, and Pepsi Foods Ltd. was required to process and distribute local fruits and vegetables. The government also mandated that Pepsi Food's products be promoted under the name "Lehar Pepsi" ("lehar" meaning "wave"). Foreign collaboration rules in force at the time prohibited the use of foreign brand names on products intended for sale inside India. Although the requirements for Pepsi's entry were considered stringent, the CEO of Pepsi-Cola International said at that time, "We're willing to go so far with India because we want to make sure we get an early entry while the market is developing."

In keeping with local tastes, Pepsi Foods launched Lehar 7UP in the clear lemon category, along with Lehar Pepsi. Marketing and distribution were focused in the north and west around the major cities of Delhi and Mumbai (formally Bombay). An aggressive pricing policy on the one-liter bottles had a severe impact on the local producer, Pure Drinks. The market leader, Parle, preempted any further pricing moves by Pepsi Foods by introducing a new 250-ml bottle that sold for the same price as its 200-ml bottle.

Pepsi Foods struggled to fight off local competition from Pure Drinks' Campa Cola, Duke's lemonade, and various brands of Parle. The fight for dominance intensified in 1993 with Pepsi Food's launch of two new brands, Slice and Teem, along with the introduction of fountain sales. At this time, market shares in the cola segment were 60 percent for Parle (down from 70 percent), 26 percent for Pepsi Foods, and 10 percent for Pure Drinks.

Coca-Cola In May 1990, Coca-Cola attempted to reenter India by means of a proposed joint venture with a local bottling company owned by the giant Indian conglomerate, Godrej. The government turned down this application just as PepsiCo's application was being approved. Undeterred, Coca-Cola made its return to India by joining forces with Britannia Industries India Ltd., a local producer of snack foods. The new venture was called "Britco Foods."

Among local producers, it was believed at that time that Coca-Cola would not take market share away from local companies because the beverage market was itself growing consistently from year to year. Yet this belief did not stop individual local producers from trying to align themselves with the market leader. Thus in July 1993, Parle offered to sell Coca-Cola its bottling plants in the four key cities of Delhi, Mumbai, Ahmedabad, and Surat. In addition, Parle offered to sell its leading brands Thums Up, Limca, Citra, Gold Spot, and Mazaa. It chose to retain ownership only of Frooti and a soda (carbonated water) called Bisleri.

FAST FORWARD TO THE NEW MILLENNIUM

Seasonal Sales Promotions—2006 Navratri Campaign

In India the summer season for soft drink consumption lasts 70 to 75 days, from mid-April to June. During this time, over 50 percent of the year's carbonated beverages are consumed across the country. The second-highest season for consumption lasts only 20 to 25 days during the cultural festival of Navratri ("Nav" means nine and "ratri" means night). This traditional Gujarati festival goes on for nine nights in the state of Gujarat, in the western part of India. Mumbai also has a significant Gujarati population that is considered part of the target market for this campaign.

As the Regional Marketing Manager for Coca-Cola India stated, "As part of the 'think local—act local' business plan, we have tried to involve the masses in Gujarat with 'Thums Up Toofani Ramjhat,' with 20,000 free passes issued, one per Thums Up bottle. ['Toofan' means a thunderstorm and 'ramjhat' means 'let's dance,' so together these words convey the idea of a 'fast dance.'] There are a number of [retail] on-site activities too, such as the 'buy one—get one free' scheme and lucky draws where one can win a free trip to Goa." (Goa is an independent Portuguese-speaking state on the west coast of India, famed for its beaches and tourist resorts.)

For its part, PepsiCo also participates in annual Navratri celebrations through massive sponsorships of "garba" competitions in selected venues in Gujarat. ("Garba" is the name of a dance, done by women during the Navratri festival.) The Executive Vice President for PepsiCo India commented: "For the first time, Pepsi has tied up with the Gujarati TV channel, Zee Alpha, to telecast 'Navratri Utsav' on all nine nights. ['Utsav' means festival.] Then there is the mega offer for the people of Ahmedabad, Baroda, Surat, and Rajkot where every refill of a case of Pepsi 300-ml. bottles will fetch one kilo of Basmati rice free." These four cities are located in the state of Gujarat. Basmati rice is considered a premium quality rice. After the initial purchase of a 300-ml. bottle, consumers can get refills at reduced rates at select stores.

The TV Campaign

Both Pepsi-Cola and Coca-Cola engage in TV campaigns employing local and regional festivals and sports events. A summer campaign featuring 7UP was launched by Pepsi with the objectives of growing the category and building brand awareness. The date was chosen to coincide with the India–Zimbabwe One-Day cricket series. The new campaign slogan was "Keep It Cool" to emphasize the product attribute of refreshment. The national campaign was to be reinforced with regionally adapted TV campaigns, outdoor activities, and retail promotions.

A 200-ml bottle was introduced during this campaign in order to increase frequency of purchase and volume of consumption. Prior to the introduction of the 200-ml bottle, most soft drinks were sold in 250-ml, 300-ml, and 500-ml bottles. In addition to 7UP, Pepsi Foods also introduced Mirinda Lemon, Apple, and Orange in 200-ml bottles.

In the past, celebrity actors Amitabh Bachchan and Govinda, who are famous male stars of the Indian movie industry, had endorsed Mirinda Lemon. This world-famous industry is referred to as "Bollywood" (the Hollywood of India based in Bombay).

Pepsi's Sponsorship of Cricket and Football (Soccer)

After India won an outstanding victory in the India–England NatWest One-Day cricket series finals, PepsiCo launched a new ad campaign featuring the batting sensation, Mohammad Kaif. PepsiCo's line-up of other cricket celebrities includes Saurav Ganguly, Rahul Dravid, Harbhajan Singh, Zaheer Khan, V.V.S. Laxman, and Ajit Agarkar. All of these players were part of the Indian team for the World Cup Cricket Series. During the two months of the Series, a new product, Pepsi Blue, was marketed nationwide. It was positioned as a "limited edition," icy-blue cola sold in 300-ml, returnable glass bottles and 500-ml plastic bottles, priced at 8 rupees (Rs) and Rs 15, respectively. In addition, commemorative, nonreturnable 250-ml Pepsi bottles priced at Rs 12 were introduced. (One rupee was equal to US 2.54 cents in 2008.)

In addition to the sponsorship of cricket events, PepsiCo has also taken advantage of World Cup soccer fever in India by featuring football heroes such as Baichung Bhutia in Pepsi's celebrity and music-related advertising communications. These ads featured football players pitted against sumo wrestlers.

To consolidate its investment in its promotional campaigns, PepsiCo sponsored a music video with celebrity endorsers including the Bollywood stars, as well as several nationally known cricketers. The new music video aired on SET Max, a satellite channel broadcast mainly in the northern and western parts of India and popular among the 15–25 year age group,

Coca-Cola's Lifestyle Advertising

While Pepsi's promotional efforts focused on cricket, soccer, and other athletic events, Coca-Cola's India strategy focused on relevant local idioms in an effort to build a "connection with the youth market." The urban youth target market, known as "India A," includes 18–24 year olds in major metropolitan areas.

Several ad campaigns were used to appeal to this market segment. One campaign was based on use of "gaana" music and ballet. ("Gaana" means to sing.)

The first ad execution, called "Bombay Dreams," featured A. R. Rahman, a famous music director. This approach was very successful among the target audience of young people, increasing sales by about 50 percent. It also won an Effi Award from the Mumbai Advertising Club. A second execution of Coke's southern strategy was "Chennai Dreams" (Chennai was formerly called Madras), a 60-second feature film targeting consumers in Tamil Nadu, a region of southern India. The film featured Vijay, a youth icon who is famous as an actor in that region of south India.

Another of the 60-second films featured actor Vivek Oberoi with Aishwarya Rai. Both are famous as Bollywood movie stars. Aishwarya won the Miss World crown in 1994 and became an instant hit in Indian movies after deciding on an acting career.

This ad showed Oberoi trying to hook up with Rai by deliberately leaving his mobile phone in the taxi that she hails, and then calling her. The ad message aimed to emphasize confidence and optimism, as well as a theme of "seize the day." This campaign used print, outdoor, point-of-sale, restaurant and grocery chains, and local promotional events to tie into the 60-second film. "While awareness of soft drinks is high, there is a need to build a deeper brand connect" in urban centers, according to the Director of Marketing for Coca-Cola India. "Vivek Oberoi—who's an up and coming star today, and has a wholesome, energetic image—will help build a stronger bond with the youth, and make them feel that it is a brand that plays a role in their life, just as much as Levi's or Ray-Ban."

In addition to promotions focused on urban youth, Coca-Cola India worked hard to build a brand preference among young people in rural target markets. The campaign slogan aimed at this market was "thanda matlab Coca-Cola" (or "cool means Coca-Cola" in Hindi). Coca-Cola India calls its rural youth target market "India B." The prime objective in this market is to grow the generic soft drinks category and to develop brand preference for Coke. The "thanda" ("cold") campaign successfully propelled Coke into the number three position in rural markets.

Continuing to court the youth market, Coke has opened its first retail outlet, Red Lounge. The Red Lounge is touted as a one-stop-destination where the youth can spend time and consume Coke products. The first Red Lounge pilot outlet is in Pune, and based on the feedback, more outlets will be rolled out in other cities. The lounge sports red color, keeping with the theme of the Coke logo. It has a giant LCD television, video games, and Internet surfing facilities. The lounge offers the entire range of Coke products. The company is also using Internet to extend its reach into the public domain through the Web site www.myenjoyzone.com. The company has created a special online "Sprite-itude" zone that provides consumers opportunities for online gaming and expressing their creativity, keeping with the no-nonsense attitude of the drink.

Coca-Cola's specific marketing objectives are to grow the per-capita consumption of soft drinks in the rural markets, capture a larger share in the urban market from competition, and increase the frequency of consumption. An "affordability plank" along with introduction of a new 5-rupee bottle, was designed to help achieve all of these goals.

The "Affordability Plank"

The purpose of the "affordability plank" was to enhance affordability of Coca-Cola's products, bringing them within arm's reach of consumers, and thereby promoting regular consumption. Given the very low per-capita consumption of soft drinks in India, it was expected that price reductions would expand both the consumer base and the market for soft drinks. Coca-Cola India dramatically reduced prices of its soft drinks by 15 percent to 25 percent nationwide to encourage consumption. This move followed an earlier regional action in North India that reduced prices by 10–15 percent for its carbonated brands Coke, Thums Up, Limca, Sprite, and Fanta. In other regions such as Rajasthan, western and eastern Uttar Pradesh, and Tamil Nadu, prices were slashed to Rs 5 for 200-ml glass bottles and Rs 8 for 300-ml bottles, down from the existing Rs 7 and Rs 10 price points, respectively.

Another initiative by Coca-Cola was the introduction of a new size, the "Mini," expected to increase total volume of sales and account for the major chunk of Coca-Cola's carbonated soft drink sales.

The price reduction and new production launch were announced together in a new television ad campaign for Fanta and Coke in Tamil. A 30-second Fanta spot featured the brand ambassador, actress Simran, well-known for her dance sequences in Hindi movies. The ad showed Simran stuck in a traffic jam. Thirsty, she tosses a 5-rupee coin to a roadside stall and signals to the vendor that she wants a Fanta Mini by pointing to her orange dress. (Fanta is an orangeade drink.) She gets her Fanta and sets off a chain reaction on the crowded street, with everyone from school children to a traditional "nani" mimicking her action. ("Nani" is the Hindi word for grandmother.) The director of marketing commented that the company wanted to make consumers "sit up and take notice."

A NEW PRODUCT CATEGORY

Although carbonated drinks are the mainstay of both Coke's and Pepsi's product line, the Indian market for carbonated drinks is not growing. It grew at a compounded annual growth rate of only 1 percent between 1999 and 2006, from $1.31 billion to $1.32 billion. However, the overall market for beverages, which includes soft drinks, juices, and other drinks, grew 6 percent from $3.15 billion to $3.34 billion.

To encourage growth in demand for bottled beverages in the Indian market, several producers, including Coke and Pepsi, have launched their own brands in a new category, bottled water. This market was valued at 1,000 Crores.[1]

Pepsi and Coke are responding to the declining popularity of soft drinks or carbonated drinks and the increased focus on all beverages that are non-carbonated. The ultimate goal is leadership in the rapidly growing packaged water market, which is growing more rapidly than any other category of bottled beverages. Pepsi is a significant player in the packaged water market with its Aquafina brand, which has a significant share of the bottled water market and is among the top three retail water brands in the country.

PepsiCo consistently has been working toward reducing its dependence on Pepsi Cola by bolstering its non-cola portfolio and other categories. This effort is aimed at making the company more broad-based in category growth so that no single product or category becomes the key determinant of the company's market growth. The non-cola segment is said to have grown to contribute one-fourth of PepsiCo's overall business in India during the past three to four years. Previously, the multinational derived a major chunk of its growth from Pepsi-Cola.

Among other categories on which the company is focusing are fruit juices, juice-based drinks, and water. The estimated fruit juice market in India is approximately 350 Crores and growing month to month. One of the key factors that has triggered this trend is the emergence of the mass luxury segment and increasing consumer consciousness about health and wellness. "Our hugely successful international brand Gatorade has gained momentum in the country with consumers embracing a lifestyle that includes sports and exercise. The emergence of high-quality gymnasiums, fitness and aerobic centres mirror the fitness trend," said a spokesperson.

Coca-Cola introduced its Kinley brand of bottled water and in two years achieved a 28 percent market share. It initially produced bottled water in 15 plants and later expanded to another 15 plants. The Kinley brand of bottled water sells in various pack sizes: 500 ml, 1 liter, 1.5 liter, 2 liter, 5 liter, 20 liter, and 25 liter. The smallest pack was priced at Rs 6 for 500 ml, while the 2-liter bottle was Rs 17.

The current market leader, with 40 percent market share, is the Bisleri brand by Parle. Other competing brands in this segment include Bailley by Parle, Hello by Hello Mineral Waters Pvt. Ltd., Pure Life by Nestlé, and a new brand launched by Indian Railways, called Rail Neer.

CONTAMINATION ALLEGATIONS AND WATER USAGE

Just as things began to look up, an environmental organization claimed that soft drinks produced in India by Coca-Cola and Pepsi contained significant levels of pesticide residue. Coke and Pepsi denied the charges and argued that extensive use of pesticides in agriculture had resulted in a minute degree of pesticide in sugar used in their drinks. The result of tests conducted by the Ministry of Health and Family Welfare showed that soft drinks produced by the two companies were safe to drink under local health standards.

Protesters in India reacted to reports that Coca-Cola and Pepsi contained pesticide residues. Some states announced partial bans on Coke and Pepsi products. When those reports appeared on the front pages of newspapers in India, Coke and Pepsi executives were confident that they could handle the situation. But they stumbled.

They underestimated how quickly events would spiral into a nationwide scandal, misjudged the speed with which local politicians would seize on an Indian environmental group's report to attack their global brands, and did not respond swiftly to quell the anxieties of their customers.

The companies formed committees in India and the United States, working in tandem on legal and public relations issues. They worked around the clock fashioning rebuttals. They commissioned their own laboratories to conduct tests and waited until the results came through before commenting in detail. Their approaches backfired. Their reluctance to give details fanned consumer suspicion. They became bogged down in the technicalities of the charges instead of focusing on winning back the support of their customers.

At the start, both companies were unprepared when one state after another announced partial bans on Coke and Pepsi products; the drinks were prevented from being sold in government offices, hospitals, and schools. Politicians exploited the populist potential.

In hindsight, the Coke communications director said she could see how the environmental group had picked Coca-Cola as a way of attracting attention to the broader problem of pesticide contamination in Indian food products. "Fringe politicians will continue to be publicly hostile to big Western companies, regardless of how eager they are for their investment," she said.

Failing to anticipate the political potency of the incident, Coke and Pepsi initially hoped that the crisis would blow over and they adopted a policy of silence. "Here people interpret silence as guilt," said an Indian public relations expert. "You have to roll up your sleeves and get into a street fight. Coke and Pepsi didn't understand that."

Coca-Cola eventually decided to go on the attack, though indirectly, giving detailed briefings by executives, who questioned the scientific credentials of their products' accusers. They directed reporters to Internet blogs full of entries that were uniformly pro-Coke, and they handed out the cell phone number for the director of an organization called the Center for Sanity and Balance in Public Life. Emphasizing that he was not being paid by the industry, Kishore Asthana, from that center, said, "One can drink a can of Coke every day for two years before taking in as much pesticide as you get from two cups of tea."

The situation continued to spin out of control. Newspapers printed images of cans of the drinks with headlines like "toxic cocktail." News channels broadcast images of protesters pouring Coke down the throats of donkeys. A vice president for Coca-Cola India said his "heart sank" when he first heard the accusations because he knew that consumers would be easily confused. "But even terminology like P.P.B.—parts per billion—is difficult to comprehend," he said. "This makes our job very challenging."

PepsiCo began a public relations offensive, placing large advertisements in daily newspapers saying, "Pepsi is one of the safest beverages you can drink today."

The company acknowledged that pesticides were present in the groundwater in India and found their way into food products in general. But, it said, "compared with the permitted levels in tea and other food products, pesticide levels in soft drinks are negligible."

After all the bad press Coke got in India over the pesticide content in its soft drinks, an activist group in California launched a campaign directed at U.S. college campuses, accusing Coca-Cola of India of using precious groundwater, lacing its drinks with pesticides, and supplying farmers with toxic waste used for fertilizing their crops. According to one report, a plant that produces 300,000 liters of soda drink a day uses 1.5 million liters of water, enough to meet the requirements of 20,000 people.

---

[1]One Crore = 10,000,000 Rupees, and US$1 = Rs48, so 1,000 Crore = US$0.2083 million.

The issue revolved around a bottling plant in Plachimada, India. Although the state government granted Coke permission to build its plant in 1998, the company was obliged to get the locally elected village council's go-ahead to exploit groundwater and other resources. The village council did not renew permission in 2002, claiming the bottling operation had depleted the farmers' drinking water and irrigation supplies. Coke's plant was closed until the corporation won a court ruling allowing them to reopen.

The reopening of the plant in 2006 led students of a major Midwestern university to call for a ban on the sale of all Coca-Cola products on campus. According to one source, more than 20 campuses banned Coca-Cola products, and hundreds of people in the United States called on Coca-Cola to close its bottling plants because the plants drain water from communities throughout India. They contended that such irresponsible practices rob the poor of their fundamental right to drinking water, are a source of toxic waste, cause serious harm to the environment, and threaten people's health.

In an attempt to stem the controversy, Coca-Cola entered talks with the Midwestern university and agreed to cooperate with an independent research assessment of its work in India; the university selected the institute to conduct the research, and Coke financed the study. As a result of the proposed research program, the university agreed to continue to allow Coke products to be sold on campus.

In 2008 the study reported that none of the pesticides were found to be present in processed water used for beverage production and that the plants met governmental regulatory standards. However, the report voiced concerns about the company's use of sparse water supplies. Coca-Cola was asked by the Delhi-based environmental research group to consider shutting down one of its bottling plants in India. Coke's response was that "the easiest thing would be to shut down, but the solution is not to run away. If we shut down, the area is still going to have a water problem. We want to work with farming communities and industries to reduce the amount of water used."

The controversies highlight the challenges that multinational companies can face in their overseas operations. Despite the huge popularity of the drinks, the two companies are often held up as symbols of Western cultural imperialism.

QUESTIONS

1. The political environment in India has proven to be critical to company performance for both PepsiCo and Coca-Cola India. What specific aspects of the political environment have played key roles? Could these effects have been anticipated prior to market entry? If not, could developments in the political arena have been handled better by each company?

2. Timing of entry into the Indian market brought different results for PepsiCo and Coca-Cola India. What benefits or disadvantages accrued as a result of earlier or later market entry?

3. The Indian market is enormous in terms of population and geography. How have the two companies responded to the sheer scale of operations in India in terms of product policies, promotional activities, pricing policies, and distribution arrangements?

4. "Global localization" (glocalization) is a policy that both companies have implemented successfully. Give examples for each company from the case.

5. How can Pepsi and Coke confront the issues of water use in the manufacture of their products? How can they defuse further boycotts or demonstrations against their products? How effective are activist groups like the one that launched the campaign in California? Should Coke address the group directly or just let the furor subside?

6. Which of the two companies do you think has better long-term prospects for success in India?

7. What lessons can each company draw from its Indian experience as it contemplates entry into other Big Emerging Markets?

8. Comment on the decision of both Pepsi and Coke to enter the bottled water market instead of continuing to focus on their core products—carbonated beverages and cola-based drinks in particular.

This case was prepared by Lyn S. Amine, Ph.D., Professor of Marketing and International Business, Distinguished Fellow of the Academy of Marketing Science, President, Women of the Academy of International Business, Saint Louis University, and Vikas Kumar, Assistant Professor, Strategic Management Institute, Bocconi University, Milan, Italy. Dr. Lyn S. Amine and Vikas Kumar prepared this case from public sources as a basis for classroom discussion only. It is not intended to illustrate either effective or ineffective handling of administrative problems. The case was revised in 2005 and 2008 with the authors' permission.

Sources: Lyn S. Amine and Deepa Raizada, "Market Entry into the Newly Opened Indian Market: Recent Experiences of US Companies in the Soft Drinks Industry," in *Developments in Marketing Science*, XVIII, proceedings of the annual conference of the Academy of Marketing Science, Roger Gomes (ed.) (Coral Gables, FL: AMS, 1995), pp. 287–92; Jeff Cioletti, "Indian Government Says Coke and Pepsi Safe," *Beverage World*, September 15, 2003; "Indian Group Plans Coke, Pepsi Protests After Pesticide Claims," AFP, December 15, 2004; "Fortune Sellers," *Foreign Policy*, May/June 2004; "International Pressure Grows to Permanently Close Coke Bottling Plant in Plachimada," *PR Newswire*, June 15, 2005; "Indian Village Refuses Coca-Cola License to Exploit Ground Water," AFP, June 14, 2005; "Why Everyone Loves to Hate Coke," *Economist Times*, June 16, 2005; "PepsiCo India To Focus on Non-Cola Segment," *Knight Ridder Tribune Business* News, September 22, 2006; "For 2 Giants of Soft Drinks, A Crisis in a Crucial Market," *The New York Times*, August 23, 2006; "Coke and Pepsi Try to Reassure India That Drinks Are Safe," *The New York Times*, August 2006; "Catalyst: The Fizz in Water" *Financial Times Limited*, October 11, 2007; "Marketing: Coca-Cola Foraying Into Retail Lounge Format," *Business Line*, "April 7, 2007; "India Ops Now in Control, Says Coke Boss," *The Times of India*, October 3, 2007; "Pepsi: Repairing a Poisoned Reputation in India; How the Soda Giant Fought Charges of Tainted Products in a Country Fixated on its Polluted Water," *Business Week*, June 11, 2007, p. 48; "Coca-Cola Asked to Shut Indian Plant to Save Water," *International Herald Tribune*, January 15, 2008.

CASE 1−4 Marketing Microwave Ovens to a New Market Segment

You are the Vice President of International Marketing for White Appliances, an international company that manufactures and markets appliances globally. The company has a line of microwave ovens—some manufactured in the United States and some in Asia—which are exported to the U.S. market and Europe. Your company markets several high-end models in India that are manufactured in the United States. Your presence in the Indian market is limited at this time.

White Appliances has traditionally sold to the high-income segment of the Indian market. However, India is in the midst of a consumer boom for everything from soda pop to scooters to kitchen appliances. Demand for microwave ovens jumped 27 percent in two years amid surging demand for kitchen conveniences. Sales have been spurred by declining import tariffs and rising salaries, as well as the influx of companies reaching to all ends of the market. India has about 17 million households—or 90 million people that belong to the country's middle class, earning between $4,500 and $22,000 annually. Another 287 million are "aspirers," those that hope to join the middle class. Their household income is between $2,000 and $4,500. By 2010, these two groups combined will number 561 million. Furthermore, significant numbers of Indians in America are repatriating to their homeland and taking their American spending habits and expectations back home with them. After preliminary analysis, you and your team have come to the conclusion that in addition to the market for high-end models, a market for microwave ovens at all price levels exists.

Several international companies like Samsung, Whirlpool, and LG Electronics India are entering the market with the idea that demand can be expanded with the right product at the right price. There are, however, several challenges in the Indian market, not the least of which is the consumer's knowledge about microwaves and the manner in which they are perceived as appliances.

In conducting research on the market, your research team put together a summary of comments from consumers and facts about the market that should give you a feel for the market and the kinds of challenges that will have to be dealt with if the market is to grow and if White Appliances is to have a profitable market share.

- Five top consumer durable companies are in the race to sell the oven, but to sell the product, they must first sell the idea. The players do not agree on the size of the market or what the oven will do for the Indian family.

- It may be a convenient and efficient way to cook, but microwave ovens were invented with European food in mind. "Only when Indian eating habits change can the microwave ovens market grow in a big way," says one market leader in appliances.

- Some companies disagree with the previous statement. Their contention is that all Indian dishes can be prepared in a microwave; people only need to know how to use one.

Consumer comments were mixed.

- One housewife commented, "The microwave oven was the first purchase after my wedding. I bought it only because I liked it and I had the money. But I must say its performance surprised me."

- "Men no longer have an excuse for not helping in cooking. My husband, who never before entered the kitchen, now uses the microwave oven to cook routinely."

- "Somebody gifted it to me but food doesn't taste the same when cooked in a microwave whatever the company people may claim."

- "Microwave ovens will be very useful and they are fast becoming as essential as a fridge."

- "Ovens are of great use to bachelors. They can make curries every day or sambhar every day. If you heat in a regular oven sambhar or dal for the second or third time it will have a burnt smell. The microwave oven will not get you any such problem. It will be heated and at the same time as fresh as if it was made now."

- "Some people say that using a microwave oven is lazy and getting away from the traditional 'Indian culture' of always fresh food. I say that microwaves are of greatest use when you are very busy and not lazy. There are times when piping hot food rapidly becomes cold, especially in winter and a microwave is the easiest, quickest and cleanest way to heat up, so it even has applications in a traditional family running on 'Indian Culture' mode."

- To the chagrin of microwave oven marketers, the Indian perception of the gadget remains gray. Yet, for the first time in the some seven years that it's been officially around optimism toward the microwave has been on the upswing.

- A microwave oven is beginning to replace the demand for a second television or a bigger refrigerator. The middle-income consumer comes looking for novelty, value, and competitive pricing.

- The penetration level of microwave ovens remains shockingly minuscule, under 1 percent. The top seven cities comprise nearly 70 percent of the market with Delhi and Mumbai (Bombay) recording the highest sales. But the good news is that the microwave is beginning to be seen in smaller towns.

- When asked about the nonurban market, one microwave oven company executive commented, "We know it's an alien concept for the rural consumer, but we want to do our homework now to reap the benefits years later. Once the consumer is convinced a microwave can actually be part of daily cooking, the category will grow immensely."

- Apart from styling and competitive pricing, marketers acknowledge that cracking the mind-set that microwaves are not suited to Indian food holds the key to future growth.

- People who own microwaves usually have cooks who may not be using the gadget in any case. Even consumers who own microwave ovens don't use them frequently; usage is confined to cooking Western food or reheating.

- With consumers still unclear on how to utilize the microwave oven for their day-to-day cooking, marketers are shifting away from mass marketing to a more direct

Exhibit 1

A Customer's Evaluation
of the LG Robogrill
Microwave

One customer's lengthy evaluation of the LG Robogrill Microwave posted on MouthShut.com, India's first, largest, and most comprehensive Person to Person (P2P) Information Exchange follows:

"We bought our LG Robogrill Microwave about 10 months ago. The microwave has all the features mentioned in the official description, in addition to many other helpful features."

For a complete review by this customer, see www.mouthshut.com and select Microwave Ovens, then select LG on the menu, then select model #LGMH-685 HD.

marketing–oriented approach to create awareness about the benefits of the product.

- The challenge in this category is to get the user to cook in the microwave oven rather than use it as a product for reheating food. Keeping this in mind, companies are expecting an increasing number of sales for microwave ovens to come from the semi urban/rural markets. We are seeing an increasing number of sales coming from the upcountry markets.

- "Elite fad or smoke-free chullah for low-fat paranthas? Which way will the microwave oven go in the Indian market?" asks one company representative.

- Most agree on a broadly similar strategy to expand the Indian market: product and design innovation to make the microwave suited to Indian cooking, local manufacturing facility to promote innovation while continuing to import high-end models, reduce import content to cut costs, boost volumes, and bring down prices.

- Even as early as 1990, the microwave was touted as a way to cook Indian food. Julie Sahni, the nation's best known authority on Indian cooking, has turned her attention to the microwave. And her new cookbook sets a new threshold for the microwave cook. Simply cooked lentils, spicy dal, even tandoori chicken—with its distinctive reddish color—come steaming from the modern microwave with the spices and scents of an ancient cuisine. Cynics who think microwave cooking is bland and unimaginative will eat their words.

For many the microwave is a complicated appliance that can be used incorrectly and thus be a failure in the mind of the user. Some companies now marketing in India appear to give poor service because they do not have a system to respond to questions that arise about the use of microwaves. It appears that consumer education and prompt reply to inquiries about microwave use is critical.

An interesting Internet site to get product comparisons and consumer comments is www.mouthshut.com. For specific comments about one brand of microwave oven, visit www.mouthshut.com/product-reviews/LG_767war-925045495.html. Another site that gives some insights into Indian cooking and microwave ovens is www.indianmirror.com/cuisine/cus2.html.

MARKET DATA

LG Electronics, the category leader, has a 41.5 percent share of the 1.6 lakh[1] units market; its eight models are priced in the range of Rs 8,500–19,000 with a marked presence in the Indian family size of 28–30 liters. LG Electronics and Samsung India dominated the segment with a collective market share of about 61 percent.

In the early days, microwave ovens did not figure at all in the consumer's purchase list. Kelvinator's Magicook made a high profile entry some seven years ago. What went wrong, according to an analyst, was the pricing, which was nothing less than Rs 20,000, and sizes which were too small to accommodate large Indian vessels.

Efforts to grow the market are concentrated in large urban areas with routine fare such as organized cookery classes, recipe contests, and in-house demos, giving away accessories such as glass bowls, aprons, and gloves as freebies and hosting co-promotions. "To change the way you look, just change the way you cook" was a recent tagline by one of the companies.

What will really spur the category's growth will be a change in eating habits. One company piggybacks on "freshness," a tactic the company adopts for all its product lines.

Even though consumer durable sales fell in the first quarter of 2005, the microwave oven segment, which accounts for 70 percent of unit sales in the consumer durable industry, bucked the overall trend. The strength of microwave oven sales is attributed to the steady price reduction from Rs 7,000 for the lowest priced to Rs 5,000 over the last two years. While sales are predominantly in the urban areas, semiurban towns have emerged as a key growth driver for the category.

There is some difference of opinion on the right price for the ovens. For the microwave market to take off, its price would have to be below Rs 7,000, says one company. Since microwave ovens were introduced locally, prices have been all over the place. For example, one company prices its ovens between Rs 7,000 and Rs 18,000, another between Rs 12,500 and 15,000, and an oven with grill functions goes for Rs 17,900.

From wooing the supermom to courting the single male, the journey of microwave ovens has just begun. Once perceived as a substitute to the toaster oven and grill (OTG), microwaves today, according to companies with large shares of this segment, are more than just a reheating device.

According to one analyst, the product category is going through a transition period, and modern consumers are more educated about an OTG than a microwave. This analyst believes there is demand for both microwave and OTG categories.

Microwave companies face a chicken-and-egg question on price and sales. Prices will not come down easily until volumes go up, while volume depends on prices.

The product is a planned purchase and not an impulse buy. Samsung has set up call centers where customers can call and get all their queries pertaining to the Samsung microwave oven answered.

Besides the basic, low-end models that lead sales, the combination models (convection and microwave) models are showing a steady increase in sales.

Although the concept of microwave ovens is Western, microwave technology has advanced to a level that even complex cooking like Indian cooking is possible.

---

[1] A lakh is a unit in a traditional number system, still widely used in India. One lakh is equal to 100,000.

One of the older company marketing managers, who has worked in microwave marketing most of his career, is somewhat skeptical about the prospects of rapid growth of the Indian market. He remarked that the microwave oven first introduced in the U.S. market in about 1950 did not become popular across all market segments until about the mid-1970s. Of course, now almost every household in the United States has at least one microwave.

One U.S. marketer of coffee makers, blenders, crock pots, and other small appliances is exploring the possibility of distributing their appliances through Reliance retail stores. Until recently, Reliance Industries Ltd. the second largest company in India, has been in industrial and petroleum products but has now entered the retail market. Reliance is modeling itself after Wal-Mart, and the U.S. marketer sees Reliance reaching the market for its appliances. India's Reliance Industries Ltd. plans to open thousands of stores nationwide over the next five years and is also building a vast network of suppliers. Reliance retail stores may offer the opportunity to get in on the ground floor of a major boom in large store retail-ing that will appeal to the growing middle income market. The retail industry in India is projected to increase from $330 billion to $892 billion from 2006 to 2015, and the share of chain store retailers, such as the proposed Reliance Retail chain, may increase from 4 percent to 27 percent.

Your task is to develop a strategy to market White Appliance's microwave ovens in India. Include target market(s), microwave oven features, price(s), promotion, and distribution in your program. You should also consider both short-term and long-term marketing programs. Some of the issues you may want to consider are:

- Indian food preparation versus Western food preparation.
- Values and customs that might affect opinions about microwave ovens.
- The effects of competition in the market.

You may also want to review the Country Notebook: A Plan for Developing a Marketing Plan, p. 583 of the text for some direction.

cases 2

THE CULTURAL ENVIRONMENT OF GLOBAL MARKETING

CASE 2–1 The Not-So-Wonderful World of EuroDisney*—Things Are Better Now at Paris Disneyland

BONJOUR, MICKEY!

In April 1992, EuroDisney SCA opened its doors to European visitors. Located by the river Marne some 20 miles east of Paris, it was designed to be the biggest and most lavish theme park that Walt Disney Company (Disney) had built to date—bigger than Disneyland in Anaheim, California; Disneyworld in Orlando, Florida; and Tokyo Disneyland in Japan.

Much to Disney management's surprise, Europeans failed to "go goofy" over Mickey, unlike their Japanese counterparts. Between 1990 and early 1992, some 14 million people had visited Tokyo Disneyland, with three-quarters being repeat visitors. A family of four staying overnight at a nearby hotel would easily spend $600 on a visit to the park. In contrast, at EuroDisney, families were reluctant to spend the $280 a day needed to enjoy the attractions of the park, including *les hamburgers* and *les milkshakes*. Staying overnight was out of the question for many because hotel rooms were so high priced. For example, prices ranged from $110 to $380 a night at the Newport Bay Club, the largest of EuroDisney's six new hotels and one of the biggest in Europe. In comparison, a room in a top hotel in Paris cost between $340 and $380 a night.

Financial losses became so massive at EuroDisney that the president had to structure a rescue package to put EuroDisney back on firm financial ground. Many French bankers questioned the initial financing, but the Disney response was that their views reflected the cautious, Old World thinking of Europeans who did not understand U.S.-style free market financing. After some acrimonious dealings with French banks, a two-year financial plan was negotiated. Disney management rapidly revised its marketing plan and introduced strategic and tactical changes in the hope of "doing it right" this time.

A Real Estate Dream Come True
The Paris location was chosen over 200 other potential sites stretching from Portugal through Spain, France, Italy, and into Greece. Spain thought it had the strongest bid based on its yearlong, temperate, and sunny Mediterranean climate, but insufficient acreage of land was available for development around Barcelona.

In the end, the French government's generous incentives, together with impressive data on regional demographics, swayed Disney management to choose the Paris location. It was calculated that some 310 million people in Europe live within two hours' air travel of EuroDisney, and 17 million could reach the park within two hours by car—better demographics than at any other Disney site. Pessimistic talk about the dismal winter weather of northern France was countered with references to the success of Tokyo Disneyland, where resolute visitors brave cold winds and snow to enjoy their piece of Americana. Furthermore, it was argued, Paris is Europe's most-popular city destination among tourists of all nationalities.

Spills and Thrills
Disney had projected that the new theme park would attract 11 million visitors and generate over $100 million in operating earnings during the first year of operation. By summer 1994, EuroDisney had lost more than $900 million since opening.

Attendance reached only 9.2 million in 1992, and visitors spent 12 percent less on purchases than the estimated $33 per head.

If tourists were not flocking to taste the thrills of the new Euro-Disney, where were they going for their summer vacations in 1992? Ironically enough, an unforeseen combination of transatlantic airfare wars and currency movements resulted in a trip to Disneyworld in Orlando being cheaper than a trip to Paris, with guaranteed good weather and beautiful Florida beaches within easy reach.

EuroDisney management took steps to rectify immediate problems in 1992 by cutting rates at two hotels up to 25 percent, introducing some cheaper meals at restaurants, and launching a Paris ad blitz that proclaimed "California is only 20 miles from Paris."

An American Icon
One of the most worrying aspects of EuroDisney's first year was that French visitors stayed away; they had been expected to make up 50 percent of the attendance figures. A park services consulting firm framed the problem in these words: "The French see EuroDisney as American imperialism—plastics at its worst." The well-known, sentimental Japanese attachment to Disney characters contrasted starkly with the unexpected and widespread French scorn for American fairy-tale characters. French culture has its own lovable cartoon characters such as Astérix, the helmeted, pint-sized Gallic warrior, who has a theme park located near EuroDisney.

Hostility among the French people to the whole "Disney idea" had surfaced early in the planning of the new project. Paris theater director Ariane Mnouchkine became famous for her description of EuroDisney as "a cultural Chernobyl." In fall 1989, during a visit to Paris, French Communists pelted Michael Eisner with eggs. The joke going around at the time was, "For EuroDisney to adapt properly to France, all seven of Snow White's dwarfs should be named Grumpy *(Grincheux)*."

Early advertising by EuroDisney seemed to aggravate local French sentiment by emphasizing glitz and size rather than the variety of rides and attractions. Committed to maintaining Disney's reputation for quality in everything, more detail was built into EuroDisney. For example, the centerpiece castle in the Magic Kingdom had to be bigger and fancier than in the other parks. Expensive trams were built along a lake to take guests from the hotels to the park, but visitors preferred walking. Total park construction costs were estimated at FFr 14 billion ($2.37 billion) in 1989 but rose by $340 million to FFr 16 billion as a result of all these add-ons. Hotel construction costs alone rose from an estimated FFr 3.4 billion to FFr 5.7 billion.

EuroDisney and Disney managers unhappily succeeded in alienating many of their counterparts in the government, the banks, the ad agencies, and other concerned organizations. A barnstorming, kick-the-door-down attitude seemed to reign among the U.S. decision makers: "They had a formidable image and convinced everyone that if we let them do it their way, we would all have a marvelous adventure." One former Disney executive voiced the opinion, "We were arrogant—it was like 'We're building the Taj Mahal and people will come—on our terms.'"

---

*The official name has been changed from "EuroDisney" to "Disneyland Resort Paris"

612

STORM CLOUDS AHEAD

Disney and its advisors failed to see signs at the end of the 1980s of the approaching European recession. Other dramatic events included the Gulf War in 1991, which put a heavy brake on vacation travel for the rest of that year. Other external factors that Disney executives have cited were high interest rates and the devaluation of several currencies against the franc. EuroDisney also encountered difficulties with regard to competition—the World's Fair in Seville and the 1992 Olympics in Barcelona were huge attractions for European tourists.

Disney management's conviction that it knew best was demonstrated by its much-trumpeted ban on alcohol in the park. This rule proved insensitive to the local culture, because the French are the world's biggest consumers of wine. To them a meal without *un verre de rouge* is unthinkable. Disney relented. It also had to relax its rules on personal grooming of the projected 12,000 cast members, the park employees. Women were allowed to wear redder nail polish than in the United States, but the taboo on men's facial hair was maintained. "We want the clean-shaven, neat and tidy look," commented the director of Disney University's Paris branch, which trains prospective employees in Disney values and culture. EuroDisney's management did, however, compromise on the question of pets. Special kennels were built to house visitors' animals. The thought of leaving a pet at home during vacation is considered irrational by many French people.

Plans for further development of EuroDisney after 1992 were ambitious. The initial number of hotel rooms was planned to be 5,200, more than in the entire city of Cannes on the Côte d'Azur. Also planned were shopping malls, apartments, golf courses, and vacation homes. EuroDisney would design and build everything itself, with a view to selling at a profit. As a Disney executive commented, "Disney at various points could have had partners to share the risk, or buy the hotels outright. But it didn't want to give up the upside."

"From the time they came on, Disney's Chairman Eisner and President Wells had never made a single misstep, never a mistake, never a failure," said a former Disney executive. "There was a tendency to believe that everything they touched would be perfect." The incredible growth record fostered this belief. In the seven years before EuroDisney opened, they took the parent company from being a company with $1 billion in revenues to one with $8.5 billion, mainly through internal growth.

Telling and Selling Fairy Tales   Mistaken assumptions by the Disney management team affected construction design, marketing and pricing policies, and park management, as well as initial financing. Disney executives had been erroneously informed that Europeans don't eat breakfast. Restaurant breakfast service was downsized accordingly, and guess what? "Everybody showed up for breakfast. We were trying to serve 2,500 breakfasts in a 350-seat restaurant [at some of the hotels]. The lines were horrendous. And they didn't just want croissants and coffee, they wanted bacon and eggs."

In contrast to Disney's American parks, where visitors typically stay at least three days, EuroDisney is at most a two-day visit. Energetic visitors need even less time. One analyst claimed to have "done" every EuroDisney ride in just five hours. Typically many guests arrive early in the morning, rush to the park, come back to their hotel late at night, and then check out the next morning before heading back to the park.

Vacation customs of Europeans were not taken into consideration. Disney executives had optimistically expected that the arrival of their new theme park would cause French parents to take their children out of school in mid-session for a short break. It did not happen unless a public holiday occurred over a weekend. Similarly, Disney expected that the American-style short but more frequent family trips would displace the European tradition of a one-month family vacation, usually taken in August. However, French office and factory schedules remained the same, with their emphasis on an August shutdown.

In promoting the new park to visitors, Disney did not stress the entertainment value of a visit to the new theme park; the emphasis was on the size of the park, which "ruined the magic." To counter this, ads were changed to feature Zorro, a French favorite, Mary Poppins, and Aladdin, star of the huge moneymaking movie success. A print ad campaign at that time featured Aladdin, Cinderella's castle, and a little girl being invited to enjoy a "magic vacation" at the kingdom where "all dreams come true." Six new attractions were added in 1994, including the Temple of Peril, Storybook Land, and the Nautilus attraction. Donald Duck's birthday was celebrated on June 9—all in hopes of positioning EuroDisney as the number 1 European destination of short duration, one to three days.

Faced with falling share prices and crisis talk among shareholders, Disney was forced to step forward in late 1993 to rescue the new park. Disney announced that it would fund EuroDisney until a financial restructuring could be worked out with lenders. However, it was made clear by the parent company, Disney, that it "was not writing a blank check."

In June 1994, EuroDisney received a new lifeline when a member of the Saudi royal family agreed to invest up to $500 million for a 24 percent stake in the park. The prince has an established reputation in world markets as a "bottom-fisher," buying into potentially viable operations during crises when share prices are low. The prince's plans included a $100 million convention center at EuroDisney. One of the few pieces of good news about EuroDisney is that its convention business exceeded expectations from the beginning.

MANAGEMENT AND NAME CHANGES

Frenchman Philippe Bourguignon took over at EuroDisney as CEO in 1993 and has navigated the theme park back to profitability. He was instrumental in the negotiations with the firm's bankers, cutting a deal that he credits largely for bringing the park back into the black.

Perhaps more important to the long-run success of the venture were his changes in marketing. The pan-European approach to marketing was dumped, and national markets were targeted separately. This new localization took into account the differing tourists' habits around the continent. Separate marketing offices were opened in London, Frankfurt, Milan, Brussels, Amsterdam, and Madrid, and each was charged with tailoring advertising and packages to its own market. Prices were cut by 20 percent for park admission and 30 percent for some hotel room rates. Special promotions were also run for the winter months.

The central theme of the new marketing and operations approach is that people visit the park for an "authentic" Disney day out. They may not be completely sure what that means, except that it entails something American. This approach is reflected in the transformation of the park's name. The "Euro" in EuroDisney was first shrunk in the logo, and the word "land" added. Then in October 1994 the "Euro" was eliminated completely; the park is now called Disneyland Paris.

In 1996, Disneyland Paris became France's most visited tourist attraction, ahead of both the Louvre Art Museum and the Eiffel Tower. In that year, 11.7 million visitors (a 9 percent increase from the previous year) allowed the park to report another profit.

THEME PARK EXPANSION IN THE TWENTY-FIRST CENTURY

With the recovery of Disneyland Paris, Disney embarked on an ambitious growth plan. In 2001 the California Adventure Park was added to the Anaheim complex at a cost of $1.4 billion, and Walt Disney Studios Theme Park was added to Disneyland Paris. Through agreements with foreign partners, Disney opened DisneySea in Tokyo and Disneyland Hong Kong in 2006, and plans are underway for a theme park in Shanghai scheduled for 2010.

A decade after being slammed for its alleged ignorance of European ways with EuroDisney, Disney is trying to prove its gotten things right the second time around. The new movie-themed park, Walt Disney Studios adjacent to Disneyland Paris, is designed to be tribute to moviemaking—but not just the Hollywood kind. The Walt Disney Studios blends Disney entertainment and attractions with the history and culture of European film since French camera-makers helped invent the motion picture. The park's general layout is modeled after an old Hollywood studio complex, and some of the rides and shows are near replicas of Disney's first film park, Disney-MGM Studios. Rather than celebrating the history of U.S. Disney characters, the characters in the new theme park speak six different languages. A big stunt show features cars and motorcycles that race through a village modeled after the French resort town of St. Tropez.

Small details reflect the cultural lessons learned. "We made sure that all our food venues have covered seating," recalling that, when EuroDisney first opened, the open-air restaurants offered no protection from the rainy weather that assails the park for long stretches of the year.

On the food front, EuroDisney offered only a French sausage, drawing complaints from the English, Germans, Italians, and everyone else about why their local sausages weren't available. This time around, the park caters to the multiple indigenous cultures throughout Europe—which includes a wider selection of sausages.

Unlike Disney's attitude with their first park in France, "Now we realize that our guests need to be welcomed on the basis of their own culture and travel habits," says Disneyland Paris Chief Executive. Disneyland Paris today is Europe's biggest tourist attraction—even more popular than the Eiffel Tower—a turnaround that showed the park operators' ability to learn from their mistakes.

The root of Disney's problems in EuroDisney may be found in the tremendous success of Japan's Disneyland. The Tokyo Park was a success from the first day, and it has been visited by millions of Japanese who wanted to capture what they perceived as the ultimate U.S entertainment experience.

Disney took the entire U.S. theme park and transplanted it in Japan. It worked because of the Japanese attachment to Disney characters. Schools have field trips to meet Mickey and his friends to the point that the Disney experience has become ingrained in Japanese life. In the book *Disneyland as Holy Land,* University of Tokyo professor Masako Notoji wrote: "The opening of Tokyo Disneyland was, in retrospect, the greatest cultural event in Japan

during the '80s." With such success, is there any wonder that Disney thought they had the right model when they first went to France? The Tokyo Disney constitutes a very rare case in that the number of visitors has not decreased since the opening.

2005 Update—Bankruptcy Pending

In early 2005, Disneyland Paris was on the verge of bankruptcy. The newest park attraction at Disneyland Paris, Walt Disney Studios, featured Hollywood-themed attractions such as a ride called "Armageddon—Special Effects" based on a movie starring Bruce Willis, flopped. Guests said it lacked attractions to justify the entrance price, and others complained it focused too much on American, rather than European, filmmaking. Disney blames other factors: the post-9/11 tourism slump, strikes in France, and a summer heat wave in 2003. The French government came to the aid of Disneyland Paris with a state-owned bank contribution of around $500 million to save the company from bankruptcy.

A new Disneyland Paris CEO, a former Burger King executive, introduced several changes in hopes of bringing the Paris park back from the edge of bankruptcy. To make Disneyland Paris a cheaper vacation destination, the CEO is lobbying the government to open up Charles de Gaulle airport to more low-cost airlines. Under his direction, Disneyland Paris created its first original character tailored for a European audience: the Halloween-themed "L'Homme Citrouille," or "Pumpkin Man." He has also introduced a one-day pass giving visitors access to both parks in place of two separate tickets. He is planning new rides, including the Tower of Terror, and other new attractions. If these changes fail to bring in millions of new visitors, Disney and the French government might once again be forced to consider dramatic measures.

Even though French President Jacques Chirac called the spread of American culture an "ecological disaster" and the French government imposes quotas on non-French movies to offset the influence of Hollywood and officially discourages the use of English words such as "e-mail," Disneyland Paris is important to the French economy. In light of France's 10 percent unemployment, Disneyland Paris is seen as a job-creation success. The company accounts for an estimated 43,000 jobs and its parks attract over 12 million visitors a year, more than the Louvre Museum and the Eiffel Tower combined. By 2008 Disneyland Paris was experiencing increases in park attendance, and the turnaround appeared to be working.

DISNEY'S GREAT LEAP INTO CHINA

Disney's record with overseas theme parks has been mixed. Tokyo Disneyland is a smash hit with 25 million visitors a year and Disneyland Paris, opened in 1992, was a financial sinkhole that just now is showing promise of a turnaround. Disney was determined not to make the same cultural and management mistakes in China that had plagued Disneyland Paris.

Disney took special steps to make Hong Kong Disneyland culturally acceptable. "Disney has learned that they can't impose the American will—or Disney's version of it—on another continent." "They've bent over backward to make Hong Kong Disneyland blend in with the surroundings." "We've come at it with an American sensibility, but we still appeal to local tastes," says one of Hong Kong Disneyland's landscape architects.

Desiring to bring Disneyland Hong Kong into harmony with local customs from the beginning, it was decided to observe feng shui in planning and construction. Feng shui is the practice of arranging objects (such as the internal placement of furniture) to achieve harmony with one's environment. It is also used for choosing a place to live. Proponents claim that feng shui has effects on health, wealth, and personal relationships.

The park's designers brought in a feng shui master who rotated the front gate, repositioned cash registers, and ordered boulders set in key locations to ensure the park's prosperity. He even chose the park's "auspicious" opening date. New construction was often begun with a traditional good-luck ceremony featuring a carved suckling pig. Other feng shui influences include the park's orientation to face water with mountains behind. Feng shui experts also designated "no fire zones" in the kitchens to try to keep the five elements of metal, water, wood, fire, and earth in balance.

Along with following feng shui principles, the park's hotels have no floors that are designated as fourth floors, because 4 is considered an unlucky number in Chinese culture. Furthermore, the opening date was set for September 12 because it was listed as an auspicious date for opening a business in the Chinese almanac.

But the park's success wasn't a sure thing. The park received more than 5 million visitors in its first year but short of its targeted 5.6 million, and the second year was equally disappointing with attendance dropping nearly 30 percent below forecasts. Many of those who came complained that it was too small and had little to excite those unfamiliar with Disney's cast of characters.

Disneyland is supposed to be "The Happiest Place on Earth," but Liang Ning isn't too happy. The engineer brought his family to Disney's new theme park in Hong Kong from the southern Chinese city of Guangzhou one Saturday in April with high hopes, but by day's end, he was less than spellbound. "I wanted to forget the world and feel like I was in a fairytale," he says. Instead, he complains, "it's just not big enough" and "not very different from the amusement parks we have" in China. Hong Kong Disneyland has only 16 attractions and only one a classic Disney thrill ride, Space Mountain, compared with 52 rides at Disneyland Paris.

After the first year's lackluster beginning, Disney management introduced five new attractions and added "It's a Small World," the ride made famous at the flagship Disneyland in Anaheim, California. A variety of other new entertainment offerings were due in 2008.

Guest's lack of knowledge of Disney characters created a special hurdle in China. Until a few years ago, hardly anyone in mainland China knew Mickey Mouse and Donald Duck even existed. Disney characters were banned for nearly 40 years, so their knowledge of Disney lore is limited. China was the first market where Disney opened a park in which there had been no long-term relationship with attendees. It was the Chinese consumer who was expected to understand Disney, or so it seemed. Chinese tourists unfamiliar with Disney's traditional stories were sometimes left bewildered by the Hong Kong park's attractions.

To compensate for the lack of awareness of Disney characters and create the mystique of a Disney experience, Disney launched numerous marketing initiatives designed to familiarize guests with Disneyland. One of the first buildings upon entering the park exhibits artwork and film footage of Disney history, from the creation of Mickey Mouse through the construction of Hong Kong Disneyland. Tour groups are greeted by a Disney host who introduces them to Walt Disney, the park's attractions, characters, and other background information. For example, the character Buzz Lightyear explains *Toy Story* and the Buzz Lightyear Astro Blaster attraction.

Even though there were complaints about the park size and the unfamilarity of Disney characters, there were unique features built with the Asian guest in mind that have proved to be very popular.

Fantasy Gardens, one of the park's original features, was designed to appeal to guests from Hong Kong and mainland China who love to take pictures. At five gazebos, photo-happy tourists can always find Mickey, Minnie, and other popular characters who will sign autographs and pose for photos and videos. Mulan has her own pavilion in the garden, designed like a Chinese temple. Mickey even has a new red-and-gold Chinese suit to wear. Restaurants boast local fare, such as Indian curries, Japanese sushi, and Chinese mango pudding, served in containers shaped like Mickey Mouse heads.

All in all, Hong Kong Disney is Chinese throughout. It's not so much an American theme park as Mickey Mouse coming to China. The atmosphere is uncomplicated and truly family oriented. It is possible to have a genuine family park experience where six-year-olds take precedence. However, early advertising that featured the family missed its mark somewhat by featuring a family consisting of two kids and two parents, which did not have the impact it was supposed to have, because China's government limits most couples to just one child. The error was quickly corrected in a new TV commercial, which the company says was designed to "forge a stronger emotional connection with Mickey." The revised ad featured one child, two parents, and two grandparents together sharing branded Disney activities, such as watching a movie and giving a plush version of the mouse as gifts. "Let's visit Mickey together!" says the father in the commercial, before scenes at the park set to traditional Chinese music.

Many other aspects of the park have been modified to better suit its Chinese visitors. The cast members are extremely diverse, understand various cultures, and, in many cases, speak three languages. Signs, audio-recorded messages, and attractions are also in several languages. For example, riders can choose from English, Mandarin, or Cantonese on the Jungle River Cruise.

Disney runs promotions throughout the year. For example, the "Stay and Play for Two Days" promotion was created mainly to give mainland tourists a chance to experience the park for a longer period of time. Because many Chinese tourists cross into Hong Kong by bus, they arrive at Disneyland mid-day. With this promotion, if a guest stays at a Disneyland hotel and purchases a one-day ticket, the guest is given a second day at the park for free.

Special Chinese holidays feature attractions and decorations unique to the holiday. For the February 7, 2008, New Year holiday (the Year of the Rat), Disney suited up its own house rodents, Mickey and Minnie, in special red Chinese New Year outfits for its self-proclaimed Year of the Mouse. The Disneyland Chinese New Year campaign, which lasts until February 24, features a logo with the kind of visual pun that only the Chinese might appreciate: the Chinese character for "luck" flipped upside-down (a New Year tradition), with mouse ears added on top. Inside the park, vendors hawk deep-fried dumplings and turnip cakes. The parade down Main Street, U.S.A., is joined by the "Rhythm of Life Procession," featuring a dragon dance and puppets of birds, flowers, and fish, set to traditional Chinese music. And of course there's the god of wealth, a relative newcomer to the regular Hong Kong Disneyland gang, joined by the gods of longevity and happiness, all major figures in Chinese New Year celebrations.

There are broader implications for Disney from the performance of the Hong Kong theme park than just its financial health. From the outset, executives at the business's Burbank headquarters viewed Hong Kong Disneyland as a springboard to promote awareness of the Disney name among the mainland Chinese population and cement ties with Beijing. The next theme park is set for

Shanghai, and the last thing they want is a "turkey" in Hong Kong that would undermine their whole China strategy. Plans have already been submitted, and once the central government approves, construction is expected to begin in 2010.

REFERENCES

"An American in Paris," *BusinessWeek,* March 12, 1990, pp. 60–61, 64; Asahi Shimbun, " Tokyo Disney Prospers In Its Own Way," *Asahi Evening News,* April 22, 2003; Chester Dawson, "Will Tokyo Embrace Another Mouse?" *BusinessWeek,* September 10, 2001; "Euro Disney Gets Its Rights Issue Thanks to Underwriting Banks but Success in Balance," *Euroweek,* February 11, 2005; "EuroDisney's Prince Charming?" *Business-Week,* June 13, 1994, p. 42; "Saudi to Buy as Much as 24% of EuroDisney," *The Wall Street Journal,* June 2, 1994, p. A4; Bernard J. Wolfson, "The Mouse That Roared Back," *Orange County Register,* April 9, 2000, p. 1; "Disney Applies Feng Shui to Hong Kong Park," *AP Online,* June 27, 2005; Michael Schuman, "Disney's Great Leap into China," *Time,* July 11, 2005; Michael Schuman, "Disney's Hong Kong Headache," *Time,* May 8, 2006; "A Bumpy Ride for Disneyland in Hong Kong; Despite Fixes, Some Observers Say Troubles Could Follow company to Shanghai," *The Washington Post,* November 20, 2006; Dikky Sinn, "Hong Kong Government Unhappy with Disneyland's Performance," *AP Worldstream,* December 4, 2007; Elaine Kurtenbach, "Reports: Shanghai Disneyland May be Built on Yangtze Island; City Officials Mum on Talks," *AP Worldstream,* December 4, 2007; Lauren Booth, "The Wonderful World of Mandarin Mickey . . . " *The Independent on Sunday,* July 22, 2007; Mark Kleinman, "Magic Kingdom Fails to Cast Its Spell in the Middle Kingdom . . . " *The Sunday Telegraph* (London), February 25, 2007; Paula M. Miller, "Disneyland in Hong Kong," *China Business Review,* January 1, 2007; Jeffrey Ng, "Hong Kong Disneyland Seeks New Magic," *The Wall Street Journal,* December 19, 2007; Geoffrey A. Fowler, "Main Street, K.K.; Disney Localizes Mickey to Boost Its Hong Kong Theme Park," *The Wall Street Journal,* January 23, 2008; "A Chinese Makeover for Mickey and Minnie," *The New York Times,* January 22, 2008.

QUESTIONS

1. What factors contributed to EuroDisney's poor performance during its first year of operation? What factors contributed to Hong Kong Disney's poor performance during its first year?

2. To what degree do you consider that these factors were (a) foreseeable and (b) controllable by EuroDisney, Hong Kong Disney, or the parent company, Disney?

3. What role does ethnocentrism play in the story of EuroDisney's launch?

4. How do you assess the cross-cultural marketing skills of Disney?

5. Why did success in Tokyo predispose Disney management to be too optimistic in their expectations of success in France? In China? Discuss.

6. Why do you think the experience in France didn't help Disney avoid some of the problems in Hong Kong?

7. Now that Hong Kong Disney is up and running, will the Shanghai development benefit from the Hong Kong experience?

8. Now that Disney has opened Hong Kong Disney and begun work on the Shanghai location, where and when should it go next? Assume you are a consultant hired to give Disney advice on the issue of where and when to go next. Pick three locations and select the one you think will be the best new location for "Disneyland *X*." Discuss.

9. Given your choice of locale *X* for the newest Disneyland, what are the operational implications of the history of EuroDisney and Disney Hong Kong for the new park?

This case was prepared by Lyn S. Amine, Ph.D., Professor of Marketing and International Business, Distinguished Fellow of the Academy of Marketing Science, and President, Women of the Academy of International Business, Saint Louis University and graduate student Carolyn A. Tochtrop, Saint Louis University, as a basis for class discussion rather than to illustrate either effective or ineffective handling of a situation. The original case appearing in prior editions has been edited and updated to reflect recent developments.

CASE 2-2 Cultural Norms, *Fair & Lovely,* and Advertising

Fair & Lovely, a branded product of Hindustan Lever Ltd. (HLL), is touted as a cosmetic that lightens skin color. On its Web site (www.hll.com), the company calls its product "the miracle worker," "proven to deliver one to three shades of change." While tanning is the rage in Western countries, skin lightening treatments are popular in Asia.

According to industry sources, the top-selling skin lightening cream in India is Fair & Lovely from Hindustan Lever Ltd. (HLL), followed by CavinKare's Fairever brand. HLL's Fair & Lovely brand dominated the market with a 90 percent share until CavinKare Ltd. (CKL) launched Fairever. In just two years, the Fairever brand gained an impressive 15 percent market share. HLL's share of market for the Fair & Lovely line generates about $60 million annually. The product sells for about 23 rupees ($0.29) for a 25-gram tube of cream.

The rapid growth of CavinKare's Fairever (www.cavinkare.com) brand prompted HLL to increase its advertising effort and to launch a series of ads depicting a "fairer girl gets the boy theme." One advertisement featured a financially strapped father lamenting his fate, saying, "If only I had a son," while his dark-skinned daughter looks on, helpless and demoralized because she can't bear the financial responsibility of her family. Fast-forward and plain Jane has been transformed into a gorgeous light-skinned woman through the use of a "fairness cream," Fair & Lovely. Now clad in a miniskirt, the woman is a successful flight attendant and can take her father to dine at a five-star hotel. She's happy and so is her father.

In another ad, two attractive young women are sitting in a bedroom; one has a boyfriend and, consequently, is happy. The darker-skinned woman, lacking a boyfriend, is not happy. Her friend's advice—Use a bar of soap to wash away the dark skin that's keeping men from flocking to her.

HLL's series of ads provoked CavinKare Ltd. to counter with an ad that takes a dig at HLL's Fair & Lovely ad. CavinKare's ad has a father–daughter duo as the protagonists, with the father shown encouraging the daughter to be an achiever irrespective of her complexion. CavinKare maintained that the objective of its new commercial is not to take a dig at Fair & Lovely but to "reinforce Fairever's positioning."

Skin color is a powerful theme in India, and much of Asia, where a lighter color represents a higher status. While Americans and Europeans flock to tanning salons, many across Asia seek ways to have "fair" complexions. Culturally, fair skin is associated with positive values that relate to class and beauty. One Indian lady commented that when she was growing up, her mother forbade her to go outdoors. She was not trying to keep her daughter out of trouble but was trying to keep her skin from getting dark.

Brahmins, the priestly caste at the top of the social hierarchy, are considered fair because they traditionally stayed inside, poring over books. The undercaste at the bottom of the ladder are regarded as the darkest people because they customarily worked in the searing sun. Ancient Hindu scriptures and modern poetry eulogize women endowed with skin made of white marble.

Skin color is closely identified with caste and is laden with symbolism. Pursue any of the "grooms" and "brides wanted" ads in newspapers or on the Web that are used by families to arrange suitable alliances, and you will see that most potential grooms and their families are looking for "fair" brides; some even are progressive enough to invite responses from women belonging to a different caste. These ads, hundreds of which appear in India's daily newspapers, reflect attempts to solicit individuals with the appropriate religion, caste, regional ancestry, professional and educational qualifications, and, frequently, skin color. Even in the growing numbers of ads that announce "caste no bar," the adjective "fair" regularly precedes professional qualifications. In everyday conversation, the ultimate compliment on someone's looks is to say someone is *gora* (fair). "I have no problem with people wanting to be lighter," said a Delhi beauty parlor owner, Saroj Nath. "It doesn't make you racist, any more than trying to make yourself look younger makes you ageist."

Bollywood (India's Hollywood) glorifies conventions on beauty by always casting a fair-skinned actress in the role of heroine, surrounded by the darkest extras. Women want to use whiteners because it is "aspirational, like losing weight."

Even the gods supposedly lament their dark complexion— Krishna sings plaintively, "*Radha kyoon gori, main kyoon kala?* (Why is Radha so fair when I'm dark?)." A skin deficient in melanin (the pigment that determines the skin's brown color) is an ancient predilection. More than 3,500 years ago, Charaka, the famous sage, wrote about herbs that could help make the skin fair.

Indian dermatologists maintain that fairness products cannot truly work as they reach only the upper layers of the skin and so do not affect melanin production. Nevertheless, for some, Fair & Lovely is a "miracle worker." A user gushes that "The last time I went to my parents' home, I got compliments on my fair skin from everyone." For others, there is only disappointment. One 26-year-old working woman has been a regular user for the past eight years but to no avail. "I should have turned into Snow White by now but my skin is still the same wheatish color." As an owner of a public relations firm commented, "My maid has been using Fair and Lovely for years and I still can't see her in the dark. . . . But she goes on using it. Hope springs eternal, I suppose."

The number of Indians who think lighter skin is more beautiful may be shrinking. Sumit Isralni, a 22-year-old hair designer in his father's salon, thinks things have changed in the last two years, at least in India's most cosmopolitan cities, Delhi, Mumbai, and Bangalore. Women now "prefer their own complexion, their natural way" Isralni says; he prefers a more "Indian beauty" himself: "I won't judge my wife on how fair her complexion is." Sunita Gupta, a beautician in the same salon, is more critical. "It's just foolishness!" she exclaimed. The premise of the ads that women could not become airline attendants if they are dark-skinned was wrong, she said. "Nowadays people like black beauty." It is a truism that women, especially in the tropics, desire to be a shade fairer, no matter what their skin color. Yet, unlike the approach used in India, advertisements elsewhere usually show how to use the product and how it works.

Commenting on the cultural bias toward fair skin, one critic states, "There are attractive people who go through life feeling inferior to their fairer sisters. And all because of charming grandmothers and aunts who do not hesitate to make unflattering comparisons. *Kalee Kalooti* is an oft-heard comment about women who happen to have darker skin. They get humiliated and mortified over the color of their skin, a fact over which they have no control. Are societal values responsible? Or advertising campaigns? Advertising moguls claim they only reflect prevailing attitudes in India. This is possibly true but what about ethics in advertising? Is it correct to make advertisements that openly denigrate a majority of Indian people—the dark-skinned populace? The advertising is blatant in their strategy. Mock anyone who is not the right color and shoot down their self-image."

A dermatologist comments, "Fairness obtained with the help of creams is short-lived. The main reason being, most of these creams contain a certain amount of bleaching agent, which whitens facial hair, and not the skin, which leads people to believe that the cream worked." Furthermore, "In India the popularity of a product depends totally on the success of its advertising."

HLL launched its television ad campaign to promote Fair & Lovely in December 2001 and withdrew it in February 2003, amid severe criticism for its portrayal of women. Activists argued that one of the messages the company sends through its "air hostess" ads demonstrating the preference for a son who would be able to take on the financial responsibility for his parents is especially harmful in a country such as India where gender discrimination is rampant. Another offense is perpetuating a culture of discrimination in a society where "fair" is synonymous with "beautiful." AIDWA (All India Women's Democratic Association) lodged a complaint in March and April 2002 with HLL about their offensive ads, but Hindustan Lever failed to respond.

The women's association then appealed to the National Human Rights Commission alleging that the ad demeaned women. AIDWA objected to three things: (1) the ads were racist, (2) they were promoting son preference, and (3) they were insulting to working women. "The way they portrayed the young woman who, after using Fair & Lovely, became attractive and therefore lands a job suggested that the main qualification for a woman to get a job is the way she looks." The Human Rights Commission passed AIDWA's complaints on to the Ministry of Information and Broadcasting, which said the campaign violated the Cable and Television Network Act of 1995—provisions in the act state that no advertisement shall be permitted which "derides any race, caste, color, creed and nationality" and that "Women must not be portrayed in a manner that emphasized passive, submissive qualities and encourages them to play a subordinate secondary role in the family and society." The government issued notices of the complaints to HLL. After a year-long campaign led by the AIDWA, Hindustan Lever Limited discontinued two of its television advertisements for Fair & Lovely fairness cold cream in March 2003.

Shortly after pulling its ads off the air, HLL launched its Fair & Lovely Foundation, vowing to "encourage economic empowerment of women across India" by providing resources in education and business to millions of women "who, though immensely talented and capable, need a guiding hand to help them take the leap forward," presumably into a fairer future.

HLL sponsored career fairs in over 20 cities across the country offering counseling in as many as 110 careers. It supported 100 rural scholarships for women students passing their 10th grade, a professional course for aspiring beauticians, and a three-month Home Healthcare Nursing Assistant course catering to young women between the ages of 18 and 30 years. According to HLL, the Fair & Lovely Academy for Home Care Nursing Assistants

offers a unique training opportunity for young women who possess no entry-level skills and therefore are not employable in the new economy job market. The Fair & Lovely Foundation plans to serve as a catalyst for the economic empowerment for women across India. The Fair & Lovely Foundation will showcase the achievements of these women not only to honor them but also to set an example for other women to follow.

AIDWA's campaign against ads that convey the message "if she is not fair in color, she won't get married or won't get promoted," also has resulted in some adjustment to fairness cream ads. In revised versions of the fairness cream ads, the "get fair to attract a groom" theme is being reworked with "enhance your self-confidence" so that a potential groom himself begs for attention. It is an attempt at typifying the modern Indian woman, who has more than just marriage on her mind. Advertising focus is now on the message that lighter skin enables women to obtain jobs conventionally held by men. She is career-oriented, has high aspirations, and, at the same time, wants to look good. AIDWA concedes that the current crop of television ads for fairness creams are "not as demeaning" as ones in the past. However, it remains against the product; as the president of AIDWA stated, "It is downright racist to denigrate dark skin."

Although AIWDA's campaign against fairness creams seems to have had a modest impact on changing the advertising message, it has not slowed the demand for fairness creams. Sales of Fair & Lovely, for example, have been growing 15 to 20 percent year over year, and the $318 million market for skin care has grown by 42.7 percent since 2001. Says Euromonitor International, a research firm: "Half of the skin care market in India is fairness creams and 60 to 65 percent of Indian women use these products daily."

In 2007, several Indian companies were extending their marketing of fairness creams beyond urban and rural markets. CavinKare's launch of Fairever, a fairness cream in a small sachet pack priced at Rs 5, aimed at rural markets where some 320 million Indians reside. Most marketers have found rural markets impossible to penetrate profitably due to low income levels and inadequate distribution systems, among other problems. However, HLL is approaching the market through Project Shakti, a rural initiative that targets small villages with populations of 2,000 people or less. It empowers underprivileged rural women by providing income-generating opportunities to sell small, lower priced packets of its brands in villages. Special packaging for the rural market was designed to provide single-use sachet packets at 50 paise for a sachet of shampoo to Rs 5 for a fairness cream (for a week's usage). The aim is to have 100,000 "Shakti Ammas," as they are called, spread across 500,000 villages in India" by 2010. CavinKare is growing at 25 percent in rural areas compared with 15 percent in urban centers.

In addition to expanding market effort into rural markets, an unexpected market arose when a research study revealed Indian men were applying girlie fairness potions in droves—but on the sly. It was estimated that 40 percent of boyfriends/husbands of girlfriends/wives were applying white magic solutions that came in little tubes. Indian companies spotted a business opportunity, and Fair & Handsome, Menz Active, Fair One Man, and a male bleach called Saka were introduced to the male market. The sector expanded dramatically when Shah Rukh Khan, a highly acclaimed Bollywood actor likened to an Indian Tom Cruise, decided to endorse Fair & Handsome. Euromonitor International forecasts that in the next five years, spending on men's grooming products will rise 24 percent to 14.5 billion rupees, or US$320 million.

A product review in www.mouthshut.com, posted February 28, 2005, praises Fair & Lovely fairness cream: "[Fair & Lovely] contains fairness vitamins which penetrate deep down our skin to give us radiant fairness." "I don't know if it can change the skin color from dark to fair, but my personal experience is that it works very well, if you have a naturally fair color and want to preserve it without much headache." "I think Riya Sen has the best skin right now in Bollywood. It appears to be really soft and tender. So, to have a soft and fair skin like her I recommend Fair & Lovely Fairness Lotion or Cream." Yet "skin color isn't a proof of greatness. Those with wheatish or dark skin are by no way inferior to those who have fair skin."

Here are a few facts from Hindustan Lever Ltd.'s homepage:

Lever Limited is India's largest Packaged Mass Consumption Goods Company. We are leaders in Home and Personal Care Products and Food and Beverages including such products as Ponds and Pepsodent. We seek to meet everyday needs of people everywhere—to anticipate the aspirations of our consumers and customers and to respond creatively and competitively with branded products and services which raise the quality of life. It is this purpose which inspires us to build brands. Over the past 70 years, we have introduced about 110 brands.

Fair & Lovely has been specially designed and proven to deliver one to three shades of change in most people. Also its sunscreen system is specially optimized for Indian skin. Indian skin, unlike Caucasian skin, tends to "tan" rather than "burn" and, hence, requires a different combination of UVA and UVB sunscreens.

You may want to visit HLLs homepage (www.hhl.com) for additional information about the company.

QUESTIONS

1. Is it ethical to sell a product that is, at best, only mildly effective? Discuss.

2. Is it ethical to exploit cultural norms and values to promote a product? Discuss.

3. Is the advertising of Fair & Lovely demeaning to women, or is it promoting the fairness cream in a way not too dissimilar from how most cosmetics are promoted?

4. Will HLL's Fair & Lovely Foundation be enough to counter charges made by AIDWA? Discuss.

5. In light of AIDWA's charges, how would you suggest Fair & Lovely promote its product? Discuss. Would your response be different if Fairever continues to use "fairness" as a theme of its promotion? Discuss.

6. Propose a promotion/marketing program that will counter all the arguments and charges against Fair & Lovely and be an effective program.

7. Now that a male market for fairness cream exists, is the strength of AIDWA's argument weakened?

8. Comment on using "Shakti Ammas" to introduce "fairness cream for the masses" in light of AIDWA's charges.

Sources: Nicole Leistikow, "Indian Women Criticize 'Fair and Lovely' Ideal," *Women's eNews,* April 28, 2003; Arundhati Parmar, "Objections to Indian Ad Not Taken Lightly," *Marketing News,* June 9, 2003, p. 4; "Fair & Lovely Launches Foundation to Promote Economic Empowerment of Women," *press release,* Fair & Lovely Foundation, http://www.hll.com (search for foundation), March 11, 2003; Rina Chandran, "All for Self-Control," *Business Line* (*The Hindu*), April 24, 2003; Khozem Merchant and Edward Luce, "Not So Fair and Lovely," *Financial Times,* March 19, 2003; "Fair & Lovely Redefines Fairness with Multivitamin Total Fairness Cream," press release, Hindustan Lever Ltd., May 3, 2005; Dr. Deepa Kanchankoti, "Do You Think Fairness Creams Work?" http://www.mid-day.com/metro, July 13, 2005; "CavinKare Launches Small Sachet Packs," *Business India,* December 7, 2006; "Analysis of Skin Care Advertising on TV During January–August 2006," *Indiantelevision.com Media, Advertising, Marketing Watch,* October 17, 2006; "Women Power Gets Full Play in CavinKare's Brand Strategy." *The Economic Times* (*New Delhi, India*), December 8, 2006; Heather Timmons, "Telling India's Modern Women They Have Power, Even Over Their Skin Tone," *The New York Times,* May 30, 2007; "The Year We Almost Lost Tall (or Short or Medium-Height), Dark and Handsome," *The Hindustan Times,* December 29, 2007; "India's Hue and Cry Over Paler Skin," *The Sunday Telegraph* (London), July 1, 2007; "Fair and Lovely?" *University Wire,* June 4, 2007; "The Race to Keep up with Modern India," *Media,* June 29, 2007.

CASE 2-3 Starnes-Brenner Machine Tool Company: To Bribe or Not to Bribe?

The Starnes-Brenner Machine Tool Company of Iowa City, Iowa, has a small one-man sales office headed by Frank Rothe in Latino, a major Latin American country. Frank has been in Latino for about 10 years and is retiring this year; his replacement is Bill Hunsaker, one of Starnes-Brenner's top salespeople. Both will be in Latino for about eight months, during which time Frank will show Bill the ropes, introduce him to their principal customers, and, in general, prepare him to take over.

Frank has been very successful as a foreign representative in spite of his unique style and, at times, complete refusal to follow company policy when it doesn't suit him. The company hasn't really done much about his method of operation, though from time to time he has angered some top company people. As President Jack McCaughey, who retired a couple of years ago, once remarked to a vice president who was complaining about Frank, "If he's making money—and he is (more than any of the other foreign offices)—then leave the guy alone." When McCaughey retired, the new chief immediately instituted organizational changes that gave more emphasis to the overseas operations, moving the company toward a truly worldwide operation into which a loner like Frank would probably not fit. In fact, one of the key reasons for selecting Bill as Frank's replacement, besides Bill's record as a top salesperson, is Bill's capacity to be an organization man. He understands the need for coordination among operations and will cooperate with the home office so that the Latino office can be expanded and brought into the mainstream.

The company knows there is much to be learned from Frank, and Bill's job is to learn everything possible. The company certainly doesn't want to continue some of Frank's practices, but much of his knowledge is vital for continued, smooth operation. Today, Starnes-Brenner's foreign sales account for about 25 percent of the company's total profits, compared with about 5 percent only 10 years ago.

The company is actually changing character, from being principally an exporter, without any real concern for continuous foreign market representation, to having worldwide operations, where the foreign divisions are part of the total effort rather than a stepchild operation. In fact, Latino is one of the last operational divisions to be assimilated into the new organization. Rather than try to change Frank, the company has been waiting for him to retire before making any significant adjustments in its Latino operations.

Bill Hunsaker is 36 years old, with a wife and three children; he is a very good salesperson and administrator, though he has had no foreign experience. He has the reputation of being fair, honest, and a straight shooter. Some back at the home office see his assignment as part of a grooming job for a top position, perhaps eventually the presidency. The Hunsakers are now settled in their new home after having been in Latino for about two weeks. Today is Bill's first day on the job.

When Bill arrived at the office, Frank was on his way to a local factory to inspect some Starnes-Brenner machines that had to have some adjustments made before being acceptable to the Latino government agency buying them. Bill joined Frank for the plant visit. Later, after the visit, we join the two at lunch.

Bill, tasting some chili, remarks, "Boy! This certainly isn't like the chili we have in America."

"No, it isn't, and there's another difference, too. The Latinos are Americans and nothing angers a Latino more than to have a 'Gringo' refer to the United States as America as if to say that Latino isn't part of America also. The Latinos rightly consider their country as part of America (take a look at the map), and people from the United States are North Americans at best. So, for future reference, refer to home either as the United States, States, or North America, but, for gosh sakes, not just America. Not to change the subject, Bill, but could you see that any change had been made in those S-27s from the standard model?"

"No, they looked like the standard. Was there something out of whack when they arrived?"

"No, I couldn't see any problem—I suspect this is the best piece of sophisticated bribe taking I've come across yet. Most of the time the Latinos are more 'honest' about their *mordidas* than this."

"What's a *mordida*?" Bill asks.

"You know, *kumshaw*, *dash*, *bustarella*, *mordida*; they are all the same: a little grease to expedite the action. *Mordida* is the local word for a slight offering or, if you prefer, bribe," says Frank.

Bill quizzically responds, "Do we pay bribes to get sales?"

"Oh, it depends on the situation, but it's certainly something you have to be prepared to deal with." Boy, what a greenhorn, Frank thinks to himself, as he continues, "Here's the story. When the S-27s arrived last January, we began uncrating them and right away the *jefe* engineer (a government official)—*jefe*, that's the head man in charge—began extra-careful examination and declared there was a vital defect in the machines; he claimed the machinery would be dangerous and thus unacceptable if it wasn't corrected. I looked it over but couldn't see anything wrong, so I agreed to have our staff engineer check all the machines and correct any flaws that might exist. Well, the *jefe* said there wasn't enough time to wait for an engineer to come from the States, that the machines could be adjusted locally, and we could pay him and he would make all the necessary arrangements. So, what do you do? No adjustment his way and there would be an order canceled; and, maybe there was something out of line, those things have been known to happen. But for the life of me, I can't see that anything had been done since the machines were supposedly fixed. So, let's face it, we just paid a bribe, and a pretty darn big bribe at that—about $1,200 per machine. What makes it so aggravating is that that's the second one I've had to pay on this shipment."

"The second?" asks Bill.

"Yeah, at the border, when we were transferring the machines to Latino trucks, it was hot and they were moving slow as molasses. It took them over an hour to transfer one machine to a Latino truck and we had ten others to go. It seemed that every time I spoke to the dock boss about speeding things up, they just got slower. Finally, out of desperation, I slipped him a fistful of pesos and, sure enough, in the next three hours they had the whole thing loaded. Just one of the local customs of doing business. Generally, though, it comes at the lower level where wages don't cover living expenses too well."

There is a pause, and Bill asks, "What does that do to our profits?"

"Runs them down, of course, but I look at it as just one of the many costs of doing business—I do my best not to pay, but when I have to, I do."

Hesitantly, Bill replies, "I don't like it, Frank. We've got good products, they're priced right, we give good service, and keep plenty of spare parts in the country, so why should we have to pay bribes? It's just no way to do business. You've already had to pay two bribes on one shipment; if you keep it up, the word's going to get around and you'll be paying at every level. Then all the profit goes out the window—you know, once you start, where do you stop? Besides that, where do we stand legally? The Foreign Bribery Act makes paying bribes like you've just paid illegal. I'd say the best policy is to never start: You might lose a few sales, but let it be known that there are no bribes; we sell the best, service the best at fair prices, and that's all."

"You mean the Foreign Corrupt Practices Act, don't you?" Frank asks, and continues, in an I'm-not-really-so-out-of-touch tone of voice, "Haven't some of the provisions of the Foreign Corrupt Practices Act been softened somewhat?"

"Yes, you're right, the provisions on paying a *mordida* or grease have been softened, but paying the government official is still illegal, softening or not," replies Bill.

Oh boy! Frank thinks to himself as he replies, "Look, what I did was just peanuts as far as the Foreign Corrupt Practices Act goes. The people we pay off are small, and, granted we give good service, but we've only been doing it for the last year or so. Before that I never knew when I was going to have equipment to sell. In fact, we only had products when there were surpluses stateside. I had to pay the right people to get sales, and besides, you're not back in the States any longer. Things are just done different here. You follow that policy and I guarantee that you'll have fewer sales because our competitors from Germany, Italy, and Japan will pay. Look, Bill, everybody does it here; it's a way of life, and the costs are generally reflected in the markup and overhead. There is even a code of behavior involved. We're not actually encouraging it to spread, just perpetuating an accepted way of doing business."

Patiently and slightly condescendingly, Bill replies, "I know, Frank, but wrong is wrong and we want to operate differently now. We hope to set up an operation here on a continuous basis; we plan to operate in Latino just like we do in the United States. Really expand our operation and make a long-range market commitment, grow with the country! And one of the first things we must avoid is unethical. . . "

Frank interrupts, "But really, is it unethical? Everybody does it, the Latinos even pay *mordidas* to other Latinos; it's a fact of life—is it really unethical? I think that the circumstances that exist in a country justify and dictate the behavior. Remember, man, 'When in Rome, do as the Romans do.'"

Almost shouting, Bill blurts out, "I can't buy that. We know that our management practices and relationships are our strongest point. Really, all we have to differentiate us from the rest of our competition, Latino and others, is that we are better managed and, as far as I'm concerned, graft and other unethical behavior have got to be cut out to create a healthy industry. In the long run, it should strengthen our position. We can't build our future on illegal and unethical practices."

Frank angrily replies, "Look, it's done in the States all the time. What about the big dinners, drinks, and all the other hanky-panky that goes on? Not to mention PACs' [Political Action Committee] payments to congressmen, and all those high speaking fees certain congressmen get from special interests. How many congressmen have gone to jail or lost reelection on those kinds of things? What is that, if it isn't *mordida* the North American way? The only difference is that instead of cash only, in the United States we pay in merchandise and cash."

"That's really not the same and you know it. Besides, we certainly get a lot of business transacted during those dinners even if we are paying the bill."

"Bull. The only difference is that here bribes go on in the open; they don't hide it or dress it in foolish ritual that fools no one. It goes on in the United States and everyone denies the existence of it. That's all the difference—in the United States we're just more hypocritical about it all."

"Look," Frank continues, almost shouting, "we are getting off on the wrong foot and we've got eight months to work together. Just keep your eyes and mind open and let's talk about it again in a couple of months when you've seen how the whole country operates; perhaps then you won't be so quick to judge it absolutely wrong."

Frank, lowering his voice, says thoughtfully, "I know it's hard to take; probably the most disturbing problem in underdeveloped countries is the matter of graft. And, frankly, we don't do much advance preparation so we can deal firmly with it. It bothered me at first; but then I figured it makes its economic contribution, too, since the payoff is as much a part of the economic process as a payroll. What's our real economic role, anyway, besides making a profit, of course? Are we developers of wealth, helping to push the country to greater economic growth, or are we missionaries? Or should we be both? I really don't know, but I don't think we can be both simultaneously, and my feeling is that, as the company prospers, as higher salaries are paid, and better standards of living are reached, we'll see better ethics. Until then, we've got to operate or leave, and if you are going to win the opposition over, you'd better join them and change them from within, not fight them."

Before Bill could reply, a Latino friend of Frank's joined them, and they changed the topic of conversation.

QUESTIONS

1. Is what Frank did ethical? By whose ethics—those of Latino or the United States?

2. Are Frank's two different payments legal under the Foreign Corrupt Practices Act as amended by the Omnibus Trade and Competitiveness Act of 1988?

3. Identify the types of payments made in the case; that is, are they lubrication, extortion, or subornation?

4. Frank seemed to imply that there is a similarity between what he was doing and what happens in the United States. Is there any difference? Explain.

5. Are there any legal differences between the money paid to the dockworkers and the money paid the *jefe* (government official)? Any ethical differences?

6. Frank's attitude seems to imply that a foreigner must comply with all local customs, but some would say that one of the

contributions made by U.S. firms is to change local ways of doing business. Who is right?

7. Should Frank's behavior have been any different had this not been a government contract?

8. If Frank shouldn't have paid the bribe, what should he have done, and what might have been the consequences?

9. What are the company interests in this problem?

10. Explain how this may be a good example of the SRC (self-reference criterion) at work.

11. Do you think Bill will make the grade in Latino? Why or why not? What will it take?

12. How can an overseas manager be prepared to face this problem?

CASE 2−4 Ethics and Airbus

One September, a fraud squad, led by Jean-Claude Van Espen, a Belgian magistrate, raided Airbus's headquarters in Toulouse. "They wanted to check whether there was possible falsification of documents, bribery or other infractions as part of the sale of Airbus aircraft to Sabena," says Van Espen's spokesman. The team of 20 Belgian and French investigators interviewed several Airbus employees during its three-day stay in Toulouse and carted away boxes of documents.

In November 1997, Sabena had approved an order for 17 Airbus A320s (narrow-bodied aircraft), which it did not need. Even more oddly, it had doubled the order at the last minute to 34, a move that helped trigger the airline's collapse four years later.

Although nominally controlled by the Belgian government, Sabena was run by the parent company of Swissair, SAirGroup, which had owned a stake of 49.5 percent since 1995 and which also went bust in 2001. A former Sabena manager, who arrived after the Airbus order was placed, says that the planes were not needed: "It was a fatal business decision." A Belgian parliamentary commission's recent report confirms that the Airbus order was a big cause of Sabena's collapse.

Van Espen's separate criminal investigation is continuing. According to the report, it started in October 2001 after Philippe Doyen, then a Sabena employee, lodged a complaint. Among other things, he suggested to Van Espen that he interview Peter Gysel, a former Swissair employee now working at Airbus, who put together Sabena's deal with Airbus. Gysel denies any impropriety. The former Sabena manager says: "I never got the slightest whiff that the decision was driven by kickbacks, side-payments, and so on. But I cannot rule anything out." Neither does Van Espen.

Today airlines are ordering about 400 aircraft a year. But in good times, 800 planes, worth around $60 billion, are sold a year. In the past ten years Airbus (originally a consortium, now owned 80 percent by EADS and 20 percent by BAE Systems) has caught up with Boeing, which had enjoyed two-thirds of the market since its 747 jumbo-jet entered commercial service in 1970.

Many aircraft are no doubt bought and sold in entirely conventional ways. But many are not. After all, lots of airlines are still state-owned and not subject to normal business rules. Commission payments (licit or illicit) on multi-million-dollar aircraft deals increase the capital cost of aircraft, which are therefore subject to higher depreciation or operating-lease charges, or both. But these extra costs are barely discernible in the pool of red ink created by the carriers' perennial losses.

Aircraft purchases drag on for years, as airlines play Boeing and Airbus off against each other. Especially in a buyer's market, deep discounts are common, performance guarantees are demanding, and manufacturers have to offer all sorts of sweeteners (e.g., aircraft trade-ins, unusual guarantees) to persuade an airline to switch to their aircraft.

Unsurprisingly, given the regulated nature of international air travel, politics plays a part. For instance, no sooner had Air Mauritius bought Airbus A340s in 1994 than it obtained an upgrade from Paris Orly to Charles de Gaulle airport, which is Air France's main base with better onward connections.

Aircraft purchases have long been associated with controversy. In the 1970s, when Lockheed was still making civil jets, it was caught bribing Japanese officials to buy its L1011 wide-bodied airliner. A Japanese prime minister was later charged and convicted in 1983 for taking a bribe. Prince Bernhard of the Netherlands was also disgraced for his involvement with Lockheed. This scandal led in 1977 to Congress passing the Foreign Corrupt Practices Act (FCPA), which forbids American companies, their officers, or their representatives from bribing foreign officials.

Critics have often pointed out that American firms can sidestep the FCPA by using foreign subsidiaries and nationals to pay bribes. Boeing says that its policy is to adhere to the spirit and letter of the FCPA, that its systems of controls ensure employees comply with this policy, and that no Boeing employee has been charged under the FCPA. In 1982 Boeing pleaded guilty to false statements about commissions on the sale of commercial aircraft prior to 1977. Boeing also says that there have been public hearings in the Bahamas over allegations of bribery in the 1990 sale of deHavilland aircraft to Bahamas Air, during Boeing's ownership of deHavilland.

Airbus has not been subject to such constraints. France ratified an OECD convention to outlaw bribery of foreign public officials in 2000. Until then the government even permitted French companies tax deductions for giving bribes.

For years, as they steadily lost market share to the European challenger, the Americans have been outspokenly critical of Airbus. In the 1980s the beef was the huge subsidies that European governments poured into the industry. Now that Airbus repays such launch aid, that is less relevant, especially as Boeing receives indirect subsidies through America's defense budget and space program.

But the American government has also spoken out on the subject of bribery. Grant Aldonas, an undersecretary for international trade, told a congressional committee: "Unfortunately this [aircraft manufacturing] is an industry where foreign corruption has a real impact . . . this sector has been especially vulnerable to trade distortions involving bribery of foreign public officials."

According to a European Parliament report, published in 2001, America's National Security Agency (NSA) intercepted faxes and phone calls between Airbus, Saudi Arabian Airlines, and the Saudi government in early 1994. The NSA found that Airbus agents were offering bribes to a Saudi official to secure a lion's share for Airbus in modernizing Saudi Arabian Airlines' fleet. The planes were in a $6 billion deal that Edouard Balladur, France's then prime minister, had hoped to clinch on a visit to see King Fahd in January 1994. He went home empty-handed.

James Woolsey, then director of the Central Intelligence Agency, recounted in a newspaper article in 2000 how the American government typically reacted to intelligence of this sort. "When we have caught you [Europeans] . . . we go to the government you're bribing and tell its officials that we don't take kindly to such corruption," he wrote. Apparently this (and a direct sales pitch from Bill Clinton to King Fahd) swung the aircraft part of the deal Boeing's and McDonnell Douglas's way.

KUWAITI KICKBACKS?

Not even the NSA, however, knows about everything in the aircraft-manufacturing industry as it actually happens. Consider the history of an Airbus order placed by Kuwait Airways Corporation (KAC), another state-owned airline.

In November 1995, Reuters reported that Kuwaiti prosecutors had questioned Bader Mallalah, KAC's then chief financial officer, over allegations of embezzlement made against him by KAC. The firm's chairman, Ahmed al Mishari, had suspended Mallalah from his job the previous month. But KAC had trumped up the allegations against Mallalah to put the lid on a story of corruption in which its then chairman was himself involved.

That story began exactly five years earlier in Cairo, where KAC had set up temporary headquarters after Iraq's invasion of Kuwait in August 1990. Most of its planes would inevitably be lost or damaged, so al Mishari was planning a shiny new postwar fleet. Naturally, both Boeing and Airbus were asked to tender. Both firms expected politics to play a part in KAC's choice, especially after an American-led coalition had liberated Kuwait.

Shortly after the liberation of Kuwait, Boeing and KAC met in London. One person present says al Mishari gave the impression that the order would be Boeing's. After all, until then, American companies had won most of the large reconstruction contracts from a grateful government.

Airbus hoped otherwise. In 1991, shortly before the Paris Air Show, Jean Pierson, the then boss of Airbus, met al Mishari at the Churchill Hotel in London. The two talked in private for part of the time, so what they discussed is not known. Two clear inferences can, however, be drawn from subsequent events: al Mishari promised the order to Airbus, and Pierson pressed for an announcement at the imminent air show.

As substantial public funds were involved, KAC was supposed to follow the formal process in Kuwait before placing the order. This process included approvals from the Ministry of Finance and the public-spending watchdog. None of these approvals was sought before the air show. In June 1991, at the show, al Mishari stunned Kuwaiti officials and Boeing when he announced a firm order for 15 Airbus aircraft, worth $1.1 billion, and options for nine more, worth up to $900 million. A delighted Pierson trumpeted the deal as Airbus's first single order for all its aircraft types.

Most unusually, Boeing was not asked for its "best and final" offer, according to a former KAC employee. Boeing's response to the announcement was to offer generous discounts to KAC—so that its package was around $100 million cheaper than its rival's—but it was too late. The upshot of a meeting in the summer of 1991 between the boss of Boeing Commercial, furious American officials, and the Crown Prince of Kuwait was a messy compromise. KAC would order the engines for the Airbuses from General Electric; Boeing would receive an order for two wide-bodied planes as a sop; and the firm order for 15 Airbus aircraft would go ahead provided that KAC bought from Boeing in future.

This compromise left al Mishari in a rather awkward spot. KAC had an option to buy nine more aircraft from Airbus. An airline is usually able to walk away from an option deal if it forfeits the modest deposit paid. But this case was far from normal. The company that was to take up the option was not KAC itself but a subsidiary, Aviation Lease and Finance Company (ALAFCO), which al Mishari had set up in Bermuda in September 1992. ALAFCO was to buy the aircraft and lease them to KAC. In late 1992 al Mishari confirmed to Pierson that ALAFCO would buy

the nine planes and sent off a $2.5 million deposit. By buying the planes through ALAFCO, al Mishari intended to bypass formal governmental approval.

There was more to the deal. Airbus chipped in a total of $450,000 between 1992 and 1994 to help with the costs of setting up and running ALAFCO. On December 15, 1992, ALAFCO appointed a part-time commercial adviser, Mohamed Habib El Fekih, a Tunisian national. His day job was then as head of sales in the Middle East—for Airbus. Under his ALAFCO contract of employment, a copy of which *The Economist* has and which was to run for three years from January 1993, El Fekih received $5,000 a month and $80,000 in back pay for "services" rendered to ALAFCO from February 1, 1990—31 months before ALAFCO's incorporation—to December 31, 1992. The $5,000 was paid each month from ALAFCO's account number 201-901-04 at the Commercial Bank of Kuwait in New York to El Fekih's personal account at Crédit Lyonnais's branch in Blagnac, France, where Airbus is based on the outskirts of Toulouse.

By 1993 three of the nine aircraft under option, all cargo planes, were nearly ready for delivery. However, Mallalah, who was also ALAFCO's chief executive, insisted that the transaction be subject to formal procedure in Kuwait. This meant competitive tenders from Airbus and Boeing. Unsurprisingly, Airbus, with inside knowledge from its two-hatted vice president, El Fekih, was able to match exactly offers from Boeing, after Boeing came in over $50 million cheaper. With nothing to choose between the offers, ALAFCO selected Airbus, on the grounds that KAC's fleet now comprised predominantly Airbus aircraft.

The deal sailed through KAC's board and the Ministry of Finance. However, Mallalah provided Kuwait's public spending watchdog with full details of ALAFCO's order for the cargo planes. It refused to sanction the deal. Consultants concluded in early 1995 that the purchase of the cargo aircraft was not justified. The Ministry of Finance told KAC not to proceed. After Mallalah submitted a report to KAC's board on the affair, El Fekih resigned from ALAFCO in March 1995.

El Fekih says that he acted in an honest way; Pierson approved his ALAFCO contract, as did the boards of KAC and ALAFCO; his ALAFCO contract had nothing to do with the sale of Airbus to KAC; KAC canceled its option; ALAFCO never bought any Airbus aircraft; he acted as a consultant to help set up ALAFCO as an aircraft-financing company; and he declared his earnings to the tax man. Airbus says that it offers this sort of support to customers, when asked. The present owners of the ALAFCO business confirm that ALAFCO bought three Airbus aircraft.

Of the other six aircraft under option, three were not converted into firm orders. Two Airbus A320s were leased to Shorouk Air in Egypt. This joint-venture between KAC and EgyptAir was specifically set up to find a home for them but is being liquidated because of massive losses. Kuwait's Ministry of Finance leased another.

Al Mishari, sacked as the chairman of KAC in 1999 after spending almost his entire career with the airline, owns a shopping complex in the Salmiya district of Kuwait, which local wags have dubbed the "Airbus Centre." Al Mishari, whose family is wealthy, suffered financial problems when the Kuwaiti stock market collapsed in the early 1980s. Al Mishari declines to comment, as does KAC.

It is not irrelevant to ask if the price of the Airbus aircraft was inflated to allow for kickbacks. No evidence of graft has ever come to light. However, no policeman, in Kuwait (or elsewhere), has looked for any.

INDIA INK

What about cases where police have carried out investigations? In March 1990 India's Central Bureau of Investigation (CBI) filed a first information report (FIR). It was investigating allegations that Airbus had bribed highly placed public servants and others to induce Indian Airlines (IA) to order its aircraft.

In March 1986 state-owned IA had ordered 19 Airbus A320s, worth $952 million, with an option for 12 more, later exercised. This order was despite the fact that, when IA set up a committee in 1983 to recommend replacement aircraft for its aging Boeing fleet, the A320 was not considered—it had not then been launched or flown. With approval from the Indian government, IA had in July 1984 paid Boeing a deposit for 12 Boeing 757s, large narrow-bodied aircraft.

Several civil servants and IA officials were named in the FIR. One name not on the list was that of Rajiv Gandhi, India's prime minister in 1984–89, who was killed in a bomb explosion in May 1991.

How has the CBI's investigation progressed in the intervening 13 years? Hardly at all, despite the hounding on public-interest grounds of the CBI in Delhi's High Court since 1998 by B. L. Wadehra, an anti-corruption lawyer based in Delhi. *The Economist* has examined the publicly available court documents—the CBI's status reports on its investigation are secret—from Wadehra's litigation.

These papers allege, first, that in October 1984, weeks before Gandhi, a former pilot, succeeded his mother, IA received an offer from Airbus for A320 aircraft, a smaller and less expensive plane than Boeing's 757. It required urgent attention. Second, in November, the aviation ministry gave IA just three days to appraise the offer for Gandhi's office.

Much later, in 1990, *Indian Express,* an Indian newspaper, reported a leaked manuscript note which showed that Gandhi had decided at a meeting on August 2, 1985, that IA "should go in for Airbus A320 aircraft."

Gandhi's correspondence file on the deal mysteriously vanished. The court papers show that civil servants reconstructed 29 pages of the missing file for the CBI by obtaining copy correspondence from government departments. Remarkably, this task took seven years—and even then the reconstruction was only partial.

After the green light from Gandhi, approvals from IA and government bodies were a formality. For instance, the IA board approved the Airbus order at a meeting on August 30, 1985, which started at noon. The quality of the analysis presented to the board on the competing offers was pitiful. The board considered only one criterion—comparative fuel efficiency. Even for that, the data were incomplete. The A320 with the engine chosen by IA had yet to be tried and tested anywhere; provisional data only were included in the report for Boeing 737s "since no technical data were supplied by the company."

But Boeing had not been asked for any, because two hours before the board meeting, at 9:50 a.m. IA's managing director, who is named in the FIR as an alleged recipient of kickbacks, received a letter from Richard Elliott, then Boeing's regional sales director. Boeing offered to supply up to 35 of its 737 aircraft, its narrow-bodied rival to the A320, with a discount of $5 million per plane. This offer would reduce IA's investment in new planes by $140 million, stated Elliott. IA's board brushed the offer aside on the grounds that "if Boeing was [sic] too serious . . . they [sic] could have made the offer earlier."

The Delhi court has a withering opinion of the help Airbus has given the CBI. It allowed Wadehra to add Airbus's Indian subsidiary to his action on the grounds that Airbus in France was not cooperating. Airbus told Wadehra that French law forbade it from answering his questions. "[Airbus] sells its aircraft on their merits," the firm insisted.

The court has castigated the CBI for its dilatory approach. It took the Indian authorities until 1995 to contact Airbus for information, only to be told that such requests should be routed through the French government. The CBI told Wadehra, despite trying Interpol and diplomatic channels, it was not getting any help from the French government. The French embassy in Delhi in effect told Wadehra to get lost when he wrote to ask why France was not cooperating.

Wadehra's case is now topical, because in March last year, IA's board approved an order for 43 Airbus planes, worth around $2 billion. The order now needs government approval. However, in September 2000, the Delhi court ruled that the Indian government should not approve further purchases from Airbus until the CBI had obtained the information it wanted from the French.

The upshot of the IA story is that no serious attempt has been made to establish whether or not Airbus paid kickbacks to Gandhi and associates. The CBI has not answered written questions.

MOUNTIES AND BANKS

But there are police forces that have shown rather more resolve and initiative than the CBI. One important case establishes that Airbus has paid "commissions" to individuals hiding behind shell companies in jurisdictions where ownership of companies is not a matter of public record, and where strict bank secrecy applies.

Airbus's first big sale in North America was a $1.5 billion deal, signed in 1988, to sell 34 aircraft to the then state-owned Air Canada. The middleman was Karlheinz Schreiber, a German-Canadian with connections to politicians in Germany and Canada. Schreiber emerged as a figure in the financing scandal that engulfed Germany's Christian Democrat party and its top politician, Helmut Kohl, a former chancellor, in the late 1990s.

In August 1999 the Royal Canadian Mounted Police, acting on a German arrest warrant, nabbed Schreiber. In 2000, Schreiber was charged in Germany with tax evasion on money he had received for the Airbus transaction and other deals. The *Süddeutsche Zeitung*, a German daily, supplied a copy of Schreiber's indictment to *The Economist*. According to this document, Airbus signed a consultancy contract (amended four times) with International Aircraft Leasing (IAL) in March 1985. IAL, which was to help with the Air Canada deal, was a shell company based in Vaduz, Liechtenstein, and a subsidiary of another Liechtenstein-registered shell, Kensington Anstalt.

According to the indictment, between September 30, 1988, and October 21, 1993 (i.e., as Air Canada took delivery of Airbus planes), Airbus paid a total of $22,540,000 in "commissions" to IAL. Then $10,867,000 was paid into IAL's account at the Verwaltungs-und Privat-Bank in Vaduz and $11,673,000 into IAL's account numberat Swiss Bank Corporation (SBC) in Zurich. During extradition proceedings against Schreiber in 1999, Airbus admitted to these payments. In October 2000 Schreiber won a suspension of execution of his case.

The court ruled that IAL belonged to Schreiber, but also that, to the extent that Schreiber had paid out the Airbus "commissions" as *Schmiergelder* ("grease monies"), these payments could be tax deductible. Schreiber's German tax lawyer later told the court: "*Schmiergelder* were not openly paid to the 'greased' person by [Airbus]. It was through third persons to make reception anonymous and the *Schmiergelder* unrecognizable as such."

So who got the commissions? After years of police investigations in at least five jurisdictions, it is still not clear. According to *The Last Amigo*, a well-researched book on the affair by Harvey Cashore and Stevie Cameron, both Canadian journalists, a lot was withdrawn in cash. Cashore, a producer on "The Fifth Estate," the Canadian Broadcasting Corporation's main investigative program, says that Schreiber's bank records and diaries showed that he usually followed a simple formula for dividing up the money: half for Canadians and half for Europeans.

The book alleges that there may have been a smaller scam within the bigger scam: an Airbus employee may have got some of the money. Some of the money was transferred into subaccounts at SBC in Zurich. One of the subaccounts, code-named "Stewardess," received as much as one-eighth of the commissions. The book suggests that this account was intended for Stuart Iddles, Airbus's senior vice president from 1986 to 1994.

Iddles's wife bought Casa Las Estacas, a luxurious beachfront villa in Puerto Vallarta, Mexico, in September 1992. Documents in *The Economist*'s possession show the price was $1.5 million. According to a person involved in the deal, the money was wired from an account in the name of the Ciclon Foundation at the Zurich branch of Lloyds, a British bank. Mrs. Iddles confirms that she bought the villa in 1992 but says she has not the "foggiest idea" how much it cost, or which bank the money came from. Mr. Iddles has denied any impropriety. Airbus says it has not been indicted in any jurisdiction over the Air Canada deal, or over any other sales. It adds that no investigator has found unethical behavior on its part.

SYRIAN SCANDALS

Only one case of Airbus's colluding with a middleman apparently to bribe officials to buy its aircraft has led to convictions. According to Syria's state news agency, three people were sentenced in Syria in October 2001 to 22 years imprisonment each (later reduced to 10 years) for "serious irregularities" in connection with state-owned Syrianair's order for six Airbus A320s in 1996. The court also imposed a fine on the three of $268 million. They were a former minister for economic affairs, a former transport minister, and Munir Abu Khaddur, the middleman. Khaddur was sentenced in absentia and is reportedly living in Spain. The court found that the men had forced the airline to buy the planes, worth $240 million, and as a result Syrianair had incurred "big financial losses."

The only inferences to be drawn are either that there was a miscarriage of justice or that bribes were paid. If the latter, the news agency did not release details of how much the men embezzled. Quite why bribes would have been necessary is puzzling. Because America deems Syria to be a sponsor of terrorism, Boeing has long been prohibited from exporting there. The Syrian government declines to comment.

The result of investigations into instances of corruption or alleged corruption by Airbus suggests that Van Espen will have a very long haul as he tries to establish whether "commissions" influenced Sabena's decision to buy Airbuses. The order for the 34 A320s could be viewed as incompetence. But nobody can predict the results of Van Espen's inquiry.

The parliamentary report says Sabena's board received some lacunary information that was misleading. The choice of Airbus supposedly meant Sabena was confident of strong sales growth. Yet a month after the order was placed, SAirGroup's chief executive, who also sat on Sabena's board, said: "We're now in the last year or years of the boom in air travel." (We do not mean to imply by inference that the chief executive was corrupt.)

Most of what is recounted in this case happened before Airbus's present top management team arrived, before it was established as a proper company, and before France adopted the OECD convention on bribery.

No one doubts the company's ability to compete across the whole product range with Boeing. By the time the Paris Air Show is over, Airbus will probably be well ahead of its rival in market share, thanks to an attractive range of planes. But if charges of corruption involving Airbus were to emerge from Van Espen's investigation of Sabena, that would deal the company's reputation a severe blow.

AIRBUS LOBBIES TO RELAX ANTI-BRIBERY RULES

Newly released documents have revealed how companies used their lobbying power to loosen official rules designed to stop corruption. In behind-the-scenes maneuvers, Rolls-Royce, BAE Systems, and the aircraft giant Airbus persuaded trade secretary Patricia Hewitt to allow them to keep secret details of the middlemen used to secure international contracts.

She brushed aside the advice of U.K. government officials who argued that these middlemen are often used to channel bribes to foreign politicians and officials to win contracts. The government's Export Credits Guarantee Department (ECGD) had proposed that exporters had to disclose the identities of middlemen when they applied for financial support from the taxpayer. The government required the details as part of tougher measures to stop the payment of bribes overseas by British companies.

The documents were released by the ECGD following a freedom of information request from *The Guardian* (a British newspaper) and a recent court case. Minutes of a meeting on August 9, 2004, show that the three companies told the ECGD that information about these middlemen was "very commercially sensitive." The minutes continued: "The network of agents/intermediaries was a valuable asset built up over a number of years and offered important commercial advantages such as being able to open doors. . . . The intermediaries themselves may have valid and justifiable reasons for wanting to remain anonymous."

The companies claimed that the names of the agents would leak from the ECGD, enabling competitors to poach them. Hewitt agreed that the companies did not have to give the names or addresses of these middlemen, provided the firms gave an explanation.

At a meeting on October 7, the companies wanted "confirmation that commercial confidentiality would be accepted as a valid reason for not identifying its agents." Hewitt has been forced to rethink the anti-bribery rules because of a legal victory by anti-corruption campaigners, the Corner House group. Susan Hawley, for the group, said: "Knowing who is the middleman is crucial to stopping corruption, otherwise the taxpayer will end up directly supporting bribery." BAE is alleged to have made corrupt payments through middlemen in Saudi Arabia, Qatar, and India. Rolls-Royce is accused of paying £15 million to win a contract in India.

According to *Reuters News,* Airbus is again being criticized regarding suspected bribery—this time regarding a hidden slush fund an payments to Emirates Airline encouraging the purchase of 43 A380 superjumbo jets.

QUESTIONS

1. In each of the cases described, who benefits and who suffers from the alleged ethical and legal lapses of Airbus?

2. How should the public relations staff at Airbus respond to the articles appearing in *The Economist*, *The Guardian*, and *Reuters News?*

3. What steps might Boeing take to defend itself from this sort of competition?

4. Do you think that Boeing and Airbus behave differently in marketing their aircraft around the globe? How and why?

5. Had France adopted the OECD convention on bribery ahead of these transactions, would the firm's behavior have differed? Why?

Sources: "Airbus' Secret Past—Aircraft and Bribery," *The Economist,* June 14, 2003, pp. 55–58; Rob Evans and David Leigh, "Firms Can Keep Secret Agents: Minister Persuaded to Ease Anti-bribery Rules," *The Guardian,* January 25, 2005, p. 18; "EADS Says Airbus Audit Shows No Wrongdoing, *Reuters News,* April 3, 2007.

CASE 2–5 Coping with Corruption in Trading with China

Corruption is a fact of life in China. In fact, Transparency International, a German organization that applies its Corruption Perception Index (CPI) globally,[1] rates China with a CPI of 3.5 and is number 72 of the 180 countries rated. Finland is rated the least corrupt at number 1 with a CPI of 9.7, the United States at 17 with a CPI of 7.5, and Haiti the most corrupt at number 180 with a CPI of 1.5. The country's press frequently has detailed cases of corruption and of campaigns to crack down on bribery and other forms of corruption. The articles primarily have focused on domestic economic crimes among Chinese citizens and on local officials who have been fired, sent to prison, or assessed other penalties.

There is strong evidence that the Chinese government is taking notice and issuing regulations to fight corruption. Newly issued Communist Party of China (CPC) regulations on internal supervision and disciplinary penalties have raised hopes that the new regulations will enhance efforts against corruption. The regulations established "10 Taboos" for acts of party members that violate political, personnel, and financial regulations and who are involved in bribery, malfeasance, and infringement of others' rights. The taboos included lobbying officials of higher rank, handing out pamphlets or souvenirs without authorization, holding social activities to form cliques, and offering or taking bribes. Also on the list were making phone calls, giving gifts, holding banquets or conducting visits to win support, covering up illicit activities, spreading hearsay against others, using intimidation or deception, and arranging jobs for others. Some believe that the execution of three bankers, for "a run-of-the-mill fraud," just before the Communist Party's annual meeting, was an indication of how serious the government was about cracking down on corruption.

Much of China's early efforts to stem corruption were focused on activities among domestic Chinese companies and not on China's foreign business community. Traders, trade consultants, and analysts have said that foreign firms are vulnerable to a variety of corrupt practices. Although some of these firms said they had no experience with corruption in China, the majority said they increasingly were asked to make payments to improve business, engage in black-market trade of import and export licenses, and bribe officials to push goods through customs or the Commodity Inspection Bureau, or engage in collusion to beat the system. The Hong Kong Independent Commission Against Corruption reports that outright bribes, as well as gifts or payment to establish *guanxi*, or "connections," average 3 to 5 percent of operating costs in the PRC, or $3 billion to $5 billion of the $100 billion of foreign investments that have been made there. The most common corrupt practices confronting foreign companies in China are examined here.

PAYING TO IMPROVE BUSINESS

Foreign traders make several types of payments to facilitate sales in China. The most common method is a trip abroad. Chinese officials, who rarely have a chance to visit overseas, often prefer foreign travel to cash or gifts. (This was especially true when few PRC officials had been abroad.) As a result, traders report that dangling foreign trips in front of their PRC clients has become a regular part of negotiating large trade deals that involve products with a technological component. "Foreign travel is always the first inducement we offer," said an executive involved in machinery trade. In most cases, traders build these costs into the product's sale price. Some trips are "reasonable and bona fide expenditures directly related to the promotion, demonstration, or explanation of products and services, or the execution of a contract with a foreign government agency" but it may be another matter when officials on foreign junkets are offered large per diems and aren't invited specifically to gain technical knowledge.

Foreign travel isn't always an inducement—it also can be extorted. In one case, a PRC bank branch refused to issue a letter of credit for a machinery import deal. The Chinese customer suggested that the foreign trader invite the bank official on an overseas inspection tour. Once the invitation was extended, the bank issued the letter of credit.

ANGLING FOR CASH

Some MNCs are asked to sponsor overseas education for the children of trading officials. One person told a Chinese source that an MNC paid for that individual's U.S. $1,500-a-month apartment, as well as a car, university education, and expenses.

Firms find direct requests for cash payments—undeniably illegal—the most difficult. One well-placed source said that a major trader, eager for buyers in the face of an international market glut, had fallen into regularly paying large kickbacks into the Honduran, U.S., and Swiss accounts of officials at a PRC foreign trade corporation. Refusing to make payments may not only hurt sales, it can also be terrifying. A U.S. firm was one of several bidders for a large sale; a Chinese official demanded the MNC pay a 3 percent kickback. When the company representative refused, the official threatened: "You had better not say anything about this. You still have to do business in China, and stay in hotels here." Not surprisingly, the U.S. company lost the deal.

Traders of certain commodities may be tempted to resort to the black market for import and export licenses that are difficult to obtain legally. A fairly disorganized underground market, for instance, exists for licenses to export China-made garments to the United States.

Some branches of the Commodity Inspection Bureau (CIB) also have posed problems for traders. Abuses have emerged in the CIB since it started inspecting imports in 1987. A Japanese company, for instance, informed CIB officials of its intention to bring heavy industrial items into China—items that had met Japanese and U.S. standards. The officials responded that they planned to dismantle the products on arrival for inspection purposes. The problem was resolved only after the firm invited the officials to visit Japan.

Some traders get around such problems by purchasing inspection certificates on the black market. According to press accounts, these forms, complete with signatures and seals, can be bought for roughly U.S. $200.

---

[1]See http://www.transparency.org for more details about its 2007 index.

Some claim that, for the appropriate compensation, customs officials in a southern province are very willing to reduce the dutiable value of imports as much as 50 percent. Because the savings can far exceed transport costs, some imports that would logically enter China through a northern port are redirected through the southern province.

The new Communist Party of China (CPC) regulations address some of these problems, but unfortunately, the new law raises more questions than answers. Two kinds of bribes are covered under the new law: The "Criminal Law of the PRC," known as common bribery, applies to the bribery of state officials and employees of state-owned enterprises, which are most of China's large companies. Anyone who demands or accepts money or property in return for benefits is guilty of bribery. The other is the "Law Against Unfair Competition of the PRC," known as commercial bribery. It prohibits businesses from giving money or property to customers to sell or purchase products.

The law is confusing in that it says nothing about punishment for gifts and benefits costing less than $600 or even whether these transactions can amount to bribes. Thus, tickets to sports events, which can cost several hundred dollars, wining and dining executives, or even pharmaceutical samples to physicians remain in a gray area. The only clue is that Communist Party guidelines prohibit members from accepting gifts exceeding $500 but that doesn't necessarily mean that gifts under $500 won't be considered a violation of the law. The trouble with China's bribery laws is that they can be interpreted to apply to any gift at all.

AN ILLUSTRATION

Here are some excerpts from a trial concerning a Chinese bank, a Chinese consultant, and several U.S. companies in which charges of bribery, among other issues, are involved. The list of charges, countercharges, and alleged bribery will give you a sample of the types of behavior that can arise in a transaction where bribery is rampant.

A Chinese company alleged that it got pushed out of a lucrative business deal because an American software company secretly funneled money to powerful Chinese government officials to ensure a profitable banking contract. In court filings, lawyers for the Chinese company said they had obtained copies of detailed e-mails and other records that show that the American company paid over a million dollars in fees to a consultant for services in addition to reimbursing the consultant about $170,000 in expenses covering an array of gifts, hotels, shopping sprees, and entertainment costs.

The suit also contends that the American company arranged through the Chinese consultant for two Chinese banking officials and family members to travel on vacation to Hong Kong, Paris, Rome, Las Vegas, and the golfing resort of Pebble Beach, California. These trips were arranged by a consultant who was reimbursed for an array of gifts given to the Chinese bankers and their families. The gifts included expensive Sony cameras, luxury outfits from Versace and Burberry, and perhaps even a $330,000 apartment in Shanghai.

The suit says an American company official e-mailed another company executive saying the chairman of China Construction Bank was interested in playing golf at "Cobble Beach" (he thought he meant Pebble Beach). Soon after, the American company paid for the chairman's hotel, car services, and green fees in Pebble Beach. After the chairman expressed an interest in seeing Florida,

the lawsuit says the American company sent its corporate jet to fly him from San Francisco, where he had been visiting with another U.S. company, to its headquarters in Florida.

The lawsuit also charges that the American company reimbursed the consultant for tickets the chairman's wife and son used to travel in China and the United States. The lawsuit claims it also paid for his son's tennis club fees in Shanghai and golfing fees in Shenzhen and for the daughter of the bank's chief information officer to travel to Europe.

The American company contended that all payments made to the consultant and all the business trips by the Chinese officials the company paid for were legitimate costs of doing business in China. It is the price the company had to pay to help secure a huge software contract with China Construction Bank worth about $176 million.

It is important to note that this is an illustration of a civil lawsuit between two companies and does not involve charges by the U.S. government and possible violations of the FCPA. However, the report indicated that the Justice Department was looking into the charges.

TWO COMMENTS ON DEALING WITH CORRUPTION

Comment of a Consultant
As the head of one U.S. consulting firm asserts, "Corruption is a huge issue, it's systemic. Whether it's self-dealing, phantom suppliers, kickbacks, intellectual property theft or inappropriate dealings with governmental officials, crime and corruption are risks companies face when operating in China. There are many instances where, unbeknownst to the U.S. company, various payments are being made under the table. The company's credo, the company's standard operating procedures, the company's code of conduct, corporate governance, best practices—all of that needs to be ingrained and it needs to be accepted. There has to be constant training and constant reminding" to the local Chinese staff. Chinese culture is "very different" from Western culture. As such, "a U.S. company cannot simply translate its compliance policies and procedures into Chinese and expect them to have the same effect as in the U.S. The entire approach must be tailored to the Chinese environment."

Comment of Former U.S. Foreign Service Agent
A retired agent of the U.S. Foreign Service raises questions about how strictly the Foreign Corrupt Practices Act is enforced. The economics officer of the U.S. Foreign Service says he intentionally subverted the intent of the Foreign Corrupt Practices Act so U.S. investors and exporters would not lose out unfairly to companies and agencies from other foreign countries.

"I figured out how business was actually done in corrupt countries, who was on the take, whether the going rate for host country cooperation in a particular type of transaction was 10 percent or 25 percent and who was good or bad as a go between."

"I would tell Americans trying to do business in the host country: 'Don't tell me about any corrupt practices you are engaged in, because I am obliged to write that up and report you to Washington, but do tell me in detail about corrupt activities by competing foreign companies. In return, if your information is interesting, I'll give you my best guess on how corruption works here.' By doing this I hope that I have helped level the playing field."

QUESTIONS

1. List all the different types of bribes, payments, or favors represented in this case under (a) FCPA, (b) Criminal Law of PRC, and (c) Law Against Unfair Competition of the PRC. Why is each either legal or illegal?

2. For those practices that you listed as illegal, classify each as lubrication, extortion, or subornation, and explain your reasoning.

3. Which of the payments, favors, or bribes are illegal under the Foreign Corrupt Practices Act (FCPA)?

4. Assuming that the FCPA did not exist, what is the ethical response to each of the payments, favors, or bribes you have identified? Read the section titled Ethical and Socially Responsible Decisions in Chapter 5 as a guide to assist you in your decision.

5. In your view, which of the expenses detailed in the lawsuit could be in violation of the FCPA, and which could be legitimate business expenses as the American Company contends? Discuss.

6. Discuss the legal/ethical issues raised by the comments by the retired Foreign Service agent and the consultant.

7. List alternatives to paying bribes in international markets and discuss the plusses and minuses of each.

Sources: Walter H. Drew, "Corrupt Thinking," *Foreign Policy,* May/June 2005; David Barboza, "Charges of Bribery in a Chinese Bank Deal," *The New York Times,* November 29, 2006; "India, China Ranked 72 out of 180 in Corruption Rankings," *The Hindustan Times,* October 8, 2007; "Take Great Care in Choosing Partners: Corruption Rampant, but Lately Its Drawing Government Attention," *Business Insurance,* March 26, 2007; "China's Communist Party Issues List of 'Taboos' Ahead of Politician Reshuffle," *International Herald Tribune,* January 4, 2008; "China Lists New Anti-Graft Rules," *BBC News,* January 4, 2008.

CASE 2−6 When International Buyers and Sellers Disagree

No matter what line of business you're in, you can't escape sex. That may have been one conclusion drawn by an American exporter of meat products after a dispute with a German customer over a shipment of pork livers. Here's how the disagreement came about.

The American exporter was contracted to ship "30,000 lbs. of freshly frozen U.S. pork livers, customary merchantable quality, first rate brands." The shipment had been prepared to meet the exacting standards of the American market, so the exporter expected the transaction to be completed without any problem. But when the livers arrived in Germany, the purchaser raised an objection: "We ordered pork livers of customary merchantable quality—what you sent us consisted of 40 percent sow livers."

"Who cares about the sex of the pig the liver came from?" the exporter asked.

"We do," the German replied. "Here in Germany we don't pass off spongy sow livers as the firmer livers of male pigs. This shipment wasn't merchantable at the price we expected to charge. The only way we were able to dispose of the meat without a total loss was to reduce the price. You owe us a price allowance of $1,000."

The American refused to reduce the price. The determined resistance may have been partly in reaction to the implied insult to the taste of the American consumer. "If pork livers, whatever the sex of the animal, are palatable to Americans, they ought to be good enough for anyone," the American thought.

It looked as if the buyer and seller could never agree on eating habits.

QUESTIONS

1. In this dispute, which country's law would apply, that of the United States or of Germany?

2. If the case were tried in U.S. courts, who do you think would win? In German courts? Why?

3. Draw up a brief agreement that would have eliminated the following problems before they could occur:

   a. Whose law applies.

   b. Whether the case should be tried in U.S. or German courts.

   c. The difference in opinion as to "customary merchantable quality."

4. Discuss how SRC may be at work in this case.

CASE 2-7 McDonald's and Obesity

THE PROBLEM

Governments and influential health advocates around the world, spooked that their nations' kids will become as fat as American kids, are cracking down on the marketers they blame for the explosion in childhood obesity. Across the globe, efforts are under way to slow the march of obesity.

In the United States, roughly 30 percent of American children are overweight or obese. According to the U.S. Centers for Disease Control and Prevention (CDC), an estimated 64.5 percent of Americans tip the scales as overweight or obese, the highest percentage of fat people of any country in the world. However, adults and kids in other countries are catching up.

THE WORLD

The World Heart Federation reports that globally there are now more than 1 billion overweight adults and that at least 400 million of those are obese. An estimated 155 million children are overweight worldwide including 30–45 million who are obese.[1]

In many countries, the worst increases in obesity have occurred in young people. About half a million children in Europe are suffering classic middle-aged health problems because they are too fat. Obesity among European children has been on the rise over the last 25 years. The number of overweight children in Europe did not change much from 1974 to 1984; then the rate started to creep up during the next 10 years, and it exploded after 1995.

In Britain, one in five children is overweight or obese; in Spain 30 percent; and in Italy, 36 percent. While less than 1 percent of the children in Africa suffer from malnutrition, 3 percent are overweight or obese.

Perhaps the most distressing data come from Asia, where the measure of being overweight used in Western countries may underestimate the seriousness of weight-related health problems faced by Asians. In Japan, for example, obesity is defined as a body mass index (BMI) level of 25 or more, not 30 as it is in Western countries. But Japanese health officials report that a BMI of 25 or more is already causing high rates of diabetes. About 290 million children in China are thought to be overweight, and researchers expect that number to double in the next 10 years. The World Health Organization has warned of an escalating global epidemic of overweight and obesity.

GLOBAL REACTIONS TO OBESITY

One of the perplexing questions is why there has been a relatively sudden increase of obesity worldwide. Some opine that fast-food portion sizes are partly to blame; the average size order of French fries has nearly tripled since 1955. Some people say advertising is to blame, particularly ads aimed at children, such as those that use celebrities to market high-calorie foods. According to *USA Today*, one study found that the average American child sees 10,000 food ads a year, mostly for high-fat or sugary foods and drinks.

Traditionally, in developing countries, the poorest people have been the thinnest, a consequence of hard physical labor and the consumption of small amounts of traditional foods. But when these people in poor countries migrate to cities, obesity rates rise fastest among those in the lowest socioeconomic group.

Even as food companies' battle U.S. lawsuits and legislators who blame them for inducing childhood obesity, they're being attacked on another front—Europe—which is threatening, among other things, to ban advertising icons such Tony the Tiger and Ronald McDonald. "I would like to see the industry not advertising directly to children," said one European health commissioner. "If this doesn't produce satisfactory results, we will proceed to legislation." The European Health Commission has called for the food industry to set its own regulations to curb so-called junk-food advertising aimed at the European Union's 450 million citizens—or face bans similar to the tobacco industry.

The ominous comparison to cigarettes is increasingly being made in the United States as well. Commenting on a McDonald's plan to send Ronald McDonald to schools to preach about nutrition, an aide to a U.S. senator said, "No matter what Ronald is doing, they are still using this cartoon character to sell fatty hamburgers to kids. Once upon a time, tobacco companies had Joe Camel and they didn't get it either."

Also under fire is TV advertising of kids' foods, as calls for curbs or bans rise around the world. "If the rise in [the] child obesity trend continues, within five years we'll be in the same situation as America is today," said a senior child nutritionist at the University of Copenhagen who sits on the board of Denmark's National Board of Nutritional Science. "Banning TV ads that are targeting kids is an important strategy to adopt." But there is an argument that those measures won't help. "In Sweden, Norway and Quebec, where food ads are banned from kids' TV, there's no evidence that obesity rates have fallen."

A new law in France will force food marketers to choose between adding a health message to commercials or paying a 1.5 percent tax on their ad budgets to fund healthy-eating messages. Other measures under consideration in Europe include banning celebrities and cartoon characters from food ads aimed at children and preventing food marketers from using cell phone jingles to reach kids.

Ireland bans celebrities from food and beverage ads aimed at children and requires confectionery and soft-drink spots broadcast in programs where half the audience is younger than 18 years of age to carry a visual or voice-over warning that snacking on sugary foods and drinks can damage teeth. Ireland is a small market, but there are fears that these measures could spread to the United Kingdom and then to the rest of Europe, especially since many advertisers run the same campaigns in the United Kingdom and Ireland.

Unlike France and Ireland, the United Kingdom is trying a more carrot-and-stick approach, encouraging self-regulation with legislation as a last but threatened resort. In November 2004, the U.K. government published health recommendations giving the food and beverage industries until early 2007 to act more responsibly or face formal legislation. The document followed a high-

---

[1] "Obesity," World Heart Federation, May 2007, http://www.world-heart-federation.org.

profile U.K. government inquiry into child obesity. Marketing and agency executives called to give evidence were grilled publicly over the use of celebrities in ads, inciting kids' "pester power" and high salt and sugar content in foods.

The paper's proposals include clamping down on using cartoon characters to appeal to kids in food and beverage ads, potentially dooming brand icons such as Kellogg's Tony the Tiger. There have also been calls for a ban, like Ireland's, on celebrity endorsement in "junk-food" advertising by 2006. In a country where the biggest grocery-store brand, PepsiCo's Walker's Crisps, relies on celebrities in its ad campaigns, that's a big deal.

The Nordic countries are the most militant about enacting laws to ban or restrict marketing of foods that they consider unhealthy to children and fighting to extend those restrictions to the rest of Europe. The toughest laws against advertising to children have long been in Scandinavia, where the health risks of obesity and diabetes from high sugar consumption are sometimes compared to tobacco. The legislatures in Sweden, Finland, and Denmark are all considering even tighter controls on marketing sugary foods. Denmark's National Consumer Council has petitioned the government to ban marketing "unhealthy food products" to anyone under 16 years of age, and Finland's legislature is hearing from health groups that want a total ban on TV ads for sugar-laden food. Commenting on such proposals, the CEO of the Finnish Food and Drink Industries Federation said, "Implementing stricter controls on advertising food and drinks will not be a quick-fix answer to all these problems."

"The European Union is on it, Washington is on it, the ball is rolling now and the food companies have to do something," said one top advertising agency executive. But he added, "I hope food companies won't be bullied into doing things that play to the politicians," noting there are other contributing factors for obesity, such as low income. He said food marketers could truly contribute to a solution by putting money into programs like the USDA's Nutrition Program for Women, Infants and Children, a subsidized food and education program that also happens to be very good at driving sales for the products approved for the list. The key is to translate the hype to real solutions like physical education in schools and parents—the most important role models according to substantiated research—reclaiming responsibility. "If a food has a right to exist, a marketer has the right to advertise it."

Marketers are struggling against a crackdown on food advertising amid growing concern over obesity throughout the world. Marketers are trying to avert a clampdown with greater self-regulation. But, despite a slew of individual company efforts to shift new-product and marketing focus to healthier offerings, the industry has, until now, largely shied away from defending itself more broadly.

MCDONALD'S RESPONSE

For the last few years, McDonald's has reacted to the obesity issues in several ways in the United Kingdom and other countries. Concerned about consumer reaction to the film *Super Size Me*,[2]

McDonald's Corp. broke a U.K. campaign called "Changes" with poster ads that omit the Golden Arches for the first time, replacing them with a question mark in the same typeface and the tagline "McDonald's. But not as you know it." Promoting ongoing menu changes, the posters feature items such as a salad, a pile of free-range eggshells, pieces of fruit, and cups of cappuccino. The effort preceded a direct-mail campaign to 17 million households touting healthier menu items and smaller portion sizes.

McDonald's aim was to cause people to think differently about McDonald's and to make the public aware of new products. "There's no intention to abandon the Arches" but only to focus attention on the "healthy" additions to the menu. Despite the new campaign, research showed the chain hadn't received the hoped-for awareness for some of the newer items on its menu, including the all-white-meat Chicken Selects and the fruit bags. More worrisome, a research study revealed that frequent users didn't like to admit to friends that they ate at McDonald's. "We don't want to have closet loyalists."

One researcher urged more time for McDonald's "Changes" campaign to get traction. "The market position and market stature of McDonald's in the U.K. is not nearly as strong as it is in the U.S. and accordingly, you have to stick with the program longer," he said. But he warned that the "Changes" campaign could backfire. "Trying to suppress the logo is not likely to change the hearts and minds of many fast-food voters in Europe."

In anticipation of the release of the documentary *Super Size Me* in the United Kingdom, McDonald's in London went on the defensive with full-page newspaper ads discussing the film. The ads, headlined "If you haven't seen the film 'Super Size Me,' here's what you're missing," have appeared in the film-review sections of six newspapers to coincide with filmmaker Morgan Spurlock's appearance at the annual Edinburgh film festival. The copy describes it as "slick and well-made," and says McDonald's actually agrees with the "core argument" of the film—"If you eat too much and do too little, it's bad for you." However, it continues: "What we don't agree with is the idea that eating at McDonald's is bad for you." The ad highlights some of McDonald's healthier menu items such as grilled chicken salad and fruit bags. A spokeswoman for McDonald's said it ran the ads to ensure there was a "balanced debate" about the film. *Super Size Me* distributor Tartan Films has retaliated by running identical-looking ads in newspapers promoting the film.

As a direct response to government calls for food marketers to promote a more active lifestyle, McDonald's U.K. launched an ad campaign aimed at kids featuring Ronald McDonald and animated fruit and vegetable characters called Yums. In two-minute singing-and-dancing animated spots, the Yums urge, "It's fun when you eat right and stay active."

Even though McDonald's plans to expand its healthier menu offerings, it does so cautiously, so people remember that the Golden Arches at its core still means burgers and fries.

McDonald's, throughout Europe and elsewhere, is testing ways to address the obesity issue. In Scandinavia, for example, popular healthy local foods have been added to the McMenu, like cod wrapped in rye bread in Finland. In Norway, some outlets sell a salmon burger wrapped in rye bread. In Sweden, no salt is added to the food served. In Australia, McDonald's took a different approach—it reduced its budget for ads directed to kids by 50 percent.

McDonald's French operation raised the ire of the parent company when it ran a print ad in a women's magazine quoting a nutritionist's suggestion that kids shouldn't eat at the restaurant more

---

[2]*Super Size Me* is a documentary about the fast-food industry and the addictiveness of fast food, its allure to children, and so forth. Scenes in the film feature Morgan Spurlock (the director, producer, and star of the documentary), whose fast-food feat consists of eating some 5,000 calories a day, twice what his doctor says he needs to maintain his starting weight of 185 pounds. He also avoids exercise because, he says, that's what most Americans do. Spurlock gains weight—nearly 25 pounds over 30 days. His cholesterol goes up, and so does his blood pressure. His doctor describes his liver function test results as "obscene." Spurlock complains of sluggishness, depression, shortness of breath, impotence, chest pressure, and headaches.

than once a week. While the ad was meant to promote McDonald's and seems reasonable since the French only visit quick-service restaurants every two weeks on average anyway, such a campaign would have been heresy in the United States. McDonald's Corp. later issued a statement claiming that "the majority of nutritionists" believe McDonald's can fit into a balanced diet. Later, the company recruited a pair of French nutritionists who declared the Big Mac and cheeseburger healthier than traditional French fare such as quiche.

Marketers in France have lobbied hard to be allowed to use positive lifestyle messages in ads—like emphasizing the importance of physical exercise and a balanced diet—rather than grim health warnings. France's Ministry of Health appears to be listening and is now expected to let marketers choose among three or four positive health messages. Industry experts say the government changed its mind out of fear that strong warnings might backfire, causing anxiety among consumers about eating. Moreover, France may hope its new law, if not too extreme, will become a blueprint for Europe.

Although McDonald's responded to the obesity issue with menu changes and reworking its advertising, McDonald's didn't stop advertising to children. The chief executive of McDonald's pooh-poohed the idea that McDonald's should "go dark on communications" to kids—two-and-a-half million U.K. customers every day, a fair portion of them under 16 years. McDonald's is keeping children firmly in its marketing sights. School's out, ads for the kids' big summer movie releases are slapped on burger boxes, and a trip to McDonald's is on the holiday menu. McDonald's defense is that McDonald's Ronnie's YumChum friends are positively bursting with healthy advice. There's even a song: "Don't let your Yum-Chums get glum, put healthy stuff in your tum."

One of the casualties of the obesity turmoil may have been the tie between McDonald's and Disney's line of cartoon characters, a marvel for attracting young children to the golden arches. Disney failed to renew its 10 year exclusive partnership with McDonald's. Both parties insist it was a mutual decision that would allow each to seek more profitable promotions. However, the growing concern over the obesity epidemic may have proved critical for Disney, which has become increasingly worried that its links to McDonald's would damage its family-friendly image. For its part, McDonald's may have wanted to avoid being linked to box-office flops such as *Treasure Planet*.

THE MARKET'S REACTION

Initially, McDonald's sales worldwide, as well as in England, suffered. However European sales growth in 2006, from restaurants open all year, was 5.8 percent, outstripping even U.S. growth. By 2007 McDonald's had recorded growth figures close to its fastest rate since the 1980s. Some 320,000 more people a day than the year before visited McDonald's in Britain. Around 90 percent of them are buying traditional products such as burgers, fries, and ice cream rather than the healthier sandwiches and salads the chain stocks. The estimates mark a big turnaround for McDonald's, which bounced back after negative publicity about fat content in its food. McDonald's changed menu—with such items as porridge, smoothies, and chicken wraps—is one reason for the growing business. But its traditional food items.

The government has spent large sums on promoting healthier diets and the message to eat five portions of fruit and vegetables a day as obesity levels continue to rise. There's been enough publicity about the relentless rise and impact of obesity, but from the figures, it seems the public is choosing to ignore them. More than 88 million visits were made to McDonald's worldwide restaurants in one month, up 10 million on the previous year.

THE PRINCE CHIMES IN

Just as the focus on obesity was giving away to concerns about anorexia and the pressure being put on young girls by so-called size zero models at a British Fashion Week, Prince Charles, Prince of Wales and future King of England, tipped the scales back in the direction of obesity. On a royal visit to the Middle East, the Prince suggested that McDonald's was to blame for an obesity epidemic among children. Charles asked: "Have you got anywhere with McDonald's? Have you tried getting it banned? That's the key." His comments were reported internationally, with reactions that were more positive for McDonald's than one would expect.

Positive comments from several sources attested to the effectiveness of the work that McDonald's had done to improve its image. Health advocates and nutritionists said a ban on McDonald's was "certainly not the answer" to Britain's obesity epidemic. Even the press ran articles favorable to McDonald's. One referred to the Prince as a hypocrite, because his company, Duchy Originals (one of the United Kingdom's leading brands of organic food and drink),[3] offered fast foods whose fat and calorie content was no better, if not worse, than McDonald's. The Duchy Originals' Cornish pasty carries 264 calories per 100g, considerably more than the 229 per 100 g of the Big Mac, and the fat content is 13.6g per 100g, which is higher than the 11.12g in the Big Mac. A medium portion of fries from McDonald's contains 298 calories per 100g; again this amount is considerably less than the 464 per 100g contained in the Duchy Original Organic Hand Cooked Vegetable Crisps. A 100g serving of Duchy Original's Organic Lemon Tart has 337 calories (one-third more than the McDonald's Apple Pie).

The Prince's comments were later downplayed, stressing that he was merely advocating a balanced diet, especially for children, and wanted to make the point that burgers and chips were not the only foods available to them.

McDonald's took a conciliatory tact stating, "The comment made by the Prince of Wales appears to be an off-the-cuff remark that, in our opinion, does not reflect either our menu or where we are at as a business. We know that other Royal Family members have visited and have probably got a more up-to-date picture of us." Prince Harry certainly does not share his father's distaste for McDonald's and often eats their burgers. He even took advantage of a "buy one get one free" offer, then wolfed down two chicken burgers outside a McDonald's in Plymstock, Devon.

QUESTIONS

1. How should McDonald's respond when ads promoting healthy lifestyles featuring Ronald McDonald are equated with Joe Camel and cigarette ads? Should McDonald's eliminate Ronald McDonald in its ads?

---

[3]In 1990, the Prince created Duchy Originals because of his belief in the clear advantages of organic farming, the production of natural and healthy foods, and sound husbandry, which helps regenerate and protect the countryside. All of the profits from Duchy Originals are donated to the Prince of Wales's Charitable Foundation.

2. Discuss the merits of the law proposed by France that would require fast-food companies either to add a health message to commercials or pay a 1.5 percent tax on their ad budgets. Propose a strategy for McDonald's to pay the tax or add health messages, and defend your recommendation.

3. If there is no evidence that obesity rates fall in those countries that ban food advertising to children, why bother?

4. The broad issue facing McDonald's U.K. is the current attitude toward rising obesity. The company seems to have tried many different approaches to deal with the problem, but the problem persists. List all the problems facing McDonald's and critique its various approaches to solve the problems.

5. Based on your response to Question 4 above, recommend both a short-range and long-range plan for McDonald's to implement.

Sources: Jardine and Laurel Wentz, "U.K. Not Feeling the Love; McD's Puts Slogan on Ice," *Advertising Age,* September 13, 2004; "Thinking Locally," *Advertising Age,* March 7, 2005; Alexandra Jardine and Laurel Wentz, "It's a Fat World After All," *Advertising Age,* March 7, 2005; Steven Gray and Janet Adamy, "McDonald's Gets Healthier—But Burgers Still Rule," *The Wall Street Journal,* February 23, 2005; Stephanie Thompson, "Europe Slams Icons as Food Fights Back," *Advertising* Age, January 3, 2005; Emma Ross, "Obesity Hurting Health of European Children," *Associated Press,* June 3, 2005; J. E. Brody, "Globesity," *The New York Times,* April 19, 2005; "Disney Drops $1 bn McDonald's Deal Amid Health Fears," *Belfast Telegraph,* May 10, 2006; "McDonald's Defies Critics With an Even Bigger Big Mac," *The Independent* (London), April 24, 2006; "McDonald's Set to Fight Message in Movie: Chain Warns Franchisees About 'Fast Food Nation,'" *Crain's Chicago Business,* April 10, 2006; "McDonald's . . . Now With Ethical Sauce. Fast-food Giant Takes on the Critics with Soft Lights, Comfy Sofas and the Promise of Great Career Prospects," *Mail on Sunday* (London), April 23, 2006; "Prince Wants McDonald's Off the Middle East Menu as Prince Charles Advises Health Workers in the Middle East to Ban McDonald's," *The Aberdeen Press and Journal,* February 28, 2007; "So Why Does Charles Think McDonald's Is the Root of All Food Evil?" *The Scotsman,* February 28, 2007; "McDonald's Health Wins Back Customers," *The Independent* (London), January 18, 2007; "Sure, McDonald's 'Health Kick' Is a Ruse—But It's Better Than Nothing," *The Independent* (London), July 23, 2007; "UK's McDonald's Outlets Selling More Burgers than Ever Before," *Hindustan Times,* January 7, 2008; "McDonald's Answer to Obesity Fears—A Boom In Burger Sales," *Evening Standard* (London), January 7, 2008.

CASE 2-8   Ultrasound Machines, India, China, and a Skewed Sex Ratio

General Electric Co. and other companies have sold so many ultrasound machines in India that tests are now available in small towns like Indergarh, where there is no drinking water, electricity is infrequent, and roads turn to mud after a March rain shower. A scan typically costs $8, or a week's wages.

GE has waded into India's market as the country grapples with a difficult social issue: the abortion of female fetuses by families who want boys. Campaigners against the practice and some government officials are linking the country's widely reported skewed sex ratio with the spread of ultrasound machines. That's putting GE, the market leader in India, under the spotlight. It faces legal hurdles, government scrutiny, and thorny business problems in one of the world's fastest-growing economies.

"Ultrasound is the main reason the sex ratio is coming down," says Kalpana Bhavre, who is in charge of women and child welfare for the Datia district government, which includes Indergarh. Having a daughter is often viewed as incurring a lifetime of debt for parents because of the dowry payment at marriage. Compared with that, the cost of an ultrasound "is nothing," she says.

For more than a decade, the Indian government has tried to stop ultrasound technology from being used as a tool to determine gender. The devices use sound waves to produce images of fetuses or internal organs for a range of diagnostic purposes. India has passed laws forbidding doctors from disclosing the sex of fetuses, required official registrations of clinics, and stiffened punishments for offenders. Nevertheless, some estimate that hundreds of thousands of girl fetuses are aborted each year.

GE, by far the largest seller of ultrasound machines in India through a joint venture with the Indian outsourcing giant Wipro Ltd., introduced its own safeguards, even though that means forsaking sales. "We stress emphatically that the machines aren't to be used for sex determination," says V. Raja, chief executive of GE Healthcare South Asia. "This is not the root cause of female feticide in India."

But the efforts have failed to stop the problem, as a growing economy has made the scans affordable to more people. The skewed sex ratio is an example of how India's strong economy has, in unpredictable ways, exacerbated some nagging social problems, such as the traditional preference for boys. Some activists are accusing GE of not doing enough to prevent unlawful use of its machines to boost sales.

"There is a demand for a boy that's been completely exploited by multinationals," says Puneet Bedi, a New Delhi obstetrician. He says GE and others market the machines as an essential pregnancy tool, though the scans often aren't necessary for mothers in low-risk groups.

Prosecutors in the city of Hyderabad brought a criminal case against the GE venture with Wipro, as well as Erbis Engineering Co., the medical-equipment distributor in India for Japan's Toshiba Corp. In the suits, the district government alleged that the companies knowingly supplied ultrasound machines to clinics that were not registered with the government and were illegally performing sex-selection tests. The penalty is up to three months in prison and a fine of 1,000 rupees.

Both companies deny wrongdoing and say they comply with Indian laws. A GE spokesman said its legal team would be looking into the charges.

Vivek Paul, who helped build the early ultrasound business in India, first as a senior executive at GE and then at Wipro, says blame should be pinned on unethical doctors, not the machine's suppliers. "If someone drives a car through a crowded market and kills people, do you blame the car maker?" says Paul, who was Wipro's chief executive before he left the company in 2005. Paul is now a managing director at private equity specialists TPG Inc., formerly known as Texas Pacific Group.

India has been a critical market to GE. Its outsourcing operations have helped the Fairfield, Connecticut, giant cut costs. The country also is a growing market for GE's heavy equipment and other products. The company won't disclose its ultrasound sales, but Wipro GE's overall sales in India, which includes ultrasounds and other diagnostic equipment, reached about $250 million in 2006, up from $30 million in 1995.

Annual ultrasound sales in India from all vendors also reached $77 million in 2006, up about 10 percent from the year before, according to an estimate from consulting firm Frost & Sullivan, which describes GE as the clear market leader. Other vendors include Siemens AG, Philips Electronics NV, and Mindray International Medical Ltd., a new Chinese entrant for India's price-sensitive customers.

India has long struggled with an inordinate number of male births, and female infanticide—the killing of newborn baby girls—remains a problem. The abortion of female fetuses is a more recent trend, but unless "urgent action is taken," it's poised to escalate as the use of ultrasound services expands, the United Nations Children's Fund said in a report. India's "alarming decline in the child sex ratio" is likely to exacerbate child marriage, trafficking of women for prostitution, and other problems, the report said.

The latest official Indian census, in 2001, showed a steep decline in the relative number of girls aged 0 to 6 years compared with the decade earlier: 927 girls for every 1,000 boys compared with 945 in 1991. In much of northwest India, the number of girls has fallen below 900 for every 1,000 boys. In the northern state of Punjab, the figure is below 800.

Only China today has a wider gender gap, with 832 girls born for every 1,000 boys among infants aged 0 to 4 years, according to UNICEF. GE sells about three times as many ultrasound machines in China as in India. In January, the Chinese government pledged to improve the gender balance, including tighter monitoring of ultrasounds. Some experts predict China will be more effective than India in enforcing its rules, given its success at other population-control measures.

Boys in India are viewed as wealth earners during life and lighters of one's funeral pyre at death. India's National Family Health Survey, released in February, showed that 90 percent of parents with two sons didn't want any more children. Of those with two daughters, 38 percent wanted to try again. Although there are restrictions on abortions in this Hindu-majority nation, the rules offer enough leeway for most women to get around them.

GE took the lead in selling ultrasounds in the early 1990s soon after it began manufacturing the devices in India. It tapped Wipro's extensive distribution and service network to deliver its products to about 80 percent of its customers. For more remote locations and lower-end machines, it used sales agents.

The company also teamed with banks to help doctors finance the purchase of their machines. GE now sells about 15 different models, ranging from machines costing $100,000 that offer sophisticated color images to basic black-and-white scanners that retail for about $7,500.

To boost sales, GE has targeted small-town doctors. The company has kept prices down by refurbishing old equipment and marketing laptop machines to doctors who travel frequently, including to rural areas. GE also offered discounts to buyers inclined to boast about their new gadgets, according to a former GE employee. "Strategically, we focused on those customers who had big mouths," said Manish Vora, who until 2006 sold ultrasounds in the western Indian state of Gujarat for the Wipro-GE joint venture.

Without discussing specific sales tactics, Raja, of GE Healthcare South Asia, acknowledges the company is "aggressive" in pursuing its goals. But he points out that ultrasound machines have broad benefits and make childbirth safer. As the machines become more available, women can avoid making long trips into cities where health care typically is more expensive, he says.

Indian authorities have tried to regulate sales. In 1994, the government outlawed sex selection and empowered Indian authorities to search clinics and seize anything that aided sex selection. Today any clinic that has an ultrasound machine must register with the local government and provide an affidavit that it will not conduct sex selection. To date, more than 30,000 ultrasound clinics have been registered in India.

GE has taken a number of steps to ensure customers comply with the law. It has educated its sales force about the regulatory regime, demanded its own affidavits from customers that they will not use the machines for sex selection, and followed up with periodic audits, say executives. They note that in 2004, the first full year it began implementing these new measures, GE's sales in India shrank by about 10 percent from the year before. The sales decline in the low-end segment, for black-and-white ultrasound machines, was especially sharp, executives say. Only in 2006 did GE return to the sales level it had reached before the regulations were implemented, according to Raja.

Complying with Indian law is often tricky. GE cannot tell if doctors sell machines to others who fail to register them. Different states interpret registration rules differently. GE also is under close scrutiny by activists battling the illegal abortion of female fetuses. Sabu George, a 48-year-old activist who holds degrees from Johns Hopkins and Cornell universities, criss-crosses the country to spot illegal clinics.

The criminal case in Hyderabad against Wipro-GE, a company representative, three doctors, and an ultrasound technician followed an inspection in 2005 that found one clinic could not produce proper registration and had not kept complete records for two years. A team of inspectors seized an ultrasound supplied by Wipro-GE. The inspection team's report said it suspected the clinic was using the machines for illegal sex determination.

The owner, Sarawathi Devi, acknowledged in an interview that her clinic, Rite Diagnostics, was not officially registered at the time of the 2005 inspection. She said the ultrasound machine was owned by a "freelance" radiologist who had obtained proper documentation for the Wipro-GE machine but was not there when the inspectors had arrived. She denied the clinic has conducted sex determination tests. Later in 2005, Dr. Devi's records show, she registered the clinic with the government and bought a Wipro-GE machine, a sale the company confirms.

The court case was part of a wider dragnet spearheaded by Hyderabad's top civil servant, District Magistrate Arvind Kumar. During an audit last year, Kumar demanded paperwork for 389 local scan centers. Only 16 percent could furnish complete address information for its patients, making it almost impossible to track women to check if they had abortions following their scans. Kumar ordered the seizure of almost one-third of the ultrasound machines in the district due to registration and paperwork problems. A suit also was lodged against Erbis, the Toshiba dealer.

GE's Raja says that, in general, if there's any doubt about the customer's intent to comply with India's laws, it doesn't make the sale. "There is no winking or blinking," he says.

A Wipro-GE representative is scheduled to appear at the Hyderabad court hearing. An Erbis spokesman said he was unaware of the case in Hyderabad. A court date for Erbis had not been set.

A visit to the clinic in Indergarh, a town surrounded by fields of tawny wheat, shows the challenges GE faces keeping tabs on its machines. Inside the clinic, a dozen women wrapped in saris awaited tests on GE's Logiq 100 ultrasound machine. The line snaked along wooden benches and down into a darkened basement. On the wall, scrawled in white paint, was the message: "We don't do sex selection."

Manish Gupta, a 34-year-old doctor, said he drives two hours each way every week to Indergarh from much larger Jhansi City, where there are dozens of competing ultrasound clinics. He said even when offered bribes, he refuses to disclose the sex of the fetus. "I'm just against that," Dr. Gupta said.

But he is not complying with Indian law. Although the law requires that clinics display their registration certificate in a conspicuous place, Dr. Gupta's was nowhere to be seen. When Dr. George, the social activist, asked for the registration, he was shown a different document, an application. But the application was for a different clinic: the Sakshi X-ray center. Dr. Gupta said the proper document wasn't with him, adding: "I must have forgotten it at home."

Asked by *The Wall Street Journal* about the clinic, the local chief magistrate of Datia district called for Dr. Gupta's dossier later in the day. When a local official arrived, "Sakshi X-Ray center" had been crossed out on the application. In blue pen was written the correct name, "Sheetal Nagar," the part of Indergarh where the clinic is located.

It's not clear how Dr. Gupta procured the GE machine. Dr. Gupta said he bought it from a GE company representative, but he declined to show documents of ownership. GE says it does not comment on individual customers.

Like the rest of India, the Datia district government has taken a number of steps to try to boost the number of girls in the district. For girls of poor families, the local government provides a place to live, free school uniforms, and books. When they enter ninth grade, the government buys bicycles for them. Yet the low ratio of girls born had not budged much over the past decade, according to Bhavre, the district government official.

Ultimately, says Raja, head of GE Healthcare in South Asia, it's the job of the government, not companies, to change the prevailing preference for boys. "What's really needed is a change in mind-sets. A lot of education has to happen and the government has to do it," he says.

India's Ministry of Health, which is now pursuing 422 different cases against doctors accused of using ultrasounds for sex selection, agrees. "Mere legislation is not enough to deal with this problem," the ministry said in a statement. "The situation could change only when the daughters are not treated as a burden and the sons as assets."

QUESTION

What should GE management do in India about this problem, if anything? In China?

Source: Peter Wonacott, "Medical Quandry: India's Skewed Sex Ratio Puts GE Sales in Spotlight," *The Wall Street Journal,* April 18, 2007, pp. A1, A8. Licensed from Dow Jones Reprint Services, Document J000000020070418e34i00032.

cases 3
ASSESSING GLOBAL MARKET OPPORTUNITIES

CASE 3-1 International Marketing Research at the Mayo Clinic

[handwritten: wrong, it's minnesota!]

The Mayo Clinic, known for treating international leaders, recently saw the president of a central Africa country in its halls. Teodoro Obiang Nguema Mbasogo, the president of the Republic of Equatorial Guinea, was in Rochester, New York, for a checkup, clinic officials confirmed. Security officers and limousines—not an uncommon sight in Rochester—signaled his visit.

[handwritten: whose president]

Nguema Mbasogo assumed the leadership of his country in 1979 with a coup that overthrew his uncle. His country recently began working with the U.S. Agency for International Development, under the leadership of a dean of the University of Minnesota's Hubert H. Humphrey Institute of Public Affairs, to improve Equatorial Guinea's social services. Dean J. Brian Atwood of the institute is overseeing this effort. He went to Equatorial Guinea in June, and a second meeting is scheduled for this month.

Nguema Mbasogo also is serving his third, seven-year term, which ends in 2009. The BBC reported in 2003 that a presidential aide announced on a radio show that Nguema Mbasogo "can decide to kill without anyone calling him to account and without going to hell because it is God himself, with whom he is in permanent contact, who gives him this strength." A 2006 movie called *Coup!*, made in the United Kingdom, was based on an incident in which the president announced a plot, which included U.S. intelligence services, to overthrow him.

[handwritten: need little marketing research to VM]

The Mayo Clinic has a long international history, providing care to international patients since its inception. Despite its history and reputation, however, the marketing staff continues to monitor the international market to gauge the level of awareness, reputation, and attractiveness of the Mayo Clinic around the world. This institution has used word-of-mouth marketing to maintain its global reputation.

Marketing, as most formally defined, historically was not a critical factor in delivering patients to Mayo Clinic. Indeed, the marketing department at Mayo Clinic has existed for only the past 15 years, and patients have been coming for care for more than a century. The Clinic believes that the marketing department provides valuable information to physicians and their support staff—information that helps them deliver better care, highlights their patients' wants and needs, and educates them as to what's going on in the marketplace.

In reality, however, it's the providers themselves—the doctors, nurses, receptionists, and all the rest of the allied health staff—who bring in business by creating positive experiences for patients. Patients who leave Mayo Clinic highly satisfied with their care will return to their communities in the United States and elsewhere and say good things to their family and friends. And these family members and friends in turn travel to Mayo Clinic when they need tertiary or quaternary medical care. Although the marketing division strives to provide excellent internal support, it is the doctors and other care providers who have created and maintained a brand of healthcare excellence.

Despite the hype surrounding what has been presented as the highly lucrative international marketplace, "international" is not something new at Mayo Clinic. Experience and research indicates that "international" is a part of who the Clinic is, as well as how the market defines it. Nearly 100 years ago, the founders, a family of physicians named "Mayo," created an international legacy by traveling around the world to compare notes and surgical approaches with physicians across the globe. In some cases, they even returned with international patients who were in need of additional expertise. As in so many other areas of medical practice, the current Mayo Clinic continues in these traditions.

In recent years, however, it has begun to study the international patient population in particular and the international marketplace in general. These studies fall into a few categories and grow in number in proportion to the organization's understanding (or perhaps greater understanding of how much it does not know) of the international marketplace.

First, the Mayo Clinic tracks international patient trends rather carefully, which seems like an obvious place to start. But as in most data tracking, the value of the concept is significantly more straightforward than the logistics of acquiring consistently reliable data. Internal data systems must be coordinated—a significant undertaking for any institution, and particularly hard when dealing with a large and complicated infrastructure. To give a simple example, data fields must be made uniform—not just on one data system, but on all of them. Rather than a free-text field, for example, that allows a registrant to enter Venzuela, or Venosuela, or Vensuala, or maybe even Venezuela, the Mayo Clinic pushes for a predefined field that provides standardized information.

The Clinic monitors international data by the quarter, carefully watching trends over time by country or region, tracking significant changes in volume, hospitalization rates, and percentage of new patients out of any given market. For example, it knows it has between 9,000 and 10,000 patients, depending on the year, from more than 160 different countries annually. Some are third-generation patients—maybe their grandfather was cured there in the 1930s—and others are brand new. Some are neighbors from Ontario or Monterrey; others come all the way from Indonesia. Some markets are significantly less predictable than others, and some countries deliver more "new" patients than others. The Mayo Clinic probes further to figure out why.

Second, it conducts research with internal salespeople—the physicians and their support staff who deliver care to international patients. Through carefully moderated focus groups, the Clinic identifies the things that are going smoothly, as well as the barriers to providing excellent care. And where appropriate, it makes recommendations for change.

Third, just as with U.S.-based patients, the healthcare institute conducts both quantitative and qualitative research in the international marketplace, including research with patients, international physicians, and international health care consumers, designed to help it understand why people choose to leave their own communities for health care, why some of them come to Mayo Clinic, and why others do not. It works hard to understand how healthcare decisions are made so it can better assist decision makers, physicians, and their staff in providing care. The Clinic positions itself to offer counsel on where to best expend valuable institutional resources, both human and financial.

GLOBAL MARKET RESEARCH

The marketing department conducts periodic and ongoing patient satisfaction studies with international patients, measuring their assessment of various aspects of the care provided. To date, the Mayo Clinic has surveyed nearly 1,500 patients in 20 countries, in four different languages. As any market researcher knows, sound patient satisfaction research requires great attention to detail to ensure reliable data. Not surprisingly, international data collection offers significant additional challenges. For example, according to the Mayo Clinic:

The quality of our own data. The name and address fields designed for clean U.S. addresses often are not sufficient to hold reliable international detail. If we want to do it right, we must manually "clean" thousands of patient records before fielding our studies.

Varying quality of international postal and telecommunications infrastructure. This variance can create significant problems for either phone or mail surveys; consequently, international studies take a lot more time than U.S.-based studies and require much more patience.

Cultural dynamics. In some countries, individuals may be suspicious of an international call; in others, they may spend a lot of time outside of their homes. In still others, a nonfamily "gatekeeper" must be diplomatically convinced to transfer the call to the targeted respondents. These cultural dynamics pose further delays and require special sensitivities.

High standards for quality. Our own standards for quality compel us to maintain high quality language- and culture-specific fielding of our various research projects. These studies, whether managed internally or through an external vendor, require more oversight than we are accustomed to with U.S.-based research.

Despite these challenges, however, this international research has taught the Mayo Clinic a lot. International patient satisfaction studies demonstrate that the key driver of patients' satisfaction seems to hold across borders. This is excellent care—manifested by listening, explaining, and thoroughness on the part of Mayo Clinic physicians.

Other factors in the healthcare experience are important—for example, quality of language interpretation and waiting times—but they do not consistently correlate with overall satisfaction.

The power of word of mouth is also confirmed in the international marketplace. Most international patients indicate that friends or relatives provided their most important influence in choosing Mayo Clinic. This finding reinforces the most powerful marketing "tool"—satisfied patients who say good things about Mayo Clinic and influence others' health care decisions. Exhibit 1 indicates the factors influencing choice of Mayo Clinic by patients from Latin America and the Middle East.

Formal focus groups with international patients and nonpatients in six cities around the world attempted to learn more about how those populations make healthcare decisions, and whether the process is the same or different from U.S. healthcare consumers. As it turns out, for most aspects of decision making, the process is very similar to that of U.S. consumers. However, for a few others, the process is quite different.

The areas with the most differences across borders relate to the role of health insurance. Three co-sponsored international research projects have provided some good lessons and demonstrated that international healthcare insurance is as different from that in the United States as it is across countries and regions. Furthermore, many assumptions taken for granted in the U.S. market—for example, name recognition—simply do not hold in certain international markets. Exhibit 2 is a graph of responses from a satisfaction study of patients from Latin America and the Middle East, showing the different history of Mayo Clinic brand awareness in those regions

Mayo Clinic awareness among patients was much more recent in the Middle East than in Latin America. Other studies, however, showed that awareness among nonpatients—even those who have purchased health insurance policies that offer them Mayo Clinic care as a benefit—is not as strong.

The international healthcare insurance market is expanding rapidly, and many providers view this expansion as a significant opportunity to glean additional patients from outside the United States. Commercial and noncommercial contracts comprise a significant body of business in U.S. healthcare. If this business could be expanded to provide patients from markets outside the United States,

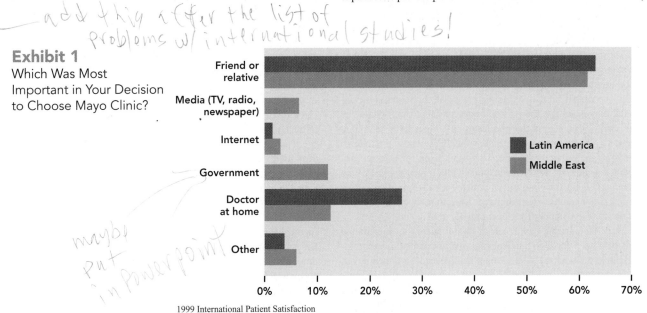

Exhibit 1
Which Was Most Important in Your Decision to Choose Mayo Clinic?

1999 International Patient Satisfaction
N = 331 Middle Eastern patients; 755 Latin American patients.

Exhibit 2
How Long Ago Did You First Hear of Mayo Clinic?

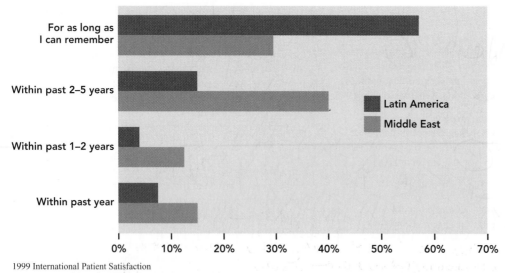

1999 International Patient Satisfaction
N = 331 Middle Eastern patients; 755 Latin American patients.

all the better. However, healthcare systems vary significantly from country to country, and the knowledge and use of health insurance vary even more. To study these differences in detail, the Mayo Clinic cosponsored two quantitative studies of healthcare insurance policyholders—in particular, holders of policies that offer some degree of coverage for care at Mayo Clinic.

The first study consisted of face-to-face interviews with 400 policyholders in a particular country and delivered a great deal of information regarding policyholders' preferences, healthcare behavior, and demographics. In this country, as throughout most of the world, the public healthcare system exists as a universal "safety net" for all citizens. Even in markets where the private insurance market has expanded, the public system continues to offer care for all citizens. Therefore, if a private insurance policy does not offer adequate coverage, especially for high-cost procedures, the public system is used to reduce the consumer's financial burden.

The private policy might cover, for example, access to primary and secondary care at private rather than public clinics as well as the price of a private room, or the option of receiving care at a more upscale facility. But for high-cost, life-threatening procedures, the co-pay or deductible for having these procedures conducted exclusively in the private sector remains significant. The end result, of course, is that the lower cost procedures are transferred to the private system, while the higher cost procedures remain in the public safety net. The implication for U.S. tertiary providers is that, while private insurance might reduce some of the financial risk for traveling out of country for care, in many cases the risk is not completely eliminated. Therefore, the policies might not deliver the volume of patients initially anticipated.

Other factors, such as a lack of brand awareness and limited perceived need for U.S. medical care, may be impediments to attracting patients in the international healthcare insurance market. In the first study, when the Clinic probed for brand awareness among those 400 consumers who had purchased a health insurance policy touting Mayo Clinic coverage as a benefit, no unaided recall of that coverage emerged as a benefit of the policy. (See Exhibit 3.)

In an aided list, Mayo Clinic coverage was ranked as the least important benefit of the policy, on a par with eyeglass coverage at the bottom of the list.

Furthermore, when asked to name a leading medical center in the United States, most policyholders (72 percent) did not know a single one. Twenty-five percent (25 percent) named Mayo Clinic, and the other 2 percent named other U.S. medical centers. It was no real surprise that citizens in the studied country were not familiar with Mayo Clinic. However, the Clinic was surprised that policyholders who had purchased an insurance product that very publicly advertised the Mayo Clinic benefit were unable to name Mayo Clinic as a leading U.S. medical center.

As it turned out, many of these policyholders had no intention of leaving their home country for medical care. They were buying insurance to facilitate care in the more desirable private system. Furthermore, most felt that the health care in their own country was very good and that there would be little if any reason to ever leave home to obtain care elsewhere. This phenomenon emerges repeatedly in research with U.S. patients. Most believe in the abilities of their own doctor and feel very confident about medical care in their own community. Even though "quality" may be regionally or culturally defined, almost everyone considers his or her doctor to be a good one.

A second cosponsored study consisted of 353 telephone interviews with individuals who had purchased a health care insurance policy specifically for international coverage. Once again, confidence in local care was very high—in fact, significantly higher than in the country of the first study. Nonetheless, this group of individuals had purchased a product that offered them coverage for medical care outside their home country, should they decide it was necessary or appropriate. In this study, aided brand recognition among policyholders was higher than in the first; when asked directly whether they had heard of Mayo Clinic, 75 percent responded affirmatively. But when asked unaided to name the best medical centers in the United States, the vast majority (nearly 70 percent) of policyholders indicated they did not know. And while the majority

Exhibit 3
Recall of Plan Benefits (unaided)

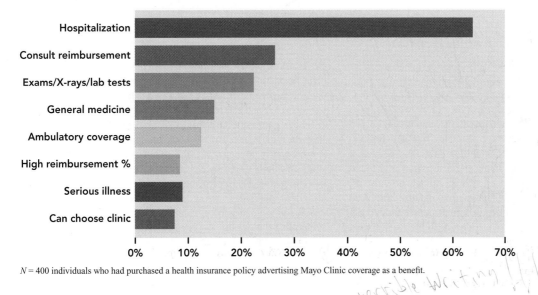

N = 400 individuals who had purchased a health insurance policy advertising Mayo Clinic coverage as a benefit.

had heard of Mayo Clinic, fewer than 10 percent were aware of any benefit of their health insurance policy that related to Mayo Clinic.

Both of these studies offered substantially more information about the nature of international insurance agreements, policyholders' wants and needs, and their disposition toward traveling out of country for medical care. But they also showed that the knowledge of the Mayo brand is limited outside the United States and that a high number of policyholders does not necessarily translate into a high number of patients. This research has taught the Clinic to be more selective, to be cautious in expending significant resources to pursue insurance arrangements, and to conduct further research to expand understanding.

THE FUTURE

"International" will continue to be part of who the Mayo Clinic is. Its doctors, hailing from all corners of the globe, will continue to collaborate with their colleagues around the world. Mayo Clinic researchers will conduct clinical trials in collaboration with researchers on many continents. Students and residents will continue to offer rich diversity, as Mayo international alumni now number 1,500, representing 67 countries. But most important, Mayo Clinic will strive to provide the best medical care possible to those patients around the world who need it the most.

To support that mission, members of the "marketing" department will continue to support the medical staff by studying patients' wants, needs, preferences, and behavior patterns and learning all that they can about the ever-changing, rich, and diverse worldwide health care market. In the end, outstanding medical care and sensitive service to patients and families will be the most productive marketing strategy, because it creates positive word of mouth about something very important—healthcare. As the stories of satisfied patients churn—sometimes for decades—in the minds of their friends and family, Mayo Clinic remains an option if they ever need the care it offers.

QUESTION

Assume you are the new marketing vice president at the Mayo Clinic. The CEO and the board have decided to expand their international sales revenues by 100 percent over the next five years. Write a memo to your staff outlining the marketing research that will be needed to support such a strategy. Be specific about sources of secondary data and the best places and media for gathering primary data. Also, be specific about the best methods to use.

Sources: Misty Hathaway and Kent Seltman, "International Marketing Research at the Mayo Clinic," *Marketing Health Services,* Winter 2001, 21(4), pp. 18–23; Jeff Kiger, "African President Gets Checkup at Mayo Clinic," *Post-Bulletin,* September 21, 2007.

CASE 3-2 Swifter, Higher, Stronger, Dearer

Television and sport are perfect partners. Each has made the other richer. But is the alliance really so good for sport?

Back in 1948, the BBC, Britain's public broadcasting corporation, took a fateful decision. It paid a princely £15,000 (£27,000 in today's money) for the right to telecast the Olympic Games to a domestic audience. It was the first time a television network had paid the International Olympic Committee (IOC, the body that runs the Games) for the privilege. But not the last. The rights to the 1996 Summer Olympics, which opened in Atlanta on July 19, 1996, raised $900 million from broadcasters round the world. And the American television rights to the Olympiads up to and including 2008 have been bought by America's NBC network for an amazing $3.6 billion (see Exhibit 1).

The Olympics are only one of the sporting properties that have become hugely valuable to broadcasters. Sport takes up a growing share of screen time (as those who are bored by it know all too well). When you consider the popularity of the world's great tournaments, that is hardly surprising. *Sportsfests* generate audiences beyond the wildest dreams of television companies for anything else. According to Nielsen Media Research, the number of Americans watching the Super Bowl, the main annual football championship, averaged 94 million. The top eight television programs in America are all sporting events. Some 3 billion people watched some part of the 2000 Olympiad—over half of mankind.

The reason television companies love sport is not merely that billions want to tele-gawk at ever-more-wonderful sporting feats. Sport also has a special quality that makes it unlike almost any other sort of television program: immediacy. Miss seeing a particular episode of, say, *ER,* and you can always catch the repeat and enjoy it just as much. Miss seeing your team beat hell out of its biggest rival, and the replay will leave you cold. "A live sporting event loses almost all its value as the final whistle goes," says Steve Barnett, author of a British book on sport. The desire to watch sport when it is happening, not hours afterward, is universal: A study in South Korea by Spectrum, a British consultancy, found that live games get 30 percent of the audience while recordings get less than 5 percent.

This combination of popularity and immediacy has created a symbiotic relationship between sport and television in which each is changing the other. As Stephen Wenn, of Canada's Wilfrid Laurier University, puts it, television and the money it brings have had an enormous impact on the Olympic Games, including on the timing of events and their location. For instance, an Asian Olympics poses a problem for American networks: Viewers learn the results on the morning news.

The money that television has brought into professional basketball has put some of the top players among the world's highest-paid entertainers: A few are getting multiyear contracts worth over $100 million. Rugby has begun to be reorganized to make it more television friendly; other sports will follow. And, though soccer and American football draw the largest audiences, television has also promoted the popularity of sports that stir more local passions: rugby league in Australia, cricket in India, table tennis in China, snooker in Britain.

Exhibit 1

Chariots for Hire: Olympic Broadcast Rights Fees,* $bn (world totals)

Source: International Olympic Committee. Used by permission of the International Olympic Committee.

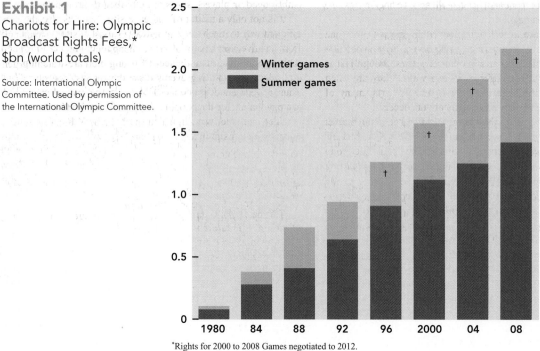

*Rights for 2000 to 2008 Games negotiated to 2012.
†Two years earlier.

What is less often realized is that sport is also changing television. To assuage the hunger for sports, new channels are being launched at a tremendous pace. In America, ESPN, a cable network owned by Capital Cities/ABC, started a 24-hour sports news network in 1997; in Britain, BSkyB, a satellite broadcaster partly owned by Rupert Murdoch, has three sports channels. Because people seem more willing to pay to watch sport on television than to pay for any other kind of programming, sport has become an essential part of the business strategy of television empire-builders such as Murdoch. Nobody in the world understands the use of sports as a bait for viewers better than he.

In particular, sport suggests an answer to one of the big problems that will face television companies in the future: How can viewers, comfortable with their old analog sets, be persuaded to part with the hefty price of a new digital set and a subscription to an untried service? The answer is to create an exclusive chance to watch a desirable event, or to use the hundreds of channels that digital television provides to offer more variety of sports coverage than analog television can offer. This ploy is not new. "Radio broadcasts of boxing were once used to promote the sale of radios, and baseball to persuade people to buy television sets," points out Richard Burton, a sports marketing specialist at the Lundquist College of Business at Oregon University. In the next few years, the main new outlet for sports programs will be digital television.

GOING FOR GOLD

To understand how these multiple effects have come about, go back to those vast sums that television companies are willing to pay. In America, according to Neal Weinstock of Weinstock Media Analysis, total spending on sports rights by television companies is about $2 billion a year. Easily the most valuable rights are for American football. One of the biggest sporting coups in the United States was the purchase by Fox, owned by Murdoch's News Corporation, of the rights to four years of National Football League games for $1.6 billion. Rights for baseball, basketball, and ice hockey are also in the billion-dollar range.

Americans are rare in following four main sports rather than one. America is also uncommon in having no publicly owned networks. As a result, bidding wars in other countries, though just as fierce as in America, are different in two ways: They are often fought between public broadcasters and new upstarts, many of them pay channels, and they are usually about soccer.

Nothing better illustrates the change taking place in the market for soccer rights than the vast deal struck in 1997 by Kirch, a German group owned by a secretive Bavarian media mogul. The group spent $2.2 billion for the world's biggest soccer-broadcasting rights: to show the finals of the World Cup in 2002 and 2006 outside America. That is over six times more than the amount paid for the rights to the World Cups of 1990, 1994, and 1998.

Such vast bids gobble up a huge slice of a television company's budget. In America, reckons London Economics, a British consultancy, sport accounts for around 15 percent of all television-program spending. For some television companies, the share is much larger. BSkyB spends £100 million ($180 million) a year on sports, about one-third of its programming budget.

This spending seems to pose a threat to public broadcasting, for, in any bidding war outside America, public broadcasting companies are generally the losers. A consortium of mainly public broadcasters bought the rights to the 1990–1998 World Cups for a total of $344 million. This time around, the consortium raised its bid to around $1.8 billion and still lost. Public broadcasters often do not have the money to compete. In Britain, the BBC spends about 4 percent of its program budget on sport in a non-Olympic year, about £15 million a year less than BSkyB.

The problem is that the value of sport to viewers ("consumer surplus," as economists would put it) is much larger than the value of most other sorts of programming. Public broadcasters have no way to benefit from the extra value that a big sporting event offers viewers. But with subscription television and with pay TV, where viewers are charged for each event, the television company will directly collect the value viewers put on being able to watch.

Therefore, many people (especially in Europe) worry that popular sports will increasingly be available only on subscription television, which could, they fear, erode the popular support upon which public broadcasters depend. In practice, these worries seem excessive. Although far more sport will be shown on subscription television, especially outside America's vast advertising market, the most popular events are likely to remain freely available for many years to come, for two reasons.

First, those who own the rights to sporting events are rarely just profit maximizers: They also have an interest in keeping the appeal of their sport as broad as possible. They may therefore refuse to sell to the highest bidder. For example, the IOC turned down a $2 billion bid from Murdoch's News Corporation for the European broadcasting rights to the Olympic Games between 2000 and 2008 in favor of a lower bid from a group of public broadcasters. Sometimes, as with the sale of World Cup rights to Kirch, the sellers may stipulate that the games be aired on "free" television.

Second, the economics of televising sport means that the biggest revenues are not necessarily earned by tying up exclusive rights. Steven Bornstein, the boss of ESPN, argues that exclusive deals to big events are "not in our long-term commercial interest." Because showing sport on "free" television maximizes the audience, some advertisers will be willing to pay a huge premium for the big occasion. So will sponsors who want their names to be seen emblazoned on players' shirts or on billboards around the field.

It is not only a matter of audience size. Sport is also the most efficient way to reach one of the world's most desirable audiences from an advertiser's point of view: young men with cash to spend. Although the biggest audiences of young men are watching general television, sporting events draw the highest concentrations. Thus, advertisers of products such as beer, cars, and sports shoes can pay mainly for the people they most want to attract.

There are other ways in which sport can be indirectly useful to the networks. A slot in a summer game is a wonderful opportunity to promote a coming autumn show. A popular game wipes out the audience share of the competition. And owning the rights to an event allows a network plenty of scope to entertain corporate grandees who may then become advertisers.

For the moment, though, advertising revenue is the main recompense that television companies get for their huge investments in sport. Overall, according to *Broadcasting & Cable,* a trade magazine, sport generates 10 percent of total television advertising revenues in America. The biggest purchasers of sports rights by far in America are the national networks. NBC alone holds more big sports rights than any other body has held in the history of television. It can obviously recoup some of the bill by selling advertising: For a 30-second slot during the Super Bowl, by most estimates networks are now asking and getting more than $3 million.

Such deals, however, usually benefit the networks indirectly rather than directly. The Super Bowl is a rarity: It has usually made a profit for the network that airs it. "Apart from the Super Bowl, the World Series and probably the current Olympics, the big sports don't usually make money for the networks," says Arthur Gruen of Wilkowsky Gruen, a media consultancy. "But they are a boon for their affiliate stations, which can sell their advertising slots for two or three times as much as other slots." Although Fox lost money on its NFL purchase, it won the loyalty of affiliate stations (especially important for a new network) and made a splash.

Almost everywhere else, the biggest growth in revenues from showing sports will increasingly come from subscriptions or pay-per-view arrangements. The versatility and huge capacity of digital broadcasting make it possible to give subscribers all sorts of new and lucrative services.

In America, DirectTV and Primestar, two digital satellite broadcasters, have been tempting subscribers with packages of sporting events from distant parts of the country. "They have been creating season tickets for all the main events, costing $100–150 per season per sport," says John Mansell, a senior analyst with Paul Kagan, a California consultancy. In Germany, DF1, a satellite company jointly owned by Kirch and BSkyB, has the rights to show Formula One motor racing. It allows viewers to choose to follow particular teams, so that Ferrari fanatics can follow their drivers, and to select different camera angles.

In Italy, Telepiu, which launched digital satellite television in 1997, offers viewers a package in September that allows them to buy a season ticket to live matches played by one or more teams in the top Italian soccer leagues. The system's "electronic turnstile" is so sophisticated that it can shut off reception for subscribers living in the catchment area for a home game, to assuage clubs' worries that they will lose revenue from supporters at the gate. In fact, top Italian clubs usually have to lock out their fanatical subscribers to avoid overcapacity.

Most skillful of all at using sports rights to generate subscription revenue is BSkyB. It signed an exclusive contract with the English Premier League that has been the foundation of its success. Some of those who know BSkyB well argue that £5 billion of the business's remarkable capital value of £8 billion is attributable to the profitability of its soccer rights.

WINNER TAKE ALL

Just as the purchase of sporting rights enriches television companies, so their sale has transformed the finances of the sports lucky enough to be popular with viewers. On the whole, the biggest beneficiaries have not been the clubs and bodies that run sports but the players. In the same way as rising revenues from films are promptly dissipated in vast salaries to stars in Hollywood, so in sport the money coming in from television soon flows out in heftier payments to players.

In America, the market for sportsmen is well developed and the cost of players tends to rise with the total revenues of the main sporting organizations. Elsewhere, the market is newer and so a bigger slice of the revenues tends to stick to the television companies. "The big difference between sports and movies is the operating margins," says Chris Akers, chairman of Caspian, a British media group, and an old hand at rights negotiations. "Hollywood majors have per-subscriber deals. No sports federation has yet done such a deal."

Guided by the likes of Akers, they soon will. Telepiu's latest three-year soccer contract gives the television firm enough revenue to cover its basic costs, guarantees the soccer league a minimum sum, and then splits the takings down the middle. In Britain, BSkyB is locked in dispute with the Premier League over the terms of the second half of its rights deal: Should the league then be able to opt for half the revenue from each subscriber on top of or instead of a fixed hunk of net profits?

The logical next step would be for some clubs or leagues to set up their own pay-television systems, distributing their games directly by satellite or cable. A few people in British soccer are starting to look with interest at America's local sports networks, such as the successful Madison Square Garden cable network, and to wonder whether Europe might move the same way.

If it does, not all teams will benefit equally. In America, football has an elaborate scheme to spread revenues from national television across teams. But in other sports, including baseball, the wealth and size of a team's local market mean large differences in rights from local television. The New York Yankees now make more than $50 million a year from local television rights. At the other end of the scale, the Milwaukee Brewers make $6 million to $7 million a year.

Not all players benefit equally, either. Television has brought to sport the "winner-take-all" phenomenon. It does not cost substantially more to stage a televised championship game than a run-of-the-week, untelevised match. But the size of the audience, and therefore the revenue generated, may be hugely different. As a result, players good enough to be in the top games will earn vastly more than those slightly less good, who play to smaller crowds.

THE REFEREE'S WHISTLE

The lure of money is already altering sport and will change it more. Increasingly, games will be reorganized to turn them into better television. British rugby-union officials are squabbling over the spoils from television rights. Rugby league, whose audiences had been dwindling, won a contract worth £87 million over five years from BSkyB in exchange for switching its games from winter to summer. Purists were aghast.

Other reorganizations for the benefit of television will surely come. Murdoch wants to build a rugby superleague, allowing the best teams around the world to play each other. A European superleague for soccer is possible. "At the moment, Manchester United plays AC Milan every 25 years: it's a joke," complains one enthusiast.

Sports traditionalists resist changing their ways for the likes of Murdoch. So far, the big sporting bodies have generally held out against selling exclusive pay-television rights to their crown jewels, and have sometimes deliberately favored public broadcasters. Regulators have helped them, intervening in some countries to limit exclusive deals with pay-television groups. Britain passed a law to stop subscription channels tying up exclusive rights to some big events, such as the Wimbledon tennis championship. In Australia, a court threw out News Corporation's attempt to build a rugby superleague as the lynchpin of its pay-television strategy.

The real monopolists are not the media companies, however, but the teams. Television companies can play off seven or eight Hollywood studios against each other. But most countries have only one national soccer league, and a public that loves soccer above all other sports. In the long run, the players and clubs hold most of the cards. The television companies are more likely to be their servants than their masters.

QUESTIONS

1. The following are the prices paid for the *American* television broadcasting rights of the summer Olympics since 1980: Moscow—NBC agreed to pay $85 million; 1984 in Los Angeles—ABC paid $225 million; 1988 in Seoul—NBC paid $300 million; 1992 in Barcelona—NBC paid $401 million; 1996 through 2008—NBC will pay $3.6 billion; 2010—NBC will pay $820 million; 2012 in London—NBC will pay $1.18 billion for its American broadcast rights. At this writing, the venue for the 2016 Games has not been awarded. However, assume you have been charged with the responsibility of determining the IOC and local Olympic Committee's asking prices for the 2016 television broadcast rights for five different markets: Japan, China, Australia, the European Union, and Brazil. Determine a price for each, and justify your decisions.

2. Your instructor may assign you to represent either the IOC or any one of the television networks in each of the five countries that have been asked to bid for the broadcast rights for the London 2016 Games. Prepare to negotiate prices and other organizational details.

Sources: Adapted from *The Economist,* July 20, 1996, pp. 17–19. Also see Mark Hyman, "The Jets: Worth a Gazillion?" *BusinessWeek,* December 6, 1999, pp. 99–100; Mark Hyman, "Putting the Squeeze on the Media," *BusinessWeek,* December 11, 2000, p. 75; Alan Abrahamson, "NBC Wins Rights to 2010, 2012 Olympics," *Los Angeles Times,* June 7, 2003, p. C1.

CASE 3-3 easyCar.com

At easyCar we aim to offer you outstanding value for money. To us value for money means a reliable service at a low price. We achieve this by simplifying the product we offer, and passing on the benefits to you in the form of lower prices.[1]

This excerpt was the stated mission of the car rental company easyCar.com. EasyCar was a member of the EasyGroup family of companies, founded by the flamboyant Greek entrepreneur Stelios Haji-Ioannou, who was known simply as Stelios to most. Stelios founded low-cost air carrier easyJet.com in 1995, after convincing his father, a Greek shipping billionaire, to loan him the £5 million (in January 2003, £1 = €1.52 = U.S.$1.61) needed to start the business.[2] EasyJet was one of the early low-cost, no-frills air carriers in the European market. It was built on a foundation of simple point-to-point flights, booked over the Internet, and the aggressive use of yield management policies to maximize the revenues it derived from its assets. The company proved highly successful, and as a result, Stelios had expanded this business model to industries with similar characteristics as the airline industry. EasyCar, founded in 2000 on a £10 million investment on the part of Stelios, was one of these efforts.

EasyCar's approach, built on the easyJet model, was quite different from the approaches used by the traditional rental car companies. EasyCar rented only a single vehicle type at each location it operated, while most of its competitors rented a wide variety of vehicle types. EasyCar did not work with agents—over 95 percent of its bookings were made through the company's Web site, with the remainder of bookings being made directly through the company's phone reservation system (at a cost to the customer of €0.95/minute for the call). Most rental car companies worked with a variety of intermediaries, with their own Web sites accounting for less than 10 percent of their total booking.[3] And like easyJet, easyCar managed prices in an attempt to have its fleet rented out 100 percent of the time and to generate the maximum revenue from its rentals. EasyCar's information system constantly evaluated projected demand and expected utilization at each site, and it adjusted price accordingly. Because of its aggressive pricing, easyCar was able to achieve a fleet utilization rate in excess of 90 percent[4]—much higher than other major rental car companies. Industry leader Avis Europe, for example, had a fleet utilization rate of 68 percent.[5]

It was January 2003. EasyCar had broken even in the fiscal year ending September 2002[6] on revenues of £27 million.[7] This figure represented a significant improvement over 2001, when easyCar had lost £7.5 million on revenues of £18.5 million.[8] While pleased that the company had broken even in only its third year in operation, Stelios had set aggressive financial goals for easyCar for the next two years. Plans called for a quadrupling of revenues in the next two years in preparation for a planned initial public offering in the second half of 2004. EasyCar's goal was to reach £100 million in revenue and £10 million in profit for the year 2004. The £100 million revenue goal and £10 million profit goal were believed necessary to obtain the desired return from an initial public offering (IPO). It was thought that with this level of performance, the company might be worth about £250 million.[9] To achieve these financial goals, the company was pushing to open an average of 2 new sites a week through 2003 and 2004 to reach a total of 180 sites by the end of 2004.[10]

THE RENTAL CAR INDUSTRY IN WESTERN EUROPE

The western European rental car industry consisted of many different national markets that were only semi-integrated. Although many companies competed within this European rental car industry, a handful of companies held dominant positions, either across a number of national markets or within one or a few national markets. Industry experts saw the sector as ripe for consolidation.[11] Several international companies—notably Avis, Europcar, and Hertz—had strong positions across most major European markets. Within most countries, a primarily national or regional company had a strong position in its home market and perhaps a moderate market share in neighboring markets. Sixt was the market leader in Germany, for example, while Atesa (in partnership with National) was the market leader in Spain. Generally these major players accounted for more than half the market. In Germany, for example, Sixt, Europcar, Avis, and Hertz had a combined 60 percent of the €2.5 billion German rental car market.[12] In Spain, the top five firms accounted for 60 percent of the €920 million Spanish rental car market. Generally, these top firms targeted both business and vacation travelers and offered a wide range of vehicles for rent. Exhibit 1 provides basic information on these market-leading companies.

Many smaller rental companies operated in each market in addition to these major companies. In Germany, for example, there were over 700 smaller companies,[13] while in Spain there were

[1] EasyCar.com Web site.

[2] "The Big Picture—An Interview with Stelios," *Sunday Herald (UK)*, March 16, 2003.

[3] "Click to Fly," *The Economist*, May 13, 2004.

[4] E. Simpkins, "Stelios Isn't Taking It Easy," *Sunday Telegraph (UK)*, December 15, 2002.

[5] Avis Europe Plc. 2002 annual report, p. 10, accessed at ir.avis-europe.com/avis/reports, August 16, 2004.

[6] Simpkins.

[7] "Marketing: Former eBay UK Chief Lands Top easyCar Position," *Financial Times Information Limited*, January 9, 2003.

[8] T. Burt, "EasyCar Agrees to Deal with Vauxhall," *Financial Times*, April 30, 2002, p. 24.

[9] N. Hodgson, "Stelios Plans easyCar Float," *Liverpool Echo*, September 24, 2002.

[10] Simpkins.

[11] "Marketing Week: Don't Write Off the Car Rental Industry," *Financial Times Information Limited*, September 26, 2002.

[12] "EasyCar Set to Shake Up German Car Rental Market," *European Intelligence Wire*, February 22, 2002.

[13] Ibid.

Exhibit 1

Information on easyCar's Major European Competitors

	easyCar	Avis Europe	Europcar	Hertz	Sixt
Number of Rental Outlets	46	3,100	2,650	7,000	1,250
2002 Fleet Size	7,000	120,000	220,000	700,000	46,700
Number of Countries	5	107	118	150	50
Largest Market	U.K.	France	France	U.S.	Germany
Company Owner	EasyGroup/ Stelios Haji-Ioannou	D'Ieteren (Belgium) is majority shareholder	Volkswagen AG	Ford Motor Company	Publicly traded
European Revenues	€41 million	€1.25 billion	€1.12 billion	€910 million	€600 million
Company Web Site	www.easyCar.com	www.avis-europe.com	www.europcar.com	www.hertz.com	ag.sixt.com

Source: Information in this table comes from each company's Web site and online annual reports. European revenues are for vehicle rental in Europe and are estimated based on market share estimates for 2001 from Avis Europe's Web site.

more than 1,600 smaller companies. Many of these smaller companies operated at only one or a few locations and were particularly prevalent in tourist locations. A number of brokers also operated in the sector, like Holiday Autos. Brokerage companies did not own their own fleet of cars but basically managed the excess inventory of other companies and matched customers with rental companies with excess fleet capacity.

Overall, the rental car market could be thought of as composed of two broad segments, a business segment and a tourist/leisure segment. Depending on the market, the leisure segment represented somewhere between 45 and 65 percent of the overall market, and a large part of this segment was very price conscious. The business segment made up the remaining 35 to 55 percent of the market. It was less price sensitive than the tourist segment and more concerned about service quality, convenience, and flexibility.

THE GROWTH OF EASYCAR

EasyCar opened its first location in London on April 20, 2000, under the name easyRentacar. In the same week, easyCar opened locations in Glasgow and Barcelona. All three locations were popular easyJet destinations. Vehicles initially could be rented for as low as €15 a day plus a one-time car preparation fee of €8. Each of these locations had a fleet consisting entirely of Mercedes A-class vehicles. It was the only vehicle that easyCar rented at the time.

EasyCar had signed a deal with Mercedes, amid much fanfare, at the Geneva Motor Show earlier in the year to purchase a total of 5,000 A-class vehicles. The vehicles, which came with guaranteed buyback terms, cost easyCar's parent company a little over £6 million.[14] Many in the car rental industry were surprised by the choice, expecting

easyCar to rely on less expensive models.[15] In describing the acquisition of the 5,000 Mercedes vehicles, Stelios had said:

> The choice of Mercedes reflects the easyGroup brand. EasyRentacar will use brand new Mercedes cars in the same way that easyJet uses brand new Boeing aircraft. We do not compromise on the hardware, we just use innovation to substantially reduces costs. The car hire industry is where the airline industry was five years ago, a cartel feeding off the corporate client. EasyRentacar will provide a choice for consumers who pay out of their own pockets and who will not be ripped off for traveling mid-week.[16]

EasyCar quickly expanded to other locations, focusing first on those locations that were popular with easyJet customers, including Amsterdam, Geneva, Nice, and Malaga. By July 2001, a little over a year after its initial launch, easyCar had fleets of Mercedes A-class vehicles in 14 locations in the United Kingdom, Spain, France, and the Netherlands. At this point, easyCar secured £27 million from a consortium of Bank of Scotland Corporate Banking and NBGI Private Equity to expand its operations. The package consisted of a combination of equity and loan stock.

Although easyCar added a few sites in the second half of 2001 and early 2002, volatile demand in the wake of the September 11 attacks forced easyCar to roll out new rental locations somewhat slower than originally expected.[17] Growth accelerated, however, in the spring of 2002. Between May 2002 and January 2003, easyCar opened 30 new locations, going from 18 sites to a total of 48. This acceleration in growth also coincided with a change in easyCar's policy regarding the makeup of its fleet. By May 2002, easyCar's fleet consisted of 6,000 Mercedes A-class vehicles

---

[14]N. Hodgson, "Stelios Plans easyCar Float," *Liverpool Echo*, September 24, 2002.

[15]A. Felsted, "EasyCar Courts Clio for Rental Fleet," *Financial Times*, February 11, 2002, p. 26.

[16]EasyCar.com Web site news release, March 1, 2000.

[17]Burt.

Exhibit 2
EasyCar Locations in
January 2003

Source: easyCar.com Web site,
January 2003.

Country	City	Number	Number Near an Airport
France	Nice	1	1
France	Paris	8	0
Netherlands	Amsterdam	3	1
Spain	Barcelona	2	0
Spain	Madrid	2	0
Spain	Majorca	1	1
Spain	Malaga	1	1
Switzerland	Geneva	1	1
UK	Birmingham	2	0
UK	Bromley	1	0
UK	Croydon	1	1
UK	Glasgow	2	1
UK	Kingston-upon-Thames	1	0
UK	Liverpool	2	1
UK	London	15	0
UK	Manchester	2	1
UK	Waterford	1	0
Total	5 countries, 17 cities	46	9

across 18 sites. Beginning in May, however, easyCar began to stock its fleet with other types of vehicles. It still maintained its policy of offering only a single vehicle at each location, but now the vehicle the customer received depended on the location. The first new vehicle easyCar introduced was the Vauxhall Corsa. According to Stelios,

> Vauxhall Corsas cost easyCar £2 a day less than Mercedes A-Class so we can pass this saving on to customers. Customers themselves will decide if they want to pay a premium for a Mercedes. EasyGroup companies benefit from economies of scale where relevant but we also want to create contestable markets among our suppliers so that we can keep the cost to our customers as low as possible.[18]

By January 2003, easyCar was also using Ford Focuses (4 locations), Renault Clios (3 locations), Toyota Yarises (3 locations), and Mercedes Smart cars (2 locations), in addition to the Vauxhall Corsas (7 locations) and the Mercedes A-Class vehicles (28 locations). Plans called for a further expansion of the fleet, from the 7,000 vehicles that easyCar had in January to 24,000 vehicles across 180 rental sites by the end of 2004.[19]

In addition to making vehicles available at more locations, easyCar had also changed its policies for 2003 to allow rentals for as little as one hour and with as little as one hour's notice of rental. By making this change, Stelios felt that easyCar could be a serious competitor to local taxis, buses, trains, and even car ownership. EasyCar expected that if it made car rental simple enough and cheap enough, some people living in traffic-congested European cities who only use their car occasionally would give up the costs and hassles of car ownership and simply rent an easyCar when they needed a vehicle. Tapping into this broader transportation market would help the company reach its ambitious future sales goals.

FACILITIES

EasyCar had facilities in a total of 17 cities in 5 European countries, as shown in Exhibit 2. It primarily located its facilities near bus and train stations in the major European cities, seeking out sites that offered low lease costs. It generally avoided prime airport locations, as the cost for space at and in some cases near airports was significantly higher than most other locations. When easyCar did locate near an airport, it generally chose sites off the airport, to reduce the cost of the lease. Airport locations also tended to require longer hours to satisfy customers arriving on late flights or departing on very early flights. EasyCar kept its airport locations open 24 hours a day, whereas its other locations were generally open only from 7:00 a.m. to 11:00 p.m.

The physical facilities at all locations were kept to a minimum. In many locations, easyCar leased space in an existing parking garage. Employees worked out of a small, self-contained cubicle within the garage. The cubicle, depending on the location, might be no more than 15 square meters and included little more than a small counter and a couple of computers at which staff processed customers as they came to pick up or return their vehicles. EasyCar also leased a number of spaces within the garage for its fleet of cars. However, because easyCar's vehicles were rented 90 percent of the time, the number of spaces required at an average site, which had a fleet of about 150 cars, was only 15–20 spaces.[20] To speed up the opening of new sites, easyCar had equipped a number of vans with all the needed computer and telephone equipment to run a site.[21] From an operational perspective, it could open a new location by simply leasing 20 or so spaces in a parking garage, hiring a small staff, driving a van to the location, and adding the location to the company's Web site. Depending on the fleet size at a location, easyCar typically had only one or two people working at a site at a time.

---

[18]EasyCar.com Web site news release, May 2, 2002.

[19]"Marketing Week: EasyCar Appoints Head of European Marketing," *Financial Times Information Limited*, January 9, 2003.

[20]Simpkins.

[21]Ibid.

VEHICLE PICKUP AND RETURN PROCESSES

Customers arrived to a site to pick up a vehicle within a prearranged one-hour time period. Each customer selected this time slot when booking the vehicle. EasyCar adjusted the first day's rental price based on the pickup time. Customers who picked their cars up early in the day or at popular times were charged more compared with customers picking up their cars late in the day or at less busy times. Customers were required to bring a printed copy of their contract, along with the credit card they used to make the booking and identification. Given the low staffing levels, customers occasionally had to wait 30 minutes or more to be processed and receive their vehicles, particularly at peak times of the day. Processing a customer began with the employee accessing the customer's contract online. If the customer was a new easyCar customer to the site, the basic policies and possible additional charges were briefly explained. The employee then made copies of the customer's identification and credit card and took a digital photo of the customer. Customers were charged an €80 refundable deposit, signed the contract, and were on their way.

All vehicles were rented with more or less empty fuel tanks; the exact level depended on how much gasoline was left in the vehicle when the previous renter returned it. Customers were provided with a small map of the immediate area around the rental site, showing the location and hours of nearby gas stations. Customers could return vehicles with any amount of gas in them as long as the low-fuel indicator light in the vehicle was not on. Customers who returned vehicles with the low-fuel indicator light on were charged a fueling fee of €16.

Customers were also expected to return the vehicle within a prearranged one-hour time period, which they also selected at the time of booking. While customers did not have to worry about refueling the car before returning it, they were expected to clean the car thoroughly. This clean-car policy had been implemented in May 2002 to reduce the price customers could pay for their vehicle. Prior to this change, all customers paid a fixed preparation fee of €11 each time they rented a vehicle (up from the €8 preparation fee when the company started operations in 2000). The new policy reduced this upfront preparation fee to €4 but required customers to either return the vehicle clean or pay an additional cleaning fee of €16. To avoid any misunderstanding about what it meant by a clean car, easyCar provided customers with an explicit description of what constituted a clean car, both for the interior and the exterior of the car. This description included the appearance that the exterior of the car had been washed prior to returning the vehicle. The map that customers were provided when they picked up their cars that showed nearby gas stations also showed nearby car washes, where they could clean the car before returning it. Although easyCar had received some bad press in relation to the policy,[22] 85 percent of customers returned their vehicles clean as a result of the policy.

When a customer returned the vehicle, an easyCar employee would check to make sure that the vehicle was clean and undamaged and that the low-fuel indicator light was not on. The employee would also check the kilometers driven. The customer would then be notified of any additional charges. These charges would be subtracted from the €80 deposit and the difference refunded to the customer's credit card (or, if additional charges exceeded the €80 deposit, the customer's credit card would be charged the difference).

PRICING

EasyCar clearly differentiated itself from its competitors with its low price. In addition, pricing played a key role in easyCar's efforts to achieve high utilization of its fleet of cars. EasyCar advertised prices as low as €5 per day plus a per-rental preparation fee of €4. Prices, however, varied by the location and dates of the rental, by when the booking was made, and by what time the car was to be picked up and returned. EasyCar's systems constantly evaluated projected demand and expected utilization at each site and adjusted prices accordingly. Achieving the €5 per day rate usually required customers to book well in advance, and these rates were typically available only on weekdays. Weekend rates, when booked well in advance, typically started a few euros higher than the weekday rates. As a given rental date approached, however, the price typically went up significantly as easyCar approached 100 percent fleet utilization for that day. Rates could literally triple overnight if there was sufficient booking activity. Generally, however, easyCar's price was less than half that of its major competitors. EasyCar, unlike most other rental car companies, required customers to pay in full at the time of booking, and once a booking was made, it was nonrefundable.

EasyCar's base price covered only the core rental of the vehicle—the total price customers paid was in many cases much higher and depended on how the customer reserved, paid for, used, and returned the vehicle. EasyCar's price was based on customers booking through the company's Web site and paying for their rental with their easyMoney credit card. EasyMoney was the easyGroup's credit and financial services company. Customers who chose to book through the company's phone reservation system were charged an additional €0.95 each minute for the call, and those who used other credit cards were charged €5 extra. All vehicles had to be paid for by a credit or debit card—cash was not accepted. The base rental price allowed customers to drive vehicles 100 kilometers per day; additional kilometers were charged at a rate of €0.12 per kilometer. In addition, customers were expected to return their cars clean and on time. Customers who returned cars that did not meet easyCar's standards for cleanliness were charged a €16 cleaning fee. Those who returned their cars late were immediately charged €120 and subsequently charged an additional €120 for each subsequent 24-hour period in which the car was not returned. EasyCar explained the high late fee as representing the cost that it would likely incur in providing another vehicle to the next customer. Customers wishing to make any changes to their bookings were also charged a change fee of €16. Changes could be made either before the rental started or during the rental period but were limited to changing the dates, times, and location of the rental and subject to the prices and vehicle availability at the time the change was being made. If the change resulted in an overall lower price for the rental, however, no refund was provided for the difference.

Beginning in 2003, all customers were also required to purchase loss-damage insurance for an additional charge of €4 each day, which eliminated the customer's liability for loss or damage to the vehicle (excluding damage to the tires or windshield of the vehicle). Through 2002, customers were able to choose whether or not to purchase additional insurance from easyCar to eliminate any financial liability in the event that the rental vehicle was damaged. The cost of this insurance had been €6 per day, and approximately 60 percent of easyCar's customers purchased this

---

[22]J. Hyde, "Travel View: Clearing Up on the Extras," *The Observer (UK)*, July 7, 2002.

optional insurance. Those not purchasing this insurance had either assumed the liability for the first €800 in damages personally or had their own insurance through some other means (e.g., some credit card companies provide this insurance to cardholders at no additional charge for short-term rentals paid for with the credit card).

EasyCar's Web site attempted to make all of these additional charges clear to customers at the time of their booking. EasyCar had received a fair amount of bad press when it first opened for business after many renters complained about having to pay undisclosed charges when they returned their cars.[23] In response, easyCar had revamped its Web site in an effort to make these charges more transparent to customers and to explain the logic behind many of these charges.

PROMOTION

EasyCar's promotional efforts had, through 2002, focused primarily on posters and press advertising. Posters were particularly prevalent in metro systems and bus and train stations in cities where easyCar had operations. All of this advertising focused on easyCar's low price. According to founder Stelios: "You will never see an advert for an easy company offering an experience—it's about price. If you create expectations you can't live up to then you will ultimately suffer as a result."[24] In 2002, easyCar spent £1.43 million on such advertising.[25]

EasyCar also promoted itself by displaying its name, phone number, and Web site address prominently on the doors and rear window of its entire fleet of vehicles, and it took advantage of free publicity when the opportunity presented itself. An example of seeking out such publicity occurred when Hertz complained that easyCar's comparative advertising campaign in the Netherlands, featuring the line "The best reason to use easyCar.com can be found at hertz.nl," violated Dutch law that required comparative advertising to be exact, not general. In response, Stelios and a group of easyCar employees, dressed in orange boiler suits and with a fleet of easyCar vehicles, protested outside the Hertz Amsterdam office with signs asking "What is Hertz frightened of?"[26]

In an effort to help reach its goal of quadrupling sales in the next two years, easyCar hired Jennifer Mowat into the new position of commercial director to take over responsibility for easyCar's European marketing. Mowat had previously been eBay's U.K. country manager and had recently completed an MBA in Switzerland. Previously, Stelios and easyCar's managing director, Andrew Fitzmaurice, had handled the marketing function themselves.[27] As part of this stepped-up marketing effort, easyCar also planned to double its advertising budget for 2003, to £3 million, and to begin to advertise on television. The television advertising campaign was to feature easyCar's founder, Stelios.[28]

LEGAL CHALLENGES

EasyCar faced several challenges to its approaches. The most significant dealt with a November 2002 ruling made by the Office of Fair Trading (OFT) that easyCar had to grant customers seven days from the time they made a booking to cancel their booking and receive a full refund. The OFT, a U.K. governmental agency, is responsible for protecting U.K. consumers from unfair and/or anticompetitive business practices. The ruling against easyCar was based on the 2000 Consumer Protection Distance Selling Regulations. These regulations stipulated that companies that sell at a distance (e.g., by Internet or phone) must provide customers with a seven-day cooling-off period, during which customers can cancel their contracts with the company and receive a full refund. The law exempted accommodation, transportation, catering, and leisure service companies from this requirement. The OFT's ruling concluded that easyCar did not qualify as a transportation service company because consumers had to drive themselves and thus were receiving not a transport service, but just a car.[29]

EasyCar appealed the OFT's decision to the U.K. High Court on the grounds that it was indeed a transportation service company and was entitled to an exemption from this requirement. EasyCar was hopeful that it would eventually win this legal challenge. EasyCar had argued that this ruling would destroy the company's book-early–pay-less philosophy and could lead to a tripling of prices.[30] Chairman Stelios said, "It is very serious. My fear is that as soon as we put in the seven-day cooling off periods our utilization rate will fall from 90% to 65%. That's the difference between a profitable company and an unprofitable one."[31] EasyCar was also concerned that prolonged legal action on this point could interfere with its plans for a 2004 IPO.

For its part, OFT had also applied to the U.K. High Court for an injunction to make the company comply with the ruling. Other rental car companies were generally unconcerned about the ruling, as few offered big discounts for early bookings or nonrefundable bookings.[32]

EasyCar's new policy of posting the pictures of customers whose cars were 15 days or more overdue was also drawing legal criticism. EasyCar had recently received public warnings from lawyers that this new policy might violate data protection, libel, privacy, confidentiality, and human rights laws.[33] Of particular concern to some lawyers was the possibility that easyCar might post the wrong person's picture, given the large number of customers with whom the company dealt.[34] Such a mistake could open the company to costly libel suits. The policy of posting the pictures of overdue customers on the easyCar Web site, initiated in November 2002, was designed to reduce the losses associated with customers renting a vehicle and never returning it. The costs were significant, according to Stelios: "These cars are expensive,

---

[23]J. Stanton, "The Empire That's Easy Money," *Edinburgh Evening News*, November 26, 2002.

[24]"The Big Picture."

[25]"Marketing Week: EasyCar Appoints Head of European Marketing."

[26]EasyCar.com Web site news release, April 22, 2002.

[27]"Marketing Week: EasyCar Appoints Head of European Marketing."

[28]"Campaigning: EasyGroup Appoints Publicist for easyCar TV Advertising Brief," *Financial Times Information Limited*, January 31, 2003.

[29]J. Macintosh, "EasyCar Sues OFT Amid Threat to Planned Flotation," *Financial Times*, November 22, 2002, p. 4.

[30]"Marketing Week: EasyCar Appoints Head of European Marketing."

[31]Mackintosh.

[32]Ibid.

[33]B. Sherwood and A. Wendlandt, "EasyCar May Be in Difficulty over Naming Ploy," *Financial Times*, November 14, 2002, p. 2.

[34]Ibid.

£15,000 each, and we have 6000 of them. At any given time we are looking for as many as several tens which are overdue. If we don't get one back, it's a write-off. We are writing off an entire car, and its uninsurable."[35]

Stelios was also convinced of the legality of the new policy. In a letter to the editor responding to the legal concerns raised in the press, Stelios wrote:

> From a legal perspective, we have been entirely factual and objective and are merely reporting the details of the overdue car and the person who collected it. In addition, our policy is made very clear in our terms and conditions and the photo is taken both overtly and with the consent of the customer. . . . I estimate the total cost of overdue cars to be 5% of total easyCar costs, or 50p on every car rental day for all customers. In 2004, when I intend to float easyCar, this cost will amount to £5 million unless we can reduce our quantity of overdue cars.[36]

In the past, easyCar had simply provided pictures to police when a rental was 15 or more days overdue. The company hoped that posting the picture would both discourage drivers from not returning vehicles and shame those drivers who currently had overdue cars into returning them. In fact, the first person who easyCar posted to its Web site did return his car two days later. The vehicle was 29 days late.[37]

THE FUTURE

At the end of 2002, Stelios had stepped down as the CEO of easy-Jet so that he could devote more of his time to the other easyGroup companies, including easyCar. He had three priorities for the new year. One was to turn around the money-losing easyInternetCafe business, which Stelios had described as "the worst mistake of my career."[38] The 22-store chain had lost £80 million in the last two years. A second was to oversee the planned launch of another new easyGroup business, easyCinema, in the spring of 2003. And the third was to oversee the rapid expansion of the easyCar chain so that it would be ready for an initial public offering.

QUESTIONS

1. What are the characteristics of the car rental industry? How do these characteristics influence the design of service delivery processes in this industry in general?

2. EasyCar obviously competes on the basis of low price. What does it do in operations to support this strategy?

3. How would you characterize the level of quality that easyCar provides?

4. Is easyCar a viable competitor to taxis, buses, and trains, as Stelios claims? How does the design of its operations currently support this form of competition? How not?

5. What are the operational implications of the changes made by easyCar.com in the last year?

6. How significant are the legal challenges that easyCar is facing?

7. What is your assessment of the likelihood that easyCar will be able to realize its goals?

Source: This case was written by John J. Lawrence (University of Idaho) and Luis Solis (Instituto de Empresa) and used with their permission.

---

[35] "e-business: Internet Fraudsters Fail to Steal Potter Movie's Magic & Other News," *Financial Times Information Limited*, November 19, 2002.

[36] S. Haji-Ioannou, "Letters to the Editor: Costly Effect of Late Car Return," *Financial Times*, November 16, 2002, p. 10.

[37] M. Hookham, "How Stelios Nets Return of His Cars," *Liverpool (UK) Daily Post*, November 14, 2002.

[38] S. Bentley, "The Worst Mistake of My Career, by Stelios," *Financial Times*, December 24, 2002.

CASE 3—4 Marketing to the Bottom of the Pyramid

Professor C. K. Prahalad's seminal publication, *The Fortune at the Bottom of the Pyramid*, suggests an enormous market at the "bottom of the pyramid" (BOP)—a group of some 4 billion people who subsist on less than $2 a day. By some estimates, these "aspirational poor," who make up three-fourths of the world's population, represent $14 trillion in purchasing power, more than Germany, the United Kingdom, Italy, France, and Japan put together. Demographically, it is young and growing at 6 percent a year or more.

Traditionally, the poor have not been considered an important market segment. "The poor can't afford most products"; "they will not accept new technologies"; and "except for the most basic products, they have little or no use for most products sold to higher income market segments"—these are some of the assumptions that have, until recently, caused most multinational firms to pay little or no attention to those at the bottom of the pyramid. Typical market analysis is limited to urban areas, thereby ignoring rural villages where, in markets like India, the majority of the population lives. However, as major markets become more competitive and in some cases saturated—with the resulting ever-thinning profit margins—marketing to the bottom of the pyramid may have real potential and be worthy of exploration.

One researcher suggested that American and European businesses should go back and look at their own roots. Sears, Roebuck was created to serve the lower-income, sparsely settled rural market. Singer sewing machines fashioned a scheme to make consumption possible by allowing customers to pay $5 a month instead of $100 at once. The world's largest company today, Wal-Mart, was created to serve the lower-income market. Here are a few examples of multinational company efforts to overcome the challenges in marketing to the BOP.

Designing products for the BOP is not about making cheap stuff but about making technologically advanced products affordable. For example, one company was inspired to invent the Freeplay, a windup self-power–generating radio, when it learned that isolated, impoverished people in South Africa were not getting information about AIDS because they had no electricity for radios and could not afford replacement batteries.

BOP MARKETING REQUIRES ADVANCED TECHNOLOGY

The BOP market has a need for advanced technology, but to be usable, infrastructure support must often accompany the technology. For example, ITC, a $2.6 billion a year Indian conglomerate, decided to create a network of PC kiosks in villages. For years, ITC conducted its business with farmers through a maze of intermediaries, from brokers to traders. The company wanted farmers to be able to connect directly to information sources to check ITC's offer price for produce, as well as prices in the closest village market, in the state capital, and on the Chicago commodities exchange. With direct access to information, farmers got the best price for their product, hordes of intermediaries were bypassed, and ITC gained a direct contact with the farmers, thus improving the efficiency of ITC's soybean acquisition. To achieve this goal, it had to do much

more than just distribute PCs. It had to provide equipment for managing power outages, solar panels for extra electricity, and a satellite-based telephone hookup, and it had to train farmers to use the PCs. Without these steps, the PCs would never have worked. The complex solution serves ITC very well. Now more than 10,000 villages and more than 1 million farmers are covered by its system. ITC is able to pay more to farmers and at the same time cut its costs because it has dramatically reduced the inefficiencies in logistics.

The vast market for cell phones among those at the BOP is not for phones costing $200 or even $100 but for phones costing less than $50. Such a phone cannot simply be a cut-down version of an existing handset. It must be very reliable and have lots of battery capacity, as it will be used by people who do not have reliable access to electricity. Motorola went thorough four redesigns to develop a low-cost cell phone with battery life as long as 500 hours for villagers without regular electricity and an extra-loud volume for use in noisy markets. Motorola's low-cost phone, a no-frills cell phone priced at $40, has a standby time of two weeks and conforms to local languages and customs. The cell-phone manufacturer says it expects to sell 6 million cell phones in six months in markets including China, India, and Turkey.

BOP MARKETING REQUIRES CREATIVE FINANCING

There is also demand for personal computers but again, at very low prices. To meet the needs of this market, Advanced Micro Devices markets a $185 Personal Internet communicator—a basic computer for developing countries—and a Taiwan Company offers a similar device costing just $100.

For most products, demand is contingent on the customer having sufficient purchasing power. Companies have to devise creative ways to assist those at the BOP to finance larger purchases. For example, Cemex, the world's third-largest cement company, recognized an opportunity for profit by enabling lower-income Mexicans to build their own homes. The company's *Patrimonio Hoy Programme*, a combination builder's "club" and financing plan that targets homeowners who make less than $5 a day, markets building kits using its premium-grade cement. It recruited 510 promoters to persuade new customers to commit to building additions to their homes. The customers paid Cemex $11.50 a week and received building materials every 10 weeks until the room was finished (about 70 weeks—customers were on their own for the actual building). Although poor, 99.6 percent of the 150,000 *Patrimonio Hoy* participants have paid their bills in full. *Patrimonio Hoy* attracted 42,000 new customers and is expected to turn a $1.5 million profit in 2005.

One customer, Diega Chavero, thought the scheme was a scam when she first heard of it, but after eight years of being unable to save enough to expand the one-room home where her family of six lived, she was willing to try anything. Four years later, she has five bedrooms. "Now I have a palace."

Another deterrent to the development of small enterprises at the BOP is available sources of adequate financing for microdistributors and budding entrepreneurs. For years, those at the bottom of the pyramid needing loans in India had to depend on local money-lenders, at interest rates up to 500 percent a year. ICICI Bank, the second-largest banking institution in India, saw these people as a potential market and critical to its future. To convert them into customers in a cost-effective way, ICICI turned to village self-help groups.

ICICI Bank met with microfinance-aid groups working with the poor and decided to give them capital to start making small loans to the poor—at rates that run from 10 percent to 30 percent. This sounds usurious, but it is lower than the 10 percent daily rate that some Indian loan sharks charge. Each group was composed of 20 women who were taught about saving, borrowing, investing, and so on. Each woman contributes to a joint savings account with the other members, and based on the self-help group's track record of savings, the bank then lends money to the group, which in turn lends money to its individual members. ICICI has developed 10,000 of these groups reaching 200,000 women. ICICI's money has helped 1 million households get loans that average $120 to $140. The bank's executive directory says the venture has been "very profitable." ICICI is working with local communities and NGOs to enlarge its reach.

BOP MARKETING REQUIRES EFFECTIVE DISTRIBUTION

When Unilever saw that dozens of agencies were lending micro-credit loans funds to poor women all over India, it thought that these would-be microentrepreneurs needed businesses to run. Unilever realized it could not sell to the bottom of the pyramid unless it found low-cost ways to distribute its product, so it created a network of hundreds of thousands of *Shakti Amma* ("empowered mothers") who sell Lever's products in their villages through an Indian version of Tupperware parties. Start-up loans enabled the women to buy stocks of goods to sell to local villagers. In one case, a woman who received a small loan was able to repay her start-up loan and has not needed to take another one. She now sells regularly to about 50 homes and even serves as a miniwholesaler, stocking tiny shops in outlying villages a short bus ride from her own. She sells about 10,000 rupees ($230) of goods each month, keeps about $26 profit, and ploughs the rest back into new stock. While the $26 a month she earns is less than the average $40 monthly income in the area, she now has income, whereas before she had nothing.

Today about 1,300 poor women are selling Unilever's products in 50,000 villages in 12 states in India and account for about 15 percent of the company's rural sales in those states. Overall, rural markets account for about 30 percent of the company's revenue.

In another example, Nguyen Van Hon operates a floating sundries distributorship along the Ke Sat River in Vietnam's Mekong Delta—a maze of rivers and canals dotted with villages. His boat is filled with boxes containing small bars of Lifebuoy soap and single-use sachets of Sunsilk shampoo and Omo laundry detergent, which he sells to riverside shopkeepers for as little as 2.5 cents each. At his first stop he makes deliveries to a half dozen small shops. He sells hundred of thousands of soap and shampoo packets a month, enough to earn about $125—five times his previous monthly salary as a junior Communist party official. "It's a hard life, but its getting better." Now, he "has enough to pay his daughter's schools fees and soon . . . will have saved enough to buy a bigger boat, so I can sell to more villages." Because of aggressive

efforts to reach remote parts of the country through an extensive network of more than 100,000 independent sales representatives such as Hon, the Vietnam subsidiary of Unilever realized a 23 percent increase in sales in 2004 to more than $300 million.

BOP MARKETING REQUIRES AFFORDABLE PACKAGING

As one observer noted, "the poor cannot be Wal-Martized." Consumers in rich nations use money to stockpile convenience. We go to Sam's Club, Costco, K-Mart, and so on, to get bargain prices and the convenience of buying shampoos and paper towels by the case. Selling to the poor requires just the opposite approach. They do not have the cash to stockpile convenience, and they do not mind frequent trips to the village store. Products have to be made available locally and in affordable units; fully 60 percent of the value of all shampoo sold in India is in single-serve packets.

Nestlé is targeting China with a blitz of 29 new ice cream brands, many selling for as little as 12 cents with take-home and multipack products ranging from 72 cents to $2.30. It also features products specially designed for local tastes and preferences of Chinese consumers, such as Nestlé Snow Moji, a rice pastry filled with vanilla ice cream that resembles dim sum, and other ice cream flavors like red bean and green tea. The ice cream products are distributed through a group of small independent saleswomen, which the company aims to expand to 4,000 women by 2006. The project is expected to account for as much as 24 percent of the company's total rural sales within the next few years.

BOP MARKETING CREATES HEALTH BENEFITS

Albeit a promotion to sell products, marketing to BOP does help improve personal hygiene. The World Health Organization (WHO) estimates that diarrhea-related diseases kill 1.8 million people a year and noted that better hand-washing habits—using soap—is one way to prevent their spread. In response to WHO urging, Hindustan Lever Company introduced a campaign called "Swasthya Chetna" or "Glowing Health," which argues that even clean-looking hands may carry dangerous germs, so use more soap. It began a concentrated effort to take this message into the tens of thousands of villages where the rural poor reside, often with little access to media.

"Lifebuoy teams visit each village several times," using a "Glo Germ" kit to show schoolchildren that soap-washed hands are cleaner. This program has reached "around 80 million rural folk," and sales of Lifebuoy in small affordable sizes have risen sharply. The small bar has become the brand's top seller.

QUESTIONS

1. As a junior member of your company's committee to explore new markets, you have received a memo from the chairperson telling you to be prepared at the next meeting to discuss key questions that need to be addressed if the company decides to look further into the possibility of marketing to the BOP segment. The ultimate goal of this meeting will be to establish a set of general guidelines to use in developing a market strategy for any one of the company's products to be marketed to the "aspirational poor." These guidelines need not be company or product specific at this time. In fact, think of the

final guideline as a checklist—a series of questions that a company could use as a start in evaluating the potential of a specific BOP market segment for one of its products.

2. Marketing to the BOP raises a number of issues revolving around the social responsibility of marketing efforts. Write a position paper either pro or con on one of the following:

   a. Is it exploitation for a company to profit from selling soaps, shampoo, personal computers, and ice cream, and so on, to people with little disposable income?

   b. Can making loans to customers whose income is less than $100 monthly at interest rates of 20 percent to purchase TVs, cell phones, and other consumer durables be justified?

   c. One authority argues that squeezing profits from people with little disposable income—and often not enough to eat—is not capitalist exploitation but rather that it stimulates economic growth.

Sources: C. K. Prahalad, *The Fortune at the Bottom of the Pyramid* (Philadelphia: Wharton School Publishing, 2004); Stefan Stern, "How Serving the Poorest Can Bring Rich Rewards," *Management Today,* August 2004; Kay Johnson and Xa Nhon, "Selling to the Poor: There Is a Surprisingly Lucrative Market in Targeting Low-Income Consumers," *Time*, April 25, 2005; Cris Prystay, "India's Small Loans Yield Big Markets," *Asian Wall Street Journal,* May 25, 2005; C. K. Prahalad, "Why Selling to the Poor Makes for Good Business," *Fortune,* November 15, 2004; Alison Maitland, "A New Frontier in Responsibility," *Financial Times,* November 29, 2004; Normandy Madden, "Nestlé Hits Mainland with Cheap Ice Cream," *Advertising Age,* March 7, 2005; Ritesh Gupta, "Rural Consumers Get Closer to Established World Brands," *Ad Age Global,* June 2002; Alison Overholt, "A New Path to Profit," *Fast Company,* January 1, 2005; Patrick Whitney, "Designing for the Base of the Pyramid," *Design Management Review,* Fall 2004; C. K. Prahalad and Stuart Hart, "Fortune at the Bottom of the Pyramid," *Strategy & Business* 26 (2002); C. K. Prahalad and Aline Hammond, "Serving the World's Poor, Profitably," *Harvard Business Review,* September 2002; "The Invisible Market," *Across the Board,* September/October 2004; Anuradha Mittal and Lori Wallach, "Selling Out the Poor," *Foreign Policy,* September/October 2004; G. Pascal Zachary, "Poor Idea," *New Republic,* March 7, 2005; "Calling an End to Poverty," *The Economist,* July 9, 2005; Susanna Howard, "P&G, Unilever Court the World's Poor," *The Wall Street Journal,* June 1, 2005; Rajiv Banerjee and N. Shatrujeet, "Shoot to the Heart," *Economic Times,* July 6, 2005; David Ignatius, "Pennies from the Poor Add Up to Fortune," *Korea Herald,* July 7, 2005; Rebecca Buckman, "Cell Phone Game Rings in New Niche: Ultra Cheap," *The Wall Street Journal,* August 18, 2005, p. B4; "It's Good Business, but a Strategy that Saves Lives as Well," *The Boston Globe,* June 10, 2007; "Global Executive: See the Poor as Entrepreneurs, Consumers," *Star Tribune* (Minneapolis, MN, July 30, 2007; "The Right Package; It Started With Shampoo but Now Sachets Have Overtaken Shop Shelves," *India Today,* December 31, 2007; "The Fortune at the Bottom of the Pyramid: Eradicating Poverty Through Profits," *South Asian Journal of Management,* April 1, 2007; "The Legacy that Got Left on the Shelf–Unilever and Emerging Markets," *The Economist,* February 2, 2008.

cases 4

DEVELOPING GLOBAL MARKETING STRATEGIES

OUTLINE OF CASES

CASE 4-1   McDonald's Great Britain—The Turnaround

New menus, improved service, advertising, opening new stores, closing others, and refurbishing others have propelled McDonald's U.S. back into an active growth cycle after experiencing a slack period in 2003 and 2004—U.S. sales climbed for 24 straight months. Sales in Great Britain did not show a similar movement. Sales at McDonald's 1,235 British outlets had been sluggish for years, and the reasons were numerous. New chains such as Yo! Sushi and Nando's Chicken Restaurants, which features spicy Portuguese chicken, have outpaced McDonald's. Operators such as U.S.-based Subway Restaurants are pulling in customers with fresh salads and sandwiches on focaccia bread. Starbucks has made McDonald's outlets look sterile and out of date. And the 2001 scare over mad cow disease, along with concerns about rising obesity, made things worse.

In part because of lackluster performance in Great Britain, McDonald's European operations—the second biggest market after America, responsible for about 30 percent of profits, have suffered. In 2005, European sales fell 0.7 percent, while U.S. sales grew 4.7 percent. Furthermore, same-store sales for European restaurants open more than a year registered a 3 percent decline.

To give you a flavor of what McDonald's U.K. faces, here are some observations about McDonald's Britain.

COMMENTS FROM VARIOUS NEWS SOURCES

- A 24-year-old advertising sales representative in West London commented, "The McDonald's near where I work is really smart, with Internet access and everything, but I only go in there as a last resort."

- "Twenty-three years ago, or thereabouts, I had my first McDonald's. I was studying at Cambridge and a group of us drove to London to watch a football match. We stopped off at McDonald's in the Strand and I experienced the joys of a Big Mac with fries, to go. It felt like the height of cool. I was from Cumbria, and McDonald's, which came to this country only in 1974, hadn't yet penetrated that far north. My friends were Londoners, hip, dead trendy. They had cars at university, they drove to see the capital's smarter teams, and they ate at McDonald's.

    "Recently, I popped into the same outlet in Strand and clearly, it's not just fashion that shifts: my taste buds have altered too—either that or after two or three pints at a football ground, anything seems delicious. Eschewing the option—as most of its customers do—to go healthy and order a salad, I went for a traditional double cheeseburger. The burger bun tasted like cotton or wool, the beef in the burger patty lacked texture. It was manufactured, processed and quick."

Some opine that like all empires, McDonald's has had its day and is now on the slippery slope to oblivion. McDonald's could go the way of Howard Johnson's, another restaurant chain that once covered America but now has all but disappeared.

Everything has been hurled at the company, from fears about contracting mad cow disease to two teenage girls suing the company for making them fat to a savagely critical best-selling book, *Fast Food Nation* (which revealed, among other things, that the beef in McDonald's patties can come from up to 100 different cows), and a hit film, *Super Size Me* (whose maker, Morgan Spurlock, did nothing except eat at McDonald's for a month with disastrous effects to his health, turning his liver into something approaching pâté). The result: Profits fell, earnings per share were down, and the firm famous for its expansion was forced to close restaurants.

A recently released documentary, called *McLibel,* reopened old wounds for McDonald's. *McLibel* recounts the story behind a decade-long court battle—the longest in British history—that pitted McDonald's against two Greenpeace activists whom the company accused of libel. In 1994, McDonald's sued five London-based Greenpeace activists after they distributed leaflets that asked, "What's Wrong with McDonald's?" Three pulled out, but two fought the chain. After initially being ordered to pay damages, the two appealed twice, then took their complaint to the U.K.'s Court of Human Rights, claiming that a lack of access to legal aid hurt their right to a fair trail. The court sided with the activists, giving the government three months to appeal. At the time of the decision, McDonald's said the world has moved on since then, and so has McDonald's.

There are some positives for McDonald's U.K. For all its perceived problems, McDonald's profits are £118 million a year. Nearly 3 million people visit its British branches every day, and among teenagers, McDonald's is still the number one food brand.

The company monitors news articles and television references to McDonald's in Britain, rating them "negative," "neutral," or "positive." In 2004, most reports were negative, but in 2005, opinion had moved to pretty much neutral ground.

STEPS TAKEN TO REVERSE THE TREND

- McDonald's has rolled out new offerings, including salads, yogurt, and other fare aimed at health-conscious diners. To develop new recipes, the company has opened a test kitchen in Europe. It is also planning facelifts for many of its 6,200 European outlets.

- McDonald's temporarily dropped its globally recognized Golden Arches logo in ads in the United Kingdom in an attempt to change customers' perception and emphasize a new "healthy menu." The two-week campaign, called "Change," carried the tag line: "McDonald's—But not as you know it." The ads show healthy meals such as fruits and salads.

- The Big Tasty, a burger on an oversized bun introduced last year, is selling well, the company says.

- In April 2004, a Salads Plus menu, which features four varieties of main-course salads topped with warm chicken, a premium chicken sandwich, and a fruit-and-yogurt dessert, was introduced in Britain.

- In response to demands for more nutritional information on McDonald's menu, tray liners were used to convey dietary information. At the top of the tray liner is an appeal for RMCC (Ronald McDonald Children's Charities), and on the flip side is a detailed breakdown of nutritional and allergy information. Every item available in a McDonald's is listed, from the obvious—a Big Mac at 493 calories, 22.9 grams of fat, and 5.9 grams of fiber—to the less obvious—mineral water comprises no nuts, no seafood, no gluten, and no egg and is suitable for vegetarians. No other restaurant chain goes in for this analytical overload. One observer's reaction to the nutritional detail was less than positive: "The amount of detail is mind-boggling, and disturbing. You come in for a fast burger and fries, knowing they aren't the healthiest foods on the planet, and you're assailed with a battery of facts and figures that merely confirm what you already know."

- McDonald's feels itself under siege from diet campaigners and food experts as well as competitors pushing "healthy" salads and even bread-free sandwiches. To some it seems that McDonald's has adopted a defensive posture, even though it is still the second best-known brand in the world, behind only Coca-Cola.

- Aiming to boost its popularity among women, McDonald's launched an ad program in April 2005 featuring the performers Destiny's Child. The campaign features its Salads Plus menu with the addition of chicken salad with pasta, which includes roast peppers, basil, and cherry tomatoes. A low-fat, grilled-chicken Caesar flatbread will replace the grilled chicken flatbread item launched six months earlier. The company has also replaced its dressing on its Salad Plus, which was criticized for its fat content, with lower-calorie, lower-fat versions.

- In response to the rise of coffee shops, McDonald's is serving coffee made from freshly ground Kenco beans. Since the restaurants started grinding beans, the response has been phenomenal. The same goes for the salads and fruit now offered. Ten percent of its profit mix is from salads, and 10 million fruit bags were sold in the first year after introduction.

COMMENTS OF A NEWLY APPOINTED CEO OF MCDONALD'S U.K.

We're not innovating the way we used to, we're not leading the way we used to. The world is changing—our customers tell us they're changing and we've not been changing.

- We will upgrade the McDonald's experience and give more value to the customer.

- We've slipped. In the area of service, it has become spartan and inconsistent. Our cleanliness didn't just used to be good, it used to be great. We need to get back to basics. The first part of back to basics is giving the customers the choice they want. The second is making sure service and cleanliness are great. I'm finding out what's important, and I'm reacting to it.

- We're the innovators, we're the leaders. Our customers are outspoken and they criticize. My job is to understand the problem and to lead. If we can get this right, our customers will reward us. We took our eye off the ball. Our customers

have been changing, and we haven't noticed. In the last four or five years, a raft of companies have come to the marketplace that have done a better job of identifying those changing tastes.

- I want McDonald's to be the U.K.'s breakfast restaurant. Households have been blitzed with new menus, including toasted bagels and toast, and sampling deals. I want people to try it, to compare us. Breakfast is a huge opportunity for us. We can use our drive-thru to offer lattes and toasted bagels to people on their way to work.

- One immediate task is to assuage the franchisees and owner-operators. If our performance is flat, they're flat. My philosophy is that we're like a three-legged stool—staff, suppliers, and owner-operators.

Does he eat at McDonald's? Not every day, but three times a week. His favorite—the double cheeseburger.

BY 2007, LIGHT AT THE END OF THE TUNNEL

After five consecutive years of sales decreases, McDonald's was selling more burgers than at any time since it arrived in Britain 34 years earlier. In 2007, sales were up 4.6 percent for the year, with a substantial increase in market share. Although still lagging the performance of other regions in the European division, the positive report seemed to signal that the steps taken by U.K. management were beginning to pay off. Menu changes, refurbishing and/or closing stores, opening new stores, and polishing the public image can all be attributed to the apparent turnaround. The most salient events follow:

- Menus were adjusted to include "healthy" choices, such as salads, fruit packets, and bottled water instead of only soft drinks for kid's meals. New items such as roast beef sandwiches, vegetable melts, onion rings with sweet chili dip, and even better coffee, including lattes, were introduced to appeal to a wider market. The burger offerings were not necessarily downplayed but were adjusted to include such seasonal items as a Bigger Big Mac, 40 percent bigger than the current Big Mac. The New Big Mac, launched for a limited period to coincide with the football World Cup, was designed to offer football (soccer) fans more of what they enjoy.

- Some felt that the nutritional value of a McDonald's meal seemed less important to its turnaround than the sheer diversity of options on the menu and the flexibility stores had in their offerings. Menus have changed more in the past three years than they did in the previous thirty, according to one source. McDonald's was seen as too much an American brand; it needed to become "more European" and more "locally relevant." A separate food factory in Munich dedicated to coming up with new menus for the different tastes in the 41 European countries where McDonald's operates was a move away from having the same menu in all its branches.

- A complete overhaul of two French stores with new designs for interiors and uniforms led to sales increases in excess of 4 percent compared with stores with traditional décor. Although considered radical at the time and not altogether consistent with McDonald's philosophy, the success of the refurbished stores resulted in a management decision to invest in the refurbishing throughout the European market, including the United Kingdom. A design studio in Paris was established to create nine different designs from which franchised restaurants could choose the design most appropriate for their location and clientele.

- The restructuring in Britain resulted in the closing of underperforming stores, new stores opened in upscale locations, and old stores refurbished. Bolted-down plastic yellow-and-white furniture got replaced with lime-green designer chairs and dark leather upholstery, modern lighting, and wireless Internet access, with rental iPods. This redecoration was the biggest revamp by the company in more than 20 years, ending a one-size-fits-all philosophy at its 1,220 U.K. outlets that had made them look decidedly dowdy. McDonald's kept its trademark Golden Arches logo but got rid of the red accompanying it. Instead, restaurants feature a warm burgundy color. The pointy roofs are being phased out and replaced by simple olive green facades, and the bright neon lights in the restaurants were dimmed.

- Compounding the problem of negative perceptions of the quality and healthiness of fast food was a negative attitude toward McDonald's as an employer. As one company executive said, "The British people don't respect those who work at McDonald's because they mix up service with being servile." Popular views of McDonald's paying bad wages to desperate teenagers led to the coining of the term "McJob" to describe someone working for low pay in a job with no future.

- To counter this negative image of McDonald's, an advertising campaign argued that a McJob is actually rather good. McDonald's says 80 percent of its managers began in the kitchens or serving counters, and half of them now earn £40,000 a year or more. Apart from specialized jobs like accountants and lawyers, every rung on the corporate ladder, from restaurant managers to chief executives, is filled by people who started out flipping burgers and mopping floors.

- The company was so worried about the use of "McJob" that it trademarked the word in 1992. As a result, the Oxford English Dictionary dropped "McJob," and Merriam-Webster, the best-selling English dictionary in the world, had to defend its definition of the word after a former McDonald's chief executive called it a "slap in the face" to the company.

- McDonald's U.K. vice president said: "The McJob campaign is not being done because we have difficulty attracting staff. It's all about tackling perceptions." The campaign is only the first step in a fight to transform the company's image.

- What looked like a disaster for McDonald's, with bad publicity created by movies such as *Super-Size Me* and books like *Fast Food Nation*, which attacked fast-food restaurants, and the worldwide concern about obesity may have proved the impetus for the rebirth of a lumbering superannuated giant that McDonald's had become.

QUESTIONS

1. Identify the problems confronting McDonald's U.K. and list them from the most to the least critical. For each problem identified, explain your reasoning.

2. Some problems you identified in Question 1 may require a "quick fix" in the short run, while others may require a major shift in company strategy. Assuming that you cannot focus on all the problems at once, suggest the order in which the issues should be addressed and suggest an approach to solving each problem.

3. By 2007, it seemed that the decisions made by McDonald's U.K. management had begun to pay off. However, McDonald's U.K. still lags behind the performance of other regions in the European division. Considering your responses to Questions 1 and 2, identify problems that may still exist and suggest actions to be taken.

Sources: Carol Matlack, Laura Cohn, and Michael Arndt, "Can McDonald's Get Cooking in Europe?" *BusinessWeek*, April 26, 2004; "Healthier Options Help McDonald's to Fatter Profits," *The Times* (London), October 14, 2004; "Film Revisits McD's Libel Suit in U.K.," *Advertising Age*, June 20, 2005; Katherine Griffiths, "McDonald's Sales Fall in Europe," *The Independent* (London), June 9, 2005; Chris Blackhurst, "Peter Beresford," *Management Today*, January 2005, p. 28; Mark Sweney, "McDonald's Unveils 8 Million Ads to Win Over Women," *Marketing (UK)*, April, 6, 2005; Eric Herman, "McDonald's Europe Chief Quits after Sales Slide," *Chicago Sun-Times*, June 8, 2005; Richard Gibson, "McDonald's Names New Head of Its European Operations," *The Wall Street Journal*, June 7, 2005; "McDonald's . . . Now With Ethical Sauce: Fast-Food Giant Takes on the Critics with Soft Lights, Comfy Sofas and the Promise of Great Career Prospects," *The Mail on Sunday* (London), April 23, 2006; "Chew On This" *Mail on Sunday* (London), April 23, 2006; "McDonald's to Refit UK Restaurants," *The Independent* (London), February 3, 2006; "Super Sizing McDonald's: How the Food Police Can Trigger a Company Turnaround," *The Grocer*, January 28, 2006; "McDonald's Health Drive Wins Back Customers," *The Independent* (London), January 18, 2007; "Burger Boss Gets a Grilling," *Evening Chronicle* (Newcastle, England), January 20, 2007; "American Instincts in a French Executive," *The New York Times*, August 25, 2007; "McDonald's Posts Robust Growth," *The New York Times*, December 11, 2007; "McDonald's Is Set to Expand Within the City," *Plymouth Evening Herald*, January 18, 2008.

CASE 4-2 Tambrands—Overcoming Cultural Resistance

Tampax, Tambrands's only product, is the best-selling tampon in the world, with 44 percent of the global market. North America and Europe account for 90 percent of those sales. Company earnings dropped 12 percent to $82.8 million on revenues of $662 million. Stakes are high for Tambrands because tampons are basically all it sells, and in the United States, which currently generates 45 percent of Tambrands' sales, the company is mired in competition with such rivals as Playtex Products and Kimberly-Clark. What's more, new users are hard to get because 70 percent of women already use tampons.

In the overseas market, Tambrands officials talk glowingly of a huge opportunity. Only 100 million of the 1.7 billion eligible women in the world currently use tampons. In planning for expansion into a global market, Tambrands divided the world into three clusters, based not on geography but on how resistant women are to using tampons. The goal is to market to each cluster in a similar way.

Most women in Cluster 1, including the United States, the United Kingdom, and Australia, already use tampons and may feel they know all they need to know about the product. In Cluster 2, which includes countries such as France, Israel, and South Africa, about 50 percent of women use tampons. Some concerns about virginity remain, and tampons are often considered unnatural products that block the flow. Tambrands enlists gynecologists' endorsements to stress scientific research on tampons. Potentially the most lucrative group—but infinitely more challenging—is Cluster 3, which includes countries like Brazil, China, and Russia. There, along with tackling the virginity issue, Tambrands must also tell women how to use a tampon without making them feel uneasy. While the advertising messages differ widely from country to country, Tambrands is also trying to create a more consistent image for its Tampax tampons. The ads in each country show consecutive shots of women standing outside declaring the tampon message, some clutching a blue box of Tampax. They end with the same tagline, "Tampax. Women Know." While marketing consultants say Tambrands' strategy is a step in the right direction, some caution that tampons are one of the most difficult products to market worldwide.

GLOBAL EXPANSION

"The greatest challenge in the global expansion of tampons is to address the religious and cultural mores that suggest that insertion is fundamentally prohibited by culture," says the managing director of a consulting company. "The third market [Cluster 3] looks like the great frontier of tampons, but it could be the seductive noose of the global expansion objective."

The company's new global campaign for Tambrands is a big shift from most feminine protection product ads, which often show frisky women dressed in white pants biking or turning cartwheels, while discreetly pushing messages of comfort. The new campaign features local women talking frankly about what had been a taboo subject in many countries. A recent Brazilian ad shows a close-up of a tampon while the narrator chirps, "It's sleek, smooth, and really comfortable to use."

For years Tambrands has faced a delicate hurdle selling Tampax tampons in Brazil because many young women fear they'll lose their virginity if they use a tampon. When they go to the beach in tiny bikinis, tampons aren't their choice. Instead, hordes of women use pads and gingerly wrap a sweater around their waist. Now, the number 1 tampon maker hopes a bold new ad campaign will help change the mindset of Brazilian women. "Of course, you're not going to lose your virginity," reassures one cheerful Brazilian woman in a new television ad. Tambrands's risky new ads are just part of a high-stakes campaign to expand into overseas markets where it has long faced cultural and religious sensitivities. The new ads feature local women being surprisingly blunt about such a personal product. In China, another challenging market for Tambrands, a new ad shows a Chinese woman inserting a tampon into a test tube filled with blue water. "No worries about leakage," declares another.

"In any country, there are boundaries of acceptable talk. We want to go just to the left of that," says the creative director of the New York advertising agency that is creating Tambrands's $65 million ad campaign worldwide. "We want them to think they have not heard frankness like this before." The agency planned to launch new Tampax ads in 26 foreign countries and the United States. However, being a single-product company, it is a risky proposition for Tambrands to engage in a global campaign and to build a global distribution network all at the same time. Tambrands concluded that the company could not continue to be profitable if its major market was the United States and that to launch a global marketing program was too risky to do alone.

PROCTER & GAMBLE ACQUIRES TAMBRANDS

The company approached Procter & Gamble about a buyout, and the two announced a $1.85 billion deal. The move puts P&G back in the tampon business for the first time since its Rely brand was pulled in 1980 after two dozen women who used tampons died from toxic shock syndrome. Procter & Gamble plans to sell Tampax as a complement to its existing feminine-hygiene products, particularly in Asia and Latin America. Known for its innovation in such mundane daily goods as disposable diapers and detergent, P&G has grown in recent years by acquiring products and marketing them internationally. "Becoming part of P&G—a world-class company with global marketing and distribution capabilities—will accelerate the global growth of Tampax and enable the brand to achieve its full potential. This will allow us to take the expertise we've gained in the feminine protection business and apply it to a new market with Tampax." Market analysts applauded the deal. "P&G has the worldwide distribution that Tampax so desperately needs," said a stock market analyst. "Tambrands didn't have the infrastructure to tap into growth in the developing countries and P&G does."

P&G CREATES A GLOBAL MODEL

Despite the early promise that Brazil seemed to offer with its beach culture and mostly urban population, P&G abandoned Tambrands's marketing efforts there as too expensive and slow-growing. Instead, it set out to build a marketing model that it could export to the rest of the globe. P&G began studying cities in Mexico and chose Monterrey, an industrial hub of 4 million people—with 1.2 million women as its target customers—as a prime test spot. Research and focus groups of Mexican women in Monterrey resulted in a new marketing approach based on education.

"Everywhere we go, women say 'this is not for senoritas,'" says Silvia Davila, P&G's marketing director for Tampax Latin America. They're using the Spanish word for unmarried women as a modest expression for young virgins. This concern crops up in countries that are predominantly Catholic, executives say. In Italy, for instance, just 4 percent of women use tampons. P&G is finding that in countries where school health education is limited, that concept is difficult to overcome. P&G marketers say they often find open boxes of tampons in stores—a sign, P&G says, that women were curious about the product but unsure as to how it worked.

Hanging out in blue jeans and tank tops and sipping Diet Pepsi on a recent afternoon, Sandra Trevino and her friends seem very much in tune with American culture. But the young women are getting a lesson in Trevino's living room on how to use a product that is commonplace in the United States—and is a mystery to them.

"We're giving you the opportunity to live differently 'those days' of the month," Karla Romero tells the group. She holds up a chart of the female body, then passes out samples to the 10 women. Tampons will bring freedom and discretion, Romero says. "For me, it's the best thing that ever happened." A few of the women giggle. Romero is on the front lines of a marketing campaign for one of the world's most in-the-closet products. Procter & Gamble Co. pays Romero to give a primer on tampons in gatherings that resemble Tupperware parties.

Romero and other counselors run through a slide show about the stages of puberty. She pours blue liquid through a stand-up model of a woman's reproductive tract so the girls can see what happens inside their bodies when they have their periods. They see the tampon absorb the blue fluid. Romero points to the hymen on the model and explains they won't lose their virginity with a tampon. Still, when Maria brought home a sample from another session a few months ago, "my mother said don't use them," she reported. While the 18-year-old can be rebellious—she wears a tiny tank top, heavy-blue eye shadow, and three gold studs in each ear—she shares her mother's doubts. "You can lose your virginity. The norm here is to marry as a virgin," she says.

In addition to in-home demonstrations, counselors in navy pantsuits or doctor's white coats embroidered with the Tampax logo speak in stores, schools, and gyms—anywhere women gather. One counselor met with 40 late-shift women workers in a cookie factory at midnight.

Counselors are taught to approach the subject in a dignified and sensitive manner. For example, they avoid using the word "tampon," which is too close to the Spanish word *tampone,* meaning plug. P&G calls its product an "internal absorbent" or simply Tampax.

Although tampons currently account for just 4 percent of the total Mexican market for feminine-protection products, early results indicate P&G's investment is paying off. Sales for Tampax tripled in the first 12 months after the new program was launched.

Based on the success in Mexico, P&G picked Venezuela to be its next market because it is relatively small—23 million people— and its population are mostly urban. P&G gathered women in Caracas for focus groups where they expressed some cultural similarities with their Mexican counterparts, emphasizing the sanctity of virginity. But the tropical weather fostered some promising

differences too. There's a party culture where women seem comfortable with their bodies in skimpy skirts and clingy pants.

This attitude led P&G marketers to conclude that Tampax advertising could be racier in Venezuela. One slogan, though, misfired. On a list of common misconceptions, headed by "will I lose my virginity?" P&G wrote, "La ignorancia es la madre de todo los mitos," which translates as "ignorance is the mother of all myths." Focus groups were offended: "In a Latin culture, ignorance and mother don't go together." The title was scrapped.

In the end, they unveiled ads like "Es Tiempo De Cambiar Las Reglas," for billboards, buses, and magazines. The company knows that Venezuelan women will catch the pun: "reglas" is the slang they use for their period, but the ad also translates as "It's time to change the rules."

GETTING THE MESSAGE ONLINE

P&G has always been an early and aggressive adopter of new media, dating back to radio and television. Continuing in this vein, Procter & Gamble is stepping up its Internet activity to use the Web as a marketing medium. P&G's idea is to attract consumers to interactive sites that will be of interest to particular target groups, with the hope of developing deeper relationships with consumers. Its first step was to launch a Web site for teenage girls with information on puberty and relationships, promoting products such as Clearasil, Sunny Delight, and Tampax. The Web site, www.beinggirl.com, was designed with the help of an advisory board of teenage girls.

This site has been expanded to include an online interactive community for teen girls between 14 and 19 years of age, which urges teenage girls to get the most out of life. The site includes a variety of subjects that interest teen girls, as well as an interactive game that lets girls pick from five available "effortless" boyfriends. Characters range from Mysterious and Arty to Sporty. The chosen boyfriend will send confidence-boosting messages and provide girls with a series of "Effortless Guides" to things like football. If the girl gets bored of her boyfriend, she can dump him using a variety of excuses, such as "It's not you, its me," and choose another. As one company source stated, "interactive Web sites have become the number one medium, and boys are the number one topic for teenage girls."

A feature of the site, "urban myths," discusses many of the concerns about the use of tampons and related products. Visit www.beinggirl.co.uk for the British market and www.beinggirl.co.in for a comparable site for India. Hindustan Lever has a similar campaign built around the Sunsilkgangofgirls community portal (www.sunsilkgangofgirls.com) for its products.

PUBLIC HEALTH FOR YOUNG GIRLS

In those markets where the Web is not readily available to the target market, a more direct and personal approach entails a health and education emphasis. The P&G brands Always and Tampax have joined forces with HERO, an awareness building and fund-raising initiative of the United Nations Association, to launch the "Protecting Futures" program (www.protectingfutures.com), designed to help give girls in Africa a better chance at an education.

Girls living in sub-Saharan Africa often miss up to four days of school each month because they lack the basic necessities of sanitary protection and other resources to manage their periods. According to research, 1 in 10 school-age African girls do not attend school during menstruation or drop out at puberty because of the lack of clean and private sanitation facilities in schools. If a girl has no access to protective materials or if the materials she has are unreliable and cause embarrassment, she may be forced to stay at home. This absence of approximately 4 days every four weeks may result in the girl missing 10 to 20 percent of her school days.

"Working with HERO, the Protecting Futures is a comprehensive care program which brings puberty education, a traveling healthcare provider for all the children at these schools, nutritious feeding programs, educational support services, a pad distribution program, and significant construction projects to add restrooms and upgrade the school buildings. Support for this program is part of the P&G corporate cause, Live, Learn, and Thrive which has helped over 50 million children in need."

In addition, Tampax and Always brands help sponsor the HERO Youth Ambassador program (www.beinggirl.com/hero) through their teen-focused Web site. Twenty-four teens from across the United States were selected to become Youth Ambassadors and travel to Namibia and South Africa to work on the Protecting Futures program. Their personal experiences were documented in a series of webisodes airing on beinggirl.com/hero to help encourage and empower all teens to become global citizens. All of this effort is done with the idea that better health education and the use of the company's products will result in fewer days absent from school and, thus, better education for female students.

QUESTIONS

1. Evaluate the wisdom of Tambrands becoming part of Procter & Gamble.

2. Tambrands indicated that the goal of its global advertising plan was to "market to each cluster in a similar way." Discuss this goal. Should P&G continue with Tambrands's original goal adapted to the new educational program? Why? Why not?

3. For each of the three clusters identified by Tambrands, identify the cultural resistance that must be overcome. Suggest possible approaches to overcoming the resistance you identify.

4. In reference to the approaches you identified in Question 3, is there an approach that can be used to reach the goal of "marketing to each cluster in a similar way"?

5. P&G is marketing in Venezuela with its "Mexican" model. Should the company reopen the Brazilian market with the same model? Discuss.

6. A critic of the "Protecting Futures" program comments, "If you believe the makers of Tampax tampons, there's a direct link between using Western feminine protection and achieving higher education, good health, clean water and longer life." Comment.

Sources: Yumiko Ono, "Tambrands Ads Aim to Overcome Cultural and Religious Obstacles," *The Wall Street Journal,* March 17, 1997, p. B8; Sharon Walsh, "Procter & Gamble Bids to Acquire Tambrands; Deal Could Expand Global Sales of Tampax," *The Washington Post,* April 10, 1997, p. C01; Ed Shelton, "P&G to Seek Web Friends," *The European,* November 16, 1998, p. 18; Emily Nelson and Miriam Jordan, "Sensitive Export: Seeking New Markets for Tampons, P&G Faces Cultural Barriers," *The Wall Street Journal,* December 8, 2000, p. A1; *Weekend Edition Sunday (NPR),* March 12, 2000; "It's Hard to Market the Unmentionable," *Marketing Week,* March 13, 2002, p. 19; Richard Weiner, "A Candid Look at Menstrual Products—Advertising and Public Relations," *Public Relations Quarterly,* Summer 2004; "Procter & Gamble and Warner Bros. Pictures Announce 'Sisterhood' between New Movie and Popular Teen Web Site," *PR Newswire,* June 1, 2005; "Tampax Aims to Attract Teens With New 'Effortless' Message," *Revolution* (London), May 2006; "It's Back; Dotcom Funding Has Jumped 10 Times to $166 Million," *Business* Today, May 2006; "Emerging Markets Force San Pro Makers to Re-examine Priorities," *Euromonitor International,* November 2007; "Tampax and Always Launch Protecting Futures Program Dedicated to Helping African Girls Stay in School," *USA, Discussion Lounge, Africa,* December 4, 2007; "Can Tampons Be Cool?" *Slate,* http://www. Slate.com, January 15; 2007; "Where Food, Water Is a Luxury, Tampons Are Low on Priorities," *Winnipeg Free Press,* February 10, 2008.

CASE 4–3 Iberia Airlines Builds a BATNA

MADRID—One day last April, two model airplanes landed in the offices of Iberia Airlines.

They weren't toys. The Spanish carrier was shopping for new jetliners, and the models were calling cards from Boeing Co. and Airbus, the world's only two producers of big commercial aircraft.

It was the first encounter in what would become a months-long dogfight between the two aviation titans—and Iberia was planning to clean up.

Airbus and Boeing may own the jetliner market, with projected sales of more than $1 trillion in the next 20 years, but right now they don't control it. The crisis in the air-travel industry makes the two manufacturers desperate to nail down orders. So they have grown increasingly dependent on airlines, engine suppliers, and aircraft financiers for convoluted deals.

Once the underdog, Airbus has closed the gap from just four years ago—when Boeing built 620 planes to Airbus's 294—and this year the European plane maker expects to overtake its U.S. rival. For Boeing, Iberia was a chance to stem the tide. For Airbus, Iberia was crucial turf to defend.

Iberia and a few other airlines are financially healthy enough to be able to order new planes these days, and they are all driving hard bargains. Enrique Dupuy de Lome, Iberia's chief financial officer and the man who led its search for widebody jets, meant from the start to run a real horse race. "Everything has been structured to maintain tension up to the last 15 minutes," he said.

Throughout the competition, the participants at Iberia, Boeing, and Airbus gave *The Wall Street Journal* detailed briefings on the pitches, meetings, and deliberations. The result is a rarity for the secretive world of aircraft orders: an inside look at an all-out sales derby with globetrotting executives, huge price tags, and tortuous negotiations over everything from seats to maintenance and cabin-noise levels. The rivals' offers were so close that on the final day of haggling, Iberia stood ready with multiple press releases and extracted last-minute concessions in a phone call between the airline's chair and the winning bidder.

By that point, both suitors felt like they'd been through the wringer. "With 200 airlines and only two plane makers, you'd think we'd get a little more respect," said John Leahy, Airbus's top salesman.

Airbus, a division of European Aeronautic Defense & Space Co., reckoned it had a big edge. It had sold Iberia more than 100 planes since 1997. Leahy thought last summer that he might even bag the contract with minimal competition. In June he had clinched a separate deal with Iberia for three new Airbus A340 widebodies.

But Dupuy made Leahy fight for the order—and so enticed Boeing to compete more aggressively. Then, "just to make things interesting," Dupuy said, he upped the pressure by going shopping for secondhand airplanes. These are spilling onto the market at cut-rate prices as the airline industry's problems force carriers to ground older jets with their higher operating costs.

Iberia is one of the industry's few highly profitable carriers, thanks to a thorough restructuring before the national carrier was privatized in early 2001. The world's number 18 in passenger traffic, with a fleet of 145 planes, it has benefited by flying few routes to North America, where air travel is in tatters, and by dominating the large Latin American market.

The Spanish carrier was looking to replace six Boeing 747-200 jumbo jets more than 20 years old. It wanted as many as 12 new planes to complete a 10-year modernization program for Iberia's long-haul fleet. Based on list prices, the 12-plane order was valued at more than $2 billion.

Iberia's Dupuy, a soft-spoken career finance man, first needed to woo Boeing to the table. The U.S. producer had last sold Iberia planes in 1995, and since then, the carrier had bought so many Airbus jets that Boeing considered not even competing. But in late July, Dupuy met Toby Bright, Boeing's top salesman for jets. Over dinner in London, according to both men, Dupuy told Bright that Iberia truly wanted two suppliers, not just Airbus.

The Boeing sales chief was skeptical, and he recalled thinking at the time, "You're running out of ways to show us." Having worked as Boeing's chief salesman in Europe, Airbus's home turf, he had heard similar lines from customers who eventually bought Airbus planes. So he wondered: "Are we being brought in as a stalking horse?"

Yet replacing Iberia's old 747s with new 777s would be Boeing's last chance for years to win back Iberia. The argument against Boeing was that an all-Airbus fleet would make Iberia's operations simpler and cheaper. Still, going all-Airbus might weaken Iberia's hand in future deals. Airbus would know that the carrier's cost of switching to Boeing would require big investments in parts and pilot training.

In early November, Airbus and Boeing presented initial bids on their latest planes. The four-engine Airbus A340-600 is the longest plane ever built. Boeing's 777-300ER is the biggest twin-engine plane.

The new A340 can fly a bit farther and has more lifting power than the 777. The new Boeing plane is lighter, holds more seats and burns less fuel. The Boeing plane, with a catalog price around $215 million, lists for some $25 million more than the A340.

Dupuy, whose conference room is decorated with framed awards for innovative aircraft-financing deals, set his own tough terms on price and performance issues including fuel consumption, reliability, and resale value. He wouldn't divulge prices, but people in the aviation market familiar with the deal say he demanded discounts exceeding 40 percent.

As negotiations began, Dupuy told both companies his rule: Whoever hits its target, wins the order. The race was on.

Bright, who had been appointed Boeing's top airplane salesperson in January 2002, pitched the Boeing 777 as a "revenue machine." He insisted that his plane could earn Iberia about $8,000 more per flight than the A340-600 because it can hold more seats and is cheaper to operate. A burly 50-year-old West Virginian, Bright joined Boeing out of college as an aerospace designer. He knew the new Airbus would slot easily into Iberia's fleet. But he also felt that Dupuy's target price undervalued his plane.

At Airbus, Leahy also fumed at Iberia's pricing demands. A New York City native and the company's highest-ranking American, he pursues one goal: global domination over Boeing. Last year he spent 220 days on sales trips.

To Iberia, he argued that his plane offered a better investment return because the A340 is less expensive to buy and is similar to Iberia's other Airbus planes. From a hodge-podge of 11 models in 1997, Iberia now flies five types, and replacing the old 747s with A340s would trim that to four—offering savings on parts, maintenance, and pilot training.

Even before presenting Airbus's offer, Leahy had flown to Madrid in October to make his case. On November 18, he once again took a chartered plane for the one-hour flight from Airbus headquarters in Toulouse, France, to Madrid. For two hours that evening, he and his team sat with Dupuy and other Iberia managers around a table in Dupuy's office, debating how many seats can fit on a 777. Those numbers were crucial to the deal because each seat represents millions of dollars in revenue over the life of a plane but also adds weight and cost.

Boeing had told Iberia that its 777 could hold 30 more seats than the 350 Iberia planned to put on the Airbus plane. Leahy argued that the Boeing carries at most five more seats. "Get guarantees from Boeing" on the seat count, Leahy prodded the Iberia managers.

At Boeing, Bright was eager to soften Iberia's pricing demand. His account manager, Steve Aliment, had already made several visits to pitch the plane, and in late November, Bright sent him once again to protest that Iberia didn't appreciate the 777's revenue potential. Boeing desperately wanted to avoid competing just on price, so Bright pushed operating cost and comfort.

On the Airbus side, Leahy also was feeling pressured because a past sales tactic was coming back to haunt him. In 1995, when Iberia was buying 18 smaller A340s and Dupuy expressed concern about their future value, Leahy helped seal the deal by guaranteeing him a minimum resale price, which kicks in after 2005. If Iberia wants to sell them, Airbus must cover any difference between the market price of the used planes and the guaranteed floor price.

The guarantee is one of the tools that Leahy has used to boost Airbus's share of world sales to about 50 percent today from 20 percent in 1995. Boeing rarely guarantees resale values.

Dupuy had wanted guarantees because they lower his risk of buying and thus cut his cost of borrowing. What mattered now was that the guarantees also freed him to sell the planes at a good price. Early in the competition, he suggested to both Airbus and Boeing that he might eventually replace all of Iberia's A340s with Boeings—and potentially stick Airbus with most of the tab.

"If we didn't have the guarantees, the position of Airbus would be very strong," Dupuy said in an interview. Instead, "we have a powerful bargaining tool on future prices."

On December 4, Leahy flew again to Madrid to try to persuade Iberia to close a deal by year's end. Running through a presentation in Dupuy's office, Leahy and five colleagues ticked off fuel and maintenance costs for their plane. They asserted that passengers prefer the plane because it is quieter than the 777 and has no middle seats in business class.

Dupuy then rattled Leahy's cage with a new scenario: Iberia managers would be flying off next week to look at used Boeing 747-400 jumbo jets. Singapore Airlines had stopped flying the planes and was offering to lease them at bargain prices.

Leahy chided Dupuy, saying that was "like buying a used car," where a bargain can easily backfire. Dupuy replied that sometimes buying used makes sense because it offers the flexibility of other options. The message: Iberia could dump its Airbus fleet.

Within Iberia, another debate was ending. Dupuy heard from his managers the results of a yearlong analysis of the rival planes.

The Airbus was cheaper than the Boeing, and the A340's four engines help it operate better in some high-altitude Latin American airports. But Iberia managers had decided they could fit 24 more seats on the Boeing, boosting revenue. And Iberia engineers calculated that the 777 would cost 8 percent less to maintain than the A340. Maintenance on big planes costs at least $3 million a year, so the savings would be huge over the life of a fleet.

Unaware of Iberia's analysis, the Boeing team arrived in Dupuy's office on the morning of December 11 with three bound selling documents. One contained Boeing's revised offer, titled "Imagine the Possibilities . . . Iberia's 777 Fleet." Knowing Dupuy as a numbers guy, the Boeing team peppered him with data showing passengers would choose Iberia because they prefer the 777.

Dupuy told the salespeople their price was still too high.

By mid-December, Iberia chairman Xabier de Irala was getting impatient and wanted a decision by the end of the year. On December 18, Boeing's Bright flew to Madrid. Over a long lunch, Dupuy reiterated his price target.

"If that's your number, let's give this up," Bright said. Talks continued cordially, but the men left doubtful they could close the gap. That Friday, December 20, Dupuy told Iberia's board that prices from Airbus and Boeing were still too high, and he would push the used-plane option harder.

By the start of the year, Airbus's Leahy, growing frustrated, arranged a Saturday meeting with Dupuy. On January 4, the Iberia executive interrupted a family skiing holiday in the Pyrenees and drove two hours along winding French roads to meet Leahy for lunch.

Leahy spent four hours trying to convince Dupuy and a colleague that Airbus couldn't offer a better deal. Dupuy argued that Airbus had just given steep discounts to British airline easyJet, so it should do the same for Iberia. Annoyed, Leahy said media reports of a 50 percent price cut for easyJet were nonsense.

"You get Boeing to give you a 50 percent discount and I'll send you a bottle of champagne," he told the Iberia executives.

Bright was frustrated too. In the first week of January, Dupuy proposed visiting Seattle, where Boeing builds passenger planes. Bright's reply: If Iberia was unwilling to budge, there was little reason to come. So when Dupuy said he would make the 14-hour journey, Bright was encouraged.

On January 14, Dupuy and two colleagues arrived in Seattle. In the private dining room of Cascadia, a high-end downtown restaurant, they met for dinner with the Boeing salespeople and Alan Mulally, the chief executive of Boeing's commercial-plane division. Dupuy was impressed by Mulally's eagerness and was pleased when he urged Bright's team to find a way to close the gap.

The next day, the Boeing salesmen offered a new proposal—including a slightly lower price, improved financing and better terms on spare parts, crew training, and maintenance support from General Electric Co., the maker of the plane's engines.

When Dupuy left Seattle on January 16, Bright felt Iberia was relenting a bit on price and that Dupuy wanted to "find a way to do the deal." Dupuy was also optimistic about striking a deal with Boeing.

Back in Madrid the next day, he raced off to join Iberia's chairman Irala for a meeting with Leahy and Airbus President Noel Forgeard. Irala, a bear of a man who is credited with saving Iberia from bankruptcy eight years ago, told the Airbus executives that Dupuy's price target remained firm. When the Airbus men relented on a few points, Irala yielded a bit too and spelled out Iberia's remaining targets for Airbus. Forgeard said a deal looked possible.

As the meeting broke up, Dupuy was pleased. He felt that Boeing and Airbus were digging deep. And no wonder. The world air-travel market was sinking deeper, and fears of war in Iraq and terrorism had slashed global bookings.

In the next few days, the sales teams from Boeing and Airbus each huddled to refine their offers. Both remained about 10 percent above Dupuy's price targets. Each called him several times daily, pushing for concessions. Dupuy didn't budge. On January 23, he told Iberia's board that both companies could do better. The board scheduled a special meeting for the following Thursday, January 30.

Energized by the Seattle meetings, Bright pushed his team "to go all out to win this bid," and they worked around the clock. Bright phoned Dupuy daily from Seattle and occasionally fielded his calls at 3:00 a.m., Pacific time. By late January, Boeing had cut its price by more than 10 percent after haggling over engine price with GE and financing with leasing firms. The 777 was now less than 3 percent above Dupuy's target—so close that Mr. Bright asked for a gesture of compromise from Iberia.

Dupuy was impressed by Boeing's new aggressiveness. But Airbus was also closing the gap so quickly, he said, that he could offer no concessions. To Leahy, he talked up Boeing's willingness to deal. "I was just talking to Toby . . . ," Dupuy told Leahy during several conversations, referring to Bright. Airbus improved its offer further.

On Wednesday, the day before the deadline, Boeing and Airbus were running about even. In Seattle, Bright threw some clothes in his briefcase and proposed to Dupuy that he hop on a plane to Madrid. Dupuy said the choice was his, but what really mattered was the price target. That day, Dupuy told Bright and Leahy that their bosses should call Irala with any final improvements before the board meeting.

On Thursday morning, Bright offered to trim Boeing's price further if Dupuy could guarantee that Boeing would win the deal. "I can't control Forgeard," Dupuy replied, referring to the Airbus president, who was due to talk soon with Irala. Bright made the price cut without the concession.

"You're very close," Dupuy told him.

Later, Forgeard got on the phone with Iberia's Irala, who said he still needed two concessions on the financial terms and economics of the deal. Airbus had already agreed to most of Dupuy's

terms on asset guarantees and, with engine maker Rolls-Royce PLC, agreed to limit Iberia's cost of maintaining the jets. Forgeard asked if relenting would guarantee Airbus the deal. Irala replied yes, pending board approval—and looked over with a grin at Dupuy, who sat nearby with his laptop open. Forgeard acquiesced. Dupuy plugged the new numbers in his spreadsheet. Airbus had hit its target.

That evening, Boeing got a call from Iberia saying the airline would soon announce it had agreed to buy nine A340-600s and taken options to buy three more. Hours later, Boeing posted on its Web site a statement criticizing Iberia's choice as "the easiest decision." Bright said later that he simply couldn't hit Dupuy's numbers and "do good business."

In the end, Airbus nosed ahead thanks to its planes' lower price and common design with the rest of Iberia's fleet. By offering guarantees on the planes' future value and maintenance costs, plus attractive financing terms, Airbus edged out Boeing's aggressive package. The deal's final financial terms remain secret.

At Airbus, Leahy was relieved, but he faced one last slap. Iberia's news release crowed about Airbus's price guarantees on the planes—a detail Leahy considered confidential. Iberia's Dupuy said he wasn't rubbing it in. But he had, he boasted, won "extraordinary conditions."

QUESTIONS

1. Critique the negotiation strategies and tactics of all three key executives involved: Dupuy, Leahy, and Bright.

2. Critique the overall marketing strategies of the two aircraft makers as demonstrated in this case.

3. What were the key factors that ultimately sent the order in Airbus's direction?

4. Assume that Iberia again is on the market for jet liners. How should Bright handle a new inquiry? Be explicit.

Source: Daniel Michaels, "Boeing and Airbus in Dogfight to Meet Stringent Terms of Iberia's Executives," *The Wall Street Journal Europe,* March 10, 2003, p. A1. Copyright 2003 by Dow Jones & Co. Inc. Reproduced with permission of Dow Jones & Co. Inc. via Copyright Clearance Center.

CASE 4—4 Sales Negotiations Abroad for MRI Systems

International sales of General Medical's Magnetic Resonance Imaging (MRI) systems have really taken off in recent months. Your representatives are about to conclude important sales contracts with customers in both Tokyo and Rio de Janeiro. Both sets of negotiations require your participation, particularly as final details are worked out. The bids you approved for both customers are identical (see Exhibits 1 and 2). Indeed, both customers had contacted you originally at a medical equipment trade show in Las Vegas, and you had all talked business together over drinks at the conference hotel. You expect your two new customers will be talking together again over the Internet about your products and prices as they had in Las Vegas. The Japanese orders are potentially larger because the doctor you met works in a hospital that has nine other units in the Tokyo/Yokohama area. The Brazilian doctor represents a very large hospital in Rio, which may require more than one unit. Your travel arrangements are now being made. Your local representatives will fill you in on the details. Best of luck!

[Note: Your professor will provide you with additional material that you will need to complete this case.]

Exhibit 1
Price Quotation

Deep Vision 2000 MRI (basic unit)	$1,200,000
Product options	
• 2D and 3D time-of-flight (TOF) angiography for capturing fast flow	150,000
• Flow analysis for quantification of cardiovascular studies	70,000
• X2001 software package	20,000
Service contract (2 years normal maintenance, parts, and labor)	60,000
Total price	$1,500,000

Exhibit 2
Standard Terms and Conditions

Delivery	6 months
Penalty for late delivery	$10,000/month
Cancellation charges	10% of contract price
Warranty (for defective machinery)	parts, one year
Terms of payment	COD

CASE 4−5   National Office Machines—Motivating Japanese Salespeople: Straight Salary or Commission?

National Office Machines of Dayton, Ohio, manufacturer of cash registers, electronic data processing equipment, adding machines, and other small office equipment, recently entered into a joint venture with Nippon Cash Machines of Tokyo, Japan. Last year, National Office Machines (NOM) had domestic sales of over $1.4 billion and foreign sales of nearly $700 million. In addition to the United States, it operates in most of western Europe, the Mideast, and some parts of the Far East. In the past, it had no significant sales or sales force in Japan, though the company was represented there by a small trading company until a few years ago. In the United States, NOM is one of the leaders in the field and is considered to have one of the most successful and aggressive sales forces found in this highly competitive industry.

Nippon Cash Machines (NCM) is an old-line cash register manufacturing company organized in 1882. At one time, Nippon was the major manufacturer of cash register equipment in Japan, but it has been losing ground since 1970 even though it produces perhaps the best cash register in Japan. Last year's sales were 9 billion yen, a 15 percent decrease from sales the prior year. The fact that it produces only cash registers is one of the major problems; the merger with NOM will give it much-needed breadth in product offerings. Another hoped-for strength to be gained from the joint venture is managerial leadership, which is sorely needed.

Fourteen Japanese companies have products that compete with Nippon; other competitors include several foreign giants such as IBM, National Cash Register, and Unisys of the United States, and Sweda Machines of Sweden. Nippon has a small sales force of 21 people, most of whom have been with the company their entire adult careers. These salespeople have been responsible for selling to Japanese trading companies and to a few larger purchasers of equipment.

Part of the joint venture agreement included doubling the sales force within a year, with NOM responsible for hiring and training the new salespeople, who must all be young, college-trained Japanese nationals. The agreement also allowed for U.S. personnel in supervisory positions for an indeterminate period of time and for retaining the current Nippon sales force.

One of the many sales management problems facing the Nippon/American Business Machines Corporation (NABMC, the name of the new joint venture) was which sales compensation plan to use. That is, should it follow the Japanese tradition of straight salary and guaranteed employment with no individual incentive program, or the U.S. method (very successful for NOM in the United States) of commissions and various incentives based on sales performance, with the ultimate threat of being fired if sales quotas go continuously unfilled?

The immediate response to the problem might well be one of using the tried-and-true U.S. compensation methods, since they have worked so well in the United States and are perhaps the kind of changes needed and expected from U.S. management. NOM management is convinced that salespeople selling its kinds of products in a competitive market must have strong incentives to produce. In fact, NOM had experimented on a limited basis in the United States with straight salary about ten years ago, and it was a

bomb. Unfortunately, the problem is considerably more complex than it appears on the surface.

One of the facts to be faced by NOM management is the traditional labor–management relations and employment systems in Japan. The roots of the system go back to Japan's feudal era, when a serf promised a lifetime of service to his lord in exchange for a lifetime of protection. By the start of Japan's industrial revolution in the 1880s, an unskilled worker pledged to remain with a company all his useful life if the employer would teach him the new mechanical arts. The tradition of spending a lifetime with a single employer survives today mainly because most workers like it that way. The very foundations of Japan's management system are based on lifetime employment, promotion through seniority, and single-company unions. There is little chance of being fired, pay raises are regular, and there is a strict order of job-protecting seniority.

Japanese workers at larger companies still are protected from outright dismissal by union contracts and an industrial tradition that some personnel specialists believe has the force of law. Under this tradition, a worker can be dismissed after an initial trial period only for gross cause, such as theft or some other major infraction. As long as the company remains in business, the worker isn't discharged, or even furloughed, simply because there isn't enough work to be done.

Besides the guarantee of employment for life, the typical Japanese worker receives many fringe benefits from the company. Bank loans and mortgages are granted to lifetime employees on the assumption that they will never lose their jobs and therefore the ability to repay. Just how paternalistic the typical Japanese firm can be is illustrated by a statement from the Japanese Ministry of Foreign Affairs that gives the example of A, a male worker who is employed in a fairly representative company in Tokyo.

> To begin with, A lives in a house provided by his company, and the rent he pays is amazingly low when compared with average city rents. The company pays his daily trips between home and factory. A's working hours are from 9:00 a.m. to 5:00 p.m. with a break for lunch, which he usually takes in the company restaurant at a very cheap price. He often brings home food, clothing, and other miscellaneous articles he has bought at the company store at a discount ranging from 10 percent to 30 percent below city prices. The company store even supplies furniture, refrigerators, and television sets on an installment basis, for which, if necessary, A can obtain a loan from the company almost free of interest.
>
> In case of illness, A is given free medical treatment in the company hospital, and if his indisposition extends over a number of years, the company will continue paying almost his full salary. The company maintains lodges at seaside or mountain resorts where A can spend the holidays or an occasional weekend with the family at moderate prices. . . . It must also be remembered that when A reaches retirement age (usually 55) he will receive a lump-sum retirement allowance or a pension, either of which will assure him a relatively stable living for the rest of his life.

Even though A is only an example of a typical employee, a salesperson can expect the same treatment. Job security is such an expected part of everyday life that no attempt is made to motivate the Japanese salesperson in the same manner as in the United States; as a consequence, selling traditionally has been primarily an order-taking job. Except for the fact that sales work offers some travel, entry to outside executive offices, the opportunity to entertain, and similar side benefits, it provides a young person with little other incentive to surpass basic quotas and drum up new business. The traditional Japanese bonuses are given twice yearly, can be up to 40 percent of base pay, and are no larger for salespeople than any other functional job in the company.

As a key executive in a Mitsui-affiliated engineering firm put it recently, "The typical salesman in Japan isn't required to have any particular talent." In return for meeting sales quotas, most Japanese salespeople draw a modest monthly salary, sweetened about twice a year by bonuses. Manufacturers of industrial products generally pay no commission or other incentives to boost their businesses.

Besides the problem of motivation, a foreign company faces other different customs when trying to put together and manage a sales force. Class systems and the Japanese distribution system, with its penchant for reciprocity, put a strain on the creative talents of the best sales managers, as Simmons, the U.S. bedding manufacturer, was quick to learn.

In the field, Simmons found itself stymied by the bewildering realities of Japanese marketing, especially the traditional distribution system that operates on a philosophy of reciprocity that goes beyond mere business to the core of the Japanese character: A favor of any kind is a debt that must be repaid. To wear another person on in business and then turn against that person is to lose face, abhorrent to most Japanese. Thus, the owner of large Western-style apartments, hotels, or developments buys his beds from the supplier to whom he owes a favor, no matter what the competition offers.

In small department and other retail stores, where most items are handled on consignment, the bond with the supplier is even stronger. Consequently, all sales outlets are connected in a complicated web that runs from the largest supplier, with a huge national sales force, to the smallest local distributor, with a handful of door-to-door salespeople. The system is self-perpetuating and all but impossible to crack from the outside.

However, there is some change in attitude taking place as both workers and companies start discarding traditions for the job mobility common in the United States. Skilled workers are willing to bargain on the strength of their experience in an open labor market in an effort to get higher wages or better job opportunities; in the United States, it's called shopping around. And a few companies are showing a willingness to lure workers away from other concerns. A number of companies are also plotting how to rid themselves of deadwood workers accumulated as a result of promotions by strict seniority.

Toyo Rayon company, Japan's largest producer of synthetic fibers, started reevaluating all its senior employees every five years with the implied threat that those who don't measure up to the company's expectations have to accept reassignment and possibly demotion; some may even be asked to resign. A chemical engineering and construction firm asked all its employees over 42 to negotiate a new contract with the company every two years. Pay raises and promotions go to those the company wants to keep. For those who think they are worth more than the company is willing to pay, the company offers retirement with something less than the $30,000 lump-sum payment the average Japanese worker receives at age 55.

More Japanese are seeking jobs with foreign firms as the lifetime-employment ethic slowly changes. The head of student placement at Aoyama Gakuin University reports that each year the number of students seeking jobs with foreign companies increases. Bank of America, Japan Motorola, Imperial Chemical Industries, and American Hospital Supply are just a few of the companies that have been successful in attracting Japanese students. Just a few years ago, all Western companies were places to avoid.

Even those companies that are successful work with a multitude of handicaps. American companies often lack the intricate web of personal connections that their Japanese counterparts rely on when recruiting. Furthermore, American companies have the reputation for being quick to hire and even quicker to fire, whereas Japanese companies still preach the virtues of lifelong job security. Those U.S. companies that are successful are offering big salaries and promises of Western-style autonomy. According to a recent study, 20- to 29-year-old Japanese prefer an employer-changing environment to a single lifetime employer. They complain that the Japanese system is unfair because promotions are based on age and seniority. A young recruit, no matter how able, has to wait for those above him to be promoted before he too can move up. Some feel that if you are really capable, you are better off working with an American company.

Some foreign firms entering Japan have found that their merit-based promotion systems have helped them attract bright young recruits. In fact, a survey done by *Nihon Keizai Shimbun*, Japan's leading business newspaper, found that 80 percent of top managers at 450 major Japanese corporations wanted the seniority promotion system abolished. But, as one Japanese manager commented, "We see more people changing their jobs now, and we read many articles about companies restructuring, but despite this, we won't see major changes coming quickly."

A few U.S. companies operating in Japan are experimenting with incentive plans. Marco and Company, a belting manufacturer and Japanese distributor for Power Packing and Seal Company, was persuaded by Power to set up a travel plan incentive for salespeople who topped their regular sales quotas. Unorthodox as the idea was for Japan, Marco went along. The first year, special one-week trips to Far East holiday spots like Hong Kong, Taiwan, Manila, and Macao were inaugurated. Marco's sales of products jumped 212 percent, and the next year, sales were up an additional 60 percent.

IBM also has made a move toward chucking the traditional Japanese sales system (salary plus a bonus but no incentives). For about a year, it has been working with a combination that retains the semiannual bonus while adding commission payments on sales over preset quotas. "It's difficult to apply a straight commission system in selling computers because of the complexities of the product," an IBM Japan official said. "Our salesmen don't get big commissions because other employees would be jealous." To head off possible ill feeling, therefore, some nonselling IBM employees receive monetary incentives.

Most Japanese companies seem reluctant to follow IBM's example because they have doubts about directing older salespeople to go beyond their usual order-taking role. High-pressure tactics are not well accepted here, and sales channels are often pretty well set by custom and long practice (e.g., a manufacturer normally deals with one trading company, which in turn sells only to customers A, B, C, and D). A salesperson or trading company, for that matter, is not often encouraged to go after customer Z and get it away from a rival supplier.

The Japanese market is becoming more competitive and there is real fear on the part of NOM executives that the traditional system

Exhibit 1
Life Goals

	(Unit: %)					
Japan	35.4	5.8	41.2	6.8	10.8	
U.S.	6.2 / 5.1	77.3		9.5		1.8
U.K.	11.2	13.9	63.4	8.6		2.9
Germany	9.0	17.8	60.6	5.5	7.5	
France	7.1	16.4	62.2	10.9		3.4
Switzerland	3.7 / 9.2	72.3		11.9		3.0
Sweden	2.5 / 1.7	84.8		7.5		3.4
Australia	6.7 / 5.1	76.0		10.5		1.6
India	22.3	33.3	16.2	26.3		1.8
Philippines	21.7	9.6	46.2	22.0		0.5
Brazil	7.7	16.7	63.2	11.9		0.5
Key:	To get rich	To acquire social position	To live as I choose	To work on behalf of society	No answer	

just won't work in a competitive market. However, the proponents of the incentive system concede that the system really has not been tested over long periods or even adequately in the short term because it has been applied only in a growing market. In other words, was it the incentive system that caused the successes achieved by the companies, or was it market growth? Other companies following the traditional method of compensation and employee relations also have had sales increases during the same period.

The problem is further complicated for NABMC because it will have both new and old salespeople. The young Japanese seem eager to accept the incentive method, but older ones are hesitant. How do you satisfy both since you must, by agreement, retain all the sales staff?

A study done by the Japanese government on attitudes of youth around the world suggests that younger Japanese may be more receptive to U.S. incentive methods than one would anticipate. In a study done by the Japanese prime minister's office, there were some surprising results when Japanese responses were compared with responses of similar-aged youths from other countries. Exhibit 1 summarizes some of the information gathered on life goals. One point that may be of importance in shedding light on the decision NOM has to make is a comparison of Japanese attitudes with young people in 11 other countries—the Japanese young people are less satisfied with their home life, school, and working situations and are more passive in their attitudes toward social and political problems. Furthermore, almost one-third of those employed said they were dissatisfied with their present jobs primarily because of low income and short vacations. Asked if they had to choose between a difficult job with responsibility and

authority or an easy job without responsibility and authority, 64 percent of the Japanese picked the former, somewhat less than the 70 to 80 percent average in other countries.

Another critical problem lies with the nonsales employees; traditionally, all employees on the same level are treated equally, whether sales, production, or staff. How do you encourage competitive, aggressive salesmanship in a market unfamiliar with such tactics, and how do you compensate salespeople to promote more aggressive selling in the face of tradition-bound practices of paternalistic company behavior?

QUESTIONS

1. What should NABMC offer—incentives or straight salary? Support your answer.

2. If incentives are out, how do you motivate salespeople and get them to compete aggressively?

3. Design a U.S.-type program for motivation and compensation of salespeople. Point out where difficulties may be encountered with your plan and how the problems are to be overcome.

4. Design a pay system you think would work, satisfying old salespeople, new salespeople, and other employees.

5. Discuss the idea that perhaps the kind of motivation and aggressiveness found in the United States is not necessary in the Japanese market.

6. Develop some principles of motivation that could be applied by an international marketer in other countries.

CASE 4—6 AIDS, Condoms, and Carnival

Worldwide, more than 2 million people died of AIDS in 2007, and more than 40 million are estimated to be living with HIV/AIDS.

BRAZIL

Half a million Brazilians are infected with the virus that causes acquired immunodeficiency syndrome (AIDS), and millions more are at high risk of contracting the incurable ailment, a federal study reported. The Health Ministry study is Brazil's first official attempt to seek an estimate of the number of residents infected with human immunodeficiency virus (HIV). Many had doubted the government's prior number of 94,997. The report by the National Program for Transmissible Diseases/AIDS said 27 million Brazilians are at high risk to contract AIDS, and another 36 million are considered to be at a medium risk. It said Brazil could have 7.5 million AIDS victims in the next decade.

"If we are going to combat this epidemic, we have to do it now," said Pedro Chequer, a Health Ministry official. Chequer said the Health Ministry would spend $300 million next year, distributing medicine and 250 million condoms and bringing AIDS awareness campaigns to the urban slums, where the disease is most rampant. Last month, Brazil became one of the few countries to offer a promising AIDS drug free to those who need it. The drug can cost as much as $12,000 a year per patient.

AIDS cases in Brazil have risen so dramatically for married women that the state of São Paulo decided that it must attack a basic cultural practice in Latin America: Their husbands don't practice safe sex. Last month, the government of Brazil's megalopolis started promoting the newly released female condom.

Many of the new AIDS cases in Brazil are married women who have children, according to a report released last month at the Pan-American Conference on AIDS in Lima, Peru. Worldwide, women constitute the fastest-growing group of those diagnosed with HIV. And of the 30.6 million people who are diagnosed with HIV, 90 percent live in poor countries.

One Brazilian mother, Rosana Dolores, knows well why women cannot count on male partners to use condoms. She and her late husband never thought of protecting their future children against AIDS. "We were married. We wanted to have kids," says Dolores, both of whose children were born HIV positive. "These days, I would advise young people to always use condoms. But married couples . . . who is going to?"

Brazil, with its 187 million people and the largest population in South America, has the second-highest number of reported HIV infections in the Americas, after the United States, according to a report released by the United Nations agency UNAIDS.

Public health officials say one reason why AIDS prevention efforts have failed is that many Brazilians just don't like condoms. Although use in Brazil has quadrupled in the past six years, it is still the least popular method of birth control—a touchy issue in the predominantly Roman Catholic country. Another reason is that condoms cost about 75 cents each, making them more expensive here than anywhere else in the world, health officials say.

Plus, Latin-style machismo leaves women with little bargaining power. Only 14 percent of Brazilian heterosexual men used condoms last year, according to AIDSCAP, an AIDS prevention program funded by the U.S. Agency for International Development. In other studies, many women said they would not ask their partner to use a condom, even if they knew he was sleeping with others.

"Women are afraid of asking their men to have safe sex, afraid of getting beaten, afraid of losing their economic support," says Guido Carlos Levi, a director at the health department at Emilio Ribas Hospital. "This is not Mexico, but we're quite a machoistic society here."

The frequency with which Latin men stray from monogamous relationships has compounded the problem. In studies conducted in Cuba by the Pan American Health Organization, 49 percent of men and 14 percent of women in stable relationships admitted they had had an affair in the past year.

In light of statistics showing AIDS as the number one killer of women of childbearing age in São Paulo state, public health officials launched a campaign promoting the female condom. The hope is that it will help women—especially poor women—protect themselves and their children. But the female condom seemed unlikely to spark a latex revolution when it hit city stores. The price is $2.50 apiece—more than three times the price of most male condoms.

The Family Health Association is asking the government to help subsidize the product and to cut the taxes on condoms that make them out of reach for many poor Brazilians. "We're looking for a pragmatic solution to prevent the transmission of HIV-AIDS," group President Maria Eugenia Lemos Fernandes said. "Studies show there is a high acceptance of this method because it's a product under the control of women."

While 75 percent of the women and 63 percent of the men in a pilot study on the female condom said they approved of the device, many women with AIDS say they would have been no more likely to have used a female condom than a conventional one.

Part of the problem is perception: 80 percent of women and 85 percent of men in Brazil believe they are not at risk of contracting HIV, according to a study conducted by the Civil Society for the Well-Being of the Brazilian Family.

Also at risk are married women, 40 percent of whom undergo sterilization as an affordable way of getting around the Catholic church's condemnation of birth control, health officials noted.

"It's mostly married women who are the victims. You just never think it could be you," says a former hospital administrator who was diagnosed with the virus after her husband had several extramarital affairs. He died two years ago. "I knew everything there was to know about AIDS—I worked in a hospital—but I never suspected he was going out like that. He always denied it," she says.

While HIV is making inroads in rural areas and among teenagers in Brazil, Fernandes says it doesn't have to reach epidemic proportions as in Uganda or Tanzania. "There is a very big window of opportunity here."

Brazil's Health Ministry has added a new ingredient to the heady mix that makes up the country's annual Carnival—condoms. The ministry will distribute 10 million condoms next month, along with free advice on how to prevent the spread of AIDS, at places like Rio de Janeiro's sambadrome, where bare-breasted dancing girls attract millions of spectators every year.

"It's considered as a period of increased sexual activity," a spokeswoman at the ministry's AIDS coordination department said on Monday. "The euphoria provoked by Carnival and the excessive consumption of alcohol make it a moment when people are more likely to forget about prevention," she explained.

It is no coincidence that Rio de Janeiro was chosen to host a Conference on HIV Pathogenesis and Treatment. Brazil's handling of the epidemic is widely regarded as exemplary. In the early 1990s, the World Bank predicted that by 2000, HIV would have infected 1.2 million Brazilians. Five years after that deadline, the total was just half the prediction, at about 600,000. So how did Brazil do it, and can other poor countries learn from what was done?

Perhaps the first lesson is don't be squeamish. Brazil, a predominantly Catholic country, hands out free condoms in abundance. Some 20 million are given away every month—a figure boosted by 50 percent in February to accommodate for the exuberance of the country's famous carnivals. Drug users, too, are treated sensibly. Those who inject are offered regular supplies of clean needles and, as a result, three-fourths of them claim never to share needles with others. Nor are prostitutes neglected. Both ladies and gentlemen of the night are the targets of campaigns intended to promote condom use.

The second lesson is to treat freely. Brazilian law gives all residents the right to the best available drug treatment at no cost. This is important, because having to pay discourages people from complying with the full treatment and thus encourages the emergence of drug-resistant viruses. Providing free treatment is, of course, expensive. This year, the government will spend $395 million on anti-HIV drugs, almost two-thirds of it on three expensive patented drugs. This has brought it into conflict with foreign drug companies. Although it has never actually broken a drug-company patent, the government has exploited every available loophole to evade patents and buy or manufacture generic versions of drugs. For those patents that cannot legally be evaded, the government has played chicken with the patent owners over prices, knowing that manufacturers are desperate to avoid a patent-breaking precedent that others might follow. So far, it has been the companies that have blinked, though the latest sparring match, with Abbott Laboratories, an American firm, over a drug combination called Kaletra, has yet to be resolved.

The third lesson is to encourage voluntary action. In 1992, Brazil had 120 charities and voluntary groups devoted to AIDS. By the turn of the century, that had risen to 500. The virtues of voluntarism were recently confirmed when the Global Fund (the main multilateral distributor of anti-AIDS money to poor countries) audited the success of its donations. It found that spending by voluntary groups usually produced the best value for the money.

The fourth lesson is to do the sums. One of the arguments that has sustained Brazil's anti-AIDS program is "if you think action is expensive, try inaction." The government spent $1.8 billion on antiretroviral drugs between 1996 and 2002 but estimates that early treatment saved it more than $2.2 billion in hospital costs over the same period. Add that to the GDP loss that Brazil would have suffered if the World Bank had been right, and an aggressive program of prevention and treatment does not seem so costly after all.

INDIA

S. Mani's small barbershop in a southern Indian city looks like any other the world over. It's equipped with all the tools of the trade: scissors, combs, razors—and condoms, too.

A blue box full of free prophylactics stands in plain view of his customers as Mani trims hair and dispenses advice on safe sex, a new dimension to his 20-year career. "I start by talking about the family and children," Mani explains, snipping a client's moustache. "Slowly, I get to women, AIDS, and condoms."

Many Indian men are too embarrassed to buy condoms at a drugstore or to talk freely about sex with health counselors and family members. There's one place where they let down their hair: the barbershop. So, the state of Tamil Nadu is training barbers to be frontline soldiers in the fight against AIDS.

Programs like the barber scheme are what make Tamil Nadu, a relatively poor Indian state that's home to 60 million people, a possible model for innovative and cost-effective methods to contain AIDS in the developing world.

Six years after it was first detected in India, the AIDS virus is quickly spreading in the world's second most populous nation. Already, up to 2.4 million of India's 1 billion people are infected with HIV—more than in any other country, according to UNAIDS, the United Nations' AIDS agency.

But faced with more immediate and widespread health woes, such as tuberculosis and malaria, officials in many Indian states are reluctant to make AIDS prevention a priority. And in some states, the acquired immunodeficiency syndrome is regarded as a Western disease of decadence; officials deny that prostitution and drug use even exist in their midst. "Some Indian states are still in total denial or ignorance about the AIDS problem," says Salim Habayeb, a World Bank physician who oversees an $84 million loan to India for AIDS prevention activities.

Tamil Nadu, the state with the third-highest incidence of HIV infection, has been open about its problem. Before turning to barbers for help, Tamil Nadu was the first state to introduce AIDS education in high school and the first to set up a statewide information hotline. Its comprehensive AIDS education program targets the overall population, rather than only high-risk groups.

In the past two years, awareness of AIDS in Tamil Nadu has jumped to 95 percent of those polled, from 64 percent, according to Operations Research Group, an independent survey group. "Just two years ago, it was very difficult to talk about AIDS and the condom," says P. R. Bindhu Madhavan, director of the Tamil Nadu State AIDS Control Society, the autonomous state agency managing the prevention effort.

The AIDS fighters take maximum advantage of the local culture to get the message across. Tamils are among the most ardent moviegoers in this film-crazed country. In the city of Madras, people line up for morning screenings even during weekdays. Half of the state's 630 theaters are paid to screen an AIDS-awareness short before the main feature. The spots are usually melodramatic musicals laced with warnings.

In the countryside, where cinemas are scarce, a movie mobile does the job. The concept mimics that used by multinationals, such as Colgate-Palmolive, for rural advertising. Bright red-and-blue trucks ply the back roads, blaring music from well-known movie soundtracks whose lyrics have been rewritten to address AIDS issues. In villages, hundreds gather for the show, on a screen that pops out of the rear of the truck.

In one six-minute musical, a young husband's infidelity leads to his death from AIDS, the financial ruin of his family, and then the death of his wife, also infected. The couple's toddler is left alone in the world. The heart-rending tale is followed by a brief lecture by an AIDS educator—and the offer of a free pack of condoms and an AIDS brochure.

Tamil Nadu's innovations have met with obstacles. It took several months for state officials to persuade Indian government television, Doordarshan, to broadcast an AIDS commercial featuring the Hindu gods of chastity and death. Even then, Madhavan says, Doordarshan "wouldn't do it as a social ad, so we have to pay a commercial rate."

Later, the network refused to air a three-minute spot in which a woman urges her husband, a truck driver, to use a condom when he's on the road. Safe infidelity was deemed "inappropriate for Indian living rooms," says Madhavan. A number of commercial satellite channels have been willing to run the ad.

Tamil Nadu has met little resistance recruiting prostitutes for the cause. For almost a year, 37-year-old prostitute Vasanthi has been distributing condoms to colleagues. With state funding, a nongovernmental agency has trained her to spread the word about AIDS and other sexually transmitted diseases. As an incentive, the state pays participants like Vasanthi, a mother of three, the equivalent of $14 a month, about what she earns from entertaining a client.

Before Vasanthi joined the plan, she didn't know that the condom could help prevent HIV infection. These days, if any client refuses to wear a condom, "I kick him out, even if it takes using my shoes," she says. "I'm not flexible about this." More men are also carrying their own condoms, she says.

Thank barbers such as Mani for that. Especially in blue-collar areas of Madras, men "trim their hair and beard before frequenting a commercial sex worker," says Madhavan. They can pick up their condom on the way out.

Tamil Nadu launched the barber program in Madras last March. So far, it has enlisted 5,000 barbers, who receive AIDS education at meetings each Tuesday—the barbers' day off. The barbers aren't paid to be AIDS counselors, but they appear to take pride in their new responsibility.

Over the generations, India's barbers have been respected as traditional healers and trusted advisers. "If you want to get to the king's ears, you tell his barber," says Madhavan, the state AIDS director. Reinforcing the image of barbers as healers, the local trade group is called the Tamil Nadu Medical Barber Association.

"I first talked about AIDS with my barber," says Thiyagrajan, an electrician in his 40s. "I don't have multiple partners, so I don't need a condom, but I take them for my friends."

One recent night, a man in his 30s walked into Aruna Hair Arts, greeted Swami, then headed out the door with a fistful of condoms scooped from the plastic dispenser. "That's OK," Swami says approvingly. "He's a regular customer."

A local nongovernmental organization helps barbers replenish condom stocks by providing each shop with self-addressed order forms. But the central government hasn't always been able to meet supply, for reasons ranging from bureaucracy to price disputes with manufacturers.

Tamil Nadu has started sourcing condoms from elsewhere. But they're too expensive to give away. So the next stage of the barber scheme, just under way, is to charge two rupees (six cents) for a two-condom "pleasure pack." The barbers will get a 25 percent commission. Thus far, the only perk of participating has been a free wall calendar listing AIDS prevention tips.

Roughly 30 percent of barbers approached by Tamil Nadu have refused to participate in the AIDS program, fearing that they would alienate customers. But those who take part insist that carrying the AIDS message hasn't hurt business. "We give the message about AIDS, but we still gossip about women," says barber N. V. Durairaj at Rolex Salon.

Multinational soft drink giants Coke and Pepsi may soon become part of the Indian government's efforts to reach out to people in far-flung areas to spread awareness about HIV/AIDS and promote the use of condoms. Where social marketing efforts have failed in reaching supplies of condoms, the idea is to reach out through the soft drink firms that have managed to set up a marketing network estimated at more than 1 million outlets across the country. "Realizing their reach, we have appealed to the cola companies PepsiCo and Coca-Cola to allow us to piggyback on their advertisement, including possible slogans on their soft drinks bottles," a senior health ministry official said. "We have also asked them to help us with the distribution of condoms through their outlets in remote areas."

The requests have elicited encouraging response from both the multinationals. "We are planning to talk to them and hope that they will soon be on board with our awareness campaign and promotion of condom use," the official said.

What led to the National AIDS Control Organisation (NACO) looking to Coke and Pepsi for support was the encouraging response they received for advertisements featuring cricket stars advising on the need for preparedness. Some campaigns even had them carrying condoms along with the cricket gear. Backed by 10 countries, including India, the International Cricket Council (ICC) has been actively supporting efforts to promote awareness about HIV/AIDS through campaigns on safe sex. "So whether it is cricket stumps bearing condoms or cricketers themselves urging the need for preparedness, we are finding good response among the public." NACO also wants to take the campaign forward with celebrity endorsement at a time when sensitive films about HIV/AIDS like *Phir Milenge* ("We'll Meet Again") and *My Brother Nikhil* have struck a responsive chord among viewers.

The effort is to ensure that the number of HIV-positive cases in the country is contained at the official estimate of 5.13 million. Besides cola companies, several other multinational and national companies with large sales networks, such as banks, are now being looked at by NACO as potential vehicles for creating mass awareness and promotion of condoms.

LONDON INTERNATIONAL GROUP

London International Group (LIG) is recognized worldwide as a leader in the development of latex and thin-film barrier technologies. The Group has built its success on the development of its core businesses: the Durex family of branded condoms, Regent medical gloves, and Marigold household and industrial gloves. These are supported by a range of noncore health and beauty products.

With operational facilities in over 40 countries, 12 manufacturing plants, either wholly or jointly owned, and an advanced research and development facility based in Cambridge, England, LIG is well placed to expand into the new emerging markets of the world.

Durex is the world's number one condom brand in terms of quality, safety, and brand awareness. The Durex family of condom brands includes Sheik, Ramses, Hatu, London, Kohinoor, Dua Lima, Androtex, and Avanti. Sold in over 130 countries worldwide and leader in more than 40 markets, Durex is the only global condom brand.

The development of innovative and creative marketing strategies is key to communicating successfully with target audiences. Consumer marketing initiatives remain focused on supporting the globalization of Durex. A series of innovative yet cost-effective projects have been used to communicate the global positioning "Feeling Is Everything" to the target young adult market, securing loyalty.

The Durex Global Survey, together with a unique multimillion-pound global advertising and sponsorship contract with MTV, has successfully emphasized the exciting and modern profile of Durex and presented significant opportunities for local public relations and event sponsorship, especially in emerging markets like Taiwan.

LIG continues to focus on education, using sponsorship of events such as the XI Annual AIDS Conference held in Vancouver and other educational initiatives to convey the safer sex message to governments, opinion formers, and educators worldwide.

JAPAN

London Okamoto Corporation, the joint venture company between London International Group and Okamoto Industries, announced the Japanese launch in Spring 1998 of Durex Avanti, the world's first polyurethane male condom.

This is the first time an international condom brand will be available in Japan, the world's most valuable condom market, which is estimated to be worth £260 million ($433 million). Durex Avanti has already been successfully launched in the United States and Great Britain and will be launched in Italy and other selected European countries within a year.

Durex Avanti condoms are made from Duron, a unique polyurethane material twice as strong as latex, which enables them to be made much thinner than regular latex condoms, thereby increasing sensitivity without compromising safety. In addition, Durex Avanti condoms are able to conduct body heat, creating a more natural feeling, and are the first condoms to be totally odorless, colorless, and suitable for use with oil-based lubricants.

Commenting on the launch, Nick Hodges, chief executive of LIG, said; "Japan is a very important condom market; with oral contraceptives still not publicly available, per capita usage rates for condoms are among the highest in the world. Our joint venture with Okamoto, Japan's leading condom manufacturer, gives us instant access to this strategically important market."

The joint venture with Okamoto, which is the market leader in Japan with a 53 percent share, was established in 1994 with the specific purpose of marketing Durex Avanti. Added Takehiko Okamoto, president of Okamoto, "We are confident that such an innovative and technically advanced product as Durex Avanti, coupled with our strong market franchise, will find significant consumer appeal in Japan's sophisticated condom market."

Durex Avanti, which is manufactured at LIG's research and development center in Cambridge, England, has taken over ten years to develop and represents an investment by LIG of approximately £15 million.

QUESTIONS

1. Comment on the Brazilian and Indian governments' strategies for the prevention of AIDS via the marketing of condoms.

2. How is the AIDS problem different in the United States compared with Brazil and India?

3. Would the approaches described in Brazil and India work in the United States? Why or why not?

4. Suggest additional ways that London International Group could promote the prevention of AIDS through the use of condoms worldwide.

5. Do you think it would be a good idea for Coke and Pepsi to participate in a condom distribution program in India, Brazil, and the United States?

Sources: "Half a Million Brazilians Are Infected with the AIDS Virus," *Associated Press,* December 21, 1996; Andrea McDaniels, "Brazil Turns to Women to Stop Dramatic Rise in AIDS Cases. São Paulo Pushes Female Condom to Protect Married Women from Husbands, but Costs of Devices Are High," *Christian Science Monitor,* January 9, 1998, p. 7; "Brazil to Hand out 10 Million Condoms during Carnival," *Chicago Tribune,* January 19, 1998, p. 2; Miriam Jordan, "India Enlists Barbers in the War on AIDS," *The Wall Street Journal,* September 24, 1996, p. A18; Caro Ezzzell, "Care for a Dying Continent," *Scientific American,* May 2000, pp. 96–105; Ginger Thompson, "In Grip of AIDS, South Africa Cries for Equity," *The New York Times,* p. 4; "Roll Out, Roll Out—AIDS in Brazil," *The Economist,* July 30, 2005, p. 376; "AIDS Campaign May Soon Piggyback on Pepsi, Coke," http://www.HindustanTimes.com, August 30, 2005; "A Portrait in Red—AIDS in Brazil," *The Economist,* March 15, 2008, p. 38. Also see the Web sites http://www.lig.com and http://www.durex.com.

CASE 4—7 Making Socially Responsible and Ethical Marketing Decisions: Selling Tobacco to Third World Countries

Strategic decisions move a company toward its stated goals and perceived success. Strategic decisions also reflect the firm's social responsibility and the ethical values on which such decisions are made. They reflect what is considered important and what a company wants to achieve.

Mark Pastin, writing on the function of ethics in business decisions, observes:

> There are fundamental principles, or ground rules, by which organizations act. Like the ground rules of individuals, organizational ground rules determine which actions are possible for the organization and what the actions mean. Buried beneath the charts of organizational responsibility, the arcane strategies, the crunched numbers, and the political intrigue of every firm are sound rules by which the game unfolds.

The following situations reflect different decisions made by multinational firms and governments and also reflect the social responsibility and ethical values underpinning the decisions. Study the following situations in the global cigarette marketplace carefully and assess the ground rules that guided the decisions of firms and governments.

EXPORTING U.S. CIGARETTE CONSUMPTION

In the United States, 600 billion cigarettes are sold annually, but sales are shrinking rapidly. Unit sales have been dropping about 1 to 2 percent a year, and sales have been down by almost 5 percent in the last six years. The U.S. Surgeon General's campaign against smoking, higher cigarette taxes, non-smoking rules in public areas, and the concern Americans have about general health have led to the decline in tobacco consumption. Faced with various class-action lawsuits, the success of states in winning lawsuits, and pending federal legislation, tobacco companies have stepped up their international marketing activities to maintain profits.

Even though companies have agreed to sweeping restrictions in the United States on cigarette marketing and secondhand smoke and to bolder cancer-warning labels, they are fighting as hard as ever in the Third World to convince the media, the public, and policymakers that similar changes are not needed. In seminars at luxury resorts worldwide, tobacco companies invite journalists, all expenses paid, to participate in programs that play down the health risks of smoking. It is hard to gauge the influence of such seminars, but in the Philippines, a government plan to reduce smoking by children was "neutralized" by a public relations campaign from cigarette companies to remove "cancer awareness and prevention" as a "key concern." A slant in favor of the tobacco industry's point of view seemed to prevail.

At a time when most industrialized countries are discouraging smoking, the tobacco industry is avidly courting consumers throughout the developing world using catchy slogans, obvious image campaigns, and single-cigarette sales that fit a hard-pressed customer's budget. The reason is clear: The Third World is an expanding market. As an example, Indonesia's per capita cigarette consumption quadrupled in less than ten years. Increasingly, cigarette advertising on radio and television is being restricted in some countries, but other means of promotion, especially to young people, are not controlled.

China, with more than 300 million smokers, produces and consumes about 1.4 trillion cigarettes per year, more than any other country in the world. Estimates are that China has more smokers than the United States has people. Just 1 percent of that 1.4 trillion cigarette market would increase a tobacco company's overseas sales by 15 percent and would be worth as much as $300 million in added revenue.

American cigarette companies have received a warm welcome in Russia, where at least 50 percent of the people smoke. Consumers are hungry for most things Western, and tobacco taxes are low. Unlike in the United States and other countries that limit or ban cigarette advertising, there are few effective controls on tobacco products in Russia. Russia, the world's fourth largest cigarette market, has proved to be an extremely profitable territory for British American Tobacco (BAT). BAT Russia, established in 1949, sold 65 billion cigarettes in Russia in 2005, giving it almost one-fifth of market share.

ADVERTISING AND PROMOTION

In Gambia, smokers send in cigarette box tops to qualify for a chance to win a new car. In Argentina, smoking commercials fill 20 percent of television advertising time. And in crowded African cities, billboards that link smoking to the good life tower above the sweltering shantytowns. Such things as baby clothes with cigarette logos, health warnings printed in foreign languages, and tobacco-sponsored contests for children are often featured in tobacco ads in Third World countries. Latin American tobacco consumption rose by more than 24 percent over a ten-year period.

Critics claim that sophisticated promotions in unsophisticated societies entice people who cannot afford the necessities of life to spend money on a luxury—and a dangerous one at that. The sophistication theme runs throughout the smoking ads. In Kinshasa, Zaire, billboards depict a man in a business suit stepping out of a black Mercedes as a chauffeur holds the door. In Nigeria, promotions for Graduate brand cigarettes show a university student in his cap and gown. Those for Gold Leaf cigarettes have a barrister in a white wig and the slogan, "A very important cigarette for very important people." In Kenya, a magazine ad for Embassy cigarettes shows an elegant executive officer with three young men and women equivalent to American yuppies. The most disturbing trend in developing countries is advertising that associates tobacco with American affluence and culture. Some women in Africa, in their struggle for women's rights, defiantly smoke cigarettes as a symbol of freedom. Billboards all over Russia feature pictures of skyscrapers and white sandy beaches and slogans like "Total Freedom" or "Rendezvous with America." They aren't advertising foreign travel but American cigarette brands.

Every cigarette manufacturer is in the image business, and tobacco companies say their promotional slant is both reasonable and common. They point out that in the Third World a lot of people cannot understand what is written in the ads anyway, so the ads zero in on the more understandable visual image. "In most of the world, the Marlboro Man isn't just a symbol of the Wild West; he's a symbol of the West." "You can't convince people that all Americans don't smoke." In Africa, some of the most effective advertising includes images of affluent white Americans with recognizable landmarks, such as the New York City skyline, in the background. In much of Africa, children as young as five are used to sell single cigarettes, affordable to other children, to support their own nicotine habits. Worldwide nearly one-fourth of all teenage smokers smoked their first cigarette before they were 10 years old.

The scope of promotional activity is enormous. In Kenya, a major tobacco company is the fourth-largest advertiser. Tobacco-sponsored lotteries bolster sales in some countries by offering as prizes expensive goods that are beyond most people's budgets. Gambia has a population of just 640,000, but a tobacco company lottery attracted 1.5 million entries (each sent in on a cigarette box top) when it raffled off a Renault car.

Evidence is strong that the strategy of tobacco companies is to target young people as a means of expanding market demand. Report after report reveals that adolescents receive cigarettes free as a means of promoting the product. For example, in Buenos Aires, a Jeep decorated with the yellow Camel logo pulls up in front of a high school. The driver, a blond woman wearing khaki safari gear, begins handing out free cigarettes to 15- and 16-year-olds on lunch recess. Teens visiting MTV's Web sites in China, Germany, India, Poland, and Latin America were given the chance to click on a banner ad that led them to a questionnaire about their exposure to cigarette ads and other marketing tools in their countries. Some 10,000 teens responded to the banner ads. "In the past week, more than 62 percent of teenagers in these countries have been exposed to tobacco advertising in some form," the 17-year-old SWAT (Students Working against Tobacco) chairman told Reuters. "The tobacco companies learned that marketing to teens and kids worked in this country, but since they can't do it here anymore, they've taken what they learned to other countries." At a video arcade in Taipei, free American cigarettes are strewn atop each game. "As long as they're here, I may as well try one," says a high school girl.

In Malaysia, *Gila-Gila,* a comic book popular with elementary school students, carries a Lucky Strike ad. Attractive women in cowboy outfits regularly meet teenagers going to rock concerts or discos in Budapest and hand them Marlboros. Those who accept a light on the spot also receive Marlboro sunglasses.

According to the American Lung Association Tobacco Policy Trend Alert, the tobacco industry is offering candy-flavored cigarettes in an attempt to continue to target teens.[1] Advertising and promotion of these products uses hip-hop imagery, attractive women, and other imagery to appeal to youth in similar ways that Joe Camel did a decade ago. Marketing efforts for candy-flavored cigarettes came after the Master Settlement Agreement prohibited tobacco companies from using cartoon characters to sell cigarettes. Researchers recently released the results of several surveys that showed that 20 percent of smokers ages 17 to 19 smoked flavored cigarettes, while only 6 percent of smokers ages 17 to 20 did.

---

[1] See "From Joe Camel to Kauai Kolada—The Marketing of Candy-Flavored Cigarettes," http://lungusa.org.

In Russia, a U.S. cigarette company sponsors disco parties where thousands of young people dance to booming music. Admission is the purchase of one pack of cigarettes. At other cigarette-sponsored parties, attractive women give cigarettes away free.

In many countries, foreign cigarettes have a status image that also encourages smoking. A 26-year-old Chinese man says he switched from a domestic brand to Marlboro because "You feel a higher social position" when you smoke foreign cigarettes. "Smoking is a sign of luxury in Czechoslovakia as well as in Russia and other Eastern countries," says an executive of a Czech tobacco firm that has a joint venture with a U.S. company. "If I can smoke Marlboro, then I'm a well-to-do man."

The global tobacco companies insist that they are not attempting to recruit new smokers. They say they are only trying to encourage smokers to switch to foreign brands. "The same number of cigarettes are consumed whether American cigarettes or not," was the comment of one executive.

Although cigarette companies deny they sell higher tar and nicotine cigarettes in the Third World, one British tobacco company does concede that some of its brands sold in developing countries contain more tar and nicotine than those sold in the United States and Europe. A recent study found three major U.S. brands with filters had 17 milligrams of tar in the United States, 22.3 in Kenya, 29.7 in Malaysia, and 31.1 in South Africa. Another brand with filters had 19.1 milligrams of tar in the United States, 28.8 in South Africa, and 30.9 in the Philippines. The firm says that Third World smokers are used to smoking their own locally made product, which might have several times more tar and nicotine. Thus, the firm leaves the tar- and nicotine-level decisions to its foreign subsidiaries, who tailor their products to local tastes.

C. Everett Koop, the retired U.S. Surgeon General, was quoted in a recent news conference as saying, "Companies' claims that science cannot say with certainty that tobacco causes cancer were flat-footed lies" and that "sending cigarettes to the Third World was the export of death, disease, and disability." An Oxford University epidemiologist has estimated that, because of increasing tobacco consumption in Asia, the annual worldwide death toll from tobacco-related illnesses will more than triple over the next two decades.

Perhaps 100 million people died prematurely during the 20th century as a result of tobacco, making it the leading preventable cause of death and one of the top killers overall. According to the World Health Organization, each year smoking causes 4 million deaths globally, and it expects the annual toll to rise to 10 million in 2030.

GOVERNMENT INVOLVEMENT

Third World governments often stand to profit from tobacco sales. Brazil collects 75 percent of the retail price of cigarettes in taxes, some $100 million a month. The Bulgarian state-owned tobacco company, Bulgartabac, contributes almost $30 million in taxes to the government annually. Bulgartabac is a major exporter of cigarettes to Russia, exporting 40,000 tons of cigarettes annually.

Tobacco is Zimbabwe's largest cash crop. One news report from a Zimbabwe newspaper reveals strong support for cigarette companies. "Western anti-tobacco lobbies demonstrate unbelievable hypocrisy," notes one editorial. "It is relatively easy to sit in Washington or London and prattle on about the so-called evils of smoking, but they are far removed from the day-to-day grind of earning a living in the Third World." It goes on to comment that it doesn't dispute the fact that smoking is addictive or that it may cause diseases, but "smoking does not necessarily lead to certain death. Nor is it any more dangerous than other habits." Unfortunately, tobacco smoking has attracted the attention of a particularly "sanctimonious, meddling sector of society. They would do better to keep their opinions to themselves."

Generally, smoking is not a big concern of governments beset by debt, internal conflict, drought, or famine. It is truly tragic, but the worse famine becomes, the more people smoke—just as with war, when people who are worried want to smoke. "In any case," says one representative of an international tobacco company, "People in developing countries don't have a long enough life expectancy to worry about smoking-related problems. You can't turn to a guy who is going to die at age 40 and tell him that he might not live up to 2 years extra at age 70." As for promoting cigarettes in the Third World, "If there is no ban on TV advertising, then you aren't going to be an idiot and impose restrictions on yourself," says the representative, "and likewise, if you get an order and you know that they've got money, no one is going to turn down the business."

Cigarette companies figure China's self-interest will preserve its industry. Tobacco provides huge revenues for Beijing because all tobacco must be sold through the China National Tobacco Company monopoly. Duty on imported cigarettes is nearly 450 percent of their value. Consequently, tobacco is among the central government's biggest source of funding, accounting for more than $30 billion in income in 2005. China is also a major exporter of tobacco.

FOCUS ON DEVELOPING MARKETS

Lawsuits, stringent legislation against advertising, laws restricting where people can smoke, and other antismoking efforts on the part of governments have caused tobacco companies to intensify their efforts in those markets where restrictions are fewer and governments more friendly. As part of a strategy to increase its sales in the developing world, Philip Morris International (PMI) was spun off from Philip Morris USA in 2008 to escape the threat of litigation and government regulation in the United States. The move frees the tobacco giant's international operations of the legal and public-relations headaches in the United States that have hindered its growth. Its practices are no longer constrained by American public opinion, paving the way for broad product experimentation.

A new product, Marlboro Intense, is likely to be part of an aggressive blitz of new smoking products PMI will roll out around the globe. The Marlboro Intense cigarette has been shrunk down by about a half inch and offers smokers seven potent puffs apiece, versus the average of eight or so milder draws. The idea behind Intense is to appeal to customers who, due to indoor smoking bans, want to dash outside for a quick nicotine hit but don't always finish a full-size cigarette. The CEO of PMI says there are "possibly 50 markets that are interested in deploying Marlboro Intense."

Other product innovations include sweet-smelling cigarettes that contain tobacco, cloves and flavoring—with twice the tar and nicotine levels of a conventional U.S. cigarette. Marlboro Mix 9, a high-nicotine, high-tar cigarette launched in Indonesia in 2007, and a clove-infused Mix 9 will be exported to other southeast Asian markets next. Another iteration of the Marlboro brand, the Marlboro Filter Plus, is being sold in South Korea, Russia, Kazakhstan, and Ukraine. It touts a special filter made of carbon, cellulose acetate, and a tobacco plug that the company claims lowers the tar level while giving smokers a smoother taste.

One of PMI's immediate goals is to harness the huge potential of China's smoking population, as well as some of that country's own brands, which it has agreed to market worldwide. With some

350 million smokers, China has 50 million more cigarette buyers than the U.S. has people, according to Euromonitor.

While smoking rates in developed countries have slowly declined, they have shot up dramatically in some developing counties where PMI is a major player. These include Pakistan (up 42 percent since 2001), Ukraine (up 36 percent), and Argentina (up 18 percent).

ANTISMOKING PROMOTIONS

Since the early 1990s, multinational tobacco companies have promoted "youth smoking prevention" programs as part of their "Corporate Social Responsibility" campaigns. The companies have partnered with third-party allies in Latin America, most notably nonprofit educational organizations and education and health ministries to promote youth smoking prevention. Even though there is no evidence that these programs reduce smoking among youths, they have met the industry's goal of portraying the companies as concerned corporate citizens.

In fact, a new study proves that youth smoking prevention ads created by the tobacco industry and aimed at parents actually increase the likelihood that teens will smoke. The study, "Impact of Televised Tobacco Industry Smoking Prevention Advertising on Youth Smoking-Related Beliefs, Intentions and Behavior," published in the December 2006 issue of the *American Journal of Public Health*, sought to understand how the tobacco industry uses "youth smoking prevention" programs in Latin America. Tobacco industry documents, so-called social reports, media reports, and material provided by Latin American public health advocates were all analyzed. The study is the first to examine the specific effect of tobacco company parent-focused advertising on youth. It found that ads that the industry claims are aimed at preventing youth from smoking actually provide no benefit to youth. In fact, the ads that are created for parental audiences but also are seen by teens are associated with stronger intentions by teens to smoke in the future.

Brazil has the world's strictest governmental laws against smoking, consisting of highly visible antismoking campaigns, severe controls on advertising, and very high tax rates on smoking products. Despite these obstacles, the number of smokers in Brazil continues to grow. In 2006, there were approximately 44 million smokers in the country, up from 38 million in 1997. Factors driving this trend include the low price of cigarettes, which are among the lowest in the world; the easy access to tobacco products; and the actions taken by the powerful tobacco companies to slow down antismoking legislation in Brazil.

ASSESSING THE ETHICS OF STRATEGIC DECISIONS

Ethical decision making is not a simplistic "right" or "wrong" determination. Ethical ground rules are complex, tough to sort out and to prioritize, tough to articulate, and tough to use.

The complexity of ethical decisions is compounded in the international setting, which comprises different cultures, different perspectives of right and wrong, different legal requirements, and different goals. Clearly, when U.S. companies conduct business in an international setting, the ground rules become further complicated by the values, customs, traditions, ethics, and goals of the host countries, which each have developed their own ground rules for conducting business.

Three prominent American ethicists have developed a framework to view the ethical implications of strategic decisions by

American firms. They identify three ethical principles that can guide American managers in assessing the ethical implications of their decisions and the degree to which these decisions reflect these ethical principles or ground rules. They suggest asking, "Is the corporate strategy acceptable according to the following ethical ground rules?"

These questions can help uncover the ethical ground rules embedded in the tobacco consumption situation described in this case. These questions lead to an ethical analysis of the degree to which this strategy is beneficial or harmful to the parties and, ultimately, whether it is a "right" or "wrong" strategy, or whether the consequences of this strategy are ethical or socially responsible for the parties involved. These ideas are incorporated in the decision tree in Exhibit 1.

Principles	**Question**
Utilitarian ethics (Bentham, Smith)	Does the corporate strategy optimize the "common good" or benefits of all constituencies?
Rights of the parties (Kant, Locke)	Does the corporate strategy respect the rights of the individuals involved?
Justice or fairness (Aristotle, Rawls)	Does the corporate strategy respect the canons of justice or fairness to all parties?

Exhibit 1

A Decision Tree for Incorporating Ethical and Social Responsibility Issues into Multinational Business Decisions

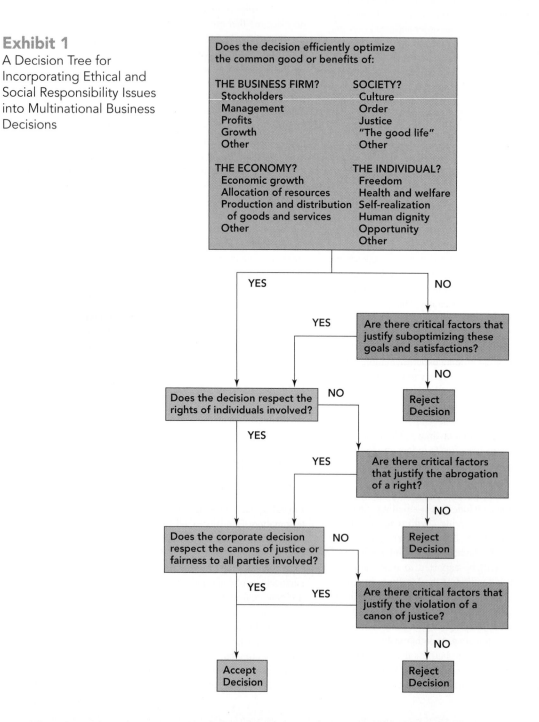

Laczniak and Naor discuss the complexity of international ethics or, more precisely, the ethical assumptions that underlie strategic decisions for multinationals.[2] They suggest that multinationals can develop consistency in their policies by using federal law as a baseline for appropriate behavior as well as respect for the host country's general value structure. They conclude with four recommendations for multinationals:

1. Expand codes of ethics to be worldwide in scope.

2. Expressly consider ethical issues when developing worldwide corporate strategies.

3. If the firm encounters major ethical dilemmas, consider withdrawal from the problem market.

4. Develop periodic ethics-impact statements, including impacts on host parties.

---

[2] Gene R. Laczniak and Jacob Naor, "Global Ethics: Wrestling with the Corporate Conscience," *Business,* July–September 1985.

See www.who.int, the World Health Organization's Web site, for more details regarding the current tobacco controversy. See also www.getswat.com for a worldwide student initiative against smoking.

QUESTIONS

1. Use the model in Exhibit 1 as a guide and assess the ethical and social responsibility implications of the situations described.

2. Can you recommend alternative strategies or solutions to the dilemmas confronting the tobacco companies? To governments? What is the price of ethical behavior?

3. Should the U.S. government support U.S. tobacco company interests abroad?

4. Should a company be forced to stop marketing a product that is not illegal, such as cigarettes?

Sources: "Smoke Over the Horizon; U.S. Gains in Tobacco Control Are Being Offset Internationally," *The Washington Post,* July 23, 2006; "Death and Taxes: England Has Become the Latest in a Series of Countries to Vote for Restrictions on Smoking in Public Places," *Financial Management (UK),* April 1, 2006; "Trick or Treat? Tobacco Industry Prevention Ads Don't Help Curb Youth Smoking," *PR Newswire,* October 31, 2006; "China Exclusive: China, With One Third of World's Smokers, Promises a 'Non-Smoking' Olympics," *Xinhua News Agency,* May 29, 2006; "Tobacco Consumption and Motives for Use in Mexican University Students," *Adolescence,* June 22, 2006; "A Change in the Air: Smoking Bans Gain Momentum Worldwide," *Environmental Health Perspectives,* August 1, 2007; "Adams Won't Kick the BAT Habit: The Head of British American Tobacco Is Stoical About the Looming Ban on Smoking in Public Spaces: BAT will Adapt," *The Sunday Telegraph London,* June 10, 2007; "Heart Disease, Stroke Plague Third World," Associated Press (Online), April 4, 2006; "Get a Detailed Picture of the Tobacco Industry in Brazil," *M2 Press Wire,* December 20, 2007; Vanessa O'Connell, "Philip Morris Readies Global Tobacco Blitz; Division Spin-off Enables Aggressive Product Push; High-Tar Smokes in Asia," *The Wall Street Journal,* January 29, 2008; "The Global Tobacco Threat," *The New York Times,* February 19, 2008; "How to Save a Billion Lives; Smoking," *The Economist* (London,) February 9, 2008; "Whether Here or There, Cigarettes Still Kill People," *The Wall Street Journal,* February 4, 2008.

GLOSSARY

a

administered pricing   The attempt to establish prices for an entire market through the cooperation of competitors, through national, state, or local governments, or by international agreement. Its legality differs from country to country and from time to time.

advanced pricing agreement (APA)   An agreement made between a company and the Internal Revenue Service covering **transfer pricing** methods used by the company. Without such an agreement, if the IRS charges the company with underreporting income through its transactions with affiliates, the burden of proof that a transfer price was fair rests with the company.

aesthetics   Philosophically, the creation and appreciation of beauty; collectively, the arts, including folklore, music, drama, and dance.

AFTA   ASEAN (Association of Southeast Asian Nations) Free Trade Area; a multinational trade group that evolved from ASEAN. *See* **APEC; ASEAN+3**

agent middlemen   In an international transaction, intermediaries who represent the principal (home manufacturer/marketer) rather than themselves; agent middlemen work on commission and arrange for sales in the foreign country but do not take title to the merchandise. *See* **home-country middlemen; merchant middlemen**

analogy   A method of market estimation that assumes that demand for a product develops in much the same way in all countries as comparable economic development occurs in each country.

APEC   The Asian-Pacific Economic Cooperation; a forum that meets annually to discuss regional economic development. See **AFTA; ASEAN+3**

arbitration   A procedure, used as an alternative to **litigation,** in which parties in a dispute may select a disinterested party or parties as referee to determine the merits of the case and make a judgment that both parties agree to honor.

ASEAN+3   A forum for ministers of the Association of Southeast Asian Nations plus ministers from China, Japan, and South Korea. *See* **AFTA; APEC**

b

back translation   The process in which a document, such as a questionnaire, or phrase is translated from one language to another and then translated by a second party into the original language. Back translations can be used to verify that the first translation, as of a marketing slogan, has the intended meeting for the targeted audience. *See* **decentering; parallel translation**

balance of payments   The system of accounts that records a nation's international financial transactions.

balance of trade   The difference in value over a period of time between a country's imports and exports.

barter   The direct exchange of goods between two parties in a transaction. *See* **compensation deals; counterpurchase; countertrade**

BATNA   Acronym for "best alternative to a negotiated agreement," a notion discussed in *Getting to Yes,* by Fisher, Ury, and Patton.

BEMs   Big emerging markets; used to describe the core group of populous nations that will account for much of the growth in world trade among developing and newly industrialized countries.

bills of exchange   A form of international commercial payment drawn by sellers on foreign buyers; in transactions based on bills of exchange, the seller assumes all risk until the actual dollars are received, making them riskier for the seller than **letters of credit.**

c

capital account   The portion of a **balance of payments** statement that shows a record of direct investment, portfolio investment, and short-tern capital movements to and from countries.

cartel   An arrangement in which various companies producing similar products or services work together to control markets for the goods and service they produce. The Organization of Petroleum Exporting Countries (OPEC) is the best-known international cartel.

client followers   Companies, often providers of services, that follow companies that first moved into a foreign market; for example, an American insurance company setting up in Mexico to serve a U.S. auto company that had previously opened a factory there.

code law   A legal system based on an all-inclusive system of written rules, or codes, of law; generally divided into three separate codes: commercial, civil, and criminal. In the United States, Louisiana is the one state to use code law. *See* **common law**

Commerce Control List (CCL)   A directory, organized by a series of **Export Control Classification Numbers,** that indicates U.S. rules for the exportability of items. Exporters must use the list to determine if there are end-use restrictions on certain items, such as uses in nuclear, chemical, and biological weapons, and determine if a product has a dual use—that is, both in commercial and restricted applications. *See* **Export Administration Regulations**

Commerce Country Chart (CCC)   A directory of information that a U.S. exporter needs to consult, along with the **Commerce Control List,** to determine if the exporter needs a license to export or reexport a product to a particular destination. *See* **Export Control Classification Numbers**

common law   The body of law based on tradition, past practices, and legal precedents set by courts through interpretations of statutes, legal legislation, and past rulings. Common law, which is used in all states in the United States except Louisiana, uses past decisions to interpret statutes and apply them to present situations. Also known as English law. *See* **code law**

common market   An agreement that eliminates all tariffs and other restrictions on internal trade, adopts a set of common external tariffs, and removes all restrictions on the free flow of capital and labor among member nations.

compensation deals   Transactions that involve payment in both goods and cash. *See* **barter; counterpurchase; countertrade**

complementary marketing   The process by which companies with excess marketing capacity in different countries or with a desire for a broader product line take on additional lines for international distribution; commonly called *piggybacking.*

conciliation   A nonbinding agreement between parties to resolve disputes by asking a third party to mediate differences. Also known as *mediation. See* **arbitration; litigation**

confiscation   The seizing of a company's assets without payment. Prominent examples involving U.S. companies occurred in Cuba and Iran. *See* **domestication; expropriation**

controllable elements   The aspects of trade over which a company has control and influence; they include marketing decisions covering product, price, promotion, distribution, research, and advertising. *See* **uncontrollable elements**

corporate planning   The formulation of long-term, generalized goals for an enterprise as a whole. *See* **strategic planning; tactical planning**

counterpurchase   A type of **countertrade** in which a seller receives payment in cash but agrees in a contract to buy goods from the buyer for the total monetary amount involved in the first transaction or for a set percentage of that amount; also known as *offset trade*. *See* **barter; compensation deals**

countertrade   A type of transaction in which goods are imported and sold by a company from a country in exchange for the right or ability to manufacture and/or sell goods in that country. Countertrade can substitute for cash entirely or partially and is used extensively in trade between U.S. firms and the former Soviet bloc, along with other emerging markets. *See* **barter; compensation deals; counterpurchase**

countervailing duty   A fee that may, under **World Trade Organization** rules, be imposed on foreign goods benefiting from subsidies, whether in production, export, or transportation; may be applied in conjunction with *minimum access volume,* which restricts the amount of goods a country will import.

cultural borrowing   The phenomenon by which societies learn from other cultures' ways and borrow ideas to solve problems or improve conditions.

cultural congruence   A marketing strategy in which products are marketed in a way similar to the marketing of products already in the market in a manner as congruent as possible with existing cultural norms.

cultural elective   *See* **elective**

cultural exclusive   *See* **exclusive**

cultural imperative   *See* **imperative**

cultural sensitivity   An awareness of the nuances of culture so that a culture can be viewed objectively, evaluated, and appreciated; an important part of foreign marketing.

cultural values   The system of beliefs and customs held by a population in a given **culture.** A book by Geert Hofstede describes a study of 66 nations and divides the cultural values of those nations into four primary dimensions: the Individualized/Collectivism Index, the Power Distance Index, the Uncertainty Avoidance Index, and the Masculinity/Femininity Index (which is not considered as useful as the other three).

culture   The human-made part of human environment—the sum total of knowledge, beliefs, arts, morals, laws, customs, and any other capabilities and habits acquired by humans as members of society.

current account   The portion of a **balance of payments** statement that shows a record of all merchandise exports, imports, and services, plus unilateral transfers of funds.

customs-privileged facilities   Areas, as in international transactions, where goods can be imported for storage and/or processing with tariffs and quota limits postponed until the products leave the designated areas. *See* **foreign-trade zones**

customs union   A stage in economic cooperation that benefits from a **free trade area**'s reduced or eliminated internal tariffs and adds a common external tariff on products imported from countries outside the union. *See* **common market; political union**

cybersquatters   Persons or businesses that buy, usually for a nominal fee, and register as Web site names descriptive nouns, celebrity names, variations on company trademarks, geographic and ethnic group names, and pharmaceutical and other descriptors and then hold them until they can be sold at an inflated price. Sometimes called *CSQ.*

d

dealers   The middlemen selling industrial goods or durable goods directly to customers; they are the last step in the **distribution channel.**

decentering   A method of translation, a variation on **back translation,** that is a successive process of translation and retranslation of a document, such as a questionnaire, each time by a different translator. The two original-language versions are then compared, and if there are differences, the process is repeated until the second original-language version is the same as the first. *See* **parallel translation**

derived demand   Demand that is dependent on another source; it can be fundamental to the success of efforts to sell capital equipment and big-ticket industrial services.

direct exporting   The type of exporting in which a company sells to a customer in another country. *See* **indirect exporting**

distribution channels   The various routes through which marketers must negotiate their goods to deliver them to the consumer. Distribution channel structures range from those with little developed marketing infrastructure, as found in many emerging markets, to those with a highly complex, multilayered systems, as found in Japan. Consideration for channel structure involves "the six Cs": cost, capital, control, coverage, character, and continuity.

distribution process   The physical handling of goods, the passage of ownership (title), and—especially important from a marketing viewpoint—the buying and selling negotiations between the producers and middlemen and between middlemen and customers. *See* **distribution structure**

distribution structure   The system, present in every country's market, through which goods pass from producer to user; within the structure are a variety of middlemen. *See* **distribution process**

domestication   A process by which a host country gradually transfers foreign investments to national control and ownership through a series of government decrees mandating local ownership and greater national involvement in company management. *See* **confiscation; expropriation**

domestic environment uncontrollables   Factors in a company's home country over which the company has little or no control or influence. They include political and legal forces, the economic climate, level of technology, competitive forces, and economic forces. *See* **uncontrollable elements**

dumping　An export practice, generally prohibited by laws and subject to penalties and fines, defined by some as the selling of products in foreign markets below the cost of production and by others as the selling of products at below the prices of the same goods in the home market.

e

economic development　Generally, an increase in national production that results in an increase in average per capita gross domestic product.

economic dualism　The coexistence of modern and traditional sectors within an economy, especially as found in less-developed countries.

ELAIN　Export License Application and Information Network; an electronic service that enables authorized exporters to submit license applications via the Internet for all commodities except supercomputers and to all free-world destinations. *See* **ERIC; SNAP; STELA**

elective　A business custom (as in a foreign country) to which adaptation is helpful but not necessary. *See* **exclusive; imperative**

EMU　The Economic and Monetary Union; formed by the **Maastricht Treaty,** which also formed the European Union.

ERIC　Electronic Request for Item Classification; a supplementary service to **ELAIN** that allows an exporter to submit commodity classification requests via the Internet to the Bureau of Export administration. *See* **SNAP; STELA**

exclusive　A business custom (as in a foreign country) in which an outsider must not participate. *See* **elective; imperative**

exclusive distribution　A practice in which a company restricts which retailers can carry its product; often used by companies to maintain high retail margins, to maintain the exclusive-quality image of a product, and to encourage retailers to provide extra service to customers.

expatriate　A person living away from his or her own country. In international sales, expatriates from the selling company's home country may be the best choice for the sales force when products are highly technical or when selling requires an extensive knowledge of the company and its product line. *See* **local nationals**

expert opinion　A method of market estimation in which experts are polled for their opinions about market size and growth rates; used particularly in foreign countries that are new to the marketer.

Export Administration Regulations (EAR)　A set of rules issued by the U.S. Department of Commerce, designed to alleviate many of the problems and confusions of exporting; they are intended to speed up the process of granting export licenses by concentrating license control on a list of specific items, most of which involve national security. Exporters must ensure that their trade activities do not violate the provisions of EAR. *See* **Commerce Control List; Export Control Classification Number**

Export Control Classification Number (ECCN)　Under the provisions of the U.S. **Export Administration Regulations (EAR),** a classification number that a U.S. exporter must select for an item to be exported; the number corresponds to a description in the **Commerce Control List,** which indicates the exportability of the item.

export documents　The various items of documentation for an international transaction, as required by the exporting government, by established procedures of foreign trade, and, in some cases, as required by the importing government.

export regulations　Restrictions placed by countries on the selling of goods abroad; among reasons they may be imposed are to conserve scarce goods for home consumption and to control the flow of strategic goods actual or potential enemies. *See* **import regulations**

Export Trading Company (ETC) Act　An act allowing producers of similar products in the United States to form an export trading company; the act created a more favorable environment for the formation of joint export ventures, in part by removing antitrust disincentives to trade activities.

expropriation　The seizure of an investment by a government in which some reimbursement is made to the investment owner; often the seized investment becomes nationalized. *See* **confiscation; domestication**

f

factual knowledge　A type of knowledge or understanding of a foreign culture that encompasses different meanings of color, different tastes, and other traits of a culture that a marketer can study, anticipate, and absorb. *See* **interpretive knowledge**

FCPA　Foreign Corrupt Practices Act. The act prohibits U.S. businesses from paying bribes openly or using middlemen as conduits for a bribe when the U.S. official knows that the middleman's payment will be used for a bribe.

foreign environment uncontrollables　Factors in the foreign market over which a business operating in its home country has little or no control or influence. They include political and legal forces, economic climate, geography and infrastructure, level of technology, structure of distribution, and level of technology. *See* **domestic environment uncontrollables**

foreign-trade zones (FTZs)　Regions or ports that act as holding areas for goods before quotas or customs duties are applied. In the United States, more than 150 FTZs allow companies to land imported goods for storage or various processing such as cleaning or packaging before the goods are officially brought into the United States or reexported to another country. *See* **customs-privileged facilities**

forfaiting　A financing technique that may be used in an international transaction in which the seller makes a one-time arrangement with a bank or other financial institution to take over responsibility for collecting the account receivable.

franchising　A form of **licensing** in which a company (the franchiser) provides a standard package of products, systems, and management services to the franchisee, which in foreign markets may have market knowledge. Franchising permits flexibility in dealing with local market conditions while providing the parent firm with a degree of control.

free trade area (FTA)　A type of regional cooperation that involves an agreement between two or more countries to reduce or eliminate customs duties and nontariff trade barriers among partner countries while members maintain individual tariff schedules for external countries. An FTA requires more cooperation than the arrangement known as the regional cooperation for development.

full-cost pricing   A method of pricing based on the view that no unit of a similar product is different from any other unit of a similar product and that each unit must bear its full share of the total fixed and variable cost, whether sold in the home market or abroad. *See* **skimming; variable-cost pricing**

g

GATT   General Agreement on Tariffs and Trade; a trade agreement signed by the United States and 22 other countries shortly after World War II. The original agreement provided a process to reduce **tariffs** and created an agency to patrol world trade; the treaty and subsequent meetings have produced agreements significantly reducing tariffs.

global awareness   A frame of reference, important to the success of a businessperson, that embodies tolerance of cultural differences and knowledge of cultures, history, world market potential, and global economic, social, and political trends.

global brand   The worldwide use of a name, term, sign, symbol (visual or auditory), design, or a combination thereof to identify goods or services of a seller and to differentiate them from those of competitors.

global marketing   The performance of business activities designed to plan, price, promote, and direct the flow of a company's goods and services to consumers or users in more than one nation for a profit. The most profound difference between global and domestic marketing involves the orientation of the company toward markets and planning activities around the world.

global marketing concept   A perspective encompassing an entire set of country markets, whether the home market and one other country or the home market and 100 other countries, and viewing them as a unit, identifying groups of prospective buyers with similar needs as a global market segment, and developing a market plan that strives for standardization wherever it is effective in cost and cultural terms.

global orientation   A means of operating by which a company acts as if all the company's markets in a company's scope of operations (including the domestic market) were approachable as a single global market, with the company standardizing the marketing mix where culturally feasible and cost effective.

green marketing   Consideration and concern for the environmental consequences of product formulation, marketing, manufacturing, and packaging.

h

home-country middlemen   In international transactions, the intermediaries, located in the producer's home country, who provide marketing services from a domestic base; also known as *domestic middlemen.* Home-country middlemen offer advantages for companies with small international sales volume or for those inexperienced in international trade. *See* **agent middlemen; merchant middlemen**

homologation   A term used to describe changes in a product that are mandated by local standards for product and service **quality.**

IMF   The International Monetary Fund. A global institution that, along with the World Bank Group, was created to assist nations in becoming and remaining economically viable.

imperative   A business custom (as in a foreign country) that must be recognized and accommodated. *See* **elective; exclusive**

import jobbers   In international transactions, business entities that purchase goods directly from the manufacturer and sell to wholesalers and retailers and to industrial customers.

import regulations   Restrictions placed by countries on the sale of goods from outside markets; among the reasons they are imposed are to protect health, conserve foreign exchange, serve as economic reprisals, protect home industry, and provide revenue from tariffs. Exporters to markets under such regulations may have to go through various steps to comply with them. *See* **export regulations**

indirect exporting   The type of exporting in which a company sells to a buyer (an importer or distributor) in the home country; the buyer in turn exports the product. *See* **direct selling**

infrastructure   The collective assortment of capital goods that serve the activities of many industries and support production and marketing.

innovation   An idea perceived as new by a group of people; when applied to a product, an innovation may be something completely new or something that is perceived as new in a given country or culture. *See* **product diffusion**

integrated marketing communications (IMCs)   The collective arrangement of efforts and methods to sell a product or service, including advertising, sales promotions, trade shows, personal selling, direct selling, and public relations.

international marketing   The performance of business activities designed to plan, price, promote, and direct the flow of a company's goods and services to consumers or users in more than one nation for a profit.

international marketing research   The form of **marketing research** involving two additional considerations: (1) the need to communicate information across national boundaries, and (2) the challenge of applying established marketing techniques in the different environments of foreign markets, some of which may be strange or vexing milieus for the marketer.

interpretive knowledge   An ability to understand and to appreciate fully the nuances of different cultural traits and patterns. *See* **factual knowledge**

Islamic law   The *Shari'ah;* the legal system based on an interpretation of the Koran. Islamic law encompasses religious duties and obligations as well as the secular aspect of law regulating human acts. Among its provisions is a prohibition of the payment of interest.

ISO 9000s   A series of international industrial standards (ISO 9000–9004) originally designed by the International Organization for Standardization to meet the need for product quality assurances in purchasing agreements.

joint venture   A partnership of two or more participating companies that join forces to create a separate legal entity. *See* **strategic international alliance**

justice or fairness   One of three principles of ethics (the others are **utilitarian ethics** and **rights of the parties**); it tests an action by asking if the action respects the canons of justice or fairness to all parties involved.

Large-Scale Retail Store Location Act   A regulatory act in Japan, implemented under pressure from the United States in 2000; it replaced the protective Large-Scale Retail Store Law and relaxed restrictions on the opening of large retailers near small shops and abolished the mandate on the number of days a store must be closed.

letters of credit   Financing devices that, when opened by a buyer of goods, allow the seller to draw a draft against the bank issuing the credit and receive dollars by presenting proper shipping document. Except for cash in advance, letters of credit afford the seller the greatest degree of protection. *See* **bills of exchange**

licensing   A contractual means by which a company grants patent rights, trademark rights, and the rights to use technology to another company, often in a foreign market; a favored strategy of small and medium-sized companies seeking a foothold in foreign markets without making large capital outlays. *See* **franchising**

linguistic distance   The measure of difference between languages; an important factor in determining the amount of trade between nations.

litigation   The process in which a dispute between parties is contested in a formal judicial setting; commonly instigated by a lawsuit asserting one party's version of the facts.

local nationals   Persons living in their home country; historically the persons preferred by **expatriate** managers to form the sales force. Local nationals are more knowledgeable about a country's business structure than an expatriate would be, and they are generally less expensive to field and maintain.

logistics management   A total systems approach to management of the distribution process that includes all activities involved in physically moving raw material, in-process inventory, and finished goods inventory from the point of origin to the point of use or consumption.

m

Maastricht Treaty   Treaty signed by 12 nations of the European Community creating the European Union.

Manifest Destiny   The notion that Americans were a chosen people ordained by God to create a model society; it was accepted as the basis for U.S. policy during much of the 19th and 20th centuries as the nation expanded its territory.

maquiladoras   Also known as *in-bond companies* or *twin plants,* a type of customs-privileged facility that originated in Mexico in the 1970s and provided U.S. companies with a favorable means to use low-cost Mexican labor. They operate through an agreement with the Mexican government allowing U.S. companies to import parts and materials into Mexico without import taxes provided the finished products are reexported to the United States or another country. *See* **customs-privileged facilities**

marketing research   The systematic gathering, recording, and analyzing of data to provide information useful in marketing decision making. *See* **international marketing research**

Marxist-socialist tenets   The set of views in which law is subordinate to prevailing economic conditions. Marxist-socialist tenets influenced the legal systems of Russia and other republics of the former Soviet Union, as well as China, forcing these nations to revamp their commercial legal code as they become involved in trade with non-Marxist countries.

merchant middlemen   In international transactions, the intermediaries, located in the foreign market, who take title to the home-country manufacturer's goods and sell on their own account. Manufacturers using merchant middlemen have less control over the **distribution process** than those using **agent middlemen.** *See* **home-country middlemen**

Mercosur   An evolving South American union, also called the Southern Cone Free Trade Area, formed in 1991 with the goal of creating a **common market** and **customs union** among the participating countries. The original signers were Argentina, Brazil, Paraguay, and Uruguay; Bolivia and Chile later signed agreements with Mercosur.

merge-in-transit   A distribution method in which goods shipped from several supply locations are consolidated into one final customer delivery point while they are in transit and then shipped as a unit to the customer.

Monroe Doctrine   A cornerstone of U.S. foreign policy as enunciated by President James Monroe, it proclaimed three basic dicta: no further European colonization in the New World, abstention of the United States from European political affairs, and nonintervention of European governments in the governments of the Western Hemisphere. *See* **Roosevelt Corollary**

M-time   Monochromatic time; describing a view of time, typical of most North Americans, Swiss, Germans, and Scandinavians, as something that is linear and can be saved, wasted, spent, and lost. M-time cultures tend to concentrate on one thing at a time and value promptness. *See* **P-time**

multicultural research   Inquiry, analysis, and study of countries and cultures that takes into account differences in language, economic structure, social structure, behavior, and attitude patterns. Different methods of research may have varying reliability in different countries.

multinational market regions   The groups of countries that seek mutual economic benefit from reducing interregional tariffs and barriers to trade.

n

NAFTA   North American Free Trade Agreement. NAFTA is a comprehensive trade agreement that addresses, and in many cases improves all aspects of doing business within North America. By eliminating trade and investment barriers among Canada, the United States, and Mexico, it created one of the largest and richest markets in the world.

nationalism An intense feeling of national pride and unity; an awakening of a nation's people to pride in their country. Nationalism can take on an antiforeign business bias.

NICs Newly industrialized countries; countries that are experiencing rapid economic expansion and industrialization.

noise The term for an impairment to communications process comprising external influences, such as competitive advertising, other sales personnel, and confusion at the "receiving end." Noise can disrupt any step of the communications process and is frequently beyond the control of the sender or the receiver.

nontariff barriers Restrictions, other than **tariffs,** placed by countries on imported products; they may include quality standards, sanitary and health standards, **quotas,** embargoes, boycotts, and antidumping penalties.

nontask sounding The part of the negotiation process in which conversation covers topics other than the business at hand; non-task sounding is commonly a preliminary phase and precedes **task-related information exchange.**

O

open account In U.S. domestic trade, the typical payment procedure for established customers, in which the goods are delivered and the customer is billed on an end-of-the-month basis.

orderly market agreements (OMAs) Agreements, similar to **quotas,** between an importing country and an exporting country for a restriction on the volume of exports. Also known as **voluntary export restraints.**

P

parallel imports International transactions in which importers buy products from distributors in one country and sell them in another to distributors that are not part of the manufacturer's regular distribution system.

parallel translation A method of translation in which two translators are used to make a **back translation;** the results are compared, differences are discussed, and the most appropriate translation is used. The method addresses the use of common idioms in the languages being translated. *See* **decentering**

physical distribution system The overall network for the physical movement of goods, including plants and warehousing, transportation mode, inventory quantities, and packaging.

planned change A marketing strategy in which a company deliberately sets out to change those aspects of a foreign culture resistant to predetermined marketing goals. *See* **unplanned change**

political union A fully integrated form of regional co-operation-that involves complete political and economic integration, either voluntary or enforced; the most notable example was the now-disbanded Council for Mutual Economic Assistance (COMECON), a centrally controlled group of countries organized by the Soviet Union.

predatory pricing A practice by which a foreign producer intentionally sells its products in another country for less than the cost of production to undermine the competition and take control of the market.

price escalation The pricing disparity in which goods are priced higher in a foreign market than in the home market; caused by the added costs involved in exporting products from one country to another.

price–quality relationship The balance between a product's price and how well the product performs. Often the price–quality of a product is ideal if it meets basic expectations and no more, allowing it to be priced competitively.

primary data Data collected, as in market research, specifically for a particular research project. *See* **secondary data**

principle of justice or fairness *See* **justice or fairness**

principle of rights of the parties *See* **rights of the parties**

principle of utilitarian ethics *See* **utilitarian ethics**

prior use versus registration The principle, as observed in the United States and other common-law nations, that ownership of intellectual property rights usually goes to whoever can establish first use.

product buyback agreement A type of **countertrade** in which the sale involves goods or services that produce other goods or services—that is, production plant, production equipment, or technology.

Product Component Model A tool for characterizing how a product may be adapted to a new market by separating the product's many dimensions into three components: support services, packaging, and core component.

product diffusion The process by which product **innovation** spreads; successful product diffusion may depend on the ability to communicate relevant product information and new product attributes.

protectionism The use by nations of legal barriers, exchange barriers, and psychological barriers to restrain entry of goods from other countries.

PSAs Political and social activists. PSAs are individuals who participate in efforts to change the practices and behaviors of corporations and governments, with tactics that can range from peaceful protest to terrorism.

P-time Polychromatic time; a view of time, as held in "high context" cultures, in which the completion of a human transaction is more important than holding to schedules. P-time is characterized by the simultaneous occurrence of many things. *See* **M-time**

public relations (PR) The effort made by companies to create positive relationships with the popular press and general media and to communicate messages to their publics, including customers, the general public, and government regulators.

Q

quality The essential character of something, such as a good or service; defined in two dimensions: market-perceived quality and performance quality. Consumer perception of a product's quality often has more to do with market-perceived quality than performance quality.

quotas Specific unit or dollar limits applied to a particular type of good by the country into which the good is imported. *See* **tariff**

r

relationship marketing   The aspect of marketing products that depends on long-term associations with customers; an important factor in business-to-business contexts and especially important in most international markets, where culture dictates strong ties between people and companies.

research process   The process of obtaining information; it should begin with a definition of the research problem and establishment of objectives, and proceed with an orderly approach to the collection and analysis of data.

reserves account   The portion of a **balance-of-trade** statement that shows a record of exports and imports of gold, increases or decreases in foreign exchange, and increases or decreases in liabilities to foreign banks.

rights of the parties   One of three principles of ethics (the others are **utilitarian ethics** and **justice or fairness**); it tests an action by asking if the action respects the rights of the individuals involved.

Roosevelt Corollary   An extension of U.S. policy applied to the Monroe Doctrine by President Theodore Roosevelt, stating that the United States would not only prohibit non-American intervention in Latin American affairs but would also police Latin America and guarantee that all Latin American nations would meet their international obligations. *See* **Monroe Doctrine**

S

sales promotion   Marketing activities that stimulate consumer purchases and improve retailer or middlemen effectiveness and cooperation.

secondary data   Data collected by an agency or individual other than the one conducting research; often useful in market research. *See* **primary data**

self-reference criterion (SRC)   An unconscious reference to one's own cultural values, experience, and knowledge as a basis for a decision.

separation allowances   Payment of overseas premiums to employees who take on short-term foreign assignments and travel without their families; allowances generally compensate for all excess expenses and any tax differential.

Silent Language   Term used by Edward T. Hall for the non-spoken and symbolic meanings of time, space, things, friendships, and agreements, and how they vary across cultures; from Hall's article "The Silent Language of Business."

Single European Act   An agreement, ratified in 1987, designed to remove all barriers to trade and to make the European Community a single internal market.

skimming   A method of pricing, generally used for foreign markets, in which a company seeks to reach a segment of the market that is relatively price insensitive and thus willing to pay a premium price for the value received; may be used to sell a new or innovative product to maximize profits until a competitor forces a lower price. *See* **full-cost pricing; variable-cost pricing**

SNAP   Simplified Network Application Process; an electronic service offered by the U.S. Department of Commerce as an alternative to paper license submissions that enables an exporter to submit export and reexport applications, high-performance computer notices, and commodity classification requests via the Internet. *See* **ELAIN; ERIC; STELA**

social institutions   The methods and systems, including family, religion, school, the media, government, and corporations, that affect the ways in which people relate to one another, teach acceptable behavior to succeeding generations, and govern themselves.

sovereignty   The powers exercised by a state in relation to other countries, as well as the supreme powers of a state as exercised over its own inhabitants.

special drawing rights (SDRs)   A means of monetary measurement that represents an average base of value derived from the value of a group of major currencies. Known as "paper gold," it is used by the **IMF** to report most monetary statistics in a unit more reliable than a single currency, such as dollars.

stage of economic development   A classification describing the (stage of) maturity and sophistication of a nation's economy as it evolves over time. The best-known model, by Walt Rostow, describes five stages, starting with the traditional society and finally reaching the age of high mass consumption.

STELA   System for Tracking Export License Applications; an automated voice response system for exporters that enables license applicants to track the status of their license and classification applications with U.S. authorities. *See* **ELAIN; ERIC; SNAP**

strategic international alliance (SIA)   A business relationship established by two or more companies to cooperate out of mutual need and to share risk in achieving a common objective.

strategic planning   A type of planning conducted at the highest levels of management, dealing with products, capital, and research and the long- and short-term goals of a company. *See* **corporate planning; tactical planning**

subornation   The giving of large sums of money—frequently not fully accounted for—designed to entice an official to commit an illegal act on behalf of the one offering the money.

sustainable development   An approach toward economic growth that has been described (by Joke Waller-Hunter) as a cooperative effort among businesses, environmentalists, and others to seek growth with "wise resource management, equitable distribution of benefits, and reduction of negative efforts on people and the environment from the process of economic growth."

t

tactical planning   A type of planning that pertains to specific actions and to the allocation of resources used to implement strategic planning goals in specific markets; also known as *market planning;* generally conducted at the local level. *See* **corporate planning; strategic planning**

tariff   A fee or tax that countries impose on imported goods, often to protect a country's markets from intrusion from foreign countries. *See* **nontariff barriers; quotas**

task-related information exchange   The point in the negotiation process at which nontask communication, or **nontask sounding,** is completed and substantial negotiations begin.

TCNs   Third-country nationals; expatriates from one country working for a foreign company in a third country. *See* **expatriate; local nationals**

terms of sale   The set of rules and costs applying to a transaction, covering such categories as price, freight, and insurance. In international trade, terms of sale often sound similar to those in domestic commerce but generally have different meanings. Also known as *trade terms.*

trading companies   Business entities that accumulate, transport, and distribute goods from many countries.

transfer pricing   The pricing of goods transferred from a company's operations or sales units in one country to its units elsewhere; also known as *intracompany pricing.* In transfer pricing, prices may be adjusted to enhance the ultimate profit of the company as a whole.

Treaty of Amsterdam   Treaty, concluded in 1997, that addressed issues left undone by the **Maastricht Treaty** and identified priority measures necessary to bring a single market in Europe fully into effect and to lay a solid foundation for both a single currency and an enlargement of the European Union into central and eastern Europe. *See* **Economic and Monetary Union; Single European Act**

24-Hour Rule   A U.S. requirement, part of the Cargo and Container Security Initiative, mandating that sea carriers and NVOCCs (Non-Vessel Operating Common Carriers) provide U.S. Customs with detailed descriptions (manifests) of the contents of containers bound for the United States 24 hours before a container is loaded on board a vessel.

U

uncontrollable elements   Factors in the business environment over which the international marketer has no control or influence; may include competition, legal restraints, government controls, weather, consumer preferences and behavior, and political events. *See* **controllable elements**

United States–Canada Free Trade Agreement   An agreement, known as CFTA, between the United States and Canada designed to eliminate all trade barriers between the two nations.

unplanned change   A marketing strategy in which a company introduces a product into a market without a plan to influence the way the market's culture responds to or resists the company's marketing message. *See* **planned change**

utilitarian ethics   One of three principles of ethics (the others are **rights of the parties** and **justice or fairness**); it tests an action by asking if it optimizes the "common good" or benefits of all constituencies.

V

variable-cost pricing   A method of pricing goods in foreign markets in which a company is concerned only with the marginal or incremental costs of producing goods for sale in those markets. Firms using variable-cost pricing take the view that foreign sales are bonus sales. *See* **full-cost pricing; skimming**

VERS   *See* **voluntary export restraints**

voluntary export restraints (VERS)   Agreements, similar to **quotas,** between an importing country and an exporting country for a restriction on the volume of exports. Also known as **orderly market agreements (OMAs).**

W

World Trade Organization   *See* **WTO**

WTO   World Trade Organization. The organization formed in 1994 that encompasses the **GATT** structure and extends it to new areas that had not been adequately covered previously. The WTO adjudicates trade disputes. All member countries have equal representation.

Page numbers with n indicate notes.

Page numbers with n indicate notes.